Masterpieces of the Orient

ENLARGED EDITION

Uniform with this volume, and also under the General Editorship of Maynard Mack

The Norton Anthology of World Masterpieces

SIXTH EDITION

Masterpieces of the Orient

ENLARGED EDITION

Edited by G. L. Anderson
UNIVERSITY OF HAWAII

General Editor
Maynard Mack
YALE UNIVERSITY

W · W · NORTON & COMPANY
New York · London

FOR JULIET

for the mole on whose cheek
I'd barter Bukhara and Samarkand

W. W. Norton & Company, Inc., 500 Fifth Avenue, New York, N.Y. 10110
W. W. Norton & Company Ltd., 10 Coptic Street, London WC1A 1PU

Library of Congress Cataloging in Publication Data
Anderson, George Lincoln, 1920– ed.
Masterpieces of the Orient.
Bibliography: p.
Includes index.
1. Oriental literature–Translations into English.
2. English literature–Translations from Oriental languages. I. Title.
PJ409.A5 1977 808.8 76–25159
ISBN 0-393-09196-1 pbk.

Book design by John Woodlock

PRINTED IN THE UNITED STATES OF AMERICA

1 2 3 4 5 6 7 8 9 0

Contents

PREFACE

The Near East

INTRODUCTION 1 WRITINGS AND CRITICISM 4

THE GOLDEN ODES (*Mu'allaqat*) 6

The Wandering King (*Mu'allaqa of Imru'-al-Qays*) 9
Whom the Gods Loved? (*Mu'allaqa of Tarafa*) 14
The Centenarian (*Mu'allaqa of Labid*) 19
The Black Knight (*Mu'allaqa of 'Antara*) 24

FIRDAUSĪ (ca. 940–1020 or 1025) 29

The Book of Kings (*Shāhnāma*) 31
The Poet's Introduction 31
The Reign of Keyumars 34
The Adventures of Sekander 34
Yazdegerd the Sinner 39

RŪMĪ (1207–1273) 56
The *Mathnawī* 58

SA'DĪ (1213/19–1292) 66
The Rose Garden (*Gulistān*) 67

HĀFIZ (ca. 1320–1389/90) 90
Poems (*Ghazals*) 91

TĀHĀ HUSSEIN (born 1889) 102
The Stream of Days 103

India

INTRODUCTION 130 — WRITINGS AND CRITICISM 132

THE RIGVEDA 134

THE SONG OF GOD (*Bhagavad Gītā*) 153

VĀLMĪKI (ca. 1st Century B.C.) 168
The Rāmāyana 170

KĀLĪDASA (ca. 5th Century A.D.) 232
Shakuntalā 234

VIDYĀKARA (ca. 1100), compiler 316
The Treasury of Well-Turned Verse (*Subhāsitaratnakosa*)

RABINDRANATH TAGORE (1861–1941) 328
The Post Office 329

R. K. NARAYAN (born 1906) 346
The Financial Expert 348

China

INTRODUCTION 367 — WRITINGS AND CRITICISM 369

THE BOOK OF SONGS (*Shih Ching*) (ca. 600 B.C.) 371

CONFUCIUS (K'UNG FU-TZU) (ca. 551–ca. 479 B.C.) 389
The Analects 391

CHUANG-TZU (ca. 369 B.C.–ca. 286 B.C.) 407
Selections 408

LU KI (291–303) 422
Rhymeprose on Literature (*Wen Fu*) 424

THREE POETS 432
T'AO CH'IEN (365–427) 434
LI PO (701–762) 455
PO CHÜ-I (722–846) 463

WU CH'ENG-EN (ca. 16th Century) 477
Monkey (*Hsi Yu Chi*) 478

LIU T'IEH-YÜN (1857–1909) 496
The Travels of Lao Ts'an (*Lao-ts'an Yu-chi*) 498

LU HSÜN (CHOU SHU-JEN) (1881–1936) 531
Three Stories
A Madman's Diary 533
Medicine 541
Soap 547

THE RED LANTERN (1965 version) 556

Japan

INTRODUCTION 593 WRITINGS AND CRITICISM 595

THE COLLECTION OF TEN THOUSAND LEAVES (*Manyōshū*) (ca. Late 8th Century) 598

SEI SHŌNAGON (965?–1025?) 625
The Pillow Book (*Makura no Sōshi*) 626

TALES OF THE MIDDLE COUNSELOR OF THE EMBANKMENT (*Tsutsumi Chunagon Monogatari*) (ca. 794–1160) 659
The Lady Who Loved Worms (*Mushi Mezruru Himegimi*) 660

TALES OF THE HEIKE (*Heike Monogatari*) 668

KAMO-NO CHŌMEI (1153?–1216) 690
Life in a Ten-Foot-Square Hut (*Hōjōki*) 691

SIX NŌ PLAYS 702
ZEAMI MOTOKIYO (1363–1443) 702
Atsumori 706
The Deserted Crone (*Obasute*) 712
The Dwarf Trees (*Hachi no Ki*) 720
Komachi at Sekidera (*Sekidera Komachi*) (attributed to Zeami) 728
ZENCHIKU UJINOBU (1414–1499?)
Princess Hollyhock (*Aoi no Uye*) 737
KOMPARU ZEMBO MOTOYASU (1453–1532)
Early Snow (*Hatsuyuki*) 742

BASHŌ AND OTHERS 745
Twenty-five *Haiku* 747

CHIKAMATSU MONZAEMON (1653–1725) 753
The Courier for Hell (*Meido no Hikyaku*) 757

FOUR MODERN MASTERS OF FICTION 786
RYŪNOSUKE AKUTAGAWA (1892–1927)
Rashōmon 790
In a Grove (*Yabu no Naka*) 795
JUNICHIRO TANIZAKI (1886–1965)
The Tattooer 802
YASUNARI KAWABATA (1899–1972)
The Moon on the Water 807
YUKIO MISHIMA (1925–1970)
The Priest and His Love 815
GUIDE TO PRONUNCIATION 828
NOTE ON PROPER NAMES 831
BIBLIOGRAPHICAL NOTE 832
INDEX 833

Preface

This volume contains extracts from the literatures of Arabia, Persia, India, China, and Japan. Their standards are not our own, and the pleasure they give to us is often different from what we get from Western literature. The word "Orient" itself is a vague term, of use only for convenience. "East" would not be better: there is an Arab literature in Morocco, which is fifteen hundred miles west of Athens, and there is Western literature in Vladivostok, almost a thousand miles east of Peking. "Asiatic"— a word frowned upon by Asians as reflecting Western nineteenth-century attitudes towards the Orient—and "Asian" will not do; the literature of the Arabs has largely been produced in Africa, but for many centuries in Europe the Near East is the "Orient." So we fall back on the word "Oriental" as useful only in labeling major civilizations not in the Western tradition. It is a very old-fashioned word. The affinities of Arabic and Persian literature are with the West and not with their Eastern relatives, especially in the Middle Ages. Arabic and Persian literature, distinct from one another in significant ways, have little to do with Indian. The great bond of Buddhism connects India with the Far East, but Indian literature exhibits little similarity to Chinese or Japanese. Japanese literature and Japanese culture generally have systematically imitated Chinese, but the Japanese genius has everywhere put its own stamp on its borrowings, and it is doubtful that Japanese literature is any closer to Chinese than French is to classical Latin. These Oriental literatures have in general less in common with one another than do the European literatures, which have a common cultural ancestry. Limitations of space preclude any notice of two dozen or more other major literatures of the Orient—national literatures taught in universities and read by millions of people, such as the Korean, Mongolian, Thai, Burmese, Indonesian, Vietnamese, and others. Here scholarship is still sparse and translations few; there is a generation of work still to be done. For the literatures included here, there has been a great increase in available translations since the first edition of

1961, translations marked by both accuracy and felicity of language, and the general reader now has a small library, rather than a shelf, to supplement this volume of selections.

Readers will find in these selections, it is hoped, new insights into the human mind and spirit, and new aesthetic experiences. They will discover the delight in intricate language of the Arab and the stately splendor of Persian. In Indian literature they will find a pervasive religious element whether the work be gay or pathetic, heroic or realistic, tragic or comic. In Chinese literature they will experience the world's best amalgam of the didactic and the poetic. And in Japanese literature they will find a restless desire for novelty and change controlled by a powerful and instinctive sense of beauty. To gain an understanding of these literatures is to gain new worlds. To ignore them is to limit and make provincial our understanding of our own.

The translations are the best available. The transliteration systems used in the introductions and in my notes are intended to be consistent and represent systems commonly used by American Orientalists. However, I have thought it wise not to attempt to make changes in the alternate systems used by some of the translators. To do so would be the height of presumption for an amateur. The variety of systems presents no obstacle to the reader. The one exception to this principle is that I have replaced the accent (´) sometimes used to indicate a long vowel in Persian and Sanskrit and replaced it with the more common and more modern macron (–).

What critical acumen is displayed in this volume I owe to an acquaintance, now going back many years, with a number of American Orientalists who have talked to me not only about the literature itself but about the difficulties of presenting it to the general reader. These scholars have everywhere received me with hospitality, spent time on my problems, and endured my most ignorant questions with fortitude. To mention all of them by name would shed a luster on the collection that it may not merit, but without them I would indeed have walked in darkness. I would like to mention two, whose labors are done. The late W. Norman Brown seemed to me to be a sage when I was an undergraduate at the University of Pennsylvania and his career in Indic scholarship spanned decades after that. His advice was invaluable. The career of the late John Lyman Bishop of Harvard University was cut short, but not before he had made substantial contributions to the study of Chinese literature, especially fiction. I remember him as a pleasant companion, a precise scholar, and a subtle critic. I also express my appreciation to the others, whose work goes on, some of whom are represented by their translations below.

G. L. Anderson

Masterpieces of the Orient

The Near East

The literatures of the Arabs and the Persians, though welded into a common tradition by the lightning flash of Islam, have differing early traditions that are separately cherished and periodically revived. The Arab world before Islam is almost a *tabula rasa;* a single great work, the *Golden Odes* (*Mu'allaqāt*), survives. This collection and the highly poetic sacred book of the prophet Muhammad, the *Koran,* stand at the dawn of Arabic literature and enforce a reverence for the poet and the seer which the writer of prose never achieves. Persian literature, on the other hand, looks back on a history rivaling that of the Greek in antiquity. The Persian sees a heroic age, which he celebrates in epic, in the days when great kings and a widespread empire challenged European rule in the eastern Mediterranean. Just as the Greek knows that there were poets before Homer, so the Persian can postulate a literary past stretching far back into pre-Islamic times.

The Arabs leap into history. In less than two hundred years they grow from an obscure tribe in the wastes of South Arabia into an empire stretching from the frontiers of India to the Pyrenees. But this violent historical process does not provide the Arab with a literary past. Behind the glories of the Baghdad court of Hārūn-al-Rashīd lies, in the Arab imagination, the Bedouin or desert nomad, a hero closer to an American cowboy or a Gaucho than to a Homeric or a Persian warrior. The Persian can see the signs of a long and indefinite past carved on the rocks of his land. It is a land of barren plains and nomadic life, as is Arabia, but the Persian is aware of his ancestors and celebrates in literature bygone empires and the culture of cities.

After the advent of Islam, the Persian clung to his non-Moslem traditions, and the Arab, in the case of the *Golden Odes,* cherished his pre-Moslem ways. A flood of borrowings from Arabic into the Persian language and the mandate to read the Prophet in his own language succeeded to a certain extent in "Arabicizing" both the Persian language and Persian thought. The unifying influence of Islam is found most notably in poetry—both court poetry and an extensive tradition of mystical poetry—and in philosophical writing. Here the Persian and the Arab spirit meet, but Persian independence often vies with Arab orthodoxy in the interpretation of religious doctrine (the Sunnite, or orthodox sect, flourishes principally in the Arab lands; the Shi'ite, the largest rival sect, is centered in Iraq and Iran).

PERSIAN LITERATURE

The Persians speak a language that is basically Indo-European or Indo-Aryan. Old Persian, the most ancient form of the language, probably goes back to at least the sixth century B.C. The great king Darius about 500 B.C. describes himself as a Persian and an Aryan.[1] The earliest literary works are the sacred scriptures of the Zoroastrian religion (sixth century B.C.) in a form of Persian (or, more properly, Iranian) known as Avestan. Little is known of Zoroaster except through his religious doctrine, the most important aspect of which is a dualistic concept of deity—there is a god of good and a god of evil, of equal powers. The *Avesta* (still the sacred scripture of the Parsis, an Iranian group in India) is a most difficult book, and in it are imbedded some seventeen poems—the actual words of Zoroaster—known as *Gáthás*, which certainly rank among the world's most untranslatable poems. The narrative material in the *Avesta* is epical. There is evidence of much other writing in the epic form, though little has survived, either in the old language or in Pahlavi or Middle Persian (first to tenth centuries A.D.), but a lengthy epic tradition existed when Firdausi (see below) sat down to incorporate the entire legendary past of Iran into one monumental poem. Doubtless the onslaught of a new religion encouraged the Persians to neglect their Zoroastrian past. The modern Persian language dates from the Arab conquest in the seventh century A.D. Its towering monument is the *Book of Kings* (*Shāh-nāma*) of Firdausī, written in the early eleventh century. Fragments of early epics in verse and prose and later imitations are insignificant beside this work.

Lyric poetry is a major type in Persian literature. The mystical lyric is best exemplified in the work of the thirteenth-century poet Jalāl al-Dīn Rūmī. His *Mathnavī* (see below) is an exciting and difficult example of a strain of religious writing common to the Arab and Persian world. It is worth noting that almost all Near Eastern lyric poetry (including 'Umār Khayyām's, which we will come to, can be interpreted allegorically or symbolically for religious purposes, as can the *Song of Songs* in the Old Testament. Two better known Persian poets are sa'di (thirteenth century) and Hafiz (fourteenth century) (see below). 'Umar Khāyyām is not, we should note in passing, considered one of Persia's great poets; his fame in Persia is that of an astronomer. But his *Rubā'iyāt*, re-created by Edward FitzGerald in Victorian England, has given him fame in English-speaking lands. FitzGerald's quatrains are easy to remember, and 'Umar's "eat, drink and be merry" philosophy is appealing.

Prose is considered by the Persians a lower kind of litera-

1. "Aryan" here or "Indo-Aryan" is a designation for a language family and has no validity as an ethnic term.

ture. Collections of stories abound, and some of the stories in the *Arabian Nights* are clearly Persian in origin (Shahrāzād—Scheherazade—is a Persian name). A special kind of anecdotal and didactic prose is employed in various manuals of guidance for young princes. How *Princes Conduct Their Lives* (*Siyar al-mulūk*) is one of these works; it provides, as it were, a complete course in personal and public behavior for the young nobleman. Another such work is the *Mirror for Princes* (*Qābūs-nāma*), compiled by an aging warrior prince to instruct his son in every aspect of a nobleman's life, not excluding the ritual of the bath, sexual etiquette, and hunting and gambling techniques.

Persian literature underwent many centuries of decline from its great days. The classical mode in poetry became fossilized, and lasted, without vitality, at least to the end of the nineteenth century. Today there are stirrings of a revival among young Persian intellectuals who read Western literature, but activity so far has been limited.

ARABIC LITERATURE

The *Golden Odes* (*Mu'allaqāt*) of pre-Islamic Arabic (see below) has already been mentioned. The odes are the epic lays of the Bedouin tribes that existed in loosely organized confederations in the Arabian peninsula before Muhammad gave these tribes a common and dynamic religion and a missionary purpose. Though these odes have always been cherished by the Arabs and have had great appeal for the Westerner, in an orthodox sense Arabic literature starts with the *Koran* (*Qur'ān*), the book of the Prophet, the text of which was standardized in 646 A.D. by the third caliph, 'Uthman. Perhaps uniquely among the sacred books of the world's great religions, the text of the *Koran* was established with a finality that modern philologists have not been able to disturb (all variant versions were destroyed), and, more importantly, the *Koran* represents the actual words of the Prophet, not his thought as set down by others. These factors have tended to put great stress on the actual language of the *Koran*: on the one hand, grammatical and lexicographical studies abound in Arab scholarship; on the other hand, the acceptance and preservation of classical Arabic as a national language was greatly encouraged by the desire to use and to preserve the actual idiom of the Prophet. To this day it is of religious value to the traditionally educated Arab to be able to recite verses from the *Koran* in classical Arabic even if he is uncertain of their meaning. Next to the *Koran*, the traditions (*hadith*) concerning the life of Muhammad and the application of the religion and philosophy of Islam to practical affairs are what the orthodox would consider to be Arabic "literature." Belles-lettres, in the narrowest Western sense of the term, are not and cannot be on a par with these other kinds of written composition.

Of the main literary types only poetry has been able to hold its head high in the Arab world. The lengthy ode (*qasīda*), simple in syntax but rich in language, persists in the literature, from the *Golden Odes* almost to the present. Variations of it, occasionally deliberately archaic in language, are used by later poets (ca. 800–1300 A.D.). The difficulty of translation into English is acute. To translate adequately the bitterly philosophical al-Ma'arrī (973–1057) G. M. Wickens says, ". . . would need the joint services of Swift and Pope, with the carefully controlled intervention of Ezra Pound."[2] Abū Nuwās (756?–?810), immortalized in the *Arabian Nights*, is perhaps easier to translate than either al-Ma'arrī or al-Mutanabbi (915–965), who is considered by many to be the greatest of the Arab lyric poets.

Drama was unknown in the Arab world until recent times, though there is now both theater and a flourishing cinema; and fiction, always the entertainment of the masses, was not considered respectable for the educated until Western admiration for such collections as the *Arabian Nights* won them a hearing. History and travel writing, on the other hand, were raised to a literary level. There is a brilliant historian and historiographer in Ibn Khaldun (1332–1406). Of more belletristic interest is the essay or epistle (*risāla*). Originating as a letter, the form became fixed, and a premium was put, as in poetic composition, on literary virtuosity. The poet al-Ma'arrī will serve as a representative author in this genre.

In the twentieth century the Arabic world has been beset both by local problems which affect literature and also by all the ills of the modern world. One of these is the problem of language—what kind of Arabic to use. The classical language is much revered, but it is argued by some that it is not suited for the modern world. If a modern dialect is to be used, Cairene, Moroccan, Syriac, and Iraqi all compete for the reader's mind. The literature has been assaulted by Western models from Ibsen and Maupassant to Sartre. The Arab-Israeli conflict and the ideological conflict between Western European ideas and Soviet Marxism has made much modern Arab writing either polemical or romantic and totally disengaged, and little has been translated into English. Tāhā Hussein's writings (see below) have received as much respect and admiration as those of any other Arab author.

2. *Literatures of the East,* edited by E. B. Ceadel, 1959, p. 37.

WRITINGS AND CRITICISM

The date of the latest edition or reprint is given. The place is New York unless otherwise indicated.

The cultural background of Arabic and Persian literature may be found in T. W. Arnold and A. Guillaume's *The Legacy of Islam* (Oxford, 1931), G. E. von Grunebaum's *Medieval Islam: A Study in Cultural Orientation* (Chicago, 2nd ed., 1953), and Carl Brockelmann's *History of the Islamic Peoples* (1947). A great deal of material is made available in Eric Schroeder's anthology *Muhammad's People* (Freeport, Maine, 1954), and with introductions and notes in Marshall G. S. Hodgson's *Islamic Civilization* (3 vols., Chicago, 1958–1959). The history of the Arabs is well surveyed by Philip K. Hitti in *The Arabs: A Short History* (1948) and in his more detailed *History of the Arabs* (5th ed. rev. 1951). Percy M. Sykes's *History of Persia* (2 vols., London, 1915) is recommended, as is also *The Legacy of Persia,* edited by A. J. Arberry (Oxford, 1953). Much valuable material on specific writers, literary forms, and religious and historical matters is contained in the *Encyclopaedia of Islam* (4 vols. and supplements, London, 1913–

1938), of which a new edition has begun to appear. R. A. Nicholson's *Translations of Eastern Poetry and Prose* (Cambridge, 1922) contains both Persian and Arabic writings.

Arabic Literature

A good, brief introduction is G. M. Wickens' "Arabic Literature," pp. 22–49 in *Literatures of the East,* ed. E. B. Ceadel (1959). H. A. R. Gibb has a short history, *Arabic Literature* (rev. ed., 1963). An extensive treatment is R. A. Nicholson's *Literary History of the Arabs* (1907). The general nature of Arabic literature is discussed in G. E. von Grunebaum's "The Aesthetic Foundations of Arabic Literature," *Comparative Literature,* IV (1952), 323–340. For anthologies see James Kritzeck's *Anthology of Islamic Literature* (1964), which contains both Arabic and Persian material, R. A. Nicholson's *Translations of Eastern Poetry and Prose* (1922), and Herbert Howarth and Ibrahim Shukrallah's *Images from the Arab World* (1944).

For a first reading of the *Koran* (*Qur'ān*), A. J. Arberry's *The Holy Koran, an Introduction with Selections* (1953), or the older translation of J. M. Rodwell (Everyman's Library) is satisfactory. Rodwell rearranges the *suras,* however, in their probable chronological order. An excellent translation is that of Richard Bell (2 vols., 1937–39). Other useful translations include N. J. Dawood (1956) and Marmaduke Pickthall's *The Meaning of the Glorious Koran,* a free interpretation by a Moslem (1953). For comment see Arthur Jeffrey's "The *Qur'ān,*" pp. 49–61 in *Approaches to the Oriental Classics,* ed. W. T. deBary (1959) and *The Koran Interpreted* by A. J. Arberry (1964), perhaps the best scholarly translation. George Sale's literal translation (1734, often reprinted) is still valuable as a very orthodox interpretation.

The nature of Arabic poetry is well analyzed in G. E. von Grunebaum's "Arabic Poetics," pp. 27–46 in *Papers of the Indiana Conference on Oriental-Western Literary Relations,* ed. Horst Frenz and G. L. Anderson (1955), and in R. B. Serjeant, "Arabic Poetry," pp. 42–47 in *Encyclopedia of Poetry and Poetics* (1965). For the *Golden Odes,* see below. A general anthology of poetry is Charles J. Lyall, *Translations of Ancient Arabian Poetry* (1930). A considerable part of a mystical poetic work (the *Poem of the Way* of Ibn-al-Fārid) has been translated by A. J. Arberry (1952). See also "The Response to Nature in Arabic Poetry" by G. E. von Grunebaum, *Journal of Near Eastern Studies,* IV (1945), 137–151.

For Arabic prose, Ibn Battūta's *Travels in Asia and Africa,* translated by H. A. R. Gibb (1929), and Ibn Khaldūn's *The Muqaddimah: An Introduction to History* (3 vols., 1958; Bollingen Series, XLIII) translated by Franz Rosenthal, especially the "Prolegomena," are important works of interest to Westerners. Al-Ma'arrī's *Letters* have been translated by D. S. Margoliouth (1898). A delightful treatise on Platonic love is Ibn Hazm's *The Ring of the Dove,* translated by A. J. Arberry (1953). Versions of the *Arabian Nights* are numerous. The old one of Edward Lane is still serviceable. Sir Richard Burton's, especially in the editions which contain his notes, is an encyclopedia of Arab lore. Selections have been done by A. J. Arberry, N. J. Dawood, and Joseph Campbell. A succinct account of the background of the *Nights* may be found in the *Encyclopaedia of Islam;* a more detailed study is M. I. Gerhardt's *The Art of Story Telling: A Literary Study of the Thousand and One Nights* (1963).

Modern Arabic literature is discussed in A. Abdel-Meguid, *The Modern Arabic Short Story* (n.d. [1955?]); P. J. E. Cachia, "Modern Arabic Literature," in *The Islamic Near East,* ed. D. Grant (1960); A. J. K. Germanus, "Trends of Contemporary Arabic Literature," *Islamic Quarterly,* III (1956) and IV (1957); and, for the early twentieth century, H. A. R. Gibb in his *Studies on the Civilization of Islam* (London, 1962). The *Atlantic Monthly* supplement on the Arabs (October, 1956) is useful. Twentieth-century Arabic poetry is translated by A. J. Arberry in *Modern Arabic Poetry: An Anthology with English Verse Translations* (1950). Taufīq al-Hakīm's *Maze of Justice,* translated by A. S. Eban (1947), is an important modern work, as are various volumes by J. K. Jibrān (Kahlil Gibran): *Nymphs of the Valley* (1948), *Spirits Rebellious* (1949), and *A Tear and a Smile* (1950), all translated by H. M. Nahmad. See also Jacob M. Landau, *Studies in the Arab Theatre and Cinema* (1958). For Tāhā Hussein, see below.

For general bibliographical aids see the Bibliographic Note at the end of this book.

Persian Literature

The pre-Islamic period is well but briefly surveyed in I. Gershevitch's "Iranian Literature," pp. 50–73, and the Moslem period in Reuben Levy's "Persian Literature," pp. 74–96 in *Literatures of the East,* edited by E. B. Ceadel (1959). A short history is Levy's *Persian Literature: An Introduction* (1923) and his somewhat longer critical account in *An Introduction to Persian Literature* (1969). A lengthy recent history which includes the other Iranian literatures as well as Persian is Jan Rypka's *History of Iranian Literature* (1968). This has an excellent bibliography. A. J. Arberry's *Classical Persian Literature* (1958) covers the great period (down to 1492) and is rich in critical comment. An extensive history is E. G. Browne's *Literary History of Persia* (4 vols., rev. ed., 1928). See also M. Farzad, *The Main Currents in Persian Literature* (1965), and C. A. Storey, *Persian Literature* (5 parts, 1927–1953). For the poets Rūmī, Sa'di, and Hāfiz, see below. FitzGerald's famous version of the *Rubā'iyāt* of 'Umār Khayyam is widely available: the edition of E. Heron-Allen (1899) gives literal translations from the Persian along with FitzGerald's renderings. Arberry has translated the quatrains in *Omar Khayyám: A New Version Based on Recent Discoveries* (1952). Persian tales are translated by Reuben Levy in *The Three Dervishes and Other Persian Tales and Legends* (1928). Levy has done the *Qābūs-nāma* as *A Mirror for Princes* (1951). For a description of Persian poetics see A. J. Arberry, "Persian Poetry," pp. 609–612 in *Encyclopedia of Poetry and Poetics* (1965).

Modern Persian literature has been little translated into English. Studies include A. J. Arberry, "Modern Persian Poetry," *Life and Letters* (December 1949); P. W. Avery, "Developments in Modern Prose," *Muslim World*, XLV (1955), 313–323; M. Ishaque, *Modern Persian Poetry* (Calcutta, 1943); H. Kamshad, *Modern Persian Prose Literature* (1966); D. G. Law, "Modern Persian Prose," *Life and Letters* (December, 1949); R. Mostafavi, "Fiction in Contemporary Persian Literature," *Middle East Affairs*, II (1951), 273–279; S. R. Shafaq, "Patriotic Poetry in Modern Iran," *Middle East Journal*, VI (1952), 417–428; and Mansour Shaki, "An Introduction to Modern Persian Literature," pp. 300–315 in *Charisteria Orientalia*, edited by Felix Tauer and others (1956). Rypka (cited above) covers the modern period.

For general bibliographical aids see the Bibliographic Note at the end of this book.

THE GOLDEN ODES. There is an elaborate critical commentary in Arberry's translation (cited below). See also Francesco Gabrieli, "Ancient Arabic Poetry," *Diogenes*, No. 40 (Winter 1962), 82–95. Anne and Wilfred S. Blount's *The Seven Golden Odes of Pagan Arabia* is still attractive as a literary rendering.

FIRDAUSĪ. Theodor Noldeke's *The Iranian National Epic, or the Shahnamah*, translated by L. Bogdanov (1930), although somewhat outdated, is still very useful. See also G. E. von Grunebaum's "Firdausī's Concept of History," pp. 168–184 in *Islamic Essays in the Nature and Growth of a Cultural Tradition* (1955). A good verse translation of the epic is by A. G. Warner and E. Warner (1926).

RŪMĪ. For criticism see the introduction to Nicholson's translation (cited below), A. J. Arberry, *Tales from the Mathnavi* (1961), and the complete translation with commentary by R. A. Nicholson, *The Mathnawi* (1925–1940).

SA'DĪ. For criticism see G. M. Wilkins' introduction to Rehatsek's translation (cited below). Other translations include *Būstān*, translated by C. S. Davie (1882); *Stories from the Bustan*, translated by Reuben Levy (1928); and *Kings and Beggars* (*Gulistān*, Chapters I and II), translated by A. J. Arberry (1945).

HĀFIZ. See the Introduction to Arberry's translation (cited below) and to P. Avery and J. Heath-Stubbs' *Hafiz of Shiraz* (1952; Wisdom of the East Series). Gertrude Bell's *Poems from the Divan of Hafiz* is a sensitive poetic rendering, first published in 1897.

TĀHĀ HUSSEIN (or HUSAYN). His *An Egyptian Childhood* has been translated by E. H. Paxton (1932). See the general studies listed above and P. Cachia, *Tāhā Huseyn* (1956).

The Golden Odes (*Mu'allaqāt*)

"A poet was a defence of their honour, a protection for their good repute; he immortalized their deeds of glory, and published their eternal fame. On three things they congratulated one another—the birth of a boy, the emergence of a poet in their midst, or the foaling of a mare." So writes Ibn Rashīq of Kairouan, an eleventh-century Arab writer, of the position of the poet in the nomadic society of the early Arab world.[1] *The Golden Odes* are the only important survivals of what must have been a considerable oral literature among the Bedouin tribes of the Arabian Desert during the sixth century A.D. They are the literary expression of a world of marches across arid wastes (more like the drier areas of the American West than the Sahara) from one water hole to another. They celebrate war and women, endurance and a life of austerity. They left a sentimental legacy in the Arab world similar to the idealization, among Jews and Christians, of the days of Abraham. The harsh, primitive world of the nomad stood in sharp contrast to the opulence of the courts of David and Solomon or of Harun-al-Rashid of the *Arabian Nights*, and to the complexities of urban life—the life of the ghetto Jews and of the Arab *fallahin*, or city dwellers.

The word *mu'allaqāt* had by the tenth century come to mean "suspended poems." The legend was that the prize-winning poems of competing poets were inscribed in letters of gold and suspended in the Kaaba, the most sacred of the Moslem shrines in Mecca. This is probably fanciful; likelier translations include "transcribed (i.e., written down) odes," "precious odes," "separated (from anthologies) odes," or something similar, but no agreement has been reached by modern scholars on the translation of the term. What is clear is that immediately after the advent of Muhammad and the fixing of the *Koran* in its final form after his death, efforts were made to collect the poetry of pre-Islamic Arabia. Working somewhat in the manner of present-day folk collectors, early Arab scholars attempted to get from the poets themselves or from professional reciters the works (*diwan* or *díván*) of the various Bedouin poets. An interest in genealogy—the desire to find illustrious ancestors—certainly stimulated the search.

The form of the ancient ode (*qasīda*) was conventionalized both in meter and in content. The poem was supposed to be of substantial length (as against many later short lyrics by Arab poets), with perhaps sixty couplets following an identical rhyme. A choice of meter was available, but, having committed himself, the poet was expected to stick to one meter. The subject matter was prescribed, and nearly all of the proper subjects were likely to appear in one ode: the nomadic life contrasted with that of the town; the passions of physical love; the extremes of physical

1. A. J. Arberry, *The Seven Odes* (New York, 1957), p. 14.

experience in the desert—cold, heat, rain, dryness, thirst, feast and famine, and danger from enemies—and the hope of receiving recognition from a patron for the poem.

The locale of the poems is southern Arabia. The place names are vague and can be conceived of as mere water holes—a few trees clustered around a well. At the time of the composing of the odes, the Byzantine Empire and Persia contested the area between present-day Baghdad and Damascus. A line drawn at the midpoint of a line between these cities brings us down to more and more remote and difficult country (the "Empty Quarter") until the desert is somewhat relieved by Yeman and Aden on the Gulf of Aden. Sometimes the Bedouin served as a vassal of Constantinople, of Ctesiphon, or of other powers infiltrating northern Arabia. Sometimes he formed alliances with other tribes. But his horizon was limited to his tribe, and into his *Mu'allaqāt* went the joys and sorrows of the tribe, and also its history.

"The Wandering King" (the English titles are the translator's) or "Ode of Imru'-al-Qays" is the poem of an unruly poet-warrior who was approached by the Byzantine king Justinian to fight against Persia and on whose shoulders fell the duty of avenging his father's death in a tribal conflict—if all of the legend is not a fiction. In any case, there is little historical material in the poem, and Imr al-Qais emerges mostly as a frontier Don Juan, sensual and indiscreet in his boasting, even by heroic standards. Tarafa's ode ("Whom the Gods Loved?") is the most casually constructed of the four printed below. The legend of his death is well known in the Arab world. He is said to have been sent with a letter from his king to a provincial governor. His traveling companion grew suspicious of the king, and, opening his letter, found that it contained instructions that they both were to be put to death. Tarafa, even on the strength of this warning, refused to violate his trust, and was put to death on his arrival. There is no proof of the truth of this legend, but it adds color to his rambling, meditative ode.

Abū 'Aqil Labīd's ode ("The Centenarian") is a love elegy, of the kind that made Sir William Jones, the eighteenth-century English orientalist, see parallels between the seven odes and the Western tradition of the pastoral. The poet laments his fruitless love, takes a long journey to forget, then returns and greets the indifference of the loved one with equal indifference. War and the desert journey are likely to take an equal place with love in the reader's mind. 'Antara, the author of "The Black Knight," if the facts are authentic, was a mulatto son of an Arab prince and a Negro slave girl from Abyssinia. His "inferior" blood kept his father from recognizing him as legitimate. In a fierce battle, his father ordered him to fight, but he refused, saying that it was not proper for a slave to fight. His father then freed him on the field, and he fought valorously. His ode is the most powerful expression of the savagery of desert battles that has survived from pre-Islamic times.

From The Golden Odes*

The Wandering King

(*Mu'allaqa of Imru'-al-Qays*)

Halt, friends both! Let us weep, recalling a love and a lodging
by the rim of the twisted sands between Ed-Dakhool and
    Haumal,
Toodih and El-Mikrât, whose trace is not yet effaced
for all the spinning of the south winds and the northern blasts;
there, all about its yards, and away in the dry hollows
you may see the dung of antelopes spattered like peppercorns.
Upon the morn of separation, the day they loaded to part,
by the tribe's acacias it was like I was splitting a colocynth;
there my companions halted their beasts awhile over me
saying, 'Don't perish of sorrow; restrain yourself decently!'
Yet the true and only cure of my grief is tears outpoured:
what is there left to lean on where the trace is obliterated?

* These four odes are from *The Seven Odes: The First Chapter in Arabic Literature* by A. J. Arberry. Translated by A. J. Arberry. Copyright by Allen & Unwin Ltd. Reprinted by permission.

2–3. *Ed-Dakhool . . . El-Mikrat:* the geography of the poem is vague. The Bedouin tribes ranged all over South Arabia. A line drawn between Bahrein, on the Persian Gulf, and Hodeida, in Yemen, separates the desert of the Bedouins with its oases and wadis from Rub'al-Khali, the "Empty Quarter," into which few men have ever ventured.

8. *colocynth:* a bitter, hard, orange-like fruit.

Even so, my soul, is your wont; so it was with Umm al-Huwairith
before her, and Umm ar-Rabát her neighbour, at Ma'sal;
when they arose, the subtle musk wafted from them
sweet as the zephyr's breath that bears the fragrance of cloves.
Then my eyes overflowed with tears of passionate yearning
upon my throat, till my tears drenched even my sword's harness.

Oh yes, many a fine day I've dallied with the white ladies,
and especially I call to mind a day at Dára Juljul,
and the day I slaughtered for the virgins my riding-beast
(and oh, how marvellous was the dividing of its loaded saddle),
and the virgins went on tossing its hacked flesh about
and the frilly fat like fringes of twisted silk.
Yes, and the day I entered the litter where Unaiza was
and she cried, 'Out on you! Will you make me walk on my feet?'
She was saying, while the canopy swayed with the pair of us,
'There now, you've hocked my camel, Imr al-Kais. Down with you!'
But I said, 'Ride on, and slacken the beast's reins,
and oh, don't drive me away from your refreshing fruit.
Many's the pregnant woman like you, aye, and the nursing mother
I've night-visited, and made her forget her amuleted one-year-old;
whenever he whimpered behind her, she turned to him
with half her body, her other half unshifted under me.'

Ha, and a day on the back of the sand-hill she denied me
swearing a solemn oath that should never, never be broken.
'Gently now, Fátima! A little less disdainful:
even if you intend to break with me, do it kindly.
If it's some habit of mine that's so much vexed you
just draw off my garments from yours, and they'll slip away.
Puffed-up it is it's made you, that my love for you's killing me
and that whatever you order my heart to do, it obeys.
Your eyes only shed those tears so as to strike and pierce
with those two shafts of theirs the fragments of a ruined heart.
Many's the fair veiled lady, whose tent few would think of seeking,

13–14. *Umm al-Huwairith . . . Umm ar-Rabat:* women whom Imru'-al-Qays has loved.
25. *Unaiza:* I'mru'al-Qays's cousin, whom he wooed for a time.
35–37. *Ha . . . Fatima!:* He boasts of having seduced the lady Fatima of the Banu'Udhra, a tribe noted for its puritanical moral code.

I've enjoyed sporting with, and not in a hurry either,
slipping past packs of watchmen to reach her, with a whole tribe
hankering after my blood, eager every man-jack to slay me,
what time the Pleiades showed themselves broadly in heaven
glittering like the folds of a woman's bejewelled scarf.
I came, and already she'd stripped off her garments for sleep
beside the tent-flap, all but a single flimsy slip;
and she cried, "God's oath, man, you won't get away with this!
The folly's not left you yet; I see you're as feckless as ever."
Out I brought her, and as she stepped she trailed behind us
to cover our footprints the skirt of an embroidered gown.
But when we had crossed the tribe's enclosure, and dark about us
hung a convenient shallow intricately undulant,
I twisted her side-tresses to me, and she leaned over me;
slender-waisted she was, and tenderly plump her ankles,
shapely and taut her belly, white-fleshed, not the least flabby,
polished the lie of her breast-bones, smooth as a burnished mirror.
She turns away, to show a soft cheek, and wards me off
with the glance of a wild deer of Wajra, a shy gazelle with its fawn;
she shows me a throat like the throat of an antelope, not ungainly
when she lifts it upwards, neither naked of ornament;
she shows me her thick black tresses, a dark embellishment
clustering down her back like bunches of a laden date-tree—
twisted upwards meanwhile are the locks that ring her brow,
the knots cunningly lost in the plaited and loosened strands;
she shows me a waist slender and slight as a camel's nose-rein,
and a smooth shank like the reed of a watered, bent papyrus.
In the morning the grains of musk hang over her couch,
sleeping the forenoon through, not girded and aproned to labour.
She gives with fingers delicate, not coarse; you might say
they are sand-worms of Zaby, or tooth-sticks of ishil-wood.
At eventide she lightens the black shadows, as if she were
the lamp kindled in the night of a monk at his devotions.
Upon the like of her the prudent man will gaze with ardour
eyeing her slim, upstanding, frocked midway between matron and maiden;
like the first egg of the ostrich—its whiteness mingled with yellow—

47–48. *slipping . . . me:* Like his nomadic counterpart, the American Indian, the Bedouin prided himself on his ability to steal into the enemy's camp.

nurtured on water pure, unsullied by many paddlers.
Let the follies of other men forswear fond passion,
my heart forswears not, nor will forget the love I bear you.
Many's the stubborn foe on your account I've turned and thwarted
sincere though he was in his reproaches, not negligent.'

Oft night like a sea swarming has dropped its curtains
over me, thick with multifarious cares, to try me,
and I said to the night, when it stretched its lazy loins
followed by its fat buttocks, and heaved off its heavy breast,
'Well now, you tedious night, won't you clear yourself off, and let
dawn shine? Yet dawn, when it comes, is no way better than you.
Oh, what a night of a night you are! It's as though the stars
were tied to the Mount of Yadhbul with infinite hempen ropes;
as though the Pleiades in their stable were firmly hung
by stout flax cables to craggy slabs of granite.'

Many's the water-skin of all sorts of folk I have slung
by its strap over my shoulder, as humble as can be, and humped it;
many's the valley, bare as an ass's belly, I've crossed,
a valley loud with the wolf howling like a many-bairned wastrel
to which, howling, I've cried, 'Well, wolf, that's a pair of us,
pretty unprosperous both, if you're out of funds like me.
It's the same with us both—whenever we get aught into our hands
we let it slip through our fingers; tillers of our tilth go pretty thin.'
Often I've been off with the morn, the birds yet asleep in their nests,
my horse short-haired, outstripping the wild game, huge-bodied,
charging, fleet-fleeing, head-foremost, headlong, all together
the match of a rugged boulder hurled from on high by the torrent,
a gay bay, sliding the saddle-felt from his back's thwart
just as a smooth pebble slides off the rain cascading.
Fiery he is, for all his leanness, and when his ardour
boils in him, how he roars—a bubbling cauldron isn't in it!
Sweetly he flows, when the mares floundering wearily
kick up the dust where their hooves drag in the trampled track;

100. *many-bairned:* A bairn is a child.

the lightweight lad slips landward from his smooth back,
he flings off the burnous of the hard, heavy rider;
very swift he is, like the toy spinner a boy will whirl
plying it with his nimble hands by the knotted thread.
His flanks are the flanks of a fawn, his legs like an ostrich's;
the springy trot of the wolf he has, the fox's gallop;
sturdy his body—look from behind, and he bars his legs' gap
with a full tail, not askew, reaching almost to the ground;
his back, as he stands beside the tent, seems the pounding-slab
of a bride's perfumes, or the smooth stone a colocynth's
broken on;
the blood of the herd's leaders spatters his thrusting neck
like expressed tincture of henna reddening combed white locks.
A flock presented itself to us, the cows among them
like Duwár virgins mantled in their long-trailing draperies;
turning to flee, they were beads of Yemen spaced with cowries
hung on a boy's neck, he nobly uncled in the clan.
My charger thrust me among the leaders, and way behind him
huddled the stragglers herded together, not scattering;
at one bound he had taken a bull and a cow together
pouncing suddenly, and not a drop of sweat on his body.
Busy then were the cooks, some roasting upon a fire
the grilled slices, some stirring the hasty stew.
Then with the eve we returned, the appraising eye bedazzled
to take in his beauty, looking him eagerly up and down;
all through the night he stood with saddle and bridle upon him,
stood where my eyes could see him, not loose to his will.
Friend, do you see yonder lightning? Look, there goes its glitter
flashing like two hands now in the heaped-up, crowned
stormcloud.
Brilliantly it shines—so flames the lamp of an anchorite
as he slops the oil over the twisted wick.
So with my companions I sat watching it between Dárij
and El-Odheib, far-ranging my anxious gaze;
over Katan, so we guessed, hovered the right of its deluge,
its left dropping upon Es-Sitár and further Yadhbul.
Then the cloud started loosing its torrent about Kutaifa
turning upon their beards the boles of the tall kanahbals;
over the hills of El-Kanán swept its flying spray
sending the white wild goats hurtling down on all sides.
At Taimá it left not one trunk of a date-tree standing,

116. *burnous:* a mantle or cloak with a hood.
126. *expressed:* pressed out.
129. *Yemen:* Imr al-Qais was once exiled to Yemen. *cowries:* shells.
150. *boles:* trunks.
153. *Taima*: Taima, if it is the same place, is about 250 miles directly west of the tip of the Sinai Peninsula. There are numerous low mountains here and all the way down the coast to Yemen.

not a solitary fort, save those buttressed with hard rocks;
and Thabeer—why, when the first onrush of its deluge came
Thabeer was a great chieftain wrapped in a striped jubba.
In the morning the topmost peak of El-Mujaimir
was a spindle's whorl cluttered with all the scum of the torrent;
it had flung over the desert of El-Ghabeet its cargo
like a Yemeni merchant unpacking his laden bags.
In the morning the songbirds all along the broad valley
quaffed the choicest of sweet wines rich with spices;
the wild beasts at evening drowned in the furthest reaches
of the wide watercourse lay like drawn bulbs of wild onion.

Whom the Gods Loved?

(*Mu'allaqa of Tarafa*)

There are traces yet of Khaula in the stony tract of Thahmad
apparent like the tattoo-marks seen on the back of a hand;
there my companions halted their beasts awhile over me
saying, 'Don't perish of sorrow; bear it with fortitude!'
The litters of the Máliki camels that morn in the broad
watercourse of Wadi Dad were like great schooners
from Adauli, or the vessels of Ibn-i Yámin
their mariners steer now tack by tack, now straight forward;
their prows cleave the streaks of the rippling water
just as a boy playing will scoop the sand into parcels.

A young gazelle there is in the tribe, dark-lipped, fruit-shaking,
flaunting a double necklace of pearls and topazes,
holding aloof, with the herd grazing in the lush thicket,
nibbling the tips of the arak-fruit, wrapped in her cloak.
Her dark lips part in a smile, teeth like a camomile
on a moist hillock shining amid the virgin sands,
whitened as it were by the sun's rays, all but her gums
that are smeared with collyrium—she gnaws not against them;
a face as though the sun had loosed his mantle upon it,
pure of hue, with not a wrinkle to mar it.

Ah, but when grief assails me, straightway I ride it off
mounted on my swift, lean-flanked camel, night and day racing,
sure-footed, like the planks of a litter; I urge her on
down the bright highway, that back of a striped mantle;
she vies with the noble, hot-paced she-camels, shank on shank

1. *Khaula:* his youthful love. *Thahmad:* Many place names throughout are unidentifiable.

15. *camomile:* a plant with very white flowers.

18. *collyrium:* a whitish medicinal salve.

nimbly plying, over a path many feet have beaten.
Along the rough slopes with the milkless shes she has pastured
in Spring, cropping the rich meadows green in the gentle rains;
to the voice of the caller she returns, and stands on guard
with her bunchy tail, scared of some ruddy, tuft-haired stallion,
as though the wings of a white vulture enfolded the sides
of her tail, pierced even to the bone by a pricking awl;
anon she strikes with it behind the rear-rider, anon
lashes her dry udders, withered like an old water-skin.
Perfectly firm is the flesh of her two thighs—
they are the gates of a lofty, smooth-walled castle—
and tightly knit are her spine-bones, the ribs like bows,
her underneck stuck with the well-strung vertebrae,
fenced about by the twin dens of a wild lote-tree;
you might say bows were bent under a buttressed spine.
Widely spaced are her elbows, as if she strode
carrying the two buckets of a sturdy water-carrier;
like the bridge of the Byzantine, whose builder swore
it should be all encased in bricks to be raised up true.
Reddish the bristles under her chin, very firm her back,
broad the span of her swift legs, smooth her swinging gait;
her legs are twined like rope uptwisted; her forearms
thrust slantwise up to the propped roof of her breast.
Swiftly she rolls, her cranium huge, her shoulder-blades
high-hoisted to frame her lofty, raised superstructure.
The scores of her girths chafing her breast-ribs are water-
courses
furrowing a smooth rock in a rugged eminence,
now meeting, anon parting, as though they were
white gores marking distinctly a slit shirt.
Her long neck is very erect when she lifts it up
calling to mind the rudder of a Tigris-bound vessel.
Her skull is most like an anvil, the junction of its two halves
meeting together as it might be on the edge of a file.
Her cheek is smooth as Syrian parchment, her split lip
a tanned hide of Yemen, its slit not bent crooked;
her eyes are a pair of mirrors, sheltering
in the caves of her brow-bones, the rock of a pool's hollow,
ever expelling the white pus mote-provoked, so they seem
like the dark-rimmed eyes of a scared wild-cow with calf.
Her ears are true, clearly detecting on the night journey
the fearful rustle of a whisper, the high-pitched cry,
sharp-tipped, her noble pedigree plain in them,

56. *Tigris-bound:* The Tigris flows through Iraq, emptying into the Persian Gulf near Basra. Southeast of Basra, in the gulf, is Bahrein, to which Tarafa was sent by his king to be treacherously slain.

pricked like the ears of a wild-cow of Haumal lone-pasturing.
Her trepid heart pulses strongly, quick, yet firm
as a pounding-rock set in the midst of a solid boulder.
If you so wish, her head strains to the saddle's pommel
and she swims with her forearms, fleet as a male ostrich,
or if you wish her pace is slack, or swift to your fancy
fearing the curled whip fashioned of twisted hide.
Slit is her upper lip, her nose bored and sensitive,
delicate; when she sweeps the ground with it, faster she runs.

Such is the beast I ride, when my companion cries
'Would I might ransom you, and be ransomed, from yonder
    waste!'
His soul flutters within him fearfully, he supposing
the blow fallen on him, though his path is no ambuscade.
When the people demand, 'Who's the hero?' I suppose
myself intended, and am not sluggish, not dull of wit;
I am at her with the whip, and my she-camel quickens pace
what time the mirage of the burning stone-tract shimmers;
elegantly she steps, as a slave-girl at a party
will sway, showing her master skirts of a trailing white gown.
I am not one that skulks fearfully among the hilltops,
but when the folk seek my succour I gladly give it;
if you look for me in the circle of the folk you'll find me there,
and if you hunt me in the taverns there you'll catch me.
Come to me when you will, I'll pour you a flowing cup,
and if you don't need it, well, do without and good luck to
    you!
Whenever the tribe is assembled you'll come upon me
at the summit of the noble House, the oft-frequented;
my boon-companions are white as stars, and a singing-wench
comes to us in her striped gown or her saffron robe,
wide the opening of her collar, delicate her skin
to my companions' fingers, tender her nakedness.
When we say, 'Let's hear from you,' she advances to us
chanting fluently, her glance languid, in effortless song.

Unceasingly I tippled the wine and took my joy,
unceasingly I sold and squandered my hoard and my patrimony
till all my family deserted me, every one of them,
and I sat alone like a lonely camel scabby with mange;
yet I saw the sons of the dust did not deny me
nor the grand ones who dwell in those fine, wide-spread tents.
So now then, you who revile me because I attend the wars

69. *trepid:* intrepid.

and partake in all pleasures, can you keep me alive forever?
If you can't avert from me the fate that surely awaits me
then pray leave me to hasten it on with what money I've got.
But for three things, that are the joy of a young fellow,
I assure you I wouldn't care when my deathbed visitors arrive—
first, to forestall my charming critics with a good swig
of crimson wine that foams when the water is mingled in;
second, to wheel at the call of the beleaguered a curved-
shanked steed
streaking like the wolf of the thicket you've startled lapping
the water;
and third, to curtail the day of showers, such an admirable
season,
dallying with a ripe wench under the pole-propped tent,
her anklets and her bracelets seemingly hung on the boughs
of a pliant, unriven gum-tree or a castor-shrub.
So permit me to drench my head while there's still life in it,
for I tremble at the thought of the scant draught I'll get when
I'm dead.
I'm a generous fellow, one that soaks himself in his lifetime;
you'll know to-morrow, when we're dead, which of us is the
thirsty one.
To my eyes the grave of the niggardly who's mean with his
money
is one with the wastrel's who's squandered his substance in
idleness;
all you can see is a couple of heaps of dust, and on them
slabs of granite, flat stones piled shoulder to shoulder.

I see Death chooses the generous folk, and takes for his own
the most prized belonging of the parsimonious skinflint;
I see Life is a treasure diminishing every night,
and all that the days and Time diminish ceases at last.
By your sweet life, though Death may miss a lad for the nonce
he's like a loosened lasso, whose loops are firmly in hand.

How is it with me, that I observe my cousin Malik,
whenever I approach him, sheers off and keeps his distance?
He scolds me—and I haven't a clue as to why he should—
just the way Kurt, A'bad's son, scolded me among the tribe.
Whatever good I've asked him for, he's disappointed me—
it's just as though we had laid him down in the hollow tomb.
I don't know of anything wrong I've said to him; the only
thing is
I searched, and not casually at that, for Ma'bad's lost baggage-
camels.

I used our kinship as a close argument; and, by your luck,
whenever there's anything requiring an effort, I'm always present;
let me be summoned in a serious fix, and I'm there to defend,
or let your enemies come against you sternly, I'm stern to help;
if they assault your honour with dirty cracks, I don't waste time
threatening, but pour down their throats draughts from the pool of Death.
There's nothing amiss I've occasioned; yet it's just as if I was cause
of my own defamation, and being complained of, and made an outcaste.
If there'd been anyone else but him involved in the case
he'd surely have eased my grief, or at least given me a day's respite;
but my fine master is a man who's forever throttling me
and I must thank him, and fawn upon him, and be his ransom.
Truly, the tyranny of kinsfolk inflicts sharper anguish
upon a man than the blow of a trenchant Indian sabre.
So leave me to my own habits; I'll always be grateful to you
even though my tent be pitched far-off, by Mount Darghad.

Had my Lord willed, I'd have been another Kais bin Khálid,
and had my Lord willed, I'd have been another Amr bin Marthad;
then I'd have been a man of much substance, visited
by all the sprigs of the nobility, chiefs and sons of chiefs.
I'm the lean, hard-bitten warrior you know of old,
intrepid, lively as the darting head of a serpent;
I have vowed my loins cease not to furnish a lining
for an Indian scimitar sharp as to both its edges,
trenchant—when I stand forth to take my revenge with it
its first blow suffices; I need no repeat stroke; it's no pruning-hook—
a trusty blade, recoiling not from its target;
say, 'Gently now!' and its edge would answer, 'Done!'
When the tribesmen hurry to arms, you'll surely find me
impregnable, let my hand but be gripping its handle.

Many's the kneeling, sleeping camel—the fear of me
stalking with naked blade has oft startled the runaways;
then some ancient she-camel with flaccid udders, huge, the pride
of an elder thin as a stick, quarrelsome, has passed me by

159–160. *Kais bin Khalid . . . Amr bin Marthad:* two wealthy and powerful relatives of Tarafa. Amr invited Tarafa to join his household when he heard the young man's verses. But a gift for both satiric verses and high living resulted in the alienation depicted in the poem.

and he remarking to me (for her pastern and shank were slit)
'Don't you see what ruination you've brought on me now?
What think you,' this to the tribesmen, 'we should do with a drunkard
whose wickedness presses hard on us, a wilful sinner?
But let him be,' he went on. 'He shall have the full benefit of her;
only if you don't halt those far-off kneelers, he'll go on killing.'
Then the maidservants set to roasting her little foal,
while the tender shredded hump was hastened to regale us.

If I should die, cry me, sweet daughter of Ma'bad,
as my deeds deserve, and rend the collar of your gown for me;
make me not out as a man whose zeal was not any way
like my zeal, who served not in battle and tumult as I have served,
one who was slow to doughty enterprises, swift to foul mouthing,
inglorious, pushed away contemptuously by men's fists.
Had I been such a poltroon in men's eyes, the enmity
of the companioned, aye, and the solitary had mischiefed me;
but my known daring, my bold demeanour, my honesty
and my high ancestry—these repelled my enemies from me.
I swear, by your life, the task that is on me perplexes me not
in the daylight hours, neither is my night an eternity.

Many's the day I've braced myself, when the foemen pressed,
guarding the threatened breaches, firm in the face of fear,
taking my stand where the cavalier dreads destruction
and the heart's muscles, rubbed together, twitch with terror.
Many's the yellow arrow, smoke-blackened, whose win I've awaited.
by the camp-fire, and then thrust it in the palm of the shuffler.

The days shall disclose to you things you were ignorant of,
and he whom you never provisioned will bring you back tidings;
one that you purchased never a scrap for will come to you
with news, though you appointed no time for him to keep tryst.

The Centenarian
(*Mu'allaqa of Labīd*)

The abodes are desolate, halting-place and encampment too,
at Miná; deserted lies Ghaul, deserted alike Rijám,

2–3. ***Mina . . . Er-Raiyan:*** **Unidentifiable.**

and the torrent-beds of Er-Raiyán—naked shows their trace,
rubbed smooth, like letterings long since scored on a stony slab;
blackened orts that, since the time their inhabitants tarried there,
many years have passed over, months unhallowed and sacrosanct.
The star-borne showers of Spring have fed them, the outpouring
of thundercloud, great deluge and gentle following rain,
the cloud that travels by night, the sombre pall of morn,
the outspread mantle of eve with muttering antiphon.
Then the branches of aihakan shot up, and the ostriches
and antelopes brought forth their young on both valley-slopes,
and the great-eyed cows that had lately calved stand over their brood
while in the spreading plain the little lambs form their flocks.
Then the torrents washed the dusty ruins, until they seem
like scrolls of writing whose text their pens have revivified,
or the back and forth of a woman tattooing, her indigo
in rings scattered, the tattooing newly revealed above them.

So I stood and questioned that site; yet how should we question rocks
set immovable, whose speech is nothing significant?
All is naked now, where once the people were all foregathered;
they set forth with dawn, leaving the trench and panic-grass behind;
and the womenfolk—how they stirred your passion, the day they climbed
and hid themselves in the curtained howdahs with creaking tents,
each litter well-upholstered, its pole overshadowed by
a brocaded hanging, with fine veil and crimson overlay.
So borne they parted in throngs, wild cows of Toodih and
gazelles of Wajra belike, their calves gathered close to them;
the troop was urged, to be swallowed up in the shimmering haze
till they seemed as tamarisk-shrubs and boulders in Bísha's vale.

But what think you still of the Lady Nawár, so far away
and every bond with her broken, new cord alike with old?
A Murrite she, who dwells now in Faid and for neighbours takes

5. *blackened orts:* literally, fragments of food. Used metaphorically here for crumbs.

24. *howdahs:* canopied seats placed on the top of camels or horses (or, in India, elephants).

the Hejázi folk: how can you aspire then to come to her?
In the eastern parts of the Two Mountains, or in Muhajjar
she lodges, surrounded by Farda and near-by Rukhám,
and Suwá'id, if she fares to the right, then presumably
the black ridge of El-Kahr, or Tilhám thereabouts.
So cut off your longing for one whom you may no more
attain—
the best knotters of friendship sever the bond at need—
and bestow your gifts in plenty on him who entreats you fair;
you can always break, when his love falters and swerves away,
with a lean camel to ride on, that many journeyings
have fined to a bare thinness of spine and shrunken hump,
one that, when her flesh is fallen away and her strength is spent
and her ankle-thongs are worn to ribbons of long fatigue,
yet rejoices in her bridle, and runs still as if she were
a roseate cloud, rain-emptied, that flies with the south wind,
or a great-uddered she-ass, pregnant of a white-bellied sire
worn lean
by the stampeding and kicking and biting of fellow-stallions.
Bitten to the bone, he mounts with her the humps of the hills
disquieted by her refractoriness and insatiable craving;
in the stony reach of Eth-Thalaboot he outclambers her
to the barren watchposts, fear lurking in every waymark.
Till, with Jumáda and the six months past, content with grass
and unwatered, a long fasting for them together,
they returned at last determined upon a firm resolve
unwavering—and success in a decision is of solid purpose—
the thorns pricking her hinder hoofs, the summer winds
swelling and swirling about them in scorching blasts.
They kicked up a long column of dust, its shadow flying
like the smoke of a bonfire, its flames soaring aloft
fanned by the north wind, stoked with fresh arfaj branches,
like the smoke of a blaze, high-billowing its ardent mass.
On he went, pushing her ahead of him as was his wont
to push her ahead whenever she threatened to swing aside;
then they plunged into the middle of a rivulet, and split through
a brimming pool, where the kalam-rods grew close together,
encompassed about by the reeds overshadowing it,
a veritable thicket, part trampled down, part upstanding.

Is such my camel? Or shall I liken her to a wild cow, whose calf
the beasts of prey have devoured, lagging, though true herd-
leader?

34. *Hejazi: The Hejaz (Hijaz)* is the area along the coast of Saudi Arabia from about the 28th parallel to south of Mecca.

Flat-nosed, she has lost her young, and therefore unceasingly
circles about the stony waste, lowing all the while
as she seeks a half-weaned white calf, whose carcase the grey robber-wolves
in greed unappeasable have dragged hither and thither;
they encountered her unawares, and seized her little one from her,
and of a truth the arrows of Fate miss not their mark.
All that night she wandered, the raindrops streaming upon her
in continuous flow, watering still the herb-strewn sands;
she crouched under the stem of a high-branched tree, apart
on the fringes of certain sand-hills, whose soft slopes trickled down
while the rain uninterruptedly ran down the line
of her back, on a night the clouds blotted the starlight out,
yet she shone radiantly in the face of the gathered murk
as the pearl of a diver shines when shaken free from its thread;
but when the shadows dispersed, and the dawn surrounded her,
forth she went, her feet slipping upon the dripping earth.
Distraught with sorrow, for seven nights and successive days
ceaselessly she wandered among the pools of Sawá'id
till at last she gave up hope, and her swelling udders shrank
that no suckling and no weaning had ever wrung so dry.
Now she heard the murmur of men's voices, that startled her
coming from the unseen—for man is her sickness of old—
and on both sides, behind and before her, so she deemed,
danger awaited, the awful apprehension of doom.
Then, when the huntsmen, despairing to come to grips, unleashed
their flap-eared hunting-dogs with collars of untanned hide,
they closed in on her, and she turned upon them with her horn
pointed and altogether like to a Samhari spear
to repel them, for she was sure that if she repelled them not
Fate inexorable was imminent, and certain death.
So Kasáb came to her doom, a fine hound, horribly smeared
in blood, and Sukhám, another, left on the battlefield.

Upon such a camel, when dances the shimmering forenoon haze
and the hills draw on their vaporous mantle, the white mirage,
I fulfil my yearning, not neglecting an inward doubt
nor leaving any handle for fault-finders to fasten on.

Did Nawár not know then, and was she not aware that I
am skilled to knot the bonds of friendship, and break them too?

I am quick to be gone from places when they're unpleasing
 to me
except, as happens, its destiny fetters my spirit there.
Ha, but you have no idea, my dear, how many nights
of agreeable warmth, delicious in sport and companionship,
I have passed chatting, how many a taverner's hoisted flag
I have visited, when the wine it proclaimed was precious dear,
and I've forked out a pretty penny for an old, brown wineskin
or a pitch-smeared jar, newly decanted and seal broken,
for the pleasure of a song on a wet morning, and a charming
 girl plucking
with nimble fingers the strings of her melodious lute;
yes, I've raced the cock bright and early, to get me my spirit's
 need
and to have my second wetting by the time the sleepers stirred.
And many's the morning of wind and cold I've kept at bay
when its reins lay in the fingers of the bitter north
and defended the knights, my bristling panoply burdening
a swift-stepper, its bridle at dawn flung about my shoulders.
I have climbed to a look-out post on the brow of a fearful ridge
the dust of whose summits hung closely about their standards
till, when the sun flung its hand into dusk's coverlet
and darkness shrouded the perilous marches of the frontiers,
I came down to the plain; my horse stood firm as the trunk
of a tall, stripped palm-tree the gatherers shrink to ascend.
Then I pricked her on, to run like an ostrich and fleeter still
until, when she was warm and her bones were light and pliant,
her saddle slipped about, and her neck streamed with sweat
and the foam of her perspiration drenched her leather girth;
she tosses her head, and strains at the rein, and rushes on
as a desert dove flutters with the flight swiftly to water.

And oft in an unfamiliar muster of many strangers
where gifts were hoped for, and the voice of reproach was
 feared,
thick-necked men, ranting together of blood-revenge
like very devils of El-Badí, feet planted firm,
I've disowned the wrong, and boldly maintained the right
as I saw it, and none of those noble gentry could glory over me.
And many a time I've called for the gambling-arrows, so like
each to each in shape, to kill a gamblers' slaughtering-beast,
called for the arrows to choose a barren or bearing camel
whose flesh was distributed to the poor relations of all;
and the guest and the poor stranger must have thought themselves

come down upon Tabála, whose valleys are ever green.
To the shelter of my tent-ropes comes every forwearied woman
starved as a tomb-tethered camel, her garments tattered and shrunk.
When the winds blow into each other's teeth, they crown canals
of heaped-up platters, and the orphans hurl themselves on them.

When the assemblies meet together, we never fail
to supply a match for the gravest issue, strong to shoulder it,
a partitioner, bestowing on all the tribe their due,
granting to some their rights, denying the claims of some
for the general good, generous, assisting liberality,
gentlemanly, winning and plundering precious prize,
sprung of a stock whose fathers laid down a code for them,
and every folk has its code of laws and its high ideal.
When alarmed to battle, there they are with their helmets on
and their coats of mail, the rings of them gleaming like stars:
unsullied is their honour, their deeds are not ineffectual,
for their prudent minds incline not after capricious lust.
They have built for us a house whose roof reaches very high
and to it have mounted alike the elders and young of the tribe.
So be satisfied with what the Sovereign has allotted;
He has divided the qualities among us, knowing them well,
and when trustworthiness came to be apportioned among a tribe
the Apportioner bestowed on us an exceeding share.
They are the strivers, whenever the tribe is visited
by distress; they are the tribe's knights and high arbiters;
to those who seek their protection they are as the bounteous Spring
as also to widows in their long year of widowhood.
Such a tribe they are, that no envier succeeds to hold back
nor any reviler assists the enemy's reviling tongue.

The Black Knight

(*Mu'allaqa of 'Antara*)

Have the poets left a single spot for a patch to be sewn?
Or did you recognise the abode after long meditation?
O abode of Abla at El-Jawá, let me hear you speak;
I give you good morning, abode of Abla, and greetings to you!

3. *Abla:* 'Antara's cousin, with whom he was in love.

3–18. *El-Jawa . . . El-Ghailam:* The place names are generally unidentifiable, although El-Hazn (line 8) may be the site with the same name at the head of the Wadi Sirhan, 150 miles east-south-east of Jerusalem.

For there I halted my she-camel, huge-bodied as a castle,
that I might satisfy the hankering of a lingerer;
while Abla lodged at El-Jawá, and our folk dwelt
at El-Hazn and Es-Sammán and El-Mutathallim.
All hail to you, ruins of a time long since gone by,
empty and desolate since the day Umm el-Haitham parted.
She alighted in the land of the bellowers; and it has become
very hard for me to seek you out, daughter of Makhram.
Casually I fell in love with her, as I slew her folk
(by your father's life, such a declaration is scarce opportune),
and you have occupied in my heart, make no doubt of it,
the place of one dearly beloved and highly honoured.
But how to visit her, now her people are in spring-quarters
at Unaizatan, while ours are dwelling in El-Ghailam?

If you were resolved upon departing, assuredly
it was a dark night your camels were bridled on;
nothing disquieted me, but that her people's burthen-beasts
were champing khimkhim-berries amid their habitations,
two and forty milch-camels among them, all black
as the inner wing-feathers of the sable raven.
When she captures you with that mouthful of sharp white
teeth,
sweet indeed the kiss of it, delicious to taste,
you might think a merchant's musk-bag borne in its basket
has outstripped the press of her side-teeth, wafted from her
mouth to you,
or an untrodden meadow that a good rain has guaranteed
shall bear rich herbage, but sparsely dunged, not known of men,
visited by every virgin raincloud bountiful in showers
that have left every puddle gleaming like a silver dirham,
deluging and decanting, so that at every eve
the water is streaming over it in unbroken flow;
and there the fly sits alone, unceasingly
humming away, like a toper raising his voice in song,
trilling, the while he rubs one leg against another
just like a one-armed man bending to strike the flint.
She lolls evening and morning lazily upon a pillow
while I rode through the night on a black, well-bridled mare
with a saddle for my cushion, laid on a stout-legged beast
very large in the flanks, generous in the girth.
Would I indeed be brought to her dwelling by a Shadani
she-camel

27. *musk-bag:* Musk is an expensive ingredient of perfume.
32. *dirham:* a coin.

cursed by an udder barren of milk and withered up,
lashing her tail after all night travelling, still a-swagger,
stamping the sand-mounds with pads heavily tramping?
At eventide it is as though I am breaking the hillocks
upon an ostrich close-footed, that lacks for ears,
to which the young ostriches flutter, as herds of Yemeni camels
flock to the call of a barbarous, incomprehensible voice;
they follow after the crest of his head; he is like a litter
laid upon a sort of bier, and tented for them,
small-headed, visiting his eggs in Dhul Ushaira,
like an ear-lopped slave swaggering in long furs.
My camel drank of the waters of Ed-Duhrudán
then swerved and fled, avoiding the pools of Ed-Dailam,
as though she twisted her right side to get away
from a big-headed beast that screams at evening,
a cat padding beside her, and every time she turns
to him in anger he wards her off with claws and teeth.
Long journeying has left her with a strong-built back,
high-hoisted, supported on props like a tent-pitcher's.
She knelt down at the waters of Er-Ridá', and you might have
said
it was upon crackling cleft reeds that she knelt down,
and it was like as if thick butter-fat or molten pitch
that is used to kindle a blaze about a boiler
welled out from the back of the neck of an angry, spirited
proud-stepping she, the match of a well-bitten stallion.

If you should lower your veil before me, what then? Why,
I am a man skilled to seize the well-armoured knight.
Praise me therefore for the things you know of me; for I
am easy to get on with, provided I'm not wronged;
but if I am wronged, then the wrong I do is harsh indeed,
bitter to the palate as the tang of the colocynth.
It may also be mentioned how often I have drunk good wine,
after the noon's sweltering calm, from a bright figured bowl
in a glittering golden glass scored with lines
partnered to a lustrous filtered flask on its left,
and whenever I have drunk, recklessly I squander
my substance, while my honour is abounding, unimpaired,
and whenever I have sobered up, I diminish not my bounty,
my qualities and my nobility being as you have known them.
And many's the good wife's spouse I have left on the floor
the blood whistling from his ribs like a harelip hissing,
my fists having beaten him to it with a hasty blow

74. *colocynth:* a fruit with a bitter taste, often used as a medicine.

and the spray of a deep thrust, dyed like dragon's blood.
I could advise you, daughter of Malik, to ask the horsemen
if you should happen to be ignorant and uninformed,
for I'm never out of the saddle of a strong swimmer,
sturdy, assaulted again and again by the warriors, wounded,
now detached for the lance-thrusting, and anon
resorting to the great host with their tight bows.
Those who were present at the engagement will acquaint you
how I plunge into battle, but abstain at the booty-sharing.
Many's the bristling knight the warriors have shunned to take
on,
one who was not in a hurry to flee or capitulate,
my hands have been right generous too with the hasty thrust
of a well-tempered, strong-jointed, straightened spear
giving him a broad, double-sided gash, the hiss of which
guides in the night-season the prowling, famished wolves;
I split through his accoutrements with my solid lance
(for even the noblest is not sacrosanct to the spear)
and left him carrion for the wild beasts to pounce on,
all of him, from the crown of his head to his limp wrists.

Many's the time I've ripped with my sword the links of a long
well-riveted mail-coat off a signal defender of the right;
nimble his hands were with the gaming-arrows in winter,
he tore down traders' inn-signs, and was much chided.
When he beheld me come down in the field against him
he bared his back-teeth, and not in a grin I may say;
so I thrust him with my lance, then I came on top of him
with a trenchant Indian blade of shining steel,
and when the sun was high in the heavens I descried him
his fingers and his head as it were dyed with indigo—
a true hero, as if he were a clothed sarha-tree,
shod in shoes of tanned leather, no weakling twin.

O lovely fawn, huntable indeed for those who may enjoy her
but to me denied—and would to God she were lawful to me—
I sent my slave-girl to her, telling her, 'Off with you now,
scout out news of her for me, and tell me truly.'
She said, 'I saw the enemy were off their guard
and the fawn was attainable to any good marksman.'
As she turned, her throat was like a young antelope's,
the throat of a tender gazelle-fawn with spotted upper lip.

117–118. *O lovely fawn . . . lawful to me:* She is of another tribe, and he is a Negro not welcomed by her parents.

I am told that Amr is ungrateful for my beneficence,
and ingratitude is a heaviness to the soul of the benefactor.
I have minded well the counsel my uncle gave me in the forenoon
when fearfully the lips drew back from the mouth's white teeth
in the thick of death, of whose agonies the true hero
utters no complaint, other than a muffled cry:
when my comrades thrust me against the lances, I did not shrink
from them, but my field of advance was narrowly choked.
When in the midst of the battle-dust I heard the cry
of Murra ascend shrill, and the two sons of Rabí'a,
and all Muhallim were striving beneath their banner
and death stalked beneath the sons of Muhallim's banner,
then I knew for sure that when the issue was joined with them
such a blow would fall as to scare the bird from its snuggling chicks.
When I beheld the people advancing in solid mass
urging each other on, I wheeled on them blamelessly;
'Antara!' they were calling, and the lances were like
well-ropes sinking into the breast of my black steed.
Continuously I charged them with his white-blazoned face
and his breast, until his body was caparisoned in blood,
and he twisted round to the spears' impact upon his breast
and complained to me, sobbing and whimpering;
had he known the art of conversation, he would have protested,
and had he been acquainted with speech, he would have spoken to me.
The horses frowning terribly plunged into the crumbling soil,
long-bodied mare along with short-haired, long-bodied stallion,
and oh, my soul was cured, and its faint sickness was healed
by the horsemen's cry, 'Ha, Antara, on with you!'

Submissive are my riding-camels; wherever I will go
my heart accompanies me, and I urge it with firm command.
I greatly feared that death might claim me, before
war's wheel should turn against the two sons of Damdam,
who blaspheme against my honour, and I have not reviled them,
who threaten to spill my blood, if I do not meet them;
and well they may, it being myself that left their father
carrion for the wild beasts and all the great vultures.

125. *Amr:* his father.

FIRDAUSĪ

(ca. 940–1020 or 1025)

The Book of Kings (*Shāhnāma*)

The greatest of the Persian poets, Firdausī, was born in Tus, near Meshed (Mashhad), in the far northwest corner of Iran, about the year 940 A.D. Early in life he conceived of a verse epic which would do no less than encompass the whole of Persian history in a single poem. There is evidence that he started this project early, but it was not completed until about 1010, by which time he was in financial difficulties, having exhausted his inheritance, and Persia itself was in political turmoil. The Sāmānid dynasty had fallen, civil war had flared intermittently, and the new royal house to which he presented his epic was of Turkish blood. Firdausi hoped for an imperial bounty from Mahmud, the ruler of this new house, who had shown great favor to science and the arts. For reasons not clear, Mahmūd was not impressed by either the epic or the panegyric preface dedicating it to him, and the poet's reward was small. To remind the monarch that poetry is a two-edged sword, Firdausi penned a savage satire[1] on the king and fled to Tabaristān, at the head of the Persian Gulf. He died in Tūs, his native city, in 1020 or 1025, his last years having been spent in writings on Koranic themes in contrast to the glories of paganism in the *Book of Kings*. A romantic legend has it that the king repented of his treatment of the poet, and that a camel-load of indigo, a most valuable gift, arrived just after the poet died. "Even as the camels entered the Rudbar Gate, the corpse of Firdausī was borne forth from the Gate of Razán."[2] So the legend goes, but it is unlikely that the royal house was so forgiving.

Firdausī's purpose in the *Book of Kings* was to chronicle the entire history of Persia from the creation of man down to the Sāsānian empire (226–641 A.D.), beginning with a largely mythical Pishdādian dynasty devoted at first to such primitive matters as the invention of agriculture and the domestication of animals. Firdausī imagined that this dynasty lasted 2.441 years, and was followed by the Kaiānian line, which is in power in the selection below. The last two Kaiānian shahs move us from myth to recorded history in the poem, and the arrival in the East of Sikander (Alexander the Great) marks the end of ancient Persia. The great capital of Firdausī's Persian world is Persepolis, the imposing ruins of which rise from the plains about thirty miles northeast of modern Shiraz in southern Iran. His geography is none too exact. He believes Iran to be the center of the earth, surrounded by the waters of the Indus, Oxus, Araks, Euxine, Bosporus, Sea of Marmara, Dardanelles, Nile, and Indian Ocean. To the northwest and west lies the Byzantine Em-

1. See A. J. Arberry, *Classical Persian Literature* (Cambridge, 1958), pp. 43–44.

2. *Ibid.*, p. 44.

pire (Rūm, the Arabic word for Rome), and to the northeast Turan (Turkestan), which includes the whole area east to China.

Though a Muslim, Firdausī sings the glories of a pagan world. The Zoroastrian deities, Urmuzd and Ahriman, gods of good and evil respectively, function as mythical forces and poetic metaphors in his poem. They are necessary simply because they are part of Persian culture. He does not hesitate to reduce Ahriman to the role of a meddling and evil demon or to abridge and recapitulate history according to his likes. His heroes grow old in the poem, disappear, and reappear later without any explanation for their continued vitality.

Both his poetic gifts and his preservation of the cultural history of Persia are responsible for Firdausī's exalted reputation. His material was on the verge of oblivion: he rescued it from forgotten written sources and a dying oral tradition, and put it in a verse form which enabled it to be read by the literate and listened to by the illiterate over the succeeding centuries. His position as a former and preserver of the language is comparable to that of Luther in Germany. (It is worth nothing that Firdausī's competitors for the literary laurels of Persia are lyric poets—Sa'dī and Hāfiz—who, by the nature of their form, have none of his scope.)

The *Book of Kings* was composed in 60,000 couplets, but not all have survived. Like the Indian *Mahābhārata* (see p. 84) it is loosely constructed and episodic compared to Western epic, though not compared to Western medieval romance. The glory of Persia, not the deeds of a single hero, is its theme, but Firdausī emphasizes the single hero or the group of lords acting as one. The hero is invariably good-humored and valiant, boastful and verbose. Firdausī depicts at length in stately verse each incident of his vast chronicle, objectively giving each its proper weight and not intruding with his own commentary. From one point of view, the poem would be superior if it were not so even, if some dramatic incidents were considerably magnified and other less important matters summarized, but this would have meant altering the sources, which the poet refused to do. Firdausī's personality emerges in lines which comment on life or death, usually in the precludes to parts of the action, and in descriptions such as begin the passage below.

Firdausī's language, says a Persian commentator, is "as solid as iron, yet smooth as running water."[3] The poet felt that the language of poetry should be dignified yet not remote from the understanding of the ordinary man. Metrically, in the original, the lines have four stresses, often with a caesura ("The *Pha*raohs of *E*gypt, the *Cae*sars of *Rome*").

We detect in the *Shāh-nāma* a sense of wonder at and nostalgia for the pagan past, by an author who sees that all of this is gone and who believes in the new faith of the Arab conquerors, but who feels like a northern European might have when the world of Christianity over-

3. *Ibid.*, p. 48.

whelmed the world of *Beowulf* and the other glories of Germanic Europe. FitzGerald's quatrain from 'Umar touches on this emotion:

They say the Lion and the Lizard keep
The Courts where Jamshyd gloried and drank deep:
And Bahram, that great Hunter—the Wild Ass
Stamps o'er his Head, but cannot break his sleep.

There is irony here in that Bahram, because of his courage and strength, was nicknamed the onager or wild ass, but once dead and the empire in ruins, he is not disturbed by the eternal frolic of his namesake.

From The Book of Kings*

The Poet's Introduction

THE OPENING OF THE BOOK

In the name of the Lord of the soul and of wisdom, than Whom thought can conceive nothing higher; the Lord of all things nameable and of all space; the Lord who grants sustenance and is our Guide; the Lord of the universe and the revolving sky, who kindles the Moon, Venus and the Sun. He is beyond all naming, indication or fancy and He is the essence of anything a limner may design.

[The poet repeats his asseveration that the mind of man has no means of attaining to a knowledge of God by any power of reason.]

IN PRAISE OF WISDOM

Wisdom is better than aught else which God has granted to you. Wisdom is the guide and is the heart's enlivener; wisdom is your helper in both worlds. From it comes happiness and all human welfare; from it you gain increase and without it you experience loss. Thou, Wisdom, art the creation of the Creator of the world and knowest all things patent or hidden. Do thou, O man, ever keep wisdom as your counsellor, whereby you may preserve your soul from all unworthiness. When you have acquired an insight into any branch of a matter, you will understand that science does not reach down to the root.

ON THE CREATION OF THE WORLD[1]

As a beginning you must know precisely what the material of the elements was in origin. God created matter out of nothingness in order that his power might be manifested; out of it was produced the substance of the four elements, without effort and without expenditure of time. Of these elements one was fire, which arose

* From *The Book of Kings*, translated by Reuben Levy. Reprinted by permission of the Persian Heritage Series.

1. Firdausī draws on Zoroastrian mythology for his account.

shining; then the wind and the water came, above the dark earth. First the fire was stirred into motion and so dryness appeared because of the heat of fire. When it was still again, cold manifested itself, and then, out of cold grew moisture.

When these four elements were once in existence they came together to form this fleeting abode of the world. Thus they were compounded each with the other to make up every genus of the proudest order of phenomena, such as this swift-moving dome [the sky], displaying ever-new marvels. It is master of the twelve [Signs] and the seven [Planets], each of which takes up its due position. Through God generosity and justice came into being and He has granted fitting reward to all who recognize Him.

The heavenly spheres were constructed one within the other and set in motion once the srtucture had been completed. With sea, mountain, desert and meadow the earth became bright as a shining lamp. With the mountain towering high, waters coalesced and the heads of growing plants reared upwards. But to the earth itself no place on high was allotted; it was a central point, dark and black. Overhead the stars displayed their wonders, casting their brightness on to the earth. Fire ascended, water poured down and the sun revolved about the earth.

Grass sprouted, together with trees of several kinds, whose tops happily grew upwards. These things grow and have no other power; they cannot move in any direction in the way that animals can. These moving creatures brought the growing things into subjection. They ever seek food, sleep and respose and find all their satisfaction in being alive; with neither tongue for utterance nor wisdom to make investigation they nurture their bodies on thorn and stubble. They do not know if the outcome of what they do is good or ill; the Lord demands no service of them.

THE CREATION OF MAN

Going beyond these creatures Man appeared, to become the key to all these close-linked things. His head was raised up like the cypress, he was endowed with good speech and applied wisdom to use. He received sense, reason and wisdom, and all animals whether wild or tame are obedient to his command. By the path of wisdom you may perceive in some small measure what the significance of man may be. Perhaps you know mankind as a distracted thing and can find no indication of its being ought else. You were produced out of two worlds and nurtured in some respects to be a go-between; although first in nature you must regard yourself as the latest in time. Thus you are; therefore do not devote yourself to triviality.

THE CREATION OF THE SUN

The blue vault of heaven is made of red coral, being composed neither of wind and water, nor of dust and smoke. With its brilliance and light is bright as a garden in the Spring. There is in it a heart-warming element which moves and from which day receives its illumination. Each dawn like a golden shield it raises its glowing head out of the East, clothing the earth in a garment of light in such fashion that the universe stands revealed. When it travels onwards from the East towards the West, dark night raises its head out of the East; neither seeks to overtake the other and nothing can be more orderly than this succession.

THE CREATION OF THE MOON

The moon is a lamp provided for the dark night (never turn to evil if it is within your power). For two days and two night it does not show its face, the circle of it fades away; then it reappears thin and yellow, its back bent like the back of a person who has suffered the torment of love. Even as the beholder gazes on it from afar it vanishes from sight. The next night it reappears larger and provides you with more light. In two weeks it becomes full and whole again and then returns to what it was at first, becoming more slender each night and moving nearer to the sun. Thus did God establish a just path for it and as long as it exists it will pursue this same course.

IN PRAISE OF THE PROPHET AND HIS COMPANIONS

[Here follows a section belauding the Prophet Mohammad and his four Companions, the 'Upright' Caliphs, of whom the poet regards the prophet's cousin Ali as the most to be revered.[2]]

HOW THE *Shah-nama* CAME TO BE COMPOSED

From early times there existed a work in which were contained an abundance of legends, and it was shared out between a number of [Magian] priests, each of whom held a portion. It happened once that a personage of high rank, belonging to Dehqan [landed gentry] stock, a man of noble character, liberal disposition and high intelligence, came to be interested in primeval days and sought for histories of times gone by. Accordingly, he assembled from their various provinces the aged priests who had learnt that work by heart and he put questions to them concerning the kings who had once possessed the world and about other famous and illustrious men.

'How did they,' he inquired, 'hold the world in the beginning, and why is it that it has been left to us in such a sorry state? And how was it that they were able to live free of care during the days of their heroic labours?'

Little by little these revered men unfolded to him the histories of

2. The Shi'ite Moslems of Iran believe especially in the holiness of 'Ali, fourth of the orthodox caliphs. The Sunnite Moslems of most of the Arab world minimize the change to a new line of caliphs following the assassination of 'Ali in 661 A.D.

the kings and told how the world's vicissitudes had come about; and when this great knight had heard all that they had to tell him, he laid the foundations of a noble book that achieved fame throughout the world and received universal adulation from all people, high and low.

'Who was it first,' that gifted Dehqan had inquired, 'who invented the crown of royalty and placed a diadem on his head?'

They answered, 'The time of that goes far back in the memory of human beings. A son learnt of it from his father, and told about it, in every detail, as he had received it from his begetter.'

And now that inquirer into ancient legend, who recounts the story of the Heroes, has this to say:

I

The Reign of Keyumars[3]

The ceremonial of throne and crown was introduced by Keyumars, who was king and ruler over the whole world. He placed his residence at first in the mountains, where his fortunes and throne were raised on high. Like his people he clothed himself in leopard-skin; nevertheless it was through him that civilization came, because clothing was something new, as also was food. He ruled the world for thirty years, benevolent as the sun everywhere and as resplendent on his throne as the two weeks old moon shining above a slender cypress. All living creatures, wild or tame, on seeing him, assembled from every part of the world and took refuge with him, bowing low before his throne. And so it was that he grew in majesty and power. All came to him in the attitude of reverence, and hence religion took its rise.

[*The Adventures of Sekandar*][4]

(IV) SEKANDAR BUILDS THE DAM OF GOG AND MAGOG[5]

Sekandar had seen the East and now went towards the West, having conceived the notion of traversing the whole of the world.

3. Or Gāya Marenta, the "first man" of the ancient Zoroastrian sacred scripture the *Avesta*. Firdausi believes that this, the Pishdādī dynasty, is the earliest pre-Islamic dynasty.

4. Sekandar is Alexander the Great (356–323 B.C.), who conquered Persia and carried his arms to the gates of India. Extensive cycles of romance grew up around him in both Western Europe and Persia, adding fabulous adventures to his many real ones. The Persian Alexander tradition is complex. Sometimes he is a conquering villain and destroyer of ancient Persian civilization, but Firdausī makes him a hero—a Persian hero—born of a Persian father and a Persian mother who had been one of the wives of Philip of Macedon, thus making Alexander wholly Persian and falsely claimed by Philip.

5. Gog and Magog (Yājuj and Mājuj) are creatures who will break forth and devestate the earth in the Last Days, until they are destroyed in the land of Israel (see Ezekiel, 38, 39; Revelation, 30:9). For the Arabic sources see the *Qur'ān*, xxi:96. Possibly there is a connection between Alexander's wall and the Great Wall of China.

On his way he saw a fine city, which was so large that neither wind nor dust could have passed across it. When the sound of Sekandar's drums was heard from the backs of his elephants, the elders came out a distance of two leagues to welcome him. He asked them if in that region there existed marvels greater than could be equalled elsewhere. But when they loosed their tongues to the monarch it was to lament the manner in which fortune's wheel had turned against them. They said,

'We are confronted by a difficult task of which we shall speak to your fortunate-starred Majesty. From that mountain there, whose summit reaches into the clouds, something comes which fills our heart with torment, anguish and blood. From Yajuj and Majuj there descend on our city creatures through whom our lot becomes one of sorrow and suffering. Their faces are those of camels, their tongues are black and their eyes the colour of blood. In their black faces are teeth like boars' tusks and none dares to encounter them. Their bodies, covered with bristles, are the colour of the Nile; their chests, bosoms and ears resemble those of elephants. When they lie down to sleep one ear forms their bed, with the other they make a covering for their bodies. Of each female a thousand young are born; but who can tell their number more or less? They come upon us in herds like horses and they charge down like the wild boar. In the Spring, when the turbulence from the clouds arrives, that green sea is stirred to effervescence, the clouds raise up serpent-like creatures out of the waves, and the aether roars like a lion. The clouds cast those serpents down onto the mountain and then great multitudes of these people appear whose food consists of these serpents, which last from one year to the next. When the weather turns cold, they become emaciated and their voices then are as weak as those of pigeons, whereas in the Spring, because of the serpents, they roar aloud. If your Majesty could devise some means of ridding us of this trouble, you would receive the blessings of us all and thereafter live long in the world.'

Sekandar was left marvelling at their story and being disturbed by it set himself to consideration. At last he said,

'Treasure will come from me but labour and other help must come from your city. I will devise a plan of cutting off this road of theirs.'

Sekandar then came to inspect the mountain, bringing with him a company of his philosophers. He commanded that smiths be brought and that copper and bronze, together with heavy hammers, should be fetched, as well as mortar, stone and timber beyond reckoning, which were to suffice for all that was required in the town. When all was ready and his ideas precise, masons, smiths and such as were masters in their trades in the world over flocked to Sekandar and worked together in that honourable task. On two sides of the mountain they built walls, the thickness of each from base to summit being a hundrd ells. There was one ell of charcoal and one of iron, between them being copper. Into the middle of all the layers sulphur was poured according to magical ideas of past kings. Thus they commingled layers of every element. When all was compact from ground to summit, naphtha and oil were mixed together and poured over these elements. Onto this again charcoal by the ass-load was thrown, and then Sekandar gave the order that all was to be set alight. The flames were fanned by a hundred thousand smiths, working at the command of the all-conquering king. From the mountain there issued an explosive roar; the very stars were overcome by the heat of the flames. For long the smiths fanned the flames and toiled, fusing together the elements which had been rapidly smelted in the fire.

So was the world liberated from Yajuj and Majuj and the earth became a place of repose and tranquillity. Because of that famous Alexandrian barrier the world was delivered from evildoers and tyranny.

[There follow accounts of adventures in which Sekandar is depicted as a sight-seeing traveller. He visits a topaz palace enshrining a corpse, comes to the Talking Tree which warns him that he has not long to live and will never see his homeland of Rūm again. He goes to China, whose king, the Faghfur, rebukes him for his proud ambition, and to Sind, where he routs an army sent against him and acquires rich booty consisting of elephants, golden crowns, scimitars and slaves in abundance. After marching thence to the Yemen, where he was received with lavish gifts, he advances on Babylon.]

(v) SEKANDAR MARCHES TO BABYLON

To Babylon then Sekandar led an army so numerous that because of its dust the world became invisible. For a whole month he and his troops rode on without finding a place to rest, and continued so until they reached the mountain whose summit lay beyond the range of sight. On it hung a black cloud which you would have said approached to Saturn. No way across the mountain appeared, so that the king and army were in difficulty about what they should do. But with great toil they at last crossed this mass of granite, which caused even the lightest-footed of them to despair. When wearily they had climbed to the other side they beheld a mighty river. As the air became clear the army's spirits were gladdened, for there they beheld not only the river but the plain and the road beyond. They drove on towards the great stream singing praises to God, seeing that on all sides were creatures wild and tame beyond counting and the troops now had an abundance of game for their victuals. As they continued their march there appeared in the distance a man of great size, covered with hair and having immense ears. Under his hair his body was blue as the Nile, while his ears were as large as those of an elephant. On seeing the man with these strange qualities the warriors dragged him into the presence of Sekandar, who was filled with amazement at the sight. He enquired of him,

'What man are you and what is your name? What do you find in the river there and what do you need?'

The man replied,

'My father and mother bestowed on me the name of *Gushbastar* [Bed-ear].'

The king asked further,

'What is that object in the middle of the river, on the other side of which the sun is rising?'

To that the man returned,

'It is a city like Paradise and you would say that no particle of earth entered into its composition. There you will see no palace or mansion that is not built and roofed with bone, and on their walls you will see the battles of Afrasiyab depicted more brilliantly than the sun. There is also there the portrait of Khosrow, that martial king, in all his greatness, valour and wisdom, clearly limned. In the city you will see neither dust nor earth. The people's nurture is nothing but fish; they have no food other than that.'

'Go,' said Sekandar to the man with the ears. 'Bring me someone from the city to tell me what novelty I can see.'

Without delay Gush-bastar departed and brought back with him a group of men, eighty in number, who had crossed the river with him. The elders amongst them held in their hands a golden goblet encrusted with pearls, while the young men held diadems. The night passed. At the time of cockcrow the roll of drums came up from the royal camp and Sekandar marched on to Babylon.

On the following night there was born to a certain woman a child whose appearance caused all who saw it to marvel. Its head was that of a lion, it had hoofs for feet, its shoulders were human and it had a cow's tail. This monster died at the moment of its birth—let no one claim origin from that woman! They brought it to the king, who gazed on it with wonderment but took it as a portent of evil. Astrologers in number were called and there was much discussion concerning the dead child. These men who told the stars were greatly troubled and concealed their uneasiness from the king, who, at their attitude, was stirred to fury and threatened that if anything was kept hidden from him he would at once sever their heads from their bodies and their only grave would be the lion's maw. Seeing the king thus roused, one of them said,

'Glorious monarch, you were in your beginnings born under the constellation of the Lion. That is established by the priests and the nobles, and you see that the child's head resembles that of a lion. It means that the head of the realm will be brought low. For a time the world will be filled with turmoil which will not cease until a new monarch ascends to the throne.'

All the astrologers in his presence said the same and showed what pointed to the truth of it. Sekandar heard and was smitten with grief. He said,

'From death there is no escape, and I feel no apprehension in my breast at the prospect. My life will continue no longer; fate grants no less than what is allotted, but also never adds to it.

(VI) SEKANDAR COUNSELS HIS MOTHER

[Sekandar dictates a letter to his mother in which he warns her that he is about to die. He continues,]

'Bury my body in the soil of Egypt; let nothing of my behest go astray. Should a son be born to Rowshanak [Roxana], without dubiety his father's name will be thus kept alive. Let none but that son become king of Rum, for he will cause that land and realm to flourish again. But should it be, in an evil moment, that a daughter is born, then betroth her to a son of Filicus, whom you will call my son, not my son-in-law.[6]

'Of the goods which I brought from India, China, Iran, Turan,[7] and the land of Makran,[8] keep what you need and bestow on others what is in excell of what you can enjoy. Of you, my dear one, my request is that you shall remain thoughtful in spirit and clear in mind. Do not let yourself be troubled by your body, for no person exists eternally in the world. Without any doubt my spirit will behold yours when the appropriate time arrives. Endurance is a nobler virtue than love; the impatient are men of a lower degree. Your love watched over my body for years; now pray to God for my pure soul.'

[Sekander died in Babylon. His corpse, after some argument, was carried to Alexandria, a city which he had founded. While recounting the words of grief he places in the mouths of Sekandar's mother and wife, Ferdowsi is reminded of his own miseries and addresses a lament to Fate complaining in particular of his old age. To this, Fate is made to reply that it acts only as God commands.]

6. Filicus is Philip of Macedon and Rūm (Rome) is the Roman world, including Greece.

7. The river Oxus in northwest Persia is the traditional boundary line between Iran and Tūrān, between the Persian-speaking world and the Turkish-speaking peoples.

8. The Persian frontier with Pakistan, the northern coast of the Gulf of Oman.

XXVII

Yazdegerd[9] *the Sinner*

[THE STORY OF BAHRAM GUR]

(1) THE BIRTH OF BAHRAM, SON OF YAZDEGERD

Seven years passed of the reign of Yazdegerd, during which time all his ministers suffered pain and outrage. At the beginning of the eighth year, in the month of Farvardin [March-April], when the Sun reveals his religion anew to the world, a son was born to him on the day of Ormazd,[10] under a goodly star and world-brightening omens. On him his father bestowed the name Bahram, rejoicing in the little child. To the Court there flocked all the astrologers—those men whose speech was deserving of attention. Amongst them was a greatly honoured man of dignity and understanding who was chief of the Hindu star-gazers and whose name was Sorush. Another was one named Hoshyar, who came from Fars and who by his science could fit a bridle on the stars.

These men were commanded to appear before the king and they did so with keen minds and eagerness to find the true paths. With their astrolabes they observed the stars and with Rumi tables they investigated the true courses. One seeker observed that the secret of the stars was that the child would one day be a monarch in the world and would be king over the seven climes. Moreover he would be of cheerful heart and pious disposition. With their findings they hastened into the Shah's court, with their astrolables and star-tables at their bosoms, and told the royal Yazdegerd that they had surveyed the whole field of science and discovered in their calculation of the sky that it was favourable towards this child, into whose possession the seven climes of the earth would come, and that he would be a mighty king enjoying the blessings of all men. When the astrologers departed from the palace, the warriors and the priests, honourable counsellors of the Shah, seated themselves to investigate plans of every kind in order that some scheme to suit the circumstances might be discovered. [They said,]

'If this boy does not inherit his father's nature he will be a just king, 'If, however, he does possess the character of his father, the whole world will be overturned from top to bottom; neither priest nro warrior will be contented nor will he himself be happy or serene of spirit.'

9. King of Persia A.D. 399–420.
10. Ahura Mazda, the supreme god of ancient Zorostrian Persia.

All these priests, sincere of heart and of good intent, came to the king and said,

'This child, so full of merit, is remote from any taint of blame. Now the whole world is under your command and in every land tribute and loyalty are owed to you. Look about therefore for some place where learning is fostered and which favours its scholars. There choose out men of dignity to be tutors, men on whom praise will be bestowed in our land. So shall this prince of happy disposition acquire talent, and the world will rejoice in his authority.'

Yazdegerd gave ear to the priests and sent envoys abroad, some to Rum[11] some to India and China and others to every other civilized realm. A man of note also departed for the land of the Arabs to spy out the advantages and defects there. So it was that lettered men came from every clime, men of experience in the world who had lived good lives and were sagacious. All these came to the court, aspiring to office under the king. He questioned them closely, paid them compliments and gave them lodgments within the city precincts. Amongst them from the Arabs went No'man, accompanied by a troop of noted spearsmen.

When all these men of distinction were assembled in Fars, they presented themselves before royal Yazdegerd. Each in his turn said,

'We are your slaves, hastening to come at the bidding of the Chosroes. Who among the great ones will find the good fortune of taking the brilliant son of the king of the world to his breast and so illumining his mind as to clear it of all darkness? All of us here, whether we come from Rum or India or Fars, whether we are astrologers or geometers, many-sided philosophers, rhetoricians, or skilled craftsmen, are without exception the dust at his feet. Seek out those of us who meet with your approval and will be of value to you.'

For his own part, however, Monzer [the Arab Prince of Yemen] said to the Shah,

'We are your slaves and live in the world only for the sake of the Shah. He knows all our qualities, for he is the shepherd and we are the flock. As for us, we are cavaliers, warriors and tamers of horses and we have power to destroy any masters of learning. Not one of us is a star-gazer or has any endowment of geometry. But our souls are devoted to the Shah and under us we have Arab steeds. We all stand in attendance on his son and we adore his greatness.'

(II) YAZDEGERD ENTRUSTS HIS SON BAHRAM TO MONZER AND NO'MAN

Yazdegerd listened to his speech from Monzer and gathered in his wit and wisdom; and so, with his eye on the outcome from the very beginning, he entrusted Bahram to him. An order came that a robe of honour was to be made and presented to him and his head

11. The Roman empire.

was exalted to the skies. From the palace of the king of the world and far out on to the open plain there extended a procession of horses and of camels with howdahs. Servants and female attendants without number stretched from the bazaars to the king's gate and thence into the king's audience-chamber, while all the bazaars were festively decorated.

When Monzer returned to the land of Yemen, every man and woman came forth to welcome him. Then, when he had reached his capital, his first act was to seek out a large number of his finest cavaliers, both owners of estates and Bedouins, men of substance, rich men, whose protection was sure. From the families of these notables he picked out four women, whose character was patent from their lineage. Two were Bedouins and two of land-owning families of royal seed who were prepared to act as nurses. They maintained Bahram as a suckling for four years, and although he was sated with milk and his body had become stout they found difficulty in weaning him, so they kept him softly at their breasts. When he reached the age of seven years, what said he, with the reason associated with maturer years? He said,

'Noble prince, do not treat me any further as a nursling. Hand me over to learned teachers, for the time has now arrived for men to instruct me.'

'My noble youth,' said Monzer to him, 'the need for instruction has not yet arrived for you. When the time comes and you determine to acquire knowledge, I will not leave you to play in the palace hall or to make a boast of your sport.'

Bahram answered,

'Do not treat me as a babe unfitted for work. I possess understanding even though my years are few and I have neither the chest nor shoulders of a warrior. You have the years, but your comprehension is too small to understand that my composition is different from what you imagine. Do you not understand that he who is seeking for the right moment decides which out of all tasks must come first? Having found that moment, you wash your mind free of care. A task performed at an inauspicious time is fruitless. Teach me those matters which are appropriate to a king; it is proper that I should know them. Amongst the principles of truth what stands first is knowledge; happy the man who from the outset looks to the end.'

Monzer gazed at him in astonishment and under his breath called on the name of God. He immediately sent a hard-riding counsellor on a racing camel to Shursan to seek out three scholars who were held in honour there. One was to teach Bahram the art of letters so as to cleanse his mind of obscurities, one to give him an understanding of the habits of hawk and hunting-panther that kindle the heart, moreover to teach him polo, the use of bow and arrow, how to wield the sword in face of the foe, how to manipulate the reins to right and left and how the head should be kept proudly raised among warriors. The third was to teach him the ways of kings, and the speech and conduct of men experienced in affairs. These learned men presented themselves before Monzer and their discourses ranged over all the sciences. He entrusted the person of the prince to them, for he was himself a man eager to increase his knowledge as well as a warrior.

Bahram of the line of Khosrow[12] steadily grew until he could give a good account of himself in skill amongst any men. When he reached the age of eighteen years he was a bold warrior, brilliant as the sun. In no pursuit now did he have need of an instructor, either in letters or at polo or in handling panther and hawk, in the manipulation of his reins on the battlefield, in the taming of horses or training them. He requested Monzer, therefore, to dismiss the skilled instructor to their homes. To each he gave many gifts and they departed in felicity from the court.

One day the young prince said to Monzer,

'My wise and clear-minded patron, it is without true reason that you watch over me as you do, never leaving me for a moment in anxiety. And yet amongst all the people you see in the world there is not one heart which does not have its secret. Men's faces become pallid with anxiety but the body of the warrior flourishes in happiness. Now the person of a beauteous maid increases man's happiness greatly, for a woman is man's refuge from pain. The young man requires to achieve his happiness through woman, whether he be the wearer of a crown or a Pahlavan.[13] Through woman, moreover, God's religion keeps its hold and she is the young man's guide to the good life. Command therefore that there shall be brought here five or six slave-girls who shall be beautiful and sunlike in their splendour. It may be that if I make my choice of one or two of them my thoughts will be directed to God's praise. Perhaps also a son will be born to me to bring comfort to my heart, the emperor too deriving pleasure from me, while I shall be complimented in every assembly.'

Monzer heard the young man's speech and he, the elder man, applauded him. In all haste he despatched a messenger to the warehouse of a slave-dealer, who brought out forty Greek slave-girls, all desirable and fitted to bring solace to the heart. Of these pretty maids he chose out two whose bones of ivory were clad in skin of roses. Their figure was cypress-like and they were compounded of all that was desirable, colourful and glorious. Of the two, one played the lyre, while the other was tulip-cheeked and beautiful as Canopus[14] in the Yemen. She too was of cypress stature and her

12. Kai Khosrow, an ancient and perhaps legendary king of the Kayanī dynasty, which Firdausī thought followed the Pishdādī.

13. I.e., from Iraq, probably of inferior blood or status.

14. A star in the constellation Carina. Presumably it shines brightest in the clear, dry desert air of Yemen.

tresses were lassos. Monzer approved of them and paid their price, while Bahram smiled and applauded and his cheeks blushed the colour of a ruby in a ring.

(III) THE ADVENTURE OF BAHRAM AND THE LYRE-PLAYING GIRL

Polo and the hunting-ground now were Bahram's sole occupations. It happened one day that he went out hunting accompanied by the lyre-player and without his retinue. The Greek girl's name was Azada and the colour of her cheeks was that of coral. She was the solace of his heart and she shared all his tastes. Her name was ever on his lips. One day when he went hunting he had asked for a racing-camel, the back of which he adorned with brocade. From the saddle four stirrups hung down and the twain galloped together over hill and dale. Under his quiver the gallant Bahram had a bow with which to cast pebbles, he being proficient in every kind [of skill]. Suddenly there came running towards them two pairs of gazelles, and the young man smilingly said to Azada,

'My pretty one, when I string the bow and put the knot in my thumbstall, which gazelle do you wish to see shot? The female is young and her mate very old.'

Azada gave answer,

'My lion-hearted prince, men of war do not go in chase of gazelles. Convert yonder female into a buck with your arrow and with another arrow let the old buck become a female. Then spur the camel on to a sharp trot as the gazelles try to escape your arrow. Shoot a pebble at the ear of one so that it will lay its head down on its shoulder. The pebble will cause the creature to scratch its ear and for the purpose it will bring its hind leg up to its shoulder. Then, with your arrow, pin head, foot and back together, if you would like me to call you the most brilliant [archer] in the world.'

Bahram Gur ['The Wild Ass'] strung his bow and raised a shout in that silent waste. In his quiver he had an arrow with two heads, which he kept for hunting on the plain. As soon as the gazelles were in flight the prince shot away the horns on the head of the fleeting buck, using the arrow with the double head, whereat the girl was filled with amazement. The buck's head being shorn of its black horns at once came to look like a doe. Then the hunter shot two arrows at the doe's head at the places where horns might grow. Instead of horns there were now two arrows, the doe's blood reddening its breast. Now he urged the camel towards the other pair while he placed two pebbles in the bow. One he shot into the ear of one of the gazelles, greatly to his pleasure, for which he had reason, seeing that the gazelle immediately scratched its ear. At that moment he fixed an arrow into his bow and with it pinned together the creature's head, ear and hind leg. Azada's heart burned with grief for the gazelle, and Bahram said to her,

'How is it, my pretty one, that you release such a stream of tears from your eyes?'

'This is not a humane deed,' she replied. 'You are no man; you have the spirit of a demon.'

Putting out his hand Bahram dashed her from the saddle headlong to the ground and drove the camel over her, bespattering her head, her breast and her arms and the lyre with her blood.

'You silly lyre player,' he called out to her. 'Why did you try thus to ensnare me? If my aim when I shot had gone astray it would have brought disgrace on my birth.'

The girl died beneath the camel's feet and never again did he take a girl with him when hunting.

[Some time elapsed and Bahram Gur returned home to his father Yazdegerd. By some misdemeanour on his part he offended the Shah, who confined him as prisoner in his own house. In the end he found release, whereupon he immediately returned to the Yemen. When in due course, the Shah died. Iran's powerful princes, priests and other notables declared themselves unwilling to be ruled over by a man of the same family as that of his evil predecessor. They therefore placed on the throne an elderly nobleman named Khosrow. He was incapable of protecting Iran from the enemies surrounding it, and appeals for help were sent to Monzer in the Yemen. Bahram learned of his father's death and the conditions prevailing in his country and was persuaded by Monzer to set out with an army to win the throne for himself. A group of Iranian nobles came out to meet him.]

(IV) THE IRANIANS COME TO WELCOME BAHRAM

Bahram addressed the nobles thus,

'Dukes, experienced and venerable princes, by inheritance from ancestor to ancestor the kingship is mine. Why should you now contest it?'

The Iranians retorted,

'We will not let you prolong our misery and we are entirely unwilling to have you for our king. Our land and home are ours, in spite of your having an army. We have been afflicted with outrage by your dynasty and suffered grief and torment; day and night we live in agony and the cold winds blow upon us.'

'Is that indeed the truth? The wish is king over every man's heart. Even if you do not desire me, why do you seat a man in my place without having consulted me?'

A priest answered,

'None can escape from the path of justice, whether he be a subject or of royal birth. Be one of us and choose a king whom all men shall bless.'

Three days were spent in argument, during which they sought to choose a sovereign for Iran. They wrote down the names of a hundred noblemen who could bring lustre to crown, throne and girdle. Of this number Bahram was one, for he was a prince who charmed the heart. The hundred names were reduced to fifty, those of resourceful men who were also, however, full of demands. First among the fifty was Bahram; and if he demanded his father's place it was only equitable that he should do so. Then out of the fifty they wrote down thirty names, the choicest in Iran for fame and achievement. Amongst those thirty also Bahram led, for he was both worthy of the crown and youthful as a prince. Of the thirty the priests picked four, and of those four Bahram was sovereign.

When the appointment of the king became imminent, the elders in Iran declared that they did not desire Bahram, as being rash, frivolous and over-ambitious. A clamour arose amongst the princes there, for they had set their hearts on their own decision. Monzer thereupon addressed the Iranians, demanding to know where the advantages and defects in this lay and why they were so aggrieved and wounded in spirit over this young and untried king. The chieftains set out their replies at length and summoned many a man of Fars[15] who had a grievance, gathering on that plain all the many in Iran on whom Yazdegerd had inflicted injuries. One man had had his arm and both feet cut off by him and another had been left alive with neither hands nor feet. Still another one he had deprived of hands, ears and tongue, leaving him like a body without a soul. No'man was stunned at sight of these mutilated men and burst into anger. Bahram too was profoundly saddened. He called out against his father's tomb,

'You man of dark fate, why did you stitch up the eyes of your happiness? Why did you destroy my spirit in the fire?'

Monzer the world-seeker then said to Bahram,

'All this may not be hidden from the princes. You have heard their words; give them an answer. Dull wits are not suited to a prince.'

(v) BAHRAM REPLIES TO THE IRANIAN NOBLES AND OFFERS TO SUBMIT TO AN ORDEAL

In answer to the princes, Bahram replied,

'You have all spoken truly but there is something worse, and it is proper for me to charge my father with it. There is tribulation within me because of it and my delicate reasoning has been clouded thereby. His castle was my prison and my palate was pierced by his hook. I escaped and made Monzer's deserts my refuge, for I had

15. Fārs or Faris is southern Persia, the home of the greatest of the Persian dynasties. *Fārs* (*pars, parsa*) was corrupted by the Greeks to *Persis*, from which we get the word *Persia*.

never enjoyed the Shah's favour. I have prayed God till this last to be my guide in His goodness and permit me to wash away from my soul and heart all the sins which the Shah committed towards mankind. From one ancestor to another the kingship descends to me, and I have understanding and goodwill.

'I will make a compact with you giving my tongue as pledge to God. Let us bring out the ivory throne of the king of kings and on it place the most precious crown. Then let two fierce lions be brought out of the forest and, the crown being placed between them, let them be tied one on each side. Then shall the man ambitious for the kingship advance and seize the crown from the ivory throne and lay the illustrious diadem on his head. He will seat himself as king between the two lions; he being in the middle with the diadem on him and the throne beneath. If you turn your backs from what I propose, choose some proud fellow who is my equal. I and Monzer with our battle-axes and sharp swords—for Arab warriors know nothing of flight—will pound the life out of your chosen king of kings and slice off your heads as high as the moon. I have spoken; give me an answer. Let me have your felicitous consent to this trial.'

After making that speech he departed and entered his tent, leaving the world stunned at what he proposed. The warrior champions, priests and all others in Iran, when they heard those words, said,

'This is divine magnificence; it does not derive from self-delusion or folly. He speaks no word but what is true and we ought to rejoice at the truth. Now, as for his proposal about fierce lions and the throne and the royal crown to be placed between them, if the male lions tear him to pieces, the just Lord does not demand his blood from us. Since he himself spoke of this plan and proposed it we shall be able to rejoice at his death. If, on the other hand, he carries off the crown, he will surpass Faridun[16] with his *Farr*. We shall not ask for any other monarch and we shall have justified his words; nothing more than that.'

[After swearing a solemn oath before the chieftains and priests that he would rule justly, Bahram is promised the kingship on condition that he submits to the ordeal he has proposed. With his bullheaded mace he slays both the lions, seats himself on the ivory throne and crowns himself king of Iran with the royal diadem. Thereafter the usurper Khosrow swears allegiance to him and all goes well during his reign of sixty-three years. Ferdowsi's narrative is little more than a selection of popular tales describing Bahram Gur's amorous adven-

16. Faridun, founder of the Kayanī dynasty, defeated a cannibalistic devil-king and chained him alive, Prometheus-like, to a tree, and hence won his crown by popular acclaim on the basis of his deeds.

tures and his prowess as a huntsman. In the tale here selected as representative of the rest there is a touch of grim humour not often encountered in this generally solemn work.]

(VI) BAHRAM GUR'S PRIEST DESTROYS AND REBUILDS A VILLAGE

At early dawn one day Bahram went out hunting on the plain accompanied by his retinue. On his right was his minister Hormaz and on his left his knee-witted priest. They told him stories, speaking much of Jamshid[17] and Faridun. Ahead of them ran hounds and panthers and over the plain king-falcons and hawks were being sent up all day long, yet when the blazing sun had reached the zenith not a trace of wild ass or gazelle had been seen. Wearied by the fiercely blazing sun, the king despondently turned back from the hunting ground. There came into view ahead of them a verdant hamlet full of houses, men and animals, and out of it on to the road there emerged a numerous crowd to view the spectacle of the cavalcade. The monarch himself was in ill-humour, being heated and desirous to rest himself in the place. But no one there saluted him. It was as though the earth had petrified those asses, until the king became enraged at the stupidity of the people there, and he cast no kindly glance upon them. To his priest the Shah said,

'Let this ill-starred place become the resort of wild beasts and may the water in its stream turn to pitch.'

The priest understood what the king's words implied and turning away from the road he addressed the inhabitants, to whom he said,

'This flourishing town, full of fruits and men and animals, has greatly pleased Shah Bahram, and he desires to establish a new order here. Every one of you is promoted to be an elder so that this fine village may be turned into a city. In this place even women and children are now elders, needing to obey no one's command; here no one is a hireling and no one master, but all walk the same path. Women, men and children—all are elevated to the headship; each single one is chieftain of the town.'

A great shout arose in that rich town out of joy that now all equally were elders. Women and men, servants and hirelings thereafter declared their opinions as heads of the town, and since the youths of the place had lost their awe of the elders they at once cut off their heads. Every man attacked his fellow and blood flowed in every direction. The inhabitants felt that Resurrection Day had arrived in that rural spot and took flight from it. Only a few ancients were left, helpless and crippled; for now all means of cultivation, work and carriage had vanished. The aspect of the whole

17. Jamshid (or Jamshyd). Successor to Keyumars (see note 3). The earliest popular hero of Persian romance.

town declined into one of desolation, the trees having withered because there was no water in the stream. The plain became a desert and the houses fell into ruin, now that all the people and animals had fled away.

A year passed and springtime arrived. Again the Shah went hunting in that direction and came to that place which had once been flourishing and happy. Now when he looked he saw it no longer existed in its old form; the trees were withered and the houses in ruins, in the whole region there was neither man nor beast. The king's cheeks paled at the sight; he felt the fear of God and was tormented with sorrow. He said to the priest,

'How sad that so pleasant a village should have become a desert. Quickly set about restoring it; spend money so that they shall no further suffer misery.'

The counsellor left the king's presence and swiftly moved about the desolate place, hastening from one empty house to another. At last he came upon an old man sitting idle. He dismounted from his horse, greeted him, made room for him by his side and said,

'My elderly master, who destroyed this once flourishing place?'

The man replied,

'One day our sovereign passed through this district of ours and a foolish priest came with him, one of those great ones whose deeds bear no fruit. He told us that we were all nobles and that we were not to pay reverence to anyone; we were all headmen in the town, even women and men were all superior to the elders. As soon as he said it the whole of the town was in turmoil, filled with looting and killing and beating. May God requite him in due measure! May grief and pain and hardship ever renew themselves upon him! The affairs of this place go from bad to worse; we are an object over which to shed tears.'

At the old man's story the good man [the priest] was grieved. He asked who the village headman was and was asked in reply who could be headman in a place where grass-seed was the only fruit. The good man said to him,

'You be the elder. In every task you are to be the diadem on the head. Demand money from the monarch's treasury as well as seed and oxen and asses and food. Drag anyone you find idle into the town; all are subject to you and you are the chief. Call no curses down on that priest; it was not of his own desire that he uttered those words. If you require aid from the royal treasures I will send it to you. Demand as much as you need.'

[The newly-appointed headman rejoiced and by the following spring the village was enjoying greater prosperity than it had ever had before. The moral of the story is then given to the king; namely, that when two conflicting ideas come into a man's mind or when a town has two chiefs, confusion and ruin are the result.]

(VII) BAHRAM GUR AND THE FOUR SISTERS

A week later the lord of the world went out to the chase accompanied by his priests and nobles, purposing to remain hunting and drinking wine with his retinue for a whole month. The time passed in the taking of great quantities of the game which roamed both on the mountains and on the plain; and then the monarch turned happily back to the town with his retinue. Night was falling and the whole world darkened as these noble men rode on reciting to each other the adventures of the kings. Suddenly a fire appeared burning in the distance, bright as the fire which the Shah kindled at the feast of Bahman[18] [January]. As the king of kings gazed at the illumination there came into view at one side a prosperous village, in front of which he saw a mill with some men seated here and there. Beyond the fire were girls, who had made themselves a festal place apart. Each wore a wreath of roses on her head, and all about were seated musicians who sang odes of the battles of Khosrow, each in turn reciting a new one. The faces of these girls were beautiful and they wore curling tresses; all were elegant of speech and they were redolent of musk. Close to the door of the mill and somewhat in front of it they had formed in line on the grass for their minstrelsy; each holding a nosegay of flowers and being in part bemused with happiness and wine. At one point a shout went up from the festal spot, and someone then called forth,

'This is to the health of Bahram the Shah, who has the *Farr* and fine shoulders, a handsome face and great affection. It is through him that the revolving firmament continues its existence. You would say that wine trickles from his cheeks and the perfume of musk is exhaled from his tresses. All he will hunt is the lion and the onager,[19] whence men call him Bahram Gur ["The Wild Ass"].'

When the emperor heard their voices he turned his rein and went in their direction, and, as he came near to the girls and looked about him he saw that the plain from end to end was peopled with lovely maidens, by whom the path of his approach was barred. He therefore ordered that the cupbearers should bring wine from the provision made for the journey and let the people there drink it. A crystal cup was brought and placed in Bahram's hands while from among the maidens there, all bearing noble names, four presented themselves to him. One was Moshknaz [Pure Musk], the second

18. Last king of the Kayanī dynasty. Perhaps Artaxerxes I, king of Persia 465–425 B.C.

19. The onager or wild ass is a small but very fast and sturdy beast.

was Meshkanak [Partridge], and the third was Nazyab [The Fondled] and the fourth Susanak [Lily]. They came forward to the Shah holding each other's hands, their faces like the spring and their stature tall. They recited odes in honour of Bahram the king of kings, the wise and triumphant. Turmoil possessed his heart because of them and he asked,

'Rosy-cheeked maidens, who are you and what do you celebrate with those fires?'

One of them replied to him,

'Our father is an old miller who is now hunting game on these mountain slopes. He is on his way home, for the night is getting dark and his eyes will be puzzled by the gloom.'

At that moment the miller with a company came down from hunting on the mountain and, catching sight of Bahram, he rubbed his face in the dust and then came forward in awe and reverence. The Shah commanded that a golden goblet be offered to the old man just returned from his journey and said to him,

'These four sunny-cheeked maids, why do you keep them? The time is ripe for them to have husbands.'

The old man called down blessings on him and said,

'There are no mates to be had for these girls. They have reached their present age as virgins, and they are pure in their virginity. Of possessions they have nought, neither gold, silver nor anything of any good at all.'

Thereupon Bahram said to him,

'Give all four of them to me and you will never more need to maintain your daughters.'

The old man retorted,

'Cavalier, do not insist on that which you have said, for I have neither raiment, nor estates, nor land, neither silver nor mansion, neither oxen nor asses.'

Bahram answered,

'All that is agreeable to me; I have no need of possessions.'

To that the answer came,

'All four are yours to be wives or servants or the dust of your inner apartments. Your eye sees them with all their defects and merits. Do you approve what it has seen?'

Bahram answered,

'I accept all four of them from their excellent parent.'

Thus saying he rose to his feet. Out in the open the neighing of led horses was to be heard and he ordered the attendants in his retinue to take the lovely maidens to the royal women's quarters. The escort filed out of the plain and all night long troops were crossing it. Meanwhile the miller remained in a state of bewilderment and in the darkness of the night he fell into thought. He said to his wife,

'That distinguished man, handsome as the moon, with his fine presence and majestic bearing, how was it that he came to this place in the night?'

His wife answered,

'He saw the fire in the distance and hearing the sound of the girls' music he seated himself amongst them bringing wine and minstrels.'

Again the miller said to her,

'Wife, give me your opinion. Will this matter end in good or in evil?'

She replied,

'This is of divine ordering. When the man saw them he asked nothing about their birth nor was there any thought of wealth in his mind. He was merely looking about in the world for a beautiful woman and he sought neither money nor a king's daughter. If the Buddhist priests in China saw anything like them the adoration given to the idols would soon cease.'

When night turned into day again the headman from the village came and said to the old man,

'My blessed champion, good fortune came to you in the darkness of the night. The green branches of that tree of yours have come to fruiting. In the darkness of last night Bahram the Shah came from the plain where he had been hunting, and seeing the festivities and the fire he turned his rein and drew in to you. Now your daughters are his wives and are safely in his women's quarters. The king of kings is now your son-in-law; in every region hereafter men will speak of you. He has granted you this province and fine estate. Pine no more, for you can turn aside from all care and fear. We are all now your vassals; nay more, we are all your slaves.'

(VIII) BAHRAM SLAYS A DRAGON: HIS ADVENTURE WITH THE GARDENER'S WIFE

For a long time the Shah lingered with his nobles, occupied with wine, goblets and minstrels. Spring arrived and the ground displayed itself a veritable paradise; the air planted tulips everywhere on the surface of the earth. The whole region was covered with game. In the channels the water flowed as though they were wine and milk; onagers and gazelles roamed the mountain slopes and pastured in herds everywhere among the herbage. Someone said to Shah Bahram Gur that the time for hunting the onager was being overlong delayed, whereupon he commanded that a thousand men be picked from amongst his mounted troops, that hunting panthers and hawks were to be got ready as well as kestrels and proud falcons. All were to journey to Turan in search of game and the chase was to be continued for a month.

Now the king set out for the land of Tur in pursuit of game and beheld the world full of colour and perfume. They cleared the land of onagers, wild sheep and gazelles and lingered for two days over their exploits, Bahram ever with the wine-cup in his hand. On the third day, when the sun lit up his throne and the world became white, mountain and sea taking on the hue of ivory, the valorous king of kings set out once more to hunt. He espied a dragon having the appearance of a male lion, on its head a mane as long as the creature's own height and on its chest two breasts like a woman's. He affixed to his bow a cord and a poplar-wood arrow which he let fly at once at the dragon's chest. Another arrow he shot through the creature's head while the blood and venom came spurting from its chest. Alighting now from his horse he drew a dagger and slit the dragon's body from end to end. It had swallowed a young man who had been congealed in the blood and venom.

Bahram wept bitterly over the dead man, but his eyes became obscured because of the venom. Bemused and staggering he went on his way, longing for sleep and water, and so continued until he reached an inhabited village. There on the plain he came to the gate of a house where a woman stood with a jar on her shoulder hiding her face from the king. He said to her,

'Will you give me a resting-place here, or must I continue onwards in suffering?'

She answered,

'Gallant knight, regard the house as your own.'

When he heard her reply he rode his horse into the garden and the hostess summoned her husband, whom she told to bring straw and to rub down the horse. If he had no comb, he was to use a woollen saddle-cloth. She herself went into her private apartment, and when she emerged she swept the house clean. She spread out a reed mat on which she laid a cushion, all the while calling down blessings on Bahram. Then she went to the tank and brought water, meanwhile quietly scolding her husband.

'This old fool,' she said, 'stands there immovable even though he sees that there is someone in the house. This is not the work for womenfolk, for I must wait on the warrior.'

Shah Bahram now went away to wash his face, for he felt unwell after his combat with the dragon, and the woman brought in a tray on which she had carefully set out chives and vinegar, bread and sour milk. He ate a little and lay down groaning, covering his face with a silken kerchief. When he woke from his sleep the woman said to her husband,

'You ugly fellow with your unwashed face, you have a lamb to kill. This cavalier is a great man and must be of royal seed. He has the chest of a warrior and the splendour of the moon; he resembles no one so much as Bahram Shah.'

The wretched husband replied to his wife,

'Why must you talk so much? You have nothing salted, nor fuel, nor bread, and you never spin thread at night as other women do. When you have killed the lamb and this cavalier has eaten and departed, what profit will you have from this action? Nothing but winter and cold and raging winds will come to you, all together, and that without a doubt.'

Thus did her helpmeet speak. But the woman gave no ear, for she was kindly and full of good sense. In the end, at the woman's bidding the lamb was killed for the knight, and when it was slaughtered she cooked a pot of wheaten meal, having made a fire of half-burnt wood. Then she brought a tray for the royal guest on which were laid eggs and water-cresses which she followed with a roasted leg of lamb and the comestibles with which to garnish it. When Bahram had washed his hands after his food he still remained sleepless and unwell so that when night came up to meet the sun the woman brought him a jug of wine and some jujube[20] fruits. The Shah said to her,

'Woman of few words, recite me some ancient story. While you are talking I shall drink the wine and chase the unhappiness out of my heart. I give you full liberty in telling your story and you may freely make complaint about this Shah of yours.'

'That is well,' said the woman of few words. 'He is the beginning and end of all things.'

Bahram inquired,

'Only that, and nothing more? Do people see no justice or kind act from him?'

That woman of stout character said to him,

'Clear-minded man, there are many people and houses in this village and there is constant coming and going of horsemen, and the agents of the Shah's revenue are many. Let anyone call one of them a robber and the end of it will be trouble in abundance for him. The agent seeks after five or six pence and for them makes a man's life a misery to him. Or he gives a pure-bodied woman a vile name and then tries to avail himself of her modesty. Great harm is done, for the reason that the money taken does not come into the treasury. That is the trouble which comes to us from the lord of the world.'

The monarch fell into musing as he heard these words, and realized that because of his agents' deeds he was acquiring an evil name. The God-fearing king said to himself that a just ruler does

20. A fruit like a plum.

not inspire fear. He determined that for a time he would control all rigorously, so that beneficience and justice could be distinguished from harshness. Tormented by his gloomy thoughts he felt unable to sleep and all night long his mind was occupied with the methods of strict government. When the sun rent its musk-perfumed veil and showed its face in the sky, the woman emerged from the house and said to her husband,

'Bring the cauldron and some fire from indoors; throw grain of all kinds into the water but without letting the sun see it. Now I will go and milk the cow. Do not neglect this matter of the cauldron.'

She brought the cow from where it had been pasturing, carried in a bundle of grass and set it down. Now she pulled the teats, uttering the words, 'In the name of God who has neither companion nor peer.' But she soon saw that her cow's udder was empty of milk, and so the heart of that young hostess became old. She said to her husband,

'Master, the mind of the king of the world has changed its purposes. The king has become a tyrant; his heart last night was secretly tormented.'

'For what reason do you say that,' he inquired. 'In what do you find an evil omen?'

'My dear husband,' she answered him. 'I do not say this without cause. The milk has dried in the teats, the musk in the pod is no longer perfumed. Fornication and hypocrisy will be openly practised; the gentle heart will become hard as granite. On the plain the wolf will eat men, and the wise man will flee before the fool. Eggs will addle under the hen when the tyrannous man becomes king.'

The monarch heard these words and quickly repented of his purposes. Now when once again the happy, chaste and pious woman touched her cow's udder, uttering the words 'In the name of God who produces milk from the hidden source', the milk poured out of her cow's teats. When the milk was boiling in the cauldron and the woman with her husband had completed their preparations she went over to her guest, the man following her with a tray. The king, having partaken of the milk, said to his worthy hostess,

'Take this whip to the gateway and hang it up in a place where men pass by. Look for a stout branch of a tree, where it will receive no damage from the wind; then see who comes in from the road.'

Quickly the master of the house ran out and hung the king's whip from the tree. For a time he watched it. Then, men without number appeared on the road and everyone who saw the whip called down blessings on Bahram. The woman said,

'This man can be none other than the Shah; that face is fitted only for someone of high rank,

[The pair ran to the Shah, begged mercy for their meagre hospitality and were rewarded by the man's being granted the province for his own.]

(IX) THE KHAQAN[21] OF CHINA INVADES IRAN

After a time the tidings came to India and Rum, to Turkestan and China and every populous land that Bahram's heart was set only on amusement and that he disregarded all mankind. He posted neither sentinel nor watchman and in his land there was no warden of the frontiers. He was ever engaged in sport and he let the world go by, knowing nothing either of what was public or hidden. These circumstances came to the hearing of the ruler of China and he mustered an army of chosen troops from China and Khotan. He paid them and set out for Iran without any man sparing a thought for Bahram.

Then from Rum, from India, from China and every populous land the rumours came to Iran that the Caesar had mustered an army and was bringing troops. Furthermore that armies had appeared from China and Khotan.[22] All men that held leadership in Iran therefore, whether elders or young men bearing great names, came in a body to Bahram Gur; they came filled with wrath and resentment and turbulence and they spoke many a harsh word to the king.

'Your brilliant fortune,' they said to him, 'has turned its back on you. The minds of those kings are intent on war, while your heart is fixed on sport and feasting. In your eyes the treasury and the army are things to be despised in the same way as the land of Iran, the throne and the crown.'

The monarch said to the priests, his counsellors,

'The Lord of the world is my ally, loftier in his knowledge than even the highest of you. With the majesty of a great king I guard Iran from the claws of the wolf; by my good fortune, my troops, my sword and my treasure I will avert this trouble and grief from the land.'

[He nevertheless clung to his frivolous ways of life and the Iranians were defeated. In the end, however, Bahram was able to summon up sufficient strength to regain all that had been lost and also to make new conquests. Although he continued to remain addicted to women and the pleasures of the chase, he did attend to the affairs of the state. Near the end of his life he invited ten thousand gypsies from India so that even the poor could enjoy music and dancing with their wine.]

21. I.e., the khan. The beginnings of Tartar and Mongol rule in China come in the Sung period (which ends 1280 A.D.). This is followed by the establishment of a Mongol dynasty, the Yüan.

22. An oasis in the southwestern Sinkiang province, in western China.

(x) BAHRAM GUR'S LIFE COMES TO AN END

So he consumed sixty-three years and no one was his equal. At the beginning of the new year his vizier came to him—namely that wise priest who was his scribe—to tell him that the royal treasuries were empty and that he had come to ask for his commands. Bahram answered,

'Do nothing further, for we no longer need to continue our activities. Resign the world to Him that created it; it is through Him that this revolving wheel is made manifest. The wheel goes on, but God remains in his place as my guide and yours to what is good.'

That night he slept. Next morning at dawn an army without number came to the palace, and an assembly in like numbers gathered about it. There his son Yazdegerd approached him, and to him in the presence of the nobles the Shah gave the crown, the necklace and collar and the ivory throne. Now he resolved to devote himself to the worship of God, for he had surrendered the crown and vacated the throne and so he hastened away from the world's affairs. When the night darkened he laid himself down to sleep. Next morning, when the sun displayed its head from below, the heart of the Shah's counsellor was stricken with fear. The king of the world could no longer be roused.

RŪMĪ

(1207–1273)

The *Mathnawī*

Jalalul'l-Dīn Rūmī is considered the greatest mystical poet of Persia. He was born at Balkh in the northern Persian province of Khorasan in 1207 of a highly respected family, which during his lifetime was forced to wander from city to city as the Mongol invaders attacked the Islamic world. The family finally settled in Turkey, where Rūmī married, and, about his twenty-fifth year, became enamored of the doctrines of the Sūfī sect. For a decade he studied the doctrines of the sect and became a master on the death of his favorite teacher, Burhānu l-Dīn, in 1240. His "real life," however, is a spiritual biography in which dates and facts play a small part, and his son, in describing it, divides it into three mystical periods. Each of the periods is marked by a relationship with a "Perfect Man," a saint whom the worshipper admires and whom he later realizes is a mirror image of himself. He finds, in the light of divine illumination, that he and his object of adoration are not two, but one. The first of these intermediaries between the spirit and the flesh was wandering dervish—a holy man not attached to an institution dedicated to a life of austerity and godliness—whom Rūmī became devoted to about 1244, with the eventual result of alienating his other disciples. This episode ended violently with his followers in revolt and the holy man's mysterious disappearance. A second similar discipleship occupied Rūmī from 1252 to 1261, and also caused friction among his followers. Finally, on the death of this holy man, Rūmī turned to one of his own disciples, Husāmu l-Dīn Hasan, for spiritual companionship. To him he gave credit for his great collection of poems, the *Mathnawī*. This relationship lasted until the end of the poet's life in 1273.

First-hand accounts of Rūmī's life come from biased sources—his dutiful son and devoted followers on the one hand, and his enemies on the other—and it is difficult to ascertain the facts of his life. In any case, many legends have grown up about him. His passionate devotion to the Sūfī doctrine of Oneness through love, a form of Platonic love in which the love for one human spirit for another finally transcends the two people and unites them as one in the love of God, is his chief obsession. In this philosophy of Oneness, God and the World are one, God is both everywhere in the universe and also transcendent and above it, and the transitory world of phenomena is simply a reminder, almost a metaphor, of the Oneness of all things in God. As in most mystical philosophies, God is unknowable, or if he were knowable, inexpressible, and the creatures of the earth give us only clues to his existence. The Perfect Man is the man who realizes his Oneness with God and himself thereby becomes the best possible proof for God's existence.

The Western reader may find a link between Rūmī and the English metaphysical poets—Donne, Herbert, Vaughn, and others—in that Rūmī's mysticism is, as R. A. Nicholson calls it, "experimental,"[1] not doctrinaire. Extravagant metaphor and simile, all of the artillery of the language, is used to storm the gates of heaven, and the poet either succeeds magnificently or fails in a mixture of extravagant language and bad taste. Like the metaphysicals at their best. Rūmī combines a powerful intellect with a rich imagination, and his work appeals to the heart and soul rather than to the mind. His poems, sung by his followers, were said to put them in a state of hypnotic fervor.

Rūmī exists, however, in a much larger tradition of metaphysical poetry than do the English metaphysicals, a tradition that permeates the ancient Near East from earliest times. All of the sensuous lyrics in the Old Testament Song of Songs as well as the symbols of 'Umar Khayyām (the rose, the wine, the tavern door) are interpreted allegorically by the religious. But while Sa'di and Hāfiz in their more worldly poems never quite escape from mystical symbolism, Rūmī is immersed in it. Direct intuition of God is what he promises, and he leads us forward in the quest by suggesting to us the untold raptures that

1. *Rūmī, Poet and Mystic*, by Reynold A. Nicholson (London, 1950), p. 24.

we will attain if we succeed in breaking through to the Oneness.

Although the title of the collection, the *Mathnawī*, means "epic poem," it is certainly not an epic in the Western or even the Indian sense, although it is epical in its sweep and variety. "The poem resembles a trackless ocean," says R. A. Nicholson, "there are no boundaries; no lines of demarcation between the literal 'husk' and the 'kernal' of doctrine in which the inner sense is conveyed and copiously expounded."[2] Blake is perhaps the English poet most in the spirit of Rūmī.

2. Ibid., p. 22.

From The Mathnawī*

*The Song of the Reed***

Harken to this Reed forlorn,
Breathing, even since 'twas torn
From its rushy bed, a strain
Of impassioned love and pain.

"The secret of my song, though near,
None can see and none can hear.
Oh, for a friend to know the sign
And mingle all his soul with mine!

'Tis the flame of Love that fired me,
'Tis the wine of Love inspired me.
Wouldst thou learn how lovers bleed,
Hearken, hearken to the Reed!"

Remembered Music†

'Tis said, the pipe and lute that charm our ears
Derive their melody from rolling spheres;
But Faith, o'erpassing speculation's bound,
Can see what sweetens every jangled sound.

* From *Rūmī, Poet and Mystic (1207–1273). Selections from his Writings Translated from the Persian with Introduction and Notes by the late Reynold A. Nicholson* (London, Allen and Unwin, 1968). Reprinted by permission of Allen & Unwin, Ltd. The notes are the translator's, unless otherwise indicated.

** The opening lines of the poem strike a keynote that recurs insistently throughout. The Persian reed-flute (*nay*) has always been associated with the religious services of the Maulawi order, in which music and dancing are prominent features. Rūmī uses it as a symbol for the soul emptied of self and filled with the divine spirit. This blessed soul, during its life on earth, remembers the union with God which it enjoyed in eternity and longs ardently for deliverance from the world where it is a stranger and exile.

7. *Oh, for a friend . . . :* i.e., a soul of its own kind. Only the mystic understands the mystic.

† The celestial spheres make celestial music when they revolve, which delights the souls of angels. Earthly music echoes this, bringing us pleasure and relief from care and sorrow, and reminders of paradise. A similar Greek view is expressed by Pythagoras. [Editor.]

We, who are parts of Adam, heard with him
The song of angels and of seraphim.
Our memory, though dull and sad, retains
Some echo still of those unearthly strains.

Oh, music is the meat of all who love,
Music uplifts the soul to realms above.
The ashes glow, the latent fires increase:
We listen and are fed with joy and peace.

"The Marriage of True Minds"

Happy the moment when we are seated in the palace, thou and I,
With two forms and with two figures but with one soul, thou and I.
The colours of the grove and the voices of the birds will bestow immortality
At the time when we shall come into the garden, thou and I.
The stars of Heaven will come to gaze upon us:
We shall show them the moon herself, thou and I.
Thou and I, individuals no more, shall be mingled in ecstasy,
Joyful and secure from foolish babble, thou and I.
All the bright-plumed birds of Heaven will devour their hearts with envy
In the place where we shall laugh in such a fashion, thou and I.
This is the greatest wonder, that thou and I, sitting here in the same nook,
Are at this moment both in 'Iraq and Khorasan, thou and I.

The Grief of the Dead

The Prince of mankind (Mohammed) said truly that no one who has passed away from this world
Feels sorrow and regret for having died; nay, but he feels a hundred regrets for having missed the opportunity,
Saying to himself, "Why did I not make death my object—death which is the store-house of all fortunes and riches,
And why, through seeing double, did I fasten my lifelong gaze upon those phantoms that vanished at the fated hour?"
The grief of the dead is not on account of death; it is because they dwelt on the phenomenal forms of existence
And never perceived that all this foam is moved and fed by the Sea.

3. *Why did I not . . . :* Here "death" signifies "dying to self" (*fanā*). Cf. the Prophet's saying, "Die before ye die."

6. *And never . . . :* God is the only real agent. All movement and life in the universe proceeds from him.

When the Sea has cast the foam-flakes on the shore, go to the graveyard and behold them!
Say to them, "Where is your swirling onrush now?" and hear them answer mutely, "Ask this question of the Sea, not of us."
How should the foam fly without the wave? How should the dust rise to the zenith without the wind?
Since you have seen the dust, see the Wind; since you have seen the foam, see the Ocean of Creative Energy.
Come, see it, for insight is the only thing in you that avails: the rest of you is a piece of fat and flesh, a woof and warp (of bones and sinews).
Dissolve your whole body into Vision: become seeing, seeing, seeing!
One sight discerns but a yard or two of the road; another surveys the temporal and spiritual worlds and beholds the Face of their King.

*The Birds of Solomon**

The eloquence of courtly birds is a mere echo: where is the speech of the birds of Solomon?
How wilt thou know their cries, when thou hast never seen Solomon for a single moment?
Far beyond East and West are spread the wings of the bird whose note thrills them that hear it:
From the Footstool of God to the earth and from the earth to the Divine Throne it moves in glory and majesty.
The bird that goes without this Solomon is a bat in love with darkness.
Make thyself familiar with Solomon, O miscreant bat, lest thou remain in darkness for ever.
Go but one ell in that direction, and like the ell thou wilt become the standard of measurement
Even by hopping lamely and limply in that direction thou wilt be freed from all lameness and limpness.

The Beauty of Death

He who deems death to be lovely as Joseph gives up his soul in ransom for it; he who deems it to be like the wolf turns back from the path of salvation.

* Solomon was taught the bird language (*Qur'ān*, xxvii:16). Here he represents the Perfect man, i.e., the Sūfī *murshid*. All artificial eloquence, such as court poets display in their panegyrics, is meaningless in comparison with the mystical utterances of those whom God has inspired.

7. *Go but one ell . . . :* The perfect man is the neasurement of all things. [Editor.]

1. *He who deems . . . :* The comparison with Joseph and the wolf alludes to the *Qur'ān*, xii:13ff.

Every one's death is of the same quality as himself, my lad: to the enemy of God an enemy, to the friend of God a friend.
In the eyes of the Turcoman the mirror is fair; in the eyes of the Ethiopian it is dark as an Ethiopian.
Your fear of death is really fear of yourself: see what it is from which you are fleeing!
'Tis your own ugly face, not the visage of Death: your spirit is like the tree, and death like the leaf.
It has grown from you, whether it be good or evil; all your hidden thoughts, foul or fair, are born from yourself.
If you are wounded by thorns, you planted them; and if you are clad in satin snd silk, *you* were the spinner.
Know that the act is not of the same complexion as its result; a service rendered is not homogeneous with the fragment given in return.
The labourer's wage is dissimilar to his work: the latter is the accident, while the former is the substance.
The latter is wholly toil and effort and sweat, the former is wholly silver and gold and viands.
When the worshipper has sown a prostration or genuflexion here, it becomes the Garden of the Blest hereafter.
When praise of God has flown from his mouth, the Lord of the Daybreak fashions it into a fruit of Paradise.

The Man Who Fled from Azrael

At morn, to Solomon in his hall of justice
A noble suitor came, running in haste,
His countenance pale with anguish, his lips blue.
"What ails, the, Khwajah?" asked the King. Then he:
"'Twas Azrael—ah, such a look he cast
On me of rage and vengeance." "Come now, ask
What boon thou wilt." "Protector of our lives,
I pray thee, bid the Wind convey me straight
To Hindustan: thy servant, there arrived,
Shall peradventure save his soul from Death."

How folk do ever flee from dervishhood
Into the jaws of greed and idle hope!
Your fear of dervishhood is that doomed man's terror,

2. *Every one's death . . . :* Death, whether physical or mystical, is like a mirror in which everyone sees the image of himself: if his nature be good and his actions righteous, he will be in love with death; otherwise he will loathe it and flee in terror from the reflection of his own wickedness. What he dreads so much is really something conceived and produced by himself.

13. *dervishhood:* spiritual poverty, which means "dying to self," i.e., abandoning every "god" or object of desire except Allah. To shrink from this death and seek satisfaction in the pursuit of worldly goods is as vain and useless as to flee from Azrael.

Greed and ambition are your Hindustan.
Solomon bade the Wind transport him swiftly
Over the sea to farthest Hindustan.
On the morrow, when the King in audience sate,
He said to Azrael, "Wherefore didst thou look
Upon that Musulman so wrathfully
His home knew him no more?" "Nay, not in wrath,"
Replied the Angel, "did I look on him;
But seeing him pass by, I stared in wonder,
For God had bidden me take his soul that day
In Hindustan. I stood there marvelling.
Methought, even if he had a hundred wings,
'Twere far for him to fly to Hindustan."

Judge all things of the world by this same rule
And ope your eyes and see! Away from whom
Shall we fly headlong? From ourselves? Absurd!
From God, then? Oh, the vain and woeful crime!

The Blind Follower

The parrot looking in the mirror sees
Itself, but not its teacher hid behind,
And learns the speech of Man, the while it thinks
A bird of its own sort is talking to it.

So the disciple full of egoism
Sees nothing in the Shaykh except himself.
The Universal Reason eloquent
Behind the mirror of the Shaykh's discourse—
The Spirit which is the mystery of Man—
He cannot see. Words mimicked, learned by rote,
'Tis all. A parrot he, no bosom-friend!

The Mystic Way

Plug thy low sensual ear, which stuffs like cotton
Thy conscience and makes deaf thine inward ear.
Be without ear, without sense, without thought,
And hearken to the call of God, "*Return!*"
Our speech and action is the outer journey,

26. *'Twere far . . . :* Cf. the Oriental story at the beginning of John O'Hara's novel *Appointment in Samarra.* [Editor.]

1–4. *The parrot . . . talking to it:* Parrots in the East are trained to talk by means of a mirror, behind which is a curtain. Allegorically the "mirror" is the holy man, who serves as a medium between the "parrot," i.e., the disciple, and God, the invisible Speaker and Teacher.

Our inner journey is above the sky
The body travels on its dusty way;
The spirit walks, like Jesus, on the sea.

Knowledge Is Power

Knowledge is the seal of the Kingdom of Solomon: the whole world is form, and knowledge is its spirit.
Because of this virtue, the creatures of the seas and those of hill and plain are helpless before Man.
Of him the pard and the lion are afraid; the crocodile of the great river trembles.
From him peri and demon take refuge, each lurks in some hiding-place.
Man hath many a secret enemy: the cautious man is wise.
There are hidden beings, evil and good: at every moment their blows are falling on the heart.
The pricks of angelic inspiration and satanic temptation come from thousands, not only from one.
Wait for your senses to be transmuted, so that you may discern these occult presences
And see whose words you have rejected and whom you have made your captain.

The Spirit of the Universe

What worlds mysterious roll within the vast,
The all-encircling ocean of the Mind!
Cup-like thereon our forms are floating fast,
Only to fill and sink and leave behind
No spray of bubbles from the Sea upcast.

The Spirit thou canst not view, it comes so nigh.
Drink of this Presence! Be not thou a jar
Laden with water, and its lip stone-dry;
Or as a horseman blindly borne afar,
Who never sees the horse beneath his thigh.

Divine Providence

Does any painter paint a beautiful picture for the sake of the picture itself?
Nay, his object is to please children or recall departed friends to the memory of those who loved them.

6. ***There are hidden . . . :*** a reference to the Moslem belief that the heart (*qalb*) is a battlefield for invisible hosts of devils and guardian angels.

Does any porter mould a jug for the jug's sake and not in hope of the water?
Does any calligrapher write for the writing's sake and not for the benefit of the reader?
'Tis like moves in chess, my son: perceive the result of each move in the next one.
By discerning cause within cause, one after another, you arrive at victory and checkmate.
The man of dull spirit knows not how to advance: he acts on trust and steps forward blindly.
Blind trust, when you are engaged in war, is as vain as a gambler's reliance on his luck.
When the barriers in front and behind are lifted, the eye penetrates and reads the tablet of the Invisible.
Such a clairvoyant looks back to the origin of existence—he sees the angels dispute with the Almighty as to making our Father (Adam) His viceregent;
And again, casting his eye forward, he beholds all that shall come to pass till the Day of Judgement.
Everyone sees the things unseen according to the measure of his illumination.
The more he polishes the heart's mirror, the more clearly will he descry them.
Spiritual purity is bestowed by the Grace of God; success in polishing is also His Gift.
Work and prayer depend on aspiration; *Man hath nothing but what he hath worked for.*
God alone is the Giver of aspiration: no churl aspires to be a King;
Yet God's assignment of a particular lot to any one does not hinder him from exercising will and choice.
When trouble comes, the ill-fated man turns his back on God, while the blessed man draws nigher unto Him.

The Universal Spirit Revealed in Prophets and Saints

Every moment the robber Beauty rises in a different shape, ravishes the soul and disappears.
Every instant the Loved One assumes a new garment, now of eld, now of youth.

10. *Such a clairvoyant . . . : Qur'ān*, II:28: "The Lord said to the angels, 'Lo, I am about to place a viceroy in the earth.' They said, 'Wilt Thou place therein one who will do evil and shed blood? We are more worthy, since we glorify Thee.' God said, 'Verily I know what ye know not."

15. *Work and prayer . . . : Qur'ān*, liii: 40.

Now He plunged into the heart of the potter's clay—the Spirit plunged like a diver.
Anon, rising from the depths of clay that is moulded and baked, He appeared in the world.
He became Noah, and went into the Ark when at His prayer the world was flooded.
He became Abraham and appeared in the midst of the fire, which bloomed with roses for His sake.
For a while He was roaming on the earth to pleasure Himself;
Then He became Jesus and ascended to Heaven and glorified God.
In brief, it was He that was coming and going in every generation thou hast known,
Until at last He appeared in the form of an Arab and gained the empire of the world.
There is no transmigration, nothing is transferred. The lovely Winner of hearts
Became a sword in the hand of 'Ali and appeared as the Slayer of the time.
No, no! 'Twas even He that cried in human shape, "*Ana 'l-Haqq.*"
The one who mounted the scaffold was not Mansūr, as the foolish imagined.
Rūmī hath not spoken and will not speak words of infidelity: do not disbelieve him!

*The Soul of the World**

I have circled awhile with the nine Fathers in each Heaven.
For years I have revolved with the stars in their signs.
I was invisible awhile, I was dwelling with Him.
I was in the Kingdom of "*or nearer,*" I saw what I have seen.
I receive my nourishment from God, as a child in the womb;
Man is born once, I have been born many times.
Clothed in a bodily mantle, I have busied myself with affairs,

3. *Now he plunged . . . :* The Divine Spirit was breathed into the clay body of Adam, which God had kneaded with His own hands for forty days.

11. *There is no transmigration . . . :* Rūmī warns us against a belief in the transmigration of souls, a heresy. There is no transmigration because the soul is all One Essence. [Editor.]

14. *Mansur:* Husayn ibn Mansūr, a mystic, executed at Baghdad 922 A.D. [Editor.]

1. *the nine Fathers:* Each of the nine celestial spheres was supposed to have a ruling Intelligence, and these spiritual powers are called "Fathers" here.

* A description of the Perfect Man as the Universal Spirit.

4. *"or nearer":* Cf. *Qur'ān,* liii:8–10: "then he approached and descended and was at a distance of two bow-lengths or nearer"—a passage which is generally interpreted as the climax of the Prophet's ascension.

And often have I rent the mantle with my own hands.
I have passed nights with ascetics in the monastery,
I have slept with infidels before the idols in the pagoda.
I am the pangs of the jealous, I am the pain of the sick.
I am both cloud and rain: I have rained on the meadows.
Never did the dust of mortality settle on my skirt, O dervish!
I have gathered a wealth of roses in the garden of Eternity.
I am not of water nor fire, I am not of the froward wind,
I am not of moulded clay: I have mocked at them all.
O son, I am not Shams-i Tabriz, I am the pure Light.
If thou seest me, beware! Tell not any one what thou hast
seen!

SA'DĪ

(1213/19–1292)

The Rose Garden (*Gulistān*)

Though biographical and hagiographical accounts if Sa'dī abound, the demonstrably true facts of his life are few. He was born about 1213–19 in the famous city of Shiraz and began early a restless life of travel, as the Mongol invaders made life intolerable in Iran. He studied in Baghdad at a famous academy, and almost certainly traveled through Mesopotamia, Asia Minor, Syria, and to the fountainhead of Moslem belief, Mecca. Probably he did not reach Kashgar and India as later legend records it. He attained fame in 1256–57 with his *Orchard* (*Būstān*), after his return to Shiraz, and issued his *Rose Garden* (*Gulistān*) a year later, both dedicated to the local ruler. We need not assume, however, that the *Rose Garden* was composed in a year, but that it is a collection of works done over a period of time. While we have few insights into Sa'dī's personal life, his fame was established by these two works and continued to grow. If Rūmī is the mystical poet *par excellence* and Hāfiz the great master of Persian lyric, Sa'dī most brings poetry down to the marketplace and the haunts of living men. Sa'dī exhibits the same intense thinking about the world of the spirit that the other two poets have, but he is less interested in expressing the mystical, and is usually didactic. He attempts to bring the teaching of the sages to play on the conduct of life in the court, in the bazaar, and in the home. His mystical love for mankind takes earthy form, and he is a master of the moral tale pointed up by verses. His observations come from everyday life —in the act of the politician, in the heat of an argument, in the gap in everyday life between the word and the deed. For this reason the reader often feels that Sa'dī is basing his observations on experiences from this own life. Justice, equity, government administration, benevolence, love (physical and mystical), contentment, self-restraint, devout meditations—these are the announced subjects of the *Orchard* and they are the themes of the *Rose Garden* too.

Sa'dī died in December 1292 in a monastery, having in the *Rose Garden* especially mirrored the particular virtues and vices of the Persian people. He gives us vivid scenes of real life, distilled to their didactic essences. His heart and mind seem at war. On the one hand there is his mystical and emotional religious self. On the other, there is his cool, analytical eye, ever observing the failings of men. He sees that if the Holy Spirit is to be felt among men that it must manifest itself as a guide to daily conduct, not only in the mystic's solitary revels or in the mosque.

From The Rose Garden*

The Manners of Kings

STORY 1

I heard a padshah[1] giving orders to kill a prisoner. The helpless fellow began to insult the king on that occasion of despair, with the tongue he had, and to use foul expressions according to the saying:

> Who washes his hands of life
> Says whatever he has in his heart.

When a man is in despair his tongue becomes long and he is like a vanquished cat assailing a dog.

> In time of need, when flight is no more possible,
> The hand grasps the point of the sharp sword.

When the king asked what he was saying, a good-natured vezier replied: 'My lord, he says: *Those who bridle their anger and forgive men; for Allah loveth the beneficent.*'[2]

The king, moved with pity, forbore taking his life but another vezier, the antagonist of the former, said: 'Men of our rank ought to speak nothing but the truth in the presence of padshahs. This fellow has insulted the king and spoken unbecomingly.' The king, being displeased with these words, said 'That lie was more acceptable to me than this truth thou hast uttered because the former proceeded from a conciliatory disposition and the latter from

* From *The Gulistan, or Rose Garden of Sa'di*. Translated by Edward Rehatsek and edited by W. G. Archer. The notes are mostly abridged from those of the translator.

2. *Qur'ān*, iii:128.

malignity; and wise men have said: "A falsehood resulting in conciliation is better than a truth producing trouble." '

He whom the shah follows in what he says,
It is a pity if he speaks anything but what is good.

The following inscription was upon the portico of the hall of Feridun:

O brother, the world remains with no one.
Bind the heart to the Creator, it is enough.
Rely not upon possessions and this world
Because it has cherished many like thee and slain them.
When the pure soul is about to depart,
What boots it if one dies on a throne or on the ground?

STORY 2

One of the kings of Khorasan had a vision in a dream of Sultan Mahmud, one hundred years after his death. His whole person appeared to have been dissolved and turned to dust, except his eyes, which were revolving in their orbits and looking about. All the sages were unable to give an interpretation, except a dervish who made his salutation and said: 'He is still looking amazed how his kingdom belongs to others.'

Many famous men have been buried under ground
Of whose existence on earth not a trace has remained
And that old corpse which had been surrendered to the earth
Was so consumed by the soil that not a bone remains.
The glorious name of Nushirvan survives in good repute
Although much time elapsed since he passed away.
Do good, O man, and consider life as a good fortune,
The more so, as when a shout is raised, a man exists no more.[3]

STORY 3

I have heard that a royal prince of short stature and mean presence, whose brothers were tall and good-looking, once saw his father glancing on him with aversion and contempt but he had the shrewdness and penetration to guess the meaning and said: 'O father, a puny intelligent fellow is better than a tall ignorant man, neither is everything bigger in stature higher in price. *A sheep is nice to eat and an elephant is carrion.*'

3. G. M. Wilkins translates thus: "O what's your name, do good, and make the most of life/Before the cry goes up that what's his name's no more" (Rehatsek's note, p. 74).

The smallest mountain on earth is Jur;[4] *nevertheless*
It is great with Allah in dignity and station.

Hast thou not heard that a lean scholar
One day said to a fat fool:
'Although an Arab horse may be weak
It is thus more worth than a stable full of asses.'

The father laughed at this sally, the pillars of the state approved of it, but the brothers felt much aggrieved.

While a man says not a word
His fault and virtue are concealed.
Think not that every desert is empty.
Possibly it may contain a sleeping tiger.

I heard that on the said occasion the king was menaced by a powerful enemy and that when the two armies were about to encounter each other, the first who entered the battlefield was the little fellow who said:

'I am not he whose back thou wilt see on the day of battle
But he whom thou shalt behold in dust and blood.
Who himself fights, stakes his own life
In battle but he who flees, the blood of his army.'

After uttering these words he rushed among the troops of the enemy, slew several warriors and, returning to his father, made humble obeisance and said:

'O thou, to whom my person appeared contemptible,
Didst not believe in the impetuosity of my valour.
A horse with slender girth is of use
On the day of battle, not a fattened ox.'

It is related that the troops of the enemy were numerous, and that the king's being few, were about to flee, but that the puny youth raised a shout, saying: 'O men, take care not to put on the garments of women.' These words augmented the rage of the troopers so that they made a unanimous attack and I heard that they gained the victory on the said occasion. The king kissed the head and eyes of his son, took him in his arms and daily augmented his affection till he appointed him to succeed him on the throne. His brothers became envious and placed poison in his food but were preceived by his sister from her apartment, whereon she closed the window violently and the youth, shrewdly guessing the significance

4. Mount Sinai is also called by this name, but in the above passage it refers to a very small mountain near Jerusalem, with the tombs of holy men on it.

of the act, restrained his hands from touching the food, and said: 'It is impossible that men of honour should die, and those who possess none should take their place.'

> No one goes under the shadow of an owl
> Even if the homa[5] should disappear from the world.

This state of affairs having been brought to the notice of the father, he severely reproved the brothers and assigned to each of them a different, but pleasant, district as a place of exile till the confusion was quelled and the quarrel appeased; and it has been said that ten dervishes may sleep under the same blanket but that one country cannot hold two padshahs.

> When a pious man eats half a loaf of bread
> He bestows the other half upon dervishes.
> If a padshah were to conquer the seven climates[6]
> He would still in the same way covet another.

STORY 4

A band of Arab brigands having taken up their position on the top of a mountain and closed the passage of caravans, the inhabitants of the country were distressed by their stratagems and the troops of the sultan foiled because the robbers, having obtained an inaccessible spot on the summit of the mountain, thus had a refuge which they made their habitation. The chiefs of that region held a consultation about getting rid of the calamity because it would be impossible to offer resistance to the robbers if they were allowed to remain.

> A tree which has just taken root
> May be moved from the place by the strength of a man
> But, if thou leavest it thus for a long time,
> Thou canst not uproot it with a windlass.
> The source of a fountain may be stopped with a bodkin
> But, when it is full, it cannot be crossed on an elephant.

The conclusion was arrived at to send one man as a spy and to wait for the opportunity till the brigands departed to attack some people and leave the place empty. Then several experienced men, who had fought in battles, were despatched to keep themselves in ambush in a hollow of the mountain. In the evening the brigands returned from their excursion with their booty, divested themselves

5. The *homa* is a fabulous bird resembling, in some respects, the phoenix. The person upon whose head the shadow of it falls is believed to be destined to occupy a throne.

6. The seven climates cover the whole world.

of their arms, put away their plunder and the first enemy who attacked them was sleep, till about a watch of the night[7] had elapsed:

> The disk of the sun went into darkness.
> Jonah went into the mouth of the fish.

The warriors leapt forth from the ambush, tied the hands of everyone of the robbers to his shoulders and brought them in the morning to the court of the king, who ordered all of them to be slain. There happened to be a youth among them, the fruit of whose vigour was just ripening and the verdure on the rose-garden of whose cheek had begun to sprout. One of the veziers, having kissed the foot of the king's throne and placed the face of intercession upon the ground, said: 'This boy has not yet eaten any fruit from the garden of life and has not yet enjoyed the pleasures of youth. I hope your majesty will generously and kindly confer an obligation upon your slave by sparing his life.' The king, being displeased with this request, answered:

> 'He whose foundation is bad will not take instruction from the good,
> To educate unworthy persons is like throwing nuts on a cupola.

'It is preferable to extirpate the race and offspring of these people and better to dig up their roots and foundations, because it is not the part of wise men to extinguish fire and to leave burning coals or to kill a viper and leave its young ones.

> 'If a cloud should rain the water of life[8]
> Never sip it from the branch of a willow-tree[9]
> Associate not with a base fellow
> Because thou canst not eat sugar from a mat-reed'[10]

The vezier heard these sentiments, approved of them *nolens volens*, praised the opinion of the king and said: 'What my lord has uttered is the very truth itself because if the boy had been brought up in the company of those wicked men, he would have become one of themselves. But your slave hopes that he will, in the society of pious men, profit by education and will acquire the disposition of wise persons. Being yet a child the rebellious and perversed temper of that band has not yet taken hold of his nature and there is a tradition of the prophet that *every inrant is born with an inclination*

7. About three hours.
8. The water of life or the fountain of youth. Alexander is said to have sought this in his Asian conquests.
9. The willow is considered a very lowly tree.
10. The branches from which mats are made can never produce sugar like the branches of the sugan cane.

for Islam but his parents make him a Jew, a Christian or a Majusi.'[11]

> The spouse of Lot became a friend of wicked persons.
> His race of prophets became extinct.
> The dog of the companions of the cave[12] for some days
> Associated with good people and became a man.

When the vezier had said these words and some of the king's courtiers had added their intercession to his, the king no longer desired to shed the blood of the youth and said: 'I grant the request although I disapprove of it.'

> Knowest thou not what Zal said to the hero Rastam:[13]
> 'An enemy cannot be held despicable or helpless.
> I have seen many a water from a paltry spring
> Becoming great and carrying off a camel with its load.'

In short, the vezier brought up the boy delicately, with every comfort, and kept masters to educate him, till they had taught him to address persons in elegant language as well as to reply and he had acquired every accomplishment. One day the vezier hinted at his talents in the presence of the king, asserting that the instructions of wise men had taken effect upon the boy and had expelled his previous ignorance from his nature. The king smiled at these words and said:

> 'At last a wolf's whelp will be a wolf
> Although he may grow up with a man.'

After two years had elapsed a band of robbers in the locality joined him, tied the knot of friendship and, when the opportunity presented itself, he killed the vezier with his son, took away untold wealth and succeeded to the position of his own father in the robber-cave where he established himself. The king, informed of the event, took the finger of amazement between his teeth and said:

> 'How can a man fabricate a good sword of bad iron?
> O sage, who is nobody becomes not somebody by education.
> The rain, in the beneficence of whose nature there is no flaw,
> Will cause tulips to grow in the garden and weeds in bad soil.
> Saline earth will not produce hyacinths.
> Throw not away thy seeds or work thereon.
> To do good to wicked persons is like
> Doing evil to good men.'

11. *Majusi* is the Arabized form of *magus* ("magician") and stands for Zoroasterian.

12. In the *Qur'ān*, chapter xviii bears the title "The Cave"; here is narrated the story of the "Companions," who are known in European tales as the "seven sleepers."

13. Or Rustam, a hero of Firdausī's *Shāh-nāma*. Zal was his father.

The Morals of Dervishes

STORY 6

A hermit, being the guest of a padshah, ate less than he wished when sitting at dinner and when he rose for prayers he prolonged them more than was his wont in order to enhance the opinion entertained by the padshad of his piety.

O Arab of the desert, I fear thou wilt not reach the Ka'bah[14]
Because the road on which thou travellest leads to Turkestan.

When he returned to his own house, he desired the table to be laid out for eating. He had an intelligent son who said: 'Father, hast thou not eaten anything at the repast of the sultan?' He replied: 'I have not eaten anything to serve a purpose.' The boy said: 'Then likewise say thy prayers again as thou hast not done anything to serve that purpose.'

O thou who showest virtues on the palms of the hand
But concealest thy errors under the armpit
What wilt thou purchase, O vain-glorious fool,
On the day of distress with counterfeit silver?

STORY 7

I remember, being in my childhood pious, rising in the night, addicted to devotion and abstinence. One night I was sitting with my father, remaining awake and holding the beloved Qur'ān in my lap, whilst the people around us were asleep. I said: 'Not one of these persons lifts up his head or makes a genuflection. They are as fast asleep as if they were dead.' He replied: 'Darling of thy father, would that thou wert also asleep rather than disparaging people.'

The pretender sees no one but himself
Because he has the veil of conceit in front.
If he were endowed with a God-discerning eye
He would see that no one is weaker than himself.

STORY 11

I spoke in the cathedral mosque of Damascus a few words by way of a sermon but to a congregation whose hearts were withered and dead, not having travelled from the road of the world of form, the physical, to the world of meaning, the moral world. I perceived that my words took no effect and that burning fire does not kindle moist

14. The sacred stone in the shrine at Mecca, the holiest of holies.

wood. I was sorry for instructing brutes and holding forth a mirror in a locality of blind people. I had, however, opened the door of meaning and was giving a long explanation of the verse *We are nearer unto Him than the jugular vein*[15] till I said:

> 'The Friend[16] is nearer to me than my self,
> But it is more strange that I am far from him.
> What am I to do? To whom can it be said that he
> Is in my arms, but I am exiled from him.'

I had intoxicated myself with the wine of these sentiments, holding the remnant of the cup of the sermon in my hand when a traveller happened to pass near the edge of the assembly, and the last turn of the circulating cup made such an impression upon him that he shouted and the others joined him who began to roar, whilst the raw portion of the congregation became turbulent. Whereon I said: 'Praise be to Allah! Those who are far away but intelligent are in the presence of Allah, and those who are near but blind are distant.'

> When the hearer understands not the meaning of words
> Do look for the effect of the orator's force
> But raise an extensive field of desire
> That the eloquent man may strike the ball of effect.

STORY 12

One night I had in the desert of Mekkah become so weak from want of sleep that I was unable to walk and, laying myself down, told the camel driver to let me alone.

> How far can the foot of a wretched pedestrian go
> When a dromedary gets distressed by its load?
> Whilst the body of a fat man becomes lean
> A weak man will be dead of exhaustion.

He replied: 'O brother, the sanctuary[17] is in front of us and brigands in the rear. If thou goest thou wilt prosper. If thou sleepest thou wilt die.'

> It is pleasant to sleep under an acacia on the desert road
> But alas! thou must bid farewell to life on the night of departure.

STORY 13

I saw a holy man on the seashore who had been wounded by a tiger. No medicine could relieve his pain; he suffered much but he

15. See *Qur'ān*, 1:15.
16. In Sūfī parlance, "the friend" means God.
17. Mecca.

nevertheless constantly thanked God the most high, saying: 'Praise be to Allah that I have fallen into a calamity and not into sin.'

If that beloved Friend decrees me to be slain
I shall not say that moment that I grieve for life
Or say: What fault has thy slave committed?
My grief will be for having offended thee.

STORY 14

A dervish who had fallen into want stole a blanket from the house of a friend. The judge ordered his hand to be amputated but the owner of the blanket interceded, saying that he had condoned the fault. The judge rejoined: 'Thy intercession cannot persuade me to neglect the provision of the law.' The man continued: 'Thou hast spoken the truth but amputation is not applicable to a person who steals some property dedicated to pious uses. Moreover *a beggar possesses nothing* and whatever belongs to a dervish is dedicated to the use of the needy.' Thereon the judge released the culprit, saying: 'The world must indeed have become too narrow for thee that thou hast committed no theft except from the house of such a friend.' He replied: 'Hast thou not heard the saying: 'Sweep out the house of friends and do not knock at the door of foes.'

If thou sinkest in a calamity be not helpless.
Strip thy foes of their skins and thy friends of their fur-coats.

STORY 15

A padshah, meeting a holy man, asked him whether he did not sometimes remember him for the purpose of getting presents. He replied: 'Yes, I do, whenever I forget God.'

Whom He drives from his door, runs everywhere.
Whom He calls, runs to no one's door.

STORY 16

A pious man saw in a dream a padshah in paradise and a devotee in hell whereon he asked for the reason of the former's exaltation and the latter's degradation, saying that he had imagined the contrary ought to be the case. He received the following answer: 'The padshah had, for the love he bore to dervishes, been rewarded with paradise and the devotee had, for associating with padshahs, been punished in hell.'

Of what use is thy frock, rosary and patched dress?
Keep thyself free from despicable practices.

Then thou wilt have no need of a cap of leaves.[18]
Have the qualities of a dervish and wear a Tatar cap.

STORY 38

A murid said to his pir:[19] 'What am I to do? I am troubled by the people, many of whom pay me visits. By their coming and going they encroach upon my precious time.' He replied: 'Lend something to every one of them who is poor and ask something from every one who is rich and they will come round thee no more.'

If a mendicant were the leader of the army of Islam,
The infidels would for fear of his importunity run as far as China.

On the Excellence of Contentment

STORY 11

A brave warrior who had received a dreadful wound in the Tatar war was informed that a certain merchant possessed a medicine which he would probably not refuse to give if asked for; but it is related that the said merchant was also well known for his avarice.

If instead of bread he had the sun in his table-cloth
No one could see daylight till the day of resurrection.

The warrior replied: 'If I ask for the medicine he will either give it or refuse it and if he gives it maybe it will profit me, and maybe not. At any rate the inconvenience of asking it from him is a lethal poison.'

Whatever thou obtainest by entreaties from base men
Will profit thy body but injure thy soul.

And philosophers have said: 'If for instance the water of life[20] were to be exchanged for a good reputation, no wise man would purchase it because it is preferable to die with honour than to live in disgrace.'

To eat coloquinth[21] from hand of a sweet-tempered man
Is better than confectionery from the hand of an
ill-humoured fellow.

18. Caps of leaves were worn by dervishes, who were supposed to dress in a humble fashion.

19. A *murid* is a religious devotee, *pir* the spiritual teacher of dervishes.

20. See note 8.

21. A bitter citrus fruit.

STORY 16

Moses,[22] to whom be salutation, beheld a dervish who had on account of his nudity concealed himself in the sand exclaiming: 'O Moses, utter a supplication to God the most high to give me an allowance because I am, on account of my distress, on the point of starvation.' Moses accordingly prayed and departed but returning a few days afterwards he saw that the dervish was a prisoner and surrounded by a crowd of people. On asking for the reason he was informed that the dervish had drunk wine, quarrelled, slain a man and was to be executed in retaliation.

> If the humble cat possessed wings
> He would rob the world of every sparrow-egg.
> It may happen that when a weak man obtains power
> He arises and twists the hands of the weak.

And if Allah were to bestow abundance upon his servants, they would certainly rebel upon earth.[23]

> What has made thee wade into danger, O fool,
> Till thou hast perished. Would that the ant[24] had not been able to fly!

> When a base fellow obtains dignity, silver and gold,
> His head necessarily demands to be knocked.
> Was not after all this maxim uttered by a sage?
> 'That ant is the best which possess no wings.'

The heavenly father has plenty of honey but the son has a hot disease.

> He who does not make thee rich
> Knows better what is good for thee than thyself.

STORY 17

I noticed an Arab of the desert sitting in a company of jewellers at Bosrah[25] and narrating stories to them. He said: 'I had once lost my road in the desert and consumed all my provisions. I considered that I must perish when I suddenly caught sight of a bag full of pearls and I shall never forget the joy and ecstasy I felt on thinking

22. Both the patriarchs of the Old Testament and Jesus Christ are revered by Moslems, for whom Muhammad is the last and greatest prophet.
23. *Qur'ān*, xlii:26.
24. The lion-ant or flying ant.
25. Basra, a major port city of Iraq.

they might be parched grain nor the bitterness and despair when I discovered them to be pearls.'

In a dry desert and among moving sand
It is the same to a thirsty man whether he has pearls
or shells in his mouth
When a man has no provisions and his strength is exhausted
It matters not whether his girdle is adorned with pearls or
potsherds.

STORY 20

A king with some of his courtiers had during a hunting party and in the winter season strayed far from inhabited places but when the night set in he perceived the house of a dehqan[26] and said: 'We shall spend the night there to avoid the injury of the cold.' One of the veziers, however, objected alleging that it was unworthy of the high dignity of a padshah to take refuge in the house of a dehqan and that it would be best to pitch tents and to light fires on the spot. The dehqan who had become aware of what was taking place prepared some food he had ready in his house, offered it, kissed the ground of service and said: 'The high dignity of the sultan would not have been so much lowered, but the courtiers did not wish the dignity of the dehqan to become high.' The king who was pleased with these words moved for the night into the man's house and bestowed a dress of honour upon him the next morning. When he accompanied the king a few paces at the departure he was heard to say:

'Nothing was lost of the sultan's power and pomp
By accepting the hospitality of a dehqan,
But the corner of the dehqan's cap reached the sun
When a sultan such as thou overshadowed his head.'

STORY 23

I heard about a wealthy man who was as well known for his avarice as Hatim Tai for his liberality. Outwardly he displayed the appearance of wealth but inwardly his sordid nature was so dominant that he would not for his life give a morsel of bread to anyone or bestow a scrap upon the kitten of Abu Harirah[27] or throw a bone to the dog of the companions of the cave.[28] In short, no one had seen the door of his house open or his table-cloth spread.

26. A *dehqan* is usually a landowner, but here the word means a peasant.

27. His appelation means "father of the kitten." He was a companion of Muhammad who always carried a kitten about.

28. See note 12.

The dervish got nothing of his food except the smell.
The fowl picked up the crumbs after his bread-dinner.

I heard that he was sailing in the Mediterranean with the pride of Pharaoh in his head—according to the words of the most high, *Until drowning overtook him*[29]—when all of a sudden a contrary wind befell the ship, as it is said:

What can thy heart do to thy distress nature for the
wind is not fair?
It is not at all times suitable for a ship.

He uplifted the hands of supplication and began to lament in vain but Allah the most high has commanded: *When they sail in a ship they call upon Allah, sincerely exhibiting unto him their religion.*[30]

Of what use is the hand of supplication to a needy worshipper
Which is uplifted to God in the time of prayer but in the
armpit in the time of bounty?

Bestow comfort with gold and with silver
And thereby also profit thyself.
As this house of thine will remain,
Build it with a silver and a gold brick.

It is narrated that he had poor relations in Egypt who became rich by the remainder of his wealth, tearing up their old cloths and cutting new ones of silk and of Damiari.[31] During the same week I also beheld one of them riding a fleet horse with a fairy-faced slave boy at his heels. I said:

'Wah! If the dead man were to return
Among his kinsfolk and connections
The refunding of the inheritance would be more painful
To the heirs than the death of their relative.'

On account of the acquaintance which had formerly subsisted between us, I pulled his sleeve, and said:

'Eat thou, O virtuous and good man,
What that mean fellow gathered and did not eat.'

STORY 26

I have seen a fat fool, dressed in a costly robe, with a turban of Egyptian linen on his head, riding on an Arab horse. Someone said: 'Sa'di, what thinkest thou of this famous brocade upon this igno-

29. *Qur'ān*, x:90.
30. *Qur'ān*, xxix:65.
31. A kind of fine linen made at Damietta, in Egypt.

rant animal?' I replied: 'It is like ugly characters scrawled with gold-water.'

A calf, a body which is bleating.
Verily he is like an ass among men,

This animal cannot be said to resemble a man
Except in his cloak, turban and outward adornment.
Examine all his property and belongs of his estate
Thou wilt find nothing lawful to take except his blood.
If a noble man becomes impoverished imagine not
That his high worth will also decrease.

On the Advantages of Silence

STORY 10

A poet went to an amir of robbers and recited a panegyric but he ordered him to be divested of his robe. As the poor man was departing naked in the world, he was attacked from behind by dogs, whereon he intended to snatch up a stone but it was frozen to the ground and, being unable to do so, he exclaimed: 'What whore-sons of men are these? They have let loose the dogs and have tied down the stones.' The amir of the robbers who heard these words from his room laughed and said: 'O philosopher, ask something from me.' He replied: 'I ask for my robe if thou wilt make me a present of it.'

We are satisfied of thy gift by departure.[32]

A man was hoping for the gifts of people.
I hope no gift from thee. Do me no evil.

The robber chief took pity upon him, ordered his robe to be restored to him and added to it a sheepskin jacket with some dirhems.

STORY 12

A preacher imagined his miserable voice to be pleasing and raised useless shouts, thou wouldst have said that the *crow of separation* had become the tune of his song;[33] and the verse—*for the most detestable of voice of asses*[34]—appears to have been applicable to him. This distich also concerns him:

32. I.e., the greatest gift you could give us would be allowing us to depart.

33. The crow is so called because he searches abandoned campsites for food and it is considered extremely unlucky to meet him.

34. *Qur'ān*, xxxi:18.

When the preacher Abu-l-Fares brays
At his voice Istakhar-Fares[35] *quakes.*

On account of the position he occupied the inhabitants of the locality submitted to the hardship and did not think proper to molest him. In course of time, however, another preacher of that region, who bore secret enmity towards him, arrived on a visit and said to him: 'I have dreamt about thee, may it end well!' 'What hast thou dreamt?' 'I dreamt that thy voice had become pleasant and that the people were comfortable during thy sermons.' The preacher meditated a while on these words and then said: 'Thou hast dreamt a blessed dream because thou hast made me aware of my defect. It has become known to me that I have a disagreeble voice and that the people are displeased with my loud reading. Accordingly I have determined henceforth not to address them except in a subdued voice':

I am displeased with the company of friends
To whom my bad qualities appear to be good.
They fancy my faults are virtues and perfection.
My thorns they believe to be rose and jessamine.
Say. Where is the bold and quick enemy
To make me aware of my defects?

He whose faults are not told him
Ignorantly thinks his defects are virtues.

STORY 13

A man used to shout superfluous calls to prayers in the mosque of Sinjar and in a voice which displeased all who heard it. The owner of the mosque, who was a just and virtuous amir, not desirous to give him pain, said: 'My good fellow, in this mosque there are old muezzins[36] to each of whom I pay five dinars monthly but to thee I shall give ten, if thou wilt go to another place.' The man agreed and went away. Some time afterwards however, he returned to the amir and said: 'My lord, thou hast injured me by turning me away for ten dinars from this place because where I next went they offered me twenty dinars to go to another locality but I refused. The amir smiled and said: 'By no means accept them because they will give thee even fifty dinars.'

No one can scrape the mud from gravel with an axe
As thy discordant shouting scrapes the heart.

35. The celebrated ruins of Persepolis.
36. The crier who calls the faithful to prayer five times a day from a minaret or tower in the mosque.

STORY 14

A fellow with a disagreeable voice happened to be reading the Qur'ān, when a pious man passed near, and asked him what his monthly salary was. He replied: 'Nothing.' He further inquired: 'Then why takest thou this trouble?' He replied: 'I am reading for God's sake.' He replied: 'For God's sake do not read.'

> If thou readest the Qur'an thus
> Thou wilt deprive the religion of splendour.

On Love and Youth

STORY 5

A schoolboy was so perfectly beautiful and sweet-voiced that the teacher, in accordance with human nature, conceived such an affection towards him that he often recited the following verses:

> I am not so little occupied with thee, O heavenly face,
> That remembrance of myself occurs to my mind.
> From thy sight I am unable to withdraw my eyes
> Although when I am opposite I may see that an arrow comes.

Once the boy said to him: 'As thou strivest to direct my studies, direct also my behavior. If thou perceivest anything reprovable in my conduct, although it may seem approvable to me, inform me thereof that I may endeavour to change it.' He replied: 'O boy, make that request to someone else because the eyes with which I look upon thee behold nothing but virtues.'

> The ill-wishing eye, be it torn out
> Sees only defects in his virtue.
> But if thou possessest one virtue and seventy faults
> A friend sees nothing except that virtue.

STORY 13

A parrot, having been imprisoned in a cage with a crow, was vexed by the sight and said: 'What a loathsome aspect is this! What an odious figure! What cursed object with rude habits! O *crow of separation,*[37] *would that the distance of the east from the west were between us.*'

> Whoever beholds thee when he rises in the morning
> The morn of a day of safety becomes evening to him.

37. See note 33.

An ill-omened one like thyself is fit to keep thee company
But where in the world is one like thee?

More strange still, the crow was similarly distressed by the proximity of the parrot and, having become disgusted, was shouting 'La haul,'[38] and lamenting the vicissitudes of time. He rubbed the claws of sorrow against each other and said: 'What ill-luck is this? What base destiny and chameleon-like times? It was befitting my dignity to strut about on a garden-wall in the society of another crow.

'It is sufficient imprisonment for a devotee
To be in the same stable with profligates.

'What sin have I committed that I have already in this life, as a punishment for it, fallen into the bonds of this calamity in company with such a conceited, uncongenial and heedless fool?'

No one will approach the foot of the wall
Upon which they paint thy portrait.
If thy place were in paradise
Others would select hell.

I have added this parable to let thee know that no matter how much a learned man may hate an ignorant man the latter hates him equally.

A hermit was among profligates
When one of them, a Balkhi[39] beauty, said:
'If thou art tired of us sit not sour
For thou art thyself bitter in our midst.'

An assembly joined together like roses and tulips!
Thou art withered wood, growing in its midst,
Like a contrary wind and unpleasant frost,
Like snow inert, like ice bound fast.

STORY 16

I remember having in the days of my youth passed through a street, intending to see a moon-faced beauty. It was in Temuz, whose heat dried up the saliva in the mouth and whose simum[40] boiled the marrow in my bones. My weak human nature being unable to

38. Figuratively, the words "La haul" are synonymous with the exclamation "God forbid!" Literally, they mean "There is no power"; they are the first two words of the phrase "There is no power or strength except by the will of Allah the most high" and are uttered by Moslems when any extraordinary event takes place.

39. From the city of Balkh in Afganistan, the ancient Bactria.

40. *Temuz* is the month of July; the *simum* is a fearfully hot wind blowing in the African desert.

endure the scorching sun, I took refuge in the shadow of a wall, wishing someone might relieve me from the summer heat and quench my fire with some water; and lo, all of a sudden, from the darkness of the porch of a house a light shone forth, namely a beauty, the grace of which the tongue of eloquence is unable to describe. She came out like the rising dawn after an obscure night or the water of immortality gushing from a dark cavern, carrying in her hand a bowl of snow-water, into which sugar had been poured and essence of roses mixed. I knew not whether she had perfumed it with rose-water or whether a few drops from her rosy face had fallen into it. In short, I took the beverage from her beautiful hands, drank it and began to live again.

The thirst of my heart cannot be quenched
By sipping limpid water even if I drink oceans of it.

Blessed is the man of happy destiny whose eye
Alights every morning on such a countenance.
One drunk of wine awakens at midnight,
One drunk of the cupbearer on the morn of resurrection.

STORY 18

A man in patched garments[41] accompanied us in a caravan to the Hejaz and one of the Arab amirs presented him with a hundred dinars to spend upon his family but robbers of the Kufatcha tribe suddenly fell upon the caravan and robbed it clean of everything. The merchants began to wail and to cry, uttering vain shouts and lamentations.

Whether thou implorest or complainest
The robber will not return the gold again.

The dervish alone had not lost his equanimity and showed no change. I asked: 'Perhaps they have not taken thy money?' He replied: 'Yes, they have but I was not so much accustomed to that money that separation therefrom could grieve my heart':

The heart must not be tied to any thing or person
Because to take off the heart is a difficult affair.

I replied: "What thou hast said resembles my case because, when I was young, my intimacy with a young man and my friendship for him were such that his beauty was the Qiblah[42] of my eye and the chief joy of my life union with him':

41. A dervish.
42. All Moslems are bound to turn towards Mecca when they say their prayers, wherever they may be on the face of the earth.

Perhaps an angel in heaven but no mortal
Can be on earth equal in beauty of form to him.
I swear by the amity, after which companionship is illicit,
No human sperm will ever become a man like him.

All of a sudden the foot of his life sank into the mire of non-existence. The smoke[43] of separation arose from his family. I kept him company on his grave for many days and one of my compositions on his loss is as follows:

Would that on the day when the thorn of fate entered thy foot
The hand of heaven had struck a sword on my head;
So that this day my eye could not see the world without thee.
Here I am on thy grave, would that it were over my head.

He who could take neither rest nor sleep
Before he had first scattered roses and narcissi.
The turns of heaven have strewn the roses of his face.[44]
Thorns and brambles are growing on his tomb.

After separation from him I resolved and firmly determined to fold up the carpet of pleasure during the rest of my life and to retire from mixing in society:

Last night I strutted about like a peacock in the garden of union
But today, through separation from my friend, I twist my head like a snake.
The profit of the sea would be good if there were no fear of waves.
The company of the rose would be sweet if there were no pain from thorns.

STORY 19

A king of the Arabs, having been informed of the relations subsisting between Laila and Mejnun,[45] with an account of the latter's insanity, to the effect that he had in spite of his great accomplishments and eloquence, chosen to roam about in the desert and to let go the reins of self-control from his hands; he ordered him to be brought to his presence, and this having been done, he began to reprove him and to ask him what defect he had discovered in the nobility of the human soul that he adopted the habits of beasts and abandoned the society of mankind. Mejnun replied:

43. I.e., grief.
44. I.e., blanched or borne away.
45. The tragic love story of Laila and Majnun is told by the Persian poet Nizāmī. When Laili, according to her father's wish, is married to a man she does not love, Majnun goes mad and retires to the desert.

'Many friends have blamed me for loving her.
Will they not see her one day and understand my excuse?'

Would that those who are reproving me
Could see thy face, O ravisher of hearts,
That instead of a lemon in thy presence
They might heedlessly cut their hands.[46]

That the truth may bear witness to the assertion: *This is he for whose sake ye blamed me.*[47]

The king expressed a wish to see the beauty of Laila in order to ascertain the cause of so much distress. Accordingly he ordered her to be searched for. The encampments of various Arab families having been visited, she was found, conveyed to the king and led into the courtyard of the palace. The king looked at her outward form for some time and she appeared despicable in his sight because the meanest handmaids of his harem excelled her in beauty and attractions. Mejnun, who shrewdly understood the thoughts of the king, said: 'It would have been necessary to look from the window of Mejnun's eye at the beauty of Laila when the mystery of her aspect would have been revealed to thee.'

If the record of the glade which entered my ears
Had been heard by the leaves of the glade they would have lamented with me.
O company of friends, say to him who is unconcerned
'Would that thou knewest what is in a pining heart!'

Who are healthy have no pain from wounds.
I shall tell my grief to no one but a sympathizer.
It is useless to speak of bees to one
Who never in his life felt their sting.
As long as thy state is not like mine
My state will be but an idle tale to thee.

On the Effects of Education

STORY 1

A vezier who had a stupid son gave him in charge of a scholar to instruct him and if possible to make him intelligent. Having been some time under instruction but ineffectually, the learned man sent one to his father with the words: 'The boy is not becoming intelligent and has made a fool of me.'

46. Zuleikha, the wife of Potiphar and the tempter of the Biblical Joseph, in order to dramatize the beauty of Joseph, provides each of her handmaidens with a sharp knife. When Joseph is presented to them, their agitation at his beauty causes them to cut their hands. (*Qur'ān*, xii:31).

47. *Qur'ān*, xii:32.

When a nature is originally receptive
Instruction will take effect thereon.
No kind of polishing will improve iron
Whose essence is originally bad.
Wash a dog in the seven oceans,
He will be only dirtier when he gets wet.
If the ass of Jesus be taken to Mekkah
He will on his return still be an ass.

STORY 2

A sage, instructing boys, said to them: 'O darlings of your fathers, learn a trade because property and riches of the world are not to be relied upon; also silver and gold are an occasion of danger because either a thief may steal them at once or the owner spend them gradually; but a profession is a living fountain and permanent wealth; and although a professional man may lose riches, it does not matter because a profession is itself wealth and wherever he goes he will enjoy respect and sit in high places, whereas he who has no trade will glean crumbs and see hardships:

It is difficult to obey after losing dignity
And to bear violence from men after being caressed.

Once confusion arose in Damascus.
Everyone left his snug corner.
Learned sons of peasants
Became the veziers of padshahs.
Imbecile sons of the veziers
Went as mendicants to peasants.

If you wanted thy father's inheritance, acquire his knowledge
Because this property of his may be spent in ten days.

STORY 8

I saw an Arab of the desert who said to his boy: 'O *son, on the day of resurrection thou wilt be asked what thou hast gained and not from whom thou art descended,* that is to say, thou wilt be asked what thy merit is and not who thy father was.'

The covering of the Ka'bah[48] which is kissed
Has not been ennobled by the silkworm.
It was some days in company with a venerable man
Wherefore it became respected like himself.

48. See note 14.

STORY 18

I noticed the son of a rich man, sitting on the grave of his father and quarrelling with a dervish-boy, saying: 'The sarcophagus of my father's tomb is of stone and its epitaph is elegant. The pavement is of marble, tesselated with turquois-like bricks. But what resembles thy father's grave? It consists of two contiguous bricks with two handfuls of mud thrown over it.' The dervish-boy listened to all this and then observed: 'By the time thy father is able to shake off those heavy stones which cover him, mine will have reached paradise.'

An ass with a light burden
No doubt walks easily.

A dervish who carries only the load of poverty
Will also arrive lightly burdened at the gate of death
Whilst he who lived in happiness, wealth and ease
Will undoubtedly on all these accounts die hard.
At all events, a prisoner who escapes from all his bonds
Is to be considered more happy than an amir taken prisoner.

On the Rules for the Conduct of Life

ADMONITION 18

Who has power over his foe and does not slay him is his own enemy.

With a stone in the hand and a snake on a stone
It is folly to consider and to delay.

Others, however, enounce a contrary opinion and say that it is preferable to respite captives because the option of killing or not killing remains; but if they be slain without delay, it is possible that some advantage may be lost, the like of which cannot be again obtained.

It is quite easy to deprive a man of life.
When he is slain he cannot be resuscitated again.
It is a condition of wisdom in the archer to be patient
Because when the arrow leaves the bow it returns no more.

MAXIM 34

When a sage comes in contact with fools, he must not expect to be honoured, and if an ignorant man overcomes a sage in an oratorical contest, it is no wonder, because even a stone breaks a jewel.

What wonder is there that the song
Of a nightingale ceases when imprisoned with a crow
Or that a virtuous man under the tyranny of vagabonds
Feels affliction in his heart and is irate.
Although a base stone may break a golden vase,
The price of the stone is not enhanced nor of the gold lost.

MAXIM 44

Transgression by whomsoever committed is blamable but more so in learned men, because learning is a weapon for combating Satan and, when the possessor of a weapon is made prisoner, his shame will be greater.

It is better to be an ignorant poor fellow
Then a learned man who is not abstemious;
Because the former loses the way by his blindness
While the latter falls into a well with both eyes open.

MAXIM 45

Whose bread is not eaten by others while he is alive, he will not be remembered when he is dead. A widow knows the delight of grapes and not the lord of fruits. Joseph the just, salutation to him, never ate to satiety in the Egyptian dearth for fear he might forget the hungry people.

How can he who lives in comfort and abundance
Know what the state of the famished is?
He is aware of the condition of the poor
Who has himself fallen into a state of distress.

O thou who art riding a fleet horse, consider
That the poor thorn-carrying ass is in water and mud.
Ask not for fire from thy poor neighbour's house
Because what passes out of his window is the smoke of his heart.

MAXIM 50

A disciple without intention is a lover without money; a traveller without knowledge is a bird without wings; a scholar without practice is a tree without fruit, and a devotee without science is a house without a door. The Qur'ān was revealed for the acquisition of a good character, not for chanting written chapters. A pious unlettered man is like one who travels on foot, whilst a negligent scholar is like a sleeping rider. A sinner who lifts his hands in supplication is better than a devotee who keeps them proudly on his head.

A good humoured and pleasant military officer
Is superior to a theologian who injures men.

One being asked what a learned man without practice resembled, replied: 'A bee without honey.'

Say to the rude and unkind bee,
'At least forbear to sting, if thou givest no honey.'

HĀFIZ

(1320?–1389/90)

Poems (*Ghazals*)

Shams al-Dīn Hāfiz was born in Shiraz, about 1320 A.D. or somewhat later, half a century after the great Mongol conqueror Hulagu Khan had ravaged the Islamic world. Persian poetry by this time had passed its zenith. The great poetical forms—the epic, the mystical *mathnawī*—had been done by Rūmī, Nizāmī, and Sa'di. Hāfiz elected to specialize in the short lyric, the *ghazal* or "ode." As a student, he had apparently learned all of the *Qur'ān* by heart as well as all of the science (i.e., philosophical and theological knowledge) of his day, for the Persian tradition in poetry required that the writer be learned as well as a wizard with language. He was evidently poor, and hoped, by his verses, to attract the patronage of the great as his predecessors had done. But the age was against him. The Mongols, although they could conquer, could not rule, and palace intrigues and revolutions, bandits in the countryside, and censorship and repression in the cities characterized the times. It was not until 1375 when Shāh Shujā assumed control over the state that a more liberal atmosphere prevailed and Hāfiz's genius blossomed. Hāfiz immortalized the great Shah in his poems. Hafiz died in or about 1389, as war clouds again gathered about his beloved city of Shīrāz, and he was buried in the famous rose garden of Musallā, which had often been the subject of his poems. While Hāfiz's great poetic gifts are not difficult to appreciate, his fame in the Persian world is nevertheless difficult for a Westerner to fully understand. He is the most beloved of all Persian poets, and after his death a wealth of legend grew up about him that is difficult to untangle from his actual life. Likewise, the canon of his works is difficult to determine, as the verses of later imitators attached themselves to the collection.

"His true mastery," says a Persian critic, "is in the lyric (*ghazal*). In Hāfiz's hands the mystical lyric on the one hand reached the summit of eloquence and beauty, and on the other manifested a simplicity of its own."[1] While we usually translate *ghazal* as "ode," the Persian form does not have the pretentiousness of the English ode, and the word "lyric" suggests something lesser, a song. An analogy has been made between their Persian form and the sonnet. Although the *ghazal* does not resemble a sonnet, the analogy is valid in so far as the sonnet has a tight formal structure and is briefer than the ode.

Hāfiz's verses express great spiritual sublety, a natural gift for language, and great variety. Although he works within a smaller compass than Rumi or Sa'di he stamps his verses with his own individual perfection. "Every beauty alike of language and meaning to be found in poetry," says another Persian critic,[2] is to be found in Hāfiz. As with Rūmī, Sūfī mysticism pervades his work, but he is more worldly oriented in his symbols, and reaches the Western reader more easily. Although he is commonly read by Persians in an entirely mystical way, his secular images and his irony add a dimension to his work which does not require allegorical interpretation to be meaningful.

1. Quoted in A. J. Arberry, *Fifty Poems of Hāfiz* (Cambridge, 1962), p. 16.

2. Ibid., p. 21.

Poems*

Love's Awakening

1

Ho, saki, haste, the beaker bring,
Fill up, and pass it round the ring;
Love seemed at first an easy thing—
But ah! the hard awakening.

2

So sweet perfume the morning air
Did lately from her tresses bear,
Her twisted, musk-diffusing hair—
What heart's calamity was there!

Within life's caravanserai
What brief security have I,
When momently the bell doth cry,
"Bind on your loads; the hour is nigh!"

* From *Fifty Poems of Hāfiz*, edited by A. J. Arberry. Reprinted by permission of Cambridge University Press. The notes are the editor's, often based on Arberry's. The translators are: Arthur J. Arberry (*Love's Awakening, The House of Hope, A Mad Heart,* and *Conversation*); Walter Leaf (*Wild of Mien* and *The Crier*); Gertrude Bell (*Red Rose, Secret Draught,* and *Spring*); R. Levy (*Dawn*); and Richard Le Gallienne (*Ismail*).

3

Let wine upon the prayer-mat flow,
An if the taverner bids so;
Whose wont is on this road to go
Its ways and manners well doth know.

4

Mark now the mad career of me,
From wilfulness to infamy;
Yet how conceal that mystery
Whereof men make festivity?

A mountain sea, moon clouded o'er,
And nigh the whirlpool's awful roar—
How can they know our labour sore
Who pass light-burthened on the shore?

5

Hafiz, if thou wouldst win her grace,
Be never absent from thy place;
When thou dost see the well-loved face,
Be lost at last to time and space.

The House of Hope

The house of hope is built on sand,
And life's foundations rest on air;
Then come, give wine into my hand,
That we may make an end of care.

Let me be slave to that man's will
Who 'neath high heaven's turquoise bowl
Hath won and winneth freedom still
From all entanglement of soul;

Save that the mind entangled be
With her whose radiant loveliness
Provoking love and loyalty
Relieves the mind of all distress.

21–24. *A mountain sea . . . shore:* The sea is the "dark night of the soul." The "light-burthened" walkers on the shore are presumably those standing on a firm foundation of religious faith.

27–28. *When . . . space:* The lover of God is constrained by his ecstasy to reveal the secret that should remain hidden.

Last night as toping I had been
In tavern, shall I tell to thee
What message from the world unseen
A heavenly angel brought to me?

"Falcon of sovereign renown,
High-nesting bird of lofty gaze,
This corner of affliction town
Befits thee ill, to pass thy days.

"Hearest thou not the whistle's call
From heaven's rampart shrills for thee?
What chanced I cannot guess at all
This snare should now thy prison be."

Heed now the counsel that I give,
And be it to thy acts applied;
For these are words I did receive
From him that was my ancient guide.
"Be pleased with what the fates bestow,
Nor let thy brow be furrowed thus;
The gate to freedom here below
Stands not ajar to such as us."

Look not to find fidelity
Within a world so weakly stayed;
This ancient crone, ere flouting thee,
A thousand bridegrooms had betrayed.

Take not for sign of true intent
Nor think the rose's smile sincere;
Sweet, loving nightingale, lament:
There is much cause for weeping here.

What envying of Hafiz' ease,
Poor poetaster, does thou moan?
To make sweet music, and to please,
That is a gift of God alone.

Wild of Mien

Wild of mien, chanting a love-song, cup in hand, locks disarrayed,
Cheek beflushed, wine-overcome, vesture awry, breast displayed.

17–18. *Falcon . . . gaze:* The bird is the spirit of Muhammad in a tree at the farthest boundary of paradise, where Muhammad has his second vision of Gabriel (*Qur'ān*, liii:13–17).

27–28. *For . . . guide:* The poet suggests that he has divine guidance for his poetry.

With a challenge in that eye's glance, with a love-charm on the lip,
Came my love, sat by my bedside in the dim midnight shade:

O'er my ear bending, my love spake in a sad voice and a low,
"It is thus, spite of the old years, lover mine, slumber-bewrayed?"

To the wise comes there a cup, fired of the night, pressed to the lip;
An he bow not to the Wine Creed, be he writ Love's renegade.

Go thy way, saint of the cell, flout not the dreg-drainer again;
In the first hour of the world's birth was the high hest on us laid.

Whatsoe'er potion His hand pours in the bowl, that will we quaff,
Heady ferment of the Soul-world, or the grape-must unallayed.

Ah, how oft' e'en as with HAFIZ, hath the red smile of the vine
And the curled ringlet on Love's cheek a repentance unmade!

Red Rose

The rose has flushed red, the bud has burst,
And drunk with joy is the nightingale—
Hail, Sufis! lovers of wine, all hail!
For wine is proclaimed to a world athirst.
Like a rock your repentance seemed to you;
Behold the marvel! of what avail
Was your rock, for a goblet has cleft it in two!

Bring wine for the king, and the slave at the gate
Alike for all is the banquet spread,
And drunk and sober are warmed and fed.
When the feast is done and the night grows late,
And the second door of the tavern gapes wide,
The low and the mighty must bow the head
'Neath the archway of Life, to meet what . . . outside?

Except thy road through affliction pass,
None may reach the halting-station of mirth;
God's treaty: Am I not Lord of the earth?
Man sealed with a sigh: Ah yes, alas!

12. *second door:* Birth is the first door of the tavern of life, and death the second.

Nor with Is nor Is Not let thy mind contend;
Rest assured all perfection of mortal birth
In the great Is Not at the last shall end.

For Assaf's pomp, and the steeds of the wind,
And the speech of birds, down the wind have fled,
And he that was lord of them all is dead;
Of his mastery nothing remains behind.
Shoot not thy feathered arrow astray!
A bow-shot's length through the air it has sped,
And then . . . dropped down in the dusty way.

But to thee, oh Hafiz, to thee, oh Tongue
That speaks through the mouth of the slender reed,
What thanks to thee when thy verses speed
From lip to lip, and the song thou hast sung?

Dawn

Thus spoke at dawn the field-bird to the newly wakened rose:
"Be kind, for many a bloom like you in this meadow grows."
The rose laughed: "You will find that we at truth show no distress,
But never did a lover with harsh words his love so press.
If ruby wine from jewelled cup it is your wish to drink,
Then pearls and corals pierced with eyelash you must strive to link.
Love's savour to his nostrils to entice he ne'er can seek,
Who on the tavern's earthy floor has not swept dusty cheek."

In Iram's garden yesternight, when, in the grateful air,
The breeze of coming day stirred the tress of hyacinth fair,
I asked: "Throne of Jamshid, where is they world-revealing cup?"
It sighed: "That waking fortune deep in sleep lies muffled up."
They are not aways words of love that from the tongue descend:
Come, bring me wine, O taverner, and to this talk put end.
His wit and patience to the waves are cast by Hafiz' tears.
What can he do, that may not hide how love his being sears?

22. *Assaf:* Solomon's minister (also spelled Asaf, Asaph). The wind was his steed and he understood the speech of birds (*Qur'ān*, xxxviii:37; xxxiv:12; xxvii:16).

9. *Iram's garden:* The garden of Iram was supposed to have been planted by the legendary king Shaddad, grandson of Iran, in Aden (*Qur'ān*, lxxxix:6–8). It was destroyed in a great flood (xxxiv:16).

11. *Jamshid:* This heroic king of ancient Persia was supposed to have a magic cup in which the whole world could be seen. (Alexander the Great is supposed to have had a mirror with the same properties.)

Secret Draught

The secret draught of wine and love repressed
Are joys foundationless—then come whate'er
May come, slave to the grape I stand confessed!
Unloose, oh friend, the knot of thy heart's care,
Despite the warning that the Heavens reveal!

For all his thought, never astronomer
That loosed the knot of Fate those Heavens conceal!

Not all the changes that thy days unfold
Sall rouse thy wonder; Time's revolving sphere
Over a thousand lives like thine has rolled.
That cup within thy fingers, dost not hear
The voices of dead kings speak through the clay
Kobad, Bahman, Djemshid, their dust is here,
"Gently upon me set thy lips!" they say.

What man can tell where Kaus and Kai have gone?
Who knows where even now the restless wind
Scatters the dust of Djem's imperial throne?
And where the tulip, following close behind
The feet of Spring, her scarlet chalice rears,
There Ferhad for the love of Shirin pined,
Dyeing the desert red with his heart's tears.

Bring, bring the cup! drink we while yet we may
To our soul's ruin the forbidden draught;
Perhaps a treasure-trove is hid away
Among those ruins where the wine has laughed!—
Perhaps the tulip knows the fickleness
Of Fortune's smile, for on her stalk's green shaft
She bears a wine-cup through the wilderness.

1–5. *The secret . . . reveal:* We are warned that the mystery of life cannot be unravelled and that sensual desires cannot be satisfied—but their lure is overwhelming.

2. *joys foundationless:* The poet rejects the solitary life of abstinence of the anchorite-like Sūfī in favor of the joys of the tavern.

15. *Kaus and Kai:* Cf. FitzGerald's *Rubā'iyāt*, xxxvii. Djemshid (Jamshīd), Bahman, [Kai-] Kubād, [Kai-] Kā ūs, and [Kai-] Khusrau are all ancient Persian kings. Djem (line 17) is Djemshid.

20. *Ferhād . . . Shīrīn:* The romance of Shīrīn and Ferhād (Farhad) is treated in Nizāmī's *Khusrau and Shirin.* The gallant Ferhād commits suicide on a report of Shīrīn's death.

24–25. *Perhaps . . . laughed:* It is a common poetic conceit that treasure lies concealed in ruins.

The murmuring stream of Ruknabad, the breeze
That blows from out Mosalla's fair pleasaunce,
Summon me back when I would seek heart's ease,
Travelling afar; what though Love's countenance
Be turned full harsh and sorrowful on me,
I care not so that Time's unfriendly glance
Still from my Lady's beauty turned be.

Like Hafiz, drain the goblet cheerfully
While minstrels touch the lute and sweetly sing,
For all that makes thy heart rejoice in thee
Hangs of Life's single, slender, silken string.

A *Mad Heart*

I

Long years my heart had made request
Of me, a stranger, hopefully
(Not knowing that itself possessed
The treasure that it sought of me),
That Jamshid's chalice I should win
And it would see the world therein.

That is a pearl far too rare
To be contained within the shell
Of time and space; lost vagrants there
Upon the ocean's margin, well
We know it is a vain surmise
That we should hold so great a prize.

II

There was a man that loved God well;
In every motion of his mind
God dwelt; and yet he could not tell
That God was in him, being blind:
Wherefore as if afar he stood
And cried, "Have mercy, O my God!"

29–30. *Ruknābād . . . Mosallā:* The river Ruknābād flows by the famous Musallā or rose garden of Shīrāz, where Hāfiz was to be buried.
5. *Jamshīd:* See note to line 11 of *Dawn.* The wine cup is a mirror of the world.
13–18. *There . . . God":* The theme of this stanza may be a Sūfī saying, "Who knows himself knows his Lord."

III

This problem that had vexed me long
Last night unto the taverner
I carried; for my hope was strong
His judgement sure, that could not err,
Might swiftly solve infallibly
The riddle that had baffled me.

I saw him standing in his place,
A goblet in his grasp, a smile
Of right good cheer upon his face,
As in the glass he gazed awhile
And seemed to view in vision clear
A hundred truths reflected there.

IV

"That friend who, being raised sublime
Upon the gallows, glorified
The tree that slew him for his crime,
This was the sin for which he died,
That, having secrets in his charge,
He told them to the world at large."

So spake he; adding, "But the heart
That has the truth within its hold
And, practicing the rosebud's art,
Conceals a mystery in each fold,
That heart hath well this comment lined
Upon the margin of the mind.

"When Moses unto Pharaoh stood,
The men of magic strove in vain
Against his miracle of wood;
So every subtlety of brain
Must surely fail and feeble be
Before the soul's supremacy.

"And if the Holy Ghost descend
In grace and power infinite
His comfort in these days to lend
To them that humbly wait on it,
Theirs too the wondrous works can be
That Jesus wrought in Galilee."

24. *riddle:* the unsolvable riddle of the universe; only the wine of unreason makes life tolerable.

V

"What season did the Spirit wise
This all-revealing cup assign
Within thy keeping?" "When the skies
Were painted by the Hand Divine
And heaven's mighty void was spanned,
Then gave He this into my hand."

"You twisted coil, you chain of hair
Why doth the lovely Idol spread
To keep me fast and fettered there?"
"Ah, Hafiz!", so the wise man said,
"'Tis a mad heart, and needs restraint
That speaks within thee this complaint."

*Conversation**

"Ah, when shall I to thy mouth and lips attain?"
"'Fore God, but speak, for thy word is sovereign."
"'Tis Egypt's tribute thy lips require for fee."
"In such transaction the less the loss shall be."
"What lip is worthy the tip of thy mouth to hold?"
"To none but initiates may this tale be told."
"Adore not idols, but sit with the One, the True!"
"In the street of Love it is lawful both to do."

"The tavern's breath is balm to the spirit's smart."
"And blessed are they that comfort the lonely heart."
"No part of faith is the dervish cloak and the wine."
"Yet both are found in this Magian faith of mine."
"What gain can coral lips to an old man bring?"
"A honeyed kiss, and his youth's recovering."

"And when shall bridegroom come to the couch of the bride?"
"The morn that Moon and Jupiter stand allied."
"Still Hafiz prays for thy yet ascending might."
"So pray and praise the angels in heaven's height."

65. *mad heart:* This reference may remind us of Husain b. Mansūr al-Hallāj, whose ecstatic utterances about God were interpreted as blasphemy, for which he was gibbeted.

* This is one of Hāfiz's few dialogues. The conversation is between an old holy man—a Sūfī—and a beautiful boy.

3. *tribute:* taxes. Egypt was the wealthiest province of the Moslem empire.

9. *tavern's breath:* The sage tries to draw the boy from the tavern into the temple.

11. *"No . . . wine":* The boy says his Magian (Zoroastrian or perhaps just heretical) faith permits wine.

Spring

Cypress and Tulip and sweet Eglantine,
Of these the tale from lip to lip is sent;
Washed by three cups oh Saki, of thy wine,
My song shall turn upon this argument.
Spring, bride of all the meadows, rises up,
Clothed in her ripest beauty: fill the cup!
Of Spring's handmaidens runs this song of mine.

The sugar-loving birds of distant Ind,
Except a Persian sweetmeat that was brought
To fair Bengal, have found nought to their mind.
See how my song, that in one night was wrought,
Defies the limits set by space and time!
O'er plains and mountain-tops my fearless rhyme,
Child of a night, its year-long road shall find.

And thou whose sense is dimmed with piety,
Thou too shalt learn the magic of her eyes;
Forth comes the caravan of sorcery
When from those gates the blue-veined curtains rise.
And when she walks the flowery meadows through,
Upon the jasmine's shamèd cheek the dew
Gathers like sweat, she is so fair to see!

Ah, swerve not from the path of righteousness
Though the world lure thee! like a wrinkled crone,
Hiding beneath her robe lasciviousness,
She plunders them that pause and heed her moan.
From Sinai Moses brings thee wealth untold;
Bow not thine head before the calf of gold
Like Samir, following after wickedness.

From the Shah's garden blows the wind of Spring,
The tulip in her lifted chalice bears
A dewy wine of Heaven's minist'ring;
Until Ghiyasuddin, the Sultan, hears,
Sing, Hafiz, of thy longing for his face.
The breezes whispering round thy dwelling-place
Shall carry thy lament unto the King.

1–7. *Cypress . . . mine:* Three is a magical number everywhere, especially in epic. Three cups of wine in the morning were thought to purge the body of ill-humors. Cyprus, Tulip, and Eglantine may refer to three maidens who nursed a Bengali prince through an illness. In any case, winter (the season of dryness and death) is departing and spring brings a quickening of life.

8–10. *birds . . . Bengal:* The sweetmeat is probably a poem Hāfiz sent to Bengal; the birds may be Bengali poets.

28. *Samir:* The Sāmirī was a magician who made a calf of "saffron hue" for the Israelites to worship (*Qur'ān*, xx:85ff). For the Biblical account of the golden calf see Exodus 32:4.

32. *Sultan:* of Bengal.

The Crier

Send the criers round the market, call the royst'rers' band to
hear,
Crying, "O yes! All ye good folk through the Loved One's
realm, give ear!

"Lost, a handmaid! Strayed a while since! Lost, the Vine's wild
daughter, lost!
Raise the hue and cry to seize her! Danger lurks where she is
near.

"Round her head she wears a foam-crown; all her garb glows
ruby-hued;
Thief of wits is she; detain her, lest ye dare not sleep for fear.

"Whoso brings me back the tart maid, take for sweetmeat all
my soul!
Though the deepest hell conceal her, go ye down, go hale her
here.

"She's a wastrel, she's a wanton, shame-abandoned, rosy-red;
If ye find her, send her forthright back to
HAFIZ, Balladier."

*Ismail**

Ismail is dead, of men and cadis best:
His pen, like its great master, takes its rest.

Much wrote he of God's law, and lived it too—
Would I could say as much for me and you!

The middle of the week he went away—
The month of Rajab it was, and the eighth day.

In this uncertain dwelling ill at ease,
To a more ordered house he went for peace.

His home is now with God, and if you write
"The mercy of God", interpreting aright

The mystic letters standing side by side,
You then shall read the year when Ismail died.

* I am unable to identify this Ismail.

6. *Rajab:* the fourth month of the Moslem year.

9–12. *if . . . died:* The poem ends with a chronogram. The numerical value of the Arabic letters in the phrase "The Mercy of God" (200 + 8 + 40 + 400 + 8 + 100) equals 756, the year of Ismali's death. Chronograms are well known also in the West.

TĀHĀ HUSSEIN

(born 1889)

The Stream of Days

Tāhā Hussein (the name is also transliterated Huseyn) is without doubt the greatest living man of letters in the Arab world. Born in 1889 in a village in Upper Egypt, he underwent the traditional education of an Arab —a kind of education that had not changed in centuries. Blind from the age of three, he learned the *Koran* by heart as a child. At the age of thirteen he was sent to the Azhar University in Cairo. This famous institution of Koranic learning—founded in, and little changed since, 970 A.D.—was a conservative citadel of Islamic thought in battle with the infiltration of Western ideas. Its curriculum included almost nothing but the *Koran* and its interpretation (*tafsīr*); *hadith*, or the traditions concerning the Prophet which are not found in the *Koran; tawhīd*, or the doctrine of one God; and study of the various orthodox schools of Islamic thought. Poetics and rhetoric—fields in which Tāhā Hussein was to cause a revolution—were included as an adjunct to the study of religious texts. Though change was in the air—largely because of a desire of some Arabs to unite intellectuals against British rule—no modern Arab thinker ever got a more conservative education. From the Azhar, he went on to the newly founded secular University of Cairo and in 1914 received the first Ph.D. granted by that institution. His westernization continued with a doctorate at the Sorbonne and with his marriage to a French woman. He has spent a lifetime of activity in education and politics in Egypt, having been dean of a university, professor of Arabic letters, and Undersecretary of State for Education. Tāhā Hussein opposed the corrupt government of King Farouk, and was instrumental in creating the atmosphere necessary for Farouk's overthrow.

In literature as well as in politics, Tāhā Hussein has been an innovator. Western literary criticism—the *explication de texte* of French education and, more recently, of the so-called New Criticism—attracted Tāhā in Paris. In applying modern methods of exegesis to classical Arab literature he ran into fierce opposition from traditional scholars. In miniature, his career has been a battleground rather like those on which Humanism and Scholasticism clashed in Renaissance Europe.

At least half a dozen novels, as yet untranslated, on aspects of contemporary Arab life flowed from Tāhā's pen between 1935 and 1950. These works were a revelation to literary men still writing verse of the traditional Arabic kind and a dynamic social force to the intellectual thirsting for a new type of literature. The depiction in prose of everyday social, religious, and psychological problems, though common in European literature for several centuries, was largely new to the Arab world. Tāhā has also written much literary criticism and philosophical and historical commentary. However, many Arabs and most Westerners acquainted with Arabic think his memoirs of his early years the most moving of his works. Part I of this, *An Egyptian Childhood,* appeared in 1929; Part II, *The Stream of Days,* in 1939.

The Stream of Days recounts the author's experiences as a student at the Azhar University in Cairo. The curriculum at such a university was largely the study of the *Koran* and the traditions of Islam (*hadīth*), with a certain amount of time spent on later medieval philosophers and religious thinkers. Nothing comparable to this type of education exists in the West, but there are —or were in the first decades of the century—similarities between it and the programs of orthodox Jewish secondary schools in the United States and Europe. The hero is blind, but blindness is sufficiently common in the Near East so that less is made of this than in a Western book. Certainly the account is not about a youth overcoming the handicap of blindness, though we who are heirs to a less fatalistic tradition are sometimes disturbed as we read that more concessions are not made to the young man because of his handicap. Being blind, the author must depend on sound, smell, and taste. The hero's youthful agonies are intense, and in a sense the memoirs are similar to the numerous novels of adolescence that we have had recently in Western literature, particularly in French. But the world of al-Azhar is a placid and timeless world in which the moribund final phase of medieval Arabia is delicately preserved. Faint echoes of a sweeping twentieth-century social and intellectual revolution drift into the account. The charm of *The Stream of Days* lies in this evocation of a dying past, with some nostalgia but with objectivity and without sentimentality. Tāhā's style is noted for its grace and beauty, which means, among other things, that he has succeeded in creating a literary language that is a happy marriage of classical and vernacular Arabic. He is also a master of sustained moods.

From The Stream of Days*

I

For the first two or three weeks of his stay in Cairo he was lost in bewilderment. All he knew was that he had left the country behind him and settled in the capital as a student attending lectures at the Azhar. It was more by imagination than by sense that he distinguished the three phases of his day.

Both the house he lived in and the path that led to it were strange and unfamiliar. When he came back from the Azhar he

* From *The Stream of Days* by Tāhā Hussein, translated by Hilary Wayment. Reprinted by permission of Longman Group Limited. The footnotes, unless otherwise indicated, are the translator's.

turned to the right through a gateway which was open during the daytime and shut at night; after evening prayer there was only a narrow opening left in the middle of the door. Once through it, he became aware of a gentle heat playing on his right cheek, and a fine smoke teasing his nostrils; while on the left he heard an odd gurgling sound which at once puzzled and delighted him.

For several days, morning and evening, he listened curiously to this sound, but lacked the courage to inquire what it might be. Then one day he gathered from a chance remark that it came from the bubbling of a *narghile*[1] smoked by tradesmen of the district. It was provided for them by the proprietor of the café from which the gentle heat and the fine smoke-cloud issued.

He walked straight on for a few steps before crossing a damp, roofed-in space in which it was impossible to stand firmly because of the slops thrown there by the café proprietor. Then he came out into an open passage-way; but this was narrow and filthy and full of strange, elusive smells, which were only moderately unpleasant early in the day and at nightfall, but as the day advanced and the heat of the sun grew stronger, became utterly intolerable.

He walked straight on through this narrow passage; but rarely did he find it smooth or easy. More often than not his friend would have to push him either this way or that so as to avoid some obstacle or other. Then he would continue in the new direction, feeling his way towards a house either to left or right, until he had passed the obstacle and taken the old direction again. He hurried along nervously at his companion's side, breathing the nauseous smells, and half-deafened by the medley of sounds that came from all sides at once, left and right, above and below, to meet in mid-air, where they seemed to unite above the boy's head, layer upon layer, into a single fine mist.

There was in fact a remarkable variety of sounds. Voices of women raised in dispute, of men shouting in anger or peaceably talking together; the noise of loads being set down or picked up; the song of the water-carrier crying his wares; the curse of a carter to his horse or mule or donkey; the grating sound of cart-wheels; and from time to time this confused whirl of sounds was torn by the braying of a donkey or the whinnying of a horse.

As he passed through this babel, his thoughts were far away, and he was scarcely conscious of himself or of what he was doing; but at a certain point on the road he caught the confused sound of conversation through a half-open door on the left; then he knew that a pace or two further on he must turn to the left up a staircase which would bring him to his lodging.

It was an ordinary sort of staircase, neither wide nor narrow, and its steps were of stone; but since it was used very frequently in both

1. a water pipe, similar to a hookah.

directions, and no one troubled to wash or sweep it, the dirt piled up thickly and stuck together in a compact mass on the steps, so that the stone was completely covered up, and whether you were going up or coming down the staircase appeared to be made of mud.

Now whenever the boy went up or down a staircase he was obliged to count the steps. But long as were the years he stayed in this place, and countless the times he negotiated this staircase, it never occurred to him to count the number of its steps. He learnt at the second or third time of climbing it that after going up a few steps he had to turn a little to the left before continuing his ascent, leaving on his right an opening through which he never penetrated, though he knew that it led to the first floor of the building in which he lived for so many years.

This floor was not inhabited by students, but by workers and tradesmen. He left the entrance to it on his right, and went on up to the second floor. There his harassed spirit found rest and relief; lungfuls of fresh air drove away the sense of suffocation with which he had been oppressed on that filthy staircase; and then too there was the parrot, whistling on without a break, as if to testify before all the world to the tyranny of her Persian master, who had imprisoned her in an abominable cage, and would sell her tomorrow or the day after to another man who would treat her in exactly the same way. And when he was rid of her and had laid hands on the cash, he would buy a successor for her who would be cooped up in the same prison pouring forth the same curses on her master, and waiting as her sister had waited to be passed on from hand to hand, and from cage to cage, while everywhere she went that plaintive cry of hers would delight the hearts of men and women.

When our friend reached the top of the staircase he breathed in the fresh air that blew on his face, and listened to the voice of the parrot calling him towards the right. He obeyed, turning through a narrow corridor, past two rooms in which two Persians lived. One of these was still a young man, while the other was already past middle age. The one was as morose and misanthropic as the other was genial and good-natured.

At last the boy was home. He entered a room like a hall, which provided for most of the practical needs of the house. This led on to another room, large but irregular in shape, which served for social and intellectual needs. It was bedroom and dining-room, reading-room and study, and a room for conversation by day or by night. Here were books and crockery and food; and here the boy had his own particular corner, as in every room he occupied or visited at all frequently.

This place of his was on the left inside the door. After advancing a pace or two he found a mat spread on the ground, and above that an old but quite serviceable carpet. Here he sat in the daytime, and here he slept at night, with a pillow for his head and a rug to cover him. On the opposite side of the room was his elder brother's pitch, a good deal higher than his own. He had a mat spread on the ground, and a decent carpet on top of that, then a felt mattress, and above that a long, wide piece of bedding stuffed with cotton, and finally, crowning all, a coverlet. Here the young sheikh[2] would sit with his close friends. They were not obliged to prop up their backs against the bare wall, as the boy did, having cushions to pile up on the rugs. At night this couch was transformed into a bed on which the young sheikh slept.

II

This was all the boy ever learnt about his immediate surroundings. The second phase of his life consisted in the tumultuous journey between his home and the Azhar. He went out through the covered passage till he felt the heat of the café on his left cheek, and heard the bubbling of the *narghile* on his right. In front of him was a shop which played an important part in his life; it belonged to El-Hagg Firûz, who supplied the neighborhood with most of the necessities of life. In the morning he sold boiled beans,[3] prepared in the usual variety of ways. But El-Hagg Firûz used to boast the special virtues of his beans—and raise their prices accordingly. He had plain beans, beans in fat, beans in butter, beans in every kind of oil; he added, if required, all sorts of spices. As for the students, they adored these beans, and often made far too large a meal of them. So by mid-morning they were already dull in the head, and at the noon lecture they slept.

When evening came El-Hagg Firûz sold his customers their supper: cheese, olives, milled sesame, or honey. To the more luxurious he supplied boxes of tunny or sardines. And to a few of them perhaps, as night approached, he sold things which have no name, and nothing to do with food, things spoken of in a whisper, yet passionately vied for.

The boy used to overhear these whisperings; sometimes he half understood, but as a rule the whole transaction was a mystery to him. As the days passed by and he grew older, he came to see through these subtle hints and ambiguities. What he learnt then obliged him to overhaul his standards of judgment, and to revise his valuation both of people and of things.

El-Hagg Firûz was a tall, jet-black fellow, and anything but talkative. But when he did speak he mumbled his words and lisped out his Arabic in a fashion which made an ineffaceable impression on the boy. He is always reminded of it by the story of Ziad and his

2. The word *sheikh* means originally "old man" or "elder." In this translation it is used in two senses: (1) as more or less equivalent to *'âlim*, "doctor," and so teacher at the Azhar; (2) "scholar" or aspirant to learning, as here.

3. *Fool*, the brown bean which is the staple diet of the Egyptian masses.

pupil in *El-Bayan wal-Tabyîn.*[4] Ziad asked his pupil to say: "We have been given a pony." Instead of which he repeated it so: "We have been given a bony." "Wretch!" said Ziad, annoyed. "If you can't say pony, say horse instead." Whereupon the boy replied: "We have been given an arse." Ziad, shocked, reverted to the "bony" as the lesser evil.

El-Hagg Firûz held a unique position in the neighborhood and amongst the students especially. It was to him that they went when their money ran out towards the end of the month, or when their remittances were overdue. He it was who gave them food on credit, lent them a piastre or two from time to time, and helped them out in all kinds of emergencies. No wonder his name was as often on their lips as those of the most learned sheikhs of the Azhar.

But this was not all. El-Hagg Firûz was essential to the students in yet another way. It was to him that were addressed all the letters bringing them news of their families, or enclosing flimsy notes which they took to the post office with empty pockets, to return with the jingle of silver falling cheerily on their ears and into their very hearts.

Naturally not a single student missed an opportunity of passing the time of day morning and evening at El-Hagg Firûz' shop, or of casting a quick furtive glance at the spot where letters were waiting to be collected. How often one of them would go home grasping a sealed envelope which was spotted with oil and butter stains; yet despite its greasiness that envelope was more precious in his eyes than any composition or text-book on law, grammar or theology.

On leaving the covered passage, then, the boy found himself in front of El-Hagg Firûz' shop; his friend would take him a few paces in that direction to greet El-Hagg Firûz and to inquire if there was a letter for him or not; the reply would bring either smiles or frowns to his face. Then he turned away to the left, and walked straight forwards down the long narrow street crowded with passers-by. It was full of students, merchants, tradesmen, labourers; carts drawn by donkeys, horses or mules; carters shouting out warnings or curses at the men, women or children blocking their path. Then on each side of the street were different kinds of shops, in many of which was prepared the meagre diet of the poor. The smells that issued from them were abominable, but that did not prevent them from delighting most of the passers-by, whether they were students, labourers or porters. Some of them turned aside to these shops and bought a scrap of food to gulp down on the spot, or take home and eat, either alone or with others. And some of them, assailed by this battery of smells, remained unmoved. They were tempted but did not yield. Their eyes saw, their nostrils smelt, their

4. Book of *Exposition and Demonstration:* a treatise on rhetoric, constituting a huge anthology of Arab eloquence, by El-Jâhiz, a prolific and original author of the Basra school (ninth century).

appetite was stirred; but, alas, their pockets were empty. They passed on with yearning in their souls and with bitterness and resentment in their hearts; yet at the same time they were content with their lot and accepted it with resignation.

In some other shops a quiet, unhurried trade was transacted, almost without any words passing at all. If anything was said, it was under the breath, so as scarcely to be heard. In spite of this—or perhaps for this very reason—the trade in question brought great wealth and prosperity to those who practised it. To all appearances the majority of these shops dealt only in coffee and soap, though some of them also sold sugar and rice.

As he passed through all this a warm interest stirred in the boy. But he would have understood practically nothing had not his friend from time to time volunteered an explanation. He continued on his way, sometimes walking firmly forwards, sometimes swerving aside. When the road was clear he marched with a sure step, but stumbled and faltered on its edges when it was crowded or twisty. At last he came to a spot where he had to turn a little to the left and then plunge into a lane as narrow and crooked and filthy as could be. Its atmosphere was foul with an abominable medley of smells, and from time to time weak, hollow voices which reflected its misery and wrong echoed back cries for charity to the footfalls of passers-by, begging at the sound of steps, as if life had only been perceptible through the ears. They were answered by other voices: the thin, harsh, strangled cries of those winged creatures which love darkness and desolation and ruins. Often enough these noises were accompanied by the flutter of wings, which sometimes, to his horror, shaved past his ear or his face. Instinctively his hand would fly up for protection, and for sometime afterwards his heart would be throbbing with apprehension.

On he walked with his friend along this narrow, dark, twisting alley, now rising, now descending, now going straight on, now turning to left or right. And all the time these loathsome sounds assailed him, sometimes from in front, and sometimes from behind, but never without dismaying him. After a time he felt his heart lighten and his lungs expand, and knew that the moment of release had come. He heaved one sigh of relief, loaded with all the weight of his anxiety and distress.

Now he breathed freely and easily, as if he were taking in great draughts of life from the fresh air which flowed over him as he left the bat-ridden alley. On he went along the road, which twisted treacherously under his feet for a few moments, then became firm again so that he could step forward easily and with confidence. His heart thrilled with joy at the strange harmony of sounds which came to his ears as he walked along the pleasant, peaceful street. On one side of him was the Mosque of Sayyidna-l-Hussein,[5] and on the other a series of small shops. How often he would stop at one of these during the days that followed, and what good things he tasted there! Soaked figs and their juice in summertime, and in winter *bassbûssa*,[6] which diffused a warm glow of well-being through the body. Sometimes he would stop at a Syrian retailer's to choose from a variety of foods, hot or cold, salt or sweet. Their taste gave him inexpressible pleasure, yet if they were offered him now he would be afraid they might make him ill, or even poison him.

He continued along this street until he came to a place where the voices grew louder and more numerous. He realised that the roads divided here and that he could branch right or left, go straight on, or turn about. "Here are the crossroads," said his companion. "If you go right you reach the Sikka El-Gadida, then the Musky, then 'Ataba El-Khadra. To the left you have Sharia El-Darrâssa. But we must go straight on into Sharia El-Halwagi, the street of learning and hard work. It is so narrow that if you stretched out your arms left and right you could almost touch both walls. Now you are walking between a number of small bookshops. There are books of every kind in them, new and old, good and bad, in print or manuscript."

How many a pleasant and rewarding halt did our friend make in that narrow street, which remained fixed in his memory later on, after his life had changed its course.

But this time he must hurry past. His guide had to be at the Azhar before the lecture began. Here they were, arrived at the Barbers' Gate. He took off his sandals, laid them one on top of the other, then picked them up in his hand as he followed his companion. A little further on he stepped over a shallow threshold into the quiet courtyard of the Azhar, and felt a cool morning breeze blow refreshingly upon his face. And so he entered the third phase of this new life of his.

III

This third phase of his existence was the one he loved best of all. In his own room he endured all the pains of exile. It was like a foreign country to him, and he never became familiar with its contents, except perhaps those nearest to him. He did not live in it in the same sense that he had lived in his country home or in other familiar rooms where nothing was unknown to him. He passed his days there in exile from people and things alike, and in such anguish

5. Sayyidna (lit. *Our Master*) Hussein was the grandson of the Prophet; he and his descendants were considered the true Caliphs by the Shi'te ("separatist") sect, as opposed to the Sunnis (traditionalists). The mosque is of the Ottoman period.

6. nut-cake of Syrian origin.

of heart that the oppressive air he breathed there brought him no rest or refreshment, but only heaviness and pain.

Nor was there any doubt of his preferring these hours in the Azhar to the agitated journey back and forth, whose hazards drove him almost to despair. It was not only his steps that were confused and unsteady; his very heart was overwhelmed by that unnerving perplexity which perverts a man's purposes and drives him blindly onwards, not only along the material road which he needs must follow, but also along the free paths of the mind, feckless and without a plan. Not only was he distracted by the hubbub and tumult that eddied around him. He was distressed at the unsteadiness of his walk and the impossibility of harmonising his own quiet, faltering steps with the firm and even brutal pace of his companion.

It was only in the third phase of his day that he found rest and security. The fresh breeze that blew across the court of the Azhar at the hour of morning prayer met him with a welcome and inspired him with a sense of security and hope. The touch of this breeze on his forehead, damp with sweat from that feverish journey, resembled nothing so much as the kisses his mother used to give him during his early years, when he chanted verses from the Koran to her, or entertained her with a story he had heard at the village school; or when, as a pale, delicate infant, he abandoned the corner in which he had been reciting the litany from the *sura* Ya-Sin to go and carry out some household task or other.

Those kisses revived his heart and filled him not only with tenderness but with hope and confidence. The breeze which welcomed him in the court of the Azhar, no less, brought rest after weariness, calm after tumult, a smile after gloomy looks. However, he as yet knew nothing of the Azhar, and had not the least idea what he would find there. But it was enough for him to brush with his bare feet the ground of that court, to feel on his face the caress of its morning breeze, and to realise that around him the Azhar was preparing to awake from its drowsiness, that its inertia would soon give place to activity. He began to recover consciousness of himself, as life returned to him. He felt the conviction of being in his own country, amongst his own people, and lost all sense of isolation, all sadness. His soul blossomed forth, and with every fibre of his being he yearned to discover . . . well, what? Something he was a stranger to, though he loved it and felt irresistibly drawn towards it—knowledge. How many times had he heard this word, and longed to find out its hidden meaning! His impression of it was vague enough, to be sure; but of this he was convinced, that knowledge had no limits and that people might spend their whole lives in acquiring a few drops of it. He too wished to devote his whole life to it and to win as much of it as he could, however little that might be. His father and the learned friends who came to visit him had spoken of knowledge as a boundless ocean, and the child had never taken this expression for a figure of speech or a metaphor, but as the simple truth. He had come to Cairo and to the Azhar with the intention of throwing himself into this ocean and drinking what he could of it, until the day he drowned. What finer end could there be for a man of spirit than to drown himself in knowledge? What a splendid plunge into the beyond!

All these thoughts suddenly thronged into his young spirit, filling it and taking possession of it, blotting out the memory of that desolate room, of the turbulent, twisty road, and even of the country and its delights. They convinced him that it was no mistake or exaggeration to be consumed with love for the Azhar as well as with regret for the country.

The boy paced on with his companion until he had crossed the court and mounted the shallow step which is the threshold of the Azhar itself. His heart was all modesty and humility, but his soul was filled with glory and pride. His feet stepped lightly over the worn-out mats that were laid out across the floor, leaving a bare patch here and there, as if on purpose to touch the feet which passed over them with something of the benediction attached to that holy ground. The boy used to love the Azhar at this moment, when worshippers were finishing their early-morning prayer and going away, with the marks of drowsiness still in their eyes, to make a circle round some column or other and wait for the teacher who was to give a lecture on tradition or exegesis, first principles or theology.[7]

At this moment the Azhar was quiet, and free from the strange intermingled murmurs that filled it from sunrise until evening prayer. You could only hear the whispered conversations of its inmates or the hushed but steady voice of some young man reciting the Koran. Or you might come upon a worshipper who had arrived too late for the common service, or had gone on to perform extra prayers after completing the statutory number. Or maybe you would hear a teacher beginning his lecture in the languid tone of a man who has awakened from sleep and said his prayers but has not yet eaten anything to give him strength and energy. He starts in a quiet, husky voice: "In the name of God, the merciful, the compassionate: Praise be to God, father of the worlds. May His peace and blessing be upon our lord Muhammad, the most noble of the prophets, upon his family and his companions. These are the words of the author of the Book, may God rest his soul and grant us the fruits of his learning. Amen!"

The students listened to the lecture with the same quiet languor in which it was given. There was a striking contrast between the

7. These are the four primary subjects of the traditional Azharite course.

different tones the sheikhs used at the early-morning and midday lectures. At dawn their voices were calm and gentle, with traces of drowsiness in them. At noon they were strong and harsh, but fraught too with a certain sluggishness induced by the lunch they had just eaten, the baked beans and pickles and so on which made up the usual fare of an Azharite at this time. At dawn the voices seemed to beg humbly for favour from the great authorities of the past, while by noon they were attacking them almost as if they were adversaries. This contrast always astonished and delighted the boy.

On he went with his friend up the two steps leading into the *liwân*.[8] There beside one of those sacred pillars, to which a chair was bound by a great chain, our friend was deposited by his companion, who left him with these words: "Wait there and you will hear a lecture on tradition; when mine is over I will return and fetch you." His companion's lecture was on the first principles of Islamic law, given by Sheikh Râdy, God rest his soul. The text-book was the *Tahrîr* of El-Kemal Ibn El-Humam. When the boy heard this sentence, every word filled him at once with awe and curiosity. First principles of law? What science was this? Sheikh Râdy? Who could he be? *Tahrîr?*[9] What was the meaning of this word? El-Kemal Ibn El-Humam? Could there be a more wonderful pair of names? How true it was that knowledge is a boundless ocean, full of unimaginable benefit for any thoughtful being who is ready to plunge into it. The boy's admiration for this lecture especially grew deeper every day as he listened to his brother and his brother's friends studying their lesson beforehand. What they read sounded very strange, but there was no doubt of its fascination.

As he listened the boy used to burn with longing to grow six or seven years older, so that he might be able to understand it, to solve its riddles and ambiguities, to be master of the whole subject as those distinguished young men were, and to dispute with the teachers about it as they did. But for the present he was compelled to listen without understanding. Time and again he would turn over some sentence or other in his mind on the chance of finding some sense in it. But he achieved nothing by all this, except perhaps a greater respect for knowledge and a deeper reverence for his teachers, together with modesty as to his own powers and a determination to work harder.

There was one sentence in particular. How many sleepless nights it cost him! How many days of his life it overcast! Sometimes it tempted him to miss an elementary lecture—for he had understood his first lessons without difficulty—and so led him on to play-

8. colonnade surrounding the central court of the mosque.

9. "Correct Reformulation" (of the first principles of law). The work was written in the fifteenth century.

ing truant from the sheikh's lecture on tradition, in order to speculate on what he had heard from the lips of those older students.

The sentence which took possession of him in this way was certainly a remarkable one. It would fall echoing in his ears as he lay on the threshold of sleep, and drag him back to a wakefulness which lasted all night through. This was the sentence: "Right is the negation of negation." What could these words mean? How could negation be negated? What might such negation be? And how could the negation of negation be right?[10] The sentence began to whirl round in his head like the ravings of delirium in a sick man's brain, until one day it was driven out of his mind by one of El-Kafrawy's[11] *Problems.* This problem he understood at once and was able to argue about. Thus he came at last to feel that he had begun to taste the water of the boundless ocean of knowledge.

The boy sat beside the pillar, toying with the chain and listening to the sheikh on tradition. He understood him perfectly, and found nothing to criticise in his lesson except the cascade of names which he poured forth on his listeners in giving the source and authorities for each tradition. It was always "so-and-so tells us" or "according to so-and-so." The boy could not see the point of these endless chains of names, or this tedious tracing of sources. He longed for the sheikh to have done with all this and come down to the tradition itself. As soon as he did so the boy listened with all his heart. He memorised the tradition and understood it, but showed not the slightest interest in the sheikh's analysis, which reminded him too well of the explanations given by the Imam of the mosque in his country village and the sheikh who used to teach him the elements of law.

While the sheikh proceeded with his lesson the Azhar began gradually to wake up, as if stirred out of its torpor by the voices of the teachers holding forth, and by the discussions which arose between them and the students, amounting sometimes almost to quarrels. The students came closer, the voices rose higher, the echoes intermingled and the sheikhs raised their voices again, so that the students might be able to hear them, ever higher and higher, up to the final climax of the words "God is all-wise." For meanwhile other students had come up to wait for a lecture on law by another sheikh, or maybe the same one; so he had no choice but to end the early-morning lecture and begin the next. Then the boy's companion would return, take him by the hand without a word and drag him off all ungently to another place, where he dumped him like a piece of luggage and abandoned him again.

10. As the context is legal, the sentence means: "Property is a counter-claim against a counter-claim," or the assertion of a right against all comers. In a different context the words might well mean: "Truth is the refutation of refutation," or the rebuttal of scepticism.

11. An Azharite grammarian of the eighteenth century.

The boy realised that he had been transferred to the law class. He would listen to this lecture until it came to an end and both sheikhs and students went off. Then he would stay rooted to the spot until his friend came back from Sayyidna-l-Hussein, where he had been attending a lecture on law given by Sheikh Bakhît, God rest his soul.

Now Sheikh Bakhît was prolix in the extreme, and his students used to harass him with objections. So he never finished the lesson until the middle of the morning. Then the boy's companion would return to where he was, take him by the hand without a word and lead him out of the Azhar. And so back he went through the second phase along the road between the Azhar and his lodgings into the third and final phase, where he was left alone in his place in the corner on the old carpet stretched out over a rotten worn-out mat.

IV

The boy sat down on this carpet in the corner of the room, resting his hand or arm on the window at his left. He had no time now to dream, but only to pass over in his mind the things that were uppermost in it: incidents on the road or in the court of the Azhar, points from lectures on tradition or on law. But these reminiscences were short-lived; for when his brother deposited him in his corner it was not with the intention of leaving him to dream or to go over his lessons, but simply of giving himself time to get the food ready for lunch.

This meal varied from day to day, not so much in its menu, which consisted always of beans cooked in butter or oil, as by the atmosphere in which it was eaten. For one day it was silent and another day clamorously noisy. When the boy was alone with his brother they lunched in oppressive gloom almost without exchanging a word; they spoke in short sentences and the boy replied to his brother in monosyllables. But what a hullabaloo when the young sheikh's friends were invited! There were sometimes three and sometimes four, even occasionally five; but the fifth was important for a different reason, and it is better not to mention him now.

These young students came to spend a pleasant hour together; they completely neglected the boy, and addressed never a word to him, so that he had no need to make any reply.

He preferred it so, for he loved listening. And what a host of things there were to listen to and wonder at! Nothing could be more varied than the conversations which took place over that low circular table. The guests sat all round it on the floor; in the centre of it was placed a huge dish full of beans cooked in butter or oil, and beside it a great bowl full of mixed pickles soaked in water. The young men took a drink from this bowl before beginning to eat; one of them drank first and then passed the bowl on to his neighbour, but it was never offered to the boy. When they had each taken their share of this tart apéritif, they started eating. The table was piled high with loaves, some of which were bought and paid for, others drawn as an allowance from the Azhar. The meal was nothing less than a competition to see which of them could eat the most, who could consume the largest quantity of loaves, gulp down the greatest number of mouthfuls, swallow the most considerable amount of beans in sauce, or devour the largest share of the turnips, peppers and cucumbers which were intended to help all this down. The din of eager laughing voices flooded through the room, burst out through the window on the left and dropped echoing into the street below; it overflowed through the door on the right and cascaded into the well of the building, where it interrupted the bickerings or whispered undertones of the workers' wives on the first floor. The women stopped to listen to the hubbub of talk and laughter wafted to them by the wind, as if they found a pleasure in it only paralleled by the delight which the young men took in swallowing their food.

The boy sat silently amongst them with his back bent like a bow. His hand travelled in a hesitant, apologetic way between the loaf laid on the table in front of him and the bowl which stood some distance away in the middle of the table. It kept colliding with a criss-cross of other hands, which moved so rapidly up and down that in a short time they had completely scoured the bowl. This aroused in the boy an astonishment mingled with disgust. He could not admit the compatibility of this passion for beans and pickles with the noble thirst for knowledge, the vivacity and penetration of mind which he recognised in these young men.

They did not let their lunch occupy any great length of time. Not a quarter of an hour passed before the bowl was empty and the table clean, apart from an odd crumb or two and half of the loaf which had been put in front of the boy. He had been unable, or unwilling, to eat more than half of it. In another moment the table had been lifted up by one of them, taken outside the room and cleared of the remains, to be brought back to its place clean and smooth except for the spots of butter and sauce which had been dropped on it. Another went to fetch some wood-charcoal and prepare the samovar—that species of tea-kettle which the Persians and Russians use. He filled it up with water, then after lighting the fire and arranging the coals round it he put it back in the place where the bowl had been, with the tea-glasses on the edge of the table in front. Then he sat down again and waited for the water to boil. Whereupon the young men resumed their conversation, but this time in a quiet, languorous tone. For their energies were occupied at the moment in digesting the mixture of hot and cold, solid and liquid, which they had just put inside them. Then suddenly the voices dropped again and were quiet. The room was possessed by a solemn stillness, broken only by a thin, feeble vibration, intermittent at first, but soon becoming continuous.

The young men were enthralled. They broke the silence all together with a single word pronounced quietly, but in a firm, sustained tone; "Allaah!" Their voices lingered over the word as if they had been stirred to ecstasy by soft music heard a long way off. There was nothing strange in this; for what they were listening to was the wheeze of the water beginning to shift uneasily above the place where, without either noise or smoke, the charcoal was burning away. The student responsible for the tea watched intently over the samovar, concentrating eye and ear and mind upon it, until when the wheezing of the water changed to a bubbling he took a china tea-pot and, putting it close to the samovar, turned the tap carefully so that a little of the boiling water ran out into the tea-pot. Then he closed the tap again and cut off the flow of water. After this he replaced the lid of the tea-pot and shook it gently to and fro so that the little hot water that was in it could warm every part of the pot. As soon as it was warm he got up and poured this water away. For the tea must never come into contact either with cold glass or cold metal, which spoil its taste. After waiting for a few seconds he poured the water gently into the pot, without filling it to the brim. Then he picked up the tin of Indian tea, took a pinch of it and dropped it into the pot, which he then filled up to the brim before picking it up very carefully and putting it on to the embers for a few seconds. Finally he raised it in triumph and invited his friends to hold out their glasses.

Throughout this process the others waited in silence, watching jealously every movement their friend made, in case he should infringe any of the regulations. When the glasses were full, the teaspoons began to circle in them with a gay tinkle of metal against glass that fell like music upon the ear. Then the company raised their glasses to their mouths and began to suck the tea in with their lips in long sips, making an unpleasant sound which drowned the noise of the spoons playing in the glasses. They continued drinking with scarcely a word, except for this invariable remark, which had to be made by one of them and assented to by the rest: "So much to quench the fire in the beans!" When they had finished the first round the glasses were filled a second time, after fresh water had been poured into the pot to replace what had been drawn off. But this time the company was taking more interest in the tea than in the unhappy water which, as it absorbed the heat of the fire, first moaned, then sang plaintively, then burst into weeping as it boiled. But the young men paid no attention to it, unmoved either by its music or its tears. They were intent on the tea, and on this second round especially. The first round was intended to quench "the fire in the beans." But as for the second, that was destined simply for their own delight and the satisfaction of their bodies as a whole. It gave refreshment not only to their mouths and throats but to their heads too; at all events when they had finished this round they recovered their wits and became intelligent again. Their tongues were loosened, their lips began to smile, their voices were once more raised in conversation. But now it was not food and drink they were discussing. They were no longer preoccupied with physical needs and could turn their attention to things of the mind. They remembered what one sheikh had said in the first lecture, or another in the second, and found something to laugh at in each. They recalled an objection one of them had made to the sheikh, and discussed it amongst themselves. One would consider it so strong as to be conclusive, while another thought it unconvincing and even nonsensical. One of them would take the place of the sheikh in question, and another that of the student who had made the objection, while a third set up as judge of the debate. The judge would interfere from time to time to bring one of the speakers back to the point or to support one of them with a forgotten argument or a proof left out. The student responsible for the tea was not debarred from the discussion, but on no account must he let his mind wander too far. He had added more tea and water to what was left in the pot, and the glasses had been drained and refilled. The tea ran at least to a third round; there were normally three glasses, but while the number might not be decreased, there was no objection to raising it.

The boy was still crouching in his corner, back bent and eyes lowered. His tea was passed to him in silence, and in silence he drank it. He paid attention to what went on and listened to what was said around him, understanding some of it, though missing more. But everything he heard, whether understood or not, enthralled him; and he asked himself yearningly how soon he would be able to talk and argue as these young men did.

Nearly an hour had gone by. Everyone had drunk his tea, but the table remained as it was, with the samovar in the middle and the glasses dotted round the edges. Noon was approaching, and the company would have to break up so that each of them might quickly look over the midday lesson before going in to hear it. They had prepared it together the night before, but there was no harm in a rapid revision to reconsider any word which was at all obscure or ambiguous. No doubt the text was clear and the commentary lucid. But El-Bannân[12] complicates the simple and ties knots where all seems plain. El-Sayyid Jurjâny's[13] penetrating mind draws dark secrets out of clarity itself; while 'Abdul-Hakîm[14] is often clear

12. A modern writer on rhetoric.

13. A fourteenth-century Arabic philosopher of Persia. To be distinguished from his more famous namesake the rhetorician 'Abdul-Qâhir Jurjâny.

14. Author of treatises on theology who lived at the court of the Mongol rulers of India in the first half of the seventeenth century.

enough, but even he creates unnecessary difficulties. As for the commentator, he's an imbecile who has no idea what he means. Now there are only a few minutes left before noon, so we must hurry to the Azhar, where the muezzins will be giving the call to prayer. The service will have begun while we are still on the way there. When we reach the Azhar it will already be over, and the students will have started forming circles round their sheikhs. No matter. We have missed the common prayer, so we will say it together after the lecture and still be praying in company. It is better not to say prayers before the lesson, when one's mind is distracted by the difficulties and problems in it requiring to be solved. When the lesson is over, when we have listened to it and discussed it, and delivered ourselves of its intricacies and puzzles, we shall be able to devote our whole hearts and minds to prayer.

The boy's brother was calling him, in a phrase which, throughout those years, he never ceased to use: "Now, sir, up with you!" So up the boy got, still rather dazed, and stumbled along at his brother's side till they reached the Azhar. His guide put him in his place for the grammar class and went off to Sheikh Sâlihy's lecture in the Chapel of the Blind.

The boy listened to the grammar lesson and understood it without effort. He found the sheikh's explanations and repetitions tedious in the extreme. When the lesson was over and the students had dispersed the boy remained in his place. Sooner or later his brother would come to drag him away all ungently without a word, out of the Azhar and along the road they had taken at dawn and in the middle of the morning, then deposit him in his place in the corner of the room, where the old carpet was stretched out on a rotten worn-out mat. From that moment the boy set himself to face the hours of agony.

IX

The building was all but empty when the boy arrived there for the first time. It was after the Ramadan holiday, and the lodgers had not yet returned. This was how the boy discovered that the students liked to delay their return to Cairo, especially after this holiday, which marked the beginning of the university year. It was as if students and sheikhs felt a certain melancholy reluctance to leave their families and their villages, and prolonged their holidays for two or three days, perhaps even for a week or more. There was no objection to this; for the Azhar was still in that happy period when work-days and rest-days were not meticulously marked out, either for students or for lecturers. There was no rigid timetable to enforce attendance daily and hourly without fail. Everything was flexible and easy. The rector would fix the official date of return, but lecturers were free to begin when it suited them, and students might come to lectures as soon as they wished or found it convenient.

At that time the regulations were pleasantly elastic.[15] They relied much more on people's goodwill and enthusiasm than on rigid discipline or compulsory rules. They were better calculated to divide the sheep from the goats and to encourage students to work out of sheer love of learning rather than in obedience to orders or for fear of punishment.

This atmosphere of freedom and tolerance was keenly appreciated by students and sheikhs alike, though they took care not to abuse it. The first two weeks of the year were left free for people to do what they liked with, and served as a rule for renewing old friendships and making new ones. Students would trickle back from their villages and begin by paying each other visits of welcome before gently settling down to work. Lecturers too were in no very great haste to return from their homes and spent some time arranging their houses for the long stay in Cairo and calling on each other by way of friendly greeting, until finally, without either undue hurry or delay, they began their lectures. However, there were many, both among lecturers and students, who set more value on learning than on their families and their homes. Some of them stayed in Cairo over the holiday, studying in their rooms, at the Azhar itself, or at some other mosque. Others hastened to return to Cairo as soon as the opportunity occurred, in the hope of securing a few private lessons before the general courses began.

For these various reasons the tenement was practically empty when the boy and his brother arrived. There was no one living there but Uncle Hagg 'Aly, two of the young sheikh's friends, and the two Persians. But scarcely had the boy installed himself in the block before the other lodgers began coming back, singly or in groups, morning or evening. Soon the building was teeming with movement and activity and voices rang out on all sides, until the place seemed full to bursting point. It was in fact distinctly overcrowded. Some of the rooms were packed with students, and one of them actually contained no less than twenty.

How could they sit down? How could they study? How could they sleep? These were questions the boy asked himself, without finding any answer. He did know, however, that the rent of a room could scarcely exceed twenty-five piastres a month, and might well be as little as twenty, so that each student would pay only one piastre for a month's lodging.

This well illustrates the situation of those sons of the country who come up to Cairo in their multitudes to study theology at the

15. This was before the tightening up of teaching conditions by the Administrative Council of the Azhar under Muhammad 'Abdu.

Azhar. They acquire as much religious knowledge as they can, but not without contracting at the same time a host of maladies, physical, moral, and even intellectual.

The room next to the boy's on the right-hand side was empty for the first week. No sound or movement was to be heard in it. A second week followed upon the first, but still the room was vacant and still not a sound came from it. The students began asking themselves what had happened to the sheikh who had lodged there before the fast. Had he perhaps moved from this block and gone to live elsewhere? But one night in the second week the boy woke up at the sound of Uncle Haag 'Aly's voice piercing the darkness, and his stick belabouring the floor. Mystified as usual, he waited for the voice of the muezzin, then silently joined in the call to prayer. The voice ceased, and the boy's thoughts began to follow the worshippers at the mosque as they arrived for the service, some with quick, lively steps, others still heavy with sleep. But hark! What was that? A strange, shrill voice came through the wall behind the boy's head, penetrating his eardrum, and sending a shiver right through his body from head to foot. The boy has never since forgotten that voice and cannot think of it without laughing to himself, even if with an effort he can keep the smile from his lips. It was an extraordinary voice. At first it terrified him, then it convulsed him with laughter such as he found it impossible to control, despite his anxiety not to wake his brother. "Al . . . Al . . . Al . . . Allahu, Allahu, Allahu Ak . . . Al . . . Al . . . Allahu Ak . . . Allahu Ak . . . Allahu Akbar."

This was what the boy heard. The beginning and the repetitions were unintelligible, though he could recognise the end. However, the voice did not break off on finishing the phrase, but repeated it once or twice more, before finally setting it straight. Each letter took its right place in the chanter's mouth, then in the air, and lastly in the boy's ear and brain. After that the voice proceeded to recite the opening chapter of the Koran, and it was only then that the boy recognised it as the voice of a man praying. It went on reciting the *fâtiha* until it came to the phrase: "Thee we worship, and in Thee is our succour," where it stuck on the final *s* and could go no further. Then it went back and started all over again: "Al . . . Al . . . Al . . . Allahu Ak . . . Al . . . Al . . ." It was at this point that the boy finally lost control and broke out into such a peal of laughter that his brother woke up with a start and asked what was the matter. The boy was incapable of replying; but as soon as his brother heard the voice on the other side of the wall no further explanation was necessary. He too could scarcely restrain his laughter. "Gently," he whispered, "that's our neighbour Sheikh So-and-so, the Shâfi'ite.[16] He has come back, and is saying his morning prayer."

The young sheikh was too sleepy to say any more, and returned to his rest. The boy succeeded in controlling himself and followed the voice of the sheikh through the wall until, after heroic efforts, he finished his prayer. But there was still something that mystified the boy. Why did this Shâfi'ite sheikh inflict such a purgatory on himself? He had only finished his prayer after facing almost unsurmountable difficulties. In the morning the boy plucked up the courage to ask his brother about it. "This sheikh," he explained, "is conscientious to the point of obsession. He wants to make sure of his will to pray and to devote all his heart and mind to God from the beginning of his prayer to the end. So if you find he hesitates, or interrupts his prayer to go back to the beginning again, you must understand that he has been distracted by some worldly consideration and is trying to drive it away in order to concentrate his whole mind on the worship of God."

This sheikh was extremely quiet and scarcely gave any sign of life except when he said his prayers at dawn. It was many days before the boy could get used to his voice or listen to it without laughing. Yet at bottom he could only pity a victim of this demon of superstition, which, whether supernatural or not, can inflict such cruel obsessions on human beings.

Apart from the memory of his voice, there remain in the boy's mind only two stories about this sheikh. In one of these he was personally concerned, but the other he learnt only by hearsay. The first incident occurred when the boy was a good deal older and had advanced much further in his studies. It was at one of the sheikh's lectures, in which he was explaining the famous phrase in the *Talkhîs*:[17] "Every word varies in meaning according to its context." What a sea of ink has been wasted on this sentence, in abridgements and expansions, in commentaries and glosses, in criticisms and objections; while all the time it is a truth as clear as daylight, as unambiguous and unequivocal as can be. The sheikh, like many an Azharite before him, embarked upon the analysis of this sentence and the sifting of all the rigmarole that has been talked about it. He put himself to such exertions that before long his voice was hoarse, his brow ran with sweat, and all his strength was gone. Loyalty to learning, without a doubt, is a burden such as none but the strongest can support.

The boy began to criticise some of the sheikh's statements, as he

16. The Shâfi'ite is one of the four orthodox schools of law, to which most Egyptian Moslems belong.

17. *Talkhîs al-Miftâh* (*Abridgement of the Key*) is an advanced book on rhetoric, of the early fourteenth century. It is abridged from a twelfth-century work entitled *Miftâh al-'Ulûm* (*The Key to the Sciences*).

used to do with all the teachers. But the sheikh pounced upon him with a crushing reply, which filled him in a moment with confusion, resentment and contempt. "Give it up, my lad," he said. "All this is too much for you. You're only fit for the husk which you'll get at the end of the morning. As for the juice, it's not for you, nor you for it." With this he laughed, and the whole class joined in. The boy was ashamed to leave the lesson in the middle, so he bore up in silence till the end, when a friend took him away. The "husk" to which the sheikh referred was a lecture on literature, at which among other books Mubarrad's *Kâmil*[18] was studied. From that day the sheikh declined in the boy's estimation and he came eventually to detest a man he had once loved and respected. The sheikh became a target for the boy's wit as he laughed and joked with his companions before and after the "husk."

The second of the two stories occasioned nothing but the most hearty laughter and amusement; it even stimulated the boy to poetry. It was indeed the simplest and most commonplace of occurrences —but what can be simpler than the laughter of youth?

The sheikh had a son who was not noticeably intelligent and had nothing about him to suggest that he had been born for a life of study. He was, nevertheless, a student. He lived in his father's room, and was just as quiet and just as unobtrusive a neighbour as his father. One day, or rather one night, a group of friends came to visit the father, and asked his son for coffee. After a while he brought the coffee, and the sheikhs took up their cups as lickerishly as ever. They took a sip at it, or rather a long, noisy suck; but scarcely had the liquid reached their throats before they spewed it out with a rush. They all began coughing and spluttering convulsively in the effort to expel it from their throats. A mixture of coffee and saliva dribbled onto their beards and ran down onto their *kuftâns* as they went on coughing in the most extreme discomfort. What they had drunk was not coffee, but snuff. The sheikh's son had made a mistake and mixed up the coffee-pot with the snuff-box.

The incident in which the boy was concerned, at the sheikh's lecture on rhetoric, had a curious sequel. He abandoned this sheikh in favour of another who had a room next to his in the block where the boy lived. This man was a Shâfi'ite too, though he did not have the same obsession. He was the quietest and gravest of men, as kind-hearted as he was niggardly of speech. Apart from an occasional greeting to himself or one of his friends, the boy had never heard him utter a word. The day after leaving the first sheikh he attended a lecture by this colleague of his under the dome of the Mosque of

18. Mubarrad (826–868) was born at Basra, studied under El-Jâhiz, and taught at Baghdad under the 'Abbasids. The *Kâmil* (lit. *Complete*) is an extremely varied medley of traditions, proverbs, poems and anecdotes, accompanied by extensive grammatical commentary, which is the main aim of the book.

Muhammad Bey Abu-l-Dhahab. The boy knew this mosque very well, as he had listened to lectures on grammar and logic in almost every corner of it. Later on in this history there will be other stories to tell of things which took place there.[19]

Here, then, the boy came at noon, after the "husk" lecture. He climbed the steps he knew so well, took off his shoes, and walked forward between two familiar lecture-groups. Then he stepped over the threshold of the dome and sat down in the circle of waiting students. It was not long before the sheikh arrived, in his usual quiet manner, and began the lesson. After glorifying God and invoking blessings on the Prophet, he started to read a text on the peculiar qualities of the indefinite subject. He eventually came to a quotation made by the author from the Koran: "A sign of approval from God is no mean thing." Then following the author, the scholiast, the marginal commentator and the editor, he discussed the indefiniteness of the phrase "a sign of approval" in terms which did not please the young man at all. He found it impossible to contain himself, and started to criticise what the sheikh had been saying. But scarcely had he begun before the sheikh interrupted him, and said in his calm, placid voice: "Be quiet, my lad. May God open your eyes and grant you pardon; and may He deliver us from mischief-makers like you. Fear the wrath of God, and cease to plague us at this lecture. Go back where you came from, to your mid-morning husk, where the blind mislead the blind."

This rebuke provoked a general roar of laughter. The young man bowed his head and remained speechless with rage as the sheikh continued his reading and commentary in the same calm, unruffled tone. He stayed sullenly where he was until the circle broke up, and then went off in a mood of bitter fury.

He was thus excluded from rhetoric lectures for the rest of the year. At noon, after the "husk," he used to go off to the library at Bab El-Khalq and stay there almost until closing-time just before sundown.

Was it a coincidence that the two sheikhs should both have dismissed the young man from their lectures, or was it a concerted plan? He never knew. In any case the recital of these two incidents is a little premature. We had best return from this digression to the tenement and its occupants, and see what was happening there when the young student first arrived.

XX

The young man became more and more disgusted with the Azhar, where he was committed to a life he loathed and cut off from all that he longed for. No sooner had he settled in Cairo at the be-

19. Muhammad Abu-l-Dhahab the Mameluke was virtual ruler of Egypt towards the end of the eighteenth century. His mosque is one of the finest examples in Cairo of the Ottoman style.

ginning of the academic year than he began to yearn for it to end. God alone can know how glad he was when the first signs of summer appeared and the whole district he lived in became rife with intolerable smells which sprang up in the heat of the sun until the air was thick with them and even breathing became unbearable. There was not a lecture, morning or afternoon, from whatever sheikh, at this time of the year at which he did not sooner or later doze off, to start up again with a brutal jerk when the students crowded round, laughing or indignant, to wake him up.

No wonder, then, that the arrival of summer made him gay and light-hearted, since it heralded the approach of the holidays when he would go back to the country and take a rest from the Azhar and everyone in it. Not for this reason alone did he look forward to the holiday, nor because he would see his people again and enjoy the good things he had missed in Cairo. Apart from all this he had one special reason for looking forward to them which outweighed all the rest: spiritually and intellectually they were far more satisfying than the whole of the academic year itself.

The holidays gave him the leisure to think; and what advantage he took of it! Then the chance to read[20] with his brothers; and how rich and varied was the reading they did!

The young men of the family came home from their schools and institutes with their satchels full of books quite unrelated to their regular studies which they had no time to read during the year. There were serious books and books for amusement, translations and originals, modern books and classics.

Before they had been at home a week they were bored with doing nothing. Shaking off their inactivity they plunged into their books and remained engrossed in them all day and half the night. Their father was delighted at this and congratulated them upon it; though sometimes he was displeased and even scolded them when they turned to folk-tales and became absorbed in the *Thousand & One Nights* or the stories of 'Antara and Saif Ibn Zhî Yazan.[21]

But whether the family liked it or not, they continued to devour such books and derived twice as much pleasure from them as from their Azharite text-books. Apart from this they read the translations of Fathy Zaghlûl from the French, and of Siba'y from the English; the articles of Jurjy Zaidan in the *Hilal*, with his novels and works on the history of literature and civilisation; Jacob Sarruf's writings in the *Maqtataf* and Sheikh Rashîd Rida's in the *Manâr*. Then they read the books of Qâsim Amîn[22] and many of the

20. By "read" he means "be read to." [Ed.]

21. Popular romances on the lives of two half-legendary pre-Islamic heroes, written down centuries after their death. (See p. 24.)

22. Recent Egyptian and Syrian writers. He read a wide variety of historical and controversial writing. *Hilal, Muqtataf,* and *Manâr* are journals appearing in Cairo.

works of the Imam, then some of the many novels translated into Arabic for a more popular taste, which fascinated them with the pictures they gave of a life utterly different from anything they had known either in town or country. All this tempted them to intensify their reading to a point where it became a menace not only to their own welfare but to the family's. They never saw an advertisement in the press for an unfamiliar book, whether new or old, but they sent the publisher an order for it. Not many days would pass before the book—or books—arrived by parcel post, and the family would be compelled willy-nilly to pay for them.

Another joy which the holidays brought the boy was the chance to think about absent friends, to write letters to them[23] and receive their answers. These exchanges gave him a zest and satisfaction far greater than he could derive from their conversation and companionship in Cairo.

Then there was the delight of meeting other young men from outside the family who belonged to the world of the tarboush. Some of them had come from secondary or higher training schools to rest at home in the country like himself. It was a joy for them to meet and talk with him, as it was for him to meet them, and they had plenty of questions to ask each other about their different courses of study. Sometimes they would read him passages from their books or he would introduce them to some literary classic.

The beginning of one of these vacations was rather less pleasant. A change in the family fortunes had obliged them to move from the town in which the boy had been born to the southernmost part of the province, in the first place; then after staying a year there they moved again to the most distant part of Upper Egypt, where they settled for a long period. Our friend bitterly regretted his home town and felt ill at ease in these strange unfamiliar places where he never knew which way to turn. But in the end he became reconciled to this town in the far south, which he learnt to know and to love like a second birth-place. Yet his first acquaintance with it had been painful in the extreme.

He went with the rest of the family to join his father, who had begun his work there alone. As soon as he had made all his arrangements and felt settled he invited his family to move there too. This occurred in the summer vacation, so that the boy travelled with them. They caught the train in the middle of the night and arrived at their destination at four o'clock the next morning. It was a newly-built town, and the train only stopped there for one minute. The family was a sizeable group, led by the eldest son, and including women and children, not to mention a mountain of baggage. As the train neared the station the elder sons attended to the women

23. He dictates letters, a common practice even among those who could see. [Ed.]

and children and piled up all the luggage close to the carriage door, so that when the train stopped at the station they were able to drag everything out onto the platform and then leap out after it themselves. No a single thing was forgotten or left behind—except the blind boy.

He was thoroughly scared to find himself alone and helpless. However, a few passengers, seeing the plight he was in, took pity on him and reassured him as best they could. When the train stopped at the next station they set him down and handed him over to the telegraph-man before returning to their carriage.

The boy learnt later on that the family had reached their new house and started looking round, inspecting all the rooms and putting everything in its place. Then their father came in and sat down to chat with his sons and daughters.

Some considerable time after the family's arrival the boy's name chanced to crop up in conversation. Immediate alarm on the part of his father, mother and brothers: the elder sons rush to the telegraph-station. Without success, however. It was some time before news came that he was at the next station, waiting for someone to come and rescue him. So one of them came and brought him home on the crupper of a most eccentric mule, which at one moment would be walking quite gently and at the next break wildly into a trot; all of which only added to his discomfiture.

The boy will never forget the time he spent with the telegraph operator. He was a spirited young man, full of mirth and pleasantry. His room was the meeting-place for a crowd of station employees, who at first resented the young man's presence there, though as soon as they had heard his story they showed him sympathy and kindness. Seeing before them a blind sheikh they assumed that he was an excellent reciter of the Koran and a first-class chanter. So they asked him to sing them something. When he protested that he was not a good singer they asked him to recite them something from the Koran, and though he swore that he had no voice for Koran-reading they insisted on hearing him and would take no refusal. So the boy was compelled to recite the Koran in shame and anguish of heart at a moment when he loathed life and cursed the day he was born. His voice stuck in his throat and the tears streamed down his cheeks. So at last they had mercy on him and left him alone with his misery until someone came to take him home.

This mishap, though it wounded the young man deeply, did not make him dislike his new home or regret coming there. On the contrary he loved it, and on the approach of summer he used to long to go back there, though the heat was well-nigh unbearable.

In the tenement at Cairo there were many changes. Of the older students two had secured their doctor's degree and the rest, including the young man's brother, had joined the newly founded[24] School for Qâdys. The young man himself had lost the cousin who had been the main relief of his solitude both at the Azhar and in the tenement; he had joined the *Dar El-'Ulûm*.[25]

The young man saw himself condemned once more to the stony solitude which long before in the first months of his life as a student had caused him so much suffering. In fact it would be a great deal worse, since there would be no one at all to look after him when he went back to Cairo at the end of the summer. His brother would be attending the School for Qâdys and his cousin the *Dar El-'Ulûm*. How could he manage alone in the tenement? What was the use, to himself or anyone else, of his going to Cairo? He had already acquired a reasonable store of knowledge. What profit was he likely to derive from the doctorate, even if he obtained it? In all probability he would fail, for success demanded an effort such as he could never make alone. So his brother argued when he spoke to the family about him one day towards the end of the summer vacation. His father would have liked to say something in reply, but he was struck dumb by these unanswerable arguments. His mother could find no answer either, and merely wept in silent misery. The young man could only stumble away and stay in one of the rooms alone, grim and heartbroken, his mind a blank.

The night was long and burdensome, and his heart ached with misery. He got up without saying a word, and no one spoke to him. The day dragged by as heavily as the night. Then in the evening his father came up to him, stroked his head and kissed him: "You shall go to Cairo," he said. "You are to have a servant of your own." It was all he could do to prevent himself bursting into tears, and his mother too was almost overcome.

The day of departure arrived and he went off with the other young men of the family to catch the train. The servant's people had agreed to meet them at the station. But the young man waited there until the train came in, and no servant arrived. So the others boarded the train and went off, leaving their brother behind. The young man and his father walked back home in gloomy silence.

That same evening the servant arrived and he recaptured all his gaiety and cheerfulness. Two days later he travelled to Cairo with his small black servant, carrying provisions for his elder brother.

Thus he returned to Cairo and settled there with the negro servant, who took him to lectures at the Azhar, prepared his food for lunch, and read to him, when he was free, in a broken, stumbling voice.

24. 1907.

25. Training College for teachers of Arabic.

Meanwhile the Egyptian University had been founded[26] and our friend went there and put his name on the rolls. His negro boy took him to lectures at the Azhar in the morning and at the University in the afternoon. He felt a new relish for life, met new kinds of people, and studied with lecturers who were in a different class from those of the Azhar. The University was a long way from the tenement, and so were the School for Qâdys and the *Dar El-'Ulûm.* There was no point in staying there any longer, and the little group moved to another new house in Darb El-Gamamîz.

So the young man started a new life which had practically no relation with the old. Once every week or two, perhaps, he felt a regret for the Azhar; now and again he met Azharite friends on their visits to the University; and from time to time he went to call upon Sheikh Marsafy.

The truth is that deep down in his heart the young man had broken with the Azhar once and for all. Yet his name remained on the registers. Nor did he reveal this final decision to his father for fear that he might feel hurt or disappointed. His father knew nothing whatsoever about the University and cared still less.

One day during the summer holidays, however, after the young man and his brothers had returned to their new home, the post came while they were reading and brought his brother a letter from one of his friends. He read it and then repeated it to the young man. It contained a most wonderful piece of news.

The boy had been studying at the Azhar for eight years, during which time the regulations had been changed many times. That summer all students on the rolls had been allowed to increase the nominal period of their enrolment if they could show that they had studied in the Azhar or the other religious institutes before reaching the minimum age for official enrolment, which was fifteen. The result would be to advance the date of their examination and graduation.

The new rule had been announced during the vacation, and their friend had immediately sent an application to the Rector in the young man's name, declaring that he had studied at the Azhar for two years before reaching the required age. He showed the application to two senior sheikhs with whom the boy had never had any sort of acquaintance either at lectures or at any other time. Nevertheless they read it through and witnessed to the truth of the young man's declaration. You could hardly blame them for that; they had hosts of students coming to their lectures, and how were they to know them all?

So it was that the boy learnt, to his great surprise, that he was

26. The Egyptian University, first founded in 1908, was reconstituted as a state university in 1925 and renamed Fuad I University in 1938. [It is now called Cairo University.—Editor.]

credited with ten years at the Azhar when in fact he had only spent eight there, and that in two years he would be qualified to take the examination for his degree.

So he had to renew the connection with the Azhar which he had broken or tried to break off, and keep a foot in both camps, that is to say in the University of the Azhar, as it was called at that time, and the Egyptian University. He had to go on living this double life, between two worlds that pulled him different ways: the old world of the Azhar, down in the age-worn streets between the Batinîya and Kafr El-Tamâ'în, and the new world of the University amidst all the modern elegance of Sharia Koubry Kasr El-Nil.

There let us leave him, with the old and the new struggling in him for mastery. Who knows? Perhaps one day we shall resume his story.

India

Sanskrit, the ancient, classical language of India, is a language of the Indo-European family and came to India with invaders from the northwest who pushed into southern India a native stock of Dravidian speakers. This linguistic dichotomy still persists in India. Most of the modern languages of India stem from Sanskrit and its descendants, but several in the south descend from the non–Indo-European Dravidian family. The literary tradition of India is largely the tradition of Sanskrit literature and its imitation in the modern languages, but some Dravidian material has been perpetuated. And greater India (including the area which is now Pakistan) has a rich Moslem literature, largely in Urdu, an Indian language written with an Arab script and powerfully influenced by Arabic and Persian models.

Sanskrit at the dawn of its history is already the literary language of a scholastic and priestly caste. The earliest works, difficult to date but perhaps going back to 1000 B.C. are the *Vedas* ("sacred lore"), a collection of hymns and ritual texts (see below). The Vedic age in Sanskrit literature is followed by the age of the great epics, the *Mahābhārata (War of the Descendants of Bharata)* and the *Rāmāyana (Story of Rāma)*. The *Mahābhārata* is of great length and embodies an encyclopedic amount of ancient legend; the *Rāmāyana* (see below) is somewhat briefer. These epics were constantly revised in later times, were redacted in all of the important vernaculars, and traveled as far afield as the isle of Java. They are important both as sacred scripture and as literary entertainment, and their artistic quality is of a high order. Except for the philosophical portion of the *Mahābhārata* known as the *Bhagavad Gītā* or *Song of Gods* (see below), the *Rāmāyana* has been the more popular of the two works.

By about the sixth century A.D. a tradition of court epic or *kāvya* was under way. Açvaghosha's *Budda-charita,* or *Doings of Buddha,* calls itself a court epic, but the greatest works in this form are by Kālidāsa, who was also a writer of major dramas (see below). His *Raghuvamsha* or *Race of Raghu* describes the life of Rāma, the epic hero, and gives an account of his ancestors. The poem is admired especially for its descriptions of nature, in rich simile and metaphor, though it is perhaps artificial in style for Western tastes. Kālidāsa's other major poem is the *Kumārasambhava* or *Birth of the War God.* This describes the wedding of the god Shiva and Parvati. It is an erotic work meant to serve as a prototype for human love and marriage. The poem is fanciful and has greater warmth of feeling than the *Race of Raghu*. For this extensive tradition of court epic, principles were laid down by Dandin in his *Mirror or Poetry* (*Kavyadarça*): the subject must be derived from epic legend, the scope must be large, and there must be elaborate descriptions of cities, seas, mountains, seasons, sunrises, weddings, battles, and so forth.

Indian drama traces its origin to a Thespis-like Bharata, the legendary author of the *Nātyashāstra*, a treatise of dramaturgy. Açvaghosha, who has already been mentioned, left fragments of dramas. Bhāsa (*ca.* 300 A.D.), an important earliest dramatist, left a number of plays on legendary subjects and was a dramatist of some skill, though neither his poetry nor his characterization is up to Kālidāsa's. Perhaps the *Mrcchakatikā* (*Little Clay Cart*), attributed to King Shūdraka, belongs also before Kālidāsa. The characters in it include a Brahman merchant who has lost his money through liberality, a rich courtesan in love with a poor young man, much description of resplendent palaces, and both comic and tragic or near-tragic emotional situations. This play and the work of Kālidāsa represent the peak of Sanskrit drama.

Sanskrit literary theorists distinguish sharply among the genres: dramatic poetry is supplemented by stage action, narrative poetry is another type, and lyric, in which Sanskrit literature is very rich, is yet another distinct genre (see below). To these forms must be added the considerable achievement of ancient India in philosophic and religious writing, law, animal fables and tales, and even, in the work of the great Panini, stylistic and linguistic investigation.

Sanskrit continued for a long time as a living language in India, and lasted long after it was no longer spoken as a first language as a court and literary vehicle as did Latin in Europe. Modern Indian literature has produced many major writers, and its difficulties have been political. At least fourteen modern Indian languages have literatures of their own and universities to perpetuate the language, and some of these, like Hindi and Bengali, are spoken and read by millions of people. Since English was learned by educated Indians from the early nineteenth century, there is a considerable Indian literature in English. Hindi will perhaps become the official and actual "standard" language of India, but the powerful cultural traditions of the other modern languages are not likely to disappear. It is impossible to note here developments in these modern literatures, but each of the major ones has been critically studied.

The two most important writers of the Indo-Pakistan world in the early twentieth century were the Hindu Rabindranath Tagore (see below), who gained world-wide fame for a variety of writings, and the Moslem Sir Mohammad Iqbal (1873-1938). But whereas Tagore's work became immediately accessible to the English-speaking world, Iqbal's equal versatility has been slower to gain readers outside of the Islamic world. Iqbal was educated at Lahore and Cambridge, and began by writing poems in Urdu to revive the ancient glories of the Islamic faith. For his philosophical writings, he chose to write in Persian, and his *Secrets of the Self* (translated by R. A. Nicholson, 1920) won him much acclaim in the Moslem world. Many volumes of passionate poetry flowed from his pen in both Urdu and Persian. He was an ardent nationalist and an early advocate of Pakistan as a separate state for Moslems.

R. K. Narayan (see below) is an excellent and typical example of the modern Indian novelist. He combines an Indian sensitivity with modern European realism.

WRITINGS AND CRITICISM

The date of the latest edition or reprint is given.

Louis Renou's *Indian Literature* (trans. Patrick Evans, 1964) is a good general introduction, as is the older work of A. A. Macdonell, *A History of Sanskrit Literature* (1900). A. B. Keith's *Sanskirt Literature* (1920), and V. H. Subramania Sastri and K. Chandrasekharan's *Sanskrit Literature* (1951); P.E.N. Books—Indian Literatures, XII) are satisfactory brief works. Longer histories are M. Winternitz, *History of Sanskirt Literature* (3 vols., 1927–33), A. B. Keith, *A History of Sanskrit Literature* (of the classical period) (1928), Krisna Chaitanya, *A New History of Sanskrit Literature* (1962), and Surendra N. Dasgupta, *History of Sanskrit Literature* (2nd ed., 1947–). A brief sketch of the earliest literature is H. W. Bailey's "Ancient Indian Literature" in *Literatures of the East,* ed. E. B. Ceadel (1953). . L. Basham's *The Wonder that Was India* (1959) is an excellent survey of the cultural history of pre-Moslem India. *The Legacy of India* by G. T. Garratt and others (1937), is useful. An extensive cultural history now appearing is R. C. Majumdar's *History and Culture of the Indian People* (1951–). Controversial and exciting are Heinrich Zimmer's *Myths and Symbols in Indian Art and Civilization* (1946) and his *Philosophies of India* (1951), both edited by Joseph Campbell. A comprehensive anthology of good translations from philosophical and religious literature is *Sources of the Indian Tradition,* ed. William T. De Bary, Stephen Hay, Royal Weiler, and Andrew Yarrow (1958). There is much useful material in V. Raghavan's *The Indian Heritage,* 2nd ed., 1958) and Lin Yutang's *Wisdom of China and India* (1946).

For the earliest poems in the *Rigveda,* see below. The *Upanishads* are translated by R. E. Hume (1931) and by Max Muller (2 vols., 1879–82; Sacred Books of the East Series). On the Upanishads see George B. Burch in *Approaches to the Oriental Classics,* ed. W. T. De Bary (1959).

The background of the age of the epics is examined in N. K. Sidhanta's *The Heroic Age of India* (1929) and E. Washburn Hopkins' *The Great Epic of India* (1901). Hopkins' *Epic Mythology* (1915; Grundriss der Indo-Arischen Philologie und Altertumskunde, III.i.B) is an indispensible reference work. For the *Ramayana* see below. An excellent new translation of the *Mahābhārata* is *The Mahabharata Book I: The Book of the Beginning* by J. A. B. van Buitenen (1973–). There is also a translation by P. B. Roy (11 vols., 1919–35), and abridgements by R. C. Dutt (with the *Rāmāyana*) (1917; Everyman's Library) and by Sir Edwin Arnold in his *Indian Idylls* (1888). See also "Indian and Greek Epics" by Robert Antoine and "Comments on the *Rāmāyana* and *Mahābhārata*" by George T. Artola in *Approaches to the Oriental Classics,* cited above. For the *Bhagavad Gītā* see below.

There are a great many works on Sanskrit drama, but A. B. Keith's *Sanskrit Drama* (1924) is authoritative. For Kālidāsa, see below. *The Little Clay Cart* (*Mrcchakatika*), attributed to King Shudraka, competes with Kālidāsa's *Shakuntala* for Western interest. Arthur Ryder's translation (1938; Harvard Oriental Series, IX—reprinted in *Genius of the Oriental Theater* [see Bibliographical Note]) is excellent. P. Lal has done a good modern version in *Great Sanskirt Plays in Modern Translation* (1964). Revilo P. Oliver's translation (1938) is very precise, with elaborate apparatus. G. K. Bhat's *Preface to Mrcchakatika* (1953) is a full-length critical study. An excellent recent translation of the *Mrcchakatika,* along with Prince Visakhadatta's *The Minister's Seal,* is by J. A. B. Van Buitenen in *Two Plays of Ancient India* (1968). The introduction to this constitutes a brief introduction to classical Sanskrit drama.

An excellent introduction to Sanskrit poetry is Daniel H. H. Ingalls' "Sanskrit Poetry and Sanskrit Poetics," in *Papers of the Indiana University Conference on Oriental-Western Literary Relations,* ed. Horst Frenz and G. L.

Anderson (1955). In expanded form, this constitutes the introduction to Ingalls' translation of Vidyahara (see below). A brief sketch of Sanskirt poetics is available in the Princeton *Encyclopedia of Poetry and Poetics* (see Bibliographical Note). See also the following works by S. K. De: *Some Problems in Sanskrit Poetics* (1959, 2 vols.), *History of Sanskrit Poetics* (1960), and *Sanskrit Poetics as a Study of Aesthetic* (1963).

Classical Indian story literature is available in Arthur Ryder's translation of the *Panchatantra* (1925), Dandin's *Adventures of the Ten Princes* (1928), and in the Indian equivalent of the *Thousand and One Nights*, the *Ocean of Story*, translated by C. H. Tawney and edited by N. M. Penzer (10 vols., 1924). A treatise on dramaturgy is Dhanamjaya's *The Dasharūpa*, translated by C. O. Haas (1912).

Much has been written in the more than a dozen modern languages of India, and a considerable selection is available in translation. The major literatures of modern India are in Assamese, Bengali, Gujarati, Hindi (the official language), Kanarese, Kashmiri, Malayalam, Marathi, Oriya, Punjabi, Sindhi, Tamil, Telugu, and Urdu, and, of course, English. All of these plus writing in classical Sanskrit are represented in *An Anthology of Indian Literatures* edited by K. Santhanam (1969). Buddhadeva Bose's *An Acre of Green Grass* (1948), is a well-written and critically oriented study of the major modern literatures. See also his "Modern Bengali Literature" in *Papers of the Indiana Conference* (see Bibliographical Note). Some histories of modern literature are: J. H. Ghosh, *Bengali Literature* (1948); F. E. Keay, *History of Hindi Literature* (1920); B. K. Barua, *Assamese Literature* (1965); various volumes on Gujarati literature by Dewan Bahadur K. M. Jhaveri; B. M. Shrinkathia, *Kannada Literature* (n.d.); E. R. Rice, *History of Kanarese Literature* (1921); Mohan Singh, *History of Panjabi Literature* (1936); K. B. Jindal, *A History of Hindi Literature* (1955). For English literature in India see K. R. Srinivasa Iyengar's *Indo-Anglian Literature* (1943) and his *The Indian Contribution to English Literature* (1944). Most Moslem Literature in India has been written in Urdu, now the official language of Pakistan. See T. Graham Bailey, *History of Urdu Literature* (1932), and Muhammad Sadiq, *A History of Urdu Literature* (1964). *Three Mughal Poets* edited by Ralph Russell and Khurshidul Islam (1968) is concerned with three major, pre-modern Islamic poets. *The Indian Literatures of Today, A Symposium*, ed. B. Kumarappa (1947) serves as a brief general introduction to the whole field of twentieth-century writing in India. See also K. R. Srinivasa Iyengar's *Literature and Authorship in India* (1943). Michigan State University publishes *Mahfil: A Quarterly of South Asian Literature.*

For general bibliographical aids see the Bibliographical Note.

RIGVEDA. A complete translation, not without some errors, is Ralph T. H. Griffith's *The Hymns of the Rigveda* (2 vols., 1920–1926), selections from which are in *Hindu Scriptures*, edited by Nicol Macnicol. The standard edition is Karl F. Geldner's *Der Rigveda* (4 vols., 1951–1957; Harvard Oriental Series, XXXIII–XXXVI), with translation and notes in German. Older translations are Max Muller's and Hermann Oldenberg's in the Sacred Books of the East Series (1891, 1897; XXXII, XLVI). The major commentary is still Arthur B. Keith's *Religion and Philosophy of the Vedas and Upanishads* (2 vols., 1925; Harvard Oriental Series, XXI, XXXII). A. A. Macdonell's *Vedic Mythology* (1897) is very useful, and his (with A. B. Keith) *Vedic Index of Names and Subjects* (2 vols., 1967) is valuable but difficult for the non-Sanskritist to use. Adolf Kaegi's *The Rigveda*, translated by R. Arrowsmith (1886; reprinted 1950, as *Life in Ancient India*) is a good general study. On the cosmology of the Rigveda see also W. Norman Brown's articles in *Journal of the American Oriental Society*, LI (1931); LXI (1941); LXII (1942).

BHAGAVAD-GĪTĀ. R. C. Zaehner's *The Bhagavad-Gītā* (1969) contains a lengthy introduction and elaborate commentary, a quite literal English translation, and the Sanskrit text. The commentary and notes to Hill's translation (cited below) are very full. Franklin Egerton's *The Bhagavad Gītā* (1944; reprinted without the Sanskrit text, 1972) has fewer notes but a substantial interpretive introduction. Other more literary renderings are the translations by: P. Lal (1965); Eliot Deutsch (1968); Juan Mascaro (1963); Swami Paramanda, reprinted in Lin Yutang's *Wisdom of China and India* (1942); Lionel Barnett (1905; in Macnicol, *Hindu Scriptures*, cited above); and Arthur Ryder (1929; in rhyme). For commentary see Zaehner, Hill, and Egerton (cited above) and Sri Aurobindo Ghose, *Essays on the Gita* (1950); Vinoba Bhave, *Talks on the Gita* (1960); Surenda Nath Dasgupta, *History of Indian Philosophy*, Vol. II (1932). On the history of the interpretation of the *Gita* see Satis Chandra Roy's *The Bhagavad-Gita and Modern Scholarship* (1941).

VĀLMĪKI. Griffith's translation (cited below) is the only adequate full-length verse translation of the *Ramayana.* A good prose translation is Hari Prasad Shastri's *The Ramayan* (3 vols., 1927). Romesh C. Dutt's *The Ramayana and the Mahabharata* (1917) is a useful abridgement of the two epics. The *Ramayana* has been much redacted over all of south and southeast Asia. The important version of Tulsidas (1532–1623) has been translated as *The Holy Lake of the Acts of Rama* by W. Douglas P. Hill (1952). An original, modern, satiric recreation is Aubrey Menon's *The Ramayana* (1954; also as *Rama Retold*, 1954). For criticism see the general works on the epic period cited above plus M. Monier Williams, *Indian Epic Poetry* (1863), and Dhairyabala P. Vora, *Evolution of Morals in the Epic* (1959).

KĀLIDĀSA. His works have been well translated by Arthur Ryder (Everyman's Library). *Shakuntala* has been often translated. The early translation of Sir William Jones (1789) still commands respect. The first adequate modern English translation (of the slightly different Bengali recension) is that of Monier Williams (1853, often reprinted). M. B. Emeneau has done a scholarly, almost literal translation (1962). P. Lal has done an attractive modern rendering of the play in *Great Sanskrit Plays in Modern Translation* (1963). For comment on Kālidāsa see Keith, *Sanskrit Drama*, cited above; G. C. Jhala, *Kālidāsa*, a Study (1943); Henry H. Wells, *The Classical Drama of India* (1963); B. S. Upadhyaya, *India in Kālidāsa* (1947); C. K. Raja, *Kālidāsa, a Critical Study* (1956): Walter Ruben, *Kālidāsa* (1956); and John D. Mitchell, "A Sanskrit Classic: *Shakuntala*," in *Approaches to the Oriental Classics*, cited above.

TAGORE. Collections include *A Tagore Reader*, ed. A. Chakravarty (1966); *Towards Universal Man* (1961); *Collected Poems and Plays* (1937); *The Housewarming and Other Selected Writings*, ed. A. Chakravarty (1965). Other works of Tagore are: *Gitanjali*, with an Introduction by W. B. Yeats (1935); *One Hundred and One Poems* (1967); *Binodini*, trans. Krishna Kripalani (1965); *Fireflies* (1951); *The Religion of Man* (1930), (1961); *Three Plays* (*Mukta-Dhara, Natir Puja, Chandalika*), trans. Marjorie Sykes (1950); and *The Diary of a Westward Voyage* (1962). Studies of Tagore by various critics are collected in *Rabindranath Tagore, a Centenary Volume 1961–1961*, edited by the Sahitya Akademi (1962). See also *The Social Thinking of Rabindranath Tagore* by Sasadhar Sinha (1962); *The Lute and the Plough* by G. D. Khanolkar, trans. Thomas Gay (1963), and *Rabindranath Tagore* by G. E. G. Catlin (1964). Tagore was also a painter; see *Drawings and Paintings of Rabindranath Tagore* (1961).

NARAYAN. His other fiction includes *Grateful to Life and Death* (1953), *Swami and Friends* and *The Bachelor of Arts* (published together, 1954), *The Printer of Malgudi* (1949), and *Waiting for the Mahatma* (1953), *The Vendor of Sweets* (1967), and *The Guide* (1958).

The *Rigveda*

(ca. 1000 B.C.)

The *Rigveda* is the oldest of the four great scriptures of ancient India. It is a collection of sacred hymns—1,028 of them—the origins of some of which may even go back to the days before the Indo-European invaders moved into the Punjab and then into northern India. The three other, later, *Vedas* are of a more liturgical character. The *Sāmaveda* consists of certain verses of the *Rigveda* rearranged for religious purposes. The two *Yajuvedas* contain ritual incantations in prose and verse to be used by priests at sacrifices. The *Atharvaveda* is a book of magic spells in verse. These four books are the basic scriptures of the Hindu religion, but only in the *Rigveda* do we have poetry which speaks clearly and easily to the modern reader and is comparable in beauty and simplicity to the Psalms of the Old Testament.

The origins of the Indian people are in Europe. The Indo-Iranian branch of the Indo-European family split early in history from the parent group in central Europe and wandered eastward, one group moving into Iran and becoming the parents of the Persian-speaking peoples, and the other moving through the Khyber Pass into India. Faint traces of the common ancestry can be found and the relations of the languages of Europe to the languages of Iran and India were systematically investigated by the nineteenth-century philologists who founded the discipline of comparative philology. The names of some of the gods who were to be important in India can be found, for instance, at the court of the King of Mitanni in Boghaz-köi, an ancient Hittite capital, about eighty miles west of Ankara in Turkey (ca. 1400 B.C.). But the poems of the *Rigveda* have a distinctly Indian stamp, and the world of nature depicted in the hymns is that of northern India, not the more arid regions to the north and west. Dating the *Rigveda* would include establishing a date for the original form of the poems, which is impossible, dating the earliest form of the collection, and dating the collection as it has come down to us. Similarities between the *Rigveda* and the earliest Persian religious text, the *Avesta,* make a date before 1200 B.C. impossible, and the latest possible date is perhaps 800 B.C. The language of the hymns is called Vedic or Vedic Sanskrit, and it is not much more different from classical Sanskrit than the Greek of Homer is from the Greek of the age of Aeschylus and Sophocles.

The people of the *Rigveda* were largely a pastoral people (there is little trace of town life in the poems) inhabiting the area later made famous as Kurusetra—the battlefield of Kuru in the *Bhagavad-Gītā,* that region between the Sarasvati (now Sarsuti) River and the Drsadvati (modern Chitang), near the modern city of Delhi, although some of the older hymns may reflect memories of life farther north. The religion depicted in the poems has reached a complex stage, with important earlier deities (like Dawn) almost eclipsed and the more familiar, later gods like Varuna, Indra, and Agni holding the center of the stage. The cult of fire (personified in Agni) was well developed, and also the ritual drinking of the juice of the *soma* plant. The hymns were memorized by the priestly caste, and not put into writing until later. While many of the hymns are specifically intended for religious ritual, many others are simply hymns of praise to a god personifying a familiar natural force in the universe, and therefore speak to all men. Among the more specifically ritualistic hymns are spells against vermin (I, 191) and disease (X, 163), to restore life to one apparently dead (X, 58; 60, lines 7–12), to fight insomnia (V, 55), to destroy enemies (X, 166), to beget children (X, 183), and even to oust a rival wife from a husband's affections (X, 145). There are also marriage hymns (X, 85) and funeral hymns (X, 14–18).

The hymns below dramatize the fact that perhaps of all religions of the world the Hindu best represents the integration of man and nature in all aspects. Nearly all of them deal admiringly and numenously with the mysterious forces that speak to man through nature; only a few of them, like "The Gambler," seem secular, but the Hindu does not make a distinction between the sacred and the secular.

From The Rigveda*

*Hymn of Creation***

X, 129

1. Non-being then existed not, nor being:
There was no air, nor sky that is beyond it.
What was concealed? Wherein? In whose protection?
And was there deep unfathomable water?

2. Death then existed not, nor life immortal;
Of neither night nor day was any token.
By its inherent force the One breathed windless:
No other thing than that beyond existed.

3. Darkness there was at first, by darkness hidden;
Without distinctive marks, this all was water.
That which, becoming, by the void was covered,
That One by force of heat came into being.

4. Desire entered the One in the beginning:
It was the earliest seed, of thought the product.
The sages searching in their hearts with widsom,
Found out the bond of being in non-being.

5. Their ray extended light across the darkness;
But was the One above or was it under?
Creative force was there, and fertile power;
Below was energy, above was impulse.

6. Who knows for certain? Who shall here declare it?
Whence was it born, and whence came this creation?
The gods were born after this world's creation:
Then who can know from whence it has arisen?

7. None knoweth whence creation has arisen;
And whether he has or has not produced it:
He who surveys it in the highest heaven,
He only knows, or haply he may know not.

* From *Hymns from the Rigveda,* selected and metrically translated by A. A. Macdonell. Copyright The Association Press, Calcutta. Reprinted by permission of The Association Press.

** In this hymn the origin of the world is explained as the evolution of the existent from the non-existent. Water came into being first; from it was evolved intelligent life by heat. This is the starting point of the natural philosophy which developed into the Sankhya system.

*Mitra and Varuna**

VII, 61

1. The beauteous eye of Varuna and Mitra,
The Sun, now rises up, his light extending,
Who with his gaze looks down upon all creatures:
He ever notes the burning zeal of mortals.

2. This pious priest, heard far away, here utters
His hymn for you, O Varuna and Mitra:
Do ye, O sages, treat his prayers with favour,
And may his autumns be replete with wisdom.

3. From wide-spread earth, O Varuna and Mitra,
Ye bounteous gods, and from the lofty heaven,
Ye have disposed your wandering spies in dwellings
And plants, ye who with watchful eye protect us.

4. Praise thou the law of Varuna and Mitra;
Their force the two worlds keeps with might asunder.
The mouths of impious men shall pass by sonless;
May those on worship bent increase their homestead.

5. Ye both are wise, O mighty ones, for you two
These lauds are sung without deceit or magic.
Avenging spies pursue men's falsehoods closely:
There are no secrets that ye cannot fathom.

6. With reverence I will consecrate your offering;
With zeal I call you, Varuna and Mitra.
These novel thoughts to praise you are intended:
May these prayers that I have offered please you.

7. For you, O gods, this service has been rendered
At sacrifices, Varuna and Mitra.
Across all dangers do ye safely take us.
Ye gods protect us evermore with blessings.

* Varuna is pre-eminent among the Vedic gods as a moral ruler. His eyes are the sun. He is angered by sin, which he severely punishes, but he forgives the penitent. Hymns addressed to him often contain prayers for forgiveness. Varuna controls order in the universe. Mitra is almost always associated with him, and emerges as a vaguely benevolent god, one also associated with the sun.

*Sūrya**

I, 115

1. The gods' refulgent countenance has risen,
The eye of Mitra, Varuna and Agni.
He has pervaded air, and earth, and heaven:
The soul of all that moves and stands is Sūrya.

2. The Sun pursues the Dawn, the gleaming goddess,
As a young man a maiden, to the region
Where god-devoted men lay on the harness
Of brilliant offerings for the brilliant godhead.

3. The brilliant steeds, bay coursers of the sun-god,
Refulgent, dappled, meet for joyful praises,
Wafting our worship, heaven's ridge have mounted,
And in one day round earth and sky they travel.

4. This is the Sun's divinity, his greatness:
In midst of action he withdraws the daylight.
When from their stand he has withdrawn his coursers,
Then straightway night for him spreads out her garment.

5. This form the Sun takes in the lap of heaven,
That Varuna and Mitra may regard him.
One glow of his appears unending, splendid;
His bay steeds roll the other up, the black one.

6. To-day, O gods, do ye at Sūrya's rising
Release us from distress and from dishonour:
This boon may Varuna and Mitra grant us,
And Aditi and Sindhu, Earth and Heaven.

*Night**

X, 127

1. When night comes on, the goddess shines
In many places with her eyes:
All glorious she has decked herself.

* Sūrya is specifically the sun-god, and the solar disc is often called the Eye of Sūrya. He is produced by the dawn, and like Apollo goes through the heavens drawn by horses, or otherwise as a bird, a gem, or a wheel. He measures the days and he stirs men into activity.

2. *Agni:* the god of fire. See note on p. 147.

23. *Aditi and Sindhu:* Aditi is a benevolent mother-goddess; Sindhu personifies a river or stream, but often the Great River, the Indus.

* Rātrī, the goddess of night, is curiously enough a bright goddess whose countless eyes, the stars, drive away darkness. She also safeguards travelers, and sends men, birds, and beasts off to their rest. This is the only *Rigveda* hymn to this goddess.

2. Immortal goddess far and wide,
She fills the valleys and the heights:
Darkness she drives away with light.

3. The goddess now, as she comes on,
Is turning out her sister, Dawn:
Far off the darkness hastes away.

4. So, goddess, come to-day to us:
At thy approach we seek our homes,
As birds their nests upon the tree.

5. The villagers have gone to rest
And footed beasts and wingèd birds;
The hungry hawk himself is still.

6. Ward off from us she-wolf and wolf,
Ward off the robber, goddess Night:
So take us safe across the gloom.

7. The darkness, thickly painting black,
Has, palpable, come nigh to me:
Like debts, O Dawn, clear it away.

8. I have brought up a hymn, like kine,
For thee, as one who wins a fight:
This, Heaven's daughter, Night, accept.

*Indra**

I, 32

1. I will proclaim the manly deeds of Indra,
The first that he performed, the lightning-wielder.
He slew the serpent, then discharged the waters,
And cleft the caverns of the lofty mountains.

2. He slew the serpent lying on the mountain:
For him the whizzing bolt has Tvastar fashioned.
Like lowing cows, with rapid current flowing,
The waters to the ocean down have glided.

3. Impetuous like a bull he chose the Soma,
And drank in threefold vessels of its juices.
The bounteous god grasped lightning for his missile;
He struck down dead that first-born of the serpents.

* Indra is the favorite national god of the Vedic people, and far more anthopomorphic than many other gods, almost resembling a mythological human hero. He is primarily a thunder-god (like Zeus) and is armed with, besides thunderbolts, a bow and arrow and a hook. He is vast in size, and, inspired by the intoxicating *soma* (see Introduction) he slays the demon Vrtra and releases the waters and the sun for mankind.

3. *Serpent:* Vrtra.

4. When thou hadst slain the first-born of the serpents,
And thwarted all the wiles of crafty schemers,
Anon disclosing sun, and dawn, and heaven,
Thou truly foundest not a foe, O Indra.

5. Indra slew Vrtra and one worse than Vrtra,
Vyamsa, with lightning, his resistless weapon;
Like trunks of trees, with axes hewn in pieces,
The serpent clinging to the earth lay prostrate.

6. He like a drunken coward challenged Indra,
The headlong, many-crushing, mighty hero.
He parried not the onset of the weapons:
The foe of Indra, falling, crushed the channels.

7. Footless and handless he with Indra battled,
Who smote him then upon his back with lightning.
But, impotent, he strove to match the hero:
He lay with scattered limbs in many places.

8. As thus he lay, like broken reed, the waters,
Now courage taking, surge across his body.
He lies beneath the very feet of rivers
Which Vrtra with his might had close encompassed.

9. The strength began to fail of Vrtra's mother,
For Indra had cast down his bolt upon her.
Above the mother was, the son was under;
And like a cow beside her calf lies Dānu.

10. The waters deep have hidden Vrtra's body,
Plunged in the midst of never-ceasing torrents
That stand not still, but ever hasten onward:
Indra's fierce foe sank down to lasting darkness.

11. Enclosed by demons, guarded by a serpent,
The waters stood like cows by Pani captured.
The waters' orifice that was obstructed,
When Vrtra he had smitten, Indra opened.

12. A horse's tail thou didst become, O Indra,
When, on his spear impaled, as god unaided,
The cows, O hero, thou didst win and Soma,
And free the seven streams to flow in torrents.

13. Him lightning then availed not nor thunder,
Nor mist, nor hailstorm which around he scattered:
When Indra and the serpent fought in battle,
The bounteous god gained victory for ever.

18. *Vyamsa:* a demon, the personification of drought.

42. *Pani:* The Panis are supernatural enemies of the gods.

14. Whom saw'st thou as avenger of the serpent,
As terror seized thy heart when thou hadst slain him,
And thou didst cross the nine and ninety rivers
And air's broad spaces, like a hawk affrighted?

15. Indra is king of all that's fixed and moving,
Of tame and horned beasts, the thunder-wielder.
He truly rules, as king of busy mortals;
Them he encompasses as spokes the felly.

Indra

II, 12

1. He who just born as chief god full of spirit
Went far beyond the other gods in wisdom:
Before whose majesty and mighty manhood
The two worlds trembled: he, O men, is Indra.

2. Who made the widespread earth when quaking steadfast,
Who set at rest the agitated mountains,
Who measured out air's middle space more widely,
Who gave the sky support: he, men, is Indra.

3. Who slew the serpent, freed the seven rivers,
Who drove the cattle out from Vala's cavern,
Who fire between two rocks has generated,
A conqueror in fights: he, men, is Indra.

4. He who has made all earthly things unstable,
Who humbled and dispersed the Dāsa colour,
Who, as the player's stake the winning gambler,
The foeman's fortune gains: he, men, is Indra.

5. Of whom, the terrible, they ask, "Where is he?"
Of him, indeed, they also say, "He is not."
The foemen's wealth, like players' stakes, he lessens.
Believe in him: for he, O men, is Indra.

6. He furthers worshippers, both rich and needy,
And priests that supplicate his aid and praise him.
Who, fair-lipped, helps the man that presses Soma,
That sets the stones at work: he, men, is Indra.

10. *Vala:* another demon (also called "Bali") killed by Indra's lightning-bolt, thus freeing cattle for mankind's use. In Roman myth, Hercules battles Cacus, a fire-breathing demon and the son of Vulcan, for the cattle of Geryon.

14. *Dāsa colour:* Dāsas are black-skinned, noseless demons who refuse to worship the Aryan gods. They may reflect an Indian attitude towards aboriginal tribes on the Indian frontier in early times.

7. In whose control are horses and all chariots,
In whose control are villages and cattle;
He who has generated sun and morning,
Who leads the waters: he, O men, is Indra.

8. Whom two contending armies vie in calling,
On both sides foes, the farther and the nearer;
Two fighters mounted on the self-same chariot
Invoke him variously: he, men, is Indra.

9. Without whose aid men conquer not in battle,
Whom fighting ever they invoke for succour,
Who shows himself a match for every foeman,
Who moves what is unmovéd: he, men, is Indra.

10. Who with his arrow slays the unexpecting
Unnumbered crew of gravely guilty sinners;
Who yields not to the boasting foe in boldness,
Who slays the demons: he, O men, is Indra.

11. He who detected in the fortieth autumn
Sambara dwelling far among the mountains;
Who slew the serpent that puts forth his vigour,
The demon as he lay: he, men, is Indra.

12. Who with his seven rays, the bull, the mighty,
Let loose the seven streams to flow in torrents;
Who, bolt in arm, spurned Rauhina, the demon,
On scaling heaven bent: he, men, is Indra.

13. Both Heaven and Earth, themselves, bow down before
him:
Before his might the very mountains tremble,
Who, famed as Soma-drinker, armed with lightning,
Is wielder of the bolt: he, men, is Indra.

14. Who with his aid helps him that presses Soma,
That bakes and lauds and ever sacrifices;
Whom swelling prayer, whom Soma pressings strengthen,
And now this offering: he, O men, is Indra.

15. Who, fierce, on him that bakes and him that presses
Bestowest booty: thou, indeed, art trusted.
May we, for ever dear to thee, O Indra,
Endowed with hero sons address the synod.

47. *Rauhina:* another demon-foe of Indra. His origin and function are obscure.

*Parjanya**

v, 83

1. Invoke the mighty god with songs of welcome;
Parjanya praise: with homage seek to win him.
He, roaring like a bull, with streams that quicken,
A seed to germinate in plants deposits.

2. The trees he shatters and he smites the demon host:
The whole world trembles at his mighty weapon's stroke,
The guiltless man himself flees from the potent god,
When miscreants Parjanya with his thunder strikes.

3. Like charioteer his horses lashing with a whip,
The god makes manifest his messengers of rain.
From far away the roaring of the lion sounds,
What time Parjanya veils the firmament with rain.

4. The winds blow forth; to earth the quivering lightnings fall,
The plants shoot up; with moisture streams the realm of light.
For all the world abundant nourishment is born,
When by Parjanya Earth is fertilized with seed.

5. O thou at whose behest the earth bows downward,
O thou at whose behest hoofed creatures quiver,
At whose behest by plants all shapes are taken:
As such, Parjanya, grant to us strong shelter.

6. The rain of heaven bestow, O Maruts, on us,
Of your strong steed pour forth the streams abundant.
With this thy thundering roar do thou come hither,
And shed the waters as our heavenly father.

7. With roar and thunder now the germ deposit,
Fly round us with thy water-bearing chariot.
Turn well thy water-skin unloosened downward,
Make, with the waters, heights and hollows level.

8. Draw the great bucket up and pour it downward,
And let the liberated streams flow forward.
On all sides drench both heaven and earth with fatness;
Let there be for the cows fair pools for drinking.

* Parjanya is a subordinate deity, a rain-god, often alluded to as an udder, a pail, or a water-skin. He is of course associated with lightning and storms, and is a nourisher of the earth. In India, the rainy and the dry season are sharply contrasted, and the monsoon rain often arrives suddenly and is torrential.

21. *Maruts:* the seven winds, each having a different effect on mortals.

9. When, O Parjanya, roaring loud,
Thou slay'st with thunder wicked men,
This universe rejoices then,
And everything that is on earth.

10. Thou hast shed rain; pray now withhold it wholly;
Thou hast made passable all desert places.
To serve as food thou hast made plants to flourish:
And hast received the gratitude of creatures.

*Vāta**

x, 168

1. Of Vāta's car I now will praise the greatness:
Rending it speeds along; its noise is thunder.
Touching the sky it flies, creating lightnings;
Scattering dust it traverses earth's ridges.

2. The hosts of Vāta onward speed together:
They haste to him as women to a concourse.
The god with them upon the same car mounted,
The king of all this universe speeds onward.

3. In air, along his pathways speeding onward,
Never on any day he tarries resting.
The first-born order-loving friend of waters:
Where was he born, and whence has he arisen?

4. Of gods the breath, and of the world the offspring,
This god according to his liking wanders.
His sound is heard, his form is never looked on:
That Vāta let us worship with oblation.

*Waters**

VII, 49

1. With ocean for their chief they flow unresting;
From the aërial flood they hasten cleansing;
For whom the mighty Indra's bolt cut out channels,
Here may those waters, goddesses, preserve me.

* A wind-god, personified as the breath of the gods.

* The gods of waters are thought of as mothers, bringing life to the earth and also cleansing away defilement, including moral guilt. They are also associated with milk, honey, and *soma*. They are presumably pre-Vedic and among the earliest gods.

2. Waters that come from heaven or run in channels
Dug out, or flow spontaneously by nature,
That, clear and pure, have as their goal the ocean:
Here may those waters, goddesses, preserve me.

3. In midst of whom king Varuna is moving,
And looking down surveys men's truth and falsehood:
Who, clear and purifying, drip with sweetness:
Here may those waters, goddesses, preserve me.

4. In whom king Varuna, in whom, too, Soma,
In whom the All-gods drink exalted vigour;
Into whom Agni, friend of all, has entered:
Here may those waters, goddesses, preserve me.

*Earth**

V, 84

1. Thou bearest truly, Pṛthivī,
The burden of the mountains' weight;
With might, O thou of many streams,
Thou quickenest, potent one, the soil.

2. With flowers of speech our songs of praise
Resound to thee, far-spreading one,
Who sendest forth the swelling cloud,
O bright one, like propelling speed;

3. Who, steadfast, holdest with thy might,
The forest-trees upon the ground,
When, from the lightning of thy cloud,
The rain-floods of the sky pour down.

*Heaven and Earth**

I, 185

1. Which of the two is earlier, which the later?
How were they born, ye sages, who discerns it?
They by themselves support all things existing.
As with a wheel the day and night roll onward.

15. *Agni:* See note to the hymn entitled "Agni."

* The goddess Earth is mostly a personification of the physical earth—"Kindly Mother Earth." This is the only *Rigveda* hymn addressed solely to her, but see the *Atharaveda*, xii.1.

* Heaven and Earth are often paired in the *Rigveda* and Heaven is not addressed alone in any hymn. A prolific bull and a cow, they grant food and wealth, fame and dominion. However, they are not anthropomorphized to the extent of the other gods and are not important in worship.

2. The two support, though moving not and footless,
Abundant offspring having feet and moving.
O Heaven and Earth, from dreadful darkness save us,
Like your own son held in his parents' bosom.

3. I crave of Aditi the gift, the matchless,
Beneficent, illustrious, and honoured:
O ye two worlds, procure that for the singer.
O Heaven and Earth, from dreadful darkness save us.

4. May we be near to both the worlds who suffer
No care, parents of gods, who aid with favour.
Both are divine, with days and nights alternate.
O Heaven and Earth from dreadful darkness save us.

5. Maidens uniting, with adjoining limits,
Twin sisters, resting in their parents' bosom,
They kiss, combined, the universe's centre.
O Heaven and Earth, from dreadful darkness save us.

6. Devoutly I the two seats wide and lofty,
The parents of the gods, invoke with fervour,
Who, fair of aspect, grant us life immortal.
O Heaven and Earth, from dreadful darkness save us.

7. Them wide and broad and great, whose bounds are distant,
Who, beautiful and fain to help, grant blessings:
I at this sacrifice invoke with homage.
O Heaven and Earth, from dreadful darkness save us.

8. If ever we have any sin committed
Against the gods, or friend, or house's chieftain,
Of that may this our hymn be expiation.
O Heaven and Earth, from dreadful darkness save us.

9. May both, as objects of men's praises, bless me;
May both attend me with their help and favour.
Give much to men more liberal than the godless.
We would be strong, ye gods, enjoying nurture.

10. This truth have I now uttered first with wisdom
To Heaven and Earth that every one may hear it.
Protect me from disgrace and peril; guard me
As Father and as Mother with your succour.

9. *Aditi:* See note to line 23 of "Surya."

11. May this my prayer come true, O Earth and Heaven,
With which I here address you, Father, Mother.
Be nearest of the gods to us with favours:
May we find food and home with flowing water.

*Agni**

vi, 6

1. The man who seeks success and aid approaches
The son of strength, with feast and newest worship.
He rends the wood and has a blackened pathway,
The brightly radiant and divine invoker.

2. The shining thunderer who dwells in lustre,
With his unaging, roaring flames, most youthful,
Refulgent Agni, frequently recurring,
Goes after many spacious woods and chews them.

3. Thy flames when driven by the wind, O Agni,
Disperse, O pure one, pure in all directions;
And thy divine Navagvas, most destructive,
Lay low the woods and devastate them boldly.

4. Thy steeds, the bright, the pure, O radiant Agni,
Let loose speed on and shave the ground beneath them.
Thy whirling flame then widely shines refulgent,
The highest ridges of earth's surface reaching.

5. When the bull's tongue darts forward like the missile
Discharged by him who fights the cows to capture,
Like hero's onset is the flame of Agni:
Resistless, dreadful, he consumes the forests.

6. Thou with the sunbeams of the great impeller,
Hast boldly overspread the earthly spaces.
So with thy mighty powers drive off all terrors;
Attack our rivals and burn down our foemen.

7. Give us, O splendid one of splendid lordship,
Wealth giving splendour, splendid, life-imparting.
Bestow bright wealth and vast with many heroes,
Bright god, with thy bright flames, upon the singer.

* Judged by the number of hymns devoted to him, Agni is second only to Indra in importance in the *Rigveda.* He is a god of fire, and is mostly concerned with the sacrificial aspects of fire. He consumes (eats) the burning sacrifices offered to the gods. His brightness is much dwelt on: he dispels the darkness. But he is also destructive and shaves the forest as a barber does a beard. Indra is called his twin brother. Agni is closely associated with human life because of the hearth —he is a guest in human dwellings and "Lord of the House."

11. *Navagvas:* priests connected with the cult of the cow.

*Soma**

VIII, 48

1. I have partaken wisely of the sweet food
That stirs good thoughts, best banisher of trouble,
The food round which all deities and mortals,
Calling it honey-mead, collect together.

2. Thou shalt be Aditi when thou hast entered
Within, appeaser of celestial anger.
May'st thou, O drop, enjoying Indra's friendship,
Like willing mare the car, to wealth advance us.

3. We have drunk Soma and become immortal;
We have attained the light the gods discovered.
What can hostility now do against us
And what, immortal god, the spite of mortals?

4. Be cheering to our heart when drunk, O Indu,
Kindly, like father to his son, O Soma.
Like friend for friend, far-famed one, wisely
Prolong our years that we may live, O Soma.

5. These glorious, freedom-giving drops, when drunk by me,
Have knit my joints together as do thongs a car.
May these protect me now from fracturing a limb.
And may they ever keep me from disease remote.

6. Like fire produced by friction, make me brilliant;
Do thou illumine us and make us richer;
For then I seem in thy carouse, O Soma,
Enriched. Now enter us for real welfare.

7. Of this thy juice pressed out with mind devoted,
We would partake as of paternal riches.
Prolong the years of life for us, King Soma,
As Sūrya lengthens out the days of spring-time.

8. King Soma, gracious be to us for welfare;
We are thy devotees; of that be mindful.
O Indu, might and anger rise against us:
Hand us not over to our foeman's mercies.

9. Thou, as the guardian of our body, Soma,
Surveying men, in every limb hast settled.
If we perchance infringed, O god, thy statutes,
As our good friend for greater wealth be gracious.

* See the headnote to the *Rigveda*.
13. *Indu:* Indra.
28. *Sūrya:* See note to the hymn entitled "Sūrya."

10. I would accompany the friend, the wholesome,
Who, Lord of Bays, imbibed, would never hurt me.
I come to Indra to prolong our life-time,
That we may relish Soma placed within us.

11. Away have fled those ailments and diseases;
The powers of darkness have been all affrighted.
With mighty strength in us has Soma mounted:
We have arrived where men prolong existence.

12. The drop drunk deeply in our hearts, O Fathers,
Us mortals that immortal god has entered.
That Soma we would worship with oblation;
We would be in his mercy and good graces.

13. Uniting with the Fathers thou, O Soma,
Hast over Heaven and Earth thyself extended.
So, Indu, we would serve thee with oblation:
Thus we would be the lords of ample riches.

14. Do ye, protecting gods, speak in our favour,
Let neither sleep nor idle talk subdue us;
May we, for evermore, beloved of Soma,
Endowed with hero sons, address the synod.

15. Thou, Soma, givest strength to us on all sides.
Light-finder, watching men, within us enter.
Do thou, O Indu, with thine aids accordant,
Behind for ever and before protect us.

*Aranyānī**

x, 146

1. O forest nymph, O forest nymph,
Thou seemest to have lost thy way:
Why dost not for the village ask?
Has fear, perchance, now entered thee?

2. When to the owl's loud-sounding hoot
The parrot makes an answering cry,
And hops, as to the cymbal's clash,
Then Aranyānī heaves with joy.

3. Sounds as of cows that graze are heard,
A dwelling house appears to loom,
And Aranyānī, forest nymph,
Creaks like a cart at eventide.

38. *Lord of Bays:* Soma is the Lord of Plants but also the Lord of Speech since he stimulates speech.

* Aranyānī is a minor goddess. The poet is here trying to depict the strange sounds of the forest at night.

4. Here some one calls his cow to him,
Another there is felling wood:
Who in the forest bides at eve
Thinks to himself, "I heard a cry."

5. Never does Aranyānī hurt,
Unless one goes too near to her;
When she has eaten of sweet fruit,
At her own will she goes to rest.

6. Sweet-scented, redolent of balm,
Replete with food, though tilling not,
Mother of beasts, the forest nymph,
Her I have magnified with praise.

The Gambler

x, 34

1. On high trees born and in a windy region
The danglers, rolling on the diceboard, cheer me.
Like Soma draught from Mūjavant's great mountain,
The rousing nut Vibhīdaka has pleased me.

2. She wrangles not with me nor is she angry:
To me and comrades she was ever kindly.
For dice that only luckless throws effected
I've driven away from home a wife devoted.

3. Her mother hates me, she herself rejects me:
For one in such distress there is no pity.
I find a gambling man is no more useful
Than is an aged horse that's in the market.

4. Others embrace the wife of him whose chattels
The eager dice have striven hard to capture;
And father, mother, brothers say about him:
"We know him not; lead him away a captive."

5. When to myself I think, "I'll not go with them,
I'll stay behind my friends that go to gamble,"
And those brown nuts, thrown down, have raised their voices,
I go, like wench, straight to the place of meeting.

4. *Vibhīdaka:* Dice were made from the nuts of a large tree called the *vibhīdaka,* still used in modern times for this purpose. Mūjavant or Mūnjavant is a mountain in northern India, where the *soma* plant grows. This is one of the few hymns with a purely didactic purpose.

6. To the assembly hall the gambler sallies,
And asking, "Shall I win?" he quakes and trembles.
And then the dice run counter to his wishes,
Giving the lucky throw to his opponent.

7. The dice attract the gambler, but deceive and wound,
Both paining men at play and causing them to pain.
Like boys they offer first and then take back their gifts:
With honey sweet to gamblers by their magic charm.

8. Their throng in triple fifties plays untrammelled,
Like Savitar the god whose laws are constant.
They yield not to the wrath of even the mighty:
A king himself on them bestows obeisance.

9. Downward they roll, then swiftly springing upward,
They overcome the man with hands, though handless.
Cast on the board like magic bits of charcoal,
Though cold themselves, they burn the heart to ashes.

10. Grieved is the gambler's wife by him abandoned,
Grieved, too, his mother as he aimless wanders.
Indebted, fearing, he desiring money
At night approaches other people's houses.

11. It pains the gambler when he sees a woman
Another's wife, and their well-ordered household.
He yokes those brown seeds early in the morning,
And when the fire is low sinks down a beggar.

12. To him who's general of your mighty forces,
As king becomes the chief of your battalions,
I hold my fingers ten extended forward:
"No money I withhold, this truth I tell thee."

13. Play not with dice, but cultivate thy tillage,
Enjoy thy riches, deeming them abundant.
There are thy cows, there is thy wife, O Gambler:
This counsel Savitar the noble gives me.

14. Make friends with us, we pray, to us be gracious;
Do not bewitch us forcibly with magic;
Let now your enmity, your anger slumber:
Let others be in brownies' toils entangled.

30. *Savitar:* another name for Sūrya (see note to the hymn of that title) but his role in the gambler's life is not clear.

Frogs

VII, 103

1. Resting in silence for a year,
Like Brahmins practising a vow,
The frogs have lifted up their voices,
Excited by Parjanya's call.
2. When heavenly waters have poured down upon them
Resting in pools, like dried up leather buckets,
The croakings of the frogs resound together,
Like noise of cows with calves in concert lowing.

3. When showers have streamed around them, eager, thirsty,
Upon the advent of the rainy season,
With joyful croak the one draws near the other
Who greets him, as a son comes near his father.

4. The one of them the other hails with welcome,
When in the flow of waters they have revelled;
When rained upon the frogs become exultant;
He that is Spotty joins his voice to Tawny's.

5. When one repeats the utterance of the other,
As those who learn the lessons of their teacher,
All this is like concordant recitation,
As eloquent ye prate upon the waters.

6. One lows like cows, one like a goat is bleating;
This one is Spotty, one of them is Tawny.
Bearing a common name they're many-coloured,
They variously adorn their voice in speaking.

7. As Brahmins at the mighty Soma offering
Sit round the large and brimming vessel talking;
So throng ye all around the pool to hallow
This annual day that, frogs, begins the rain-time.

8. These Soma-pressing Brahmins raise their voices
And offer their recurrent year's devotion;
And these Adhvaryu priests with kettles sweating
Come forth to view, and none of them are hidden.

4. *Parjanya:* See note on p. 143, above.

26. *Vessel:* The frogs are likened to heated sacrificial vessels. They raise their voices together as the rains come.

31. *Adhvaryu priests:* five priests, and perhaps the five planets which move around the sky as do priests in performing a sacrifice. They are mentioned in the *Rigveda*, iii.7,7.

9. The twelve months' god-sent order they have guarded,
And never do these men infringe the season.
When in the year the rainy time commences,
Those who were heated milk-pots gain deliverance.

10. Both Lowing Cow and Bleating Goat have given,
Spotty and Tawny, too, have given us riches.
The frogs give kine by hundreds; they for pressings
Of Soma thousandfold, prolong existence.

The Song of God (*Bhagavad Gītā*)

The *Bhagavad Gītā* is an episode from the vast medieval Indian epic known as the *Great War of the Bhāratas* (*Mahābhārata*). The *Mahābhārata* and its shorter sister epic the *Lay of Rāma* (*Rāmāyana*) are more encyclopedias of Indian religious legend than epics in the manner of Homer and Virgil. They constitute an ocean of story and didactic material which has flowed through all levels of Indian life. Though sacred, they have been constantly remade in vernacular versions from the Punjab to Indonesia. Many of the incidents (such as the story of Nala and Damayantī) are long enough to be epics in themselves and have led independent existences. They have provided the Indian with everything from material for folk plays to sophisticated fiction (in modern times) and exempla for religious and philosophical "sermons." A comparison with the Western epic is only valid if we imagine the *Iliad* and the *Odyssey* as episodes in a much larger epic which contained the whole corpus of Greek legend and maintained its sacred character into the twentieth century.

The *Mahābhārata* runs to some 100,000 couplets. It is traditionally ascribed to the sage Vyāsa, but its present recension is in early classical Sanskrit of the period 300–500 A.D. The locale of the war of the Bhāratas is the plain of Kūru, not far from modern Delhi in north central India. The cause of the war is a quarrel with origins almost as trivial as those which cause the break between Achilles and Menelaus at the beginning of the *Iliad:* there is a princess involved, a gambling match, insults, and finally, epic strife in the domain of King Hastināpura. The Kauravas are the king's hundred sons and the Pāndavas their five cousins. The eighteen-day battle on the plain of Kūru which ends with the rout of the Kauravas is the focal point, in terms of action, of the *Mahābhārata.* The Western reader, with his strongly secular tradition of the epic from early classical times, will be surprised to find that the *Bhagavad Gītā*—the work which is regarded by the Hindus in somewhat the same way as the Gospels are by Christians—is inserted at the high point of suspense and intensity in the *Mahābhārata*. The dialogue which opens the *Gītā* takes place as the two armies are drawn up for battle. It is as if Christ preached the Sermon on the Mount from a war chariot. The Hindu would not find a contradiction in this.

The religious and philosophical background of the *Gītā* embraces the entire history of Hinduism and can only be touched on here. Briefly, the development of Hinduism can be described as a Brahmanical or "orthodox" tradition, deriving its authority from the earliest sacred scriptures, the four Vedas, and somewhat later elaborations of the scriptures, the Upanishads, and the addition to this tradition of less orthodox elements, sometimes in the form of "Hinduizing" local religious movements, a process with analogies in Christianity. Sometimes deities or demigods in the Hindu pantheon were elevated in certain areas or among certain cultural groups in India to a position where in the popular imagination they tended to eclipse the high gods. However, a common reverence for the authority of the Vedas united the most unorthodox splinter groups with the mainstream of Hinduism. Also, the Hindu mind is synthetic, prone to stress areas of agreement in matters of faith rather than differences.

Somewhere in western and central India the cult of the god Krishna originated. The doctrines of the cult merged with versions of the bardic lays of the war of the Bhāratas, and the result became incorporated into the *Mahābhārata*. The religion of Krishna had a different emphasis from that of the Vedic-Upanishadic tradition. It focused on man in society. Vedic-Upanishadic doctrine was that essentially man is concerned with his individual salvation. The phenomenal world not being real, the goal of the individual was to have as little to do with worldly things as possible in order to free the soul for unity with the Universal Soul. (This doctrine is, of course, shared by the Buddhists and has affinities with some interpretations of Christianity.) The sage, the recluse, and the ascetic obviously have the best chance of reducing the burden of the flesh to a minimum, and the Brahman—the priest or monk—has no other function in society but this attempt at union with the Universal Soul through renunciation. The Brahman's sacrifices and rituals benefit society as a whole, but they benefit him most of all. The *Gītā* accepts unequivocally the unreal character of the world, but sees that society as a whole cannot accept the Brahman's abnegation of action, and it proposes a combination of action and renunciation for the various casts. Every man must perform certain actions; these have an effect (*karma*) upon him, whether in this life or in a reincarnation. But he cannot escape his *sve-dharma*, the set of duties of his social level. He desires ultimate release and liberation (*moksha*), but he must—unless he is a seer or sage—do his work (*yoga* is the term for work or self-discipline). The *Gītā* is concerned not with ceremony, ritual, or devotion, but with *karma-yoga*, the actions that one must perform in one's daily tasks.

The solution in the *Gītā* to the dilemma of *karma-yoga* versus *moksha* is twofold: one must perform one's tasks in life with fidelity, and one must not be concerned with the goals and rewards of a well-performed task. One fights in a battle with the utmost courage and skill, but one is not really concerned with the outcome and certainly not with the reward of glory or the alternative of pain and death. The village baker carries out the task of his guild faithfully but without lust for gain. He does not wish to be a soldier, or a soldier a Brahman. This kind of doctrine is obviously conducive to a solid and stable social structure: like the class system of the European Middle Ages, it could make a man satisfied with his lot and proud of his fidelity to his walk of life. But the devotee of Krishna cannot really be satisfied or vain, for he knows that all worldly life is unreal: he must renounce in advance the goal he seems to be seeking. This doctrine of work has consoled such people as Gandhi in the dark hours of their lives. It provides purpose for the necessary activities of both the king and his nobles and also for the thief and the prostitute. The member of the outlawed caste who faithfully performs his necessary but unclean duties presumably accumulates more "good time" than the warrior who wishes to be king and is unhappy with his lot. Thus, the reason for the popularity of the doctrine expressed in the *Gītā* is its "democracy" of appeal. It has a message for all castes and justifies their existence in the social structure. Moreover, since it is a poem rather than a carefully organized system of philosophy, it has the power to animate and console. Hindus dip into it the way Christians do the Bible; it provides spiritual strength and solace in a more available form than the older scriptures.

The beginning of the *Gītā*, which is printed here, is an exciting moment in the history of the Bhārata wars, a moment familiar in Western epic and saga. The two contending sides are drawn up for battle. In the stillness before they lock in combat, Prince Arjuna of the Pāndavas (who later becomes king) surveys the lines and is overcome—is unmanned—by the futility of war. In this atmosphere of hideous tension, his charioteer convinces him of the necessity of doing his duty, his *dharma*. The charioteer is the god Krishna in mortal guise.

From The Song of God*

Reading the First

Dhritarāstra said:

1. On the Field of Right, the Kuru-Field,[1] assembled, eager to fight, what did my warriors and the warriors of Pāndu, O Samjaya?

Samjaya said:

2. When be beheld the host of Pāndu's warriors in array, then did king Duryodhana approach his master[2] and speak a word:

3. See, O master, this great host of Pāndu's sons, set in array by thy wise pupil, the son of Drupada!

4. Here are men of prowess, bearing great bows, peers in the fight with Bhīma and with Arjuna[3]—Yuyudhāna and Virāta and Drupada, lord of the mighty car,

5. Dhristaketu, Cekitāna, and the strong king of the Kāśis, Purujit, Kuntibhoja, and the mighty Sibian chief,

6. Yudhāmanyu the lusty, and strong Uttamaujas, Subhadrā's son and the sons of Draupadī, all, yea all, lords of the mighty car.

7. Now of our host the chiefest learn, O noblest of the Twiceborn[4], the captains of my army; that thou mayest know them I declare them to thee.

8. Thyself, and Bhīsma[5] and Karna and Kripa, victor in battle, Aśvatthāman and Vikarna and the son of Somadatta too,

9. And many another hero for my sake surrendering life; various the weapons and the arms they bear, and all are versed in war.

10. Guarded by Bhīsma, this our force is all too weak; and all too strong that force of theirs, by Bhīma guarded.

11. So stand in all the ranks according to your companies, and guard only Bhīsma, every one of you!

12. To give him cheer the aged Kuru lord[6], the glorious sire, blew his shell, raising on high a roar as of a lion.

---

* From *The Bhagavadgītā*, translated by W. D. P. Hill. Reprinted by permission of Oxford University Press, Indian Branch. The notes are mostly abridged from Hill.

1. The Kuru Field (Kuruksetra) is a plain not far from Delhi, the ancient Hastināpura, and an area of particular sanctity.

2. Drona, who has taught the art of war to the princes of both sides, identifies the warriors for the blind king. Sanjaya narrates the episode.

3. Bhīma and Arjuna are the two great heroes of the Pandavas, and Subhadra's son is Arjuna's child. Bhīma is a man of great strength and fights with a club.

4. A high Brahman, who has been invested with the sacred thread, symbolizing his rebirth in sanctity.

5. Bhīsma will lead the Kauravas troops. Karna, Arjuna's half-brother, will kill him in the battle.

6. Bhīsma.

13. Thereupon shells and kettledrums, cymbals and drums and trumpets, suddenly were sounded; tumultuous was that din.

14. Then standing in their mighty car yoked with white horses, did Mādhava and the son of Pāndu[7] blow their shells divine.

15. Hrisikeśa blew Pāñcajanya, Dhanamjaya blew Devadatta, insatiable Bhīma, whose deeds are dread, blew the great shell Paundra.

16. Yudhisthira the king, the son of Kuntī, blew Anantavijaya; Nakula and Sahadeva blew Sughosa and Manipuspaka.

17. And Kāśī's king, bowman supreme, and Sikhandin of the mighty car, Dhristadyumna and Virāta and Sātyaki unsubdued,

18. Drupada and the sons of Draupadī, O lord of earth, and the strong-armed son of Subhadrā—on every side blew each his several shell.[8]

19. That uproar rent the hearts of Dhritarāstra's men; it made both sky and earth tumultuously resound.

20. Then Pāndu's son, who bare the banner of the ape,[9] beholding in array the host of Dhritarāstra, when now the arrows had begun to fly, took up his bow,

21. And straightway spake, O lord of earth, this word to Hrisīkeśa:

Arjuna said:

Between the armies set my car, O thou that fallest not,[10]

22. While I behold them as they stand lusting for the fight, while I behold with whom must be my conflict in this hard toil of war,

23. And gaze on those assembled here to strive, eager in battle to fulfil the pleasure of Dhritarāstra's perverse son.[11]

Samjaya said:

24. Thus addressed by Gūdakeśa,[12] Hrisīkeśa set the best of cars between the armies, Bhārata,

25. Before the face of Bhīsma and Drona and all the rulers of the earth, and said, 'O son of Prithā, behold these Kurus assembled!'

7. Mādhaya is one of the many names of Krisna, the divine charioteer of Arjuna; Arjuna is the son of Pāndu.

8. Articles of military equipment are given formal names in many cultures. Western ships are named individually; airplanes have class names ("Spitfire," "Marauder," etc.). Japanese swords have names. King Arthur's sword was named Excaliber. Hrisīkeśa here is Krisna and his conch horn is made of the bone of the demon Pāñcajanya. Devadatta means "gift of the *deva* (god)." Anantavijaya means "Everlasting Victory." Sughosa and Manipuspaka mean "Sweet-toned" and "Gem-flowered," respectively.

9. The monkey and the ape are thought to have great strength and intelligence and often assist the hero in battle. Pāndu's son is Arjuna.

10. Kriśna (Hrisīkeśa), Arjuna's charioteer, is immortal.

11. Duryodhana, who was mainly responsible for the war.

12. Another name for Arjuna, as are Prithā and Kuntī, below. Bhārata is Dhritarāstra.

26. There as they stood the son of Prithā saw fathers and grandfathers, masters, uncles, brothers, sons, and grandsons, ay, and comrades,

27. Fathers-in-law, and friends, in both armies.
When he saw all these kinsmen in array, the son of Kuntī
28. Was filled with deep compassion, and in despair he spoke this word[13]:

Arjuna said:
O Kriśna, when I see these kinsmen present here in act to fight,
29. My limbs grow faint, my mouth is parched, trembling lays hold upon my body, and my hair stands erect;

30. Gāndīva slips from my hand, and my skin is afire; I cannot stand; my brain seems to reel.

31. Adverse omens I behold, O Keśava, nor if I kill my kinsmen in the fight do I foresee aught good.

32. I desire not victory, O Kriśna, nor yet sovereignty, nor pleasures. What have we to do with sovereignty, Govinda?[14] What with delights or life?

33. Those for whose sake we do desire sovereignty, delights, and pleasures, stand here in readiness to fight, surrendering life and wealth—

34. Master, fathers and sons and grandsires too, uncles, fathers-in-law, grandsons, brothers-in-law, and other kin.

35. Them would I not slay, O Madhusūdana,[15] though they slay me; not even to win the sovereignty of the three worlds[16]—how much less for earth!

36. 'If we slew Dhritarāstra's men, what pleasure should we win, Janārdana? Guilt, guilt, would make its home with us, did we slay these criminals!

37. Therefore we must not slay Dhritarāstra's men, who are our kin; for if we slew our kinsmen, how, Mādhava, should we be happy?

38. Though these, whose wits are blind with greed, see not the sin that lies in the destruction of a family, nor crime in treachery,

39. Yet how should we not know avoidance of this guilt, we who see clearly the sin that lies in the destruction of a family, Janārdana?

40. With the destruction of a family perish the family's eternal laws; and when the law has perished, the whole family yields to lawlessness.

13. A civil war is always more of a tragedy than a war against foreign invaders, but Arjuna fears that the structure of society, the caste system, will break down if brother fights brother.

14. Gāndīva is Arjuna's great bow; Keśava and Govinda are yet other names for Kriśna.

15. Kriśna is the slayer of Madhu, a demon. He is also called Janārdana ("Troubler of Men," i.e., of foes) below.

16. Heaven, earth, and patala, the abode of demons.

41. When lawlessness prevails, O Krisna, the women of the family become corrupt; when women are corrupted, son of Vrisni, there appears caste-confusion.[17]

42. To hell does this confusion bring the family and those who slay it; for when the ritual offerings of rice and water fail, their Fathers fall degraded.[18]

43. By these sins of those who slay the family, these caste confounding sins, are brought to naught the everlasting laws of clan and family.

44. For men whose family laws have been brought to naught there is ordained an abode in hell, Janārdana; so have we heard.

45. Alas, a grievous sin have we determined to commit, in that for greed of sovereignty and pleasure we are prepared to slay our kin!

46. If Dhritarāstra's men, with weapons in their hands, should slay me in the fight, unresisting and unarmed, that were happier for me!

Samjaya said:

47. Thus spoke Arjuna on the field of battle, and sat down upon the chariot seat, dropping his arrows and his bow, his soul o'erwhelmed with grief.

Here Endeth the First Reading in
The Glorious Song of the Blessed Lord,
The Mystical Lesson,
The Wisdom of the Absolute,
The Scripture of Control,
The Converse of Lord Krisna and Arjuna;
And Its Name[19] Is
Arjuna's Despair.

Reading the Second

Samjaya said:

1. To him thus filled with compassion, his eyes distressed and full of tears, despairing, spoke Madhusūdana this word:

The Blessed Lord said:

2. Whence comes on thee in peril this despondency, unmeet for nobles, leading not to heaven, whose end is disrepute, O Arjuna?

3. Yield not to cowardice, O son of Prithā: it becomes thee not. Cast off poor impotence of heart, and rise, Paramtapa![1]

17. Presumably caused by inter-marriage, not simply by immortality.

18. Water and rice are offered to departed fathers. If these duties are neglected, the fathers in the spirit world would fall from blessedness to a lower state.

19. The names of the Readings vary in different manuscripts.

1. Paramtapa (Arjuna) means "Harasser of Foes"; Arisūdana (Krisna) means "Slayer of Enemies."

Arjuna said:

4. How shall I fight, O Madhusūdana, with arrows against Bhīsma and Drona in battle? Worthy of reverence are they, O Arisūdana.

5. For better were it, slaying not most reverend masters, even to eat the bread of beggary in this world: were I to slay my masters, greedy though they be for wealth, I should but here enjoy blood-sullied joys!

6. Nor know we which is better for us, whether that we should conquer them, or that they should conquer us; here stand in array before us Dhritarāstra's men, and if we slay them, we shall not wish to live.

7. My soul is vexed by the fault of weak compassion; my mind perplexed knows not where duty lies; I ask thee, then; tell me with no uncertain voice which would be better. I am thy disciple; teach me; I come to thee.

8. For I see not clearly aught that may dispel the grief that withers up my senses, though I should win on earth broad sovereignty unrivalled, and lordship even of Heaven's Lords.

Samjaya said:

9. Thus to Hrisīkeśa spoke Gudākeśa Paramtapa; 'I will not fight!' said he to Govinda, and fell silent.

10. This word, O Bhārata, spoke Hrisīkeśa, as one smiling, to him between the armies stricken with despair:

The Blessed Lord said:

11. For them hast thou grieved for whom no grief should be; yet speakest thou words of wisdom. The wise grieve not for dead nor yet for living.

12. Verily never was I not, never wast thou not, nor were these princes not; nor yet henceforth shall any one of us not be.[2]

13. As in this body the embodied soul knows childhood, youth, and eld, so too another body doth he win; herein the steadfast man is not perplexed.

14. The touchings of the world of sense, O son of Kunti, which bring cold and heat, pleasure and pain—these come and go, impermanent; endure them, Bhārata.[3]

15. For he whom these do not disturb and to whom pain and pleasure are alike, that steadfast man, O prince of men, is fit for deathlessness.

16. Of what is not there is no being, and no not-being of what is; and of these two is seen the boundary by seers of the truth.

17. Know verily that cannot be destroyed whereby all this is pervaded; of this immutable none can work destruction.

2. Here begins the expounding of the doctrine of the Self and the not-Self.

3. Here Bhārata (and below, verse 18) is a name for Arjuna.

18. They have an end, 'tis said, these bodies of the embodied soul; but permanent is he and indestructible, incomprehensible.[4] Fight therefore, Bhārata!

19. He who thinks of him as slayer, he who deems him slain—these both are void of judgement; he doth not slay, nor is he slain.[5]

20. Never is he born or dies; he came not into being, nor shall come hereafter; unborn, abiding, eternal, ancient, he is not slain when the body is slain.

21. If a man knows him to be indestructible, abiding, unborn, and immutable, how and whom does he cause to be slain, or slay, O son of Prithā?

22. As a man puts off worn-out raiment and takes other new, so does the embodied soul put off his worn-out bodies, and enter other new.

23. Him no weapons cleave, him no fire burns. him no waters wet, and no wind dries.

24. Not to be cleft is he, not to be burned is he, not to be wetted nor yet to be dried; abiding he and all-pervading, stable, unmoved, from everlasting;

25. Unmanifested is he called, beyond conception, beyond change; therefore, when thus thou knowest him, thou shouldst not grieve.

26. And even if thou deemest him ever born and ever dying, yet, O thou strong of arm, for him thou shouldst not grieve.

27. For of the born the death is sure, and sure the birth of the dead; therefore for what none can prevent thou shouldst not grieve.

28. In the beginning, Bhārata, are beings unmanifest; their middle state is manifest; their final state, unmanifest; what place therein for lamentation?[6]

29. Marvellous is one who sees him; marvellous, likewise, another who declares him; marvellous another who hears of him; yet even though one hear of him, one knows him not.

30. Never can this embodied soul be slain in the body of any, O Bharata; therefore for no being shouldst thou grieve.

31. Again, if thou considerest thy duty, thou shouldst not waver; for than a fight decreed by duty is naught better for a Ksatriya.[7]

32. Happy the Ksatriyas, O son of Prithā, who find a fight like this, that comes without their seeking! It is heaven's gate thrown wide!

4. The Self is immortal and cannot be destroyed with the body. Destruction of the body merely releases the soul from the cycle of birth and death.

5. Cf. Emerson's *Brahma*:

If the red slayer think he slays,
  Or if the slain think he is slain,
They know not well the subtle ways
  I keep, and pass, and turn again.

6. The Self comes from the unseen (into the world of the body) and departs into the unseen.

7. It is the holy duty of the warrior caste to fight. The other castes have other functions. The warriors (*ksatriyas*) are below the Brahman or priestly caste (see p. 238, note 7).

33. But if thou wilt not wage this war, as duty bids, then wilt thou cast aside thy duty and thine honour, and gather to thee guilt.

34. Yea, and the world will tell of thine imperishable dishonour: and for a knight of fame dishonour is worse than death.

35. 'Tis fear has held thee from the battle—so will the lords of great cars think; and where thou hast been highly honoured, thou wilt come to light esteem.

36. And many words ill to speak will they speak who wish thee hurt, and mock thy prowess. What can cause greater pain than this?

37. Slain, thou shalt win heaven; victorious, thou shalt enjoy the earth; therefore arise, O son of Kuntī, with no uncertain spirit for the fight!

38. Hold equal pleasure and pain, gain and loss, victory and defeat; then gird thyself for the battle; thus shalt thou not gather to thee guilt.

39. In Sāmkhya mode has this wisdom been set before thee; hear it now in Yoga; if thou dost put this wisdom into practice, son of Prithā, thou shalt cast off the bond of work.[8]

40. Here is no loss of enterprise nor going back; even a very little of this Rule delivers from the Great Fear.[9]

41. Here, O son of Kuru,[10] the judgement is resolution and one; many-branched are the judgements of the irresolute, and without bounds.

42. A flowery speech there is fools utter, O son of Prithā; in the words of the Veda they rejoice and say, 'There is naught else!'

43. Their soul is all desire, their goal is heaven; their speech gives birth as fruit of work, and prescribes many varied rites that lead to joys and lordship.

44. Nor resolute nor fit for contemplation is the judgement of those who cling to joys and lordship, robbed by that speech of wit.

45. The Vedas have three Strands for their province; free from the three Strands, Arjuna, be thou, free from the pairs, abiding in eternal truth,[11] free from all gain and guardianship of wealth, and master of thy soul.

46. As much use as there is in a tank flooded with waters from all

8. *Sāmkhya* is theory and *yoga* practice. If Arjuna fights in the spirit of this wisdom—not for glory, and not from lust for battle—it will not make him guilty of sin and hold up the release of his spirit.

9. *Samsāra,* "the Great Fear," is the cycle of birth and death.

10. The poet calls Arjuna "Kuru" here to remind us that he descends from the same stock as his present enemies.

11. The three Strands *(guna)* are *sattva*, the white strand, that which in nature is pure, light-giving, and good; *rajas*, the red strand, that of energy, that which causes restlessness and passion; and, *tamas*, the black strand, all that is dark, heavy, indifferent, and inert. They are interwoven like the strands of a rope, and in action cause the differences in character and function of men. The pairs are pleasure and pain, cold and heat, etc.

sides, so much there is in all the Vedas for a Brāhmana of wisdom.[12]

47. In work thy rightful interest should lie, nor even in its fruits; let not thy motive be the fruit of work; to no-work let not thine attachment be.

48. Steadfast in control, abandoning attachment, Dhanamjaya, do works, viewing with balanced mind success and failure. To be of balanced mind is called control.

49. For lower far is work than is the method of discernment, O Dhanamjaya; seek refuge in discernment. Miserable are they whose motive is fruit![13]

50. Here in this world a man who practices discernment discards both good and evil deeds; then practise thou control; control is skill in work.

51. For practising discernment prudent men abandon the fruit work bears, and from the bond of birth released go to the region where no sickness is.

52. When thy reason shall pass beyond the thicket of delusion, then shalt thou feel disgust for what thou shalt hear and hast heard.[14]

53. When thy reason, perplexed by what is heard, shall stand unmoved and firm in contemplation, then to control shalt thou attain.

Arjuna said:

54. What, O Keśava, is the man of steadfast wisdom, who abides in contemplation? How should the man of steadfast thought converse? How sit? How move?

The Blessed Lord said:

55. When one does put away, O son of Prithā, all the desires that enter the mind, in Self alone by Self well satisfied, then is he called a man of steadfast wisdom.

56. Whose mind in pains is not disturbed, who is in pleasures void of longing, free from love and fear and wrath, that man is called the man of steadfast thought, the saint.[15]

57. Who feels for nothing tender love, who, when he finds or good or bad, rejoices not nor hates, firm set is that man's wisdom.

12. A difficult passage. Probably the *Vedas* are unnecessary for an enlightened Brahman, who is beyond them. Arjuna, however, is a *ksatriya*, a warrior, and work (fighting and guarding) is his function and also his sacrament.

13. I.e., work with a desire for gain is low; work with discernment is without desire for gain.

14. The wisdom he has heard from Krisna or perhaps that which he has heard from other people.

15. A *muni*, a recluse who has taken the vow of silence—a sage or ascetic.

58. And when he draws his senses in from things of sense on every side, as a tortoise draws in its limbs, firm set is that man's wisdom.

59. When the embodied soul refuses food, then turn from him the things of sense, but not the relish; the relish also turns from him when it beholds the Highest.[16]

60. For even though a wise man strive, O son of Kuntī, the froward senses carry away perforce his mind.

61. Holding all these in check let him sit, controlled, intent on me: for he whose senses are restrained possesses steadfast wisdom.

62. When a man ponders on the things of sense, springs up attachment to them; of attachment is born desire; of desire is born wrath;

63. From wrath there comes delusion, and from delusion a wandering of memory; from memory wrecked the ruin of reason;[17] with reason's ruin the man is lost.

64. But he who approaches the things of sense with sense from love and hate disjoined and under Self's control, with governed self, comes to serenity.

65. For him serenity begets the loss of every pain; for soon his reason becomes steadfast whose mind is serene.

66. There is no judgement in the uncontrolled, and in the uncontrolled is no reflection; the unreflecting man can know no peace; he that has no peace—whence has he pleasure?

67. For when the mind of a man is governed by wandering senses, it carries away his wisdom, as the wind a ship on the waters.

68. Therefore whose senses are on all sides held from things of sense, O thou strong of arm, steadfast is his wisdom.

69. When it is night for all the world, the austere man is awake; when the world is awake, that is the night of the saint who sees.

70. He whom all desires enter as the waters enter the full and firm-established sea, wins peace; not so the desirer of desires.

71. That man who puts off all desires, and walks without longing, knowing that Mine and I are naught—he comes to peace.

72. This, O son of Prithā, is the Brahman-state.[18] Attaining this none is deluded. He who abides therein even at the hour of death passes to the Calm of Brahman.

16. Food here means, metaphorically, all sense objects. Enlightenment makes one turn away from sense objects, but first one continues to enjoy their recollected flavor. Further enlightenment makes this disappear.

17. Inner reason, like the Christian conscience, not logical power.

18. The Brahman-state of one who has achieved peace but is still alive and waits only for release from the flesh. Cf. Plato, *Phaedo*, 68.

Thus Endeth the Second Reading in
The Glorious Song of the Blessed Lord,
The Mystical Lesson,
The Wisdom of the Absolute,
The Scripture of Control,
The Converse of Lord Kriśna and Arjuna;
And Its Name Is
Sāmkhya.[19]

Reading the Third

Arjuna said:

1. If, O Janārdana, discernment be held by thee more excellent than work, then why, O Keśava, dost thou set me to do a work of violence?

2. Thou dost, meseems, perplex my judgement with words that appear confused; tell me with no uncertain voice that single course whereby I may attain the better.

The Blessed Lord said:

3. In this world the twofold system was of old declared by me, O sinless one—that of the Sāmkhyas with the method of knowledge, and that of the Yogins with the method of work.[1]

4. Not by abstaining from works does a man enjoy worklessness, nor yet by mere renunciation does he attain perfection.

5. For no one ever, even for a moment, remains without doing work; for every man is caused to work perforce by the Strands born of Nature.[2]

6. He who sits holding his organs of action in restraint, but with his mind remembering the things of sense, is called bemused and hypocrite.

7. But he, O Arjuna, is more excellent who checks the senses with the mind, and with the organs of action undertakes, free from attachment, the practice of the method of work.

8. Do thou the work thou art obliged to do; for work is better than no-work; not even thy body from no-work can win its sustenance.

9. This world is bound by bonds of work, save where that work is done for sacrifice;[3] work to this end do thou perform, O son of Kuntī, from attachment freed.

19. *Sāmkhya* here means "wisdom" or "knowledge."

1. See note 8, Second Reading.

2. "Nature" may be translated as "Not-Self."

3. I.e., work done in actually performing a sacrifice.

10. Thus spake of old the Lord of men,[4] creating men and, with them, sacrifice: 'By this shall ye increase; draw from this Cow the milk of your desires!

11. With this support the Lords of Heaven, and let these Lords of Heaven support you; by mutual support shall ye obtain the highest good;

12. For, by sacrifice supported, shall Heaven's Lords give you the food you crave; he who gives naught to them, and yet consumes the food they give, is but a thief.'[5]

13. Good men who eat the remnants of the sacrifice are from all guilt released; but those are sinners, and eat sin, who cook for their own sakes.

14. Food is the life of beings; from rain[6] is the birth of food; from sacrifice comes rain; sacrifice is sprung of work.

15. Know thou that work arises from Brahman, and Brahman from the Imperishable; therefore ever on sacrifice firm-founded is Brahman[7] all pervading.

16. He who in this world turns not with the wheel thus turned lives in vain a life of sin, O son of Pritha, satisfying sense.

17. Now that man whose delight is but in Self, whose pleasure is in Self, whose satisfaction is in Self alone, has no work that he must do;

18. For him there is no purpose here in work done or left undone, and he has no reliance on any being for any end.

19. Therefore without attachment ever perform the work that thou must do; for if without attachment a man works, he gains the Highest.

20. For by work only Janaka[8] and others reached perfection. Even if thou regardest only the guidance of the world, thou shouldest work.

21. Whatever the best man does, that too do other men; that which he makes his standard the world follows.

22. For me, O son of Prithā, is no work at all in the three worlds that I must do; nor aught ungained that I must gain; yet I abide in work.

23. For if I were not, tireless, to abide ever in work—my path men follow altogether, son of Prithā—

4. Brahma the Creator, or Prajāpati. The sacred cow Kāmaduh granted all desires.

5. Gods are supported, not merely honored, by man's sacrifices, and in turn support man.

6. "The oblation, duly cast upon the fire, ascends to the sun; of the sun is born the rain; of rain, food; thence creatures" (*Mānava-dharma-śātra*, iii, 76).

7. Brahman here can mean both the Absolute and the *Veda* itself. See Hill, p. 130, note 2; Zaehner, p. 167.

8. Janaka, philosopher-king of Videha, and known for his generosity. He is prominent in the *Brhadāranyaka Upanishad* (see iv, 1–4). The world must be guided by the work of rulers.

24. Did I not work my work, these worlds would fall in ruin, and I should be the worker of confusion, and should destroy these creatures.

25. Just as, to work attached, the ignorant work, O Bhārata, so too, but unattached, should the wise work, wishing to effect the guidance of the world.

26. The wise man should not raise a doubt in the minds of those that have no knowledge and are attached to work; rather should he approve all works, fulfilling them with control.

27. Entirely by the Strands of Nature are works done; he whose Self is deluded by the I thinks, 'I am the doer'.

28. But he who knows the truth about the distribution of Strands and works, O thou strong of arm, thinks, 'Strands abide in Strands,' and so escapes attachment.[9]

29. Deluded by the Strands of Nature are men attached to the works of the Strands; he, then, who knows the whole should not shake these dull men who know in part.

30. Cast off all works on me, and fix thy thought on the Essential Self; hope thou for naught, and have no thought of Mine; put off thy fever! Fight!

31. The men who ever practise this my teaching, without calumny, men of faith—these are released from works.

32. But know that those calumnious men who practise not this my teaching are deluded in all knowledge, witless, lost.

33. As is a man's own nature, so he acts, even a man of knowledge; all creatures follow Nature; what will restraint effect?

34. Towards the object of each sense is ordered love or hate; one should not fall into their power; for these two block one's path.

35. Better a man's own duty, though ill-done, than another's duty well-performed; beter it is to die in one's own duty—another's duty is fraught with dread.

Arjuna said:

36. Then what impels this man to do sin, all unwilling, O son of Vriśni, as though by force constrained?

The Blessed Lord said:

37. It is desire, it is wrath, born of the Strand of Energy; greatly devouring, greatly sinning; know this to be the enemy here!

38. As a fire is obscured by smoke, as a mirror by dirt, as the embryo by the womb, so by this is this world obscured.

39. Knowledge is obscured by this, the perpetual foe of him who knows, changing its shape at will, O son of Kunti, a fire insatiable.

9. I.e., the not-Self in man is concerned with the not-Self without; therefore it is not the Self which acts.

40. The senses, the mind, and the reason are said to be its base; by these it obscures knowledge, and deludes the embodied soul.

41. Checking the sense, therefore, in the beginning, cast off, O prince of Bharatas, this thing of sin, that destroys both knowledge and experience.

42. High, they say, are the senses; higher than the senses is the mind; and higher than the mind is the reason; but one who is higher than the reason is He.[10]

43. Thus understanding Him to be higher than the reason, steadying self by Self,[11] O thou strong of arm, slay thou the enemy that changes shape at will, so hard to reach!

Thus Endeth the Third Reading in
The Glorious Song of the Blessed Lord,
The Mystical Lesson,
The Wisdom of the Absolute,
The Scripture of Control,
The Converse of Lord Krišna and Arjuna;
And Its Name Is
Work.

VĀLMĪKI

(ca. 1st Century B.C.)

The *Rāmāyana*

The *Rāmāyana* is the later and perhaps the more popular of the two great epics of ancient India. Whereas the *Mahābhārata* is largely concerned with the great civil wars of the kingdom of the Kurus (see below) and has many heroes, the *Rāmāyana* is largely concerned with Prince Rāma, who is not only a great warrior but also an ideal of youthful conduct and the loyal husband of the beautiful bride Sītā. What we in the West would call a "romantic" element adds to the appeal of the work, although we should note that neither "romantic" nor religious themes are excluded from the Indian epic, and that, moreover, it is not in any way confined to the conventions of classical Western epic. Homeric epic, as Aristotle points out in the *Poetics*, is confined to a single episode in the life of a single hero—in the *Iliad* the wrath of Achilles and its consequences and in the *Odyssey* the last stages of the hero's journey home from the Trojan war. The Indian epic is exactly the opposite of what Aristotle defined as a good epic. It can not only depict the entire life of the hero but it may go back to his father

10. The Great Self. "Reason" here may be also translated as "Soul."

11. The Self of man must be steadied by the Great Self.

and go on to his sons. The *Mahābhārata* contains nearly 90,000 verses and may be the longest poem in world literature. The *Rāmāyana* is only slightly more than a quarter as long, but the concept of the unity of time is not a part of Indian epic theory in either.

The traditional author of the *Rāmāyana* is the sage Valmiki, and while the poem is later than the *Mahābhārata*, some events in the earlier poem reflect a knowledge of the later one. The date may be shortly before the beginning of the Christian era. There is no question that later additions were made to the Ramayana, especially the identification of the hero with the god Visnu and the second ending.

The story is not just about Rāma, but about the dynasty of King Daśaratha and his four sons by three different wives: Rāma and his brother Lakhsmana, and his half-brothers Bharata and Satrughna. In the first episode printed below, Rāma as a young prince lifts the giant bow which no other man can lift and in so doing shakes the heavens and proves that he will be a great king. Because of this deed, he wins the hand of Sītā, daughter of King Janaka. The episode is similar to the feats of other heroes in world literature such as Odysseus stringing the bow at the end of the *Odyssey* and the young Arthur drawing the sword from the stone, whereby by magic or strength the untried young man exhibits his power to lead the people. But Rāma is cheated out of his right to the throne by one of Dásaratha's jealous queens, and Bharata, against his wishes, ascends the throne as regent for Rāma who is sent into exile because of a vow his father made.

With his wife and his brother Lakhsmana Rāma dwells as a hermit in the forest doing his pious duty as a member of the warrior caste by defending the villages against enemies and demons, and he does his job exceedingly well. The arch-demon Rāvana, king of Lankā (Ceylon) retaliates by kidnapping Rāma's wife Sītā. It is an important part of the epic that Sita keeps her chastity while imprisoned by Rāvana in Lankā. Most of the epic concerns Rāma's search for Sītā, and this makes Rāma's heroic deeds a quest for love as well as for valor. His scouts find Sītā, and with the aid of an army of friendly bears and monkeys Rāma constructs a bridge from India to Ceylon, storms Rāvana's stronghold, and in a furious battle slays Rāvana and his cohorts.

But the rescued Sītā, having lived however chastely in the home of another man, is impure under the sacred law, and Rāma can do nothing but repudiate her. She throws herself, like a widow into the fire but the god Agni rejects her and thus her innocence is proved. Rāma and Sītā return to the capital and Rāma ascends the throne, to rule long and gloriously. Here the epic should end. Or it should go on, as *Shakuntalā* does, to the coming greatness of the hero's son.

The last book of the *Rāmāyana* is probably an addition, composed by someone not convinced of the miraculous redemption of Sītā. It depicts a resentful population insisting that Sīta had, intentionally or not, broken the marriage vow. Though convinced of her innocence, Rāma banishes her again. Years later he acknowledges their children, and he finally ascends to heaven as an incarnation of the god Viśnu. This grim ending did not please all of the later redactors of this most popular poem, and some versions reconcile Rāma and Sītā fully.

In the episodes below, Rāma first performs the feat of lifting the great bow. In the second episode, the events leading up to his banishment are depicted, and here his exemplary character is revealed more in the manner of medieval Christian romance than in classical western epic. In the third episode, near the end of the poem, Rāma fights and kills Rāvana, king of the demons.

From The Rāmāyana*

Book One: [The Breaking of the Bow]

CANTO LXVI

With cloudless lustre rose the sun;
The king, his morning worship done,
Ordered his heralds to invite
The princes and the anchorite.
With honour, as the laws decree,
The monarch entertained the three.
Then to the youths and saintly man
Videha's lord this speech began:
'O blameless Saint, most welcome thou!
If I may please thee tell me how.
Speak, mighty lord, whom all revere,
'Tis thine to order, mine to hear.'

Thus he on mighty thoughts intent;
Then thus the sage most eloquent:
'King Daśaratha's sons, this pair
Of warriors famous everywhere,
Are come that best of bows to see
That lies a treasure stored by thee.
This, mighty Janak, deign to show,
That they may look upon the bow.
And then, contented, homeward go.'

* From *The Rámáyana of Válmiki.* Translated by Ralph T. H. Griffith. Benares, 1895.

9. *Saint:* The sage Viśvāmitra, a semi-divine holy man.

15. *King Daśaratha's sons:* Rāma and his devoted half-brother Lakshmana.

Then royal Janak spoke in turn:
'O best of Saints, the story learn
Why this famed bow, a noble prize,
A treasure in my palace lies.
A monarch, Devarāt by name,
Who sixth from ancient Nimi came,
Held it as ruler of the land,
A pledge in his successive hand.
This bow the mighty Rudra bore
At Daksha's sacrifice of yore,
When carnage of the Immortals stained
The rite that Daksha had ordained.
Then as the Gods sore wounded fled,
Victorious Rudra, mocking, said:
'Because, O Gods, ye gave me naught
When I my rightful portion sought,
Your dearest parts I will not spare,
But with my bow your frames will tear.'

The Sons of Heaven, in wild alarm,
Soft flatteries tried his rage to charm.
Then Bhava, Lord whom Gods adore,
Grew kind and friendly as before,
And every torn and mangled limb
Was safe and sound restored by him.
Thenceforth this bow, the gem of bows,
That freed the God of Gods from foes,
Stored by our great forefathers lay
A treasure and a pride for aye.
Once, as it chanced, I ploughed the ground,
When sudden, 'neath the share was found
An infant springing from the earth,
Named Sītā from her secret birth.
In strength and grace the maiden grew,
My cherished daughter, fair to view.
I vowed her, of no mortal birth,
Meet prize for noblest hero's worth.
In strength and grace the maiden grew,

26 *Devarāt:* Ancient king of Nimi, the land of Mithila, over which Janaka now reigns.

30–31. *Rudra . . . sacrifice:* Rudra (also called Bhava below) is the god Śiva, and Daksha is an ancient god created by Brahmā. Śiva threatened harm to the other gods because he had not been invited to a sacrifice.

53. Sītā means "furrow"; she was obviously once associated with a goddess of vegetation and fertility. Her story resembles that of the Persephone myth of the Greeks. In the *Iliad* (II, 547) Erechtheus, hero of Athens, is described as being born in a furrow.

And many a monarch came to woo.
To all the princely suitors I
Gave, mighty Saint, the same reply:
'I give not thus my daughter, she
Prize of heroic worth shall be.
To Mithilā the suitors pressed
Their power and might to manifest.
To all who came with hearts aglow
I offered Śiva's wondrous bow.
Not one of all the royal band
Could raise or take the bow in hand.
The suitors' puny might I spurned,
And back the feeble princes turned.
Enraged thereat, the warriors met,
With force combined my town beset.
Stung to the heart with scorn and shame,
With war and threats they madly came,
Besieged my peaceful walls, and long
To Mithilā did grievous wrong.
There, wasting all, a year they lay,
And brought my treasures to decay,
Filling my soul, O Hermit chief,
With bitter woe and hopeless grief.
At last by long-wrought penance
Won favour with the Gods on high,
Who with my labours well content
A four-fold host to aid me sent.
Then swift the baffled heroes fled
To all the winds discomfited—
Wrong-doers, with their lords and host,
And all their valour's idle boast.
This heavenly bow, exceeding bright,
These youths shall see, O Anchorite.
Then if young Rāma's hand can string
The bow that baffled lord and king,
To him I give, as I have sworn,
My Sītā, not of woman born.'

CANTO LXVII

Then spoke again the great recluse:
'This mighty bow, O King, produce.
King Janak, at the saint's request,
This order to his train addressed:
'Let the great bow be hither borne,

Which flowery wreaths and scents adorn.'
Soon as the monarch's words were said,
His servants to the city sped:
Five thousand youths in number, all
Of manly strength and stature tall,
The ponderous eight-wheeled chest that held
The heavenly bow, with toil propelled.
At length they brought that iron chest,
And thus the godlike king addressed:
'This best of bows, O lord, we bring,
Respected by each chief and king,
And place it for these youths to see,
If, Sovereign, such thy pleasure be.'

With suppliant palm to palm applied
King Janak to the strangers cried:
'This gem of bows, O Brāhman Sage,
Our race has prized from age to age,
Too strong for those who yet have reigned,
Though great in might each nerve thev strained,
Titan and fiend its strength defies,
God, spirit, minstrel of the skies.
And bard above and snake below
Are baffled by this glorious bow.
Then how may human prowess hope
With such a bow as this to cope?
What man with valour's choicest gift
This bow can draw, or string, or lift?
Yet let the princes, holy Seer,
Behold it: it is present here.'

Then spoke the hermit pious-souled:
'Rāma, dear son, the bow behold.'
Then Rāma at his word unclosed
The chest wherein its might reposed,
Thus crying, as he viewed it: 'Lo!
I lay mine hand upon the bow:
May happy luck my hope attend
Its heavenly strength to lift or bend.'
'Good luck be thine,' the hermit cried:
'Assay the task!' the king replied.
Then Raghu's son, as if in sport,
Before the thousands of the court,

45. *Raghu:* a god of healing, Rāma's ancestor, his father only metaphorically.

The weapon by the middle raised
That all the crowd in wonder gazed.
With steady arm the string he drew
Till burst the mighty bow in two.
As snapped the bow, an awful clang,
Loud as the shriek of tempests, rang.
The earth, affrighted, shook amain
As when a hill is rent in twain.
Then, senseless at the fearful sound,
The people fell upon the ground:
None save the king, the princely pair,
And the great saint, the shock could bear.

When woke to sense the stricken train,
And Janak's soul was calm again,
With suppliant hands and reverent head,
These words, most eloquent, he said:
'O Saint, Prince Rāma stands alone:
His peerless might he well has shown.
A marvel had the hero wrought
Beyond belief, surpassing thought.
My child, to Royal Rāma wed,
New glory on our line will shed:
And true my promise will remain
That hero's worth the bride should gain.
Dearer to me than light and life,
My Sītā shall be Rāma's wife.
If thou, O Brāhman, leave concede,
My counsellors, with eager speed,
Borne in their flying cars, to fair
Ayodhyā's town the news shall bear,
With courteous message to entreat
The king to grace my royal seat.
This to the monarch shall they tell,
The bride is his who won her well:
And his two sons are resting here
Protected by the holy seer.
So, at his pleasure, let them lead
The sovereign to my town with speed.'

The hermit to his prayer inclined
And Janak, lord of virtuous mind,
With charges, to Ayodhyā sent
His ministers: and forth they went.

87. *Ayodhyā:* Rāma's own country.

Book Two: [*Rāma Exiled*]

CANTO VII

It chanced a slave-born handmaid, bred
With Queen Kaikeyī, fancy-led,
Mounted the stair and stood upon
The terrace like the moon that shone.
Thence Mantharā at ease surveyed
Ayodhyā to her eyes displayed,
Where water cooled the royal street,
Where heaps of flowers were fresh and sweet,
And costly flags and pennons hung
On roof and tower their shadow flung;
With covered ways prepared in haste,
And many an awning newly placed;
With sandal-scented streams bedewed,
Thronged by a new bathed multitude:
Whose streets were full of Brahman bands
With wreaths and sweetmeats in their hands.
Loud instruments their music raised,
And through the town, where'er she gazed,
The doors of temples glittered white,
And the maid marvelled at the sight.

Of Rāma's nurse who, standing by,
Gazed with a joy-expanded eye,
In robes of purest white attired,
The wondering damsel thus inquired:

'Does Rāma's mother give away
Rich largess to the crowds to-day,
On some dear object fondly bent,
Or blest with measureless content?
What mean these signs of rare delight
On every side that meet my sight?
Say, will the king with joy elate
Some happy triumph celebrate?'

The nurse, with transport uncontrolled,
Her glad tale to the hump-back told:
'Our lord the king to-morrow morn
Will consecrate his eldest-born,

1. *handmaid:* Queen Kaikeyī's handmaiden, Mantharā, urges her mistress to insist on the king holding to a vow he made her years before in the heat of battle with an army of demons. The demand will be that Rāma be sent into exile for a period of years and that his son, Bharata, be appointed to the throne.

And raise in Pushya's favouring hour,
Prince Rāma to the royal power.'
As thus the nurse her tidings spoke,
Rage in the hump-back's breast awoke.
Down from the terrace, like the head
Of high Kailāsa's hill, she sped.
Sin in her thoughts, her soul aflame,
Where Queen Kaikeyī slept, she came:
'Why sleepest thou?' she cried, 'arise,
Peril is near, unclose thine eyes.
Ah, heedless Queen, too blind to know
What floods of sin above thee flow!
Thy boasts of love and grace are o'er:
Thine is the show and nothing more.
His favour is an empty cheat,
A torrent dried by summer's heat.'

Thus by the artful maid addressed
In cruel words from raging breast,
The queen, sore troubled, spoke in turn;
'What evil news have I to learn?
That mournful eye, that altered cheek
Of sudden woe or danger speak.'

Such were the words Kaikeyī said:
Then Mantharā, her eyeballs red
With fury, skilled with threacherous art
To grieve yet more her lady's heart,
From Rāma, in her wicked hate,
Kaikeyī's love to alienate,
Upon her evil purpose bent
Began again most eloquent:
'Peril awaits thee swift and sure,
And utter woe defying cure;
King Daśaratha will create
Prince Rāma Heir Associate.
Plunged in the depths of wild despair,
My soul a prey to pain and care,
As though the flames consumed me, zeal
Has brought me for my lady's weal,
Thy grief, my Queen, is grief to me:
Thy gain my greatest gain would be.

37. *Pushya:* the name of a constellation (also called Naksatra and Tisya).

42. *Kailāsa:* a mountain in northern India, sacred to both Siva and Kuvera.

Proud daughter of a princely line,
The rights of consort queen are thine.
How art thou, born of royal race,
Blind to the crimes that kings debase?
Thy lord is gracious, to deceive,
And flatters, but thy soul to grieve,
While thy pure heart that thinks no sin
Knows not the snares that hem thee in.
Thy husband's lips on thee bestow
Soft soothing word, an empty show:
The wealth, the substance, and the power
This day will be Kauśalyā's dower.
With crafty soul thy child he sends
To dwell among thy distant friends,
And, every rival far from sight,
To Rāma gives the power and might.
Ah me! for thou, unhappy dame,
Deluded by a husband's name.
With more than mother's love hast pressed
A serpent to thy heedless breast.
And cherished him who works thee woe,
No husband but a deadly foe.
For like a snake, unconscious Queen,
Or enemy who stabs unseen,
King Daśaratha all untrue
Has dealt with thee and Bharat too.
Ah, simple lady, long beguiled
By his soft words who falsely smiled!
Poor victim of the guileless breast,
A happier fate thou meritest.
For thee and thine destruction waits
When he Prince Rāma consecrates.
Up, lady, while there yet is time;
Preserve thyself, prevent the crime.
Up, from thy careless ease, and free
Thyself, O Queen, thy son, and me!'

Delighted at the words she said,
Kaikeyī lifted from the bed,
Like autumn's moon, her radiant head,
And joyous at the tidings gave
A jewel to the hump-back slave;
And as she gave the precious toy

88. *Kauśalyā:* Queen Kauśalyā is Rāma's mother.

She cried in her exceeding joy:
"Take this, dear maiden, for thy news
Most grateful to mine ear, and choose
What grace beside most fitly may
The welcome messenger repay.
I joy that Rāma gains the throne:
Kauśalyā's son is as mine own.'

CANTO VIII

The damsel's breast with fury burned:
She answered, as the gift she spurned:
'What time, O simple Queen, is this
For idle dreams of fancied bliss?
Hast thou not sense thy state to know,
Engulfed in seas of whelming woe;
Sick as I am with grief and pain
My lips can scarce a laugh restrain
To see thee hail with ill-timed joy
A peril mighty to destroy.
I mourn for one so fondly blind:
What woman of a prudent mind
Would welcome, e'en as thou hast done,
The lordship of a rival's son,
Rejoiced to find her secret foe
Empowered, like death, to launch the blow;
I see that Rāma still must fear
Thy Bharat, to his throne too near.
Hence is my heart disquieted,
For those who fear are those we dread.
Lakshman, the mighty bow who draws,
With all his soul serves Rāma's cause;
And chains as strong to Bharat bind
Satrughna, with his heart and mind,
Now next to Rāma, lady fair,
Thy Bharat is the lawful heir:
And far remote, I ween, the chance
That might the younger two advance.
Yes, Queen, 'tis Rāma that I dread,
Wise, prompt, in warlike science bred;
And oh, I tremble when I think
Of thy dear child on ruin's brink.
Blest with a lofty fate is she,
Kauśalyā; for her son will be

24. *Satrughna:* another son of Daśaratha.

Placed, when the moon and Pushya meet,
By Brāhmans on the royal seat.
Thou as a slave in suppliant guise
Must wait upon Kauśalyā's eyes,
With all her wealth and bliss secured
And glorious from her foes assured.
Her slave with us who serve thee, thou
Wilt see thy son to Rāma bow,
And Sītā's friends exult o'er all,
While Bharat's wife shares Bharat's fall.'

As thus the maid in wrath complained,
Kaikeyī saw her heart was pained,
And answered eager in defence
Of Rāma's worth and excellence:
'Nay, Rama, born the monarch's heir,
By holy fathers trained with care,
Virtuous, grateful, pure, and true,
Claims royal sway as rightly due.
He, like a sire, will long defend
Each brother, minister, and friend.
Then why, O hump-back, art thou pained
To hear that he the throne has gained?
Be sure when Rāma's empire ends,
The kingdom to my son descends,
Who, when a hundred years are flown,
Shall sit upon his fathers' throne.
Why is thine heart thus sad to see
The joy that is and long shall be,
This fortune by possession sure
And hopes which we may count secure?
Dear as the darling son I bore
Is Rama, yea, or even more.
Most duteous to Kauśalyā, he
Is yet more dutiful to me.
What though he rule, we need not fear:
His brethren to his soul are dear.
And if the throne Prince Rāma fill
Bharat will share the empire still.'

She ceased. The troubled damsel sighed
Sighs long and hot, and thus replied:
'What madness has possessed thy mind,
To warnings deaf, to dangers blind?
Canst thou not see the floods of woe
That threaten o'er thine head to flow:

First Rāma will the throne acquire,
Then Rāma's son succeed his sire,
While Bharat will neglected pine
Excluded from the royal line.
Not all his sons, O lady fair,
The kingdom of a monarch share:
All ruling when a sovereign dies
Wild tumult in the state would rise.
The eldest, be he good or ill,
Is ruler by the father's will.
Know, tender mother, that thy son
Without a friend and all undone,
Far from the joyous ease of home
An alien from his race will roam.
I sped to thee for whom I feel,
But thy fond heart mistakes my zeal,
Thy hand a present would bestow
Because thy rival triumphs so.
When Rāma once begins his sway
Without a foe his will to stay,
Thy darling Bharat he will drive
To distant lands if left alive.
By thee the child was sent away
Beneath his grandsire's roof to stay.
Even in stocks and stones perforce
Will friendship spring from intercourse.
The young Śatrughna too would go
With Bharat, for he loved him so.
As Lakshman still to Rāma cleaves,
He his dear Bharat never leaves.
There is an ancient tale they tell:
A tree the foresters would fell
Was saved by reeds that round it stood,
For love that sprang of neighbourhood.
So Lakshman Rāma will defend,
And each on each for aid depend.
Such fame on earth their friendship wins
As that which binds the Heavenly Twins.
And Rāma ne'er will purpose wrong
To Lakshman, for their love is strong.
But Bharat, Oh, of this be sure,
Must evil at his hands endure.
Come, Rāma from his home expel
An exile in the woods to dwell.
The plan, O Queen, which I advise
Secures thy weal if thou be wise.

So we and all thy kith and kin
Advantage from thy gain shall win.
Shall Bharat, meet for happier fate,
Born to endure his rival's hate,
With all his fortune ruined cower
And dread his brother's mightier power?
Up, Queen, to save thy son, arise;
Prostrate at Rama's feet he lies.
So the proud elephant who leads
His trooping consorts through the reeds
Falls in the forest shade beneath
The lion's spring and murderous teeth.
Scorned by thee in thy bliss and pride
Kauśalyā was of old defied,
And will she now forbear to show
The vengeful rancour of a foe?
  O Queen, thy darling is undone
  When Rama's hand has once begun
    Ayodhta's realm to sway.
  Come, win the kingdom for thy child
  And drive the alien to the wild
    In banishment to-day.

CANTO IX

As fury lit Kaikeyī's eyes
She spoke with long and burning sighs:
'This day my son enthroned shall see,
And Rāma to the woods shall flee.
But tell me, damsel, if thou can,
A certain way, a skilful plan
That Bharat may the empire gain,
And Rāma's hopes be nursed in vain.'

The lady ceased. The wicked maid
The mandate of her queen obeyed,
And darkly plotting Rāma's fall
Responded to Kaikeyī's call.

'I will declare, do thou attend,
How Bharat may his throne ascend.
Dost thou forget what things befell?
Or dost thou feign, remembering well?
Or wouldst thou hear my tongue repeat
A story for thy need so meet?
Gay lady, if thy will be so,

Now hear the tale of long ago,
And when my tongue has done its part
Ponder the story in thine heart.
When Gods and demons fought of old,
Thy lord, with royal saints enrolled,
Sped to the war with thee to bring
His might to aid the Immortals' King.
Far to the southern land he sped
Where Dandaks mighty wilds are spread,
To Vaijayanta's city swayed
In Śambara, whose flag displayd
The hugest monster of the sea.
Lord of a hundred wiles was he;
With might which Gods could never blame
Against the King of Heaven he came.
Then raged the battle wild and dread,
And mortal warriors fought and bled;
The fiends by night with strength renewed
Charged, slew the sleeping multitude.
Thy lord, King Daśaratha, long
Stood fighting with the demon throng,
But long of arm, unmatched in strength,
Fell wounded by their darts at length.
Thy husband, senseless, by thine aid
Was from the battle field conveyed,
And wounded nigh to death thy lord
Was by thy care to health restored.
Well pleased the grateful monarch sware
To grant thy first and second prayer.
Thou for no favour then wouldst sue,
The gifts reserved for season due;
And he, thy high-souled lord, agreed
To give the boons when thou shouldst need.
Myself I knew not what befell,
But oft the tale have heard thee tell,
And close to thee in friendship knit
Deep in my heart have treasured it.
Remind thy husband of his oath,
Recall the boons and claim them both,
That Bharat on the throne be placed
With rites of consecration graced,
And Rāma to the woods be sent
For twice seven years of banishment.

27–31. *Far . . . sea:* King Daśaratha had aided the gods in a battle against forest demons (*Dandaka*), associated with Rāvana's brother, Sambara is the "demon of a hundred illusions." He was killed by Indra, one of whose cities was Vaijayanta.

Go, Queen, the mourner's chamber seek,
With angry eye and burning cheek;
And with disordered robes and hair
On the cold earth lie prostrate there.
When the king comes still mournful lie,
Speak not a word nor meet his eye,
But let thy tears in torrent flow,
And lie enamoured of thy woe.
Well do I know thou long hast been,
And ever art, his darling queen.
For thy dear sake, O well-loved dame,
The mighty king would brave the flame,
But ne'er would anger thee, or brook
To meet his favourite's wrathful look.
The loving lord would even die
Thy fancy, Queen, to gratify,
And never could he arm his breast
To answer nay to thy request.
Listen and learn, O dull of sense,
Thine all-resistless, influence.
Gems he will offer, pearly and gold:
Refuse his gifts, be stern and cold.
Those proffered boons at length recall,
And claim them till he grants thee all.
And O my lady, high in bliss,
With heedful thought forget not this.
When from the ground his queen he lifts
And grants again the promised gifts,
Bind him with oaths he cannot break
And thy demands unflinching, make,
That Rāma travel to the wild
Five years and nine from home exiled,
And Bharat, best of all who reign,
The empire of the land obtain.
For when this term of years has fled
Over the banished Rāma's head,
Thy royal son to vigour grown
And rooted firm will stand alone.
The king, I know, is well inclined,
And this the hour to move his mind.
Be bold: the threatened rite prevent,
And force the king from his intent.'

64. ***mourner's chamber:*** a small, sparsely furnished chamber in the palace, happily translated by Griffith as a "growlery"—a place where women betook themselves to be offended and sulky.

She ceased. So counseled to her bane
Disguised beneath a show of gain,
Kaikeyī in her joy and pride
To Mantharā again replied:
'Thy sense I envy, prudent maid;
With sagest lore thy lids persuade.
No hump-back maid in all the earth,
For wise resolve, can match thy worth.
Thou art alone with constant zeal
Devoted to thy lady's weal.
Dear girl, without thy faithful aid
I had not marked the plot he laid.
Full of all guile and sin and spite
Misshapen hump-backs shock the sight:
But thou art fair and formed to please,
Bent like a lily by the breeze.
I look thee o'er with watchful eye,
And in thy frame no fault can spy;
The chest so deep, the waist so trim,
So round the lines of breast and limb.
Thy cheeks with moonlike beauty shine,
And the warm wealth of youth is thine.
Thy legs, my girl, are long and neat,
And somewhat long thy dainty feet,
While stepping out before my face
Thou seemest like a crane to pace.
The thousand wiles are in thy breast
Which Śambara the fiend possessed,
And countless others all thine own,
O damsel sage, to thee are known.
Thy very hump becomes thee too,
O thou whose face is fair to view,
For there reside in endless store
Plots, wizard wiles, and warrior lore.
A golden chain I'll round it fling
When Rāma's flight makes Bharat king:
Yea, polished links of finest gold,
When once the wished for prize I hold
With naught to fear and none to hate,
Thy hump, dear maid, shall decorate.
A golden frontlet wrought with care,
And precious jewels shalt thou wear:
Two lovely robes around thee fold,
And walk a Goddess to behold,
Bidding the moon himself compare
His beauty with a face so fair.

With scent of precious sandal sweet
Down to the nails upon thy feet,
First of the household thou shalt go
And pay with scorn each baffled foe.'

Kaikeyī's praise the damsel heard,
And thus again her lady stirred,
Who lay upon her beauteous bed
Like fire upon the altar fed:
'Dear Queen, they build the bridge in vain
When swollen streams are dry again.
Arise, thy glorious task complete,
And draw the king to thy retreat.'

The large-eyed lady left her bower
And with the hump-back sought the gloom
And silence of the mourner's room.
The string of priceless pearls that hung
Around her neck to earth she flung,
With all the wealth and lustre lent
By precious gem and ornament,
Then, listening to her slave's advice,
Lay, like a nymph from Paradise.
As on the ground her limbs she laid
Once more she cried unto the maid:
'Soon must thou to the monarch say
Kaikeyī's soul has past away,
Or, Rāma banished as we planned,
My son made king shall rule the land.
No more for gold and gems I care,
For brave attire or dainty fare.
If Rāma should the throne ascend,
That very hour my life will end.'

  The royal lady wounded through
The bosom with the darts that flew
  Launched from the hump-back's tongue
Pressed both her hands upon her side,
And o'er and o'er again she cried
  With wildering fury stung:
'Yes, it shall be thy task to tell
That I have hurried hence to dwell
  In Yama's realms of woe,

191. *Yama:* lord of the world of death, having dominion over the heroes who die in battle.

Or happy Bharat shall be king,
And doomed to years of wandering
   Kauśalyā's son shall go.
I heed not dainty viands now
Fair wreaths of flowers to twine my brow,
   Soft balm or precious scent:
My very life I count as naught,
Nothing on earth can claim my thought
   But Rāma's banishment.'
   She spoke these words of cruel ire;
Then stripping off her gay attire,
   The cold bare floor she pressed.
So, falling from her home on high,
Some lovely daughter of the sky
   Upon the ground might rest.
With darkened brow and furious mien,
Stripped of her gems and wreath, the queen
   In spotless beauty lay,
Like heaven obscured with gathering cloud,
When shades of midnight darkness shroud
   Each star's expiring ray.

CANTO X

As Queen Kaikeyī thus obeyed
The sinful counsel of her maid
She sank upon the chamber floor,
As sinks in anguish, wounded sore,
An elephant beneath the smart
Of the wild hunter's venomed dart.
The lovely lady in her mind
Revolved the plot her maid designed,
And prompt the gain and risk to scan
She step by step approved the plan.
Misguided by the hump-back's guile
She pondered her resolve awhile,
As the fair path that bliss secured
The miserable lady lured,
Devoted to her queen, and swayed
By hopes of gain and bliss, the maid
Rejoiced her lady's purpose known,
And deemed the prize she sought her own.
Then bent upon her purpose dire,
Kaikeyī with her soul on fire,
Upon the floor lay, languid, down,

Her brows contracted in a frown.
The bright-hued wreath that bound her hair,
Chains, necklets, jewels rich and rare,
Stripped off by her own fingers lay
Spread on the ground in disarray,
And to the floor a lustre lent
As stars light up the firmament.
Thus prostrate in the mourner's cell,
In gerb of woe the lady fell,
Her long hair in a single braid,
Like some fair nymph of heaven dismayed.

The monarch, Rāma to install,
With thoughtful care had ordered all,
And now within his home withdrew,
Dismissing first his retinue.
Now all the town had heard, thought he,
What joyful rite the morn will see,
So turned he to her bower to cheer
With the glad news his darling's ear.
Majestic, as the Lord of Night,
When threatened by the Dragon's might,
Bursts radiant on the evening sky
Pale with the clouds that wander by,
So Daśaratha, great in fame,
To Queen Kaikeyī's palace came.
There parrots flew from tree to tree,
And gorgeous peacocks wandered free,
While ever and anon was heard
The note of some glad water-bird.
Here loitered dwarf and hump-backed maid,
There lute and lyre sweet music played.
Here, rich in blossom, creepers twined
O'er grots with wondrous art designed,
There champac and aśoka flowers
Hung glorious o'er the summer bowers,
And mid the waving verdure rose
Gold, silver, ivory porticoes.
Through all the months in ceaseless store
The trees both fruit and blossom bore.
With many a lake the grounds were graced;
Seats, gold and silver, here were placed;

55. *champac and aśoka:* The *champac* (*campaka*) tree has yellow-red flowers; the *aśoka,* tiny red flowers (see p. 318, note to lines 3–6).

Here every viand wooed the taste.
It was a garden meet to vie
E'en with the home of Gods on high.
Within the mansion rich and vast
The mighty Daśaratha passed:
Not there was his beloved queen
On her fair couch reclining seen,
With love his eager pulses beat
For the dear wife he came to meet,
And in his blissful hopes deceived,
He sought his absent love and grieved.
For never had she missed the hour
Of meeting in her sumptuous bower,
And never had the king of men
Entered the empty room till then.
Still urged by love and anxious thought
News of his favourite queen he sought,
For never had his loving eyes
Found her or selfish or unwise.
Then spoke at length the warder maid,
With hands upraised and sore afraid:
'My Lord and King, the queen has sought
The mourner's cell with rage distraught.'

The words the warder maiden said
He heard with soul disquieted,
And thus as fiercer-grief assailed,
His troubled senses wellnigh failed.
Consumed by torturing fires of grief
The king, the world's imperial chief,
His lady lying on the ground
In most unqueenly posture, found.
The aged king, all pure within,
Saw the young queen resolved on sin,
Low on the ground his own sweet wife,
To him far dearer than his life,
Like some fair creeping plant uptorn,
Or like a maid of heaven forlorn,
A nymph of air or Goddess sent
From Swarga down in banishment.

As some wild elephant who tries
To soothe his consort as she lies

101. *Swarga:* Heaven (also spelled *Svarga*).

Struck by the hunter's venomed dart,
So the great king, disturbed in heart,
Strove with soft hand and fond caress
To soothe his darling queen's distress,
And in his love addressed with sighs
The lady of the lotus eyes:
'I know not, Queen, why thou shouldst be
Thus angered to the heart with me.
Say, who has slighted thee, or whence
Has come the cause of such offence
That in the dust thou liest low,
And rendest my fond heart with woe,
As if some goblin of the night
Had struck thee with a deadly blight,
And cast foul influence on her
Whose spells my loving bosom stir?
I have Physicians famed for skill,
Each trained to cure some special ill:
My sweetest lady, tell thy pain,
And they shall make thee well again.
Whom, darling, wouldst thou punished see?
Or whom enriched with lordly fee?
Weep not, my lovely Queen, and stay
This grief that wears thy frame away.
Speak, and the guilty shall be freed,
The guiltless be condemned to bleed,
The poor enriched, the rich abased,
The low set high, the proud disgraced.
My lords and I thy will obey,
All slaves who own thy sovereign sway;
And I can ne'er my heart incline
To check in aught one wish of thine.
Now by my life I pray thee tell
The thoughts that in thy bosom dwell.
The power and might thou knowest well
Should from thy breast all doubt expel.
I swear by all my merit won,
Speak, and thy pleasure shall be done.
Far as the world's wide bounds extend
My glorious empire knows no end.
Mine are the tribes in eastern lands.
And those who dwell on Sindhu's sands:

145–152. *Sindhu's . . . domain:* These are regions of north central India named after the gods who are worshipped there.

Mine is Surāshtra, far away,
Suvira's realm admits my sway.
My hest the southern nations fear,
The Angas and the Vangas hear.
And as lord paramount I reign
O'er Magadh and the Matsyas' plain,
Kośal and Kāśi's wide domain;
All rich in treasures of the mine.
In golden corn, sheep, goats, and kine.
Choose what thou wilt, Kaikeyī, thence:
But tell me, O my darling, whence
Arose thy grief, and it shall fly
Like hoar-frost when the sun is high.'

She, by his loving words consoled,
Longed her dire purpose to unfold.
And sought with sharper pangs to wring
The bosom of her lord the king.

CANTO XI

To him enthralled by love, and blind,
Pierced by his darts who shakes the mind,
Kaikeyī with remorseless breast
Her cruel purpose thus expressed:
'O King, no insult or neglect
Have I endured, or disrespect
One wish I have, and fain would see
That longing granted, lord, by thee.
Now pledge thy word if thou incline
To listen to this prayer of mine,
Then I with confidence will speak,
And thou shalt hear the boon I seek.'

Ere she had ceased, the monarch fell
A victim to the lady's spell.
And to the deadly snare she set
Sprang, like a roebuck to the net.
Her lover raised her drooping head,
Smiled, playing with her hair, and said:
'Hast thou not learnt, wild dame, till now
That there is none so dear as thou
To me thy loving husband, save

2. *who shakes the mind:* Manmatha ("Mind Disturber") is another name for Kāma, the god of love.

My Rāma bravest of the brave?
By him my race's high-souled heir,
By him whom none can match, I swear,
Now speak the wish that on thee weighs:
By him whose right is length of days,
Whom if my fond paternal eye
Saw not one hour I needs must die,—
I swear by Rāma my dear son,
Speak, and thy bidding shall be done.
Speak, darling; if thou choose, request
To have the heart from out my breast;
Regard my words, sweet love, and name
The wish thy mind thinks fit to frame.
Nor let thy soul give way to doubt:
My power should drive suspicion out.
Yea, by my merits won I swear,
Speak, darling, I will grant thy prayer.'

The queen, ambitious, overjoyed
To see him by her plot decoyed.
More eager still her aims to reach,
Spoke her abominable speech:
'A boon thou granted, nothing loth,
And swearest with repeated oath.
Now let the thirty Gods and three
My witnesses, with Indra, be.
Let sun and moon and planets hear,
Heaven, quarters, day and night, give ear.
The mighty world, the earth outspread,
With bards of heaven and demons dread;
The ghosts that walk in midnight shade,
And household Gods, our present aid,
And every being great and small
To hear and mark the oath I call.'

When thus the archer king was bound
With treacherous arts and oaths enwound,
She to her bounteous lord subdued
By blinding love, her speech renewed:
'Remember, King, that long-past day
Of Gods' and demons' battle fray,
And how thy foe in doubtful strife

46. *Thirty gods and three*: The traditional number of the Indian gods, but there are many more gods than this. Indra is the most revered god of classical India, and a prototype for the great human hero. See p. 139, note.

Had nigh bereft thee of thy life.
Remember, it was only I
Preserved thee when about to die,
And thou for watchful love and care
Wouldst grant my first and second prayer.
Those offered boons, pledged with thee then,
I now demand, O King of men.
Of thee, O Monarch, good and just,
Whose righteous soul observes each trust,
If thou refuse thy promise sworn,
I die, despised, before the morn.
These rites in Rāma's name begun—
Transfer them, and enthrone my son.
The time is come to claim at last
That double boon of days long-past,
When Gods and demons met in fight,
And thou wouldst fain my care requite.
Now forth to Dandak's forest-drive
Thy Rāma for nine years and five,
And let him dwell a hermit there
With deerskin coat and matted hair,
Without a rival let my boy
The empire of the land enjoy,
And let mine eyes ere morning see
Thy Rāma to the forest flee.'

CANTO XII

The monarch, as Kaikeyī pressed
With cruel words her dire request,
Stood for a time absorbed in thought
While anguish in his bosom wrought.
'Does some wild dream my heart assail?
Or do my troubled senses fail?
Does some dire portent scare my view?
Or frenzy's stroke my soul subdue?'
Thus as he thought, his troubled mind
In doubt and dread no rest could find,
Distressed and trembling like a deer
Who sees the dreaded tigress near.
On the bare ground his limbs he threw,
And many a long deep sigh he drew,
Like a wild snake, with fury blind,

80. *Dandak:* here the leader of the demons of the forest. See note for Canto VIII, 27–30.

By charms within a ring confined.
Once as the monarch's fury woke
'Shame on thee!' from his bosom broke,
And then in sense-bewildering pain
He fainted on the ground again.
At length, when slowly strength returned,
He answered as his eyeballs burned
With the wild fury of his ire
Consuming her, as 'twere, with fire:
'Fell traitress, thou whose thoughts design
The utter ruin of my line,
What wrong have I or Rāma done?
Speak murderess, speak thou wicked one,
Seeks he not evermore to please
Thee with all sonlike courtesies?
By what persuasion art thou led
To bring this ruin on his head?
Ah me, that fondly unaware
I brought thee home my life to snare,
Called daughter of a king, in truth
A serpent with a venomed tooth!
What fault can I pretend to find
In Rāma praised by all mankind,
That I my darling should forsake?
No, take my life, my glory take:
Let either queen be from me torn,
But not my well-loved eldest-born.
Him but to see is highest bliss,
And death itself his face to miss.
The world may sunless stand, the grain
May thrive without the genial rain,
But if my Rama be not nigh
My spirit from its frame will fly.
Enough, thine impious plan forgo,
O thou who plottest sin and woe.
My head before thy feet, I kneel,
And pray thee some compassion feel.
O wicked dame, what can have led
Thy heart to dare a plot so dread?
Perchance thy purpose is to sound
The grace thy son with me has found;
Perchance the words that, all these days,
Thou still hast said in Rāma's praise,
Were only feigned, designed to cheer
With flatteries a father's ear.
Soon as thy grief, my Queen, I knew,

My bosom felt the anguish too.
In empty halls art thou possessed,
And subject to anothers' hest?
Now on Ikshavāku's ancient race
Falls foul disorder and disgrace,
If thou, O Queen, whose heart so long
Has loved the good should choose the wrong
Not once, O large-eyed dame, hast thou
Been guilty of offence till now,
Nor said a word to make me grieve,
Nor will I now thy sin believe.
With thee my Rāma used to hold
Like place with Bharat lofty-souled.
As thou so often, when the pair
Were children yet, wouldst fain declare.
And can thy righteous soul endure
That Rāma glorious, pious, pure,
Should to the distant wilds be sent
For fourteen years of banishment?
Yea, Rāma Bharat's self exceeds
In love to thee and sonlike deeds,
And, for deserving love of thee,
As Bharat, even so is he.
Who better than that chieftain may
Obedience, love, and honour pay,
Thy dignity with care protect,
Thy slightest word and wish respect?
Of all his countless followers none
Can breathe a word against my son;
Of many thousands not a dame
Can hint reproach or whisper blame.
All creatures feel the sweet control
Of Rāma's pure and gentle soul.
The pride of Manu's race he binds
To him the people's grateful minds,
He wins the subjects with his truth,
The poor with gifts and gentle ruth,
His teachers with his docile will,
The foemen with his archer skill.
Truth, purity, religious zeal,
The hand to give, the heart to feel.
The love that ne'er betrays a friend,
The rectitude that naught can bend,

65. *Ikshvāku:* a son of Manu (line 95), who is a son of Brahman—Rāma's ancestry goes back to the gods.

Knowledge, and meek obedience grace
My Rāma pride of Raghu's race.
Canst thou thine impious plot design
'Gainst him in whom these virtues shine,
Whose glory with the sages vies.
Peer of the Gods who rule the skies?
From him no harsh or bitter word
To pain one creature have I heard,
And how can I my son address,
For thee, with words of bitterness?
Have mercy, Queen: some pity show
To see my tears of anguish flow,
And listen to my mournful cry,
A poor old man who soon must die.
Whate'er this sea-girt land can boast
Of rich and rare from coast to coast,
To thee, my Queen, I give it all:
But O, thy deadly words recall:
O see, my suppliant hands entreat,
Again my lips are on thy feet:
Save Rāma, save my darling child,
Nor kill me with this sin defiled.'
He grovelled on the ground, and lay
To burning grief a senseless prey,
And ever and anon, assailed
By floods of woe he wept and wailed,
Striving with eager speed to gain
The margent of his sea of pain.

With fiercer words she fiercer yet
The hapless father's pleading met:
'O Monarch, if thy soul repent
The promise and thy free consent,
How wilt thou in the world maintain
Thy fame for truth unsmirched with stain?
When gathered kings with thee converse,
And bid thee all the tale rehearse,
What wilt thou say, O truthful King,
In answer to their questioning?
'She to whose love my life I owe,
Who saved me smitten by the foe,
Kaikeyī, for her tender care,
Was cheated of the oath I sware.'
Thus wilt thou answer, and forsworn
Wilt draw on thee the princes' scorn.

Learn from that tale, the Hawk and Dove,'
How strong for truth was Saivya's love.
Pledged by his word the monarch gave
His flesh the suppliant bird to save.
So King Alarka gave his eyes,
And gained a mansion in the skies.
The Sea himself his promise keeps,
And ne'er beyond his limit sweeps.
My deeds of old again recall,
Nor let thy bond dishonoured fall.
The rights of truth thou wouldst forget,
Thy Rāma on the throne to set,
And let thy days in pleasure glide,
Fond King, Kauśalyā by thy side.
Now call it by what name thou wilt,
Justice, injustice, virtue, guilt,
Thy word and oath remain the same,
And thou must yield what thus I claim.
If Rāma be anointed, I
This very day will surely die,
Before thy face will poison drink,
And lifeless at thy feet will sink.
Yea, better far to die than stay
Alive to see one single day
The crowds before Kauśalyā stand
And hail her queen with reverent hand.
Now by my son, myself, I swear,
No gift, no promise whatsoe'er
My steadfast soul shall now content,
But only Rāma's banishment.'

So far she spake by rage impelled,
And then the queen deep silence held.
He heard her speech full fraught with ill,
But spoke no word bewildered still,
Gazed on his love once held so dear
Who spoke unlovely rede to hear;
Then as he slowly pondered o'er
The queen's resolve and oath she swore,

149–154. *Learn . . . skies:* A dove being pursued by a hawk landed on King Saivya's arm, and the king offered the dove protection. The hawk, however, decided to argue about this on moral principles, pointing out that doves are meant for hawks to eat. But the king had sworn to protect the dove, and offered the hawk cows, a deer, a ram and a lamb. The hawk was adamant, and insisted that the king either give up the dove or give some of his own flesh to the hawk for food. True to his vow, the king sliced off his own flesh and offered it to the hawk, and won renown with the gods. (This story is in the *Mahābhārata* (xx, 110–118). King Alarka, like St. Teresa, gave up his eyes for spiritual insight. (See Canto XIV, 13–16).

Once sighing forth. Ah Rāma! he
Fell prone as falls a smitten tree.
His senses lost like one insane,
Faint as a sick man weak with pain,
Or like a wounded snake dismayed,
So lay the king whom earth obeyed.
Long burning sighs he slowly heaved,
As, conquered by his woe, he grieved,
And thus with tears and sobs between
His sad faint words addressed the queen:

'By whom, Kaikeyī, wast thou taught
This flattering hope with ruin fraught?
Have goblins seized thy soul, O dame,
Who thus canst speak and feel no shame.
Thy mind with sin is sicklied o'er,
From thy first youth ne'er seen before.
A good and loving wife wast thou,
But all, alas! is altered now.
What terror can have seized thy breast
To make thee frame this dire request,
That Bharat o'er the land may reign,
And Rāma in the woods remain?
Turn from thine evil ways, O turn,
And thy perfidious counsel spurn,
If thou would fain a favour do
To people, lord, and Bharat too.
O wicked traitress, fierce and vile,
Who lovest deeds of sin and guile,
What crime or grievance dost thou see,
What fault in Rāma or in me?
Thy son will ne'er the throne accept
If Rāma from his rights be kept.
For Bharat's heart more firmly yet
Than Rāma's is on justice set.
How shall I say, Go forth, and brook
Upon my Rāma's face to look,
See his pale cheek and ashy lips
Dimmed like the moon in sad eclipse?
How see the plan so well prepared
When prudent friends my counsels shared,
All ruined, like a host laid low
Beneath some foeman's murderous blow
What will these gathered princes say,
From regions near and far away?
'O'erlong endures the monarch's reign,

For now he is a child again.'
When many a good and holy sage
In Scripture versed, revered for age,
Shall ask for Rāma, what shall I
Unhappy, what shall I reply?
'By Queen Kaikeyī long distressed
I drove him forth and dispossessed.'
Although herein the truth I speak,
They all will hold me false and weak.
What will Kauśalyā say when she
Demands her son exiled by me?
Alas! what answer shall I frame,
Or how console the injured dame?
She like a slave on me attends,
And with a sister's care she blends
A mother's love, a wife's, a friend's.
In spite of all her tender care,
Her noble son, her face most fair,
Another queen I could prefer
And for thy sake neglected her.
But now, O Queen, my heart is grieved
For love and care by thee received,
E'en as the sickening wretch repents
His dainty meal and condiments.
And how will Queen Sumitrā trust
The husband whom she finds unjust,
Seeing my Rāma driven hence
Dishonoured, and for no offence?
Ah! the Videhan bride will hear
A double woe, a double fear,
Two whelming sorrows at one breath,
Her lord's disgrace, his father's death.
Mine aged bosom she will wring
And kill me with her sorrowing,
Sad as a fair nymph left to weep
Deserted on Himalaya's steep,
For short will be my days, I ween,
When I with mournful eyes have seen
My Rāma wandering forth alone
And heard dear Sītā sob and moan.
Ah me! my fond belief I rue,
Vile traitress, loved as good and true,
As one who in his thirst has quaffed,
Deceived by looks, a deadly draught.

256. *Queen Sumitrā:* another wife of Daśaratha, and Lakshmana's mother.

Ah! thou hast slain me, murderess, while
Soothing my soul with words of guile,
As the wild hunter kills the deer
Lured from the brake his song to hear.
Soon every honest tongue will fling
Reproach on the dishonest king;
The people's scorn in every street
The seller of his child will meet,
And such dishonour will be mine
As whelms a Brāhman drunk with wine,
Ah me, for my unhappy fate,
Compelled thy words to tolerate!
Such woe is sent to scourge a crime
Committed in some distant time.
For many a day with sinful care
I cherished thee, thou sin and snare,
Kept thee, unwitting, like a cord
Destined to bind its hapless lord.
Mine hours of ease I spent with thee,
Nor deemed my love my death would be.
While like a heedless child I played,
On a black snake my hand I laid.
A cry from every mouth will burst
And all the world will hold me curst,
Because I saw my high-souled son
Unkinged, unfathered, and undone:
'The king by power of love beguiled
Is weaker than a foolish child,
His own beloved son to make
An exile for a woman's sake.
By chaste and holy vows restrained,
By reverend teachers duly trained,
When he his virtue's fruit should taste
He falls by sin and woe disgraced.'
Two words will all his answer be
When I pronounce the stern decree,
'Hence, Rāma, to the woods away,'
All he will say is, I obey.
O, if he would my will withstand
When banished from his home and land,
This were a comfort in my woe;
But he will ne'er do this, I know.
My Rāma to the forest fled,
And curses thick upon my head,
Grim Death will bear me hence away,
His world-abominated prey.

When I am gone and Rāma too,
How wilt thou those I love pursue?
What vengeful sin will be designed
What vengeful sin will be designed
When thou hast slain her son and me
Kauśalyā soon will follow: she
Will sink beneath her sorrows' weight,
And die like me disconsolate.
Exult, Kaikeyī, in thy pride,
And let thy heart be gratified,
When thou my queens and me hast hurled,
And children, to the under world.
Soon wilt thou rule as empress o'er
My noble house unvext before,
But then to wild confusion left,
Of Rāma and of me bereft,
If Bharat to thy plan consent
And long for Rāma's banishment,
Ne'er let his hands presume to pay
The funeral honours to my clay.
Vile foe, thou cause of all mine ill,
Obtain at last thy cursed will.
A widow soon shalt thou enjoy
The sweets of empire and thy boy.
O Princess, sure some evil fate
First brought thee here to devastate,
In whom the night of ruin lies
Veiled in a consort's fair disguise.
The scorn of all and deepest shame
Will long pursue my hated name,
And dire disgrace on me will press,
Misled by thee to wickedness.
How shall my Rāma, whom, before,
His elephant or chariot bore,
Now with his feet, a wanderer, tread
The forest wilds around him spread?
How shall my son, to please whose taste,
The deftest cooks, with earrings graced,
With rivalry and jealous care
The dainty meal and cates prepare—
How shall he now his life sustain
With acid fruit and woodland grain?
He spends his time unvext by cares,
And robes of precious texture wears;
How shall he, with one garment round

His limbs recline upon the ground?
Whose was this plan, this cruel thought
Unheard till now, with ruin fraught,
To make thy son Ayodhyā's king,
And send my Rāma wandering?
Shame, shame on women! Vile, untrue,
Their selfish ends they still pursue.
Not all of womankind I mean,
But more than all this wicked queen.
O worthless, cruel, selfish dame,
I brought thee home, my plague and woe.
What fault in me hast thou to blame,
Or in my son who loves thee so?
Fond wives may from their husbands flee,
And fathers may their sons desert,
But all the world would rave to see
My Rāma touched with deadly hurt.
I joy his very step to hear,
As though his godlike form I viewed;
And when I see my Rāma near
I feel my youth again renewed.
There might be life without the sun,
Yea, e'en if Indra sent no rain,
But, were my Rāma banished, none
Would, so I think, alive remain.
A foe that longs my life to take,
Brought thee here my death to be,
Caressed thee long, a venomed snake,
And through my folly die, Ah me!
Rāma and me and Lakshman slay,
And then with Bharat rule the state;
So bring the kingdom to decay,
And fawn on those thy lord who hate,
Plotter of woe, for evil bred,
For such a speech why do not all
Thy teeth from out thy wicked head
Split in a thousand pieces fall?
My Rāma's words are ever kind,
He knows not how to speak in ire:
Then how canst thou presume to find
A fault in him whom all admire?
Yield to despair, go mad, or die,
Or sink within the rifted earth;
Thy fell request will I deny,
Thou shamer of thy royal birth,

Thy longer life I scarce can bear,
  Thou ruin of my home and race,
Who wouldst my heart and heartstrings tear,
  Keen as a razor, false and base.
My life is gone, why speak of joy?
  For what, without my son, were sweet?
Spare, lady, him thou canst destroy;
  I pray thee as I touch thy feet.'
He fell and wept with wild complaint,
  Heart-struck by her presumptuous speech,
But could not touch, so weak and faint,
  The cruel feet he strove to reach.

CANTO XIII

Unworthy of his mournful fate,
The mighty king, unfortunate,
Lay prostrate in unseemly guise,
As, banished from the blissful skies,
Yayāti, in his evil day,
His merit all exhausted, lay.
The queen, triumphant in the power
Won by her beauty's fatal dower,
Still terrible and unsubdued,
Her dire demand again renewed:
'Great Monarch, 'twas thy boast till now
To love the truth and keep the vow;
Then wherefore would thy lips refuse
The promised boon 'tis mine to choose?'

King Daśaratha, thus addressed,
With anger raging in his breast,
Sank for a while beneath the pain,
Then to Kaikeyī spoke again:
'Childless so long, at length I won,
With mighty toil from Heaven a son,
Rāma, the mighty-armed; and how
Shall I desert my darling now?
A scholar wise, a hero bold,
Of patient mood, with wrath controlled,
How can I bid my Rāma fly,
My darling of the lotus eye?
In heaven itself I scarce could bear,
When asking of my Rāma there,

5. *Yayāti:* King Yayāti attained heaven but was later ejected because of pride, though he subsequently regained his heavenly place. Only the highest merit wins a permanent place in heaven.

To hear the Gods his griefs declare,
And O, that death would take me hence
Before I wrong his innocence!'

As thus the monarch wept and wailed,
And maddening grief his heart assailed,
The sun had sought his resting place,
And night was closing round apace.
But yet the moon-crowned night could bring
No comfort to the wretched king.
As still he mourned with burning sighs
And fixed his gaze upon the skies:
'O Night whom starry fires adorn,
I long not for the coming morn.
Be kind and show some mercy: see,
My suppliant hands are raised to thee.
Nay, rather fly with swifter pace;
No longer would I see the face
Of Queen Kaikeyī, cruel, dread,
Who brings this woe upon mine head.'
Again with suppliant hands he tried
To move the queen, and wept and sighed:
'To me, unhappy me, inclined
To good, sweet dame, thou shouldst be kind;
Whose life is well-nigh fled, who cling
To thee for succour, me thy king.
This, only this, is all my claim:
Have mercy, O my lovely dame.
None else have I to take my part:
Have mercy: thou art good at heart.
Hear, lady, of the soft black eye.
And win a name that ne'er shall die:
Let Rāma rule this glorious land,
The gift of thine imperial hand.
O lady of the dainty waist,
With eyes and lips of beauty graced.
Please Rāma, me, each saintly priest,
Bharat, and all from chief to least.'

She heard his wild and mournful cry,
  She saw the tears his speech that broke,
Saw her good husband's reddened eye,
  But, cruel still, no word she spoke.
His eyes upon her face he bent,
  And sought for mercy, but in vain:
She claimed his darling's banishment,
  He swooned upon the ground again.

CANTO XIV

The wicked queen her speech renewed,
When rolling on the earth she viewed
Ikshavāku's son, Ayodhyā's king,
For his dear Rāma sorrowing:
'Why, by a simple promise bound,
Liest thou prostrate on the ground,
As though a grievous sin dismayed
Thy spirit? Why so sore afraid!
Keep still thy word. The righteous deem
That truth, mid duties, is supreme:
And now in truth and honour's name
I bid thee own the binding claim.
Śaivya, a king whom earth obeyed,
Once to a hawk a promise made,
Gave to the bird his flesh and bone,
And by his truth made heaven his own.
Alarka, when a Brāhmam famed
For Scripture lore his promise claimed,
Tore from his head his bleeding eyes
And unreluctant gave the prize.
His narrow bounds prescribed restrain
The Rivers' Lord, the mighty main,
Who, though his waters boil and rave,
Keeps faithful to the word he gave.
Truth all religion comprehends,
Through all the world its might extends:
In truth alone is justice placed,
On truth the words of God are based:
A life in truth unchanging past
Will bring the highest bliss at last
If thou the right would still pursue,
Be constant to thy word and true:
Let me thy promise fruitful see,
For boons, O King, proceed from thee.
Now to preserve thy righteous fame,
And yielding to my earnest claim—
Thrice I repeat it—send thy child,
Thy Rāma, to the forest wild.
But if the boon thou still deny,
Before thy face, forlorn, I die.'

Thus was the helpless monarch stung
By Queen Kaikeyī's fearless tongue,

As Bali strove in vain to loose
His limbs from Indra's fatal noose.
Dismayed in soul and pale with fear,
The monarch, like a trembling steer
Between the chariot's wheel and yoke,
Again to Queen Kaikeyī spoke,
With sad eyes fixt in vacant stare,
Gathering courage from despair:
'That hand I took, thou sinful dame,
With texts, before the sacred flame,
Thee and thy son, I scorn and hate,
And all at once repudiate.
The night is fled: the dawn is near:
Soon will the holy priests be here
To bid me for the rite prepare
That with my son the throne will share,
The preparation made to grace
My Rama in his royal place—
With this, e'en this, my darling for
My death the funeral flood shall pour.
Thou and thy son at least forbear
In offerings to my shade to share,
For by the plot thy guile has laid
His consecration will be stayed.
This very day how shall I brook
To meet each subject's altered look?
To mark each gloomy joyless brow
That was so bright and glad but now?'

While thus the high-souled monarch spoke
To the stern queen, the morning broke,
And holy night had slowly fled,
With moon and stars engarlanded.
Yet once again the cruel queen
Spoke words in answer fierce and keen,
Still on her evil purpose bent,
Wild with her rage and eloquent:
'What speech is this? Such words as these
Seem sprung from poison-sown disease.
Quick to thy noble Rāma send
And bid him on his sire attend.
When to my son the rule is given;
When Rāma to the woods is driven;
When not a rival copes with me,
From chains of duty thou art free.'

43. *Bali:* a demon slain by Indra (see p. 141, note 10).

Thus goaded, like a generous steed
Urged by sharp spurs to double speed,
'My senses are astray,' he cried,
'And duty's bonds my hands have tied.
I long to see mine eldest son,
My virtuous, my beloved one.'

And now the night had past away;
Out shone the Maker of the Day,
Bringing the planetary hour
And moment of auspicious power.
Vāśishtha, virtuous, far renowned,
Whose young disciples girt him round,
With sacred things without delay
Through the fair city took his way.
He traversed, where the people thronged.
And all for Rāma's coming longed,
The town as fair in festive show
As his who lays proud cities low.
He reached the palace where he heard
The mingled notes of many a bird,
Where crowded thick high-honoured bands
Of guards with truncheons in their hands.
Begirt by many a sage, elate,
Vāśishtha reached the royal gate,
And standing by the door he found
Sumantra, for his form renowned,
The king's illustrious charioteer
And noble counsellor and peer.
To him well skilled in every part
Of his hereditary art
Vasishtha said: 'O charioteer,
Inform the king that I am here.
Here ready by my side behold
These sacred vessels made of gold,
Which water for the rite contain
From Gangā and each distant main.
Here for installing I have brought
The seat prescribed of fig-wood wrought,
All kinds of seed and precious scent
And many a gem and ornament;
Grain, sacred grass, the garden's spoil,

97. *Vāśishtha:* a priest and advisor to King Daśaratha.

104. *who lays proud cities low:* Indra, also called Purandara ("Town Destroyer").

122. *Ganga:* the Ganges.

Honey and curds and milk and oil;
Eight radiant maids, the best of all
War elephants that feed in stall;
A four-horse car, a bow and sword,
A litter, men to bear their lord;
A white umbrella bright and fair
That with the moon may well compare;
Two chouries of the whitest hair;
A golden beaker rich and rare;
A bull high-humped and fair to view,
Girt with gold bands and white of hue;
A four-toothed steed with flowing mane,
A throne which lions carved sustain;
A tiger's skin, the sacred fire,
Fresh kindled, which the rites require;
The best musicians skilled to play,
And dancing girls in raiment gay;
Kine, Brāhmans, teachers fill the court,
And bird and beast of purest sort.
From town and village, far and near,
The noblest men are gathered here;
Here merchants with their followers crowd,
And men in joyful converse loud,
And kings from many a distant land
To view the consecration stand.
The dawn is come, the lucky day;
Go bid the monarch haste away,
That now Prince Rāma may obtain
The empire, and begin his reign.'

Soon as he heard the high behest
The driver of the chariot pressed
Within the chambers of the king,
His lord with praises honouring.
And none of all the warders checked
His entrance for their great respect
Of him well known, in place so high,
Still fain their king to gratify.
He stood beside the royal chief,
Unwitting of his deadly grief,
And with sweet words began to sing
The praises of his lord and king:
'As, when the sun begins to rise,
The sparkling sea delights our eyes,
Wake, calm with gentle soul, and thus
Give rapture, mighty King, to us.

As Mātali this self-same hour
Sang lauds of old to Indra's power,
When he the Titan hosts o'erthrew,
So hymn I thee with praises due.
The Vedas, with their kindred lore,
Brahma their soul-born Lord adore,
With all the doctrines of the wise,
And bid him, as I bid thee, rise.
As with the moon, the Lord of Day
Wakes with the splendour of his ray
Prolific Earth, who neath him lies,
So, mighty King, I bid thee rise.
With blissful words, O Lord of men,
Rise, radiant in thy form, as when
The sun ascending darts his light
From Meru's everlasting height.
May Śiva, Agui, Sun, and Moon
Bestow on thee each choicest boon,
Kuvera, Varun, Indra bless
Kakutstha's son with all success.
Awake, the holy night is fled,
The happy light abroad is spread;
Awake, O best of kings, and share
The glorious task that claims thy care.
The holy sage Vāśishtha waits,
With all his Brāhmans, at the gates.
Give thy decree, without delay,
To consecrate thy son to-day.
As armies, by no captain led,
As flocks that feed unshepherded,
Such is the fortune of a state
Without a king and desolate.'

Such were the words the bard addressed,
With weight of sage advice impressed;
And, as he heard, the hapless king
Felt deeper yet his sorrow's sting.
At length, all joy and comfort fled,
He raised his eyes with weeping-red,
And, mournful for his Rāma's sake,

174. *Matali:* Indra's charioteer.

189–193. *From . . . success:* Meru is a mountain believed to be the source of the Ganges. For Śiva, Agni, and Varuna, see pp. 235, 147, 137. Kuvera (Kubera) is a god of productivity and wealth, and immanent in kings. Kakutstha is another name for the dynasty of Rāma.

The good and glorious monarch spake:
'Why seek with idle praise to greet
The wretch for whom no praise is meet?
Thy words mine aching bosom tear,
And plunge me deeper in despair.'

Sumantra heard the sad reply,
And saw his master's tearful eye.
With reverent palm to palm applied
He drew a little space aside.
Then, as the king, with misery weak,
With vain endeavour strove to speak,
Kaikeyī, skilled in plot and plan,
To sage Sumantra thus began:
'The king, absorbed in joyful thought
For his dear son, no rest has sought:
Sleepless to him the night has past,
And now o'erwatched he sinks at last.
Then go, Sumantra, and with speed
The glorious Rāma hither lead:
Go, as I pray, nor longer wait;
No time is this to hesitate.'
  'How can I go, O Lady fair,
Unless my lord his will declare?'
  'Fain would I see him,' cried the king,
'Quick, quick, my beauteous Rāma bring.'
  Then rose the happy thought to cheer
The bosom of the charioteer,
'The king, I ween, of pious mind,
The consecration has designed.'
Sumantra for his wisdom famed,
Delighted with the thought he framed,
From the calm chamber, like a bay
Of crowded ocean, took his way.
  He turned his face to neither side,
    But forth he hurried straight;
Only a little while he eyed
The guards who kept the gate.
He saw in front a gathered crowd
  Of men of every class,
Who, parting as he came, allowed
  The charioteer to pass.

218. *Sumantra:* Rāma's charioteer.

CANTO XV

There slept the Brāhmans, deeply read
In Scripture, till the night had fled;
Then, with the royal chaplains, they
Took each his place in long array.
There gathered fast the chiefs of trade,
Nor peer nor captain long delayed,
Assembling all in order due
The consecrating rite to view.

The morning dawned with cloudless ray
On Pushya's high auspicious day,
And Cancer with benignant power
Looked down on Rāma's natal hour.
The twice-born child, with zealous heed,
Made ready what the rite would need.
The well-wrought throne of holy wood
And golden urus in order stood.
There was the royal car whereon
A tiger's skin resplendent shone;
The water, brought for sprinkling thence
Where, in their sacred confluence,
Blend Jumnā's waves with Gangā's tide,
From many a holy flood beside,
From brook and fountain far and near,
From pool and river, sea and mere.
And there were honey, curd, and oil,
Parched rice and grass, the garden's spoil,
Fresh milk, eight girls in bright attire,
An elephant with eyes of fire;
And urns of gold and silver made,
With milky branches overlaid,
All brimming from each sacred flood,
And decked with many a lotus bud.
And dancing-women fair and free,
Gay with their gems, were there to see,
Who stood in bright apparel by
With lovely brow and witching eye.
White flashed the jewelled *chouri* there,
And shone like moonbeams through the air;
The white umbrella overhead
A pale and moonlike lustre shed,

21. *Blend . . . :* The Jumna River flows into the Ganges near Allahabad in north central India.

37. *chouri:* a fly-swatter, often jewelled or otherwise decorated.

Went in pure splendour to precede,
And in such rites the pomp to lead.
There stood the charger by the side
Of the great bull of snow-white hide;
There was all music soft and loud,
And bards and minstrels swelled the crowd.
For now the monarch bade combine
Each custom of his ancient line
With every rite Ayodhyā's state
Observed, her kings to consecrate.

Then, summoned by the king's behest,
The multitudes together pressed,
And, missing still the royal sire,
Began, impatient, to inquire:
'Who to our lord will tidings bear
That all his people throng the square?
Where is the king? the sun is bright,
And all is ready for the rite.'

As thus they spoke, Sumantra, tried
In counsel, to the chiefs replied,
Gathered from lands on every side:
'To Rāma's house I swiftly drave,
For so the king his mandate gave.
Our aged lord and Rāma too
In honour high hold all of you:
I in your words (be long your days!)
Will ask him why he thus delays.'

Thus spoke the peer in Scripture read,
And to the ladies' bower he sped.
Quick through the gates Sumantra hied,
Which access ne'er to him denied.
Behind the curtained screen he drew,
Which veiled the chamber from the view.
In benediction loud he raised
His voice, and thus the monarch praised:
'Sun, Moon, Kuvera, Śiva bless
Kakutstha's son with high success!
The Lords of air, flood, fire decree
The victory, my King, to thee!
The holy night has past away,
Auspicious shines the morning's ray.
Rise, Lord of men, thy part to take
In the great rite, awake! awake!

Brāhmans and captains, chiefs of trade,
All wait in festive garb arrayed;
For thee they look with eager eyes:
O Raghu's son, awake! arise.'

To him in holy Scripture read,
Who hailed him thus, the monarch said,
Upraising from his sleep his head:
'Go, Rāma hither lead as thou
Wast ordered by the queen but now.
Come, tell me why my mandate laid
Upon thee thus is disobeyed.
Away! and Rāma hither bring;
I sleep not: make no tarrying.'

Thus gave the king command anew:
Sumantra from his lord withdrew;
With head in lowly reverence bent,
And filled with thoughts of joy, he went.
The royal street he traversed, where
Waved flag and pennon to the air,
And, as with joy the car he drove,
He let his eyes delighted rove,
On every side, where'er he came,
He heard glad words, their theme the same,
As in their joy the gathered folk
Of Rama and the throning spoke.
Then saw he Rāma's palace bright
And vast as Mount Kailāsa's height,
That glorious in its beauty showed
As Indra's own supreme abode:
With folding doors both high and wide;
With hundred porches beautified:
Where golden statues towering rose
O'er gemmed and coralled porticoes:
Bright like a cave in Meru's side,
Or clouds through Autumn's sky that ride:
Festooned with length of bloomy twine,
Flashing with pearls and jewels' shine,
While sandal-wood and aloe lent
The mingled riches of their scent;
With all the odorous sweets that fill
The breezy heights of Dardak's hill.
There by the gate the sāras screamed,
And shrill-toned peacocks' plumage gleamed.
Its floors with deftest art inlaid,

Its sculptured wolves in gold arrayed,
With its bright sheen the palace took
The mind of man and chained the look,
For like the sun and moon it glowed,
And mocked Kuvera's loved abode.
Circling the walls a crowd he viewed
Who stood in reverent attitude,
With throngs of countrymen who sought
Acceptance of the gifts they brought.
The elephant was stationed there,
Appointed Rāma's self to bear;
Adorned with pearls, his brow and cheek
Were sandal-dyed in many a streak,
While he, in stature, bulk, and pride,
With Indra's own Airāvat vied.
Sumantra, borne by coursers fleet,
Flashing a radiance o'er the street,
  To Rāma's palace flew,
And all who lined the royal road,
Or thronged the prince's rich abode,
  Rejoiced as near he drew.
And with delight his bosom swelled
As onward still his course he held
  Through many a sumptuous court
Like Indra's palace nobly made,
Where peacocks revelled in the shade,
  And beasts of silvan sort.
Through many a hall and chamber wide,
That with Kailaśa's splendour vied,
  Or mansions of the Blest,
While Rāma's friends, beloved and tried,
Before his coming stepped aside,
  Still on Sumantra pressed.
He reached the chamber door, where stood
Around his followers young and good,
Bard, minstrel, charioteer,
Well skilled the tuneful chords to sweep,
With soothing strain to lull to sleep,
  Or laud their master dear.
Then, like a dolphin darting through
Unfathomed depths of ocean's blue
  With store of jewels decked,
Through crowded halls that rock-like rose,
Or as proud hills where clouds repose,
  Sumantra sped unchecked—

142. *Airāvat:* Indra's elephant.

Halls like the glittering domes on high
Reared for the dwellers of the sky
By heavenly architect.

CANTO XVI

So through the crowded inner door
Sumantra, skilled in ancient lore,
On to the private chambers pressed
Which stood apart from all the rest.
There youthful warriors, true and bold,
Whose ears were ringed with polished gold,
All armed with trusty bows and darts,
Watched with devoted eyes and hearts.
And hoary men, a faithful train,
Whose aged hands held staves of cane,
The ladies' guard, apparellel fair
In red attire, were stationed there.
Soon as they saw Sumantra nigh,
Each longed his lord to gratify,
And from his seat beside the door
Up sprang each ancient servitor.
Then to the warders quickly cried
The skilled Sumantra, void of pride:
'Tell Rāma that the charioteer
Sumantra waits for audience here.'
The ancient men with one accord
Seeking the pleasure of their lord,
Passing with speed the chamber door
To Rāma's ear the message bore.
Forthwith the prince with duteous heed
Called in the messenger with speed,
For 'twas his sire's command, he knew,
That sent him for the interview.
Like Lord Kuvera, well arrayed,
He pressed a couch of gold,
Wherefrom a covering of brocade
Hung down in many a fold.
Oil and sandal's fragrant dust
Had tinged his body o'er
Dark as the stream the spearman's thrust
Drains from the wounded boar.
Him Sītā watched with tender care,
A *chouri* in her hand,

38. ***chouri:*** See note for Canto XV, 37.

As Chitra, ever fond in fair,
Beside the Moon will stand.
Him glorious with unborrowed light,
A liberal lord of sunlike might,
Sumantra hailed in words like these,
Well skilled in gentle courtesies,
As, with joined hands in reverence raised,
Upon the beauteous prince he gazed:
'Happy Kauśalyā! Blest is she,
The Mother of a son like thee.
Now rise, O Rāma, speed away,
Go to thy sire without delay;
For he and Queen Kaikeyī seek
And interview with thee to speak.'

The lion-lord of men, the best
Of splendid heroes, thus addressed,
To Sītā spake with joyful cheer:
'The king and queen, my lady dear,
Touching the throning, for my sake
Some salutary counsel take.
The lady of the full black eye
Would fain her husband gratify,
And, all his purpose understood,
Counsels the monarch to my good.
A happy fate is mine, I ween,
When he, consulting with his queen,
Sumantra on this charge, intent
Upon my gain and good, has sent.
An envoy of so noble sort
Well suits the splendour of the court.
The consecration rite this day
Will join me in imperial sway.
To meet the lord of earth, for so
His order bids me, I will go.
Thou, lady, here in comfort stay,
And with thy maidens rest or play.'

Thus Rāma spake. For meet reply
The lady of the large black eye
Attended to the door her lord,
And blessings on his head implored:
'The majesty and royal state

39. *Chitrā:* a star in the constellation Virgo, which gives the name to the Hindu month Chaitra.

Which holy Brāhmans venerate,
The consecration and the rite
Which sanctifies the ruler's might,
And all imperial powers should be
Thine by thy father's high decree,
As He, the world who formed and planned,
The kingship gave to Indra's hand.
Then shall mine eyes my king adore
When lustral rites and fast are o'er,
And black deer's skin and roebuck's horn
Thy lordly limbs and hand adorn.
May He whose hands the thunder wield
Be in the east thy guard and shield;
May Yama's care the south befriend,
And Varun's arm the west defend;
And let Kuvera, Lord of Gold,
The north with firm protection hold.'

Then Rāma spoke a kind farewell,
And hailed the blessings as they fell
From Sītā's gentle lips; and then,
As a young lion from his den
Descends the mountain's stony side,
So from the hall the hero hied.
First Lakshman at the door he viewed
Who stood in reverent attitude,
Then to the central court he pressed
Where watched the friends who loved him best.
To all his dear companions there
He gave kind looks and greeting fair.
On to the lofty car that glowed
Like fire the royal tiger strode.
Bright as himself its silver shone:
A tiger's skin was laid thereon.
With cloudlike thunder, as it rolled,
It flashed with gems and burnished gold,
And, like the sun's meridian blaze,
Blinded the eye that none could gaze.
Like youthful elephants, tall and strong,
Fleet coursers whirled the car along:
In such a car the Thousand-eyed
Borne by swift horses loves to ride.
So like Parjanya, when he flies

119, 121. *Thousand-eyed:* Panjanya, the rain god. See p. 143, note.

Thundering through the autumn skies,
The hero from the palace sped,
As leaves the moon some cloud o'erhead.
Still close to Rāma Lakshman kept,
Behind him to the car he leapt,
And, watching with fraternal care,
Waved the long *chouri's* silver hair,
As from the palace gate he came
Up rose the tumult of acclaim,
While loud huzza and jubilant shout
Pealed from the gathered myriads out.
Then elephants, like mountains vast,
And steeds who all their kind surpassed,
Followed their lord by hundreds, nay
By thousands, led in long array.
First marched a band of warriors trained,
With sandal dust and aloe stained;
Well armed was each with sword and bow,
And every breast with hope aglow,
And ever, as they onward went,
    Shouts from the warrior train,
And every sweet-toned instrument
    Prolonged the minstrel strain.
On passed the tamer of his foes,
While well clad dames, in crowded rows,
Each chamber lattice thronged to view,
And chaplets on the hero threw.
Then all of peerless face and limb,
Sang Rāma's praise for love of him,
And blent their voices, soft and sweet,
From palace high and crowded street:
'Now, sure, Kausalya's heart must swell
To see the son she loves so well,
Thee, Rāma, thee, her joy and pride,
Triumphant o'er the realm preside'
Then—for they knew his bride most fair
Of all who part the soft dark hair,
His love, his life, possessed the whole
Of her young hero's heart and soul:—
'Be sure the lady's fate repays
Some mighty vow of ancient days,

128. *chouri:* See note for Canto XV, 37.

162. *of ancient days:* i.e., in a former life.

For blest with Rāma's love is she
As, with the Moon's, sweet Rohini.'
Such were the witching words that came
From lips of many a peerless dame
Crowding the palace roofs to greet
The hero as he gained the street.

CANTO XVII

As Rāma, rendering blithe and gay
His loving friends, pursued his way,
He saw on either hand a press
Of mingled people numberless.
The royal street he traversed, where
Incense of aloe filled the air,
Where rose high palaces, that vied
With paly clouds, on either side;
With flowers of myriad colours graced,
And food for every varied taste,
Bright as the glowing path o'erhead
Which feet of Gods celestial tread.
Loud benedictions, sweet to hear,
From countless voices soothed his ear.
While he to each gave due salute
His place and dignity to suit:
'Be thou,' the joyful people cried,
'Be thou our guardian, lord and guide.
Throned and anointed king to-day,
Thy feet set forth upon the way
Wherein, each honoured as a God,
Thy fathers and forefathers trod.
Thy sire and his have graced the throne,
And loving care to us have shown:
Thus blest shall we and ours remain,
Yea still more blest in Rāma's reign.
No more of dainty fare we need,
And but one cherished object heed.
That we may see our prince to-day
Invested with imperial sway.'

Such were the words and pleasant speech
That Rāma heard, unmoved, from each
Of the dear friends around him spread,
As onward through the street he sped.

164. *Rohinī:* a favorite wife of the moon-god, Chandra, for whom he neglected his other wives. For this he was sentenced to regular bouts of ill-health, his cycle of wasting away and being reborn.

For none could turn his eye or thought
From the dear form his glances sought,
With fruitless ardour forward cast
Even when Raghu's son had past.
And he who saw not Rāma nigh,
Nor caught a look from Rāma's eye,
A mark for scorn and general blame,
Reproached himself in bitter shame.
For to each class his equal mind
With sympathy and love inclined
Most fully of the princely four,
So greatest love to him they bore.

His circling course the hero bent
Round shrine and altar; reverent,
Round homes of Gods, where cross-roads met,
Where many a sacred tree was set.
Near to his father's house he drew
Like Indra's beautiful to view,
And with the light his glory gave
Within the royal palace drave.
Through three broad courts, where bowmen kept
Their watch and ward, his coursers swept.
Then through the two remaining went
On foot that prince preëminent.
Through all the courts the hero passed,
And gained the ladies' bower at last;
Then through the door alone withdrew,
And left without his retinue.
When thus the monarch's noble boy
    Had gone his sire to meet,
The multitude, elate with joy,
    Stood watching in the street,
And his return with eager eyes
    Expected at the gates,
As for his darling moon to rise
    The King of Rivers waits.

CANTO XVIII

With hopeless eye and pallid mien
There sat the monarch with the queen.
His father's feet with reverence due
He clasped, and touched Kaikeyī's too.

70. *King of Rivers:* the sea, which rises and falls under the influence of the moon.

The king, with eyes still brimming o'er,
Cried Rāma! and could do no more.
His voice was choked, his eye was dim,
He could not speak or look on him.
Then sudden fear made Rāma shake
As though his foot had roused a snake,
Soon as his eyes had seen the change
So mournful, terrible, and strange.
For there, his reason well-nigh fled,
Sighing, with soul disquieted,
To torturing pangs a prey,
Dismayed, despairing, and distraught,
In a fierce whirl of wildering thought
The hapless monarch lay,
Like Ocean wave-engarlanded
Storm-driven from his tranquil bed,
The Sun-God in eclipse,
Or like a holy seer, heart-stirred
With anguish, when a lying word
Has passed his heedless lips.
The sight of his dear father, pained
With woe and misery unexplained,
Filled Rāma with unrest,
As Ocean's pulses rise and swell
When the great moon he loves so well
Shines full upon his breast.
So grieving for his father's sake,
To his own heart the hero spake:
'Why will the king my sire to-day
No kindly word of greeting say?
At other times, though wroth he be,
His eyes grow calm that look on me.
Then why does anguish wring his brow
To see his well-beloved now?'
Sick and perplexed, distraught with woe,
To Queen Kaikeyī bowing low,
While pallor o'er his bright cheek spread,
With humble reverence he said:
'What have I done, unknown, amiss
To make my father wroth like this?
Declare it, O dear Queen, and win
His pardon for my heedless sin.
Why is the sire I ever find
Filled with all love to-day unkind?
With eyes cast down and pallid cheek

This day alone he will not speak.
Or lies he prostrate neath the blow
Of fierce disease or sudden woe?
For all our bliss is dashed with pain,
And joy unmixt is hard to gain.
Does stroke of evil fortune smite
Dear Bharat charming to the sight,
Or on the brave Śatrughna fall,
Or consorts, for he loves them all?
Against his words when I rebel,
Or fail to please the monarch well,
When deeds of mine his soul offend,
That hour I pray my life may end.
How should a man to him who gave
His being and his life behave?
The sire to whom he owes his birth
Should be his deity on earth.
Hast thou, by pride and folly moved,
With bitter taunt the king reproved?
Has scorn of thine or cruel jest
To passion stirred his gentle breast?
Speak truly, Queen, that I may know
What cause has changed the monarch so.'

Thus by the high-souled prince addressed,
Of Raghu's sons the chief and best,
She cast all ruth and shame aside,
And bold with greedy words replied:
'Not wrath, O Rāma, stirs the king,
Nor misery stabs with sudden sting;
One thought that fills his soul has he,
But dares not speak for fear of thee.
Thou art so dear, his lips refrain
From words that might his darling pain.
Bur thou, as duty bids, must still
The promise of thy sire fulfil.
He who to me in days gone by
Vouchsafed a boon with honours high,
Dares now, a king, his word regret,
And caitiff-like disowns the debt.
The lord of men his promise gave
To grant the boon that I might crave,
And now a bridge would idly throw

57. *Satrughna:* See note for Canto VIII, 24.

When the dried stream has ceased to flow.
His faith the monarch must not break
In wrath, or e'en for thy dear sake.
From faith, as well the righteous know,
Our virtue and our merits flow.
Now, be they good or be they ill,
Do thou thy father's words fulfil:
Swear that his promise shall not fail,
And I will tell thee all the tale.
Yes, Rāma, when I hear that thou
Hast bound thee by thy father's vow,
Then, not till then, my lips shall speak,
Nor will he tell what boon I seek.'

He heard, and with a troubled breast
This answer to the queen addressed:
'Ah me, dear lady, canst thou deem
That words like these thy lips beseem?
I, at the bidding of my sire,
Would cast my body to the fire,
A deadly draught of poison drink,
Or in the waves of ocean sink:
If he command, it shall be done,—
My father and my king in one.
Then speak and let me know the thing
So longed for by my lord the king.
It shall be done: let this suffice;
Rāma ne'er makes a promise twice.'

He ended. To the princely youth
Who loved the right and spoke the truth,
Cruel, abominable came
The answer of the ruthless dame:
'When Gods and Titans fought of yore,
Transfixed with darts and bathed in gore
Two boons to me thy father gave
For the dear life 'twas mine to save.
Of him I claim the ancient debt,
That Bharat on the throne be set,
And thou, O Rāma, go this day
To Dandak forest far away.
Now, Rāma, if thou wilt maintain
Thy father's faith without a stain,
And thine own truth and honour clear,

130. *Dandak:* See note for Canto IX, 27–30.

Then, best of men, my bidding hear.
Do thou thy father's word obey,
Nor from the pledge he gave me stray.
Thy life in Dandak forest spend
Till nine long years and five shall end.
Upon my Bharat's princely head
Let consecrating drops be shed,
With all the royal pomp for thee
Made ready by the king's decree.
Seek Dandak forest and resign
Rites that would make the empire thine.
For twice seven years of exile wear
The coat of bark and matted hair.
Then in thy stead let Bharat reign
Lord of his royal sire's domain,
Rich in the fairest gems that shine,
Cars, elephants, and steeds, and kine.
The monarch mourns thy altered fate
And vails his brow compassionate:
Bowed down by bitter grief he lies
And dares not lift to thine his eyes.
Obey his word: be firm and brave,
And with great truth the monarch save.'
    While thus with cruel words she spoke,
      No grief the noble youth betrayed;
But forth the father's anguish broke,
    At his dear Rāma's lot dismayed.

CANTO XIX

Calm and unmoved by threatened woe
The noble conqueror of the foe
Answered the cruel words she spoke,
Nor quailed beneath the murderous stroke:
'Yea, for my father's promise sake
I to the wood my way will take,
And dwell a lonely exile there
In hermit dress with matted hair.
One thing alone I fain would learn,
Why is the king this day so stern?
Why is the scourge of foes so cold,
Nor gives me greeting as of old?
Now let not anger flush thy cheek:
Before thy face the truth I speak.
In hermit's coat with matted hair
To the wild wood will I repair.

How can I fail his will to do,
Friend, master, grateful sovereign too?
One only pang consumes my breast,
That his own lips have not expressed
His will, nor made his longings known
That Bharat should ascend the throne.
To Bharat I would yield my wife,
My realm and wealth, mine own dear life.
Unasked I fain would yield them all:
More gladly at my father's call,
More gladly when the gift may free
His honour and bring joy to thee.
Thus, lady, his sad heart release
From the sore shame, and give him peace.
But tell me, O, I pray thee, why
The lord of men, with downcast eye,
Lies prostrate thus, and one by one
Down his pale cheek the tear-drops run.
Let couriers to thy father speed
On horses of the swiftest breed,
And, by the mandate of the king,
Thy Bharat to his presence bring.
My father's words I will not stay
To question, but this very day
To Dandak's pathless wild will fare,
For twice seven years an exile there.'

When Rāma thus had made reply
Kaikeyī's heart with joy beat high.
She, trusting to the pledge she held,
The youth's departure thus impelled:
'Tis well. Be messengers despatched
On coursers ne'er for fleetness matched,
To seek my father's home and lead
My Bharat back with all their speed.
And, Rāma, as I ween that thou
Wilt scarce endure to linger now,
So surely it were wise and good
This hour to journey to the wood.
And if, with shame cast down and weak,
No word to thee the king can speak.
Forgive, and from thy mind dismiss
A trifle in an hour like this.
But till thy feet in rapid haste
Have left the city for the waste,
And to the distant forest fled,
He will not bathe nor call for bread.'

'Woe! woe!' from the sad monarch burst,
In surging floods of grief immersed;
Then swooning, with his wits astray,
Upon the gold-wrought couch he lay.
And Rāma raised the aged king:
But the stern queen, unpitying,
Checked not her heedless words, nor spared
The hero for all speed prepared,
But urged him with her bitter tongue
Like a good horse with lashes stung.
She spoke her shameful speech. Serene
He heard the fury of the queen,
And to her words so vile and dread
Gently, unmoved in mind, he said:
'I would not in this world remain
A grovelling thrall to paltry gain,
But duty's path would fain pursue,
True as the saints themselves are true.
From death itself I would not fly
My father's wish to gratify.
What deed soe'er his loving son
May do to please him, think it done.
Amid all duties, Queen, I count
This duty first and paramount,
That sons, obedient, aye fulfil
Their honoured fathers' word and will.
Without his word, if thou decree,
Forth to the forest will I flee,
And there shall fourteen years be spent
Mid lonely wilds in banishment.
Methinks thou couldst not hope to find
One spark of virtue in my mind,
If thou, whose wish is still my lord,
Hast for this grace the king implored.
This day I go, but, ere we part,
Must cheer my Sītā's tender heart,
To my dear mother bid farewell;
Then to the woods, a while to dwell.
With thee, O Queen, the care must rest
That Bharat hear his sire's behest,
And guard the land with righteous sway,
For such the law that lives for aye.'

In speechless woe the father heard,
Wept with loud cries, but spoke no word.
Then Rāma touched his senseless feet,
And hers, for honour most unmeet;

Round both his circling steps he bent,
Then from the bower the hero went.
Soon as he reached the gate he found
His dear companions gathered round.
Behind him came Sumitrā's child
With weeping eyes so sad and wild.
Then saw he all that rich array
Of vases for the glorious day.
Round them with reverent steps he paced,
Nor vailed his eye, nor moved in haste.
The loss of empire could not dim
The glory that encompassed him.
So will the Lord of Cooling Rays
On whom the world delights to gaze,
Through the great love of all retain
Sweet splendour in the time of wane.
Now to the exile's lot resigned
He left the rule of earth behind:
As though all worldly cares he spurned
No trouble was in him discerned.
The chouries that for kings are used,
And white umbrella, he refused,
Dismissed his chariot and his men,
And every friend and citizen.
He ruled his senses, nor betrayed
The grief that on his bosom weighed,
And thus his mother's mansion sought
To tell the mournful news he brought.
Nor could the gay-clad people there
Who flocked round Rāma true and fair,
One sign of altered fortune trace
Upon the splendid hero's face.
Nor had the chieftain, mighty-armed,
Lost the bright look all hearts that charmed,
As e'en from autumn moons is thrown
A splendour which is all their own.
With his sweet voice the hero spoke
Saluting all the gathered folk,
Then righteous-souled and great in fame
Close to his mother's house he came.
Lakshman the brave, his brother's peer
In princely virtues, followed near,
Sore troubled, but resolved to show

113. *Sumitrā:* i.e., Lakshmana.

121. *Lord of Cooling Rays:* the moon.

No token of his secret woe.
Thus to the palace Rāma went
  Where all were gay with hope and joy;
But well he knew the dire event
  That hope would mar, that bliss destroy.
So to his grief he would not yield
  Lest the sad change their hearts might rend,
And, the dread tiding unrevealed,
  Spared from the blow each faithful friend.

Book Six: [The Death of Rāvan]

CANTO CVI

There faint and bleeding fast, apart
Stood Rāvan raging in his heart.
Then, moved with ruth for Rāma's sake,
Agastya came and gently spake:
'Bend, Rāma, bend thy heart and ear
The everlasting truth to hear
Which all thy hopes through life will bless
And crown thine arms with full success.
The rising sun with golden rays,
Light of the worlds, adore and praise:
The universal king, the lord
By hosts of heaven and fiends adored.
He tempers all with soft control:
He is the Gods' diviner soul;
And Gods above and fiends below
And men to him their safety owe.
He Brahmā, Vishnu, Śiva, he
Each person of the glorious Three,
Is every God whose praise we tell,
The King of Heaven, the Lord of Hell:
Each God revered from times of old,
The Lord of War, the King of Gold:
Mahendra, Time and Death is he,
The Moon, the Ruler of the Sea.
He hears our praise in every form,—

2. *Rāvan:* See the headnote to the *Rāmāyana.*
4. *Agastya:* a saint who had assisted Rāma on former occasions.
20–22. *King of Heaven . . . King of Gold:* Indra is the King of Heaven, Yama the Lord of Hell, and Kārttkeya Lord of War. Kuvera (see note for Canto XIV, 189–193) is King of Wealth and Gold.
24–25. *Mahendra . . . Sea:* Mahendra is a sacred mountain in northern India. Varuna is ruler of the sea.

The manes, Gods who ride the storm,
The Ásvins, Manu, they who stand
Round Indra, and the Sādhyas' band
He is the air, and life and fire,
The universal source and sire:
He brings the seasons at his call,
Creator, light, and nurse of all.
His heavenly course he joys to run,
Maker of Day, the golden sun,
The steeds that whirl his car are seven,
The flaming steeds that flash through heaven.
Lord of the sky, the conqueror parts
The clouds of night with glistering darts.
He, master of the Vedas' lore,
Commands the clouds' collected store:
He is the rivers' surest friend;
He bids the rains, and they descend,
Stars, planets, constellations own
Their monarch of the golden throne.
Lord of twelve forms, to thee I bow,
Most glorious King of heaven art thou.
O Rāma, he who pays aright
Due worship to the Lord of Light
Shall never fall oppressed by ill,
But find a stay and comfort still.
Adore with all thy heart and mind
This God of Gods, to him resigned;
And thou his saving power shalt know
Victorious o'er thy giant foe.'

CANTO CVIII

He spoke, and vanished: Rāma raised
His eyes with reverence meet, and praised
The glorious Day-God full in view:
Then armed him for the fight anew.
Urged onward by his charioteer
The giant's foaming steeds came near,
And furious was the battle's din
Where each resolved to die or win.

26–28. *manes . . . band:* The Manes or Maruts are storm-gods; the Asvins, the constellation Castor and Pollux, the heavenly twins; Manu is the "first man," the Hindu Adam; "they who stand round Indra" are the Vasus, gods personifying natural phenomena; the Sādhyas are celestial beings who dwell between the heaven and the earth.

35. *seven:* The seven steeds probably symbalize the days of the week.

45. *twelve forms:* The twelve months of the year.

The Rakshas host and Vānar bands
Stood with their weapons in their hands,
And watched in terror and dismay
The fortune of the awful fray.
The giant chief with rage inflamed
His darts at Rāma's pennon aimed;
But when they touched the chariot made
By heavenly hands their force was stayed.
Then Rāma's breast with fury swelled;
He strained the mighty bow he held,
And straight at Rāvan's banner flew
An arrow as the string he drew—
A deadly arrow swift of flight,
Like some huge snake ablaze with light,
Whose fury none might e'er repel,—
And, split in twain, the standard fell.
At Rāma's steeds sharp arrows, hot
With flames of fire, the giant shot.
Unmoved the heavenly steeds sustained
The furious shower the warrior rained,
As though soft lotus tendrils smote
Each haughty crest and glossy coat.
Then volleyed swift by magic art,
Tree, mountain peak and spear and dart,
Trident and pike and club and mace
Flew hurtling straight at Rāma's face.
But Rāma with his steeds and car
Escaped the storm which fell afar
Where the strange missiles, as they rushed
To earth, a thousand Vānars crushed.

CANTO CIX

With wondrous power and might and skill
The giant fought with Rāma still.
Each at his foe his chariot drove,
And still for death or victory strove.
The warriors' steeds together dashed,
And pole with pole reëchoing clashed.
Then Rāma launching dart on dart
Made Rāvan's coursers swerve and start.
Nor was the lord of Lanka slow
To rain his arrows on the foe,

9. *Rāksha:* a general name for a demon. Vanar bands are forest demons, savages, or robber bands.

9. *Lankā: Ceylon,* now again called Sri Lanka.

Who showed, by fiery points assailed,
No trace of pain, nor shook nor quailed.
Dense clouds of arrows Rāma shot
With that strong arm which rested not,
And spear and mace and club and brand
Fell in dire rain from Rāvan's hand.
The storm of missiles fiercely cast
Stirred up the oceans with its blast,
And Serpent-Gods and fiends who dwell
Below were troubled by the swell.
The earth with hill and plain and brook
And grove and garden reeled and shook:
The very sun grew cold and pale,
And horror stilled the rising gale.
God and Gandharva, sage and saint
Cried out, with grief and terror faint:
O may the prince of Raghu' line
Give peace to Brāhmans and to kine,
And, rescuing the worlds, o'erthrow
The giant king our awful foe.'

Then to his deadly string the pride
Of Raghu's race a shaft applied.
Sharp as a serpent's venomed fang
Straight to its mark the arrow sprang,
And from the giant's body shred
With trenchant steel the monstrous head.
There might the triple world behold
That severed head adorned with gold.
But when all eyes were bent to view,
Swift in its stead another grew.
Again the shaft was pointed well:
Again the head divided fell;
But still as each to earth was cast
Another head succeeded fast.
A hundred, bright with fiery flame,
Fell low before the victor's aim,
Yet Rāvan by no sign betrayed
That death was near or strength decayed.
The doubtful fight he still maintained,
And on the foe his missiles rained.
In air, on earth, on plain, on hill,
With awful might he battled still;
And through the hours of night and day
The conflict knew no pause or stay.

25. *Gandharva:* holy men associated with the Gandharva area of northwest India and Afghanistan.

CANTO CX

Then Mātali to Rāma cried:
'Let other arms the day decide.
Why wilt thou strive with useless toil
And see his might thy efforts foil?
Launch at the foe thy dart whose fire
Was kindled by the Almighty Sire.'
He ceased: and Raghu's son obeyed:
Upon his string the hero laid
An arrow, like a snake that hissed,
Whose fiery flight had never missed:
The arrow Saint Agastya gave
And blessed the chieftain's life to save:
That dart the Eternal Father made
The Monarch of the Gods to aid;
By Brahmā's self on him bestowed
When forth to fight Lord Indra rode.
'Twas feathered with the rushing wind;
The glowing sun and fire combined
To the keen point their splendour lent;
The shaft, ethereal element,
By Meru's hill and Mandar, pride
Of mountains, had its weight supplied.
He laid it on the twisted cord,
He turned the point at Lanka's lord,
And swift the limb-dividing dart
Pierced the huge chest and cleft the heart,
And dead he fell upon the plain
Like Vritra by the Thunderer slain.
The Rākshas host when Rāvan fell
Sent forth a wild terrific yell,
Then turned and fled, all hope resigned,
Through Lankā's gates, nor looked behind
His voice each joyous Vānar raised,
And Rāma, conquering Rāma, praised.
Soft from celestial minstrels came
The sound of music and acclaim.
Soft, fresh, and cool, a rising breeze
Brought odours from the heavenly trees,
And ravishing the sight and smell
A wondrous rain of blossoms fell:
And voices breathed round Raghu's son:
'Champion of Gods, well done, well done.'

1. *Mātali:* Indra's charioteer.

21. *Meru's Hill:* See note for Canto XIV, 189–193.

28. *Vritra:* a demon slain by Indra, and one of his most formidable opponents.

KĀLIDĀSA

(ca. 5th Century A.D.)

Shakuntalā[1]

Shakuntalā is regarded as the major achievement of India's foremost dramatist, Kālidāsa, who probably flourished in the fifth century in Gwalior Province in north central India. For the general reader and critic, his dates are less important than they would be if we were writing about a Western dramatist of similar stature. He wrote for a sophisticated court society. He was heir to a dramatic tradition and also a tradition of dramatic theory (very elaborately expressed) which encouraged a highly formal dramatic art with no great literary revolutions to mark off eras or movements; at least there was nothing comparable to the violent fluctuations of European dramatic taste from Aeschylus to Ibsen. His audience, thoroughly instructed in this formal mode, brought to his plays the attention of the connoisseur; it was the kind of audience that Racine perhaps had occasionally and that Yeats and Pound believed to be the audience of the Nō play—an audience which appreciated all refinements in both theatrical and verbal skill because it had become accustomed to a tradition. This tradition included the codification (and perhaps fossilization) of a body of dramatic theory to which some attention must be paid if we are to appreciate *Shakuntalā* properly.

Sanskrit dramatic theory at first sight has some strikingly Aristotelian features. It stresses the elements of spectacle in drama. It assumes that the plot will be drawn from Indian legend and the scene laid in India. It provides that painful or offensive episodes—bloodshed, battles, religious rites, amorous play—are not to be depicted on the stage. It calls for unity of action in the play as a whole, and, though this is more like the Aristotelians than like Aristotle, for unity of time—a day's span—within the individual scene. (There is no objection to as much as a year between one act and the next.)

What is not Aristotelian in Sanskrit dramatic theory is, however, more important. To Aristotle the soul of a tragedy is its plot, and the successful writer of tragedy must be a good plotmaker. Sanskrit theory is that the drama is not the imitation of an action or actions, but the imitation of states of being. The Aristotelian drama can be depicted graphically as a solid line ascending as the plot develops, undergoing various fluctuations, and descending after a denouement. The Sanskrit play does not offer a linear graph of action, but a series of overlapping color

1. The full title of the play is *Shakuntalā and the Ring of Recognition* (*Abhijñānashakuntalā*).

washes depicting emotions evoked in the audience. We do not have to analyze Western drama in Aristotle's fashion, to be sure. We have experiments in modern criticism in which plays are regarded as complexes of recurring verbal patterns. Such a study as R. B. Heilman's *Magic in the Web* sees *Othello* predominantly as clusters of images, the development of the image clusters having far more aesthetic force than what has been described as the "Italian opera plot" of the play. But no Western theory has ever placed so much weight upon the audience as Sanskrit theory does. The quality of the play is held to lie in the emotional flavor or *rasa* which it evokes in the audience. The great early text of dramatic theory, the *Nātyashāstra*, recognizes eight dominant emotions under which drama may be classified: love, mirth, energy (the heroic emotion), terror, disgust, and astonishment. Moreover, each scene of the play is expected to engender in the audience some emotional flavor which will provide variety but not run counter to the dominant *rasa*, which in *Shakuntalā* is the erotic. Each phrase and each gesture in the drama establishes mood by stirring the audience to an emotional response. The highly formalized gestures are immediately decipherable by the audience as vehicles of particular states of feeling. All of this tends to minimize plot: plot is always satisfactory if it does not interfere with *rasa*.

Like the Greek, Sanskrit drama is immersed in a complex of myth and legend. Just as the Greek spectator knew at the opening lines of the *Agamemnon* that Agamemnon was to be killed by Clytemnestra and that his son Orestes would kill her in turn, so the Indian audience knows that Dushyanta was a descendant of Puru, a great king of the lunar dynasty, and that Dushyanta's son by Shakuntalā would be Bharata, for whom India is still called *Bharatavarsha*. The audience knew also that the descendants of Bharata would engage in the wars chronicled in the *Mahābhārata*, just as we know that the passion of Zeus for Leda led to the birth of Helen of Troy and the passion which started the Trojan War. We must remind ourselves, however, that whereas the Greek legends became rapidly secularized, the Hindu ones remained sacred.

Kālidāsa draws his material for *Shakuntalā* from the *Mahābhārata*. He takes a simple story, which is hardly more than a legal wrangle over the recognition of the king's child—a story with no subtlety of character or development—and makes it a tender drama of dawning love in a young girl and of the vicissitudes of a king whose conduct is irreproachable, but who is cursed. The erotic *rasa* dominates the play, but we get the entire spectrum of love from the sensual appeal of the early scenes to the dignity and purification that come to the couple through separation and trial. We would be wrong, of course, to impute to Dushyanta or Shakuntalā any romantic love in the Western sense. The girl's appeal to the king is sensual, but his conduct, from the beginning, is extremely proper. Kālidāsa skillfully keeps out of our mind's eye Dushyanta's other wives; although there is a poignant scene in which we hear of Queen Hansavati, we are not permitted to become emotionally involved with her. The *vidūshaka* or clown, after serving the purpose of emphasizing the sportsman facet of the king's personality, is dismissed early so that he will not spoil the mood of the love scenes. The other characters are as skillfully drawn, from the fierce holy man Durvāsas to the police, who seem like the police in all countries and at all times. The supernatural is held in check: it is employed only in the last scene in which the Indian theatregoer would want a celestial atmosphere for the reunion of two such faithful lovers after so arduous an ordeal.

Kālidāsa's genius manifests itself both in the dramatic and in the poetic elements of the play. Love, as we have said, is the ruling sentiment, but other emotions or flavors supplement it. The heroic sentiment appears in Act II when the hermits extol the king and in the vigor of the hunting scene in Act I. The dusk at the close of Act III is supposed to fill the audience with foreboding or even terror. The menacing of the *vidūshaka* or clown by Mātali in Act VI evokes horror. Pathos is an important supplement to the emotion of love: from Kanva's arrival in Act IV to the departure of Shakuntalā, the plight of the young mother saddens the audience. The marvelous appears both in the supernatural voyage at the end and also when the king, by chance, picks up the bracelet of recognition.

Finally, all of the play is immersed in that love of nature that characterizes both Hinduism and Buddhism. There is constant interplay between actual description of nature and the symbolic overtones attributed to it.

Shakuntalā*

Characters

KING DUSHYANTA

BHARATA, *nicknamed* ALL-TAMER, *his son*

MADHAVYA, *a clown, his companion*

HIS CHARIOTEER

RAIVATAKA, *a door-keeper*

BHADRASENA, *a general*

KARABHAKA, *a servant*

PARVATAYANA, *a chamberlain*

SOMARATA, *a chaplain*

KANVA, *hermit-father*

SHARNGARAVA, SHARADVATA, HARITA, } *his pupils*

* From *Shakuntalā* by Kalidāsā, translated by Arthur Ryder. An Everyman's Library Edition, published in the United States by E. P. Dutton & Co., Inc. Reprinted by permission of E. P. Dutton & Co., Inc., and J. M. Dent & Sons Ltd.

DURVASAS, *an irascible sage*

THE CHIEF OF POLICE
SUCHAKA, JANUKA, } *policemen*
A FISHERMAN

SHAKUNTALA, *foster-child of Kanva*
ANUSUYA, PRIYAMVADA, } *her friends*
GAUTAMI, *hermit-mother*

KASHYAPA, *father of the gods*
ADITI, *mother of the gods*
MATALI, *charioteer of heaven's king*
GALAVA, *a pupil in heaven*
MISHRAKESHI, *a heavenly nymph*

STAGE-DIRECTOR and ACTRESS (*in the prologue*), HERMITS *and* HERMIT-WOMEN, TWO COURT POETS, PALACE ATTENDANTS, INVISIBLE FAIRIES

The first four acts pass in KANVA'S *forest hermitage; acts five and six in the king's palace; act seven on a heavenly mountain. The time is perhaps seven years.*

Prologue

BENEDICTION UPON THE AUDIENCE

Eight forms has Shiva, lord of all and king:
And these are water, first created thing;
And fire, which speeds the sacrifice begun;
The priest; and time's dividers, moon and sun;
The all-embracing ether, path of sound;
The earth, wherein all seeds of life are found;
And air, the breath of life: may he draw near,
Revealed in these, and bless those gathered here.[1]

THE STAGE-DIRECTOR. Enough of this! [*Turning toward the dressing-room*] Madam, if you are ready, pray come here.

[*Enter an* ACTRESS.]

ACTRESS. Here I am, sir. What am I to do?

DIRECTOR. Our audience is very discriminating, and we are to offer them a new play, called *Shakuntala and the Ring of Recognition*, written by the famous Kalidasa. Every member of the cast must be on his mettle.

ACTRESS. Your arrangements are perfect. Nothing will go wrong.

DIRECTOR. [*Smiling*] To tell the truth, madam,

1. Most Sanskirt plays begin with an invocation to a god, a Brahman (holy man), or a king. Shiva ("The Destroyer") is one of three major Hindu gods, the others being Brahma ("The Creator") and Vishnu ("The Preserver"). Different sects within the faith and different localities tend to selest one or the other of these or some less important god for special devotion. There was a large shrine to Shiva near Ujjayini. He had eight different manifestations (*rudras*): aether conveys sound; air has for its properties sound and feeling; fire has sound, feeling and color; water has sound, feeling, color and taste; earth has all of these plus smell. Shiva is also the sun, the moon, and the priest.

Until the wise are satisfied,
  I cannot feel that skill is shown;
The best-trained mind requires support,
  And does not trust itself alone.

ACTRESS. True. What shall we do first?

DIRECTOR. First, you must sing something to please the ears of the audience.

ACTRESS. What season[2] of the year shall I sing about?

DIRECTOR. Why, sing about the pleasant summer which has just begun. For at this time of year

A mid-day plunge will temper heat;
  The breeze is rich with forest flowers;
To slumber in the shade is sweet;
  And charming are the twilight hours.

ACTRESS. [*Sings*]

The siris-blossoms fair,
  With pollen laden,
Are plucked to deck her hair
  By many a maiden,
But gently; flowers like these
Are kissed by eager bees.

DIRECTOR. Well done! The whole theatre is captivated by your song, and sits as if painted. What play shall we give them to keep their good-will?

ACTRESS. Why, you just told me we were to give a new play called *Shakuntala and the Ring.*

DIRECTOR. Thank you for reminding me. For the moment I had quite forgotten.

Your charming song had carried me away
As the deer enticed the hero of our play.

[*Exeunt.*]

Act I

THE HUNT

[*Enter, in a chariot, pursuing a deer,* KING DUSHYANTA,[3] *bow and arrow in hand; and a* CHARIOTEER.]

CHARIOTEER. [*Looking at the king and the deer*] Your Majesty,

2. Plays were acted on festival days, at lunar holidays, and at the change of seasons.

3. The end of the prologue should usher in a major character. Dushyanta, a great king of the Lunar dynasty, has as his ancestor the legendary Puru. The charioteer calls Dushyanta the "*Pināka*-Bearer," thus comparing him to the god Shiva, whose bow was called the *pināka.*

I see you hunt the spotted deer
  With shafts to end his race,
As though God Shiva should appear
  In his immortal chase.

KING. Charioteer, the deer has led us a long chase. And even now

His neck in beauty bends
As backward looks he sends
At my pursuing car
That threatens death from far.
Fear shrinks to half the body small;
See how he fears the arrow's fall!

The path he takes is strewed
With blades of grass half-chewed
From jaws wide with the stress
Of fevered weariness.
He leaps so often and so high,
He does not seem to run, but fly.

[*In surprise*] Pursue as I may, I can hardly keep him in sight.

CHARIOTEER. Your Majesty, I have been holding the horses back because the ground was rough. This checked us and gave the deer a lead. Now we are on level ground, and you will easily overtake him.

KING. Then let the reins hang loose.

CHARIOTEER. Yes, your Majesty.
[*He counterfeits rapid motion.*] Look, your Majesty!

The lines hang loose; the steeds unreined
  Dart forward with a will.
Their ears are pricked; their necks are strained;
  Their plumes lie straight and still.
They leave the rising dust behind;
They seem to float upon the wind.

KING. [*Joyfully*] See! The horses are gaining on the deer.

As onward and onward the chariot flies,
The small flashes large to my dizzy eyes.
What is cleft in twain, seems to blur and mate;
What is crooked in nature, seems to be straight.
Things at my side in an instant appear
Distant, and things in the distance, near.[4]

4. The effect depicted here is like that of a speeding train.

A VOICE BEHIND THE SCENES. O King, this deer belongs to the hermitage, and must not be killed.

CHARIOTEER. [*Listening and looking*] Your Majesty, here are two hermits, come to save the deer at the moment when your arrow was about to fall.

KING. [*Hastily*] Stop the chariot.

CHARIOTEER. Yes, your Majesty.

[*He does so. Enter a* HERMIT *with his* PUPIL.]

HERMIT. [*Lifting his hand*] O King, this deer belongs to the hermitage.

Why should his tender form expire,
As blossoms perish in the fire?
How could that gentle life endure
The deadly arrow, sharp and sure?

Restore your arrow to the quiver;
To you were weapons lent
The broken-hearted to deliver,
Not strike the innocent.

KING. [*Bowing low*] It is done.

[*He does so.*]

HERMIT. [*Joyfully*] A deed worthy of you, scion of Puru's race, and shining example of kings. May you beget a son to rule earth and heaven.[5]

KING. [*Bowing low*] I am thankful for a Brahman's blessing.

THE TWO HERMITS. O King, we are on our way to gather firewood. Here, along the bank of the Malini, you may see the hermitage of Father Kanva[6] over which Shakuntala presides, so to speak, as guardian deity. Unless other duties prevent, pray enter here and receive a welcome. Besides,

Beholding pious hermit-rites
Preserved from fearful harm,
Perceive the profit of the scars
On your protecting arm.[7]

KING. Is the hermit father there?

5. "To rule earth and heaven" is literally "wheel-turner," one who turns the wheel of domination. Dushyanta's son by Shakuntalā does become a "world ruler," (i.e., he rules from sea to sea). The hermit is a priest or Brahman.

6. a descendant of Kashyapa, whom the Hindus consider to be the father of the inferior gods, demons, man, fish, reptiles. and all animals, by his twelve wives. His hermitage is on the Malīnī River. Shakuntalā as we shall see, is not his daughter but his ward.

7. Dushyanta, a warrior king, is in the class immediately below the Brahman or priestly caste. It is the duty of the warrior class to protect hermitages, and religious shrines and persons. The scars are from the bowstring.

THE TWO HERMITS. No, he has left his daughter to welcome guests, and has just gone to Somatirtha[8], to avert an evil fate that threatens her.

KING. Well, I will see her. She shall feel my devotion, and report it to the sage.

THE TWO HERMITS. Then we will go on our way.

[*Exit* HERMIT *with* PUPIL.]

KING. Charioteer, drive on. A sight of the pious hermitage will purify us.

CHARIOTEER. Yes, your Majesty.

[*He counterfeits motion again.*]

KING. [*Looking about*] One would know, without being told, that this is the precinct of a pious grove.

CHARIOTEER. How so?

KING. Do you not see? Why, here

Are rice-grains, dropped from bills of parrot chicks
Beneath the trees; and pounding-stones where sticks
A little almond-oil;[9] and trustful deer
That do not run away as we draw near;
And river-paths that are besprinkled yet
From trickling hermit-garments, clean and wet.

Besides,

The roots of trees are washed by many a stream
That breezes ruffle; and the flowers' red gleam
Is dimmed by pious smoke; and fearless fawns
Move softly on the close-cropped forest lawns.[10]

CHARIOTEER. It is all true.

KING. [*After a little*] We must not disturb the hermitage. Stop here while I dismount.

CHARIOTEER. I am holding the reins. Dismount, your Majesty.

KING. [*Dismounts and looks at himself*] One should wear modest garments on entering a hermitage. Take these jewels and the bow.

[*He gives them to the charioteer.*] Before I return from my visit to the hermits, have the horses' backs wet down.

CHARIOTEER. Yes, your Majesty.

[*Exit.*]

KING. [*Walking and looking about*] The hermitage! Well, I will enter.

[*As he does so, he feels a throbbing in his arm.*][11]

8. a shrine in west India on the coast of Gujarat.

9. The pounding stones are used for grinding nuts. The oil is used for both lighting and ointment.

10. The grass (*kusha*) also is used to strew sacred places.

11. The throbbing of an arm or eyelid is considered a good omen if on the right side, an evil one if on the left (reversed for women). Specifically, the omen signifies union with a beautiful woman.

A tranquil spot! Why should I thrill?
  Love cannot enter there—
Yet to inevitable things
  Doors open everywhere.

A VOICE BEHIND THE SCENES. This way, girls!

KING. [*Listening*] I think I hear some one to the right of the grove. I must find out.

[*He walks and looks about.*]

Ah, here are hermit-girls, with watering-pots just big enough for them to handle. They are coming in this direction to water the young trees. They are charming!

The city maids, for all their pains,
  Seem not so sweet and good;
Our garden blossoms[12] yield to these
  Flower-children of the wood.

I will draw back into the shade and wait for them.

[*He stands, gazing toward them. Enter* SHAKUNTALA, *as described, and her* TWO FRIENDS.]

FIRST FRIEND. It seems to me, dear, that Father Kanva cares more for the hermitage trees than he does for you. You are delicate as a jasmine blossom, yet he tells you to fill the trenches about the trees.

SHAKUNTALA. Oh, it isn't Father's bidding so much. I feel like a real sister to them.

[*She waters the trees.*]

PRIYAMVADA. Shakuntala, we have watered the trees that blossom in the summer-time. Now let's sprinkle those whose flowering-time is past. That will be a better deed, because we shall not be working for a reward.

SHAKUNTALA. What a pretty idea!

[*She does so.*]

KING. [*To himself*] And this is Kanva's daughter, Shakuntala. [*In surprise*] The good Father does wrong to make her wear the hermit's dress of bark.

The sage who yokes her artless charm
  With pious pain and grief,
Would try to cut the toughest vine
  With a soft, blue lotus-leaf.

Well, I will step behind a tree and see how she acts with her friends.

[*He conceals himself.*]

12. I.e., the girls of the palace seraglio.

SHAKUNTALA. Oh, Anusuya! Priyamvada has fastened this bark dress so tight that it hurts. Please loosen it.

[ANUSUYA *does so.*]

PRIYAMVADA. [*Laughing*] You had better blame your own budding charms for that.

KING. She is quite right.

Beneath the barken dress
Upon the shoulder tied,
In maiden loveliness
Her young breast seems to hide,

As when a flower amid
The leaves by autumn tossed—
Pale, withered leaves—lies hid,
And half its grace is lost.

Yet in truth the bark dress is not an enemy to her beauty. It serves as an added ornament. For

The meanest vesture glows
On beauty that enchants:
The lotus lovelier shows
Amid dull water-plants;

The moon in added splendour
Shines for its spot of dark;
Yet more the maiden slender
Charms in her dress of bark.

SHAKUNTALA. [*Looking ahead*] Oh, girls, that mango-tree is trying to tell me something with his branches that move in the wind like fingers. I must go and see him.

[*She does so.*]

PRIYAMVADA. There, Shakuntala, stand right where you are a minute.

SHAKUNTALA. Why?

PRIYAMVADA. When I see you there, it looks as if a vine were clinging to the mango-tree.

SHAKUNTALA. I see why they call you the flatterer.

KING. But the flattery is true.

Her arms are tender shoots; her lips
Are blossoms red and warm;
Bewitching youth begins to flower
In beauty on her form.

ANUSUYA. Oh, Shakuntala! Here is the jasmine-vine that you named Light of the Grove. She has chosen the mango-tree as her husband.[13]

SHAKUNTALA. [*Approaches and looks at it, joyfully*] What a pretty pair they make. The jasmine shows her youth in her fresh flowers, and the mango-tree shows his strength in his ripening fruit.

[*She stands gazing at them.*]

PRIYAMVADA. [*Smiling*] Anusuya, do you know why Shakuntala looks so hard at the Light of the Grove?

ANUSUYA. No. Why?

PRIYAMVADA. She is thinking how the Light of the Grove has found a good tree, and hoping that she will meet a fine lover.

SHAKUNTALA. That's what you want for yourself.

[*She tips her watering-pot.*]

ANUSUYA. Look, Shakuntala! Here is the spring-creeper that Father Kanva tended with his own hands—just as he did you. You are forgetting her.

SHAKUNTALA. I'd forget myself sooner.

[*She goes to the creeper and looks at it, joyfully.*] Wonderful! Wonderful! Priyamvada, I have something pleasant to tell you.

PRIYAMVADA. What is it, dear?

SHAKUNTALA. It is out of season, but the spring-creeper is covered with buds down to the very root.

THE TWO FRIENDS. [*Running up*] Really?

SHAKUNTALA. Of course. Can't you see?

PRIYAMVADA. [*Looking at it joyfully*] And I have something pleasant to tell *you*. You are to be married soon.

SHAKUNTALA. [*Snappishly*] You know that's just what you want for yourself.

PRIYAMVADA. I'm not teasing. I really heard Father Kanva say that this flowering vine was to be a symbol of your coming happiness.

ANUSUYA. Priyamvada, that is why Shakuntala waters the spring-creeper so lovingly.

SHAKUNTALA. She is my sister. Why shouldn't I give her water?

[*She tips her watering-pot.*]

KING. May I hope that she is the hermit's daughter by a mother of a different caste? But it *must* be so.

Surely, she may become a warrior's bride;
  Else, why these longings in an honest mind?
The motions of a blameless heart decide
  Of right and wrong, when reason leaves us blind.

13. There is suggestion here of the ceremony of *svayamvara*, in which a princess was allowed to choose her own suitor from a selected group of young gentlemen.

Yet I will learn the whole truth.[14]

SHAKUNTALA. [*Excitedly*] Oh, oh! A bee has left the jasmine-vine and is flying into my face.

[*She shows herself annoyed by the bee.*]

KING. [*Ardently*]

As the bee about her flies,
Swiftly her bewitching eyes
Turn to watch his flight.
She is practising to-day
Coquetry and glances' play
Not from love, but fright.

[*Jealously*]

Eager bee, you lightly skim
O'er the eyelid's trembling rim
Toward the cheek aquiver.
Gently buzzing round her cheek,
Whispering in her ear, you seek
Secrets to deliver.

While her hands that way and this
Strike at you, you steal a kiss,
Love's all, honeymaker.
I know nothing but her name,
Not her caste, nor whence she came—
You, my rival, take her.

SHAKUNTALA. Oh, girls! Save me from this dreadful bee!

THE TWO FRIENDS. [*Smiling*] Who are we, that we should save you? Call upon Dushyanta. For pious groves are in the protection of the king.

KING. A good opportunity to present myself. Have no—

[*He checks himself. Aside*] No, they would see that I am the king. I prefer to appear as a guest.

SHAKUNTALA. He doesn't leave me alone! I am going to run away.

[*She takes a step and looks about.*] Oh, dear! Oh, dear! He is following me. Please save me.

KING. [*Hastening forward*] Ah!

A king of Puru's mighty line
Chastises shameless churls;
What insolent is he who baits
These artless hermit-girls?

14. Dushyanta, being a religious man, wants Shakuntalā only to marry her, and he cannot do this unless she is of the right caste. If she were of pure Brahman caste, as would be the case if Kanva were her father, he could not press his suit. But if she is of mixed caste, as it turns out, he will be eligible.

[*The girls are a little flurried on seeing the* KING.]

ANUSUYA. It is nothing very dreadful, sir. But our friend [*Indicating* SHAKUNTALA] was teased and frightened by a bee.

KING. [*To* SHAKUNTALA] I hope these pious days are happy ones.

[SHAKUNTALA'S *eyes drop in embarrassment.*]

ANUSUYA. Yes, now that we receive such a distinguished guest.

PRIYAMVADA. Welcome, sir. Go to the cottage, Shakuntala, and bring fruit. This water will do to wash the feet.[15]

KING. Your courteous words are enough to make me feel at home.

ANUSUYA. Then, sir, pray sit down and rest on this shady bench.

KING. You, too, are surely wearied by your pious task. Pray be seated a moment.

PRIYAMVADA. [*Aside to* SHAKUNTALA] My dear, we must be polite to our guest. Shall we sit down?

[*The three girls sit.*]

SHAKUNTALA. [*To herself*] Oh, why do I have such feelings when I see this man? They seem wrong in a hermitage.

KING. [*Looking at the girls*] It is delightful to see your friendship. For you are all young and beautiful.

PRIYAMVADA. [*Aside to* ANUSUYA] Who is he, dear? With his mystery, and his dignity, and his courtesy? He acts like a king and a gentleman.

ANUSUYA. I am curious too. I am going to ask him. [*Aloud*] Sir, you are so very courteous that I make bold to ask you something. What royal family do you adorn, sir? What country is grieving at your absence? Why does a gentleman so delicately bred submit to the weary journey into our pious grove?

SHAKUNTALA. [*Aside*] Be brave, my heart. Anusuya speaks your very thoughts.

KING. [*Aside*] Shall I tell at once who I am, or conceal it?

[*He reflects.*] This will do. [*Aloud*] I am a student of Scripture. It is my duty to see justice done in the cities of the king. And I have come to this hermitage on a tour of inspection.[16]

ANUSUYA. Then we of the hermitage have some one to take care of us.

[SHAKUNTALA *shows embarrassment.*]

THE TWO FRIENDS. [*Observing the demeanour of the pair*] [*Aside to* SHAKUNTALA] Oh, Shakuntala! If only Father were here to-day.

SHAKUNTALA. What would he do?

THE TWO FRIENDS. He would make our distinguished guest happy, if it took his most precious treasure.

15. The rites of hospitality are formalized and obligatory. Grass, flowers, fruits, and water are necessary. The water for the feet was the first important thing. There are similar rites in Homer.

16. That is, to see that nothing interferes with the rituals.

SHAKUNTALA. [*Feigning anger*] Go away! You mean something. I'll not listen to you.

KING. I too would like to ask a question about your friend.

THE TWO FRIENDS. Sir, your request is a favour to us.

KING. Father Kanva lives a lifelong hermit. Yet you say that your friend is his daughter. How can that be?

ANUSUYA. Listen, sir. There is a majestic royal sage named Kaushika——

KING. Ah, yes. The famous Kaushika.

ANUSUYA. Know, then, that he is the source of our friend's being. But Father Kanva is her real father, because he took care of her when she was abandoned.

KING. You waken my curiosity with the word "abandoned." May I hear the whole story?

ANUSUYA. Listen, sir. Many years ago, that royal sage was leading a life of stern austerities, and the gods, becoming strangely jealous, sent the nymph Menaka to disturb his devotions.

KING. Yes, the gods feel this jealousy toward the austerities of others. And then——

ANUSUYA. Then in the lovely spring-time he saw her intoxicating beauty——

[*She stops in embarrassment.*]

KING. The rest is plain. Surely, she is the daughter of the nymph.[17]

ANUSUYA. Yes.

KING. It is as it should be.

To beauty such as this
  No woman could give birth;
The quivering lightning flash
  Is not a child of earth.

[SHAKUNTALA *hangs her head in confusion.*]

KING. [*To himself*] Ah, my wishes become hopes.

PRIYAMVADA. [*Looking with a smile at* SHAKUNTALA] Sir, it seems as if you had more to say.

[SHAKUNTALA *threatens her friend with her finger.*]

KING. You are right. Your pious life interests me, and I have another question.

PRIYAMVADA. Do not hesitate. We hermit people stand ready to answer all demands.

KING. My question is this:

17. The Hindu gods sent the nymph not to test the holy man, but because excessive devotions give men compulsive power over inferior gods. Kaushika (also called Vishvāmitra) was in the Kshatriya caste, the same caste as Dushyanta. It would therefore be perfectly proper for the king to marry the child of a member of his own caste and a nymph, but he does not know yet whether she is pledged to a holy life or is already betrothed.

Does she, till marriage only, keep her vow
  As hermit-maid, that shames the ways of love?
Or must her soft eyes ever see, as now,
  Soft eyes of friendly deer in peaceful grove?

PRIYAMVADA. Sir, we are under bonds to lead a life of chastity. But it is her father's wish to give her to a suitable lover.

KING. [*Joyfully to himself*]

O heart, your wish is won!
All doubt at last is done;
The thing you feared as fire.
Is the jewel of your desire.

SHAKUNTALA. [*Pettishly*] Anusuya, I'm going.

ANUSUYA. What for?

SHAKUNTALA. I am going to tell Mother Gautami that Priyamvada is talking nonsense.

[*She rises.*]

ANUSUYA. My dear, we hermit people cannot neglect to entertain a distinguished guest, and go wandering about.

[SHAKUNTALA *starts to walk away without answering.*]

KING. [*Aside*] She is going! [*He starts up as if to detain her, then checks his desires.*] A thought is as vivid as an act, to a lover.

Though nurture, conquering nature, holds
  Me back, it seems
As had I started and returned
  In waking dreams.

PRIYAMVADA. [*Approaching* SHAKUNTALA] You dear, peevish girl! You mustn't go.

SHAKUNTALA [*Turns with a frown*] Why not?

PRIYAMVADA. You owe me the watering of two trees. You can go when you have paid your debt.[18]

[*She forces her to come back.*]

KING. It is plain that she is already wearied by watering the trees. See!

Her shoulders droop; her palms are reddened yet;
  Quick breaths are struggling in her bosom fair;
The blossom o'er her ear hangs limply wet;
  One hand restrains the loose, dishevelled hair.

I therefore remit her debt.

[*He gives* THE TWO FRIENDS *a ring. They take it, read the name engraved on it, and look at each other.*]

18. Doing humble tasks at a hermitage is a form of religious service which ideally every Hindu owes to the faith. This is Shakuntalā's "debt."

KING. Make no mistake. This is a present—from the king.

PRIYAMVADA. Then, sir, you ought not to part with it. Your word is enough to remit the debt.

ANUSUYA. Well, Shakuntala, you are set free by this kind gentleman —or rather, by the king himself. Where are you going now?

SHAKUNTALA. [*To herself*] I would never leave him if I could help myself.

PRIYAMVADA. Why don't you go now?

SHAKUNTALA. I am not *your* servant any longer. I will go when I like.

KING. [*Looking at* SHAKUNTALA. *To himself*] Does she feel toward me as I do toward her? At least, there is ground for hope.

Although she does not speak to me,
 She listens while I speak;
Her eyes turn not to see my face,
 But nothing else they seek.

A VOICE BEHIND THE SCENES. Hermits! Hermits! Prepare to defend the creatures in our pious grove. King Dushyanta is hunting in the neighbourhood.

The dust his horses' hoofs have raised,
 Red as the evening sky,
Falls like a locust-swarm on boughs
 Where hanging garments dry.

KING. [*Aside*] Alas! My soldiers are disturbing the pious grove in their search for me.

THE VOICE BEHIND THE SCENES. Hermits! Hermits! Here is an elephant who is terrifying old men, women, and children.[19]

One tusk is splintered by a cruel blow
Against a blocking tree; his gait is slow,
For countless fettering vines impede and cling;
He puts the deer to flight; some evil thing
He seems, that comes our peaceful life to mar,
Fleeing in terror from the royal car.

[*The girls listen and rise anxiously.*]

KING. I have offended sadly against the hermits. I must go back.

THE TWO FRIENDS. Your Honour, we are frightened by this alarm of the elephant. Permit us to return to the cottage.

ANUSUYA. [*To* SHAKUNTALA] Shakuntala dear, Mother Gautami will be anxious. We must hurry and find her.

SHAKUNTALA. [*Feigning lameness*] Oh, oh! I can hardly walk.

19. The elephant has been frightened into the hermitage by Dushyanta's hunting party.

KING. You must go very slowly. And I will take pains that the hermitage is not disturbed.

THE TWO FRIENDS. Your honour, we feel as if we knew you very well. Pray pardon our shortcomings as hostesses. May we ask you to seek better entertainment from us another time?

KING. You are too modest. I feel honoured by the mere sight of you.

SHAKUNTALA. Anusuya, my foot is cut on a sharp blade of grass, and my dress is caught on an amaranth twig. Wait for me while I loosen it.

[*She casts a lingering glance at the king, and goes out with her* TWO FRIENDS.]

KING. [*Sighing*] They are gone. And I must go. The sight of Shakuntala has made me dread the return to the city. I will make my men camp at a distance from the pious grove. But I cannot turn my own thoughts from Shakuntala.

It is my body leaves my love, not I;
My body moves away, but not my mind;
For back to her my struggling fancies fly
Like silken banners borne against the wind.

[*Exit.*]

Act II

THE SECRET

[*Entering the* CLOWN.]

CLOWN. [*Sighing*] Damn! Damn! Damn! I'm tired of being friends with this sporting king. "There's a deer!" he shouts, "There's a boar!" And off he chases on a summer noon through woods where shade is few and far between. We drink hot, stinking water from the mountain streams, flavoured with leaves—nasty! At odd times we get a little tepid meat to eat. And the horses and the elephants make such a noise that I can't even be comfortable at night. Then the hunters and the bird-chasers—damn 'em—wake me up bright and early. They do make an ear-splitting rumpus when they start for the woods. But even that isn't the whole misery. There's a new pimple growing on the old boil. He left us behind and went hunting a deer. And there in a hermitage they say he found—oh, dear! oh, dear! he found a hermit-girl named Shakuntala. Since then he hasn't a thought of going back to town. I lay awake all night, thinking about it. What can I do? Well, I'll see my friend when he is dressed and beautified.

[*He walks and looks about.*] Hello! Here he comes, with his bow in his hand, and his girl in his heart. He is wearing a wreath of wild flowers! I'll pretend to be all knocked out. Perhaps I can get a rest that way.

[*He stands, leaning on his staff. Enter the* KING, *as decribed.*]

KING. [*To himself*]

Although my darling is not lightly won,
  She seemed to love me, and my hopes are bright;
Though love be balked ere joy be well begun,
  A common longing is itself delight.

[*Smiling*] Thus does a lover deceive himself. He judges his love's feelings by his own desires.

Her glance was loving—but 'twas not for me;
Her step was slow—'twas grace, not coquetry;
Her speech was short—to her detaining friend.
In things like these love reads a selfish end!

CLOWN. [*Standing as before*] Well, king, I can't move my hand. I can only greet you with my voice.

KING. [*Looking and smiling*] What makes you lame?

CLOWN. Good! You hit a man in the eye, and then ask him why the tears come.

KING. I do not understand you. Speak plainly.

CLOWN. When a reed bends over like a hunchback, do you blame the reed or the river-current?

KING. The river-current, of course.

CLOWN. And you are to blame for my troubles.

KING. How so?

CLOWN. It's a fine thing for you to neglect your royal duties and such a sure job—to live in the woods! What's the good of talking? Here I am, a Brahman, and my joints are all shaken up by this eternal running after wild animals, so that I can't move. Please be good to me. Let us have a rest for just one day.

KING. [*To himself*] He says this. And I too, when I remember Kanva's daughter, have little desire for the chase. For

The bow is strung, its arrow near;
  And yet I cannot bend
That bow against the fawns who share
  Soft glances with their friend.

CLOWN. [*Observing the* KING] He means more than he says. I might as well weep in the woods.

KING. [*Smiling*] What more could I mean? I have been thinking that I ought to take my friend's advice.

CLOWN. [*Cheerfully*] Long life to you, then.

[*He unstiffens.*]

KING. Wait. Hear me out.

CLOWN. Well, sir?

KING. When you are rested, you must be my companion in another task—an easy one.

CLOWN. Crushing a few sweetmeats?

KING. I will tell you presently.

CLOWN. Pray command my leisure.

KING. Who stands without?

[*Enter the* DOOR-KEEPER.]

DOOR-KEEPER. I await your Majesty's commands.

KING. Raivataka, summon the general.

DOOR-KEEPER. Yes, your Majesty.

[*He goes out, then returns with the* GENERAL.] Follow me, sir. There is his Majesty, listening to our conversation. Draw near, sir.

GENERAL. [*Observing the* KING, *to himself*] Hunting is declared to be a sin, yet it brings nothing but good to the king. See!

He does not heed the cruel sting
Of his recoiling, twanging string;
The mid-day sun, the dripping sweat
Affect him not, nor make him fret;
His form, though sinewy and spare,
Is most symmetrically fair;
No mountain-elephant could be
More filled with vital strength than he.

[*He approaches*] Victory to your Majesty! The forest is full of deer-tracks, and beasts of prey cannot be far off. What better occupation could we have?

KING. Bhadrasena, my enthusiasm is broken. Madhavya has been preaching against hunting.

GENERAL. [*Aside to the* CLOWN] Stick to it, friend Madhavya. I will humour the king a moment. [*Aloud*] Your Majesty, he is a chattering idiot. Your Majesty may judge by his own case whether hunting is an evil. Consider:

The hunter's form grows sinewy, strong, and light;
He learns, from beasts of prey, how wrath and fright
Affect the mind; his skill he loves to measure
With moving targets. 'Tis life's chiefest pleasure.

CLOWN. [*Angrily*] Get out! Get out with your strenuous life! The king has come to his senses. But you, you son of a slave-wench, can go chasing from forest to forest, till you fall into the jaws of some old bear that is looking for a deer or a jackal.

KING. Bhadrasena, I cannot take your advice, because I am in the vicinity of a hermitage. So for to-day

The hornèd buffalo may shake
The turbid water of the lake;
Shade-seeking deer may chew the cud,
Boars trample swamp-grass in the mud;
The bow I bend in hunting, may
Enjoy a listless holiday.

GENERAL. Yes, your Majesty.

KING. Send back the archers who have gone ahead. And forbid the soldiers to vex the hermitage, or even to approach it. Remember:

There lurks a hidden fire in each
Religious hermit-bower;
Cool sun-stones[20] kindle if assailed
By any foreign power.

GENERAL. Yes, your Majesty.

CLOWN. Now will you get out with your strenuous life?

[*Exit* GENERAL.]

KING. [*To his attendants*] Lay aside your hunting dress. And you, Raivataka, return to your post of duty.

RAIVATAKA. Yes, your Majesty.

[*Exit.*]

CLOWN. You have got rid of the vermin. Now be seated on this flat stone, over which the trees spread their canopy of shade. I can't sit down till you do.

KING. Lead the way.

CLOWN. Follow me.

[*They walk about and sit down.*]

KING. Friend Madhavya, you do not know what vision is. You have not seen the fairest of all objects.

CLOWN. I see you, right in front of me.

KING. Yes, every one thinks himself beautiful. But I was speaking of Shakuntala, the ornament of the hermitage.

CLOWN. [*To himself*] I mustn't add fuel to the flame. [*Aloud*] But you can't have her because she is a hermit-girl. What is the use of seeing her?

KING. Fool!

And is it selfish longing then,
That draws our souls on high
Through eyes that have forgot to wink,
As the new moon climbs the sky?

20. Crystals. Properly shaped, they gather the rays of the sun like a lens.

Besides, Dushyanta's thoughts dwell on no forbidden object.

CLOWN. Well, tell me about her.

KING.

Sprung from a nymph of heaven
  Wanton and gay,
Who spurned the blessing given,
  Going her way;

By the stern hermit taken
  In her most need:
So fell the blossom shaken,
  Flower on a weed.

CLOWN. [*Laughing*] You are like a man who gets tired of good dates and longs for sour tamarind. All the pearls of the palace are yours, and you want this girl!

KING. My friend, you have not seen her, or you could not talk so.

CLOWN. She must be charming if she surprises *you*.

KING. Oh, my friend, she needs not many words.

She is God's vision, of pure thought
  Composed in His creative mind;
His reveries of beauty wrought
  The peerless pearl of womankind.
So plays my fancy when I see
How great is God, how lovely she.

CLOWN. How the women must hate her!

KING. This too is in my thought.

She seems a flower whose fragrance none has tasted,
  A gem uncut by workman's tool,
A branch no desecrating hands have wasted,
  Fresh honey, beautifully cool.

No man on earth deserves to taste her beauty,
  Her blameless loveliness and worth,
Unless he has fulfilled man's perfect duty—
  And is there such a one on earth?

CLOWN. Marry her quick, then, before the poor girl falls into the hands of some oily-headed hermit.

KING. She is dependent on her father, and he is not here.

CLOWN. But how does she feel toward you?

KING. My friend, hermit-girls are by their very nature timid. And yet

When I was near, she could not look at me;
  She smiled—but not to me—and half denied it;
She would not show her love for modesty,
  Yet did not try so very hard to hide it.

CLOWN. Did you want her to climb into your lap the first time she saw you?

KING. But when she went away with her friends, she almost showed that she loved me.

> When she had hardly left my side,
> "I cannot walk," the maiden cried,
> And turned her face, and feigned to free
> The dress not caught upon the tree.

CLOWN. She has given you some memories to chew on. I suppose that is why you are so in love with the pious grove.

KING. My friend, think of some pretext under which we may return to the hermitage.

CLOWN. What pretext do you need? Aren't you the king?

KING. What of that?

CLOWN. Collect the taxes on the hermits' rice.

KING. Fool! It is a very different tax which these hermits pay—one that outweighs heaps of gems.

> The wealth we take from common men,
> Wastes while we cherish;
> These share with us such holiness
> As ne'er can perish.

VOICES BEHIND THE SCENES. Ah, we have found him.

KING. [*Listening*] The voices are grave and tranquil. These must be hermits.

[*Enter the* DOOR-KEEPER.]

DOOR-KEEPER. Victory, O King. There are two hermit-youths at the gate.

KING. Bid them enter at once.

DOOR-KEEPER. Yes, your Majesty.

[*He goes out, then returns with the* YOUTHS.] Follow me.

FIRST YOUTH. [*Looking at the* KING] A majestic presence, yet it inspires confidence. Nor is this wonderful in a king who is half a saint.[21] For to him

> The splendid palace serves as hermitage;
> His royal government, courageous, sage,
> Adds daily to his merit; it is given
> To him to win applause from choirs of heaven
> Whose anthems to his glory rise and swell,
> Proclaiming him a king, and saint as well.

21. Indra and other inferior gods are forever battling with their half-brothers, the demons called Daityas (somewhat similar to the Titans of Greek mythology). They depend on the help of mortal heroes in these battles.

SECOND YOUTH. My friend, is this Dushyanta, friend of Indra?

FIRST YOUTH. It is.

SECOND YOUTH.

> Nor is it wonderful that one whose arm
> Might bolt a city gate, should keep from harm
> The whole broad earth dark-belted by the sea;
> For when the gods in heaven with demons fight,
> Dushyanta's bow and Indra's weapon bright
> Are their reliance for the victory.

THE TWO YOUTHS. [*Approaching*] Victory, O King!

KING. [*Rising*] I salute you.

THE TWO YOUTHS. All hail! [*They offer fruit.*]

KING. [*Receiving it and bowing low*] May I know the reason of your coming?

THE TWO YOUTHS. The hermits have learned that you are here, and they request——

KING. They command rather.

THE TWO YOUTHS. The powers of evil[22] disturb our pious life in the absence of the hermit-father. We therefore ask that you will remain a few nights with your charioteer to protect the hermitage.

KING. I shall be most happy to do so.

CLOWN. [*To the* KING] You rather seem to like being collared this way.

KING. Raivataka, tell my charioteer to drive up, and to bring the bow and arrows.

RAIVATAKA. Yes, your Majesty.

[*Exit.*]

THE TWO YOUTHS.

> Thou art a worthy scion of
> The kings who ruled our nation
> And found, defending those in need,
> Their truest consecration.

KING. Pray go before. And I will follow straightway.

THE TWO YOUTHS. Victory, O King!

[*Exeunt.*]

KING. Madhavya, have you no curiosity to see Shakuntala?

CLOWN. I *did* have an unending curiosity, but this talk about the powers of evil has put an end to it.

KING. Do not fear. You will be with me.

CLOWN. I'll stick close to your chariot-wheel.

[*Enter the* DOOR-KEEPER.]

22. Evil spirits called Rakshasas were believed to interfere with religious ritual. The holy men frequently needed the physical force of the warrior caste to fight off demons, and the warrior gained piety by aiding them.

DOOR-KEEPER. Your Majesty, the chariot is ready, and awaits your departure to victory. But one Karabhaka has come from the city, a messenger from the queen-mother.

KING. [*Respectfully*] Sent by my mother?

DOOR-KEEPER. Yes.

KING. Let him enter.

DOOR-KEEPER. [*Goes out and returns with* KARABHAKA] Karabhaka, here is his Majesty. You may draw near.

KARABHAKA. [*Approaching and bowing low*] Victory to your Majesty. The queen-mother sends her commands——

KING. What are her commands?

KARABHAKA. She plans to end a fasting ceremony on the fourth day from to-day. And on that occasion her dear son must not fail to wait upon her.

KING. On the one side is my duty to the hermits, on the other my mother's command. Neither may be disregarded. What is to be done?

CLOWN. [*Laughing*] Stay half-way between, like Trishanku.[23]

KING. In truth, I am perplexed.

> Two inconsistent duties sever
> My mind with cruel shock,
> As when the current of a river
> Is split upon a rock.

[*He reflects.*] My friend, the queen-mother has always felt toward you as toward a son. Do you return, tell her what duty keeps me here, and yourself perform the offices of a son.

CLOWN. You don't think I am afraid of the devils?

KING. [*Smiling*] O mighty Brahman, who could suspect it?

CLOWN. But I want to travel like a prince.

KING. I will send all the soldiers with you, for the pious grove must not be disturbed.

CLOWN. [*Strutting*] Aha! Look at the heir-apparent!

KING. [*To himself*] The fellow is a chatterbox. He might betray my longing to the ladies of the palace. Good, then! [*He takes the clown by the hand. Aloud.*] Friend Madhavya, my reverence for the hermits draws me to the hermitage. Do not think that I am really in love with the hermit-girl. Just think:

> A king, and a girl of the calm hermit-grove,
> Bred with the fawns, and a stranger to love!
> Then do not imagine a serious quest;
> The light words I uttered were spoken in jest.

23. King Trishanku in the epic *Rāmāyana* (see p. 168) was suspended between heaven and earth in a dispute between the sage Vishwamitra and the gods.

CLOWN. Oh, I understand that well enough.
[*Exeunt.*]

Act III

THE LOVE-MAKING

[*Enter a* PUPIL, *with sacred grass for the sacrifice.*]

PUPIL. [*With meditative astonishment*] How great is the power of King Dushyanta! Since his arrival our rites have been undisturbed.

He does not need to bend the bow;
  For every evil thing,
Awaiting not the arrow, flees
  From the twanging of the string

Well, I will take this sacred grass to the priests, to strew the altar.

[*He walks and looks about, then speaks to some one not visible.*] Priyamvada, for whom are you carrying this cuscus-salve and the fibrous lotus-leaves?[24]

[*He listens.*] What do you say? That Shakuntala has become seriously ill from the heat, and that these things are to relieve her suffering? Give her the best of care, Priyamvada. She is the very life of the hermit-father. And I will give Gautami the holy water for her.

[*Exit. Enter the lovelorn* KING.]

KING. [*With a meditative sigh*]

I know that stern religion's power
  Keeps guardian watch my maiden o'er;
Yet all my heart flows straight to her
  Like water to the valley-floor.

Oh, mighty Love, thine arrows are made of flowers.[25] How can they be so sharp?

[*He recalls something.*] Ah, I understand.
Shiva's devouring wrath still burns in thee,
As burns the eternal fire beneath the sea;
  Else how couldst thou, thyself long since consumed,
Kindle the fire that flames so ruthlessly?[26]

Indeed, the moon and thou inspire confidence, only to deceive the host of lovers.

24. These are medicinal materials.

25. The Hindu diety *Kāma* or God of Love is armed with a bow made of sugarcane, the string of which consists of bees. His arrows are tipped with flowers. His sacred book is the *Kāmasūtra.*

26. The God of Love was blasted into a cinder by a flash from the eyes of the god Shiva, who was angered by being reminded of his love for his wife while he was practicing austerities. His wrath is compared to the perpetual fire kindled by Urva, an ascetic, who would have destroyed the world had not Brahma banished him beneath the sea. Some undersea volcano must have been the source of this myth.

Thy shafts are blossoms; coolness streams
  From moon-rays: thus the poets sing;
But to the lovelorn, falsehood seems
  To lurk in such imagining;
The moon darts fire from frosty beams;
  Thy flowery arrows cut and sting.

And yet

If Love will trouble her
  Whose great eyes madden me,
I greet him unafraid,
  Though wounded ceaselessly.

O mighty god, wilt thou not show me mercy after such reproaches?

With tenderness unending
  I cherished thee when small,
In vain—thy bow is bending;
  On me thine arrows fall.
My care for thee to such a plight
Has brought me; and it serves me right.

I have driven off the powers of evil, and the hermits have dismissed me. Where shall I go now to rest from my weariness?

[*He sighs.*] There is no rest for me except in seeing her whom I love.

[*He looks up.*] She usually spends these hours of midday heat with her friends on the vine-wreathed banks of the Malini. I will go there.

[*He walks and looks about.*] I believe the slender maiden has just passed through this corridor of young trees. For

The stems from which she gathered flowers
  Are still unhealed;
The sap where twigs were broken off
  Is uncongealed.

[*He feels a breeze stirring.*] This is a pleasant spot, with the wind among the trees.

Limbs that love's fever seizes,
  Their fervent welcome pay
To lotus-fragrant breezes
  That bear the river-spray.

[*He studies the ground.*] Ah, Shakuntala must be in this reedy bower. For

In white sand at the door
  Fresh footprints appear,
The toe lightly outlined,
  The heel deep and clear.[27]

I will hide among the branches, and see what happens. [*He does so. Joyfully*] Ah, my eyes have found their heaven. Here is the darling of my thoughts, lying upon a flower-strewn bench of stone, and attended by her two friends. I will hear what they say to each other.

[*He stands gazing. Enter* SHAKUNTALA *with her two* FRIENDS.]

THE TWO FRIENDS. [*Fanning her*] Do you feel better, dear, when we fan you with these lotus-leaves?

SHAKUNTALA. [*Wearily*] Oh, are you fanning me, my dear girls?

[*The two* FRIENDS *look sorrowfully at each other.*]

KING. She is seriously ill. [*Doubtfully*] Is it the heat, or is it as I hope? [*Decidedly*] It *must* be so.

With salve upon her breast,
  With loosened lotus-chain,
My darling, sore oppressed,
  Is lovely in her pain.

Though love and summer heat
  May work an equal woe,
No maiden seems so sweet
  When summer lays her low.

PRIYAMVADA. [*Aside to* ANUSUYA] Anusuya, since she first saw the good king, she has been greatly troubled. I do not believe her fever has any other cause.

ANUSUYA. I suspect you are right. I am going to ask her. My dear, I must ask you something. You are in a high fever.

KING. It is too true.

Her lotus-chains that were as white
As moonbeams shining in the night,
Betray the fever's awful pain,
And fading, show a darker stain.

SHAKUNTALA. [*Half rising*] Well, say whatever you like.

ANUSUYA. Shakuntala dear, you have not told us what is going on in your mind. But I have heard old, romantic stories, and I can't help thinking that you are in a state like that of a lady in love. Please tell us what hurts you. We have to understand the disease before we can even try to cure it.

27. Shakuntalā's gait suggests large hips, considered a characteristic of great beauty in Hindu women. Dushyanta's interest is not spiritual.

KING. Anusuya expresses my own thoughts.

SHAKUNTALA. It hurts me terribly. I can't tell you all at once.

PRIYAMVADA. Anusuya is right, dear. Why do you hide your trouble? You are wasting away every day. You are nothing but a beautiful shadow.

KING. Priyamvada is right. See!

> Her cheeks grow thin; her breast and shoulders fail;
> Her waist is weary and her face is pale:
> She fades for love; oh, pitifully sweet!
> As vine-leaves wither in the scorching heat.

SHAKUNTALA. [*Sighing*] I could not tell any one else. But I shall be a burden to you.

THE TWO FRIENDS. That is why we insist on knowing, dear. Grief must be shared to be endured.

KING. To friends who share her joy and grief
> She tells what sorrow laid her here;
> She turned to look her love again
> When first I saw her—yet I fear!

SHAKUNTALA. Ever since I saw the good king who protects the pious grove——

[*She stops and fidgets.*]

THE TWO FRIENDS. Go on, dear.

SHAKUNTALA. I love him, and it makes me feel like this.

THE TWO FRIENDS. Good, good! You have found a lover worthy of your devotion. But of course, a great river always runs into the sea.

KING. [*Joyfully*] I have heard what I longed to hear.

> 'Twas love that caused the burning pain;
> 'Tis love that eases it again;
> As when, upon a sultry day,
> Rain breaks, and washes grief away.

SHAKUNTALA. Then, if you think best, make the good king take pity upon me. If not, remember that I was.

KING. Her words end all doubt.

PRIYAMVADA. [*Aside to* ANUSUYA] Anusuya, she is far gone in love and cannot endure any delay.

ANUSUYA. Priyamvada, can you think of any scheme by which we could carry out her wishes quickly and secretly?

PRIYAMVADA. We must plan about the "secretly." The "quickly" is not hard.

ANUSUYA. How so?

PRIYAMVADA. Why, the good king shows his love for her in his tender glances, and he has been wasting away, as if he were losing sleep.

KING. It is quite true.

The hot tears, flowing down my cheek
All night on my supporting arm
And on its golden bracelet, seek
To stain the gems and do them harm.

The bracelet slipping o'er the scars
Upon the wasted arm,[28] that show
My deeds in hunting and in wars,
All night is moving to and fro.

PRIYAMVADA. [*Reflecting*] Well, she must write him a love-letter. And I will hide it in a bunch of flowers and see that it gets into the king's hand as if it were a relic of the sacrifice.

ANUSUYA. It is a pretty plan, dear, and it pleases me. What does Shakuntala say?

SHAKUNTALA. I suppose I must obey orders.

PRIYAMVADA. Then compose a pretty little love-song, with a hint of yourself in it.

SHAKUNTALA. I'll try. But my heart trembles, for fear he will despise me.

KING.

Here stands the eager lover, and you pale
For fear lest he disdain a love so kind:
The seeker may find fortune, or may fail;
But how could fortune, seeking, fail to find?

And again:

The ardent lover comes, and yet you fear
Lest he disdain love's tribute, were it brought,
The hope of which has led his footsteps here—
Pearls need not seek, for they themselves are sought.

THE TWO FRIENDS. You are too modest about your own charms. Would anybody put up a parasol to keep off the soothing autumn moonlight?

SHAKUNTALA. [*Smiling*] I suppose I shall have to obey orders.
[*She meditates.*]

KING. It is only natural that I should forget to wink when I see my darling. For

28. Love has emaciated the king's strong arms so that his bracelet slips up and down.

One clinging eyebrow lifted,
  As fitting words she seeks,
Her face reveals her passion
  For me in glowing cheeks.

SHAKUNTALA. Well, I have thought out a little song. But I haven't anything to write with.

PRIYAMVADA. Here is a lotus-leaf, glossy as a parrot's breast. You can cut the letters in it with your nails.

SHAKUNTALA. Now listen, and tell me whether it makes sense.

THE TWO FRIENDS. Please.

SHAKUNTALA. [*Reads*]

I know not if I read your heart aright;
  Why, pitiless, do you distress me so?
I only know that longing day and night
  Tosses my restless body to and fro,
  That yearns for you, the source of all its woe.

KING. [*Advancing*]

Though Love torments you, slender maid,
  Yet he consumes me quite,
As daylight shuts night-blooming flowers
  And slays the moon outright.

THE TWO FRIENDS. [*Perceive the* KING *and rise joyfully*] Welcome to the wish that is fulfilled without delay.

[SHAKUNTALA *tries to rise.*]

KING. Do not try to rise, beautiful Shakuntala.

Your limbs from which the strength is fled,
That crush the blossoms of your bed
And bruise the lotus-leaves, may be
Pardoned a breach of courtesy.

SHAKUNTALA. [*Sadly to herself*] Oh, my heart, you were so impatient, and now you find no answer to make.

ANUSUYA. Your Majesty, pray do this stone bench the honour of sitting upon it.

[SHAKUNTALA *edges away.*]

KING. [*Seating himself*] Priyamvada, I trust your friend's illness is not dangerous.

PRIYAMVADA. [*Smiling*] A remedy is being applied and it will soon be better. It is plain, sir, that you and she love each other. But I love her too, and I must say something over again.

KING. Pray do not hesitate. It always causes pain to leave unsaid what one longs to say.

PRIYAMVADA. Then listen, sir.

KING. I am all attention.

PRIYAMVADA. It is the king's duty to save hermit-folk from all suffering. Is not that good Scripture?

KING. There is no text more urgent.

PRIYAMVADA. Well, our friend has been brought to this sad state by her love for you. Will you not take pity on her and save her life?

KING. We cherish the same desire. I feel it a great honour.

SHAKUNTALA. [*With a jealous smile*] Oh, don't detain the good king. He is separated from the court ladies, and he is anxious to go back to them.

KING.
Bewitching eyes that found my heart,
You surely see
It could no longer live apart,
Nor faithless be.
I bear Love's arrows as I can;
Wound not with doubt a wounded man.

ANUSUYA. But, your Majesty, we hear that kings have many favourites. You must act in such a way that our friend may not become a cause of grief to her family.

KING. What more can I say?

Though many queens divide my court,
But two support the throne;
Your friend will find a rival in
The sea-girt earth alone.

THE TWO FRIENDS. We are content.

[SHAKUNTALA *betrays her joy.*]

PRIYAMVADA. [*Aside to* ANUSUYA] Look, Anusuya! See how the dear girl's life is coming back moment by moment—just like a peahen in summer when the first rainy breezes come.

SHAKUNTALA. You must please ask the king's pardon for the rude things we said when we were talking together.

THE TWO FRIENDS. [*Smiling*] Anybody who says it was rude, may ask his pardon. Nobody else feels guilty.

SHAKUNTALA. Your Majesty, pray forgive what we said when we did not know that you were present. I am afraid that we say a great many things behind a person's back.

KING. [*Smiling*]

Your fault is pardoned if I may
Relieve my weariness
By sitting on the flower-strewn couch
Your fevered members press.

PRIYAMVADA. But that will not be enough to satisfy him.

SHAKUNTALA. [*Feigning anger*] Stop! You are a rude girl. You make fun of me when I am in this condition.

ANUSUYA. [*Looking out of the arbour*] Priyamvada, there is a little fawn, looking all about him. He has probably lost his mother and is trying to find her. I am going to help him.

PRIYAMVADA. He is a frisky little fellow. You can't catch him alone. I'll go with you.

[*They start to go.*]

SHAKUNTALA. I will not let you go and leave me alone.

THE TWO FRIENDS. [*Smiling*] You alone, when the king of the world is with you!

[*Exeunt.*]

SHAKUNTALA. Are my friends gone?

KING. [*Looking about*] Do not be anxious, beautiful Shakuntala. Have you not a humble servant here, to take the place of your friends? Then tell me:

Shall I employ the moistened lotus-leaf
To fan away your weariness and grief?
Or take your lily feet upon my knee
And rub them till you rest more easily?

SHAKUNTALA. I will not offend against those to whom I owe honour.

[*She rises weakly and starts to walk away.*]

KING. [*Detaining her*] The day is still hot, beautiful Shakuntala, and you are feverish.

Leave not the blossom-dotted couch
  To wander in the midday heat,
With lotus-petals on your breast,
  With fevered limbs and stumbling feet.

[*He lays his hand upon her.*]

SHAKUNTALA. Oh, don't! Don't! For I am not mistress of myself. Yet what can I do now? I had no one to help me but my friends.

KING. I am rebuked.

SHAKUNTALA. I was not thinking of your Majesty. I was accusing fate.

KING. Why accuse a fate that brings what you desire?

SHAKUNTALA. Why not accuse a fate that robs me of self-control and tempts me with the virtues of another?

KING. [*To himself*]

Though deeply longing, maids are coy
  And bid their wooers wait;
Though eager for united joy
  In love, they hesitate.

Love cannot torture them, nor move
 Their hearts to sudden mating;
Perhaps they even torture love
 By their procrastinating.

[SHAKUNTALA *moves away.*]

KING. Why should I not have my way?

[*He approaches and seizes her dress.*]

SHAKUNTALA. Oh, sir! Be a gentleman. There are hermits wandering about.

KING. Do not fear your family, beautiful Shakuntala. Father Kanva knows the holy law. He will not regret it.

For many a hermit maiden who
 By simple, voluntary rite[29]
Dispensed with priest and witness, yet
 Found favour in her father's sight.

[*He looks about.*] Ah, I have come into the open air.

[*He leaves* SHAKUNTALA *and retraces his steps.*]

SHAKUNTALA. [*Takes a step, then turns with an eager gesture*] O King, I cannot do as you would have me. You hardly know me after this short talk. But oh, do not forget me.

KING.

When evening comes, the shadow of the tree
 Is cast far forward, yet does not depart;
Even so, belovèd, wheresoe'er you be,
 The thought of you can never leave my heart.

SHAKUNTALA. [*Takes a few steps. To herself*] Oh, oh! When I hear him speak so, my feet will not move away. I will hide in this amaranth hedge and see how long his love lasts.

[*She hides and waits.*]

KING. Oh, my belovèd, my love for you is my whole life, yet you leave me and go away without a thought.

Your body, soft as siris-flowers,
Engages passion's utmost powers;
How comes it that your heart is hard
As stalks that siris-blossoms guard?

SHAKUNTALA. When I hear this, I have no power to go.

KING. What have I to do here, where she is not?

[*He gazes on the ground.*] Ah, I cannot go.

29. There is a Hindu form of marriage (*Gandharva*) without the usual ceremonies; it was supposed to be the form of marriage prevailing among the nymphs in heaven.

The perfumed lotus-chain
  That once was worn by her
Fetters and keeps my heart
  A hopeless prisoner.

[*He lifts it reverently.*]

SHAKUNTALA. [*Looking at her arm*] Why, I was so weak and ill that when the lotus-bracelet fell off, I did not even notice it.

KING. [*Laying the lotus-bracelet on his heart*] Ah!

Once, dear, on your sweet arm it lay,
And on my heart shall ever stay;
Though you disdain to give me joy,
I find it in a lifeless toy.

SHAKUNTALA. I cannot hold back after that. I will use the bracelet as an excuse for my coming.

[*She approaches.*]

KING. [*Seeing her. Joyfully*] The queen of my life! As soon as I complained, fate proved kind to me.

No sooner did the thirsty bird
  With parching throat complain,
Than forming clouds in heaven stirred
  And sent the streaming rain.

SHAKUNTALA. [*Standing before the* KING] When I was going away, sir, I remembered that this lotus-bracelet had fallen from my arm, and I have come back for it. My heart seemed to tell me that you had taken it. Please give it back, or you will betray me, and yourself too, to the hermits.

KING. I will restore it on one condition.

SHAKUNTALA. What condition?

KING. That I may myself place it where it belongs.

SHAKUNTALA. [*To herself*] What can I do?

[*She approaches.*]

KING. Let us sit on this stone bench.

[*They walk to the bench and sit down.*]

KING. [*Taking* SHAKUNTALA'S *hand*] Ah!

When Shiva's anger burned the tree
  Of love in quenchless fire,
Did heavenly fate preserve a shoot
  To deck my heart's desire?

SHAKUNTALA. [*Feeling his touch*] Hasten, my dear, hasten.

KING. [*Joyfully to himself*] Now I am content. She speaks as a wife to her husband. [*Aloud*] Beautiful Shakuntala, the clasp of the bracelet is not very firm. May I fasten it in another way?

SHAKUNTALA. [*Smiling*] If you like.

KING. [*Artfully delaying before he fastens it*] See, my beautiful girl!

> The lotus-chain is dazzling white
> As is the slender moon at night.
> Perhaps it was the moon on high
> That joined her horns and left the sky,
> Believing that your lovely arm
> Would, more than heaven, enhance her charm.

SHAKUNTALA. I cannot see it. The pollen from the lotus over my ear has blown into my eye.

KING. [*Smiling*] Will you permit me to blow it away?

SHAKUNTALA. I should not like to be an object of pity. But why should I not trust you?

KING. Do not have such thoughts. A new servant does not transgress orders.

SHAKUNTALA. It is this exaggerated courtesy that frightens me.

KING. [*To himself*] I shall not break the bonds of this sweet servitude.

[*He starts to raise her face to his.* SHAKUNTALA *resists a little, then is passive.*]

KING. Oh, my bewitching girl, have no fear of me.

[SHAKUNTALA *darts a glance at him, then looks down. The* KING *raises her face. Aside*]

> Her sweetly trembling lip
> With virgin invitation
> Provokes my soul to sip
> Delighted fascination.

SHAKUNTALA. You seem slow, dear, in fulfilling your promise.

KING. The lotus over your ear is so near your eye, and so like it, that I was confused.

[*He gently blows her eye.*]

SHAKUNTALA. Thank you. I can see quite well now. But I am ashamed not to make any return for your kindness.

KING. What more could I ask?

> It ought to be enough for me
> To hover round your fragrant face;
> Is not the lotus-haunting bee
> Content with perfume and with grace?

SHAKUNTALA. But what does he do if he is not content?

KING. This! This!

[*He draws her face to his.*]

A VOICE BEHIND THE SCENES. O sheldrake bride, bid your mate farewell. The night is come.[30]

SHAKUNTALA. [*Listening excitedly*] Oh, my dear, this is Mother Gautami, come to inquire about me. Please hide among the branches.

[*The* KING *conceals himself. Enter* GAUTAMI, *with a bowl in her hand.*]

GAUTAMI. Here is the holy water, my child.

[*She sees* SHAKUNTALA *and helps her to rise.*] So ill, and all alone here with the gods?

SHAKUNTALA. It was just a moment ago that Priyamvada and Anusuya went down to the river.

GAUTAMI. [*Sprinkling* SHAKUNTALA *with the holy water*] May you live long and happy, my child. Has the fever gone down?

[*She touches her.*]

SHAKUNTALA. There is a difference, mother.

GAUTAMI. The sun is setting. Come, let us go to the cottage.

SHAKUNTALA. [*Weakly rising. To herself*] Oh, my heart, you delayed when your desire came of itself. Now see what you have done.

[*She takes a step, then turns around. Aloud*] O bower that took away my pain, I bid you farewell until another blissful hour.

[*Exeunt* SHAKUNTALA *and* GAUTAMI.]

KING. [*Advancing with a sigh*] The path to happiness is strewn with obstacles.

> Her face, adorned with soft eye-lashes,
> Adorable with trembling flashes
> Of half-denial, in memory lingers;
> The sweet lips guarded by her fingers,
> The head that drooped upon her shoulder—
> Why was I not a little bolder?

Where shall I go now? Let me stay a moment in this bower where my belovèd lay.

[*He looks about.*]

> The flower-strewn bed whereon her body tossed;
> The bracelet, fallen from her arm and lost;
> The dear love-missive, in the lotus-leaf
> Cut by her nails: assuage my absent grief
> And occupy my eyes—I have no power,
> Though she is gone, to leave the reedy bower.

[*He reflects.*] Alas! I did wrong to delay when I had found my love. So now

30. The sheldrake or *chakwa* duck and its mate were supposed to be models of connubial bliss during the daytime, but, because of a curse, forced to spend their nights apart piteously crying on opposite sides of the river.

If she will grant me but one other meeting,
I'll not delay; for happiness is fleeting;
So plans my foolish, self-defeated heart;
But when she comes, I play the coward's part.

A VOICE BEHIND THE SCENES. O King!

The flames rise heavenward from the evening altar;
And round the sacrifices, blazing high,
Flesh-eating demons stalk, like red cloud-masses,
And cast colossal shadows on the sky.

KING. [*Listens. Resolutely*] Have no fear, hermits. I am here.
[*Exit.*]

Act IV

SHAKUNTALA'S DEPARTURE

SCENE I

[*Enter* THE TWO FRIENDS, *gathering flowers.*]

ANUSUYA. Priyamvada, dear Shakuntala has been properly married by the voluntary ceremony and she has a husband worthy of her. And yet I am not quite satisfied.

PRIYAMVADA. Why not?

ANUSUYA. The sacrifice is over and the good king was dismissed today by the hermits. He has gone back to the city and there he is surrounded by hundreds of court ladies. I wonder whether he will remember poor Shakuntala or not.

PRIYAMVADA. You need not be anxious about that. Such handsome men are sure to be good. But there is something else to think about. I don't know what Father will have to say when he comes back from his pilgrimage and hears about it.

ANUSUYA. I believe that he will be pleased.

PRIYAMVADA. Why?

ANUSUYA. Why not? You know he wanted to give his daughter to a lover worthy of her. If fate brings this about of itself, why shouldn't Father be happy?

PRIYAMVADA. I suppose you are right.
[*She looks at her flower-basket.*] My dear, we have gathered flowers enough for the sacrifice.

ANUSUYA. But we must make an offering to the gods that watch over Shakuntala's marriage. We had better gather more.

PRIYAMVADA. Very well.
[*They do so.*]

A VOICE BEHIND THE SCENES. Who will bid me welcome?

ANUSUYA. [*Listening*] My dear, it sounds like a guest announcing himself.

PRIYAMVADA. Well, Shakuntala is near the cottage. [*Reflecting*] Ah, but to-day her heart is far away. Come, we must do with the flowers we have.

[*They start to walk away.*]

THE VOICE. Do you dare despise a guest like me?

> Because your heart, by loving fancies blinded,
> Has scorned a guest in pious life grown old,
> Your lover shall forget you though reminded,
> Or think of you as of a story told.

[*The two girls listen and show dejection.*]

PRIYAMVADA. Oh, dear! The very thing has happened. The dear, absent-minded girl has offended some worthy man.

ANUSUYA. [*Looking ahead*] My dear, this is no ordinary somebody. It is the great sage Durvasas,[31] the irascible. See how he strides away!

PRIYAMVADA. Nothing burns like fire. Run, fall at his feet, bring him back, while I am getting water to wash his feet.

ANUSUYA. I will.

[*Exit.*]

PRIYAMVADA. [*Stumbling*] There! I stumbled in my excitement, and the flower-basket fell out of my hand.

[*She collects the scattered flowers.* ANUSUYA *returns.*]

ANUSUYA. My dear, he is anger incarnate. Who could appease him? But I softened him a little.

PRIYAMVADA. Even that is a good deal for him. Tell me about it.

ANUSUYA. When he would not turn back, I fell at his feet and prayed to him. "Holy sir," I said, "remember her former devotion and pardon this offence. Your daughter did not recognise your great and holy power to-day."

PRIYAMVADA. And then——

ANUSUYA. Then he said: "My words must be fulfilled. But the curse shall be lifted when her lover sees a gem which he has given her for a token." And so he vanished.

PRIYAMVADA. We can breathe again. When the good king went away, he put a ring, engraved with his own name, on Shakuntala's finger to remember him by. That will save her.

ANUSUYA. Come, we must finish the sacrifice for her.

[*They walk about.*]

PRIYAMVADA. [*Gazing*] Just look, Anusuya! There is the dear girl, with her cheek resting on her left hand. She looks like a painted picture. She is thinking about him. How could she notice a guest when she has forgotten herself?

ANUSUYA. Priyamvada, we two must keep this thing to ourselves. We

31. The sage Durvasas had a reputation for fierce anger and for enacting severe penalties from those who offended him. On one occasion he cursed the god Indra because an elephant let fall a garland he had offered as a sacrifice. His punishment of Shakuntalā is obviously excessive for her unthinking, girlish offence.

must be careful of the dear girl. You know how delicate she is.

PRIYAMVADA. Would any one sprinkle a jasmine-vine with scalding water?

[*Exeunt.*]

SCENE II.—*Early Morning*

[*Enter a* PUPIL *of* KANVA, *just risen from sleep.*]

PUPIL. Father Kanva has returned from his pilgrimage, and has bidden me find out what time it is. I will go into the open air and see how much of the night remains.

[*He walks and looks about.*] See! The dawn is breaking. For already

The moon behind the western mount is sinking;
 The eastern sun is heralded by dawn;
From heaven's twin lights, their fall and glory linking,
 Brave lessons of submission may be drawn.

And again:

Night-blooming lilies, when the moon is hidden,
 Have naught but memories of beauty left.
Hard, hard to bear! Her lot whom heaven has bidden
 To live alone, of love and lover reft.

And again:

On jujube-trees the blushing dewdrops falter;
 The peacock wakes and leaves the cottage thatch;
A deer is rising near the hoof-marked altar,
 And stretching, stands, the day's new life to catch.

And yet again:

The moon that topped the loftiest mountain ranges,
 That slew the darkness in the midmost sky,
Is fallen from heaven, and all her glory changes:
 So high to rise, so low at last to lie!

ANUSUYA. [*Entering hurriedly. To herself*] That is just what happens to the innocent. Shakuntala has been treated shamefully by the king.

PUPIL. I will tell Father Kanva that the hour of morning sacrifice is come.

[*Exit.*]

ANUSUYA. The dawn is breaking. I am awake bright and early. But what shall I do now that I am awake? My hands refuse to attend to the ordinary morning tasks. Well, let love take its course. For the dear, pure-minded girl trusted him—the traitor! Perhaps it is not the good king's fault. It must be the curse of Durvasas.

Otherwise, how could the good king say such beautiful things, and then let all this time pass without even sending a message? [*She reflects.*] Yes, we must send him the ring he left as a token. But whom shall we ask to take it? The hermits are unsympathetic because they have never suffered. It seemed as if her friends were to blame and so, try as we might, we could not tell Father Kanva that Shakuntala was married to Dushyanta and was expecting a baby. Oh, what shall we do?

[*Enter* PRIYAMVADA.]

PRIYAMVADA. Hurry, Anusuya, hurry! We are getting Shakuntala ready for her journey.

ANUSUYA. [*Astonished*] What do you mean, my dear?

PRIYAMVADA. Listen. I just went to Shakuntala, to ask if she had slept well.

ANUSUYA. And then——

PRIYAMVADA. I found her hiding her face for shame, and Father Kanva was embracing her and encouraging her. "My child," he said, "I bring you joy. The offering fell straight in the sacred fire, and auspicious smoke rose toward the sacrificer. My pains for you have proved like instruction given to a good student; they have brought me no regret. This very day I shall give you an escort of hermits and send you to your husband."

ANUSUYA. But, my dear, who told Father Kanva about it?

PRIYAMVADA. A voice from heaven that recited a verse when he had entered the fire-sanctuary.

ANUSUYA. [*Astonished*] What did it say?

PRIYAMVADA. Listen. [*Speaking in good Sanskrit*]

Know, Brahman, that your child,
  Like the fire-pregnant[32] tree,
Bears kingly seed that shall be born
  For earth's prosperity.

ANUSUYA. [*Hugging* PRIYAMVADA] I am so glad, dear. But my joy is half sorrow when I think that Shakuntala is going to be taken away this very day.

PRIYAMVADA. We must hide our sorrow as best we can. The poor girl must be made happy to-day.

ANUSUYA. Well, here is a cocoa-nut casket, hanging on a branch of the mango-tree. I put flower-pollen in it for this very purpose. It keeps fresh, you know. Now you wrap it in a lotus-leaf, and I will get yellow pigment and earth from a sacred spot and blades of panic grass for the happy ceremony.

[PRIYAMVADA *does so. Exit* ANUSUYA.]

32. The goddess Pārvatī, under the influence of love, rested on the trunk of a tree. A sympathetic warmth developed in the wood and the tree thereafter burst into sacred flame if touched.

A VOICE BEHIND THE SCENES. Gautami, bid the worthy Sharngarava and Sharadvata make ready to escort my daughter Shakuntala.

PRIYAMVADA. [*Listening*] Hurry, Anusuya, hurry! They are calling the hermits who are going to Hastinapura.[33]

[*Enter* ANUSUYA, *with materials for the ceremony.*]

ANUSUYA. Come, dear, let us go.

[*They walk about.*]

PRIYAMVADA. [*Looking ahead*] There is Shakuntala. She took the ceremonial bath at sunrise, and now the hermit-women are giving her rice-cakes and wishing her happiness. Let's go to her.

[*They do so. Enter* SHAKUNTALA *with* ATTENDANTS *as described, and* GAUTAMI.]

SHAKUNTALA. Holy women, I salute you.

GAUTAMI. My child, may you receive the happy title "queen," showing that your husband honours you.

HERMIT-WOMEN. My dear, may you become the mother of a hero.

[*Exeunt all but* GAUTAMI.]

THE TWO FRIENDS. [*Approaching*] Did you have a good bath, dear?

SHAKUNTALA. Good morning, girls. Sit here.

THE TWO FRIENDS. [*Seating themselves*] Now stand straight, while we go through the happy ceremony.

SHAKUNTALA. It has happened often enough, but I ought to be very grateful to-day. Shall I ever be adorned by my friends again?

[*She weeps.*]

THE TWO FRIENDS. You ought not to weep, dear, at this happy time.

[*They wipe the tears away and adorn her.*]

PRIYAMVADA. You are so beautiful, you ought to have the finest gems. It seems like an insult to give you these hermitage things.

[*Enter* HARITA, *a hermit-youth, with ornaments.*]

HARITA. Here are ornaments for our lady.

[*The women look at them in astonishment.*]

GAUTAMI. Harita, my son, whence come these things?

HARITA. From the holy power of Father Kanva.

GAUTAMI. A creation of his mind?

HARITA. Not quite. Listen. Father Kanva sent us to gather blossoms from the trees for Shakuntala, and then

> One tree bore fruit, a silken marriage dress
> That shamed the moon in its white loveliness;
> Another gave us lac-dye for the feet;[34]
> From others, fairy hands extended, sweet
> Like flowering twigs, as far as to the wrist,
> And gave us gems, to adorn her as we list.

33. Dushyanta's capital, about fifty miles east of modern Delhi on the Ganges in north central India.

34. Hindu women dyed the soles of their feet with red coloring obtained from the bodies of the tiny cochineal insect.

PRIYAMVADA. [*Looking at* SHAKUNTALA] A bee may be born in a hole in a tree, but she likes the honey of the lotus.

GAUTAMI. This gracious favour is a token of the queenly happiness which you are to enjoy in your husband's palace.

[SHAKUNTALA *shows embarrassment.*]

HARITA. Father Kanva has gone to the bank of the Malini, to perform his ablutions. I will tell him of the favour shown us by the trees.

[*Exit.*]

ANUSUYA. My dear, we poor girls never saw such ornaments. How shall we adorn you?

[*She stops to think, and to look at the ornaments.*] But we have seen pictures. Perhaps we can arrange them right.

SHAKUNTALA. I know how clever you are.

[THE TWO FRIENDS *adorn her. Enter* KANVA, *returning after his ablutions.*]

KANVA

Shakuntala must go to-day;
I miss her now at heart;
I dare not speak a loving word
Or choking tears will start.

My eyes are dim with anxious thought;
Love strikes me to the life:
And yet I strove for pious peace—
I have no child, no wife.

What must a father feel, when come
The pangs of parting from his child at home?

[*He walks about.*]

THE TWO FRIENDS. There, Shakuntala, we have arranged your ornaments. Now put on this beautiful silk dress.

[SHAKUNTALA *rises and does so.*]

GAUTAMI. My child, here is your father. The eyes with which he seems to embrace you are overflowing with tears of joy. You must greet him properly.

[SHAKUNTALA *makes a shamefaced reverence.*]

KANVA. My child,

Like Sharmishtha, Yayati's wife,
Win favour measured by your worth;
And may you bear a kingly son
Like Puru, who shall rule the earth.[35]

35. Sharmishtha was the mother of Puru, Dushyanta's great ancestor. Her lineage, like Shakuntalā's, was partly supernatural, her father being King of the Demons. Her husband, Yayāti, was a prince of the Lunar dynasty. The son of Dushyanta and Shakuntalā is destined to be the greatest hero of India.

GAUTAMI. My child, this is not a prayer, but a benediction.

KANVA. My daughter, walk from left to right about the fires in which the offering has just been thrown.

[*All walk about.*]

The holy fires around the altar kindle,
And at their margins sacred grass is piled;
Beneath their sacrificial odours dwindle
Misfortunes. May the fires protect you, child!

[SHAKUNTALA *walks about them from left to right.*]

KANVA. Now you may start, my daughter.

[*He glances about.*] Where are Sharngarava and Sharadvata?

[*Enter* THE TWO PUPILS.]

THE TWO PUPILS. We are here, Father.

KANVA. Sharngarava, my son, lead the way for your sister.

SHARNGARAVA. Follow me.

[*They all walk about.*]

KANVA. O trees of the pious grove, in which the fairies dwell,

She would not drink till she had wet
Your roots, a sister's duty,
Nor pluck your flowers; she loves you yet
Far more than selfish beauty.

'Twas festival in her pure life
When budding blossoms showed;
And now she leaves you as a wife—
Oh, speed her on her road!

SHARNGARAVA. [*Listening to the songs of koïl-birds*][36] Father,

The trees are answering your prayer
In cooing cuckoo-song,
Bidding Shakuntala farewell,
Their sister for so long.

INVISIBLE BEINGS.

May lily-dotted lakes delight your eye;
May shade-trees bid the heat of noonday cease;
May soft winds blow the lotus-pollen nigh;
May all your path be pleasantness and peace.

[*All listen in astonishment.*]

GAUTAMI. My child, the fairies of the pious grove bid you farewell. For they love the household. Pay reverence to the holy ones.

SHAKUNTALA. [*Does so. Aside to* PRIYAMVADA] Priyamvada, I long to

36. The Indian cuckoo, called poetically the "Messenger of Spring." It is as much a favorite in Indian poetry as the nightingale is in the West.

see my husband, and yet my feet will hardly move. It is hard, hard to leave the hermitage.

PRIYAMVADA. You are not the only one to feel sad at this farewell. See how the whole grove feels at parting from you.

> The grass drops from the feeding doe;
> The peahen stops her dance;
> Pale, trembling leaves are falling slow,
> The tears of clinging plants.

SHAKUNTALA. [*Recalling something*] Father, I must say good-bye to the spring-creeper, my sister among the vines.

KANVA. I know your love for her. See! Here she is at your right hand.

SHAKUNTALA. [*Approaches the vine and embraces it*] Vine sister, embrace me too with your arms, these branches. I shall be far away from you after to-day. Father, you must care for her as you did for me.

KANVA.

> My child, you found the lover who
> Had long been sought by me;
> No longer need I watch for you;
> I'll give the vine a lover true,
> This handsome mango-tree.

And now start on your journey.

SHAKUNTALA. [*Going to* THE TWO FRIENDS] Dear girls, I leave her in your care too.

THE TWO FRIENDS. But who will care for poor us?

[*They shed tears.*]

KANVA. Anusuya! Priyamvada! Do not weep. It is you who should cheer Shakuntala.

[*All walk about.*]

SHAKUNTALA. Father, there is the pregnant doe, wandering about near the cottage. When she becomes a happy mother, you must send some one to bring me the good news. Do not forget.

KANVA. I shall not forget, my child.

SHAKUNTALA. [*Stumbling*] Oh, oh! Who is that keeps pulling at my dress, as if to hinder me?

[*She turns round to see.*]

KANVA.

> It is the fawn whose lip, when torn
> By kusha-grass, you soothed with oil;
> The fawn who gladly nibbled corn
> Held in your hand; with loving toil
> You have adopted him, and he
> Would never leave you willingly.

SHAKUNTALA. My dear, why should you follow me when I am going away from home? Your mother died when you were born and I brought you up. Now I am leaving you, and Father Kanva will take care of you. Go back, dear! Go back!

[*She walks away, weeping.*]

KANVA. Do not weep, my child. Be brave. Look at the path before you.

> Be brave, and check the rising tears
> That dim your lovely eyes;
> Your feet are stumbling on the path
> That so uneven lies.

SHARNGARAVA. Holy Father, the Scripture declares that one should accompany a departing loved one only to the first water. Pray give us your commands on the bank of this pond, and then return.

KANVA. Then let us rest in the shade of this fig-tree.

[*All do so.*] What commands would it be fitting for me to lay on King Dushyanta?

[*He reflects.*]

ANUSUYA. My dear, there is not a living thing in the whole hermitage that is not grieving to-day at saying good-bye to you. Look!

> The sheldrake does not heed his mate
> Who calls behind the lotus-leaf;
> He drops the lily from his bill
> And turns on you a glance of grief.

KANVA. Son Sharngarava, when you present Shakuntala to the king, give him this message from me.

> Remembering my religious worth,
> Your own high race, the love poured forth
> By her, forgetful of her friends,
> Pay her what honour custom lends
> To all your wives. And what fate gives
> Beyond, will please her relatives.

SHARNGARAVA. I will not forget your message, Father.

KANVA. [*Turning to* SHAKUNTALA] My child, I must now give you my counsel. Though I live in the forest, I have some knowledge of the world.

SHARNGARAVA. True wisdom, Father, gives insight into everything.

KANVA. My child, when you have entered your husband's home,

> Obey your elders; and be very kind
> To rivals; never be perversely blind
> And angry with your husband, even though he

Should prove less faithful than a man might be;
Be as courteous to servants as you may,
Not puffed with pride in this your happy day:
Thus does a maiden grow into a wife;
But self-willed women are the curse of life.

But what does Gautami say?

GAUTAMI. This is advice sufficient for a bride. [*To* SHAKUNTALA] You will not forget, my child.

KANVA. Come, my daughter, embrace me and your friends.

SHAKUNTALA. Oh, Father! Must my friends turn back too?

KANVA. My daughter, they too must some day be given in marriage. Therefore they may not go to court. Gautami will go with you.

SHAKUNTALA. [*Throwing her arms about her father*] I am torn from my father's breast like a vine stripped from a sandal-tree on the Malabar hills. How can I live in another soil?

[*She weeps.*]

KANVA. My daughter, why distress yourself so?

A noble husband's honourable wife,
You are to spend a busy, useful life
In the world's eye; and soon, as eastern skies
Bring forth the sun, from you there shall arise
A child, a blessing and a comfort strong—
You will not miss me, dearest daughter, long.

SHAKUNTALA. [*Falling at his feet*] Farewell, Father.

KANVA. My daughter, may all that come to you which I desire for you.

SHAKUNTALA. [*Going to her* TWO FRIENDS] Come, girls! Embrace me, both of you together.

[THE TWO FRIENDS *do so.*] Dear, if the good king should perhaps be slow to recognise you, show him the ring with his own name engraved on it.

SHAKUNTALA. Your doubts make my heart beat faster.

THE TWO FRIENDS. Do not be afraid, dear. Love is timid.

SHARNGARAVA. [*Looking about*] Father, the sun is in mid-heaven. She must hasten.

SHAKUNTALA. [*Embracing* KANVA *once more*] Father, when shall I see the pious grove again?

KANVA. My daughter,

When you have shared for many years
  The king's thoughts with the earth,
When to a son who knows no fears
  You shall have given birth,

When, trusted to the son you love,
  Your royal labours cease,
Come with your husband to the grove
  And end your days in peace.[37]

GAUTAMI. My child, the hour of your departure is slipping by. Bid your father turn back. No, she would never do that. Pray turn back, sir.

KANVA. Child, you interrupt my duties in the pious grove.

SHAKUNTALA. Yes, Father. You will be busy in the grove. You will not miss me. But oh! I miss you.

KANVA. How can you think me so indifferent?

[*He sighs.*]

My lonely sorrow will not go,
  For seeds you scattered here
Before the cottage door, will grow;[38]
  And I shall see them, dear.

Go. And peace go with you.

[*Exit* SHAKUNTALA, *with* GAUTAMI, SHARNGARAVA, *and* SHARADVATA.]

THE TWO FRIENDS. [*Gazing long after her. Mournfully*] Oh, oh! Shakuntala is lost among the trees.

KANVA. Anusuya! Priyamvada! Your companion is gone. Choke down your grief and follow me.

[*They start to go back.*]

THE TWO FRIENDS. Father, the grove seems empty without Shakuntala.

KANVA. So love interprets.

[*He walks about, sunk in thought.*] Ah! I have sent Shakuntala away, and now I am myself again. For

A girl is held in trust, another's treasure;
  To arms of love my child to-day is given;
And now I feel a calm and sacred pleasure;
  I have restored the pledge that came from heaven.

[*Exeunt omnes.*]

Act V

SHAKUNTALA'S REJECTION

[*Enter a* CHAMBERLAIN.]

CHAMBERLAIN. [*Sighing*] Alas! To what a state am I reduced!

37. It was usual for kings to abdicate in their old age and retire to the seclusion of a religious life, sometimes with their wives.

38. Shakuntalā has thrown rice or other grain at the door to honor the household deities, accompanying this offering with prayer. Some of these seeds have grown.

I once assumed the staff of reed
For custom's sake alone,
As officer to guard at need
The ladies round the throne.
But years have passed away and made
It serve, my tottering steps to aid.

The king is within. I will tell him of the urgent business which demands his attention.

[*He takes a few steps.*] But what is the business?

[*He recalls it.*] Yes, I remember. Certain hermits, pupils of Kanva, desire to see his Majesty. Strange, strange!

The mind of age is like a lamp
Whose oil is runinng thin;
One moment it is shining bright,
Then darkness closes in.

[*He walks and looks about.*] Here is his Majesty.

He does not seek—until a father's care
Is shown his subjects—rest in solitude;
As a great elephant recks not of the sun
Until his herd is sheltered in the wood.

In truth, I hesitate to announce the coming of Kanva's pupils to the king. For he has this moment risen from the throne of justice. But kings are never weary. For

The sun unyokes his horses never;
Blows night and day the breeze;
Shesha upholds the world forever:[39]
And kings are like to these.

[*He walks about. Enter the* KING, *the* CLOWN, *and retinue according to rank.*]

KING. [*Betraying the cares of office*] Every one is happy on attaining his desire—except a king. His difficulties increase with his power. Thus:

Security slays nothing but ambition;
With great possessions, troubles gather thick;
Pain grows, not lessens, with a king's position,
As when one's hand must hold the sunshade's stick.

TWO COURT POETS BEHIND THE SCENES. Victory to your Majesty.

39. A mythological serpent who holds up the world on one of his many heads.

FIRST POET.

The world you daily guard and bless,
Not heeding pain or weariness;
Thus is your nature made.
A tree will brave the noonday, when
The sun is fierce, that weary men
May rest beneath its shade.

SECOND POET.

Vice bows before the royal rod;
Strife ceases at your kingly nod;
You are our strong defender.
Friends come to all whose wealth is sure,
But you, alike to rich and poor,
Are friend both strong and tender.

KING. [*Listening*] Strange! I was wearied by the demands of my office, but this renews my spirit.

CLOWN. Does a bull forget that he is tired when you call him the leader of the herd?

KING. [*Smiling*] Well, let us sit down.

[*They seat themselves, and the retinue arranges itself. A lute is heard behind the scenes.*]

CLOWN. [*Listening*] My friend, listen to what is going on in the music-room. Some one is playing a lute, and keeping good time. I suppose Lady Hansavati is practising.

KING. Be quiet. I wish to listen.

CHAMBERLAIN. [*Looks at the* KING] Ah, the king is occupied. I must await his leisure.

[*He stands aside.*]

A SONG BEHIND THE SCENES.

You who kissed the mango-flower,
Honey-loving bee,
Gave her all your passion's power,
Ah, so tenderly!

How can you be tempted so
By the lily, pet?
Fresher honey's sweet, I know;
But can you forget?

KING. What an entrancing song!

CLOWN. But, man, don't you understand what the words mean?

KING. [*Smiling*] I was once devoted to Queen Hansavati. And the rebuke comes from her. Friend Madhavya, tell Queen Hansavati in my name that the rebuke is a very pretty one.

CLOWN. Yes, sir.

[*He rises.*] But, man, you are using another fellow's fingers to grab a bear's tail with. I have about as much chance of salvation as a monk who hasn't forgotten his passions.

KING. Go. Soothe her like a gentleman.

CLOWN. I suppose I must.

[*Exit.*]

KING. [*To himself*] Why am I filled with wistfulness on hearing such a song? I am not separated from one I love. And yet

In face of sweet presentment
Or harmonies of sound,
Man e'er forgets contentment,
By wistful longings bound.

There must be recollections
Of things not seen on earth,
Deep nature's predilections,
Loves earlier than birth.

[*He shows the wistfulness that comes from unremembered things.*]

CHAMBERLAIN. [*Approaching*] Victory to your Majesty. Here are hermits who dwell in the forest at the foot of the Himalayas. They bring women with them, and they carry a message from Kanva. What is your pleasure with regard to them?

KING. [*Astonished*] Hermits? Accompanied by women? From Kanva?

CHAMBERLAIN. Yes.

KING. Request my chaplain Somarata in my name to receive these hermits in the manner prescribed by Scripture, and to conduct them himself before me. I will await them in a place fit for their reception.

CHAMBERLAIN. Yes, your Majesty.

[*Exit.*]

KING. [*Rising*] Vetravati, conduct me to the fire-sanctuary.

PORTRESS. Follow me, your Majesty.

[*She walks about.*] Your Majesty, here is the terrace of the fire-sanctuary. It is beautiful, for it has just been swept, and near at hand is the cow that yields the milk of sacrifice. Pray ascend.

KING. [*Ascends and stands leaning on the shoulder of an attendant*] Vetravati, with what purpose does Father Kanva send these hermits to me?

Do leaguèd powers of sin conspire
To balk religion's pure desire?
Has wrong been done to beasts that roam
Contented round the hermits' home?

Do plants no longer bud and flower,
To warn me of abuse of power?
These doubts and more assail my mind,
But leave me puzzled, lost, and blind.

PORTRESS. How could these things be in a hermitage that rests in the fame of the king's arm? No, I imagine they have come to pay homage to their king, and to congratulate him on his pious rule.

[*Enter the* CHAPLAIN *and the* CHAMBERLAIN, *conducting the* TWO PUPILS *of* KANVA, *with* GAUTAMI *and* SHAKUNTALA.]

CHAMBERLAIN. Follow me, if you please.

SHARNGARAVA. Friend Sharadvata,

The king is noble and to virtue true;
None dwelling here commit the deed of shame;
Yet we ascetics view the worldly crew
As in a house all lapped about with flame.

SHARADVATA. Sharngarava, your emotion on entering the city is quite just. As for me,

Free from the world and all its ways,
I see them spending worldly days
As clean men view men smeared with oil,
As pure men, those whom passions soil,
As waking men view men asleep,
As free men, those in bondage deep.

CHAPLAIN. That is why men like you are great.

SHAKUNTALA. [*Observing an evil omen*] Oh, why does my right eye throb?[40]

GAUTAMI. Heaven avert the omen, my child. May happiness wait upon you.

[*They walk about.*]

CHAPLAIN. [*Indicating the* KING] O hermits, here is he who protects those of every station and of every age. He has already risen, and awaits you. Behold him.

SHARNGARAVA. Yes, it is admirable, but not surprising. For

Fruit-laden trees bend down to earth;
The water-pregnant clouds hang low;
Good men are not puffed up by power—
The unselfish are by nature so.

PORTRESS. Your Majesty, the hermits seem to be happy. They give you gracious looks.

KING. [*Observing* SHAKUNTALA] Ah!

40. See note 11.

Who is she, shrouded in the veil
That dims her beauty's lustre,
Among the hermits like a flower
Round which the dead leaves cluster?

PORTRESS. Your Majesty, she is well worth looking at.

KING. Enough! I must not gaze upon another's wife.

SHAKUNTALA. [*Laying her hand on her breast. Aside*] Oh, my heart, why tremble so? Remember his constant love and be brave.

CHAPLAIN. [*Advancing*] Hail, your Majesty. The hermits have been received as Scripture enjoins. They have a message from their teacher. May you be pleased to hear it.

KING. [*Respectfully*] I am all attention

THE TWO PUPILS. [*Raising their right hands*] Victory, O King.

KING. [*Bowing low*] I salute you all.

THE TWO PUPILS. All hail.

KING. Does your pious life proceed without disturbance?

THE TWO PUPILS.

How could the pious duties fail
While you defend the right?
Or how could darkness' power prevail
O'er sunbeams shining bright?

KING. [*To himself*] Indeed, my royal title is no empty one. [*Aloud*] Is holy Kanva in health?

SHARNGARAVA. O King. those who have religious power can command health. He asks after your welfare and sends this message.

KING. What are his commands?

SHARNGARAVA. He says: "Since you have met this my daughter and have married her, I give you my glad consent. For

You are the best of worthy men, they say;
And she, I know, Good Works personified;
The Creator wrought for ever and a day,
In wedding such a virtuous groom and bride.

She is with child. Take her and live with her in virtue."

GAUTAMI. Bless you, sir. I should like to say that no one invites me to speak.

KING. Speak, mother.

GAUTAMI.

Did she with father speak or mother?
Did you engage her friends in speech?
Your faith was plighted each to other;
Let each be faithful now to each.

SHAKUNTALA. What will my husband say?

KING. [*Listening with anxious suspicion*] What is this insinuation?

SHAKUNTALA. [*To herself*] Oh, oh! So haughty and so slanderous!

SHARNGARAVA. "What is this insinuation?" What is your question? Surely you know the world's ways well enough.

> Because the world suspects a wife
> Who does not share her husband's lot,
> Her kinsmen wish her to abide
> With him, although he love her not.

KING. You cannot mean that this young woman is my wife.

SHAKUNTALA. [*Sadly to herself*] Oh, my heart, you feared it, and now it has come.

SHARNGARAVA. O King,

> A king, and shrink when love is done,
> Turn coward's back on truth, and flee!

KING. What means this dreadful accusation?

SHARNGARAVA. [*Furiously*]

> O drunk with power! We might have known
> That you were steeped in treachery.

KING. A stinging rebuke!

GAUTAMI. [*To* SHAKUNTALA] Forget your shame, my child. I will remove your veil. Then your husband will recognise you.

[*She does so.*]

KING. [*Observing* SHAKUNTALA. *To himself*]

> As my heart ponders whether I could ever
> Have wed this woman that has come to me
> In tortured loveliness, as I endeavour
> To bring it back to mind, then like a bee
>
> That hovers round a jasmine flower at dawn,
> While frosty dews of morning still o'erweave it,
> And hesitates to sip ere they be gone,
> I cannot taste the sweet, and cannot leave it.

PORTRESS. [*To herself*] What a virtuous king he is! Would any other man hesitate when he saw such a pearl of a woman coming of her own accord?

SHARNGARAVA. Have you nothing to say, O King?

KING. Hermit, I have taken thought. I cannot believe that this woman is my wife. She is plainly with child. How can I take her, confessing myself an adulterer?

SHAKUNTALA. [*To herself*] Oh, oh, oh! He even casts doubt on our marriage. The vine of my hope climbed high, but it is broken now.

SHARNGARAVA. Not so.

> You scorn the sage who rendered whole
> His child befouled, and choked his grief,
> Who freely gave you what you stole
> And added honour to a thief!

SHARADVATA. Enough, Sharngarava. Shakuntala, we have said what we were sent to say. You hear his words. Answer him.

SHAKUNTALA. [*To herself*] He loved me so. He is so changed. Why remind him? Ah, but I must clear my own character. Well, I will try. [*Aloud*] My dear husband—

[*She stops.*] No, he doubts my right to call him that. Your Majesty, it was pure love that opened my poor heart to you in the hermitage. Then you were kind to me and gave me your promise. Is it right for you to speak so now, and to reject me?

KING. [*Stopping his ears*] Peace, peace!

> A stream that eats away the bank,
> Grows foul, and undermines the tree.
> So you would stain your honour, while
> You plunge me into misery.

SHAKUNTALA. Very well. If you have acted so because you really fear to touch another man's wife, I will remove your doubts with a token you gave me.

KING. An excellent idea!

SHAKUNTALA. [*Touching her finger*] Oh, oh! The ring is lost. [*She looks sadly at* GAUTAMI.]

GAUTAMI. My child, you worshipped the holy Ganges at the spot where Indra descended. The ring must have fallen there.

KING. Ready wit, ready wit!

SHAKUNTALA. Fate is too strong for me there. I will tell you something else.

KING. Let me hear what you have to say.

SHAKUNTALA. One day, in the bower of reeds, you were holding a lotus-leaf cup full of water.

KING. I hear you

SHAKUNTALA. At that moment the fawn came up, my adopted son. Then you took pity on him and coaxed him. "Let him drink first," you said. But he did not know you, and he would not come to drink water from your hand. But he liked it afterwards, when I held the very same water. Then you smiled and said: "It is true. Every one trusts his own sort. You both belong to the forest."

KING. It is just such women, selfish, sweet, false, that entice fools.

GAUTAMI. You have no right to say that. She grew up in the pious grove. She does not know how to deceive.

KING. Old hermit woman,

> The female's untaught cunning may be seen
> In beasts, far more in women selfish-wise;
> The cuckoo's eggs are left to hatch and rear
> By foster-parents, and away she flies.

SHAKUNTALA. [*Angrily*] Wretch! You judge all this by your own false heart. Would any other man do what you have done? To hide behind virtue, like a yawning well covered over with grass!

KING. [*To himself*] But her anger is free from coquetry, because she has lived in the forest. See!

> Her glance is straight; her eyes are flashing red;
> Her speech is harsh, not drawlingly well-bred;
> Her whole lip quivers, seems to shake with cold;
> Her frown has straightened eyebrows arching bold.

No, she saw that I was doubtful, and her anger was feigned. Thus

> When I refused but now
> Hard-heartedly, to know
> Of love or secret vow,
> Her eyes grew red; and so,
> Bending her arching brow,
> She fiercely snapped Love's bow.

[*Aloud*] My good girl. Dushyanta's conduct is known to the whole kingdom, but not this action.

SHAKUNTALA. Well, well. I had my way. I trusted a king, and put myself in his hands. He had a honey face and a heart of stone.

[*She covers her face with her dress and weeps.*]

SHARNGARAVA. Thus does unbridled levity burn.

> Be slow to love, but yet more slow
> With secret mate;
> With those whose hearts we do not know,
> Love turns to hate.

KING. Why do you trust this girl, and accuse me of an imaginary crime?

SHARNGARAVA. [*Disdainfully*] You have learned your wisdom upside down.

> It would be monstrous to believe
> A girl who never lies;
> Trust those who study to deceive
> And think it very wise.

KING. Aha, my candid friend! Suppose I were to admit that I am such a man. What would happen if I deceived the girl?

SHARNGARAVA. Ruin.

KING. It is unthinkable that ruin should fall on Puru's line.

SHARNGARAVA. Why bandy words? We have fulfilled our Father's bidding. We are ready to return.

Leave her or take her, as you will;
She is your wife;
Husbands have power for good or ill
O'er woman's life.

Gautami, lead the way.

[*They start to go.*]

SHAKUNTALA. He has deceived me shamelessly. And will you leave me too?

[*She starts to follow.*]

GAUTAMI. [*Turns around and sees her*] Sharngarava, my son, Shakuntala is following us, lamenting piteously. What can the poor child do with a husband base enough to reject her?

SHARNGARAVA. [*Turns angrily*] You self-willed girl! Do you dare show independence?

[SHAKUNTALA *shrinks in fear.*] Listen.

If you deserve such scorn and blame,
What will your father with your shame?
But if you know your vows are pure,
Obey your husband and endure.

Remain. We must go.

KING. Hermit, why deceive this woman? Remember:

Night-blossoms open to the moon,
Day-blossoms to the sun;
A man of honour ever strives
Another's wife to shun.

SHARNGARAVA. O King, suppose you had forgotten your former actions in the midst of distractions. Should you now desert your wife—you who fear to fail in virtue?

KING. I ask *you* which is the heavier sin:

Not knowing whether I be mad
Or falsehood be in her,
Shall I desert a faithful wife
Or turn adulterer?

CHAPLAIN. [*Considering*] Now if this were done——

KING. Instruct me, my teacher.

CHAPLAIN. Let the woman remain in my house until her child is born.

KING. Why this?

CHAPLAIN. The chief astrologers have told you that your first child was destined to be an emperor. If the son of the hermit's daughter is born with the imperial birthmarks,[41] then welcome her and introduce her into the palace. Otherwise, she must return to her father.

KING. It is good advice, my teacher.

CHAPLAIN. [*Rising*] Follow me, my daughter.

SHAKUNTALA. O mother earth, give me a grave!

[*Exit weeping, with the* CHAPLAIN, *the* HERMITS, *and* GAUTAMI. *The* KING, *his memory clouded by the curse, ponders on* SHAKUNTALA.]

VOICES BEHIND THE SCENES. A miracle! A miracle!

KING. [*Listening*] What does this mean?

[*Enter the* CHAPLAIN.]

CHAPLAIN. [*In amazement*] Your Majesty, a wonderful thing has happened.

KING. What?

CHAPLAIN.

When Kanva's pupils had departed,
She tossed her arms, bemoaned her plight,
Accused her crushing fate——

KING. What then?

CHAPLAIN.

Before our eyes a heavenly light
In woman's form, but shining bright,
Seized her and vanished straight.

[*All betray astonishment.*]

KING. My teacher, we have already settled the matter. Why speculate in vain? Let us seek repose.

CHAPLAIN. Victory to your Majesty.

[*Exit.*]

KING. Vetravati, I am bewildered. Conduct me to my apartment.

PORTRESS. Follow me, your Majesty.

KING. [*Walks about. To himself*]

With a hermit-wife I had no part,
All memories evade me;
And yet my sad and stricken heart
Would more than half persuade me.

[*Exeunt omnes.*]

41. When the lines on the right hand of the child formed a circle, this was thought to be a discus or mark of a future emperor or hero.

Act VI

SEPARATION FROM SHAKUNTALA

SCENE I.—*In the street before the Palace*

[*Enter the* CHIEF OF POLICE, TWO POLICEMEN, *and a man with his hands bound behind his back.*]

THE TWO POLICEMEN. [*Striking the man*] Now, pickpocket, tell us where you found this ring. It is the king's ring, with letters engraved on it, and it has a magnificent great gem.

FISHERMAN. [*Showing fright*] Be merciful, kind gentlemen. I am not guilty of such a crime.

FIRST POLICEMAN. No, I suppose the king thought you were a pious Brahman, and made you a present of it.

FISHERMAN. Listen, please. I am a fisherman, and I live on the Ganges, at the spot where Indra came down.

SECOND POLICEMAN. You thief, we didn't ask for your address or your social position.

CHIEF. Let him tell a straight story, Suchaka. Don't interrupt.

THE TWO POLICEMEN. Yes, chief. Talk, man, talk.

FISHERMAN. I support my family with things you catch fish with—nets, you know, and hooks, and things.

CHIEF. [*Laughing*] You have a sweet trade.[42]

FISHERMAN. Don't say that, master.

You can't give up a lowdown trade
  That your ancestors began;
A butcher butchers things, and yet
  He's the tenderest-hearted man.

CHIEF. Go on. Go on.

FISHERMAN. Well, one day I was cutting up a carp. In its maw I see this ring with the magnificent great gem. And then I was just trying to sell it here when you kind gentlemen grabbed me. That is the only way I got it. Now kill me, or find fault with me.

CHIEF. [*Smelling the ring*] There is no doubt about it, Januka. It has been in a fish's maw. It has the real perfume of raw meat. Now we have to find out how he got it. We must go to the palace.

THE TWO POLICEMEN. [*To the* FISHERMAN] Move on, you cutpurse, move on.

[*They walk about.*]

CHIEF. Suchaka, wait here at the big gate until I come out of the palace. And don't get careless.

42. The occupation of catching or slaughtering fish or animals was considered very lowly.

THE TWO POLICEMEN. Go in, chief. I hope the king will be nice to you.

CHIEF. Good-bye. [*Exit.*]

SUCHAKA. Januka, the chief is taking his time.

JANUKA. You can't just drop in on a king.

SUCHAKA. Januka, my fingers are itching [*Indicating the* FISHERMAN] to kill this cutpurse.

FISHERMAN. Don't kill a man without any reason, master.

JANUKA. [*Looking ahead*] There is the chief, with a written order from the king. [*To the* FISHERMAN] Now you will see your family, or else you will feed the crows and jackals.

[*Enter the* CHIEF.]

CHIEF. Quick! Quick!

[*He breaks off.*]

FISHERMAN. Oh, oh! I'm a dead man.

[*He shows dejection.*]

CHIEF. Release him, you. Release the fishnet fellow. It is all right, his getting the ring. Our king told me so himself.

SUCHAKA. All right, chief. He is a dead man come back to life.

[*He releases the* FISHERMAN.]

FISHERMAN. [*Bowing low to the* CHIEF] Master, I owe you my life.

[*He falls at his feet.*]

CHIEF. Get up, get up! Here is a reward that the king was kind enough to give you. It is worth as much as the ring. Take it.

[*He hands the* FISHERMAN *a bracelet.*]

FISHERMAN. [*Joyfully taking it*] Much obliged.

JANUKA. He *is* much obliged to the king. Just as if he had been taken from the stake and put on an elephant's back.

SUCHAKA. Chief, the reward shows that the king thought a lot of the ring. The gem must be worth something.

CHIEF. No, it wasn't the fine gem that pleased the king. It was this way.

THE TWO POLICEMEN. Well?

CHIEF. I think, when the king saw it, he remembered somebody he loves. You know how dignified he is usually. But as soon as he saw it, he broke down for a moment.

SUCHAKA. You have done the king a good turn, chief.

JANUKA. All for the sake of this fish-killer, it seems to me.

[*He looks enviously at the* FISHERMAN.]

FISHERMAN. Take half of it, masters, to pay for something to drink.

JANUKA. Fisherman, you are the biggest and best friend I've got. The first thing we want, is all the brandy we can hold. Let's go where they keep it.

[*Exeunt omnes.*]

SCENE II.—*In the Palace Gardens*

[*Enter* MISHRAKESHI, *flying through the air.*]

MISHRAKESHI. I have taken my turn in waiting upon the nymphs. And now I will see what this good king is doing. Shakuntala is like a second self to me, because she is the daughter of Menaka. And it was she who asked me to do this.

[*She looks about.*] It is the day of the spring festival.[43] But I see no preparations for a celebration at court. I might learn the reason by my power of divination. But I must do as my friend asked me. Good! I will make myself invisible and stand near these girls who take care of the garden. I shall find out that way.

[*She descends to earth. Enter a* MAID, *gazing at a mango branch, and behind her, a second.*]

FIRST MAID.

First mango-twig, so pink, so green,
First living breath of spring,
You are sacrificed as soon as seen,
A festival offering.

SECOND MAID. What are you chirping about to yourself, little cuckoo?

FIRST MAID. Why, little bee, you know that the cuckoo goes crazy with delight when she sees the mango-blossom.

SECOND MAID. [*Joyfully*] Oh, has the spring really come?

FIRST MAID. Yes, little bee. And this is the time when you too buzz about in crazy joy.

SECOND MAID. Hold me, dear, while I stand on tiptoe and offer this blossom to Love, the divine.

FIRST MAID. If I do, you must give me half the reward of the offering.

SECOND MAID. That goes without saying, dear. We two are one.

[*She leans on her friend and takes the mango-blossom.*] Oh, see! The mango-blossom hasn't opened, but it has broken the sheath, so it is fragrant.

[*She brings her hands together.*] I worship mighty Love.

O mango-twig I give to Love
As arrow for his bow,
Most sovereign of his arrows five,
Strike maiden-targets low.

[*She throws the twig. Enter the* CHAMBERLAIN.]

CHAMBERLAIN. [*Angrily*] Stop, silly girl. The king has strictly for-

43. In celebration of the god Krishna and his son Kāma, the God of Love. A joyous festival or carnival, with flowers the chief decoration.

bidden the spring festival. Do you dare pluck the mango-blossoms?

THE TWO MAIDS. [*Frightened*] Forgive us, sir. We did not know.

CHAMBERLAIN. What! You have not heard the king's command, which is obeyed even by the trees of spring and the creatures that dwell in them. See!

> The mango branches are in bloom,
> Yet pollen does not form;
> The cuckoo's song sticks in his throat,
> Although the days are warm;
>
> The amaranth-bud is formed, and yet
> Its power of growth is gone;
> The love-god timidly puts by
> The arrow he has drawn.

MISHRAKESHI. There is no doubt of it. This good king has wonderful power.

FIRST MAID. A few days ago, sir, we were sent to his Majesty by his brother-in-law Mitravasu to decorate the garden. That is why we have heard nothing of this affair.

CHAMBERLAIN. You must not do so again.

THE TWO MAIDS. But we are curious. If we girls may know about it, pray tell us, sir. Why did his Majesty forbid the spring festival?

MISHRAKESHI. Kings are fond of celebrations. There must be some good reason.

CHAMBERLAIN. [*To himself*] It is in everybody's mouth. Why should I not tell it? [*Aloud*] Have you heard the gossip concerning Shakuntala's rejection?

THE TWO MAIDS. Yes, sir. The king's brother-in-law told us, up to the point where the ring was recovered.

CHAMBERLAIN. There is little more to tell. When his Majesty saw the ring, he remembered that he had indeed contracted a secret marriage with Shakuntala, and had rejected her under a delusion. And then he fell a prey to remorse.

> He hates the things he loved; he intermits
> The daily audience, nor in judgment sits;
> Spends sleepless nights in tossing on his bed;
> At times, when he by courtesy is led
> To address a lady, speaks another name,
> Then stands for minutes, sunk in helpless shame.

MISHRAKESHI. I am glad to hear it.

CHAMBERLAIN. His Majesty's sorrow has forbidden the festival.

THE TWO MAIDS. It is only right.

A VOICE BEHIND THE SCENES. Follow me.

CHAMBERLAIN. [*Listening*] Ah, his Majesty approaches. Go, and attend to your duties.

[*Exeunt the* TWO MAIDS. *Enter the* KING, *wearing a dress indicative of remorse; the* CLOWN, *and the* PORTRESS.]

CHAMBERLAIN. [*Observing the* KING] A beautiful figure charms in whatever state. Thus, his Majesty is pleasing even in his sorrow. For

All ornament is laid aside; he wears
  One golden bracelet on his wasted arm;
His lip is scorched by sighs; and sleepless cares
  Redden his eyes. Yet all can work no harm
On that magnificent beauty, wasting, but
Gaining in brilliance, like a diamond cut.

MISHRAKESHI. [*Observing the* KING] No wonder Shakuntala pines for him, even though he dishonoured her by his rejection of her.

KING. [*Walks about slowly, sunk in thought*]

Alas! My smitten heart, that once lay sleeping,
  Heard in its dreams my fawn-eyed love's laments,
And wakened now, awakens but to weeping,
  To bitter grief, and tears of penitence.

MISHRAKESHI. That is the poor girl's fate.

CLOWN. [*To himself*] He has got his Shakuntala-sickness again. I wish I knew how to cure him.

CHAMBERLAIN. [*Advancing*] Victory to your Majesty. I have examined the garden. Your Majesty may visit its retreats.

KING. Vetravati, tell the minister Pishuna in my name that a sleepless night prevents me from mounting the throne of judgment. He is to investigate the citizens' business and send me a memorandum.

PORTRESS. Yes, your Majesty.

[*Exit.*]

KING. And you, Parvatayana, return to your post of duty.

CHAMBERLAIN. Yes, your Majesty.

[*Exit.*]

CLOWN. You have got rid of the vermin. Now amuse yourself in this garden. It is delightful with the passing of the cold weather.

KING. [*Sighing*] My friend, the proverb makes no mistake. Misfortune finds the weak spot. See!

No sooner did the darkness lift
  That clouded memory's power,
Than the god of love prepared his bow
  And shot the mango-flower.

No sooner did the ring recall
  My banished maiden dear,
No sooner do I vainly weep
  For her, than spring is here.

CLOWN. Wait a minute, man. I will destroy Love's arrow with my stick.

[*He raises his stick and strikes at the mango branch.*]

KING. [*Smiling*] Enough! I see your pious power. My friend, where shall I sit now to comfort my eyes with the vines? They remind me somehow of her.

CLOWN. Well, you told one of the maids, the clever painter, that you would spend this hour in the bower of spring-creepers. And you asked her to bring you there the picture of the lady Shakuntala which you painted on a tablet.

KING. It is my only consolation. Lead the way to the bower of spring-creepers.

CLOWN. Follow me.

[*They walk about.* MISHRAKESHI *follows.*] Here is the bower of spring-creepers, with its jewelled benches. Its loneliness seems to bid you a silent welcome. Let us go in and sit down.

[*They do so.*]

MISHRAKESHI. I will hide among the vines and see the dear girl's picture. Then I shall be able to tell her how deep her husband's love is.

[*She hides.*]

KING. [*Sighing*] I remember it all now, my friend. I told you how I first met Shakuntala. It is true, you were not with me when I rejected her. But I had told you of her at the first. Had you forgotten, as I did?

MISHRAKESHI. This shows that a king should not be separated a single moment from some intimate friend.

CLOWN. No, I didn't forget. But when you had told the whole story, you said it was a joke and there was nothing in it. And I was fool enough to believe you. No, this is the work of fate.

MISHRAKESHI. It must be.

KING. [*After meditating a moment*] Help me, my friend.

CLOWN. But, man, this isn't right at all. A good man never lets grief get the upper hand. The mountains are calm even in a tempest.

KING. My friend, I am quite forlorn. I keep thinking of her pitiful state when I rejected her. Thus:

When I denied her, then she tried
To join her people. "Stay," one cried,
Her father's representative.

She stopped, she turned, she could but give
A tear-dimmed glance to heartless me—
That arrow burns me poisonously.

MISHRAKESHI. How his fault distresses him!

CLOWN. Well, I don't doubt it was some heavenly being that carried her away.

KING. Who else would dare to touch a faithful wife? Her friends told me that Menaka was her mother. My heart persuades me that it was she, or companions of hers, who carried Shakuntala away.

MISHRAKESHI. His madness was wonderful, not his awakening reason.

CLOWN. But in that case, you ought to take heart. You will meet her again.

KING. How so?

CLOWN. Why, a mother or a father cannot long bear to see a daughter separated from her husband.

KING. My friend,

And was it phantom, madness, dream,
  Or fatal retribution stern?
My hopes fell down a precipice
  And never, never will return.

CLOWN. Don't talk that way. Why, the ring shows that incredible meetings do happen.

KING. [*Looking at the ring*] This ring deserves pity. It has fallen from a heaven hard to earn.

Your virtue, ring, like mine,
  Is proved to be but small;
Her pink-nailed finger sweet
  You clasped. How could you fall?

MISHRAKESHI. If it were worn on any other hand, it would deserve pity. My dear girl, you are far away. I am the only one to hear these delightful words.

CLOWN. Tell me how you put the ring on her finger.

MISHRAKESHI. He speaks as if prompted by my curiosity.

KING. Listen, my friend. When I left the pious grove for the city, my darling wept and said: "But how long will you remember us, dear?"

CLOWN. And then you said——

KING. Then I put this engraved ring on her finger, and said to her——

CLOWN. Well, what?

KING.

> Count every day one letter of my name;
> Before you reach the end, dear,
> Will come to lead you to my palace halls
> A guide whom I shall send, dear.

Then, through my madness, it fell out cruelly.

MISHRAKESHI. It was too charming an agreement to be frustrated by fate.

CLOWN. But how did it get into a carp's mouth, as if it had been a fish-hook?

KING. While she was worshipping the Ganges at Shachitirtha, it fell.

CLOWN. I see.

MISHRAKESHI. That is why the virtuous king doubted his marriage with poor Shakuntala. Yet such love does not ask for a token. How could it have been?

KING. Well, I can only reproach this ring.

CLOWN. [*Smiling*] And I will reproach this stick of mine. Why are you crooked when I am straight?

KING. [*Not hearing him*]

> How could you fail to linger
> On her soft, tapering finger,
> And in the water fall?

And yet

> Things lifeless know not beauty;
> But I—I scorned my duty,
> The sweetest task of all.

MISHRAKESHI. He has given the answer which I had ready.

CLOWN. But that is no reason why I should starve to death.

KING. [*Not heeding*] O my darling, my heart burns with repentance because I abandoned you without reason. Take pity on me. Let me see you again.

[*Enter a* MAID *with a tablet.*]

MAID. Your Majesty, here is the picture of our lady.

[*She produces the tablet.*]

KING. [*Gazing at it*] It is a beautiful picture. See!

> A graceful arch of brows above great eyes;
> Lips bathed in darting, smiling light that flies
> Reflected from white teeth; a mouth as red
> As red karkandhu-fruit; love's brightness shed
> O'er all her face in bursts of liquid charm—
> The picture speaks, with living beauty warm.

CLOWN. [*Looking at it*] The sketch is full of sweet meaning. My eyes seem to stumble over its uneven surface. What more can I say? I expect to see it come to life, and I feel like speaking to it.

MISHRAKESHI. The king is a clever painter. I seem to see the dear girl before me.

KING. My friend,

> What in the picture is not fair,
>   Is badly done;
> Yet something of her beauty there,
>   I feel, is won.

MISHRAKESHI. This is natural, when love is increased by remorse.

KING. [*Sighing*]

> I treated her with scorn and loathing ever;
>   Now o'er her pictured charms my heart will burst:
> A traveller I, who scorned the mighty river,
>   And seeks in the mirage to quench his thirst.

CLOWN. There are three figures in the picture, and they are all beautiful. Which one is the lady Shakuntala?

MISHRAKESHI. The poor fellow never saw her beauty. His eyes are useless, for she never came before them.

KING. Which one do you think?

CLOWN. [*Observing closely*] I think it is this one, leaning against the creeper which she has just sprinkled. Her face is hot and the flowers are dropping from her hair; for the ribbon is loosened. Her arms droop like weary branches; she has loosened her girdle, and she seems a little fatigued. This, I think, is the lady Shakuntala, the others are her friends.

KING. You are good at guessing. Besides, here are proofs of my love.

> See where discolorations faint
>   Of loving handling tell;
> And here the swelling of the paint
>   Shows where my sad tears fell.

Chaturika, I have not finished the background. Go, get the brushes.

MAID. Please hold the picture, Madhavya, while I am gone.

KING. I will hold it.

[*He does so. Exit* MAID.]

CLOWN. What are you going to add?

MISHRAKESHI. Surely, every spot that the dear girl loved.

KING. Listen, my friend.

The stream of Malini, and on its sands
The swan-pairs resting; holy foot-hill lands
Of great Himalaya's sacred ranges, where
The yaks are seen; and under trees that bear
Bark hermit-dresses on their branches high,
A doe that on the buck's horn rubs her eye.

CLOWN. [*Aside*] To hear him talk, I should think he was going to fill up the picture with heavy-bearded hermits.

KING. And another ornament that Shakuntala loved I have forgotten to paint.

CLOWN. What?

MISHRAKESHI. Something natural for a girl living in the forest.

KING.

The siris-blossom, fastened o'er her ear,
  Whose stamens brush her cheek;
The lotus-chain like autumn moonlight soft
  Upon her bosom meek.

CLOWN. But why does she cover her face with fingers lovely as the pink water-lily? She seems frightened.

[*He looks more closely.*] I see. Here is a bold, bad bee. He steals honey, and so he flies to her lotus-face.

KING. Drive him away.

CLOWN. It is your affair to punish evil-doers.

KING. True. O welcome guest of the flowering vine, why do you waste your time in buzzing here?

Your faithful, loving queen,
  Perched on a flower, athirst,
Is waiting for you still,
  Nor tastes the honey first.

MISHRAKESHI. A gentlemanly way to drive him off!

CLOWN. This kind are obstinate, even when you warn them.

KING. [*Angrily*] Will you not obey my command? Then listen:

'Tis sweet as virgin blossoms on a tree,
The lip I kissed in love-feasts tenderly;
Sting that dear lip, O bee, with cruel power,
And you shall be imprisoned in a flower.

CLOWN. Well, he doesn't seem afraid of your dreadful punishment. [*Laughing. To himself*] The man is crazy, and I am just as bad, from associating with him.

KING. Will he not go, though I warn him?

MISHRAKESHI. Love works a curious change even in a brave man.

CLOWN. [*Aloud*] It is only a picture, man.

KING. A picture?

MISHRAKESHI. I too understand it now. But to him, thoughts are real experiences.

KING. You have done an ill-natured thing.

> When I was happy in the sight,
> And when my heart was warm,
> You brought sad memories back, and made
> My love a painted form.

[*He sheds a tear.*]

MISHRAKESHI. Fate plays strangely with him.

KING. My friend, how can I endure a grief that has no respite?

> I cannot sleep at night
> And meet her dreaming;
> I cannot see the sketch
> While tears are streaming.

MISHRAKESHI. My friend, you have indeed atoned—and in her friend's presence—for the pain you caused by rejecting dear Shakuntala.

[*Enter the maid* CHATURIKA.]

MAID. Your Majesty, I was coming back with the box of paint-brushes——

KING. Well?

MAID. I met Queen Vasumati with the maid Pingalika. And the queen snatched the box from me, saying: "I will take it to the king myself."

CLOWN. How did you escape?

MAID. The queen's dress caught on a vine. And while her maid was setting her free, I excused myself in a hurry.

A VOICE BEHIND THE SCENES. Follow me, your Majesty.

CLOWN. [*Listening*] Man, the she-tiger of the palace is making a spring on her prey. She means to make one mouthful of the maid.

KING. My friend, the queen has come because she feels touched in her honour. You had better take care of this picture.

CLOWN. "And yourself," you might add.

[*He takes the picture and rises.*] If you get out of the trap alive, call for me at the Cloud Balcony.[44] And I will hide the thing there so that nothing but a pigeon could find it.

[*Exit on the run.*]

MISHRAKESHI. Though his heart is given to another, he is courteous to his early flame. He is a constant friend.

[*Enter the* PORTRESS *with a document.*]

PORTRESS. Victory to your Majesty.

KING. Vetravati, did you not meet Queen Vasumati?

44. This alludes poetically to the height of Dushyanta's palace.

PORTRESS. Yes, your Majesty. But she turned back when she saw that I carried a document.

KING. The queen knows times and seasons. She will not interrupt business.

PORTRESS. Your Majesty, the minister sends word that in the press of various business he has attended to only one citizen's suit. This he has reduced to writing for your Majesty's perusal.

KING. Give me the document.

[*The* PORTRESS *does so.*]

KING. [*Reads*] "Be it known to his Majesty. A seafaring merchant named Dhanavriddhi has been lost in a shipwreck. He is childless, and his property, amounting to several millions, reverts to the crown. Will his Majesty take action?" [*Sadly*] It is dreadful to be childless. Vetravati, he had great riches. There must be several wives. Let inquiry be made. There may be a wife who is with child.

PORTRESS. We have this moment heard that a merchant's daughter of Saketa is his wife. And she is soon to become a mother.

KING. The child shall receive the inheritance. Go, inform the minister.

PORTRESS. Yes, your Majesty.

[*She starts to go.*]

KING. Wait a moment.

PORTRESS. [*Turning back*] Yes, your Majesty.

KING. After all, what does it matter whether he have issue or not?

> Let King Dushyanta be proclaimed
> To every sad soul kin
> That mourns a kinsman loved and lost,
> Yet did not plunge in sin.

PORTRESS. The proclamation shall be made.

[*She goes out and soon returns.*] Your Majesty, the royal proclamation was welcomed by the populace as is a timely shower.

KING. [*Sighing deeply*] Thus, when issue fails, wealth passes, on the death of the head of the family, to a stranger. When I die, it will be so with the glory of Puru's line.

PORTRESS. Heaven avert the omen!

KING. Alas! I despised the happiness that offered itself to me.

MISHRAKESHI. Without doubt, he has dear Shakuntala in mind when he thus reproaches himself.

KING.

> Could I forsake the virtuous wife
> Who held my best, my future life
> And cherished it for glorious birth,
> As does the seed-receiving earth?

MISHRAKESHI. She will not long be forsaken.

MAID. [*To the* PORTRESS] Mistress, the minister's report has doubled our lord's remorse. Go to the Cloud Balcony and bring Madhavya to dispel his grief.

PORTRESS. A good suggestion.

[*Exit.*]

KING. Alas! The ancestors of Dushyanta are in a doubtful case.

For I am childless, and they do not know,
When I am gone, what child of theirs will bring
The scriptural oblation; and their tears
Already mingle with my offering.

MISHRAKESHI. He is screened from the light, and is in darkness.

MAID. Do not give way to grief, your Majesty. You are in the prime of your years, and the birth of a son to one of your other wives will make you blameless before your ancestors. [*To herself*] He does not heed me. The proper medicine is needed for any disease.

KING. [*Betraying his sorrow*] Surely,

The royal line that flowed
A river pure and grand,
Dies in the childless king,
Like streams in desert sand.

[*He swoons.*]

MAID. [*In distress*] Oh, sir, come to yourself.

MISHRAKESHI. Shall I make him happy now? No, I heard the mother of the gods consoling Shakuntala. She said that the gods, impatient for the sacrifice, would soon cause him to welcome his true wife. I must delay no longer. I will comfort dear Shakuntala with my tidings.

[*Exit through the air.*]

A VOICE BEHIND THE SCENES. Help, help!

KING. [*Comes to himself and listens*] It sounds as if Madhavya were in distress.

MAID. Your Majesty, I hope that Pingalika and the other maids did not catch poor Madhavya with the picture in his hands.

KING. Go, Chaturika. Reprove the queen in my name for not controlling her servants.

MAID. Yes, your Majesty.

[*Exit.*]

THE VOICE. Help, help!

KING. The Brahman's voice seems really changed by fear. Who waits without?

[*Enter the* CHAMBERLAIN.]

CHAMBERLAIN. Your Majesty commands?

KING. See why poor Madhavya is screaming so.

CHAMBERLAIN. I will see.

[*He goes out, and returns trembling.*]

KING. Parvatayana, I hope it is nothing very dreadful.

CHAMBERLAIN. I hope not.

KING. Then why do you tremble so? For

> Why should the trembling, born
> Of age, increasing, seize
> Your limbs and bid them shake
> Like fig-leaves in the breeze?

CHAMBERLAIN. Save your friend, O King!

KING. From what?

CHAMBERLAIN. From great danger.

KING. Speak plainly, man.

CHAMBERLAIN. On the Cloud Balcony, open to the four winds of heaven——

KING. What has happened there?

CHAMBERLAIN.

> While he was resting on its height,
> Which palace peacocks in their flight
> Can hardly reach, he seemed to be
> Snatched up—by what, we could not see.

KING. [*Rising quickly*] My very palace is invaded by evil creatures. To be a king, is to be a disappointed man.

> The moral stumblings of mine own,
> The daily slips, are scarcely known;
> Who then that rules a kingdom, can
> Guide every deed of every man?

THE VOICE. Hurry, hurry!

KING. [*Hears the voice and quickens his steps*] Have no fear, my friend.

THE VOICE. Have no fear! When something has got me by the back of the neck, and is trying to break my bones like a piece of sugar-cane!

KING. [*Looks about*] A bow! a bow!

[*Enter a* GREEK WOMAN *with a bow.*]

GREEK WOMAN. A bow and arrows, your Majesty. And here are the finger-guards.

[*The king takes the bow and arrows.*]

ANOTHER VOICE BEHIND THE SCENES.

Writhe, while I drink the red blood flowing clear
And kill you, as a tiger kills a deer;
Let King Dushyanta grasp his bow; but how
Can all his kingly valour save you now?

KING. [*Angrily*] He scorns me too! In one moment, miserable demon, you shall die. [*Stringing his bow*] Where is the stairway, Parvatayana?

CHAMBERLAIN. Here, your Majesty.

[*All make haste.*]

KING. [*Looking about*] There is no one here.

THE CLOWN'S VOICE. Save me, save me! I see you, if you can't see me. I am a mouse in the claws of the cat. I am done for.

KING. You are proud of your invisibility. But shall not my arrow see you? Stand still. Do not hope to escape by clinging to my friend.

My arrow, flying when the bow is bent,
Shall slay the wretch and spare the innocent;
When milk is mixed with water in a cup,
Swans leave the water, and the milk drink up.

[*He takes aim. Enter* MATALI[45] *and the* CLOWN.]

MATALI. O King, as Indra, king of the gods, commands,

Seek foes among the evil powers alone;
For them your bow should bend;
Not cruel shafts, but glances soft and kind
Should fall upon a friend.

KING. [*Hastily withdrawing the arrow*] It is Matali. Welcome to the charioteer of heaven's king.

CLOWN. Well! He came within an inch of butchering me. And you welcome him.

MATALI. [*Smiling*] Hear, O King, for what purpose Indra sends me to you.

KING. I am all attention.

MATALI. There is a host of demons who call themselves Invincible—the brood of Kalanemi.[46]

KING. So Narada has told me.

MATALI.

Heaven's king is powerless; you shall smite
His foes in battle soon;
Darkness that overcomes the day,
Is scattered by the moon.

45. The charioteer of the god Indra.

46. A demon or *daitya* with a hundred arms and as many heads, of whom the king has been told by Narada, a celebrated sage; one of the ten patriarchs first created by Brahma; and a messenger of the gods.

Take your bow at once, enter my heavenly chariot, and set forth for victory.

KING. I am grateful for the honour which Indra shows me. But why did you act thus toward Madhavya?

MATALI. I will tell you. I saw that you were overpowered by some inner sorrow, and acted thus to rouse you. For

> The spurnèd snake will swell his hood;
> Fire blazes when 'tis stirred;
> Brave men are roused to fighting mood
> By some insulting word.

KING. Friend Madhavya, I must obey the bidding of heaven's king. Go, acquaint the minister Pishuna with the matter, and add these words of mine:

> Your wisdom only shall control
> The kingdom for a time;
> My bow is strung; a distant goal
> Calls me, and tasks sublime.

CLOWN. Very well.

[*Exit.*]

MATALI. Enter the chariot.

[*The* KING *does so. Exeunt omnes.*]

Act VII

[*Enter, in a chariot that flies through the air, the* KING *and* MATALI.]

KING. Matali, though I have done what Indra commanded, I think myself an unprofitable servant, when I remember his most gracious welcome.

MATALI. O King, know that each considers himself the other's debtor. For

> You count the service given
> Small by the welcome paid,
> Which to the king of heaven
> Seems mean for such brave aid.

KING. Ah, no! For the honour given me at parting went far beyond imagination. Before the gods, he seated me beside him on his throne. And then

> He smiled, because his son Jayanta's heart
> Beat quicker, by the self-same wish oppressed,
> And placed about my neck the heavenly wreath
> Still fragrant from the sandal on his breast.[47]

47. The breast of Indra was dyed yellow with a fragrant sandalwood cosmetic.

MATALI. But what do you not deserve from heaven's king? Remember:

> Twice, from peace-loving Indra's sway
> The demon-thorn was plucked away:
> First, by Man-lion's crooked claws;[48]
> Again, by your smooth shafts to-day.

KING. This merely proves Indra's majesty. Remember:

> All servants owe success in enterprise
> To honour paid before the great deed's done;
> Could dawn defeat the darkness otherwise
> Than resting on the chariot of the sun?

MATALI. The feeling becomes you. [*After a little*] See, O King! Your glory has the happiness of being published abroad in heaven.

> With colours used by nymphs of heaven
> To make their beauty shine,
> Gods write upon the surface given
> Of many a magic vine,
> As worth their song, the simple story
> Of those brave deeds that made your glory.

KING. Matali, when I passed before, I was intent on fighting the demons, and did not observe this region. Tell me. In which path of the winds are we?

MATALI.

> It is the windpath sanctified
> By holy Vishnu's second stride;
> Which, freed from dust of passion, ever
> Upholds the threefold heavenly river;
> And, driving them with reins of light,
> Guides the stars in wheeling flight.

KING. That is why serenity pervades me, body and soul.

[*He observes the path taken by the chariot.*] It seems that we have descended into the region of the clouds.

MATALI. How do you perceive it?

KING.

> Plovers that fly from mountain-caves,
> Steeds that quick-flashing lightning laves,
> And chariot-wheels that drip with spray—
> A path o'er pregnant clouds betray.

48. Vishnu took the form of half-man, half-lion to deliver the three worlds (earth, heaven, and the lower regions) from the demon Hiranya-Kashipu.

MATALI. You are right. And in a moment you will be in the world over which you bear rule.

KING. [*Looking down*] Matali, our quick descent gives the world of men a mysterious look. For

The plains appear to melt and fall
From mountain peaks that grow more tall;
The trunks of trees no longer hide
Nor in their leafy nests abide;
The river network now is clear,
For smaller streams at last appear:
It seems as if some being threw
The world to me, for clearer view.

MATALI. You are a good observer, O King.

[*He looks down, awe-struck.*] There is a noble loveliness in the earth.

KING. Matali, what mountain is this, its flanks sinking into the eastern and into the western sea? It drips liquid gold like a cloud at sunset.

MATALI. O King, this is Gold Peak,[49] the mountain of the fairy centaurs. Here it is that ascetics most fully attain to magic powers. See!

The ancient sage, Marichi's son,[50]
Child of the Uncreated One,
Father of superhuman life,
Dwells here austerely with his wife.

KING. [*Reverently*] I must not neglect the happy chance. I cannot go farther until I have walked humbly about the holy one.

MATALI. It is a worthy thought, O King.

[*The chariot descends.*] We have come down to earth.

KING. [*Astonished*] Matali,

The wheels are mute on whirling rim;
  Unstirred, the dust is lying there;
We do not bump the earth, but skim:
  Still, still we seem to fly through air.

MATALI. Such is the glory of the chariot which obeys you and Indra.

KING. In which direction lies the hermitage of Marichi's son?

MATALI. [*Pointing*] See!

Where stands the hermit, horridly austere,
Whom clinging vines are choking, tough and sere;
Half-buried in an ant-hill that has grown
About him, standing post-like and alone;

49. A sacred range of mountains apparently in the Himalaya connected with the God of Wealth.

50. Marichi's son was Kashyapa, a patriarch created by Brahma to fill the universe with inhabitants. He is the father of all animals and also of the demons.

Sun-staring with dim eyes that know no rest,
The dead skin of a serpent on his breast:
So long he stood unmoved, insensate there
That birds build nests within his mat of hair.

KING. [*Gazing*] All honour to one who mortifies the flesh so terribly.

MATALI. [*Checking the chariot*] We have entered the hermitage of the ancient sage, whose wife Aditi[51] tends the coral-trees.

KING. Here is deeper contentment than in heaven. I seem plunged in a pool of nectar.

MATALI. [*Stopping the chariot*] Descend, O King.

KING. [*Descending*] But how will you fare?

MATALI. The chariot obeys the word of command. I too will descend. [*He does so.*] Before you, O King, are the groves where the holiest hermits lead their self-denying life.

KING. I look with amazement both at their simplicity and at what they might enjoy.

Their appetites are fed with air[52]
Where grows whatever is most fair;
They bathe religiously in pools
Which golden lily-pollen cools;
They pray within a jewelled home,
Are chaste where nymphs of heaven roam:
They mortify desire and sin
With things that others fast to win.

MATALI. The desires of the great aspire high.

[*He walks about and speaks to some one not visible.*] Ancient Shakalya, how is Marichi's holy son occupied?

[*He listens.*] What do you say? That he is explaining to Aditi, in answer to her question, the duties of a faithful wife? My matter must await a fitter time.

[*He turns to the* KING.] Wait here, O King, in the shade of the ashoka tree, till I have announced your coming to the sire of Indra.

KING. Very well.

[*Exit* MATALI. *The* KING'S *arm throbs, a happy omen.*][53]

I dare not hope for what I pray;
  Why thrill—in vain?
For heavenly bliss once thrown away
  Turns into pain.

A VOICE BEHIND THE SCENES. Don't! You mustn't be so foolhardy. Oh, you are always the same.

51. Aditi is Marichi's wife.

52. The height of asceticism is to be so far removed from need of food and drink as to live on air.

53. See note 11.

KING. [*Listening*] No naughtiness could feel at home in this spot. Who draws such a rebuke upon himself?

[*He looks towards the sound. In surprise*] It is a child, but no child in strength. And two hermit-women are trying to control him.

He drags a struggling lion cub,
The lioness' milk half-sucked, half-missed,
Towzles his mane, and tries to drub
Him tame with small, imperious fist.

[*Enter a small* BOY, *as described, and two* HERMIT-WOMEN.]

BOY. Open your mouth, cub. I want to count your teeth.

FIRST WOMAN. Naughty boy, why do you torment our pets? They are like children to us. Your energy seems to take the form of striking something. No wonder the hermits call you All-tamer.

KING. Why should my heart go out to this boy as if he were my own son?

[*He reflects.*] No doubt my childless state makes me sentimental.

SECOND WOMAN. The lioness will spring at you if you don't let her baby go.

BOY. [*Smiling*] Oh, I'm dreadfully scared.

[*He bites his lip.*]

KING. [*In surprise*]

The boy is seed of fire
Which, when it grows, will burn;
A tiny spark that soon
To awful flame may turn.

FIRST WOMAN. Let the little lion go, dear. I will give you another plaything.

BOY. Where is it? Give it to me.

[*He stretches out his hand.*]

KING. [*Looking at the hand*] He has one of the imperial birthmarks![54]

For

Between the eager fingers grow
The close-knit webs together drawn,
Like some lone lily opening slow
To meet the kindling blush of dawn.

SECOND WOMAN. Suvrata, we can't make him stop by talking. Go. In my cottage you will find a painted clay peacock that belongs to the hermit-boy Mankanaka. Bring him that.

54. See note 41.

FIRST WOMAN. I will.

[*Exit.*]

BOY. Meanwhile I'll play with this one.

HERMIT-WOMAN. [*Looks and laughs*] Let him go.

KING. My heart goes out to this wilful child. [*Sighing*]

They show their little buds of teeth
  In peals of causeless laughter;
They hide their trustful heads beneath
  Your heart. And stumbling after
Come sweet, unmeaning sounds that sing
  To you. The father warms
And loves the very dirt they bring
  Upon their little forms.

HERMIT-WOMAN. [*Shaking her finger*] Won't you mind me?

[*She looks about.*] Which one of the hermit-boys is here?

[*She sees the* KING.] Oh, sir, please come here and free this lion cub. The little rascal is tormenting him, and I can't make him let go.

KING. Very well.

[*He approaches, smiling.*] O little son of a great sage!

Your conduct in this place apart,
  Is most unfit;
'Twould grieve your father's pious heart
  And trouble it.

To animals he is as good
  As good can be;
You spoil it, like a black snake's brood
  In sandal tree.[55]

HERMIT-WOMAN. But sir, he is not the son of a hermit.

KING. So it would seem, both from his looks and his actions. But in this spot, I had no suspicion of anything else.

[*He loosens the boy's hold on the cub, and touching him, says to himself.*]

It makes me thrill to touch the boy,
  The stranger's son, to me unknown;
What measureless content must fill
  The man who calls the child his own!

HERMIT-WOMAN. [*Looking at the two*] Wonderful! wonderful!

KING. Why do you say that, mother?

55. The highly perfumed sandalwood tree was supposed to be infested with serpents.

HERMIT-WOMAN. I am astonished to see how much the boy looks like you, sir. You are not related. Besides, he is a perverse little creature and he does not know you. Yet he takes no dislike to you.

KING. [*Caressing the* BOY] Mother, if he is not the son of a hermit, what is his family?

HERMIT-WOMAN. The family of Puru.

KING. [*To himself*] He is of one family with me! Then could my thought be true? [*Aloud*] But this is the custom of Puru's line:

> In glittering palaces they dwell
> While men, and rule the country well;
> Then make the grove their home in age,
> And die in austere hermitage.

But how could human beings, of their own mere motion, attain this spot?

HERMIT-WOMAN. You are quite right, sir. But the boy's mother was related to a nymph, and she bore her son in the pious grove of the father of the gods.

KING. [*To himself*] Ah, a second ground for hope. [*Aloud*] What was the name of the good king whose wife she was?

HERMIT-WOMAN. Who would speak his name? He rejected his true wife.

KING. [*To himself*] This story points at me. Suppose I ask the boy for his mother's name.

[*He reflects.*] No, it is wrong to concern myself with one who may be another's wife.

[*Enter the* FIRST WOMAN, *with the clay peacock.*]

FIRST WOMAN. Look, All-tamer. Here is the bird, the *shakunta.* Isn't the *shakunta* lovely?

BOY. [*Looks about*] Where is my mamma?

[*The* TWO WOMEN *burst out laughing.*]

FIRST WOMAN. It sounded like her name, and deceived him. He loves his mother.

SECOND WOMAN. She said: "See how pretty the peacock is." That is all.

KING. [*To himself*] His mother's name is Shakuntala! But names are alike. I trust this hope may not prove a disappointment in the end, like a mirage.

BOY. I like this little peacock, sister. Can it fly?

[*He seizes the toy.*]

FIRST WOMAN. [*Looks at the* BOY. *Anxiously*] Oh, the amulet is not on his wrist.

KING. Do not be anxious, mother. It fell while he was struggling with the lion cub.

[*He starts to pick it up.*]

THE TWO WOMEN. Oh, don't, don't!

[*They look at him.*] He has touched it!

[*Astonished, they lay their hands on their bosoms, and look at each other.*]

KING. Why did you try to prevent me?

FIRST WOMAN. Listen, your Majesty. This is a divine and most potent charm, called the Invincible. Marichi's holy son gave it to the baby when the birth-ceremony was performed. If it falls on the ground, no one may touch it except the boy's parents or the boy himself.

KING. And if another touch it?

FIRST WOMAN. It becomes a serpent and stings him.

KING. Did you ever see this happen to any one else?

BOTH WOMEN. More than once.

KING. [*Joyfully*] Then why may I not welcome my hopes fulfilled at last?

[*He embraces the* BOY.]

SECOND WOMAN. Come, Suvrata. Shakuntala is busy with her religious duties. We must go and tell her what has happened.

[*Exeunt.*]

BOY. Let me go. I want to see my mother.

KING. My son, you shall go with me to greet your mother.

BOY. Dushyanta is my father, not you.

KING. [*Smiling*] You show I am right by contradicting me.

[*Enter* SHAKUNTALA, *wearing her hair in a single braid.*[56]]

SHAKUNTALA. [*Doubtfully*] I have heard that All-tamer's amulet did not change when it should have done so. But I do not trust my own happiness. Yet perhaps it is as Mishrakeshi told me. [*She walks about.*]

KING. [*Looking at* SHAKUNTALA. *With plaintive joy*] It is she. It is Shakuntala.

> The pale, worn face, the careless dress,
>   The single braid,
> Show her still true, me pitiless,
>   The long vow paid.

SHAKUNTALA. [*Seeing the* KING *pale with remorse. Doubtfully*] It is not my husband. Who is the man that soils my boy with his caresses? The amulet should protect him.

BOY. [*Running to his mother*] Mother, he is a man that belongs to other people. And he calls me his son.

56. The single braid was a sign of mourning, either for a dead or for a long-absent husband.

KING. My darling, the cruelty I showed you has turned to happiness. Will you not recognise me?

SHAKUNTALA. [*To herself*] Oh, my heart, believe it. Fate struck hard, but its envy is gone and pity takes its place. It is my husband.

KING.

Black madness flies;
Comes memory;
Before my eyes
My love I see.

Eclipse flees far;
Light follows soon;
The loving star
Draws to the moon.

SHAKUNTALA. Victory, victo——

[*Tears choke her utterance.*]

KING.

The tears would choke you, sweet, in vain;
My soul with victory is fed,
Because I see your face again—
No jewels, but the lips are red.

BOY. Who is he, mother?

SHAKUNTALA. Ask fate, my child. [*She weeps*]

KING.

Dear, graceful wife, forget;
Let the sin vanish;
Strangely did madness strive
Reason to banish.

Thus blindness works in men,
Love's joy to shake;
Spurning a garland, lest
It prove a snake.

[*He falls at her feet.*]

SHAKUNTALA. Rise, my dear husband. Surely, it was some old sin of mine that broke my happiness—though it has turned again to happiness. Otherwise, how could you, dear, have acted so? You are so kind.

[*The king rises.*] But what brought back the memory of your suffering wife?

KING. I will tell you when I have plucked out the dart of sorrow.

'Twas madness, sweet, that could let slip
A tear to burden your dear lip;
On graceful lashes seen to-day,
I wipe it, and our grief, away.

[*He does so.*]

SHAKUNTALA. [*Sees more clearly and discovers the ring*] My husband, it is the ring!

KING. Yes. And when a miracle recovered it, my memory returned.

SHAKUNTALA. That was why it was so impossible for me to win your confidence.

KING. Then let the vine receive her flower, as earnest of her union with spring.

SHAKUNTALA. I do not trust it. I would rather you wore it.

[*Enter* MATALI.]

MATALI. I congratulate you, O King, on reunion with your wife and on seeing the face of your son.

KING. My desires bear sweeter fruit because fulfilled through a friend. Matali, was not this matter known to Indra?

MATALI. [*Smiling*] What is hidden from the gods? Come. Marichi's holy son, Kashyapa, wishes to see you.

KING. My dear wife, bring our son. I could not appear without you before the holy one.

SHAKUNTALA. I am ashamed to go before such parents with my husband.

KING. It is the custom in times of festival. Come.

[*They walk about.* KASHYAPA *appears seated, with* ADITI.]

KASHYAPA. [*Looking at the* KING] Aditi,

'Tis King Dushyanta, he who goes before
  Your son in battle, and who rules the earth,
Whose bow makes Indra's weapon seem no more
  Than a fine plaything, lacking sterner worth.

ADITI. His valour might be inferred from his appearance.

MATALI. O King, the parents of the gods look upon you with a glance that betrays parental fondness. Approach them.

KING. Matali,

Sprung from the Creator's children, do I see
Great Kashyapa and Mother Aditi?
The pair that did produce the sun in heaven,
To which each year twelve changing forms[57] are given;
That brought the king of all the gods to birth,
Who rules in heaven, in hell, and on the earth;

57. The twelve months (*adityas*) were born of Kashyapa and Aditi.

That Vishnu, than the Uncreated higher,[58]
Chose as his parents with a fond desire.

MATALI. It is indeed they.

KING. [*Falling before them*] Dushyanta, servant of Indra, does reverence to you both.

KASHYAPA. My son, rule the earth long.

ADITI. And be invincible.

[SHAKUNTALA *and her son fall at their feet.*]

KASHYAPA. My daughter,

Your husband equals Indra, king
Of gods; your son is like his son;
No further blessing need I bring:
Win bliss such as his wife has won.

ADITI. My child, keep the favour of your husband. And may this fine boy be an honour to the families of both parents. Come, let us be seated.

[*All seat themselves.*]

KASHYAPA. [*Indicating one after the other*]

Faithful Shakuntala, the boy,
And you, O King, I see
A trinity to bless the world—
Faith, Treasure, Piety.

KING. Holy one, your favour shown to us is without parallel. You granted the fulfilment of our wishes before you called us to your presence. For, holy one,

The flower comes first, and then the fruit;
The clouds appear before the rain;
Effect comes after cause; but you
First helped, then made your favour plain.

MATALI. O King, such is the favour shown by the parents of the world.

KING. Holy one, I married this your maid-servant by the voluntary ceremony.[59] When after a time her relatives brought her to me, my memory failed and I rejected her. In so doing, I sinned against Kanva, who is kin to you. But afterwards, when I saw the ring, I perceived that I had married her. And this seems very wonderful to me.

Like one who doubts an elephant,
Though seeing him stride by,
And yet believes when he has seen
The footprints left; so I.

58. Vishnu as the Supreme Spirit (*nārāyana*) moved over the waters before the creation of the world.
59. See note 29.

KASHYAPA. My son, do not accuse yourself of sin. Your infatuation was inevitable. Listen.

KING. I am all attention.

KASHYAPA. When the nymph Menaka descended to earth and received Shakuntala, afflicted at her rejection, she came to Aditi. Then I perceived the matter by my divine insight. I saw that the unfortunate girl had been rejected by her rightful husband because of Durvasas' curse. And that the curse would end when the ring came to light.

KING. [*With a sigh of relief. To himself*] Then I am free from blame.

SHAKUNTALA. [*To herself*] Thank heaven! My husband did not reject me of his own accord. He really did not remember me. I suppose I did not hear the curse in my absent-minded state, for my friends warned me most earnestly to show my husband the ring.

KASHYAPA. My daughter, you know the truth. Do not now give way to anger against your rightful husband. Remember:

> The curse it was that brought defeat and pain;
> The darkness flies; you are his queen again.
> Reflections are not seen in dusty glass,
> Which, cleaned, will mirror all the things that pass.

KING. It is most true, holy one.

KASHYAPA. My son, I hope you have greeted as he deserves the son whom Shakuntala has borne you, for whom I myself have performed the birth-rite and the other ceremonies.

KING. Holy one, the hope of my race centres in him.

KASHYAPA. Know then that his courage will make him emperor.

> Journeying over every sea,
> His car will travel easily;
> The seven islands of the earth[60]
> Will bow before his matchless worth;
> Because wild beasts to him were tame,
> All-tamer was his common name;
> As Bharata he shall be known,
> For he will bear the world alone.

KING. I anticipate everything from him, since you have performed the rites for him.

ADITI. Kanva also should be informed that his daughter's wishes are fulfilled. But Menaka is waiting upon me here and cannot be spared.

60. According to the mythical geography of the Hindus, the earth is the central one of these islands. The others are legendary islands surrounded by seas of wine, butter, etc.

SHAKUNTALA. [*To herself*] The holy one has expressed my own desire.

KASHYAPA. Kanva knows the whole matter through his divine insight.

[*He reflects.*] Yet he should hear from us the pleasant tidings, how his daughter and her son have been received by her husband. Who waits without?

[*Enter a* PUPIL.]

PUPIL. I am here, holy one.

KASHYAPA. Galava, fly through the air at once, carrying pleasant tidings from me to holy Kanva. Tell him how Durvasas' curse has come to an end, how Dushyanta recovered his memory, and has taken Shakuntala with her child to himself.

PUPIL. Yes, holy one.

[*Exit.*]

KASHYAPA. [*To the king*] My son, enter with child and wife the chariot of your friend Indra, and set out for your capital.

KING. Yes, holy one.

KASHYAPA. For now

May Indra send abundant rain,
Repaid by sacrificial gain;
With aid long mutually given,
Rule you on earth, and he in heaven.

KING. Holy one, I will do my best.

KASHYAPA. What more, my son, shall I do for you?

KING. Can there be more than this? Yet may this prayer be fulfilled.

May kingship benefit the land,
And wisdom grow in scholars' band;
May Shiva see my faith on earth
And make me free of all rebirth.[61]

[*Exeunt omnes.*]

VIDYĀKARA

(ca. 1100)

Treasury of Well-Turned Verse (*Subhāsitaratnakosa*)

Lyric poetry occupies a prominent place in Sanskrit literature, and the critics, even in early times, distinguish it sharply from other kinds of verse. It is called *kāvya* and is regarded as different from didactic and philosophical verse and also from the narrative verse of drama and epic, although lyric inter-

61. He hopes that by good works he will rid his body of temporal desires and impurities and escape reincarnation (see pp. 160–161).

ludes decorate both epics and plays. The Sanskrit language is even more elaborately inflected than Greek and Latin, and permits great variety in word order. It employs frequent compounding, reminiscent of German. Thus it has a succinctness that is not readily translated into English. Also, classical (i.e., post-epic) Sanskrit is a highly artistic language not used as a first language by the poet but used rather like Latin in Europe in post-Roman times, learned for the special purposes of aristocratic literature and not subject to the constant pressure for change of the spoken, utilitarian language of everyday use. It is thus "artificial" and has true synonyms which natural languages rarely have.[1] Both the philological principles of the Sanskrit language and the critical principles of lyric poetry were formalized early by Indian scholars and critics, and we are dealing with a highly sophisticated literature in the lyrics that follow. If the poet seems to be warbling his native woodnotes wild, he is working within a set of rigid conventions that leave little room for the kind of incongruity that is often either a brilliant juxtaposition or a lapse of taste in English poets.

The anthology of "well-turned" verse that Vidyākara compiled shortly before 1100 A.D. came from the volumes of a large library in the monastery of Jagaddala. The ruins of this monastery are still visible in the Malda district near the present border between East and West Bengal. Vidyākara included selections from over two hundred poets, some going back as far as the eighth century, in his collection. Two kinds of critical concepts help us approach the poetry. The poet works not to vividly restructure "real life," though he sometimes seems to be doing so, but to create moods (the Sanskrit *rasa*). As with the dramatic application of *rasa* theory (see below), the poet accepts the psychology of his tradition and sees the human emotions that create moods as systematically classified into such categories as laughter, grief, sexual excitement, anger, energy, fear, loathing, and wonder, and these affected by a counterpoint of transitory experiences such as embarrassment, reminiscence, and worry. The poet's aim is to transmit a "decoction," as Ingalls term it,[2] of these moods. Each verse of a poem must do this.

Within the formal conventions of their art, the Sanskrit poets in Vidyākara's collection succeed in depicting scenes from the broadest perspective of Indian life. There are poems about the Buddha and about the gods, a panorama of the seasons and of natural phenomena, a spectrum of the love of man and woman, and, indeed, of all of the other basic experiences of mankind—good men and bad, poverty and riches, heroes and villains, old age and death. There are often subtle classifications within these subjects. Love is not divided into only pre- and post-marital, but we have poems on love in general and on the God of Love, Kāma; on the first budding of adolescence; on young women; on their female

1. See the "General Introduction" to Ingalls' translation, p. 6.

2. Ibid., p. 14.

go-betweens in the courtship relation; on the maturing of passion; on marriage; on the ills of love—jealousy, separation, wantonness. These are all common human emotions but are elaborately classified and distilled into their essences by the poets. Along with all this, we have in many of the poems the staggering effects of the passage of the seasons on the rituals of everyday life. India does not have a temperate climate. The spring is pleasant, but the summer is dry and hot—the earth bakes and the relations of human beings are affected in every way. Autumn brings the monsoon rains, which are so welcome that floods and a sea of mud are signs to rejoice at. The winters, even in northern India, are not as cold as in Europe, but houses are fragile and the fire gives off little heat and life slows down in winter. Gorgeous flowers, colorful birds and animals appear and depart in this panorama of violent seasons, and festivals, replete with elaborate costumes, dancing and music, perfumed ladies, and colored powder strewn on the earth, mark the sacred transitions of life. The selections below represent mostly the everyday life of the people heightened by the poet's vision, rather than poems of gods and heroes, but Vidyākara's collection includes the whole cycle of celestial and terrestial life.

From The *Treasury of Well-Turned Verse**

Spring

The lotus pond is bristling with pink buds;
the nights grow shorter while the empyrean's gem,
its cloak of frost unloosed, grows bold.
Now comes the days resounding with the cukoo
and sweet mango scent
to cut the hearts of ladies separated from their lovers.

Samghaśrī. 152.

Our flesh uprises at the twang of Kama's bow,
his arrows set in motion by the amorous note
that pours forth from the cuckoo's bride.[1]
Not only we, my fair one: see upon these trees, the buds,
their petals still enwrapped within the rosy tips,
burst forth with the departure of withered leaves.

Vinayedeva. 153.

* From *An Anthology of Sanskrit Court Poetry: Vidyākara's "Subhāsitaratnakosa,"* translated by Daniel H. Ingalls. Cambridge, Mass.: Harvard University Press. Copyright © 1965 by the President and Fellows of Harvard College. (Harvard Oriental Series, 44.) The notes are abridged from the translator's. The poet's name, if known, follows each poem. If it is ascribed to a source other than Vidyākara, the name is in brackets. The numbers refer to Ingalls' edition above.

1. *Kāma's bow . . . cuckoo's bride:* There is a play on words here in that the flowered arrows of the love god Kāma are five in number and are set in motion by the fifth note sung by the cuckoo. Furthermore, the fifth note on the musical scale is the tonic of the amorous mood.

The wind that blows
from the sandal-trees of Malabar,
the sweet sound of cukoos, and the bower vines
raise waves within the hearts of men,
raise yearning.[2]

Srīkantha. 154.

Bright chains of amaranth about their hips,
fresh mango blossoms at their ears,
the red *aśoka* on their breasts
and *mādhāvi* within their hair,
their bodies roughed all over
with yellow pollen of the *bakula*:[3]
such is our lasses' costume; may its advent
bring joy to lusty lads.

Sāvarni. 177.

Summer

The embrace of fawn-eyed damsels
just bathed and moist with sandal paste,[4]
their hair decked out with new-born flowers,
slowly makes love rise again,
whose strength had withered in the summer beams.

Mangalārjuna. 192.

In this summer month which blasts all hope,
burns the vines, is angry at the deer,
is tree-wilting, bee-distressing, jasmine-hating,
dries up lakes, heats dust and fries the sky;
in this month that glows with cruel rays,
how can you, traveler, walk and live?

Bāna. 194.

With flames of saffron-colored forest fire,
broad and narrow, low and high,
spreading, stretching, then cutting back,
and with draughts of smoke for aloe paste[5]
the wind, turned lady's maid, now paints the faces here and
there
of the nymphs, the four directions.

Anon. 196

2. "Wave" and "yearning" here are the same word in the original.

3. *aśoka . . . bakula:* The *aśoka* bears red flowers along its entire branch, often likened to a placard inscribed with red letters. It is regularly associated with fertility and love. It was in an *aśoka* grove that Rāvana imprisoned Sītā in the *Rāmāyana*, and its blooming signaled a festival as long ago as the *Kāmasūtra* (I,i,42). The *mādhāvi* is a delicate, pale flower. The *bakula* is a flower which must be sprinkled with wine from a maiden's mouth.

4. Sandalwood is fragrant and is used in perfumes and cosmetics. [Ingalls' note.]

5. *saffron-colored . . . aloe paste:* Aloe paste (*agallochum*) was used to paint ornamental designs on the face, often applied over a base of saffron or turmeric, to perfume the body and to create a pleasing effect.

A herd of innocent gazelles has gathered close
at the singing of the girl who tends the well,
charmed by its sweetly rocking lullaby.[6]
Beside the road the trees arouse our longing
with gentle breezes that fan the drops of sweat
from weary travelers.

Anon. 197.

The Rains

The water of the arbor brooks carries the scent of the can
flowers[7]
and on the banks a latticework of jasmine buds has opened.
The clouds upon the mountain tops have formed a canopy
for the dancing of the peacocks on the slopes
that laugh with opening flowers.

Bhavabhūti. 215.

The peacock calls gently to his mate who tarries,
and glances once again toward the sky;
then, leaping from his stagem the earth,
making a parasol of his unfolded tail,
to the sound of thunder sweet as loud reverberations of a drum
he performs his joyful dance.

Anon. 222.

Rich is he who drinks his bride's red-lotus lip
in a roof pavilion screened by mats against the rain,
their amorous murmurs mingling with the sound of moorhens[8]
wakened in their baskets by the driving downpour.

[Subhānga?]. 225.

Now the great cloud cat,
darting out his lightning tongue,
licks the creamy moonlight
from the saucepan of the sky.

Yogeśvara. 257.

Autumn

The flights of geese make a semblance of white clouds
and, by reflections in the water, of a hundred lotuses:
as if the fall had not enamored us already
with its river waves ringing sweet and sharp
like women's jeweled anklets.

Manovinoda. 270.

6. The song is a cradle song, the musical *rāga* "Hindola."
7. That is, the flowers are the audience and the clouds and mountaintops the stage for the performance.
8. *Datyuha*, a shy aquatic bird, the size of a small duck, which makes a guttural cry that sounds like "kek-kek-kek-kek."

The sun gives sharp pain
like a low man newly rich.
The deer drops his horns
like a thankless friend.
The waters grow lucid
like a saint's pious thought;
and the mud is squeezed dry
like a poor man who keeps a mistress.

[Bhāsa]. 276.

Mourning with the soft complaint of wild geese,
dressed in skies as white as snowy hills,
her cloud breasts pale and cumulous,
the autumn is like a bride whose husband is abroad.

[Anon]. 277.

Fieldbreaks are set with platforms by the farmers
to repel wild boars who come to eat the crop;
trees are now decked with doves' nests built firm to rear their
young
and anthills have been dug out by the sharp claws of jackals.[9]

Satānanda. 285.

Early Winter

Now are the days when the winter wind[10] sets forth,
friendly days to the jasmine
but death to the beauty of the lotus ponds.
Now women, suffering from the cold,
although their lovers' faults be deep,
welcome by feigning sleep a tight embrace.

Anon. 293.

The peasants now grow haughty,
being flattered by a hundred travelers for their straw;
at night the cows in calf, chewing the cud,
keep warm the herdsmen with their breath;
at dawn the first rays of the sun play on the great bull's back
as he lies covered with mustard flower
and eyelids thick with frost upon the village common.

Yogeśvara. 297.

9. *Fieldbreaks . . . jackels:* Winter rice is planted in the fall for a January harvest. The platforms are manned by farmers who shout or sling stones to drive off wild animals.

10. There is an overtone suggesting that the winter wind is setting forth on its journey or pilgrimage.

With rags upon her back, holding her hands
over the chaff fire placed between her fire-scarred thighs
and pressing her shivering elbows to her sides,
the old woman leaves the house now
neither day nor night.

Vaiśya. 301.

The fire of cow dung, which though mostly smoke
by constant stirring is made to give off flame,
comes into honor with the winter season.
At end of day it shines for the enjoyment
of peasant women, at the stretching of whose arms
the graceful robes fall back
from the contours of their breasts.

Anon. 302.

Late Winter

In the rites of January Jasmine Festival
the women are not so prized, despite their care,
for their worship of the jasmine or their decking of themselves
or their preparation of the pastry cakes,
as they are for stirring up of young men's hearts
with their cry 'ulū ulū ulū' that calls for love.[11]

Anon. 306.

The path of the mountain gorge at dawn,
filling with mist from the slender stream below,
teaches the traveler suddenly to slow his pace,
for though the path runs high above the chasm
it seems, to his frightened gaze that seeks the other side,
to be flooded with the torrent.

Anon. 309.

The cold beauty of the moonlight fades as though
from lack of luck in love;[12]
for no more is it met by laughter of the waterlilies;
its darling moonstone, overlaid by frost,
no longer sweats with yearning;
nor is it welcomed by the eyes of lovers
between their bouts of love.

Anon. 310.

11. *Jasmine . . . love:* A love festival celebrated in Bengal in January, and later in western India. *Ulūlukā* is a warbled woman's cry used as a provocation to love or an auspicious cry at weddings.

12. *cold . . . love:* The moonstone is supposed to weep or sweat in the moon's rays, and the poet hints at lovers sweating in their passion. The winter moon is not even glanced at by the lovers.

The moon bears likeness
to a frightened woman's face;
the sun's weak glow
is a like a bankrupt's order.
The dung fire[13] is as gentle
as a new bride's wrath,
the winter wind as cruel
as a hypocrite's embrace.

Abhinanda? 317.

Kāma

Shot from a stretched eyebrow-bow;
more beautiful than bees on waterlilies,
and swift as spotted antelope;
with pupils for their cruel tips to pierce the hearts of men;
feathered with the long angle of an eye
and hurtful with smiling venom:
may these, a woman's sidelong glances from thick lashes,
these hero-quelling, world-subduing arrows
of the five-arrowed god, protect you.[14]

Manovinoda. 324.

Hail to the family priest of womankind,
who consecrates them for the sport;
to the disembodied boon companion of the moon,
who with his flowered arrows
overcame the god of gods;
hail to the stage director of the play of sex.

Rājaśekhara. 327.

I praise the god, who though bodiless,
by using the lotus eyes of women
has roped the world securely in his far-flung noose;
who forces even upon Siva,
though he wears the ascetic skull and ashes,
consecration in the ritual of bowing
before the feet of the love-angered Pārvatī.[15]

Lalitoka. 328.

13. A dung fire gives off much smoke but little flame.

14. *Shot . . . you:* The chain of sidelong glances is likened to a series of black bees (i.e., the pupils of the eye) on white waterlilies (the white of the eye.) Likewise, the spotted antelope has black spots on a white background. For the love god Kāma see p. 256, notes 25, 26.

15. *I . . . Pārvāti:* Kāma once dared to shoot his arrows of love at the god Śiva and was consumed by fire for his insolence. Hence he is called "bodiless." But Śiva was later smitten and wed to Pārvatī (Umā). On Siva see p. 235.

Behold the skill
of the bowman, Love;
that leaving the body whole,
he breaks the heart within.

Anon. 330.

Adolescence

Now comes a certain grace of eyebrow,
a new development of eye,
and the curve of the breast appears
at youth's commencement;
while in the child's voice
the note of love sounds clear,
composed, one knows not which to say,
of nectar, honey, or of bliss.

Vīryamitra. 334.

No longer do they leave their locks disheveled,
but study how to braid their hair;
they tend their teeth and knot their skirts,
grow fond of amorous practice with their brows;
the motions of their eyes become oblique;
their words acquire ambiguity:
each moment shows a progress in coquetry
as childhood slips to youth.

Rājaśekhara. 335.

This is no budding breast
with standing nipple and expanding sphere,
but rather, say, a saffron-colored cymbal
used by the actor Adolescence
as prologue to the play.

Anon. 340.

Her buttocks vie on their appearance
with an altar made of polished pearl;
her cheek grows somewhat pale,
equaling *madhūka* buds in beauty.
As she enters on young womanhood
how perfect is her body just rising from a sea
of loveliness compounded of thick saffron.

Anon. 341.

Behold the risen face-moon of my darling,
wherein the only blemish is
that I've compared it to the blemished moon.[16]

Anon. 396.

16. The blemish in the moon is a rabbit, or deer, not the Western "man in the moon."

If her plump thighs, her charming lip, her close-set breasts,
if her face-lotus, play the conquerors;
then killed are a pair of plantain stems, killed the *bandhūka*[17] flower,
destroyed are two gold jars, and broken is the moon.

Anon. 400.

The Blossoming of Love

Lady, send forth in waves your glances,
and the bright waterlily fades;
let shine the color of your lip
and coral will grow pale.
Disclose a fraction of your limbs
and gold itself grows black;
lift up your face, and lo,
the sky will bear two moons.

[Rājaśekhara. 518.]

The speed of the dance has shaken loose
the circled blade of palmleaf,[18] which escapes,
as from Love's quiver, from the slender maiden's ear
that, goldened with saffron paste to steal our hearts,
is like the stem, bent in a graceful loop,
of the waterlily flower of her eye.

Rājaśekhara. 524.

The damsel of arched eyebrows,
gracefully circling as she whirls the yo-yo,
constructs three parasols:
with her skirt of southern silk,
with her beautiful pearl necklace,
and with her whirling braid of hair.

Rājaśekhara. 525.

Delicious is ambrosia beyond doubt,
and honey ever tastes like honey;
sweet also is the ripened fruit
of mangoes.
But let a neutral expert say is anything on earth
is half as sweet as my beloved's lip.

Anon. 529.

17. A red tree-flower which blooms in the autumn. It is often a symbol for a girl's red lips.

18. The girl is performing a dance with a yo-yo (*kanduka*), and the blade of palmleaf, which has been wound around her ear, comes untied and sticks out like an arrow.

The Lover Separated from His Mistress

The woods are as lonely
and the rivers have grown as thin as I,
while the days are as long and as hot
as are my sighs.

Anon. 782.

My love rests in my mind
as if melted therein
or reflected or painted or sculpted
or set therein as a jewel or mortised with cement or engraved;
as if nailed thereto by Love's five arrows
or as if tightly sewn into the very threads
of its continuum of thought.

[Bhavabhūti. 783.]

If my absent bride were but a pond,
her eyes the waterliles and her face the lotus,
her brows the rippling waves, her arms the lotus stems;
then might I dive into the water of her loveliness
and cool of limb escape the mortal pain
exacted by the flaming fire of love.

Anon. 784.

Gold necklace, dampened couch and lotus petals,
the wind from the Himālaya bringing drops of sleet:
when these and even liquid sandal are but fuel to Love
how shall his fire ever be extinguished?

[Bana. 803.]

Sunset

The holes of serpents blaze now with the jewels of their hoods;
from sunstones [19] fire has migrated to the sheldrakes' hearts;
and lamps, spearing the darkness, shine in rivalry
of these fragments of the sunset, powdered
in the fierece encounter between day and night.

[Murāri. 861.]

The lion sun, resplendent with wide-flaming mane,
has slain the elephant of day and entered
the cave within the Western Mountain.
Forthwith the bears of darkness drink the sunset blood
and stars shine forth in heaven as the pearls
scattered from the victim's head.

Anon. 864.

19. Sunstones are said to cast off sparks at the touch of the sun.

The darkness wears the guise of rising smoke
and the sky is filled with opening stars for sparks
as the sun descends into the sunset fire.
As his loves, the lot uses, bow down in grief,
lamenting with the cry of struggling bees,[20]
the goddess of the day turns west and joins him in his death.

Malayarāja. 867.

As the sun sets red as an old crane's head
by the western peak
and the vault of the sky is painted with night
as black as crow's harsh throat,
the East, with its darkness fading
as it waits for the rise of the moon,
grows as pale as the cheek of a Sabari[21] girl
long parted from her love.

Acalasimha? 875.

The Moon

He who manages love's theater,
chaplain of the Bowman's[22] grove,
chief god of women, famed in the three worlds,
high priest of passion's kingdom;
he who performs our moonlight mass
and sleeps in the peak of Siva's crown:
victorious is that god born of the sea of milk,
the white-rayed lover of the waterlilies.

Vasukalpa. 897.

The cat, thinking its rays are milk,
licks them from the dish;
the elephant, seeing them woven through the lattice of the
trees,
takes them for lotus stems;
the damsel after love would draw them from her couch
as if thy were her dress:
see how the moon in its pride of light
has cozened all the world.

[Bhāsa? 905.]

The East has borne the Moon.
Love dances and the nymphs of the directions laugh,
while the wind scatters holiday powder,[23]
the pollen of waterlilies, through heaven's court.

Dharmakīrti. 919.

20. The bees are pictured as trying to escape as the petals of flowers close at dusk.

21. Here probably used loosely as "foreigner."

22. Kāma.

23. A sweet-smelling red powder, *patavāsa*, is scattered on occasions of rejoicing and at festivals.

"The moon pours milk down in a thousand steady streams."
"The waterlilies raise their thirsty necks to drink the milk of moonlight."
"The earth, worn out by daytime labor, sinks within a sea of milk."
"From the splash it makes, the cast-up bubbles form the stars."[24]

"By Four Authors." 927.

24. *moon . . . stars:* A capping verse. Each poet supplies a line on a given idea, here that the moon pours forth milk. The authors are unidentified. The Japanese have a similar convention in their *renga,* "linked verse."

RABINDRANATH TAGORE

(1861–1941)

The Post Office

Sir Rabindranath Tagore was certainly the leading early twentieth-century writer of India. A figure of world renown, he received the Nobel Prize in 1913. Rabindranath came from a famous Indian family known for their interest in the arts and for their modern religious and social views. He began to write poetry at an early age and drew his inspiration both from the Bengali poets of the land of his birth and the standard English authors, especially Shelley and Keats. His first volume of poetry was *The Mind's Embodiment* (*Mānasi*) published in 1890. A most versatile writer, Tagore tried his hand at poetry, journalism, drama, and the novel. Among his early works *Beauty* (*Chitrā*) is outstanding. Ezra Pound and Yeats were both impressed with Tagore and Yeats did an introduction to what was perhaps Tagores' most popular work, *Gitanjali* (1912). A major drama, *The King of the Dark Chamber,* was published in 1913. Tagore, it has often been said, reads better in his native Bengali, but nevertheless he made himself a master of English letters and gained a wide reputation in English-speaking countries. His reputation as an intellect and as an educator equaled his literary fame. He travelled widely, including to the United States, and was knighted in 1915. But in 1919 he resigned this honor to protest against British policy in India.

The Post Office is a deceptively simple play, but one with many subtle emotional overtones, and, though modern, continues the Indian tradition of literature as the depiction of emotion rather than of action.

The Post Office*

Characters

MADHAV	GAFFER
AMAL, *his child*	THE VILLAGE HEADMAN
SUDHA, *a flower girl*	THE KING'S HERALD
THE DOCTOR	THE ROYAL PHYSICIAN
A WATCHMAN	A TROOP OF BOYS

Act 1

MADHAV'S HOUSE

MADHAV. What a state I am in! Before he came, nothing mattered; I felt so free. But now that he has come, goodness knows from where, my heart is filled with his dear self, and my home will be no home to me when he leaves. Doctor, do you think he—

PHYSICIAN. If there's life in his fate, then he will live long. But what the medical scriptures say, it seems—

MADHAV. Great heavens, what?

PHYSICIAN. The scriptures have it: "Bile or palsy, cold or gout spring all alike."

MADHAV. Oh, get along, don't fling your scriptures at me; you only make me more anxious; tell me what I can do.

PHYSICIAN. [*Taking snuff*] The patient needs the most scrupulous care.

MADHAV. That's true; but tell me how.

PHYSICIAN. I have already mentioned, on no account must he be let out of doors.

MADHAV. Poor child, it is very hard to keep him indoors all day long.

PHYSICIAN. What else can you do? The autumn sun and the damp are both very bad for the little fellow—for the scriptures have it:

> "In wheezing, swooning, or in nervous fret,
> In jaundice or leaden eyes—"

MADHAV. Never mind the scriptures, please. Eh, then we must shut the poor thing up. Is there no other method?

PHYSICIAN. None at all: for "In the wind and in the sun—"

MADHAV. What will your "in this and in that" do for me now? Why don't you let them alone and come straight to the point? What's to be done, then? Your system is very, very hard for the

* From *Collected Poems and Plays* by Rabindranath Tagore, copyright 1914 by Macmillan Publishing Co., Inc., renewed 1942 by Rabindranath Tagore. Reprinted by permission of Macmillan Publishing Co., Inc., and Macmillan London and Basingstoke.

poor boy; and he is so quiet too with all his pain and sickness. It tears my heart to see him wince, as he takes your medicine.

PHYSICIAN. The more he winces, the surer is the effect. That's why the sage Chyabana observes: "In medicine as in good advice, the least palatable is the truest." Ah, well! I must be trotting now.

[*Exit.*]

[GAFFER *enters.*]

MADHAV. Well, I'm jiggered, there's Gaffer now.

GAFFER. Why, why, I won't bite you.

MADHAV. No, but you are a devil to send children off their heads.

GAFFER. But you aren't a child, and you've no child in the house; why worry then?

MADHAV. Oh, but I have brought a child into the house.

GAFFER. Indeed, how so?

MADHAV. You remember how my wife was dying to adopt a child?

GAFFER. Yes, but that's an old story; you didn't like the idea.

MADHAV. You know, brother, how hard all this getting money has been. That somebody else's child would sail in and waste all this money earned with so much trouble—Oh, I hated the idea. But this boy clings to my heart in such a queer sort of way—

GAFFER. So that's the trouble! and your money goes all for him and feels jolly lucky it does go at all.

MADHAV. Formerly, earning was a sort of passion with me; I simply couldn't help working for money. Now, I make money, and as I know it is all for this dear boy, earning becomes a joy to me.

GAFFER. Ah, well, and where did you pick him up?

MADHAV. He is the son of a man who was a brother to my wife by village ties. He has had no mother since infancy; and now the other day he lost his father as well.

GAFFER. Poor thing; and so he needs me all the more.

MADHAV. The doctor says all the organs of his little body are at loggerheads with each other, and there isn't much hope for his life. There is only one way to save him and that is to keep him out of this autumn wind and sun. But you are such a terror! What with this game of yours at your age, too, to get children out of doors!

GAFFER. God bless my soul! So I'm already as bad as autumn wind and sun, eh! But, friend, I know something, too, of the game of keeping them indoors. When my day's work is over I am coming in to make friends with this child of yours.

[*Exit.*]

[AMAL *enters.*]

AMAL. Uncle, I say, Uncle!

MADHAV. Hullo! Is that you, Amal?

AMAL. Mayn't I be out of the courtyard at all?

MADHAV. No, my dear, no.

AMAL. See there, where Auntie grinds lentils in the quern, the squirrel is sitting with his tail up and with his wee hands he's picking up the broken grains of lentils and crunching them. Can't I run up there?

MADHAV. No, my darling, no.

AMAL. Wish I were a squirrel!—it would be lovely. Uncle, why won't you let me go about?

MADHAV. The doctor says it's bad for you to be out.

AMAL. How can the doctor know?

MADHAV. What a thing to say! The doctor can't know and he reads such huge books!

AMAL. Does his book-learning tell him everything?

MADHAV. Of course, don't you know!

AMAL. [*With a sigh*] Ah, I am so stupid! I don't read books.

MADHAV. Now, think of it; very, very learned people are all like you; they are never out of doors.

AMAL. Aren't they really?

MADHAV. No, how can they? Early and late they toil and moil at their books, and they've eyes for nothing else. Now, my little man, you are going to be learned when you grow up; and then you will stay at home and read such big books, and people will notice you and say, "He's a wonder."

AMAL. No, no Uncle; I beg of you, by your dear feet—I don't want to be learned; I won't.

MADHAV. Dear, dear; it would have been my saving if I could have been learned.

AMAL. No, I would rather go about and see everything that there is.

MADHAV. Listen to that! See! What will you see, what is there so much to see?

AMAL. See that far-away hill from our window—I often long to go beyond those hills and right away.

MADHAV. Oh, you silly! As if there's nothing more to be done but just get up to the top of that hill and away! Eh! You don't talk sense, my boy. Now listen, since that hill stands there upright as a barrier, it means you can't get beyond it. Else, what was the use in heaping up so many large stones to make such a big affair of it, eh!

AMAL. Uncle, do you think it is meant to prevent us crossing over? It seems to me because the earth can't speak it raises its hands into the sky and beckons. And those who live far off and sit alone by their windows can see the signal. But I suppose the learned people—

MADHAV. No, they don't have time for that sort of nonsense. They are not crazy like you.

AMAL. Do you know, yesterday I met some one quite as crazy as I am.

MADHAV. Gracious me, really, how so?

AMAL. He had a bamboo staff on his shoulder with a small bundle at the top, and a brass pot in his left hand, and an old pair of shoes on; he was making for those hills straight across that meadow there. I called out to him and asked, "Where are you going?" He answered, "I don't know; anywhere!" I asked again, "Why are you going?" He said, "I'm going out to seek work." Say, Uncle, have you to seek work?

MADHAV. Of course I have to. There are many about looking for jobs.

AMAL. How lovely! I'll go about like them too, finding things to do.

MADHAV. Suppose you seek and don't find. Then—

AMAL. Wouldn't that be jolly? Then I should go farther! I watched that man slowly walking on with his pair of worn-out shoes. And when he got to where the water flows under the fig tree, he stopped and washed his feet in the stream. Then he took out from his bundle some gram-flour, moistened it with water and began to eat. Then he tied up his bundle and shouldered it again; tucked up his cloth above his knees and crossed the stream. I've asked Auntie to let me go up to the stream, and eat my gram-flour just like him.

MADHAV. And what did your Auntie say to that?

AMAL. Auntie said, "Get well and then I'll take you over there." Please, Uncle, when shall I get well?

MADHAV. It won't be long, dear.

AMAL. Really, but then I shall go right away the moment I'm well again.

MADHAV. And where will you go?

AMAL. Oh, I will walk on, crossing so many streams, wading through water. Everybody will be asleep with their doors shut in the heat of the day and I will tramp on and on seeking work far, very far.

MADHAV. I see! I think you had better be getting well first; then—

AMAL. But then you won't want me to be learned, will you, Uncle?

MADHAV. What would you rather be, then?

AMAL. I can't think of anything just now; but I'll tell you later on.

MADHAV. Very well. But mind you, you aren't to call out and talk to strangers again.

AMAL. But I love to talk to strangers!

MADHAV. Suppose they had kidnaped you?

AMAL. That would have been splendid! But no one ever takes me away. They all want me to stay in here.

MADHAV. I am off to my work—but, darling, you won't go out, will you?

AMAL. No, I won't. But, Uncle, you'll let me be in this room by the roadside.

[*Exit* MADHAV.]

DAIRYMAN. Curds, curds, good nice curds.

AMAL. Curdseller, I say, Curdseller.

DAIRYMAN. Why do you call me? Will you buy some curds?

AMAL. How can I buy? I have no money.

DAIRYMAN. What a boy! Why call out then? Ugh! What a waste of time!

AMAL. I would go with you if I could.

DAIRYMAN. With me?

AMAL. Yes, I seem to feel homesick when I hear you call from far down the road.

DAIRYMAN. [*Lowering his yoke-pole*] Whatever are you doing here, my child?

AMAL. The doctor says I'm not to be out, so I sit here all day long.

DAIRYMAN. My poor child, whatever has happened to you?

AMAL. I can't tell. You see, I am not learned, so I don't know what's the matter with me. Say, Dairyman, where do you come from?

DAIRYMAN. From our village.

AMAL. Your village? Is it very far?

DAIRYMAN. Our village lies on the river Shamli at the foot of the Panch-mura hills.

AMAL. Panch-mura hills! Shamli river! I wonder. I may have seen your village. I can't think when, though!

DAIRYMAN. Have you seen it? Been to the foot of those hills?

AMAL. Never. But I seem to remember having seen it. Your village is under some very old big trees, just by the side of the road—isn't that so?

DAIRYMAN. That's right, child.

AMAL. And on the slope of the hill cattle grazing.

DAIRYMAN. How wonderful! Cattle grazing in our village! Indeed there are!

AMAL. And your women with red saris fill their pitchers from the river and carry them on their heads.

DAIRYMAN. Good, that's right! Women from our dairy village do come and draw their water from the river; but then it isn't everyone who has a red sari to put on. But, my dear child, surely you must have been there for a walk some time.

AMAL. Really, Dairyman, never been there at all. But the first day the doctor lets me go out, you are going to take me to your village.

DAIRYMAN. I will, my child, with pleasure.

AMAL. And you'll teach me to cry curds and shoulder the yoke like you and walk the long, long road?

DAIRYMAN. Dear, dear, did you ever? Why should you sell curds? No, you will read big books and be learned.

AMAL. No, I never want to be learned—I'll be like you and take my curds from the village by the red road near the old banyan tree, and I will hawk it from cottage to cottage. Oh, how do you cry —"Curds, curds, fine curds"? Teach me the tune, will you?

DAIRYMAN. Dear, dear, teach you the tune; what a notion!

AMAL. Please do. I love to hear it. I can't tell you how queer I feel when I hear you cry out from the bend of that road, through the line of those trees! Do you know I feel like that when I hear the shrill cry of kites from almost the end of the sky?

DAIRYMAN. Dear child, will you have some curds? Yes, do.

AMAL. But I have no money.

DAIRYMAN. No, no, no, don't talk of money! You'll make me so happy if you take some curds from me.

AMAL. Say, have I kept you too long?

DAIRYMAN. Not a bit; it has been no loss to me at all; you have taught me how to be happy selling curds.

[*Exit.*]

AMAL. [*Intoning*] Curds, curds, fine curds—from the dairy village —from the country of the Panch-mura hills by the Shamli bank. Curds, good curds; in the early morning the women make the cows stand in a row under the trees and milk them, and in the evening they turn the milk into curds. Curds, good curds. Hello, there's the watchman on his rounds. Watchman, I say, come and have a word with me.

WATCHMEN. What's all this row about? Aren't you afraid of the likes of me?

AMAL. No, why should I be?

WATCHMAN. Suppose I march you off, then?

AMAL. Where will you take me to? Is it very far, right beyond the hills?

WATCHMAN. Suppose I march you straight to the King?

AMAL. To the King! Do, will you? But the doctor won't let me go out. No one can ever take me away. I've got to stay here all day long.

WATCHMAN. The doctor won't let you, poor fellow! So I see! Your face is pale and there are dark rings round your eyes. Your veins stick out from your poor thin hands.

AMAL. Won't you sound the gong, Watchman?

WATCHMAN. The time has not yet come.

AMAL. How curious! Some say the time has not yet come, and some say the time has gone by! But surely your time will come the moment you strike the gong!

WATCHMAN. That's not possible; I strike up the gong only when it is time.

AMAL. Yes, I love to hear your gong. When it is midday and our meal is over, Uncle goes off to his work and Auntie falls asleep reading her Ramayana, and in the courtyard under the shadow of the wall our doggie sleeps with his nose in his curled-up tail; then your gong strikes out, "Dong, dong, dong!" Tell me, why does your gong sound?

WATCHMAN.. My gong sounds to tell the people, Time waits for none, but goes on for ever.

AMAL. Where, to what land?

WATCHMAN. That none knows.

AMAL. Then I suppose no one has ever been there! Oh, I do wish to fly with the time to that land of which no one knows anything.

WATCHMAN. All of us have to get there one day, my child.

AMAL. Have I too?

WATCHMAN. Yes, you too!

AMAL. But the doctor won't let me out.

WATCHMAN. One day the doctor himself may take you there by the hand.

AMAL. He won't; you don't know him. He only keeps me in.

WATCHMAN. One greater than he comes and lets us free.

AMAL. When will this great doctor come for me? I can't stick in here any more.

WATCHMAN. Shouldn't talk like that, my child.

AMAL. No, I am here where they have left me—I never move a bit. But, when your gong goes off, dong, dong, dong, it goes to my heart. Say, Watchman?

WATCHMAN. Yes, my dear.

AMAL. Say, what's going on there in that big house on the other side, where there is a flag flying high up and the people are always going in and out?

WATCHMAN. Oh, there? That's our new Post Office.

AMAL. Post Office? Whose?

WATCHMAN. Whose? Why, the King's, surely!

AMAL. Do letters come from the King to his office here?

WATCHMAN. Of course. One fine day there may be a letter for you in there.

AMAL. A letter for me? But I am only a little boy.

WATCHMAN. The King sends tiny notes to little boys.

AMAL. Oh, how splendid! When shall I have my letter? How do you know he'll write to me?

WATCHMAN. Otherwise why should he set his Post Office here right in front of your open window, with the golden flag flying?

AMAL. But who will fetch me my King's letter when it comes?

WATCHMAN. The King has many postmen. Don't you see them run about with round gilt badges on their chests?

AMAL. Well, where do they go?

WATCHMAN. Oh, from door to door, all through the country.

AMAL. I'll be the King's postman when I grow up.

WATCHMAN. Ha! ha! Postman, indeed! Rain or shine, rich or poor, from house to house delivering letters—that's very great work!

AMAL. That's what I'd like best. What makes you smile so? Oh, yes, your work is great too. When it is silent everywhere in the heat of the noonday, your gong sounds, Dong, dong, dong,—and sometimes when I wake up at night all of a sudden and find our lamp blown out, I can hear through the darkness your gong slowly sounding, Dong, dong, dong!

WATCHMAN. There's the village headman! I must be off. If he catches me gossiping there'll be a great to-do.

AMAL. The headman? Whereabouts is he?

WATCHMAN. Right down the road there; see that huge palm-leaf umbrella hopping along? That's him!

AMAL. I suppose the King's made him our headman here?

WATCHMAN. Made him? Oh, no! A fussy busybody! He knows so many ways of making himself unpleasant that everybody is afraid of him. It's just a game for the likes of him; making trouble for everybody. I must be off now! Mustn't keep work waiting, you know! I'll drop in again tomorrow morning and tell you all the news of the town.

[*Exit.*]

AMAL. It would be splendid to have a letter from the King every day. I'll read them at the window. But, oh! I can't read writing. Who'll read them out to me, I wonder! Auntie reads her *Ramayama;* she may know the King's writing. If no one will, then I must keep them carefully and read them when I'm grown up. But if the postman can't find me? Headman, Mr. Headman, may I have a word with you?

HEADMAN. Who is yelling after me on the highway? Oh, it's you, is it, you wretched monkey?

AMAL. You're the headman. Everybody minds you.

HEADMAN. [*Looking pleased*] Yes, oh yes, they do! They must!

AMAL. Do the King's postmen listen to you?

HEADMAN. They've got to. By Jove, I'd like to see—

AMAL. Will you tell the postman it's Amal who sits by the window here?

HEADMAN. What's the good of that?

AMAL. In case there's a letter for me.

HEADMAN. A letter for you! Whoever's going to write you?

AMAL. If the King does.

HEADMAN. Ha! Ha! what an uncommon little fellow you are! Ha! ha! the King, indeed; aren't you his bosom friend, eh! You haven't met for a long while and the King is pining for you, I am sure. Wait till tomorrow and you'll have your letter.

AMAL. Say, Headman, why do you speak to me in that tone of voice? Are you cross?

HEADMAN. Upon my word! Cross, indeed! You write to the King! Madhav is a devilish swell nowadays. He's made a little pile; and so kings and padishahs are everyday talk with his people. Let me find him once and I'll make him dance. Oh, you—you snipper-snapper! I'll get the King's letter sent to your house—indeed I will!

AMAL. No, no, please don't trouble yourself about it.

HEADMAN. And why not, pray! I'll tell the King about you and he won't be long. One of his footmen will come presently for news of you. Madhav's impudence staggers me. If the King hears of this, that'll take some of his nonsense out of him.

[*Exit.*]

AMAL. Who are you walking there? How your anklets tinkle! Do stop a while, won't you?

[A GIRL *enters.*]

GIRL. I haven't a moment to spare; it is already late!

AMAL. I see, you don't wish to stop; I don't care to stay on here either.

GIRL. You make me think of some late star in the morning! Whatever's the matter with you?

AMAL. I don't know; the doctor won't let me out.

GIRL. Ah me! Don't go, then! Should listen to the doctor. People will be cross with you if you're naughty. I know, always looking out and watching must make you feel tired. Let me close the window a bit for you.

AMAL. No, don't, only this one's open! All the others are shut. But will you tell me who you are? I don't seem to know you.

GIRL. I am Sudha.

AMAL. What Sudha?

SUDHA. Don't you know? Daughter of the flower-seller here.

AMAL. What do *you* do?

SUDHA. I gather flowers in my basket.

AMAL. Oh, flower-gathering! That is why your feet seem so glad and your anklets jingle so merrily as you walk. Wish I could be out too. Then I would pick some flowers for you from the very top-most branches right out of sight.

SUDHA. Would you really? Do you know as much about flowers as I?

AMAL. Yes, I *do*, quite as much. I know all about Champa of the fairy tale and his six brothers. If only they let me, I'll go right into the dense forest where you can't find your way. And where the honey-sipping humming-bird rocks himself on the end of the thinnest branch, I will blossom into a *champa*. Would you be my sister *parul*?[1]

SUDHA. You are silly! How can I be sister *parul* when I am Sudha and my mother is Sasi, the flower-seller? I have to weave so many garlands a day. It would be jolly if I could lounge here like you!

AMAL. What would you do then, all the day long?

SUDHA. I could have great times with my doll Benay the bride, and Meni the pussy-cat, and—but I say, it is getting late and I mustn't stop, or I won't find a single flower.

AMAL. Oh, wait a little longer; I do like it so!

SUDHA. Ah, well—now don't be naughty. Be good and sit still, and on my way back home with the flowers I'll come and talk with you.

AMAL. And you'll let me have a flower, then?

SUDHA. No, how can I? It has to be paid for.

AMAL. I'll pay when I grow up—before I leave to look for work on the other side of that stream.

SUDHA. Very well, then.

AMAL. And you'll come back when you have your flowers?

SUDHA. I will.

AMAL. You will, really?

SUDHA. Yes, I will.

AMAL. You won't forget me? I am Amal, remember that.

SUDHA. I won't forget you, you'll see.

[*Exit.*]

[A TROOP OF BOYS *enter.*]

AMAL. Say, brothers, where are you all off to? Stop here a little.

A BOY. We're off to play.

AMAL. What will you play at, brothers?

A BOY. We'll play at being plowmen.

ANOTHER BOY. [*Showing a stick*] This is our plowshare.

ANOTHER BOY. We two are the pair of oxen.

AMAL. And you're going to play the whole day?

A BOY. Yes, all day long.

AMAL. And you will come home in the evening by the road along the river bank?

BOY. Yes.

AMAL. Do you pass our house on your way home?

1. He invites her to become a fairy-tale princess and live in the forest, as a companion (sister *parul*) rather than a lover. A *champa* is a scented magnolia.

A BOY. Come out and play with us; yes, do.

AMAL. The doctor won't let me out.

A BOY. The doctor! Do you mean to say you mind what the doctor says? Let's be off; it is getting late.

AMAL. Don't go. Play on the road near this window. I could watch you, then.

A BOY. What can be play at here?

AMAL. With all these toys of mine that are lying about. Here you are; have them. I can't play alone. They are getting dirty and are of no use to me.

BOYS. How jolly! What fine toys! Look, here's a ship. There's old mother Jatai. Isn't this a gorgeous *sepoy*? And you'll let us have them all? You don't really mind?

AMAL. No, not a bit; have them by all means.

A BOY. You don't want them back?

AMAL. Oh, no, I shan't want them.

A BOY. Say, won't you get a scolding for this?

AMAL. No one will scold me. But will you play with them in front of our door for a while every morning? I'll get you new ones when these are old.

A BOY. Oh, yes, we will. I say, put these *sepoys* into a line. We'll play at war; where can we get a musket? Oh, look here, this bit of reed will do nicely. Say, but you're off to sleep already.

AMAL. I'm afraid I'm sleepy. I don't know, I feel like it at times. I have been sitting a long while and I'm tired; my back aches.

A BOY. It's hardly midday now. How is it you're sleepy? Listen! The gong's sounding the first watch.

AMAL. Yes, Dong, dong, dong; it tolls me to sleep.

A BOY. We had better go, then. We'll come in again tomorrow morning.

AMAL. I want to ask you something before you go. You are always out—do you know of the King's postmen?

BOYS. Yes, quite well.

AMAL. Who are they? Tell me their names.

A BOY. One's Badal.

ANOTHER BOY. Another's Sarat.

ANOTHER BOY. There's so many of them.

AMAL. Do you think they will know me if there's a letter for me?

A BOY. Surely, if your name's on the letter they will find you out.

AMAL. When you call in tomorrow morning, will you bring one of them along so that he'll know me?

A BOY. Yes, if you like.

CURTAIN

Act II

AMAL IN BED

AMAL. Can't I go near the window today, Uncle? Would the doctor mind that too?

MADHAV. Yes, darling; you see you've made yourself worse squatting there day after day.

AMAL. Oh, no, I don't know if it's made me more ill, but I always feel well when I'm there.

MADHAV. No, you don't; you squat there and make friends with the whole lot of people round here, old and young, as if they are holding a fair right under my eaves—flesh and blood won't stand that strain. Just see—your face is quite pale.

AMAL. Uncle, I fear my fakir will pass and not see me by the window.

MADHAV. Your fakir; whoever's that?

AMAL. He comes and chats to me of the many lands where he's been. I love to hear him.

MADHAV. How's that? I don't know of any fakirs.

AMAL. This is about the time he comes in. I beg of you, by your dear feet, ask him in for a moment to talk to me here.

[GAFFER *enters in a fakir's guise.*]

AMAL. There you are. Come here, Fakir, by my bedside.

MADHAV. Upon my word, but this is—

GAFFER. [*winking hard*] I am the Fakir.

MADHAV. It beats my reckoning what you're not.

AMAL. Where have you been this time, Fakir?

GAFFER. To the Isle of Parrots. I am just back.

MADHAV. The Parrots' Isle!

GAFFER. Is it so very astonishing? I am not like you. A journey doesn't cost a thing. I tramp just where I like.

AMAL. [*Clapping*] How jolly for you! Remember your promise to take me with you as your follower when I'm well.

GAFFER. Of course, and I'll teach you so many travelers' secrets that nothing in sea or forest or mountain can bar your way.

MADHAV. What's all this rigmarole?

GAFFER. Amal, my dear, I bow to nothing in sea or mountain; but if the doctor joins in with this uncle of yours, then I with all my magic must own myself beaten.

AMAL. No. Uncle won't tell the doctor. And I promise to lie quiet; but the day I am well, off I go with the Fakir, and nothing in sea or mountain or torrent shall stand in my way.

MADHAV. Fie, dear child, don't keep on harping upon going! It makes me so sad to hear you talk so.

AMAL. Tell me, Fakir, what the Parrots' Isle is like.

GAFFER. It's a land of wonders; it's a haunt of birds. No men are there; and they neither speak nor walk, they simply sing and they fly.

AMAL. How glorious! And it's by some sea?

GAFFER. Of course. It's on the sea.

AMAL. And green hills are there?

GAFFER. Indeed, they live among the green hills; and in the time of the sunset when there is a red glow on the hillside, all the birds with their green wings go flocking to their nests.

AMAL. And there are waterfalls!

GAFFER. Dear me, of course; you don't have a hill without its waterfalls. Oh, it's like molten diamonds; and, my dear, what dances they have! Don't they make the pebbles sing as they rush over them to the sea! No devil of a doctor can stop them for a moment. The birds looked upon me as nothing but a man, merely a trifling creature without wings—and they would have nothing to do with me. Were it not so I would build a small cabin for myself among their crowd of nests and pass my days counting the sea-waves.

AMAL. How I wish I were a bird! Then—

GAFFER. But that would have been a bit of a job; I hear you've fixed up with the dairyman to be a hawker of curds when you grow up; I'm afraid such business won't flourish among birds; you might land yourself into serious loss.

MADHAV. Really this is too much. Between you two I shall turn crazy. Now, I'm off.

AMAL. Has the dairyman been, Uncle?

MADHAV. And why shouldn't he? He won't bother his head running errands for your pet fakir, in and out among the nests in his Parrots' Isle. But he has left a jar of curds for you saying that he is busy with his niece's wedding in the village, and has to order a band at Kamlipara.

AMAL. But he is going to marry me to his little niece.

GAFFER. Dear me, we are in a fix now.

AMAL. He said she would be my lovely little bride with a pair of pearl drops in her ears and dressed in a lovely red sari and in the morning she would milk with her own hands the black cow and feed me with warm milk with foam on it from a brand-new earthen cruse; and in the evenings she would carry the lamp round the cow-house, and then come and sit by me to tell me tales of Champa and his six brothers.

GAFFER. How charming! It would even tempt me, a hermit! But never mind, dear, about this wedding. Let it be. I tell you that when you marry there'll be no lack of nieces in this household.

MADHAV. Shut up! This is more than I can stand. [*Exit.*]

AMAL. Fakir, now that Uncle's off, just tell me, has the King sent me a letter to the Post Office?

GAFFER. I gather that his letter has already started; it is on the way here.

AMAL. On the way? Where is it? Is it on that road winding through the trees which you can follow to the end of the forest when the sky is quite clear after rain?

GAFFER. That is where it is. You know all about it already.

AMAL. I do, everything.

GAFFER So I see, but how?

AMAL. I can't say; but it's quite clear to me. I fancy I've seen it often in days long gone by. How long ago I can't tell. Do you know when? I can see it all: there, the King's postman coming down the hillside alone, a lantern in his left hand and on his back a bag of letters; climbing down for ever so long, for days and nights, and where at the foot of the mountain the waterfall becomes a stream he takes to the footpath on the bank and walks on through the rye; then comes the sugar-cane field and he disappears into the narrow lane cutting through the tall stems of sugar-canes; then he reaches the open meadow where the cricket chirps and where there is not a single man to be seen, only the snipe wagging their tails and poking at the mud with their bills. I can feel him coming nearer and nearer and my heart becomes glad.

GAFFER. My eyes are not young; but you make me see all the same.

AMAL. Say, Fakir, do you know the King who has this Post Office?

GAFFER. I do; I go to him for my alms every day.

AMAL. Good! When I get well I must have my alms too from him, mayn't I?

GAFFER. You won't need to ask, my dear; he'll give it to you of his own accord.

AMAL. No, I will go to his gate and cry, "Victory to thee, O King!" and dancing to the tabor's sound, ask for alms. Won't it be nice?

GAFFER. It will be splendid, and if you're with me I shall have my full share. But what will you ask?

AMAL. I shall say, "Make me your postman, that I may go about, lantern in hand, delivering your letters from door to door. Don't let me stay at home all day!"

GAFFER. What is there to be sad for, my child, even were you to stay at home?

AMAL. It isn't sad. When they shut me in here first I felt the day was so long. Since the King's Post Office was put there I like more and more being indoors, and as I think I shall get a letter one day, I feel quite happy and then I don't mind being quiet and alone. I wonder if I shall make out what'll be in the King's letter?

GAFFER. Even if you didn't, wouldn't it be enough if it just bore your name?

[MADHAV *enters.*]

MADHAV. Have you any idea of the trouble you've got me into, between you two?

GAFFER. What's the matter?

MADHAV. I hear you've let it get rumored about that the King has planted his office here to send messages to both of you.

GAFFER. Well, what about it?

MADHAV. Our headman Panchanan has had it told to the King anonymously.

GAFFER. Aren't we aware that everything reaches the King's ears?

MADHAV. Then why don't you look out? Why take the King's name in vain? You'll bring me to ruin if you do.

AMAL. Say, Fakir, will the King be cross?

GAFFER. Cross, nonsense! And with a child like you and a fakir such as I am? Let's see if the King be angry, and then won't I give him a piece of my mind!

AMAL. Say, Fakir, I've been feeling a sort of darkness coming over my eyes since the morning. Everything seems like a dream. I long to be quiet. I don't feel like talking at all. Won't the King's letter come? Suppose this room melts away all on a sudden, suppose—

GAFFER. [*Fanning* AMAL] The letter's sure to come today, my boy.

[DOCTOR *enters.*]

DOCTOR. And how do you feel today?

AMAL. Feel awfully well today, Doctor. All pain seems to have left me.

DOCTOR. [*Aside to* MADHAV] Don't quite like the look of that smile. Bad sign, his feeling well! Chakradhan has observed—

MADHAV. For goodness' sake, Doctor, leave Chakradhan alone. Tell me what's going to happen?

DOCTOR. Can't hold him in much longer. I fear! I warned you before—this looks like a fresh exposure.

MADHAV. No, I've used the utmost care, never let him out of doors; and the windows have been shut almost all the time.

DOCTOR. There's a peculiar quality in the air today. As I came in I found a fearful draught through your front door. That's most hurtful. Better lock it at once. Would it matter if this kept your visitors off for two or three days? If some one happens to call unexpectedly—there's the back door. You had better shut this window as well, it's letting in the sunset rays only to keep the patient awake.

MADHAV. Amal has shut his eyes. I expect he is sleeping. His face tells me—Oh, Doctor, I bring in a child who is a stranger and love him as my own, and now I suppose I must lose him!

DOCTOR. What's that? There's your headman sailing in!—What a bother! I must be going, brother. You had better stir about and see to the doors being properly fastened. I will send on a strong dose directly I get home. Try it on him—it may save him at last, if he can be saved at all.

[*Exeunt* MADHAV *and* DOCTOR.]

[THE HEADMAN *enters.*]

HEADMAN. Hello, urchin!—

GAFFER. [*Rising hastily*] 'Sh, be quiet.

AMAL. No, Fakir, did you think I was asleep? I wasn't. I can hear everything; yes, and voices far away. I feel that mother and father are sitting by my pillow and speaking to me.

[MADHAV *enters.*]

HEADMAN. I say, Madhav, I hear you hobnob with bigwigs nowadays.

MADHAV. Spare me your jokes, Headman; we are but common people.

HEADMAN. But your child here is expecting a letter from the King.

MADHAV. Don't you take any notice of him, a mere foolish boy!

HEADMAN. Indeed, why not! It'll beat the King hard to find a better family! Don't you see why the King plants his new Post Office right before your window? Why, there's a letter for you from the King, urchin.

AMAL. [*Starting up*] Indeed, really!

HEADMAN. How can it be false? You're the King's chum. Here's your letter. [*Showing a blank slip of paper*] Ha, ha, ha! This is the letter.

AMAL. Please don't mock me. Say, Fakir, is it so?

GAFFER. Yes, my dear. I as Fakir tell you it is his letter.

AMAL. How is it I can't see? It all looks so blank to me. What is there in the letter, Mr. Headman?

HEADMAN. The King says, "I am calling on you shortly; you had better have puffed rice for me.—Palace fare is quite tasteless to me now." Ha! ha! ha!

MADHAV. [*With folded palms*] I beseech you, Headman, don't you joke about these things—

GAFFER. Joking indeed! He would not dare.

MADHAV. Are you out of your mind too, Gaffer?

GAFFER. Out of my mind; well then, I am; I can read plainly that the King writes he will come himself to see Amal, with the State Physician.

AMAL. Fakir, Fakir, shh, his trumpet! Can't you hear?

HEADMAN. Ha! ha! ha! I fear he won't until he's a bit more off his head.

AMAL. Mr. Headman, I thought you were cross with me and didn't love me. I never could have believed you would fetch me the King's letter. Let me wipe the dust off your feet.

HEADMAN. This little child does have an instinct of reverence. Though a little silly, he has a good heart.

AMAL. It's hard on the fourth watch now, I suppose. Hark, the gong, "Dong, dong, ding—Dong, dong, ding." Is the evening star up? How is it I can't see—

GAFFER. Oh, the windows are all shut; I'll open them.

[*A knocking outside.*]

MADHAV. What's that?—Who is it?—What a bother!

VOICE. [*From outside*] Open the door.

MADHAV. Headman—I hope they're not robbers.

HEADMAN. Who's there?—It is Panchanan, the headman, who calls.—Aren't you afraid to make that noise? Fancy! The noise has ceased! Panchanan's voice carries far.—Yes, show me the biggest robbers!—

MADHAV. [*Peering out of the window*] No wonder the noise has ceased. They've smashed the outer door.

[THE KING'S HERALD *enters.*]

HERALD. Our Sovereign King comes tonight!

HEADMAN. My God!

AMAL. At what hour of the night, Herald?

HERALD. On the second watch.

AMAL. When my friend the watchman will strike his gong from the city gates, "Ding dong ding, ding dong ding"—then?

HERALD. Yes, then. The King sends his greatest physician to attend his young friend.

[STATE PHYSICIAN *enters.*]

STATE PHYSICIAN. What's this? How close it is here! Open wide all the doors and windows. [*Feeling* AMAL'*s body*] How do you feel, my child?

AMAL. I feel very well, Doctor, very well. All pain is gone. How fresh and open! I can see all the stars now twinkling from the other side of the dark.

PHYSICIAN. Will you feel well enough to leave your bed when the King comes in the middle watches of the night?

AMAL. Of course, I'm dying to be about for ever so long. I'll ask the King to find me the polar star.—I must have seen it often, but I don't know exactly which it is.

PHYSICIAN. He will tell you everything. [*To* MADHAV] Arrange flowers through the room for the King's visit. [*Indicating* THE HEADMAN] We can't have that person in here.

AMAL. No, let him be, Doctor. He is a friend. It was he who brought me the King's letter.

PHYSICIAN. Very well, my child. He may remain if he is a friend of yours.

MADHAV. [*Whispering into* AMAL'*s ear*] My child, the King loves you. He is coming himself. Beg for a gift from him. You know our humble circumstances.

AMAL. Don't you worry, Uncle.—I've made up my mind about it.

MADHAV. What is it, my child?

AMAL. I shall ask him to make me one of his postmen that I may wander far and wide, delivering his message from door to door.

MADHAV. [*Slapping his forehead*] Alas, is that all?

AMAL. What'll be our offerings to the King, Uncle, when he comes?

HERALD. He has commanded puffed rice.

AMAL. Puffed rice. Say, Headman, you're right. You said so. You knew all we didn't.

HEADMAN. If you would send word to my house I could manage for the King's advent really nice—

PHYSICIAN. No need at all. Now be quiet, all of you. Sleep is coming over him. I'll sit by his pillow; he's dropping asleep. Blow out the oil-lamp. Only let the starlight stream in. Hush, he sleeps.

MADHAV. [*Addressing* GAFFER] What are you standing there for like a statue, folding your palms?—I am nervous.—Say, are there good omens? Why are they darkening the room? How will starlight help?

GAFFER. Silence, unbeliever!

[SUDHA *enters*.]

SUDHA. Amal!

PHYSICIAN. He's asleep.

SUDHA. I have some flowers for him. Mayn't I give them into his own hand?

PHYSICIAN. Yes, you may.

SUDHA. When will he be awake?

PHYSICIAN. Directly the King comes and calls him.

SUDHA. Will you whisper a word for me in his ear?

PHYSICIAN. What shall I say?

SUDHA. Tell him Sudha has not forgotten him.

CURTAIN

R. K. NARAYAN

(born 1906)

The Financial Expert

R. K. Narayan combines an Indian outlook on life with a technique of the novel which draws its inspiration from modern England and the United States. The novels of Somerset Maugham, Sinclair Lewis, and John Steinbeck are among his models. Steinbeck's *Tortilla Flat* and the *Grapes of Wrath* he has called "desirable patterns" in fiction. But the greatest influence from the West has come from his friend Graham Greene, to whom he says he owes his literary career. Some of the precision and economy of expression of Greene's earlier work is evident in Narayan, but the tortuous spiritual problems of Greene's more recent work are alien to him and to the Hindu spirit in general. The world of Narayan's villages is a world where good and bad blend and where there are no absolutes. In the *Financial Expert* the hero's worship of the Goddess of Money causes him to be rewarded with a valuable pornographic manuscript. But the work does not end here; the hero's elaborate system of banking fails, leaving him, at the end of the work as he was at the beginning, a moneychanger sitting under a banyan tree. A Western writer might have made the story a triumph or a tragedy. Narayan does neither: the ending is happy and the indestructible Margayya will start again. Narayan mixes the tragic and the comic with gentle irony and with no editorializing.

A typical Southern Indian village in the neighborhood of Madras, Narayan's birthplace, is the scene of most of his stories. In such villages the middle ages and the twentieth century live side by side—the family craft shop lies in the shadow of the steel mill, and the ascetic, living like a holy man of old, preaches in a world of socialists, Marxists, and modern government officialdom. Narayan has covered various aspects of this scene in his works. He depicts a professor's life at a boys' school in *Grateful to Life and Death* (1953). *Swami and Friends* (1954), a short novel, chronicles the adventures of two Tom Sawyer-like Indian moppets. In *Waiting for the Mahatma* (1955) Narayan has as a hero a dissolute youth who becomes a follower of Gandhi merely to be with a girl he is wooing. His portrait of Gandhi and his followers is objective: he can admire the holy man but at the same time see his errors and his human qualities. The impact of industrialism is poetically revealed in *The Guide* (1958); its hero is a boy whose imagination is overwhelmed by the arrival of the first locomotive in Malgudi and who by accident becomes a holy man responsible for performing a miracle.

For his buoyant humor Narayan has been compared to Gogol. The financial expert, Margayya, has been called a "modern Babbitt." There is more truth in the first of these observations than in the second. Margayya has go-getter, Babbitt-like qualities, to be sure, and the village of Malgudi is as typical of India as Sinclair Lewis's town is typical of America. But Margayya is shrewder and more resilient than Babbitt; he is Babbitt, but an entrepreneur as well as just a businessman. His combination of modern business acumen, age-old wisdom and superstition is characteristic of the Indian village mind. His problems, especially his difficulties with his son, are a microcosm of the problems of India today.

The Financial Expert is written in English. There exists in India an Anglo-Indian literary tradition at least a hundred years old, and of the fourteen or so major languages of India, English competes favorably for its share of the reading audience. Despite certain anti-English pressures developing from independence and increased nationalism, only Bengali and Hindi are superior to English in securing a writer a large Indian audience.

From The Financial Expert*

From time immemorial people seemed to have been calling him "Margayya." No one knew, except his father and mother, who were only dimly recollected by a few cronies in his ancestral village, that he had been named after the enchanting god Krishna. Everyone called him Margayya and thought that he had been called so at his naming ceremony. He himself must have forgotten his original name: he had gradually got into the habit of signing his name "Margayya" even in legal documents. And what did it mean? It was purely derivative: "Marga" meant "The Way" and "Ayya" was an honorific suffix: taken together it denoted one who showed the way. He showed the way out to those in financial trouble. And in all those villages that lay within a hundred-mile radius of Malgudi, was there anyone who could honestly declare that he was not in financial difficulties? The emergence of Margayya was an unexpected and incalculable offshoot of a co-operator's zeal. This statement will be better understood if we watch him in his setting a little more closely.

One of the proudest buildings in Malgudi was the Central Co-operative Land Mortgage Bank, which was built in the year 1914 and named after a famous Registrar of Co-operative Societies, Sir ——, who had been knighted for his devotion to Co-operation after he had, in fact, lost his voice explaining co-operative principles to peasants in the village at one end and to the officials in charge of the files at the Secretariat end. It was said that he died while serving on a Rural Indebtedness Sub-committee. After his death it was discovered that he had left all his savings for the construction of the bank. He now watched, from within a teak frame suspended on the central landing, all the comings and goings, and he was said to be responsible for occasional poltergeist phenomena, the rattling of paperweights, flying ledgers, and sounds like the brisk opening of folios, the banging of fists on a table, and so on—evidenced by successive night watchmen. This could be easily understood, for the ghost of the Registrar had many reasons to feel sad and frustrated. All the principles of co-operation for which he had sacrificed his life

* From *The Financial Expert* by R. K. Narayan. Copyright 1953 by The Michigan State University Press. Reprinted by permission of The Michigan State University Press.

were dissolving under his eyes, if he could look beyond the portals of the bank itself, right across the little stretch of lawn under the banyan tree, in whose shade Margayya sat and transacted his business. There was always a semi-circle of peasants sitting round him, and by their attitude and expression one might easily guess that they were suppliants. Margayya, though very much their junior (he was just forty-two), commanded the respect of those who sat before him. He was to them a wizard who enabled them to draw unlimited loans from the co-operative bank. If the purpose of the co-operative movement was the promotion of thrift and the elimination of middlemen, those two were just the objects that were defeated here under the banyan tree: Margayya didn't believe in advocating thrift: his living depended upon helping people to take loans from the bank opposite and from each other.

His tin box, a grey, discoloured, knobby affair, which was small enough to be carried under his arm, contained practically his entire equipment: a bottle of ink, a pen and a blotter, a small register whose pages carried an assortment of names and figures, and above all—the most important item—loan application forms of the co-operative bank. These last named were his greatest asset in life, and half his time was occupied in acquiring them. He had his own agency at work to provide him with these forms. When a customer came, the very first question Margayya asked was, "Have you secured the application form?"

"No."

"Then go into that building and bring one—try and get one or two spare forms as well." It was not always possible to secure more than one form, for the clerks there were very strict and perverse. They had no special reason to decline to give as many forms as were required except for the impulse to refuse anything that is persistently asked for. All the same, Margayya managed to gather quite a lot of forms and kept them handy. They were taken out for use on special occasions. Sometimes a villager arrived who did not have a form and who could not succeed in acquiring one by asking for it in the bank. On such occasions Margayya charged a fee for the blank form itself, and then another for filling in the relevant details.

The clerks of the bank had their own methods of worrying the villagers. A villager who wanted to know his account had to ask for it at the counter and invariably the accounts clerk snapped back, "Where is your pass-book?" A pass-book was a thing the villager could never keep his hand on. If it was not out of sight it was certain to be out of date. This placed the villager fully at the mercy of the clerk, who would say: "You will have to wait till I get through all the work I have now on hand. I'm not being paid to look after only your business here." And then the peasant would have to hang about for a day or two before getting an answer to his question, which would only be after placating the clerk with an offering in cash or kind.

It was under such circumstances that Margayya's help proved invaluable. He kept more or less parallel accounts of at least fifty of the members of the bank. What its red-tape obstructed, he cleared up by his own contrivance. He carried most of the figures in his head. He had only to sight a customer (for instance Mallanna of Koppal, as it now happened to be) to say at once: "Oh! you have come back for a new loan, I suppose. If you pay seventy-five rupees more, you can again take three hundred rupees within a week! The bye-law allows a new loan when fifty per cent is paid up."

"How can I burden myself with a further loan of three hundred, Margayya? It's unthinkable."

Now would begin all the persuasiveness that was Margayya's stock-in-trade. He asked point blank, "What difference is it going to make? Are you not already paying a monthly instalment of seventeen rupees eight annas? Are you or are you not?"

"Yes . . . I'm paying. God knows how much I have to——"

"I don't want all that," Margayya said, cutting him short. "I am not concerned with all that—how you pay or what you do. You may perhaps pledge your life or your wife's sarees. It is none of my concern: all that I want to know is whether you are paying an instalment now or not."

"Yes, master, I do pay."

"You will continue to pay the same thing, that is all. Call me a dog if they ask you for even one anna more. You fool, don't you see the difference? You pay seventeen rupees eight annas now for nothing, but under my present plan you will pay the same seventeen rupees eight annas but with another three hundred rupees in your purse. Don't you see the difference?"

"But what's the use of three hundred rupees, master?"

"Oh! I see, you don't see a use for it. All right, don't come to me again. I have no use for nincompoops like you. You are the sort of fellow who won't——" He elaborated a bawdy joke about him and his capacity, which made the atmosphere under the tree genial all round. The other villagers sitting around laughed. But Margayya assumed a stern look, and pretended to pass on to the next question in hand. He sat poring over some papers, with his spectacles uneasily poised over his nose. Those spectacles were a recent acquisition, the first indication that he was on the wrong side of forty. He resisted them as long as he could—he hated the idea of growing old, but "long-sight" does not wait for approval or welcome. You cannot hoodwink yourself or anyone else too long about it—the strain of holding a piece of paper at arm's length while reading stretches the nerves of the forearm and invites comments from others. Margayya's wife laughed aloud one day and asked: "Why don't you buy a pair of glasses like other young men of your age? Otherwise you will sprain your hand." He acted upon this advice and obtained a pair of glasses mounted in silver from the V.N. Stores in the Market. He and the proprietor of the shop had been playmates once, and Margayya took the glasses on trial, and forgot to go that way again. He was accosted about it on the road occasionally by the rotund optician, who was snubbed by Margayya: "Haven't you the elementary courtesy to know the time and place for such reminders?"

"Sorry, sorry," the other hastened to apologize, "I didn't intend to hurt or insult you."

"What greater insult can a man face than this sort of thing? What will an onlooker think? I am busy from morning to night—no time even for a cup of coffee in the afternoon! All right, it doesn't matter. Will you send someone to my house? I'm not able to use those glasses either. I wanted to come and exchange them if possible, but— —" it trailed off into indefiniteness, and the optician went away once again and soon ceased to bother about it. It was one of his many bad debts, and very soon he changed his commodity; gradually his show-case began to display powder-puffs, scents, chocolate bars—and the silver-rimmed glasses sat securely on Margayya's nose.

He now took off his spectacles and folded the sides as if disposing once and for all of the problem of Mallanna. He looked away at a man on his right and remarked: "You may have to wait for a week more before I can take up your affair."

"Brother, this is urgent, my daughter's marriage is coming off next month."

"Your daughter's marriage! I have to find you the money for it, but the moment my service is done, you will forget me. You will not need your Margayya any more?" The other made several deprecating noises, as a protestation of his loyalty. He was a villager called Kanda who had come walking from his village fifteen miles away. He owned about twenty acres of land and a house and cattle, but all of it was tied up in mortgages—most through Margayya's advice and assistance. He was a gambler and drank heavily, and he always asked for money on the pretext of having to marry his daughters, of whom he had a good number. Margayya preferred not to know what happened to all the money, but helped him to borrow as much as he wanted. "The only course now left is for you to take a joint-loan, but the difficulty will be to find someone as a partner." He looked round at the gathering before him and asked, "All of you are members of the Co-operative Society. Can't someone help a fellow-creature?" Most of them shook their heads. One of them remarked, "How can you ask for our joint-signature? It's risky to do it even for one's own brother."

"It's most risky between brothers," added Margayya. "But I'm not suggesting it for brothers now. I am only suggesting it between human beings." They all laughed and understood that he was referring to an elder brother of his with whom he was known to be on throat-cutting terms. He prepared to deliver a speech: "Here is a great man, a big man, you cannot find a more important man round about Somanur. He has lands, cattle, yes, he's a big man in every way. No doubt, he has certain habits: no use shutting our eyes to it: but I guarantee he will get over them. He must have a joint loan because he needs at least five hundred rupees immediately to see him through his daughter's marriage. You know how it is with the dowry system——" Everybody made a sympathetic noise and shook their heads. "Very bad, very bad. Why should we criticize what our ancestors have brought into existence?" someone asked.

"Why not?" another protested.

"Some people are ruined by the dowry."

"Why do you say some people?" Margayya asked. "Why am I here? Three daughters were born to my father. Five cart-loads of paddy came to us every half year, from the fields. We just heaped them upon the floor of the hall, we had five halls to our house; but where has it all gone? To the three daughters. By the time my father found husbands for them there was nothing left for us to eat at home!"

"But is it not said that a man who begets a son is blessed in three lives, because he gives away the greatest treasure on earth?" said someone.

"And how much more blessed is he that gives away three daughters? He is blessed no doubt, but he also becomes a bankrupt," Margayya said.

The talk thus went on and on, round and round, always touching practical politics again at some point or other. Margayya put his spectacles on, looked fixedly at Mallanna, and said: "Come and sit near me." The villager moved up. Margayya told the gathering, "We have to talk privately." And they all looked away and pretended not to hear although all their attention was concentrated on the whispering that now started between the two. Margayya said: "It's going to be impossible for Kanda to get a joint-loan, but he ought to be ready to accept whatever is available. I know you can help him and help yourself—you will lose nothing. In fact, you will gain a little interest. You will clear half your present loan by paying seventy-five rupees and apply for a fresh one. Since you don't want it, give it to Kanda. He will pay you seven and a half per cent. You give the four and a half per cent to that father-in-law" (Margayya always referred to the Co-operative Bank with a fresh sobriquet) "and take the three per cent yourself. He will pay back the instalments to you. I will collect and give them to you." Mallanna took time to grasp all the intricacies of this proposition, and then asked: "Suppose he doesn't?" Margayya looked horrified at this doubt. "What is there to be afraid of when I am here?" At this one of the men who were supposed to be out of earshot remarked: "Ah, what is possible in this world without mutual trust?" Margayya added, "Listen to him. He knows the world."

The result of all this talk was that Mallanna agreed to the proposal. Margayya grew busy filling up a loan application form with all the details of Mallanna's heritage, etc. He read it out aloud, seized hold of Mallanna's left thumb, pressed it on a small ink pad he carried in his box and pressed it again on the application form and endorsed it. He took out of the box seventy-five rupees in cash, and handed them to Mallanna with: "Why should I trust you with this without a scrap of paper? Now credit this to your account and halve your loan; and then present that application."

"If they refuse to take it?"

"Why should they refuse? They have got to accept it. You are a shareholder, and they have got to accept your application. It's not their grand-father's money that they are giving you but your own. Bye-law— —" He quoted the bye-law, and encouraged by it, the other got up and moved on.

It is impossible to describe more clearly than this Margayya's activity under the tree. He advanced a little loan (for interest) so that the little loan might wedge out another loan from the Co-operative Bank; which in its turn was passed on to someone in need for a higher interest. Margayya kept himself as the centre of all the complex transaction, and made all the parties concerned pay him for his services, the bank opposite him being involved in it willy-nilly. It was as strenuous a job as any other in the town and he felt that he deserved the difficult income he ground out of a couple of hundred rupees in his box, sitting there morning till evening. When the evening sun hit him on the nape of the neck he pulled down the lid of his box and locked it up, and his gathering understood that the financial wizard was closing his office for the day.

Margayya deposited the box under a bench in the front room of his house. His little son immediately came running out from the kitchen with a shout: "*Appa!*— —" and gripped his hand, asking: "What have you brought today?" Margayya hoisted him up on his shoulder: "Well, tomorrow, I will buy you a new engine, a small engine." The child was pleased to hear it. He asked, "How small will the engine be? Will it be so tiny?" He indicated with his thumb and first finger a minute size. "All right," said Margayya and put him down. This was almost a daily ritual. The boy revelled in visions of miniature articles—a tiny engine, tiny cows, tiny table, tiny everything, of the maximum size of a mustard seed. Margayya put him down and briskly removed his upper cloth and shirt, picked up a towel that was hanging from a nail on the wall, and moved to the backyard. Beyond a small clump of banana trees, which waved their huge fan-like leaves in the darkness, there was a single well of crumbling masonry, with a pulley over its cross-bar. Margayya paused for a moment to admire the starry sky. Down below at his feet the earth was damp and marshy. All the drain water of two houses flowed into the banana beds. It was a common backyard for his house and the one next door, which was his brother's. It was really a single house, but a partition wall divided it into two from the street to the back yard.

No. 14 D, Vinayak Street had been a famous land-mark, for it was the earliest house to be built in that area. Margayya's father was considered a hero for settling there in a lonely place where there was supposed to be no security for life or property. Moreover it was built on the fringe of a cremation ground, and often the glow of a burning pyre lit up its walls. After the death of the old man the brothers fell out, their wives fell out, and their children fell out. They could not tolerate the idea of even breathing the same air or being enclosed by the same walls. They got involved in litigation and partitioned everything that their father had left. Everything that could be cut in two with an axe or scissors or a knife was divided between them, and the other things were catalogued, numbered and then shared out. But one thing that could neither be numbered nor cut up was the back yard of the house with its single well. They could do nothing about it. It fell to Margayya's share, and he would willingly have seen his brother's family perish without water by closing it to them, but public opinion prevented the exercise of his right. People insisted that the well should remain common property, and so the dividing wall came up to it, and stopped there, the well acting as a blockade between the two brothers, but accessible from either side.

Now Margayya looked about for the small brass pot. He could not see it anywhere.

"Hey, little man!" he called out, "where is the well-pot?" He liked to call his son out constantly. When he came home, he could not bear to be kept away from him even for a moment. He felt uneasy and irritated when the child did not answer his call. He saw the youngster stooping over the lamp, trying to thrust a piece of paper into the chimney. He watched him from the doorway. He suppressed the inclination to call him away and warn him. The child thrust a piece of paper into the lamp, and when it burned brightly he recoiled at the sudden spurt of fire. But when it blackened and burnt out he drew near the lamp again, gingerly putting his finger near the metal plate on the top. Before Margayya could stop him, he had touched it. He let out a shriek. Margayya was beside him in a moment. His shriek brought in Margayya's wife, who had gone to a neighbouring shop. She came rushing into the house with cries of "What is it? What is it? What has happened?" Margayya felt embarrassed, like a man caught shirking a duty. He told his wife curtly, "Why do you shout so much, as if a great calamity had befallen this household—so that your sister-in-law in the neighbourhood may think how active we are, I suppose!"

"Sister-in-law—how proud you are of your relatives!" Her further remarks could not be continued because of the howling set up by the child, whose burnt finger still remained unattended. At this the mother snatched him up from her husband's arms, and hugged him close to her, hurting him more, whereupon he shouted in a new key. Margayya tried to tear him out of his wife's arms, crying: "Quick, get that ointment. Where is it? You can keep nothing in its place."

"You need not shout!" the wife answered, running about and rummaging in the cupboard. She grumbled: "You can't look after him even for a second without letting him hurt himself."

"You need not get hysterical about it, gentle lady, I had gone for a moment to the well."

"Everyone gets tap-water in this town. We alone——" she began, attacking on a new front.

"All right, all right," he said, curbing her, and turning his attention to the finger. "You must never, never go near fire again, do you understand?"

"Will you buy me a little elephant tomorrow?" the child asked, his cheeks still wet with tears. By now they had discovered a little wooden crucible containing some black ointment in the cupboard, hidden behind a small basket containing loose cotton (which Margayya's wife twisted into wicks for the lamp in God's niche). She applied the ointment to the injured finger, and set the child roaring in a higher key. This time he said "I want a big peppermint."

At night when the lights were put out and the sound of Vinayak Street had quieted, Margayya said to his wife, lying on the other side of their sleeping child: "Do you know—poor boy! I could have prevented Balu from hurting himself. I just stood there and watched. I wanted to see what he would do alone by himself." His wife made a noise of deprecation: "It is as I suspected. You were at the bottom of the whole trouble. I don't know . . . I don't know . . . that boy is terribly mischievous . . . and you are . . . you are . . ." She could not find the right word for it. Her instinct was full of foreboding, and she left the sentence unfinished. After a long pause she added: "It's impossible to manage him during the afternoons. He constantly runs out of the house into the street. I don't have a moment's peace or rest."

"Don't get cantankerous about such a small child," said Margayya, who disliked all these adverse remarks about his son. It seemed to him such a pity that that small bundle of man curled beside him like a tiny pillow should be so talked about. His wife retorted: "Yes, I wish you could stay at home and look after him instead of coming in the evening and dandling him for a moment after he has exhausted all his tricks."

"Yes, gladly, provided you agree to go out and arrange loans for all those village idiots."

Next to the subject of money, the greatest burden on his mind was his son. As he sat in his shop and spoke to his clients, he forgot for the time being the rest of the world, but the moment he was left alone he started thinking of his son: the boy had failed in his matriculation exam, and that embittered him very much. He wondered what he should do with him now. Whenever he thought of it, his heart sank within him. "God has blessed me with everything under the sun; I need not bother about anything else in life, but . . . but. . . ." He could not tell people "My son is only fifteen and he has already passed into college." The son had passed that stage two years ago. Two attempts and yet no good. Margayya had engaged three home tutors, one for every two subjects, and it cost him quite a lot in salaries. He arranged to have him fed specially with nutritive food during his examination periods. He bought a lot of fruits, and compelled his wife to prepare special food, always saying, "The poor boy is preparing for his examination. He must have enough stamina to stand the strain." He forbade his wife to speak loudly at home. "Have you no consideration for the young man who is studying?"

He was in agonies on examination days. He escorted him up to the examination hall in Albert College. Before parting from him at the sounding of the bell he always gave him advice: "Don't get frightened; write calmly and fearlessly . . . and don't come away before it is time," but all this was worth nothing because the boy had nothing to write after the first half hour, which he spent in scrawling fantastic designs on his answer book. He hated the excitement of an examination and was sullenly resentful of the fact that he was being put through a most unnecessary torment. He abruptly rose from his seat and went over to a restaurant near by. His father had left with him a lot of cash in view of the trying times he was going through. He ate all the available things in the restaurant, bought a packet of cigarettes, sought a secluded corner away from the prying eyes of his elders on the bank of the river behind the college, sat down and smoked the entire packet, dozed for a while, and returned home at five in the evening. The moment he was sighted his mother asked, "Have you written your examination well?"

He made a wry face and said, "Leave me alone." He hated to be reminded of the examination. But they would not let him alone. His mother put before him milk, and fruits, and the special edibles she had made to sustain him in his ordeal. He made a wry face and said, "Take it away, I cannot eat anything." At this she made many sounds of sympathy and said that he must get over the strain by feeding himself properly.

It was at this moment that his father returned home, after closing his office early, and hastening away in a jutka. All day as he counted money, his and other peoples', a corner of his mind was busy with the examination. "Oh, God, please enlighten my son's mind so that he may answer and get good marks," he secretly prayed. The moment he saw his son he said, "I am sure you have done very well my boy. How have you done?" The boy sat in a corner of the house with a cheerless look on his face. Margayya put it down to extreme strain, and said soothingly, "You stayed in the hall throughout?" That was for him an indication of his son's performance.

Whatever was the son's reply, he got the correct answer very soon, in less than eight weeks, when the results came out. At first Margayya raved, "Balu has done very well, I know. Someone has been working off a grudge." Then he felt like striking his son, but restrained himself for the son was four inches taller as he stood hanging his head with his back to the wall, and Margayya feared that he might retaliate. So he checked himself; and from a corner the mother watched, silently with resignation and fear, the crisis developing between father and son. She had understood long before that the boy was not interested in his studies and that he attached no value to them, but it was no use telling that to her husband. She pursued what seemed to her the best policy and allowed events to shape themselves. She knew that matters were coming to a conclusion now and she was a helpless witness to a terrific struggle between two positive-minded men, for she no longer had any doubt that the son was a grown-up man. She covered her mouth with her fingers, and with her chin on her palms stood there silently watching.

Margayya said, "Every little idiot has passed his S.S.L.C. exam. Are you such a complete fool?"

"Don't abuse me, father," said the boy, whose voice had recently become gruff. It had lost, as his mother noticed, much of the original softness. The more she saw him, the more she was reminded of her own father in his younger days; exactly the same features, the same gruffness, and the same severity. People had been afraid to speak to her father even when he was in the sweetest temper, for his face had a severity without any relation to his mood. She saw the same expression on the boy's face now. The boy's look was set and grim. His lips were black with cigarettes which she knew he smoked: he often smelt of them when he came home . . . But she kept this secret knowledge to herself since she didn't like to set up her husband against him. She understood that the best way to attain some peace of mind in life was to maintain silence; ultimately, she found that things resolved themselves in the best manner possible or fizzed out. She found that it was only speech which made existence worse every time. Lately, after he had become affluent, she found that her husband showed excessive emphasis, rightly or wrongly, in all matters; she realized that he had come to believe that whatever he did was always right. She did her best not to contradict him: she felt that he strained himself too much in his profession, and that she ought not to add to his burden. So if he sometimes raved over the mismanagement of the household, she just did not try to tell him that it was otherwise. She served him his food silently, and he himself discovered later what was right and what was wrong and confessed it to her. Now more than in any other matter she practised this principle where their son was concerned. She knew it would be no use telling her husband not to bother the son over his studies, that it would be no use asking him to return home at seven-thirty each day to sit down to his books with his home teachers . . . he simply would not return home before nine. It was no use shouting at him for it. It only made one's throat smart and provided a scene for the people next door to witness. She left it all to resolve itself. Once or twice she attempted to tell the son to be more mindful of his father's wishes and orders, but he told her to shut up. She left him alone. And she left her husband alone. She attained thereby great tranquillity in practical everyday life.

Now she watched the trouble brewing between the two as if it all happened behind a glass screen. The father asked in a tone full of wrath: "How am I to hold up my head in public?" The boy looked up detached, as if it were a problem to be personally solved by the father, in which he was not involved. Margayya shouted again: "How am I to hold up my head in public? What will they think of me? What will they say of my son?"

The boy spoke with a quiet firmness, as if expressing what immediately occurred to the mother herself. She felt at once a great admiration for him. He said in a gruff tone: "How is it their concern?"

Margayya wrung his hands in despair and clenched his teeth. What the boy said seemed to be absolutely correct. "You are no son of mine. I cannot tolerate a son who brings such disgrace on the family."

The boy was pained beyond words. "Don't talk nonsense, father," he said.

Margayya was stupefied. He had no idea that the boy could speak so much. Talking till now was only a one way business, and he had taken it for granted that the boy could say nothing for himself. He raved: "You are talking back to me, are you mad?"

The boy burst into tears and wailed: "If you don't like me send me out of the house."

Margayya studied him with surprise. He had always thought of Balu as someone who was spoken to and never one who could speak with the same emphasis as himself. He was offended by the boy's aggressive manner. He was moved by the sight of the tears on his face. He was seized with a confusion of feelings. He found his eyes smarting with tears and felt ashamed of it before his son and before that stony-faced woman who stood at the doorway of the kitchen and relentlessly watched. Her eyes seemed to watch unwaveringly, with a fixed stare. So still was she that Margayya feared lest she should be in a cataleptic state. He now turned his wrath on her. "It's all your doing. You have been too lenient. You have spoilt him beyond redemption. You with your— —"

The boy checked his tears and interrupted him. "Mother has not spoilt me, nor anyone else. Why should anyone spoil me?"

"There is too much talk in this house. That's what's wrong here," Margayya declared, and closed the incident by going in to change and attend to his other activities. The boy slunk away, out of sight. In that small house it was impossible to escape from one another, and the boy slipped out of the front door. The mother knew he would return, after his father had slept, bringing into the home the smell of cigarette smoke.

Margayya stayed awake almost all night. When the boy sneaked back after his rounds and pushed the door open, it creaked slightly on its hinges and he at once demanded: "Who is there? Who is there?"

Balu answered mildly: "It's myself, father."

Margayya was pleased with the softening that now seemed to be evident in his tone, but he wished at the same time that the boy had not disgraced him by failing. He said: "You have been out so long?"

"Yes," came the reply.

"Where?" he asked.

There was no further reply. Margayya felt that failing the Matric seemed to have conferred a new status on his son, and unloosened his tongue. He felt in all this medley a little pride at the fact that his son had acquired so much independence of thought and assertiveness. He somehow felt like keeping him in conversation and asked, with a slight trace of cajolery in his voice: "Was the door left open without the bolt being drawn?"

"Yes," replied the boy from somewhere in the darkness.

"That's very careless of your mother. Does she do it every day?"

There was once again a pause and silence. His wife seemed to have fallen asleep too, for there was no response from her. He somehow did not wish the conversation to lapse. He said as a stop gap: "What'll happen if a thief gets in?" There was no response from the son. After blinking in the dark for a few minutes, Margayya asked: "Boy, are you sleep?" And the boy answered: "Yes, I am." And Margayya, feeling much more at peace with himself at heart for having spoken to him, fell asleep at once, forgetting for a few hours the Matriculation examination and his other worries.

They got into a sort of live and let live philosophy. He hoped that when the schools reopened he could put the boy back at school, prepare him intensively for his examination, and if necessary see some of the examiners and so on. Margayya had a feeling that he had of late neglected his duties in this direction. He had unqualified faith in contacting people and getting things done that way. He could get at anybody through Dr. Pal. That man had brought into his business a lot of people known to him. Margayya's contacts were now improving socially. People were indebted to him nowadays, and would do anything to retain his favour. Margayya hoped that if he exerted himself even slightly in the coming year he would see his son pull through Matriculation without much difficulty. Of course the boy would have to keep up a show of at least studying the books and would have to write down his number correctly in the answer book and not merely scribble and look out of the door. It was extremely necessary that he should at least write one page of his answer and know what were the subjects he ought to study.

Margayya felt that if he could persuade Balu to make at least a minimum of effort for his own sake, his mind would be easier. He proposed it very gently to him about a fortnight later as they sat down to their dinner together. Margayya showed him extreme consideration nowadays; it was born out of fear and some amount of respect. The boy was always taciturn and grim. He recollected that it seemed ages since he had seen any relaxation in his face. He had a gravity beyond his years. That frightened Margayya. Except the one instance when he saw tears in his eyes on the day of the results, he had always found him sullen. He hoped to soften him by kindness, or, at least, outward kindness, for he still smarted inside at the results of the examination. He looked for a moment at the face of his son and said: "Balu, you must make another attempt. I'll see that you get through the examination without the least difficulty."

Balu stopped eating and asked: "What do you mean, father?"

Margayya sensed danger, but he had started the subject. He could not stop it now under any circumstances. So he said: "I mean about the Matriculation examination."

"I will not read again," said the boy definitely, defiantly. "I have already spoken to mother about it."

"H'm." Margayya turned to his wife who was serving him and said: "He has spoken to you, has he? What has he said?"

"Just what he has told you," she answered promptly, and went back to the fire-place to fetch something.

"Why didn't you tell me about it?" Margayya asked, eagerly looking for some lapse on her part to justify him in letting off steam.

She merely replied: "Because I knew he was going to tell you about it himself."

Margayya burst out at her: "What do you mean by discussing all sorts of things with the boy and not telling me anything? These are matters— —"

His son interrupted him: "Father, if you hate me and want to make me miserable, you will bother me with examinations and studies. I hate them."

Margayya went on arguing with him all through the meal till the boy threatened to abandon his dinner and walk out of the dining room. Margayya assumed a sullen silence, but the atmosphere ached with tension. Everyone was aware that the silence was going to be broken in a violent manner next moment, as soon as dinner was over. Father and son seemed to be in a race to finish eating first. Balu gobbled up his food and dashed to the back yard. He poured a little water on his hand, wiped it on a towel near by and moved towards the street door. Margayya jumped up from his seat, with his hand unwashed, dashed to the street door and shut and bolted it. Frustrated, the boy stood still. Margayya asked: "Where are you going? I have still much to tell you. I have not finished speaking yet." The boy withdrew a few steps in response.

Meanwhile his mother had brought in a vessel of water; Margayya snatched a moment to wash his hand at the little open yard. He said, "Wait" to his son. He opened his office box and brought from it the boy's S.S.L.C. Register. He had secured it on the previous day from the headmaster of the school. The S.S.L.C. Register is a small calico-bound note-book with columns marked in it, containing a record of a high-school boy's marks, conduct, handwriting and physical fitness. Margayya had got the register from the headmaster and studied its pages keenly the whole of the previous day. Matters did not now appear to him so hopeless. The headmaster had marked "Fair" both for his handwriting and drill attendance. Margayya had no idea that his son could shine in anything. So this was an entirely happy surprise. . . . His marks in almost all subjects were in single digits. The highest mark he had obtained was twelve out of a hundred in hygiene, and he had maintained his place as the last in the class without a variation.

One would have expected Margayya to be shocked by this, but the effect was unexpected. He was a fond and optimistic father, and he fastened on the twelve marks for hygiene. It seemed so high after all the diminutive marks the boy had obtained in other subjects. Margayya hoped that perhaps he was destined to be a doctor, and that was why his inclination was so marked for hygiene. What a wonderful opening seemed to be before him as a doctor! Doctor Balu—it would be very nice indeed. If only he could get through the wretched S.S.L.C. barrier, he'd achieve great things in life. Margayya would see to it that he did so; Margayya's money and contacts would be worth nothing if he could not see his son through . . .

He had prepared himself to speak to Balu about all this gently and persuasively. He hoped to lead up to the subject with encouraging talk, starting with hygiene, and then to ask him if he wished to be a doctor. What a glorious life opened before a doctor! He would send him to England to study surgery. He could tell him all that and encourage him. Margayya had great faith in his own persuasiveness. He sometimes had before him a tough customer who insisted upon withdrawing all his deposits and winding up the account: a most truculent client. But Margayya remembered that if he had about an hour with him, he could always talk him out of it. The deposit would remain with him, plus any other money that the man possessed. . . . Now Margayya wanted to employ his capacity for a similar purpose with his son. That's why he had come armed with the S.S.L.C. Register. He could read out to him the headmaster's remarks "Fair," etc., and prove to him how hopeful everything was if only he would agree to lend his name and spare time to go through the formality of an examination in the coming year.

At the sight of the note-book the boy asked: "What is this? Why have you brought it from school?" as if it were the most repulsive article he had seen in the whole of his life. His face went a shade darker. It symbolized for him all the wrongs that he had suffered in his life: it was a chronicle of all the insults that had been heaped upon him by an ungracious world—a world of schools, studies and examinations. What did they mean by all this terrible torment invented for young men? It had been an agony for him every time the headmaster called him up and made him go through the entries and sign below. Such moments came near his conception of hell. Hell, in his view, was a place where a torturing God sat up with your scholastic record in his hand and lectured you on how to make good and told you what a disgrace you were to society. His bitterness overwhelmed him suddenly, as his father opened a page and started: "Here is your hygiene— —"

The boy made a dash for the book, snatched it from his father's hand before he knew what was happening, tore its entire bulk into four pieces (it had been made of thick ledger paper and only his fury gave him the necessary strength to tear it up at one effort), and ran out into the street and threw the pieces into the gutter. And Vinayak Mudali Street gutter closed on it and carried the bits out of sight. Margayya ran up and stood on the edge of the gutter woefully looking into its dark depth. His wife was behind him. He was too stunned to say anything. When he saw the last shred of it gone, he turned to his wife and said: "They will not admit him in any school again, the last chance gone." And then he turned to tackle his son—but the boy had gone.

The only sign of prosperity about him now was the bright handle of the umbrella which was hooked to his right forearm whenever he went out. He was a lover of umbrellas, and the moment he could buy anything that caught his fancy, he spent eight rupees and purchased this bright-handled umbrella with "German ribs," in the parlance of the umbrella dealers. Hitherto he had carried for years an old bamboo one, a podgy thing with discoloured cloth which had been patched up over and over again. He protected it like his life for several years. He had his own technique of holding an umbrella which assured it a long lease of life and kept it free from fractures. He never twisted the handle when he held an umbrella over his head. He never lent it to anyone. Margayya, if he saw anyone going out in the rain in imminent danger of catching and perishing of pneumonia, would let him face his fate rather than offer him the protection of his umbrella. He felt furious when people thought that they could ask for an umbrella. "They will be asking for my skin next," he often commented when his wife found fault with him for his attitude. Another argument he advanced was, "Do people ask for each other's wives? Don't they manage to have one for themselves? Why shouldn't each person in the country buy his own umbrella?" "An umbrella does not like to be handled by more than one person in its lifetime," he often declared, and stuck to it. He had to put away his old umbrella in the loft, carefully rolled up, because its ribs had become too rickety and it could not maintain its shape any longer. It began to look like a shot-down crow with broken wings. Though for years he had not noticed it, suddenly one day when he was working under the tree in the Co-operative Bank compound, someone remarked that he was looking like a wayside umbrella repairer and that he had better throw it away; he felt piqued and threw it in the loft, but he could never bring himself to the point of buying a new one and had more or less resigned himself to basking in the sun until the time came when he could spend eight rupees without calculating whether he was a loser or a gainer in the bargain. That time had come, now that thousands of rupees were passing through his hands—thousands which belonged to others as well as to him.

Except for this umbrella, he gave no outward sign of his affluence. He hated any perceptible signs of improvement. He walked to his office every day. His coat was of spun silk, but he chose a shade that approximated to the one he had worn for years so that no one might notice the difference. He whitewashed the walls of his house inside only, and built a small room upstairs. He bought no furniture except a canvas deckchair at a second-hand shop. On this he lounged and looked at the sky from his courtyard. He told his wife to buy any clothes she liked, but she was more or less in mourning and made no use of the offer. She merely said, "Tell me about Balu. That is what I need, not clothes."

Margayya replied: "Well, I can only offer you what is available. If you are crying for the moon, I can't help you much there."

"I am asking for my son, not crying for the moon," she said.

She was always on the verge of hysteria nowadays. She spoke very little and ate very little; and Margayya felt that at a time when he had a right to have a happy and bright home, he was being denied the privilege unnecessarily. He felt angry with his wife. He felt that it was her sulking which ruined the atmosphere of the home. They had so much accustomed themselves to the disappearance of their son that he ceased to think of it as a primary cause: the more immediate reasons became perceptible. He tried in his own clumsy manner to make her happy. He told her, "Ask for any money you want."

"What shall I do with money?" she said. "I have no use for it."

He disliked her for making such a statement. It was in the nature of a seditious speech. He merely frowned at her and went on with his business. What was that business? When at home he carried about him the day's financial position finely distilled into a statement, and was absorbed in studying the figures. When he wanted relaxation he bought a paper and went through its pages. Nowadays he did not borrow the paper from the newspaper dealer but subscribed for a copy himself. He read with avidity what was happening in the world: the speeches of statesmen, the ravings of radicals, the programme for this and that, war news, and above all the stocks and shares market. He glanced through all this because a certain amount of world information seemed to be an essential part of his equipment when he sat in his office. All kinds of people came in and it was necessary that he should be able to take part in their conversation. To impress his clients, he had to appear as a man of all round wisdom.

He walked to his work every day soon after his morning meal. The house was in suspense till he was seen safely off. He did not believe in employing servants at home and so his wife had to do all the work. He often said, "Why should we burden ourselves with servants when we are like a couple of newly-weds? Ours is not a very big family." The lady accepted it meekly because she knew it would not be much use arguing it out with Margayya. She knew, as he himself did, that he did not employ a cook because he did not like to spend money on one. But he was sure to give some other reason if he was asked. He would in all probability say, "Where is the need to show off?" She knew that he viewed money as something to accumulate and not to be spent on increasing one's luxuries in life. She knew all his idioms even before he uttered them. Sometimes when he saw her sitting at the fireplace, her eyes shrunken and swollen with the kitchen smoke, he felt uneasy and tried to help her with the kitchen work, keeping up the pretence of being newly-weds. He picked up a knife here and a green vegetable there, cut it up in a desultory manner, and vaguely asked, "Is there anything I can do?" She hardly ever answered such a question. She merely said, "Please come in half an hour, and I will serve you your meal." She had become very sullen and reserved nowadays.

She brooded over her son Balu night and day. She lost the taste for food. Margayya behaved wildly whenever he was reminded of their son. "He is not my son," he declared dramatically. "A boy who has an utter disregard for his father's feelings is no son. He is a curse that the Gods have sent down for us. He is not my son." It all sounded very theatrical, but the feeling was also very real. When he remembered the floating bits of calico in the street gutter, he felt sorry that his son was no longer there to be slapped. His fingers itched to strike him. He reflected: "If he had at least disappeared after receiving the slap I aimed, I would not have minded much." He discouraged his wife from mentioning their son again and had grandly ordered that the household must run on as if he had not been born. When he spoke in that tone his wife fully understood that he meant it. His affluence, his bank balance, buoyed him up and made him bear the loss of their son. He lived in a sort of radiance which made it possible for him to put up with anything. When he sat at his desk from early in the day till sunset, he had to talk, counsel, wheedle out, and collect money; in fact go through all the adventures of money-making. At the end of the day as he walked back home his mind was full of the final results, and so there was practically no time for him to brood over Balu.

Late at night when the voices of the city had died down and when the expected sleep came a little late, he speculated on Balu. Perhaps he had drowned himself. There was no news of him, although several days and weeks had passed. His wife accused him at first of being very callous and not doing anything about it. He did not know what was expected of him. He could not go and tell the police. He could not announce a reward for anyone who traced him. He could not. . . . He hated to make a scene about it, and solved the whole thing by confiding in Dr. Pal. Dr. Pal had promised to keep an eye on the matter and tell him if anything turned up. No one could do more than that. Margayya had generally given out that his son had gone on a holiday to Bombay or Madras, and lightly added: "Young boys of his age must certainly go out by themselves and see a bit of the world: I think that's the best education."

"But boys must have a minimum of S.S.L.C.," someone remarked.

Margayya dismissed it as a foolish notion. "What is there in Matriculation? People can learn nothing in schools. I have no faith in our education. Who wants all this nonsense about A squared plus B squared. If a boy does not learn these, so much the better. To be frank, I have got on without learning the A squared and B squared business, and what is wrong with me? Boys must learn things in the rough school of life." Whatever he said sounded authoritative and mature nowadays, and people listened to him with respectful attention. These perorations he delivered as he sat in his office.

China

The Chinese are often content to say that their literature proper begins with the Confucian classics (ca. 500 B.C.), a body of works containing not only philosophical and religious doctrine but poetry, narrative, anecdote, and aphorism. But the classical Chinese language is fixed by at least a century earlier than this, and we must assume a long literary tradition before Confucius. The origins of the Chinese script go back perhaps as far as the eighteenth century B.C.—specimens have survived on bones used for divination and on bronze ritual vessels. The language is ideographic—each character represents not a sound but a word—and because pictographic character is gradually lost it is not easy to see, even with early classical Chinese, the original picture on which the graph was based, except with a small number of characters. The spoken language of China, however, has various dialects, not mutually intelligible, of which Peking or Mandarin (the official language) and Cantonese are spoken by the largest number of people today. But the written language unified the cultural and intellectual world of China from the earliest times and remained the literary norm until the twentieth century. No other culture boasts such a continuous literary tradition. It became divorced from the language of common speech (as did Sanskrit and Latin), and an increasingly important parallel literature in the spoken languages developed.

To begin Chinese literature with the Confucian classics is analogous to beginning Greek literature with Homer. Much earlier writing, now lost, must have preceded these sophisticated works. The Confucian classics are books incorporating the wisdom of Confucius and books which he and his followers were thought to have written or edited. One of these is the *Book of Songs* or *Odes* (*Shih Ching*), an anthology of poetry which represents the earliest extant purely literary efforts of the Chinese people. It is sufficient to say here that lyric poetry is the first prestigious literary form in China and that the short or moderate-length poem (rather than, in some Western literatures, epic or drama) remains literature par excellence for the Chinese. The other manifestation of Chinese literature which makes it different from Western literature is the popularity and prestige of literary and evocative philosophical prose. The very fact that there is no term in Western criticism for this genre accentuates the difference between the arid logic of an Aristotle, a Spinoza, or a Kant, and the Chinese philosophers, both Confucian and later.

As an example of the reverence for poetry which the Chinese exhibit, one can cite the official establishment in 120 B.C. of a Music Bureau, attached to the Han court, to subsidize poetry and music. An unbroken tradition of Chinese lyric poetry characterizes the literature down to the present. Some Chinese would argue that the allusive and difficult-to-translate Tu Fu (712–770) is China's greatest poet.[1] For the major poets T'ao Ch'ien, Li Po, and Po Chü-i, see below. The forms range from lengthy *fu*, sometimes running to two hundred lines and including satiric and narrative material, to a form of song, the *t'zü*, which is written to be set to music.

Though a written language may be "frozen" by a literary elite so that it remains unchanged for centuries (Latin and Sanskrit are examples), the spoken language inevitably slowly changes. A demand for literature in the spoken language resulted in a tradition of popular literature in a mixture of colloquial and classical Chinese. During the T'ang and Sung dynasties (618–1279) the short story flourished, at first mostly concerned with the supernatural and with love. By Ming times (fourteenth to seventeenth centuries) the colloquial novel had come into its own. Wu Ch'eng-en's *Monkey* (*Hsi Yu Chi*) (see below) is highly imaginative fantasy, but a tradition of realism and even naturalism was established also. Among the major novels, romantic in plot but relatively realistic in technique, are *The Romance of the Three Kingdoms* (*San-Kuo-Chih Yen-i*) and *Water Margin* (*Shui Hu Chuan*). The somewhat later *Golden Lotus* (*Chin P'ing Mei*) is a bitterly naturalistic chronicle of the amorous adventures of a prince of a great Chinese household.

During the Yuan period, under Mongol rule, the drama became popular and the so-called Peking opera has remained to this day a standing-room-only phenomenon wherever Chinese communities exist. These musical dramas are often long and are romantic in plot. Though exciting theatrically, they are not comparable to the drama of India and the *nō* play of Japan, and have not enjoyed the prestige in China of the other literary forms. But their popularity has been enormous. Also, a folk or village drama has always existed in China, and the theater in Maoist China (see below) incorporates elements of the early folk play, the Peking opera, and modern Western realistic drama.

Chinese literature is vast. Much has been done in other forms—the essay, history, the travel book, and in a special genre of metrical prose.

The nineteenth century brought China into convulsive contact with the West. The literary relations between China and the West in this period have not yet been thoroughly studied, at least in comparison with the period after the revolution of Sun Yat-sen. Mass translation programs were under-

1. William Hung's *Tu Fu, China's Greatest Poet* (Cambridge, Mass., 1952) is the most comprehensive study of this poet.

taken, and the Chinese proved both very receptive to and critical of ideas from the West. The problem of foreign influence in literature and of what form of the vernacular to use plagued the creative writer. A successful compromiser of these problems is Liu T'ieh-yün (see below). The early twentieth century brought with it a political revolution which overthrew the Manchu dynasty and brought with it a literary revolution closely allied to it. A leading figure in the literary revolution was Hu Shih (born 1891). Among the many writers of magnitude are Lu Hsün (see below), Lao Shë (Lao Shaw), and Kuo Mo-jo. We may note in closing that Mao Tse-tung himself is a writer of poetry and fiction.

WRITINGS AND CRITICISM

The date of the latest edition or reprint is given.

For a brief sketch of Chinese literature see A. R. Davis, pp. 131–160 in *Literatures of the East*, ed. E. R. Ceadel (1959). A short history is that of Odile Kaltenmark, *Chinese Literature* (1964). More lengthy treatments are Liu Wu-chi's *An Introduction to Chinese Literature* (1966), Lai Ming's *A History of Chinese Literature* (1964) and Shou-yi Ch'ên's *Chinese Literature, a Historical Introduction* (1961). The earliest period is well-covered in Burton Watson's *Early Chinese Literature* (1962). Herbert A. Giles's *A History of Chinese Literature* (1923, often reprinted) is now out of date. There is much useful material in James Robert Hightower's *Topics in Chinese Literature* (rev. ed., 1953). See also his "Chinese Literature in the Context of World Literature," *Comparative Literature,* V (1953), 117–124. For the Chinese language see Bernhard Karlgren's *Philology and Ancient China* (1926) and his *The Chinese Language* (1949), and the longer study by R. A. D. Forrest, *The Chinese Language* (1948).

For background, an excellent collection of material mostly from philosophical and religious sources in *Sources of Chinese Tradition,* ed. W. H. de Bary, Wingtsit Chan, and Burton Watson (1960). L. Carrington Goodrich's *Short History of the Chinese People* (1951) emphasizes cultural history; René Grousset's *Chinese Art and Culture* (1959), the arts. Herrlee Creel's *Chinese Thought from Confucius to Mao Tse-tung* (1953) surveys the intellectual accomplishment.

An extensive collection of Chinese literature in translation is in Cyril Birch's *Anthology of Chinese Literature* (2 vols., 1965–72). Another large anthology is *Chinese Literature,* ed. William McNaughton (1974). See also Lin Yutang's *Wisdom of China and India* (1948).

The earliest literary and philosophical achievements of China were edited and translated in the late nineteenth century by James Legge in *The Confucian Classics* (5 vols. in 8, 1893–95) and *The Texts of Confucianism* (1879–85; Sacred Books of the East Series, III, XVI, XXVII, XXVIII). While Legge's translations have usually been superseded, his works are often cited and are a convenient place to locate passages in the early classics. Various early texts are translated in Lin Yutang (cited above). For the *Book of Songs* (or *Poems* or *Odes*) (*Shih Ching*) and the *Analects* (*Wun Yü*) of Confucius, see below. *The Book of Changes* (*I Ching*) has been translated by C. F. Baynes (1960). The work of Lao Tzu, the *Tao te Ching*—the great Taoist classic—has been done by a number of translators: D. C. Lau (1973); R. B. Blakney, *The Way of Life* (1955); Archie J. Baum (1958); J. J. L. Duyvendak (1954; Wisdom of the East Series); Lin Yutang (1948); Arthur Waley, *The Way and Its Power* (1958); Paul Carus (1913); John C. H. Wu (1961). For Mencius (Meng Tzu) see D. C. Lau (1970; Leonard A. Lyall (1932); and I. A. Richards, *Mencius on the Mind* (1932). For the *Chuang-ztu* see below.

There are a number of volumes of Chinese poetry translated by Arthur Waley, including *Translations from the Chinese* (1954). Other collections include the *Penguin Book of Chinese Verse*, ed. A. R. Davis (1962); *Poems of the Late T'ang,* tr. A. C. Graham (1965); *Poems of Solitude*, tr. Jerome Ch'en and Michael Bullock (1960); *Chinese Lyricism: Shih Poetry from the Second to the Twelfth Century* (1971) and *Chinese Rhyme-Prose* (1971), both by Burton Watson; H. H. Hart, *Poems of the Hundred Names* (1954); Shih-Shun Liu, *One Hundred and One Chinese Poems* (1968); *A Collection of Chinese Lyrics*, ed. Duncan MacIntosh

(1965). Older anthologies are Robert Payne's *The White Pony* (1947) and Witter Bynner's *The Jade Mountain* (1929).

For the poets Li Po, T'ao Ch'ien, and Po Chü-i see below. For other major poets see: William Hung, *Tu Fu, China's Greatest Poet* (1952); Florence Ayscough, *Tu Fu, The Autobiography of a Chinese Poet* (2 vols., 1929–34); *The Poems of Wang Wei,* G. W. Robinson (1974); *Li Po and Tu Fu,* Arthur Cooper (1974); *Yuan Mei, Eighteenth Chinese Poet,* by Arthur Waley (1956); *The Poet Kao Ch'i,* by F. W. Mote (1962); and, *The Murmuring Stream: The Life and Works of the Chinese Nature Poet Hsieh Ling-yun* (2 vols., 1967) and *The Poems of Li Ho* (1970), both by J. D. Prodsham.

The *Princeton Encyclopedia of Poetry and Poetics* has a good brief article on Chinese poetics. An excellent longer treatment is John L. Bishop's "Prosodic Elements in T'ang Poetry," pp. 49–63 in *Papers of the Indiana Conference on Oriental-Western Literary Relations,* ed. Horst Frenz and G. L. Anderson (1955). A book-length study is James J. Y. Liu's *The Art of Chinese Poetry* (1962). Ezra Pound's fascination with Chinese poetry and the written character is well known. Besides his *Cantos,* see his *The Chinese Written Character as a Medium for Poetry* (1936) and *Cathay* (1915). More specialized studies are *The Four Seasons of T'ang Poetry* by John C. H. Wu (1972) and Kōjirō Yoshikawa's *An Introduction to Sung Poetry,* Burton Watson (1967).

Chinese prose, including fiction and drama, are collected in Ch'u Chai's *Treasury of Chinese Literature* (1965). A number of translations of works of fiction are available. *Water Margin* (*Shui hu chuan*) has been translated by J. H. Jackson (1937) and by Pearl Buck under the title *All Men Are Brothers* (1957). Richard G. Irwin has written a study of this novel in *The Evolution of a Chinese Novel* (1953). Stories from the *Chin ku ch'i kuan,* an early collection, may be found in E. B. Howell's *The Inconstancy of Madame Chuang* (1924) and *The Restitution of the Bride* (1926). Clement Egerton has translated the *Chin p'ing mei* as *The Golden Lotus,* (4 vols., 1954); an abridged version is Bernard Miall's *Chin Ping Mei* (1940). Ts'ao Hsueh-ch'in's *Hung Lou Mêng* has been translated by Chi-chen Wang (1958) as *The Dream of the Red Chamber.* A new translation of this work is by David Hawkes under the title *The Story of the Stone* (1974). (Hawkes uses the modern system of transliterating Chinese—the author's name appears as Cao Xueqin.) C. H. Brewitt-Taylor has translated *The Romance of the Three Kingdoms* (*San kuo yen i*) (2 vols., 1959). For the *Hsi Yu Chi* (*Monkey*), see below.

Studies of the fiction are *The Classic Chinese Novel* by C. T. Hsia (1968) and John L. Bishop's *The Colloquial Short Story in China* (1956). For the theory of fiction see Bishop's "The Limitations of Chinese Fiction," *Far Eastern Quarterly,* XV (1956), 239–247 (reprinted in *Studies in Chinese Literature,* ed. J. L. Bishop, (1965), and Yi-ste Mei Feuerwerker, "The Chinese Novel," pp. 169–185 in *Approaches to the Oriental Classics,* ed. W. T. De Bary (1959). Popular Chinese literature has been extensively studied by Jaroslav Průšek in articles mostly appearing in *Archiv Orientálni* (Prague). See also H. C. Chang, *Chinese Literature: Popular Fiction and Drama* (1973). For literary criticism, see Lu Chi, below, and *The Literary Mind and the Carving of Dragons* by Liu Hsieh, translated by Vincent Yu-chung Shih (1959). Tien-yi Li's *Chinese Fiction: A Bibliography of Books and Articles in Chinese and English* (1968) is useful.

A useful recent work on the Chinese theater is A. C. Scott's *The Classical Theatre of China* (1957), Roger P. Bailey's *Guide to Chinese Poetry and Drama* (1973) includes considerable commentary. Other works on the theatre include: A. E. Zucker, *The Chinese Theater* (1925); A. C. Arlington, *The Chinese Drama* (1930); Cecilia S. L. Zung, *Secrets of the Chinese Drama* (1937; reprinted 1964); Kate Buss, *Studies in the Chinese Drama* (1922); R. F. Johnson. *The Chinese Drama* (1921). A more specialized study is Josephine Huang Hung's *Ming Drama* (1966). For collections of plays see L. C. Arlington, ed., *Famous Chinese Plays* (1937; reprinted 1963); Josephine Huang Hung, ed., *Classical Chinese Plays* (1971); Liu Jung-en, ed. *Six Yuan Plays* (1972); and *The West Chamber,* Henry H. Hart (1936). For a Chinese play that has enjoyed a limited vogue in the West see Liu Wu-chi's "The Original *Orphan of China,*" *Comparative Literature,* V (1953), 193ff.

Modern Chinese literature divides into three periods: from the entrance of large-scale Western influence in the late nineteenth century to the Sun Yat-sen revolution which resulted in the founding of the Republic in 1911, with its attendent literary revolution, and from 1911 until the establishment of the People's Republic under Mao. The twentieth century has received much attention; the following works are representative: "Tradition and Experiment in Modern Chinese Literature" by Yi-tse Mei, pp. 107–121 in *Papers of the Indiana Conference* (cited above); "People, Places and Time in the Modern Chinese Novel" by Chun-jo Liu, pp. 15–25 in *Asia and the Humanities,* ed. Horst Frenz (1959); *Chinese Communist Literature* (1963) by Cyril Birch; *Literature and Politics in Contemporary China* (1960) by Howard L. Boorman; *A History of Modern*

Chinese Fiction (1961) by Chih-tsing Hsia; *A Short History of Modern Chinese Literature* (1959), by I Ting. (See Bibliographical Note for further sources). For translations of and comment on recent Chinese drama see Walter J. and Ruth I. Meserve's *Modern Drama from Communist China* (1970) and Lois Wheeler Snow's *China on Stage* (1972). Much useful information on recent Chinese literature can be found in the journal *Chinese Literature*, published in Peking.

The most satisfactory study of the influence of Chinese literature is in W. W. Appleton's *A Cycle of Cathay* (1951).

THE BOOK OF SONGS. Arthur Waley's translation is the most satisfactory literary version and has explanatory notes. For the metrics and style of the *Songs* see Burton Watson, *Early Chinese Literature* (cited above), pp. 201ff., and Bernhard Karlgren's *The Book of Odes* (Stockholm, 1950), which provides a literal translation and elaborate commentary. Other translations include one by L. Cranmer-Byng (London, 1927) and an imaginative one by Ezra Pound, *The Classic Anthology Defined by Confucius* (Cambridge, Mass., 1954).

CONFUCIUS. The *Analects* and other works in the Confucian canon are included in James Legge's editions (cited above), which are often referred to. In addition to Arthur Waley's translation, there are modern versions by Lionel Giles (London, 1927), Lin Yutang (1938), James R. Ware (1955), and Ezra Pound (1956). For the history of Confucian thought in China see Fung Yu-lan, *A History of Chinese Philosophy* (Vol. I., Princeton, 1952); Arthur Waley, *Three Ways of Thought in Ancient China* (cited above); Herrlee Creel, *Chinese Thought* (cited above); and Wu-chi Liu, *Confucius, His Life and Times* (1955).

CHUANG-TZU. The Complete Works of Chuang-Tzu has been translated by Burton Watson (1968). Arthur Waley's *Three Ways of Thought* includes excerpts with commentary. There is also a translation by Herbert A. Giles (London, 1926). See also Watson, *Early Chinese Literature*, pp. 160ff.

LU KI. Achilles Fang's translation first appeared in *Harvard Journal of Asiatic Studies*, XIV (1951) and is reprinted in *Studies in Chinese Literature*, ed. John L. Bishop (cited above). Other translations of the *Wen Fu* are *Essay on Literature*, translated by Shih-hsiang Chen (rev. ed., Portland, Maine: Anthoensen Press, 1953) and *The Art of Letters*, translated by E. R. Hughes (1951; Bollingen Series, XXIX). All three of these translations have commentary.

THREE POETS. The basic work on Li Po is Arthur Waley's *Poetry and Career of Li Po* (London, 1950). Another translation is *The Works of Li Po* by Shigeyoshi Obata (1922). The most satisfactory translations of T'ao Ch'ien are in *The Poetry of T'ao Ch'ien* by James Robert Hightower (Oxford, 1970), with elaborate commentary. There are attractive translations in William Acker's *Tao the Hermit* (1952) and in Lily Pao-hu Chang and Marjorie Sinclair's *Poems* (Honolulu, 1953). On Po (or Pai) Chü-i see Arthur Waley, *The Life and Times of Po Chü-i* (London, 1949).

MONKEY. See the introduction to Arthur Waley's translation (1958). The journey of the monk Hsuan Tsang which forms the historical basis for the tale is discussed by Waley in *The Real Tripitaka* (London, 1951). See also S. Beal's *Buddhist Records of the Western World* (2 vols., London, 1906).

LIU T'IEH-YUN. Harold Shadick's translation *The Travels of Lao Ts'an* has an excellent introduction and very full notes.

The Book of Songs (*Shih Ching*)
(ca. 600 B.C.)

The Book of Songs (or *Odes*) is an anthology of 305 poems, compiled about 600 B.C., although some of the songs included go back to much earlier. Confucius is supposed to have made this selection from an earlier collection of some three thousand poems and is supposed to have arranged them in their present order. As we shall see from his *Analects*, he certainly valued them highly. There is also a tradition that the poems were first collected by an early king, who ordered them presented to him so that he might find out the aspirations and the discontents of his people—this in itself is a Confucian ideal for poetry. Many of the poems do express discontent against the government, hard times, and military service. Many of the poems were intended to be sung to musical accompaniment, but nothing is known now about the music.

The heart of the collection consists of poems from folk tradition later revised by men of letters. They deal with common human themes—courtship and marriage, travel and its dangers, separation from loved ones, festivals, the weariness of war, and the occupations of daily life. These poems are close to the people and the metaphors are often drawn from nature. The ancientness of the language and the difficulties of interpreting the symbols of a culture distant even from later China make understanding some of the poems a problem. Also, they are often very musical, and the repetitions, alliterations, and rhyme schemes are difficult to translate into English. Another group of poems, clearly from the court, may satirize court affairs or complain about corruption in government, but these too are often disguised as folk songs. Also, there are poems based on historical themes, about the great rulers and events of early China, especially the Chou dynasty, much revered in later times as a kind of Golden Age.

The great place of lyric poetry in Chinese literature was established by this anthology. Metaphors that connect the problems of the human heart with the world of nature are not common in early Western poetry, and the broad range of topics in The *Book of Songs* is extraordinary. The ode is the vehicle for all sorts of social and political comment as well as for what we associate the lyric with, the expression of emotional relations and situations. The topics that are the concern of epic, tragedy, and satire in early Western literature are treated in briefer form in the Chinese ode. As in later times Homer's epics were considered to be works worth reading for their ancient wisdom, so *The Book of Songs*, associated with the name of Confucius, was held to be a source of wisdom, both general wisdom and a knowledge of specific men and events in the past.

The basic form of the poems consists of a line of four characters, most often rhymed at the end of the lines, although internal rhyme (and alliteration) occurs. Sometimes, as with Western ballads, there are four-line stanzas with the second and fourth rhyming, but couplets are also used. Again, like Western odes, the structure of the longer poems is often irregular. The poems have a traditional numbering following an edition named after an early scholar, Mao, which is often used by modern scholars to identify the poems. Arthur Waley's translation supplies a conversion table which will enable the reader to locate any poem in Waley's rearrangement of the traditional order.

The *Book of Songs* represents a small selection of what must have been a much larger body of early Chinese poetry, but it is presumably a careful selection reflecting what later admirers of the poetry thought was most valuable of the songs of the past.

From The Book of Songs*

24

I beg of you, Chung Tzu,
Do not climb into our homestead,
Do not break the willows we have planted.
Not that I mind about the willows,
But I am afraid of my father and mother.
Chung Tzu I dearly love;
But of what my father and mother say
Indeed I am afraid.

I beg of you, Chung Tzu,
Do not climb over our wall,
Do not break the mulberry-trees we have planted.
Not that I mind about the mulberry-trees,
But I am afraid of my brothers.
Chung Tzu I dearly love;
But of what my brothers say
Indeed I am afraid.

I beg of you, Chung Tzu,
Do not climb into our garden,
Do not break the hard-wood we have planted.
Not that I mind about the hard-wood,
But I am afraid of what people will say.
Chung Tzu I dearly love;
But of all that people will say
Indeed I am afraid.

28

Cold blows the northern wind,
Thick falls the snow.
Be kind to me, love me,
Take my hand and go with me.
Yet she lingers, yet she havers!
There is not time to lose.

* From *The Book of Songs*, translated by Arthur Waley. Copyright 1960 by Grove Press, Inc. Copyright under the Berne Convention. Reprinted by permission of Grove Press, Inc., and Allen & Unwin Ltd. The poems reprinted here are numbered as in that edition, to which the reader is referred for additional critical material. The notes are derived from Waley's.

2. *Do not . . . :* Poems 1–63 are poems of courtship. The situation—the lover visiting his beloved secretly at night, and often, as in *Romeo and Juliet*, lamenting the coming of dawn, is a commonplace in world literature.

5. *havers:* talks foolishly.

The north wind whistles,
Whirls the falling snow.
Be kind to me, love me,
Take my hand and go home with me.
Yet she lingers, yet she havers!
There is no time to lose.

Nothing is redder than the fox,
Nothing blacker than the crow.
Be kind to me, love me,
Take my hand and ride with me.
Yet she lingers, yet she havers!
There is no time to lose.

42

Look at that little bay of Ch'i,
Its kitesfoot so delicately waving.
Delicately fashioned is my lord,
As thing cut, as thing filed,
As thing chiselled, as thing polished.
Oh, the grace, the elegance!
Oh, the lustre, oh, the light!
Delicately fashioned is my lord;
Never for a moment can I forget him.

Look at that little bay of the Ch'i,
Its kitesfoot so fresh.
Delicately fashioned is my lord,
His ear-plugs are of precious stones,
His cap-gems stand out like stars.
Oh, the grace, the elegance!
Oh, the lustre, the light!
Delicately fashioned is my lord;
Never for a moment can I forget him.

Look at that little bay of the Ch'i,
Its kitesfoot in their crowds.
Delicately fashioned is my lord,
As a thing of bronze, a thing of white metal,
As a sceptre of jade, a disc of jade.
How free, how easy

13–14. *Nothing . . . crow:* i.e., and no one truer than I.

2. *kitesfoot:* a kind of reed-like grass.

13. *earplugs:* worn when elaborate ear-rings were not called for; but he is especially elegant in that his inferior ear-rings are of precious stones.

23. *disc of jade:* Jade discs (with a hole in the center) are found among the most ancient Chinese sacred objects. Probably the disc symbolizes the sun.

He leant over his chariot-rail!
How cleverly he chaffed and joked,
And yet was never rude!

49

Heigh, Po is brave;
Greatest hero in the land!
Po, grasping his lance,
Is outrider of the king.

Since Po went to the east
My head has been touzled as the tumbleweed.
It is not that I lack grease to dress it with;
Bur for whom should I want to look nice?

Oh, for rain, oh, for rain!
And instead the sun shines dazzling.
All this longing for Po
Brings weariness to the heart, aching to the head.

Where can I get a day-lily
To plant behind the house?
All this longing for Po
Can but bring me heart's pain.

57

By the willows of the Eastern Gate,
Whose leaves are so thick,
At dusk we were to meet;
And now the morning star is bright.

By the willows of the Eastern Gate,
Whose leaves are so close,
At dusk we were to meet;
And now the morning star is pale.

63

In the wilds there is a dead doe;
With white rushes we cover her.
There was a lady longing for the spring;
A fair knight seduced her.

13. *day-lily:* the herb of forgetfulness; the *wasuragusa* of Japanese love poetry. Flowers were worn at the belt.

1. *doe:* The pursued deer is an obvious symbol for a lady chased and seduced by a man. When an actual dead deer is found, the Chinese piously cover it with rushes.

In the wood there is a clump of oaks,
And in the wilds a dead deer
With white rushes well bound;
There was a lady fair as jade.

'Heigh, not so hasty, not so rough;
Heigh, do not touch my handkerchief.
Take care, or the dog will bark.'

74

SHE. Spray rises from those waters;
The white rocks are rinsed.
White coat with red lappet,
I followed you to Wo;
And now that I have seen my lord,
Happy am I indeed.

Spray rises from those waters;
The white rocks are washed clean.
White coat with red stitching,
I followed you to Hu;
And now that I have seen my lord,
How can I be sad?

HE. Spray rises from those waters;
The white rocks are dabbled.
I hear that you are pledged;
I dare not talk to your people.

84

Gorgeous in their beauty
Are the flowers of the cherry,
Are they not magnificent in their dignity,
The carriages of the royal bride?

Gorgeous in her beauty
As flower of peach or plum,
Granddaughter of King P'ing,
Child of the Lord of Ch'i.

10. *handkerchief:* which was worn at the girdle.

2. *white rocks:* Poems 74–95 are poems of marriage. The white rocks symbolize the man's clear, fresh appearance, but also, in the final stanza, his tears at finding that the lady has been pledged by her parents to someone else.

4. *Wo:* Wo and Hu are in central-southern Shansi province.

4. *bride:* Little is known about this royal marriage, which must have taken place about the middle of the eighth century.

Wherewith does she angle?
Of silk is her fishing-line,
This child of the Lord of Ch'i,
Granddaughter of King P'ing.

86

A splendid woman and upstanding;
Brocade she wore, over an unlined coat,
Daughter of the Lord of Ch'i,

Wife of the Lord of Wei,
Sister of the Crown Prince of Ch'i,
Called sister-in-law by the Lord of Hsing,
Calling the Lord of T'an her brother-in-law.

Hands white as rush-down,
Skin like lard,
Neck long and white as the tree-grub,
Teeth like melon seeds,
Lovely head, beautiful brows.
Oh, the sweet smile dimpling,
The lovely eyes so black and white.

This splendid lady takes her ease;
She rests where the fields begin.
Her four steeds prance,
The red trappings flutter.
Screened by fans of pheasant-feather she is led to Court.
Oh, you Great Officers, retire early,
Do not fatigue our lord.

Where the water of the river, deep and wide,
Flows northward in strong course,
In the fish-net's swish and swirl
Sturgeon, snout-fish leap and lash.
Reeds and sedges tower high.
All her ladies are tall-coiffed;
All her knights, doughty men.

10. *fishing-line:* The fish is a world-wide symbol of fertility and prosperity. Possibly, as was true in India, the ancient Chinese bridal couple performed a ritual act of fishing.

3. *Daughter of the Lord of Ch'i:* This poem celebrates the most famous wedding of Chinese antiquity, that of Chuang Chiang, daughter of the Lord of Ch'i (northern Shantung) to the Lord of Wei, whose domains centered around the modern Weihwei in northern Honan and southern Hopei. T'an was the modern Ch'eng-tzu-ai, near Lungshan in central Shantung. It is possible that the song was later sung at ordinary weddings—the idea that the bridegroom and bride are king and queen for a day is a commonplace.

95

GUESTS. Slim and fine is the axle-pin of a coach,
And lovely the young girl that has come.
Of hunger we made light, of thirst;
For her fair fame had reached us.

HOST. Though I have no fine friends to meet you,
Pray feast and rejoice.

GUESTS. Such shelter gives that wood on the plains
That the pheasants all roost there.
Truly of this great lady
The magic Powers are strong.
HOST. Pray feast and be at ease,
Good friends, of whom I cannot weary.

Although this wine is not good,
Try to drink just a little.
Although these meats are not fine,
Try to eat just a little.
Although I have no Power that I can impart to you,
Pray sing and dance.

GUESTS. We climbed that high ridge
To cut firewood from the oak-tree,
To cut firewood from the oak-tree.
And ah, its leaves so wet!
But now that in the end we have seen you,
All our sorrows are at rest.

High hills we breasted,
Long ways we went,
Our four steeds prancing,
Six reins like zithern strings.
But the sight of your new bride
Brings good comfort to our hearts.

126

The wild geese are flying;
Suk, suk go their wings.
The soldiers are on the march;
Painfully they struggle through the wilds.
In dire extremity are the strong men;
Sad are their wives, left all alone.

10. *Powers:* The *tê* or powers of the lady. "Virtue" is a possible translation, but in the sense that we speak of the "virtues" of a drug (there is bad as well as good *tê*). See Waley, p. 346.

3. *Soldiers:* Poems 126–140 are of warriors and battles.

The wild geese are flying;
They have lighted in the middle of the marsh.
The soldiers are walling a fort;
The hundred cubits have all risen.
Though they struggle so painfully,
At last they are safely housed.

The wild geese are flying;
Dolefully they cry their discontent.
But these were wise men
Who urged us in our toil,
And those were foolish men
Who urged us to make mischief and rebel.

127

Minister of War,
We are the king's claws and fangs.
Why should you roll us on from misery to misery,
Giving us no place to stop in or take rest?

Minister of War,
We are the king's claws and teeth.
Why should you roll us from misery to misery,
Giving us no place to come to and stay?

Minister of War,
Truly you are not wise.
Why should you roll us from misery to misery?
We have mothers who lack food.

129

Jagged are the rocks.
Oh, how high!
These hills and rivers go on and on.
Oh, how toilsome!
But soldiers fighting in the east
Have no time to pause.

Jagged are the rocks.
Oh, how steep!
These hills and rivers go on and on.
It seems as though they would never end.
But soldiers fighting in the east
Have no time to halt.

9. *fort:* wooden frames to hold the earth—they are constructing an earthern fortification.

We met swine with white trotters
Plunging in a herd through the waves.
The moon is caught in the Net.
There will be deluges of rain.
Soldiers fighting in the east
Have no time to rest.

132

We bring out our carts
On to those pasture-grounds.
From where the Son of Heaven is
Orders have come that we are to be here.
The grooms are told
To get the carts loaded up.
The king's service brings many hardships;
It makes swift calls upon us.

We bring out our carts
On to those outskirts.
Here we set up the standards,
There we raise the ox-tail banners,
The falcon-hunter and the standards
That flutter, flutter.
Our sad hearts are very anxious;
The grooms are worn out.

The king has ordered Nan-chung
To go and build a fort on the frontier.
To bring out the great concourse of chariots,
With dragon banners and standards so bright.
The Son of Heaven has ordered us
To build a fort on that frontier.
Terrible is Nan-chung;
The Hsien-yün are undone.

Long ago, when we started,
The wine-millet and cooking-millet were in flower.
Now that we are on the march again
Snow falls upon the mire.

13–15. *swine . . . Net:* The net is the constellation called the Hyades, connected by the Chinese and also in the West with rain (rain falling looks like a net cast on the landscape). Swine with white trotters are also an omen of rain. The Chinese characters for "net" and "rain" are in their oldest forms very similar.

17. *Nan-chung:* This poem deals with the campaign of the kings of the Chou dynasty, whose homeland was Shensi, against the fierce Hsien-yün tribes, about whom little is known. General Nan-chung is traditionally put in the reign of King Hsüan (827–782 B.C.).

The king's service brings many hardships.
We have no time to rest or bide.
We do indeed long to return;
But we fear the writing on the tablets.

'Dolefully cry the cicadas,
Hop and skip go the grasshoppers.
Before I saw my lord
My heart was full of grief.
But now that I have seen my lord
My heart is still.'
Terrible is Nan-chung;
Lo, he has stricken the warriors of the West!

The spring days are drawn out;
All plants and trees are in leaf.
Tuneful is the oriole's song.
The women gather aster in crowds.
We have bound the culprits; we have captured
the chieftains,
And here we are home again!
Terrible is Nan-chung;
The Hsien-yün are levelled low.

140

The fourth month was summer weather;
The sixth month, blistering heat.
Have our ancestors no compassion
That they can bear to see us suffer?

The autumn days were bitterly cold;
All plants and grasses withered.
I am sick of turmoils and troubles;
When shall we go home?

The winter days were stormy and wild;
The whirlwinds, blast on blast!
Other people are all in comfort;
Why should we alone be harmed?

32. *writing on the tablets:* the king's orders.

33-38. *'Dolefully . . . still:* a bridal hymn formula, spoken by the wives.

44. *aster:* for use in the ancestral temple.

45. *culprits:* Enemies are criminals; they will be "tried" briefly but certainly put to death.

On the hill were lovely trees,
Both chestnut-trees and plum-trees.
Cruel brigands tore them up;
But no one knew of their crime.

Look at that spring water;
Sometimes clear, sometimes foul.
But we every day meet fresh disaster.
How can we be expected to feed?

On flow the Kiang and the Han,
Main-threads of this southern land.
We are worn out with service;
Why does no one heed us?

Would that I were an eagle or a falcon
That I might soar to heaven.
Would I were a sturgeon or snout-fish
That I might plunge into the deep.

On the hill grows the bracken,
In the lowlands, the red-thorn.
A gentleman made this song
That his sorrows might be known.

159

In the seventh month the Fire ebbs;
In the ninth month I hand out the coats.
In the days of the First, sharp frosts;
In the days of the Second, keen winds.
Without coats, without serge,
How should they finish the year?
In the days of the Third they plough;
In the days of the Fourth out I step
With my wife and children,
Bringing hampers to the southern acre
Where the field-hands come to take good cheer.

In the seventh month the Fire ebbs;
In the ninth month I hand out the coats.

20. *feed:* i.e., our parents.

1. *seventh month:* This poem is a song (eighth or seventh century B.C.) made out of sayings about "works and days," about the occupations belonging to the different seasons of the year, but not in an orderly progression. Two calendars are used: "the seventh month," "the ninth month," etc., are the months of the traditional popular calendar which begins its year with spring; "days of the first," "days of the second," etc., refer to the Chou calendar, which begins its year at the winter solstice. *Fire ebbs:* This is explained as meaning that Scorpio is sinking behind the horizon at the moment of its first visibility at dusk.

But when the spring days grow warm
And the oriole sings
The girls take their deep baskets
And follow the path under the wall
To gather the soft mulberry-leaves:
'The spring days are drawing out;
They gather the white aster in crowds.
A girl's heart is sick and sad
Till with her lord she can go home.'

In the seventh month the Fire ebbs;
In the eighth month they pluck the rushes,
In the silk-worm month they gather the mulberry-leaves,
Take that chopper and bill
To lop the far boughs and high,
Pull towards them the tender leaves.
In the seventh month the shrike cries;
In the eighth month they twist thread,
The black thread and the yellow:
'With my red dye so bright
I make a robe for my lord.'

In the fourth month the milk wort is in spike,
In the fifth month the cidada cries.
In the eighth month the harvest is gathered,
In the tenth month the boughs fall.
In the days if the First we hunt the racoon,
And take those foxes and wild-cats
To make furs for our Lord.
In the days of the Second is the great Meet;
Practice for deeds of war.
The one-year-old we keep;
The three-year-old we offer to our Lord.

In the fifth month the locust moves its leg,
In the sixth month the grasshopper shakes its wing,
In the seventh month, out in the wilds;
In the eighth month, in the farm,
In the ninth month, at the door.
In the tenth month the cricket goes under my bed.
I stop up every hole to smoke out the rats,
Plugging the windows, burying the doors:
'Come, wife and children,
The change of the year is at hand.
Come and live in this house.'

43. *one-year-old:* i.e., boar.
60. *life:* Wine increases one's *tê* (inner power) and consequently the probability of one's prayers being answered.

In the sixth month we eat wild plums and cherries,
In the seventh month we boil mallows and beans.
In the eighth month we dry the dates,
In the tenth month we take the rice
To make with it the spring wine,
So that we may be granted long life.
In the seventh month we eat melons,
In the eighth month we cut the gourds,
In the ninth month we take the seeding hemp,
We gather bitter herbs, we cut the ailanto for firewood,
That our husbandsmen may eat.

In the ninth month we make ready the stackyards,
In the tenth month we bring in the harvest,
Millet for wine, millet for cooking, the early and the late,
Paddy and hemp, beans and wheat.
Come, my husbandmen,
My harvesting is over,
Go up and begin your work in the house,
In the morning gather thatch-reeds,
In the evening twist rope;
Go quickly on to the roofs.
Soon you will be beginning to sow your many grains.

In the days of the Second they cut the ice with tingling blows;
In the days of the Third they bring it into the cold shed.
In the days of the Fourth very early
They offer lambs and garlic.
In the ninth month are shrewd frosts;
In the tenth month they clear the stackgrounds.
With twin pitchers they hold the village feast,
Killing for it a young lamb.
Up they go into their lord's hall,
Raise the drinking-cup of buffalo-horn:
'Hurray for our lord; may he live for ever and ever!'

178

A guest, a guest,
And white his horse.
Rich in adornment, finely wrought
The carving and chiselling of his spear-shafts.

A guest so venerable,
A guest of great dignity.
Come, give him a tether
To tether his team.

1. *guest:* Poems 178 and 183 are poems of hospitality and welcome.

Here we follow him,
To left and right secure him.
Prodigal is he in his courtesies;
He will bring down blessings very joyful.

183

Yu, yu, cry the deer
Nibbling the black southernwood in the fields.
I have a lucky guest.
Let me play my zithern, blow my reed-organ,
Blow my reed-organ, trill their tongues,
Take up the baskets of offerings.
Here is a man that loves me
And will teach me the ways of Chou.

Yu, yu, cry the deer
Nibbling the white southernwood of the fields.
I have a lucky guest,
Whose fair fame is very bright.
He sees to it that the common people do not waver,
Of all gentlemen he is the pattern and example.
I have good wine;
Let my lucky guest now feast and play.

Yu, yu, cry the deer
Nibbling the wild garlic of the fields.
I have a lucky guest.
I play my zitherns, small and big,
Play my zitherns, small and big.
Let us make music together, let us be merry,
For I have good wine
To comfort and delight the heart of a lucky guest.

197

They are sprouting, those wayside reeds.
Let not the oxen or sheep trample them.
They are forming stem-shoots, they are branching;
Now the leaves are clustering.
Tender to one another should brothers be,
None absenting himself, all cleaving together.

3. *lucky guest:* For the "luckiness" of guests, compare *Odyssey*, VI,207: "All guests and beggars are envoys of Zeus."

Spread out the mats for them,
Offer them stools.
Spread the mats and the over-mats,
Offer the stools with shuffling step.
Let the host present the cup, the guest return it;
Wash the beaker, set down the goblet.

Sauces and pickles are brought
For the roast meat, for the broiled,
And blessed viands, tripe and cheek;
There is singing and beating of drums.

The painted bows are strong,
The four arrows well balanced.
They shoot, all with like success;
The guests are arranged according to their merits.
The painted bows are bent,
The four arrows, one after another, are aimed.
The four arrows are as though planted;
The guests must be arranged according to their deportment.

It is the descendant of the ancestors who presides;
His wine and spirits are potent.
He deals them out with a big ladle,
That he may live till age withers him,

Till age withers him and back is bent;
That his life may be prolonged and protected,
His latter days be blessed;
That he may secure eternal blessings.

239

Stalwart was Liu the Duke,
Not one to sit down or take his ease.
He made borders, made balks,
He stacked, he stored,
He tied up dried meat and grain
In knapsacks, in bags;
Far and wide he gathered his stores.
The bows and arrows he tested,
Shield and dagger, halberd and battle-axe;
And then began to march.

10. *step:* This poem concerns feasting as well as honoring guests. The shuffling step is a sign of respect—the heel of one foot is not allowed to get beyond the toes of the other.

20. *merits:* i.e., by their military prowess.

1. *Liu the Duke:* The poem recounts the exploits of the legendary Duke Liu. The place names are not identifiable, but Pin (line 50) may have been the area around Sanshui.

Stalwart was Liu the Duke;
He surveyed the people,
They were numerous and flourishing,
He made his royal progress, proclaimed his rule;
There were no complaints, no murmurings
Either high up in the hills
Or down in the plains.
What did they carve for him?
Jade and greenstone
As pairs and ends for his sheath.
Stalwart was Liu the Duke.
He reached the Hundred Springs
And gazed at the wide plain,
Climbed the southern ridge,
Looked upon the citadel,
And the lands for the citadel's army.
Here he made his home,
Here he lodged his hosts,
Here they were at peace with one another,
Here they lived happily with one another.

Stalwart was Liu the Duke
In his citadel so safe.
Walking deftly and in due order
The people supplied mats, supplied stools.
He went up to the dais and leant upon a stool.
Then to make the pig-sacrifice
They took a swine from the sty;
He poured out libation from a gourd,
Gave them food, gave them drink;
And they acknowledged him as their prince and founder.

Stalwart was Liu the Duke.
In his lands broad and long
He noted the shadows and the height of the hills,
Which parts were in the shade, which in the sun,
Viewed the streams and the springs.
To his army in three divisions
He allotted the low lands and the high,
Tithed the fields that there might be due provision,
Reckoning the evening sunlight,
And took possession of his home in Pin.

Stalwart was Liu the Duke.
He made his lodging in Pin,
But across the Wei River he made a ford,
Taking whetstones and pounding-stones.

20. ***pairs:*** Stones that hung in pairs.

He fixed his settlement and set its boundaries;
His people were many and prosperous
On both sides of the Huang Valley,
And upstream along the Kuo Valley.
The multitudes that he had settled there grew dense;
They went on to the bend of the Jui.

257

Ceaseless flows that beck,
Far stretch the southern hills.
May you be sturdy as the bamboo,
May you flourish like the pine,
May elder brother and younger brother
Always love one another,
Never do evil to one another.

To give continuance to foremothers and forefathers
We build a house, many hundred cubits of wall;
To south and west its doors.
Here shall we live, here rest,
Here laugh, here talk.

We bind the frames, creak, creak;
We hammer the mud, tap, tap,
That it may be a place where wind and rain cannot enter,
Nor birds and rats get in,
But where our lord may dwell.

As a halberd, even so plumed,
As an arrow, even so sharp,
As a bird, even so soaring,
As wings, even so flying
Are the halls to which our lord ascends.

Well levelled is the courtyard,
Firm are the pillars,
Cheerful are the rooms by day,
Softly gloaming by night,
A place where our lord can be at peace.

Below, the rush-mats; over them the bamboo-mats.
Comfortably he sleeps,
He sleeps and wakes
And interprets his dreams.

60. *Jui:* The modern Black Water River, which flows into the Ching from the west, in Shenshi province.

18–22. This verse is corrupt, and its meaning is not clear.

'Your lucky dreams, what were they?'
'They were of black bears and brown,
Of serpents and snakes.'

The diviner thus interprets it:
'Black bears and brown
Mean men-children.
Snakes and serpents
Mean girl-children.'

So he bears a son,
And puts him to sleep upon a bed,
Clothes him in robes,
Gives him a jade sceptre to play with.
The child's howling is very lusty;
In red greaves shall he flare,
Be lord and king of house and home.

Then he bears a daughter,
And puts her upon the ground,
Clothes her in swaddling-clothes,
Gives her a loom-whorl to play with.
For her no decorations, no emblems;
Her only care, the wine and food,
And how to give no trouble to father and mother.

44. *lusty:* The child is "lusty" enough so that he will later wear the red greaves, which could be worn only at the king's command. This was an honor similar to the Garter in England.

CONFUCIUS (K'UNG FU-TZU)

(ca. 551 B.C.–ca. 479 B.C.)

The Analects (*Lun Yü*)

If anything remains of the actual words of Confucius it is in the work known as the *Analects* or *Sayings* (*Lun Yü*). But the reputation of this great sage caused his name to be associated with a group of works in ancient China which we now call the Confucian canon or classics. By the time of the Han dynasty six works were accepted as by Confucius or his disciples. These are: (1) the *Book of Changes* (*I Ching*), a work of divination; (2) the *Book of Documents* (*Shu Ching*); (3) the *Book of Songs* (*Shih Ching*) (see above); (4) the *Spring and Autumn* (*Ch'un-ch'iu*), also known as the *Annals of Lu*; (5) the *Book of Rites* (*Li Ching*); and (6) the *Book of Music*

(*Yüeh Ching*). To these were later added the *Analects*; the work of Mencius (Meng Tzu); the three commentaries on the *Spring and Summer* [*Annals*]; and a lexical work, the *Erh ya*. Finally two parts of the *Book of Ritual* were singled out as being of especial importance to Confucian doctrine. These had an independent existence as the *Grate Learning* (*Ta Hsüeh*) and the *Doctrine of the Mean* (*Chung Yung*). These works constituted, as it were, the curriculum for Chinese education. Obviously, Confucius did not write most of them. Some are later than he is, and others he himself quotes as wisdom ancient even in his time.

Even all of the *Analects* is clearly not by Confucius; put together after his death, it likely represents the essence of his doctrine as reported by his disciples. Books III–IX perhaps best represent the earliest stratum. Other books report sayings of his followers and wisdom from other sources. Confucius probably lived at the end of the sixth and the beginning of the fifth century B.C. He was apparently a private person (he complains of a lack of official recognition) who spent his life as a tutor to the sons of the ruling class. He was not content with this life and longed for public office where he would be able to put into practice the "Way of Goodness," which he regarded as the philosophy of the great kings of the past. It is possible that he did hold an intermediate office at court, but he traveled, as did many sages and teachers, from province to province seeking a just state and a ruler who would follow his way. He says that he was brought up under humble circumstances, and a daughter and a son are mentioned, though he does not discuss his marriage. He says at one place (II, 4) that he is over seventy, so he apparently lived to a ripe old age.

Beginning with the Han dynasty, he is regarded as the great sage and utterer of divine wisdom, but during his lifetime he denied that he had divine wisdom or any secret knowledge, that he was inspired, or even that he was especially gifted. Self-improvement through love of learning is his message, a Way of Goodness open to all men. One attains virtue, he maintains, by the study of ancient wisdom. The *Analects* presumably embody his own words, fragments of wisdom he had learned from the ancients, and additions and interpretations by his disciples and later editors.

In mid-twentieth-century America, Oriental wisdom has been a popular and often a serious subject of study. Zen Buddhism and Indian *yoga* have been much discussed and sometimes practiced, and the *Book of Changes* has almost become a cult object in our lives. But is hard to imagine a philosopher less suited to the temper of contemporary Americans interested in Eastern philosophy than Confucius. He tells us that the way to wisdom is through study. One endlessly reads the ancient classics, because wisdom is in them and is reflected in good government in early times. This kind of view was held in the West into the eighteenth century. The Greek and Latin classics were regarded as sources of wisdom and a key to understanding nature, i.e., human nature. Also, Confucius sees wisdom as a key to a better society—better relationships with your friends and associates and better government, but not as a way to personal self-fulfillment or mystical illumination. He is a conservative, standing for the status quo and the traditions of the past. Part of his conservatism, respect for one's parents, is a part of Chinese religion, but one's father and mother represent not just the people who gave you birth but the transmitters of the cultural and moral traditions of the people. Confucius, if he were alive today, might stand for saluting the flag and Bible reading in public schools and for the restoring of Presidents' Day to celebrations of Washington and Lincoln's birthday on the grounds that not all presidents are equally worthy of honor. Finally, Confucius obviously had no notion that the uneducated classes are equal to the educated, and he does not imagine them participating in the affairs of government. The affairs of the state are both the prerogative and duty of the educated classes, made wise by study, not by meditation. However undemocratic this may seem to be, Confucius would argue that the educated man has the harder road to follow: he must learn, he must apply his wisdom without fear or favor, and he must be disciplined. Everything he does must be a moral example to others; he must put personal desires aside and in his every act serve society and the state.

Confucian ideas become interwoven into the very fabric of Chinese society and lasted for centuries after his death. One result was a civil service system of qualification and advancement by study of the classics, and Confucius' ideas were profoundly influential in Japan. The idea of a country ruled by philosophers is, of course, the main thesis of Plato's *Republic*, and the Chinese version of it, though imperfectly understood, captured the imagination of Europeans at least as early as the seventeenth century. To many Europeans, the Chinese mandarin, trained and disciplined by years of study, seemed the ideal statesman, and so Confucius became a myth both in his own country and in the world at large.

From The Analects*

The Master said, To learn and at due times to repeat what one has learnt, is that not after all[1] a pleasure? That friends should come to one from afar, is this not after all delightful? To remain unsoured even though one's merits are unrecognized by others, is that not after all what is expected of a gentleman? (I, 1)

* From *The Analects of Confucius*, translated by Arthur Waley. © 1938 by George Allen & Unwin Ltd. Reprinted by permission of Macmillan Publishing Co., Inc., and Allen & Unwin Ltd. The notes are abridged from Waley's; when they are quoted verbatim it is so indicated.

1. The "after all" implies "even though one does not hold office." [Waley's note.]

The Master said, While a man's father is alive, you can only see his intentions; if is when his father dies that you discover whether or not he is capable of carrying them out. If for the whole three years of mourning he manages to carry on the household exactly as in his father's day, then he is a good son indeed. (I, 11)

Master Yu said, In the usages of ritual it is harmony[2] that is prized; the Way of the Former Kings from this[3] got its beauty. Both small matters and great depend upon it. If things go amiss, he who knows the harmony[4] will be able to attune them. But if harmony itself is not modulated by ritual, things will still go amiss. (I,12)

The Master said, He who rules by moral force (*tê*)[5] is like the pole-star, which remains in its place while all the lesser stars do homage to it. (II, 1)

The Master said, If out of the three hundred *Songs* I had to take one phrase to cover all my teaching, I would say 'Let there be no evil in your thoughts.' (II, 2)

The Master said, Govern the people by regulations, keep order among them by chastisements, and they will flee from you, and lose all self-respect. Govern them by moral force, keep order among them by ritual and they will keep their self-respect and come to you of their own accord. (II, 3)

The Master said, At fifteen I set my heart upon learning. At thirty, I had planted my feet firm upon the ground. At forty, I no longer suffered from perplexities. At fifty, I knew what were the biddings of Heaven. At sixty, I heard them with docile ear. At seventy, I could follow the dictates of my own heart; for what I desire no longer overstepped the boundaries of right. (II, 4)

Mêng Wu Po asked about the treatment of parents. The Master said, Behave in such a way that your father and mother have no anxiety about you, except concerning your health. (II, 6)

Duke Ai[6] asked, What can I do in order to get the support of the common people? Master K'ung[7] replied, If you 'raise up the straight and set them on top of the crooked,' the commoners will support you. But if you raise the crooked and set them on top of the straight, the commoners will not support you. (II, 19)

2. Harmony between man and nature; playing the musical mode that harmonizes with the season, wearing seasonable clothes, eating seasonable food, and the like. [Waley's note.]

3. I.e., from harmony. [Waley's note.]

4. I.e, the act that harmonizes with the moment. [Waley's note.]

5. I.e., "instincts." See Waley, *Analects*, p. 33.

6. Duke of Lu from 494 to 468. [Waley's note].

7. Master K'ung is Confucius (K'ung Fu-tzu).

Chi K'ang-tzu[8] asked whether there were any form of encouragement by which he could induce the common people to be respectful and loyal. The Master said, Approach them with dignity, and they will respect you. Show piety towards your parents and kindness toward your children, and they will be loyal to you. Promote those who are worthy, train those who are incompetent; that is the best form of encouragement. (II, 20)

Someone, when talking to Master K'ung, said, How is it that you are not in the public service? The Master said, The Book[9] says: 'Be filial, only be filial and friendly towards your brothers, and you will be contributing to government.' There are other sorts of service quite different from what you mean by 'service.' (II, 21)

The Master said, Gentlemen never compete. You will say that in archery they do so. But even then they bow and make way for one another when they are going up to the archery-ground, when they are coming down and at the subsequent drinking-bout. Thus even when competing, they still remain gentlemen. (III, 7)

The Master said, The Ospreys![10] Pleasure not carried to the point of debauch; grief not carried to the point of self-injury. (III, 20)

Duke Ai asked Tsai Yü[11] about the Holy Ground. Tsai Yü replied, The Hsia sovereigns marked theirs with a pine, the men of Yin used a cypress, the men of Chou used a chestnut-tree, saying, 'This will cause the common people to be in fear and trembling.'[12] The Master hearing of it said, What is over and done with, one does not discuss. What has already taken its course, one does not criticize; what already belongs to the past, one does not censure.[13] (III, 21)

The Master spoke of the Succession Dance[14] as being perfect beauty and at the same time perfect goodness; but of the War Dance as being perfect beauty, but not perfect goodness. (III, 25)

8. Head of the three families who were *de facto* rules of Lu. Died 469 B.C. [Waley's note.]

9. The *Book of History* (*Shu Ching*), one of the five Confucian classics. "The passage does not occur in the genuine books. . . . What it meant in its original context no doubt was 'Be pious to your ancestors . . . be generous in rewarding your officers of State.' Confucius 'reanimates' the ancient text, in order to prove that a virtuous private life makes a real contribution towards the public welfare." [Waley's note.]

10. From the *Book of Songs* (Waley, No. 87). This is a love poem which begins with the cry of the birds.

11. A disciple in whom Confucius was much disappointed. [Waley's note.]

12. Pun on *li* "a chestnut-tree" and *li* "to be in awe." [Waley's note.]

13. It is ill-bred of Tsai Yu to make fun of the Chou dynasty for taking so inauspicious a name, especially to Duke Ai, their direct descendent.

14. The dance (at any rate according to the later Confucian theory mimed the peaceful accession of the legendary emperor Shun; the War Dance mimed the accession by conquest of the Emperor Wu, who overthrew the Yin. [Waley's note.]

The Master said, High office filled by men of narrow views, ritual performed without reverence, the forms of mourning observed without grief—these are things I cannot bear to see! (III, 26)

Wealth and rank are what every man desires; but if they can only be retained to the detriment of the Way he professes, he must relinquish them. Poverty and obscurity are what every man detests; but if they can only be avoided to the detriment of the Way he professes, he must accept them. The gentleman who ever parts company with Goodness does not fulfil that name. Never for a moment[15] does a gentleman quit the way of Goodness. He is never so harried but that he cleaves to this; never so tottering but that he cleaves to this. (IV, 5)

The Master said, I for my part have never yet seen one who really cared for Goodness, nor one who really abhorred wickedness. One who really cared for Goodness would never let any other consideration come first. One who abhorred wickedness would be so constantly doing Good that wickedness would never have a chance to get at him. Has anyone ever managed to do Good with his whole might even as long as the space of a single day? I think not. Yet I for my part have never seen anyone give up such an attempt because he had not the *strength* to go on. It may well have happened, but I for my part have never seen it. (IV, 6)

The Master said, In the morning, hear the Way; in the evening, die content![16] (IV, 8)

Tsai Yü used to sleep during the day. The Master said, Rotten wood cannot be carved, nor a wall of dried dung be trowelled.[17] What use is there in my scolding him any more?

The Master said, There was a time when I merely listened attentively to what people said, and took for granted that they would carry out their words. Now I am obliged not only to give ear to what they say, but also to keep an eye on what they do. It was my dealings with Tsai Yü that brought about the change. (V, 9)

Chi Wên Tzu used to think thrice before acting. The Master hearing of it said, Twice is quite enough.[18] (V, 19)

Once when Yen Hui and Tzu-lu were waiting upon him the Master said, Suppose each of you were to tell his wish. Tzu-lu said, I should like to have carriages and horses, clothes and fur rugs,

15. Cf. Mencius, II, 1; VII, 2. [Waley's note.]

16. The well-known saying *Vedi Napoli e poi mori* follows the same pattern. The meaning is, you will have missed nothing. [Waley's note.]

17. I.e., patterned with the trowel. To translate "be plastered" destroys the parallelism. [Waley's note.] For Tsai Yu see III, 21.

18. Ch'êng Hao (A.D. 1032–1085) says that if one thinks more than twice, self-interest begins to come into play. [Waley's note.]

share them with my friends and feel no annoyance if they were returned to me the worse for wear. Yen Hui said, I should like never to boast of my good qualities nor make a fuss about the trouble I take on behalf of others. Tzu-lu said, A thing I should like is to hear the Master's wish. The Master said, In dealing with the aged, to be of comfort to them; in dealing with friends, to be of good faith with them; in dealing with the young, to cherish them. (V, 25)

The Master said, Incomparable indeed was Hui! A handful[19] of rice to eat, a gourdful of water to drink, living in a mean street—others would have found it unendurably depressing, but to Hui's cheerfulness it made no difference at all. Incomparable indeed was Hui! (VI, 9)

Jan Ch'iu said, It is not that your Way does not commend itself to me, but that it demands powers I do not possess. The Master said, He whose strength gives out collapses during the course of the journey (the Way); but you deliberately draw the line. (VI, 10)

The Master said to Tzu-hsia, 'You must practise the *ju*[20] of gentlemen, not that of the common people. (VI, 11)

The Master said, Mêng Chih-fan is no boaster. When his people were routed[21] he was the last to flee; but when they neared the city-gate, he whipped up his horses, saying, It was not courage that kept me behind. My horses were slow. (VI, 13)

The Master said, The wise man delights in water, the Good man delights in mountains. For the wise move; but the Good stay still. The wise are happy; but the Good, secure. (VI, 21)

The Master said, I have 'transmitted what was taught to me without making up anything of my own.'[22] I have been faithful to and loved the Ancients. In these respects, I make bold to think, not even our old P'êng[23] can have excelled me. The Master said, I have listened in silence and noted what was said, I have never grown tired of learning nor wearied of teaching others what I have learnt. These at least are merits which I can confidently claim. The Master said, The thought that 'I have left my moral power (*tê*) untended, my learning unperfected, that I have heard of righteous men, but been unable to go to them; have heard of evil men, but been unable

19. Literary, a split-bamboo sectionful. [Waley's note.]

20. The meaning of the saying may be "The unwarlikeness of gentlemen means a preference for *te* (moral force), that of inferior people is mere cowardice." [Waley's note.]

21. The gentleman is a nonchalant hero and belittles his own achievements.

22. Cf. *Mo Tzu*, 46. "A gentleman does not make anything up; he merely transmits." [Waley's note.]

23. The Chinese Nestor. It is the special business of old men to transmit traditions. [Waley's note.]

to reform them'[24]—it is these thoughts that disquiet me. (VII, 1-3)

The Master said, How utterly have things gone to the bad with me! It is long now indeed since I dreamed that I saw the Duke of Chou.[25] (VII, 5)

The Master said, He who seeks only coarse food to eat, water to drink and bent arm for pillow, will without looking for it find happiness to boot. Any thought of accepting wealth and rank by means that I know to be wrong is as remote from me as the clouds that float above. (VII, 15)

The Master fished with a line but not with a net; when fowling he did not aim at a roosting bird.[26] (VII, 26)

When Master Tsêng was ill, Mêng Ching Tzu came to see him. Master Tsêng spoke to him saying, When a bird is about to die, its song touches the heart.[27] When a man is about to die, his words are of note. There are three things that a gentleman, in following the Way, places above all the rest: from every attitude, every gesture that he employs he must remove all trace of violence or arrogance; every look that he composes in his face must betoken good faith; from every word that he utters, from every intonation, he must remove all trace of coarseness or impropriety. As to the ordering of ritual vessels and the like, there are those whose business it is to attend to such matters. (VIII, 4)

Master Tsêng said, Clever, yet not ashamed to consult those less clever than himself; widely gifted, yet not ashamed to consult those with few gifts; having, yet seeming not to have; full, yet seeming empty; offended against, yet never contesting—long ago I had a friend whose ways were such as this. (VIII, 5)

The Master said, Let a man be first incited by the Songs,[28] then given a firm footing by the study of ritual, and finally perfected by music. (VIII, 8)

The Master said, Learn as if you were following someone whom you could not catch up, as though it were someone you were frightened of losing. (VIII, 17)

24. Confucius is presumably quoting an old saying here, in rhymed couplets.

25. Tan, Duke of Chou, brother of the legendary founder of the Chou dynasty, and to Confucius a great ruler and sage.

26. Sport is always somewhat ritualized, and was so in ancient China. Modern sportsmen sometimes take trout with deliberately fragile tackle, which must be manipulated with great skill by the fisherman. Some states regulate by law the number of shells a hunter may have in his gun: he is restricted either to a double-barreled shotgun or must put a plug, limiting himself to two shots, in an automatic shotgun. Confucius may be thinking about both the sportsman's code, so revered by Hemingway, and the creatures of nature, which are there for man to hunt and enjoy but are not to be slaughtered without regulation.

27. Cf. our belief concerning "swan-songs." [Waley's note.] In many cultures, dying words are considered of great significance.

28. I.e., the *Book of Songs.*

The Master said, Sublime were Shun and Yü! All that is under Heaven was theirs, yet they remaind aloof from it. (VIII, 18)

The Master said, Greatest, as lord and ruler, was Yao[29] Sublime, indeed, was he. 'There is no greatness like the greatness of Heaven,' yet Yao could copy it. So boundless was it[30] yet sublime were his achievements, dazzling the insignia of his culture! (VIII, 19)

Shun had five ministers and all that is under Heaven was well ruled. King Wu[31] said, I have ten ministers. Master K'ung said, True indeed is the saying that 'the right material is hard to find'; for the turn of the T'ang and Yü dynasties was the time most famous for this. (As for King Wu), there was a woman among his ten, so that in reality there were only nine men. Yet of all that is under Heaven he held two parts in three, using them in submissive service to the dynasty of Yin. The moral power (*tê*) of Chou may, indeed, be called an absolutely perfect moral power! (VIII, 20)

The Master said, In Yü I can find no semblance of a flaw. Abstemious in his own food and drink, he displayed the utmost devotion in his offerings to spirits and divinities.[32] Content with the plainest clothes for common wear, he saw to it that his sacrificial apron and ceremonial head-dress were of the utmost magnificence. His place of habitation was of the humblest, and all his energy went into draining and ditching. In him I can find no semblance of a flaw. (VIII, 20)

When the Master was trapped in K'uang,[33] he said, When King Wên perished, did that mean that culture (*wên*) ceased to exist? If Heaven had really intended that such culture as his should disappear, a latter-day mortal would never have been able to link himself to it as I have done. And if Heaven does not intend to destroy such culture, what have I to fear from the people of K'uang? (IX, 5)

The Grand Minister (of Wu?) asked Tzu-kung saying, Is your Master a Divine Sage? If so, how comes it that he has many practical accomplishments?[34] Tzu-kung said, Heaven certainly intended him to become a Sage;[35] it is also true that he has many accomplishments. When the Master heard of it he said, The Grand Minister is quite right about me. When I was young I was in humble

29. A legendary sage.

30. See note 5, p. 392.

31. King Wu was the Warrior King, founder of the Chou dynasty. Perhaps the ten ministers are his mother and his nine brothers. The "right material" is good ministers.

32. To ancestors, and spirits of hill, stream, etc. [Waley's note]. Yü the Great was, along with Yao and Shun, one of the three divine sages. He is associated with a Deluge Myth like that of the Near East and is a patron of agriculture.

33. The people of K'uang were supposed to have mistaken Confucius for an adventurer who had created a disturbance because Confucius' carriage was being driven by a man who had associated with the criminal.

34. Gentlemen do not get their hands dirty with practical accomplishments; sages even less.

35. But the wickedness of the world prevented it. [Waley's note.]

circumstances; that is why I have many practical accomplishments in regard to simple, everyday accomplishments? No, he is in no need of them at all.

Lao says that the Master said, It is because I have not been given a chance[36] that I have become so handy. (IX, 6)

When the Master was very ill, Tzu-lu caused some of the disciples to get themselves up as official retainers.[37] Coming to himself for a short while, the Master said, How like Yu, to go in for this sort of imposture! In pretending to have retainers when I have none, whom do I deceive? Do I deceive Heaven? Not only would I far rather die in the arms of you disciples than in the arms of retainers, but also as regards my funeral—even if I am not accorded a State Burial, it is not as though I were dying by the roadside.[38] (IX, 11)

Tzu-kung said, Suppose one had a lovely jewel, should one wrap it up, put it in a box and keep it, or try to get the best price one can for it? The Master said, Sell it! Most certainly sell it! I myself am one who is waiting for an offer.[39] (IX, 12)

The Master wanted to settle among the Nine Wild Tribes of the East.[40] Someone said, I am afraid you would find it hard to put up with their lack of refinement. The Master said, Were a true gentleman to settle among them there would soon be no trouble about lack of refinement. (IX, 13)

Once when the Master was standing by a stream, he said, Could one but go on and on[41] like this, never ceasing day or night! (IX, 16)

The Master said, I have never yet seen anyone whose desire to build up his moral power was as strong as sexual desire. (IX, 17)

The Master said, The case is like that of someone raising a mound. If he stops working, the fact that it perhaps needed only one more basketful makes no difference; I stay where I am. Whereas even if he has not got beyond levelling the ground, but is still at work, the fact that he has only tilted one basketful of earth makes no difference. I go to help him. (IX, 18)

36. To hold public office.

37. Such as he would have been entitled to, had he held office. [Waley's note.]

38. He assumes that his friends will see that he gets a decent burial and is not worried about being buried with public honors.

39. The point of this is that a talented person should be eager to perform public service.

40. There is a certain idealization in early Chinese literature of the "noble savage," as there was in the West. There is a Chinese saying: "When the Emperor no longer functions, learning must be sought among the Four Barbarians" (i.e., to the north, west, east, and south). (See Waley, p. 108)

41. In one's moral striving; cf. Mencius, IV, 2; XVIII. [Waley's note.]

The Master said, There are shoots whose lot it is to spring up but never to flower; others whose lot it is to flower, but never bear fruit. (IX, 21)

The Master said, Respect the young. How do you know that they will not one day be all that you are now? But if a man has reached forty or fifty and nothing has been heard of him, then I grant there is no need to respect him. (IX, 22)

The Master said, 'Wearing a shabby hemp-quilted gown, yet capable of standing unabashed with those who wore fox and badger.' That would apply quite well to Yu, would it not?

> Who harmed none, was foe to none,
> Did nothing that was not right.[42]

Afterwards Tzu-lu (Yu) kept on continually chanting those lines to himself. The Master said, Come now, the wisdom contained in them is not worth treasuring[43] to that extent! (IX, 26)

The Master said, Only when the year grows cold do we see that the pine and cypress are the last[44] to fade. (IX, 27)

At home in his native village his manner is simple and unassuming, as though he did not trust himself to speak. But in the ancestral temple and at Court he speaks readily, though always choosing his words with care. (X, 1)

At Court when conversing with the Under Ministers his attitude is friendly and affable; when conversing with the Upper Ministers, it is restrained and formal. When the ruler is present it is wary, but not cramped. (X, 2)

When the ruler summons him to receive a guest, a look of confusion comes over his face and his legs seem to give beneath his weight. When saluting his colleagues he passes his right hand to the left, letting his robe hang down in front and behind; and as he advances with quickened step, his attitude is one of majestic dignity.

When the guest has gone, he reports the close of the visit, saying, 'The guest is no longer looking back.' (X, 3)

On entering the Palace Gate he seems to shrink[45] into himself,

42. These lines are quoted from the *Book of Songs* (Waley, No. 67).

43. Pun on two senses of *tsang* (1) excellent; (2) treasure, to treasure up, to store. [Waley's note.]

44. This is an ancient proverb.

45. All cultures have bodily movements which reflect social situations—stooping, standing erect, bowing, various facial expressures, gestures, etc., which are learned almost from birth. However, these are in the subconscious minds of most Westerners. The Chinese, from early times, delighted in formalizing these social signals and made them into a ritual which could be studied and imitated.

as though there were not room. If he halts, it must never be in the middle of the gate, nor in going through does he ever tread on the threshold. As he passes the Stance[46] a look of confusion comes over his face, his legs seem to give way under him and words seem to fail him. While, holding up the hem of his skirt, he ascends the Audience Hall, he seems to double up and keeps in his breath, so that you would think he was not breathing at all. On coming out, after descending the first step his expression relaxes into one of satisfaction and relief. At the bottom of the steps he quickens his pace, advancing with an air of majestic dignity. On regaining his place he resumes his attitude of wariness and hesitation. (X, 4)

When carrying the tablet of jade,[47] he seems to double up, as though borne down by its weight. He holds it at the highest as though he were making a bow,[48] at the lowest, as though he were proffering a gift. His expression, too, changes to one of dread and his feet seem to recoil, as though he were avoiding something. When presenting ritual-presents, his expression is placid. At the private audience his attitude is gay and animated. (X, 5)

A gentleman does not wear facings of purple or mauve, nor in undress does he use pink or roan.[49] In hot weather he wears an unlined gown of fine thread loosely woven, but puts on an outside garment before going out-of-doors. With a black robe he wears black lambskin; with a robe of undyed silk, fawn. With a yellow robe, fox fur. On his undress robe the fur cuffs are long; but the right is shorter than the left. His bedclothes must be half as long again as a man's height. The thicker kinds of fox and badger are for home wear. Except when in mourning, he wears all his girdle-ornaments. Apart from his Court apron, all his skirts are wider at the bottom that at the waist. Lambskin dyed black and a hat of dark-dyed silk must not be worn when making visits of condolence. At the Announcement[50] of the New Moon he must go to Court in full Court dress. (X, 6)

When preparing himself for sacrifice he must wear the Bright Robe,[51] and it must be of linen. He must change his food and also

46. Thresholds are traditionally unlucky places in various parts of the world from ancient times, perhaps because in some cultures the dead were buried under thresholds. The bride is carried across the threshold so that she cannot trip and attract bad luck.

47. Symbol of the ruler's feudal investiture; the *kuei*. [Waley's note.]

48. On a level with his forehead. [Waley's note.]

49. He does not use color associated with fasting and mourning. He puts on his jacket when he goes out. The yellow robe and fox fur are formal, like our "black tie." His right sleeve is shorter to permit freedom of movement. He wears his talisman, medals, symbols of rank. Fancy dress is not proper for funerals and mourning.

50. The Announcement is made to the ancestors, who are kept informed or civic and religious activity.

51. A robe worn when one was dealing with spirits.

the place where he commonly sits. But there is no objection to his rice being of the finest quality, nor to his meat being finely minced. Rice affected by the weather or turned he must not eat, nor fish that is not sound, nor meat that is high. He must not eat anything discoloured or that smells bad. He must not eat what is overcooked nor what is undercooked, nor anything that is out of season. He must not eat what has been crookedly cut, nor any dish that lacks its proper seasoning. The meat that he eats must at the very most not be enough to make his breath smell of meat rather than of rice. As regards wine, no limit is laid down; but he must not be disorderly. He may not drink wine bought at a shop or eat dried meat from the market. He need not refrain from such articles of food as have ginger sprinkled over them; but he must not eat much of such dishes.

After a sacrifice in the ducal palace, the flesh must not be kept overnight. No sacrificial flesh may be kept beyond the third day. If it is kept beyond the third day, it may no longer be eaten. While it is being eaten, there must be no conversation, nor any word spoken while lying down after the repast. Any article of food, whether coarse rice, vegetables, broth or melon, that has been used as an offering must be handled with due solemnity. (X, 7-8)

Nan Jung in reciting the *I* Song repeated the verse about the sceptre of white jade three times.[52] (In consequence of which) Master K'ung gave him his elder brother's daughter to marry. (XI, 5)

When Yen Hui died the Master wailed without restraint. His followers said, Master, you are wailing without restraint! He said, Am I doing so? Well, if any man's death could justify abandoned wailing, it would surely be this man's! (XI, 9)

Once when Tzu-lu, Tsêng Hsi, Jan Ch'iu and Kung-hsi Hua were seated in attendance upon the Master, he said, you consider me as a somewhat older man than yourselves. Forget for a moment that I am so. At present you are out of office and feel that your merits are not recognized. Now supposing someone were to recognize your merits, what employment would you choose? Tzu-lu promptly and confidently replied, Give me a country of a thousand war-chariots, hemmed in by powerful enemies, or even invaded by hostile armies, with drought and famine to boot; in the space of three years I could endow the people with courage and teach them in what direction right conduct lies.

52. "Be always mild and good-tempered
A scratch on a sceptre of white jade
Can be polished away;
A slip of the tongue
Can never be repaired."—*Book of Songs* (Waley, No. 271)

Our Master smiled at him. What about you, Ch'iu? he said. Ch'iu replied saying, Give me a domain of sixty to seventy or say fifty to sixty (leagues), and in the space of three years I could bring it about that the common people should lack for nothing. But as to rites and music, I should have to leave them to a real gentleman.

What about you, Ch'ih?

(Kung-hsi Hua) answered saying, I do not say I could do this; but I should like at any rate to be trained for it. In ceremonies at the Ancestral Temple or at a conference or general gathering of the feudal princes I should like, clad in the Straight Gown and Emblematic Cap, to play the part of junior assistant.

Tien, what about you?

The notes of the zithern he was softly fingering died away; he put it down, rose and replied saying, I fear my words will not be so well chosen as those of the other three. The Master said, What harm is there in that? All that matters is that each should name his desire.

Tsêng Hsi said, At the end of spring, when the making of the Spring Clothes has been completed, to go with five times six newly-capped youths and six times seven uncapped boys, perform the lustration in the river I, take the air[53] at the Rain Dance altars, and then go home singing. The Master heaved a deep sigh and said, I am with Tien. (XI, 25)

Jan Jung asked about Goodness.[54] The Master said, Behave when away from home as though you were in the presence of an important guest. Deal with the common people as though you were officiating at an important sacrifice. Do not do to others what you would not like yourself. Then there will be no feelings of opposition to you, whether it is the affairs of a State that you are handling or the affairs of a Family.[55] Jan Yung said, I know that I am not clever; but this is a saying that, with your permission, I shall try to put into practice. (XII, 2)

Ssu-ma Niu grieved, saying, Everyone else has brothers; I alone have none. Tzu-hsia said, I have heard this saying, 'Death and life are the decree of Heaven; wealth and rank depend upon the will of Heaven. If a gentleman attends to business and does not idle away his time, if he behaves with courtesy to others and observes the rulers of ritual, then all within the Four Seas[56] are his brothers.' How can any true gentleman grieve that he is without brothers? (XII, 5)

53. Expose oneself to the wind, the elements. Tien and Tseng Hsi are the same person.

54. Ruling by goodness, not abstract goodness.

55. A ruling clan, not the family in our sense.

56. The four seas bound the universe.

Tzu-kung asked about government. The Master said, sufficient food, sufficient weapons, and the confidence of the common people. Tzu-kung said, Suppose you had no choice but to dispense with one of these three, which would you forgo? The Master said, Weapons. Tzu-kung said, Suppose you were forced to dispense with one of the two that were left, which would you forgo? The Master said, Food. For from of old death has been the lot of all men; but a people that no longer trusts its rulers is lost indeed. (XII, 7)

Tzu-chang asked what was meant by 'piling up moral force' and 'deciding when in two minds.'[57] The Master said, 'by piling up moral force' is meant taking loyalty and good faith as one's guiding principles, and migrating to places where right prevails. Again, to love a thing means wanting it to live, to hate a thing means wanting it to perish. But suppose I want something to live and at the same time want it to perish; that is 'being in two minds.'

> Not for her wealth, oh no!
> But merely for a change.[58] (XII, 10)

Duke Ching of Ch'i[59] asked Master K'ung about government. Master K'ung replied saying, Let the prince be a prince, the minister a minister, the father a father and the son a son. The Duke said, How true! For indeed when the prince is not a prince, the minister not a minister, the father not a father, the son not a son, one may have a dish of millet in front of one and yet not know if one will live to eat it. (XII, 11)

Chi K'ang-tzu was troubled by burglars. He asked Master K'ung what he should do. Master K'ung replied saying, If only you were free from desire, they would not steal even if you paid them to. (XII, 18)

Chi K'ang-tzu asked Master K'ung about government, saying, Suppose I were to slay those who have not the Way in order to help on those who have the Way, what would you think of it? Master K'ung replied saying, You are there to rule, not to slay. If you desire what is good, the people will at once be good. The

57. Confucius is being asked to explain a proverb or ancient text.

58. Couplet from *Song* 105,5 [Waley, *Book of Songs*, No. 105, last lines] in which a lady says: I came all this long way to marry you, and you do not give me enough to eat. I shall go back to my country and home. Your thoughts are occupied with a new mate. If it is true that it not because of her riches, then it is simply for the sake of a change. The last phrase ("only for a change") is susceptible of many interpretations. But is clearly thus that Confucius understands it, and he uses this story of a man who got a wife from a far country, and then promptly neglected her in favour of someone taken up "simply for a change," as an example of "being in two minds," "not knowing one's own mind." [Waley's note.]

59. A powerful and successful duke who died in 490 B.C., the last of his line. His career was clouded at the end by fights among his sons over the succession.

essence of the gentleman is that of wind; the essence of small people is that of grass. And when a wind passes over the grass, it cannot choose but bend. (XII, 19)

Tzu-lu asked about government. The Master said, Lead them; encourage them! Tzu-lu asked for a further maxim. The Master said, Untiringly. (XIII, 1)

Tzu-lu said, If the prince of Wei were waiting for you to come and administer his country for him, what would be your first measure? The Master said, It would certainly be to correct language. Tzu-lu said, Can I have heard you aright? Surely what you say has nothing to do with the matter. Why should language be corrected? The Master said, Yu! How boorish you are! A gentleman, when things he does not understand are mentioned, should maintain an attitude of reserve. If language is incorrect, then what is said does not concord with what was meant; and if what is said does not concord with what was meant, what is to be done cannot be effected. If what is to be done cannot be effected, then rites and music will not flourish. If rites and music do not flourish, then mutilations and lesser punishments will go astray. And if mutilations and lesser punishments go astray, then the people have nowhere to put hand or foot.

Therefore the gentleman uses only such language as is proper for speech, and only speaks of what it would be proper to carry into effect. The gentleman, in what he says, leaves nothing to mere chance. (XIII, 3)

The Master said, If only someone were to make use of me, even for a single year, I could do a great deal; and in three years I could finish off the whole work. (XIII, 10)

The Master said, 'Only if the right sort of people had charge of a country for a hundred years would it become really possible to stop cruelty and do away with slaughter.' How true the saying is! (XIII, 11)

The Master said, If a Kingly Man were to arise, within a single generation Goodness would prevail. (XIII, 12)

Tzu-kung asked, What must a man be like in order that he may be called a true knight (of the Way)? The Master said, He who

> In the furtherance of his own interests
> Is held back by scruples,
> Who as an envoy to far lands
> Does not disgrace his prince's commission

may be called a true knight.

Tzu-kung said, May I venture to ask who would rank next? The Master said, He whom his relatives commend for filial piety, his fellow-villagers, for deference to his elders. Tzu-kung said, May I venture to ask who would rank next? The Master said, He who always stands by his word, who undertakes nothing that he does not bring to achievement. Such a one may be in the humblest possible circumstances, but all the same we must give him the next place.

Tzu-kung said, What would you say of those who are now conducting the government? The Master said, Ugh! A set of peck-measures, not worth taking into account. (XIII, 20)

Tzu-kung asked, saying, What would you feel about a man who was loved by all his fellow-villagers? The Master said, That is not enough.

What would you feel about a man who was hated by all his fellow-villagers? The Master said, That is not enough. Best of all would be that the good people in his village loved him and the bad hated him. (XIII, 24)

The Master said, The truth is, no one knows me![60] Tzu-kung said, What is the reason that you are not known? The Master said, I do not 'accuse Heaven, nor do I lay the blame on men.'[61]

But the studies[62] of men here below are felt on high, and perhaps after all I am known; not here, but in Heaven! (XIV, 37)

Yüan Jang sat waiting for the Master in a sprawling position.[63] The Master said, Those who when young show no respect to their elders achieve nothing worth mentioning when they grow up. And merely to live on, getting older and older, is to be a useless pest.

And he struck him across the shins with his stick. (XIV, 46)

The Master said, Ssu, I believe you look upon me as one whose aim is simply to learn and retain in mind as many things as possible. He replied, That is what I thought. Is it not so? The Master said, No; I have one (thread) upon which I string them all. (XV, 2)

The Master said, Among those that 'ruled by inactivity' surely Shun may be counted. For what action did he take? He merely placed himself gravely and reverently with his face due south;[64] that was all. (XV, 4)

60. No ruler recognizes my merits and employs me. [Waley's note.]

61. "A gentleman neither accuses Heaven nor blames men." Mencius, II, 2; XIII, 1. [Waley's note.]

62. The self-training consisting in the study of antiquity. [Waley's note.]

63. In many parts of the world, not only in China, students stand until their teacher has arrived and asked them to be seated.

64. He practices Taoist self-hypnosis and places himself in the position of the ruler. "Shun was a divine sage (*shêng*) whose *tê* was so great that it sufficed to guide and transform the people." [Waley's note.]

The Master said, Straight and upright indeed was the recorder Yü![65] When the Way prevailed in the land he was (straight) as an arrow; when the Way ceased to prevail, he was (straight) as an arrow. A gentleman indeed is Ch'ü Po Yü.[66] When the Way prevailed in his land, he served the State; but when the Way ceased to prevail, he knew how to 'wrap it up and hide it in the folds of his dress.'[67] (XV, 6)

The Master said, I once spent a whole day without food and a whole night without sleep, in order to meditate. It was no use. It is better to learn. (XV, 30)

Master K'ung said, When the Way prevails under Heaven all orders concerning ritual, music and punitive expeditions are issued by the Son of Heaven himself. When the Way does not prevail, such orders are issued by the feudal princes; and when this happens, it is to be observed that ten generations rarely pass before the dynasty falls. If such orders are issued by State Ministers, five generations rarely pass before they lose their power. When the retainers of great Houses seize a country's commission, three generations rarely pass before they lose their power. When the Way prevails under Heaven, policy is not decided by Ministers; when the Way prevails under Heaven, commoners do not discuss public affairs. (XVI, 2)

Master K'ung said, There are three sorts of pleasure that are profitable, and three sorts of pleasure that are harmful. The pleasure got from the due ordering of ritual and music, the pleasure got from discussing the good points in the conduct of others, the pleasure of having many wise friends is profitable. But pleasure got from profligate enjoyments, pleasure got from idle gadding about, pleasure got from comfort and ease is harmful. (XVI, 5)

When the Master went to the walled town of Wu, he heard the sound of stringed instruments and singing. Our Master said with a gentle smile, 'To kill a chicken one does not use an ox-cleaver.'[68] Tzu-yu replied saying, I remember once hearing you say, 'A gentleman who has studied the Way will be all the tenderer towards his fellow-men; a commoner who has studied the Way will be all the easier to employ.' The Master said, My disciples, what he says is quite true. What I said just now was only meant as a joke. (XVIII, 4)

65. Having failed to persuade Duke Ling of Wei to use the services of Ch'ü Po Yü, the recorder Yü gave directions that when he (the recorder) died his body should not receive the honours due to a minister, as a posthumous protest against the Duke Ling's offences. [Waley's note.]

66. Ch'ü Po Yü left Wei owing to the tyrannical conduct of Duke Hsieh in 559 B.C. [Waley's note.]

67. His jewel; i.e., his talents. [Waley's note.]

68. A proverbial saying like our "casting pearls before swine."

The Master said, Little ones, Why is it that none of you study the *Songs?*[69] For the *Songs* will help you to incite people's emotions, to observe their feelings, to keep company, to express your grievances. They may be used at home in the service of one's father; abroad, in the service of one's prince. Moreover, they will widen your acquaintance with the names of birds, beasts, plants and trees. (XVII, 9)

69. I.e., the *Book of Songs.*

CHUANG-TZU

(ca. 369 B.C.–ca. 286 B.C.)

Selections

The Chinese philosopher-essayist Chuang Tzu is almost a legendary figure. The book which bears his name and in which he is the chief speaker dates from the fourth century B.C. Early biographies say that he was born about 369 B.C. in present-day Honan province in east-central China. He was apparently a minor government official and left a large body of writings. He seems to have been a recluse, which is a departure from the official Confucian idea of philosophy with its emphasis on social order and active involvement in government. His writings—"sayings" would be a better term—are uneven in quality and may represent both his own thoughts and those of his followers. Traditionally the seven "inner chapters" of the thirty-three in the work are thought to be by the master himself.

While, as we have noted earlier, Chinese philosophy is generally written in an anecdotal style and is more "literary" than most Western philosophy, Chuang-Tzu especially distrusts logic and hard definition and is the wittiest and most imaginative of the classical philosophers of China. He does not pretend that the stories and legends he uses are historical fact but employs them as a device to storm the mind and the spirit of the reader. "No single work of any other school of thought can approach the *Chuang Tzu* for sheer literary brilliance," says a modern scholar-critic of his work.[1] He tries to stir up his reader and to draw him out of the humdrum conventional modes of daily existence into the world of imagination. He likes the bizarre and the useless in life and finds wisdom in the doings of criminals and cripples, and the deformed and the ugly. The *Tao* or "The Way" is not to be found through logic, piety or tradition, and it is not definable in words, for to define it by words would be to limit it and it is limitless.

Taoism, especially in the work of Chuang-Tzu, adds a

1. Burton Watson, *Early Chinese Literature* (New York, 1962), p. 161.

mystical vision to Chinese life. Taoism did not and perhaps could not become the official religion-philosophy of a people, but it provided an antidote to the common-sense based conventional morality of Confucianism. *Tao* means simply "the Way." It includes the source and operating principles of the universe—human and natural—and supposes a basic unity of all things which is undividable and which reconciles all the opposites and variety of existence. In practice, Taoism suggested a life of contemplation and self-cultivation, and it had great appeal to the Chinese gentleman retired from the strife and coercion of office. Chunag-Tzu is even more free of human society and its problems than Lao Tzu, the other great Taoist. The free man is one aware of the *Tao*, and consequently he regards human affairs as artificial and inconsequential. He is a skeptic in society and a mystic in private. Thus Chuang-Tzu is anti-establishment and anti-Confucian at a time when Confucian doctrine dominated Chinese life.

The variety of literary devices used by Chuang-Tzu, his fertile wit, and his far-ranging imagination make him perhaps the world's greatest literary philosopher.

Selections from Chuang-tzu*

I

Hui Tzu[1] said to Chuang-tzu, 'Your teachings are of no practical use.' Chuang-tzu said, 'Only those who already know the value of the useless can be talked to about the useful. This earth we walk upon is of vast extent, yet in order to walk a man uses no more of it than the soles of his two feet will cover. But suppose one cut away the ground round his feet till one reached the Yellow Springs,[2] would his patches of ground still be of any use to him for walking?' Hui Tzu said, 'They would be of no use.' Chuang-tzu said, 'So then the usefulness of the useless is evident.'

Hui Tzu recited to Chuang-tzu the rhyme:

'I have got a big tree
That men call the *chü*.
Its trunk is knotted and gnarled,
And cannot be fitted to plumb-line and ink;
Its branches are bent and twisted,
And cannot be fitted to compass or square.

* From *Three Ways of Thought in Ancient China* by Arthur Waley, translated by Arthur Waley.

1. Hui Tzu (Hui Shih) was a logician and friend of Chuang-tzu.

2. the world of the dead. [Waley's note.]

It stands by the road-side,
And no carpenter will look at it.'

'Your doctrines,' said Hui Tzu, 'are grandiose, but useless, and that is why no one accepts them.' Chuang-tzu said, 'Can it be that you have never seen the pole-cat, how it crouches waiting for the mouse, ready at any moment to leap this way or that, high or low, till one day it lands plump on the spring of a trap and dies in the snare? Again there is the yak, "huge as a cloud that covers the sky." It can maintain this great bulk and yet would be quite incapable of catching a mouse. . . . As for you and the big tree which you are at a loss how to use, why do you not plant it in the realm of Nothing Whatever, in the wilds of the Unpastured Desert, and aimlessly tread the path of Inaction by its side, or vacantly lie dreaming beneath it?

'What does not invite the axe
No creature will harm.
What cannot be used
No troubles will befall.'

Hui Tzu said to Chuang-tzu, 'The king of Wei[3] gave me the seed of one of his huge gourds. I planted it, and it bore a gourd so enormous that if I had filled it with water or broth it would have taken several men to lift it, while if I had split it into halves and made ladles out of it they would have been so flat that no liquid would have lain in them. No one could deny that it was magnificently large; but I was unable to find any use for it, and in the end I smashed it up and threw it away.' Chuang-tzu said, 'I have noticed before that you are not very clever at turning large things to account. There was once a family in Sung[4] that possessed a secret drug which had enabled its members for generations past to steep silk floss without getting chapped hands. A stranger hearing of it offered to buy the recipe for a hundred pieces of gold. The head of the family pointed out to his kinsmen that if all the money that the family had made in successive generations through the use of the drug were added together it would not come to more than one or two pieces of gold, and that a hundred pieces would amply repay them for parting with their secret. The stranger carried off the recipe and spoke of it to the king of Wu,[5] whose country was being harried by the battleships of Yüeh. The stranger was put in command of the Wu fleet, and so efficacious was the remedy that despite the bitter cold (for it was a winter's day) the fingers of the Wu sailors never once grew

3. Wei was near Honan province, Chuang-tzu's birthplace. It is north of the Yellow River (Huang Ho) near modern Lo-yang.

4. area to the southeast of Honan and west of present-day Nanking.

5. Both the Wu and Yüeh states are south of the area where the Yangtze River meets the East China Sea near present-day Shanghai.

chapped or numbed, and the fleet of Yüeh was entirely destroyed. The land of Yüeh was divided and the stranger rewarded with a fief.

'The sole property of the drug was that it prevented hands from getting chapped. Yet so much depends on the user that, if it had stayed with the man of Sung, it would never have done more than help him to steep floss; while no sooner had it passed into the stranger's possession than it gained him a fief. As for you and your large gourd, why did you not tie it as a buoy at your waist, and, borne up by it on the waters, float to your heart's content amid the streams and inland seas? Instead, you grumble about its gigantic dimensions and say that ladles made from it would hold nothing; the reason being, I fear, that your own thoughts have not learnt to run beyond the commonplace.'

When Chuang-tzu's wife died, Hui Tzu came to the house to join in the rites of mourning. To his surprise he found Chuang-tzu sitting with an inverted bowl on his knees, drumming upon it and singing a song.[6] 'After all,' said Hui Tzu, 'she lived with you, brought up your children, grew old along with you. That you should not mourn for her is bad enough; but to let your friends find you drumming and singing—that is going too far!' 'You misjudge me,' said Chuang-tzu. 'When she died, I was in despair, as any man well might be. But soon, pondering on what had happened, I told myself that in death no strange new fate befalls us. In the beginning we lack not life only, but form. Not form only, but spirit. We are blended in the one great featureless indistinguishable mass. Then a time came when the mass evolved spirit, spirit evolved form, form evolved life. And now life in its turn has evolved death. For not nature only but man's being has its seasons, its sequence of spring and autumn, summer and winter. If some one is tired and has gone to lie down, we do not pursue him with shouting and bawling. She whom I have lost has lain down to sleep for a while in the Great Inner Room. To break in upon her rest with the noise of lamentation would but show that I knew nothing of nature's Sovereign Law. That is way I ceased to mourn.'

Once when Chuang-tzu was walking in a funeral procession, he came upon Hui Tzu's tomb, and turning to those who were with him he said, 'There was once a wall-plasterer who when any plaster fell upon his nose, even a speck no thicker than a fly's wing, used to get the mason who worked with him to slice it off. The mason brandished his adze with such force that there was a sound of rushing wind; but he sliced the plaster clean off, leaving the plasterer's nose completely intact; the plasterer, on his side, standing stock still, without the least change of expression.

6. Both his attitude and his occupation were the reverse of what the rites of mourning demand. [Waley's note.]

'Yüan, prince of Sung, heard of this and sent for the mason, saying to him, "I should very much like to see you attempt this performance." The mason said, "It is true that I used to do it. But I need the right stuff to work upon, and the partner who supplied such material died long ago."

'Since Hui Tzu died I, too, have had no proper stuff to work upon, have had no one with whom I can really talk.'

What is meant by Three in the morning? In Sung[7] there was a keeper of monkeys. Bad times came and he was obliged to tell them that he must reduce their ration of nuts. 'It will be three in the morning and four in the evening,' he said. The monkeys were furious. 'Very well then,' he said, 'you shall have four in the morning and three in the evening.' The monkeys accepted with delight.

One day when Confucius went to see Lao Tzu, it was evident that Lao Tzu had been washing his hair, which was spread out to dry. Lao Tzu himself sat so utterly motionless that one could not believe a human being was there at all. Confucius withdrew, and waited. After a while he presented himself again, and said, 'Did it really happen or was it an enchantment? A little while ago this body, these limbs of yours seemed stark and lifeless as a withered tree. It was as though you had severed yourself from men and things, and existed in utter isolation.' 'Yes,' said Lao Tzu, 'I had voyaged to the World's Beginning.' 'Tell me what that means,' said Confucius. 'The mind is darkened by what it learns there and cannot understand; the lips are folded, and cannot speak. But I will try to embody for you some semblance of what I saw. I saw Yin, the Female Energy, in its motionless grandeur; I saw Yang, the Male Energy, rampant in its fiery vigour.[8] The motionless grandeur came up out of the earth; the fiery vigour burst out from heaven. The two penetrated one another, were inextricably blended and from their union the things of the world were born.'

Confucius was on friendly terms with the sage Liu-hsia Hui.[9] Liu-hsia Hui had a younger brother who was known as the brigand Chih. This brigand and the nine thousand followers who formed his band swept through the country, pillaging and despoiling every kingdom under Heaven, burrowing their way into houses, wrenching doors, driving off men's cattle and horses, seizing their wives and daughters. In his greed for gain the brigand forgot all ties of kinship, paid no heed to father, mother, or brothers young and old,

7. I have added a few details from the better version of the story in *Lieh Tzu*, II, *q*. [Waley's note.]

8. *Yin*, the female energy, symbolized by the deep and by water in general, and *Yang*, the male energy, symbolized by the mountain and by fire, are the two creative principles in the universe. They are graphically symbolized by a circle representing unity divided by an "S"-shaped line indicating the intermingling of *Yang* and *Yin*.

9. Little is known of Liu-hsia except that he was an associate of Confucius.

and made no offerings to his ancestors. Whenever he approached a town, if it was a big place the people manned the city-walls and if it was a small place they ensconced themselves behind their barrows. The whole countryside groaned under the affliction.

Confucius said to Liu-hsia Hui, 'A father who is worthy of the name ought to be able to correct his son; an elder brother who is worthy of the name ought to be capable of instructing his younger brother. If it is not the duty of fathers to call their sons to order and of elder brothers to instruct their younger brothers, the whole importance that we attach to those relationships at once disappears. But here are you, admittedly one of the most gifted men of your generation; yet your younger brother is known as "the brigand Chih," has become a curse to the whole land, and you have failed to teach him better ways. Forgive me for saying so, but I blush on your behalf. I hope you will not take it amiss if I go in your stead and have a talk with him.' 'You say,' replied Liu-hsia Hui, 'that a father ought to be able to correct his son, that an elder brother ought to be capable of instructing his younger brother. But suppose the son does not listen to his father, suppose the younger brother does not accept the elder brother's advice? In the present case even such eloquence as yours cannot possibly have the slightest effect. My brother Chih is a remarkable man. His passions, once aroused, leap like a fountain; his calculations are swift as a whirlwind. Not only is he strong enough to defy every foe; he is also clever enough to justify every crime. Humour him, and he is friendly; thwart him and he flies into a rage. On such occasions the language he uses is far from flattering; I certainly advise you not to go near him.'

Confucius did not listen to this warning, but taking his disciple Yen Hui[10] to drive the carriage and putting Tzu-kung on his right, he set off to visit the brigand Chih. The brigand and his men happened at the time to be resting on the southern slopes of the T'ai-shan, and were enjoying a supper of minced human liver. Confucius got down from his carriage and went towards the camp. Being confronted by a sentinel he said to him: 'Pray inform the General that K'ung Ch'iu[11] of the land of Lu, having heard of his Excellency as a champion of morality, has come to pay his respects.' And so saying he prostrated himself twice before the sentinel with solemnity. When the message was brought, the brigand Chih fell into a mighty rage. His eyes blazed like fiery comets, his hair stood on end so that his hat was lifted off his head. 'Why this is that crafty fraud from Lu, K'ung Ch'iu, isn't it? Tell him from me that it is mere talk for the sake of talking—all this random chatter about his heroes king Wên and king Wu.[12] Dresses up in a forked hat that

10. Both Yen Hui and Tzu-kung were disciples of Confucius.

11. *i.e.,* Confucius. [Waley's note.]

12. Wên was king in western China from 1184–1157 B.C.; Wu from 1156–1116 B.C. They founded the great Chou dynasty.

looks as though a tree had taken root on his head, puts the whole flank of a dead ox round his belly and then chatters unceasingly, heaping nonsense upon nonsense; eats what others have grown, wears what others have woven, wags his lips and drums his tongue, deluding all the rulers under heaven with his own private notions of right and wrong and preventing the scholars who come to him from every corner of the land from using the powers that are in them! Pretends to be interested only in filial piety and brotherly obedience, but spends his time currying favour with landed lords, with the rich and great! Tell the fellow that he is a scoundrel for whom no punishment would be too great, and that if he does not clear out of here at once, we shall add his liver to our morning stew.'

The message was delivered; but Confucius again asked for an interview. 'Being fortunate enough to know your brother Liu-hsia Hui,' he said, 'I desire to look at your feet beneath the curtain.'[13]

The sentinel brought in the message, and this time the brigand Chih said, 'Bring him in!' Confucius advanced at a brisk trot,[14] carefully avoided treading upon the brigand's mat, ran backwards a few steps, and prostrated himself twice.

The brigand was evidently in a great rage. His feet were planted wide apart, he was fingering the blade of his sword, his eyes glared, and finally with a voice like that of a suckling tigress he roared out, 'Come here, Ch'iu! And remember, if what you say is acceptable to me, you live; if it is not acceptable, you die!'

'I have heard,' said Confucius, 'that there are among the men of the world three kinds of personal power (*tê*). To grow to a stature so commanding, to possess beauty and grace so incomparable as to delight the eyes of all men, high or humble, young or old—this is the highest sort of power. To have a knowledge that embraces heaven above and earth below, to have abilities that can cope with every possible situation—this is the second and lower sort of power. To be bold, ruthless, undeterred by any hazard, a gatherer of multitudes and a causer of wars—this is the third and lowest kind of personal power. To possess any one of these three is sufficient to set a man with his face turned to the south and to give him the title of Lonely One.[15] You, my General, possess all three. Your stature is 8 feet 2 inches,[16] your countenance is dazzling, your lips are as though smeared with cinnabar, your teeth are like a row of shells, your voice booms like the tone-note of the scale. And yet for all this, men call you the brigand Chih! I confess I am ashamed on your

13. *i.e.*, "to be allowed even the most cursory contact with you." [Waley's note.]

14. a sign of respect. [Waley's note.]

15. When the ruler faces his subjects, he alone faces to the south; his subjects face north. He is the Lonely One (Orphan) because his position is unique and perhaps also because the father whom he succeeded is necessarily dead. [Waley's note.]

16. about 5 feet 8 inches in our measurement. [Waley's note.]

behalf and cannot reconcile myself to this. But if you will listen to me, I will go as your ambassador to the courts of Wu and Yüeh in the south, of Ch'i and Lu in the north, of Sung and Wei in the east, of Chin and Ch'u in the west,[17] and arrange that a great walled city shall be built for you, several hundred leagues in circumference, with quarters for many hundred thousand inhabitants. You shall be raised to the dignity of a feudal prince, and under your sway the whole world shall begin anew. You will lay down your arms, disband your followers, gather about you brothers old and young, and see to it that they lack nothing; and make due offering to your ancestors. You will thus be behaving like a Sage and Hero and at the same time giving to the world that for which it ardently longs.'

'Listen here,' cried the brigand Chih, in a great rage. 'It is only the ignorant low rabble who allow themselves to be beguiled by promises of gain or scolded into altering their ways. My tall stature and my good looks which delight the eyes of all who see me—these are advantages that I inherited from my parents. I am the person most likely to be aware of them and stand in no need of your approbation. Moreover, it is commonly said that those who are prone to praise men to their faces, are quick to speak ill of them behind their backs.

'And now as to your talk of a great city and a multitude of inhabitants—this is merely an attempt to dazzle me by promises of gain, and is treating me as though I were a common, witless peasant. And even if such success were attainable, how long would it be secured? The biggest city cannot be larger than the world. The Emperors Yao and Shun[18] possessed the whole world, yet their sons and grandsons had not so much as a pin-point of land. T'ang of the Yin dynasty, Wu of the Chou dynasty rose to be Sons of Heaven; but their posterity is extinct. Was not this just because what they sought and won was far too large a prize? . . . Neither Yao nor Shun could set a son upon the throne; both made way for subjects. T'ang of Yin banished his sovereign; king Wu of Chou slew Chieh[19] of Yin. And from that day onward the strong have crushed the weak, the many have maltreated the few; nor since the time of T'ang and Wu has there been a single ruler who was not as great a ruffian as they. Yet here come you, earnestly applying yourself to the Way of king Wên and king Wu and using every sophistry under heaven in order to inculcate it upon generations to come. You dress up in a wide cloak and belt of clipped bull's hide, and by your cant and humbug delude the princes of the world into giving you the wealth and honours that are your only real ambition. There can be no

17. The geography of this promise is somewhat confused. [Waley's note.]

18. legendary "good kings." [Waley's note.]

19. semi-legendary tyrant. [Waley's note.]

greater brigand than you, and instead of talking so much about the brigand Chih, I wonder people do not call you the brigand Confucius! . . .

'There is no need for you to say a word more. If you could tell me about the affairs of ghosts or hobgoblins, it would be another matter. About them I admit I know nothing at all. But concerning human affairs nothing you say can possibly carry me any further. I shall have heard it all before. I, on the other hand, intend to tell you something about man and his natural desires. He has an eye that longs for beauty, an ear that longs for music, a mouth that longs for sweet flavours, ambitions and energies that crave fulfilment. Some few may live to eighty years, some fewer to a hundred; but one who lives till sixty has still not died young. And during these sixty years, if we take away the time that is spent in sickness, mourning and trouble, in all this time there will not be more than four or five days in each month when his lips are opened and laughter comes.

'Heaven and earth are illimitable; to man a term is set. Furnished only with the scrap of time that is his span, he is committed to a place amid the illimitables. A flash, and all is over, like a racehorse seen through a crack. He who by the enjoyment of his senses can use this brief moment to the full alone can claim to have found the Way. All that you acclaim, I utterly discard. Be off with you as fast as you can, and never dare prate to me again! This Way of yours is nothing but noise and babble, humbug and empty fraud, such as could never help any man to perfect the unalloyed that is within him; is in fact not worth a moment's discussion.'

Confucius prostrated himself twice, and retired at full speed. When he had reached the gate of the camp and regained his carriage, his hands were trembling to such an extent that three times the reins fell out of them, there was a cloud before his eyes and his face was ashen grey. He leant over the fore-rail with sunken head, gasping for breath. At last he reached Lu, and outside the eastern gate happened to meet Liu-hsia Hui. 'What has become of you lately?' asked Liu-hsia Hui. 'I have not seen you for several days. Judging by the appearance of your horses and carriage, I should think you have been on a journey. Is it possible that, despite my warning, you have been to see my brother Chih?' Confucius gazed upwards at the sky and sighed. 'I have indeed,' he said. 'And Chih,' said Liu-hsia Hui, 'did not take to your ideas any more kindly than I predicted?' 'That is true,' said Confucius. 'I must confess that, as the saying goes, I poulticed myself with moxa[20] when there was nothing wrong with me. I rushed off to dress a tiger's head and plait its beard. Small wonder if I nearly landed in the tiger's maw!'

20. an ointment burned in minute quantities on the skin for medicinal purposes.

When Chuang-tzu was going to Ch'u he saw by the roadside a skull, clean and bare, but with every bone in its place. Touching it gently with his chariot-whip he bent over it and asked it saying, 'Sir, was it some insatiable ambition that drove you to transgress the law and brought you to this? Was it the fall of a kingdom, the blow of an executioner's axe that brought you to this? Or had you done some shameful deed and could not face the reproaches of father and mother, of wife and child, and so were brought to this? Was it hunger and cold that brought you to this, or was it that the springs and autumns of your span had in their due course carried you to this?'

Having thus addressed the skull, he put it under his head as a pillow and went to sleep. At midnight the skull appeared to him in a dream and said to him, 'All that you said to me—your glib, commonplace chatter—is just what I should expect from a live man, showing as it does in every phrase a mind hampered by trammels from which we dead are entirely free. Would you like to hear a word or two about the dead?'

'I certainly should,' said Chuang-tzu.

'Among the dead,' said the skull, 'none is king, none is subject, there is no division of the seasons; for us the whole world is spring, the whole world is autumn. No monarch on his throne has joy greater than ours.'

Chuang-tzu did not believe this. 'Suppose,' he said, 'I could get the Clerk of Destinies to make your frame anew, to clothe your bones once more with flesh and skin, send you back to father and mother, wife and child, friends and home, I do not think you would refuse.'

A deep frown furrowed the skeleton's brow. 'How can you imagine,' it asked, 'that I would cast away joy greater than that of a king upon his throne, only to go back again to the toils of the living world?'

Kung-sun Lung[21] said to the recluse, Prince Mou of Wei, 'When I was young I studied the Way of the Former Kings; when I grew up, I became versed in the dictates of goodness and duty. From the dialecticians I learnt how to blend identity and difference, the so and the not-so, the possible and the impossible. I exhausted the wisdom of the Hundred Schools,[22] could confute the arguments of countless mouths, and believed that I had nothing left to learn. But recently I heard Chuang-tzu speaking, and was reduced to helpless amazement. I do not know why it was—perhaps the right arguments did not occur to me, perhaps he really knows more than I do. But in any case, "my beak was jammed"; I had not a word to say. Please

21. a famous pacifist and dialectician; lived *ca.* 300 B.C. [Waley's note.]

22. a vague number meaning "all schools of philosophy."

tell me how one deals with him.' Prince Mou leant over his arm-rest and heaved a deep sigh, then looked up to Heaven and laughed aloud saying, 'Do you not know the story of the frog that lived in the abandoned[23] well? "How you must envy my delightful existence!" it said to the giant turtle of the Eastern Sea. "When I feel inclined I can come out and hop about on the railing; then I go back into the pit and rest where a tile has fallen out of the wall. When I go into the water I can make it hold me up under the armpits and support my chin; when I jump into the mud, I can make it bury my feet and cover my ankles. As for the baby crabs and tadpoles, none of them can compete with me. To have the use of all the waters of an entire pool, to have at one's command all the delights of a disused well, that surely is the most that life can give. Why don't you, just as an experiment, come down here and see for yourself?"

'The giant turtle of the Eastern Sea attempted to get into the well, but before its left foot was well in, its right foot had got wedged fast. Whereupon it wiggled itself free and retreated, saying, "As you have been kind enough to tell me about your well, allow me to tell you about the sea. Imagine a distance of a thousand leagues, and you will still have no idea of its size; imagine a height of a thousand times man's stature, and you will still have no notion of its depth. In the time of the Great Yü,[24] in ten years there were nine floods; but the sea became no deeper. In the time of T'ang the Victorious there were seven years of drought in eight years; yet the sea did not retreat from its shores. Not to be harried by the moments that flash by nor changed by the ages that pass; to receive much, yet not increase, to receive little, yet not diminish, this is the Great Joy of the Eastern Sea."

'Knowledge such as yours gives no standard by which to set the boundaries between false and true; yet you take it upon yourself to scrutinize Chuang-tzu's teaching. As well might a gnat try to carry the Great Mountain on its back or an ant try to change the course of the River. The task is utterly beyond your powers.

'Priding yourself upon a wisdom that is unable to confute the transcendant mysteries of Chuang-tzu's doctrine merely because your cleverness has brought you a few short-lived victories, are you not indeed a Frog in the Well?

'Thoughts such as his, that can cross the Dark Streams of death, mount to the Royal Empyrean, that know neither east nor west, south nor north, but plunge into the bottomless chasms; thoughts from which all boundaries have loosened and dropped away, that begin in the Secret Darkness, that go back to the time when all was

23. Abandoned because it had dried up. [Waley's note.]

24. Legendary king, perhaps about the year 2000 B.C.

one—how can you hope to reach them by the striving of a petty intelligence or ransack them by the light of your feeble sophistries? You might as well look at Heaven through a reed or measure earth with the point of a gimlet. Your instruments are too small.

'Be off with you! But before you go I should like to remind you of what happened to the child from Shou-ling that was sent to Han-tan to learn the "Han-tan walk."[25] He failed to master the steps, but spent so much time in trying to acquire them that in the end he forgot how one usually walks, and came home to Shou-ling crawling on all fours.

'I advise you to keep away; or you will forget what you know already and find yourself without a trade.'

Kung-sun Lung's mouth gaped and would not close; his tongue stuck to the roof of his mouth and would not go down. He made off as fast as his legs would carry him.

Shih-nan I-liao visited the lord of Lu,[26] and found him looking sad. 'Why do you look so sad?' he asked. 'I study the Way of former kings,' said the lord of Lu, 'carry on the work of my ancestors, humble myself before the spirits of the dead, give honour to the wise. All this I do in my own person, never for a moment abating in my zeal. Yet troubles beset my reign. That is why I am sad.' 'My lord,' said Shih-nan I-liao, 'your method of avoiding troubles is a superficial one. The bushy-coated fox and the striped panther, though they lodge deep in the mountain woods, hide in caverns on the cliff-side, go out at night but stay at home all day, and even when driven desperate by thirst and hunger keep always far from the rivers and lakes where food might easily be had—despite their quietness, caution, and the mastery of their desires, do not escape misfortune, but fall an easy prey to the trapper's net and snare. And this, not through any fault of theirs; it is the value of their fur that brings them to disaster. And in your case, my lord, is it not the land of Lu itself that is your lordship's fur, and the cause of your undoing?

'I would have you strip away not your fine fur only, but every impediment of the body, scour your heart till it is free from all desire, and travel through the desolate wilds. For to the south there is a place called the Land where Tê Rules.[27] Its people are ignorant and unspoiled, neglgent of their own interests, and of few desires. They know how to make, but do not know how to hoard. They give, but seek no return. The suitabilities of decorum, the solemnities of ritual are alike unknown to them. They live and move thoughtlessly and at random, yet every step they take tallies with

25. Probably a way of walking gracefully rather than a dance step.

26. Lu is that land on the coast of the Yellow Sea northwest of present-day Nanking. Shih-nan I-liao cannot be identified.

27. The word *Tê* means "instincts." Early China is north of the Yangtze River; the land south of the Yangtze was conquered later and the people there—of different stock—subjugated.

the Great Plan. They know how to enjoy life while it lasts, are ready to be put away when death comes.

'I would have you leave your kingdom and its ways, take Tao as your guide and travel to this land.'

'It is a long way to go,' said the prince of Lu, 'and dangerous. There are rivers too swift for any boat, mountains that no chariot can cross. What am I to do?' 'Humility,' said Shih-nan I-liao, 'shall be your boat. Pliancy shall be your chariot.' 'It is a long way to go,' said the prince, 'and the lands through which it passes are not inhabited. There would be no villages where I could buy provisions or take a meal. I should die long before I reached my journey's end.' 'Lessen your wants, husband your powers,' said Shih-nan I-liao, 'and you will have no need to buy provisions on your way. You will cross many rivers and come at last to a lake so wide that, gaze as you will, you cannot see the further shore. Yet you will go on, without knowing whether it will ever end. At the shores of this lake all that came with you will turn back. But you will still have far to go. What matter? "He who needs others is for ever shackled; he who is needed by others is for ever sad." . . . I would have you drop these shackles, put away your sadness, and wander alone with Tao in the kingdom of the Great Void.'

II

In the time of king Mu of Chou[28] there came from a land in the far west a wizard who could go into water and fire, pierce metals and stone, turn mountains upside down, make rivers flow backwards, move fortifications and towns, ride on the air without falling, collide with solids without injury. There was indeed no limit to the miracles that he could perform. And not only could he change the outward shape of material things; he could also transform the thoughts of men. King Mu reverenced him like a god, served him like a master, put his own State chambers at the wizard's disposal, gave him for sustenance the animals reared for Imperial sacrifice, and for his entertainment chose girls skilled in music and dancing.

But the wizard found the king's palace too cramped and sordid to live in; the choicest delicacies from the king's kitchen he pronounced to be coarse and rancid, and he would not eat them. The ladies from the king's harem he would not look at, so foul and hideous did he find them.

The king accordingly set about building a completely new palace, employing all the most skillful workers in clay and wood, the most accomplished decorators in whitewash and ochre; expending indeed so much upon the work that by the time it was complete all his

28. Perhaps that king of the Chou dynasty, 1001–947 B.C.

Treasuries were empty. The towers were six thousand feet high, and from them one looked down upon the top of the Chung-nan hills.[29] It was named The Tower that hits Heaven. The king chose, from among the virgins of Chêng and Wei, girls of the most transcendant beauty and charm, anointed them with fragrant oils, straightened the curve of their eyebrows, decked them with combs and ear-rings, clothed them in jackets of the softest gauze, skirts of the thinnest floss, beautified them with white powder and with black, set jade rings at their girdles, strewed the floors with scented herbs, and brought these ladies to the palace till it was full. For the wizard's pleasure continual music was played, Receiving the Clouds, The Six Gems, The Nine Songs of Succession, The Morning Dew; every month he received a supply of costly garments, and every morning he was provided with costly food. But he was still far from content and could only with the greatest difficulty be persuaded to approach this new abode. After some time had passed, during which the magician frequently absented himself, he one day invited the king to accompany him upon a journey. Whereupon the magician began to rise from the ground and the king, clutching at his sleeve, was carried up and up, till they reached the sky. Here they halted, just in front of the magician's house, which was moated with dust of silver and gold and looped with festoons of jade and pearl. It stood out far above the rain and clouds. What it rested upon was hard to say, but it seemed to be supported by a coil of cloud. In this house nothing that his ears and eyes heard or saw, nothing that his nose and mouth smelt or tasted was in the least like what the king was accustomed to in the world of men. This, he thought, must surely be Stainless City, Purple Mystery, Level Sky, Wide Joy—one of the palaces of God. Looking down at the world below he saw what seemed like a hummock in the ground, with some piles of brushwood lying around it, and suddenly realized that this was his own palace with its arbours. Here as it seemed to him he lived for twenty or thirty years without a thought for his kingdom. At last the wizard again invited him to make a journey, and once more they travelled, till they had reached a place where looking up one could not see the sun or moon, looking down one saw neither river nor lake. So fierce a light blazed and flashed that the king's eyes were dazzled and he could not look; so loud a noise jangled and echoed that his ears were deafened and he could not listen. His limbs loosened, his entrails were as though dissolved within him, his thoughts were confused, his energy extinct. 'Let us go back,' he cried to the wizard, who gave him a push and soon they were falling through space.

The next thing that he knew was that he was sitting just where

29. All of the place names are in the area of present-day Honan.

he had sat when the magician summoned him; the same attendants were still at his side, the wine that they had just served to him was still warm, the food still moist. 'Where have I been?' he asked. 'Your Majesty,' one of his servants answered, 'has been sitting there in silence.'

It was three days before the king was completely himself again. On his recovery he sent for the wizard and asked him to explain what had happened. 'I took you,' the wizard replied, 'upon a journey of the soul. Your body never moved. The place where you have been living was none other than your own palace; the grounds in which you strolled were in fact your own park.

'Your Majesty, between himself and the understanding of such things, interposes habitual doubts. Could you for a moment divest yourself of them, there is no miracle of mine, no trick with time, that you could not imitate.'

The king was very pleased, paid no further heed to affairs of State, amused himself no more with ministers or concubines, but devoted himself henceforth to distant journeys of the soul.

King Hui of Wei had a carver named Ting. When this carver Ting was carving a bull for the king, every touch of the hand, every inclination of the shoulder, every step he trod, every pressure of the knee, while swiftly and lightly he wielded his carving-knife, was as carefully timed as the movements of a dancer in the *Mulberry Wood*. . . . 'Wonderful,' said the king. 'I could never have believed that the art of carving could reach such a point as this.' 'I am a lover of Tao,' replied Ting, putting away his knife, 'and have succeeded in applying it to the art of carving. When I first began to carve I fixed my gaze on the animal in front of me. After three years I no longer saw it as a whole bull, but as a thing already divided into parts. Nowadays I no longer see it with the eye; I merely apprehend it with the soul. My sense-organs are in abeyance, but my soul still works. Unerringly my knife follows the natural markings, slips into the natural cleavages, finds its way into the natural cavities. And so by conforming my work to the structure with which I am dealing, I have arrived at a point at which my knife never touches even the smallest ligament or tendon, let alone the main gristle.

'A good carver changes his knife once a year; by which time the blade is dented. An ordinary carver changes it once a month; by which time it is broken. I have used my present knife for nineteen years, and during that time have carved several thousand bulls. But the blade still looks as though it had just come out of the mould. Where part meets part there is always space, and a knife-blade has no thickness. Insert an instrument that has no thickness into a structure that is amply spaced, and surely it cannot fail to have plenty of room. That is why I can use a blade for nineteen years, and yet it still looks as though it were fresh from the forger's mould.

'However, one has only to look at an ordinary carver to see what a difficult business he finds it. One sees how nervous he is while making his preparations, how long he looks, how slowly he moves. Then after some small, niggling strokes of the knife, when he has done no more than detach a few stray fragments from the whole, and even that by dint of continually twisting and turning like a worm burrowing through the earth, he stands back, with his knife in his hand, helplessly gazing this way and that, and after hovering for a long time finally curses a perfectly good knife and puts it back in its case.'

'Excellent,' said the king of Wei. 'This interview with the carver Ting has taught me how man's vital forces can be conserved.'

When Chuang-tzu was angling in the river P'u, the king of Ch'u sent two high officers of state, who accosting Chuang-tzu announced that the king wished to entrust him with the management of all his domains. Rod in hand and eyes still fixed upon his line, Chuang-tzu replied, 'I have been told that in Ch'u there is a holy tortoise that died three thousand years ago. The king keeps it in the great hall of his ancestral shrine, in a casket covered with a cloth. Suppose that when this tortoise was caught, it had been allowed to choose between dying and having its bones venerated for centuries to come or going on living with its tail draggling in the mud, which would it have preferred?' 'No doubt,' said the two officers, 'it would have preferred to go on living with its tail draggling in the mud.' 'Well then, be off with you,' said Chuang-tzu, 'and leave me to drag my tail in the mud.'

LU KI

(291–303)

Rhymeprose on Literature (*Wen Fu*)

As in many other countries, literary criticism in China begins with estimates of specific works or authors, proceeds to definition—such as the very early one in China that poetry has a didactic purpose—and culminates in the full-fledged theoretical treatise. Of these, Lu Ki's essay is one of the earliest and one of the most brilliant.

The age in which the author lived provided everything except the tranquillity thought necessary for speculative contemplation of the nature of literature. Lu Ki was born in 291 at Hua T'ing in the Yangtze River delta, the grandson of one of the great military geniuses of China. Though the grandfather won a great victory for the Emperor of Wu in 229 the barbarian threat from the north continued to menace a weak and ineffectual government in the south. Lu grew up on a great estate, and for a time fortune favored him. For five years he trained in the military as a captain of his father's personal troops. Then a powerful rival force brought the dynasty to an end and misfortune to Lu's family—his two eldest brothers were killed, he and his younger brother escaped. A work which may be partly Lu's, the *Dialect of Destruction,* studies the reasons for the downfall of the Wu dynasty. The future critic was most aghast at the bungling incompetence of the authorities, who, despite clear warnings from experts like his father, permitted the military debacle.

About 290, Lu Ki and his brother decided to throw in their lot with the northern court at Loyang, partly because a reformed government seemed to be flourishing there, but more because Loyang was now the center for intellectuals and writers. Both the brothers were quickly successful. Lu Ki was awarded a position as a literary scholar at the court and later as a literary secretary attached to the household; his brother became a magistrate. In 286 we find Lu again in the field with the army. The overthrow of the government by one of the several warring clans resulted in Lu's imprisonment, and he barely escaped execution. After this, Lu returned to Hua T'ing and during a tranquil period of less than two years composed the *Rhymeprose on Literature.* When the next insurrection occurred Lu refused military service, but his sovereign prince insisted, and in an attack on Loyang Lu's troops were badly defeated. His enemies conspired to have Lu blamed for the disaster and Lu was put to death. Perhaps Lu was a less than enthusiastic soldier, a victim of a family tradition who missed his proper role, that of a civil servant.

Lu Ki's *Wen Fu* (literally, "*fu* on literature") is one of those poetic discussions of literature which demonstrates what it is discussing. English literature has a similar tradition: two conspicuous examples are Alexander Pope's *Essay on Criticism* and Archibald MacLeish's *Ars Poetica.* Horace's *Ars Poetica* is of course the great example in Western literature. Lu Ki discusses form and content and sees literature as the expression of feeling (this separates it from at least some other kinds of writing). He also defines the genres, listing ten of them. He is early in Chinese literature in insisting that euphony is a major quality. Lu also implies that artistic writing aims at encouraging virtue and discouraging vice.

While these principles do emerge from the work, the *Rhymeprose on Literature* is metaphorical, and it is an evocative and difficult poem, constructed as much to move the reader as to convice him of the logic of the analysis.

"Rhymeprose" is a good term but masks the controversy as to whether the *fu* is verse or prose. The writer uses rhyme, but the *fu* is like prose in that it has no regular meter. "Rhymeprose" has no counterpart in English literature—"free verse" is as close as we can come.

Rhymeprose on Literature (*Wen Fu*) *

Preface

Whenever I study the works of gifted writers I flatter myself that I know how their minds moved.

Certainly expression in language and the charging of words with meaning can be done variously.

And yet beauty and ugliness, good and bad can be distinguished.

By writing again and again myself, I obtain more and more insight.

My worry is that my ideas may not equal their subjects and my style may fall short of my ideas.[1]

The difficulty, then, lies not so much in the knowing as in the doing.[2]

I have written this rhymeprose on literature to tell of the consummate art of past writers and to present the why and how of good and bad writing as well.

I hope it will prove in time to be a comprehensive essay.

Surely, hewing an ax handle with a handle in hand, the pattern should not be far to seek.

However, as each artist has his own way to magic, I despair of doing him justice.

Nevertheless, whatever I can say I have set down here.—*Lu Ki*

* Translated by Achilles Fang. Reprinted from *New Mexico Quarterly, 22* (1952), 269–281. Copyright by Achilles Fang. Reprinted by permission of Dr. Fang. Dr. Fang's note to this translation is as follows: "This is not the first translation of the *Wen-fu*; a number of sinologists (including E. R. Hughes in *The Art of Letters*, Bollingen Series XXIX, 1951) have already worked on Lu Ki's *ars poetica*. If it is true that the translator has to bring over not what a man says but what he means, then these sinologists have failed. In my opinion, they have not managed to convey what Lu Ki means, nor sometimes even to comprehend what he says. This is understandable, for it is not easy to translate from the Chinese, a language supposed to have been invented by the Devil to prevent the spread of the Gospel. Whether the present version can meet Bernard Berenson's challenge (after detailing the difficulty of rendering words like Gemüt and sophrosyne: 'Then dare to translate the ancient Chinese and Indian thinkers'), I am not the one to say; I have done what I could. Previously, in the *Harvard Journal of Asiatic Studies* (Vol. 14, 1951), I published a sinological translation, with text and *apparatus criticus*. I consider this present translation my definite version, and refer the reader to the *HJAS* for sinological footnotes." The notes are much abridged from the version in *HJAS* and, when printed verbatim, with the Chinese characters omitted, are so indicated. I am indebted to Dr. Fang for corrections he has made in the translation. The name "Lu Ki" is also transliterated "Lu Chi."

1. Essentially a restatement of the Confucian saying in the *Book of Changes* (Legge, *The Sacred Books of the East* 16.376–77: "The written characters are not the full exponent of speech, and speech is not the full expression of ideas.") [Fang's note.]

2. Here is expressed the Chinese idea of the gulf between knowledge and action. Many Western thinkers, beginning with Socrates, have identified knowledge with action, but this concept was not frequently expressed in China until later times.

Preparation

Standing at the center of things, the poet contemplates the enigma of the universe,[3] he nourishes his feelings and his intellect on the great works of the past.

Concurring with the four seasons, he sighs at the passage of time; gazing at the myriad things, he thinks of the world's complexity.

He grieves for the falling leaves of lusty autumn; he rejoices in the frail bud of fragrant spring.

He senses awe in his heart as at the touch of the frost; his spirit reaches for the vast as he lifts his eyes to the clouds.[4]

He chants the splendid achievement of his forebears; he sings the clean fragrance of his predecessors.

He wanders in the forest of letters, and hymns the order[5] of great art.

Moved, he puts his books aside and takes the writing brush, to express himself in letters.

Process

At first, he shuts his eyes, listening inwardly; he is lost in thought, questioning everywhere.

His spirit rides to the eight ends of the universe;[6] his mind travels thousands of cubits up and down.

At last, his mood draws clearer and clearer; objects, clear-limned, push one another forth.

He pours out the essence of letters; he savors the extract of the six arts.[7]

He floats on the heavenly lake; he steeps himself in the nether spring.

Thereupon, submerged words squirm up, as when a flashing fish, hook in its gills, leaps from water's depth; hovering beauties flutter down, as when a soaring bird, harpoon-string about its wings, falls from a crest of cloud.

He gathers words untouched by a hundred generations; he plucks rhythms unsung for a thousand years.

He spurns the morning blossom, now full blown; he spreads the evening bud, yet unopen.

3. Seems to allude to the line in *Tao-tê ching,* chapter 10. ("When he has cleansed away the mysterious sights [of his imagination], he can become without a flaw.—Legge, *Sacred Books of the East* 39.54). [Fang's note.]

4. This more or less baffling couplet means, according to Li Shan, the sublime and the pure. [Fang's note.]

5. "Symmetry" may be understood as a correct balance between form and content, derived from Confucius, *Analects,* 6.16 (Legge, *Chinese Classics* 1.190). But it may also mean "due proportion."

6. Extremities of the eight directions (N, S, E, W, and NE, NW, SE, SW). [Fang's note.]

He sees past and present in a moment; he reaches for the four seas in the twinkling of an eye.

Words, Words, Words

Now, he selects his ideas and puts them in order; he examines his words and fits them into place.

He sounds all that is colorful; he twangs everything that rings.

Often he shakes the foilage by tugging the twig; often he traces the current to the source.

Sometimes he brings to light what was hidden; sometimes he traps a hard prey while seeking an easy one.[8]

Now the tiger puts on new stripes, to the consternation of other beasts; now the dragon emerges, and terrifies all the birds.[9]

Maybe things fit, are easy to manage; maybe they jar, are awkward to manipulate.

He empties his mind completely to concentrate his thoughts; he collects from the forest of writing-brushes.

Genres

Figures vary in a thousand ways; things are not of one measure.

Confusing and fleeting, shapes are hard to capture.

Words vie with words for mastery, but it is mind that disposes them.[10]

Faced with creating something or leaving it unborn, he groans; caught between light touch and deep incision, he chooses boldly.[11]

He may depart from the square and deviate from the compasses; for he is bent on exploring the shape and exhausting the reality.

And so, he who would dazzle the eyes exploits splendor; he who intends to satisfy the mind values cogency.

He whose reasoning is rarefied should not be fettered by details; he whose discourse is noble may unbind his language.[12]

7. Li Shan explains *liu-i* as the six arts of the *Chou-li* (ceremonies, music, archery, horsemanship, calligraphy, and mathematics); Ho Ch'o takes them to mean the six Confucian arts (the Books of *Odes, History,* and *Changes, Ceremonies, Music,* and the *Spring and Autumn.*) [Fang's note.]

8. Like Saul, who sought his father's asses, and found a kingdom. [Fang's note.]

9. This may mean that when a main item is obtained, all subsidiary ones come by themselves.

10. Probably refers to *Tao-te ching,* chapter 79. "[So,] he who has the attributes [of the Tao] regards [only] the conditions of the engagement."—Legge, *Sacred Books of the East* 39.121; "For he who has the 'power' of Tao is the Grand Almoner."—Waley, *The Way and Its Power,* 239.) [Fang's note.]

11. Patterned after Confucius (*Analects* 15.35: "When it comes to acting humanely, you need not be so modest about it as to let your teacher take precedence." Cf. Legge, *Chinese Classics,* 1.304; Waley, *Analects of Confucius,* 200.) [Fang's note.]

12. This couplet is difficult to understand and seems out of place here.

Shih[13] (lyric poetry) traces emotions daintily; *Fu* (rhymeprose) depicts things brightly.

Pei (epitaph) balances facts with fancy; *Lei* (dirge) is gripping and mournful. *Ming* (inscription) is comprehensive and concise, gentle and generous; *Chen* (admonition) praises or blames, is clear-cut and nervous.

Sung (eulogy) is natural and free, rich and full; *Lun* (disquisition) is complex and subtle, bright and smooth.

T'sou (memorial to the throne) is quiet and penetrating, genteel and decorous; *Shuo* (discourse) is dazzling and extravagant.

Different as these forms are, they all shun depravity and interdict license.[14]

Essentially, language must communicate, and reason must dominate; prolixity and verbosity are not commended.[15]

The Music of Poetry

Literature is a thing that assumes various shapes and undergoes many changes in form.[16]

Ideas should be skillfully brought together; language should be beautifully expressed.

The mutation of sounds and tones should be like the five colors of embroidery sustaining each other.

True, moods come and go, and embarrass us by their capriciousness.

But if we can rise to all emergencies and know the correct order, it will be like opening a channel from a spring.

If, however, proper juxtaposition is not made at the proper point, we will be putting the tail at the head.

The sequence of azure and yellow being disturbed, the color scheme will be blurred and vague.

The Art of Rewriting

Now you glance back and are constrained by an earlier line; now you look ahead and are coerced by the anticipated passage.

Sometimes your words jar though your reasoning is clear; sometimes your language is smooth while your ideas are lame.

13. These are not all of the literary genres in existence in Lu Chi's time, but they are the most important ones.

14. Alludes to Confucius's "having no depraved thoughts" (Legge, *Chinese Classics* 1.146).

15. Another Confucian dictum (Legge, *Chinese Classics*, 1.305) which can be interpreted in a dozen different ways. [Fang's note.]

16. The phrase occurs in the *Book of Changes* ("The Yi is a book which should not be let slip from the mind. Its method [of teaching] is marked by the frequent changing [of its lines] . . . , so that an invariable and compendious rule cannot be derived from them;—it must vary as their changes indicate."—Legge, *Sacred Books of the East* 16.399). [Fang's note.]

Such collisions avoided, both will gain; forced together, both will suffer.

Weigh merit or demerit by the milligram; decide rejection or retention by a hairbreadth.

If your idea or word has not the correct weight, it has to go, however comely it may look.[17]

Key Passages

It may be that your language is ample and your reasoning rich, yet your ideas do not round out.

If what must go on cannot be ended, what has been said in full cannot be added to.

Put down terse phrases at key positions; they will invigorate the whole piece.

Your words will acquire their intended values in the light of such phrases.

This useful device will spare you the pain of deleting and excising.

Originality

It may be that language and thought blend into perfect tapestry—fresh, gay, and exuberantly lush.

Flaming like many-colored broidery, mournful as multiple chords;[18]

But there is nothing novel in my thinking, if it tallies with earlier masterpieces.

True, the shuttle has plied my heart; what a pity, that others preceded.

As my integrity would be impaired and my probity damaged, I must renounce the piece, however proud I am of it.[19]

Purple Patches

Perhaps one ear of the stalk has opened, its tip prominent, solitary, and unsurpassingly exquisite.

But shadows cannot be caught; echoes are hard to hold.

Standing forlorn, your purple passage juts out; it can't be woven into ordinary music.

17. Literally, "Whatever is rejected by your balance deserves to be rejected, even if the things conform to the carpenter's marking-line."

18. It may be here remarked that a tragic note seems to have prevailed in Chinese poetics since the last days of the Han dynasty; in fact, it seems to have become a frame of reference with which to judge poetry. As gaiety was a quality not excluded in Confucian poetics (cf. *Analects* 3.20) it would be worth investigating how and exactly since what time sadness has become the key tune in Chinese poetry. [Fang's note.]

19. Cf. the *Book of Mencius* 4B 23: "When to take and not to take are equally correct, you will be impairing your personal integrity by taking." [Fang's note.]

Your mind, out of step, finds no mate for it; your spirit, desperately wandering, will not surrender it.

When the rock embeds jade, the mountain glows; when the stream is impregnated with pearls, the river becomes alluring.[20]

When the arrow-thorn bush is spared from the sickle, it will glory in its foliage.

Let's weave the market ditty into the classical melody; perhaps we may hold on to what we find beautiful.

Five Criteria

MUSIC

Perhaps you are toying with anemic rhythms: living in a desert, you only amuse yourself.

When you look down into silence, you see no friend; when you lift your gaze to space, you hear no echo.

It is like striking a single chord—it rings out, but there is no music.

HARMONY

Perhaps you fit your words to a feeble music; merely gaudy, your language is not charming.

As beauty and ugliness are commingled, what is good suffers.

Like the harsh note of a wind instrument below in the courtyard, there is music but no harmony.

SADNESS

Perhaps you forsake reason to strive for novelty; you go after the inane and pursue the trivial.

Your language wants sincerity and is deficient in love; your words wash back and forth, and never come to the point.

They are like thin chords reverberating—there is harmony, but they are not sad.

DECORUM

Possibly by galloping unbridled, you make your poem sound well; it is loud and seductive.

Merely pleasing to the eye, it mates with vulgarity—a fine voice but an unworthy song.

Like *Fang-lu* and *Sang-kien*, it is sad but not decorous.

20. Cf. *Hsün-tzu*, *Ssu-pu ts'ung-k'an*, ed. (1)1.11a: 'f there is jade in the mountain, the trees on it will be flourishing; if there are pearls in the pool the bank will not be parched." (Homer H. Dubs, *Hsüntze's Works*, 36). [Fang's note.]

RICHNESS

Perhaps your poem is clean and pared, all superfluities removed.

So much so that it lacks even the lingering flavor of a sacrificial broth; it resembles the limpid tune of the vermillion chord.[21]

One man sings, and three men carry the refrain; it is decorous, but it is not rich.[22]

Variability

As to whether your work should be full or close-fitting, whether you should shape it by gazing down or looking up,

You must accommodate necessary variation, if you would bring out the latent qualities.

When your language is uncouth, your conceits can be clever; when your reasoning is awkward, your words can be supple.

You may follow the well-worn path to attain novelty; you may wade the muddy water to reach the clear stream.

Perspicacity comes after examination; subtlety demands refining.

It is like dancers flinging their sleeves in harmony with the beat, or singers throwing their voices in tune with the chord.

All this is what the wheelwright P'ien[23] despaired of explaining; nor can mere language describe it.

Masterpieces

I have been paying tribute to laws of language and rules of style.

I have come to know what the world blames, and am aware of what the masters praised.

Originality is a thing often looked at askance by the fixed eye.

Emerald and jade, they say, can be picked as so many beans in the middle of the field,[24]

As timeless as the universe and growing co-eternally with heaven and earth.[25]

The world may abound with gems; yet they do not fill my two hands.[26]

21. Sacrificial broth was neither salted nor spiced; vermillion chords" refers to the zithers played in ancestral temples. [Fang's note.]

22. The last term rendered "beauty", properly means "gaudiness." If Lu Chi is pleased to pay the highest tribute to an aesthetic standard frowned upon nowadays, it is a case of *de gustibus*. . . . [Fang's note.]

23. For the wheelwright P'ien, see *Chuang-tzü* (Legge, *Sacred Books of the* East, 39.343). [Fang's note.]

24. Cf. *Book of Odes* (no. 196): "In the midst of the plain there is pulse, and the common people gather it." (Legge, *Chinese Classics*, 4.334). [Fang's note.]

25. This couplet can be understood only with reference to *Tao-tê ching,* chapter 5: "May not the space between heaven and earth be compared to a bellows? (Legge, *Sacred Books of the East,* 39.50); "Yet Heaven and Earth and all that lies between/ Is like a bellows/ In that it is empty, but gives a supply that never fails." (Waley, *The and Its Power,* 147.) [Fang's note.]

26. Refers to the *Book of Odes* (no. 266), "All the morning I gather the king-grass, / And do not collect enough to fill my hands." (Legge, *Chinese Classics,* 4.411). [Fang's note.]

The Poet's Despair

How I grieve that the bottle is often empty; how I sorrow that True Word is hard to emulate.

And so I limp along with anemic rhythms and make indifferent music to complete the song.

I always conclude a piece with lingering regret; how can I be self-satisfied?

I fear to be a drummer of an earthen jug; the players of jade instruments will laugh at me.

Inspiration

FLOW

As for the interaction of stimulus and response, and the principle of the flowing and ebbing of inspiration,

You cannot hinder its coming or stop its going.

It vanishes like a shadow and it returns like echoes.

When the heavenly arrow is at its fleetest and sharpest, what confusion cannot be brought to order?

The wind of thought bursts from the heart; the stream of words gushes through the lips and teeth.

Luxuriance and magnificence wait the command of the brush and the silk.

Shining and glittering, language fills your eyes; abundant and overflowing, music drowns your ears.

EBB

When the six emotions[27] become sluggish and stagnant, the mood gone but the psyche remaining,

You will be as abject as a dead stump, as empty as the bed of a dry river.

You probe into the hidden depth of your animal soul; you spur your spirit to reveal itself.

But your reason, darkened, is crouching lower and lower; your thought must be dragged out by force, wriggling and struggling.

So it is that you make many errors by straining your emotions, and commit fewer mistakes when you let your ideas run freely.

True, the thing lies within me, but it is not in my power to force it out.

And so, time and again I beat my empty breast and groan; I really do not know the causes of the flowing and the not flowing.

27. The six emotions are "like" and "dislikes" plus the four emotions mentioned in the *Doctrine of the Mean* ("pleasure, anger, sorrow, joy." Legge, *Chinese Classics* 1.384).

Coda: The Use of Poetry

Literature is the embodiment of our thought.

It travels over endless miles, sweeping all obstructions aside; it spans innumerable years, acting as a bridge.

Looking down, it bequeaths patterns to the future; gazing up, it contemplates the examples of the ancients.

It preserves the way of Wen and Wu, about to crumble;[28] it propagates good ethos, never to perish.

No realm is too far for it to reach; no thought is too subtle for it to comprehend.

It is the equal of clouds and rain in yielding sweet moisture; it is like spirits and ghosts in effecting metamorphoses.[29]

It inscribes bronze and marble, to make virtue known; it breathes through flutes and strings, and is new always.[30]

28. Alludes to *Analects* 19.22: "The doctrines of Wan and Wu have not yet fallen to the ground." (Legge, *Chinese Classics*, 1.346. [Fang's note.]

29. The couplet refers to the *Book of Changes*: the first half compares style with the omnipotent Ch'ien principle, by virtue of which "the clouds move and the rain is distributed," (Legge, *Sacred Books of the East*, 16.213); the second half may allude to a Confucian saying, "He who knows the method of change and transformation may be said to know what is done by that spiritual (power)." (Legge, *Sacred Books of the East* 16.336). [Fang's note.]

30. Cf. in the *Book of Changes*, "The daily renovation which it produces is what is meant by 'the abundance of its virtue.' " (Legge, *Sacred Books of the East* 16.356). Cf. also the inscription on the bathtub of T'ang: "If you can one day renovate yourself, do so from day to day. Yea, let there be daily renovation." (Legge, *Chinese Classics*, 1.361.) [Fang's note.]

THREE POETS

T'AO CH'IEN (365–427) LI PO (701–762) PO CHU-I (772–846)

Chinese poetry is usually in the middle-length forms. While there are long poems, there are no epics, and the great Chinese poets do not ordinarily work in very abbreviated forms like the Japanese *haiku* and *tanka*. Since the Chinese language is essentially monosyllabic, there are many homophones, and rhyme, while it is extensively used, is not capable of the variety that it attains in, say, English or German. But since the Chinese language has tone—syllables differentiated in meaning by being "sung" with a rising, level, falling, or other pitch—this becomes an important prosodic feature. Many of the longer pieces are in a form called the *fu*, in long (six- or seven-word) lines, and use the caesura, rhyme, and balanced parallel phrases. Some of these pieces are elaborate and strain the resources of the language in their search for synonyms. There is also a form called "regulated verse" (*lü-shih*), with its arrangements as proscribed as the sonnet. It too is in five- or seven-word lines, with an eight-line stanza, but with its rhyme scheme and tonal sequence rigidly proscribed and with strict rules of parallelism. The critic Shen Yo (441-513) provides the poet with "eight defects" he must be aware of to do the form successfully. Some kinds of poetry in China go back to folk song (see the *Book of Songs*, above) and there are many freer forms for the poet's use. But when a particular type of poetry became popular with the literati, it was likely to be formalized into a "school," and there are many proscriptive treatises on writing poetry.

The three poets included here are among the most popular in Chinese literature, though they differ markedly from one another. T'ao Ch'ien represents the early flowering of Chinese poetry. He is a poet of retirement, a Taoist recluse who lived close to nature in the Six Dynasties period (222–589), an age in which China was spilt into warring factions. T'ao Ch'ien is philosophical in that he distills into his poetry the essence of his troubled times, but always against a background of the concrete details of his personal life—his garden, his vineyard, and his village. His experiences as a government official in minor posts convinced him that integrity and government service were not easily combined. While Confucian ideals were theoretically the philosophy of government, they were not so in practice. China at this time barely managed to keep the northern barbarians at bay, and palace revolutions, banditry, and civil war were the order of the day. He is said to have given up government work so as not to have to "cringe for five pecks of rice" and to have spent his remaining years as a farmer. His poetry appeals because he bares his personality to the reader and gives us the concerns of his heart directly. He clearly worried about fame and mortality—he keeps mentioning his age and we watch the years pass with him. His direct human appeal did not make him a model of poetry in his own time, however. Official literature in the period affected a baroque and artificial style. A testimony to his humanity is that he provides few barriers for readers from other cultures. Western readers at home with poets of nature from Wordsworth to Frost will be at home with T'ao Ch'ien.

Li Po had an entirely different kind of poetic career. He is perhaps the best known of Chinese poets. He began to write poetry at a very early age in Szechuan, but his reputation grew slowly. He travelled much in northern and central China; at Ch'ang-an he won the patronage of the emperor, was made a member of the Han-ling Academy, and was asked to compose poems for the imperial court. By this time he had studied Taoism, had experimented much in poetry, and had filled his mind with the most imaginative literature. Some of his early work he later regarded as pretentious, and he sought to discard it. In the big city, he found the whirl of court life, and especially the tavern, much to his liking, and some of his exploits with wine got him into trouble. An anecdote, which if not true is at least appropriate, is that he died by drowning—he was drunk and leaned too far over a boat's rail to look at the reflection of the moon on the water. He is sometimes melancholy—drinking alone is one of his themes, and drinking in China was customarily convivial. When he is at his happiest, love and romance are his themes, and the Tartar women of the north and the white-skinned girls of Wu interest him equally.

Po Chü-i is the best known of the mid T'ang poets. He is an essentially serious poet who had a long and excellent record in government service—in the Han-lin academy and in other official posts. Despite this, he is a serious critic of government and society and uses poetry to attack the evils of his age. Poetry, he said, had become in his time playing with the wind and the moon, the flowers and the grass; it should instead use its eloquence to expose corruption, superstition, militarism, and the oppression of the people. Some of his themes are curiously modern—an old man breaks his arm to avoid military service, a poor man's supply of charcoal is seized for taxes, a bouquet of flowers in the market sells for a price equal to the entire tax burden of a poor family. Frustrated by corruption and exploited by officialdom, the people nevertheless solace themselves with meaningless superstitions, believe in omens and idols, and fancy they will end up in some celestial paradise in the presence of the Jade Emperor. Po Chü-i's attacks on these prevailing evils naturally brought down upon him the wrath of those important people in society who depend on the ignorance of the people and on bad government for their own livelihood and position, and demotion and banishment were the poet's reward. Po wrote in a language which the people could understand, and his verses were hung in taverns and learned even by sing-song girls. He represents a poet dedicated to the idea that poetry should have a moral and social purpose. He spoke out bravely, at considerable risk, on the conditions of his day. Many other poets were too cautious to imitate him.

T'AO CH'IEN*

*Hovering Clouds***

'Hovering Clouds' is a poem on thinking about a friend. My cup is filled with new wine and the trees in the garden are now in bloom. I have no way of getting what I yearn for, and sighs fill my breast.

* From *The Poetry of T'ao Ch'ien,* translated by James Robert Hightower. The notes are based on the translator's verv full annotations.

** This poem and the one following are unusual for T'ao Ch'ien in that they imitate the archaic style and structure of the *Book of Songs*, though the poet's efforts have a naturalness and a lyrical tone which sets them off from those of other imitators of the ancients.

I

Dense, dense the hovering clouds
Fine, fine the seasonable rain.
In the eight directions, the same dusk,
The level roads impassable.
Quietly I sit at the east window,
Spring wine—alone I take it.
The good friend is far away
I scratch my head and linger on.

II

The hovering clouds are dense, dense
The seasonable rain fine fine.
In the eight directions, the same dusk,
The level ways are turned to rivers.
Wine I have, wine I have—
By the east window I drink it idly,
Yearning for some one.
Neither boat nor carriage help.

III

The trees there in the eastern garden—
Their branches now begin to blossom.
There are new attractions vying
Each to draw my feelings out.
Among the people is the saying,
Sun and moon are on the march.
Where to find me a companion
To reminisce about the past?

IV

Flap, flap the flying birds
Come to rest on my courtyard tree.
They fold their wings and take their ease
Calling out with pleasant voices.
Not that there is no one else

1–3. *Dense . . . dusk:* A spring rain is falling—this makes things grow. It is not evening but the sky is dark from the rainclouds. East is the direction of spring.

14. *I drink:* While T'ao often writes about drinking alone, drinking wine always suggests the presence of friends in China.

15–16. *Yearning . . . help:* The poet is not thinking of going out; he is expecting and hoping for a visitor.

25. *birds:* Flying birds come home to rest is a common symbol for T'ao, but the birds are happy in one another's company, while the poet is lonely. The birds heighten his sense of disappointment.

But it's you I think of most.
I long for what I cannot get
What sorrow do I harbor!

Progression of the Seasons

'Progression of the Season' is a poem about an outing in late springtime. The spring clothes are made, and all nature is mild. I stroll along, my shadow for companion, joy and sadness mingled in my heart.

I

Pell-mell the seasons revolve
Still and calm is this morning.
I put on my springtime clothes
And set out for the eastern suburbs.
The hills are scoured by last night's clouds
The sky is dimmed by a film of mist.
From the south there blows a breeze
Winging over the new grain.

II

The wide waters of the level lake—
I rinse my mouth, I bathe myself;
Endlessly into the distance stretching—
I rejoice while I gaze.
Among the people is the saying,
It's easy to please a contented man.
I raise this cup to my lips
Happy and self-satisfied.

III

Toward midstream I strain my eyes
Yearning for the clear Yi River,
Where youths and men study together
And singing idly go back home.
It's their tranquility I love—
Awake or sleeping I would join them;

3. *Springtime clothes:* an allusion to the *Analects of Confucius* (see p. 389). William Empson (*Seven Types of Ambiguity,* 1930 pp. 30–32) points out that the contrast between the hurried rush of the seasons and the tranquil calm of the spring morning invites the reader to reconcile the apparent incompatability of the two time scales, one emphasizing the shortness of human life and the other the placidity of the spring morning.

7. *From* . . . . This line is almost identical to one in the *Book of Songs* (Waley, *Book of Songs,* No. 78).

18. *Yi River:* the same one referred to in the *Analects* (note to "springtime clothes," above).

19–22. *Where . . . them:* "The spring clothes are made" of the Preface is echoed here in a ritual renewal of life through spring activities.

But the times alas are different,
Too far away to be revived.

IV

All morning and in evening too
In my house I take my ease.
Herbs and flowers grow in rows,
Trees and bamboo cast their shade.
A cither lies across the bench,
Unstrained wine fills half a jug.
There's no reaching the ancient rulers
All I have is melancholy.

*An Exhortation to Farmers**

I

In the most distant past
When the people first were born,
Proud and self-sufficient
They embraced the plain and held the true.
Once clever learning sprouted
Essentials were out of reach;
And who supplied their needs?
They relied on the sage's help.

II

And that sage, who was he?
Lord Millet, Hou Chi himself.
And how did he supply their needs?
By sowing and planting—this was the way.
The Emperor Shun with his own hands plowed
The Emperor Yü, he sowed and reaped.
According to the ancient statutes of Chou
Of the eight tasks of rule, food comes first.

31. *ancient rulers:* specifically Huang and T'ang, the legendary Yellow Emperor and Yao, and the joy of the peaceful life is contrasted with the sad times of the present.

* This is a rather impersonal and didactic poem in which the poet looks to myth and legend to find justification for the importance and prestige of agriculture. [The Western pastoral tradition from the Greeks through the eighteenth century is even more removed from reality than is T'ao Ch'ien, who at least mentions hunger and cold as part of the consequences of any interruption of the endless labor of the farmer.—Editor.]

2. *When . . . born:* This echoes a line in the *Book of Songs* (Waley No. 238, line 1). "Embraced the plain" is from the *Tao te Ching* (19). The poet contrasts Taoist primitivism with the "clever learning" of line 5. Lao Tzu in the *Tao te Ching* advises us, in the same passage, to "get rid of sages and throw away learning . . . get rid of cleverness and throw away gain."

13–14. *Emperor Shun . . . reaped:* Emperor Shun did his plowing on Mount Li before he became emperor. Emperor Yü's farming is mentioned in Confucius's *Analects*, XIV, 6. Food is one of the eight tasks or responsibilities of the ruler according to the *Classic of Documents* (*Shu Ching*), one of the Confucian classics.

III

Harmonious the natural order
Fruitful and flourishing the level land.
Plants and trees are covered with blossoms
A gentle breeze blows fresh and softly.
Many are the girls and boys
Vying to make the most of time:
Mulberry pickers rise before dawn,
Farmer lads dwell in the fields.

IV

The seasons quickly hurry past
Warm and moist will not last long.
Ch'üeh of Chi worked with his wife
Chang-chü and Chieh-ni pulled their plow.
Behold those men, both wise and good,
Who made the fields their task.
How much the less can common men
Trail their robes and fold their hands!

V

The people's livelihood lies in work
Through work they shall not suffer want.
If you live a life of idleness
What can you expect at the year's end?
When no bushel of grain is stored
Hunger comes, along with cold.
When I look at my companions
How can I not be ashamed?

VI

Confucius stuck to morality
And thought Fan Hsü was vulgar.
Tung was happy with books and cither,
And never stepped inside his garden.

27–28. *Ch'üeh of Chi . . . plow:* Ch'üeh was tilling his field when his wife brought him his lunch. She was respectful and they treated one another as if they were guests. This so impressed Duke Wen of Chin that he made Chüeh an officer. Chang-chu and Chieh-ni were recluse farmers who criticized Confucius (*Analects*, XVIII, 6). Obviously the poet has a different attitude towards the lower classes than did Confucius.

42. *Fan Hsü:* Fan Hsü had the audacity to ask Confucius to teach him farming. Confucius advised him to find an old farmer and later described him as a "mean man" (*Analects*, XIII, 4).

If you can be that superior
Then take your lofty stand.
I will stand at attention
And respectfully sing your praises.

*On Naming My Son**

I

Far, far back our ancestral line
Began with the Lord of T'ao-t'ang.
In remote past as guests in Yü,
Through generations repeated glory:
Dragon-Driver served the Hsia,
Boar-Throng supported Shang.
Imposing was the Minister
Through him our clan gained fame.

II

In the turmoil of warring states
With the collapse of declining Chou,
The phoenix hid in the grove
The recluse took to the hills.
Plunging dragons circled the clouds,
Dashing whales cowed the waters.
Heaven had hit on the Han house
And looked with love on our Lord Min.

III

How glorious was that Lord Min!
He had the chance to cling to the dragon,
Sword in hand he charged like the wind
To manifest his martial deeds.

* This poem was written on the occasion of the birth of the poet's eldest son, T'ao Yen. Fifteen years later he was to write that "for laziness he has no match," but the present occasion is one for rejoicing, remembrance of his distinguished ancestors, and also awareness of his responsibility that the family line continue and prosper.

1–6. *Far . . . Shang:* T'ao Ch'ien believed his line descended from the sage Emperor Yao (the Lord of T'ao-t'ang). Dragon River and Boar Thong were heroes of two different clans serving the emperor.

9–16. *In the turmoil . . . Lord Min:* This stanza reflects the chaos in China after the downfall of the Chou dynasty (1122–255 B.C.) and the reestablishment of order under the Han (206 B.C.–A.D. 221). The phoenix, an auspicious symbol, flees, and figures of violence, the dragon and the whale, symbolize a period of conflict. Lord Min assumed power in 196 B.C.).

His ruler swore by River and Mountain
And granted him a fief in Kaifeng.
Unflagging his son the Prime Minister,
In truth he followed the way of his predecessor.

IV

Gushing forth the constant spring—
Proliferating the vast trunk—
All the streams trace back to it,
The multitude of boughs range from it.
As times demand, mute or voluble,
Following chance, now up, now down.
In our own Eastern Chin Dynasty
The heritage shone out from Changsha.

V

Oh, the valorous Lord of Changsha!
He was deserving, he was virtuous.
The Son of Heaven rewarded him.
Made him sole charge of the southern march.
His task once done, he came back home,
Enjoying favor, he did no wrong.
Who will say a heart like his
Can anywhere be found today?

VI

Full of dignity was my grandfather,
Careful to end as he began.
Straight and square inside and out
His benefits reached a thousand miles.
Oh kindly was my late father,
Retiring and unpretentious
He cast his lot with wind-blown clouds,
He never showed joy or anger.

VII

I alas am lone and lowly,
I look up but cannot reach them.

21. *River and Mountain:* the Yellow River and Mount T'ai.

25–32. This stanza reduces the history of T'ao's ancestors to generalities. They prospered but did not lead a conspicuous role in public life. T'ao K'an, Lord of Ch'ang-sha (fourth century) was the next truly outstanding member of the family.

I was ashamed of my white temples
And stood alone with my shadow.
Of all the three thousand crimes
The worst is to fail to have a successor.
This I have truly thought about
When I heard your infant cry.

VIII

I divine; the day is auspicious
Cast lots: the time is lucky.
To you I give the name Yen
With it the appellation Ch'iu-ssu.
Mild and reverent, day and night
Reflect on it, ponder it
Still bearing in mind K'ung Chi—
May you aspire to be like him.

IX

The leper whose child is born at night
Rushes out to fetch a torch.
Everyone has such an impulse,
I am not the only one.
Once you have seen him born in the world
It is natural to want him to be able.
Others have said the same before,
These are not feigned feelings.

X

As the days and the months go by
You will grow out of infancy.
Fortune comes not undeserved,
Trouble is also easily found.
'Early to rise and late to bed'—
I pray you may have the capacity.
And if you have not the capacity—
Well, there's no helping it.

54. Here the poet contemplates his responsibility to continue his illustrious line.

61. This line comes from the *Book of Songs* (Waley, No. 213). K'ung Chi was Confucius' grandson.

65–66. I.e., to see that his son is not afflicted like himself. This line is from the *Chuang Tzu*, 33.12.94.

*Substance, Shadow, and Spirit**

Nobel or base, wise or stupid, none but cling tenaciously to life. This is a great delusion. I have put in the strongest terms the complaints of Substance and Shadow and then, to resolve the matter, have made Spirit the spokesman for naturalness. Those who share my tastes will all get what I am driving at.

I

SUBSTANCE TO SHADOW

Earth and heaven endure forever,
Streams and mountains never change.
Plants observe a constant rhythm,
Withered by frost, by dew restored.
But man, most sentient being of all,
In this is not their equal.
He is present here in the world today,
Then leaves abruptly, to return no more.
No one marks there's one man less—
Not even friends and family think of him;
The things that he once used are all that's left
To catch their eye and move them to grief.
I have no way to transcend change,
That it must be, I no longer doubt.
I hope you will take my advice:
When wine is offered, don't refuse.

II

SHADOW TO SUBSTANCE

No use discussing immortality
When just to keep alive is hard enough.
Of course I want to roam in paradise,
But it's a long way there and the road is lost.
In all the time since I met up with you
We never differed in our grief and joy.

* This is a Buddhist poem. Substance focuses on the fact of human mortality—life can be made acceptable only by recourse to the wine bottle. Perhaps he believes in Taoist practices which tried alchemy, diet, and breath-control in a search for long life. Shadow is clearly Confucian in desiring a reputation for good deeds that will live after him. Spirit comes out for a stoical acceptance of life and death that has affinities with Taoism. Though the bias is for Spirit's position, all of the attitudes are held by one person—an internal conflict. The Preface states the point of departure for the poem: everyone is attached to life and this attachment is irreconcilable with the inevitability of death.

In shade we may have parted for a time,
But sunshine always brings us close again.
Still this union cannot last forever—
Together we will vanish into darkness.
The body goes; that fame should also end
Is a thought that makes me burn inside.
Do good, and your love will outlive you;
Surely this is worth your every effort.
While it is true, wine may dissolve care
That is not so good a way as this.

III

SPIRIT'S SOLUTION

The Great Potter cannot intervene—
All creation thrives of itself.
That Man ranks with Earth and Heaven
Is it not because of me?
Though we belong to different orders,
Being alive, I am joined to you.
Bound together for good or ill
I cannot refuse to tell you what I know:
The Three August Ones were great saints
But where are they living today?
Though P'eng-tsu lasted a long time
He still had to go before he was ready.
Die old or die young, the death is the same,
Wise or stupid, there is no difference.
Drunk every day you may forget,
But won't it shorten your life span?
Doing good is always a joyous thing
But no one has to praise you for it.
Too much thinking harms my life;
Just surrender to the cycle of things,
Give yourself to the waves of the Great Change
Neither happy nor yet afraid.
And when it is time to go, then simply go
Without any unnecessary fuss. .

28. ***burn inside:*** Confucius has a similar statement in the *Analects*, XV, 19.

41. *Three August Ones:* These cannot be identified with certainty. Various suggestions have been made by Chinese commentators.

43. *a long time:* Traditionally, he lived eight-hundred years, a record even in Chinese, and he died regretting that he had not lived out his span.

45. *Die old . . . :* These lines reflect still a passage in the *Lieh Tzu* (7.2a): "Among the living there are wise and foolish, noble and mean: this is how they differ. Dead there is corruption and extinction: it is in this that they are the same. . . . Ten-year-olds die and centenarians die, the good and the saintly die and the wicked and the stupid die."

An Outing on Hsieh Brook

On the fifth day of the first month of the year *hsin-yu* (421), when the sky was clear, the air was mild, and all nature genial, I went for an outing on Hsieh Brook with a couple of my neighbors. Standing beside the ever-flowing stream we gazed at Tiered Wall in the distance. Mullet and carp leaped out of the water as twilight came on; sea gulls soared in the still air. The Southern Hill has long been celebrated, and need not now be exclaimed over. But Tiered Wall, rising sharp up out of the water with nothing on either side, by its happy name reminds one of the far-off Magic Mountains. Not content simply to enjoy the sight, I wrote a hasty poem in which I bemoaned the inexorable passage of days and months and lamented that our years cannot be held back. Each of us wrote down his age and birthplace to commemorate the occasion.

With this one, fifty years have slipped away,
My life proceeds apace to its final rest.
This is the thought that moves my heart within;
Today's occasion should not be missed.
The air is mild, the sky perfectly clear,
As we sit together by the far-flowing stream.
Striped mullet race through weak rapids,
Crying gulls soar over the quiet valley.
The wandering gaze across distant waters
Descries Tiered Wall Hill, far away.
It may fall short of Ninefold Peak's perfection,
Still nothing else in sight can equal it.
I offer my companions wine from the flask,
Filled to the brim, each cup in turn is empied.
There is no knowing whether after today
It will ever be like this again.
The wine half gone, we let our fancy roam
Forgetting these thousand-year cares.
Let us make the most of today's pleasure—
We need not worry now about tomorrow.

*Begging for Food**

Hunger came and drove me out
To go I had no notion where.
I walked until I reached this town,

14. *each cup:* They drink toasts to one another.

18. *cares:* These are both the cares of everyday life and the specific fear of dying.

* Some Chinese commentators have tried to interpret this poem allegorically, feeling that it was beneath the dignity of a poet and philosopher to beg for food.

3. *town:* The setting of the poem is vague, but the poet is obviously not in his own home town. There is no explanation as to why he is in this predictament.

Knocked at a door and fumbled for words
The owner guessed what I was after
And gave it, but not just the gift alone.
We talked together all day long,
And drained our cups as the bottle passed.
Happy in our new acquaintance
We sang old songs and wrote new poems.
You are as kind as the washerwoman,
But to my shame I lack Han's talent.
I have no way to show my thanks
And must repay you from the grave.

An Outing Under the Cypress Trees at the Chou Family Graves

The weather today is perfect,
Clear flute and singing cither.
Moved at the men under the cypress trees
What else can we do but be merry?
To the high song we sing fresh words
Clear wine relaxes the youthful face.
No telling what the morrow brings—
All our feelings are used up here.

*A Lament in the Ch'u Mode**

TO SHOW TO SECRETARY P'ANG AND SCRIBE TENG

Dark and distant is the Way of Heaven,
The Spirits shrouded in obscurity.
Since childhood I have tried to do right.
The best I could, these fifty-four years.
At twenty I met with troubled times,
When thirty I lost my first wife;
More than once bright fire burned down my house,
Weevils had their way with the grain I grew,
Wind and rain came from every quarter
And the yield would not suffice a single man.
Through summer days we often bore our hunger,
Winter nights we slept without covers;
In the evening we would long for cockcrow,

11. ***washer woman:*** Han Hsin, a poor young man, was fed and befriended by a washerwoman, who indignantly denied that she expected a reward. Later, he became a famous general. His life is told in *Records of the Grand Historian of China*, translated by Burton Watson (I, 208–232).

3. ***men:*** The men are the dead in their graves. The setting may seem inappropriate, but the weather is responsible for their high spirits.

* This is one of T'ao's most personal poems. The troubled times may be personal or national (the age was one of great instability) or both.

14. ***Crow:*** the sun.

At dawn we prayed the crow would quickly cross.
It is my own doing, no fault of Heaven,
That grief and trouble embitter my life.
Alas, a name left to posterity
Is no more to me than floating mist.
With deep feeling I sing my lonely song—
Chung Tzu-ch'i in truth was a good man.

Written on the First Day of the Fifth Month to Match a Poem by Secretary Tai

It is an empty boat, cast adrift
Back and forth with never any end.
It seems but a moment since the year began
Yet nearly half the star's course is run.
The Double Luminaries make things flourish,
The north grove puts out blossoms and grows thick.
The Spirit Spring pours out the timely rain,
Early dawn plays a summer breeze.
Once here, who has ever failed to leave?
Human life comes always to its end.
Accept your lot and wait until it's over,
To stay free, crook an elbow for a pillow.
Accord with change, whatever its ups and downs—
Follow your bent, no matter the heights and depths.
If what I serve is high enough already,
'What need have I to climb Mt. Hua or Sung?

To Liu, Prefect of Ch'ai-sang

To this out-of-the-way place few people come
And sometimes I forget the seasons' passage.
Fallen leaves cover the empty courtyard
And with a pang I see that fall is come.

17–18. This echoes Confucius' saying "Undeserved riches and honor are no more to me than floating clouds" (*Analects*, XIV, 35).

20. *Chung:* A music lover and the model of a sympathetic friend.

2. *Back and forth:* Presumably this means we go back and forth in life, carefree, empty of emotions.

5. *Double Luminaries:* the sun and moon. The stars run their courses around Polaris, the Pole Star.

12. *crook an elbow:* See Confucius, *Analects,* VII, 15 (p. 000, above). If you are content with bare essentials, you are doing nothing to disturb your harmony with nature.

16. *Mt. Hua or Sung:* These mountains are associated with the Taoist Immortals.

4. *pang:* There is an implication here of the passing years, not just of the end of summer.

The new hibiscus blooms by the north window
Excellent grain grows in the southern field.
Must I not enjoy myself today?
How do I know there will be another year?
I tell my wife to bring along the children—
This is a perfect day to make an outing.

*To Clerk Yang**

Clerk Yang Sung-ling, attached to the staff of the General of the Left, was sent on a mission to Ch'in-ch'uan, and I wrote these lines to give him.

Having been born in a time of decadence
I think with longing of the ancient kings.
To learn of an age a thousand years ago
All we have are the books the ancients wrote.
The relics that are left of the saints and sages
Are one and all to be found in the Middle Region.
I never lost my wish to wander there,
But the road was blocked by rivers and passes.
Now that all Nine Regions are united
I had thought of getting boat and carriage ready.
I hear that you will have to go ahead
While I am sick and cannot go along.
If your journey takes you past Mt. Shang
Do me a favor: stop there long enough
To pay my deep respects to Ch'i and Lu.
Is their spirit still vigorous these days?
Does anyone pick the purple mushrooms now?
Their hidden valley is long since overgrown.
No coach-and-four will buy you free from care,
It's poverty and low estate bring joy.
Their pure song is kept fast in my heart's recesses,
But the men are distant, time puts us apart.
I press my breast, so many ages after;
I've said what I can, there is more I cannot express.

* General Liu Yü's campaign against the Later Ch'in ended in 417 with the capture of Ch'ang-an, and Yang Sung-ling was sent to carry congratulations on the victory.

13. *Mt. Shang:* Four sages retired to Mt. Shang, near Lo-yang. Two of these, who were admired by the poet, were Ch'i and Lu, mentioned below.

24. *I cannot express:* T'ao Ch'ien lived all of his life in the south, at a time when the Yellow River basin, the center of ancient Chinese culture, was under alien rule. Now that this region was again in the hands of a Chinese army, there should be rejoicing, but the government is still oppressive. He hints he would say more if he dared.

*A Lament for My Cousin, Chung-te**

Filled with grief I visit your old dwelling
And let fall these tears of heartfelt sorrow.
You want to know who it is I grieve for?
He is dwelling down below the Nine Springs.
My mourning dress proclaims another cousin
But in love we were more nearly brothers.
When we last clasped hands before the gate
I did not think that you would go ahead.
It was a fate's decree, there's no escape—
The hill you never got to finish building.
Your mother lies immobile, ill with grief,
Your two children but a few years old.
The pair of tablets in an empty room—
At night and dawn no sound of weeping there.
On empty seats the drifting dust collects
The front courtyard is overgrown with grass.
The stairs are empty of strolling footsteps' marks
In grove and garden all that's left are feelings.
In the dark you went, borne on the wings of change,
To the end of time your form will not return.
I slowly, slowly turn my steps around
Shattered by the grief that fills my heart.

*The Ninth of the Ninth Month, 409**

Little by Little autumn has come to an end
Chill, chill the wind and dew combine.
The creeping vines put out no blossoms now
Already courtyard trees have lost their leaves.
The crisp air scours summer's dregs away,
The distant boundary of heaven is high.

* Nothing is known of this cousin, but the Nine Springs is the underworld of the dead.

5. *mourning dress:* The type of mourning dress is proscribed by ritual, but he was closer to the cousin than the family relationship would make one assume.

13. *empty room:* Since there is no one to weep, there is an implication that the cousin's wife is dead.

16. *Grass:* The grass suggests that a year has elapsed since his cousin's death. Traditionally, he should not have to mourn longer than a year. The Confucian *Book of Rites* (*Li Chi*) tell us "when the grass planted last year grows green on the grave of a friend, one weeps for him no more" (III, 8).

* The Double Ninth is the ninth day of the ninth lunar month, a festival celebrated by climbing a hill and drinking wine. It is associated with longevity (the Chinese word for "nine" is a homonym of a word meaning "long-lasting"). The stoic acceptance of the human condition is the theme here.

The sad cicada's cry is heard no more
Geese fly honking through the empyrean.
The myriad changes are all interconnected
Is human life anything but hard?
From earliest time all have had to die—
The thought sets my heart inside afire.
How am I to do my feelings justice?
Unstrained wine will serve to cheer my up.
I do not know about a thousand years,
So I had better just prolong today.

*Twenty Poems After Drinking Wine**

PREFACE

Living in retirement here I have few pleasures, and now the nights are growing longer, so, as I happen to have some excellent wine, not an evening passes without a drink. All alone with my shadow I empty a bottle until suddenly I find myself drunk. And once I am drunk I write a few verses for my own amusement. In the course of time the pages have multiplied, but there is no particular sequence in what I have written. I have had a friend make a copy, with no more in mind than to provide a diversion.

IV

Anxious, seeking, the bird lost from the flock—
The sun declines, and still he flies alone,
Back and forth without a place to rest;
From night to night, his cry becomes more sad,
A piercing sound of yearning for the dawn,
So far from home, with nothing for support
Until at last he finds the lonely pine
And folds his wings at this his journey's end.
In that harsh wind no tree can keep its leaves
This is the only shade that will not fail.
The bird has refuge here and resting place,
And in a thousand years will never leave.

* See John Robert Hightower, "T'ao Ch'ien's 'Drinking Wine' Poems," *Wen-li*, 1968, pp. 3–44.

1. *bird:* T'ao Ch'ien is fond of bird symbols, especially the homing bird that always comes back to its nest at the day's end after an excursion out into the world. Here the bird stands for the man who is out of touch with his fellows or has lost his place in society. T'ao finds refuge from the chaotic world in his farm; the pine tree is a symbol both for constancy amidst uncertainty and for a refuge in times of hardship.

V*

I built my hut beside a traveled road
Yet hear no noise of passing carts and horses.
You would like to know how it is done?
With the mind detached, one's place becomes remote.
Picking chrysanthemums by the eastern hedge
I catch sight of the distant southern hills:
The mountain air is lovely as the sun sets
And flocks of flying birds return together.
In these things is a fundamental truth
I would like to tell, but lack the words.

VI

A thousand myriad ways to act
And who can tell the right and wrong?
Once wrong and right are given shape
All will echo blame or praise.
When times were bad this often happened,
But not with men of understanding:
Contemptuous of the vulgar clods
They chose to follow Huang and Ch'i.

VII

The fall chrysanthemums have lovely colors.
I pluck the petals that are wet with dew
And float them in the Care Dispelling Thing
To strengthen my resolve to leave the world.

* This is one of T'ao Ch'ien's most famous poems. It conveys the detachment and repose of the Great Recluse who maks his home among men yet remains uncontaminated by the world and in easy communion with nature.

5. *Chrysanthemums:* He is picking chrysanthemums to use as a medicine, probably in a wine infusion, to prolong life. The southern mountains are a prime symbol of longevity; he echoes the *Book of Songs* (Waley, No. 167). Also, this particular mountain (perhaps Lu Shan), the poet had selected as a site for his grave.

8. *birds:* The enduring mountain and the birds take the poet away from men into a harmony with nature. The poet's feelings are beyond words in the last line. The commentators find echoes here of the *Chuang Tzu* (9.11a), "Once you have grasped the meaning, you may forget the words," and (1.36b), "The Great Way applies no labels, the greatest explanation employs no words."

1. *ways to act:* People generally have no standards of conduct and are content to call that right which is popular or convenient, especially in decadent times like now. Only men of understanding like the sages conduct themselves otherwise, and prefer to retire rather than court the favor of the mob. Perhaps the poet is making a statement on the decline of the age.

8. *Huang and Ch'i:* two of the four sages or "White Heads" who retired to Mt. Shang in disapproval of the tyranny of Ch'in. But ever after a new dynasty was founded by Han Kao-tsu, they refused to serve because they doubted the legitimacy of the new dynasty. (See "To Clerk Yang," p. 447.)

3. *Care Dispelling Thing:* Drinking chrysanthemum wine has been referred to elsewhere as part of the autumn festival ritual of prolonging life. By losing the world through drinking wine the poet finds himself.

I drink my solitary cup alone
And when it's empty, pour myself another.
The sun goes down, and all of nature rests
Homing birds fly chirping toward the grove.
I sit complacent on the east veranda
Having somehow found my life again.

X

Once I made a distant trip
Right to the shore of the Eastern Sea
The road I went was long and far,
The way beset by wind and waves.
Who was it made me take this trip?
It seems that I was forced by hunger.
I gave my all to eat my fill
When just a bit was more than enough.
Since this was not a famous plan
I stopped my cart and came back home.

XV

Through poverty I am short of hands
And bushes make my yard a wilderness.
Here and there are flying birds,
The place is quiet, no one comes.
How endlessly vast is the universe
And how few men will live to be a hundred!
The months and years jostle one another—
The hair at my temples long ago turned white.
Unless we resign ourselves to whims of fate
It's just too bad for what we started with.

XVI

When young I had no taste for worldly things—
My whole delight was in the Classic Books.

5. *alone:* Drinking is usually done with friends, and somewhat more ritualistically than in the West. Normally, his friend would fill his cup.

10. *found my life:* I.e., found satisfaction in life again.

3. *road:* T'ao is no doubt referring to a real trip, but the journey is also symbolic. "Distant trip" and "Eastern Sea" are deliberately vague, and "wind and waves" refer to civil wars rather than physical hazards.

9. *famous plan:* Perhaps a plan to become famous. The last line suggests that he is home permanently.

1–4. There is no obvious connection between the first four lines and the rest of the poem. Poverty does not permit him to hire help for his farm.

5. *vast:* In time as well as in space.

9. *whims of fate:* Literally, "failure and success." This echoes the *Chuang Tzu* (5.43): "Failure and success, poverty and riches, these are vicissitudes of events, the operation of fate."

So it went and now I am nearly forty
With nothing done to show for all those years.
I clung to firmness in adversity—
Of cold and hunger I have had my fill.
A dismal wind blows round my wretched shack
And a waste of weeds engulfs the courtyard.
In coat of felt I sit the long nights out
When morning cocks refuse to start to crow.
There is no Meng-kung here to understand,
And so I keep my feelings to myself.

*On Stopping Wine**

My dwelling stops beside the city wall,
Rambling about I stop in idleness.
Sitting I stop beneath the high shade trees,
I stroll and stop inside my rustic gate.
My favorite food stops with garden mallows,
My greatest pleasure stops with my youngest son.
All my life long I never stopped drinking:
When I stopped there was no pleasure left.
If I stopped in the evening I could not sleep,
If mornings I stopped I could not get out of bed.
Every day I would be about to stop,
But if I stopped my pulse became erratic.
I only knew that stopping was no fun,
I did not know that stopping could be good.
Then I saw it would be good to stop,
And this morning stop I really did.
Starting now and from this final stop
I shall stop in the Land of the Immortals.
On my new face will stop the bloom of youth
And for a million years will never stop.

7. *dismal wind . . .*: A Chinese commentator finds political allegory in the expressions "a dismal wind," "a waste of weeds," "the long night," and "morning cocks refuse to start to crow." The times were very troubled, but T'ao is also being literal. The Classic Books may mean the arts (ritual, music, archery, charioteering, letters, and mathematics) or the Confucian classics.

9. *The long nights:* See *Analects*, II,4 (p. 392).

11. *Meng-kung:* Liu Kung, whose polite name was Meng-kung, alone among his contemporaries recognized Chang Chung-wei, a poet living in poverty. This poem ends the sequence "Twenty Poems After Drinking Wine."

* This poem is an elaborate *tour de force* on the Chinese word *chih*, here translated as "stop." The poem is light-hearted; we don't really believe that the poet will give up wine.

18. *Land of the Immortals:* Fu-sang, a mythical island in the Eastern Sea, and originally the tree where the sun rises. When he says that stopping wine will make him immortal he is joking—the tradition is exactly the opposite.

The Return

I was poor, and what I got from farming was not enough to support my family. The house was full of children, the rice-jar was empty, and I could not see any way to supply the necessities of life. Friends and relatives kept urging me to become a magistrate, and I had at last come to think I should do it, but there was no way for me to get such a position. At the time I happened to have business abroad and made a good impression on the grandees as a conciliatory and humane sort of person. Because of my poverty an uncle offered me a job in a small town, but the region was still unquiet and I trembled at the thought of going away from home. However, P'eng-tse was only thirty miles from my native place, and the yield of the fields assigned the magistrate was sufficient to keep me in wine, so I applied for the office. Before many days had passed, I longed to give it up and go back home. Why, you may ask. Because my instinct is all for freedom, and will not brook discipline or restraint. Hunger and cold may be sharp, but this going against myself really sickens me. Whenever I have been involved in official life I was mortgaging myself to my mouth and belly, and the realization of this greatly upset me. I was deeply ashamed that I had so compromised my principles, but I was still going to wait out the year, after which I might pack up my clothes and slip away at night. Then my sister who had married into the Ch'eng family died in Wu-ch'ang, and my only desire was to go there as quickly as possible. I gave up my office and left of my own accord. From mid-autumn to winter I was altogether some eighty days in office, when events made it possible for me to do what I wished. I have entitled my piece 'The Return'; my preface is dated the eleventh moon of the year *i-ssu* (405).

To get out of this and go back home!
My fields and garden will be overgrown with weeds—
  I must go back.
It was my own doing that made my mind my body's slave
Why should I go on in melancholy and lonely grief?
I realize that there's no remedying the past
But I know that there's hope in the future.
After all I have not gone far on the wrong road
And I am aware that what I do today is right, yesterday wrong.
My boat rocks in the gentle breeze
Flap, flap, the wind blows my gown;
I ask a passerby about the road ahead,
Grudging the dimness of the light at dawn.

Then I catch sight of my cottage—
  Filled with joy I run.
The servant boy comes to welcome me
  My little son waits at the door.
The three paths are almost obliterated
  But pines and chrysanthemums are still here.
Leading the children by the hand I enter my house
  Where there is a bottle filled with wine.
I draw the bottle to me and pour myself a cup;
Seeing the trees in the courtyard brings joy to my face.
I lean on the south window and let my pride expand,
I consider how easy it is to be content with a little space.
Every day I stroll in the garden for pleasure,
There is a gate there, but it is always shut.
Cane in hand I walk and rest
Occasionally raising my head to gaze into the distance.
The clouds aimlessly rise from the peaks,
The birds, weary of flying, know it is time to come home.
As the sun's rays grow dim and disappear from view
I walk around a lonely pine tree, stroking it.

Back home again!
May my friendships be broken off and my wanderings come to
    an end.
The world and I shall have nothing more to do with one
    another.
If I were again to go abroad, what should I seek?
Here I enjoy honest conversation with my family
And take pleasure in books and cither to dispel my worries.
The farmers tell me that now spring is here
There will be work to do in the west fields.
Sometimes I call for a covered cart
Sometimes I row a lonely boat
Following a deep gully through the still water
Or crossing the hill on a rugged path.
The trees put forth luxuriant foliage,
The spring begins to flow in a trickle.
I admire the seasonableness of nature
And am moved to think that my life will come to its close.
  It is all over—
So little time are we granted human form in the world!
Let us then follow the inclinations of the heart:
Where would we go that we are so agitated?
I have no desire for riches
And no expectations of Heaven.
Rather on some fine morning to walk alone

Now planting my staff to take up a hoe,
Or climbing the east hill and whistling long
Or composing verses behind the clear stream:
So I manage to accept my lot until the ultimate homecoming.
Rejoicing in Heaven's command, what is there to doubt?

LI PO*

Exile's Letter

Do you remember how once at Lo-yang
Tung Tsao-ch'iu built us a wine-tower south of the T'ien-ching Bridge?
With yellow gold and tallies of white jade we bought songs and laughter
And we were drunk month after month, scorning princes and rulers.
Among us were the wisest and bravest within the Four Seas, with thoughts high as the clouds.
(But with you above all my heart was at no cross-purpose.)
Going round mountains, skirting lakes was as nothing to them,
All their feelings, all their thoughts were ours to share; they held nothing back.
Then I went off to Huai-nan to pluck my laurel-branch
And you stayed north of the Lo, sighing over your memories and dreams.
But we could not long bear the separation—were soon together again exploring the Fairy Castle.
We followed the thirty-six banks of the twisting stream
And all the way the waters were bright with a thousand flowers.
We passed through a myriad valleys
And in each heard the voice of wind among the pines.
At last, on a silver saddle with tassels of gold that reached to the ground
The Governor of Han-tung came out to meet us,
And the Holy Man of Tzu-yang summoned us, blowing on his jade reed-pipe,
And when we came to him he made for us unearthly music, high up in the tower that he had built—
A hubbub of sound, as when the phoenix cries to its mate.

* From *The Poetry and Career of Li Po* by Arthur Waley. Copyright Allen and Unwin Ltd., 1956. Reprinted by permission of Allen and Unwin, Ltd.

1. *Lo-yang:* now Honan-fu, in northwestern Honan province.

9. *laurel-branch:* Perhaps to marry Miss Hsu. [Waley's note.] The Lo River meets the Hwang-Ho west of Lo-yang, on the boundaries of Shenshi and Shanshi.

11. *Fairy Castle:* A mountain near Han-tung. [Waley's note.]

18. *Holy Man:* The Taoist priest Hu Tzu-yang, fourteenth patriarch of the Shang-ch'ing school. He died in or soon after 742 and his grave inscription was composed by Li Po. [Waley's note.]

And the Governor of Han-tung, because his long sleeves would
not keep still when the flutes called to him
Rose and did a drunken dance.
Then he brought his embroidered coat and covered me with it
And I slept with my head on his lap.
At that feast our spirits had soared to the Nine Heavens,
But by evening we had scattered like stars or rain,
Away over the hills and rivers to the frontiers of Ch'u.
I went back to my old mountain-nest
And you too went home, crossing the bridge over the Wei.

[*On Ho Chih-Chang's Death*]*

At Ch'ang-an the first time we met
He gave to me the name of 'Banished Immortal.'
Then he loved the thing within the cup;
Now he is turned to dust beneath the pines.
I remember how once he pawned his golden tortoise
To buy me wine, and tears wet my scarf.

*Fighting South of the Ramparts***

Last year we were fighting at the source of the Sang-kan;
This year we are fighting on the Onion River road.
We have washed our swords in the surf of Parthian seas;
We have pastured our horses among the snows of the T'ien
Shan,
The King's armies have grown grey and old
Fighting ten thousand leagues away from home.

21. *Governor:* See note to line 11.

27. *Ch'u:* south of Lo-yang, with its southern border on the Yangtze River.

29. *Wei:* north of Lo-yang, immediately across the Yellow River (Huang Ho).

* In a prose note attached to the poem Li Po explains: "As soon as he set eyes on me in the temple of Lao Tzu at Ch'ang-an the Crown Prince's Social Secretary, Lord Ho, called me the Banished Immortal. Then he untied the golden tortoise that he wore at his belt and brought wine with it, that we might be happy together." [Waley's note.] Li had been a member of a group of distinguished poets in the capital of Ch'ang-an. He made many friends, including Ho Chieh-chang (659–745), an important civil servant but also a drinker, conversationalist, calligrapher, and eccentric. Ho ended his career as a Taoist monk, with many poems written for him on the occasion of his departure for the monastery and on his death.

2. *'Banished Immortal':* It was commonly believed that immortals who misbehaved in heaven were as a punishment banished to earth for a fixed period, where they figured as wayward and extraordinary human beings. [Waley's note.]

** Written to an old tune, the original words of which are translated in Waley's *Chinese Poems* (1946), p. 52. If the poem was written about 751, it may reflect two great defeats of the Chinese army in northern central Yünnan and in Turkestan. [Waley's note.]

1. *Sang-kan:* The river runs west to east through northern Shansi and Hopei, north of the Great Wall. [Waley's note.]

2. *Onion River:* The Kashgar-darya, in Turkestan. [Waley's note.]

4. *T'ien Shan:* mountains in the remote frontier region of Kansu province, where the Great Wall parallels the Huang Ho River.

The Huns have no trade but battle and carnage;
They have no fields or ploughlands,
But only wastes where white bones lie among yellow sands.
Where the House of Ch'in built the great wall that was to keep away the Tartars.
There, in its turn, the House of Han lit beacons of war.
The beacons are always alight, fighting and marching never stop.
Men die in the field, slashing sword to sword;
The horses of the conquered neigh piteously to Heaven.
Crows and hawks peck for human guts,
Carry them in their beaks and hang them on the branches of withered trees.
Captains and soldiers are smeared on the bushes and grass;
The General schemed in vain.
Know therefore that the sword is a cursed thing
Which the wise man uses only if he must.

Hardships of Travel

The clear wine in my golden cup cost five thousand a gallon;
The choice meats in my jade dish are worth a myriad cash.
Yet I stop drinking and throw down my chopsticks, I cannot bring myself to eat.
I draw my sword and gaze round with mind darkened and confused.
I want to cross the Yellow River, but ice-blocks bar my way;
I was going to climb Mount T'ai-hang when snow filled the hills.
So I sat quietly dropping my hook, on the banks of a grey stream.
Suddenly again I mounted a ship, dreaming of the sun's horizon.
Oh the hardships of travel!
The hardships of travel and the many branchings of the way,
Where are they now?
A steady wind breaks the waves, the time will soon have come
When I shall hoist my cloudy sail and cross the open sea.

11. *Han:* the district surrounding Lo-yang. See the first note to *Exile's Letter.*

19. *The sword . . .:* A quotation from the *Tao Te Ching.* [Waley's note.] Section XXXI.

4. *darkened and confused:* The poet has grown tired of his profligate existence as a spendthrift aristocrat. He looks round him and feels he must strike a blow to save his country from the dangers that beset it. [Waley's note.]

13. *Sail:* But the time has come and he retires from the world. Here he mounts the ship of Taoist mysticism. [Waley's note.]

*The Sparrow Song**

When you fly abroad do not chase the halcyon of Hainan,
When you need a rest do not perch near the swallows in the Palace of Wu.
For fire may start in the Palace of Wu and burn the swallows' nest;
If you follow the halcyon of Hainan you will fall into the fowler's net.
Stay all alone, with your wings deep down among the daisies of the field.
Kestrel and kite still may come; nothing will happen to *you*!

[*Note of Thanks*]**

The wine of Lu is like amber, the fish of Wên River
Have scales of dark brocade. Noble the spirit
Of these generous clerks in the province of Shan-tung.
With your own hands you brought these things as a present to a stranger from afar.
We have found much to agree about and feel regard for one another.
The gallons of wine, these two fish are tokens of deep feeling.
See how their gills suck and puff, their fins expand
Lashing against the silver dish, as though they would fly away.
I call the boy to clean the board, to wield the frosty blade.
The red entrails fall like flowers, the white flesh like snow.
Reeling I fix my golden saddle, mount and ride for home.

[*On Drinking with Friends*] †

See the waters of the Yellow River leap down from Heaven,
Roll away to the deep sea and never turn again!
See at the mirror in the High Hall
Aged men bewailing white locks—
In the morning, threads of silk,
In the evening flakes of snow.

* An allegory on the dangers of associating with the great. The sparrow is warned against associating with the "halcyon of Hainan," the fisher who is snared for his beautiful plumage. [Waley's note.]

3. *Fire:* In 236 2.3. a night-watchman, holding up a torch to look at a swallow's nest, burned down the ancient palace of Soochow. [Waley's note.]

** This poem is simply a poetic note of thanks to a local clerk who had brought to Li Po's inn two fish and two gallons of wine. [Waley's note.]

3. *Shan-tung:* The whole of northeast Ching, including the modern province of Shantung. [Waley's note.]

† This is an interpretation of an old song sung to the accompaniment of flutes and drums, perhaps of the first century A.D. [Waley's note.]

Snatch the joys of life as they come and use them to the full;
Do not leave the silver cup idly glinting at the moon.
The things that Heaven made
Man was meant to use;
A thousand guilders scattered to the wind may come back again.
Roast mutton and sliced beef will only taste well
If you drink with them at one sitting three hundred cups.
Great Master Ts'ên,
Doctor Tan-ch'iu,
Here is wine, do not stop drinking
But listen, please, and I will sing you a song.
Bells and drums and fine food, what are they to me
Who only want to get drunk and never again be sober?
The Saints and Sages of old times are all stock and still,
Only the mighty drinkers of wine have left a name behind.
When the prince of Ch'ên gave a feast in the Palace of P'ing-lo
With twenty thousand gallons of wine he loosed mirth and play.
The master of the feast must not cry that his money is all spent;
Let him send to the tavern and fetch wine to keep our tankards filled.
His five-flower horse and thousand-guilder coat—
Let him call the boy to take them along and pawn them for good wine,
That drinking together we may drive away the sorrows of a thousand years.

*Song of the Crows Roosting at Night**

On the royal terrace at Soochow the crows are going to rest;
The King of Wu sitting in his palace drinks with Hsi Shih.
With songs of Wu, dances of Ch'u the feast does not lag;
Half only of the sun sticks out from the jaw of the green hills.
The silver arrow on the water-clock has marked many hours;
They rise to watch the autumn moon sink into the river waves.
What if daylight mounts the east? Need morning end their sport?

14. *Master T'sên:* he cannot be identified. Doctor Tan-ch'iu was Yüan Tan-ch'iu, a Taoist adept to whom Li Po addressed many poems. [Waley's note.]

22. *Sh'ên:* In 232 A.D. Ch'ên is central Honan.

* This is about the carousals of the King of Wu with the legendary Hsi Shih, the most beautiful of women. Moralists claim it is also a satire upon Tsung for his consort Yang Kuei-fei, which would date it after 745 A.D., but this is impossible to determine. [Waley's note.]

[*Inscription for Li Yung*]*

In this monastery that stands on the banks of the southern river
Once lived my kinsman, the Governor of Pei-hai!
In the empty courtyards genius no longer dwells;
In the high hall melancholy hermits sit.
As a relic of learning, the book-thong garlic grows.
His zither-stand is veiled with white dust.
The flowering trees that he planted during his life
Are sunk into Nirvana and are not touched by Spring.

*Two Poems to His Wife***

I

You on your visit to the nun Rise-in-the-Air
Must have reached by now her home in the grey hills,
Where the river works the mica-pounding pestles
And the wind sweeps through the flowers of the rose-bay tree.
If you find yourself loth to leave this pleasant retreat
Invite me also to enjoy the sunset glow.

II

I respect you for this—that though descended from a Minister
You study Tao and love Spirits and Immortals,
In your white hands scooping the blue clouds,
Your gauze skirt trailing through the purple mists,
And that now you have gone to the Folding Screen Hill
Mounted on a phoenix and wielding a whip of jade.

Ballad of Yü-chang†

A foreign wind has stirred the horsemen of Tai;
To the north they are blocking the pass of Lu-yang.

* The highly talented writer friend of Li Po, Li Yung, was put to death in 746 on a charge of conspiracy, although he was innocent of the charge. Some years later, Li Po visited the Hsiu-chêng monastery at Wu-ch'ang, which had been Li Yung's house, and wrote this inscription. [Waley's note.]

2. *kinsman:* The relationship was probably very remote. [Waley's note.]

5. *garlic:* Its leaves were supposed to resemble the thongs which held together the covers of books. [Waley's note.]

** Li Po's fourth wife, a high-born woman, became a Taoist nun in a convent in the Lu Shan mountains. Her companion, another nun, is Miss Rise-in-the-Air. [Waley's note.]

3. *mica:* Mica was pounded by a water mill and used for medicine. [Waley's note.]

† Probably written in the winter of 756, to an old ballad tune of the third century A.D. The original is translated by Waley, *Chinese Poems,* pp. 75–76. Evidently Li Po saw raw levees for eastern China (Wu) crossing the Fêng River and then embarking in transport-ships, on their way to the war in southern Honan. [Waley's note.]

1. *Tai:* Shansi.

2. *Lu-yang:* In southern Honan.

Weapons of Wu glint on the snowy lake;
From their march to the West will the soldiers ever come home?
They are half way over the Shang-liao Ford;
Blank and grim the yellow clouds hang.
An old mother is parting from her son,
She cries to heaven, standing in the wild scrub.
She gets through the banners to the captain on his white horse,
She clutched at him, and this is her mournful cry:
'*On the white poplar the autumn moon shines cold;*
Soon it will fall, in the hills of Yü-chang.
He whom you're taking was always a man of peace;
He was not trained to kill foreign foes.'
'Mother, I do not mind being killed in the fight;
For our sovereign's sake these monsters must be swept away.
When the soul is strong an arrow can plunge into a rock;
One must not shrink from things because they are hard.'
The towered ships soar like whales in flight;
The waves leap high in the Bay of the Fallen Star.
This song has a tune, but the tune cannot be played;
If the soldiers heard it, itwould make their hair go grey.

*The Szechwan Road**

Eheu! How dangerous, how high!
It would be easier to climb to Heaven
Than walk the Szechwan Road.
Since Ts'an Ts'ung and Yü Fu ruled the land
Forty-eight thousand years have gone by,
And still from the kingdom of Shu to the frontiers of Ch'in
No human hearth was lit.
To the west, starting from the great White Mountains, it was said
There was a bird-track that cut across the mountains of Szechwan;
But the earth of the hill crumbled and heroes perished.
So afterwards they made sky-ladders and hanging-bridges.

5. ***Shang-liao Ford:*** Forty miles south of Yü-chang.

20. *Bay of One Fallen Star:* In the northeast corner of Lake P'o-yang. The transports packed with men may suggest also barges loaded with timber, and connect with "white poplar" mentioned earlier. [Waley's note.]

* This is an old travel song reinterpreted by Li Po. It has been allegorically interpreted but perhaps it expresses only the poet's lack of desire, considering the dangers of travel, to go farther than the rugged country of northern Szechwan to Ch'eng-tu, where friends were expecting him. [Waley's note.]

6. *Ch'in:* in Shensi and Kansu province west of the northern arm of the Huang Ho. Shu is the old name for Szechwan. [Waley's note.]

10. *heroes:* The heroes were five strong men sent by the King of Shu to fetch the five daughters of the King of Ch'in. We must suppose they went via the Yangtze and Han Rivers and perished in attempting to return by land. [Waley's note.]

Above, high beacons of rock that turn back the chariot of the sun;
Below, whirling eddies that meet the clashing torrent and turn it away.
The crane's wing fails, the monkeys grow weary of such climbing.
How the road curls in the Pass of Green Mud!
With nine turns in a hundred steps it twists up the hills.
Clutching at Orion, passing the Well Star, I look up and gasp;
Then beating my breast sit and groan aloud.
I fear I shall never return from my westward wandering;
The way is steep and the rocks cannot be climbed.
Sometimes the voice of a bird calls among the ancient trees—
A male calling to its wife, up and down through the woods;
Sometimes a cuckoo sings to the moon, weary of empty hills.
It would be easier to climb to Heaven than walk the Szechwan Road,
And those who hear the tale of it turn pale with fear.
Between the hill-tops and the sky there is not a cubit's space;
Withered pines hang leaning over precipitious walls.
Flying waterfalls and rolling torrents blend their din,
Pounding the cliffs and circling the rocks they thunder in a thousand valleys.
Alas, traveller, why did you come to so fearful a place?
The Sword Gate is high and jagged,
If one man stood in the Pass he could hold it against ten thousand.
At the sight of a stranger, the guardians of the Pass leap on him like wolves.
In the day time one hides from ravening tigers, in the night from long serpents
That sharpen their fangs and suck blood, wreaking havoc among men.
They say the Damask City is a pleasant place;
I had rather go quietly home.
For it is easier to climb to Heaven than to walk the Szechwan Road.
I look over my shoulder, gazing to the West, and heave a deep sigh.

*Waking from Drunkenness on a Spring Day**

'Life in the world is but a big dream;
I will not spoil it by any labour or care.'
So saying, I was drunk all day,

36. *Damask City:* Ch'êng-tu, the capital of Szechwan.

* Undated but published in 753. [Waley's note.]

Lying helpless at the porch in front of my door.
When I woke up I looked into the garden court;
A single bird was singing amid the flowers.

I asked myself, what season is this?
Restless the oriole chatters in the spring breeze.
Moved by its song I soon begin to sigh
And as wine was there, I filled my own cup.
Noisily singing I waited for the moon to rise;
When my song was over, all my senses had gone.

PO CHÜ-I

*At the End of Spring**

TO YUAN CHEN** (A.D. 810)

The flower of the pear-tree gathers and turns to fruit;
The swallows' eggs have hatched into young birds.
When the Seasons' changes thus confront the mind
What comfort can the Doctrine of Tao give?
It will teach me to watch the days and months fly
Without grieving that Youth slips away;
If the Fleeting World is but a long dream,
It does not matter whether one is young or old.
But ever since the day that my friend left my side
And has lived an exile in the City of Chiang-ling,
There is one wish I cannot quite destroy:
That from time to time we may chance to meet again.

The Poem on the Wall

(A.D. 810)

[*Yüan Chēn wrote that on his way to exile he had discovered a poem inscribed by Po Chü-i, on the wall of the Lo-k'ou Inn.*]

My clumsy poem on the inn-wall none cared to see.
With bird-droppings and moss's growth the letters were
    blotched away.
There came a guest with heart so full, that though a page
    to the Throne,
He did not grudge with his broidered coat to wipe off the
    dust, and read.

* This and the following selections are from *Translations from the Chinese,* translated by Arthur Waley. Copyright 1919 and renewed 1947 by Arthur Waley. Copyright 1941 and renewed 1969 by Alfred A. Knopf, Inc. Reprinted by permission of Alfred A. Knopf, Inc., Allen & Unwin Ltd., and Constable & Co., Ltd.

** Po Chü-i's great friend, whom he met in his twenties, and who was banished in 805 for provocative behavior toward a high official.

Chu-ch'ēn Village

(A.D. 811)

In Hsü-chou, in the District of Ku-fēng
There lies a village whose name is Chu-ch'ēn—
A hundred miles away from the county-town,
Amid fields of hemp and green of mulberry-trees.
Click, click goes the sound of the spinning-wheel;
Mules and oxen pack the village-streets.
The girls go drawing the water from the brooks;
The men go gathering fire-wood on the hill.
So far from the town Government affairs are few;
So deep in the hills, man's ways are simple.
Though they have wealth, they do not traffic with it;
Though they reach the age, they do not enter the Army.
Each family keeps to its village trade;
Grey-headed, they have never left the gates.

Alive, they are the people of Ch'ēn Village;
Dead, they become the dust of Ch'ēn Village.
Out in the fields old men and young
Gaze gladly, each in the other's face.
In the whole village there are only two clans;
Age after age Chus have married Ch'ēns.
Near or distant, they have kinsmen in every house;
Young or old, they have friends wherever they go.
On white wine and roasted fowl they fare
At joyful meetings more than "once a week."
While they are alive, they have no distant partings;
To choose a wife they go to a neighbour's house.
When they are dead,—no distant burial;
Round the village graves lie thick.
They are not troubled either about life or death;
They have no anguish either of body or soul.
And so it happens that they live to a ripe age
And great-great-grandsons are often seen.

I was born in the Realms of Etiquette;
In early years, unprotected and poor.
Alone, I learnt to distinguish between Evil and Good;
Untutored, I toiled at bitter tasks.
The World's Law honours Learning and Fame;
Scholars prize marriages and Caps.

1. *Hsü-chou:* Soochow, near Shanghai.

With these fetters I gyved my own hands;
Truly I became a much-deceived man.
At ten years old I learnt to read books;
At fifteen, I knew how to write prose.
At twenty I was made a Bachelor of Arts;
At thirty I became a Censor at the Court.
Above, the duty I owe to Prince and parents;
Below, the ties that bind me to wife and child.
The support of my family, the service of my country—
For these tasks my nature is not apt.
I reckon the time that I first left my home;
From then till now,—fifteen Springs!
My lonely boat has thrice sailed to Ch'u;
Four times through Ch'in my lean horse has passed.
I have walked in the morning with hunger in my face;
I have lain at night with a soul that could not rest.
East and West I have wandered without pause,
Hither and thither like a cloud astray in the sky.
In the civil-war my old home was destroyed;
Of my flesh and blood many are scattered and lost.
North of the River, and South of the River—
In both lands are the friends of all my life;
Life-friends whom I never see at all,—
Whose deaths I hear of only after the lapse of years.
Sad at morning, I lie on my bed till dusk;
Weeping at night, I sit and wait for dawn.
The fire of sorrow has burnt my heart's core;
The frost of trouble has seized my hair's roots.
In such anguish has my whole life passed;
Long I have envied the people of Ch'ēn Village.

The Dragon of the Black Pool

[A SATIRE]

Deep the waters of the Black Pool, coloured like ink;
They say a Holy Dragon lives there, whom men have never seen.
Beside the Pool they have built a shrine; the authorities have established a ritual;
A dragon by itself remains a dragon, but men can make it a god.

51. *Ch'u:* an ancient state that occupied the area on both sides of the Yangtze River almost to the coast.
52. *Ch'in:* a frontier state north and west of Ch'u and west of the Huang Ho River.
59. *River:* the Yangtze.

Prosperity and disaster, rain and drought, plagues and pestilences—
By the village people were all regarded as the Sacred Dragon's doing.
They all made offerings of sucking-pig and poured libations of wine;
The morning prayers and evening gifts depended on a "medium's" advice.
When the dragon comes, ah!
The wind stirs and sighs
Paper money thrown, ah!
Silk umbrellas waved.
When the dragon goes, ah!
The wind also—still.
Incense-fire dies, ah!
The cups and vessels are cold.
Meats lie stacked on the rocks of the Pool's shore;
Wine flows on the grass in front of the shrine.
I do not know, of all those offerings, how much the dragon eats;
But the mice of the woods and the foxes of the hills are continually drunk and sated.
Why are the foxes so lucky?
What have the sucking-pigs done,
That year by year *they* should be killed, merely to glut the foxes?
That the foxes are robbing the Sacred Dragon and eating His sucking-pig,
Beneath the nine-fold depths of His pool, does He know or not?

The Prisoner

(WRITTEN IN A.D. 809)

Tartars led in chains,
Tartars led in chains!
Their ears pierced, their faces bruised—they are driven into the land of Ch'in.
The Son of Heaven took pity on them and would not have them slain.
He sent them away to the south-east, to the lands of Wu and Yüeh.

9–16. *When the dragon . . . vessels are cold:* parody of a famous Han dynasty hymn. [Waley's note.]

3. *Wu and Yüeh:* seacoast states in the vicinity of modern Shanghai and Nanking.

A petty officer in a yellow coat took down their names
and surnames.
They were led from the city of Ch'ang-an under escort of
an armed guard.
Their bodies were covered with the wounds of arrows,
their bones stood out from their cheeks.
They had grown so weak they could only march a single
stage a day.
In the morning they must satisfy hunger and thirst with
neither plate nor cup:
At night they must lie in their dirt and rags on beds that
stank with filth.
Suddenly they came to the Yangtze River and remembered
the waters of Chiao.
With lowered hands and levelled voices they sobbed a
muffled song.
Then one Tartar lifted up his voice and spoke to the
other Tartars,
"*Your* sorrows are none at all compared with *my* sorrows."
Those that were with him in the same band asked to hear
his tale:
As he tried to speak the words were choked by anger.
He told them "I was born and bred in the town of
Liang-yüan.
In the frontier wars of Ta-li I fell into the Tartars' hands.
Since the days the Tartars took me alive forty years have passed:
They put me into a coat of skins tied with a belt of rope.
Only on the first of the first month might I wear my
Chinese dress.
As I put on my coat and arranged my cap, how fast the
tears flowed!
I made in my heart a secret vow I would find a way home:
I hid my plan from my Tartar wife and the children she had
borne me in the land.
I thought to myself, 'It is well for me that my limbs are
still strong,'
And yet, being old, in my heart I feared I should never live
to return.
The Tartar chieftains shoot so well that the birds are afraid
to fly:

10. *Chiao:* in Turkestan. [Waley's note.]

16. *Liang-yüan:* north of Ch'ang-an. [Waley's note.] Not far from present-day Siking in Shensi province in west-central China.

17. *Ta-li:* the period Ta-li, 766–780 A.D. [Waley's note.]

From the risk of their arrows I escaped alive and fled swiftly home.
Hiding all day and walking all night I crossed the Great Desert.
Where clouds are dark and the moon black and the sands eddy in the wind.
Frightened, I sheltered at the Green Grave, where the frozen grasses are few:
Stealthily I crossed the Yellow River, at night, on the thin ice,
Suddenly I heard Han drums and the sound of soldiers coming:
I went to meet them at the road-side, bowing to them as they came.
But the moving horsemen did not hear that I spoke the Han tongue:
Their Captain took me for a Tartar born and had me bound in chains.
They are sending me away to the south-east, to a low and swampy land:
No one now will take pity on me: resistance is all in vain.
Thinking of this, my voice chokes and I ask of Heaven above,
Was I spared from death only to spend the rest of my years in sorrow?
My native village of Liang-yüan I shall not see again:
My wife and children in the Tartars' land I have fruitlessly deserted.
When I fell among Tartars and was taken prisoner, I pined for the land of Han:
Now that I am back in the land of Han, they have turned me into a Tartar.
Had I but known what my fate would be, I would not have started home!
For the two lands, so wide apart, are alike in the sorrow they bring.
Tartar prisoners in chains!
Of all the sorrows of all the prisoners mine is the hardest to bear!
Never in the world has so great a wrong befallen the lot of man,—
A Han heart and a Han tongue set in the body of a Turk."

28. *Great Desert:* the Gobi Desert. [Waley's note.]

30. *Green Grave:* the grave of Chao-chün, a Chinese girl who in 33 B.C. was "bestowed upon the Khan of the Hsiung-nu as a mark of Imperial Regard" [Giles]. Hers was the only grave in this desolate district on which grass would grow. [Waley's note.]

32. *Han:* i.e., Chinese. [Waley's note.]

Releasing a Migrant "Yen"

(WILD GOOSE)

At Nine Rivers, in the tenth year, in winter,—heavy snow;
The river-water covered with ice and the forests broken with
their load.
The birds of the air, hungry and cold, went flying east and west;
And with them flew a migrant "yen" loudly clamouring
for food.
Among the snow it pecked for grass; and rested on the surface
of the ice:
It tried with its wings to scale the sky; but its tired flight
was slow.
The boys of the river spread a net and caught the bird
as it flew;
They took it in their hands to the city-market and sold it
there alive.
I that was once a man of the North am now an exile here:
Bird and man, in their different kind, are each strangers
in the south.
And because the sight of an exiled bird wounded an exile's
heart,
I paid your ransom and set you free, and you flew away to
the clouds.
Yen, Yen, flying to the clouds, tell me, whither shall you go?
Of all things I bid you, do not fly to the land of the north-west;
In Huai-hsi there are rebel bands that have not been subdued;
And a thousand thousand armoured men have long been
camped in war.
The official army and the rebel army have grown old in their
opposite trenches;
The soldiers' rations have grown so small, they'll be glad
of even you.
The brave boys, in their hungry plight will shoot you and
eat your flesh;
They will pluck from your body those long feathers and make
them into arrow-wings!

1. *Nine Rivers:* Kiukiang, the poet's place of exile. [Waley's note.] On the Yangtze River some three hundred miles south-southwest of Shanghai. *tenth year:* 815 A.D. His first winter at Kiukiang. [Waley's note.]

2. *with their load:* by the weight of snow. [Waley's note.]

15. *rebel bands:* the revolt of Wu Yüan-chi. [Waley's note.] This took place in 815–817. Wu, a military governor, seized the river and canal transport lines near Lo-yang, on the Yellow River in Honan province.

Going to the Mountains with a Little Dancing Girl, Aged Fifteen

(WRITTEN WHEN THE POET WAS ABOUT SIXTY-FIVE)

Two top-knots not yet plaited into one.
Of thirty years—just beyond half.
You who are really a lady of silks and satins
Are now become my hill and stream companion!
At the spring fountains together we splash and play:
On the lovely trees together we climb and sport.
Her cheeks grow rosy, as she quickens her sleeve-dancing:
Her brows grow sad, as she slows her song's tune.
Don't go singing the song of the Willow Branches,
When there's no one here with a heart for you to break!

The Old Man with the Broken Arm

[A SATIRE ON MILITARISM]

At Hsin-fēng an old man—four-score and eight;
The hair on his head and the hair of his eyebrows—white as the new snow.
Leaning on the shoulders of his great-grandchildren, he walks in front of the Inn;
With his left arm he leans on their shoulders; his right arm is broken.
I asked the old man how many years had passed since he broke his arm;
I also asked the cause of the injury, how and why it happened?
The old man said he was born and reared in the District of Hsin-fēng;
At the time of his birth—a wise reign; no wars or discords.
"Often I listened in the Pear-Tree Garden to the sound of flute and song;
Naught I knew of banner and lance; nothing of arrow or bow.
Then came the wars of T'ien-pao and the great levy of men;
Of three men in each house,—one man was taken.
And those to whom the lot fell, where were they taken to?
Five months' journey, a thousand miles—away to Yün-nan.

9. *song of the Willow Branches:* a plaintive love song, to which Po Chü-i had himself written words. [Waley's note.]

11. *wars of T'ien-pao:* 742–755 A.D. [Waley's note.]

We heard it said that in Yün-nan there flows the Lu River;
As the flowers fall from the pepper-trees, poisonous vapours rise.
When the great army waded across, the water seethed like a cauldron;
When barely ten had entered the water, two or three were dead.
To the north of my village, to the south of my village the sound of weeping and wailing,
Children parting from fathers and mothers; husbands parting from wives.
Everyone says that in expeditions against the Min tribes
Of a million men who are sent out, not one returns.
I, that am old, was then twenty-four;
My name and fore-name were written down in the rolls of the Board of War.
In the depth of the night not daring to let any one know
I secretly took a huge stone and dashed it against my arm.
For drawing the bow and waving the banner now wholly unfit;
I knew henceforward I should not be sent to fight in Yün-nan.
Bones broken and sinews wounded could not fail to hurt;
I was ready enough to bear pain, if only I got back home.
My arm—broken ever since; it was sixty years ago.
One limb, although destroyed,—whole body safe!
But even now on winter nights when the wind and rain blow
From evening on till day's dawn I cannot sleep for pain.
Not sleeping for pain
Is a small thing to bear,
Compared with the joy of being alive when all the rest are dead.
For otherwise, years ago, at the ford of Lu River
My body would have died and my soul hovered by the bones that no one gathered.
A ghost, I'd have wandered in Yün-nan, always looking for home.
Over the graves of ten thousand soldiers, mournfully hovering."
So the old man spoke,
And I bid you listen to his words
Have you not heard
That the Prime Minister of K'ai-yüan, Sung K'ai-fu,
Did not reward frontier exploits, lest a spirit of aggression should prevail?

45. *Prime Minister of K'ai-yüan:* 713–742 A.D. [Waley's note.]

And have you not heard
That the Prime Minister of T'ien-Pao, Yang Kuo-chung
Desiring to win imperial favour, started a frontier war?
But long before he could win the war, people had lost their temper;
Ask the man with the broken arm in the village of Hsin-fēng!

After Passing the Examination

(A.D. 800)

For ten years I never left my books;
I went up . . . and won unmerited praise.
My high place I do not much prize;
The joy of my parents will first make me proud.
Fellow students, six or seven men,
See me off as I leave the City gate.
My covered couch is ready to drive away;
Flutes and strings blend their parting tune.
Hopes achieved dull the pains of parting;
Fumes of wine shorten the long road . . .
Shod with wings is the horse of him who rides
On a Spring day the road that leads to home.

Escorting Candidates to the Examination Hall

(A.D. 805)

At dawn I rode to escort the Doctors of Art;
In the eastern quarter the sky was still grey.
I said to myself, "You have started far too soon,"
But horses and coaches already thronged the road.
High and low the riders' torches bobbed;
Muffled or loud, the watchman's drum beat.
Riders, when I see you prick
To your early levée, pity fills my heart.
When the sun rises and the hot dust flies
And the creatures of earth resume their great strife,
You, with your striving, what shall you each seek?
Profit and fame, for that is all your care.
But I, you courtiers, rise from my bed at noon
And live idly in the city of Ch'ang-an.
Spring is deep and my term of office spent;
Day by day my thoughts go back to the hills.

The beams of her light shone in every place,
On towers and halls dancing to and fro.
Till day broke we sat in her clear light
Laughing and singing, and yet never grew tired.
In Ch'ang-an, the place of profit and fame,
Such moods as this, how many men know?

Watching the Reapers

(A.D. 806)

Tillers of the soil have few idle months;
In the fifth month their toil is double-fold.
A south-wind visits the fields at night:
Suddenly the hill is covered with yellow corn.
Wives and daughters shoulder baskets of rice;
Youths and boys carry the flasks of wine.
Following after they bring a wage of meat
To the strong reapers toiling on the southern hill,
Whose feet are burned by the hot earth they tread,
Whose backs are scorched by flames of the shining sky.
Tired they toil, caring nothing for the heat,
Grudging the shortness of the long summer day.
A poor woman follows at the reapers' side
With an infant child carried close at her breast.
With her right hand she gleans the fallen grain;
On her left arm a broken basket hangs.
And *I* to-day . . . by virtue of what right
Have I never once tended field or tree?
My government-pay is three hundred tons;
At the year's end I have still grain in hand.
Thinking of this, secretly I grew ashamed;
And all day the thought lingered in my head.

Going Alone to Spend a Night at the Hsien-yu Temple

(A.D. 806)

The crane from the shore standing at the top of the steps;
The moon on the pool seen at the open door;
Where these are, I made my lodging-place
And for two nights could not turn away.
I am glad I chanced on a place so lonely and still
With no companion to drag me early home.

Now that I have tasted the joy of being alone
I will never again come with a friend at my side.

Planting Bamboos

(A.D. 806)

Unrewarded, my will to serve the State;
At my closed door autumn grasses grow.
What could I do to ease a rustic heart?
I planted bamboos, more than a hundred shoots.
When I see their beauty, as they grow by the stream-side,
I feel again as though I lived in the hills,
And many a time on public holidays
Round their railing I walk till night comes.
Do not say that their roots are still weak,
Do not say that their shade is still small;
Already I feel that both in garden and house
Day by day a fresher air moves.
But most I love, lying near the window-side,
To hear in their branches the sound of the autumn-wind.

An Early Levée

[ADDRESSED TO CH'ĒN, THE HERMIT]

At Ch'ang-an—a full foot of snow;
A levée at dawn—to bestow congratulations on the Emperor.
Just as I was nearing the Gate of the Silver Terrace,
After I had left the súburb of Hsin-ch'ang
On the high causeway my horse's foot slipped;
In the middle of the journey my lantern suddenly went out.
Ten leagues riding, always facing to the North;
The cold wind almost blew off my ears.
I waited for the bell outside the Five Gates;
I waited for the summons within the Triple Hall.
My hair and beard were frozen and covered with icicles;
My coat and robe—chilly like water.
Suddenly I thought of Hsien-yu Valley
And secretly envied Ch'ēn Chü-shih,
In warm bed-socks dozing beneath the rugs
And not getting up till the sun has mounted the sky.

Being on Duty all Night in the Palace and Dreaming of Hsien-yu Temple

At the western window I paused from writing rescripts;
The pines and bamboos were all buried in stillness.

The moon rose and a calm wind came;
Suddenly, it was like an evening in the hills.
And so, as I dozed, I dreamed of the South West
And thought I was staying at the Hsien-yu Temple.
When I woke and heard the dripping of the Palace clock
I still thought it the murmur of a mountain stream.

The Letter

Preface: After I parted with Yüan Chēn, I suddenly dreamed one night that I saw him. When I awoke, I found that a letter from him had just arrived and, enclosed in it, a poem on the *paulovnia* flower.

We talked together in the Yung-shou Temple;
We parted to the north of the Hsin-ch'ang dyke.
Going home—I shed a few tears,
Grieving about things,—not sorry for you.
Long, long the road to Lan-t'ien;
You said yourself you would not be able to write.
Reckoning up your halts for eating and sleeping—
By this time you've crossed the Shang mountains.
Last night the clouds scattered away;
A thousand leagues, the same moonlight scene.
When dawn came, I dreamt I saw your face;
It must have been that you were thinking of me.
In my dream, I thought I held your hand
And asked you to tell me what your thoughts were.
And *you* said: "I miss you bitterly,
But there's no one here to send to you with a letter."
When I awoke, before I had time to speak,
A knocking on the door sounded "Doong, doong!"
They came and told me a messenger from Shang-chou
Had brought a letter,—a single scroll from you!
Up from my pillow I suddenly sprang out of bed,
And threw on my clothes, all topsy-turvy.
I undid the knot and saw the letter within;
A single sheet with thirteen lines of writing.
At the top it told the sorrows of an exile's heart;
At the bottom it described the pains of separation.
The sorrows and pains took up so much space
There was no room left to talk about the weather!

6. *Hsien-yu Temple:* where the poet used to spend his holidays. [Waley's note.]

4. *paulovnia:* a purple flower like the foxglove.

9. *road to Lan-t'ien:* the road from Ch'ang-an to Shang-chou to the southeast.

But you said that when you wrote
You were staying for the night to the east of Shang-chou;
Sitting alone, lighted by a solitary candle
Lodging in the mountain hostel of Yang-Ch'ēng.
Night was late when you finished writing,
The mountain moon was slanting towards the west.
What is it lies aslant across the moon?
A single tree of purple *paulovnia* flowers,
Paulovnia flowers just on the point of falling
Are a symbol to express "thinking of an absent friend."
Lovingly—you wrote on the back side,
To send in the letter, your "Poem of the Paulovnia Flower."
The "Poem of the Paulovnia Flower" has eight rhymes;
Yet these eight couplets have cast a spell on my heart.
They have taken hold of this morning's thoughts
And carried them to yours, the night you wrote your letter.
The whole poem I read three times;
Each verse ten times I recite.
So precious to me are the fourscore words
That each letter changes into a bar of gold!

Passing T'ien-mēn Street in Ch'ang-an and Seeing a Distant View of Chung-nan Mountain

The snow has gone from Chung-nan; spring is almost come.
Lovely in the distance its blue colours, against the brown of the streets.
A thousand coaches, ten thousand horsemen pass down the Nine Roads;
Turns his head and looks at the mountains,—not one man!

Golden Bells

When I was almost forty
I had a daughter whose name was Golden Bells.
Now it is just a year since she was born;
She is learning to sit and cannot yet talk.
Ashamed,—to find that I have not a sage's heart:
I cannot resist vulgar thoughts and feelings.
Henceforward I am tied to things outside myself:
My only reward,—the pleasure I am getting now.
If I am spared the grief of her dying young,
Then I shall have the trouble of getting her married.
My plan for retiring and going back to the hills
Must now be postponed for fifteen years!

1. *Chung-nan:* part of the great Nan Shan range, fifteen miles south of Ch'ang-an. [Waley's note.]

Remembering Golden Bells

Ruined and ill,—a man of two score;
Pretty and guileless,—a girl of three.
Not a boy,—but still better than nothing:
To soothe one's feeling,—from time to time a kiss!
There came a day,—they suddenly took her from me;
Her soul's shadow wandered I know not where.
And when I remember how just at the time she died
She lisped strange sounds, beginning to learn to talk,
Then I know that the ties of flesh and blood
Only bind us to a load of grief and sorrow.
At last, by thinking of the time before she was born,
By thought and reason I drove the pain away.
Since my heart forgot her, many days have passed
And three times winter has changed to spring.
This morning, for a little, the old grief came back,
Because, in the road, I met her foster-nurse.

WU CH'ENG-EN
(ca. 16th Century)
Monkey (*Hsi Yu Chi*)

Wu Ch'eng-en seems to have lived in Kiangsu Province at Huai-an, some one hundred miles north of Nanking, in the sixteenth century A.D. Some of his poems survive in Ming anthologies. He tells of his interest in stories about monsters in a preface to a book of tales, apparently composed in classical Chinese to imitate the stylists of the T'ang period (618–906 A.D.). The sixteenth century in Chinese literature was a period of classical revival and return to T'ang models. Wu, however, read and enjoyed the literature of the people, which was written in the colloquial language and consisted of tales of heroes, ghost stories, detective stories, and fantasy. Two rambling and episodic novels of large scale, the *Romance of the Three Kingdoms* (*San-Kuo-Chih Yen-i*) and *The Story of the Water Margin* (*Shui-hu Chuan*) had attained their present form by the end of the fifteenth century, and there was a considerable vogue of fiction in the colloquial language, though it was frowned on by the upper classes and children were punished for reading such books. Wu did not sign his name to *Monkey* (the title literally means *Record of a Journey to the West*); it would have brought disgrace to any man of letters to acknowledge such a work.

Monkey is an extravagant fantasy, especially compared to the pedestrian realism of the two novels mentioned above. In its one hundred chapters it takes as its main subject matter the journey of the Buddhist priest Hsüan-tsang to India to collect sacred texts in the seventh century A.D. Hsüan-tsang, also known as Tripitaka, left an important account of India and central Asia. But by the tenth century he had become the subject of legends, many of them fantastic, and from the thirteenth century on is represented on the Chinese stage, his deeds much romanticized. In Wu Ch'eng-en's version, the great sage is beset by supernatural obstacles as he makes his holy journey and is helped out of his predicaments by the fabulous stone monkey who is, dramatically at least, the main character of the work.

Monkey combines several elements. It is the story of a pilgrimage with the religious connotations all such journeys have, a journey in search of spiritual salvation symbolized by the overcoming of physical obstacles. Tripitaka seems to stand for the ordinary man, and Monkey for the instability of genius. The society in which Monkey travels, no matter how spiritual it may seem to be, is an imitation of earthly society with all its bureaucracy and unreasonable ritual. But the work is also meant to be humorous: religion is satirized, but this does not signify that the author is anti-religious. The Chinese do not think that some amusement at the expense of religion constitutes a repudiation of it. Thus, Monkey's training at the hands of the master in Chapter I is a satire on such training as is given by holy men in monasteries even to this day. But Monkey does benefit from the training, nevertheless, and moves towards enlightenment and great deeds. The work is a mixture of satire and folk tale, fictionized history and religious allegory. Though it should be read as a fantasy, not as a profound religious treatise, there is serious meaning in Wu's treatment of society and bureaucracy.

From Monkey*

I

There was a rock that since the creation of the world had been worked upon by the pure essences of Heaven and the fine savours of Earth, the vigour of sunshine and the grace of moonlight, till at last it became magically pregnant and one day split open, giving birth to a stone egg, about as big as a playing ball. Fructified by the wind it developed into a stone monkey, complete with every organ and limb. At once this monkey learned to climb and run; but its first act was to make a bow towards each of the four quarters. As it did so, a steely light darted from this monkey's eyes and flashed as far as the Palace of the Pole Star. This shaft of light astonished the

Jade Emperor as he sat in the Cloud Palace of the Golden Gates, in the Treasure Hall of the Holy Mists, surrounded by his fairy Ministers. Seeing this strange light flashing, he ordered Thousand-league Eye and Down-the-wind Ears to open the gate of the Southern Heaven and look out. At his bidding these two captains went out to the gate and looked so sharply and listened so well that presently they were able to report, 'This steely light comes from the borders of the small country of Ao-lai, that lies to the east of the Holy Continent, from the Mountain of Flowers and Fruit. On this mountain is a magic rock, which gave birth to an egg. This egg changed into a stone monkey, and when he made his bow to the four quarters a steely light flashed from his eyes with a beam that reached the Palace of the Pole Star. But now he is taking a drink, and the light is growing dim.'

The Jade Emperor condescended to take an indulgent view. 'These creatures in the world below,' he said, 'were compounded of the essence of heaven and earth, and nothing that goes on there should surprise us.' That monkey walked, ran, leapt and bounded over the hills, feeding on grasses and shrubs, drinking from streams and springs, gathering the mountain flowers, looking for fruits. Wolf, panther and tiger were his companions, the deer and civet[1] were his friends, gibbons and baboons his kindred. At night he lodged under cliffs of rock, by day he wandered among the peaks and caves. One very hot morning, after playing in the shade of some pine-trees, he and the other monkeys went to bathe in a mountain stream. See how those waters bounce and tumble like rolling melons!

There is an old saying, 'Birds have their bird language, beasts have their beast talk.' The monkeys said, 'We none of us know where this stream comes from. As we have nothing to do this morning, wouldn't it be fun to follow it up to its source?' With a whoop of joy, dragging their sons and carrying their daughters, calling out to younger brother and to elder brother, the whole troupe rushed along the streamside and scrambled up the steep places, till they reached the source of the stream. They found themselves standing before the curtain of a great waterfall.

All the monkeys clapped their hands and cried aloud, 'Lovely water, lovely water! To think that it starts far off in some cavern below the base of the mountain, and flows all the way to the Great Sea! If any of us were bold enough to pierce that curtain, get to where the water comes from and return unharmed, we would make him our king!' Three times the call went out, when suddenly one of them leapt from among the throng and answered the challenge in a loud voice. It was the Stone Monkey. 'I will

1. a wild, catlike creature which grows to a length of several feet.

go,' he cried, 'I will go!' Look at him! He screws up his eyes and crouches; then at one bound he jumps straight through the waterfall. When he opened his eyes and looked about him, he found that where he had landed there was no water. A great bridge stretched in front of him, shining and glinting. When he looked closely at it, he saw that it was made all of burnished iron. The water under it flowed through a hole in the rock, filling in all the space under the arch. Monkey climbed up on to the bridge and, spying as he went, saw something that looked just like a house. There were stone seats and stone couches, and tables with stone bowls and cups. He skipped back to the hump of the bridge and saw that on the cliff there was an inscription in large square writing which said, 'This cave of the Water Curtain in the blessed land of the Mountain of Flowers and Fruit leads to Heaven.'[2] Monkey was beside himself with delight. He rushed back and again crouched, shut his eyes and jumped through the curtain of water.

'A great stroke of luck,' he cried, 'A great stroke of luck!' 'What is it like on the other side?' asked the monkeys, crowding round him. 'Is the water very deep?' 'There is no water,' said the Stone Monkey. 'There is an iron bridge, and at the side of it a heaven-sent place to live in.' 'What made you think it would do to live in?' asked the monkeys. 'The water,' said the Stone Monkey, 'flows out of a hole in the rock, filling in the space under the bridge. At the side of the bridge are flowers and trees, and there is a chamber of stone. Inside are stone tables, stone cups, stone dishes, stone couches, stone seats. We could really be very comfortable there. There is plenty of room for hundreds and thousands of us, young and old. Let us all go and live there; we shall be splendidly sheltered in every weather.' 'You go first and show us how!' cried the monkeys, in great delight. Once more he closed his eyes and was through at one bound. 'Come along, all of you!' he cried. The bolder of them jumped at once; the more timid stretched out their heads and then drew them back, scratched their ears, rubbed their cheeks, and then with a great shout the whole mob leapt forward. Soon they were all seizing dishes and snatching cups, scrambling to the hearth or fighting for the beds, dragging things along or shifting them about, behaving indeed as monkeys with their mischievous nature might be expected to do, never quiet for an instant, till at last they were thoroughly worn out. The Stone Monkey took his seat at the head of them and said, 'Gentlemen! "With one whose word cannot be trusted there is nothing to be

2. This inscription is translated by Hu Shih to read: "The Blessed Land of the Mountain of Flower and Fruit and the Heavenly Grotto of the Water Curtain Cave." [Waley's note.]

done!"[3] You promised that any of us who managed to get through the waterfall and back again, should be your king. I have not only come and gone and come again, but also found you a comfortable place to sleep, put you in the enviable position of being householders. Why do you not bow down to me as your king?'

Thus reminded, the monkeys all pressed together the palms of their hands and prostrated themselves, drawn up in a line according to age and standing, and bowing humbly they cried, 'Great king, a thousand years!' After this the Stone Monkey discarded his old name and became king, with the title 'Handsome Monkey King.' He appointed various monkeys, gibbons and baboons to be his ministers and officers. By day they wandered about the Mountain of Flowers and Fruit; at night they slept in the Cave of the Water Curtain. They lived in perfect sympathy and accord, not mingling with bird or beast, in perfect independence and entire happiness.

The Monkey King had enjoyed this artless existence for several hundred years when one day, at a feast in which all the monkeys took part, the king suddenly felt very sad and burst into tears. His subjects at once ranged themselves in front of him and bowed down, saying, 'Why is your Majesty so sad?' 'At present,' said the king, 'I have no cause for unhappiness. But I have a misgiving about the future, which troubles me sorely.' 'Your Majesty is very hard to please,' said the monkeys, laughing. 'Every day we have happy meetings on fairy mountains, in blessed spots, in ancient caves, on holy islands. We are not subject to the Unicorn or Phoenix,[4] nor to the restraints of any human king. Such freedom is an immeasurable blessing. What can it be that causes you this sad misgiving?' 'It is true,' said the Monkey King, 'that to-day I am not answerable to the law of any human king, nor need I fear the menace of any beast or bird. But the time will come when I shall grow old and weak. Yama, King of Death, is secretly waiting to destroy me. Is there no way by which, instead of being born again on earth, I might live forever among the people of the sky?'

When the monkeys heard this they covered their faces with their hands and wept, each thinking of his own mortality. But look! From among the ranks there springs out one monkey commoner, who cries in a loud voice 'If that is what troubles your Majesty, it shows that religion has taken hold upon your heart. There are indeed, among all creatures, three kinds that are not subject to Yama, King of Death.' 'And do you know which they are?' asked the Monkey King. 'Buddhas, Immortals[5] and Sages,' he said. 'These three are

3. *Analects* of Confucius, II, xxii. [Waley's note.]

4. as in western legend, two creatures with supernatural powers.

5. The immortals are Bodhisattvas who could become Buddhas but prefer to act as mediators between ordinary men and the Buddha.

exempt from the Turning of the Wheel, from birth and destruction. They are eternal as Heaven and Earth, as the hills and streams.' 'Where are they to be found?' asked the Monkey King. 'Here on the common earth,' said the monkey, 'in ancient caves among enchanted hills.'

The king was delighted with this news. 'To-morrow,' he said, 'I shall say good-bye to you, go down the mountain, wander like a cloud to the corners of the sea, far away to the end of the world, till I have found these three kinds of Immortal. From them I will learn how to be young forever and escape the doom of death.' This determination it was that led him to leap clear of the toils of Reincarnation and turned him at last into the Great Monkey Sage, equal of Heaven. The monkeys clapped their hands and cried aloud, 'Splendid! Splendid! To-morrow we will scour the hills for fruits and berries and hold a great farewell banquet in honour of our king.'

Next day they duly went to gather peaches and rare fruits, mountain herbs, yellow-sperm, tubers, orchids, strange plants and flowers of every sort, and set out the stone tables and benches, laid out fairy meats and drinks. They put the Monkey King at the head of the table, and ranged themselves according to their age and rank. The pledge-cup passed from hand to hand; they made their offerings to him of flowers and fruit. All day long they drank, and next day their king rose early and said, 'Little ones, cut some pine-wood for me and make me a raft; then find a tall bamboo for pole, and put together a few fruits and such like. I am going to start.' He got on to the raft all alone and pushed off with all his might, speeding away and away, straight out to sea, till favoured by a following wind he arrived at the borders of the Southern World. Fate indeed had favoured him; for days on end, ever since he set foot on the raft, a strong south-east wind blew and carried him at last to the north-western bank, which is indeed the frontier of the Southern World. He tested the water with his pole and found that it was shallow; so he left the raft and climbed ashore. On the beach were people fishing, shooting wild geese, scooping oysters, draining salt. He ran up to them and for fun began to perform queer antics which frightened them so much that they dropped their baskets and nets and ran for their lives. One of them, who stood his ground, Monkey caught hold of, and ripping off his clothes, found out how to wear them himself, and so dressed up went prancing through towns and cities, in market and bazaar, imitating the people's manners and talk. All the while his heart was set only on finding the Immortals and learning from them the secret of eternal youth. But he found the men of the world all engrossed in the quest of profit or fame; there was not one who had any care for the end that was in store for him. So Monkey went looking for the way of Immortality, but found no chance of meeting it. For eight or nine years he went from city to city and town to town till suddenly he came to the Western Ocean. He was sure that beyond this ocean there would certainly be Immortals, and he made for himself a raft like the one he had before. He floated on over the Western Ocean till he came to the Western Continent, where he went ashore, and when he had looked about for some time, he suddenly saw a very high and beautiful mountain, thickly wooded at the base. He had no fear of wolves, tigers or panthers, and made his way up to the very top. He was looking about him when he suddenly heard a man's voice coming from deep amid the woods. He hurried towards the spot and listened intently. It was some one singing, and these were the words that he caught:

I hatch no plot, I scheme no scheme;
Fame and shame are one to me,
A simple life prolongs my days.
Those I meet upon my way
Are Immortals, one and all,
Who from their quiet seats expound
The Scriptures of the Yellow Court.

When Monkey heard these words he was very pleased. 'There must then be Immortals somewhere hereabouts,' he said. He sprang deep into the forest and looking carefully saw that the singer was a woodman, who was cutting brushwood. 'Reverend Immortal,' said Monkey, coming forward, 'your disciple raises his hands.' The woodman was so astonished that he dropped his axe. 'You have made a mistake,' he said, turning and answering the salutation, 'I am only a shabby, hungry woodcutter. What makes you address me as an "Immortal"?' 'If you are not an Immortal,' said Monkey, 'why did you talk of yourself as though you were one?' 'What did I say,' asked the woodcutter, 'that sounded as though I were an Immortal?' 'When I came to the edge of the wood,' said Monkey, 'I heard you singing "Those I meet upon my way are Immortals, one and all, who from their quiet seats expound the Scriptures of the Yellow Court." Those scriptures are secret, Taoist[6] texts. What can you be but an Immortal?' 'I won't deceive you,' said the woodcutter. 'That song was indeed taught to me by an Immortal, who lives not very far from my hut. He saw that I have to work hard for my living and have a lot of troubles; so he told me when I was worried by anything to say to myself the words of that song. This, he said, would comfort me and get me out of my difficulties. Just now I was upset about something and so I was singing that song. I had no idea that you were listening.'

6. For Taoism, see p. 407. Taoist sects, when they degenerated in later times, emphasized the practice of "white" and "black" magic.

'If the Immortal lives close by,' said Monkey, 'how is it that you have not become his disciple? Wouldn't it have been as well to learn from him how never to grow old?' 'I have a hard life of it,' said the woodcutter. 'When I was eight or nine I lost my father. I had no brothers and sisters, and it fell upon me alone to support my widowed mother. There was nothing for it but to work hard early and late. Now my mother is old and I dare not leave her. The garden is neglected, we have not enough either to eat or wear. The most I can do is to cut two bundles of firewood, carry them to market and with the penny or two that I get buy a few handfuls of rice which I cook myself and serve to my aged mother. I have no time to go and learn magic.' 'From what you tell me,' said Monkey, 'I can see that you are a good and devoted son, and your piety will certainly be rewarded. All I ask of you is that you will show me where the Immortal lives; for I should very much like to visit him.'

'It is quite close,' said the woodcutter. 'This mountain is called the Holy Terrace Mountain, and on it is a cave called the Cave of the Slanting Moon and Three Stars. In that cave lives an Immortal called the Patriarch Subodhi.[7] In his time he has had innumerable disciples, and at this moment there are some thirty or forty of them studying with him. You have only to follow that small path southwards for eight or nine leagues,[8] and you will come to his home.' 'Honoured brother,' said Monkey, drawing the woodcutter towards him, 'come with me, and if I profit by the visit I will not forget that you guided me.' 'It takes a lot to make some people understand,' said the woodcutter. 'I've just been telling you why I can't go. If I went with you, what would become of my work? Who would give my old mother her food? I must go on cutting my wood, and you must find your way alone.'

When Monkey heard this, he saw nothing for it but to say goodbye. He left the wood, found the path, went uphill for some seven or eight leagues and sure enough found a cave-dwelling. But the door was locked. All was quiet, and there was no sign of anyone being about. Suddenly he turned his head and saw on top of the cliff a stone slab about thirty feet high and eight feet wide. On it was an inscription in large letters saying, 'Cave of the Slanting Moon and Three Stars on the Mountain of the Holy Terrace.' 'People here,' said Monkey, 'are certainly very truthful. There really is such a mountain, and such a cave!' He looked about for a while, but did not venture to knock at the door. Instead he jumped up into a pinetree and began eating the pine-seed and playing among the branches. After a time he heard someone call; the door of the cave opened and a fairy boy of great beauty came out, in appearance utterly

7. *Bodhi* is Sanskrit for "supreme enlightenment." This is the sage's honorary name.

8. A "league" was 360 steps. [Waley's note.]

unlike the common lads that he had seen till now. The boy shouted, 'Who is making a disturbance out there?' Monkey leapt down from his tree, and coming forward said with a bow, 'Fairy boy, I am a pupil who has come to study Immortality. I should not dream of making a disturbance.' '*You* a pupil!' said the boy laughing. 'To be sure,' said Monkey. 'My master is lecturing,' said the boy. 'But before he gave out his theme he told me to go to the door and if anyone came asking for instruction, I was to look after him. I suppose he meant you.' 'Of course he meant me,' said Monkey. 'Follow me this way,' said the boy. Monkey tidied himself and followed the boy into the cave. Huge chambers opened out before them, they went on from room to room, through lofty halls and innumerable cloisters and retreats, till they came to a platform of green jade, upon which was seated the Patriarch Subodhi, with thirty lesser Immortals assembled before him. Monkey at once prostrated himself and bumped his head three times upon the ground, murmuring, 'Master, master! As pupil to teacher I pay you my humble respects.' 'Where do you come from?' asked the Patriarch. 'First tell me your country and name, and then pay your respects again.' 'I am from the Water Curtain Cave,' said Monkey, 'on the Mountain of Fruit and Flowers in the country of Ao-lai.' 'Go away!' shouted the Patriarch. 'I know the people there. They're a tricky, humbugging set. It's no good one of them supposing he's going to achieve Enlightenment.' Monkey, kowtowing violently, hastened to say, 'There's no trickery about this; it's just the plain truth I'm telling you.' 'If you claim that you're telling the truth,' said the Patriach, 'how is it that you say you came from Ao-lai? Between there and here there are two oceans and the whole of the Southern Continent. How did you get here?' 'I floated over the oceans and wandered over the lands for ten years and more,' said Monkey, 'till at last I reached here.' 'Oh well,' said the Patriarch, 'I suppose if you came by easy stages, it's not altogether impossible. But tell me, what is your *hsing*?'[9] 'I never show *hsing*,' said Monkey. 'If I am abused, I am not at all annoyed. If I am hit, I am not angry; but on the contrary, twice more polite than before. All my life I have never shown *hsing*.'

'I don't mean that kind of *hsing*,' said the Patriarch. 'I mean what was your family, what surname had they?' 'I had no family,' said Monkey, 'neither father nor mother.' 'Oh indeed!' said the Patriarch. 'Perhaps you grew on a tree!' 'Not exactly,' said Monkey. 'I came out of a stone. There was a magic stone on the Mountain of Flowers and Fruit. When its time came, it burst open and I came out.'

'We shall have to see about giving you a school-name,' said the Patriarch. 'We have twelve words that we use in these names, ac-

9. This is a pun on *hsing*, "surname," and *hsing*, "temper." [Waley's note.]

cording to the grade of the pupil. You are in the tenth grade.' 'What are the twelve words?' asked Monkey. 'They are Wide, Big, Wise, Clever, True, Conforming, Nature, Ocean, Lively, Aware, Perfect and Illumined. As you belong to the tenth grade, the word Aware must come in your name. How about Aware-of-Vacuity?' 'Splendid!' said Monkey, laughing. 'From now onwards let me be called Aware-of-Vacuity.'

So that was his name in religion. And if you do not know whether in the end, equipped with this name, he managed to obtain enlightenment or not, listen while it is explained to you in the next chapter.

II

Monkey was so pleased with his new name that he skipped up and down in front of the Patriarch, bowing to express his gratitude. Subodhi then ordered his pupils to take Monkey to the outer rooms and teach him how to sprinkle and dust, answer properly when spoken to, how to come in, go out, and go round. Then he bowed to his fellow-pupils and went out into the corridor, where he made himself a sleeping place. Early next morning he and the others practised the correct mode of speech and bearing, studied the Scriptures, discussed doctrine, practised writing, burnt incense. And in this same way he passed day after day, spending his leisure in sweeping the floor, hoeing the garden, growing flowers and tending trees, getting firewood and lighting the fire, drawing water and carrying it in buckets. Everything he needed was provided for him. And so he lived in the cave, while time slipped by, for six or seven years. One day the Patriarch, seated in state, summoned all his pupils and began a lecture on the Great Way. Monkey was so delighted by what he heard that he tweaked his ears and rubbed his cheeks; his brow flowered and his eyes laughed. He could not stop his hands from dancing, his feet from stamping. Suddenly the Patriarch caught sight of him and shouted, 'What is the use of your being here if, instead of listening to my lecture, you jump and dance like a maniac?' 'I am listening with all my might,' said Monkey. 'But you were saying such wonderful things that I could not contain myself for joy. That is why I may, for all I know, have been hopping and jumping. Don't be angry with me.' 'So you recognize the profundity of what I am saying?' said the Patriarch. 'How long, pray, have you been in the cave?' 'It may seem rather silly,' said Monkey, 'but really I don't know how long. All I can remember is that when I was sent to get firewood, I went up the mountain behind the cave, and there I found a whole slope covered with peach-trees. I have eaten my fill of those peaches seven times.' 'It is called the Hill of Bright Peach Blossom,' said the Patriarch. 'If you have eaten there seven times, I suppose you have been here seven years. What sort of wisdom are you now hoping to learn from me?' 'I leave that to you,' said Monkey. 'Any sort of wisdom—it's all one to me.'[10]

'There are three hundred and sixty schools of wisdom,' said the Patriarch, 'and all of them lead to Self-attainment. Which school do you want to study?' 'Just as you think best,' said Monkey. 'I am all attention.' 'Well, how about Art?' said the Patriarch. 'Would you like me to teach you that?' 'What sort of wisdom is that?' asked Monkey. 'You would be able to summon fairies and ride the Phoenix,' said the Patriarch, 'divine by shuffling the yarrow-stalks and know how to avoid disaster and pursue good fortune.' 'But should I live forever?' asked Monkey. 'Certainly not,' said the Patriarch. 'Then that's no good to me,' said Monkey. 'How about natural philosophy?' said the Patriarch. 'What is that about?' asked Monkey. 'It means the teaching of Confucius,' said the Patriarch, 'and of Buddha and Lao Tzu, of the Dualists and Mo Tzu and the Doctors of Medicine; reading scriptures, saying prayers, learning how to have adepts and sages at your beck and call.' 'But should I live forever?' asked Monkey. 'If that's what you are thinking about,' said the Patriarch, 'I am afraid philosophy is no better than a prop in the wall.' 'Master,' said Monkey, 'I am a plain, simple man, and I don't understand that sort of patter. What do you mean by a prop in the wall?' 'When men are building a room,' said the Patriarch, 'and want it to stand firm, they put a pillar to prop up the walls. But one day the roof falls in and the pillar rots.' 'That doesn't sound much like long life,' said Monkey. 'I'm not going to learn philosophy!' 'How about Quietism?' asked the Patriarch. 'What does that consist of?' asked Monkey. 'Low diet,' said the Patriarch, 'inactivity, meditation, restraint of word and deed, yoga practised prostrate or standing.' 'But should I live forever?' asked Monkey. 'The results of Quietism,' said the Patriarch, 'are no better than unbaked clay in the kiln.' 'You've got a very poor memory,' said Monkey. 'Didn't I tell you just now that I don't understand that sort of patter? What do you mean by unbaked clay in the kiln?' 'The bricks and tiles,' said the Patriarch, 'may be waiting, all shaped and ready, in the kiln; but if they have not yet been fired, there will come a day when heavy rain falls and they are washed away.' 'That does not promise well for the future,' said Monkey. 'I don't think I'll bother about Quietism.'

'You might try exercises,' said the Patriarch. 'What do you mean by that,' asked Monkey. 'Various forms of activity,' said the Patriarch, 'such as the exercises[11] called "Gathering the Yin and patch-

10. This statement seems naïve and comical, but it is also profoundly philosophical. To experience true wisdom or enlightenment is to make all things one.

11. These are exercises comparable to present-day *yoga* practice in India. For *Yang* and *Yin*, see p. 411, footnote 8. The other activities satirize the occult philosophers, who, like Faust, are busy in the laboratory.

ing the Yang," "Drawing the Bow and Treading the Catapult," "Rubbing the Navel to pass breath." Then there are alchemical practices such as the Magical Explosion, Burning the Reeds and Striking the Tripod, Promoting Red Lead, Melting the Autumn Stone, and Drinking Bride's Milk.' 'Would these make me live forever?' asked Monkey. 'To hope for that,' said the Patriarch, 'would be like trying to fish the moon out of the water.' 'There you go again!' said Monkey. 'What pray do you mean by fishing the moon out of the water?' 'When the moon is in the sky,' said the Patriarch, 'it is reflected in the water. It looks just like a real thing, but if you try to catch hold of it, you find it is only an illusion.' 'That does not sound much good,' said Monkey; 'I shan't learn exercises.' 'Tut!' cried the Patriarch, and coming down from the platform, he caught hold of the knuckle-rapper and pointed it at Monkey, saying, 'You wretched simian! You won't learn this and you won't learn that! I should like to know what it is you do want.' And so saying he struck Monkey over the head three times. Then he folded his hands behind his back and strode off into the inner room, dismissing his audience and locking the door behind him. The pupils all turned indignantly upon Monkey. 'You villainous ape,' they shouted at him, 'do you think that is the way to behave? The Master offers to teach you, and instead of accepting thankfully, you begin arguing with him. Now he's thoroughly offended and goodness knows when he'll come back.' They were all very angry and poured abuse on him; but Monkey was not in the least upset, and merely replied by a broad grin. The truth of the matter was, he understood the language of secret signs. That was why he did not take up the quarrel or attempt to argue. He knew that the Master, by striking him three times, was giving him an appointment at the third watch; and by going off with his hands folded behind his back, meant that Monkey was to look for him in the inner apartments. The locking of the door meant that he was to come round by the back door and would then receive instruction.

The rest of the day he frolicked with the other pupils in front of the cave, impatiently awaiting the night. As soon as dusk came, like the others, he went to his sleeping place. He closed his eyes and pretended to be asleep, breathing softly and regularly. In the mountains there is no watchman to beat the watches or call the hours. The best Monkey could do was to count his incoming and outgoing breaths. When he reckoned that it must be about the hour of the Rat[12] (11 p.m.–1 a.m.) he got up very quietly and slipped on his clothes, softly opened the front door, left his companions and went round to the back door. Sure enough, it was only half shut. 'The Master certainly means to give me instruction,' said Monkey to himself.

12. The hours of the day and the years of a dynasty are given animal names.

'That is why he left the door open.' So he crept in and went straight to the Master's bed. Finding him curled up and lying with his face to the wall, Monkey dared not wake him, and knelt down beside the bed. Presently the Patriarch woke, stretched out his legs and murmured to himself:

> Hard, very hard!
> The Way is most secret.
> Never handle the Golden Elixir as though it were a mere toy!
> He who to unworthy ears entrusts the dark truths
> To no purpose works his jaws and talks his tongue dry.

'Master, I've been kneeling here for some time,' said Monkey, when he saw the Patriarch was awake. 'You wretched Monkey,' said Subodhi, who on recognizing his voice pulled off the bed-clothes and sat up. 'Why aren't you asleep in your own quarters, instead of coming round behind to mine?' 'At the lecture to-day,' said Monkey, 'you ordered me to come for instruction at the third watch, by way of the back gate. That is why I ventured to come straight to your bed.' The Patriarch was delighted. He thought to himself 'This fellow must really be, as he says, a natural product of Heaven and Earth. Otherwise he would never have understood my secret signs.' 'We are alone together,' said Monkey, 'there is no one to overhear us. Take pity upon me and teach me the way of Long Life. I shall never forget your kindness.' 'You show a disposition,' said the Patriarch. 'You understood my secret signs. Come close and listen carefully. I am going to reveal to you the Secret of Long Life.' Monkey beat his head on the floor to show his gratitude, washed his ears and attended closely, kneeling beside the bed. The Patriarch then recited:

> To spare and tend the vital powers, this and nothing else
> Is sum and total of all magic, secret and profane.
> All is comprised in these three, Spirit, Breath and Soul;
> Guard them closely, screen them well; let there be no leak.
> Store them within the frame;
> That is all that can be learnt, and all that can be taught.
> I would have you mark the tortoise and snake, locked in tight embrace.
> Locked in tight embrace, the vital powers are strong;
> Even in the midst of fierce flames the Golden Lotus[13] may be planted,
> The Five Elements compounded and transposed, and put to new use.
> When that is done, be which you please, Buddha or Immortal.

By these words Monkey's whole nature was shaken to the founda-

13. symbol of wisdom and beauty. One of the great *sutras* (sacred books) of Buddhism is called the *Lotus Sutra*.

tions. He carefully committed them to memory; then humbly thanked the Patriarch, and went out again by the back door.

A pale light was just coming into the eastern sky. He retraced his steps, softly opened the front door and returned to his sleeping place, purposely making a rustling noise with his bed-clothes. 'Get up!' he cried. 'There is light in the sky.' His fellow pupils were fast asleep, and had no idea that Monkey had received Illumination.

Time passed swiftly, and three years later the Patriarch again mounted his jewelled seat and preached to his assembled followers. His subject was the parables and scholastic problems of the Zen[14] Sect, and his theme, the tegument[15] of outer appearances. Suddenly he broke off and asked, 'Where is the disciple Aware-of-Vacuity?' Monkey knelt down before him and answered 'Here!' 'What have you been studying all this time?' asked the Patriarch. 'Recently,' said Monkey, 'my spiritual nature has been very much in the ascendant, and my fundamental sources of power are gradually strengthening.' 'In that case,' said the Patriarch, 'all you need learn is how to ward off the Three Calamities.' 'There must be some mistake,' said Monkey in dismay. 'I understood that the secrets I have learnt would make me live forever and protect me from fire, water and every kind of disease. What is this about three calamities?' 'What you have learnt,' said the Patriarch, 'will preserve your youthful appearance and increase the length of your life; but after five hundred years Heaven will send down lightning which will finish you off, unless you have the sagacity to avoid it. After another five hundred years Heaven will send down a fire that will devour you. This fire is of a peculiar kind. It is neither common fire, nor celestial fire, but springs up from within and consumes the vitals, reducing the whole frame to ashes, and making a vanity of all your thousand years of self-perfection. But even should you escape this, in another five hundred years, a wind will come and blow upon you. Not the east wind, the south wind, the west wind or the north wind; not flower wind, or willow wind, pine wind or bamboo wind. It blows from below, enters the bowels, passes the midriff and issues at the Nine Apertures.[16] It melts bone and flesh, so that the whole body dissolves. These three calamities you must be able to avoid.' When Monkey heard this, his hair stood on end, and prostrating himself he said, 'I beseech you, have pity upon me, and teach me how to avoid these calamities. I shall never forget your kindness.' 'There would be no difficulty about that,' said the Patriarch, 'if it were not for your peculiarities.' 'I have a round head sticking up to Heaven

14. Zen (or *Ch'an*, as it is called in China) Buddhism favors sudden enlightenment through the imaginative solving of verbal paradoxes and puts less emphasis on the study of scripture than does traditional Buddhism.

15. covering.

16. Each nostril and the eyes are counted in the nine apertures.

and square feet treading Earth,' said Monkey. 'I have nine apertures, four limbs, five upper and six lower internal organs, just like other people.' 'You are like other men in most respects,' said the Patriarch, 'but you have much less jowl.' For monkeys have hollow cheeks and pointed nozzles. Monkey felt his face with his hand and laughed saying, 'Master, I have my debits, but don't forget my assets. I have my pouch, and that must be credited to my account, as something that ordinary humans haven't got.' 'True enough,' said the Patriarch. 'There are two methods of escape. Which would you like to learn? There is the trick of the Heavenly Ladle, which involves thirty-six kinds of transformation, and the trick of the Earthly Conclusion, which involves seventy-two kinds of transformation.' 'Seventy-two sounds better value,' said Monkey. 'Come here then,' said the Patriarch, 'and I will teach you the formula.' He then whispered a magic formula into Monkey's ear. That Monkey King was uncommonly quick at taking things in. He at once began practising the formula, and after a little self-discipline he mastered all the seventy-two transformations, whole and complete. One day when master and disciples were in front of the cave, admiring the evening view, the Patriarch said, 'Monkey, how is that business going?' 'Thanks to your kindness,' said Monkey, 'I have been extremely successful. In addition to the transformations I can already fly.' 'Let's see you do it,' said the Patriarch. Monkey put his feet together, leapt about sixty feet into the air, and riding the clouds for a few minutes dropped in front of the Patriarch. He did not get more than three leagues in the whole of his flight. 'Master,' he said, 'that surely is cloud-soaring?' 'I should be more inclined to call it cloud-crawling,' said the Patriarch laughing. 'The old saying runs, "An Immortal wanders in the morning to the Northern Sea, and the same evening he is in Ts'ang-wu." To take as long as you did to go a mere league or two hardly counts even as cloud-crawling.' 'What is meant by that saying about the Northern Sea and Ts'ang-wu?' asked Monkey. 'A real cloud-soarer,' said the Patriarch, 'can start early in the morning from the Northern Sea, cross the Eastern Sea, the Western Sea and the Southern Sea, and land again at Ts'ang-wu. Ts'ang-wu means Ling-ling, in the Northern Sea. To do the round of all four seas in one day is true cloud-soaring.' 'It sounds very difficult,' said Monkey. 'Nothing in the world is difficult,' said the Patriarch, 'it is only our own thoughts that make things seem so.' 'Master,' said Monkey, prostrating himself, 'You may as well make a good job of me. While you're about it, do me a real kindness and teach me the art of cloud-soaring. I shall never forget how much I owe to you.' 'When the Immortals go cloud-soaring,' said the Patriarch, 'they sit cross-legged and rise straight from that position. You do nothing of the kind. I saw you just now put your feet together and jump. I must really take this opportunity of teaching you how to do it properly. You shall learn the Cloud Trapeze.' He then taught him the magic formula, saying, 'Make the pass, recite the spell, clench your fists, and one leap will carry you head over heels a hundred and eight thousand leagues.'

When the other pupils heard this, they all tittered, saying, 'Monkey is in luck. If he learns this trick, he will be able to carry dispatches, deliver letters, take round circulars—one way or another he will always be able to pick up a living!'

It was now late. Master and pupils all went to their quarters; but Monkey spent all night practising the Cloud Trapeze, and by the time day came he had completely mastered it, and could wander through space where he would.

One summer day when the disciples had for some time been studying their tasks under a pine-tree, one of them said, 'Monkey, what can you have done in a former incarnation to merit that the Master should the other day have whispered in your ear the secret formula for avoiding the three calamities? Have you mastered all those transformations?' 'To tell you the truth,' said Monkey, 'although of course I am much indebted to the Master for his instruction, I have also been working very hard day and night on my own, and I can now do them all.' 'Wouldn't this be a good opportunity,' said one of the pupils, 'to give us a little demonstration?' When Monkey heard this, he was all on his mettle to display his powers. 'Give me my subject,' he said. 'What am I to change into?' 'How about a pine-tree?' they said. He made a magic pass, recited a spell, shook himself, and changed into a pine-tree.

The disciples clapped and burst into loud applause. 'Bravo, Monkey, bravo,' they cried. There was such a din that the Patriarch came running out with his staff trailing after him. 'Who's making all this noise?' he asked. The disciples at once controlled themselves, smoothed down their dresses and came meekly forward. Monkey changed himself back into his true form and slipped in among the crowd, saying, 'Reverend Master, we are doing our lessons out here. I assure you there was no noise in particular.' 'You were all bawling,' said the Patriarch angrily. 'It didn't sound in the least like people studying. I want to know what you were doing here, shouting and laughing.' 'To tell the truth,' said someone, 'Monkey was showing us a transformation just for fun. We told him to change into a pine-tree, and he did it so well that we were all applauding him. That was the noise you heard. I hope you will forgive us.' 'Go away, all of you!' the Patriarch shouted, 'And you, Monkey, come here! What were you doing, playing with your spiritual powers, turning into—what was it? A pine-tree? Did you think I taught you in order that you might show off in front of other people? If you saw someone else turn into a tree, wouldn't you at once ask how it was done? If others see you doing it, aren't they certain to ask you? If you are frightened to refuse, you will give the secret away; and if you refuse, you're very likely to be roughly handled. You're putting yourself in grave danger.' 'I'm terribly sorry,' said Monkey. 'I won't punish you,' said the Patriarch, 'but you can't stay here.' Monkey burst into tears. 'Where am I to go to?' he asked. 'Back to where you came from, I should suppose,' said the Patriarch. 'You don't mean back to the Cave of the Water Curtain in Ao-lai!' said Monkey. 'Yes,' said the Patriarch, 'go back as quickly as you can, if you value your life. One thing is certain in any case; you can't stay here.' 'May I point out,' said Monkey, 'that I have been away from home for twenty years and should be very glad to see my monkey-subjects once more. But I can't consent to go till I have repaid you for all your kindness.' 'I have no desire to be repaid,' said the Patriarch. 'All I ask is that if you get into trouble, you should keep my name out of it.' Monkey saw that it was no use arguing. He bowed to the Patriarch, and took leave of his companions. 'Wherever you go,' said the Patriarch, 'I'm convinced you'll come to no good. So remember, when you get into trouble, I absolutely forbid you to say that you are my disciple. If you give a hint of any such thing I shall flay you alive, break all your bones, and banish your soul to the Place of Ninefold Darkness,[17] where it will remain for ten thousand aeons.' 'I certainly won't venture to say a word about you,' promised Monkey. 'I'll say I found it all out for myself.' So saying he bade farewell, turned away, and making the magic pass rode off on his cloud trapeze, straight to the Eastern Sea. In a very little while he reached the Mountain of Flowers and Fruit, where he lowered his cloud, and was picking his way, when he heard a sound of cranes calling and monkeys crying. 'Little ones,' he shouted, 'I have come back.' At once from every cranny in the cliff, from bushes and trees, great monkeys and small leapt out with cries of 'Long live our king!' Then they all pressed round Monkey, kowtowing and saying, 'Great King, you're very absent-minded! Why did you go away for so long, leaving us all in the lurch, panting for your return, as a starving man for food and drink? For some time past a demon has been ill-using us. He has seized our cave, though we fought desperately, and now he has robbed us of all our possessions and carried off many of our children, so that we have to be on the watch all the time and get no sleep day or night. It's lucky you've come now, for if you had waited another year or two, you'd have found us and everything hereabouts in another's hands.' 'What demon can dare commit such crimes?' cried Monkey.

17. Popular Buddhism includes in its concepts heavens, hells, and purgatory regions.

'Tell me all about it and I will avenge you.' 'Your majesty,' they said, 'he is called the Demon of Havoc, and he lives due north from here.' 'How far off?' asked Monkey. 'He comes like a cloud,' they said, 'and goes like a mist, like wind or rain, thunder or lightning. We do not know how far away he lives.' 'Well, don't worry,' said Monkey; just go on playing around, while I go and look for him.' Dear Monkey King! He sprang into the sky straight northwards and soon saw in front of him a high and very rugged mountain. He was admiring the scenery, when he suddenly heard voices. Going a little way down the hill, he found a cave in front of which several small imps were jumping and dancing. When they saw Monkey, they ran away. 'Stop!' he called, 'I've got a message for you to take. Say that the master of the Water Curtain Cave is here. The Demon of Havoc, or whatever he is called, who lives here, has been ill-treating my little ones and I have come on purpose to settle matters with him.' They rushed into the cave and cried out, 'Great King, a terrible thing has happened!' 'What's the matter?' said the demon. 'Outside the cave,' they said, 'there is a monkey-headed creature who says he is the owner of the Water Curtain Cave. He says you have been ill-using his people and he has come on purpose to settle matters with you.' 'Ha, ha,' laughed the demon. 'I have often heard those monkeys say that their king had gone away to learn religion. This means that he's come back again. What does he look like and how is he armed?' 'He carries no weapon at all,' they said. 'He goes bare-headed, wears a red dress, with a yellow sash, and black shoes—neither priest nor layman nor quite like a Taoist. He's waiting naked-handed outside the gate.' 'Bring me my whole accoutrement,' cried the demon. The small imps at once fetched his arms. The demon put on his helmet and breastplate, grasped his sword, and going to the gate with the little imps, cried in a loud voice, 'Where's the owner of the Water Curtain Cave?' 'What's the use of having such large eyes,' shouted Monkey, 'if you can't see old Monkey?' Catching sight of him the demon burst out laughing. 'You're not a foot high or as much as thirty years old. You have no weapon in your hand! How dare you strut about talking of settling accounts with me?' 'Cursed demon,' said Monkey. 'After all, you have no eyes in your head! You say I am small, not seeing that I can make myself as tall as I please. You say I am unarmed, not knowing that these two hands of mine could drag the moon from the ends of Heaven. Stand your ground, and eat old Monkey's fist!' So saying he leapt into the air and aimed a blow at the demon's face. The demon parried the blow with his hand. 'You such a pigmy and I so tall!' said the demon. 'You using your fists and I my sword—No! If I were to slay you with my sword I should make myself ridiculous. I am going to throw away my sword and use my naked fists.' 'Very good,' said Monkey. 'Now, my fine fellow, come on!' The demon relaxed his guard and struck. Monkey closed with him, and the two of them pommelled and kicked, blow for blow. A long reach is not so firm and sure as a short one. Monkey jabbed the demon in the lower ribs, pounded him in the chest, and gave him such a heavy drubbing that at last the demon stood back, and picking up his great flat sword, slashed at Monkey's head. But Monkey stepped swiftly aside, and the blow missed its mark. Seeing that the demon was becoming savage, Monkey now used the method called Body Outside the Body. He plucked out a handful of hairs, bit them into small pieces and then spat them out into the air, crying 'Change!' The fragments of hair changed into several hundred small monkeys, all pressing round in a throng. For you must know that when anyone becomes an Immortal, he can project his soul, change his shape and perform all kinds of miracles. Monkey, since his Illumination, could change every one of the eighty-four thousand hairs of his body into whatever he chose. The little monkeys he had now created were so nimble that no sword could touch them or spear wound them. See how they leap forward and jump back, crowd round the demon, some hugging, some pulling, some jabbing at his chest, some swarming up his legs. They kicked him, beat him, pommelled his eyes, pinched his nose, and while they were all at it, Monkey slipped up and snatched away the Demon's sword. Then pushing through the throng of small monkeys, he raised the sword and brought it down with such tremendous force upon the demon's skull, that he clove it in twain. He and the little monkeys then rushed into the cave and made a quick end of the imps, great and small. He then said a spell, which caused the small monkeys to change back into hairs. These he put back where they had come from; but there were still some small monkeys left—those that the Demon had carried off from the Cave of the Water Curtain. 'How did you get here?' he asked. There were about thirty or forty of them, and they all said with tears in their eyes, 'After your Majesty went away to become an Immortal, we were pestered by this creature for two years. In the end he carried us all off, and he stole all the fittings from our cave. He took all the stone dishes and the stone cups.' 'Collect everything that belongs to us and bring it with you,' said Monkey. They then set fire to the cave and burnt everything in it. 'Now follow me!' said Monkey. 'When we were brought here,' they said, 'we only felt a great wind rushing past, which whirled us to this place. We didn't know which way we were coming. So how are we to find the way home?' 'He brought you here by magic,' said Monkey. 'But what matter? I am now up to all that sort of thing, and if he could do it, I can. Shut your eyes, all of you, and don't be frightened.' He then recited a spell which produced a fierce wind. Suddenly it dropped, and Monkey shouted, 'You may look now!' The monkeys found that they were standing on firm ground quite close to their home. In high delight they all followed a familiar path back to the door of their cave. They and those who had been left behind all pressed into the cave, and lined up according to their ranks and age, and did homage to their king, and prepared a great banquet of welcome. When they asked how the demon had been subdued and the monkeys rescued, he told them the whole story; upon which they burst into shouts of applause. 'We little thought,' they said, 'that when your Majejsty left us, you would learn such arts as this!' 'After I parted from you,' said Monkey, 'I went across many oceans to the land of Jambudvipa, where I learnt human ways, and how to weaı clothes and shoes. I wandered restless as a cloud for eight or nine years, but nowhere could I find Enlightenment. At last after crossing yet another ocean, I was lucky enough to meet an old Patriarch who taught me the secret of eternal life. 'What an incredible piece of luck!' the monkeys said, all congratulating him. 'Little ones,' said Monkey, 'I have another bit of good news for you. Your king has got a name-in-religion. I am called Aware-of-Vacuity.' They all clapped loudly, and presently went to get date-wine and grape-wine and fairy flowers and fruit, which they offered to Monkey. Everyone was in the highest spirits. . . .

LIU T'IEH-YÜN

(1857–1909)

The Travels of Lao Ts'an (*Lao-ts'an yu-chi*)

Liu T'ieh-yün (also known as Liu E) was one of the most original literary minds among the Chinese intellectuals who saw in the late nineteenth and twentieth centuries the impact of the West on Chinese life and institutions. Born in 1857 at Liuho in Kiangsu province on the eastern coast of China, Liu had the benefits of a classical Chinese education. His restless and inquiring mind caused him to refuse to take the traditional examinations for office, but he read widely in the Sung philosophers and engaged in debate with learned friends on such subjects as military science, economics, music, poetry, astronomy, and medicine. Most of these interests are reflected in the *Travels*. One of them is flood control, a perpetual engineering and economic problem in China, especially in the area surrounding the Huang Ho, the Yellow River; Liu became something of a specialist in this science. In his youth, Liu had many occupations: he failed in the tobacco business; he underwent a kind of religious conversion to a sect that combined Confucianist, Taoist, and Buddhist beliefs; he attempted traditional Chinese medicine, and also printing. In 1888 when the Yellow River went on a rampage, he so impressed the chief engineer of the river valley with a flood-control scheme that he received a responsible position. His later career included advising on railroad construction, negotiating with the Russians for foodstuffs during the Boxer Rebellion (1900), diplomacy connected with the treaty that concluded the foreign occupation at the end of the Rebellion, archaeological scholarship, and failures in business almost too frequent to enumerate: water works, street car lines, salt refining, foreign trade, and real-estate speculation. Liu died in August 1909, characteristically embroiled in a battle with governmental authorities.

It was not until 1904 that Liu T'ieh-yün began to write the *Travels of Lao Ts'an*. His varied career is everywhere evident in the book. The curiosity and practicality of the entrepreneur and the imagination of the creative artist are inextricably mixed in the *Travels,* and the tone of a man weary with the insolence and ineptitude of officialdom is frequently heard. The *Travels* is a record of Liu's disillusionment, a disillusionment shared by many Chinese, because the late nineteenth century was a period of heartbreaking attempts, almost all of them doomed to failure, to push China precipitately into the twentieth century through the use of Western technology. Liu and the type of person he was are the beginnings of the westernized Chinese character. In an earlier generation Liu would have been content to be a government official in the Confucianist pattern. But though the *Travels* starts with both the wail of the newborn baby and the moans of the mourners at a funeral, the mood of the book is a genial, if reluctant, acceptance of man's lot, which contains the attitude that most suffering is brought about through man's ignorance and thoughtlessness. The honest but bigoted and narrow bureaucrat, the eccentric sage, the prostitute received in a nunnery, any traveler one might fall in with on a journey—all of these interest Liu T'ieh-yün.

There is neither unity of plot or subject matter—in the Western sense of this concept—in the *Travels.* Part of this deficiency may have been caused by desultory, serial publication (the work first appeared in installments in a magazine of fiction), but the traditional Chinese novel is likewise rambling. The narrator's personality holds the work together, along with his interest in people and his good humor. Various traditions of Chinese fiction are imitated by Liu. Many Chinese novels have supernatural prologues such as we find in Chapter I. There is a murder-mystery episode (the detective story is popular in China) said to have been inspired by Sir Arthur Conan Doyle's Sherlock Holmes stories. Shen Tzu-p'ing's visit to the Peach Blossom Mountain is in a popular tradition of fantasy. Liu's descriptions of scenery and of music have won the praise of the eminent Chinese critic, Dr. Hu Shih. The style of the work is direct and imaginative as against the prevailing vice of the times—the pedantic and bookish style. Liu's vivid recording of life on the great north China plain in Shantung Province came as a breath of fresh air into the literature of his age.

From The Travels of Lao Ts'an*

Author's Preface

When a baby is born, he weeps, *wa-wa;* and when a man is old and dying, his family form a circle around him and wail, *hao-t'ao.* Thus weeping is most certainly that with which a man starts and finishes his life. In the interval, the quality of a man is measured by his much or little weeping, for weeping is the expression of a spiritual nature. Spiritual nature is in proportion to weeping: the weeping is not dependent on the external conditions of life being favorable or unfavorable.

Horse and ox toil and moil the year round. They eat only hay and corn and are acquainted with the whip from start to finish. They can be said to suffer, but they do not know how to weep; this is because spiritual nature is lacking to them. Apes and monkeys are creatures that jump about in the depths of the forest and fill themselves with pears and chestnuts. They live a life of ease and pleasure, yet they are given to screaming. This screaming is the monkey's way of weeping. The naturalists say that among all living things monkeys and apes are nearest to man, because they have a spiritual nature. The old poem says:

> Of the three gorges of Eastern Pa, the Sorcerer's Gorge is
> the longest;
> Three sounds of monkeys screaming there cut through a
> man's bowels.

Just think what feelings they must have!

Spiritual nature gives birth to feeling; feeling gives birth to weeping. There are two kinds of weeping. One kind is strong; one kind is weak. When an addlepated boy loses a piece of fruit, he cries; when a silly girl loses a hairpin, she weeps. This is the weak kind of weeping. The sobbing of Ch'i's wife that caused the city wall to collapse,[1]

* From *The Travels of Lao Ts'an* by Liu T'ieh-yün, translated by Harold Shadick. Copyright 1952 by Cornell University. Reprinted by permission of Cornell University Press, Ithaca, N. Y. The footnotes are abridged from those of the translator.

1. In the *Records of Exemplary Women* (*Lieh Nü Chuan*) the story is told that the wife of Chi' Liang mourned her husband's death (in battle) so much that she slept with her head on his corpse at the foot of the city wall. After ten days the city wall fell down and buried the corpse. She ran to the river and drowned herself. The daughters of the mythical emperor Yao became the concubines of his successor, Shun. When Shun died, they wept so violently that their tears mottled the bamboo around them. There is a variety of mottled bamboo called "Hsiang Concubine Bamboo."

the tears of the Imperial Concubines Hsiang that stained the bamboo—these were the strong kind of weeping. Moreover the strong kind of weeping divides into two varieties. If weeping takes the form of tears, its strength is small. If weeping does not take the form of tears, its strength is great: it reaches farther.

The poem, *Encountering Sorrow,* was Lord Ch'ü's weeping.[2] The book called *Chuang Tzu* was the weeping of the Old Man of Meng.[3] The book called *Historical Records* was the weeping of the Grand Astrologer.[4] The *Poems of the Thatched Hut* were the weeping of the *Kung Pu,* Tu.[5] Prince Li[6] wept in lyric verse. The Man of the Eight Great Mountains[7] wept with paintings. Wang Shih-fu put his tears into the *Story of the Western Chamber.*[8] Ts'ao Hsüeh-chin put his tears into the *Dream of the Red Chamber.*[9] Wang's words are: "Hatred of separation and sadness at parting fill my inward parts—it is hard to give vent to them. Without paper and pen as substitutes for throat and tongue, to whom can I tell my thousand thoughts?" Ts'ao's words are: "Paper covered with wild words; a handful of bitter tears. All say the writer is mad. Who understands his meaning!" When he says of his tea, "a thousand fragrances in one hollow," and of his wine, "ten thousand beauties in one cup," he means "a thousand lovely ones weeping together" and "ten thousand beauties mourning together."[10]

We of this age have our feelings stirred about ourselves and the world, about family and nation, about society, about the various races and religions. The deeper the emotions, the more bitter the weeping. This is why the Scholar of a Hundred Temperings from Hungtu[11] has made this book, *The Travels of Lao Ts'an.*

The game of chess is finished. We are getting old. How can we not weep? I know that "a thousand lovely ones" and "ten thousand beauties" among mankind will weep with me and be sad with me.

2. Ch'ü Yüan of the third century B.C. He committed suicide because of disgrace brought about by the scheming of rivals in the ministry. His autobiographical poem, *Encountering Sorrow* (*Li Sao*) is the most important early Chinese poem outside the *Book of Odes* (*Shih King*). There is a translation in Robert Payne, *The White Pony* (New York, 1947).

3. Meng Son is a name for Chuang Tzu (see p. 204) because he was said to be a native of the city of Meng in modern Anhwei Province in east central China, west of Nanking.

4. Ch'ien Ssu-ma (145–186 A.D.).

5. Tu Fu, a great Chinese poet (see Note 29).

6. Li Hou-chu or Li Yü, the second and last ruler of the southern T'ang state, which flourished 937–974. He was greater as a poet than as a ruler. Translations of his poems are in *Chinese Lyrics* by Ch'u Ta-kao (Cambridge, 1937) and in Robert Payne, *The White Pony.*

7. Chu Ta of the royal house of Ming, who, after the fall of the dynasty in 1644, became a monk and devoted himself to wine, painting, and calligraphy.

8. His poetic drama the *Story of a Western Chamber* (*Hsi Hsiang Chi*) (English translation by S. I. Hsiung, London, 1935) is a development of an earlier T'ang-period story.

9. the great seventeenth-century Chinese novel of domestic life, the *Hung Lou Meng.*

10. The word for "hollow," *k'u* (vessel), has the same sound as the word for "sob," *k'u.* Similarly, the word for "cup," *pei,* has the same sound as the word for "sad" or "sadness," *pei.*

11. The author, Lieh T'ieh-yün, puns on his family name, *T'ieh,* which means "iron." *Hungtu* refers to no specific place; it means "the great centers of population."

I

The land does not hold back the water; every year comes disaster;
The wind beats up the waves; everywhere is danger.[12]

The story tells that outside the East Gate of Tengchoufu, in Shantung, there is a big hill called P'englai Hill,[13] and on this hill a pavilion called the P'englai Pavilion. It is most imposing with its "painted roof-tree flying like a cloud" and its "bead screens rolled up like rain."[14] To the west it overlooks the houses in the town, with mist hanging over ten thousand homes; to the east it overlooks the waves of the sea, undulating for a thousand li. It is a regular custom for the gentlemen of the town to take wine cups and wine with them to the pavilion and spend the night there, to be ready the next morning before it is light to watch the sun come up out of the sea.

However, no more of this for the present.

It is further told that there was once a traveler called Lao Ts'an. His family name was T'ieh, his *ming* was of one character, Ying, and his *hao*, Pu-ts'an. He chose Ts'an as his *hao* because he liked the story of the monk Lan Ts'an roasting taros.[15] Since he was a pleasant sort of person, people deferred to his wish and began to call him Lao Ts'an, which eventually became a regular nickname. He was a Chiangnan[16] man. By the time he was thirty he had studied quite a lot of prose and poetry, but because he was not good at writing eight-legged essays,[17] he had taken no degrees and therefore nobody wanted him as a tutor. He was too old to learn a business and therefore did not attempt it. His father had been an official of the third or fourth rank but was too stubbornly honest to make

12. Each chapter is prefaced by a couplet consisting of two lines of six to eight characters, each parallel in form. They refer to the contents of the chapter. This couplet refers to the annual flooding of the Yellow River (Huang Ho) and in the clause "everywhere is danger," to the precariousness of the ship of state in a country of perpetual disaster. Thus the first chapter introduces two main themes, flood control and political reform.

13. a city on the extreme north shore of Shantung Peninsula. The pavilion, originally built in the Sung dynasty, was a vantage point for a marvelous view. Mirages occasionally gave the effect of offshore islands, and the Han Emperor Wu (reigned 140–186 B.C.) is said to have seen the "Isles of the Blessed," a country where men never grow old or die, similar to that of the Western versions of this myth.

14. an abridged quotation from the poet Wang Po (647–675). The complete lines are:

In the morning the painted roof-tree [seems to] fly [like] a cloud over the South Bank;
In the evening the bead screens [seem to] roll up [like] rain from the Western Hills.

15. The *ming* is his personal name, given by his family; the *hao* is a "fancy" name assumed by the man himself or given to him by his friends (see p. 257). *Taros* are edible roots.

16. the provinces of Chiangsu and Anhwei; Chiangsu is on the coast of the Yellow Sea, east of Anhwei; the name is sometimes used for the territory south of the Yangtze River.

17. "Essays with eight thighs (or sections)." These had to be written, in a rigid, artificial style, in the official examinations for governmental office.

money for himself, and after twenty years of office-holding he could only afford to travel home by selling his official clothes! How do you suppose he could have anything to give his son?

Since Lao Ts'an had nothing from his family and no definite occupation, he began to see cold and hunger staring him in the face. Just when he was at his wits' end, Heaven took pity on him, for along came a Taoist priest, shaking a string of bells, who said that he had been taught by a wonderful healer and could treat a hundred diseases. He said that when people met him and asked him to heal their diseases he had a hundred cures to every hundred treatments. So Lao Ts'an made obeisance to him as his teacher, learned the patter, and from that time on went about shaking a string of bells and filling his bowl of gruel by curing diseases. Thus he wandered about by river and lake for twenty years.

When our story begins, he had just come to an old Shantung town called Ch'iench'eng,[18] where there was a great house belonging to a man whose family name was Huang (Yellow) and whose *ming* was Jui-ho. This man suffered from a strange disease which caused his whole body to fester in such a way that every year several open sores appeared, and if one year these were healed, the next year several more would appear elsewhere. Now for many years no one had been found who could cure this disease. It broke out every summer and subsided after the autumn equinox.

Lao Ts'an arrived at this place in the spring, and the major-domo of the Huang household asked him if he had a cure for the disease. He said, "I have many cures; the only thing is that you may not do as I tell you. This year I will apply a mild treatment to try my skill. But if you want to prevent the disease from ever breaking out again, this too is not difficult; all we need do is to follow the ancients whose methods hit the target every time. For other diseases we follow the directions handed down from Shen Nung and Huang Ti, but in the case of this disease we need the method of the great Yü.[19] Later, in the Han period, there was a certain Wang Ching[20] who inherited his knowledge, but after that nobody seems to have known his method. Fortunately I now have some understanding of it."

The Huang household therefore pressed him to stay in the house and to give his treatment. Strange to say, although this year there was a certain amount of festering, not one open sore appeared, and this made the household very happy.

After the autumn equinox the state of the disease was no longer

18. a Han-period center about a hundred miles northwest of present-day Tsinan, which is near the Yellow River in Shantung Province, north of Anhwei and Chiangsu.

19. legendary figures. Shen Nung was said to have invented agriculture and medicine. Huang Ti was the reputed author of the ancient *Classic of Internal Medicine*. Yü invented flood control and supposedly succeeded the mythical Emperor Shun. The symbolic connection between flood control and internal medicine is obvious.

20. In the time of Ming Ti (reigned 58–76) he practiced flood control.

serious, and everybody was delighted because for the first time in more than ten years Mr. Huang had had no open sores. The family therefore engaged a theatrical company to sing operas for three days in thanksgiving to the spirits. They also built up an artificial hill of chrysanthemums in the courtyard of the west reception hall. One day there was a feast, the next a banquet, all very gay and noisy.

On the day when our story begins Lao Ts'an had finished his noon meal, and having drunk two cups of wine more than usual, felt tired and went to his room, where he lay down on the couch to rest. He had just closed his eyes when suddenly two men walked in, one called Wen Chang-po, the other Te Hui-sheng.[21] These two men were old friends of his. They said, "What are you doing at this time of day, hiding away in your room?" Lao Ts'an quickly got up and offered them seats saying, "I have been feasting so hard these two days that I needed a change." They said, "We are going to Tengchou to see the famous view from the P'englai Pavilion and have come especially to invite you. We have already hired a cart. Put your things together quickly and we will go right away."

Lao Ts'an's baggage did not amount to much—not more than a few old books and some instruments—so that packing was easy, and in a short time the three men were getting into the cart. After an uneventful journey they soon reached Tengchou and there found lodging beside the P'englai Pavilion. Here they settled and prepared to enjoy the phantasmagoria of a "market in the sea" and the magic of "mirage towers."[22]

The next day Lao Ts'an said to his two friends Wen and Te, "Everyone says the sunrise is worth seeing. Why shouldn't we stay up to see it instead of sleeping? What do you say?" They answered, "If you are so inclined, we will certainly keep you company."

Although autumn is that time of year when day and night are about equal in length, the misty light that appears before sunrise and lingers after sunset makes the night seem shorter. The three friends opened two bottles of wine, took out the food they had brought with them, and, what with drinking and talking, before they were aware of it the east had gradually become bright. Actually it was still a long time before sunrise; the effect was due to the diffusion of the light through the air.

The three friends continued to talk for a while. Then Te Hui-sheng said, "It's nearly time now. Why don't we go and wait upstairs?" Wen Chang-po said, "The wind is whistling so, and there is such an expanse of windows upstairs that I'm afraid it will be much colder than this room. We'd better put on extra clothes."

They all followed this advice and taking telescopes and rugs went

21. *Wen Chang-po* means "Leader in Literary Composition"; *Te Hui-sheng* means "Student of Morals and Wisdom."

22. See Note 13.

up the zigzag staircase at the back. When they entered the pavilion, they sat at a table by a window and looked out toward the east. All they could see were white waves like mountains stretching away without end. To the northeast were several flecks of blue mist. The nearest was Long Hill Island; farther off were Big Bamboo, Great Black, and other islands. Around the pavilion the wind rushed and roared until the whole building seemed to be shaking. The clouds in the sky were piled up, one layer upon another. In the north was one big bank of cloud that floated to the middle of the sky and pressed down upon the clouds that were already there, and then began to crowd more and more upon a layer of cloud in the east until the pressure seemed insufferable. The whole spectacle was most ominous. A little later the sky became a shining strip of red.

Hui-sheng said, "Brother Ts'an, judging from the look of things the actual rising of the sun will be invisible." Lao Ts'an said, "The winds of heaven and the waters of the sea are sufficient to move me; even if we do not see the sunrise the journey will not have been in vain."

Chang-po meanwhile had been looking through his telescope. Now he exclaimed, "Look! There is a black shadow in the east that keeps rising and falling with the waves; it must be a steamship passing." They all took their telescopes and looked in that direction. After a while they said, "Yes! Look! There is a fine black thread on the horizon. It must be a ship."

They all watched for a while until the ship had passed out of sight. Hui-sheng continued to hold up his telescope and looked intently to right and left. Suddenly he cried, "Ayah! Ayah! Look at that sailing boat among the great waves. It must be in danger." The others said, "Where?" Hui-sheng said, "Look toward the northeast. Isn't that line of snow-white foam Long Hill Island? The boat is on this side of the island and is gradually coming nearer." The other two looked through their telescopes and both exclaimed, "Ayah! Ayah! It certainly is in terrible danger. Luckily it's coming in this direction. It has only twenty or thirty li to go before it reaches the shore."

After about an hour the boat was so near that by looking closely through their telescopes the three men could see that it was a fairly large boat, about twenty-three or twenty-four chang long.[23] The captain was sitting on the poop, and below the poop were four men in

23. This description is symbolic of the Chinese ship of state. There are twenty-three or twenty-four provinces. The captain is the emperor and his four helmsmen are his chief ministers. The six masts are the six governmental departments. The new mast with slightly worn sails is probably the Foreign Office, created in 1861, and the new mast with new sails, the Board of Admiralty, created in 1890. A Chinese and a Manchu looked after each department: they are the two men looking after each mast (for the Manchus, see Note 37). A *chang* is ten feet.

charge of the helm. There were six masts with old sails and two new masts, one with a completely new sail and the other with a rather worn one, in all eight masts. The ship was very heavily loaded; the hold must have contained many kinds of cargo. Countless people, men and women, were sitting on the deck without any awning or other covering to protect them from the weather—just like the people in third-class cars on the railway from Tientsin to Peking. The north wind blew in their faces; foam splashed over them; they were wet and cold, hungry and afraid. They all had the appearance of people with no means of livelihood. Beside each of the eight masts were two men to look after the rigging. At the prow and on the deck were a number of men dressed like sailors.

It was a great ship, twenty-three or twenty-four chang long, but there were many places in which it was damaged. On the east side was a gash about three chang long, into which the waves were pouring with nothing to stop them. Farther to the east was another bad place about a chang long through which the water was seeping more gradually.[24] No part of the ship was free from scars. The eight men looking after the sails were doing their duty faithfully, but each one looked after his own sail as though each of the eight was on a separate boat: they were not working together at all. The other seamen were running about aimlessly among the groups of men and women; it was impossible at first to tell what they were trying to do. Looking carefully through the telescope, you discovered that they were searching the men and women for any food they might be carrying and also stripping them of the clothes that they wore.

Chang-po looked intently and finally couldn't help crying out wildly, "The damnable blackguards! Just look, the boat is going to capsize any moment, and they don't even make a show of trying to reach the shore, but spend their time maltreating decent people. It's outrageous!" Hui-sheng said, "Brother Chang, don't get excited; the ship is not more than seven or eight li away from us; when it reaches land, we will go on board and try to make them stop, that's all."

While he was speaking, they saw several people on the boat killed and thrown into the sea. The helm was put about, and the ship went off toward the east. Chang-po was so angry that he stamped his feet and shouted, "A shipload of perfectly good people! All those lives! For no reason at all being killed at the hands of this crowd of navigators! What injustice!" He thought for a while and then said, "Fortunately there are lots of fishing boats at the bottom of our hill. Why don't we sail out in one of them, kill some of that crew, and replace the others? That would mean the salvation of a whole shipload of people. What a meritorious act! What satisfaction!" Hui-

24. The gash is Manchuria, threatened by Japan and Russia. The bad place "farther to the east" is Shantung Province, threatened by Germany and England.

sheng said, "Although it might be satisfying to do this, still it would be very rash, and I'm afraid not safe. What does Brother Ts'an think?"

Lao Ts'an smiled at Chang-po and said, "Brother Chang, your plan is excellent, only I wonder how many companies of soldiers you are going to take with you." Chang-po answered angrily, "How can Brother Ts'an be so blind! At this very moment the lives of these people are in the balance. In this emergency we three should go to rescue them without delay. Where are there any companies of soldiers to take with us?" Lao Ts'an said, "In that case, since the crew of that ship is not less than two hundred men, if we three try to kill them won't we only go to our own deaths and accomplish nothing? What does your wisdom think of that?"

Chang-po thought for a while and decided that Lao Ts'an's reasoning was sound; then he said, "According to you, what should we do? Helplessly watch them die?"

Lao Ts'an answered, "As I see it the crew have not done wrong intentionally; there are two reasons why they have brought the ship to this intolerable pass. What two reasons? The first is that they are accustomed to sailing on the 'Pacific' Ocean and can only live through 'pacific' days. When the wind is still and the waves are quiet, the conditions of navigation make it possible to take things easy. But they were not prepared for today's big wind and heavy sea and therefore are bungling and botching everything. The second reason is that they do not have a compass. When the sky is clear, they can follow traditional methods, and when they can see the sun, moon, and stars they don't make serious mistakes in their course. This might be called 'depending on heaven for your food.'[25] Who could have told that they would run into this overcast weather with the sun, moon, and stars covered up by clouds, leaving them nothing to steer by? It is not that in their hearts they do not want to do the right thing, but since they cannot distinguish north, south, east, and west, the farther they go, the more mistakes they make. As to our present plan, if we take Brother Chang's suggestion to follow them in a fishing boat, we can certainly catch them, because their boat is heavy and ours will be light. If when we have reached them we give them a compass, they will then have a direction to follow and will be able to keep their course. If we also instruct the captain in the difference between navigating in calm and stormy weather and they follow our words, why shouldn't they quickly reach the shore?" Hui-sheng said, "What Lao Ts'an has suggested is the very thing! Let us carry it out quickly; otherwise the shipload of people will certainly be doomed."

The three men descended from the pavilion and told the servants

25. a Confucian saying.

to watch their baggage. They took nothing with them except a reliable compass, a sextant, and several other nautical instruments. At the foot of the hill they found the mooring place of the fishing boats. They chose a light, quick boat, hoisted the sail, and set out in pursuit of the ship. Luckily the wind was blowing from the north so that whether the boat went east or west there was a thwart wind and the sail could be used to the full.

After a short time they were not far from the big boat. The three men continued to watch carefully through their telescopes. When they were a little more than ten chang away, they could hear what the people on the boat were saying. They were surprised to find that while the members of the crew were searching the passengers another man was making an impassioned speech in a loud voice.

They only heard him say, "You have all paid your fares to travel on this boat. In fact, the boat is your own inherited property which has now been brought to the verge of destruction by the crew. All in your families, young and old, are on this boat. Are you all going to wait to be killed? Are you not going to find a way of saving the situation? You deserve to be killed, you herd of slaves!"

The passengers at whom he was railing said nothing at first. Then a number of men got up and said, "What you have said is what we all in our hearts want to say but cannot. Today we have been awakened by you and are truly ashamed of ourselves and truly grateful to you. We only ask you, 'What are we to do?' "

The man then said, "You must know that nowadays nothing can be done without money. If you will all contribute some money, we will give our energy and lifeblood for you and will lay the foundations of a freedom which is eternal and secure. What do you say to this?" The passengers all clapped their hands and shouted with satisfaction.

Chang-po hearing this from the distance said to his two companions, "We didn't know there was a splendid hero like this on the boat. If we had known earlier, we needn't have come." Hui-sheng said, "Let us lower part of our sails for the time being. We don't need to catch up with the ship. We'll just watch what he does. If he really has a sound scheme, then we can very well go back." Lao Ts'an said, "Brother Hui is right. In my poor opinion this man is probably not the sort who will really do anything. He will merely use a few fine-sounding phrases to cheat people of their money—that's all!"

The three then lowered their sails and slowly trailed after the big boat. They saw the people on the boat collect quite a lot of money and hand it over to the speaker. Then they watched to see what he would do. Who could have known that when the speaker had taken the money he would seek out a place where the crowd could not touch him, stand there, and shout to them loudly, "You lot of spineless creatures! Cold-blooded animals! Are you still not going to attack those helmsmen?" And further, "Why don't you take those seamen and kill them one by one?"

Sure enough, some inexperienced young men, trusting his word, went to attack the helmsmen, while others went to upbraid the captain; they were all slaughtered by the sailors and thrown into the sea.

The speaker again began to shout down at them, "Why don't you organize yourselves? If all you passengers on the boat act together, won't you get the better of them?"

But an old and experienced man among the passengers cried out, "Good people! On no account act in this wild way! If you do this, the ship will sink while you are still struggling. I'm certain no good will come of it."

When Hui-sheng heard this he said to Chang-po, "After all, this hero was out to make money for himself while telling others to shed their blood." Lao Ts'an said, "Fortunately there are still a few respectable and responsible men; otherwise the ship would founder even sooner."

When he had spoken, the three men put on full sail and very soon were close to the big boat. Their poleman pulled them alongside with his hook, and the three then climbed up and approached the poop. Bowing very low, they took out their compass and sextant and presented them. The helmsmen looked at them and asked them politely, "How do you use these things? What are they for?"

They were about to reply when suddenly among the lower ranks of seamen arose a howl, "Captain! Captain! Whatever you do don't be tricked by these men. They've got a foreign compass. They must be traitors sent by the foreign devils! They must be Catholics! They have already sold our ship to the foreign devils, and that's why they have this compass. We beg you to bind these men and kill them to avoid further trouble. If you talk with them any more or use their compass, it will be like accepting a deposit from the foreign devils, and they will come to claim our ship."

This outburst aroused everybody on the ship. Even the great speech-making hero cried out, "These are traitors who want to sell the ship! Kill them! Kill them!"

When the captain and the helmsmen heard the clamor, they hesitated. A helmsman who was the captain's uncle said, "Your intentions are very honest, but it is difficult to go against the anger of the mob. You had better go away quickly."

With tears in their eyes the three men hurriedly returned to their little boat. The anger of the crowd on the big ship did not abate, and when they saw the three men getting into their boat, they picked up broken timbers and planks damaged by the waves and hurled them at the small boat. Just think! How could a tiny fishing boat bear up against several hundred men using all their force to destroy it? In a short time the fishing boat was broken to bits and began to sink to the bottom of the sea.

If you don't know what happened to the three men, then hear the next chapter tell.

II

At the foot of Mount Li the traces of an ancient emperor;
By the side of Lake Ming the song of a beautiful girl.

It has been told how the fishing boat Lao Ts'an was in was damaged by the mob and sank with him into the depths of the sea. He realized that there was no hope for his life. All he could do was to close his eyes and wait. He felt like a leaf falling from a tree, fluttering to and fro. In a short time he had sunk to the bottom. He could hear a voice at his side calling to him, "Wake up, Sir! It is already dark. The food has been ready in the dining hall for quite a long time." Lao Ts'an opened his eyes in great confusion, stared around him, and said, "Ay! After all it was but a dream."

Some days later Lao Ts'an said to the major-domo, "The weather is now getting colder; your honorable master is no longer ill and the disease will not break out again. Next year if you need my advice I will come again to serve him. Now your humble servant wishes to go to Tsinanfu to enjoy the scenery of the Ta Ming Lake."[26] The major-domo repeatedly urged him to stay, but without success, so that night he prepared a farewell feast and presented Lao Ts'an with a packet containing a thousand ounces of silver as an honorarium.

Lao Ts'an said a few words of thanks and put it away in his baggage. Then he said good-by, got into his cart, and started off. The road was among autumn hills covered with red leaves and gardens full of chrysanthemums so that he did not feel at all lonely. When he reached Tsinanfu and entered the city gate, the houses with their springs and the courtyards with their weeping willows seemed to him even more attractive than the scenery of Chiangnan. He found an inn called Promotion Inn on Treasury Street, took his baggage off the cart, paid the carter his fare and wine money, had a hasty evening meal, and went to bed.

The next day he got up early, had a light breakfast, and then took a turn up and down the streets shaking his string of bells in pursuit of his calling. In the afternoon he walked over to the Magpie Bridge[27] and hired a small boat. After rowing north for a short dis-

26. a large lake which occupies the whole north section of the city of Tsinan.
27. The magpie is a bird of good omen.

tance, he reached the Lihsia Pavilion,[28] where he stopped the boat and went in. Entering the main gate, he found a pavilion from which most of the paint and lacquer had peeled. On the wall hung a pair of *tui-lien* [vertical plaques] with the inscription:

In Lihsia this pavilion is the oldest;
In Tsinan there are many famous scholars.

In the upper right corner was written: "Composed by the *Kung Pu*, Tu."[29] In the lower left was, "Written by Ho Shao-chi of Taochou."[30] There were several buildings near the pavilion, none of any great interest. He returned to his boat and, rowing to the west, before very long reached the enclosure of the memorial temple to T'ieh Kung.[31]

Do you know who T'ieh Kung was? He was the T'ieh Hsüan who at the beginning of the Ming period caused a lot of trouble to the Prince of Yen. Later generations have honored him for his loyalty to the lawful emperor. For this reason even today at the spring and autumn festivals the inhabitants come to this place to burn incense.

When he reached the T'ieh Kung Temple Lao Ts'an looked toward the south and saw facing him on the Thousand Buddha Hill groups of monastic buildings among the gray-green pines and blue-green cypresses. The trees were crowded together, some red with a fiery red, others white with the white of snow, some indigo blue, others jade green, a few patches of maple red showing among the rest. It was as though a great painting by the Sung artist Chao Ch'ien-li had been made into a screen several tens of li long.

He sighed with sheer delight. Suddenly the sound of a fisherman's song reached him. He bent his head to see where the sound came from and found that the Ming Lake had become as smooth and clear as a mirror. The Thousand Buddha Hill was reflected in the lake and appeared with perfect clarity. The buildings, the terraces, and the trees down there were extraordinarily gay and varied and seemed even more beautiful and clear than the hill above. He knew that beyond the south shore of the lake was a busy street, but a bank of reeds completely concealed it. It was now their blossom time, and the stretch of white bloom reflecting the vapor-filled beams of the setting sun was like a rose-colored velvet carpet forming a cushion

28. Tsinan was formerly known as Lihsia, "beneath Li." Lishan is the old name of the mountain which rises about two miles south of the city.

29. The *Kung Pu* is the "Official of the Board of Works," here the great Chinese poet Tu Fu. The lines of the poem are misquoted; the first should read "In the west of the lake this pavilion is the oldest." Tu Fu visited Tsinan in 745, and the poem is supposed to have been written in the Lihsia Pavilion. It is translated in full by Florence Ayscough in her *Tu Fu, An Autobiography* (London, 1929).

30. (1799–1873), a distinguished calligrapher and principal of the academy at Tsinan, 1858–1860.

31. governor of Shantung under the second Ming emperor, Hui Ti (reigned 1399–1403). He was martyred for his loyalty to the legitimate emperor.

between the hill above and the hill below. It was indeed a fascinating sight.

Lao Ts'an thought to himself, "Such an enchanting scene! How is it there are no visitors to enjoy it?" He looked for a while longer and then turned round and read the *tui-lien* on the columns of the great gate. The inscriptions were:

> On four sides lotus blossoms, on three sides willows;
> A city of mountain scenery, half a city of lake.

He quietly bowed his head and said, "It's absolutely true!" He then entered the great gate, and immediately opposite him was the ceremonial hall of T'ieh Kung. To the east was a lotus pond, round which went a zigzag gallery, and at the east end of the lotus pond was a circular gate. Beyond this was an old three-*chien* [three-unit] building with a weatherworn *pien* [horizontal plaque] on which were four characters forming the name "Ancient Water Spirit Shrine." In front of the shrine were a pair of weatherworn *tui-lien* on which was written:

> A cup of cold spring water is offered to the autumn
> chrysanthemums;
> At midnight the painted boat pushes its way through
> the lotuses.

Leaving the Water Spirit Shrine, he went down to his boat and rowed to the back of the Lihsia Pavilion. On both sides the lotus leaves and lotus flowers crowded around the boat. The lotus leaves, which were beginning to shrivel, brushed against the boat with a sound, *ch'ih ch'ih*. Water birds, startled by the coming of people, flew cawing into the air, *k'e-k'e*. The ripe lotus pods kept catching on the side of the boat and scattering through the windows.

Lao Ts'an casually picked several pods, and while he was eating the seeds the boat reached the Magpie Bridge. Here he felt himself back in the press of human life. There were men carrying loads and men pushing small carts. There was a blue felt sedan chair carried by two bearers and behind the chair a yamen runner wearing a hat with a red tassel and carrying a folder full of letters under his arm. He was running with his head down as though his life depended on it and mopped his brow with a handkerchief as he went. Several five- or six-year-old children in the road did not know how to keep out of people's way. One of them was accidentally knocked over by a chair-bearer and got up crying, "Wa, wa!" His mother quickly ran up asking, "Who knocked you down? Who knocked you down?" The child could only cry, "Wa, wa!" She asked him again and again. At last through his tears he got out the words, "The chair bearer!" The mother raised her head and saw that the chair had already gone two or three li. She therefore took her child by the hand and muttering imprecations, *chi-chi, ku-ku,* went home.

As Lao Ts'an walked slowly south from the Magpie Bridge to Treasury Street, he happened to look up and saw pasted on a wall a strip of yellow paper about a foot long and seven or eight inches wide. In the middle of it were written three characters, "Recital of Drum Tales."[32] At the side was a line of small characters, "On the Twenty-Fourth at the Ming Lake House." The paper was not yet quite dry, so he guessed it had only just been put up. He did not know what it was about since he had never seen anywhere else an announcement of this kind. As he went along the road, he continued to puzzle over it. He heard two carriers talking, "Tomorrow the Fair Maid is telling stories. Let's leave our work and go to listen." And when he reached the main street he overheard a conversation behind a shop counter, "Last time you had a holiday to go and hear the Fair Maid sing; tomorrow it's my turn." Along his whole path the gossip was mostly on this subject. He wondered to himself: "What sort of person is this Fair Maid? What sort of tales are they? Why is the whole town so excited about this announcement?" He allowed his feet to lead him and very soon reached the door of Promotion Inn. He entered the inn and the servant asked him, "What will you have for supper, Sir?"

Lao Ts'an gave his order and then took the chance to ask, "What sort of local entertainment are these Drum Tales? Why is everyone so excited about them?" The servant replied, "You don't know, Sir! Drum Tales used to be a sort of popular country music in Shantung. Old stories were recited to the accompaniment of a drum and a pair of pear-blossom castanets, together called 'pear blossom and big drum.' There was nothing unusual about it. But recently Fair Maid and Dark Maid, two sisters from the Wang family have appeared. The Fair Maid's personal name is Little Jade Wang. She is the most amazing creature you ever heard of. When she was twelve or thirteen years old she learned this art of storytelling, but she soon began to despise the country tunes and said they were dull. She started going to the theater, and as soon as she heard a tune, she could sing it, whether it was a *hsi-p'i* or an *erh-huang* or a *pang-tzu-ch'iang*.[33] When she heard Yü San-sheng's, Ch'eng Chang-keng's, or Chang Erh-k'uei's[34] tunes, she could sing them right off. When she sings, she can go as high as you like. She can hold a note as long as you

32. a form of entertainment in which a story is recited to the accompaniment of stringed instruments and a small drum. This art is still quite popular in Peking and other northern cities. See Lau Shaw's novel *The Drum Singers* (New York, 1952).

33. *Hsi-p'i* is a shrill melody; *erh-huang,* softer and more melodious. *Pang-tzu-ch'iang* is a style of opera music characterized by the use of the *pang-tzu,* a piece of wood which is struck violently to emphasize the rhythm. This opera music was in favor about 1900.

34. three famous opera actors still referred to today.

want. She got hold of those southern—what-do-you-call-'em—***k'un-ch'iang***[35] melodies as well. No matter what sort of style or melody, she puts them all into the singing of Drum Tales. In two or three years' time she created this kind of singing, and now, when people hear her sing, whether they are northerners or southerners, gentry or ordinary folk, there is nobody who is not stirred to the depths of his soul. The notices are up, so tomorrow she will sing. If you don't believe what I say, go and hear her and then you will see. Only if you want to hear her, you'd better go early. Although the performance starts at one o'clock, if you go at ten o'clock there won't be any seats."

Lao Ts'an heard what he said but did not take it very seriously. The next day he got up at six o'clock and first went to see the Shun Well[36] inside the South Gate. Then he went out of the South Gate to the foot of Lishan to see the place where, according to the tradition, the great Shun ploughed the fields in ancient times. When he returned to his inn, it was already about nine o'clock, so he made a hasty breakfast and then went to the Ming Lake House, where he arrived before ten o'clock. It turned out to be a large theater. In front of the stage were more than a hundred tables, and to his surprise when he entered the gate he found all the seats taken, except for seven or eight empty tables in the middle section. These tables had red paper slips pasted on them which said, "Reserved by the Governor," "Reserved by the Director of Education," and so on.

Lao Ts'an looked for a long time but could not find a place. Finally he slipped two hundred cash to an attendant, who arranged a short bench for him in a gap between the tables. On the stage he saw an oblong table on which was placed a flat drum. On the drum were two pieces of iron and he knew that these must be the so-called pear-blossom castanets. Beside them was a three-stringed banjo. Two chairs stood behind the table, but no one was on the stage. When you saw this huge stage, quite bare except for these few things, you couldn't help wanting to laugh. Ten or twenty men were walking up and down among the audience with baskets on their heads, selling sesame-seed cakes and *yu-t'iao* [fritters] to those who had come to the theater without having breakfast.

By eleven o'clock sedan chairs began to crowd at the door. Numerous officials in informal dress came in one after another, followed by their servants. Before twelve o'clock the empty tables in the front were all full. People still kept coming to see if there were seats, and short benches had to be wedged into the narrow spaces

35. a quieter, more refined kind of singing than those mentioned above.

36. named after the legendary Emperor Shun, who is supposed to have farmed the land at the foot of Mount Li or Lishan.

that were left. As this crowd of people arrived there were mutual greetings, many genuflections, and a few low bows.[37] Loud and animated conversation, free and easy talk, and laughter prevailed. Apart from those at the ten or so tables in front, the rest of the audience was made up of tradespeople, except for a few who looked like the scholars of the place. They all gossiped away, *ch'i-ch'i, ts'a-ts'a,* but since there were so many people, you couldn't hear clearly what they were saying. In any case, it was nobody's business.

At half-past twelve a man wearing a long blue cloth gown appeared through the curtained door at the back of the stage. He had a longish face, covered with lumps, like the skin of a Foochow orange dried by the wind. But ugly as he was, you felt that he was quiet and sober. He came out on the stage and said nothing but sat down on the chair to the left, behind the oblong table. Slowly he took up the three-stringed banjo, in a leisurely way tuned up the strings, and then played one or two little melodies, to which, however, the audience did not listen with much attention. After this he played a longer piece, but I don't know the name of the tune. I only remember that as it went on he began to pluck the strings in a circular motion, with all his fingers one after another, until the sounds now high, now low, now simple, now intricate, entered the ears and stirred the hearts of the listeners so with their variety that there might have been several tens of strings and several hundreds of fingers playing on them. And now continuous shouts of approval were heard, not interfering, however, with the sound of the banjo. When he had finished this piece, he rested, and a man from the wings brought him a cup of tea.

After a pause of several minutes a girl came out from behind the curtains. She was about sixteen or seventeen years old with a long duck's egg face, hair done into a knot, and silver earrings in her ears. She wore a blue cotton jacket and a pair of blue cotton trousers with black piping. Although her clothes were of coarse material, they were spotlessly clean. She came to the back of the table and sat down on the chair to the right. The banjo player then took up his instrument and began to pluck the strings, *chen-chen, ts'ung-ts'ung.* The girl stood up, took the pear-blossom castanets between the fingers of her left hand and began to clap them, *ting-ting, tang-tang,* in time with the banjo. With her right hand she took up the drumstick and then, after listening carefully to the rhythm of the banjo, struck the drum a sharp blow and began to sing. Every word was clear-cut and crisp; every note smooth-flowing like a young oriole flying out of a valley or a young swallow returning to the nest. Every

37. The genuflection in which one knee is bent and the other leg stretched behind is the salutation of the Manchu; the Chinese bow low. The Manchus, foreign invaders from the north, conquered China with Mongol, Korean, and Manchu troops, and established the Ching dynasty in 1644. The dynasty lasted until 1912.

phrase had seven words and every part several tens of phrases, now slow, now fast, sometimes high, sometimes low. There were endless changes of tune and style so that the listener felt that no song, tune, melody, or air ever invented could equal this one piece, that it was the peak of perfection in song.

There were two men sitting at Lao Ts'an's side, one of whom asked the other in a low voice, "I suppose this must be the Fair Maid?" The other man said, "No, this is the Dark Maid, the Fair Maid's younger sister. All her songs were taught her by the Fair Maid. If you compare her with the Fair Maid, it's impossible to estimate the distance that separates them! You can talk about her skill, but the Fair Maid's can't be put into words. The Dark Maid's skill can be learned by others, but the Fair Maid's can't possibly be learned. For several years now everybody has tried to sing like them. Even the singsong girls have tried! And the most anyone has done is to sing two or three phrases as well as the Dark Maid. As to the Fair Maid's merits, why there's never been anybody who could do a tenth as well as she."

While they were talking, the Dark Maid had already finished singing and went out at the back. And now all the people in the theater began to talk and laugh. Sellers of melon seeds, peanuts, red fruit, and walnuts shouted their wares in a loud voice. The whole place was filled with the sound of human voices. Just when the uproar was at its height, another girl appeared at the back of the stage. She was about eighteen or nineteen years old, and her costume differed in no detail from that of the first. She had a melon-seed face and a clear white complexion. Her features were not particularly beautiful; she was attractive without being seductive, pure but not cold. She came out with her head slightly bent, stood behind the table, took up the pear-blossom castanets and clapped them together several times, *ting-tang*. It was most amazing! They were just two bits of iron, and yet in her hand they seemed to contain all the five notes and the twelve tones. Then she took up the drumstick, lightly struck the drum twice, lifted her head, and cast one glance at the audience. When those two eyes, like autumn water, like winter stars, like pearls, like two beads of black in quicksilver, glanced left and right, even the men sitting in the most distant corners felt: Little Jade Wang is looking at me! As to those sitting nearer, nothing need be said. It was just one glance, but the whole theater was hushed, quieter than when the Emperor comes forth. Even a needle dropped on the ground could have been heard.

Little Jade Wang then opened her vermilion lips, displaying her sparkling white teeth, and sang several phrases. At first the sound was not very loud, but you felt an inexpressible magic enter your ears, and it was as though the stomach and bowels had been passed over by a smoothing iron, leaving no part unrelaxed. You seemed to absorb ambrosia through the thirty-six thousand pores of the skin until every single pore tingled with delight. After the first few phrases her song rose higher and louder till suddenly she drew her voice up to a sharp high-pitched note like a thread of steel wire thrown into the vault of the sky. You could not help secretly applauding. Still more amazing, she continued to move her voice up and down and in and out at that great height. After several turns her voice again began to rise, making three or four successive folds in the melody, each one higher than the last. It was like climbing T'aishan[38] from the western face of the Aolai Peak. First you see the thousand-fathom cleft wall of Aolai Peak and think that it reaches the sky. But when you have wound your way up to the top, you see Fan Peak far above you. And when you have got to the top of Fan Peak, again you see the South Gate of Heaven far above Fan Peak. The higher you climb, the more alarming it seems—the more alarming, the more wonderful.

After Little Jade Wang had sung her three or four highest flourishes, suddenly her voice dropped, and then at a powerful spirited gallop, in a short time, with a thousand twists and turns she described innumerable circles like a flying serpent writhing and turning among the thirty-six peaks of The Yellow Mountains.[39] After this the more she sang, the lower her voice became; the lower she sang, the more delicate it was, until at last the sound could be heard no more. Every person in the theater held his breath and sat intently, not daring to move. After two or three minutes it was as though a small sound came forth from under the ground. And then the voice again rose like a Japanese rocket which shoots into the sky, bursting and scattering with innumerable strands of multicolored fire. The voice soared aloft until endless sounds seemed to be coming and going. The banjo player too plucked his strings with a circular movement of all his fingers, now loud, now soft, in perfect accompaniment to her voice. It was like the wanton singing of sweet birds on a spring morning in the garden. The ears were kept so busy that you couldn't decide which note to listen to. Just as it was becoming most intricate, one clear note sounded, and then voice and instrument both fell silent. The applause from the audience was like the rumbling of thunder.

After a while the uproar abated slightly and from the front row one could hear a young man of about thirty say with a Hunan accent, "When I was a student and came across that passage where the ancient writer describes the merits of good singing in the words 'The sound circles the beams and stops not for three days,'[40] I could not understand what was meant. If you think of it in the abstract,

38. Located in Shantung Province, it is the most famous sacred mountain in China. A pilgrim path leading up the mountain is noted for its temples.

39. In Anhwei Province, two hundred miles west of Hangchow.

40. From Lao Tsu, Chapter V. See p. 408.

how can sound go round and round the beams? And how can it go on for three days? It was not until I heard Little Jade Wang sing that I realized how appropriate the words of the ancient writer are. Every time I hear her sing, her song echoes in my ears for many days. No matter what I'm doing my attention wanders. Rather I feel that the 'three days' of 'stops not for three days' is too short. The 'three months' of the saying about Confucius, 'For three months he knew not the taste of meat'[41] would describe it much more adequately." Those around him all said, "Mr. Meng Hsiang[42] expresses it so aptly that he arouses my envy."

While they were talking, the Dark Maid again came on to sing. After her the Fair Maid appeared again. Lao Ts'an heard a man near him say that this piece was called "The Black Donkey." It merely told the story of a scholar who saw a beautiful maiden riding by on a black donkey. Before describing the girl, it told all about the good parts of the black donkey, and when at last it came to tell about the maiden, in a few words it was finished. It was sung entirely in "rapid recitative"; the further it went, the faster it got. The poem by Po Hsiang-shan[43] expresses it perfectly,

Big pearls and little pearls fall into the jade platter.

The marvelous thing about it was that though she recited so quickly that you would have thought the listeners could not follow, every word was clear; not one was lost to their ears. Only she could obtain this clarity. But even this piece, it must be owned, was inferior to the preceding one. . . .

VIII

. . . .

In a very short time they had come to the lights, which turned out to belong not to a market town, but to the houses of several families who lived on the mountain side. Because of the slope they looked like high buildings with several stories. When they arrived here, they talked things over and decided that nothing would make them go any further, that the only thing was to be brazen and knock on a door and ask for lodging.

By this time they had reached a gate in a "tiger-skin" stone wall. It belonged to a house that seemed to consist of quite a number of

41. from the *Analects* of Confucius, VII, xiii. The passage is: "When the Master was in Ch'i, he heard the *Shao* (music in the style of the legendary Emperor Shun), and for three months he knew not the taste of meat. He said, 'I thought not that music could be made as excellent as this!' "

42. probably the contemporary poet Wang I-min.

43. also known as Chü-i (772–846). The line quoted is from a poem called *Song of the Guitar* (*P'i Pa Hsing*), which is translated by Witter Bynner and Kiang Kang-hu in *The Jade Mountain* (New York. 1929).

buildings, probably about ten or so *chien*.[44] One of the men went forward and knocked on the door. After several knocks an old man with gray hair and beard came out, holding in his hand a candlestick with a lighted candle of white wax. He said, "What do you want?"

Shen Tzu-p'ing hurried forward and told him in his most pleasant manner about their troubles, saying, "I fully realize that this is not an inn, but unfortunately my attendants are absolutely unable to go on. I should like to ask you, Sir, to do a good deed." The old man inclined his head and said, "Please wait a while. I will go and ask our young lady." So saying, and without closing the gate, he went in.

Tzu-p'ing watched him and greatly surprised, asked himself, "Surely this family can't be without a master? Why does he go to ask a young lady? Surely the head of the family can't be a girl!" Then he thought, "I must be wrong! The family must be governed by an old lady. This old fellow must be her nephew; *ku niang* (young lady), must mean *ku mu* (paternal aunt). This is the only sensible explanation; I'm sure it can't be wrong."

Almost immediately the old man, still holding a candlestick in his hand, came out accompanied by a middle-aged fellow and said, "Will the guest please come in." On entering the gate of this house, a building of five *chien* in a row appeared, with a flight of about ten steps leading to a door in the middle. The middle-aged fellow held a candlestick in his hand and lighted the way for Shen Tzu-p'ing. Shen Tzu-p'ing ordered his men, "Wait in the courtyard for a bit while I go in to see how things are, and then I will call you."

Tzu-p'ing went up the steps; the old man was standing inside the door of the middle *chien* and said, "There is a slope on the north side. Tell them to push the wheelbarrows and lead the donkey up there and come into this building that way."

Now the main gate they had come through faced west. They all went into the building. The three *chien* in the middle formed one room which was separated by a partition from a one-*chien* room at each end. At the north end of the three *chien* there was a *k'ang*;[45] the south end was empty. They put the barrows and the donkey at the south end, and the five men settled on the *k'ang*. Then the old man asked Tzu-p'ing his name and said, "Will the guest please go inside."

He passed through the middle *chien* and there was another flight of steps. It led to a level plot of ground planted with flowers and trees, which gleamed in the moonlight, strangely secluded and beautiful. Little gusts of elusive fragrance soaked the lungs and bowels with their freshness. To the north was a fine three-*chien* apartment that faced south, completely surrounded by a gallery with posts and

44. rooms. 45. a built-in brick bed with flues under it for heating.

railings of untrimmed fir. Upon entering the building Tzu-p'ing saw, hanging from the roof, four paper lanterns with cleverly made, mottled bamboo frames. Two *chien* were thrown together; one *chien* was separated off into another room. The tables, chairs, stands, and desks were all correctly placed. Between the two rooms was hung a *lientzu*[46] of dull brown cloth.

When the old man reached the door of the inner room he called out, "Young lady, the guest, Mr. Shen, has come." Then the *lientzu* was lifted, and a maiden of eighteen or nineteen came out. She was dressed in cotton, a jacket of light blue, and a dark blue skirt. Her appearance was dignified and calm, attractive and graceful. Seeing the guest she bowed. Tzu-p'ing hastened to make a deep bow to return the greeting. The maiden said, "Please sit down." Then she said to the old man, "Hurry up and prepare the food; the guest is hungry." The old man went out.

The maiden said, "What is your honorable name? What brings you here?" Tzu-p'ing then told how his cousin had sent him specially to find Liu Jen-fu. The maiden said, "Mr. Liu used to live just to the east of this village. Now he has moved to Cypress Tree Valley." Tzu-p'ing asked, "Where is Cypress Tree Valley?" The maiden replied, "About thirty or more li west of the village. The path that leads there is much more out of the way than this and much rougher going too. The day before yesterday when my father came off duty he told us that today there would be a guest from afar who would have had a scare on the road, and told us to stay up late and prepare some food and wine for his entertainment. He further told us to ask you not to blame us if we do less than one should do for an honored guest."

When Tzu-p'ing heard this he was extremely surprised. "What sort of 'on duty' and 'off duty' can there be in a wild mountain where there is no yamen?[47] How could anyone know about my coming the day before yesterday? How does this maiden have such dignity and grace? Surely this is exactly what the ancients meant by 'a silvan air.' I must find out more about her."

If you don't know whether or not Shen Tzu-p'ing will be able to solve the mystery of who the maiden is, then hear the next chapter tell.

IX

A guest chants poems, hands behind back, facing a wall;
Three people sip tea, knee to knee, in intimate talk.

It has been told that Shen Tzu-p'ing was just wondering at this

46. a curtain, usually of cloths or reeds.

47. a general name for the headquarters of an official. The "sylvan air" is an air of refinement from living on a country estate. Not "rustic"!

maiden's dignity and grace of manner, so unlike that of a country girl, and at where her father could hold office. He was about to question her when he saw the outside *lientzu* move, and a middle-aged man come in carrying a tray of food. The maiden said, "Just put it down on the *k'ang* table in the west room."

In the west room under the south window, there was a heated brick *k'ang*. Against the window was a long *k'ang* shelf and at each end a short one. In the middle was a square *k'ang* table with places for people to sit on three sides. In the west wall was a big, round moon-window with a pane of glass let into the middle, and in front of the window was a desk. Although the room was not partitioned off from the central room, there was a carved wooden arch separating them. The man arranged the food on the *k'ang* table. It was only a plate of steamed bread, a pot of wine, a crock of millet gruel, and four dishes; no doubt some kind of rough mountain-vegetable food—no meat or fish. The maiden said, "Please have something to eat; I will come back in a little while," and went into the east room.

Tzu-p'ing really felt very cold and hungry, so he sat on the *k'ang*, drank some cups of wine, and then proceeded to eat some steamed bread. Although it was vegetable food, the fresh flavor which filled his mouth was much pleasanter than that of meat. When he had eaten the bread and finished the gruel, the man filled a basin of water and he washed his face. He then got up, and walked up and down the room to stretch his limbs. Lifting his head he saw a set of four large scrolls hanging on the north wall. They were covered with "grass" characters, very free, like flying dragons and dancing phoenixes, so unusual as to startle one. On the scroll at the extreme left were two names. At the top was written: "Presented for correction[48] to the Pillar Official of the Western Peak." At the bottom was written: "Yellow Dragon offers this writing." Although he could not decipher all of the characters, he could get eight or nine out of ten. On close examination it turned out to be six *chüeh-chu*[49] poems of seven characters to each line. They were neither purely Buddhist nor Taoist writings, but when digested they had a good deal of flavor: they were not all "extinction of desire and emptying of the mind,"[50] nor were they only about "lead and mercury" and "dragons and tigers."[51] On the desk below the moon-window he saw paper and pen ready for use so he copied down the poems to take back

48. This is a polite formula for submitting one's poems to a dedicatee.

49. a verse form of four lines, each line consisting of five or seven words. A difficult form because of the conciseness required. (Ed.)

50. mystical absorption or Buddhist Nirvana.

51. Lead and mercury could be mixed, the Taoists claimed, to make an elixir of immortality. Dragons and tigers symbolize water and fire, the two opposite forces (*yin* and *yang*) that produce the life of the universe.

to the yamen to read as you would a newspaper. Do you know what sort of verses they were? Please look. The poems[52] said:

(1)

I have worshipped the nine lotus-enthroned of the Jasper
Pool,
Hsi-i has taught me the *Chih Yüan P'ien;*
Five centuries passed unnoticed like the grass:
The ocean now rolls where mulberries grew.

(2)

Tzu-yang bade me emulate the *Ts'ui Hsü Yin,*
It resounded like the Thunderclap Lute in empty hills;
I still could not remove the "Thee" and "Me":
Heaven-sent flowers clung to my encircling cloud.

52. These difficult, symbolic poems have a philosophical theme. Brief paraphrases are these: (1) "While I was being taught the truth of things by my teacher (Li Ling-ch'uan), I was so absorbed that I did not notice the passage of time." The "nine-lotus enthroned" are nine ranks of Buddhas. The Jasper Pool is in the house of the Western Queen mother, the Taoist cult-leader Hsi Wang Mu, but is also identifiable with the sacred lake in a legendary "Western paradise." Hsi-i (lit., "inaudible and invisible"—taken from the *Tao Te Ching,* see p. 205) is the name of honor of a recluse, Ch'en T'uan, whose book of Taoist techniques, the *Chih Yüan P'ien,* is mentioned. (2) "When my friend Huang Hsi-p'eng had started to teach, he humbly admitted that his knowledge was not great and that sometimes he still could not understand the doctrine." (Chang) Tzu-yang was a priest of the Sung dynasty; the *Ts'ui Hsü Yin* (*Song of Verdant Vacuity*) is a Taoist hymn. The lute has been made out of wood from a tree struck by lightning. The last line refers to the reward of a sage who gave a correct explanation of doctrine: a heavenly maid scattered flowers over him and his assemblage. The flowers clung only to lesser holy men who had not eliminated the distinctions between all things from their minds. (3) "Many men who are filled with earthly desires, when they find a teacher to lead them, become heavenly natures." "Sky of lust," "sea of sense," and "river of desire" are all Buddhist expressions. "River of righteousness" is the water in the seven pools of the Western Paradise. The lotus (Buddha is often depicted sitting on a throne of lotuses) is the *Man T'o Lo* flower. A symbol of purity, it grows out of the mud of the pond's depths. (4) The teaching of the master (Chou T'ai-ku) is unique and incomparable like a sudden awakening after a deep sleep. The author, after studying under his teacher (Li Lung-ch'uan) felt a sudden and complete enlightenment. The first line is a metaphorical description of harp playing modeled on a poem by Li Ho (791–817) (see Robert Payne, *The White Pony,* New York, 1947, p. 308). "Three nights under one mulberry tree" refers to the Buddhist ideal that one should not spend long enough in any one place to develop attachments. (5) "The universe is a confused cycle of life and death, but when you have received this teaching, from a state of calm you pass to a state of emptiness and formlessness." The "wild horses" metaphor and the "life teems, plants throng" image are from the *Chuang Tzu* (see *Texts of Taoism,* translated by James Legge, Oxford, 1861; Sacred Books of the East series, vols. XXXIX, XL, 1, 165) and p. 204. Condor Peak (Ch'iu Ling) is a mountain in India where the Buddha is reputed to have preached. Hu Kung is mentioned in *Chuang Tzu* in connection with acts of magic (see *Texts of Taoism,* I, 263–265). (6) "When the teachers (Chiang Wen't'ien and Huang Hsi-p'eng) were together teaching in Soochow, disciples from the north and south were united and had no divisions. How commendable that was!" *Peepul* (*P'u T'i*) is a transliteration of a Sanskrit world, *bodhi,* which means "wisdom" or "enlightenment." The *bo* tree is the one under which the Buddha became enlightened. The third and fourth lines refer to a story in the *Travels of Fa Chuan* (translated by James Legge, London, 1900, pp. 73–74) which has to do with a miraculous giving of breast milk simultaneously to a thousand sons.

(3)

The sky of lust and sea of sense are full of wind and wave:
Vast and uncrossable is the river of desire;
Led into the garden as River of Righteousness,
It is everywhere planted with Man T'o Lo flowers.

(4)

With cracking of rock and trembling of heaven a single
crane flies aloft,
Blackness filled the night, at the fifth watch crows the cock;
The precept "Never three nights under one mulberry tree"
once learned,
One sees not in the world of men distinctions of right and
wrong.

(5)

"Wild horses" gallop night and day with clouds of dust,
Life teems, plants throng.
Steal into the joy of Condor Peak Nirvana;
Seize from Hu Kung his life-suspending power.

(6)

The peepul leaf is old; the *Lotus Sutra* is new.
North and south transmit the same true light;
Five hundred Heavenly Babes all received milk,
Incense flowers are offered to Hsiao Fu Jen.

Tzu-p'ing finished copying the poems and turned his head to look out of the moon-window. The moonlight, clear and bright, lighted up the mountains which rose, layer on layer, tier on tier, ever higher and higher. It was indeed a fairy land, far removed from the every-day world. And now he felt not at all tired. Why not go out and wander on the mountains a little? Wouldn't that be still better? He was about to start when he thought, "But aren't these mountains the mountains we have just come through? Isn't this moon the very moon under which we trudged? Why did it seem so gloomy and fearsome when we came, making us nervous and afraid? The mountain and the moon are still the same. How is it they now bring me a feeling of liberation and delight?" And then he thought of what General Wang[53] says, "Alas, our feelings change according

53. Wang Hsi-chih (321–379), a great calligrapher. The quotation is from his *Preface to the Party at the Orchid Pavilion* (*Lan T'ing Chi Hsu*), translated by Lin Yutang in *The Importance of Living* (New York, 1937). The complete sentence is "But when that which we have enjoyed fatigues us, our feelings change according to our surroundings, and melancholy follows."

to our surroundings; and melancholy follows." How completely true! For a moment he was undecided about what to do next and thought of writing one or two poems, but he heard behind him a musical voice saying, "Have you finished eating? How neglectful I am!" He hurriedly turned his head and found that the maiden had changed into a pale-green padded gown of printed cloth and loose black trousers, and now her eyebrows were even more like spring mountains, and her eyes like autumn water; her two cheeks were plump and as though the vermilion were sheathed in silk. From under the white the color barely showed through—not like the presentday kind of make-up you see everywhere, where they plaster themselves with that rouge stuff until they look like a monkey's rump! A smile played about her mouth and cheeks, and her eyes and eyebrows had a look of grave dignity, arousing mingled feelings of love and respect. The maiden said, "Won't you please sit on the *k'ang?* It's much warmer there."

Then they both sat down. The old grayhead came in and asked the maiden, "Where shall Mr. Shen's things be put?" The maiden replied, "When the master went away the day before yesterday, he ordered that the guest was to sleep in his bed in this building. You don't need to unpack his bedding. Have his men all had something to eat? Tell them to go to bed early. Has the donkey been fed?" The grayhead replied to all the questions, "Everything has been arranged properly." The maiden further said, "Bring us some tea." The grayhead said "Yes" several times.

Tzu-p'ing protested, "I wouldn't dare to rest my dusty and profane body here. On the way in I saw a big *k'ang*; let me sleep in that room with the others." The maiden replied, "You don't need to be so polite. These are my father's orders; otherwise a simple mountain girl like me wouldn't presume to entertain a guest alone." "You have shown me far too much kindness," Tzu-p'ing said, "I am deeply grateful. Only I have not yet asked your honorable name. What is your esteemed father's office? Where does he perform his duty?" "My name is T'u," said the girl. "My father does duty at the Palace of Colored Clouds.[54] He serves for five days at a time; this means half the month at home, half the month at the Palace."

Tzu-p'ing asked, "Who composed the poems on this set of scrolls? To look at them one would suppose it was an immortal." The maiden answered, "It was my father's friend. He often comes here for a talk, and he wrote them when he was here once last year. He is a man who goes about 'without gown or shoes.'[55] He is very intimate with my father." Tzu-p'ing said, "Well, then, is he a Buddhist monk or a Taoist priest? Why does he put into his poems

54. an imaginary and legendary place. 55. i.e., an unconventional person.

a sort of Taoistic language? And isn't there also a lot of Buddhist lore?" The maiden said, "He is neither a Taoist priest nor a Buddhist monk; in fact he wears the clothes of a layman. He always says, 'The three schools—Confucianism, Buddhism, Taoism—are like the signboards hung outside three shops. In reality they are all sellers of mixed provisions; they all sell fuel, rice, oil, salt. But the shop belonging to the Confucian family is bigger; the Buddhist and Taoist shops are smaller. There is nothing they don't stock in all the shops.' He further says, 'All teachings have two layers: one can be called the surface teaching, one the inner teaching. The inner teachings are all the same; the surface teachings are all different. So Buddhist monks shave their heads; Taoist priests do their hair up into a coil; you can tell at a glance which is Buddhist and which is Taoist. If you ask the Buddhist monk to keep his hair and do it up in a coil and wear a feather-trimmed coat, and the Taoist priest to shave his hair and put on a gown of camlet, then people will call them by the opposite names. That is how people use their eyes, ears, nose and tongue, isn't it?' Again he says, 'Surface teachings differ; inner teachings are really the same.' For this reason Mr. Yellow Dragon doesn't hold to any one teaching, but freely chants them all."

"Listening to these wonderful arguments," Tzu-p'ing said, "I am filled with admiration. But I am extremely stupid, and since you say the inner teaching of the three schools is the same, I want to ask you where the similarities are and where the differences. Also why is one greater than the other? If the Confucian school is the greatest, wherein lies its greatness? I venture to ask you to explain."

The maiden said, "Their similarity consists in encouraging man to be good, leading man to be disinterested. If all men were disinterested, the Empire would have peace. If all men scheme for private advantage, then the Empire is in chaos. Only Confucianism is thoroughly disinterested. Consider! In his life Confucius met many dissenters such as Ch'ang-chü, Chieh-ni, and the 'old man with a basket of weeds,'[56] none of whom respected him very much, but he on the contrary praised them without end. This is his disinterestedness; this is his greatness. And so he said, 'To attack heterodoxy, this is truly injurious.'[57] Now the Buddhists and Taoists indeed were narrow-minded. They feared lest later generations should not honor their teachings, so they talked a lot about heaven and hell in order to frighten people. This was partly intended to spur people to well-doing, and to this extent they were disinterested.

56. Ch'ang-chü, "the long rester," and Chieh-ni, "the firm recluse," were two recluses who condemned Confucius as a busybody. See Confucius' *Analects*, XVII, vi. The "old man" was another recluse (see *Analects*, XVIII, vii).

57. *Analects*, II, xvi. The orthodox interpretation is "The study of strange doctrines is injurious indeed" (Legge, *Chinese Classics*, I, 150), but there is ambiguity in that *kung* means both "to attack" and "to study."

But when they teach that even to say that you believe their teachings is to have all your sins blotted out, while not to believe their teachings is to be possessed by devils and when dead to go down to hell—in this they are narrow and self-interested. As to all the foreign sects, they go even further and on account of doctrinal differences raise troops and war continuously, killing men as though cutting hemp. I ask you, does this agree with their original intention? This is where they are still more narrow than others. Islam, for instance, when it says that blood shed in a religious war shines like a rosy-red precious stone, cheats man to the extreme! Now Confucianism, unfortunately, has for a long time ceased to be taught. The Han-period scholars paid attention to chapter and verse, but they lost sight of the main thought; by the T'ang dynasty there was simply nobody who propounded it. Han Ch'ang-li[58] was a charlatan who understood the letter but did not understand the spirit and talked a lot of nonsense. He even wrote an essay called *In Search of the Original Tao*, but his search led him to the opposite of the original teaching! He said, 'If the King does not give commands, he loses his kingship; if the people do not supply grain, rice, silk, and hemp and offer them to their superiors, they should be executed!' If this is true, shouldn't we say that since Chieh and Chou[59] were good at giving orders and good at executing people, therefore Chieh and Chou were good kings and the subjects of Chieh and Chou were bad? Isn't this to upset the whole idea of right and wrong? He also wanted to oppose Buddhism and Taoism and yet became the friend of a monk. Therefore later students of Confucianism felt that it was too much trouble to follow the principles of Confucius and Mencius—not as easy as to throw together a few sentences of jargon attacking the Buddhists and Taoists, and so to count as disciples of the Sage. How much simpler that was! Even Chu Fu-tzu[60] couldn't escape this limitation. Merely on the authority of Han Ch'ang-li's *In Search of the Original Tao*, he changed the meaning of the *Analects* of Confucius, taking the 'attack' in 'to attack heterodoxy' and twisting it about in a hundred ways and in the end making no sense of it at all. Finally the Sung scholars made the Confucianism of Confucius and Mencius more and more narrow until it was quite destroyed."

As Tzu-p'ing listened, he was filled with respect and admiration, and he said, "An evening's talk with you is better than ten years'

58. An important prose writer and ardent Confucian, his dates are 768–824. His essay (translated by Herbert A. Giles in *Gems of Chinese Literature*, Shanghai, 1923) upholds Confucianism against Taoism and Buddhism.

59. two bloodthirsty tyrants. Their rule showed that the imperial mandate from heaven had been exhausted.

60. Chiu Fu Tzu, also known as Chu Hsi (1130–1200), greatest of the Sung philosophers. His interpretation of Confucianism was considered authoritative until the twentieth century. The passage shows how even the diligent scholar can corrupt an ancient text by relying excessively on commentators.

reading! Truly I am hearing what I have never heard before! But I still don't understand how Ch'ang-chü and Chieh-ni can be heterodox (*i tuan*), and Buddhism and Taoism not heterodox. How do you explain that?" The maiden answered, "They are all *i tuan*. You must know that the character *i* ought to be read to mean 'not alike,' and the character *tuan* must be read 'an extremity.' Thus 'To hold the two *tuan*' expresses the idea 'hold the two extremities.' If *i tuan* is explained as 'heterodox,' then won't the 'two *tuan*' have to be explained as 'a forked teaching.' And in that case won't 'Hold the two *tuan*' then mean 'grasp a forked teaching'? What sort of sense does that make? The meaning of the Sage is that different roads may lead to the same goal; different melodies may achieve the same effect. If a doctrine sets out to persuade men to be good and lead men to take an unselfish view of life, there is nothing wrong with it. This is what is meant by: 'The greater virtue allows no overstepping of its limits; the lesser virtues permit some liberty.'[61] But if it sets out to make attacks on people, it may begin by attacking Buddhism and Taoism, but later when such differences as those between Chu and Lu[62] appear, members of the same family will take arms against each other. All being children of Confucius and Mencius, why did Chu's followers want to attack Lu, and Lu's followers want to attack Chu? This is what is called, 'losing one's proper nature,'[63] and is firmly condemned by the above-quoted words of Confucius, 'This is truly injurious.' "

When Tzu-p'ing had heard all this he sighed again and again in admiration and said, "I am indeed fortunate to meet you today; it is like meeting a distinguished teacher! But even though there are places where the Sung scholars may have misunderstood the Sage's intention, still, their development of the orthodox doctrine was an achievement beyond the reach of others. Thus, although the two terms *li* (reason) and *yü* (desire) and such expressions as *chu ching* (pay respect) and *ts'un ch'eng* (maintain sincerity), all come from the ancient sages, later men really received a great deal of gain from the Sung scholars' development of these conceptions. Men's sentiments were set right by them; customary morality was mellowed by them."

The girl smiled in a captivating manner and sent a glance in the direction of Tzu-p'ing like the seductive movement of autumn ripples. Tzu-p'ing felt the charm of her winged eyebrows and the grace of her parted red lips, and it seemed as though a subtle fragrance soaked into his flesh and bones. He couldn't prevent his spirit from

61. lit., "with the greater there is no stepping beyond the door bar; with the lesser virtue passing in and out is allowed." See *Analects,* XIX, xi.

62. In 1175 the two philosophers Chu Hsi and Lu Hsiang-shan had a famous meeting in Kiangsu at which a philosophical controversy started which their followers continued.

63. This is from Mencius, VI, x, 8 (see Legge, *Chinese Classics,* II, 414).

fluttering about in the air. The girl put forth a hand, white as jade, soft as cotton wool, reached across the *k'ang* table, and took hold of Tzu-p'ing's hand. After she had taken it, she said, "I should like to ask you, how does this compare with the time when you were a boy in the study, and your esteemed tutor took your hand and 'beating was the school punishment'?"[64]

Tzu-p'ing was silent and could make no reply. The girl again said, "Tell me honestly, how do you like me compared with your esteemed tutor? The Sage says, 'What is meant by "making the thoughts sincere" is the allowing no self-deception, as when we hate a bad smell, and when we love a beautiful woman.'[65] Confucius speaks of 'Loving virtue as you love a woman.'[66] Mencius says 'It is the nature of man to eat and love.'[67] Tzu Hsia speaks of 'transferring your esteem from women to virtue.'[68] So this love of woman is fundamental to man's nature. The Sung scholars try to say that we should love virtue and not love women. Surely this is self-deception? To deceive yourself and to deceive others is the extreme of insincerity! But they perversely want to call it 'maintaining sincerity'—isn't that hateful? The Sage made a distinction between *ch'ing* (feeling) and *li* (good manners)—he did not consider *li* (reason) and *yü* (desire) opposed to each other; and he rearranged the *Book of Odes* so as to put the 'Kuan Chü'[69] at the head. Consider:

Lovely is this noble lady,
Fit bride for our lord!

and

Sought her and could not get her

and

Now on his back, now tossing onto his side.

Can we really say this only illustrates heavenly reason (*t'ien li*) and not a mere human desire (*jen yü*)? From this we can see that the Sage did not deceive people. The *Preface* says on the 'Kuan Chü,' 'It arises from feeling; but stops within the limits of decorum and righteousness.' 'Arising from feeling' is in the realm of the spontaneous. Thus tonight an honorable guest is bestowed upon us: I cannot help being happy: this arises from spontaneous feeling. When you came, you were tired and exhausted. A good deal of time has passed, and

64. from the punishments authorized by the Emperor Shun in the *Book of History* (see Legge, *Chinese Classics*, III, 38, 39).
65. from *The Great Learning* (Legge, *Chinese Classics*, I, 366).
66. from the *Analects*, IX, xvii.
67. from Mencius, VIa, iv (Legge, *Chinese Classics*, II, 397).
68. from the *Analects*, I, vii.
69. the first poem of the *Book of Odes*, lines 3, 4, 9, 12. See No. 87 in Arthur Waley, *Book of Songs* (London, 1937; reprinted New York, 1960).

you ought to be still more tired. But instead, your spirit is bright and sparkling, and you seem very happy; this also arises from spontaneous feeling. When a young girl and a grown man sit together deep into the night, and they indulge in no improper talk, they have remained 'within the limits of decorum.' This indeed is in harmony with the Sage's teaching. As to the Sung scholars' various deceptions they are too many to be recounted. Yet although the Sung scholars made many mistakes they were right in some places. As to the present-day disciples of the Sung school, they are really nothing but hypocrites; Confucius and Mencius would hate them deeply and would disown them."

They had barely finished talking when the grayhead brought in the tea—two old porcelain cups and pale green tea. As soon as they were put on the table a fragrance assailed the nostrils. The girl took her tea, rinsed her mouth, rinsed it again, and spat it all out into the pit under the *k'ang*, saying with a laugh, "What made us discuss these ethical questions tonight? You have made me pollute my mouth with these perverted doctrines. After this let us 'only talk about wind and moon.' "[70]

Tzu-p'ing readily agreed. He raised his cup and took a sip of tea. It was unusually refreshing. He swallowed it and felt purified to the very pit of his stomach. Around the root of his tongue the juices came in waves, fragrant and sweet. He swallowed two mouthfuls one after another, and it was as though the fragrant vapor stole up from his mouth to his nose, unspeakably pleasant to experience. He asked, "What tea leaves are these? Why is it so good?" The maiden replied, "The tea leaves are nothing wonderful; it is wild tea that grows on the mountain, and therefore has quite a full flavor. Luckily, too, our water is drawn from a spring on the east summit of the mountain. The higher the spring, the more delicious is the flavor of the water. Also we use pine cones as fuel and boil the water in an earthenware container. These three advantages combine to make the result good. Where you live, all the tea is brought from outside—you have no good varieties—and the flavor is bound to be thin. Add to this that your water and fuel are not right, and the taste naturally is inferior."

At this point somebody was heard outside the window, calling, "Yü Ku (Miss Jade), why didn't you tell me that you have a distinguished guest today?" When the girl heard this, she quickly got up and said, "Uncle Dragon, how is it you have come at this time of night?"

While she was still talking, the man had already come in. He was wearing a dark blue, cotton padded gown "of a hundred patches,"[71]

70. a way of saying that one should not talk about business at pleasurable social gatherings.

71. a name for the gown of a Buddhist monk.

was bareheaded and beltless, and had no jacket. He was something more than fifty years old; he had a ruddy complexion, and his whiskers and beard were pitch black. When he saw Tzu-p'ing, he saluted him with his hands together and said, "Mr. Shen, how long have you been here?" Tzu-p'ing replied, "About two or three hours. May I ask your honorable name?" The man said, "I keep my name hidden and use Yellow Dragon as a *hao*." Tzu-p'ing said, "What good fortune to meet you! I was reading and admiring your poems sometime ago." The maiden said, "Won't you come and sit on the *k'ang*?"

Yellow Dragon then sat on the *k'ang*, taking the inside place at the table, and said, "Yü Ku, you said you would invite me to eat bamboo shoots. Where are the bamboo shoots? Bring them in and I will eat." Yü Ku answered, "Some time ago I was planning to dig some up, but I forgot, and they were taken by Mr. T'eng Liu.[72] If Uncle Dragon wants to eat some, he had better find Mr. T'eng Liu himself and argue it out with him." Yellow Dragon raised his head to heaven and laughed aloud.

Tzu-p'ing said to the maiden, "I don't want to be rude, but I take it that the two words Yü Ku must be your honorable personal name?" The maiden replied, "My humble name is Yü, the Second Daughter. My older sister is called Fan, the First Daughter, and people of my father's generation are all accustomed to call me Yü Ku (Miss Jade)."

Yellow dragon said to Tzu-p'ing, "Are you sleepy, Mr. Shen? If you are not, we are such a good company that we had better stay up tonight, and get up late tomorrow. In the Cypress Tree Valley region the paths are extremely steep and dangerous and very bad for traveling. Besides, this heavy fall of snow has made the roads hard to follow. If you slip, your life is in danger. Liu Jen-fu has been packing his bags tonight and will be at the fair at the Temple of Kuan Ti by noon tomorrow. If you start after breakfast tomorrow, you will be just in time to meet him."

Hearing this Tzu-p'ing was very happy. "To have chanced to meet you two immortals today is fortune enough for three incarnations," he said. "Please, Honorable Immortal, tell me the time of your birth; was it in T'ang or Sung?" Yellow Dragon again laughed very loud. "How do you know so much about me?" The answer was: "In your poem you say clearly:

> Five centuries passed unnoticed like the grass;
> The ocean now rolls where mulberries grew.

From this we can tell that you are certainly more than five or six hundred years old." Yellow Dragon said, " 'To believe everything in the *Book of History* would be worse than to have no *Book of History*

72. the "Snowman" or Snow Spirit.

at all.'[73] I was only playing with my pen and ink. You should read my poems as you read the *Story of the Peach Blossom Fountain,*[74] Sir!" With this, he lifted his teacup to taste the freshly made tea.

Yü Ku saw that the tea in Tzu-p'ing's cup was almost finished, so she took the little teapot to fill it for him. Tzu-p'ing half-rose several times and saying, "Please don't disturb yourself!" lifted his cup and tasted it like a connoisseur. Just then he heard a sound, "*Wu,*" outside in the distance, and noticed that the paper in the windows was moving with a slight rustling sound and the dust on the beams was coming down in a shower. He recalled what had happened on the road and unconsciously his hair stood up on end, his bones became stiff with fright, and his color suddenly changed. Yellow Dragon said, "This is a tiger's roar; nothing to worry about. Mountain folk look on this sort of animal as you city-dwellers look on donkeys and horses. Although you know they can kick a man, you are not afraid of them, for having been used to them for a long time you know that it is very unusual for them to harm people. Mountain folk and tigers are used to each other; the men usually avoid the tigers, and the tigers also avoid the men, so it is not often that a man is attacked. You don't need to be afraid of them."

Tzu-p'ing said, "You can tell from the sound that it is still far away; how is it that it makes the paper of the windows vibrate and the dust from the beams shower down?" "This is simply what is called 'the majesty of the tiger,' "[75] Yellow Dragon replied. "Since there are mountains on all four sides, the air is enclosed—one roar of a tiger and the four mountains all reply. It is like this for twenty to forty li around the tiger. If a tiger goes down to the plain, he no longer has this majestic power. For this reason the ancients said, 'If dragon leaves water or tiger leaves mountain, he suffers contempt of man!' It is just the same as when an official in the Imperial Court has experienced some difficulty, or been censured for something and goes home to vent his feelings on his wife and children. Outside his home he is afraid to utter a single determined word, nor has he the courage to give up his office. It is for the same reason that the tiger doesn't dare leave the mountains and the dragon doesn't dare leave the water."

Tzu-p'ing nodded his head several times, "That's true enough. But I still don't quite understand. When the tiger is in the mountains, how does he have such majestic power? What is the reason for it?" Yellow Dragon answered, "Haven't you read the *Thousand-Character Essay?*[76] It is for the same reason that 'Hollow ravine

73. from Mencius, VII, iii (Legge, *Chinese Classics,* II, 479).

74. by T'ao Ch'ien (365–427). Translated in Giles, *Gems of Chinese Literature.*

75. In an ancient story the fox borrows the "majesty of the tiger" simply by telling the tiger he is a divine being.

76. a work, reputedly of the sixth century, used in Chinese elementary schools. It contains one thousand characters (ideographs), not one of which is repeated.

transmits sound; in empty hall hearing is easy.' An empty hall is just a small hollow ravine. A hollow ravine is just a big empty hall. If you let off a cannon cracker outside this door, it will reverberate for half a day. For the same reason thunder in a mountain town sounds many times as loud as on the plain." He then turned his head and said to the maiden, "Yü Ku, I haven't heard you play the lute for a long time. Today we have the unwonted pleasure of a distinguished guest here; bring your lute and play him a tune! It will give me a chance to hear you, too." "Uncle Dragon, why suggest it?" Yü Ku said. "You know how I play my lute. It will make a laughingstock of me! When Mr. Shen is in the city, he hears lots of good lute players! Why should he have to listen to our rustic 'welcoming drum'?[77] However I will go and fetch a zither. If Uncle Dragon plays a melody on the zither, that will be something more rare." Yellow Dragon said, "All right. All right. Then I'll play the zither, and you play the lute. But to carry them back and forth is a lot of trouble. It's better for us to go and play in your cave. Fortunately a mountain maid is not like a young miss in a yamen, whose room may not be visited by other people." With this he got down from the *k'ang*, put on his shoes, took a candle, and beckoned to Tzu-p'ing, "Please come along; Yü Ku will lead the way."

Yü Ku then got down from the *k'ang*, took the candle, and went first. Tzu-p'ing was second, Yellow Dragon third. They went through the middle *chien*, lifted the *lientzu*, and entered the inner *chien*. It had two couches, one at each end; the one to the left had quilts and pillows in place; the one to the right was piled with books and pictures. There was a window looking out to the east, and under the window a square table. In front of the couch on the left was a small door. Yü Ku said to Tzu-p'ing, "This is my father's bedroom." They went through the little door beside the couch. It was a sort of zigzag gallery, but had windows and a roof. You walked on wooden planks over a hollow space. A turn to the north, then a turn to the east. On the north and east it was all glass windows. If you looked out of the north windows, the mountain was very close—a sheer cliff that shot up into space; if you looked down, it seemed to be very deep, just as they were going forward they suddenly heard the sound of falling rocks, *p'ing-p'eng, huo-lo;* as though the mountain were toppling over. Underfoot was a shaking and quaking. Tzu-p'ing was so frightened that his souls fled from his body.

If you don't know what happened afterwards, then hear the next chapter tell.

77. a particular type of melody.

LU HSÜN (CHOU SHU-JEN)

(1881–1936)

Three Stories

Lu Hsün has been called "the earliest practitioner of Western-style fiction"[1] in China. Certainly he is one of the greatest of modern Chinese writers. His reputation has grown steadily in China and he was famous at least a decade before his death in 1936. He was born Chou Shu-jen in Shaohsing in 1881 to a poor family which had clung to the ancient Chinese respect for education and learning. He studied at the Naval Academy at Nanking and then went to Japan to study medicine. But he soon decided that the Chinese soul needed more attention than the body, and he found himself steadily drawn towards the intellectual life. An incident in the Russo-Japanese war of 1904–5 triggered in him a desire to rouse his people from their backwardness and their apathy. Lu Hsün saw a film of a Chinese, allegedly a spy for the Russians, being decapitated by the Japanese. The execution itself did not affect him so much as the total apathy of his countrymen, the Chinese spectators at the scene. China, once the teacher of Japan, and the supreme cultural and political power in Asia for centuries, was now backward, verging on political chaos, and at the mercy of any upstart power—East or West—which chose to humiliate China. Lu Hsün learned both Japanese and German, and read such authors as Nietzsche, Gogol, and Chekhov. He determined to write to bring about change in China—not so much the kind of change the Japanese had brought to themselves with their mastery of Western technology, but a change of spirit for China.

He began by starting a magazine, *New Life*, in Tokyo, and urged on his countrymen the study of such thinkers as Darwin and Nietzsche. At the same time he also read widely in the ancient classics. But it was not until 1918 that he found a literary movement to identify himself with. Sun Yat-sen's political revolution had been followed by Hu Shih's literary revolution. China was now alive with literary activity, and Lu Hsün poured out stories, poems, and critical essays, including "The Diary of a Madman," a highly original early work. He quickly became well known as a writer and became a lecturer in literature at the National Peking University. From this point on his career was wholly that of a writer.

When he moved to Peking, Lu Hsün went back to his home town to get his mother. What he found there colors much of his work. Despite the overthrow

1. C. T. Hsia, *A History of Modern Chinese Fiction* (New Haven, 1961), p. 28.

of the Manchu dynasty and the establishment of the Republic, nothing had changed, he decided, in the small town and the countryside. Life was mean and poor. The people were superstitious, money-grubbing, cruel, oppressed, and following dead, feudal modes of conduct. Cannibalism is one of the metaphors he uses to describe this world, and his early stories depict this grim world. His most popular story, however, was "The Story of Ah Q," the earliest of his works to gain popularity in the West. "Ah Q" is satirical — the main character, though constantly humiliated by both intellectual and physical bullies, pretends to be superior to his surroundings. In him, of course, Lu Hsün was satirizing China, pretending to age-old wisdom but a laughingstock in the modern world. As a final irony, Ah Q wishes to become a revolutionary. But he is executed, with the help of the revolutionaries, for a crime he did not commit.

By 1929 Lu Hsün had accepted a new revolution, that of the Communists, not that of Sun Yat-sen and the Republic. His stories up to now had been bitter and biting pictures of life but not in any sense socialist or communist. As a new Communist, he became a cultural hero, and his canvas widened, though his work did not improve. Much of his later work is in political papers and translations, and he did not often again reach the height of his early stories. His *Old Legends Retold* (1935) is an amusing satirical attack on Confucius, Lao Tze, and Chuang Tzu, but he is less successful at this kind of intellectual satire than he was with his earlier realistic stories or with "Ah Q." By and large, Lu Hsün has retained a position of eminence in modern China, despite the ideological shifts of the Maoist revolution.

"The Diary of a Madman" demonstrates that Chinese life is hard and cruel through the fantasies of a madman who imagines that other people, including his family, are going to eat him. The virtues and principles of traditional Chinese life have given way to a philosophy of cannibalism. Lu Hsün's model here was Gogol. "Medicine" is more complicated in plot, but conveys the same message of hopelessness. The story ends with the meeting of two mothers at the graves of their sons, recently dead. One son has been executed for taking part in a revolutionary conspiracy, and for him, at least, the revolution has failed. The other son has also died uselessly, a symbol of the bankruptcy of Chinese feudalism. Dying of consumption, he has been given some of the executed man's blood, but this ancient medicine no longer works. "Soap" is somewhat less stark as a story, but though one may be amused at incidents in it, one cannot escape the picture of a life so dirty and poverty-stricken that a bar of soap is enough of a luxury to momentarily change the lives of the husband and wife.

A Madman's Diary*

Two brothers, whose names I need not mention here, were both good friends of mine in high school; but after a separation of many years we gradually lost touch. Some time ago I happened to hear that one of them was seriously ill, and since I was going back to my old home I broke my journey to call on them. I saw only one, however, who told me that the invalid was his younger brother.

"I appreciate your coming such a long way to see us," he said, "but my brother recovered some time ago and has gone elsewhere to take up an official post." Then, laughing, he produced two volumes of his brother's diary, saying that from these the nature of his past illness could be seen, and that there was no harm in showing them to an old friend. I took the diary away, read it through, and found that he had suffered from a form of persecution complex. The writing was most confused and incoherent, and he had made many wild statements; moreover he had omitted to give any dates, so that only by the colour of the ink and the differences in the writing could one tell that it was not written at one time. Certain sections, however, were not altogether disconnected, and I have copied out a part to serve as a subject for medical research. I have not altered a single illogicality in the diary and have changed only the names, even though the people referred to are all country folk, unknown to the world and of no consequence. As for the title, it was chosen by the diarist himself after his recovery, and I did not change it.

Tonight the moon is very bright.

I have not seen it for over thirty years, so today when I saw it I felt in unusually high spirits. I begin to realize that during the past thirty-odd years I have been in the dark; but now I must be extremely careful. Otherwise why should that dog at the Chao house have looked at me twice?

I have reason for my fear.

Tonight there is no moon at all, I know that this bodes ill. This morning when I went out cautiously, Mr. Chao had a strange look in his eyes, as if he were afraid of me, as if he wanted to murder me. There were seven or eight others, who discussed me in a whisper. And they were afraid of my seeing them. All the people I passed were like that. The fiercest among them grinned at me; whereupon I shivered from head to foot, knowing that their preparations were complete.

* This and the following stories are reprinted from *Selected Stories of Lu Hsun.* Translated by Yang Hsien-yi and Gladys Yang. Peking, Foreign Languages Press, 1963. The notes, except for bracketed material, are the translators'. This story was written April 1918.

I was not afraid, however, but continued on my way. A group of children in front were also discussing me, and the look in their eyes was just like that in Mr. Chao's while their faces too were ghastly pale. I wondered what grudge these children could have against me to make them behave like this. I could not help calling out: "Tell me!" But then they ran away.

I wonder what grudge Mr. Chao can have against me, what grudge the people on the road can have against me. I can think of nothing except that twenty years ago I trod on Mr. Ku Chiu's[1] account sheets for many years past, and Mr. Ku was very displeased. Although Mr. Chao does not know him, he must have heard talk of this and decided to avenge him, so he is conspiring against me with the people on the road. But then what of the children? At that time they were not yet born, so why should they eye me so strangely today, as if they were afraid of me, as if they wanted to murder me? This really frightens me, it is so bewildering and upsetting.

I know. They must have learned this from their parents!

I can't sleep at night. Everything requires careful consideration if one is to understand it.

Those people, some of whom have been pilloried by the magistrate, slapped in the face by the local gentry, had their wives taken away by bailiffs, or their parents driven to suicide by creditors, never looked as frightened and as fierce then as they did yesterday.

The most extraordinary thing was that woman on the street yesterday who spanked her son and said, "Little devil! I'd like to bite several mouthfuls out of you to work off my feelings!" Yet all the time she looked at me. I gave a start, unable to control myself; then all those green-faced, long-toothed people began to laugh derisively. Old Chen hurried forward and dragged me home.

He dragged me home. The folk at home all pretended not to know me; they had the same look in their eyes as all the others. When I went into the study, they locked the door outside as if cooping up a chicken or a duck. This incident left me even more bewildered.

A few days ago a tenant of ours from Wolf Cub Village came to report the failure of the crops, and told my elder brother that a notorious character in their village had been beaten to death; then some people had taken out his heart and liver, fried them in oil and eaten them, as a means of increasing their courage. When I interrupted, the tenant and my brother both stared at me. Only today have I realized that they had exactly the same look in their eyes as those people outside.

1. Ku Chiu means "Ancient Times." Lu Hsun had in mind the long history of feudel oppression in China.

Just to think of it sets me shivering down the crown of my head to the soles of my feet.

They eat human beings, so they may eat me.

I see that woman's "bite several mouthfuls out of you," the langhter of those green-faced, long-toothed people and the tenant's story the other day are obviously secret signs. I realize all the poison in their speech, all the daggers in their laughter. Their teeth are white and glistening: they are all man-eaters.

It seems to me, although I am not a bad man, ever since I trod on Mr. Ku's accounts it has been touch-and-go. They seem to have secrets which I cannot guess, and once they are angry they will call anyone a bad character. I remember when my elder brother taught me to write compositions, no matter how good a man was, if I produced arguments to the contrary he would mark that passage to show his approval; while if I excused evil-doers, he would say: "Good for you, that shows originality." How can I possibly guess their secret thoughts—especially when they are ready to eat people?

Everything requires careful consideration if one is to understand it. In ancient times, as I recollect, people often ate human beings, but I am rather hazy about it. I tried to look this up, but my history has no chronology, and scrawled all over each page are the words: "Virtue and Morality." Since I could not sleep anyway, I read intently half the night, until I began to see words between the lines, the whole book being filled with the two words—"Eat people."

All these words written in the book, all the words spoken by our tenant, gaze at me strangely with an enigmatic smile.

I too am a man, and they want to eat me!

In the morning I sat quietly for some time. Old Chen brought lunch in: one bowl of vegetables, one bowl of steamed fish. The eyes of the fish were white and hard, and its mouth was open just like those people who want to eat human beings. After a few mouthfuls I could not tell whether the slippery morsels were fish or human flesh, so I brought it all up.

I said, "Old Chen, tell my brother that I feel quite suffocated, and want to have a stroll in the garden." Old Chen said nothing but went out, and presently he came back and opened the gate.

I did not move, but watched to see how they would treat me, feeling certain that they would not let me go. Sure enough! My elder brother came slowly out, leading an old man. There was a murderous gleam in his eyes, and fearing that I would see it he lowered his head, stealing glances at me from the side of his spectacles.

"You seem to be very well today," said my brother.

"Yes," said I.

"I have invited Mr. Ho here today," said my brother, "to examine you."

"All right," said I. Actually I knew quite well that this old man was the executioner in disguise! He simply used the pretext of feeling my pulse to see how fat I was; for by so doing he would receive a share of my flesh. Still I was not afraid. Although I do not eat men, my courage is greater than theirs. I held out my two fists, to see what he would to. The old man sat down, closed his eyes, fumbled for some time and remained still for some time; then he opened his shifty eyes and said, "Don't let your imagination run away with you. Rest quietly for a few days, and you will be all right."

Don't let your imagination run away with you! Rest quietly for a few days! When I have grown fat, naturally they will have more to eat; but what good will it do me, or how can it be "all right"? All these people wanting to eat human flesh and at the same time stealthily trying to keep up appearances, not daring to act promptly, really made me nearly die of laughter. I could not help roaring with laughter, I was so amused. I knew that in this laughter were courage and integrity. Both the old man and my brother turned pale, awed by my courage and integrity.

But just because I am brave they are the more eager to eat me, in order to acquire some of my courage. The old man went out of the gate, but before he had gone far he said to my brother in a low voice, "To be eaten at once!" And my brother nodded. So you are in it too! This stupendous discovery, although it came as a shock, is yet no more than I had expected: the accomplice in eating me is my elder brother!

The eater of human flesh is my elder brother!

I am the younger brother of an eater of human flesh!

I myself will be eaten by others, but none the less I am the younger brother of an eater of human flesh!

These few days I have been thinking again: suppose that old man were not an executioner in disguise, but a real doctor; he would be none the less an eater of human flesh. In that book on herbs, written by his predecessor Li Shih-chen,[2] it is clearly stated that men's flesh can be boiled and eaten; so can he still say that he does not eat men?

As for my elder brother, I have also good reason to suspect him. When he was teaching me, he said with his own lips, "People exchange their sons to eat." And once in discussing a bad man, he said that not only did he deserve to be killed, he should "have his flesh eaten and his hide slept on."[3] I was still young then, and my heart beat faster for some time, he was not at all surprised by the

2. A famous pharmacologist (1518–1593), author of *Pen-tsao-kang-mu*, the *Materia Medica*.

3. These are quotations from the old classic, *Tso Chuan*. [An extensive commentary on the *Ch'un Ch'iu*, the *Spring and Autumn Annals*, one of the Confucian classics.]

story that our tenant from Wolf Cub Village told us the other day about eating a man's heart and liver, but kept nodding his head. He is evidently just as cruel as before. Since it is possible to "exchange sons to eat," then anything can be exchanged, anyone can be eaten. In the past I simply listened to his explanations, and let it go at that; now I know that when he explained it to me, not only was there human fat at the corner of his lips, but his whole heart was set on eating men.

Pitch dark. I don't know whether it is day or night. The Chao family dog has started barking again.

The fierceness of a lion, the timidity of a rabbit, the craftiness of a fox. . . .

I know their way; they are not willing to kill anyone outright, nor do they dare, for fear of the consequences. Instead they have banded together and set traps everywhere, to force me to kill myself. The behavior of the men and women in the street a few days ago, and my elder brother's attitude these last few days, make it quite obvious. What they like best is for a man to take off his belt, and hang himself from a beam; for then they can enjoy their heart's desire without being blamed for murder. Naturally that sets them roaring with delighted laughter. On the other hand, if a man is frightened or worried to death, although that makes him rather thin, they still nod in approval.

They only eat dead flesh! I remember reading somewhere of a hideous beast, with an ugly look in its eye, called "hyena" which often eats dead flesh. Even the largest bones it grinds into fragments and swallows: the mere thought of this is enough to terrify one. Hyenas are related to wolves, and wolves belong to the canine species. The other day the dog in the Chao house looked at me several times; obviously it is in the plot too and has become their accomplice. The old man's eyes were cast down, but that did not deceive me!

The most deplorable is my elder brother. He is also a man, so why is he not afraid, why is he plotting with others to eat me? Is it that when one is used to it he no longer thinks it a crime? Or is it that he has hardened his heart to do something he knows is wrong?

In cursing man-eaters, I shall start with my brother, and in dissuading man-eaters, I start with him too.

Actually, such arguments should have convinced them long age. . . .

Suddenly someone came in. He was only about twenty years old and I did not see his features very clearly. His face was wreathed in smiles, but when he nodded to me his smile did not seem genuine. I asked him: "Is it right to eat human beings?"

Still smiling, he replied, "When there is no famine how can one eat human beings?"

I realized at once, he was one of them; but still I summoned up courage to repeat my question:

"Is it right?"

"What makes you ask such a thing? You really are . . . fond of a joke. . . . It is very fine today."

"It is fine, and the moon is very bright. But I want to ask you: Is it right?"

He looked disconcerted, and muttered: "No. . . ."

"No? Then why do they still do it?"

"What are you talking about?"

"What am I talking about? They are eating men now in Wolf Cub Village, and you can see it written all over the books, in fresh red ink."

His expression changed, and he grew ghastly pale. "It may be so," he said, staring at me. "It has always been like that. . . ."

"Is it right because it has always been like that?"

"I refuse to discuss these things with you. Anyway, you shouldn't talk about it. Whoever talks about it is in the wrong!"

I leaped up and opened my eyes wide, but the man had vanished. I was soaked with perspiration. He was much younger than my elder brother, but even so he was in it. He must have been taught by his parents. And I am afraid he has already taught his son: that is why even the children look at me so fiercely.

Wanting to eat men, at the same time afraid of being eaten themselves, they all look at each other with the deepest suspicion. . . .

How comfortable life would be for them if they could rid themselves of such obsessions and go to work, walk, eat and sleep at ease. They have only this one step to take. Yet fathers and sons, husbands and wives, brothers, friends, teachers and students, sworn enemies and even strangers, have all joined in this conspiracy, discouraging and preventing each other from taking this step.

Early this morning I went to look for my elder brother. He was standing outside the hall door looking at the sky, when I walked up behind him, stood between him and the door, and with exceptional poise and politeness said to him;

"Brother, I have something to say to you."

Well, what is it?" he asked, quickly turning towards me and nodding.

"It is very little, but I find it difficult to say. Brother, probably all primitive people ate a little human flesh to begin with. Later, because their outlook changed, some of them stopped, and because they tried to be good they changed into men, changed into real men. But some are still eating—just like reptiles. Some have changed into fish, birds, monkeys and finally men; but some do not try to be good and remain reptiles still. When those who eat men compare themselves with those who do not, how ashamed they must be. Probably much more ashamed than the reptiles are before monkeys.

"In ancient times Yi Ya boiled his son for Chieh and Chou to eat; that is the old story.[4] But actually since the creation of heaven and earth by Pan Ku men have been eating each other, from the time of Yi Ya's son to the time of Hsu Hsi-lin,[5] and from the time of Hsu Hsi-lin down to the man caught in Wolf Cub Village. Last year they executed a criminal in the city, and a consumptive soaked a piece of bread in his blood and sucked it.[6]

"They want to eat me, and of course you can do nothing about it single-handed; but why should you join them? As man-eaters they are capable of anything. If they eat me, they can eat you as well; members of the same group can still eat each other. But if you will just change your ways immediately, then everyone will have peace. Although this has been going on since time immemorial, today we could make a special effort to be good, and say this is not to be done! I'm sure you can say so, brother. The other day when the tenant wanted the rent reduced, you said it couldn't be done."

At first he only smiled cynically, then a murderous gleam came into his eyes, and when I spoke of their secret his face turned pale. Outside the gate stood a group of people, including Mr. Chao and his dog, all craning their necks to peer in. I could not see all their faces, for they seemed to be masked in cloths; some of them looked pale and ghastly still, concealing their laughter. I knew they were one band, all eaters of human flesh. But I also knew that they did not all think alike by any means. Some of them thought that since it had always been so, men should be eaten. Some of them knew that they should not eat men, but still wanted to; and they were afraid people might discover their secret; thus when they heard me they became angry, but they still smiled their cynical, tight-lipped smile.

Suddenly my brother looked furious, and shouted in a loud voice:

"Get out of here, all of you! What is the point of looking at a madman?"

Then I realized part of their cunning. They would never be willing to change their stand, and their plans were all laid; they had stigmatized me as a madman. In future when I was eaten, not only

4. According to ancient records, Yi Ya cooked his son and presented him to Duke Huan of Chi, who reigned from 685 to 643 B.C. Chieh and Chou were tyrants of an earlier age. The madman has made a mistake here.

5. A revolutionary at the end of the Ching dynasty (1644–1911), Hsu Hsi-lin, was executed in 1907 for assassinating a Ching official. His heart and liver were eaten.

6. It was believed that human blood cured consumption. Thus after the execution of a criminal, the executioner would sell steamed bread dipped in blood.

would there be no trouble, but people would probably be grateful to them. When our tenant spoke of the villagers eating a bad character, it was exactly the same device. This is their old trick.

Old Chen came in too, in a great temper, but they could not stop my mouth, I had to speak to those people:

"You should change, change from the bottom of your hearts!" I said. "You must know that in future there will be no place for man-eaters in the world.

"If you don't change, you may all be eaten by each other. Although so many are born, they will be wiped out by the real men, just like wolves killed by hunters. Just like reptiles!"

Old Chen drove everybody away. My brother had disappeared. Old Chen advised me to go back to my room. The room was pitch dark. The beams and rafters shook above my head. After shaking for some time they grew larger. They piled on top of me.

The weight was so great, I could not move. They meant that I should die. I knew that the weight was false, so I struggled out, covered in perspiration. But I had to say:

"You should change at once, change from the bottom of your hearts! You must know that in future there will be no place for man-eaters in the world. . . ."

The sun does not shine, the door is not opened, every day two meals.

I took up my chopsticks, then thought of my elder brother; I know now how my little sister died: it was all through him. My sister was only five at the time. I can still remember how lovable and pathetic she looked. Mother cried and cried, but he begged her not to cry, probably because he had eaten her himself, and so her crying made him feel ashamed. If he had any sense of shame. . . .

My sister was eaten by my brother, but I don't know whether mother realized it or not.

I think mother must have known, but when she cried she did not say so outright, probably because she thought it proper too. I remember when I was four or five years old, sitting in the cool of the hall, my brother told me that if a man's parents were ill, he should cut off a piece of his flesh and boil it for them if he wanted to be considered a good son; and mother did not contradict him. If one piece could be eaten, obviously so could the whole. And yet just to think of the mourning then still makes my heart bleed; that is the extraordinary thing about it!

I can't bear to think of it.

I have only just realized that I have been living all these years in a place where for four thousand years they have been eating human flesh. My brother had just taken over the charge of the house when our sister died, and he may well have used her flesh in our rice and dishes, making us eat it unwittingly.

It is possible that I ate several pieces of my sister's flesh unwittingly and now it is my turn. . . .

How can a man like myself, after four thousand years of man-eating history—even though I knew nothing about it at first—ever hoped to face real men?

Perhaps there are still children who have not eaten men?

Save the children. . . .

Medicine*

I

It was autumn, in the small hours of the morning. The moon had gone down, but the sun had not yet risen, and the sky appeared a sheet of darkling blue. Apart from night-prowlers, all was asleep. Old Chuan suddenly sat up in bed. He struck a match and lit the grease-covered oil lamp, which shed a ghostly light over the two rooms of the tea-house.

"Are you going now, dad?" queried an old woman's voice. And from the small inner room a fit of coughing was heard.

"H'm."

Old Chuan listened as he fastened his clothes, then stretching out his hand said, "Let's have it."

After some fumbling under the pillow his wife produced a packet of silver dollars which she handed over. Old Chuan pocketed it nervously, patted his pocket twice, then lighting a paper lantern and blowing out the lamp went into the inner room. A rustling was heard, and then more coughing. When all was quiet again, Old Chuan called softly: "Son! . . . Don't you get up! . . . Your mother will see to the shop."

Receiving no answer, Old Chuan assumed his son must be sound asleep again; so he went out into the street. In the darkness nothing could be seen but the grey roadway. The lantern light fell on his pacing feet. Here and there he came across dogs, but none of them barked. It was much colder than indoors, yet Old Chuan's spirits rose, as if he had grown suddenly younger and possessed some miraculous life-giving power. He lengthened his stride. And the road became increasingly clear, the sky increasingly bright.

Absorbed in his walking, Old Chuan was startled when he saw distinctly the cross-road ahead of him. He walked back a few steps to stand under the eaves of a shop, in front of its closed door. After some time he began to feel chilly.

* Written April 1919.

"Uh, an old chap."

"Seems rather cheerful. . . ."

Old Chuan started again and, opening his eyes, saw several men passing. One of them even turned back to look at him, and although he could not see him clearly, the man's eyes shone with a lustful light, like a famished person's at the sight of food. Looking at his lantern, Old Chuan saw it had gone out. He patted his pocket—the hard packet was still there. Then he looked round and saw many strange people, in twos and threes, wandering about like lost souls. However, when he gazed steadily at them, he could not see anything else strange about them.

Presently he saw some soldiers strolling around. The large white circles on their uniforms, both in front and behind, were clear even at a distance; and as they drew nearer, he saw the dark red border too. The next second, with a trampling of feet, a crowd rushed past. Thereupon the small groups which had arrived earlier suddenly converged and surged forward. Just before the crossroad, they came to a sudden stop and grouped themselves in a semi-circle.

Old Chuan looked in that direction too, but could only see people's backs. Craning their necks as far as they would go, they looked like so many ducks held and lifted by some invisible hand. For a moment all was still; then a sound was heard, and a stir swept through the on-lookers. There was a rumble as they pushed back, sweeping past Old Chuan and nearly knocking him down.

"Hey! Give me the cash, and I'll give you the goods!" A man clad entirely in black stood before him, his eyes like daggers, making Old Chuan shrink to half his normal size. This man thrust one huge extended hand towards him, while in the other he held a roll of steamed bread, from which crimson drops were dripping to the ground.

Hurriedly Old Chuan fumbled for his dollars, and trembling he was about to hand them over, but he dared not take the object. The other grew impatient and shouted: "What are you afraid of? Why not take it?" When Old Chuan still hesitated, the man in black snatched his lantern and tore off its paper shade to wrap up the roll. This package he thrust into Old Chuan's hand, at the same time seizing the silver and giving it a cursory feel. Then he turned away, muttering, "Old fool. . . ."

"Whose sickness is this for?" Old Chuan seemed to hear someone ask; but he made no reply. His whole mind was on the package, which he carried as carefully as if it were the sole heir to an ancient house. Nothing else mattered now. He was about to transplant this new life to his own home, and reap much happiness. The sun had risen, lighting up the broad highway before him, which led straight home, and the worn tablet behind him at the cross-road with its faded gold inscription: "Ancient Pavilion."

II

When Old Chuan reached home, the shop had been cleaned, and the rows of tea-tables shone brightly; but no customers had arrived. Only his son sat eating at a table by the wall. Beads of sweat stood out on his forehead, his lined jacket clung to his spine, and his shoulder blades stuck out so sharply, an inverted V seemed stamped there. At this sight, Old Chuan's brow, which had been clear, contracted again. His wife hurried in from the kitchen, with expectant eyes and a tremor to her lips:

"Get it?"

"Yes."

They went together into the kitchen, and conferred for a time. Then the old woman went out, to return shortly with a dried lotus leaf which she spread on the table. Old Chuan unwrapped the crimson-stained roll from the lantern paper and transferred it to the lotus leaf. Little Chuan had finished his meal, but his mother exclaimed hastily:

"Sit still, Little Chuan! Don't come over here."

Mending the fire in the stove, Old Chuan put the green package and the red and white lantern paper into the stove together. A red-black flame flared up, and a strange odour permeated the shop.

"Smells good! What are you eating?" The hunchback had arrived. He was one of those who spend all their time in tea-shops, the first to come in the morning and the last to leave. Now he had just stumbled to a corner table facing the street, and sat down. But no one answered his question.

"Puffed rice gruel?"

Still no reply. Old Chuan hurried out to brew tea for him.

"Come here, Little Chuan!" His mother called him into the inner room, set a stool in the middle, and sat the child down. Then, bringing him a round black object on a plate, she said gently:

"Eat it up . . . then you'll be better."

Little Chuan picked up the black object and looked at it. He had the oddest feeling, as if he were holding his own life in his hands. Presently he split it carefully open. From within the charred crust a jet of white vapour escaped, then scattered, leaving only two halves of a steamed white flour roll. Soon it was all eaten, the flavour completely forgotten, only the empty plate being left. His father and mother were standing one on each side of him, their eyes apparently pouring something into him and at the same time extracting something. His small heart began to beat faster, and, putting his hands to his chest, he began to cough again.

"Have a sleep; then you'll be all right," said his mother.

Obediently, Little Chuan coughed himself to sleep. The woman waited till his breathing was regular, then covered him lightly with a much patched quilt.

III

The shop was crowded, and Old Chuan was busy, carrying a big copper kettle to make tea for one customer after another. There were dark circles under his eyes.

"Aren't you well, Old Chuan? . . . What's wrong with you?" asked one greybeard.

"Nothing."

"Nothing? . . . No, I suppose from your smile, there couldn't be. . . ." The old man corrected himself.

"It's just that Old Chuan's busy," said the hunchback. "If his son. . . ." But before he could finish, a heavy-jowled man burst in. Over his shoulders he had a dark brown shirt, unbuttoned and fastened carelessly by a broad dark brown girdle at his waist. As soon as he entered, he shouted to Old Chuan:

"Has he eaten it? Any better? Luck's with you, Old Chuan. What luck! If not for my hearing of things so quickly. . . ."

Holding the kettle in one hand, the other straight by his side in an attitude of respect, Old Chuan listened with a smile. In fact, all present were listening respectfully. The old woman, dark circles under her eyes too, came out smiling with a bowl containing tea-leaves and an added olive, over which Old Chuan poured boiling water for the newcomer.

"This is a guaranteed cure! Not like other things!" declared the heavy-jowled man. "Just think, brought back warm, and eaten warm!"

"Yes indeed, we couldn't have managed it without Uncle Kang's help." The old woman thanked him very warmly.

"A guaranteed cure! Eaten warm like this. A roll dipped in human blood like this can cure any consumption!"

The old woman seemed a little disconcerted by the word "consumption," and turned a shade paler; however, she forced a smile again at once and found some pretext to leave. Meanwhile the man in brown was indiscreet enough to go on talking at the top of his voice until the child in the inner room was woken and started coughing.

"So you've had a great stroke of luck for your Little Chuan! Of course his sickness will be cured completely. No wonder Old Chuan keeps smiling." As he spoke, the greybeard walked up to the man in brown, and lowered his voice to ask:

"Mr. Kang, I heard the criminal executed today came from the Hsia family. Who was it? And why was he executed?"

"Who? Son of Widow Hsia, of course! Young rascal!"

Seeing how they all hung on his words, Mr. Kang's spirits rose even higher. His jowls quivered, and he made his voice as loud as he could.

"The rogue didn't want to live, simply didn't want to! There was nothing in it for me this time. Even the clothes stripped from him were taken by Red-eye, the jailer. Old Old Chuan was luckiest, and after him Third Uncle Hsia. He pocketed the whole reward—twenty-five taels of bright silver—and didn't have to spend a cent!"

Little Chuan walked slowly out of the inner room, his hands to his chest, coughing repeatedly. He went to the kitchen, filled a bowl with cold rice, added hot water to it, and sitting down started to eat. His mother, hovering over him, asked softly:

"Do you feel better, son? Still as hungry as ever?"

"A guaranteed cure?" Kang glanced at the child, then turned back to address the company. "Third Uncle Hsia is really smart. If he hadn't informed, even *his* family would have been executed, and their property confiscated. But instead? Silver! That young rogue was a real scoundrel! He even tried to incite the jailer to revolt!"

"No! The idea of it!" A man in his twenties, sitting in the back row, expressed indignation.

"You know, Red-eye went to sound him out, but he started chatting with him. He said the great Ching empire belongs to us. Just think: is that kind of talk rational? Red-eye knew he had only an old mother at home, but had never imagined he was so poor. He couldn't squeeze anything out of him; he was already good and angry, and then the young fool would 'scratch the tiger's head,' so he gave him a couple of slaps."

"Red-eye is a good boxer. Those slaps must have hurt!" The hunchback in the corner by the wall exulted.

"The rotter was not afraid of being beaten. He even said how sorry he was."

"Nothing to be sorry about in beating a wretch like that," said Greybeard.

Kang looked at him superciliously and said disdainfully: "You misunderstood. The way he said it, he was sorry for Red-eye."

His listeners' eyes took on a glazed look, and no one spoke. Little Chuan had finished his rice and was perspiring profusely, his head steaming.

"Sorry for Red-eye—crazy! He must have been crazy!" said Greybeard, as if suddenly he saw light.

"He must have been crazy!" echoed the man in his twenties.

Once more the customers began to show animation, and conversation was resumed. Under cover of the noise, the child was seized by a paroxysm of coughing. Kang went up to him, clapped him on the shoulder, and said:

"A guaranteed cure! Don't cough like that, Little Chuan! A guaranteed cure!"

"Crazy!" agreed the hunchback, nodding his head.

IV

Originally, the land adjacent to the city wall outside the West Gate had been public land. The zigzag path running across it, trodden out by passers-by seeking a short cut, had become a natural boundary line. Left of the path were buried executed criminals or those who had died of neglect in prison. Right of the path were paupers' graves. The serried ranks of grave mounds on both sides looked like the rolls laid out for a rich man's birthday.

The Ching Ming Festival that year was unusually cold. Willows were only just beginning to put forth shoots no larger than grains. Shortly after daybreak, Old Chuan's wife brought four dishes and a bowl of rice to set before a new grave in the right section, and wailed before it. When she had burned paper money she sat on the ground in a stupor as if waiting for something; but for what, she herself did not know. A breeze sprang up and stirred her short hair, which was certainly whiter than the previous year.

Another woman came down the path, grey-haired and in rags. Carrying an old, round, red-lacquered basket with a string of paper money hanging from it, she walked haltingly. When she saw Old Chuan's wife sitting on the ground watching her, she hesitated, and a flush of shame spread over her pale face. However, she summoned up courage to cross over to a grave in the left section, where she set down her basket.

That grave was directly opposite Little Chuan's, separated only by the path. As Old Chuan's wife watched the other woman set out four dishes of food and a bowl of rice, then stand up to wail and burn paper money, she thought: "It must be her son in that grave too." The older woman took a few aimless steps and stared vacantly around, then suddenly she began to tremble and stagger backwards, as though giddy.

Fearing sorrow might send her out of her mind, Old Chuan's wife got up and stepped across the path, to say quietly: "Don't grieve, let's go home."

The other nodded, but she was still staring fixedly, and she muttered: "Look! What's that?"

Looking where she pointed, Old Chuan's wife saw that the grave in front had not yet been overgrown with grass. Ugly patches of soil still showed. But when she looked carefully, she was surprised to see at the top of the mound a wreath of red and white flowers.

Both of them suffered from failing eyesight, yet they could see these red and white flowers clearly. There were not many, but they were placed in a circle; and although not very fresh, were neatly set out. Little Chuan's mother looked round and found her own son's grave, like most of the rest, dotted with only a few little, pale flowers shivering in the cold. Suddenly she had a sense of futility and stopped feeling curious about the wreath.

In the meantime the old woman had gone up to the grave to look more closely. "They have no roots," she said to herself. "They can't have grown here. Who could have been here? Children don't come here to play, and none of our relatives ever come. What could have happened?" She puzzled over it, until suddenly her tears began to fall, and she cried aloud:

"Son, they all wronged you, and you do not forget. Is your grief still so great that today you worked this wonder to let me know?"

She looked all around, but could see only a crow perched on a leafless bough. "I know," she continued. "They murdered you. But a day of reckoning will come, Heaven will see to it. Close your eyes in peace. . . . If you are really here, and can hear me, make that crow fly on to your grave as a sign."

The breeze had long since dropped, and the dry grass stood stiff and straight as copper wires. A faint, tremulous sound vibrated in the air, then faded and died away. All around was deathly still. They stood in the dry grass, looking up at the crow; and the crow, on the rigid bough of the tree, its head drawn in, perched immobile as iron.

Time passed. More people, young and old, came to visit the graves.

Old Chuan's wife felt somehow as if a load had been lifted from her mind and, wanting to leave, she urged the other:

"Let's go."

The old woman sighed, and listlessly picked up the rice and dishes. After a moment's hesitation she started off slowly, still muttering to herself:

"What does it mean?"

They had not gone thirty paces when they heard a loud caw behind them. Startled, they looked round and saw the crow stretch its wings, brace itself to take off, then fly like an arrow towards the far horizon.

Soap*

With her back to the north window in the slanting sunlight, Ssu-min's wife with her eight-year-old daughter, Hsiu-erh, was pasting paper money for the dead when she heard the slow, heavy footsteps of someone in cloth shoes and knew her husband was back.

* Written March 22, 1924.

Paying no attention, she simply went on pasting coins. But the tread of cloth shoes drew nearer and nearer, till it finally stopped beside her. Then she could not help looking up to see Ssu-min before her, hunching his shoulders and stooping forward to fumble desperately under his cloth jacket in the inner pocket of his long gown.

By dint of twisting and turning at last he extracted his hand with a small oblong package in it, which he handed to his wife. As she took it, she smelt an indefinable fragrance rather reminiscent of olive. On the green paper wrapper was a bright golden seal with a network of tiny designs. Hsiu-erh bounded forward to seize this and look at it, but her mother promptly pushed her aside.

"Been shopping? . . ." she asked as she looked at it.

"Er—yes." He stared at the package in her hand.

The green paper wrapper was opened. Inside was a layer of very thin paper, also sunflower-green, and not till this was unwrapped was the object itself exposed—glossy and hard, besides being sunflower-green, with another network of fine designs on it. The thin paper was a cream colour, it appeared. The indefinable fragrance rather reminiscent of olive was stronger now.

"My, this is really good soap!"

She held the soap to her nose as gingerly as if it were a child, and sniffed at it as she spoke.

"Er—yes. Just use this in future. . . ."

As he spoke, she noticed him eyeing her neck, and felt herself flushing up to her cheekbones. Sometimes when she rubbed her neck, especially behind the ears, her fingers detected a roughness; and though she knew this was the accumulated dirt of many years, she had never given it much thought. Now, under his scrutiny, she could not help blushing as she looked at this green, foreign soap with the curious scent, and this blush spread right to the tips of her ears. She mentally resolved to have a thorough wash with this soap after supper.

"There are places you can't wash clean just with honey locust pods,"[1] she muttered to herself.

"Ma, can I have this?" As Hsiu-erh reached out for the sunflower-green paper, Chao-erh, the younger daughter who had been playing outside, came running in too. Mrs. Ssu-min promptly pushed them both aside, folded the thin paper in place, wrapped the green paper round it as before, then leaned over to put it on the highest shelf of the wash-stand. After one final glance, she turned back to her paper coins.

"Hsueh-cheng!" Ssu-min seemed to have remembered something.

1. In many parts of China, honey locust pods were used for washing. They were cheaper than soap, but not so effective.

He gave a long-drawn-out shout, sitting down on a high-backed chair opposite his wife.

"Hsueh-cheng!" she helped him call.

She stopped pasting coins to listen, but not a sound could she hear. When she saw him with upturned head waiting so impatiently, she felt quite apologetic.

"Hsueh-cheng!" she called shrilly at the top of her voice.

This call proved effective, for they heard the tramp of leather shoes draw near, and Hsueh-cheng stood before her. He was in shirt sleeves, his plump round face shiny with perspiration.

"What were you doing?" she asked disapprovingly. "Why didn't you hear your father call?"

"I was practising Hexagram Boxing. . . ." He turned at once to his father and straightened up, looking at him as if to ask what he wanted.

"Hsueh-cheng, I want to ask you the meaning of *o-du-fu*."[2]

"*O du fu?* Isn't it a very fierce woman?"

"What nonsense! The idea!" Ssu-min was suddenly furious. "Am I a woman, pray?"

Hsueh-cheng recoiled two steps, and stood straighter than ever. Though his father's gait sometimes reminded him of the way old men walked in Peking opera, he had never considered Ssu-min as a woman. His answer, he saw now, had been a great mistake.

"As if I didn't know *o-du-fu* means a very fierce woman. Would I have to ask you that?—This isn't Chinese, it's foreign devils' language, I'm telling you. What does it mean, do you know?"

"I . . . I don't know." Hsueh-cheng felt even more uneasy.

"Pah! Why do I spend all that money to send you to school if you don't even understand a little thing like this? Your school boasts that it lays equal stress on speech and comprehension, yet it hasn't taught you anything. The ones speaking this devils' language couldn't have been more than fourteen or fifteen, actually a little younger than you, yet they were chattering away in it, while you can't even tell me the meaning. And you have the face to answer 'I don't know.' Go and look it up for me at once!"

"Yes," answered Hsueh-cheng deep down in his throat, then respectfully withdrew.

"I don't know what students today are coming to," declared Ssu-min with emotion after a pause. "As a matter of fact, in the time of Kuang Hsu,[3] I was all in favour of opening schools; but I never foresaw how great the evils would be. What 'emancipation' and 'freedom' have we had? There is no true learning, nothing but absurdities. I've spent quite a bit of money on Hsueh-cheng, all to

2. In Chinese this means "vicious wife."

3. I.e., 1875–1908.

no purpose. It wasn't easy to get him into this half-Western, half-Chinese school, where they claim they lay equal stress on 'speaking and comprehending English.'[4] You'd think all should be well. But —bah!—after one whole year of study he can't even understand *o-du-fu*! He must still be studying dead books. What use is such a school, I ask you? What I say is: Close the whole lot of them!"

"Yes, really, better close the whole lot of them," chimed in his wife sympathetically, pasting away at the paper money.

"There's no need for Hsiu-erh and her sister to attend any school. As Ninth Grandpa said, 'What's the good of girls studying?' When he opposed girls' schools I attacked him for it; but now I see the old folk were right after all. Just think, it's already in very poor taste the way women wander up and down the streets, and now they want to cut their hair as well. Nothing disgusts me so much as these short-haired schoolgirls. What I say is; There's some excuse for soldiers and bandits, but these girls are the ones who turn everything upside down. They ought to be very severely dealt with indeed. . . ."

"Yes, as if it wasn't enough for all men to look like monks, the women are imitating nuns."[5]

"Hsueh-cheng!"

Hsueh-cheng hurried in holding a small, fat, gilt-edged book, which he handed to his father.

"This looks like it," he said, pointing to one place. "Here. . . ."

Ssu-min took it and looked at it. He knew it was a dictionary, but the characters were very small and horizontally printed too. Frowning, he turned towards the window and screwed up his eyes to read the passage Hsueh-cheng had pointed out.

" 'A society founded in the eighteenth century for mutual relief.' —No, that can't be it.—How do you pronounce this?" He pointed to the devils' word in front.

"Oddfellows."

"No, no, that wasn't it." Ssu-min suddenly lost his temper again. "I told you it was bad language, a swear-word of some sort, to abuse someone of my type. Understand? Go and look it up!"

Hsueh-cheng glanced at him several times, but did not move.

"This is too puzling. How can he make head or tail of it? You must explain things clearly to him first, before he can look it up properly." Seeing Hsueh-cheng in a quandary, his mother felt sorry for him and intervened rather indignantly on his behalf.

"It was when I was buying soap at Kuang Jun Hsiang on the

4. English was taught in nearly all the new schools at that time, and learning to speak was considered as important as learning to read.

5. Monks and nuns in China shaved their heads. Hence, at the end of the Ching dynasty and later, conservatives laughed at the men who cut their queues, claiming they looked like monks.

main street," signed Ssu-min, turning to her. "There were three students shopping there too. Of course, to them I must have seemed a little pernickety. I looked at five or six kinds of soap all over forty cents, and turned them down. Then I looked at some priced ten cents a cake, but it was too poor, with no scent at all. Since I thought it best to strike a happy mean, I chose that green soap at twenty-four cents a cake. The assistant was one of those supercilious young fellows with eyes on the top of his head, so he pulled a long dog's face. At that those impudent students started winking at each other and talking devil's language. I wanted to unwrap the soap and look at it before paying—for with all that foreign paper round it, how could I tell whether it was good or bad? But that supercilious young fellow not only refused, but was very unreasonable and passed some offensive remarks, at which those whippersnappers laughed. It was the youngest of the lot who said that, looking straight at me, and the rest of them started laughing. So it must have been some bad word." He turned back to Hsueh-cheng. "Look for it in the section headed Bad Language!"

"Yes," answered Hsueh-cheng deep down in his throat, then respectfully withdrew.

"Yet they still shout 'New Culture! New Culture!' when the world's in such a state! Isn't this bad enough?" His eyes on the rafters, Ssu-min continued. "The students have no morals, society has no morals. Unless we find some panacea, China will really be finished. How pathetic she was. . . ."

"Who?" asked his wife casually, not really curious.

"A filial daughter. . . ." His eyes came round to her, and there was respect in his voice. "There were two beggars on the main street. One was a girl who looked eighteen or nineteen. Actually, it's most improper to beg at that age, but beg she did. She was with an old woman of about seventy, who had white hair and was blind. They were begging under the eaves of that clothes shop, and everybody said how filial she was. The old one was her grandmother. Whatever trifle the girl received, she gave it to her grandmother, choosing to go hungry herself. But do you think people would give alms even to such a filial daughter?"

He fixed her with his eye, as if to test her intelligence.

She made no answer, but fixed him with *her* eye, as if waiting for him to elucidate.

"Bah—no!" At last he supplied the answer himself. "I watched for a long time, and saw one person only give her a copper. Plenty of others gathered round, but only to jeer at them.There were two low types as well, one of whom had the impertinence to say:

" 'Ah-fa! Don't be put off by the dirt on this piece of goods. If you buy two cakes of soap, and give her a good scrubbing, the result won't be bad at all!' Think, what a way to talk!"

She snorted and lowered her head. After quite a time, she asked rather casually: "Did *you* give her any money?"

"Did I?—No. I'd have felt ashamed to give just one or two coins. She wasn't an ordinary beggar, you know. . . ."

"Mm." Without waiting for him to finish she stood up slowly and walked to the kitchen. Dusk was gathering, and it was time for supper.

Ssu-min stood up too, and walked into the courtyard. It was lighter out than in. Hsueh-cheng was practising Hexagram Boxing in a corner by the wall. This constituted his "home education," and he used the economical method of employing the hour between day and night for this purpose. Hsueh-cheng had been boxing now for about half a year. Ssu-min nodded very slightly, as if in approval, then began to pace the courtyard with his hands behind his back. Before long, the broad leaves of the evergreen which was the only potted plant they had were swallowed up in the darkness, and stars twinkled between white clouds which looked like torn cotton. Night had fallen. Ssu-min could not repress his growing indignation. He felt called on to do great deeds, to declare war on all bad students about and on this wicked society. By degrees he grew bolder and bolder, his steps became longer and longer, and the thud of his cloth soles grew louder and louder, waking the hen and her chicks in the coop so that they cheeped in alarm.

A light appeared in the hall—the signal that supper was ready—and the whole household gathered round the table in the middle. The lamp stood at the lower end of the table, while Ssu-min sat alone at the head. His plump, round face was like Hsueh-cheng's, with the addition of two sparse whiskers. Seen through the hot vapour from the vegetable soup, he looked like the God of Wealth you find in temples. On the left sat Mrs. Ssu-min and Chao-erh, on the right Hsueh-cheng and Hsiu-erh. Chopsticks pattered like rain against the bowls. Though no one said a word, their supper table was very animated.

Chao-erh upset her bowl, spilling soup over half the table. Ssu-min opened his narrow eyes as wide as he could. Only when he saw she was going to cry did he stop glaring at her and reach out with his chopsticks for a tender morsel of cabbage he had spotted. But the tender morsel had disappeared. He looked right and left, and discovered Hsueh-cheng on the point of stuffing it into his wide-open mouth. Disappointed, Ssu-min ate a mouthful of yellowish leaves instead.

"Hsueh-cheng!" He looked at his son. "Have you found that phrase or not?"

"Which phrase?—No, not yet!"

"Pah! Look at you, not a good student and with no sense either—all you can do is eat! You should learn from that filial daughter:

although she's a beggar, she still treats her grandmother very respectfully, even if it means going hungry herself. But what do you impudent students know of such things? You'll grow up like those low types. . . ."

"I've thought of one possibility, but I don't know if it's right. . . . I think, perhaps, they may have said *o-du-fu-la*."[6]

"That's right! That's it exactly! That's exactly the sound it was: *o-du-fu-la*. What does that mean? You belong 'to the same group: you must know."

"Mean?—I'm not sure what it means."

"Nonsense. Don't try to deceive me. You're all a bad lot."

" 'Even thunder won't strike folk at meat,' " burst out Mrs. Ssu-min suddenly. "Why do you keep losing your temper today? Even at supper you can't stop hitting the hen while pointing at the dog. What do boys that age understand?"

"What?" Ssu-min was on the point of answering back when he saw her sunken cheeks were quivering with anger, her colour had changed, and a fearful glint had come into her eyes. He hastily changed his tune. "I'm not losing my temper. I'm just telling Hsueh-cheng to learn a little sense."

"How can he understand what's in *your* mind?" She looked angrier than ever. "If he had any sense, he'd long since have lit a lantern or a torch and gone out to fetch that filial daughter. You've already bought her one cake of soap: all you have to do is buy another. . . ."

"Nonsense! That's what that low type said."

"I'm not so sure. If you buy another cake and give her a good scrubbing, then worship her, the whole world will be at peace."

"How can you say such a thing? What connection is there? Because I remembered you'd no soap. . . ."

"There's a connection all right. You bought it specially for the filial daughter; so go and give her a good scrubbing. I don't deserve it. I don't want it. I don't want to share her glory."

"Really, how can you talk like that?" mumbled Ssu-min. "You women. . . ." His face was perspiring like Hsueh-cheng's after Hexagram Boxing, probably mostly because the food had been so hot.

"What about us women? We women are much better than you men. If you men aren't praising eighteen or nineteen-year-old girl beggars: such dirty minds you have! Scrubbing, indeed!—Disgusting!"

"Didn't you hear? That's what one of those low types said."

"Ssu-min!" A thundering voice was heard from the darkness outside.

"Tao-tung? I'm coming!"

6. Chinese transliteration of "old fool."

Ssu-min knew this was Ho Tao-tung, famed for his powerful voice, and he shouted back as joyfully as a criminal newly reprieved.

Ssu-min knew this was Ho Tao-tung, famed for his powerful voice, and he shouted back as joyfully as a criminal newly reprieved.

"Hsueh-cheng, hurry up and light the lamp and show Uncle Ho into the library!"

Hsueh-cheng lit a candle, and ushered Tao-tung into the west room. They were followed by Pu Wei-yuan.

"I'm sorry I didn't welcome you. Excuse me." With his mouth still full of rice, Ssu-min went in and bowed with clasped hands in greeting. "Won't you join us at our simple meal? . . ."

"We've already eaten," Wei-yuan stepped forward and greeted him. "We've hurried here at this time of night because of the eighteenth essay and poem contest of the Moral Rearmament Literary League. Isn't tomorrow the seventeenth?"

"What? Is it the sixteenth today?" asked Ssu-min in surprise.

"See how absent-minded you are!" boomed Tao-tung.

"So we'll have to send something in tonight to the newspaper office, to make sure they print it tomorrow."

"I've already drafted the title of the essay. See whether you think it will do or not." As he was speaking, Tao-tung produced a slip of paper from his handkerchief and handed it to Ssu-min.

Ssu-min stepped up to the candle, unfolded the paper, and read it word by word: "We humbly suggest an essay in the name of the whole nation to beg the President to issue an order for the promotion of the Confucian classics and the worship of the mother of Mencius,[7] in order to revive this moribund world and preserve our national character.' Very good. Very good. Isn't it a little long, though?"

"That doesn't matter," answered Tao-tung loudly, "I've worked it out, and it won't cost more to advertise. But what about the title for the poem?"

"The title for the poem?" Ssu-min suddenly looked most respectful. "I've thought of one. How about The Filial Daughter? It's a true story, and she deserves to be eulogized. On the main street today. . . ."

"Oh, no, that won't do," put in Wei-yuan hastily, waving his hand to stop Ssu-min. "I saw her too. She isn't from these parts, and I couldn't understand her dialect, nor she mine. I don't know where she's from. Everyone says she's filial; but when I asked her if she could write poems, she shook her head. If she could, that would be fine."[8]

7. A woman famous for her virtue. According to tradition, she moved house three times to avoid undesirable companions for her son.

8. In old China, it was considered romantic for women to exchange ideas with men through the medium of poems. The fashionable courtesans could write poetry.

"But since loyalty and filial piety are so important, it doesn't matter too much if she can't write poems. . . ."

"That isn't true. Quite otherwise." Wei-yuan raised his hands and rushed towards Ssu-min, to shake and push him. "She'd only be interesting if she could write poems."

"Let's use this title." Ssu-min pushed him aside. "Add an explanation and print it. In the first place, it will serve to eulogize her; in the second, we can use this to criticize society. What is the world coming to anyway? I watched for some time, and didn't see anybody give her a cent—people are utterly heartless! . . ."

"Aiya, Ssu-min!" Wei-yuan rushed over again. "You're cursing baldheads to a monk. I didn't give her anything because I didn't happen to have any money on me."

"Don't be so sensitive, Wei-yuan." Ssu-min pushed him aside again. "Of course you're an exception. Let me finish. There was quite a crowd around them, showing no respect, just jeering. There were two low types as well, who were even more impertinent. One of them said: 'Ah-fa! If you buy two cakes of soap and give her a good scrubbing, the result won't be bad at all!' Just think. . . ."

"Ha, ha! Two cakes of soap!" Tao-tung suddenly bellowed with laughter, nearly splitting their ear-drums. "Buy soap! Ho, ho, ho!"

"Tao-tung! Tao-tung! Don't make such a noise!" Ssu-min gave a start, panic-stricken.

"A good scrubbing! Ho, ho, ho!"

"Tao-tung!" Ssu-min looked stern. "We're discussing serious matters. Why should you make such a noise, nearly deafening everyone? Listen to me: we'll use both these titles, and send them straight to the newspaper office so that they come out without fail tomorrow. I'll have to trouble you both to take them there."

"All right, all right. Of course," agreed Wei-yuan readily.

"Ha, ha! A good scrubbing! Ho, ho!"

"Tao-tung!" shouted Ssu-min furiously.

This shout made Tao-tung stop laughing. After they had drawn up the explanation, Wei-yuan copied it on the paper and left with Tao-tung for the newspaper office. Ssu-min carried the candle to see them out, then walked back to the door of the hall feeling rather apprehensive. After some hesitation, though, he finally crossed the threshold. As he went in, his eyes fell on the small, green, oblong package of soap in the middle of the central table, the gold characters with fine designs around them glittering in the lamplight.

Hsiu-erh and Chao-erh were playing on the floor at the lower end of the table, while Hsueh-cheng sat on the right side looking up something in his dictionary. Last of all, on the high-backed chair in the shadows far from the lamp, Ssu-min discovered his wife. Her impassive face showed neither joy nor anger, and she was staring at nothing.

"A good scrubbing indeed! Disgusting!"

Faintly, Ssu-min heard Hsiu-erh's voice behind him. He turned, but she was not moving. Only Chao-erh put both small hands to her face as if to shame somebody.

This was no place for him. He blew out the candle, and went into the yard to pace up and down. Because he forgot to be quiet, the hen and her chicks started cheeping again. At once he walked more lightly, moving further away. After a long time, the lamp in the hall was transferred to the bedroom. The moonlight on the ground was like seamless white gauze, and the moon—quite full—seemed a jade disc among the bright clouds.

He felt not a little depressed, as if he, like the filial daughter, were "utterly forlorn and alone." That night he did not sleep till very late.

By the next morning, however, the soap was being honoured by being used. Getting up later than usual, he saw his wife leaning over the wash-stand rubbing her neck, with bubbles heaped up over both her ears like those emitted by great crabs. The difference between these and the small white bubbles produced by honey locust pods was like that between heaven and earth. After this, an indefinable fragrance rather reminiscent of olives always emanated from Mrs. Ssu-min. Not for nearly half a year did this suddenly give place to another scent, which all who smelt it averred was like sandalwood.

The Red Lantern
(1965 version)

Adapted by Wong Ou-hung and Ah Chia from the Shanghai Opera version

The traditional Chinese opera-drama, the so-called Peking opera, has been a favorite diversion for the Chinese people for a hundred years. Romantic in subject matter and brilliant in its stylized theatricals, the Peking opera still draws large audiences wherever there are Chinese communities. In such diverse places as Taipei, Honolulu, New York, and Paris it also draws enthusiastic westerners who are perhaps more interested in its charm and its stage techniques than in the often lengthy and episodic plots. Most Western books on the Chinese theater have concentrated on the acting and the unique staging rather than on the texts. From a Maoist point of view, such drama is naturally decadent, providing entertainment devoid of social issues to the aristocracy, the *demi-monde*, and the misguided middle classes. However, certain techniques of the classical theatre are so essentially Chinese that they are used effectively in the modern theater. The hero may kill the villain in ballet style—ballet is very popular in modern China. The hero may lapse into verse as he encounters dramatic situations. So the Chinese have not thrown away all of the techniques of the past for a Marxist realism based on naturalistic Western models, but have endeavored to use what was good of the old tradition. Also, as the Maoists themselves have pointed out, there has always been a tradition of people's drama in China—folk or village drama. Elements of this have been borrowed for the modern stage, but, more important, the philosophy of the modern drama is that the drama must be immediately understandable to the people and reflect situations in life which they have experienced or know of and with which they can identify.

Though drama in modern China reflects the cultural revolution of Chairman Mao, there is much variety in it. It has been sensitive to political shifts as much as any other literary form, but it has also been experimental and innovative.

The *Red Lantern* is an excellent melodrama that has gone through several revisions and has withstood ideological shifts to remain one of the most popular plays on the Chinese stage today. Activist drama, drama in which the characters are pitted against formidable enemies of the Revolution, is likely to be the norm for some time to come, and the *Red Lantern* displays a broad spectrum of characters confronting an implacable enemy and emerging victorious not only through courage but also through discipline and "right thinking." Other dramas which have withstood the test of time and the ideological test are *Shachaipang, Raid on the White Tiger Regiment*, and *On the Docks*. Attempts to shift the Chinese opera to more general human themes have so far been resisted by Maoist theoreticians. The *Red Lantern* is perhaps the best of the popular dramas now in vogue.

The Red Lantern

Characters

LI YU-HO, *a switchman*
TIEH-MEI, *his daughter*
GRANNY, TIEH-MEI'S *grandmother*
OLD CHOU, *a worker*
AUNT LIU, LI'S *neighbor*
KUEI-LAN, *her daughter*
The LIAISON MAN
The KNIFE-GRINDER
GUERRILLA COMMANDER LIU
The GRUEL-WOMAN
The CIGARETTE-VENDOR
HATOYAMA, *chief of the Japanese military police*
HOU HSIEN-PU, *his Chinese lieutenant.*
A *Japanese* SERGEANT
INSPECTOR WANG, *underground agent for the guerrillas*
The PEDDLER, *a spy for the Japanese*
The COBBLER, *a spy for the Japanese*
JAPANESE GENDARMES, THUGS, TOWNSPEOPLE, GUERRILLAS, ETC.

Scene 1

THE LIAISON MAN IS RESCUED

[*A late autumn night during the War of Resistance Against Japan. A siding near Lungtan Station in northeast China. It is dark and the wind is howling. Four Japanese gendarmes march past on a tour of inspection. There is a slope near by, with hills in the distance. A train passes on the other side of the slope.*]

[*Enter* LI YU-HO, *quietly, with a signal lantern.*]

LI.

Red lantern in hand, I look round;
The Party is sending a man here from the north;
The time fixed is half past ten. [*Looks at his watch.*]
The next train should bring him.

[*Enter* TIEH-MEI *with a basket.*]

TEIH-MEI. Dad!

LI. Well, Tieh-mei, how was business today?

TIEH-MEI. [*Angrily*] The gendarmes and their thugs kept searching people and made them too jittery to buy anything.

LI. Those gangsters!

TIEH-MEI. Do be careful, Dad.

LI. Don't worry. Go home and tell Granny that an uncle is coming. Ask her to have a meal ready.

TIEH-MEI. Right.

LI. Come over here [*Wraps his scarf around her neck.*]

TIEH-MEI. Dad, I'm not cold.

LI. No, you have it.

TIEH-MEI. Where's he from, this uncle?

LI. [*Kindly*] Children shouldn't bother their heads about such things.

TIEH-MEI. [*To herself*] I'll go and ask Granny. Take good care of yourself, Dad. I'm off now. [*Exit.*]

LI. Our girl is doing all right.

She can peddle goods, collect cinders,
Carry water and chop wood.
A poor man's child soon learns to cope
With all tasks at home and outside.
Different trees bear different fruit,
Different seeds grow different flowers.

[*Enter* INSPECTOR WANG.]

WANG. Who's that?

LI. It's Li.

WANG. The Japanese are keeping a close watch today, Old Li. They must be up to something.

[*Enter two Japanese soldiers.* WANG *and* LI *step apart. Exeunt the Japanese.*]

WANG. [*Taking out a ciagrette*] Got a light?

LI. Here. [*He goes over to light his cigarette, bending close to* WANG.] Things are tense, Old Wang. We must take special care. Let's get in touch once every ten days from now on. I'll let you know where to meet.

WANG. Right.

[*A whistle sounds in the distance and a train roars past. When it nears the station* THE LIAISON MAN *jumps off. The Japanese police on the train fire two shots.* LI *and* WANG *step back.*]

[THE LIAISON MAN, *wounded in the chest, staggers in and falls by the track.* LI *and* WANG *rush over to him.*]

LI. [*Helping him up*] Well, mate.

LIAISON. [*Regaining consciousness, looks around*] What's this place?

LI. The fifty-first siding, Lungtan Station. You. . . .

[*With an effort* THE LIAISON MAN *puts a blue glove on his left hand and raises this. Then he faints.*]

LI. [*To himself*] The left hand gloved. [*To* WANG] He's our man.

[*Not far off Japanese yell and whistles are blown.*]

WANG. Get him away, quick. I'll cover you.

LI. [*Carrying off the man on his back*] Be careful, Old Wang. [*Exit.*]

[*The shouts and whistles come nearer.*]

[WANG *draws his pistol and fires two shots in the direction opposite to that taken by* LI. *Pounding footsteps can be heard and angry yells. To fox the enemy,* WANG *clenches his teeth and shoots himself in the arm. As he falls to the ground in come the Japanese sergeant,* HOU HSIEN-PU, *and several gendarmes.*]

SERGEANT. [*To* WANG] Where's the man from that train?

WANG. [*Pointing towards the opposite direction and groaning*] Over there.

SERGEANT. [*In alarm*] Down! [*All the Japanese flop to the ground.*]

Scene 2

THE SECRET CODE

[*The same evening. The road where* LI*'s house stands. The house, in the center of the stage, has a door on the right and by the door a window. In the middle of the room is a square* *table with a lamp on it. Behind is a kang.*[1] *The north wind howls. The room is dark.* GRANNY *strikes a match and lights the lamp. Wind rustles the window paper.*]

GRANNY.

Fishermen brave the wind and waves,
Hunters fear neither tigers nor wolves;
The darkest night must end at last
In the bright blaze of revolution.

[GRANNY *draws back the curtain and looks out. Shaking her head she mutters, "Still not back." She goes to the table and takes up her needlework. Enter* TIEH-MEI *with a basket.*]

TIEH-MEI. Granny.

GRANNY. You must be cold, child.

TIEH-MEI. I'm not. Granny, Dad told me to let you know there's an uncle coming. He wants you to get a meal ready. [*Puts down the basket.*]

GRANNY. Oh, just coming, are they? I've rice and dishes ready.

TIEH-MEI. Why do I have so many uncles, Granny?

GRANNY. Your father has so many sisters, of course you have lots of uncles.

TIEH-MEI. Which one is this coming today?

GRANNY. Why ask? You'll know when he arrives.

TIEH-MEI. Even if you won't tell me, Granny, I know.

GRANNY. What do you know?

TIEH-MEI. Listen.

I've more uncles than I can count;
They only come when there's important business.
Though we call them relatives we have never met,
Yet they're closer to us than our own family.
Both you and Dad call them your own folk;
Well, I can guess the secret—
They're all men like my dad,
Men with fine, loyal hearts.

GRANNY. [*Smiling*] You smart girl.

[*Sound of a police siren. Enter* LI *with the wounded man on his back. He pushes open the door and staggers in.* GRANNY *and* TIEH-MEI *hurry to help the* LIAISON MAN *to a chair.*]

TIEH-MEI. [*Frightened*] Oh!

LI. [*To* TIEH-MEI] Watch the street.

[*With a sigh the girl goes to the window.* GRANNY *brings a towel.* LI *cleans the man's wound and gives him a drink of water.*]

1. A brick stove, often large enough for people to sleep on the top.

LIAISON. Can you tell me if there's a switchman here named Li?

LI. That's me.

[*The* LIAISON MAN'S *eye lights on* GRANNY *and he hesitates.*]

LI. It's all right. You can speak.

LIAISON. [*Using the password*] I sell wooden combs.

LI. Any made of peach-wood?

LIAISON. [*Eagerly*] Yes, for cash down.

LI. [*With a pleased glance at* GRANNY] Fine.

[GRANNY *lights the small square lantern to show the* LIAISON MAN *that one side is pasted with red paper.*]

LIAISON. [*Not seeing the right lantern, struggles to get up*] I must go. . . .

LI. [*Holding high the other lantern*] Look, comrade!

LIAISON. [*Grasping* LI'S *hand*] Comrade, I've found you at last. [*He faints away.*]

[TIEH-MEI *is puzzled by this business with the lantern.*]

LI. Comrade. . . .

GRANNY. Comrade, comrade. . . .

[*The* LIAISON MAN *comes to.*]

LIAISON. Comrade Li, I'm . . . the liaison man . . . sent . . . from the north. [*With difficulty he tears open the lining of his padded jacket, produces the code and hands it to* LI.] This is . . . a secret code. [*Panting*] Send it . . . quickly . . . to the guerrillas in the north hills. [*Gasping for breath*] Tomorrow afternoon, the gruel stall in the junk market. . . .

LI. Yes, comrade, What about the junk market?

LIAISON. A knife-grinder will get in touch with you there.

LI. So a knife-grinder will get in touch with me.

LIAISON. Same password as before.

LI. The same, yes.

LIAISON. The task must be carried out. . . . [*He dies.*]

[TIEH-MEI *cries.* GRANNY *quickly stops her.* LI *takes off his cap and looks at the code in his hand. All three bow their heads before the dead man.*]

LI. I swear to carry out the task.

[*The siren of the police car wails.* GRANNY *hastily blows out the light.*]

Scene 3

A COMMOTION AT THE GRUEL STALL

[*The next afternoon. The gruel stall in the junk market. To the right of the shabby booth is a rickety table at which three men,* A, B, *and* C, *are eating gruel. At the foot of the pillar on the left squats a woman selling cigarettes. As the curtain rises the market hums with noise.]*

[*Enter* LI *with his lantern in one hand and a canteen in the other.*]

LI.

Come to find our man in the junk market
I have hidden the code in my canteen;
No obstacles can stop me,
I must send it up to the hills.

[*He enters the booth and greets the people there.*] A bowl of gruel, please, mum. [*Hangs his lantern on the right-hand pillar.*] How is business?

GRUEL-WOMAN. So-so. [*She serves him.*]

[C *finishes his gruel and pays for it.*]

GRUEL-WOMAN. Another bowl, brother?

C. No more, thanks.

GRUEL-WOMAN. Is one bowl enough for you?

C. Enough? It's all I can afford. We work all day but don't earn enough to buy gruel. It's a hell of a life. [*Exit.*]

[*Enter another man,* D.]

D. A bowl of gruel, please.

[*The woman serves him.*]

D. [*Stirring the gruel with his chopsticks*] This is thin, watery stuff.

A. It's government rice. What can we do?

[*With a sigh* D *takes the bowl to the left pillar to drink. He then squats down and buys a cigarette.*]

B. Hey, what's this in the gruel? Nearly broke one of my teeth.

A. It's full of stones.

GRUEL-WOMAN. You'd better put up with it.

B. The swine just don't treat us as human.

A. Keep quiet, or you'll find yourself in trouble.

B. [*Sighing*] How are we to live?

LI. Let's have another bowl, mum.

Our people are fuming with discontent,
Trampled by iron hoofs they seethe with fury
And wait for the first rumble of spring thunder.
China's brave sons will never bow their heads;
May our guerillas come soon from the north hills!

[*Enter the* KNIFE-GRINDER *with a carrying-pole.*]

KNIFE-GRINDER.

Glancing around in search of my man,
I see the red lantern hanging high to greet me.
[*Raising his gloved left hand to his ear he cries.*]
Any knives or scissors to grind?

LI.

> The knife-grinder has his eye on my red lantern
> And he raised his hand to accost me.
> I shall casually give him the password.

[*Before* LI *can speak the siren wails and Japanese gendarmes charge in.*]

GENDARMES. Don't move. This is a search.

[*The* KNIFE-GRINDER *deliberately drops his tools to divert the attention of the Japanese.*]

LI. Good man.

> He draws their fire in order to cover me.

[*He empties his bowl of gruel into his canteen and asks for another helping. The gendarmes finish searching the* KNIFE-GRINDER, *wave him angrily away and turn towards* LI. *He offers them his canteen and lantern but they push them aside.* LI *puts them on the table and lets himself be* searched.]

GENDARME A. [*Having searched him*] Clear out.

[LI *picks up his canteen and lantern and goes out.*]

Scene 4

WANG TURNS RENEGADE

[*The following afternoon,* HATOYAMA'S *office. On his desk and a medal, a medical report and a telephone. Beside the desk stands a screen.*]

[*Enter* HOU HSIEN-PU *with* WANG'S *file.*]

HOU.

> The man from the train fired a shot
> And wounded Inspector Wang's arm;
> The damage done is not serious
> But Hatoyama is making much of it.
> No doubt he has his reasons.

[*The telephone rings.* HOU *takes the call.*]

HOU. Yes? [*Standing to attention*] Yes, sir. [*He puts the receiver down.*] A call for you, Captain Hatoyama.

[*Enter* HATOYAMA *from behind the screen.*]

HATOYAMA. Where from?

HOU. From the commander.

HATOYAMA. You should have said so. [*Takes the phone.*] Hatoyama speaking. What? Got away? Eh? Hmm. . . . Don't worry, sir, I promise to get the code. Yes, sir. What? An order from the

Kwan-tung Army Headquarters. [*He stands to attention.*] The deadline for clearing this up. . . . Yes, sir. [*Rings off, muttering to himself.*] Those Reds are the devil. Headquarters discovered some clues in the north, but now they've covered their tracks again. The Communists are the very devil.

HOU. Report! Here is the dossier on Inspector Wang. [*Presents the file.*]

HATOYAMA. Good. [*He takes it and looks through it casually.*]

SERGEANT. [*Off*] Report!

HATOYAMA. Come in.

[*Enter the* SERGEANT.]

HATOYAMA. Find him?

SERGEANT. We searched all the hotels, bath-houses, theaters and gambling dens but found no trace of the man from the train. We arrested a few suspects. Would you like to see them, sir?

HATOYAMA. What's the use of arresting suspects? This is urgent. Headquarters have just notified us that this man from the train is a liaison officer for the Communists in the north. He has a very important secret code with him.

HOU *and* SERGEANT. [*Standing at attention*] Yes, sir.

HATOYAMA. This code has been sent from the Reds' headquarters in the north to the guerrillas in the northern hills, who are waiting for this to get in touch with them. If this code reaches the guerrillas it will be like fitting several thousand tigers with wings, and that would be most detrimental to our empire.

HOU *and* SERGEANT. [*Standing at attention*] Most detrimental. Yes, sir.

HATOYAMA. How could you let such an important Red slip through your fingers?

[*The* SERGEANT *and* HOU *look at each other.*]

HATOYAMA. Fools!

HOU *and* SERGEANT. Yes, sir.

HATOYAMA. How about Inspector Wang?

HOU. He was shot in the left arm, but the bone. . . .

HATOYAMA. That's not what I was asking. Tell me his background.

HOU. Very good, sir. His name is Wang Hung-chang, otherwise known as Wang Lien-chu. His grandfather used to sell opium, his father kept a tavern, and he was one of the first graduates from the Manchukuo police school. He has one wife, one son, and one father.

HATOYAMA. So he comes from a good family. This time he did his best. Bring him here.

HOU. Yes, sir. [*Calling*] Inspector Wang.

[*Enter* WANG *with one arm in a sling. He salutes* HATOYAMA.]

WANG. Captain.

HATOYAMA. Well, young man.

> You have paid for your courage, young fellow,
> Stopping the enemy's bullet with your body
> And fearlessly defending our great empire.
> On behalf of headquarters I give you this medal, third class.

WANG. [*Surprised and pleased*] Ah!

> My ill luck has changed to good,
> Hatoyama does not suspect me.
> Thank you, sir, for your goodness,
> This is too great an honor.

HATOYAMA. Young man,

> Provided you serve the empire loyally
> You have every chance to rise high;
> One who repents can leave the sea of troubles,
> The choice is up to you.

WANG. I don't follow you, sir.

HATOYAMA. You should understand. You are not an actor, so why try to fool me? I'm afraid I can't compliment you on your performance.

WANG. Sir. . . .

HATOYAMA. I don't suppose you have followed my career. Let me tell you that when you were still a baby I was already a surgeon of some reputation. Though you fired that shot accurately enough, you forgot one thing. How could the man from the train get within three centimeters of your arm to fire?

WANG. I'm sorry you should think such a thing, sir.

HATOYAMA. [*Chuckling*] Sorry. I'm sure you are. Sorry that I wasn't taken in by your trick. You can't fox me so easily, young fellow. So now, out with the truth. Who was your accomplice?

WANG. Accomplice?

HATOYAMA. Does that word surprise you? It's obvious enough. That man who jumped off the train was badly wounded. Without an accomplice to help him and another to cover their escape, could he have grown wings and flown away?

WANG. Sir, you can investigate what happened. I was shot and fell to the ground. How could I know where that man went?

HATOYAMA. You knew all right. Why else should you shoot yourself? Don't try to outsmart me, young fellow. Tell me the truth. Who's in the underground Communist Party? Who were your accomplices? Where is the liaison man hiding? Who's got the secret code now? Make a clean breast of things and I have ready plenty of medals and rewards.

WANG. You're making my brain whirl, sir.

HATOYAMA. [*Laughing derisively*] In that case we shall have to sober you up. Hou Hsien-pu!

HOU. Yes, sir.

HATOYAMA. Take this young man out and help to sober him.

HOU. Very good, sir. Guards!

[*Enter two gendarmes.*]

WANG. I've done nothing, sir. Nothing wrong.

HATOYAMA. Take him away.

WANG. Don't punish an innocent man, sir.

[HATOYAMA *jerks his head in dismissal.*]

HOU. Come on.

[*The guards march* WANG *out, followed by* HOU.]

HATOYAMA. [*Smiling cynically after them*]

Iron hoofs trample the whole northeast,
Human skulls are used for goblets;
The crack of whips, the sound of sobs
And drumming on bones make music.
No matter how tough the fellow,

[*His singing is punctuated by the sound of blows and cries.*]

He must break down under torture.

[*Enter* HOU.]

HOU. If you please, sir, he has confessed.

HATOYAMA. Who was his accomplice?

HOU. Li Yu-ho, the switchman of the No. 51 Siding.

HATOYAMA. Li Yu-ho! [*He takes off his glasses.*] Well, well. . . .

Scene 5

THE FAMILY'S REVOLUTIONARY HISTORY

[*The next afternoon.* LI's *house.* GRANNY *is sewing and worrying about* LI.]

GRANNY.

Already dusk, but my son is still not back.

[*In the distance sound shouts and the wail of the siren.* TIEH-MEI *rushes fearfully in with her basket and locks the door.*]

TIEH-MEI. It looks bad, Granny.

GRANNY. What's happening?

TIEH-MEI. Granny,

The streets are in confusion
With sentries at every crossroad;
They are searching and arresting men right and left,

It's even worse at the station.
I ran home because I'm worried about Dad.

GRANNY. Don't worry, child.

Your dad is brave and wary,
He knows the way to deal with the Japanese.

[*She tries to calm herself.*]

TIEH-MEI. Yes, of course, Granny.

[*Enter* LI *with the red lantern and canteen.*]

LI. [*Knocking at the door*] Mother.

TIEH-MEI. It's Dad. [*She quickly opens the door.*] At last you're back, Dad.

LI. Yes. . . . Mother.

GRANNY. So you're back, son. You had me really worried.

LI. It was a near thing, Mother. [*He walks toward the pillar by the bed and signs to her to take the canteen.*] Let me have the thing in that, quick.

GRANNY. [*Signing to* TIEH-MEI *to watch the street while she opens the canteen*] There's nothing here but gruel.

LI. It's underneath, Mother.

[*She empties out the gruel, produces the code which is wrapped in cellophane and hands it to* LI.]

GRANNY. What is this?

[TIEH-MEI, *standing guard by the window, keeps an eye on her father.*]

LI. [*Hiding the code in a crack in the pillar by the bed*] Mother,

I'd just met the knife-grinder by the gruel stall
When a police car came and the Japanese started a search;
They didn't find the code hidden under the gruel,
I smiled calmly while they searched.

TIEH-MEI. Trust you, Dad. But what are we to do with this?

LI. Don't worry. We'll think of some way to send it, Tieh-mei. [*He makes her sit down opposite him and speaks gravely.*] You've seen everything. I can't keep this from you any longer. This is something more important than our own lives. We must keep it a secret even if it costs us our heads.

[GRANNY *lights the paraffin.*]

TIEH-MEI. [*Naïvely yet earnestly*] I understand.

LI. Hah, I suppose you think you're the smartest girl in the world.

TIEH-MEI. [*Pouting*] Dad!

GRANNY. Look at you both.

TIEH-MEI. Granny.

LI. [*Consulting his watch*] It's getting late. I must go out.

TIEH-MEI. Wait till you've had supper, Dad.

LI. I'll eat when I come back.

GRANNY. Don't be too late.

LI. I won't. [*He gets up to go.*]

TIEH-MEI. [*Giving him the scarf*] Take this, Dad. [*She wraps the scarf round his neck.*] Come back early.

LI. I will. [*Exit.*]

[GRANNY *polishes the lantern with care.*]

TIEH-MEI. [*Struck by an idea*] Polishing the red lantern again, Granny?

GRANNY. [*Deciding to satisfy her curiosity*] Tieh-mei, the time has come to tell you something. Sit down and listen to the story of the red lantern.

TIEH-MEI. Yes.

GRANNY. We've had this lantern for thirty years. For thirty years it has lighted the way for us poor people, for workers. Your grandad carried this lantern, and now you dad carries it. It's bound up with all that happened last night and today, which you saw for yourself. I tell you, the red lantern is our family treasure.

TIEH-MEI. Ah, the red lantern is our family treasure. I'll remember that.

GRANNY. It's dark, time to get supper. [*She puts the lantern carefully down and goes to the kitchen.*]

[TIEH-MEI *picks up the lantern to examine it carefully and then puts it gently down. She pensively turns up the paraffin lamp.*]

TIEH-MEI.

Granny has told me the story of the red lantern,
Only a few words, yet how much it means.
I have seen my father's courage,
My uncles' willingness to die for it.
What are they working for?
To save China, save the poor and defeat the Japanese invaders.
I know they are in the right,
They are examples for the rest of us.
You are seventeen, Tieh-mei, no longer a child,
You should lend your father a hand.
If his load weighs a thousand pounds,
You should carry eight hundred.

[*Enter* GRANNY. *She calls* TIEH-MEI, *who does not hear.*]

GRANNY. What were you thinking about, child?

TIEH-MEI. Nothing.

GRANNY. The food will soon be ready. When your dad comes, we'll start.

TIEH-MEI. Right.

[*The child next door cries.*]

GRANNY. Listen, is that Lung-erh crying next door?

TIEH-MEI. [*Looking towards the curtain behind the kang*] Yes, it is.

GRANNY. Poor child, he's hungry I'll be bound. Have we any of that acorn flour left?

TIEH-MEI. Not much.

[*The child cries again.*]

TIEH-MEI. [*Eager to help*] There's a little, Granny. Shall I take them a bowl? [*She gets the flour.*]

GRANNY. Yes, do.

[*Enter* KUEI-LAN.]

KUEI-LAN. [*Knocking at the door*] Aunty Li.

TIEH-MEI. It's Sister Kuei-lan. [*Opens the door.*] I was just going to call on you, sister.

GRANNY. Is Lung-erh any better?

KUEI-LAN. Yes, but . . . we've nothing at home to eat.

TIEH-MEI. Sister Kuei-lan, this is for you. [*Gives her the bowl of flour.*]

KUEI-LAN. [*Hesitating to accept it*] Well. . . .

GRANNY. Take it. I heard Lung-erh crying and thought you probably had nothing he could eat. Tieh-mei was just going to take this over.

TIEH-MEI. [*To* KUEI-LAN] Go on, take it.

KUEI-LAN. [*Accepting the bowl*] I don't know what to say, Aunty. You're too good to us.

GRANNY. Well, with the wall between us we're two families. If we pulled the wall down we'd be one family, wouldn't we?

TIEH-MEI. We are one family even with the wall.

GRANNY. That's true.

[*The child next door cries again.*]

[*Enter* AUNT LIU *and she opens the door.*]

AUNT LIU. Kuei-lan, the child is crying. [*Sees the bowl in her hand.*] Aunty, Tieh-mei, you. . . . How can we accept it? You haven't got much yourselves.

GRANNY. Never mind. In times like these we must help each other and make do as best we can. You'd better go and fix a meal for the child.

AUNT LIU. I don't know how to thank you. [*She starts out with* KUEI-LAN.]

GRANNY. It's nothing. [*She sees them to the door.*]

TIEH-MEI. [*Closing the door*] Granny, look at Kuei-lan's family. Her husband out of work and the little boy ill. How are they going to manage?

GRANNY. We'll do our best to help them.

TIEH-MEI. Yes.

[*An enemy agent posing as a peddler comes to the door and knocks lightly three times.*]

PEDDLER. Is Old Li in?

TIEH-MEI. Someone wants Dad.

GRANNY. Open the door.

TIEH-MEI. Right. [*Opens the door.*]

GRANNY You want. . . .

[*Enter the* PEDDLER. *He looks around and closes the door behind him.*]

PEDDLER. [*Raising his gloved left hand*] I sell wooden combs.

GRANNY. [*Observing him carefully*] Have you any peach-wood combs?

PEDDLER. Yes, for cash down.

TIEH-MEI. [*Eagerly*] Wait! [*She turns to pick up the red lantern.*]

[GRANNY *coughs.* TIEH-MEI *stops.* GRANNY *strikes a match and lights the small square lantern while* TIEH-MEI, *understanding, catches her breath.*]

PEDDLER. [*Raises the curtain and looks out as if on his guard. Then he eyes the small lantern*] Thank goodness, I've found you at last.

TIEH-MEI. [*Realizing that this is a trick, angrily*] You. . . .

GRANNY. [*Throwing her a warning glance*] Well, let me see your combs.

PEDDLER. [*Pretending to be in earnest*] This is no time for jokes, old lady. I've come for the code. That's important to the communist cause. The revolution depends on it. Every minute is more precious than gold to the revolution. Give it me quickly, without any more delay.

TIEH-MEI. [*Vehemently*] What nonsense are you talking? Get out.

PEDDLER. Now then. . . .

TIEH-MEI. Are you going? [*She pushes him.*]

GRANNY. Tieh-mei, call the police.

TIEH-MEI. If you won't go, I'll call the police.

PEDDLER. Don't do that. I'll go, I'll go.

TIEH-MEI. Get out quickly.

[*The spy gives her a dirty look and shuffles out.* TIEH-MEI *closes the door with a bang. Two plainclothes men enter, making signs to each other, and stand outside the door.*]

TIEH-MEI. He nearly fooled me, Granny. Where did that mangy dog come from?

GRANNY. Child, this is a bad business.

Never mind that mangy dog,
A poisonous snake will be following behind;
It's clear that someone
Has talked.

TIEH-MEI. We must send the secret code away at once.

GRANNY. It's too late. They'll have laid a trap.

TIEH-MEI. Ah! [*Runs to the window and looks out.*] Granny. [*She comes back to her.*] There's a man by the telegraph pole watching our door.

GRANNY. You see? Hurry up and paste the sign on the window.

TIEH-MEI. What sign?

GRANNY. The paper butterfly I told you to cut out.

TIEH-MEI. It's in the box of patterns.

GRANNY. Get it out then.

TIEH-MEI. Right. [*Hurries behind the bed-curtain and fetches the paper.*] How shall I paste it, Granny?

GRANNY. Open the door to keep the window dark before you start. I'll sweep the ground outside so that they can't see you.

[TIEH-MEI *opens the door and* GRANNY *gets a broom. Before she can go out* LI *enters and walks in.*]

TIEH-MEI. [*Startled*] Why, Dad. [*The paper butterfly falls to the ground. The old woman drops her broom.*]

LI. [*Seeing the paper butterfly on the ground*] Has something happened, Mother? [*Closes the door.*]

GRANNY. There are agents outside.

[*They fall silent.* GRANNY *is thinking hard.* TIEH-MEI *waits for her father to speak.* LI *paces thoughtfully up and down.*]

[*Enter* HOU HSIEN-PU *and he knocks at the door.*]

LI. Mother, they may be coming to arrest me. I went to look for Old Chou just now but couldn't find him. If you need any help, get in touch with Old Chou at No. 36 West Bank. You must be careful.

GRANNY. I know. Don't worry.

LI. Tieh-mei, open the door.

[LI *calmly sits down.* HOU *enters the room beaming.* GRANNY *makes a show of sweeping the floor.* TIEH-MEI *takes this chance to paste up the paper sign.*]

HOU. Are you Mr. Li?

LI. Yes, sir. Take a seat.

HOU. [*With an awkward laugh presenting an invitation card.*] Mr. Li, Mr. Hatoyama is celebrating his birthday today. He wants you to go and have a cup of wine with him.

[GRANNY *and* TIEH-MEI *are startled.*]

LI. [*Calmly*] What, is Mr. Hatoyama inviting me to a feast?

HOU. Just to be friendly.

LI. He wants to make friends with me?

HOU. You'll understand when you see him. Come along.

LI. All right. Mother, [*gravely*] I'm going now.

GRANNY. Wait, Tieh-mei, bring some wine.

TIEH-MEI. Yes. [*She fetches wine from the table.*]

HOU. There'll be plenty for him to drink at the feast, old lady.
GRANNY. [*With a contemptuous glance*] Pah.

> The poor refer their own wine,
> Each drop of it warms the heart.

You like wine, son, but I don't usually encourage you to drink. Today I want you to drink up this bowl. [*She passes him the wine.*]

LI. [*Taking the bowl*] Right. With this to put heart into me I can cope with whatever's coming. Watch me drink, Mother.

GRANNY. I'm watching you.

LI. [*Looking at her as if to reassure her with his strength. He grasps the bowl hard and drains it in one breath. His cheeks are flushed, his eyes gleam*] Thank you, Mother.

GRANNY. [*Proudly*] That's my fine son.

LI. Mother,

> I drink your wine at parting
> And it fills me with courage and strength.
> The Japanese is offering me a feast,
> Well, I can manage even a thousand cups.
> This is stormy, treacherous weather,
> Be ready for squalls.

TIEH-MEI. Dad. [*Clasps him and sobs.*]

LI. Tieh-mei.

> Keep your weather eye open outside,
> Don't forget our unsettled accounts;
> Keep watch for wild dogs at the door,
> And listen for the magpie's lucky cry.
> You must help at home
> And share your granny's troubles.

TIEH-MEI. Dad. [*Clasps him and sobs.*]

GRANNY. Don't cry, Tieh-mei. Our family has this rule: when one of us leaves, nobody must cry.

LI. Always do as Granny says, Tieh-mei. Don't cry.

TIEH-MEI. [*Wiping her tears*] I won't.

GRANNY. Open the door, child, and let your father go to the feast.

LI. Mother, look after yourself.

[*Grasping* LI's *hands,* GRANNY *gazes at him while* TIEH-MEI *opens the door. A gust of wind.* LI *strides out into the wind. Huddled up in his coat* HOU *follows.* TIEH-MEI *runs after them with the scarf.*]

TIEH-MEI. Dad!

[*Four* ENEMY THUGS *bar her way.*]

THUG A. Go back. [*He forces her back through the door. Then he enters and tells* GRANNY] We're making a search.

[*The* THUGS *give the place a professional going over.* TIEH-MEI *nestles up to* GRANNY *as they turn everything upside down. They discover an almanac and toss it away but fail to find anything incriminating.*]

THUG A. Come on. [*He signs to the others to leave. Exeunt.*]

TIEH-MEI. [*Closes the door, draws the curtain and looks at the chaos in the room*] Granny! [*She falls into her arms and sobs.*]

GRANNY. [*Weeping despite herself*] All right, cry, child. Have a good cry.

TIEH-MEI. Granny, will Dad ever come back?

GRANNY. [*Restraining her own tears. She knows there is little hope of his returning but does not want to say so. She takes up* LI's *scarf and strokes it.*] Tears won't help him, child. [*Looks at her.*]

TIEH-MEI. The time has come to tell you about our family.

TIEH-MEI. Yes, Granny?

GRANNY. Sit down. I'll tell you.

TIEH-MEI. Yes. [*Sits down on a stool.*]

GRANNY. Tell me: Is your dad good?

TIEH-MEI. Well . . . he's not your real father.

TIEH-MEI. [*Incredulously*] Ah! What do you mean, Granny?

GRANNY. Neither am I your real granny.

TIEH-MEI. [*Startled*] What's come over you, Granny? Have you taken leave of your senses?

GRANNY. No, child. We don't belong to one family. Your surname is Chen, mine is Li and your dad's is Chang.

TIEH-MEI. [*Blankly*] Oh.

GRANNY.

For seventeen storm-tossed years I held my peace,
Eager to speak but afraid you were not ready for the truth.

TIEH-MEI. You can tell me, Granny. I won't cry.

GRANNY.

Your father can hardly escape
And they may imprison me too;
Then the work for the revolution will fall to you.
When I tell you the truth, Tieh-mei,
Don't break down but take it bravely,
Like a girl of iron.

TIEH-MEI. Tell me. I won't cry.

GRANNY. It's a long story. When the railway was seized by the Japanese at the end of the Ching dynasty, my husband fled to the south and became a maintenance man in Kiangan. He had two apprentices. One was your real father, Chen Chih-hsing.

TIEH-MEI. My father, Chen Chih-hsing.

GRANNY. The other was your present dad, Chang Yu-ho.

TIEH-MEI. Chang Yu-ho.

GRANNY. [*Standing up*] The country was torn by the fighting between warlords. But then the Chinese Communist Party was born to lead the Chinese people's revolution. In February, 1923, workers of the Peking-Hankow Railway set up a trade union in Chengchow. One of the warlords, Wu Pei-fu, was a stooge of the foreign invaders. When he tried to suppress the union, it called on all the workers on the line to strike. More than ten thousand men in Kiangan demonstrated. That was another cold, dark night. I was so worried about your grandfather that I couldn't rest or sleep. I was mending clothes by the lamp when I heard someone knocking at the door, calling, "Aunty, Aunty, quickly open the door." I opened the door, and he came in.

TIEH-MEI. Who was it?

GRANNY. Your dad.

TIEH-MEI. [*Surprised*] My dad?

GRANNY. Yes, your present dad. Dripping with blood and all gashed with wounds, in his left hand he held this red lantern. . . .

TIEH-MEI. Ah, the red lantern.

GRANNY. In his right arm he held a baby.

TIEH-MEI. A baby?

GRANNY. A mite less than one year old.

TIEH-MEI. That baby. . . .

GRANNY. That baby was none other. . . .

TIEH-MEI. Than who?

GRANNY. Than you.

TIEH-MEI. Me. . . .

GRANNY. [*Quickly*] Hugging you tight to his chest, with tears in his eyes your dad stood before me and said, "Aunty, Aunty. . . ."

[TIEH-MEI *gazes expectantly at her.*]

GRANNY. For some minutes he just stared at me and couldn't go on. In a panic, I begged him to speak. He said, "They've murdered . . . my master and brother. This is Brother Chen's child, a child of the revolution. I must bring her up to carry on our work." He said, "Aunty, from now on I am your son and this child is your granddaughter." Then I took you in my arms.

TIEH-MEI. Granny! [*She buries her head in the old woman's lap.*]

[GRANNY *holds and comforts her.*]

GRANNY. Ah! You mustn't cry. Take a grip on yourself and listen.

In the strike those devils murdered your father and mother,
Li Yu-ho went east and west for the revolution;

He swore to tread in their steps, keep the red lantern burning;
He staunched his wounds, buried the dead, and went back to
the fight.
Now the Japanese brigands are burning, killing, and looting,
Before our eyes your dad was taken away;
Remember this debt of blood and tears,
Be brave and make up your mind to settle scores,
A debt of blood must be paid for with enemy blood.

TIEH-MEI.

Granny tells a stirring tale of the revolution,
They brought me up in wind and grain and storm,
How much I owe you, Granny, for all these years!
My mind is made up now, I see my way clear;
Blood must be shed for our blood,
I must carry on the task my father began.
Here I raise the red lantern, let its light shine far.
My father is as dauntless as the pine,
The Communist Party fears nothing under the sun,
I shall follow it and never, never waver.
The red lantern's light
Shines on my father fighting those wild beasts.
Generation shall fight on after generation,
Never leaving the field until the victory is won.

[GRANNY *and* TIEH-MEI *hold high the red lantern.*]

Scene 6

HATOYAMA IS DEFIED

[*That evening.* HATOYAMA's *house. A sumptuous feast is spread. Through the lattice windows glittering lights can be seen. Jazz sounds and girls dance past the window.*]

[*Enter* HOU *with* LI YU-HO.]

HOU. Please wait a minute. [*He starts off to report* LI's *attitude to* HATOYAMA.]

LI. As you like. [*He stands there looking round, puffiing his cigarette, disgusted by the surroundings.*]

HOU [*Off*] Captain Hatoyama.

HATOYAMA. [*Hurrying in*] Ah, my old friend, it's good to see you again. Have you been keeping well?

LI. How are you, Mr. Hatoyama?

HATOYAMA. So we meet again after all this time. Do you remember when we were both working on the railway in Harbin?

LI. [*Drily*] You were a celebrated Japanese doctor while I was a poor Chinese worker. We were like two trains running on different tracks, not traveling the same road.

HATOYAMA. Well, brother, there's not all that difference between a surgeon and a worker. We're old friends, not strangers, right?

LI. In that case can I hope for good treatment from you?

HATOYAMA. That's why I asked you over for a chat. Do sit down, please. [*They sit down.*] Today is my birthday, friend, a time to celebrate. Suppose we just talk of friendship and leave politics out of it?

LI. I'm a switchman. I don't understand politics. You can say whatever you like.

HATOYAMA. Fine, I like your frankness. Come on [*Pours wine.*] Just a cup of wine for friendship's sake. Now, drink up. [*Raises the cup.*]

LI. You are too polite, Mr. Hatoyama. Sorry, but I've given up drinking. [*He pushes the cup away.*]

HATOYAMA. Well, friend. [*Taking up his own cup.*] If you won't oblige me, I can't force you. [*He drinks and then starts his offensive.*] Why take things so seriously? There's an old Chinese saying, "Life is over in a flash like a dream. We should drink and sing, for who knows how soon life will end?"

LI. Yes, listening to songs and watching dances is living like an immortal. I wish you long life, Mr. Hatoyama, and all prosperity.

HATOYAMA. [*Frustrated, lamely*] Thank you, thank you.

LI. [*Eyeing him contemptuously*] You are too ceremonious. [*He laughs.*]

HATOYAMA. [*With a hollow laugh*] My friend, I am a believer in Buddhism. A Buddhist sutra tells us, "Boundless the sea of sorrow, yet a man who will turn back can reach the shore."

LI. [*Jokingly*] For myself, I don't believe in Buddhism but I've heard the saying, "A butcher who lays down his knife can become a Buddha, too."

HATOYAMA. Good. [*On the defensive*] Well said. But both add up to the same thing. In fact we can sum up all human beliefs in two words.

LI. What are they?

HATOYAMA. "For me."

LI. "For you," eh?

HATOYAMA. No. "Each for himself."

LI. "Each for himself." [*He laughs.*]

HATOYAMA. [*Earnestly*] Old friend, you know the saying, "Heaven destroys men who won't look out for themselves."

LI. Oh? Heaven destroys men who won't look out for themselves?

HATOYAMA. That's the secret of life.

LI. So life has a secret. I'm afraid it's too difficult for a blockhead like me to grasp. [*He laughs.*]

HATOYAMA. [*To himself*] What a stubborn fool!

His heart is hard to fathom;
He parries my thrusts
With no thought of his own safety,
Impervious to both praise and flattery.
I must be patient.
With my experience and tact
I'll get hold of that secret code.

Let's stop this shadow-boxing, friend. I want your help.

LI. [*With an air of surprise*] What do you mean? How can a poor switchman help you.

HATOYAMA. [*Unable to keep his temper*] Quit joking. Hand it over.

LI. What is it you want?

HATOYAMA. [*coldly and distinctly*] The secret code.

LI. What's that? All I can do is work switches. I've never used any such thing as a code.

HATOYAMA. [*Rising abruptly*] If you choose to do things the hard way instead of the easy way, friend, don't blame me if we get rough.

LI. Do as you like.

HATOYAMA. All right. [*Beats his plate with a chopstick.*]

[*Enter* INSPECTOR WANG *in army uniform wearing his medal.*]

HATOYAMA. My old friend, look, who is this?

LI. [*Shocked by the sight of* WANG] Ah!

WANG. Take my advice, brother. . . .

LI. You shameless renegade!

Only a coward would bend his knees in surrender,
A cur afraid of death and clinging to life.
How often did I warn you
Against enemy threats and bribes?
You swore you would gladly die for the revolution;
How could you sell out and help the Japanese?
They are treating you like a dog,
Yet you count disgrace an honor.
Come here and look me in the eyes,
Shame on you, you sneaking slave.

[HATOYAMA *waves* WANG *away and he slinks out.*]

HATOYAMA. Steady on, my friend. I didn't want to play my trump card but you forced me to.

LI. [*Laughing derisively*] I expected as much. Your trump card is nothing but a mangy dog with a broken back. You'll get no satisfaction out of me.

HATOYAMA. I can give you some satisfaction. Let's hear your terms.

LI. Terms?

HATOYAMA. Here's your chance to strike a good bargain.

LI. Bargain?

HATOYAMA. Yes, bargain. I understand you Communists very well; you have your beliefs. But beliefs can be bought or sold. The main thing is to make a profit.

LI. That's frank enough. It follows that there's nothing you wouldn't sell if you could make a profit. [*He laughs.*]

HATOYAMA. [*Furious*] You. . . . [*Fuming*] You go too far, friend. You must know my job. I'm the one who issues passes to Hell.

LI. You don't seem to know my job. I'm the one who takes your pass and destroys your Hell.

HATOYAMA [*Impressed by* LI's *spirit, makes a show of sympathy*] Take my advice and recant before your bones are broken.

LI. I'd sooner have my bones broken than recant.

HATOYAMA. Our police are rough. They think nothing of killing people.

LI. We Communists are tough. We look on death as nothing.

HATOYAMA. Even if you are made of iron, I'll force you to speak.

LI. Even if you have hills of swords and a forest of knives, you'll get nothing out of me, Hatoyama.

> The Japanese militarists are wolves
> Hiding their savagery under a smile;
> You kill our people and invade our land
> In the name of "Co-prosperity in East Asia."
> The Communists lead the people's revolution;
> We have hundreds of millions of heroes in the resistance;
> For you to rely on renegades
> Is like fishing for the moon in the lake.

HATOYAMA.

> I'll let you taste the leg-screws.

[*Enter the* SERGEANT *and two gendarmes.*]

LI.

> I need to take the weight off my feet.

SERGEANT. Get moving.

[*The gendarmes grasp* LI's *arms.*]

LI. I can do without your help. [*He throws them off and calmly picks up his cap, blows the dust off it, shakes it, and walks out with dignity.*]

[*The* SERGEANT *and gendarmes follow* LI *out.*]

HATOYAMA. [*Pacing to and fro, very put out, scratches his head and mutters*] Quite mad, these Reds.

My eyes are dim, my head is ready to burst;
My blood pressure has risen, my hands are cold;
The Reds are flesh and blood like us,
What makes them tougher than steel?
He refuses to say where the code is hidden, curse him!
What shall I do if I can't get hold of it?

[*The telephone rings.*]

HATOYAMA. [*Talking the call*] Hatoyama here. Yes, sir, we are still searching for the code. Quite so, sir. Certainly, certainly. Yes, sir. I'll stake my life on it. [*He replaces the receiver and shouts.*] Here. How are you doing?

[*Enter the* SERGEANT.]

SERGEANT. We have tried all the tortures, but Li Yu-ho would rather die than speak.

HATOYAMA. Rather die than speak?

SERGEANT. Let me take some men to search his house, sir.

HATOYAMA. That's no use. Judging by my experience, ten thousand men can't find something which a Communist has hidden. Fetch him in.

SERGEANT. Bring Li Yu-ho here!

[*Two gendarmes push* LI *in. Blood-stained and battered, he stands there defiantly.*]

LI.

You cur with the heart of a wolf.

HATOYAMA. The code! Give me the code!

LI. Hatoyama!

You have tried every torture to break me;
Though my body is mangled I clench my teeth,
I shall never bow my head. [*He laughs.*]

Scene 7

THE CODE FINDS A NEW HIDING-PLACE

[*One morning several days later.* LI'*s house. By the telegraph pole not far from the door is an enemy agent disguised as a cobbler. While pretending to mend shoes he watches the house.*]

TIEH-MEI. [*Just out of bed and emerging from behind the curtain*]. Why isn't Dad back yet, Granny?

Ever since Dad was arrested—

GRANNY.

We've been worrying and cannot rest.

[*The* KNIFE-GRINDER *offstage cries, "Any knives or scissors to grind?"*]

TIEH-MEI. Granny, listen.

[*Enter the* KNIFE-GRINDER.]

KNIFE-GRINDER. Any knives or scissors to grind?

[GRANNY *pulls* TIEH-MEI *to the window and they look out.*]
[*The* KNIFE-GRINDER *comes up to the window and sees the butterfly sign. He hesitates, then nods and starts shouting again.*]

COBBLER. There's no business for you in this poor part of town. Why do your caterwauling here?

KNIFE-GRINDER. [*In a loud, friendly voice*] You stick to your business, friend, and I'll stick to mine. We knife-grinders have to call out. If you make me keep quiet, how am I to find customers?

COBBLER. You clear out if you don't want to run into trouble.

KNIFE-GRINDER. All right, all right. I get it. I'll try my luck somewhere else. [*As he leaves he raises his left hand to his ear and yells.*] Any knives or scissors to grind?

[*Exit.*]

COBBLER. Still caterwauling, blast him.

GRANNY. [*Pulling* TIEH-MEI *close*] Did you hear that, child?

TIEH-MEI. What?

GRANNY. That knife-grinder probably came to make contact with us. He went away after seeing the sign on the window. Run after him quickly with the code and lantern and see whether he's our man or not. I'll get the code.

TIEH-MEI. All right. [*Goes to the window.*]

GRANNY. It won't do, child, not with those agents outside. You can't go.

TIEH-MEI. What shall we do, then?

> I want to run after the knife-grinder,
> But I can't leave the house and am worried.
> I wish I could grow wings and fly like a bird.

[*The child next door cries.*]

TIEH-MEI. Granny, I have an idea.

GRANNY. What is it?

TIEH-MEI. Granny.

> I know a way out.

Look. [*Points to the kang.*] There's only a wall between this and Liu's kang. I can make a hole and slip through.

GRANNY. [*Pleased*] That's a good idea. Go ahead.

[TIEH-MEI *disappears behind the curtain.* GRANNY *starts chopping cabbage to hide the noise she makes.*]

TIEH-MEI. [*Coming back*] It's done, Granny.

GRANNY. [*Takes the code from the crack in the pillar and gives it to her with the red lantern. Solemnly*] Make sure he's the right man, Tieh-mei. He must get the password correct. Be very careful.

TIEH-MEI. I will [*She disappears behind the curtain.*]

COBBLER. [*Calling outside*] Open the door.

GRANNY. Who's that?

COBBLER. It's me. The cobbler.

GRANNY. Wait, I'll open the door. [*Opens the door.*]

COBBLER. [*Sees the knife in her hand*] What are you doing?

GRANNY. Tomorrow is my son's birthday. We are going to have some vegetable rolls.

COBBLER. Ah, vegetable rolls.

GRANNY. What do you want?

COBBLER. I want to borrow a light.

GRANNY. [*Indicating the match-box on the table*] Help yourself.

COBBLER. How many of you are there, old lady?

GRANNY. You've been squatting outside our door the last few days; you should know all about us. One has gone, there are two of us left.

COBBLER. Where's the girl?

GRANNY. She's not well.

COBBLER. Not well? Where is she?

GRANNY. She's lying down in bed.

COBBLER. Lying down, eh? [*He walks towards the kang.*]

GRANNY. [*Stopping him*] Keep away. Don't frighten the child.

COBBLER. [*Sniggering*] If she's ill, old lady, why isn't she whimpering?

GRANNY. My granddaughter never whimpers when she's ill.

COBBLER. That means she isn't ill. But perhaps you feel sick at heart?

GRANNY. Seems to me you're the one who is sick.

COBBLER. Me sick? How?

GRANNY. There's a canker gnawing at your bones—they're moldering.

COBBLER. That's nothing that a little sun won't cure.

GRANNY. You're too rotten to face the sun.

COBBLER. Never mind. Men's bones have got to rot some day, so let them be rotten. Tell your girl to sit up for a bit, old lady. It's no good lying down all the time. [*He tries to lift the curtain.*]

GRANNY. What d'you think you're doing? Asking all these foolish questions, throwing your weight about in other people's houses, and insulting women. What's the idea? Clear off. Get out!

COBBLER. All right, just wait. [*Enter two* ENEMY AGENTS. *They whisper together and the* AGENTS *open the door.*]

GRANNY. Who are you?

AGENTS. We are checking up. How many people live here?

GRANNY. Three.

AGENTS. Where are the other two?

GRANNY. You should know where my son is now.

AGENTS. Where's your granddaughter?

GRANNY. She's ill.

AGENTS. Where is she? Where is she? [*Goes to lift the curtain.*]

[*Voice from behind the curtain: "Granny. Who's there?"*]

GRANNY. Police checking up.

[*The* AGENTS *grunt, shrug and go out.* GRANNY *closes the door behind them.*]

AGENTS. [*To the* COBBLER] What a fuss over nothing. She was on the kang all the time. She didn't go out.

COBBLER. All right. That old bitch tried to make a fool of me.

[*Exeunt.*]

GRANNY. What a near thing! When did you come back, Tieh-mei?

[*She lifts the curtain and* KUEI-LAN *sits up.*]

GRANNY. So it's you, Kuei-lan.

KUEI-LAN. [*Getting off the kang to catch hold of* GRANNY] Granny Li.

After Tieh-mei slipped away from our house
My mother sent me to tell you.
When I heard those spies questioning you
I pretended to be Tieh-mei lying ill in bed.
When Tieh-mei comes, she can come through our house,
With me helping, you don't have to worry.

GRANNY. You've saved us. We shall never forget what you've done.

TIEH-MEI. [*Emerging from behind the curtain*] Granny. Sister Kuei-lan.

GRANNY. So you're back at last.

KUEI-LAN. Your granny was worried about you.

GRANNY. My heart nearly jumped out of my mouth. If not for Kuei-lan we'd have been in serious trouble.

TIEH-MEI. Thank you, Sister Kuei-lan. What would we have done without you?

KUEI-LAN. It was nothing. Why thank me for such a little thing? It's good that you're back. I must be going now.

TIEH-MEI. Won't you stay a while?

GRANNY. You go and tidy up the kang.

TIEH-MEI. Yes.

[KUEI-LAN *points at the door and they understand. She steps behind the curtain and leaves.* TIEH-MEI *straightens the bedding and pulls the curtain back.*]

GRANNY. Did you find the knife-grinder?

TIEH-MEI. [*In a low voice*] I searched several streets but couldn't find him. Then I looked for Uncle Chou but he wasn't at home. So I hurried back for fear those spies might discover that I was out.

GRANNY. Where is the code?

TIEH-MEI. I thought it would be safer outside, so I hid it under a pier of Short Bridge.

GRANNY. [*Relieved*] Ah, you made me break into a cold sweat, child. You've done right. I shan't worry provided the code's in a safe place.

[*Enter* HATOYAMA *in a Chinese gown and hat with a walking stick. He is followed by* HOU *carrying two boxes of cakes. They knock at the door.*]

GRANNY. Who's there?

HOU. Captain Hatoyama is paying you a visit.

GRANNY. [*Grasping* TIEH-MEI] Child, if your granny is arrested now, you must find Uncle Chou and give him the code, then go to the north hills.

TIEH-MEI. Granny! [*She cries.*]

GRANNY. Don't cry. Go and open the door.

[TIEH-MEI *opens the door.*]

HATOYAMA. [*Entering with a show of sympathy*] How are you, madam? I am Li Yu-ho's old friend, but I have been too busy to call before. [*Signs to* HOU *to leave after he has put the cakes on the table.*] This is a trifling present.

GRANNY. So you are Mr. Hatoyama?

HATOYAMA. Yes. I'm Hatoyama, Hatoyama.

GRANNY. Will you let me tidy up a bit before I come with you?

HATOYAMA. Don't misunderstand. That's not what I came for. Please sit down.

[GRANNY *ignores him.* HATOYAMA *takes a seat.*]

HATOYAMA. You must be longing to see your son, madam.

GRANNY. Of course, a mother naturally thinks of her son.

HATOYAMA. You needn't worry. He'll come back very soon safe and sound.

GRANNY. So much the better.

HATOYAMA. This wasn't our doing. We had orders from above. As a matter of fact we are looking after him very well.

GRANNY. Thank you.

HATOYAMA. We heard from Li, madam, that he left something with you.

GRANNY. Left what?

HATOYAMA. [*Casually*] Some code.

GRANNY. I don't know what you mean. [*To* TIEH-MEI] What does he mean, child?

HATOYAMA. A code. A book.

GRANNY. A book? My son can't read, Mr. Hatoyama. My granddaughter has never been to school and I can't tell one character from another. Our family has never bought books.

HATOYAMA. Since Li Yu-ho has told us about that book, old lady, why try to hide it?

GRANNY. If he told you, why not let him come and find it? Wouldn't that be simpler?

HATOYAMA. [*To himself*] She's a crafty old bitch. [*To* GRANNY] Don't try to fool me, old lady. Let's make a bargain. You give me that book and I'll send your son straight back. If he wants a job, the railway can make him a vice-section-chief. If he wants money, he can have five thousand dollars.

GRANNY. Five thousand dollars and the job of a vice-section-chief? What book can be worth that much?

HATOYAMA. You have to sell to someone who knows its value.

GRANNY. If that book means so much to you, I'll have a look for it. Wait a minute. Tieh-mei, help me find it.

HATOYAMA. Take your time. There's no hurry.

[GRANNY *takes* TIEH-MEI *behind the curtain.*]

HATOYAMA. [*Waiting expectantly, to himself*] So after all money can work miracles.

[GRANNY *comes back with* TIEH-MEI *carrying a bundle.*]

HATOYAMA. [*Very pleased*] You've found it, madam?

GRANNY. Yes. This is what my son brought back.

HATOYAMA. Right, that must be it. That's it.

GRANNY. You can have it. [*Gives him an almanac.*]

HATOYAMA. [*Furiously*] Bah, an almanac. [*He wants to throw it away but thinks better of it, fuming.*] I'll take it back anyway. Ah. . . . You must be worried about your son. Suppose I take you to see him and find out about the book. We are bound to find it. There's no hurry.

GRANNY. That's very good of you. Thank you. [*To* TIEH-MEI] Look after the house, child.

HATOYAMA. She had better come as well to see her father.

GRANNY. [*Startled*] But she's only a child.

HATOYAMA. [*Beckoning*] Come along.

TIEH-MEI. All right, I want to see my dad.

HATOYAMA. You'd like to help your father, wouldn't you?

TIEH-MEI. Yes.

HATOYAMA. Fine. Come on.

[*Enter* HOU *with several gendarmes.*]

HATOYAMA. Look after them well. [*He strides out. To the agents.*] Keep an eye on the house. [*Exit.*]

HOU. [*To* GRANNY *and* TIEH-MEI *with a sinister smile*] Come on, old lady. Come on, miss.

[*They leave the house together. The agents seal up the door.*]

TIEH-MEI. [*Upset to see the door sealed*] Granny!

GRANNY. [*Putting one hand through* TIEH-MEI'*s arm and wrapping the scarf round her neck*] Come on.

[*A gust of wind.*]

Scene 8

THE EXECUTION GROUNDS

[*Night. The Japanese police headquarters outside the prison. Enter* HATOYAMA, HOU HSIEN-PU *and the* SERGEANT.]

HATOYAMA. It doesn't look as if we shall get anywhere with our interrogation. Hurry up and get the tape recorder ready. We'll hear what the old woman says when she meets her son. We may find out something.

HOU and SERGEANT. Yes, sir.

HATOYAMA. Bring the old woman in.

HOU. Yes, sir. Fetch the old woman.

[*Two Japanese gendarmes bring* GRANNY *in.*]

HATOYAMA. Do you know this place, madam?

GRANNY. It's the police headquarters.

HATOYAMA. [*Pointing*] And over there?

[GRANNY *glances in that direction.*]

HATOYAMA. [*With a menacing smile*] That's the gate to paradise, where your son will mount to heaven.

[GRANNY *shivers.*]

HATOYAMA. When a man has committed a crime, madam, and his mother refuses to save his life, don't you think she is rather cruel?

GRANNY. What do you mean, Mr. Hatoyama? You've arrested my son for no reason and thrown him into prison. Now you want to kill him. You are the ones that are committing a crime, you are the ones that are cruel. How can you shift the blame for his murder on to me?

HATOYAMA. Have you thought what will come of talking like that, old lady?

GRANNY. The lives of our family are in your hands. You can do whatever you like.

HATOYAMA. [*Controlling himself*] All right, go and see your son. [GRANNY *starts off.*] This is his last chance, old lady. I hope you will all decide to steer clear of trouble and be reunited as one family.

GRANNY. I know what's right.

HATOYAMA. Take her away.

[*Exit* HOU *with* GRANNY.]

HATOYAMA. Here. Take Li to the execution grounds.

SERGEANT. Bring Li Yu-ho.

[*The scene changes. On the left is the path to the prison. In the center is a stone. In the rear on the left a slope leading to the execution grounds is backed by a high wall covered with barbed wire. It is dark. Offstage the Japanese gendarmes yell: "Fetch Li Yu-ho!" Chains clank.*]

[*Enter* LI.]

LI.

At the jailers' blood-thirsty cry I leave my cell;
Though my hands and feet are manacled and fettered
They cannot chain my soaring spirit.
Hatoyama has tortured me to get the code;
My bones are broken, my flesh torn, but firm my will.
Walking boldly to the execution grounds
I look up and see the red flag of revolution,
The flames of the resistance.
Not for long will these invaders lord it over us,
And once the storm is past fresh flowers will bloom;
New China will shine like the morning sun,
Red flags will flutter over all the country—
I smile through tears of joy at the thought of it.
I have done very little for the Party,
Worst of all, I failed to send the code to the hills;
That renegade Wang's only contact was with me,
The wretch can betray no one else;
And my mother and daughter are as staunch as steel,
So Hatoyama may search heaven and earth,
But he will never find the secret code.

[*Enter* GRANNY *and she looks round.*]

GRANNY. [*Seeing* LI, *cries*] Yu-ho!

LI. Mother.

[GRANNY *runs over to put her arms around him.*]

Again I live through that day seventeen years ago,
And burn with hate for the foe of my class and country.
The cruel Japanese devils
Have beaten and tortured you, my son, my son!

LI. Don't grieve for me, mother.

GRANNY.

I shouldn't grieve to have such a fine son.

LI.

Brought up in a hard school
I'll fight and never give ground;
Though they break every bone in my body,
Though they lock me up until I wear through my chains.
As long as our country is ravaged my heart must bleed;
As long as the war lasts my family is in danger;
However hard the road to revolution,
We must press on in the steps of the glorious dead.
My one regret if I die today
Is the debt I have left unpaid.
I long to soar like an eagle through the sky,

Borne on the wind above the mountain passes
To rescue our millions of suffering countrymen—
Then how gladly would I die for the revolution!

GRANNY.

That unpaid debt is in good hands,
Cost what it may, we shall pay it.

[*Enter* HOU *with the guards.*]

HOU. I'll say this for you: You certainly know how to keep your mouths shut and not give anything away. Come on, old woman. Captain Hatoyama wants you.

LI. Mother. . . .

GRANNY. Don't worry, son. I know what he wants. [*She goes out fearlessly, followed by the guards.*]

HOU. Bring Tieh-mei here!

[*Exit.*]

LI. [*Calling*] Tieh-mei!

TIEH-MEI. Dad.

I hoped day and night to see my dad again,
Yet I hardly know you, so battered and drenched with blood
I wish I could break your chains,
Dear father. . . .

LI. [*Smiling*] Silly child.

TIEH-MEI. [*Sobbing*] If you have anything to say to me, Dad, tell me quickly.

LI. Child,

One thing I have wanted many times to tell you,
It's been hidden in my heart for seventeen years. . . .

TIEH-MEI [*Quickly stopping him*] Don't say it. You are my own true father.

Don't say it, Father,
I know the bitter tale of these seventeen years.
You are so good, our country needs you;
Why can't I die in your stead?
Ah, Dad. [*She kneels and clasps* LI'*s knees, sobbing.*]

LI.

Nurse your hatred in your heart.
Men say that family love outweighs all else,
But class love is greater yet.
Listen, child, your dad is a poor man,
With no money at home to leave you;
All I have is a red lantern,
I entrust it to your safe keeping.

TIEH-MEI.

You have left me a priceless treasure,
How can you speak of money?
You have left me your integrity
To help me stand firm as a rock;
You have left me your wisdom
To help me see clearly through the enemy's wiles;
You have left me your courage
To help me fight those brutes;
This red lantern is our heirloom,
A treasure to great
That a thousand carts and boats
Could not hold it all.
I give you my word I shall keep the lantern safe.

LI.

As wave follows wave in the great Yangtse River,
Our red lantern will be passed from hand to hand.
If they let you go home,
Find friends to help settle that debt and I'll be content.

TIEH-MEI. I will, father.

LI. Good child.

[*Enter* HOU.]

HOU. [*To* TIEH-MEI] What about the secret code, girl?

[*She ignores him.*]

HOU. Why don't you speak?

TIEH-MEI. My dad and my grandmother have said all there is to say. I've nothing to add.

HOU. Even this child is so pig-headed, confound her! Here. Being that old woman back.

[*The guards bring in* GRANNY.]

HOU. Now your whole family is here. Think well. If you don't give us the code, not one of you will leave this place alive.

[*Exit.*]

[LI *and* TIEH-MEI *help* GRANNY *to the stone.*]

LI. They've tortured you, mother. The swine!

GRANNY. It doesn't matter if my old bones ache a little, my heart is still sound.

[TIEH-MEI *sobs with her head on* GRANNY'*s lap. Enter the sergeant.* TIEH-MEI *looks up.*]

SERGEANT. Captain Hatoyama gives you five more minutes to think it over. If you still won't give up the secret code, you will all be shot.

GRANNY. [*Indignantly*] You brutes, won't you even let the child go?

SERGEANT. We'll spare no one.

[LI *and* GRANNY *look at* TIEH-MEI, *who meets their eyes and straightens up.*]

SERGEANT. [*Dragging* TIEH-MEI *away*] Only five minutes left, girl. Give up the code and save your whole family. Speak!

[TIEH-MEI *shakes off his hand and walks back to stand between* GRANNY *and* LI.]

SERGEANT. Where is the code?

TIEH-MEI. I don't know.

SERGEANT. [*Looking at his watch*] Firing squad!

LI. There's no need for such a commotion. This is nothing much.

GRANNY. That's right, child, let's go together, the three of us.

LI. Tieh-mei, mother, I'll lead the way. [*He holds himself proudly.*]

[*They walk up the slope. Enter* HATOYAMA.]

HATOYAMA. Wait! I want to give you every chance. You can have another minute to think it over.

LI. Hatoyama, you can never kill all the Chinese people or Chinese Communists. I advise you to think that over.

HATOYAMA. [*Frustratedly to himself*] These Reds are the very devil. Carry out your orders.

SERGEANT. Shoot them!

[*The three disappear from the slope followed by the* SERGEANT *and guards.*]

LI. [*Off*] Down with Japanese imperialism! Long live the Chinese Communist Party!

[*Two shots are heard. Then two guards push* TIEH-MEI *back.*]

TIEH-MEI. [*Walking down the slope in a daze, turns to call*] Dad! Granny!

HATOYAMA. [*Entering behind her, followed by* HOU] Where is the code book? Tell me quick.

[TIEH-MEI *says nothing but stares at him with loathing.*]

HATOYAMA. Here. Let her go.

HOU. What? Let her go? [*He looks at* HATOYAMA *in surprise.*]

HATOYAMA. Yes, let her go.

HOU. Very good, sir. [*He grabs* TIEH-MEI.] Get out, get out. [*He pushes her away. Exit* TIEH-MEI.] Why are you letting her off, sir?

HATOYAMA. [*Smiling coldly*] If I kill them all, how can I find the code? This is called using a long line to catch a big fish.

Scene 9

THE NEIGHBORS HELP

[*Immediately after the last scene.* LI*'s house. The door is sealed. The room is unchanged but wears an air of desolation.*]

[TIEH-MEI *walks slowly in. She stares at the house, quickens her steps and pushing the door open steps inside. She looks around, crying! "Dad! Granny!" then rests her head on the table and sobs. Slowly rising, she sees the red lantern and picks it up.*]

TIEH-MEI. Ah, red lantern, I've found you again but I shall never see Granny or Dad again. Granny, Dad, I know what you died for. I shall carry on your work. I've inherited the red lantern. That scoundrel Hatoyama has only let me go in the hope that I will lead them to the code. [*Pause.*] Never mind whether you arrest me or release me, you'll never get the code. [*She puts down the red lantern and smooths her hair.*]

My heart is bursting with anger,
I grind my teeth with rage;
Hatoyama has tried every trick to get the code,
He has killed my granny and dad.
In desperation he threatened me,
But I defy his threats,
Nursing hatred in my heart;
No cry shall escape me,
No tears wet my cheeks,
But the sparks of my smoldering fury
Will blaze up in flames of anger
To consume this black reign of night.
Nothing can daunt me now:
Arrest, release, torture, imprisonment. . . .
I shall guard the code with my life.
Wait, Hatoyama! This is Tieh-mei's answer.

[*She polishes the red lantern and rearranges her peddler's basket.*]

[*Sadly*] Granny, Dad, I'm leaving now. This isn't our home any more. Only the red lantern will be ours for ever. I promise to take the code to the north hills. I promise to avenge you. Don't you worry. [*She puts on her scarf and picks up the lantern and basket.*]

[AUNT LIU *and* KUEI-LAN *have heard* TIEH-MEI*'s sobbing and slipped in through the hole in the wall.*]

AUNT LIU. Tieh-mei!

TIEH-MEI. Aunty. Sister Kuei-lan.

AUNT LIU. Where are your dad and granny?

TIEH-MEI. Aunty. . . . [*She learns her head on* AUNT LIU*'s shoulder and cries.*]

AUNT LIU. I see. It'll soon be their turn, the devils. There's a spy outside, Tieh-mei, so you mustn't leave by the door. You can slip out again from our house. Hurry up now and change clothes with Kuei-lan.

KUEI-LAN. Yes, quick. [*She takes off her jacket.*]

TIEH-MEI. No, Aunty, Sister, I mustn't bring you into this.

AUNT LIU. [*Helping* TIEH-MEI *to change*] Tieh-mei,

> None but the poor will help the poor,
> Two bitter gourds grow on a single vine;
> We must save you from the tiger's jaws,
> And then you can press on.

TIEH-MEI. But what if something happens to you?

AUNT LIU. Tieh-mei, your people were good people. I may not understand much, but that I know. No matter how risky it is, I must see you safely away. [*She weeps.*]

TIEH-MEI. Aunty. [*Kneels.*]

[AUNT LIU *hastily helps her up.*]

KUEI-LAN. Go quickly. [*Gives her the red lantern.*]

TIEH-MEI. I shall never forget you, sister.

AUNT LIU. Hurry, child. [TIEH-MEI *slips behind the curtain.*] Be very careful, Kuei-lan. [AUNT LIU *in turn leaves from behind the curtain.*]

[KUEI-LAN *wraps* TIEH-MEI'*s scarf round her head and steps out of the door with the basket.* ENEMY AGENT C *comes up and follows her. Enter the* KNIFE-GRINDER. *He is about to call out when he notices the* AGENT *trailing a girl who looks like* TIEH-MEI. *He follows them.*]

Scene 10

THE END OF THE RENEGADE

[*Immediately after the last scene. The street.*]

[*Enter* INSPECTOR WANG *with two agents.* A THIRD AGENT *comes in from the other side.*]

THIRD AGENT. Inspector, I've lost Tieh-mei.

WANG. What!

THIRD AGENT. She got away.

WANG. You fool! [*Slaps his face.*] Well, she must be making for the north hills. Ring up Captain Hatoyama and ask him to send reinforcements to the road to the north hills. The rest of you come with me to catch her. I'll see that you don't escape me, Li Tieh-mei.

[*Black-out. The scene changes to the north suburb of Lungtan and the road to the hills. Enter* CHOU *with three guerrillas.*]

[*Enter* TIEH-MEI *with the lantern. She greets the men.*]

TIEH-MEI. Uncle Chou!

CHOU. Tieh-mei!

TIEH-MEI. At last I've found you. [*Cries.*] My granny and dad. . . .

CHOU. We know. [*Pause.*] Don't give way. Take a grip on yourself. Have you got the code with you?

TIEH-MEI. Yes, I took it from under Short Bridge where I'd hidden it.

CHOU. Good.

[*The* KNIFE-GRINDER *hurries in.*]

KNIFE-GRINDER. Old Chou. Ah, Tieh-mei, so you're here. How was it I missed you?

TIEH-MEI. It was thanks to the help of my neighbors, Uncle. Kuei-lan disguised herself as me and led the agent off on the wrong track so that I could get the code and bring it here.

KNIFE-GRINDER. So I was chasing the wrong girl.

CHOU. They'll start suspecting Kuei-lan's family now. [*To one of the guerrillas*] Old Feng, go and help them move away at once.

FENG. Right. Just leave it to me.

[*Exit.*]

[*The police car's siren is heard.*]

CHOU. [*To the* KNIFE-GRINDER] The enemy's coming. Old Chao. You deal with them while I take Tieh-mei to the north hills. [*Exit with* TIEH-MEI.]

KNIFE-GRINDER. Look, comrades, there aren't too many of them. I'll handle their leader. You take care of the rest.

GUERRILLAS. Right.

[*Enter* INSPECTOR WANG *with four enemy agents.*]

WANG. Now, where is Tieh-mei?

[*The* KNIFE-GRINDER *kicks the pistol out of* WANG'S *hand and they start fighting.* WANG *and the agents are killed. The police siren wails in the distance.*]

Scene 11

THE TASK IS ACCOMPLISHED

[*The north hills, which rise steep and sheer. The guerrillas have formed a line stretching behind the hills. Halfway up the slope is a big red flag and scouts there are keeping a lookout.*]

[LIU *and other guerrilla officers come up the slope. Enter the* KNIFE-GRINDER. *He salutes* LIU *and points behind him.* CHOU *comes in with* TIEH-MEI. *A bugle blows.* TIEH-MEI *salutes* LIU *and gives him the code.*]

Curtain

Japan

It is a cliché that Japanese culture is an imitation of Chinese. Like most clichés, this one has some truth in it, but the Japanese genius everywhere puts its stamp on its importations. In literature there are many Japanese forms which are not found in China and a number of forms—especially in fiction—improved upon by the Japanese. As if to point up the independence of the Japanese spirit, there is from time to time a Chinese literature written by Japanese in Japan which exists side by side with writing in the Japanese language. Even the reader of works in translation will usually have little trouble differentiating Japanese literature from Chinese.

The earliest monuments of Japanese literature are two eighth-century chronicles, the *Record of Ancient Matters* (*Kojiki*) and the *Chronicles of Japan* (*Nihongi*). Though not stylistically attractive, they are repositories of legend which feed later literature. They also include poems in a form called *waka.* The *waka* is a poem alternating five- and seven-syllable lines; this prosodic feature of alternation and of counting syllables is tpical of Japanese prosody, and continues with variations through later poetry. A major collection of *waka* was made about 760 A.D. This is the *Collection of Ten Thousand Leaves* (*Manyōshū*), containing about 4,500 poems by many different poets. There are good many long poems, but none of the length of the Western epic or epic lay. The collection, standing at the beginning of Japanese literature, is marvelous for its variety and its high quality.

A second great anthology, the *Collection of Poems Old and New* (*Kokinshū*), moves away from the long poem towards a subtle and evocative short poem, the forerunner of the very brief *tanka* and *haiku,* discussed below. Poetry, especially the short forms, is the major form of Japanese literature and a necessary accomplishment in earlier times of members of the nobility. On the other hand, the short forms are often casually used, with innumerable examples tossed off for social purposes. Masters of the short form—poets like Bashō and Buson—found in its compression the necessary challenge to say—or rather suggest—much in a small compass; the best *tanka* and *haiku* are rich in meaning both aesthetically and philosophically and are a major accomplishment of Japanese poetry.

Early prose in Japan was in

Chinese, because Chinese was for a long while the language of the court. Ironically, this put a stigma on writing Japanese which discouraged men but did not disqualify women, who were not trained in Chinese. As a result of this, some of the major early writings are by women. The *Tosa Diary* (*Tosa Nikki*) pretends to be by a woman. though it is not. It is an early example of a form in which the Japanese excell, the diary-memoir. The court lady Sei Shōnagon (d. 1025?) has left us sensitive autobiographical sketches in her *Pillow Book* (*Makura no Sōshi*. Lady Murasaki (d. 1031), the author of what must be the greatest work of Japanese fiction, the *Tale of Genji*, left us a diary of her services in the court at Kyoto which stresses the nuances of life more than the events. Diaries are a major genre in Japan earlier than in most other parts of the world. One masterpiece of this kind is Kamo no Chōmei's *Life in a Ten-Foot-Square Hut* (*Hōjōki*).

Besides the diary and memoir, Japanese literature offers much excellent fiction. As has been mentioned, Lady Murasaki's *Tale of Genji* is the masterpiece, the first psychological novel in world literature. It is polished in style and sensitive to the emotions of a complex court society. Somewhat in Murasaki's manner is the tale of an eccentric, *The Lady Who Loved Worms* (see below). The depiction of court life is frequently, with lesser writers, oversubtle and drawn out, and this type of fiction often ran to erotic themes. In direct contrast to this are the various narratives (*monogatari*) of the feudal wars, of which the best example may be the *Tales of the Heike* (see below). The battles between the rival clans in the middle ages provided the Japanese with many a hero for later literature and recent cinema. Poetic influences are evident in some of these works: the *Heike* is composed in alternating five- and seven-syllable phrases.

Drama is a major form in Japan, its crowning achievement being the *nō* play (see below), which bloomed in the fourteenth century under the aegis of the great dramatist and theoretician Zeami (or Seami) and his father. The form is subtle verbally and also subtle in its theatricals, and has intrigued Western writers since Yeats and Pound first evinced interest in it in the early years of this century. A major competing form is *kabuki*, the popular drama of the seventeenth and eighteenth centuries, and a parallel form, the *jōrūri* or puppet-play. The outstanding author in these modes is Chikamatsu Monzaemon (d. 1725); see below. Both battle and adventure plays and plays of domestic life are in the repertoire, which is popular to this day. Of the same period, there is a new popular fiction which reaches artistic heights in the work of Saikaku Ihara (see the bibliography below).

Japanese literature since the opening of Japan to the West in 1868 has been beset by foreign influences, but an effective compromise was made early, and twentieth-century Japanese writing demonstrates the ability of the writers to blend Western concepts and the native tradition. Soseki Natsume (d. 1916) is a major later-nineteenth-century figure, and among twentieth-century masters are Ryunosuke Akutagawa, Junichiro Tanizaki, the Nobel Prize winner Yasunari Kawabata, and Yuko Mishima (see below). Outspoken criticism of the present age and coldly objective glances at the Japanese past characterize many of the writers of today's flourishing literary renaissance.

WRITINGS AND CRITICISM

The date of the latest edition or reprint is given if known.

A good brief account of Japanese literature is Eric B. Ceadel's in *Literatures of the East*, ed. Eric B. Ceadel (1959), pp. 161–188. An excellent general introduction is Donald Keene's *Japanese Literature* (1955). There is no extensive reference history in English. W. G. Aston's *History of Japanese Literature* (1899; various reprints) is antequated but still useful. Recent guides are *Japanese Literature, an Historical Outline* by Edward Putzar (1973) and Effie B. Rogers' *An Outline of the History of Early Japanese Literature* (1966). More specialized studies are Makota Ueda, *Literature and Art Theories in Japan* (1967); John Meskill, *Japanese Viewpoints expressed in Fiction, Poetry, Drama, Thought* (1962); and E. V. Gatenby, *The Cloud Men of Yamato, Being an Outline of Mysticism in Japanese Literature* (1929).

Donald Keene's *Anthology of Japanese Literature* (1960) is an excellent collection. Yoshinobu Hakutani's *The World of Japanese Fiction* (1973) contains material from earliest to modern times. Frank J. Daniels has edited *Selections from Japanese Literature (12th to 19th Centuries)* (1959) with the original texts and translations. The *Introduction to Classical Japanese Literature* (1948) done by the Kokusai Bunka Shinkokai contains summaries of earlier works. A comprehensive volume of translations mostly from philosophical and religious works is *Sources of the Japanese Tradition* (1958), ed. Ryusaku Tsunoda, W. T. de Bary, and Donald Keene. For historical background see George Sansom's *Japan, a Short Cultural History* (1946) and Edwin O. Reischauer's *Japan, Past and Present* (1946). See also Donald Keene's *Landscapes and Portraits* (Tokyo, 1971). As in China, the graphic arts are closely allied to literature in Japan. Inexpensive collections are available in *Japanese Art* by Alain Lemière (4 vols., 1958; Petite Encyclopedie de l'Art) and in the numerous volumes of the Kodansha Library of Japanese Art.

Various anthologies of Japanese poetry are available. For the earlier material see Frederick V. Dickins, *Primitive and Medieval Japanese Texts* (2 vols., 1906). General anthologies are A. Miyamori's *Masterpieces of Japanese Poetry, Ancient and Modern* (1936); the *Penguin Book of Japanese Verse* (1964), tr. Geoffrey Bownas and Anthony Thwaite; and Arthur Waley's *Japanese Poetry* (1960). A more specialized study is *Fujiwara Teika's Superior Poems of Our Times: A Thirteenth-Century Poetic Treatise and Sequence*, tr. Robert H. Brower and Earl Miner (1967). Brower and Miner have also done two studies: *Japanese Court Poetry* (1961) and *An Introduction to Japanese Court Poetry* (1968). For the *Manyōshū*, see below, See also Earl Miner, "The Technique of Japanese Poetry," *Hudson Review*, VIII (1955), 350–366, and Brower and Miner's "Formative Elements in the Japanese Poetic Tradition," *Journal of Asian Studies*, XVI (1957), 503–527. A good brief article on the poetics is in the *Princeton Encyclopedia of Poetry and Poetics*. Selections from the early anthology the *Kokinshū* are in Keene's *Anthology* and Dickins, above. For the short poetic forms, see "Haiku," below.

An excellent introduction to the world of early Japanese court life as it is depicted in the *Tale of Genji* and many other works is Ivan Morris' *The World of the Shining Prince* (1964). Numerous memoirs and diaries characterize Japanese literature. For Sei Shōnagon's "pillow book" and Kamo no Chōmei see below. Lady Murasaki's diary has been translated by A. E. Omori and Kochi Doi in *Diaries of the Court Ladies of Old Japan* (1920); *The Tosa Diary* (Tosa Nikki) by W. N. Porter (1912); the *Tsurezuregusa* of Kenko by Donald Keene as *Essays in Idleness* (1968) and by Ryukichi Kurata as *The Harvest of Leisure* (1931, reprinted 1960). Other diaries are the *Sarashina Nikki*, translated by Ivan Morris as *I Crossed the Bridge of Dreams* (1971); *The Gossamer Years*, tr. Edward Seidensticker (1965); *Nakanoin Mastada no Musume* (*The Confessions of Lady Nijo*) tr. Karen

Brazell (1973); and *The Izumi Shikubu Diary, a Romance of the Heian Court,* tr. E. A. Cranston.

Early narrative literature (*monogatari*) is often concerned with historical events and feudal wars. For works in this category see "Tales of Heike," below. Murasaki's *Tale of Genji* as translated by Arthur Waley (1939) is available in paperback. It is discussed by Donald Keene in *Approaches to the Oriental Classics,* ed. W. T. de Bary (1959), pp. 186–195. Some important pieces of earlier fiction are translated in Edwin O. Reischauer and Joseph K. Yamagiwa's *Translations from Early Japanese Literature* (1951). The *Ochikubo Monogatari or Tale of the Lady Ochikubo* has been translated by Wilfrid Whitehouse (1934).

For the classical *nō* drama and later popular drama see "*Nō* Plays" and "Kabuki," below.

The most important early writer of fiction is Saikaku Ihara (1642–1693). Translations of his work include: *Five Japanese Love Stories,* tr. William T. de Bary (1958); *Life of an Amorous Woman,* tr. Ivan Morris (1963); *The Japanese Family Storehouse,* tr. G. W. Sargent (1959); *This Scheming World,* tr. Masanorni Takatsuka and David D. Snubbs (1965); *The Way to Wealth,* tr. Soji Mizuno (1961); and *The Life of an Amorous Man,* tr. Kenji Hamada (1964). Studies include Howard Hibbett's "Saikaku and Burlesque Fiction," *Harvard Journal of Asiatic Studies,* XX (1957), 53–73. For the background of the period see also his *The Floating World in Japanese Fiction* (1959) and James T. Araki, "The Dream Pillow in Edo Fiction," *Monumenta Nipponica,* XXV (1970), 43–105. Richard Lane has written on "Saikaku and the Japanese Novel of Realism," *Japan* Quarterly, IV (1957), 178–188. An important precursor of the modern novel is Sōseki Natsume (1867–1916). Translations of his work include: *Botchan,* tr. Umeji Sasaki (1968) and Alan Turney (1973); *Grass on the Wayside (Michikusa)* tr. Edwin McClellan (1969); *I am a Cat,* tr. Katsue Shibata and Motonari Kai (1902; reprinted); *Within My Glass Door,* tr. Twao Matsuhara (1928); *Kokoro,* tr. Edwin McClellan (1957); *Light* and Darkness, tr. V. H. Viglielmo (1971); *Wayfar* (*Kojin*), tr. Beongcheon Yu (1967). Sōseki's *Kusamakura* has been translated as *The Three Cornered World* by Alan Turney (1965), and as *Unhuman Tour* by Kazutomo Takahasi (1927). Studies include *Sōseki and Tōson* by Edwin McClelland (1969) and *Natsume Sōseki* by Beongcheon Yu (1969). A very useful outline of Sōseki's literary career is Edwin McClelland's "An Introduction to Sōseki," *Harvard Journal of Asiatic Studies,* XXII (1959), 150–208. See also Jun Eto's "Natsume Sōseki, a Japanese Meiji Intellectual," *American Scholar,* XXXIV (1965), 603–619.

For early modern literature see *Japanese Literature in the Meiji Era* by Yoshie Okasaki, tr. V. H. Viglielmo (1955); *Japanese Music and Drama in the Meiji Era* by Toyotaka Komiya, tr. Edward G. Seidensticker and Donald Keene (1956); *Japanese Literature, Manners, and Customs in the Meiji-Taisho Era* by Ki Kumur, tr. Philip Yampolsky (1957); and Tadao Kunitomi, *Japanese Literature Since 1868* (1938). Summaries of works and biographical information are available in two volumes published by the Kokusai Bunka Shinkōkai: *Introduction to Contemporary Japanese Literature 1902–1935* (1939) and *1936–1955* (1970). A continuation *1956–1970,* is edited by F. Tsuneari (Tokyo, 1972). A good anthology of the modern period is Donald Keene's *Modern Japanese Literature* (1960). A useful specialized study is Marleigh Ryan's *Japan's First Modern Novel: The Ukigumo of Futabatei Shimei* (1967).

For references to the main critical articles on contemporary Japanese literature see the Bibliographical Note at the end of this volume. For Akutagawa, Tanizaki, Kawabata, and Mishima, see below. Collections of modern writing, besides Keene's, above, include *New Writing in Japan,* ed. Yukio Mishima and Geoffrey Bownas (1972); *Post-War Japanese Poetry,* ed. Harry and Lynn Guest and Kajima Shozo (1972), and *Poetry of Living Japan,* ed. Takamichi Ninomiya and D. J. Enright (1958). Ivan Morris has edited *Modern Japanese Short Stories, an Anthology* (1962). For modern drama in Japan see J. Thomas Rimer's *Towards a Modern Japanese Theatre: Kishida Kunio* (1974), which focuses mostly on the playwright-director-critic (1890–1954) who pioneered Western theater in Japan. For plays see Y. T. Iwasaki and Glenn Hughes, *New Plays from Japan* (1930) and these authors' *Three Modern Japanese Plays* (1923). Some useful studies are: Masao Miyoshi, *Accomplices of Silence: The Modern Japanese Novel* (1974); Arthur G. Kimball, *Crisis in Identity and Contemporary Japanese Novels* (1973); Donald Keene, *Modern Japanese Novels and the West* (1961); Earl Miner, "Traditions and Individual Talents in Recent Japanese Fiction," *Hudson Review,* X (1957), 302–308; Howard Hibbett, "Tradition and Trauma in the Contemporary Japanese Novel," *Daedalus,* XCV (1966), 925–940; and Joseph K. Yamagiwa, "The Old and the New in Twentieth-Century Japanese Literature," in *Papers of the Indiana Conference,* 1955, pp. 87–104.

Earl Miner's *The Japanese Tradition in British and American Literature* (1958) is an excellent study of Japanese influence. Among comparative studies are Armando Martins Janeira's *Japanese and Western Literature, a Comparative Study* (1970); Hiro Ishibashi's *Yeats and the Noh* (1966); and Makoto Ueda's *Zeami, Bashō, Yeats, Pound: A Study in Japanese Poetics* (1965).

MANYŌSHŪ. Translations include *The Manyoshu: The Nippon Gakujutsu Kinkōkai Translation,* with a foreword by Donald Keene (reprinted 1965) and *The Manyōshū, a New and Complete Translation* by H. H. Honda (1967). The edition and translation of J. L. Pierson, *The Manyōśū* (1943-) is the most scholarly available, with extensive linguistic notes. An attractive selection is in *Land of the Reed Plains: Ancient Japanese Lyrics from the Manyōshū,* tr. Sanko Inoue and Kenneth Yasuda (1960).

TALES OF HEIKE. For a forerunner to the popular narratives of intrigue and civil war in Japan see *The Ōkagami, a Japanese Historical Tale,* tr. Joseph K. Yamagiwa (1967). *Tales of Ise (Ise Monogatari)* has been translated by Helen Clark McCullough (1968), and with full apparatus as *A Study of the Ise Monogatari* by Fritz Vos (2 vols., 1957). Another translation is by H. Jay Harris (1972). McCullough has also done the *Taiheiki, a Chronicle of Medieval Japan* (1959). Her *Yoshitsune* (1966) is a translation of yet another war narrative with a valuable introduction on the type including accounts of the various heroes who appear not only in the *monogatari* but later in the *nō* plays and *kabuki.* The *Heiji Monogatari* is translated by Reischauer and Yamagiwa, cited above, and the *Ugetsu Monogatari* by Ueda Akinari (1974). James T. Araki has written "A Critical Approach to the *Ugetsu Monogatari,*" in *Monumenta Nipponica,* XXII (1967), 49–64. The historical background for the period is well covered in George Sansom's *A History of Japan, 1615–1867* (3 vols., 1958–63).

FIVE *NŌ* PLAYS. Collections of *nō* plays include the three volumes of *Japanese Noh Drama* published by the Nippon Gakujutsu Shinkokai (1955–60); Arthur Waley, *The Nō Plays of Japan* (1957); Makoto Ueda, *The Old Pine Tree and Other Noh Plays* (1962); and Donald Keene, *Twenty Plays of the Nō Theatre* (1970). Ezra Pound and Ernest Fenollosa did a pioneering work which helped to introduce the form to Europe in *The Classic Noh Theatre of Japan* (1916; rpt. 1959), but later translations are preferable. P. G. O'Neill's *A Guide to Nō* (1953) summarizes all the repertoire, and his *Early Nō Drama* (1959) is an important study. James T. Araki has studied the origin of the plays in early folk dance-drama in *The Ballad Drama of Early Japan* (1964). Other useful works are Donald Keene's *Nō: The Classical Theatre of Japan* (1966), which is elaborately illustrated; Toyoichiro Nagami's *Japanese Noh Plays, How to See Them* (1935); and Yasuo Nakamura, *Noh, The Classical Theatre,* tr. Don Kenny (1971). On Zeami (or Seami) see Toyochiro Nagami's *Zeami and the Treatises on Noh* (1955), the work of Ueda cited at the end of this list, and Zeami's *Sixteen Treatises* (see below). Richard McKinnon has written two important articles on Zeami: "Zeami on the Art of Training," *Harvard Journal of Asiatic Studies,* XVI (1953), 200–225, and "The *Nō* and Zeami," *Far Eastern Quarterly,* XI (1952), 355–361. Earle Ernst's "A Theatre . . . of Beauty Without Tears," *Hudson Review,* XI (1958), 262–270, is general appreciation of the form. *Kyōgen* or comic interludes were customarily played along with *nō* plays. For these see Don Kenny, *A Guide to Kyōgen* (1968).

CHIKAMATSU. What we call *kabuki* drama includes performances by live actors (*kabuki*) and puppet-plays (*jōrūri, bunraku*) often of the same plays. Aubrey and G. M. Halford's *The Kabuki Handbook* (1956) summarizes the plots of the extensive repertoire. Especially recommended general studies are Earle Ernst's *Kabuki Theatre* (1956), A. C. Scott's *The Kabuki Theatre of Japan* (1958), Masakatsu Gunji's *Kabuki* (1969), and Donald Keene's *Bunraku, the Art of the Japanese Puppet Theatre* (1965), the last two lavishly illustrated. Other studies include Yonezo Hamamura et al., *Kabuki* (1956) and Shigetoshi Kawatake's *Kabuki: Japanese Drama* (1958). Besides his important translation of *The Major Plays of Chikamatsu* (1961), Donald Keene has translated Izumo Takeda's popular *Chūshingura (The Treasury of the Loyal Retainers* (1971). A. C. Scott's translation of the *Subscription List* (*Kanjinchō*) (1953) is reprinted in *Genius of the Oriental Theatre,* ed. G. L. Anderson (1966) and also translated by James Brandon and Tamako Niwa in *Evergreen Review* IV, no. 14 (September–October 1960), 28–57. Charles J. Dunn's *The Early Japanese Puppet Drama* (1966) studies the development of this popular middle-class form.

HAIKU. Harold Henderson's *An Introduction to Haiku* (1958) is an excellent critical introduction to the shortest of the poetic forms. Two extensive anthologies are A. Miyamori's *An Anthology of Haiku, Ancient and Modern* (1932) and its revision, *Haiku, Ancient and Modern* (1940); and R. H. Blyth's *Haiku* (4 vols., 1949–52). In the latter the poems are arranged by subject matter. Blyth has also written *A Hisory of Haiku* (2 vols., 1963–64). See also Kenneth Yasuda's The *Japanese Haiku, Its Essential Nature* (1957). Poetic theory is discussed by Richard N. Mc-

Kinnon in "*Tanka* and *Haiku:* Some Aspects of Classical Japanese Poetry," in *Papers of the Indiana Conference,* pp. 67–84, cited above. The short satiric Japanese poem is studied by Blyth in *Japanese Life and Character in Senryū* (1960). See also Howard Hibbett's "The Japanese Comic Linked-Verse Tradition," *Harvard Journal of Asiatic Studies,* XXIII (1966), 76–92. Bashō's *The Monkey's Raincoat* has been translated by Maeda Cana (1973).

FOUR MASTERS OF MODERN FICTION. Translations of the work of Akutgawa, with the name of the translator following, include: *Exotic Japanese Tales, the Beautiful and the Grotesque,* 1964 (Takashi Kojima and John McVittie); *A Fool's Life,* 1970 (Will Petersen); *Hell Screen and Other Stories,* 1971 (W. H. H. Norman); *Japanese Short Stories,* 1961 (Takashi Kojima); *Kappa,* 1947 (Seiichi Shiojiro); *Rashomon and Other Stories,* 1952 (Takashi Kojima); *Tales Grotesque and Curious,* 2nd ed., 1938 (Glenn W. Shaw); *The Three Treasures,* 2nd enlarged ed., 1951 (Sasaki Takamasa); *Tutze-Chun,* 1965 (Dorothy Britton).

Translations of Tanizaki include: *Ashikari and the Story of Shunkin,* 1970 (Roy Humpherson and Hajime Okita); *Diary of a Mad Old Man,* 1965 (Howard Hibbett); *The Key,* 1961 (Howard Hibbett); *The Makioka Sisters,* 1957 (Edward G. Seidensticker); *Seven Japanese Tales,* 1963 (Howard Hibbett); *Some Prefer Nettles,* 1955 (Edward G. Seidensticker); *A Spring-Time Case,* 1927? (Zenchi Iwado).

Translations of Kawabata include: *The Existence and Discovery of Beauty,* 1969 (V. H. Viglielmo); and the following, all translated by Edward G. Seidensticker: *The House of the Sleeping Beauties* (1969); *Japan the Beautiful and Myself* (1969); *The Master of Go* (1972); *Snow Country* (1957); *The Sound of the Mountain* (1970); *A Thousand Cranes* (1959.)

Translations of Mishima include: *After the Banquet,* 1963 (Donald Keene); *Confessions of a Mask,* 1958 (Meredith Weatherby); *Death in Midsummer and Other Stories,* 1966 (Ivan Morris); *Five Modern Nō Plays,* 1957 (Donald Keene); *Forbidden Colours,* 1968 (Alfred H. Marks); *Madame De Sade,* 1967 (Donald Keene); *The Sea of Fertility:* Part I, *Spring Snow,* 1972; Part II, *Runaway Horses,* 1973 (both Michael Gallagher); *The Sailor Who Fell from Grace with the Sea,* 1965 (John Nathan); *The Sound of Waves,* 1956 (Meredith Weatherby); *The Temple of Dawn,* 1973 (E. Dale Saunders and Cecilia Segawa Seigle); *The Temple of the Goldon Pavillion,* 1959 (Ivan Morris); *Sun and Steel,* 1970 (John Bester); *Thirst for Love,* 1969 (Alfred H. Marks).

The Collection of Ten Thousand Leaves (*Manyōshū*) (ca. Late 8th Century)

The *Manyōshū* is the oldest and greatest of many collcetions of early Japanese poetry. Many of them were compiled by imperial edict to preserve the treasures of the past. It reflects the life and civilization of the Fujiwara and Nara periods (the seventh and eighth centuries) and contains both "court" poetry and poems by more humble poets. The collection was probably compiled over a period of time and was substantially complete by the late eighth century. The period of its composition was followed by a period of neglect of Japanese poetry for writing in the Chinese language, which serves to isolate its contents from the poetry which follows. It would be reasonable to compare it with the early Chinese collection, the *Book of Songs* (*Shih King*). Many of the themes are the same: love and duty, departures for distant lands and the grief of exile and separation. Perhaps the Chinese collection has more strength and the Japanese one more subtlety. The Chinese poems had long been known in Japan and certainly influenced the Japanese poems, but the reader who plays a guessing game with the two collections may have less trouble than he suspects he will have in deciding which is Chinese and which is Japanese.

The metrical form is usually lines of five or seven syllables. This includes the *tanka* of 5–7–5–7–7 syllables (which is still popular) and the long poem or *chōka* which consists of an indefinite number of five- and seven-syllable lines in alternation ending with two seven-syllable lines. The longest poems run only to 150 lines. Rhyme is not employed for poetic effects perhaps because the simple consonant-plus-vowel structure of the language plus the large number of homophones make rhyme monotonous. Wordplay and deliberate ambiguity by punning is a popular device.

Most of the poems printed below have been selected from the earlier parts of the *Manyōshū* and reflect the brilliant court society of medieval times. The wittiest and the most modern are perhaps the exchanges between ladies and gentlemen on the subject of love. The more somber themes are eternal—the death of a loved one or a long separation whether imposed by the pressure of imperial duties or by exile for political reasons. Often the reflections are immersed in the spirit of nature. Finally, places constantly intrude. Japan is a small country, and scarcely a foot of it escapes identification as a site known to either history or romance or both. The *Manyōshū* reflects the first flowering of a brilliant court society—a flower which blooms uneasily in the face of the misfortunes common to all mankind but also the particular ones caused by political unrest. The gods breathe heavily on the neck of man in some of these poems and manifest themselves in natural symbols.

From The *Manyōshū**

EMPEROR TENJI**

The Three Hills

Mount Kagu strove with Mount Miminashi
        For the love of Mount Unebi.
Such is love since the age of the gods;
As it was thus in the early days,
So people strive for spouses even now.

* From *The Manyōshū*. Copyright 1965 by Columbia University Press. Reprinted by permission of Columbia University Press. Unless otherwise indicated, the notes are the translators', sometimes abridged.

** Composed by the emperor while he was still crown prince during the reign of the Empress Saimei. [Tenchi reigned 661–672.—Editor.]

1–2. The mountains are in Yamato, the west central area of the peninsula which includes Nara, Wakayama, and Ise. Nara is the most northern part of the ancient province of Yamato. The theme is an old legend. [Editor.]

3. *This plain:* In Inami district, Harima province, west of Kobe on the Inland Sea. Legend has it that at the quarrel of the Three Hills, the God of Abo, intending to compose the dispute, left Izumi Province and came as far as the plain, where he settled, on hearing of the end of the strife.

ENVOYS

When Mount Kagu and Mount Miminashi wrangled,
A god came over and saw it
Here—on this plain of Inami!

On the rich banner-like clouds
That rim the waste of waters
The evening sun is glowing,
And promises to-night
The moon in beauty!

EMPRESS YAMATO-HIME

Presented to the Emperor Tenji on the Occasion of His Majesty's Illness

On the vast lake of Ōmi
    You boatmen that come rowing
From the far waters,
And you boatmen that come rowing
Close by the shore,
Ply not too hard your oars in the far waters,
Ply not too hard your oars by the shore,
Lest you should startle into flight
The birds beloved of my dear husband!

PRINCE SHŌTOKU

*On Seeing a Man Dead on Mount Tatsuta during His Trip to the Well of Takahara**

Had he been at home, he would have slept
    Upon his wife's dear arm;
Here he lies dead, unhappy man,
On his journey, grass for pillow.

9–13. This poem does not seem to be an envoy, but as it is so often given in an older book it is retained here.

1. *Ōmi:* Today Lake Biwa, the largest lake in Japan, east of Kyoto. [Editor.]

* Located near the sea on the route to the hot springs.

PRINCE ARIMA

Lamenting His Plight, and Binding Pine Branches

At Iwashiro I bind
    The branches of a shore pine.
If fortune favors me,
I may come back
And see the knot again.

Now that I journey, grass for pillow,
They serve rice on the *shii* leaves,
Rice they would put in a bowl,
Were I at home!

PRINCE IKUSA

*Seeing the Mountains when the Emperor Jomei Sojourned in Aya District, Sanuki Province**

Not knowing that the long spring day—
    The misty night—is spent,
Like the 'night-thrush' I grieve within me,
As sorely my heart aches.
Then across the hills where our Sovereign sojourns,
Luckily the breezes blow
And turn back my sleeves with morn and eve,
As I stay alone;
But, being on a journey, grass for pillow,
Brave man as I deem me,
I know not how to cast off
My heavy sorrow;
And like the salt-fires the fisher-girls
Burn on the shore of Ami,
I burn with the fire of longing
In my heart.

1. ***bind:*** Binding tree branches was practiced as a sort of charm.

7. ***shii leaves:*** *Castanopsis cuspidata*, an evergreen tree with thick oblong leaves.

* According to the original note, the emperor visited Sanuki presumably on the occasion of his journey to the hot springs of Iyo in the twelfth month of the eleventh year of his reign (639).

3. ***'night-thrush':*** The ***nue***, identified with the ***tora-tsugumi***, a kind of thrush which sings in a mournful tone at night or in cloudy weather. Its back is yellowish-brown.

7. ***Turn back one's sleeves:*** an auspicious happening for travellers anticipating a safe journey home.

ENVOY

Fitful gusts of wind are blowing
Across the mountain-range,
And night after night I lie alone,
Yearning for my love at home.

EMPEROR TEMMU*

On the peak of Mimiga of fair Yoshinu
The snow is falling constantly,
The rain is falling ceaselessly;
Constantly as falls the snow,
Ceaselessly as falls the rain,
Ever thinking I have come,
Missing not one turning
Of that mountain path!

EMPEROR TEMMU and LADY FUJIWARA

BY THE EMPEROR

Magnificent snow
Has fallen here at my place.
But at your tumble-down old village of Ōhara,
If ever, later it will fall.

BY THE LADY

It was I who did command
The Dragon God of these hills
To send down the snow,
Whereof a few fragments, perchance,
Were sprinkled over your home.

PRINCE ŌTSU

Composed in Tears when He Died by Imperial Order on the Bank of Iware Pond

To-day, taking my last sight of the mallards
Crying on the pond of Iware,
Must I vanish into the clouds!

* Temmu Tennō usurped the throne in 627. [Editor.]

1. *Yoshinu: i.e.,* Yoshino, the mountainous district occupying the southern half of Yamato.

PRINCE ŌTSU and LADY ISHIKAWA

BY THE PRINCE

Waiting for you,
In the dripping dew of the hill
I stood,—weary and wet
With the dripping dew of the hill.

BY THE LADY

Would I have been, beloved,
The dripping dew of the hill,
That wetted you
While for me you waited.

PRINCE SHIKI

*Composed after the Empress Jitō Had Removed from the Palace of Asuka to That of Fujiwara**

The gentle winds at Asuka
That fluttered the ladies' sleeves—
Now that the court is far removed,
Those breezes blow in vain.

PRINCE ŌMI and AN ANONYMOUS PERSON

*Composed in Sympathy for Prince Ōmi When He Was Exiled to the Isle of Irago** in the Province of Ise*

Is the Prince of Ōmi a fisherman?
Alas! he gathers the seaweed
At the isle of Irago.

* The removal of the court to Fujiwara Palace took place in the twelfth month of the eighth year of the Shuchō (694).

2. *ladies: Uneme*, young women serving at court, chiefly at the imperial table. They were selected from among the daughters of influential families, or of higher officials in the provinces.

** In Mikawa Province. But it was often regarded as belonging to Ise because of its proximity to that province. [Ise is separated by Ise Bay from Mikawa.—Editor.]

REPLY BY THE PRINCE, GRIEVING AT HIS LOT

Clinging to this transient life
I live on seaweed,
Which I, drenched with the Waves,
Gather at the isle of Irago.

KAKINOMOTO HITOMARO

*On Passing the Ruined Capital of Ōmi**

Since the era of that sage Sovereign
At the palace of Kashihara
Under the hill of Unebi,
All the Sovereigns born to the Throne,
Reign after reign, ruled the under-heaven,
Remaining in Yamato;
Then the Emperor, a god,
Forsaking the ancient land,
Crossed the hills of Nara,
And, though I know not what he meant,
Held court at Ōtsu of Sasanami
In the land of Ōmi,
Remote place as it was.

But now, though I am told his royal palace towered here,
And they say here rose its lofty halls,
Only the spring weeds grow luxuriantly
And the spring sun is dimmed with mists.
As I see these ruins of the mighty palace
My heart is heavy with sorrows!

ENVOYS

Although it lies unchanged,
The cape of Karasaki
Of Shiga in Sasanami,
It waits and waits in vain
For the courtiers' barges.
Though the vast waters stand still
At Shiga in Sasanami,
Could they ever meet again
The people of the former days?

* The Emperor Tenji removed his court to Ōtsu [at the southern end of Lake Biwa, east of Kyoto—Editor] in Ōmi in 667. The city was laid waste by the war of the Jinshin in 672. In the following year a new capital was established again in Yamato.

1. *Sovereign:* the Emperor Jimmu, the first emperor.

11. *Sasanami:* a district comprising Shiga and Ōtsu.

KAKINOMOTO HITOMARO

On Leaving His Wife as He Set out from Iwami from the Capital

Along the coast of Tsunu
  On the sea of Iwami
One may find no sheltering bay,
One may find no sequestered lagoon.
O well if there be no bay!
O well if there be no lagoon!
Upon Watazu's rocky strand,
Where I travel by the whale-haunted sea,
The wind blows in the morning,
And the waves wash at eve
The sleek sea-tangle and the ocean weed,
All limpid green.

Like the sea-tangle, swaying in the wave
Hither and thither, my wife would cling to me,
As she lay by my side.
Now I have left her, and journey on my way,
I look back a myriad times
At each turn of the road.
Farther and farther my home falls behind,
Steeper and steeper the mountains I have crossed.
My wife must be languishing
Like drooping summer grass.
I would see where she dwells—
Bend down, O mountains!

ENVOYS

From between the trees that grow
On Takasunu's mountain-side
In the land of Iwami
I waved my sleeve to her—
Did she see me, my dear wife?
The leaves of bamboo grass
Fill all the hill-side
With loud rustling sounds;
But I think only of my love,
Having left her behind.

1. *Tsunu:* in western Honshu, facing the Japan Sea. Present-day Tsunotsu.
7. *Watazu:* presumably the vicinity of present-day Watatsu Village, Naka district.

KAKINOMOTO HITOMARO

In the sea of Iwami,
By the cape of Kara,
There amid the stones under sea
Grows the deep-sea *miru* weed;
There along the rocky strand
Grows the sleek sea-tangle.

Like the swaying sea-tangle,
Unresisting would she lie beside me—
My wife whom I love with a love
Deep as the *miru*-growing ocean.
But few are the nights
We two have lain together.

Away I have come, parting from her
Even as the creeping vines do part.
My heart aches within me;
I turn back my gaze—
But because of the yellow leaves
Of Watari Hill,
Flying and fluttering in the air,
I cannot see plainly
My wife waving her sleeve to me.
Now as the moon, sailing through the cloud rift
Above the mountain of Yakami,
Disappears, leaving me full of regret,
So vanishes my love out of sight;
Now sinks at last the sun,
Coursing down the western sky.

I thought myself a strong man,
But the sleeves of my garment
Are wetted through with tears.

ENVOYS

My black steed,
Galloping fast
Away have I come,
Leaving under distant skies
The dwelling-place of my love.

Oh, yellow leaves
Falling on the autumn hill,

2. *Kara:* a headland of Takuno, Nima District, jutting out towards an island called Karashina. *Miru* is an edible seaweed.

23. *Yakami:* unknown, though sometimes identified with Mount Takazen.

Cease a while
To fly and flutter in the air
That I may see my love's dwelling-place!

KAKINOMOTO HITOMARO

*Presented to Princess Hatsusebe and Prince Osakabe**

Dainty water-weeds, growing up-stream
  In the river of the bird-flying Asuka,
Drift down-stream, gracefully swaying.
Like the water-weeds the two would bend
Each toward the other, the princess and her consort.

But now no longer can she sleep,
With his fine smooth body clinging
Close to hers like a guardian sword.
Desolate must be her couch at night.
Unable to assuage her grief,
But in the hope of finding him by chance,
She journeys to the wide plain of Ochinu,
There, her skirt drenched with the morning dew
And her coat soaked with the fog of evening,
She passes the night—a wayfarer with grass for pillow—
Because of him whom she nevermore will meet!

ENVOY

Her lord and husband with whom she had slept,
The sleeves of their robes overlapping,
Has passed away to the plain of Ochinu.
How can she ever meet him again!

KAKINOMOTO HITOMARO

*On the Death of an Uneme from Tsu, Kibi Province***

Beauty was hers that glowed like autumn mountains
And grace as of the swaying bamboo stem.
How was it that she died—she who should have lived

* On the occasion of the burial of the Prince Kawashima. Both the prince and the princess were the children of the Emperor Temmu.

2. *bird-flying:* A pillow word for Asuka, now Takaichi District.

** An *uneme* (see note to line 2 of *Composed after the Empress Jito . . .*) was known by the name of the place and province from which she came. Tsu of Kibi Province was situated in the Tsu District of that time—now Tsububo District, Okayama Prefecture. Since she had a husband, the lady was evidently a former *umene.*

A life long as the coil of *taku* rope,
Though the dew falls at morn
To perish at dusk,
Though the mists that rise at eve
Vanish with the daybreak.
On learning her fate I grieve—
I who saw her but casually.
But her husband, tender as young grass,
Who with her soft white arm for pillow
Lay at her side close like a guard an sword—
How lonely must he lie—he in his widowed bed!
What anguish must fill his love-lorn heart,
Yearning for her who all too soon has gone—
Like morning dew—like mists of evening!

ENVOYS

How sorrowful to see
The road across the river-shallows
By which departed the lady
Of Shigatsu of Sasanami!

When we met, I only took—
And how I regret it now!—
A vague careless glance
At the lady of Otsu.

KAKINOMOTO HITOMARO

*Composed when the Empress Climbed the Thunder Hill**

Lo, our great Sovereign, a goddess,
Tarries on the Thunder
In the clouds of heaven!

KAKINOMOTO HITOMARO

*At a Royal Hunt Held by Prince Naga at Lake Kariji**

Our noble Prince, child of the Bright One on high,
Holds a royal hunt, horses birdle to bridle,
On the field of Kariji, thick with tender reeds,
There the boars and deer crouch and adore him,

* This poem is based on the idea that the sovereigns are the offspring of Amaterasu Ōmikami, and that their proper sphere is heaven. Here the Thunder Hill is regarded as the actual embodiment of thunder. The hill is in Yamato Province; the Empress was Jito.

* Naga was the son of the Emperor Temmu. The lake is in Yamato.

And the quails run bending low about him,
Like the quails we run bending low about him,
Tendering our loyal service;
And when we look up to him
As we look up to the sunny sky,
His freshness ever increases
Like the grass in spring—
Oh, our mighty lord!

ENVOY

Our mighty lord,
Having caught the sky-traversing moon
In his net,
Makes it his silken canopy!

KAKINOMOTO HITOMARO

O plovers flying over the evening waves,
On the lake of Ōmi,
When you cry, my heart grows heavy,
With memories of by-gone days.

FROM THE "HITOMARO COLLECTION"

On the Sky

On the sea of heaven the waves of cloud arise,
And the moon's ship is seen sailing
To hide in a forest of stars.

Composed on the Spot

Like the bubbles on the water
That echoing by the hill of Makimuku,
Frail human thing, am I.

By the River Uji

The inlet of Ōkura is echoing;
To the fields of Fushimi
The wild geese are passing.

16. *canopy:* The poem must have been composed on the way home from hunting, when the full moon seemed to follow the prince, as though it were his canopy.
2. midway between Asuka and Nara, and north of them, in the vicinity of Kyoto. [Editor.]
1. *Ōkura:* now called Ogura, which is formed by the Uji River. Situated to the north of Uji, where the town of Fushima now stands [near Kyoto, to the south—Editor.].

Love in Autumn

Let none, born after me,
Ever, ever meet, as I did,
Such ways of love!

I have lost a true man's mettle,
Day to night and night to day
I waste with thoughts of love.

Strong man as I am,
Who force my way even through the rocks,
In love I rue in misery.

Sleepless with longing for my love,
Now I see the morning break;
O the mandarin-ducks flying by—
Are they the couriers from my girl?

I will tread the sharpness of the double-edged sword
And die with a good heart
If it be for your sake.

FURU TAMUKE

Leaving the Province of Tsukushi

Would my love were a bracelet!
Tying her to my left arm,
I would start on my journey!

TAKECHI KUROHITO

Poems of Travel

When on my travels I pine for home,
I see a vermilion ship sailing
Far out on the waters.

Cranes fly calling towards Sakurada Fields;
The tide, it seems, has ebbed from Ayuchi Lagoon;
Look where the cranes fly calling.

12. *mandarin-ducks:* a symbol of affectionate love.

2. *Vermilion ship:* Ships in government employ were painted red. The poet, an official, felt homesick at the sight of a red-painted ship.

4. *Sakurada Fields:* In the province of Owari, facing Ayuchi Beach, which is near Atsuta in Aichi District [near Nagoya—Editor.].

As we row round the jutting beaches,
Cranes call in flocks at every inlet
Of the many-harboured lake of Ōmi.

Our boat shall harbour at the port of Hira;
Row not far from shore,—
It is night and late!

Where shall I seek shelter,
If, in Takashima, on the plain of Kachinu,
This day is spent?

TAKECHI KUROHITO

In the Old Capital of Ōmi

So I refused to see them:
Yet you show me over the ruins
Of the Imperial City of Sasanami,
Saddening me in vain!

OKISOME AZUMABITO

On the Death of Prince Yuge

Tread not the snow
Around the palace;
It is not a fall
We often see;
Only on the mountains
We have such snow.
Away, away, away—
Tread not the snow.

ENVOY

Our lord will view it later
Where it lies;
Tread not the snow
Around the palace.

The above verses were sung by Mikata Shami, in compliance with the order of Fujiwara Fusasaki, Minister of the Left by posthumous appointment.

10. *Hira:* On the west side of Lake Biwa, as is Takashima, below.

ANONYMOUS

On the Well at the Palace of Fujiwara

Our great Sovereign who rules in peace,
　　Offspring of the Bright One on high,
Has begun to build her Palace
On the plan of Fujii;
And standing on the dyke of Lake Haniyasu
She looks around her:
The green hill of Kagu of Yamato
Stands at the eastern gate,
Ever fresh and flourishing;
Mininashi, the green sedgy mount,
Rears at the northern gate
Its form divine;
And the mountains of Yoshinu, of lovely name,
Soar into the sky,
Far from the southern gate.
At this towering Palace,
The shelter from the sun,
The shelter from the sky,
The waters will be everlasting,
These clear waters of the sacred well!

ENVOY

The bevies of maidens who will be born
And come in succession into service
At the mighty Palace of Fujiwara,
How I envy their happy lot!

ANONYMOUS

The Old Bamboo-Cutter

Once upon a time there lived an old man. He was called 'Old Bamboo-Cutter' (Taketori no Oji). In the last month of spring he went up a hill to view the country-side. Suddenly he discovered nine girls who were cooking soup, and who were all possessed of an unrivaled beauty and charm. One of the damsels called to the old man,

4. ***Fujii:*** Fujii-ga-hara (Plain of Wisteria Well) may have been an earlier name for Fujiwara (Wisteria Plain). [The court moved to Fujiwara in 694—Editor.]

laughed and said: 'Uncle, come blow up the fire under the kettle!' 'Very well, very well,' he replied. Hobbling slowly, he reached the spot where the girls were, and seated himself among them. After a while, all the girls, with smiles on their faces, began to question one another, saying, 'Who called this old man?' Thereupon the Bamboo-Cutter apologized and said, 'Most unexpectedly I have met you fairy maidens. My mind is perplexed beyond endurance. Let me redeem with a poem the offense of having intruded myself upon your company!' So saying, he made the following poem and envoys.

When I was a new-born babe
    My mother carried me in her arms;
When an infant still tied with a band
To the back of my nurse, I wore
A sleeveless gown with lining sewed in;
When a boy with hair trimmed at the neck
I was clad in a dappled robe with sleeves.
At the age of you dear maidens
My hair was black as the bowels of the mud-snail.
I would comb it down to the shoulders,
Or have it bound up in knots
Or sometimes let it hang loose like a boy.

I had a vest of thin silk with large woven figures
Of purple matching well with its reddish tint,
And a robe of fabric dyed with the *hagi*-flower
Of Tōzato Onu in Siminoe,
To which was attached a cord of *Koma* brocade—
These I wore one over the other.

There was the cloth of *tahe* tissue
And the hand-woven cloth of sun-dried hemp,
Made with rare skill by girl hemp-spinners
And by girls who were treasured like precious robes;
When I put these on together like a double skirt,
Many a country lass from her lowly cottage
Would come, asking me to marry her.

The double-patterned stockings from a far country,
And the shoes fashioned by the men of Asuka,
Shunning the damp of the rainy season,—
I would put them on and stand under the eaves;
Then maidens who had heard of men somewhere,
Would come to me, bidding me not to walk away.

17. *Koma:* Same as *kara,* below; i.e., Korean.

19. *Tahe: Taku,* paper mulberry, from the inner bark of which cloth was made.

I would arrange my silken girdle of azure
In the manner of a *Kara* girdle like a pendant sash,
And so bedeck my waist slim as a wasp
Flying above the tiled roof of the Sea God's Temple;
Then would I hang up clear mirrors side by side,
And turn back to them again and again
To see my face therein.
When in spring I sauntered forth afield,
The pheasants of the moor, delighting in me,
Came flying and crowing merrily.
When I went to the hills in autumn
The enamoured clouds of heaven hovered low above me.
When I started for home, all along the way
The gay ladies of the palace and the court gallants
Would all look back on me in admiration,
And ask one another, saying, 'Who is he?'
So did I do and live in days gone by.

Though to-day you dear damsels may wonder
Who I am and say: 'We don't know the man,'
I was once the talk of the town—
Thus did I do and live in days gone by.

Did not the wise man of ancient times
Bring back, to set an example for after ages,
The cart in which the old man was sent away?

ENVOYS

Can it be that grey hair
Will never grow on you maidens
If you live long, unless death
Spares you from seeing it?

When grey hair has grown
On you, may it not be then
That you too will be mocked
By young folk as I am now?

54–56. The three lines allude to the old Chinese story of a man by the name of Kuan Ku. When he was fifteen years old his parents, in spite of his tearful protests, took his aged grandparent to the mountains in a cart, and there abandoned him. The boy went and brought back the cart. Being questioned by his father as to why he had done so, Yuan Ku replied: "You may not be able to make a cart by yourself when you are old." The father, much ashamed of his misdeed, brought back the old parent and took good care of him thereafter.

REPLIES BY THE MAIDENS

The dear old man's verse
Has stunned us,
We fairy maidens nine—
Are we humbled by his word?

My shame I will bear,
My shame I will ignore;
And before he speaks another word,
To his counsel mutely will I yield.

Shall I be false to friends
To whose hearts mine is bound
In life and death?
To his counsel I also will yield.

EMPRESS KŌKEN

A Poem and Envoy Granted to Fujiwara Kiyokawa, Ambassador to China, Together with Food and Drink, by Her Messenger, Koma Fukushin, of the Lower Fourth Rank Senior, Whom She Sent Down to Naniwa

The spacious land of Yamato
Is a land guarded by the gods;
You go upon the waters
As upon the land;
You sit in the ship
As on the floor at home.

In your four ships, prow by prow,
You travel in safety,
Return in haste,
Then make your reports;
On that day we shall take this wine—
This bounteous wine.

ENVOY

That your four ships may soon come back
I pray to the gods,
Tying white hemp,
To my skirt.

4. *skirt:* A woman's skirt (Japanese *mo*) was believed in ancient times to have magic power.

PRINCE HOZUMI

Ah, that rascal love
    I have put away at home,
Locked in a coffer—
Here he comes, pouncing on me!

The above was a favourite poem of Prince Hozumi, who used to always recite it at banquets when the merry-making was at its height.

PRINCE AKI

*On an Imperial Visit to the Province of Ise**

Would that they were flowers,
    The white surges far upon the sea of Ise—
I would wrap and bring them home
As a souvenir for my beloved wife.

PRINCE ICHIHARA

On the Occasion of Men Ascending the Hill of Ikuji to Drink Under a Pine-Tree

O solitary pine, how many
Generations of man have you known?
Is it because of your great age
That the passing winds sing in so clear a tone?

PRINCESS TAKATA

To Prince Imaki

This world is so full
    Of men with slanderous tongues.
May we not meet in the life to come—
If we may not now, my dearest?

* The visit was said to have taken place in the second year of Yoro (718), in the reign of the Empress Gensho.

All over the meadow,
Where the yellow roses bloom,
Multitudes of violets have opened
With this spring rain.

PRINCESS HIROKAWA

The sheaves of my love-thoughts
Would fill seven carts—
Carts huge and heavy-wheeled.
Such a burden I bear
Of my own choice.

I thought there could be
No more love left anywhere.
Whence then is come this love,
That has caught me now
And holds me in its grasp?

TAJIHI KASAMARO

On His Journey to Tsukushi

By the sea-shore of Mitsu, that reminds one
Of the mirror standing on a girl's comb-case,
I linger, longing for my wife, and sleep alone,
My scarlet sash untied.

I can but weep aloud like the crane crying
In the morning mist at the twilight hour of dawn.
Seeking to relieve me of my sorrow,
If only by a thousandth part,
I go out to gaze toward my home,
Which is—alas!—lost in the white clouds,
That trail across the green mountain of Kazuraki.

I journey on to the far-off land—
Passing Awaji Island now lying before,
And leaving behind me the island of Awashima.
I hear the shouts of sailors in the morning calm,
And in the calm of evening the plash of oars.

1. *Mitsu:* Naniwazu, the original name of the present port of Osaka.

11. *Kazuraki:* a mountain between the provinces of Yamato and Settsu. Awashima, below, is unidentified, perhaps near Awaji.

Labouring over the waters,
Circling about amid the rocks,
And past the beach of Inabizuma,
I wonder on like a bird
Till Ie-no-shima, the 'Home Island,' comes into sight,
Where thick and swaying on the stony shore
Grows the weed men call 'Speak-not'—
Ah, why have I come away from my wife
Without a word of farewell?

ENVOY

Would that my wife and I,
Unfastening our girdles for each other
And with out snow-white sleeves overlapping,
Had reckoned the day of my return
Before I came away upon my journey!

KASA KANAMURA

Composed at the Request of a Young Lady for Sending to a Member of the Emperor's Retinue on a Journey to Ki, in Winter, in the Tenth Month of the First Year of Jinki

You, dear husband, who have gone forth
    With the many men of the eighty clans
Accompanying the Emperor on his journey—

You who went by the highway of Karu,
Admiring the view of the Unebi Mountain,
And now having entered the province of Ki
Are crossing, perhaps, the mountain of Matsuchi—

You may find your journey a pleasant thing.
As you watch the autumn leaves fly and scatter,
Yet never a tender thought give to me.
Though this may be an empty fear,
I cannot stay at peace at all.
A thousand times over I wish
To follow you on your track.

19. *Inabizuma:* presumably a small island at the mouth of the Kako River [on the Inland Sea at present-day Takasage in Hyōgo Prefecture—Editor]; Ie-no-Shima, now Ejima, is in the Harima Channel.

23. *'Speak-not':* Originally *nanoriso,* now known as *hondawara* (Sargassum). The word may be translated literally as "speak-not."

7. *Matsuchi:* A mountain in Kii lying just over the border from Yamato and to the north of the Ki River. [Editor.]

And yet, young and helpless girl that I am.
I should not know what answer to give,
If a road-guard should challenge me—
So here I stand, faltering.

ENVOYS

Rather than remain behind
To pine after you,
I would we were the Imo-Se Mountains of Ki—
The Man and Wife' for ever.

If I go seeking after you,
Following your footmarks,
Will the guard of the pass
In Ki bid me halt?

FUJIWARA HIROTSUGU and A YOUNG LADY

Poem Sent with Sherry-Flowers to a Young Lady by Fujiwara Hirotsugu

Slight not these flowers!
Each single petal contains
A hundred words of mine.

REPLY BY THE YOUNG LADY

Were these flowers broken off,
Unable to hold in each petal
A hundred words of yours?

IKEDA —— and ŌMIWA OKIMORI

Poem of Ridicule by Ikeda Addressed to Ōmiwa Okimori

Thus say the famished she-devils
In the temples far and near:
'Grant me Ōmiwa, the he-devil,
That I may bear him
A litter of baby devils!'

22. *'Man and Wife'*: The twin mountain peaks seem like man and wife. [Editor.]

REPLY BY ŌMIWA OKIMORI

If you lack, makers of Buddhas,
 The vermeil clay
For your idols,
Go dig the nose-top
Of my Lord of 'Pond-Field'!

Poems in Praise of Sake*

Instead of wasting thoughts on unavailing things,
It would seem wiser
To drink a cup of raw *sake*.

How true is his saying,
That great sage of old who gave *sake*
The name of 'sage.'

Even with the seven wise men of the days of old,
Sake was, it seems,
The crown of their desire.

Far better, it seems, than uttering pompous words
And looking wise,
To drink *sake* and weep drunken tears.

I know not how to name it, how to define it,
Ten thousand times precious
Is *sake* to me!

Ceasing to live this wretched life of man
O that I were a *sake*-jar;
Then should I be soaked with *sake*!

Grotesque! When I look upon a man
Who drinks no *sake*, looking wise,
How like an ape he is!

Even a treasure priceless in the world—
How could it surpass
A cup of raw *sake*?

If there were a gem shining in the darkness of night,
How could it excel
Sake that kills all care?

10. *'Pond-Field'*: a literal translation of *Ikeda*.

* *Sake* is a white wine made from rice, often drunk warmed. New or "raw" *sake* is often preferred to aged. [Editor.]

3. *'sage'*: In ancient China, the Emperor Taitsung of Wei prohibited the use of *sake*, but those who drank it secretly called white *sake* "wise man" and pure *sake* "sage."

1. *seven wise men*: The "seven wise men of the bamboo wood" who lived under the Chin dynasty were all good drinkers.

Among the countless ways of pleasure
What refreshes most
Is weeping drunken tears!

If I could but be happy in this life,
What should I care if in the next
I become a bird or a worm!

All living things die in the end:
So long as I live here
I want the cup of pleasure.

Silence with the airs of wisdom
Is far worse
Than weeping drunken tears!

LADY ŌTOMO OF SAKANOE

Love's Complaint

At wave-bright Naniwa
    The sedges grow, firm-rooted—
Firm were the words you spoke,
And tender, pledging me your love,
That it would endure through all the years;
And to you I yielded my heart,
Spotless as a polished mirror.
Never, from that day, like the sea-weed
That sways to and fro with the waves,
Have I faltered in my fidelity,
But have trusted in you as in a great ship.
Is it the gods who have divided us?
Is it mortal men who intervene?
You come no more, who came so often,
Nor yet arrives a messenger with your letter.
There is—alas!—nothing I can do.
Though I sorrow the black night through
And all day till the red sun sinks,
It avails me nothing. Though I pine,
I know not how to soothe my heart's pain.
Truly men call us 'weak women.'
Crying like an infant,
And lingering around, I must still wait,
Wait impatiently for a message from you!

2–3. The second and third lines are alternately construed, i.e.: "And when we are melancholy, / Better take to weeping drunken tears."

ENVOY

If from the beginning
You had not made me trust you,
Speaking of long, long years,
Should I have known now
Such sorrow as this?

LADY ŌTOMO OF SAKANOE

*Sent to Her Elder Daughter from the Capital**

I cherished you, my darling,
    As the Sea God the pearls
He treasures in his comb-box.
But you, led by your lord husband—
Such is the way of the world—
And torn from me like a vine,
Left for distant Koshi;
Since then, your lovely eyebrows
Curving like the far-off waves,
Ever linger in my eyes,
My heart unsteady as a rocking boat;
Under such a longing
I, now weak with age,
Come near to breaking.

ENVOY

If I had foreknown such longing
I would have lived with you,
Gazing on you every hour of the day
As in a shining mirror.

ŌTOMO YAKAMOCHI

*Elegy on the Death of Prince Asaka***

My thought is held with awe—
    My lord and prince, leading
All the captains of eighty clans,

* Composed in the second year of Tempyō-Shoho (750).

** Son of the Emperor Shōmu. He died at the age of seventeen on the thirteenth day of the 1st month, in the sixteenth year of Tempyō (744).

Would rouse deer in the morning chase,
And start birds in the evening hunt;
Then halting his horse by the bit,
Joyously he would gaze far
From the hills of Ikuji.

But now on this hill the blossoms
That filled the leafy trees
All are scattered away.
So it is with the world;
His servitors who, warrior-hearted,
Gathered at the prince's palace,
Noisy as the flies of May,
With swords at their waists,
Birchwood bows in hand,
And full quivers on their backs,
Trusting their service would last
Long as heaven and earth endured,
For a myriad ages,
Now go in doleful white;
And daily fade their wonted smiles
And their ways grow less gay;
Which rends my heart!

ENVOYS

The path he traced, my dear prince,
The path to Ikuji where he admired the view,
Lies wild and desolate!

My heart, that bears the fame of Ōtomo,
My trust to serve, quiver on back,
For a myriad ages,
Where shall I take it now?

ŌTOMO YAKAMOCHI

On the New Moon

When I look up and gaze
    At the young moon afar
I remember the painted eyebrows
Of her whom only once I saw.

8. *Ikuji:* One of the Wazuka hills in the Sōraku district, Yamashiro.

ŌTOMO YAKAMOCHI

*On the Arrival of the Wife, Who Came by Herself Without Waiting for a Messenger from Her Husband**

At the house where the Saburu girl
Worships her lover,
There has arrived a post-horse without bells,
Upsetting the whole town.

ŌTOMO YAKAMOCHI

*Admonition to His Clansmen***

In the remote age of the gods
When the Imperial Ancestor, opening heaven's gate,
Descended upon the peak of Takachiho,
It was the founder of our clan,
Who, gripping in his hand a wax-tree bow
And grasping withal arrows for the deer hunt,
Made advance the brave troops
Of Ōkume with quivers on their backs;
Forced his way across mountains and rivers,
Trampling under foot rocks and stones;
And who, seeking for a good habitable land,
Subdued the fierce gods
And pacified unruly tribes—
Sweeping and cleansing thus the country,
He rendered a loyal service to his lord.

Thereafter, under the successive reigns
Of the sovereigns on the Celestial Throne,
Descended from that First Emperor
Who, raising the stout-pillared Unebi Palace
Of Kashihara in the land of Yamato,
Ruled the under-heaven,
Our forefathers served the Imperial House
With all their hearts faithful and true.

* Composed on the seventeenth day of the fifth month, 749. The horse without bells indicated that the wife had come privately on her own account. Government post-horses had bells.

** Composed on the occasion of the dismissal from office of Ōtomo Kojihi, Governor of Izumo, through false accusations made to the court by Ōmi Mifunē (in 756).—Note by the poet.

17. *Emperor:* Jimmu.

20. *Kashihara:* now pronounced Kashiwara.

Ours is the ancestral office of the clan,
So proclaimed and bestowed upon us,
To be handed down from father to son,
Generation after generation—
Those who see will tell of it from mouth to mouth;
Those who hear will hold it up as a mirror.

So cherished and clean is the name of our clan.
Neglect it never, lest even a false word
Should destroy this proud name of our fathers.
You clansmen all, who bear the name of Ōtomo.

ENVOYS

Beware, you leaders of our clan
Which bears a most illustrious name
In this wide land of Yamato!

Polish it like a double-edged sword,
Make it ever bright—the name
Borne through the ages, clean and without spot!

SEI SHŌNAGON

(965?–1025?)

The Pillow Book (*Makura no Sōshi*)

Little is known about the life of the woman who left us the extensive diary known as the *Makura no Sōshi*, that is, little about the external circumstances of her life, though we have a most intimate picture of her desires and frustrations, and even minor likes and dislikes, in her journal. She served as lady-in-waiting to the Empress Sadako during the last years of the tenth century. Her father was a provincial official who was also a scholar and a poet. Nothing at all is known about the later years of her life, after she left the imperial service. "Sei" refers to the Kiyowara family, to which she belonged. Perhaps her name was Nagiko, but in the palace she was called Shōnagon. Such, except for some references to her by contemporaries, are the meager facts of her life.

The diary covers the ten or so years she served at court. She was, as her modern translator Ivan Morris says, "a complicated, intelligent, well-informed woman who was quick, impatient, kneely observant of detail, high-spirited, emulative, sensitive to the charms and beauties of the world and to the pathos of things, yet intolerant and callous about people whom she regarded as her social or intellectual inferiors."[1] To this apt and condensed characterization might be added a trivial but endearing quality, the ability to deal with trivia precisely. If she were alive today, she might be jotting down "ten things I dislike about opening night at the Metroplitan Opera" or "the two gentlemen who arrived at the reception wearing brown shoes." Her casual likes and dislikes are as alive to us as her estimates of more serious social situations. What emerges is a portrait of an extraordinary woman and a vivid panorama of the Heian court, the most glorious period of early Japanese history.

This is the age of the *Tale of Genji*, and it is revealed to us not only in that work and in Sei Shōnagon's diary but in many other poems and diaries. But perhaps these two works together give us the best picture of the period. Murasaki's art may function at a higher emotional and artistic level, but this includes artistic reordering of the experiences. Sei Shōnagon is closer to the pulse-beat of the daily scene. Even her limits interest and amuse us. She worships the imperial family and both the essence and the show of rank and position, and scorns the newly rich and the lower orders, the pretenders to class and the intruders into it. Her position is consistent, and, if it would be deplorable today, was not then, and need not trouble us now, as it has some modern Japanese critics.

The poetry included in the diary is of the first quality, and Sei Shōnagon ranks high as a poet. The *Pillow Book* has long been regarded as a model of linguistic purity and rhythmic, easy style, and is recommended as such to schoolchildren in Japan.

1. Ivan Morris, "Introduction" to his translation (cited below), p. xiv.

From The Pillow Book of Sei Shōnagon*

1. *In Spring It Is the Dawn*

In spring it is the dawn that is most beautiful.[1] As the light creeps over the hills, their outlines are dyed a faint red and wisps of purplish cloud trail over them.

In summer the nights. Not only when the moon shines, but on dark nights too, as the fireflies flit to and fro, and even when it rains, how beautiful it is!

* From *The Pillow Book of Sei Shōnagon*, translated and edited by Ivan Morris. Copyright 1967 by Ivan Morris. Reprinted by permission of Ivan Morris, Columbia University Press, and Oxford University Press, Oxford. Unless otherwise indicated, the notes, sometimes abridged, are the translator's.

1. The famous opening lines of *The Pillow Book* (*haru wa akebono*) constitute an elliptical sentence. Their literal meaning is "As for spring the dawn," but some predicate like "is the most beautiful time of the day" must be understood. The same applies to the opening phrases of each of the four paragraphs in this section.

In autumn the evenings, when the glittering sun sinks close to the edge of the hills and crows fly back to their nests in threes and fours and twos; more charming still is a file of wild geese, like specks in the distant sky. When the sun has set, one's heart is moved by the sound of the wind and the hum of the insects.

In winter the early mornings. It is beautiful indeed when snow has fallen during the night, but splendid too when the ground is white with frost; or even when there is no snow or frost, but it is simply very cold and the attendants hurry from room to room stirring up the fires and bringing charcoal, how well this fits the season's mood! But as noon approaches and the cold wears off, no one bothers to keep the braziers alight, and soon nothing remains but piles of white ashes.

2. *These Are the Months*[2]

These are the months that I like best: the First Month, the Third, the Fourth, the Fifth, the Seventh, the Eighth, the Ninth, the Eleventh, and the Twelfth. In fact each month has its own particular charm, and the entire year is a delight.

3. *Especially Delightful Is the First Day*

Especially delightful is the first day of the First Month, when the mists so often shroud the sky. Everyone pays great attention to his appearance and dresses with the utmost care. What a pleasure it is to see them all offer their congratulations to the Emperor and celebrate their own new year![3]

2. The 2nd, 6th, and 10th Months were associated with relatively few of the annual observations (*nenjū gyōji*) which played a major part in the lives of the Heian aristocrats; also, these months offered less in the way of aesthetic delights than the other nine. There was a discrepancy, varying from seventeen to forty-five days, between the Japanese (lunar) calendar and the Western (Julian) calendar, the Japanese calendar being on an average about one month in advance of the Western. The names of the months are their conjectural meanings are as follows: 1st, Mutsuki (Social Month) or Moyotsuki (Sprouting Month); 2nd, Kisaragi (Clothes-Lining); 3rd, Yayoi (Ever-Growing, Germinal); 4th, Uzuki (U no Hana [white shrub] Month); 5th, Satsuki (Rice-Sprouting Month); 6th, Minazuki (Watery Month); 7th, Fumizuki (Poem-Composing Month, or [Rice Ears] Swelling Month); 8th, Hazuki (Leaf [i.e., leaf-turning] Month); 9th, Nagatsuki (Long [i.e., long nights] Month); 10th, Kaminazuki (Gods-Absent Month); 11th, Shimotsuki (Frost Month); 12th, Shiwasu (End of the Year. The seasons were as follows: spring (*haru*) 1st–3rd Months; summer (*natsu*) 4th–6th Months; autumn (*aki*) 7th–9th Months; winter (*fuyu*) 10th–12th Months.

3. New Year's Day was, and still is, an occasion for paying one's respects to the Emperor and to other superiors. It also marked an increase in one's age, thus corresponding in some ways to the Western birthday. New Year's Day in the Heian calendar came at some time between 21 January and 19 February.

I also enjoy the seventh day, when people pluck the young herbs that have sprouted fresh and green beneath the snow. It is amusing to see their excitement when they find such plants growing near the Palace, by no means a spot where one might expect them.[4]

This is the day when members of the nobility who live outside the Palace arrive in their magnificently decorated carriages to admire the blue horses. As the carriages are drawn over the ground-beam of the Central Gate, there is always a tremendous bump, and the heads of the women passengers are knocked together; the combs fall out of their hair, and may be smashed to pieces if the owners are not careful. I enjoy the way everyone laughs when this happens.

I remember one occasion when I visited the Palace to see the procession of blue horses.[5] Several senior courtiers were standing outside the guard-house of the Left Division; they had borrowed bows from the escorts, and, with much laughter, were twanging them to make the blue horses prance. Looking through one of the gates of the Palace enclosure, I could dimly make out a garden fence, near which a number of ladies, several of them from the Office of Grounds, went to and fro. What lucky women, I thought, who could walk about the Nine-Fold Enclosure[6] as though they had lived there all their lives! Just then the escorts passed close to my carriage—remarkably close, in fact, considering the vastness of the Palace grounds—and I could actually see the texture of their faces. Some of them were not properly powdered; here and there their skin showed through unpleasantly like the dark patches of earth in a garden where the snow has begun to melt. When the horses in the procession reared wildly, I shrank into the back of my carriage and could no longer see what was happening.

4. *Wakana no Sekku* (the Festival of Young Herbs) was one of the seven national festivals listed in the code of 718. The "seven herbs" (parsley, borage, etc.) were plucked and made into a gruel (*nanakusa no kayu*) which was supposed to ward off evil spirits and to protect one's health throughout the year. In the Palace a bowl of this gruel was ceremoniously presented to the Emperor. Normally the grounds near the Palace were kept clear of plants, weeds, etc.; but at this time of the year it was possible to find "young herbs," since they were hidden by the snow. (In this translation "Palace" with a capital *P* invariably refers to the Imperial Palace in Heian Kyō [the vicinity of present-day Kyoto.—Editor.].)

5. A large proportion of the Court Nobles normally resided in the Palace, which was itself a small, self-contained town. *Aouma no Sechie* (the Festival of the Blue Horses) was an annual ceremony in which twenty-one horses from the Imperial stables were paraded before the Emperor. Originally the horses were steel-grey (hence the name "blue"); but since such horses were very rare and since white was the colour of purity in Shintō ritual, they were replaced in the early tenth century by white horses. To add to the confusion, the word used to describe the horses was written with the character for "white" but continued to be pronounced "blue" (*ao*). Horses in general were connected with the Yang or Male principle and were therefore regarded as auspicious; the fact that their colour was, theoretically, *ao* also made them auspicious, since *ao* (in the sense of "green") was the traditional New Year and spring colour. A great wooden cross-beam (*tojikomi*) was fixed on the ground and joined the two main pillars of the gate. For the visit described, 987 is a likely date.

6. *Kokonoe* (Nine-Fold Enclosure): a standard figure of speech suggesting the vast extent of the Greater Imperial Palace.

On the eighth[7] day there is great excitement in the Palace as people hurry to express their gratitude, and the clatter of carriages is louder than ever—all very fascinating.

The fifteenth day is the festival of the full-moon gruel, when a bowl of gruel is presented to His Majesty. On this day all the women of the house carry gruel-sticks, which they hide carefully from each other. It is most amusing to see them walking about, as they await an opportunity to hit their companions. Each one is careful not to be struck herself and is constantly looking over her shoulder to make sure that no one is stealing up on her. Yet the precautions are useless, for before long one of the women manages to score a hit. She is extremely pleased with herself and laughs merrily. Everyone finds this delightful—except, of course, the victim, who looks very put out.

In a certain household a young gentleman had been married during the previous year to one of the girls in the family. Having spent the night with her, he was now, on the morning of the fifteenth, about to set off for the Palace. There was a woman in the house who was in the habit of lording it over everyone. On this occasion she was standing in the back of the room, impatiently awaiting an opportunity to hit the man with her gruel-stick as he left.[8] One of the other women realized what she had in mind and burst out laughing. The woman with the stick signalled excitedly that she should be quiet. Fortunately the young man did not notice what was afoot and he stood there unconcernedly.

'I have to pick up something over there,' said the woman with the stick, approaching the man. Suddenly she darted forward, gave him a great whack, and made her escape. Everyone in the room burst out laughing; even the young man smiled pleasantly, not in the least annoyed. He was not too startled; but he did blush a little, which was charming.

Sometimes when the women are hitting each other the men also join in the fun. The strange thing is that, when a woman is hit by one of the men, she often gets angry and bursts into tears; then she will upbraid the man and say the most awful things about him—most amusing. Even in the Palace, where the atmosphere is usually so solemn, everything is in confusion on this day, and no one stands on ceremony.

7. On the 8th day of the 1st Month presents of silk and brocade were given to the Imperial consorts, and many of the Court ladies were promoted in rank. All those who had been so favoured went to present their formal thanks to the Emperor. *Mochigayu* (full-moon gruel): a special gruel eaten on the 15th day of the 1st Month. A stick of peeled elder-wood (*kayu no ki*) was used to stir the gruel, and it was believed that, if a woman was struck on the loins with such a stick, she would soon give birth to a male child.

8. According to some of the commentators, the woman was Shōnagon herself. The important political influence that Court ladies exerted at this time is illustrated at the end of the passage.

It is fascinating to see what happens during the period of appointments. However snowy and icy it may be, candidates of the Fourth and Fifth Ranks come to the Palace with their official requests. Those who are still young and merry seem full of confidence. For the candidates who are old and white-haired things do not go so smoothly. Such men have to apply for help from people with influence at Court; some of them even visit ladies-in-waiting in their quarters and go to great lengths in pointing out their own merits. If young women happen to be present, they are greatly amused. As soon as the candidates have left, they mimic and deride them—something that the old men cannot possibly suspect as they scurry from one part of the Palace to another, begging everyone, 'Please present my petition favourably to the Emperor' and 'Pray inform Her Majesty about me'. It is not so bad if they finally succeed, but it really is rather pathetic when all their efforts prove in vain.

4. *On the Third Day of the Third Month*

On the third day of the Third Month[9] I like to see the sun shining bright and calm in the spring sky. Now is the time when the peach trees come into bloom, and what a sight it is! The willows too are most charming at this season, with the buds still enclosed like silkworms in their cocoons. After the leaves have spread out, I find them unattractive; in fact all trees lose their charm once the blossoms have begun to scatter.

It is a great pleasure to break off a long, beautifully flowering branch from a cherry tree and to arrange it in a large vase. What a delightful task to perform when a visitor is seated nearby conversing! It may be an ordinary guest, or possibly one of Their Highnesses, the Empress's elder brothers; but in any case the visitor will wear a cherry-coloured Court cloak,[10] from the bottom of which his under-robe emerges. I am even happier if a butterfly or a small bird flutters prettily near the flowers and I can see its face.

5. *How Delightful Everything Is!*

How delightful everything is at the time of the Festival![11] The leaves, which still do not cover the trees too thickly, are green and fresh. In the daytime there is no mist to hide the sky and, glancing up, one is overcome by its beauty. On a slightly cloudy evening, or

9. This was the day known as Jōmi, which was associated with Winding Water banquets and the display of dolls; it was also called the Peach Festival (*Momo no Sekku*). "Empress" in this translation always refers to Fujiwara no Sadako, Michitaka's daughter, in whose Court Sei Shōnagon served as lady-in-waiting.

10. Colours of clothes in Heian literature frequently referred, not to single colours, but to certain fashionable combinations produced by lining the costume with material of a different colour from the outside.

11. *Matsuri* (the Festival): refers to the Kamo Festival, the main Shintō celebration of the year, which was observed in the middle of the 4th Month.

again at night, it is moving to hear in the distance the song of a *hototogisu*[12]—so faint that one doubts one's own ears.

When the Festival approaches, I enjoy seeing the men go to and fro with rolls of yellowish green and deep violet material which they have loosely wrapped in paper and placed in the lids of long boxes.[13] At this time of the year, border shading, uneven shading, and rolled dyeing all seem more attractive than usual.[14] The young girls who are to take part in the procession have had their hair washed and arranged; but they are still wearing their everyday clothes, which sometimes are in a great mess, wrinkled and coming apart at the seams. How excited they are as they run about the house, impatiently awaiting the great day, and rapping out orders to the maids: 'Fit the cords on my clogs' or 'See that the soles of my sandals are all right'. Once they have put on their Festival costumes, these same young girls, instead of prancing about the rooms, become extremely demure and walk along solemnly like priests at the head of a procession. I also enjoy seeing how their mothers, aunts, and elder sisters, dressed according to their ranks, accompany the girls and help keep their costumes in order.

6. *Different Ways of Speaking*[15]

A priest's language.

The speech of men and of women.

The common people always tend to add extra syllables to their words.

7. *That Parents Should Bring up Some Beloved Son*

That parents should bring up some beloved son of theirs to be a priest is really distressing. No doubt it is an auspicious thing to do,[16] but unfortunately most people are convinced that a priest is

12. Usually translated as "cuckoo," but the *hototogisu* (*cuculus poliocephalus*) is a far more poetic type of bird with none of the cuckoo's cheeky associations. The name, *hototogisu*, is an onomatopoeia derived from the bird's characteristic cry of *ho-to-to*; in Heian times people accordingly described the *hototogisu* as "announcing its name."

13. A long, narrow chest with legs, carried on a pole by two men. In Shōnagon's time lids were frequently used for carrying books, clothing, and other objects.

14. Dyeing was one of the great arts of the Heian period, as well as a pastime for women of quality. It was done with particular care when the clothes were to be worn during the Kamo Festival. The three forms mentioned here are: *susogo* (border shading), in which the material becomes darker towards the bottom of the garment; *murago* (uneven shading), in which the material is dyed unevenly all over; and, *makizome* (rolled dyeing, in which the material is rolled up before being immersed in the dye.

15. Women's language was traditionally far less influenced by Chinese and contained a much larger proportion of "pure" Japanese words and constructions.

16. Popular Buddhist beliefs at the time included the following: "If a man becomes a priest, his father and mother are saved until the seventh generation" and "When a child takes the Vows, nine of his relations are reborn in Heaven." (*Hyoshaku*, p. 30). People consider that a priest should spend the night in prayer and religious austerities. *Sōjimono* (maigre food) was a diet from which meat, fish, wine, and strong vegetables like onions and radishes were excluded.

as unimportant as a piece of wood, and they treat him accordingly. A priest lives poorly on maigre food, and cannot even sleep without being criticized. While he is young, it is only natural that he should be curious about all sorts of things, and, if there are women about, he will probably peep in their direction (though, to be sure, with a look of aversion on his face). What is wrong about that? Yet people immediately find fault with him for even so small a lapse.

The lot of an exorcist is still more painful. On his pilgrimages to Mitake, Kumano,[17] and all the other sacred mountains he often undergoes the greatest hardships. When people come to hear that his prayers are effective, they summon him here and there to perform services of exorcism: the more popular he becomes, the less peace he enjoys. Sometimes he will be called to see a patient who is seriously ill and he has to exert all his powers to cast out the spirit that is causing the affliction. But if he dozes off, exhausted by his efforts, people say reproachfully, 'Really, this priest does nothing but sleep.' Such comments are most embarrassing for the exorcist, and I can imagine how he must feel.

That is how things used to be; nowadays priests have a somewhat easier life.

9. *The Cat Who Lived in the Palace*[18]

The cat who lived in the Palace had been awarded the head-dress of nobility and was called Lady Myōbu. She was a very pretty cat, and His Majesty saw to it that she was treated with the greatest care.

One day she wandered on the veranda, and Lady Uma, the nurse in charge of her, called out, 'Oh, you naughty thing! Please come inside at once.' But the cat paid no attention and went on basking sleepily in the sun. Intending to give her a scare, the nurse called for the dog, Okinamaro.

17. In order to purify themselves spiritually, exorcists (*genza*) travelled about the country visiting the many sacred Buddhist mountains. One of the most important pilgrimages was to Mt. Kimbu, also known as Mitake, the highest peak in Yoshino. Another pilgrimage was to the Three Shrines of Kumano, south of Yoshino. The gods of these ancient Shinto shrines had come to be considered as avatars of various Buddhist deities. Travel in the Heian period was both uncomfortable and dangerous.

18. Cats had been imported from the continent, and there are several references to them in Heian chronicles and literature. The diary of Fujiwara no Sanesuke, for instance, contains the momentous entry (on the 19th day of the 9th Month in 999) that one of the Palace cats gave birth to a litter of kittens, that the birth-ceremony was attended by no lesser dignitaries than the Ministers of the Left and of the Right, and that Uma no Myōbu was appointed nurse to the litter. Myōbu no Omoto may well have been one of the kittens born on this occasion. Readers of *The Tale of Genji* will recall the important part played by a cat in the Kashiwagi-Nyosan story. Emperor Ichijō was known to be particularly fond of cats, and there were several in his Palace; few, however, were elevated to the nobility. The events take place in the 3rd Month of 1000. The scene is Ko Ichijō In (Smaller Palace of the First Ward), where the Emperor had been residing for some months owing to a fire in Seiryō Palace.

'Okinamaro[19] where are you?' she cried. 'Come here and bite Lady Myōbu!' The foolish Okinamaro, believing that the nurse was in earnest, rushed at the cat, who, startled and terrified, ran behind the blind in the Imperial Dining Room,[20] where the Emperor happened to be sitting. Greatly surprised, His Majesty picked up the cat and held her in his arms. He summoned his gentlemen-in-waiting. When Tadataka, the Chamberlain, appeared, His Majesty ordered that Okinamaro be chastised and banished to Dog Island. The attendants all started to chase the dog amid great confusion. His Majesty also reproached Lady Uma. 'We shall have to find a new nurse for our cat,' he told her. 'I no longer feel I can count on you to look after her.' Lady Uma bowed; thereafter she no longer appeared in the Emperor's presence.

The Imperial Guards quickly succeeded in catching Okinamaro and drove him out of the Palace grounds. Poor dog! He used to swagger about so happily. Recently, on the third day of the Third Month, when the Controller First Secretary[21] paraded him through the Palace grounds, Okinamaro was adorned with garlands of willow leaves, peach blossoms on his head, and cherry blossoms round his body. How could the dog have imagined that this would be his fate? We all felt sorry for him. 'When Her Majesty was having her meals,' recalled one of the ladies-in-waiting, 'Okinamaro always used to be in attendance and sit opposite us. How I miss him!'

It was about noon, a few days after Okinamaro's banishment, that we heard a dog howling fearfully. How could any dog possibly cry so long! All the other dogs rushed out in excitement to see what was happening. Meanwhile a woman who served as a cleaner in the Palace latrines ran up to us. 'It's terrible,' she said. 'Two of the Chamberlains are flogging a dog. They'll surely kill him. He's being punished for having come back after he was banished. It's Tadataka and Sanefusa who are beating him.' Obviously the victim was Okinamaro. I was absolutely wretched and sent a servant to ask the men to stop; but just then the howling finally ceased. 'He's dead,' one of the servants informed me. 'They've thrown his body outside the gate.'

That evening, while we were sitting in the Palace bemoaning Okinamaro's fate, a wretched-looking dog walked in; he was trembling all over, and his body was fearfully swollen.

'Oh dear,' said one of the ladies-in-waiting. 'Can this be Okinamaro? We haven't seen any other dog like him recently, have we?'

We called to him by name, but the dog did not respond. Some of us insisted that it was Okinamaro, others that it was not. 'Please

19. Roughly translated as "Silly Old Boy."

20. This was the room in which ceremonial meals were served to the Emperor in the mornings and evenings; his real meals were eaten in another room.

21. Fujiwara no Yukinari (971–1027), a successful official and noted calligrapher, with whom Shōnagon was on friendly (if not intimate) terms.

send for Lady Ukon,'[22] said the Empress, hearing our discussion. 'She will certainly be able to tell.' We immediately went to Ukon's room and told her she was wanted on an urgent matter.

'Is this Okinamaro?' the Empress asked her, pointing to the dog.

'Well,' said Ukon, 'it certainly looks like him, but I cannot believe that this loathsome creature is really our Okinamaro. When I called Okinamaro, he always used to come to me, wagging his tail. But this dog does not react at all. No, it cannot be the same one. And besides, wasn't Okinamaro beaten to death and his body thrown away? How could any dog be alive after being flogged by two strong men?' Hearing this, Her Majesty was very unhappy.

When it got dark, we gave the dog something to eat; but he refused it, and we finally decided that this could not be Okinamaro.

On the following morning I went to attend the Empress while her hair was being dressed and she was performing her ablutions. I was holding up the mirror for her when the dog we had seen on the previous evening slunk into the room and crouched next to one of the pillars. 'Poor Okinamaro!' I said. 'He had such a dreadful beating yesterday. How sad to think he is dead! I wonder what body he has been born into this time. Oh, how he must have suffered!'

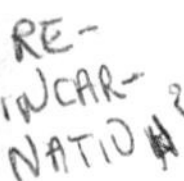

At that moment the dog lying by the pillar started to shake and tremble, and shed a flood of tears. It was astounding. So this really was Okinamaro! On the previous night it was to avoid betraying himself that he had refused to answer to his name. We were immensely moved and pleased. 'Well, well, Okinamaro!' I said, putting down the mirror. The dog stretched himself flat on the floor and yelped loudly, so that the Empress beamed with delight. All the ladies gathered round, and Her Majesty summoned Lady Ukon. When the Empress explained what had happened, everyone talked and laughed with great excitement.

The news reached His Majesty, and he too came to the Empress's room. 'It's amazing,' he said with a smile. 'To think that even a dog has such deep feelings!' When the Emperor's ladies-in-waiting heard the story, they too came along in a great crowd. 'Okinamaro!' we called, and this time the dog rose and limped about the room with his swollen face. 'He must have a meal prepared for him,' I said. 'Yes,' said the Empress, laughing happily, 'now that Okinamaro has finally told us who he is.'

The Chamberlain, Tadataka,[23] was informed, and he hurried along from the Table Room. 'Is it really true?' he asked. 'Please let me see for myself.' I sent a maid to him with the following reply: 'Alas, I am afraid that this is not the same dog after all.' 'Well,'

22. One of the ladies in the Palace Attendant's Office, a bureau of female officials who waited on the Emperor. Almost certainly Ukon recognizes Okinamaro, but pretends that it is a different dog in order to spare him further punishment.

23. I.e., Minamoto no Tadataka, who was responsible for the punishment. He does not enter the Empress's room, but stands outside the blinds, where he cannot actually see the dog.

answered Tadataka, 'whatever you say, I shall sooner or later have occasion to see the animal. You won't be able to hide him from me indefinitely.'

Before long, Okinamaro was granted an Imperial pardon and returning to his former happy state. Yet even now, when I remember how he whimpered and trembled in response to our sympathy, it strikes me as a strange and moving scene; when people talk to me about it, I start crying myself.

10. *On the First Day of the First Month*[24]

On the first day of the First Month and on the third of the Third I like the sky to be perfectly clear.

On the fifth of the Fifth Month I prefer a cloudy sky.

On the seventh day of the Seventh Month[25] it should also be cloudy; but in the evening it should clear, so that the moon shines brightly in the sky and one can almost see the shape of the stars.

On the ninth of the Ninth Month there should be a drizzle from early dawn. Then there will be heavy dew on the chrysanthemums, while the floss silk that covers them will be wet through and drenched also with the precious scent of blossoms. Sometimes the rain stops early in the morning, but the sky is still overcast, and it looks as if it may start raining again at any moment. This too I find very pleasant.

22. *The Sliding Screen in the Back of the Hall*

The sliding screen in the back of the hall in the north-east[26] corner of Seiryō Palace is decorated with paintings of the stormy sea and

24. In this section Shōnagon lists the Five Festivals (*Gosekku*), which in her day were as follows: 1st day of the 1st Month, New Year's Day; 3rd day of the 3rd Month, Peach Festival; 5th day of the 5th Month, Iris Festival; 7th day of the 7th Month, Weaver Festival [see note 25 Ed.]; 9th day of the 9th Month, Chrysanthemum Festival.

25. The Weaver Festival (*Tanabata Matsuri*) is derived from a Chinese legend about the love of the Weaver (Chih-nü) and the Herdsman (Ch'ien-niu), represented by the stars Vega and Altair respectively. Because of her love for the Herdsman, the Weaver neglected her work on the clothes for the gods, while the Herdsman neglected his cattle. As a punishment the Heavenly Emperor put the two stars on opposite sides of the Milky Way, decreeing that they should be allowed to meet only once a year, namely on the 7th day of the 7th Month, when a company of heavenly magpies use their wings to form a bridge that the Weaver can cross to join her lover. The magpies, however, will not make the bridge unless it is a clear night; if it rains, the lovers must wait until the next year. During the Tanabata Festival poems are written in dedication to the two starry lovers, and women pray to the Weaver for skill in weaving, sewing, music, poetry, and other arts. Altars with offerings and incense were set up outside the palaces and private houses in the night of the 7th.

26. *Ushitora* (north-east), lit. ox-tiger, was the unlucky direction according to traditional Chinese beliefs. Directions were frequently named by reference to the Chinese Zodiac. Seiryo Palace, lit. Pure and Fresh Palace, was the normal residence of the reigning Emperor. The Empress's was used when she came from her own palace, the Koki Den, to stay with the Emperor; the sliding screen "protected" the room from the northern veranda of the Palace by scaring away any evil spirits that might be lurking in the vicinity. The terrifying creatures with long arms and legs were, of course, imaginary; they were of Chinese origin.

of the terrifying creatures with long arms and long legs that live there. When the doors of the Empress's room were open, we could always see this screen. One day we were sitting in the room, laughing at the paintings and remarking how unpleasant they were. By the balustrade of the veranda stood a large celadon vase, full of magnificent cherry branches; some of them were as much as five foot long, and their blossoms overflowed to the very foot of the railing. Towards noon the Major Counsellor, Fujiwara no Korechika,[27] arrived. He was dressed in a cherry-coloured Court cloak, sufficiently worn to have lost its stiffness, a white under-robe, and loose trousers of dark purple; from beneath the cloak shone the pattern of another robe of dark red damask. Since His Majesty was present, Korechika knelt on the narrow wooden platform before the door and reported to him on official matters.

A group of ladies-in-waiting was seated behind the bamboo blinds. Their cherry-coloured Chinese jackets hung loosely over their shoulders with the collars pulled back; they wore robes of wistaria, golden yellow, and other colours, many of which showed beneath the blind covering the half-shutter. Presently the noise of the attendants' feet told us that dinner was about to be served in the Daytime Chamber, and we heard cries of 'Make way. Make way.'

The bright, serene day delighted me. When the Chamberlains had brought all the dishes into the Chamber, they came to announce that dinner was ready, and His Majesty left by the middle door. After accompanying the Emperor, Korechika returned to his previous place on the veranda beside the cherry blossoms. The Empress pushed aside her curtain of state and came forward as far as the threshold. We were overwhelmed by the whole delightful scene. It was then that Korechika slowly intoned the words of the old poem,

> The days and the months flow by,
> But Mount Mimoro lasts forever.[28]

Deeply impressed, I wished that all this might indeed continue for a thousand years.

As soon as the ladies serving in the Daytime Chamber had called

27. The elder brother of the Empress. In 996 he was exiled from the capital, ostensibly because of a scandal involving a former Emperor, but in fact because of the rivalry of his uncle, Michinaga. Korechika was noted for his good looks, and many commentators have regarded him as a (or even the) model for the Shining Prince, the hero of *The Tale of Genji*. Korechika figures frequently in Shōnagon's book, but she makes no overt reference to his disgrace.

28. Taken from the *Manyō Shū*, but with a few minor changes. Mimoro, in eastern Yamato, is the site of an ancient Shinto shrine mentioned in the *Kojiki*. The mountain is associated with the idea of the everlasting power promised to the Japanese Imperial line by Shintō deities. Korechika no doubt has in mind the continued prosperity of the Empress, his sister.

for the gentlemen-in-waiting to remove the trays, His Majesty returned to the Empress's room. Then he told me to rub some ink on the inkstone. Dazzled, I felt that I should never be able to take my eyes off his radiant countenance. Next he folded a piece of white paper. 'I should like each of you', he said, 'to copy down on this paper the first ancient poem that comes into your head.'

'How am I going to manage this?' I asked Korechika, who was still out on the veranda.

'Write your poem quickly,' he said, 'and show it to His Majesty. We men must not interfere in this.' Ordering an attendant to take the Emperor's inkstone to each of the women in the room, he told us to make haste. 'Write down any poem you happen to remember,' he said, 'The Naniwazu[29] or whatever else you can think of.'

For some reason I was overcome with timidity; I flushed and had no idea what to do. Some of the other women managed to put down poems about the spring, the blossoms, and such suitable subjects; then they handed me the paper and said, 'Now it's your turn.' Picking up the brush, I wrote the poem that goes,

> The years have passed
> And age has come my way.
> Yet I need only look at this fair flower
> For all my cares to melt away.[30]

I altered the third line, however, to read, 'Yet I need only look upon my lord.'

When he had finished reading, the Emperor said, 'I asked you to write these poems because I wanted to find out how quick you really were.

'A few years ago,' he continued, 'Emperor Enyū[31] ordered all his courtiers to write poems in a notebook. Some excused themselves on the grounds that their handwriting was poor; but the Emperor insisted, saying that he did not care in the slightest about their handwriting or even whether their poems were suitable for the season. So they all had to swallow their embarrassment and produce something for the occasion. Among them was His Excellency, our

29. A Famous poem attributed to the Korean scholar, Wani (who is said to have introduced Chinese writing into Japan), and later to Emperor Nintoku (c. 400). The poem is as follows:

> Ah, this flower that bloomed
> In the port of Naniwa
> And was hidden in the winter months!
> Now that spring is here
> Once more it blossoms forth.

Naniwa is the old name of Osaka; the flower in question is the early-blooming plum blossom. Children in the Heian period were taught the poem for writing practice; accordingly the word *naniwa (zu)* was often used as an equivalent of ABC (e.g., in *The Tale of Genji:* "She still does not know her *naniwazu* properly"); and by extension it could mean "elementary," "uninformed."

30. The original poem is in the *Kokin Shū.*

31. Father and predecessor of Emperor Ichijō.

present Chancellor,[32] who was then Middle Captain of the Third Rank. He wrote down the old poem,

Like the sea that beats
Upon the shores of Izumo
As the tide sweeps in,
Deeper it grows and deeper—
The love I bear for you.[33]

But he changed the last line to read, "The love I bear my lord!", and the Emperor was full of praise.'

When I heard His Majesty tell this story, I was so overcome that I felt myself perspiring. It occurred to me that no younger woman would have been able to use my poem[34] and I felt very lucky. This sort of test can be a terrible ordeal: it often happens that people who usually write fluently are so overawed that they actually make mistakes in their characters.

Next the Empress placed a notebook of *Kokin Shū* poems before her and started reading out the first three lines of each one, asking us to supply the remainder.[35] Among them were several famous poems that we had in our minds day and night; yet for some strange reason we were often unable to fill in the missing lines. Lady Saishō,[36] for example, could manage only ten, which hardly qualified her as knowing her *Kokin Shū*. Some of the other women, even less successful, could remember only about half-a-dozen poems. They would have done better to tell the Empress quite simply that thye had forgotten the lines; instead they came out with great lamentations like 'Oh dear, how could we have done so badly in answering the questions that Your Majesty was pleased to put to us?'—all of which I found rather absurd.

When no one could complete a particular poem, the Empress continued reading to the end. This produced further wails from the women: 'Oh, we all knew that one! How could we be so stupid?'

'Those of you', said the Empress, 'who had taken the trouble to copy out the *Kokin Shū* several times would have been able to complete every single poem I have read. In the reign of Emperor

32. Fujiwara no Michitaka (953–95). The Kampaku [Chancellor] who was invariably the head of the northern branch of the Fujiwara family, was the real ruler of Japan during most of the tenth and eleventh centuries. He was the elder brother of Michinaga and the father of the Empress Sadako.

33. The origin of this old love-poem is unknown. There is a play on words on *Izumo* (province on the Japan Sea) and *itsu mo* (ever). *Kimi* has the double meaning of (i) you (intimate), (ii) Lord, Emperor.

34. Because of its reference to having grown old. Shōnagon had now reached the ripe age of about thirty and was therefore, by Heian standards, well into her middle years.

35. Guessing games of this type were extremely popular.

36. Granddaughter of Fujiwara no Akitada; she was a lady-in-waiting to Empress Sadako. Despite her difficulties with the *Kokin Shū*, Saishō rivalled Sei Shōnagon in readiness of wit and she frequently appears in *The Pillow Book* (see *Pillow Book*, p. 129).

Murakami there was a woman at Court known as the Imperial Lady of Senyo Palace. She was the daughter of the Minister of the Left who lived in the Smaller Palace of the First Ward, and of course you have all heard of her. When she was still a young girl, her father gave her this advice: "First you must study penmanship. Next you must learn to play the seven-string zither better than anyone else. And also you must memorize all the poems in the twenty volumes of the *Kokin Shū*."

'Emperor Murakami,'[37] continued Her Majesty, 'had heard this story and remembered it years later when the girl had grown up and become an Imperial Concubine. Once, on a day of abstinence, he came into her room, hiding a notebook of *Kokin Shū* poems in the folds of his robe. He surprised her by seating himself behind a curtain of state; then, opening the book, he asked, "Tell me the verse written by such-and-such a poet, in such-and-such a year and on such-and-such an occasion."[38] The lady understood what was afoot and that it was all in fun, yet the possibility of making a mistake or forgetting one of the poems must have worried her greatly. Before beginning the test, the Emperor had summoned a couple of ladies-in-waiting who were particularly adept in poetry and told them to mark each incorrect reply by a *go* stone.[39] What a splendid scene it must have been! You know, I really envy anyone who attended that Emperor even as a lady-in-waiting.

'Well,' Her Majesty went on, 'he then began questioning her. She answered without any hesitation, just giving a few words or phrases to show that she knew each poem. And never once did she make a mistake. After a time the Emperor began to resent the lady's flawless memory and decided to stop as soon as he detected any error or vagueness in her replies. Yet, after he had gone through ten books of the *Kokin Shū*, he had still not caught her out. At this stage he declared that it would be useless to continue. Marking where he had left off, he went to bed. What a triumph for the lady!

'He slept for some time. On waking, he decided that he must have a final verdict and that if he waited until the following day to examine her on the other ten volumes, she might use the time to

37. Grandfather of the reigning Emperor. The woman in question was Fujiwara no Yoshiko, a great favorite of the Emperor Murakami; she was noted both for her poetic talents and for her beauty, especially her long hair.

38. The poems in the anthologies were usually provided with short notes or introductions (*kotobagaki*) explaining the circumstances in which they had been written. It was these that Emperor Murakami read to Yoshiko. In identifying the poem, Lady Yoshiko simply recited a few words to show that she recognized it; this was regarded as far more elegant than repeating the entire poem.

39. A fascinating, complicated game, introduced from China in the eighth century. It is played with black and white stones on a board with 361 intersections (19 x 19). The two players take their turns placing their stone on any suitable intersection. Once a stone has been placed, it cannot be moved to another intersection; stones that have been encircled by the enemy, however, are forfeit unless they are so placed that they themselves enclose at least two independent and viable openings or "eyes" (*me*). *Go* stones were frequently used as counters for scoring games and contests.

refresh her memory. So he would have to settle the matter that very night. Ordering his attendants to bring up the bedroom lamp, he resumed his questions. By the time he had finished all twenty volumes, the night was well advanced; and still the lady had not made a mistake.

'During all this time His Excellency, the lady's father, was in a state of great agitation. As soon as he was informed that the Emperor was testing his daughter, he sent his attendants to various temples to arrange for special recitations of the Scriptures. Then he turned in the direction of the Imperial Palace and spent a long time in prayer. Such enthusiasm for poetry is really rather moving.'

The Emperor, who had been listening to the whole story, was much impressed. 'How can he possibly have read so many poems?' he remarked when Her Majesty has finished. 'I doubt whether I could get through three or four volumes. But of course things have changed. In the old days even people of humble station had a taste for the arts and were interested in elegant pastimes. Such a story would hardly be possible nowadays, would it?'

The ladies in attendance on Her Majesty and the Emperor's own ladies-in-waiting who had been admitted into Her Maejsty's presence began chatting eagerly, and as I listened I felt that my cares had really 'melted away.'[40]

24. *Depressing Things*

A dog howling in the daytime. A wickerwork fish-net in spring.[41] A red plum-blossom dress in the Third or Fourth Months. A lying-in room when the baby has died. A cold, empty brazier. An ox-driver who hates his oxen. A scholar whose wife has one girl child after another.

One has gone to a friend's house to avoid an unlucky direction,[42] but nothing is done to entertain one; if this should happen at the time of a Seasonal Change, it is still more depressing.

A letter arrives from the provinces, but no gift accompanies it. It would be bad enough if such a letter reached one in the provinces

40. Shōnagon refers to the poem from the *Kokin Shū* that she had quoted earlier.

41. These nets were designed for catching whitebait (*hio*) during the winter; in spring-time they were useless. Scholarly activities, like most other specialized occupations, tended to run in families; and they were not considered suitable for girls.

42. *Katatagae* (avoidance of an unlucky direction): when a Master of Divination informed one that a certain direction (e.g. north) was "blocked up" by one of the invisible moving deities that were central to Heian superstition, one might circumvent the danger by first proceeding in a different direction (e.g. west); after stopping on the way at an intermediate place and staying there at least until midnight, one would continue to one's intended destination (e.g. by going north-east). People would also leave their house for a *katatagae* because they wished to obtain release from some future taboo, abstinence, or prohibition, even though they had no particular desire to go anywhere at the time.

from someone in the capital; but then at least it would have interesting news about goings-on in society, and that would be a consolation.

One has written a letter, taking pains to make it as attractive as possible,[43] and now one impatiently awaits the reply. 'Surely the messenger should be back by now,' one thinks. Just then he returns; but in his hand he carries, not a reply, but one's own letter, still twisted or knotted as it was sent, but now so dirty and crumpled that even the ink-mark on the outside has disappeared. 'Not at home,' announces the messenger, or else, 'They said they were observing a day of abstinence and would not accept it.' Oh, how depressing!

Again, one has sent one's carriage to fetch someone who had said he would definitely pay one a visit on that day. Finally it returns with a great clatter, and the servants hurry out with cries of 'Here they come!' But next one hears the carriage being pulled into the coach-house, and the unfastened shafts clatter to the ground. 'What does this mean?' one asks. 'The person was not at home,' replies the driver, 'and will not be coming.' So saying, he leads the ox back to its stall, leaving the carriage in the coach-house.

With much bustle and excitement a young man has been adopted into a family as the daughter's husband. One day he fails to come home, and it turns out that some high-ranking Court lady has taken him as her lover. How depressing! 'Will he eventually tire of the woman and come back to us?' his wife's family wonder ruefully.

The nurse who is looking after a baby leaves the house, saying that she will be back presently. Soon the child starts crying for her. One tries to comfort it by games and other diversions, and even sends a message to the nurse telling her to return immediately. Then comes her reply; 'I am afraid that I cannot be back this evening.' This is not only depressing; it is no less than hateful. Yet how much more distressed must be the young man who has sent a messenger to fetch a lady friend and who awaits her arrival in vain!

It is quite late at night and a woman has been expecting a visitor. Hearing finally a stealthy tapping, she sends her maid to open the gate and lies waiting excitedly. But the name announced by the maid is that of someone with whom she has absolutely no connexion. Of all the depressing things this is by far the worst.

With a look of complete self-confidence on his face an exorcist prepares to expel an evil spirit from his patient. Handing his mace,

43. Apart from official correspondence the two main types of formal letters were *musubibumi* (knotted) and *tatebumi* (twisted). Both were folded lengthwise into a narrow strip; but, whereas the *musubibumi* was knotted in the middle or at one end, sometimes with a sprig of blossoms stuck into the knot, the latter was twisted at both ends and tended to be narrower. A few thick lines of ink were drawn over the knot or fold by way of a seal.

rosary, and other paraphernalia to the medium who is assisting him, he begins to recite his spells in the special shrill tone that he forces from his throat on such occasions. For all the exorcist's efforts, the spirit gives no sign of leaving, and the Guardian Demon fails to take possession of the medium.[44] The relations and friends of the patient, who are gathered in the room praying, find this rather unfortunate. After he has recited his incantations for the length of an entire watch, the exorcist is worn out. 'The Guardian Demon is completely inactive,' he tells his medium. 'You may leave.' Then, as he takes back his rosary, he adds, 'Well, well, it hasn't worked!' He passes his hand over his forehead, then yawns deeply (he of all people) and leans back against a pillar for a nap.

Most depressing is the household of some hopeful candidate who fails to receive a post during the period of official appointments. Hearing that the gentleman was bound to be successful, several people have gathered in his house for the occasion; among them are a number of retainers who served him in the past but who since then have either been engaged elsewhere or moved to some remote province. Now they are all eager to accompany their former master on his visit to the shrines and temples, and their carriages pass to and fro in the courtyard. Indoors there is great commotion as the hangers-on help themselves to food and drink. Yet the dawn of the last day of the appointments arrives and still no one has knocked at the gate. The people in the house are nervous and prick up their ears.

Presently they hear the shouts of fore-runners and realize that the high dignitaries are leaving the Palace. Some of the servants were sent to the Palace on the previous evening to hear the news and have been waiting all night, tremling with cold; now they come trudging back listlessly. The attendants who have remained faithfully in the gentleman's service year after year cannot bring themselves to ask what has happened. His former retainers, however, are not so diffident. 'Tell us,' they say, 'what appointment did his Excellency receive?' 'Indeed,' murmur the servants, 'His Excellency was Governor of such-and-such a province.'[45] Everyone was counting on his receiving a new appointment, and is desolated by this failure. On the following day the people who had crowded into the house begin to slink away in twos and threes. The old attendants,

44. The aim of the exorcist was to transfer the evil spirit from the afflicted person to the medium (*yorimashi*), who was usually a young girl or woman, and to force it to declare itself. He made use of various spells and incantations so that the medium might be possessed by the Guardian Demon of Buddhism (*Gohō-dōji*). When he was successful, the medium would tremble, scream, have convulsions, faint, or behave as if in a hypnotic trance. The spirit would then declare itself through her mouth. The final step was to drive the spirit out of the medium. On watch is two hours.

45. The messengers cannot bear to announce in so many words that their master has failed to obtain an appointment; instead they answer by giving his existing title.

however, cannot leave so easily. They walk restlessly about the house, counting on their fingers the provincial appointments that will become available in the following year. Pathetic and depressing in the extreme!

One has sent a friend a verse that turned out fairly well. How depressing when there is no reply-poem![46] Even in the case of love poems, people should at least answer that they were moved at receiving the message, or something of the sort; otherwise they will cause the keenest disappointment.

Someone who lives in a bustling, fashionable household receives a message from an elderly person who is behind the times and has very little to do; the poem, of course, is old-fashioned and dull. How depressing!

One needs a particularly beautiful fan for some special occasion and instructs an artist, in whose talents one has full confidence, to decorate one with an appropriate painting. When the day comes and the fan is delivered, one is shocked to see how badly it has been painted. Oh, the dreariness of it!

A messenger[47] arrives with a present at a house where a child has been born or where someone is about to leave on a journey. How depressing for him if he gets no reward! People should always reward a messenger, though he may bring only herbal balls or hare-sticks. If he expects nothing, he will be particularly pleased to be rewarded. On the other hand, what a terrible let-down if he arrives with a self-important look on his face, his heart pounding in anticipation of a generous reward, only to have his hopes dashed!

A man has been adopted as a son-in-law; yet even now, after some five years of marriage, the lying-in room has remained as quiet as on the day of his arrival.

An elderly couple who have several grown-up children, and who may even have some grandchildren crawling about the house, are

46. When one received a poem, it was *de rigueur* to reply promptly by a "return" poem (*kaeshiuta*) in which one would normally ring the changes on some central image. A failure to reply (or at least to have a friend, relation, colleague, etc. make a reply in one's place) was regarded as the height of rudeness. It was socially permissible not to answer love poems, but this of course signified that one was totally uninterested in the sender.

47. On the 3rd, 5th, and 7th days after a child's birth it was customary for the grandparents and other members of the family to send presents of swaddling-clothes, etc., known as *ubuyashinai*. Presents were also given to people leaving on a journey. Messengers were originally rewarded by having a gift of clothing. *Kusudama* (herbal balls): during the Iris Festival various kinds of herbs were bound into balls and put into round cotton or silk bags, which were hung on the pillars, curtains, etc., to protect the inhabitants of the house from illness and other misfortunes. A close Western equivalent is the asafoetida bag, worn around the neck to ward off illness. *Uzuchi* (hare-sticks) were three-inch sticks with long, coloured tassels presented at the New Year to keep away evil spirits. They were hung on pillars in the Palace and in the houses of the nobility on the 4th of the month which corresponded to the 1st Day of the Hare. Both the herbal balls and the hare-sticks were of Chinese origin.

taking a nap in the daytime.[48] The children who see them in this state are overcome by a forlorn feeling, and for other people it is all very depressing.

To take a hot bath when one has just woken is not only depressing; it actually puts one in a bad humour.

Persistent rain on the last day of the year.[49]

One has been observing a period of fast, but neglects it for just one day—most depressing.[50]

A white under-robe in the Eighth Month.[51]

A wet-nurse who has run out of milk.

27. *Hateful Things*

One is in a hurry to leave, but one's visitor keeps chattering away. If it is someone of no importance, one can get rid of him by saying, 'You must tell me all about it next time'; but, should it be the sort of visitor whose presence commands one's best behaviour, the situation is hateful indeed.

One finds that a hair has got caught in the stone on which one is rubbing one's inkstick, or again that gravel is lodged in the inkstick, making a nasty, grating sound.

Someone has suddenly fallen ill and one summons the exorcist. Since he is not at home, one has to send messengers to look for him. After one has had a long fretful wait, the exorcist finally arrives, and with a sigh of relief one asks him to start his incantations. But perhaps he has been exorcizing too many evil spirits recently; for hardly has he installed himself and begun praying when his voice becomes drowsy. Oh, how hateful!

A man who has nothing in particular to recommend him discusses all sorts of subjects at random as though he knew everything.

An elderly person warms the palms of his hands over a brazier and stretches out the wrinkles. No young man would dream of behaving in such a fashion; old people can really be quite shameless. I have seen some dreary old creatures actually resting their feet on the brazier and rubbing them against the edge while they speak. These are the kind of people who in visiting someone's house first use their fans to wipe away the dust from the mat and, when they finally sit on it, cannot stay still but are forever spreading out the

48. There was a strong prejudice against taking naps in the daytime; the practice was considered especially undignified and unaesthetic for elderly people.

49. Because it interferes with many New Year's celebrations.

50. Fasting was enjoined by the Buddhist church on the 8th, 14th, 15th, 23rd, 29th, and 30th of each month. People who wished to expiate serious offenses would take longer fasts. The efficiacy of the entire fast was sacrificed if one violated the restrictions for a single day.

51. A white under-robe was normally only worn in the summer months. As a rule Shōnagon and her contemporaries strongly disapproved of anything that deviated from the seasonal or diurnal routines.

front of their hunting costume or even tucking it up under their knees. One might suppose that such behaviour were restricted to people of humble station; but I have observed it in quite well-bred people, including a Senior Secretary of the Fifth Rank in the Ministry of Ceremonial and a former Governor of Suruga.[52]

I hate the sight of men in their cups who shout, poke their fingers in their mouths, stroke their beards, and pass on the wine to their neighbours with great cries of 'Have some more! Drink up!' They tremble, shake their heads, twist their faces, and gesticulate like children who are singing, 'We're off to see the Governor,'[53] I have seen really well-bred people behave like this and I find it most distasteful.

To envy others and to complain about one's own lot; to speak badly about people; to be inquisitive about the most trivial matters and to resent and abuse people for not telling one, or, if one does manage to worm out some facts, to inform everyone in the most detailed fashion as if one had known all from the beginning—oh, how hateful!

One is just about to be told some interesting piece of news when a baby starts crying.

A flight of crows circle about with loud caws.

An admirer has come on a clandestine visit, but a dog catches sight of him and starts barking. One feels like killing the beast.

One has been foolish enough to invite a man to spend the night in an unsuitable place—and then he starts snoring.

A gentleman has visited one secretly. Though he is wearing a tall, lacquered hat, he nevertheless wants no one to see him. He is so flurried, in fact, that upon leaving he bangs into something with his hat. Most hateful! It is annoying too when he lifts up the Iyo blind[54] that hangs at the entrance of the room, then lets it fall with a great rattle. If it is a head-blind, things are still worse, for being more solid it makes a terrible noise when it is dropped. There is no excuse for such carelessness. Even a head-blind does not make any noise if one lifts it up gently on entering and leaving the room; the same applies to sliding-doors. If one's movements are rough, even a paper door will bend and resonate when opened; but, if one lifts the door a little while pushing it, there need be no sound.

One has gone to bed and is about to doze off when a mosquito appears, announcing himself in a reedy voice. One can actually feel the wind made by his wings and, slight though it is, one finds it hateful in the extreme.

52. Province in the Tōkaidō corresponding to modern Shizuoka Prefecture.

53. The song, though evidently popular in Shōnagon's time, is no longer extant. It was apparently sung by children to the accompaniment of certain conventional gestures.

54. The Iyo blind was a rough type of reed blind; the head blind was a more elegant type of blind that was decorated with strips of silk on the top and edges and was heavier than ordinary blinds.

A carriage passes with a nasty, creaking noise. Annoying to think that the passengers may not even be aware of this! If I am travelling in someone's carriage and I hear it creaking, I dislike not only the noise but also the owner of the carriage.

One is in the middle of a story when someone butts in and tries to show that he is the only clever person in the room. Such a person is hateful, and so, indeed, is anyone, child or adult, who tries to push himself forward.

One is telling a story about old times when someone breaks in with a little detail that he happens to know, implying that one's own version is inaccurate—disgusting behaviour!

Very hateful is a mouse that scurries all over the place.

Some children have called at one's house. One makes a great fuss of them and gives them toys to play with. The children become accustomed to this treatment and start to come regularly, forcing their way into one's inner rooms and scattering one's furnishings and possessions. Hateful!

A certain gentleman whom one does not want to see visits one at home or in the Palace, and one pretends to be asleep. But a maid comes to tell one and shakes one awake, with a look on her face that says, 'What a sleepyhead!' Very hateful.

A newcomer pushes ahead of the other members in a group; with a knowing look, this person starts laying down the law and forcing advice upon everyone—most hateful.

A man with whom one is having an affair keeps singing the praises of some woman he used to know. Even if it is a thing of the past, this can be very annoying. How much more so if he is still seeing the woman! (Yet sometimes I find that it is not as unpleasant as all that.)

A person who recites a spell himself after sneezing.[55] In fact I detest anyone who sneezes, except the master of the house.

Fleas, too, are very hateful. When they dance about under someone's clothes, they really seem to be lifting them up.

The sound of dogs when they bark for a long time in chorus is ominous and hateful.

I cannot stand people who leave without closing the panel behind them.

How I detest the husbands of nurse-maids! It is not so bad if the child in the maid's charge is a girl, because then the man will keep his distance. But, if it is a boy, he will behave as though he were the father. Never letting the boy out of his sight, he insists on managing everything. He regards the other attendants in the house as

55. Sneezing was a bad omen, and it was normal to counteract its effects by reciting some auspicious formula, such as wishing long life to the person who had sneezed (cf. "Bless you!" in the West). Shōnagon does not like the sneezer himself to utter the auspicious words.

less than human, and, if anyone tries to scold the child, he slanders him to the master. Despite this disgraceful behaviour, no one dare accuse the husband; so he strides about the house with a proud, self-important look, giving all the orders.

I hate people whose letters show that they lack respect for worldly civilities, whether by discourtesy in the phrasing or by extreme politeness to someone who does not deserve it. This sort of thing is, of course, particularly odious should the letter be addressed to oneself.

As a matter of fact, most people are too casual, not only in their letters but in their direct conversation. Sometimes I am quite disgusted at noting how little decorum people observe when talking to each other. It is particularly unpleasant to hear some foolish man or woman omit the proper marks of respect when addressing a person of quality; and, when servants fail to use honorific forms of speech in referring to their masters, it is very bad indeed. No less odious, however, are those masters who, in addressing their servants, use such phrases as 'When you were good enough to do such-and-such' or 'As you so kindly remarked'. No doubt there are some masters who, in describing their own actions to a servant, say, 'I presumed to do so-and-so'!

Sometimes a person who is utterly devoid of charm will try to create a good impression by using very elegant language; yet he only succeeds in being ridiculous. No doubt he believes this refined language to be just what the occasion demands, but, when it goes so far that everyone bursts out laughing, surely something must be wrong

It is most improper to address high-ranking courtiers, Imperial Advisers, and the like simply by using their names without any titles or marks of respect; but such mistakes are fortunately rare.

If one refers to the maid who is in attendance on some lady-in-waiting as 'Madam' or 'that lady', she will be surprised, delighted, and lavish in her praise.

When speaking to young noblemen and courtiers of high rank, one should always (unless Their Majesties are present) refer to them by their official posts. Incidentally, I have been very shocked to hear important people use the word 'I' while conversing in Their Majesties' presence.[56] Such a breach of etiquette is really distressing, and I fail to see why people cannot avoid it.

A man who has nothing in particular to recommend him but who speaks in an affected tone and poses as being elegant.

56. Etiquette demanded that in the presence of the Emperor or Empress one referred to oneself by one's name rather than by the first person singular. One referred to other people by their real names; if Their Majesties were not present, however, one referred to these people by their offices. On the whole, personal pronouns were avoided, and this added to the importance of correct honorific usage.

An inkstone with such a hard, smooth surface that the stick glides over it without leaving any deposit of ink.

Ladies-in-waiting who want to know everything that is going on.

Sometimes one greatly dislikes a person for no particular reason —and then that person goes and does something hateful.

A gentleman who travels alone in his carriage to see a procession or some other spectacle. What sort of a man is he? Even though he may be a person of the greatest quality, surely he should have taken along a few of the many young men who are anxious to see the sights. But no, there he sits by himself (one can see his silhouette through the blinds), with a proud look on his face, keeping all his impressions to himself.

A lover who is leaving at dawn announces that he has to find his fan and his paper.[57] 'I know I put them somewhere last night,' he says. Since it is pitch dark, he gropes about the room, bumping into the furniture and muttering, 'Strange' Where on earth can they be?' Finally he discovers the objects. He thrusts the paper into the breast of his robe with a great rustling sound; then he snaps open his fan and busily fans away with it. Only now is he ready to take his leave. What charmless behaviour! 'Hateful' is an understatement.

Equally disagreeable is the man who, when leaving in the middle of the night, takes care to fasten the cord of his head-dress. This is quite unnecessary; he could perfectly well put it gently on his head without tying the cord. And why must he spend time adjusting his cloak or hunting costume? Does he really think someone may see him at this time of night and criticize him for not being impeccably dressed?

A good lover will behave as elegantly at dawn as at any other time. He drags himself out of bed with a look of dismay on his face. The lady urges him on: 'Come, my friend, it's getting light. You don't want anyone to find you here.' He gives a deep sigh, as if to say that the night has not been nearly long enough and that it is agony to leave. Once up, he does not instantly pull on his trousers. Instead he comes close to the lady and whispers whatever was left unsaid during the night. Even when he is dressed, he still lingers, vaguely pretending to be fastening his sash.

Presently he raises the lattice, and the two lovers stand together by the side door while he tells her how he dreads the coming day, which will keep them apart; then he slips away. The lady watches him go, and this moment of parting will remain among her most charming memories.

57. *Futokorogami* (paper): elegant coloured paper that gentlemen carried in the folds of their clothes. It served for writing and was used like a *hanagami* in more recent times (see Saikaku Ihara, *The Life of an Amorous Woman*, tr. Ivan Morris, note 134).

Indeed, one's attachment to a man depends largely on the elegance of his leave-taking. When he jumps out of bed, scurries about the room, tightly fastens his trouser-sash, rolls up the sleeves of his Court cloak, over-robe, or hunting costume, stuffs his belongings into the breast of his robe and then briskly secures the outer sash—one really begins to hate him.

30. *Things That Arouse a Fond Memory of the Past*

Dried hollyhock. The objects used during the Display of Dolls. To find a piece of deep violet or grape-coloured material that has been pressed between the pages of a notebook.[58]

It is a rainy day and one is feeling bored. To pass the time, one starts looking through some old papers. And then one comes across the letters of a man one used to love.

Last year's paper fan.[59] A night with a clear moon.

31. *Things That Give a Pleasant Feeling*

A set of well-executed pictures of women, accompanied by interesting texts.[60]

The return journey from a festival, with a large number of escorts in attendance. The costumes of the women passengers spill out at the sides of the carriage, and, thanks to the skill of the ox-drivers, the carriages run smoothly along the road.

On a pretty sheet of white Michinoku paper someone has written a letter with a brush that would not seem capable of making such delicate strokes.

The sight of a boat as it glides downstream.

Well-blackened teeth.[61]

58. The Kamo Festival was also known as the Hollyhock Festival (Aoi Matsuri). During the celebrations, hollyhock was attached to pillars, blinds, etc. and left there until it withered and fell off. Hollyhock was also used to decorate people's hair and headdresses. The piece of material which turns up in the notebook has been used in years past at the Festival.

59. *Kawahori* (paper fan): a fan covered with paper on one side of the frame and used in the summer months. It looked like a bat with spread-out wings. Coming upon this fan, perhaps during the winter, Shōnagon is reminded of something that happened in the summer. In Japan, as in China, the moon traditionally evokes memories of the past.

60. *Onnae* (pictures of women) possibly refers to erotic drawings, but we have no extant examples from the Heian period.

61. *Hagurome* (blackened teeth): the earliest mention of the curious custom dates from the tenth century, but it is far older and may have its origins in the South Sea Islands. At first it was practised only by women of the aristocracy, but later it spread to men and to the lower classes. In the Muromachi period girls who had reached the age of eight blackened their teeth as a sign of adulthood. In Edo times it became the mark of a married woman. The custom persisted among women in rural districts until quite recently. The usual method of producing the dye was to soak bits of iron in a solution of tea or vinegar mixed with powdered gallnut. For such readers as may be interested in practising the fashion, A. B. Mitford (Lord Redesdale) gives the prescription in detail (*Tales of Old Japan,* London, 1888, p. 374). [See p. 662—Editor.]

To throw equal numbers repeatedly in a game of dice.[62]

Fine strands of silk that have been entwined.

A skilled Master of Divination performs a purification service on a river bank.[63]

A drink of water when one wakes up at night.

One is in a rather bored mood when a visitor arrives—a man with whom one's relations are neither too intimate nor too distant. He tells one what has been happening in society, things pleasant and disagreeable and strange; moving from one topic to another, he discusses matters both public and private—and all in so clear a fashion that there is no possibility of misunderstanding. This gives one a very pleasant feeling.

One has visited a shrine or a temple with the request that certain prayers be said on one's behalf. What a pleasure to hear the ritualist or priest intone them in a better voice, and more fluently, than one had expected!

33. *Oxen Should Have Very Small Foreheads*

Oxen should have very small foreheads with white hair; their underbellies, the ends of their legs, and the tips of their tails should also be white.

I like horses to be chestnut, piebald, dapple-grey, or black roan, with white patches near their shoulders and feet; I also like horses with light chestnut coats and extremely white manes and tails—so white, indeed, that their hair looks like mulberry threads.

I like a cat whose back is black and all the rest white.

35. *A Preacher Ought to Be Good-Looking*

A preacher ought to be good-looking. For, if we are properly to understand his worthy sentiments, we must keep our eyes on him while he speaks; should we look away, we may forget to listen. Accordingly an ugly preacher may well be the source of sin. . . .

But I really must stop writing this kind of thing. If I were still young enough, I might risk the consequence of putting down such impieties, but at my present stage of life I should be less flippant.[64]

Some people, on hearing that a priest is particularly venerable and pious, rush off to the temple where he is preaching, determined

62. *Chōbami* (dice) was played with the dice normally used in *sugoroku* (backgammon). If a player threw dice of the same number, he won the turn and picked up the dice-box for another throw; if the numbers were different, his opponent picked up the box.

63. Purification services (*suso no harae*) were performed to ward off bad luck that might otherwise ensue as the result of some enemy's curse (*suso*); they often took place by rivers, because it was believed that the current would carry away the evil.

64. Lit., "If my age were [more] appropriate, I should probably write words that would expose me to such sin."

to arrive before anyone else. They, too, are liable to bring a load of sin on themselves and would do better to stay away.

In earlier times men who had retired from the post of Chamberlain[65] did not ride at the head of Imperial processions; in fact, during the year of their retirement they hardly ever appeared outside their houses, and did not dream of showing themselves in the precincts of the Palace. Things seem to have changed. Nowadays they are known as 'Fifth Rank Chamberlains' and given all sorts of official jobs.

Even so, time often hangs heavily on their hands, especially when they recall their busy days in active service. Though these Fifth Rank Chamberlains keep the fact to themselves, they know they have a good deal of leisure. Men like this frequently repair to temples and listen to the popular priests, such visits eventually becoming a habit. One will find them there even on hot summer days, decked out in bright linen robes, with loose trousers of light violet or bluish grey spread about them. Sometimes they will have taboo tags[66] attached to their black lacquered headdresses. Far from preferring to stay at home on such inauspicious days, they apparently believe that no harm can come to anyone bent on so worthy an errand. They arrive hastily, converse with the priest, look inside the carriages that are being lined up outside the temple, and take an interest in everything.

Now a couple of gentlemen who have not met for some time run into each other in the temple, and are greatly surprised. They sit down together and chat away, nodding their heads, exchanging funny stories, and opening their fans wide to hold before their faces so as to laugh the more freely. Toying with their elegantly decorated rosaries, they glance about, criticizing some defect they have noticed in one of the carriages or praising the elegance of another. They discuss various services that they have recently attended and compare the skill of different priests in performing the Eight Lessons or the Dedication of Sutras.[67] Meanwhile, of course, they pay not the slightest attention to the service actually in progress. To be sure, it would not interest them very much; for they have heard it

65. Shōnagon refers here to relatively low-ranking members of the Emperor's Private Office.

66. A sign made of willow-wood and hung outside one's house on days of abstinence to warn possible visitors. If one was obliged to venture abroad on one of these days, one would wear such a tag on one's head-dress (men) or sleeve (women).

67. *Hakkō* (Eight Lessons): a series of eight services in which the eight volumes of the *Lotus Sutra* were expounded. The commentary normally took the form of a catechism, in which one priest would ask questions about important sections of the sutra and another would reply. *Kyō Kuyō* (Dedication of Sutras) refers to the practice of ordering copies of the sutra to be made and dedicated to some person or institution or to the Three Treasures (*Sambō*), the Buddha, the Law, and the Priesthood. The Chinese characters were usually written in silver or gold on heavy white or dark-blue paper. After the copy was completed, the sutra would be recited in a special service of dedication.

all so often that the priest's words could no longer make any impression.

After the priest has been on his dais for some time, a carriage stops outside the temple. The outriders clear the way in a somewhat perfunctory fashion, and the passengers get out. They are slender young gentlemen, clad either in hunting costumes or in Court cloaks that look lighter than a cicada's wings, loose trousers, and unlined robes of raw silk. As they enter the temple, accompanied by an equal number of attendants, the worshippers, including those who have been there since the beginning of the service, move back to make room for them; the young men install themselves at the foot of a pillar near the dais. As one would expect from such people, they now make a great show of rubbing their rosaries and prostrating themselves in prayer. The priest, convinced by the sight of the newcomers that this is a grand occasion, launches out on an impressive sermon that he presumes will make his name in society. But no sooner have the young men settled down and finished touching their heads on the floor than they begin to think about leaving at the first opportunity. Two of them steal glances at the women's carriages outside, and it is easy to imagine what they are saying to each other. They recognize one of the women and admire her elegance; then, catching sight of a stranger, they discuss who she can be. I find it fascinating to see such goings-on in a temple.

Often one hears exchanges like this: 'There was a service at such-and-such a temple where they did the Eight Lessons.' 'Was Lady So-and-So present?' 'Of course. How could she possibly have missed it?' It is really too bad that they should always answer like this.

One would imagine that it would be all right for ladies of quality to visit temples and take a discreet look at the preacher's dais. After all, even women of humble station may listen devoutly to religious sermons. Yet in the old days ladies almost never walked to temples to attend sermons; on the rare visits that they did undertake they had to wear elegant travelling costume, as when making proper pilgrimages to shrines and temples. If people of those times had lived long enough to see the recent conduct in the temples, how they would have criticized the women of our day!

38. *It Is So Stiflingly Hot*

It is so stiflingly hot in the Seventh Month that even at night one keeps all the doors and lattices open. At such times it is delightful to wake up when the moon is shining and to look outside. I enjoy it even when there is no moon. But to wake up at dawn and see a pale sliver of a moon in the sky—well, I need hardly say how perfect that is.

I like to see a bright new straw mat that has just been spread out on a well-polished floor.[68] The best place for one's three-foot curtain of state is in the front of the room near the veranda. It is pointless to put it in the rear of the room, as it is most unlikely that anyone will peer in from that direction.

It is dawn and a woman is lying in bed after her lover has taken his leave. She is covered up to her head with a light mauve robe that has a lining of dark violet; the colour of both the outside and the lining is fresh and glossy. The woman, who appears to be asleep, wears an unlined orange robe and a dark crimson skirt of stiff silk whose cords hang loosely by her side, as if they have been left untied.[69] Her thick tresses tumble over each other in cascades, and one can imagine how long her hair must be when it falls freely down her back.

Near by another woman's lover is making his way home in the misty dawn. He is wearing loose violet trousers, an orange hunting costume, so lightly coloured that one can hardly tell whether it has been dyed or not, a white robe of stiff silk, and a scarlet robe of glossy, beaten silk. His clothes, which are damp from the mist, hang loosely about him. From the dishevelment of his side locks one can tell how negligently he must have tucked his hair into his black lacquered head-dress when he got up. He wants to return and write his next-morning letter before the dew on the morning glories has had time to vanish;[70] but the path seems endless, and to divert himself he hums 'the sprouts in the flax fields'.[71]

68. In the Heian period rooms were not covered with straw mats (*tatami*) as became normal in later times; instead mats were spread out when and where they were needed for sleeping, sitting, etc.

69. It was customary in Shōnagon's time to use clothes as bed-covers; also it was normal to sleep fully dressed. The two sets of clothing described in this paragraph are, respectively, the woman's bedclothes and her dress. Heian women usually let their long, thick hair hang loosely down their backs. The closer it reached the floor, the more beautiful they were considered. For the aesthetic significance of women's hair, see Morris, *The World of the Shining Prince*, London, 1964, p. 203.

70. It was an essential part of Heian etiquette for the man to write a love-letter to the lady with whom he had spent the night; it usually included a poem and was attached to a spray of some appropriate flower. The letter had to be sent as soon as the man returned home or, if he was on duty, as soon as he reached his office. The lady was expected of course to send a prompt reply. If the man failed to send the letter, it normally meant that he had no desire to continue the liaison.

71. From a *Kokin Rokujō* poem:

> The sprouts of the cherry-flax,
> In the flax fields
> Are heavy now with dew.
> I shall stay with you till dawn
> Though your parents be aware.

The expression "cherry-flax" is found in a similar poem in the *Manyō Shū* and refers (i) to the fact that flax was sown at the same time that the cherries blossomed, (ii) to the similarity in appearance between cherry blossoms and the leaves of flax. The gallant declares that he will stay with the girl until daylight, though this probably means that her parents will find out about his visit. His ostensible reason is that it is hard to make his way through the heavy morning dew (a standard euphemism); the real motive, of course, is his reluctance to leave the partner of his night's pleasures. "Dew on the sprouts" (*shitakusa tsuyu*) may have a secondary erotic implication such as one frequently finds in early Japanese love poems.

As he walks along, he passes a house with an open lattice. He is on his way to report for official duty, but cannot help stopping to lift up the blind and peep into the room.[72] It amuses him to think that a man has probably been spending the night here and has only recently got up to leave, just as happened to himself. Perhaps that man too had felt the charm of the dew.

Looking round the room, he notices near the woman's pillow an open fan with a magnolia frame and purple paper; and at the foot of her curtain of state he sees some narrow strips of Michinoku paper and also some other paper of a faded colour, either orange-red or maple.[73]

The woman senses that someone is watching her and, looking up from under her bedclothes, sees a gentleman leaning against the wall by the threshold, a smile on his face. She can tell at once that he is the sort of man with whom she need feel no reserve. All the same, she does not want to enter into any familiar relations with him, and she is annoyed that he should have seen her asleep.[74]

'Well, well, Madam,' says the man, leaning forward so that the upper part of his body comes behind her curtains, 'what a long nap you're having after your morning adieu! You really are a lie-abed!'

'You call me that, Sir,' she replied, 'only because you're annoyed at having had to get up before the dew had time to settle.'

Their conversation may be commonplace, yet I find there is something delightful about the scene.

Now the gentleman leans further forward and, using his own fan, tries to get hold of the fan by the woman's pillow. Fearing his closeness, she moves further back into her curtain enclosure, her heart pounding. The gentleman picks up the magnolia fan and, while examining it, says in a slightly bitter tone, 'How standoffish you are!'

But now it is growing light; there is a sound of people's voices, and it looks as if the sun will soon be up. Only a short while ago this same man was hurrying home to write his next-morning letter before the mists had time to clear. Alas, how easily his intentions have been forgotten!

While all this is afoot, the woman's original lover has been busy with his own next-morning letter, and now, quite unexpectedly, the messenger arrives at her house. The letter is attached to a spray of clover, still damp with dew, and the paper gives off a delicious aroma of incense. Because of the new visitor, however, the woman's servants cannot deliver it to her.

72. I.e., the house of the woman with the long hair and the orange robe.

73. See note 57.

74. As a rule, a Heian woman of the upper class would not let herself be seen by a man unless she was actually having an affair with him—and not always then. They were usually protected by curtains of state, screens, fans, etc., and above all by the darkness of the rooms.

Finally it becomes unseemly for the gentleman to stay any longer. As he goes, he is amused to think that a similar scene may be taking place in the house he left earlier that morning.

43. *Birds*

The parrot[75] does not belong to our country, but I like it very much. I am told that it imitates whatever people say.

The *hototogisu*, the water-rail, and the snipe; the starling, the siskin, and the fly-catcher. They say when the copper pheasant cries for its mate it can be consoled if one puts a mirror before it—a very moving thought. What misery these birds must suffer if they are separated from each other by a gorge or a ravine!

If I were to write down all my thoughts about the crane, I should become tiresome. How magnificent when this bird lets out its cry, which reaches up to the very heavens!

The red-headed sparrow, the male grosbeak, the kinglet.

The heron is an unpleasant-looking bird with a most disagreeable expression in its eyes. Yet, though it has nothing to recommend it, I am pleased to think that it does not nest alone in Yurugi Wood.[76]

The box bird.

Among water fowl it is the mandarin duck[77] that affects me most. How charming to think that the drake and his mate take turns in brushing the frost 'from each other's wings'!

The gull. The river plover[78]—alas, that he should have lost his mate!

The distant cry of wild geese is a most moving sound.

75. Parrots had been imported from Korea in earlier times as a tribute, but they appear to have died out by Shōnagon's time and it is unlikely that she had ever actually seen one; hence the vagueness of this sentence. The copper pheasant (*yamadori*) is said to have been introduced from China. It was recommended for its beautiful voice, but on arrival at the Palace (so the story goes) it refused to sing. A certain Court lady explained that this was because the pheasant missed its mate. She ordered that a mirror be hung in the cage, and the bird immediately began singing. For the *hototogisu* see note 12.

76. Shōnagon is thinking of the following *Rokujō* poem:

In Takashima even the herons of Yurugi Wood,
Where the branches quiver in the wind,
Refuse to nest alone
And keenly seek a partner for the night.
Yet . . . [I, alas, must spent the night alone].

Hakedori (box bird) is mentioned in contemporary poetry and also in *The Tale of Gęnji*; but its identity is unclear. Its name may be an onomatopoeia derived from a characteristic cry of *hayako-hayako*.

77. The *Oshi(dori)* (mandarin duck) is a traditional symbol of conjugal love in the Far East. Cf. the *Rokujō* poem:

The mandarin ducks, the husband and his mate,
Brush from each other's wings the frost.
How sad if one is left to sleep alone!

78. A poem by Ki no Tomonori, included in the *Rokujō:*

Autumn is here
And with it comes the plover's cry—
The plover who has lost his mate
On Sao River's misty banks.

It is charming to think of the wild duck sweeping the frost from its wings.[79]

The poets have extolled the *uguisu*[80] as a splendid bird, and so indeed it is; for both its voice and its appearance are most elegant and beautiful. Alas that it does not sing in the Ninefold Enclosure of the Palace! When I first heard people say this, I thought they must be mistaken; but now I have served for ten years in the Palace,[81] and, though I have often listened for it, I have never yet heard its song. The bamboos in the Palace gardens and the plum trees with red blossoms should certainly attract these birds. Yet not one of them comes here, whereas outside the Palace, in the paltry plum tree of some commoner's house, one hears the *uguisu* warbling away joyfully.

At night the *uguisu* is silent. Obviously this bird likes its sleep, and there is nothing we can do about that.

In the summer and autumn the *uguisu's* voice grows hoarse. Now the common people change its name to 'insect eater' or something of the kind, which strikes me as both unpleasant and unseemly. I should not mind if it were an ordinary bird like the sparrow; but this is the magnificent *uguisu*, whose song in the spring has moved writers to praise that season in both poetry and prose.[82] How splendid it would be if the *uguisu* would sing only in the spring. Yet it is wrong to despise this bird just because its voice deteriorates in the later seasons. After all, should we look down on men or women because they have been ravaged by age and are scorned by the world? There are certain birds, like the kite and the crow, that people disregard entirely and would never bother to criticize; it is precisely because the *uguisu* is usually held in such high regard that people find fault with it when they can.

I remember that on a certain occasion, when we had decided to watch the return of the High Priestess's procession from the Kamo Festival and had ordered the attendants to stop our carriages in front of Urin and Chisoku Temples,[83] a *hototogisu* began to sing, not wanting to be hidden on this festive day. An *uguisu* sang in unison, perfectly imitating his voice. I was surprised by what lovely

79. *Sedōka* from the *Manyō Shū*:

In Saitama
In Osaki Marsh
The wild duck flaps its wings,
Striving to sweep away the frost
That has settled on its tail.

Shōnagon has substituted wing (*hane*) for tail (*o*).

80. *Uguisu*: usually translated "nightingale," but this is misleading since the *uguisu* does not sing at night and is far closer to the Western bush warbler.

81. This passage was probably written in the summer of 999, when Shōnagon was about thirty-four. It is likely that she entered the service of Empress Sadako about 990.

82. Perhaps Shōnagon is thinking of the following poem, which can be found in the *Shūi Shū*:

Since the morning of this day
That ushered in the fresh New Year
I have waited for one sound alone—
The sound of the *uguisu's* song.

In the traditional calendar the year began in the spring.

83. Temples near the Kamo Shrines on Murasaki Plain north-east of the capital.

music these two birds can make when they sing together high in the trees.

Having written so many good things about the *uguisu*, how can I properly praise the *hototogisu*? What a joy it is in the Fifth Month to hear its voice ring out triumphantly as if to say, 'My season has come!' The poets describe the *hototogisu* as lurking in the *u no hana* and the orange tree; and there is something so alluring about the picture of this bird half hidden by the blossoms that one is almost overcome with envy. During the short summer nights in the rainy season one sometimes wakes up and lies in bed hoping to be the first person to hear the *hototogisu*. Suddenly towards dawn its song breaks the silence; one is charmed, indeed one is quite intoxicated. But alas, when the Sixth Month comes, the *hototogisu* is silent. I really need say no more about my feelings for this bird. And I do not love the *hototogisu* alone; anything that cries out at night delights me—except babies.

44. *Elegant Things*

A white coat worn over a violet waistcoat.
Duck eggs.[84]
Shaved ice mixed with liana syrup and put in a new silver bowl.
A rosary of rock crystal.
Snow on wistaria or plum blossoms.
A pretty child eating strawberries.

53. *It Is Hateful When a Well-Bred Young Man*

It is hateful when a well-bred young man who is visiting a woman of lower rank calls out her name in such a way as to make everyone realize that he is on familiar terms with her. However well he may know her name, he should slur it slightly as though he had forgotten it. On the other hand, this would be wrong when a gentleman comes at night to visit a lady-in-waiting. In such a situation he should bring along a man who can call out the lady's name for him —a servant from the Office of Grounds if she is in the Imperial Palace, or else someone from the Attendants' Hall; for his voice will be recognized if he calls her name himself. But, when he is visiting a mere under-servant or girl attendant, such a precaution is unnecessary.

84. But *kari no ko* could mean "duckling" or (less likely) "gosling." Ice was stored in ice chambers and eaten during the summer (for instance in sherbets) or used to preserve perishable food. The stems and leaves of the liana (*amazura*) were used for mild sweetening; sugar was not introduced into Japan until the Ashikaga period.

67. *Things That Cannot Be Compared*

Summer and winter. Night and day. Rain and sunshine. Young and age. A person's laughter and his anger. Black and white. Love and hatred. The little indigo plant and the great philodendron. Rain and and mist.

When one has stopped loving somebody, one feels that he has become someone else, even though he is still the same person.[85]

In a garden full of evergreens the crows[86] are all asleep. Then, towards the middle of the night, the crows in one of the trees suddenly wake up in a great flurry and start flapping about. Their unrest spreads to the other trees, and soon all the birds have been startled from their sleep and are cawing in alarm. How different from the same crows in daytime!

68. *To Meet One's Lover*

To meet one's lover summer is indeed the right season. True, the nights are very short, and dawn creeps up before one has had a wink of sleep. Since all the lattices have been left open, one can lie and look out at the garden in the cool morning air. There are still a few endearments to exchange before the man takes his leave, and the lovers are murmuring to each other when suddenly there is a loud noise. For a moment they are certain that they have been discovered; but it is only the caw of a crow flying past in the garden.

In the winter, when it is very cold and one lies buried under the bedclothes listening to one's lover's endearments, it is delightful to hear the booming of a temple gong, which seems to come from the bottom of a deep well. The first cry of the birds, whose beaks are still tucked under their wings, is also strange and muffled. Then one bird after another takes up the call. How pleasant it is to lie there listening as the sound becomes clearer and clearer!

221. *Things That Fall from the Sky*

Snow. Hail. I do not like sleet, but when it is mixed with pure white snow it is very pretty.

Snow looks wonderful when it has fallen on a roof of cypress bark.

85. Note the *Rokujō* poem:

He whom I loved
And that same lover when my love has gone—
How can I say that both are one?

86. But see Section 43 for Shōnagon's usual opinion about crows.

When snow begins to melt a little, or when only a small amount has fallen, it enters into all the cracks between the bricks, so that the roof is black in some places, pure white in others—most attractive.

I like drizzle and hail when they come down on a shingle roof. I also like frost on a shingle roof or in a garden.

222. *The Sun*[87]

After the sun has set behind the mountain, a red glow still lingers over the ridge and pale yellow clouds trail into the distance. It is a very moving sight.

223. *The Moon*

I am very moved when I see the thin crescent of a pale moon hanging above the eastern hills.

224. *Stars*

The Pleiads. Altair. The morning star and the evening star.

If only there were no shooting stars[88] to come visiting us at night.

87. Compare Shōnagon's description of the corresponding scene at dawn (Section 1) when the clouds are purplish.

88. According to a current superstition (of Chinese origin), it was dangerous for women to see shooting stars. Also there is a pun on *yobai*—(i) shooting star (in *yobaiboshi*), (ii) clandestine visit by a man to a woman's room at night.

Tales of the Middle Counselor of the Embankment (*Tsutsumi Chūnagon Monogatari*)

(ca. 794–1160)

The ten short stories in the collection called *Tales of the Middle Counselor of the Embankment* (*Tsutsumi Chūnagon Monogatari*) date in the later Heian period (794–1160) and are thus among the earliest short stories in the world. The author or authors are unknown. The society depicted is that of a literary and sophisticated court, existing in peaceful magnificence, and more aesthetic than any similar society in the West. The feudal wars which are frequently the subject of the later fiction (see p. 668) had not yet disrupted Japanese life. The world of the Heian court was one in which one's social fate depended on the wearing of a robe in a certain manner or on the successful accomplishment of a court ritual, or even more likely, on the effect on a loved one of a poem—including the skill of its calligraphy.

In the tale reprinted here, "The Lady Who Loved Worms" —or caterpillars—is an eccentric. Her attitudes are argumentative and non-conformist, far from the ideal of the Heian society to which she belongs. In her physical appearance she is at variance with other women of her class, who live only to be well-groomed and adored by men. Her unplucked eyebrows and unblackened teeth are very unfashionable (indeed, to those around her, the white teeth are frightening); the robe worn high at her neck is not modish. Furthermore, it is highly improper for the Lady to reveal herself to strange men as she does in her search for worms; it is unladylike for her to employ boys in the search; and it is unladylike for her to quote Chinese poetry, because Chinese is a language for men. Finally, when she writes a poem, she disregards two other important conventions—the paper she uses is rough and mannish and her script is the angular *katagana* rather than the flowing and decorative *hiragana*, which was supposed always to be used for poetry.

In the theme that emerges from these details, there is evidence of Buddhist influence. It is easy, the Lady thinks, to love flowers and butterflies, but they are superficial. One must find the true nature of things (*honchi*, a Buddhist term for the origin or essence of a thing) by penetrating appearance to something more basic. The lowly caterpillar is the true and basic form of that ephemeral creature, the butterfly.

The story is a loosely strung series of encounters between the personalities involved. It is undramatic because the nature of a woman's life is the subtle, but not very powerful, emotions of domesticity. Gentle pathos and mild humor can arise in the Lady's life, but not stronger emotions. It is in the nuances of the bizarre situation that the author is interested. The author's style is casual and seemingly repetitious: an idle tale for the entertainment of the court is the tone. But below this surface the author hopes to delineate emotions that reflect the essence of the strange Lady's personality.

From Tales of the Middle Counselor of the Embankment

The Lady Who Loved Worms (Mushi Mezuru Himegimi) *

Next to the place where lived the lady who loved butterflies, [dwelled] the daughter of the Inspector Great Counselor. Boundless was the devotion her parents lavished on her, and far beyond the ordinary.

* From *Translations from Early Japanese Literature* by Edwin O. Reischauer and Joseph K. Yamagiwa, 2nd ed., abridged. Cambridge, Mass: Harvard University Press. Copyright 1951 by The Harvard-Yenching Institute. (Harvard-Yenching Institute Studies, XXXIX.) The notes are abridged from the translators'.

This lady used to say, "People's love for such things as flowers and butterflies is indeed superficial and strange. It is when man has sincerity and seeks out the true nature [of things] that his spirit is good." And so, she collected a myriad frightful worms and put them into all sorts of baskets and boxes that she might see what they would grow into. Among these, she was entranced by the pensive air of the caterpillars, and both dawn and dusk, with her hair pushed behind her ears,[1] she would lay them in her hand and watch them intently.

Since the girls[2] were frightened [of her pets] and puzzled by them, she summoned some boys of no standing who were afraid of nothing and had them pick up the worms in the boxes. She would ask them the names [of the worms] and, when she found a new one, would delight in giving it a name.

She felt that all the artificial ways of people were evil, and she would not pluck her eyebrows at all. She claimed that to blacken one's teeth was even more of a nuisance and was dirty, and she would not do it, and so she doted over her worms both morning and evening, smiling a most [ghastly] white smile. People were frightened and disquieted by her and would run away from her, whereupon she would rebuke them most severely. Such timid persons she would call no-good commoners and would glare at from under her very black eyebrows, at which they would feel all the more ill at ease.

Her parents felt it to be a very strange and eccentric business, but she seemed to have a mind of her own. When they spoke to her because they found her conduct strange, she would contradict[3] them strongly, so that they were all the more frightened by her, and this too they found most embarrassing. "This is all very well," they told her, "but gossip is a queer matter. People like things of pleasing appearance. If they were to hear that you delight in frightful caterpillars, it would be most unpleasant."

"There is nothing wrong with that," [she replied]. "Only when one inquires into the myriad things and perceives their outcome do things have meaning. This is a very childish matter. Caterpillars turn into butterflies." She took out some in a state of transition and showed them [to her parents]. "What people wear, calling it silk," she told them, "is produced by the silkworm before its wings grow. When it has become a butterfly, it is at its very end and has become useless." There was nothing they could reply to this, and they were dumbfounded.

1. This was a very unconventional coiffure.
2. her maids and attendants.
3. The pressure of the Japanese family code makes this disobedience so unusual that it confounds the parents.

[Being a lady] after all, she would not meet even her parents face to face, reasoning that "Devils and girls are best not seen by others," and she would hold forth with them in this sagacious manner from behind her standing curtains and with the hanging screens of her room rolled up only a little.

Hearing about this, the girls said, "Though she is extremely clever, what with these diversions her mind is wandering. [We wonder] what sort of girls are serving the lady who loves butterflies."[4] She who was known as Hyōe said,

Ika de ware
togamu kata naku
ideshi ka mo
Kawamushi nagara
miru waza wa seshi

"How is it that I have come here without
objections,
And have been working, looking at such
things as caterpillars."

Then she who was known as Little Taifu laughed and said,

Urayamashi
hana ya choo ya to
yuumeredo
Kawamushi kusaki
yo o mo miru kana

"How enviable! They[5] seem to speak of flowers and
butterflies,
But we look upon a world which stinks of
caterpillars."

Then, laughing, she said, "How bitter! Even her eyebrows seem like caterpillars, and her teeth might be [creatures which have] shed their skins."[6]

She known as Sakon said,

Fuyu kureba
koromo tanomoshi
samuku to mo
Kawamushi ooku
miyuru atari wa

4. i.e., the (normal) lady who lives next door.

5. i.e., the maids ("girls") mentioned above.

6. being white, that is, instead of black. The Westerner who is not used to regarding black teeth as beautiful might consider how *his* beloved would look to one not used to regarding an oily red smear on the lips as beautiful.

"If winter comes, though it be cold, we shall
be well off for clothes
Hereabouts where we see so many worms [clothed]
in furs."[7]

"There will indeed be [enough], even if we ourselves wear no clothes."

Hearing them talking together thus, a [certain] caustic lady[8] said, "What are you young people saying? I see nothing so wonderful about those who love butterflies. I find it even absurd. Now is there indeed anyone who would line caterpillars up and call them butterflies? [The latter] have merely sloughed off [their skins]. She in truth inquires into these matters and is indeed profound in her thinking. When you catch butterflies, their dust[9] gets on your hands, which is most unpleasant. Furthermore, if you catch butterflies, they may give you the ague. Oh! they are more than loathsome." At this, their tempers rose all the more as they argued with one another.

To the boys who caught the worms for her, she gave nice things and the things for which they longed, and so they collected for her all sorts of frightful worms. The caterpillars had pretty hair, but she found them dull, for she remembered no [interesting poems or stories about them], and so she [also] collected such things as praying-mantes and snails. She would have the songs [about them] shouted out to her and would raise her own voice and sing such things as, "Does one fight over the horns of a snail?"[10]

She claimed that it would be tiresome for her boys' names to be like the usual ones, so she gave them the names of the lesser creatures and ordered them about under such names as Kerao ("mole-cricket boy"), Hisamaro ("toad man"), Inakadachi,[11] Inagomaro ("locust man"), and Amabiko ("centipede").

People heard of such matters and told most unusual things about her. Among them was the son-in-law of a certain high noble, who was a spirited man, afraid of nothing and quite attractive. Hearing about this lady, he said, "Whatever she may be like, she will be afraid of this," and he skillfully made the very pretty fringe of a sash into the semblance of a snake, fashioned so that it would move, and, placing it in a bag of scale-like pattern, [sent it to her] with the attached message:

7. *Kawamushi* ("fur worm") is an ancient word for caterpillar.
8. another member of the household or a neighbor.
9. from their wings.
10. a quotation from Po Chü-i. The verse refers to a story in the *Chuang-tzu* (see pp. 407 and 408.) The allegorical snail has one horn ruled over by Aggression and the other by Violence. The choice implied is between tyranny and war.
11. The meaning of this word is unknown.

Hau hau mo
kimi ga atari ni
shitagawan
Nagaki kokoro no
kagiri naki mi wa

"Though only crawling, I shall follow at
my lord's side,
I who am limitlessly long-faithful of
heart."[12]

When [her attendants] saw this, they brought it to her in all innocence, remarking even as they opened the bag that it was strangely heavy. When they opened it, the snake raised its head. They all screamed in great confusion, but the lady, with complete composure, recited, "Hail to the Buddha Amida.[13] Hail to the Buddha Amida," and then said in a quavering voice, "It may be one of our ancestors in a former life. Be not so disturbed." Turning away from them, she murmured, "Charming creature, to me you are a blood-relative. Are we to be suspicious of you?"

She drew [the bag] to her, but, since she could not help finding it frightening, she [fluttered about it] like a butterfly, now standing, now sitting, and she spoke to it in a strained voice, which was so extremely amusing that the others all rushed pell-mell out [of the room] in fits of laughter.

His lordship,[14] hearing all about the matter, said, "This is most shameful. What a hideous affair to hear of. How strange that you would all leave her when you could see perfectly well what the situation was." So saying, he took his sword and ran to her, but when he looked carefully [at the snake he saw that] it was an exceedingly clever imitation, so he picked it up in his hand and said, "What an extremely skillful man he is. He may have heard that you admired [these creatures] in your learned way. Make a reply to him and quickly get rid of this." So saying, he departed.

When the others heard that it had been an imitation, they said spitefully that the man had played an outrageous trick, but she said that he would be put out if she did not reply, so she wrote him on a very stiff and sturdy [piece of] paper. Since she did not as yet write in [*hira*]*gana*, she inscribed in *katakana*,

Chigiri araba
yoki gokuraku ni
ikiawan
Matsuware nikushi
mushi no sugata wa

12. There is a pun here in that "long" also refers to the length of the snake.
13. Lord of the "Pure Land," the Buddhist paradise. 14. her father

"If we are related in fate, we shall perhaps meet
in the good Paradise,
Hateful is it to be entwined by a serpent's form."

"In the garden of happiness."[15]

The Vice-Director of the Stables of the Right[16] saw it and thought it a very unusual and different sort of letter. Wishing that somehow he might see her, he conferred with a [certain] Middle Commander. Making themselves up as low-born women, they went there at a time when the Inspector Great Counselor was out. Watching from behind a lattice-work fence on the north side of the lady's residence, they saw some plain-looking boys standing and walking about among the grasses and trees. Then [one of the boys] said, "Any number of them are crawling all over this tree. It is very interesting. Please look here."

"There are some very fine caterpillars," they told her, raising the hanging screen [before her room].

"How very interesting," she called out in a brisk voice. "Bring them here."

"We cannot pick them off," they replied. "Please just look at them here." Whereupon she strode forth roughly and, pushing aside the hanging curtain, peered into the branches.

[The young men] saw that her robe was jerked up toward her head[17] and the ends of hair at her forehead were pretty but appeared to be unkempt, probably because they had not been combed and made up. Her eyebrows were very black and showily luxuriant, giving her a fresh air. Her mouth too was charming and pretty, but, since her teeth were unblackened, it looked most unusual. She would have been quite pretty, if she had been made up. They felt this to be indeed sad. But unkempt as she was, she was not unpleasing to behold and had quite a distinguished air, characterized by a fine dignity and beauty. It was indeed too bad. She was wearing an under-robe of white damask tinged with pale yellow and another smaller woven one with a white skirt to suit her fancy.

She leaned out, hoping to see the worms better, and said, "How wonderful! They have come here because they do not like being broiled in the sun. Boy, drive them over here without knocking one of them off."

[But the boy] did push some of them off, and they fell bouncing down. She held out a white fan on which some jet black characters had been drawn as writing practice and said, "Pick them up on this," and the boy picked them up.

The [two young] lords, looking on, were horrified and felt that

15. the "place" of writing at the end of the message.

16. a position of honor in the imperial service.

17. See p. 661.

[such a daughter] was too much in addition to all the calamities [of this household]. And they watched, appalled at the thought of her.

A boy, seeing them standing there and thinking it odd, said, "Some handsome men, very strangely decked out, are standing by yonder fence peeping in."

She who was known as Lady Taifu[18] came, thinking to herself, "How awful! Her Ladyship has become excited over those worms of hers and has exposed herself.[19] I shall tell her about this." [Her mistress] was, as usual, outside the hanging screens and was fussing over the caterpillars and having them brushed down to her. Without drawing closer, since she was very much afraid [of the creatures, Lady Taifu] called to her, "Oh, please come back in. You are exposed."

"That is all right," [her mistress] replied, presuming that she had said this in order to stop her from what she was doing. "There is nothing to be ashamed of."

"Ah, alas! Will you think I am lying? Some very grand men are over there by the fence, so please look at [your worms] inside."

"Kerao," she ordered, "go over there and see."

The boy hurried off and [soon] reported, "They are in truth there," whereupon she rushed over, picked up the caterpillars in her sleeve, and went inside.

She was of good stature, and her hair was most luxuriant, falling the length of her robe. The ends [of her hair] were bushy for lack of trimming but were properly arranged and quite beautiful. Though she was no outstanding [beauty], if she were to have fixed herself up like other people, would there have been aught to complain of [in her appearance]? By nature she was most indifferent, but she was very pretty and dignified, and only this one annoying quality made her different from others. What a pity it was. "Why does she have such disagreeable ideas, when she [really] is so [pretty]?" [the young men] thought.

The Vice-Director of the Stables of the Right felt it would be very dreary simply to go home, so he resolved to let her know at least that he had seen her. He wrote on a piece of folded paper with the juice from a bush,

Kawamushi no
ke fukaki sama o
mitsuru yori
Torimochite nomi
mamorubeki kana

18. i.e., "Little Taifu" (see above), one of the Lady's serving-women.
19. in improper and disarrayed dress.

"Since seeing you with hair thick as the caterpillar's
I shall carry [that picture] with me and preserve
it always."[20]

He tapped with his fan, and a boy came out. "Present this [to your mistress]," he said and had [the boy] take it, but [the latter went to] her who was known at Lady Taifu and said, "The man standing over there told me to present this to Her Ladyship."

[Lady Taifu] took it, saying, "How awful! This seems to be the doing of the Vice-Director of the Stables of the Right. He must have seen her face as she amused herself with those miserable worms."

When she kept talking in this vein, [her mistress] made reply, saying, "If you think it through, there is really nothing to be ashamed of. In this dreamlike, illusory world, which of us may remain both to see the evil and to note the good?" Having nothing worth saying [in reply to this], each one of the girls felt depressed.

The [two] men stood around for a while, thinking there would be a reply, but, when the boys were all called in, [the two men realized there would be no answer and] said to each other, "How miserable!"

[But] some of those [in the house] must have remembered [what was proper] and out of pity for them [sent the following reply]:

Hito ni ninu
kokoro no uchi wa
kawamushi no
Na o toite koso
iwamahoshikere

"In my heart, unlike that of others
The caterpillar's name I wish to say, [but first]
I must ask it."[21]

The Vice-Director of the Stables of the Right [then] recited,

Kawamushi ni
magiruru mayu no
ke no sue ni
Ataru bakari no
hito wa naki kana

"Not distinguishable from a caterpillar, the
tips of your eyebrows—
Alas, there is no man who measures up to them."

And laughing, they returned home. [What follows] is in the second scroll.

20. *Torimochite* ("carry with me") contains a play on words in that *torimichi* means "bird-lime," used for catching insects.

21. This poem in essence is merely an inquiry into the man's name, and his reply is an excuse for not giving it.

Tales of the Heike (*Heike Monogatari*)

The elegant fastidiousness of Heian court society, as depicted in the *Tsutsumi Chūnagon* and the *Genji Monogatari* ended abruptly in the middle of the twelfth century in a bitter war between two strong provincial clans, the Minamoto and the Taira (Heike). When the Minamoto finally crushed the Taira in 1185, the culture of the Heian court was in ashes and the first Shogunate, or feudal government, was established. The Kamakura period (1185–1333), as this period of military feudalism is called, gave rise to what in Japanese literature is closest to the Western epic. Three *monogatari* give us vivid narratives of the Minamoto-Taira wars: the *Hōgen*, which recounts a brief war of 1156; the *Heiji*, which depicts an uprising in the winter of 1159–1160, in which the Taira defeated, for a moment, the Minamoto; and the *Heike*, which chronicles the great wars of 1180–1185 in which the Minamoto finally triumphed.

The *Heike Monogatari* has always been the most popular of the three mentioned above. All of the three are pro-Minamoto and must date from after the triumph of that clan in 1185. The *Heike*, if it was originally composed by one man, which is unlikely, has been added to, and the seams and joints smoothed out by generations of story tellers and writers—some ninety different versions are known to have existed, and its legends have fed later Japanese literature, including the *nō* play. The style of the *Heike* is direct and lively, especially in comparison with that of the writers of the Heian court. It does not depend on sophisticated emotional nuances or literary allusion. Although the characters are idealized and perhaps—by our standards—romanticized, the rush and tumult of battle emerge from the *Heike* as they do from the *Iliad*, and personal feelings, though poignant and moving, occupy a small part of the narrative. Highly popular from the beginning, the war tales were chanted by minstrels to the accompaniment of the lute and recited by storytellers. The oral recitation of these stories is facilitated by their diction, which often falls into the traditional five-syllable and seven-syllable phrases of Japanese poetic rhythm.

From Tales of the Heike*

Departure of the Emperor from the Capital

As the Chinese poet says: "The Imperial Capital[1] is a place ever busy with fame and gain; after cockcrow it has no rest." If this

* From *The Ten Foot Square Hut and Tales of the Heike,* translated by A. L. Sadler; Angus and Robertson, Sydney, 1928. Copyright 1928 by A. L. Sadler. Reprinted by permission of A. L. Sadler.

1. Kyoto. The reader need not burden himself with the numerous place names in the story. The general area of activity is Kyoto down to the Inland Sea.

is so when it is quietly governed, what must it be when all is confusion? Doubtless they [The Heike] would have liked to flee to the innermost recesses of Mount Yoshino, but their enemies were in possession of all the highroads and all the provinces were hostile, so that they could only find refuge by the sea. As we read in the golden words of the Hokke Sutra;[2] "In the Three Worlds there is no rest; it is even as a house that has taken fire." Not otherwise was the state of the Capital at this time. On the twenty-fourth day at dusk Munemori went to the Ikedono at Rokuhara[3] where the Empress Kenrei-mon-in was staying and said: "Kiso Yoshinaka is coming up to attack the Capital with fifty thousand horsemen, and has already arrived in Higashi-Sakamoto in Ōmi, where the monks of Hiezan have joined him; we must stay here at all events, but as it would be most unfortunate if either yourself or your august mother the Nii Dono came to any harm, we think it best that you, with the Emperor and the Hō-ō,[4] should for a while return to the Western Provinces." "As affairs now are," replied the Empress, "that will be perhaps the best plan;" and as she spoke her feelings overcame her and she sobbed unrestrainedly into the sleeve of her Imperial Robe. Munemori also moistened the sleeve of his garment with his tears.

Now when the Hō-ō heard privately of this design of the Heike to take him away to the Western Provinces, he departed secretly from his Palace at midnight, attended only by Uma-no-kami Suketoki, and made an Imperial Progress by himself to some place the whereabouts of which remained augustly unknown. And no one was aware of it.

When it was known that the Hō-ō was no longer in the city the excitement was extraordinary, and the flurry and confusion of the Heike was such that it seemed that it could have hardly been greater if the enemy had actually been entering the houses of the Capital. As they had thus made preparations to send the Emperor and the Hō-ō to the Western Provinces and then found that their plan was already upset, they felt like one who takes refuge under a tree that does not keep off the rain. However they determined to carry out their design in the case of the Emperor at least, so at the hour of the Hare (6 a.m.) the Imperial Palanquin was made ready, His Majesty being at this time a child of six years old, and knowing nothing of what was taking place.

His Imperial Mother Kenrei-mon-in rode also in the same Palanquin. Hei-Dainagon Tokitada-no-Kyō had given orders that all the Treasures of the Imperial House should be taken with them, the Sacred Jewel, the Sword, the Mirror, the Imperial Seal and Key,

2. Sanskrit *Pundarika.* One of the three important Buddhist *sutras,* or sacred books.

3. in Kyoto. Munemori is a Heike warrior.

4. the retired emperor, now a monk.

the Tablet for marking the hours, and the Imperial *Biwa* and *Koto*,[5] but such was the flurry and excitement that many of them were left behind. His Majesty's own sword was also forgotten in the hurry. Tokitada-no-Kyō and his two sons Kura-no-kami Nobu-moto and Sanuki-no-Chūjō Tokizane accompanied the procession in full court robes, while the Imperial Guard of the Konoe-tsukasa and the Mitsuna-no-suke escorted them in armour, carrying their bows and quivers. So they proceeded along the Shichijō to the west and the Shujaku to the south.

When the Heike fled from the Capital they set fire to all their mansions, and Rokuhara, Ikedono, Komatsudono, Hachijō Nishi-hachijō and others, in all twenty mansions, beside some forty or fifty thousand houses of their retainers in the city and in Shirakawa, went up in flames.

Thus the places that the Emperor used to frequent were reduced to ashes, and nought but the foundation-stones was left of his residences; the Imperial Car was his only refuge. Of the gardens of the Princesses but the site remains, and on the place of their elegant chambers the dew falls like tears and the blasts whine mournfully. The splendid apartments where the ladies tired themselves behind the long curtains, the hunting-lodges and fishing-pavilions, the residence of the Regent, the mansions of the Courtiers, the labour of many years made vain in an hour, what now remained of them but charred logs? How much more the lodgings of their retainers and the houses of the common people? In all the area that the fire devoured was a score of *chō*[6] and more. Not otherwise, when the power of Wu[7] was overthrown, the terraces of Ku Su were suddenly abandoned to the thistles and dew, and when the might of Ts'in was at last laid low, the smoke of the palace of Hien Yang obscured the land. Though the slopes of the pass of Han Ku were made strong, the northern barbarians broke through, and though they relied on the deep waters of the Yellow River the eastern marauders took possession of it.

Departure of Tadanori from Kyoto

Satsuma-no-kami Tadanori,[8] who had already left the Capital, wishing to see Gojō-no-sammi once again, rode back again to the city with a small train of five retainers and a page, all, like himself, in full armour. When he came to the gate of the mansion, however, he found it shut fast, and even when he called his name, it was not opened, though there was a sound of people running about within crying out that one of the fugitives had returned.

5. the *biwa* is a lute; the *koto*, a harp or lyre.

6. about two and a half acres.

7. traditional founder of the Chinese Chou Dynasty, which began one of the longest periods of cultural advancement in Chinese history. Barbarians (the Ts'in or Ch'in) overthrew the old order in 221 B.C.

8. a Heike warrior.

Then Satsuma-no-kami hastily dismounted from his horse and himself cried out with a loud voice: "It is I, Tadanori, who have come; I have something to say to Sammi-dono; if you will not open the gate, at least beg him to come forth here that I may speak with him." "If it is indeed Tadanori," replied Shunsei, "you need have no fear, but admit him." Then they opened the gate and he entered, and the meeting between the two was most moving and pathetic. "Ever since I became your pupil in the art of poetry years ago," said Tadanori, "I have never forgotten you, but for the last few years the disorder of the Capital and the risings in the provinces have prevented me from coming to see you.

"Now the final scene in the fall of our house hurries on apace, and the Emperor has already departed from the Capital. But there is one thing that I very greatly desire. Some time ago I heard that an Anthology of Poems was to be made by the Imperial Command, and I wished to ask you if you would condescend to submit one of my poor verses for consideration, that my name may be remembered in time to come; and I felt great regret when the Collection was postponed owing to the unsetled state of the country. If, however, at some time in the future, when peace is restored to the Empire, this Anthology should be made, I would beg your favour for one of the stanzas in this scroll, that my spirit may rejoice under the shade of the long grass, and from that far-off world may come and aid you."

And with these words he drew out from beneath the sleeve of his armour a scroll containing a hundred verses that he considered to be the best he had so far composed and handed them to Shunsei. "Truly does this memento show that you have not forgotten me," replied Shunsei as he opened and perused it, "and I find it hard to keep back my tears when I think of the manner of your coming.[9] Verily the sadness of it is unutterable and your affection to me most deep."

"Whether my bones will bleach on the hills or my name be echoed by the billows of the Western Sea, I care not," answered Tadanori, "for I feel no regret for this fleeting world; and so, as it must be, farewell;" and he sprang upon his horse, and, replacing his helmet on his head, rode away to the westward. Sammi-dono stood looking after him a long while until he was out of sight, and as he looked the words of the following Chinese verse were borne back to his ears in the voice, as it seemed, of Tadanori:

Far is the road I must travel; so do I gallop
into the evening mists of Yen Shan.

9. Both the lack of attendant ceremony and the state of the nation are meant here.

Overcome by his melancholy thoughts, Shunsei controlled his feelings with difficulty as he slowly returned to his mansion.

In after days, when the Empire was once more at peace, an Imperial Order was issued to make an Anthology called the Senzai-shū, and Shunsei remembered the request of Tadanori and his conversation, but though there were many verses worthy of immortality in the scroll that he had written, as at that time he and all Heike had been declared to be rebels against the Throne, all that he could do for the memory of his unhappy disciple was to include one of them under the title of "A flower of my native land," by "An unknown author." The stanza runs thus:

See the rippling waves
Lapping over Omi's strand
Where once Shiga stood.
'Tis no more, but on the hills
Still the mountain cherry blooms.[10]

Departure of Tsunemasa[11] from Kyoto

Kōgō-gū-no-suke Tsunemasa, the eldest son of Shūri-no-taiyū Tsunemori, had, as a child, served as page to the Imperial Abbot of the temple of Omuro Ninnaji, and still felt so deeply attached to him that he determined to pay him a farewell visit, even in spite of their great haste; so he took five or six retainers with him, and, riding off thither at great speed, hurriedly alighted from his horse and knocked at the gate.

"Our Sovereign has already departed from the Capital," he said, "and the doom of our house is at hand but all I regret in this fleeting world is that I must part from my lord. Since I first entered this Palace Cloister at the age of eight until my Gempuku[12] at the age of thirteen, except for a slight interval of sickness, never did I leave my lord's side; but to-day, alas, I must go forth to the wild waves of the Western Sea, not knowing when, if ever, I shall return. So I have come, wishing to see his face more, though I feel ashamed to enter his presence in this rough soldier's garb."

When he heard this, the Imperial Abbot, moved with compassion, replied: "Bid him enter as he is, without changing his dress." Tsunemasa was that day attired in a hitatare[13] of purple brocade and body armour laced with green silk. A gold-mounted sword hung at his side and a quiver of twenty-four arrows with black and white feathers at his back, and under his arm he carried his bow of black lacquer with red binding. Taking off his helmet and hanging it from his shoulder, he reverently entered the little garden before the apartment of the Abbot. His Reverence immediately appeared and

10. Omi is east of Kyoto and is mentioned in numerous Japanese poems.
11. A Heike warrior prince.
12. a ceremony of fidelity to the lord.
13. Tsunemasa deprecates his garb for politeness. A *hitatare* is a ceremonial robe.

bade them raise the curtain before the veranda, on which he invited Tsunemasa to be seated.

When Tsunemasa had seated himself he beckoned to Tōhyōye-no-Jō who attended on him, and he brought a bag of red brocade containing his master's lute, which Tsunemasa laid before the Abbot. "I have brought back this famous *Biwa* 'Seizan,'[14] which Your Reverence presented to me last year, with deep regret, for it is not proper that I should take such a thing, one of the most precious treasures of our land, into the rude wilds of the country. May I then deposit it with Your Reverence, that if a happier day should perchance dawn again for our family, and we should return to the Capital, I may receive it from your hand once more?" At this the Abbot was much moved and replied with the following stanza:

Since you cannot stay,
Leave the *Biwa* here with me
In its bag apart.
Untouched by another hand,
'Twill recall the love you feel.

Tsunemasa, borrowing his master's inkstone, then wrote the following:

Though the trickling stream
That runs from this bamboo spout
Changes ceaselessly,
Never changing is my wish
In these halls to stay with you.

When he had said farewell and retired from the presence of the Imperial Abbot, all those who were living in the monastery, acolytes, monks, and priests of all ranks, flocked round him, clinging to his sleeves and bedewing them with their tears, so sad were they at parting with him.

Among them was a certain young priest named Dainagon-no-Hoshi Gyōkei, a son of Hamuro-no-Dainagon Mitsuyori-no-Kyō, who had been much attached to him ever since his boyhood; and he was so loath to part with him that he went to see him off as far as the banks of the Katsuragawa, where he bade him farewell and returned to the monastery. As he parted with him, weeping he composed the following verse:

Nature too is sad.
See the mountain cherry-tree,
Whether old or young,
Whether late or early bud,
Cannot keep its blossom long.

14. "Green Mountain."

To which Tsunemasa made reply:

> In our traveller's garb,
> As we wend our weary way,
> Each night's bivouac
> Fills our hearts with saddening thoughts
> As we ever farther go.

Then his samurai, who had been waiting in groups here and there, unfurled their red banners and formed into a company of about a hundred horsemen in all, and as he took his place at their head they all whipped up their horses and galloped on after the Imperial Procession.

Concerning "Seizan"

It was when he was seventeen years old that Tsunemasa was presented with the *Biwa* "Seizan," and about the same time he was sent as Imperial Envoy to the shrine of Hachiman at Usa. When he arrived there he played certain secret pieces of great beauty on it before the abode of the deity, and all the assembled priests were so touched that the sleeves of their ritual garments were wet with their tears. Even those without any discrimination, who had never had any opportunity of hearing good music, were delighted, thinking it sounded like showers of rain. And the story of this *Biwa* is that, when in the time of Nimmyō Tennō, in the third month of the third year of the period of Ka-shō, Kamon-no-kami Sadatoshi went to China, he learned three styles of playing from Renshō-bu, a very reknowned master of the *Biwa*, and before he came back to Japan he was presented with three *Biwas* called "Genshō," "Shishi-maru,"[15] and "Seizan." But while he was returning over the sea, the Dragon god of the waters was moved by envy to raise a great storm, so they cast Shishi-maru into the waves to appease him, and brought back only two to this country, which were presented to the Emperor.

Many years after, in the period Ō-wa, the Emperor Murakami Tennō was sitting in the Seiryōden[16] one autumn at midnight, when the moon was shining brightly and a cool breeze was blowing, and was playing on the *Biwa* called Genshō, when suddenly a shadowy form appeared before him and began to sing in a loud and sonorous voice. On the Emperor asking him who he was and whence he had come, he answered thus.

"I am Renshō-bu, that master of the *Biwa* who in China taught the three secret styles of playing to Fujiwara Sadatoshi; but in my teaching there was one tune that I concealed and did not transmit

15. Genshō was a monk who wrote a book on poetry; a *shishi-maru* is a lion.
16. "Imperial Hall."

to him, and for this fault I have been cast into the place of devils. Having this night heard the wondrous beauty of your playing, I have come to ask Your Majesty if I may transmit the one remaining tune to you, and thus be permitted to enter the perfect enlightenment of Buddha." Then, taking Seizan which was standing before His Majesty also, he tuned the strings and taught the melody to the Emperor. And this is that which is called "Jogen" and "Sekijo."[17]

After this apparition the Emperor and his Ministers feared to play on this *Biwa*, and it was presented to the Imperial Temple of Ninnaji, and Tsunemasa received it because he was so much beloved by the Imperial Abbot. The front of it was made of a rare wood, and on it was a picture of the moon of dawn coming forth from among the green foliage of summer mountains, hence its name Seizan.

The Death of Kiso Yoshinaka[18]

Now Kiso had brought with him from Shinano two beautiful girls named Tomoe and Yamabuki, but Yamabuki had fallen sick and stayed behind in the Capital. Tomoe had long black hair and a fair complexion, and her face was very lovely; moreover she was a fearless rider whom neither the fiercest horse nor the roughest ground could dismay, and so dexterously did she handle sword and bow that she was a match for a thousand warriors, and fit to meet either god or devil. Many times had she taken the field, armed at all points, and won matchless renown in encounters with the bravest captains, and so in this last fight, when all the others had been slain or had fled, among the last seven there rode Tomoe.

At first it was reported that Kiso had escaped to the north either through Nagasaka by the road to Tamba, or by the Ryūge Pass, but actually he had turned back again and ridden off toward Seta, to see if he could hear aught of the fate of Imai Kanehira. Imai had long valiantly held his position at Seta till the continued assaults of the enemy reduced his eight hundred men to but fifty, when he rolled up his banner and rode back to Miyaki to ascertain the fate of his lord; and thus it happened that the two fell in with each other by the shore at Ōtsu. Recognizing each other when they were yet more than a hundred yards away, they spurred their horses and came together joyfully.

Seizing Imai by the hand, Kiso burst forth: "I was so anxious about you that I did not stop to fight to the death in the Rokujō-kawara, but turned my back on a host of foes and hastened off here to find you." "How can I express my gratitude for my lord's con-

17. The reader should be reminded of the magical power of music in the Western tradition beginning with the legend of Orpheus, founder of Greek (and hence Western) music.

18. a powerful general of the Minamoto (Taira) clan.

sideration?" replied Imai; "I too would have died in the defence of Seta, but I feared for my lord's uncertain fate, and thus it was that I fled hither." "Then our ancient pledge will not be broken and we shall die together," said Kiso, "and now unfurl your banner, for a sign to our men who have scattered among these hills."

So Imai unfurled the banner, and many of their men who had fled from the Capital and from Seta saw it and rallied again, so that they soon had a following of three hundred horse. "With this band our last fight will be a great one," shouted Kiso joyfully, "who leads yon great array?" "Kai-no-Ichijō Jirō, my lord." "And how many has he, do you think?" "About six thousand, it seems." "Well matched!" replied Yoshinaka, "if we must die, what death could be better than to fall outnumbered by valiant enemies? Forward then!"[19]

That day Kiso was arrayed in a hitatare of red brocade and a suit of armour laced with Chinese silk; by his side hung a magnificent sword mounted in silver and gold, and his helmet was surmounted by long golden horns. Of his twenty-four eagle-feathered arrows, most had been shot away in the previous fighting, and only a few were left, drawn out high from the quiver, and he grasped his rattan-bound bow by the middle as he sat his famous grey charger, fierce as a devil, on a saddle mounted in gold. Rising high in his stirrups he cried with a loud voice: "Kiso-no-Kwanja you have often heard of; now you see him before your eyes! Lord of Iyo and Captain of the Guard, Bright Sun General, Minamoto Yoshinaka am I! Come! Kai-no-Ichijō Jirō! Take my head and show it to Hyōye-no-suke Yoritomo!"

"Hear, men!" shouted Ichijō-no-Jirō in response; "On to the attack! This is their great Captain! See that he does not escape you now!" And the whole force charged against Kiso to take him. Then Kiso and his three hundred fell upon their six thousand opponents in the death fury, cutting and slashing and swinging their blades in every direction until at last they broke through on the farther side, but with their little band depleted to only fifty horsemen, when Doi-no-Jirō Sanehira came up to support their foes with another force of two thousand. Flinging themselves on these they burst through them also, after which they successively penetrated several other smaller bands of a hundred or two who were following in reserve.

But now they were reduced to but five survivors, and among these Tomoe still held her place. Calling her to him Kiso said: "As you are a woman, it were better that you now make your escape. I have made up my mind to die, either by the hand of the enemy or by mine own, and how would Yoshinaka be shamed if in his last fight

19. Compare the episode which follows to the Sarpedon-Glaucus episode in Homer's *Iliad* (XII, 387–389).

he died with a woman?" Even at these strong words, however, Tomoe would not forsake him, but still feeling full of fight, she replied: "Ah, for some bold warrior to match with, that Kiso might see how fine a death I can die." And she drew aside her horse and waited. Presently Onda-no-Hachirō Moroshige of Musashi, a strong and valiant samurai, came riding up with thirty followers, and Tomoe, immediately dashing into them, flung herself upon Onda and grappling with him dragged him from his horse, pressed him calmly against the pommel of her saddle and cut off his head. Then stripping off her armour she fled away to the Eastern Provinces.

Tezuka-no-Tarō was killed and Tezuka-no-Bettō took to flight, leaving Kiso alone with Imai-no-Shirō. "Ah," exclaimed Yoshinaka, "my armour that I am never wont to feel at all seems heavy on me to-day." "But you are not yet tired, my lord, and your horse is still fresh, so why should your armour feel heavy? If it is because you are discouraged at having none of your retainers left, remember that I, Kanehira, am equal to a thousand horsemen, and I have yet seven or eight arrows left in my quiver; so let me hold back the foe while my lord escapes to that pinewood of Awazu that we see yonder, that there under the trees he may put an end to his life in peace."

"Was it for this that I turned my back on my enemies in Rokujō-kawara and did not die then?" returned Yoshinaka; "by no means will we part now, but meet our fate together." And he reined his horse up beside that of Imai towards the foe, when Kanehira, alighting from his horse, seized his master's bridle and burst into tears: "However great renown a warrior may have gained," he pleaded, "an unworthy death is a lasting shame. My lord is weary and his charger also, and if, as may be, he meet his death at the hands of some low retainer, how disgraceful that it should be said that Kiso Dono, known through all Nippon as the 'Demon Warrior,' had been slain by some nameless fellow, so listen to reason, I pray you, and get away to the pines over there."

So Kiso, thus persuaded, rode off toward the pinewood of Awazu. Then Imai-no-Shirō, turning back charged into a party of fifty horsemen, shouting: "I am Imai Shiro Kanehira, foster-brother of Kiso Dono, aged thirty-three. Even Yoritomo at Kamakura knows my name; so take my head and show it to him, anyone who can!" And he quickly fitted the eight shafts he had left to his bow and sent them whirring into the enemy, bringing down eight of them from their horses, either dead or wounded. Then, drawing his sword, he set on at the rest, but none would face him in combat hand-to-hand: "Shoot him down! Shoot him down!" they cried as they let fly a hail of arrows at him, but so good was his armour that none could pierce it, and once more he escaped unwounded.

Meanwhile Yoshinaka rode off alone toward Awazu, and it was the twenty-third day of the first month. It was now nearly dark and all the land was coated with thin ice, so that none could distinguish the deep rice fields, and he had not gone far before his horse plunged heavily into the muddy ooze beneath. Right up to the neck it floundered, and though Kiso plied whip and spur with might and main, it was all to no purpose, for he could not stir it. Even in this plight he still thought of his retainer, and was turning to see how it fared with Imai, when Miura-no-Ishida Jirō Tamehisa of Sagami rode up and shot an arrow that struck him in the face under his helmet. Then as the stricken warrior fell forward in the saddle so that his crest bowed over his horse's head, two of Ishida's retainers fell upon him and struck off his head.

Holding it high on the point of a sword Ishida shouted loudly: "Kiso Yoshinaka, known through the length and breadth of Nippon as the 'Demon Warrior,' has been killed by Miura-no-Ishida Jirō Tamehisa." Imai was still fighting when these words fell on his ears, but when he saw that his master was indeed slain he cried out: "Alas, for whom now have I to fight? See, you fellows of the East Country, I will show you how the mightiest champion in Nippon can end his life!" And he thrust the point of his sword in his mouth and flung himself headlong from his horse, so that he was pierced through and died.

Now the Heike had departed from the coast of Yashima in Sanuki the winter of the year before, and crossed over to the bay of Naniwa in Settsu and took up a position between Ichi-no-tani[20] on the west, where they built a strong fortification, and the wood of Ikuta on the east, where the entrance to the fort was made. Between these points, at Fukuhara, Hyogo, Itayado and Suma were encamped all the forces of the eight provinces of the Sanyōdō and the six provinces of the Nankaidō, a total of a hundred thousand men in all.

The position at Ichi-no-tani had a narrow entrance with cliffs on the north and the sea on the south, while within it was very spacious. The cliffs rose high and steep, perpendicular as a standing screen, and from them to the shallows of the beach a strong breastwork was erected of wood and stone, well protected by palisades, while beyond it, in the deep water rode their great galleys like a floating shield. In the towers of the breastwork were stationed the stout soldiery of Shikoku and Kyūshū in full armour with bows and arrows in their hands, dense as the evening mists, while in front of the towers, ten or twelve deep, stood their horses, fully accoutred with saddle and trappings. Ceaseless was the roll of their war-drums; the might of their bows was like the crescent moon, and the gleam of their blades was as the shimmer of the hoar-frost in autumn, while their myriad red banners that flew aloft in the spring breezes rose to heaven like the flames of a conflagration.

20. a stronghold near Kyoto to the southwest in Settsu province.

About dusk on the fifth day the Genji started from Koyano and pressed on to attack the wood at Ikuta, and as the Heike looked out over Suzume-no-matsubara, Mikage-no-matsu and Koyano, they could see them pitching their camps everywhere, while the glow of their thousand watch-fires reddened the sky like the the moon rising over the mountains. The fires that the Heike kindled also showed up the dark outline of the wood of Ikuta, and twinkled as they flared up like stars in the brightening sky; they reminded them of the glimmering fire-flies on the river-bank, so often the subject of their verse in the happy days gone by. So, as they beheld the Genji thus deliberately pitching their camps here and there, and feeding and resting their horses, they watched and wondered when they would be attacked, their hearts filled with disquiet.

At dawn on the sixth day Kurō Onzōshi Yoshitsune, dividing his ten thousand men into two companies, ordered Doi-no-Jirō Sanehira to make an attack on the western outlet of Ichi-no-tani with seven thousand, while he himself with the remaining three thousand horsemen went round by Tango road to descend the pass of Hiyodorigoe to take them in the rear.

At this his men began to murmur to each other: "Every one knows the dangers of that place; if we must die, it were better to die facing the foe than to fall over a cliff and be killed. Does anyone know the way among these mountains?" "I know these mountains very well;" exclaimed Hirayama-no-Mushadokoro of Musashi, in answer to these mutterings. "But you were brought up in the Eastern Provinces, and this is the first time you have seen the mountains of the West," objected Yoshitsune, "so how can you guide us?" "That may be even as your Excellency says," replied Hirayama, "but just as a poet knows the cherry-blossoms of Yoshino and Hatsuse without seeing them, so does a proper warrior know the way to the rear of an enemy's castle!"

After this most audacious speech, a young samurai of eighteen years old named Beppu-no-Kotarō Kiyoshige of Musashi spoke up and said: "I have often been told by my father Yoshishige that whether you are hunting on the mountains or fighting an enemy, if you lose your way you must take an old horse, tie the reins and throw them on his neck, and then drive him on in front, and he will always find a path." "Well spoken," said Yoshitsune, "they say an old horse will find the road even when it is buried in snow!" So they took an old grey horse, trapped him with a silver-plated saddle and a well-polished bit, and tying the reins and throwing them on his neck, drove him on in front of them, and so plunged into the unknown mountains.

As it was the beginning of the second month, the snow had melted here and there on the peaks and at times they thought they saw flowers, while at times they heard the notes of the bush-warbler of the valleys, and were hidden from sight in the mist. As they ascended, the snow-clad peaks towered white and glistening on either side of them, and as they descended again into the valleys, the cliffs rose green on either hand. The pines hung down under their load of snow, and scarcely could they trace the narrow and mossy path. When a sudden gust blew down a cloud of snow-flakes, they almost took them for the falling plum-blossom. Whipping up their steeds to their best pace they rode on some distance, until the falling dusk compelled them to bivouac for the night in the depth of the mountains.

As they were thus halted, Musashi-bō Benkei suddenly appeared with an old man he had intercepted. In answer to the questions of Yoshitsune he declared that he was a hunter who lived in these mountains, and that he knew all that country very well. "Then," said Yoshitsune, "what do you think of my plan of riding down into Ichi-no-tani, the stronghold of the Heike?" "Ah," replied the old man, "that can hardly be done. The valley is a hundred yards deep, and of that about half is steep cliff where no one can go. Besides, the Heike will have dug pitfalls and spread caltrops[21] inside the stronghold to make it impossible for your horses."

"Indeed?" returned Yoshitsune, "but is it possible for a stag to pass there?" "That stags pass there is certain," replied the hunter, "for in the warm days of spring they come from Harima to seek the thick pasture of Tamba, and when the winter grows cold they go back towards Inamino in Harima where the snow lies lighter." "Forsooth!" ejaculated Yoshitsune, "then a horse can do it, for where a stag may pass, there a horse can go also. Will you then be our guide?" "I am an old man now; how can I go so far?" replied the hunter. "But you have a son?" "I have." And Kumaō Maru, a youth of eighteen, soon appeared before the Genji leader.

Then Yoshitsune performed the ceremony of Gempuku for the young man, giving him the name of Washio Saburō Yoshihisa, the name of his father being Washio Shōji Takehisa, and he accompanied them, going on in front to guide them down into Ichi-no-tani. And after the Heike had been overthrown and the Genji obtained the supremacy, and his lord Yoshitsune fell into disfavour with his brother and fled to Mutsu and fell there, Washio Saburō Yoshihisa was one of those who followed him to the death.

The Descent of the Hill

Thereafter the battle became general and the various clans of the Gen and Hei surged over each other in mixed and furious combat. The men of the Miura, Kamakura, Chichibu, Ashikaga, Noiyo,

21. spiked traps to ensnare horses.

Yokoyama, Inomata, Kodama, Nishi Tsuki and Kisaichi clans charged against each other with a roar like thunder, while the hills re-echoed to the sound of their war-cries, and the shafts they shot at each other fell like rain. Some were wounded slightly and fought on, some grappled and stabbed each other to death, while others bore down their adversaries and cut off their heads; everywhere the fight rolled forward and backward, so that none could tell who were victors or vanquished.

Thus it did not appear that the main body of the Genji had been successful in their attack, when at dawn on the seventh day Kurō Onzōshi Yoshitsune with his force of three thousand horsemen, having climbed to the top of the Hiyodorigoe, was resting his horses before the descent. Just then, startled by the movements of his men, two stags and a doe rushed out and fled over the cliff straight into the camp of the Heike.

"That is strange," exclaimed the Heike men-at-arms, "for the deer of this part ought to be frightened at our noise and run away to the mountains. Ah! it must be the enemy who is preparing to drop on us from above!" And they began to run about in confusion, when forth strode Takechi-no-Mushadokoro of the province of Iyo, and drawing his bow transfixed the two stags, though letting the doe escape. "Thus," he cried, "will we deal with any who try that road, and none are likely to pass it alive!" "What useless shooting of stags is this?" said Etchū Zenji Moritoshi when he saw it; "one of those arrows might have stopped ten of the enemy, so why waste them in that fashion?"

Then Yoshitsune, looking down on the Heike position from the top of the cliff, ordered some horses to be driven down the declivity, and of these, though some missed their footing half-way, and breaking their legs, fell to the bottom and were killed, three saddled horses scrambled down safely and stood, trembling in every limb, before the residence of Etchū Zenji. "If they have riders to guide them," said Yoshitsune, "the horses will get down without damage, so let us descend, and I will show you the way;" and he rode over the cliff at the head of his thirty retainers, seeing which the whole force of three thousand followed on after him.

For more than a hundred yards the slope was sandy with small pebbles, so that they slid straight down it and landed on a level place, from which they could survey the rest of the descent. From thence downwards it was all great mossy boulders, but steep as a well, and some fifty yards to the bottom. It seemed impossible to go on any farther, neither could they now retrace their steps, and the soldiers were recoiling in horror, thinking that their end had come, when Miura-no-Sahara Jūrō Yoshitsura sprang forward and shouted: "In my part we ride down places like this any day to catch a bird; the Miura would make a race course of this;" and down he went, followed by all the rest.

So steep was the descent that the stirrups of the hinder man struck against the helmet or armour of the one in front of him, and so dangerous did it look that they averted their eyes as they went down. "Ei! Ei!" they ejaculated under their breath as they steadied their horses, and their daring seemed rather that of demons than of men. So they reached the bottom, and as soon as they found themselves safely down they burst forth with a mighty shout, which echoed along the cliffs so that it sounded rather like the battle-cry of ten thousand men than of three.

Then Murakami-no-Hangwan-dai Yasukuni seized a torch and fired the houses and huts of the Heike so that they went up in smoke in a few moments, and when their men saw the clouds of black smoke rising they at once made a rush toward the sea, if haply they might find a way of escape. There was no lack of ships drawn up by the beach, but in their panic four or five hundred men in full armour and even a thousand all crowded into one ship, so that when they had rowed out not more than fifty or sixty yards from the shore, three large ships turned over and sank before their eyes.

Moreover those in the ships would only take on board those warriors who were of high rank, and thrust away the common soldiers, slashing at them with their swords and halberds, but even though they saw this, rather than stay and be cut down by the enemy, they clung to the ships and strove to drag themselves on board, so that their hands and arms were cut off and they fell back into the sea, which quickly reddened with their blood.

Thus, both on the main front and on the sea-shore did the young warriors of Musashi and Sagami strain every nerve in the fight, caring nothing for their lives as they rushed desperately to the attack. What must have been the feelings of Noto-no-kami Noritsune, who in all his battles had never been vanquished until now? Mounting his charger Usuzumi, he galloped away toward the west, and taking ship from Takasago in Harima, crossed over to Yashima in Sanuki.

The Death of Tadanori

Satsuma-no-kami Tadanori, the Commander of the western army, clad in a dark-blue hitatare and a suit of armour with black silk lacing, and mounted on a great black horse with a saddle enriched with lacquer of powdered gold, was calmly withdrawing with his following of a hundred horsemen, when Okabe-no-Rokuyata Tadazumi of Musashi espied him and pursued at full gallop, eager to bring down so noble a prize.

"This must be some great leader!" he cried. "Shameful! to turn your back to the foe!" Tadanori turned in the saddle; "We are friends! We are friends!" he replied, as he continued on his way. As he had turned, however, Tadazumi had caught a glimpse of his face and noticed that his teeth were blackened. "There are none of our side who have blackened teeth," he said, "this must be one of the Heike Courtiers." And overtaking him, he ranged up to him to grapple. When his hundred followers saw this, since they were hired retainers drawn from various provinces, they scattered and fled in all directions, leaving their leader to his fate.

But Satsuma-no-kami, who had been brought up at Kumano, was famous for his strength, and was extremely active and agile besides, so clutching Tadazumi he pulled him from his horse, dealing him two stabs with his dirk while he was yet in the saddle, and following them with another as he was falling. The first two blows fell on his armour and failed to pierce it, while the third wounded him in the face but was not mortal, and as Tadanori sprang down upon him to cut off his head, Tadazumi's page, who had been riding behind him, slipped from his horse and with a blow of his sword cut off Tadanori's arm above the elbow.

Satsuma-no-kami, seeing that all was over and wishing to have a short space to say the death-prayer, flung Tadazumi from him so that he fell about a bow's length away. Then turning toward the west he repeated: "Kōmyō Henjō Jippō Sekai, Nembutsu Shujō Sesshu Fusha; O Amida Nyorai, who sheddest the light of Thy Presence through the ten quarters of the world, gather into Thy Radiant Heaven all who call upon Thy Name!" And just as his prayer was finished, Tadazumi from behind swept off his head.

Not doubting that he had taken the head of a noble foe, but quite unaware who he might be, he was searching his armour when he came across a piece of paper fastened to his quiver, on which was written a verse with this title: "The Traveller's Host, a Flower."

> Now the daylight dies,
> And the shadow of a tree
> Serves me for an inn.
> For the host to welcome me
> There is but a wayside flower.

Wherefore he knew that it could be none but Satsuma-no-kami. Then he lifted up the head on his sword's point and shouted with a loud voice: "Satsuma-no-kami Dono, the demon-warrior of Nippon, slain by Okabe-Rokuyata Tadazumi of Musashi!" And when they heard it, all, friends and foes alike, moistened the sleeves of their armour with their tears exclaiming: "Alas! what a great captain has passed away! Warrior and artist and poet; in all things he was pre-eminent."

Shigehira Is Taken Alive

Hon-sammi Chūjō Shigehira was second in command at Ikuta no-mori, and he was attired that day in a hitatare of dark-blue cloth on which a pattern of rocks and sea-birds was embroidered in light yellow silk, and armour with purple lacing deepening in its hue toward the skirts. On his head was a helmet with tall golden horns, and his sword also was mounted in gold. His arrows were feathered with black and white falcon plumes, and in his hand he carried a "Shigeto" bow. He was mounted on a renowned war-horse called Dōji-kage, whose trappings were resplendent with ornaments of gold. With him was his foster-brother Gotō Hyōye Morinaga in a hitatare of dyed brocade and a suit of armour with scarlet lacing, and he too was mounted on a splendid cream-coloured charger named Yomenashi.

As they were riding along the shore to take ship and escape, Shō-no-Shirō Takaie and Kajiwara Genda Kagesue, thinking they looked a fine prize, spurred on their horses and bore down upon them. Now there were many ships ranged along the shore, but the enemy pressed on them so hard from behind that there was no opportunity to embark, so the two, crossing the Minatogawa and the Karumogawa, and leaving Hasu-no-ike on the right and Koma-no-hayashi on the left, rode hard through Itayado and Suma and endeavoured to make their escape to the west.

As Shigehira was mounted on such a famous charger as Dōji-kage it seemed unlikely that any ordinary horse would overhaul him, and the pursuers mounts were already weakening, when Kajiwara drew his bow to the head and sent an arrow whizzing after them. Though a long venture the shaft flew true to its mark, and buried itself deeply in the hind-leg of the Chūjō's steed, just above the root of the tail. Seeing its pace slacken his foster-brother Morinaga, thinking that the Chūjō might demand his mount, whipped it up and made good his escape. "Ah!" exclaimed the Chūjō, "why do you desert me thus? Have you forgotten all your promises?" But he paid no heed, and tearing off the red badge from his armour, thought of nothing but saving himself by flight. Then the Chūjō, seeing that his horse could go no farther, plunged headlong into the sea to die by drowning, but the water was so shallow that there was no time, and as he started to cut himself open, Shō-no-Shirō Takaie rode up, and springing from his horse, called out to him: "Desist I pray you; allow me to take you with me." And placing him on his own horse, he bound him to the pommel of his saddle and escorted him back to the Genji camp.

The Chūjō's foster-brother Morinaga, who had ridden away and deserted him, fled to seek refuge with Onaka Hōkyō, one of the priests of Kumano, but after his death returned again to the Capital with his widow, when she came up on account of a lawsuit that she had. There he was recognized by many of his associates who had known him in past times, and they pointed the finger of scorn at him saying: "How disgraceful! There is Gotō Hyōye Morinaga, who deserted the Chūjō in his need and refused to aid him. He has come back again with the widow of the Hōkyō." And Morinaga, when he heard it was so ashamed that he hid his face with his fan.

The Death of Atsumōri

Now when the Heike were routed at Ichi-no-tani, and their Nobles and Courtiers were fleeing to the shore to escape in their ships, Kumagai Jirō Naozane came riding along a narrow path on to the beach, with the intention of intercepting one of their great captains. Just then his eye fell on a single horseman who was attempting to reach one of the ships in the offing, and had swum his horse out some twenty yards from the water's edge.

He was richly attired in a silk hitatare embroidered with storks, and the lacing of his armour was shaded green; his helmet was surmounted by lofty horns, and the sword he wore was gay with gold. His twenty-four arrows had black and white feathers, and he carried a black-lacquered bow bound with rattan. The horse he rode was dappled grey, and its saddle glittered with gold-mounting. Not doubting that he was one of the chief captains, Kumagai beckoned to him with his war-fan, crying out: "Shameful! to show an enemy your back. Return! Return!"

Then the warrior turned his horse and rode him back to the beach, where Kumagai at once engaged him in mortal combat. Quickly hurling him to the ground, he sprang upon him and tore off his helmet to cut off his head, when he beheld the face of a youth of sixteen or seventeen, delicately powdered and with blackened teeth, just about the age of his own son, and with features of great beauty. "Who are you?" he inquired; "Tell me your name, for I would spare your life." "Nay, first say who you are"; replied the young man. "I am Kumagai Jirō Naozane of Musashi, a person of no particular importance." "Then you have made a good capture"; said the youth. "Take my head and show it to some of my side and they will tell you who I am."

"Though he is one of their leaders," mused Kumagai, "if I slay him it will not turn defeat into victory, and if I spare him, it will not turn victory into defeat. When my son Kojirō was but slightly wounded at Ichi-no-tani, did it not make my heart bleed? How pitiful then to put this youth to death." And so he was about to set him free, when, looking behind him, he saw Doi and Kajiwara coming up with fifty horsemen. "Alas! look there," he exclaimed, the tears running down his face, "though I would spare your life, the whole countryside swarms with our men, and you cannot escape them. If you must die, let it be by my hand, and I will see that prayers are said for your rebirth in bliss." "Indeed it must be," said the young warrior, "so take off my head at once."

Then Kumagai, weeping bitterly, and so overcome by his compassion for the fair youth that his eyes swam and his hand trembled so that he could scarcely wield his blade, hardly knowing what he did, at last cut off his head. "Alas!" he cried, "what life is so hard as that of a soldier? Only because I was born of a warrior family must I suffer this affliction! How lamentable it is to do such cruel deeds!" And he pressed his face to the sleeve of his armour and wept bitterly. Then, wrapping up the head, he was stripping off the young man's armour, when he discovered a flute in a brocade bag that he was carrying in his girdle.

"Ah," he exclaimed, "it was this youth and his friends who were diverting themselves with music within the walls this morning. Among all our men of the Eastern Provinces I doubt if there is any who has brought a flute with him. What esthetes are these Courtiers of the Heike!" And when he brought them and showed them to the Commander, all who saw them were moved to tears; and he then discovered that the youth was Taiyū-Atsumōri, the youngest son of Shūri-no-taiyū Tsunemori, aged seventeen years. From this time the mind of Kumagai was turned toward the religious life and he eventually became a recluse.

The flute of Atsumōri was one which his grandfather Tadanori, who was a famous player, had received as a present from the Emperor Toba, and had handed down to his father Tsunemori, who had given it to Atsumōri because of his skill on the instrument. It was called "Saeda."[22] Concerning this story of Kumagai we may quote the saying that "even in the most droll and flippant farce there is the germ of a Buddhist Psalm."[23]

Thus as the day wore on both Genji and Heike fell in great numbers at the eastern and western barriers, and before the towers and beneath the barricades the bodies of men and horses lay in heaps, while the green grass of Ichi-no-tani and Osasahara was turned to crimson. Countless were those who fell by arrow and sword at Ichi-no-tani and Ikuta-no-mori, by the hillside and by the strand of the sea. Two thousand heads did the Genji take in this battle, and of the Courtiers of the Heike, Echizen-no-Sammi Michimori, his younger brother Kurando-no-taiyū Narimori, Satsuma-no-kami Tadanori, Musashi-no-kami Tomoakira, Bitchū-no-kami Moromori, Owari-no-kami Kiyosada, Awaji-no-kami Kiyofusa, Kōgō-gū-no-suke

22. "Little Branch." [Sadler's note.]
23. I.e., how much more does a serious incident like this turn the mind to religion. [Sadler's note.]

Tsunemasa the eldest son of Tsunemori, his younger brother Wakasa-no-kami Tsunetoshi, and his younger brother Taiyū Atsumōri, beside ten others, all fell at Ichi-no-tani.

When their stronghold was thus captured, the Heike were compelled to put to sea once more, taking the child Emperor with them. Some of their vessels were driven by wind and tide toward the province of Kii, while others rowed and tossed about, buffeted by the waves, in the offing of Ashiya. Some rocked on the billows off Suma and Akashi, steering aimlessly hither and thither, their crews weary and dispirited as they turned on their hard plank couches, and viewed the moon of spring mistily through their tear-dimmed eyes.

Some crossed the straits of Awaji and drifted along by Ejima-ga-Iso, likening their lot to the sad sea-birds that fly there seeking by twilight the mate they have lost, while others still lay off Ichi-no-tani uncertain of where to steer. Yesterday, with a host of a hundred thousand, feared and obeyed by fourteen provinces, they lay with high hopes but one day's journey from the Capital, and now, after the defeat of Ichi-no-tani, they were scattered and dispersed along the coast, each unaware of the fate of his friend.

Michimori's Wife Drowns Herself

Now Kenda Takiguchi Tokikazu, a retainer of Echizen-no-Sammi Michimori, fled in haste to the ship in which was the wife of Michimori, and said to her: "This morning my lord was surrounded by seven horsemen at the Minatogawa and fell fighting, and among them were Sasaki-no-Kimura Saburō Naritsuna of Ōmi, and Tamai-no-Shirō Sukekage of Musashi. I too would have stayed with him to the end and died, but he had strictly charged me before, saying that if anything should happen to him I must at all costs escape to look after my mistress; and so it is that I have saved my worthless life and come to you."

On hearing these tidings his mistress uttered no word, but covered her face and fell prostrate. Though she had already heard that he was dead, she had not at first believed it, but for two or three days had waited as for one who had gone out for a short time and would soon come back. However, when four or five days had passed, her confidence was shaken, and she fell into deep melancholy. Her feelings were shared by her foster-mother who alone accompanied her and shared the same pillow.

From the seventh day, on which the news was brought to her, until the evening of the thirteenth she did not rise from her bed. At dawn on the fourteenth day the Heike were starting to cross again to Yashima, and until the evening before she still lay on her couch. Then as night drew on and all was quiet in the ship, she turned to her foster-mother and said: "Though I had been told it, until this morning I did not realize that my husband was dead, but now, this evening, I know it is true. Every one says he was killed at the Minatogawa, and after that there is none who says he has seen him alive. And what grieves me most is that when I saw him for a short while on the night before the battle he was sad and said to me: 'I am certain to be slain in to-morrow's battle, and I wonder what will become of you after I am gone.' As there have been so many battles I did not pay any special heed to it, but if I had thought that it was the last time indeed, I would have promised to follow him to the after world.

"Then, fearing that he might think me too reserved, I told him what I had up till that time concealed, that I was 'not alone.' He was extremely pleased to hear it and said: 'Ah, I have reached thirty years of age without having any children; I hope you will make it a boy if you can, for that will be a good memento of myself to leave behind in this fleeting world.' Then he went on to ask me how many months it was, and how I felt, and bade me keep as quiet as was possible in this ever-rolling ship that the birth might be easy.

"Ah, how sad it all is! If women die at that time it is a most shameful and melancholy end that they suffer, and yet, if I bear this child and bring it up so that it may recall to me the features of him who is gone, every time I look on it it will bring back the memory of my former love, and that will cause me grief without end. Death is the road that none may avoid. Even if I should by good luck pass scatheless through these dangerous times, can I trust myself to escape the common fate of being entangled in some other passion? That too is a melancholy prospect. To behold him in my dreams when I sleep, and to awake only to look on his features! Better to drown in the depths of the sea than to live on thus bereft of my love. My heart is full of sorrow at leaving you thus alone, but I pray you send to Miyako this letter which I have written, and take my robes to some priest, that his prayers may hasten the enlightenment of my husband, and may assist me too in the after world."

When she had made an end of speaking, the older woman, repressing her tears, replied: "How can you thus resolve to forsake your little one and leave your mother alone in her old age? Is your loss any greater than that of the other wives of the nobles of our house who have fallen at Ichi-no-tani? Though you may think you will sit on the same lotus as your husband, yet after rebirth you must both pass through the Six Ways and the Four Births, and in which of these can you be sure of meeting? And if you fail to meet, of what use is it to cast away your life? So be brave and calm your mind until your child is born, and strive to bring it up, whatever hardships may threaten. Then you may become a nun and spend your days in prayer for the happy rebirth of your departed husband.

Moreover, as for Miyako, who is there who can carry such a letter?"

Then the lady, wishing to comfort and reassure her weeping parent, replied: "If I seem strange, you must remember that under the stress of misfortune or the pain of parting to think of ending one's life is a natural thing, though really to nerve oneself to do so is not so easy; and if I should indeed resolve to carry out this intention I will be sure to let you know. But now it is late and I would sleep."

Now her foster-mother, seeing that the lady had not even taken a bath for the last four or five days, concluded that her mind was indeed made up, and had herself determined that if she did so she would follow her even to the bottom of the sea, for she did not wish to live a day longer if her daughter was dead, so for some time she remained awake watching by her side, but at last she fell asleep, whereupon the lady, who had been awaiting this opportunity, slipped out quietly and ran to the bulwarks of the ship.

Gazing out over the wide expanse of waters, she was uncertain in which direction lay the western quarter, but turning toward the setting moon as it was sinking behind the mountains, calmly she repeated the Nembutsu.[24] The melancholy cry of the sea-birds on the distant sand-spits and the harsh creaking of the rudder mingled with her voice as she repeated it a hundred times. "Namu Amida Nyorai, Saviour who leadest us to the Western Paradise, according to Thy True Vow unite on the same lotus flower an inseparable husband and wife!" And with the last invocation still on her lips she cast herself into the waves.

It was about midnight of the day on which they were to start for Yashima, and all aboard the ship were sleeping soundly, so no one perceived her. But as she plunged into the waves she attracted the attention of the helmsman, who alone of the crew was not asleep, and he cried out loudly that a woman had gone overboard from the ship, whereon the foster-mother, suddenly awakening, felt by her side, and finding nothing, was overcome by sorrow and amazement. Then, though all did their utmost to get her out of the water and save her life, as usual in the spring, the sky was cloudy and the moon obscured so that they could not see where she was, and when at last they did discover her and pull her out of the water, her life was already departing.

Thus they laid her on the deck with the salt water streaming from her white hakama[25] and the thick double layers of her Court costume, and dripping from her long black hair, and her foster-mother, taking her hands in hers and pressing her face to her cold features, exclaimed: "Why did you not let me know your resolve,

24. an invocation to the Buddha, the words of which are given below. *Namu Amida Nyorai* means "Praise to Amida Buddha." The mere repetition of such prayers was believed by some sects to insure salvation.

25. a skirt.

and let me follow you to the bottom of the sea? Woe is me, now I am left here all alone! At least will you not speak to me once more?" But though she thus addressed her daughter in tones of agonized entreaty, she was already destined for that other world, and her breath, which until now had just barely fluttered in her body, at last departed for ever.

KAMO-NO CHŌMEI

(1153?–1216)

Life in a Ten-Foot-Square Hut *(Hōjōki)*

Life in a Ten-Foot-Square Hut is one of the masterpieces in a great tradition of fugitive essays (*zuhitsu*) in Japanese literature. Earthly existence, to the Buddhist, is transitory, and events blow by like smoke, but the recording of even the trivial details of this "floating" world has occupied Japanese diarists, writers of travel literature, and essayists since earliest times.

Though the authorship has been disputed, the *Hōjōki* is probably the work of Kamo-no Chōmei (1153?–1216). He was born into a family of Shinto priests in the service of the Kamojinja shrine in Kyoto. The emperor admired his poetic talents and appointed him to the Imperial Poetry Bureau. Apparently he failed to become a Shinto priest and instead entered a Buddhist order, but even after a religious renunciation of the world he maintained an interest in art and poetry and made occasional visits to Kamakura to visit the emperor. From his thirtieth year, Kamo-no Chōmei lived in a tiny hut, writing and living the life of a hermit with only sporadic visits to the world. He did not seek austerity for its own sake, however. He devoted his days to saying his prayers and reading the Buddhist sacred books, but also to playing the lute and harp and to making friends with the children who lived in the village near him.

Kamo makes an interesting contrast with Henry David Thoreau, who also recorded, in *Walden*, a retreat from the clutter and trivial busyness of American life for the purpose of meditation. The essential requirements of such meditation, whether it be for Kamo, Thoreau, or for an anchorite in a Christian religious order, are world of affairs must be eliminated—one cannot think if one is interrupted by the desire for business success, the operation of a large household, the necessity to be elaborately dressed, fed, or entertained, or by a wife and children, Bacon's "hostages to fortune." Also, the recluse is animated by a desire to think of ultimate realities, not merely by the desire to simplify his life. Thoreau gives us a Yankee solution to the problem. He does various things at Walden: he meditates philosophically, drawing his inspiration frequently from great literature; he builds his cottage with a Westerner's eye for the mechanics of carpentry and a pride in the physical accomplishment of the enterprise; he engages in scientific observation—a true Westerner, he is not in practice convinced that the world is evanescent, mere smoke or foam; and, finally, he makes forays into the world of men to observe their doings and to have discourse with them. The Christian anchorite, on his part, operates in a world of much more rigorous rules than those of Buddhism or Shinto. His religious world exists in a spectrum of time from the birth of Christ to the Second Coming of the Messiah, and his life as a recluse, no matter how far he retreats, is a role played against a background of an activist, proselytizing to a religion that includes few recluses and many clergy embroiled in worldly affairs for the sake of the faith. Kamo does not have these pressures. He can sit in his hut and contemplate eternity and at the same time poetically observe the passing of the world of the here and now. His God is a world soul that is impersonal, and his world is an insubstantial pageant that brings joy and pain (even to the recluse in the hut) but in which events are finally of not enough importance to produce tragedy or ecstasy, but only transitory beauty and pathos.

The style of the *Hōjōki* is lofty and dignified, and the work is somewhat more systematically organized than that of most of the other essayists.

From Life in a Ten-Foot-Square Hut*

Ceaselessly the river flows, and yet the water is never the same, while in the still pools the shifting foam gathers and is gone, never staying for a moment. Even so is man and his habitation.

In the stately ways of our shining Capital[1] the dwellings of high and low raise their roofs in rivalry as in the beginning, but few indeed there are that have stood for many generations. This year falling into decay and the next built up again, how often does the mansion of one age turn into the cottages of the next. And so, too, are they who live in them. The streets of the city are thronged as of old, but of the many people we meet there how very few are those that we knew in our youth. Dead in the morning and born at night, so man goes on forever, unenduring as the foam on the water.

And this man that is born and dies, who knows whence he came and whither he goes? And who knows also why with so much labour he builds his house, who knows which will survive the other? The

* From *The Ten Foot Square Hut and Tales of the Heike,* translated by A. L. Sadler. Angus and Robertson, Sydney, 1928. Copyright 1928 by A. L. Sadler. Reprinted by permission of A. L. Sadler.

1. Kyoto.

dew may fall and the flower remain, but only to wither in the morning sun, or the dew may stay on the withered flower, but it will not see another evening.

During the forty years or so that I have lived since I began to understand the meaning of things I have seen not a few strange happenings.

In the third year of the era Angen,[2] and the twenty-eighth day of the fourth month I think it was, the wind blew a gale, and at the hour of the Dog (8 p.m.) a fire started in the south-east of the Capital and was blown across to the north-west. And everything as far as the Shujaku Gate, the Daikyoku Hall and the Office of Internal Affairs was reduced to ashes in a single night. They say it started at Higuchi Tominokōji in a temporary structure used as a hospital. Now as the flames came on they spread out like an opened fan, and the remoter houses were smothered in smoke while those nearer roared up in flames. The sky was dark with ashes and against this black background the fire glowed red like early dawn, while everywhere the flames driven by the wind went leaping on over a space more than a hundred yards wide. And of those caught by it some fell choked in the smoke, while others were overtaken by the flames and perished suddenly. And those few who managed with difficulty to escape were quite unable to take their goods with them, and how many precious treasures were thus lost none can tell.

Of the Palaces of the Great Nobles sixteen were entirely destroyed, and of the houses of lesser people the number is unknown. One third of the city was burnt and many thousands must have perished, and cattle and horses beyond reckoning. The handiwork of man is a vain thing enough in any place, but to spend money and time on building houses in such a dangerous spot as the Capital is foolish indeed beyond measure.

Then again in the fourth year of the era Jisho, the fourth month and about the twenty-ninth day, a great typhoon blew with immense violence from the neighborhood of Naka-no-Mikado and Kyōgoku toward Rokujō. For the space of near a quarter of a mile it raged, and of the houses within its reach there were none, great or small, that it did not throw down. Of some the whole house fell flat, and of others the roof of the gate was taken off and blown it may be some five hundred yards. Others again had their boundary walls levelled, so that there was nothing between them and their neighbor's premises. Household treasures were blown up into the air and destroyed and pieces of board and shingles filled the air like driven leaves in winter. The dust was as thick as smoke, and the roar of the wind so loud that none could hear the other speak. I suppose the bitter wind of Karma[3] that blows us to Hell could not be more savage or fearsome.

2. 1175 A.D. [Sadler's note.]

3. See pp. 154–155.

And not only were the houses damaged, but a number of people were lamed and hurt in trying to repair them. This whirlwind eventually veered round to the south-west and fresh shouts of distress arose. It is true these winds are not infrequent, but yet there were very many who said: "Ah, this must be the portent of some dreadful happening."

And in the Waterless Month (sixth) of the same year suddenly and without warning the Capital was changed.[4] And this was a most extraordinary thing, for they say that the Capital was first fixed here in the August Age of the Mikado Saga, and so it has remained for all these centuries. And thus to change it without any good reason was a very great mistake, and it was no wonder that the people should complain and lament. Still that was, of course, quite unavailing, and all the inhabitants, beginning with His August Majesty the Mikado, and the Ministers and Great Nobles of the Court, had perforce to remove to the new Capital at Naniwa in Settsu.

And of those who wished to get on in the world who would stay in the former Capital? All who coveted Court Rank, or were the expectant clients of some great lord, bustled about to get away as soon as possible. It was only a few unadaptable people who had nothing to hope for, who stayed behind in the ancient Capital.

And those mansions that stood so proudly side by side from day to day became more ruinous. Many were broken up and floated down the river Yodo, while their pleasure grounds were turned into ricefields. And the fashions changed also in these days, so that every one came to ride on horseback, while the more dignified ox-car was quite forsaken. And everybody was scrambling to get land by the Western Sea and none cared for manors in the north and east.

Now it happened at this time that I chanced to go down myself to the new Capital in the province of Settsu. And when I came to look at it the site was cramped and too narrow to lay out the Avenues properly. And the mountains towered over it to the north while the sea hemmed it in on the south and the noise of the waves and the scent of the brine were indeed too much to be borne.

The Palace was right up against the hills, a "Log-hut Palace" built of round timbers. It all seemed so very strange and rough, and yet somehow not a little elegant. And as for all those houses that had been broken up and brought down, so that the river was almost dammed up by them, I wondered wherever they were going to put them, for still there was so much empty ground, and very few dwellings had been built. So the old Capital was already a waste and the new one not yet made. Every one felt as unsettled as drifting clouds. And the natives of the place were full of complaints over losing

4. These disturbances took place during the Minamoto-Taira feuds depicted in the *Heike Monogatari*. The Minamoto gained power, and their stronghold in Settsu became the capital when the emperor (the mikado) went there for protection.

their land, while the new inhabitants grumbled at the difficulty of building on such a site. And of the people one met in the streets those who ought to have been riding in carriages were on horseback and those who usually wore court costume were in military surcoats. The whole atmosphere of the Capital was altered and they looked like a lot of country samurai. And those who said that these changes were a portent of some civil disturbance seemed to be not without reason, for as time went on things became more and more unquiet and there was a feeling of unrest everywhere.

But the murmurings of the people proved of some effect, for in the following winter they were ordered back to the Ancient Capital. But all the same the houses that had been destroyed and removed could not at once be restored to their former condition.

Now we learn that in the dim ages of the past, in the August Era of a certain most revered Mikado, the Empire was ruled with great kindness: that the Palace was thatched with reeds and its eaves were not repaired, because it was seen that little smoke went up from the houses, and the taxes were on that account remitted. So did the sovereign have pity on his people and help them in their distress. When we compare it with these ancient days we can well understand what a time we live in. And if this were not enough, in the era Yōwa[5] I think it was, but so many years have elapsed that I am not certain, there were two years of famine, and a terrible time indeed it was. The spring and summer were scorching hot, and autumn and winter brought typhoons and floods, and as one bad season followed another the Five Cereals[6] could not ripen. In vain was the spring plowing, and the summer sowing was but labour lost. Neither did you hear the joyous clamour of the harvest and storing in autumn and winter.

Some deserted their land and went to other provinces, and others left their houses and dwelt in the hills. Then all sorts of prayers were said and special services recited, but things grew no better. And since for everything the people of the Capital had to depend on the country around it, when no farmers came in with food how could they continue their usual existence? Though householders brought out their goods into the street and besought people to buy like beggars with no sense of shame, yet no one would even look at them, and if there should be any ready to barter they held money cheap enough, but could hardly be brought to part with grain. Beggars filled the streets and their clamour was deafening to the ears.

So the first year passed and it was difficult enough to live, but when we looked for some improvement during the next it was even worse, for a pestilence followed, and the prayers of the people were of no effect. As the days passed they felt like fish when the water

5. 1181 A.D. [Sadler's note.]
6. a general expression for grain. Rice and corn are chiefly meant.

dries up, and respectable citizens who ordinarily wore hats and shoes now went barefooted begging from house to house. And while you looked in wonder at such a sight they would suddenly fall down and die in the road. And by the walls and in the highways you could see everywhere the bodies of those who had died of starvation. And as there was none to take them away, a terrible stench filled the streets, and people went by with their eyes averted. The ordinary roads were bad enough, but in the slums by the River-bed there was not even room for carts and horses to pass.

As for the poor labourers and woodcutters and such like, when they could cut no more firewood and there was none to help them, they broke up their own cottages and took the pieces into the city to sell. And what one man could carry was hardly enough to provide him with food for one day.

And it was a shocking thing to see among these scraps of firewood fragments with red lacquer and gold and silver foil still sticking to them. And this because those who could get nothing else broke into the mountain temples and stole the images and utensils and broke them up for kindling. It must be a wretched and degenerate age when such things are done.

Another very sad thing was that those who had children who were very dear to them almost invariably died before them, because they denied themselves to give their sons and daughters what they needed. And so these children would always survive their parents. And there were babies who continued to feed at their mother's breast, not knowing she was already dead.

Now there was a noble recluse of the Jison-in Hall of the Ninnaji temple called Ryūgyō Hō-in and entitled Lord of the Treasury, who out of pity for the endless number of dead arranged for some monks to go round the city and write the syllable "A" on the foreheads of all they found, that they might receive enlightenment and enter Amida's Paradise.[7] And the number that they counted within the city, in the space of four or five months, between the First and Ninth Avenues on the north and south and between Kyōgoku and Shujaku on the east and west, was at least forty-two thousand three hundred. And when there is added to this those who perished before and after this period, and also those in the River-bed and Shirakawa and Western City quarters, they must have been almost beyond count. And then there were all the other provinces of the Empire. It is said that not long ago in the August Age of the Mikado Sutoku-in in the era Chōshō[8] there was such a visitation. But of that I know nothing. What I have seen with my own eyes was strange and terrible enough.

7. The spirits of the dead linger for varying lengths of time on earth. These "ghosts" frequently make their appearance in fiction. Amida is the Buddha. Souls go to his paradise only after freeing themselves of earthly desires.

8. 1132 A.D. [Sadler's note.]

Then in the second year of the era Gen-ryaku[9] there was a great earthquake. And this was no ordinary one. The hills crumbled down and filled the rivers, and the sea surged up and overwhelmed the land. The earth split asunder and water gushed out. The rocks broke off and rolled down into the valleys, while boats at sea staggered in the swell and horses on land could find no sure foothold. What wonder that in the Capital, of all the temples, monasteries, pagodas and mausoleums, there should not be one that remained undamaged. Some crumbled to pieces and some were thrown down, while the dust rose in clouds like smoke around them, and the sound of the falling buildings was like thunder. Those who were in them were crushed at once, while those who ran out did so to find the ground yawning before them. If one has no wings he cannot fly, and unless one is a Dragon he will find it difficult to ride the clouds. For one terror following on another there is nothing equal to an earthquake.

Among those who suffered was the child of a warrior some six or seven years old. He had made a little hut under the eaves of the earthen wall and was playing there when the whole wall fell and buried him. And it was very sad to see how his parents cried aloud in their grief as they picked him up all battered and with his eyes protruding from his head. Even a stern samurai at such a time thought it no shame to show signs of his deep feelings. And indeed I think it quite natural.

The worst shocks soon ceased, but the after tremors continued for some time. Every day there were some twenty or thirty that were beyond the ordinary. After the tenth and twentieth day they gradually came at longer intervals, four or five, and then two or three in a day. Then there would be a day and then several without any shock at all, but still these after shocks lasted, it may be three months.

Of the four elements, water, fire, and wind are always doing damage, but with the earth this is comparatively rare. It was in the era Saiko,[10] I think, that there was a great earthquake and the head of the Great Buddha in the Tōdaiji at Nara fell, which I consider a very sad loss indeed, but it is said to have been not so severe as the one I have described.

On these occasions it is the way of people to be convinced of the impermanence of all earthly things, and to talk of the evil of attachment to them, and of the impurity of their hearts, but when the months go by and then the years, we do not find them making mention of such views any more.

Thus it seems to me that all the difficulties of life spring from this fleeting evanescent nature of man and his habitation. And in other ways too the opportunities he has of being troubled and

9. 1184 A.D. [Sadler's note.]

10. 540 A.D. [Sadler's note.]

annoyed by things connected with his locality and rank are almost infinite.

Suppose he is a person of little account and lives near the mansion of a great man. He may have occasion to rejoice very heartily over something, but he cannot do so openly, and in the same way, if he be in trouble, it is quite unthinkable that he should lift up his voice and weep. He must be very circumspect in his deportment and bear himself in a suitably humble manner, and his feelings are like those of a sparrow near a hawk's nest. And if a poor man lives near a wealthy one he is continually ashamed of his ill appearance and has to come and go always with an apologetic air. And when he sees the envious glances of his wife and the servants, and hears the slighting way in which his neighbor refers to him, he is always liable to feel irritable and ill at ease. And if a man has little land round his house he is likely to suffer in a conflagration, while if he lives in an out of the way place it is awkward for travelling and he is very liable to be robbed.

Men of influence are usually greedy of place and power, while those of none are apt to be despised. If you have a lot of property you have many cares, while if you are poor there is always plenty to worry you. If you have servants, you are in their power, and if you compassionate others then that feeling masters you. If you follow the fashions around you, you will have little comfort, and if you do not you will be called crazy. Wherever you go and whatever you do it is hard to find rest for mind and body.

I inherited the estate of my great-grandmother on the father's side, and there I lived for a while. But then I left home and came down in the world and as there were very many reasons why I wished to live unnoticed, I could not remain where I was, so I built a cottage just suited to my wants. It was only a tenth of the size of my former home and contained only a living-room for myself, for I could not build a proper house. It had rough plastered walls and no gate, and the pillars were of bamboo, so it was really nothing more than a cart-shed. And as it was not far from the River-bed there was some peril from floods as well as anxiety about thieves.

So I went on living in this unsympathetic world amid many difficulties for thirty years, and the various rebuffs that I met left me with a poor opinion of this fleeting life. So when I arrived at the age of fifty I abandoned the world and retired, and since I had no wife or child it was by no means difficult to leave it, neither had I any rank or revenue to be a tie to hold me. And so it is that I have come to spend I know not how many useless years hidden in the mists of Mount Ohara. I am now sixty years old, and this hut in which I shall spend the last remaining years of my dew-like existence is like the shelter that some hunter might build for a night's lodging in the hills, or like the cocoon some old silkworm might spin. If I compare it to the cottage of my middle years it is not a hundredth of the size. Thus as old age draws on my hut has grown smaller and smaller. It is a cottage of quite a peculiar kind, for it is only ten feet square and less than seven feet high, and as I did not decide to fix it in any definite place I did not choose the site by divination as usual. The walls are of rough plastered earth and the roof is of thatch. All the joints are hinged with metal so that if the situation no longer pleases me I can easily take it down and transport it elsewhere. And this can be done with very little labour, for the whole will only fill two cart-loads, and beyond the small wage of the carters nothing else is needed.

Now hidden deep in the fastnesses of Mount Hino, I have put up eaves projecting on the south side to keep off the sun and a small bamboo veranda beneath them. On the west is the shelf for the offerings of water and flowers to Buddha, and in the middle, against the western wall is a picture of Amida Buddha so arranged that the setting sun shines from between his brows as though he were emitting his ray of light, while on the doors of his shrine are painted pictures of Fugen and Fudō.[11] Over the sliding doors on the north side is a little shelf on which stand three or four black leather cases containing some volumes of Japanese poems and music and a book of selections from the Buddhist Sutras. Beside these stand a harp and a lute of the kind called folding harp and jointed lute. On the eastern side is a bundle of fern fronds and a mat of straw on which I sleep at night. In the eastern wall there is a window before which stands my writing-table. A fire-box beside my pillow in which I can make a fire of broken brushwood completes the furniture. To the north of my little hut I have made a tiny garden surrounded by a thin low brushwood fence so that I can grow various kinds of medicinal herbs. Such is the style of my unsubstantial cottage.

As to my surroundings, on the south there is a little basin that I have made of piled-up rocks to receive the water that runs down from a bamboo spout above it, and as the forest trees reach close up to the eaves it is easy enough to get fuel.

The place is called Toyama. It is almost hidden in a tangled growth of evergreens. But though the valley is much overgrown it is open toward the west, so that I can contemplate the scenery and meditate on the enlightenment that comes from the Paradise in that quarter. In the spring I behold the clusters of wistaria shining like the purple clouds on which Amida Buddha comes to welcome his elect. In the summer I hear the cuckoo, and his note reminds me that he will soon guide me over the Hills of Death of which they call him the Warden. In autumn I hear everywhere the shrilling of the Evening Cicada and inquire of him if he is bewailing the

11. the Bodhisattvas Samanta Bhadra and Akshobya. [Sadler's note.] The former is a Buddhist deity of love; the latter, also a compassionate deity in whose honor a temple for lepers was erected at Nara in the eighth century.

vanity of this fleeting life, empty as his own dried up husk, while in winter the snow as it piles up and melts seems like an allegory of our evil Karma.

If I get tired of repeating the Invocation to Buddha or feel disinclined to read the Sutras,[12] and go to sleep or sit idly, there is none to rebuke me, no companion to make me feel ashamed. I may not have made any special vow of silence, but as I am all alone I am little likely to offend with the tongue, and even without intending to keep the Buddhist Commandments, separated from society it is not easy to break them.

In the morning, as I look out at the boats on the Uji River[13] by Ōkanoya, I may steal a phrase from the monk Mansei and compare this fleeting life to the white foam in their wake, and association may lead me to try a few verses myself in his style. Or in the evening, as I listen to the rustling of the maples in the wind the opening lines of the "Lute Maiden" by the great Chinese poet Po-chü-i[14] naturally occur to my mind, and my hand strays to the instrument and I play perhaps a piece or two in the style of Minamoto Tsunenobu.[15] And if I am in the mood for music I may play the piece called "Autumn Wind" to the accompaniment of the creaking of the pine-trees outside, or that entitled "Flowing Waters" in harmony with the purling of the stream. I have little skill in verse or music, but then I only play and compose for my own amusement, and not for the ears of other people.

At the foot of the hill there is a little cottage of brushwood where lives the keeper of these hills. And he has a boy who sometimes comes to bear me company, and when time is heavy on my hands we go for a walk. He is sixteen and I am sixty and though the difference in age is so great, we find plenty of amusement in each other's society.

Sometimes we gather the Lalong grass or the rock-pear or help ourselves to wild potatoes or parsley, or we may go as far as the ricefields at the foot of our hills and glean a few ears to make an offering to the deities. If the day is fine we may climb up some high peak and look out over the Capital in the distance and enjoy the views of Mt. Kobata, Fushimi, Toba or Hatsukashi. Fine scenery has no landlord, so there is nothing to hinder our pleasure.

When I feel in the mood for a longer walk we may go over the hills by Sumiyama past Kasatori and visit the temple of Kwannon[16] of the Thousand Arms at Iwama. Or it may take our fancy to go and worship at the famous temple of Ishiyama by Lake Biwa. Or

12. the sacred writings of Buddhism.

13. The Uji River is south of Lake Biwa near Kyoto.

14. A sad poem about a weeping wife who will not explain the reason for her grief. See Arthur Waley, *The Life and Times of Li Po* (New York, 1949), p. 105, and above, p. 434.

15. a famous musician.

16. Buddhist goddess of mercy (Chinese Kwan Yin).

again, if we go by Awazu, we may stop to say a prayer for the soul of Semi Maru[17] at his shrine on Ausaka Hill, and from thence may cross the River Tagami and visit the grave of Saru Maru Taiyu.[18]

Then on our way back, according to the season, there will be the cherry-blossoms to pluck and the maple or the bracken or some sort of berries to gather. And of these some we can offer to the Buddha and some we can eat ourselves.

In the quiet evenings I look out of my window at the moon and think over the friends of other days, and the mournful cry of the monkey often makes me moisten my sleeve with tears. I might imagine the cloud of fire-flies to be the fishing-fires at Makinoshima, or the rain at dawn to be the patter of the leaves driven by the wind. When I hear the hollow cry of the pheasant that might be mistaken for a father or a mother hallooing to their children, as Gyogi Basatsu's verse has it, or see the mountain deer approach me without any fear, then I understand how remote I am from the world. And I stir up the embers of my smouldering fire, the best friend an old man can find by him when he wakes. The mountains themselves are not at all awesome, though indeed the hooting of the owls is sometimes melancholy enough, but of the beauties of the ever-changing scenery of the hills one never becomes weary. And to one who thinks deeply and has a good store of knowledge such pleasure is indeed inexhaustible.

When I first came to live in this place I thought it would be but for a little space, but five years have already passed. This temporary hut of mine looks old and weatherbeaten and on the roof the rotting leaves lie deep, while the moss has grown thick on the plastered wall. By occasional tidings that reach me from the Capital, I learn that the number of distinguished people who have passed away is not small, and as to those of no consequence it must be very great indeed. And in the various fires I wonder how many houses have been burnt.

But in this little impermanent hut of mine all is calm and there is nothing to fear. It may be small, but there is room to sleep at night, and to sit down in the day-time, so that for one person there is no inconvenience. The hermit-crab chooses a small shell and that is because he well knows the needs of his own body. The fishing-eagle chooses a rough beach because he does not want man's competition. Just so am I. If one knows himself and knows what the world is he will merely wish for quiet and be pleased when he has nothing to grieve about, wanting nothing and caring for nobody.

It is the way of people when they build houses not to build them for themselves, but for their wives and family and relations, and to entertain their friends, or it may be their patrons or teachers, or to accommodate their valuables or horses or oxen.

17. famous lute player, tenth century. [Sadler's note.]

18. poet of the same period. [Sadler's note.]

But I have built mine for my own needs and not for other people. And for the good reason that I have neither companion nor dependent, so that if I built it larger who would there be to occupy it? And as to friends they respect wealth and prefer those who are hospitable to them, but think little of those who are kindly and honest. The best friends one can have are flowers and moon, strings and pipe. And servants respect those who reward them, and value people for what they get. If you are merely kind and considerate and do not trouble them they will not appreciate it. So the best servant you can have is your own body, and if there is anything to be done, do it yourself. It may be a little troublesome perhaps, but it is much easier than depending on others and looking to them to do it.

If you have to go anywhere, go on your own feet. It may be trying, but not so much so as is the bother of horses and carriages. Every one with a body has two servants, his hands and feet, and they will serve his will exactly. And since the mind knows the fatigue of the body it works when it is vigorous and allows it to rest when it is tired. The mind uses the body, but not to excess, and when the body tires it is not vexed. And to go on foot and do one's own work is the best road to strength and health. For to cause trouble and worry to our fellows is to lay up evil Karma. And why should you use the labour of others?

Clothes and food are just the same. Garments woven from wistaria-vines, and bed-clothes of hemp, covering the body with what comes nearest to hand, and sustaining one's life with the berries and fruits that grow on the hills and plains, that is best. If you do not go into society you need not be ashamed of your appearance, and if your food is scanty it will have the better relish. I do not say these things from envy of rich people, but only from comparison of my early days with the life I live now.

Since I forsook the world and broke off all its ties, I have felt neither fear nor resentment. I commit my life to fate without special wish to live or desire to die. Like a drifting cloud I rely on none and have no attachments. My only luxury is a sound sleep and all I look forward to is the beauty of the changing seasons.

Now the Three Phenomenal Worlds,[19] the World of Desire, the World of Form, and the World of No-form, are entirely of the mind. If the mind is not at rest, horses and oxen and the Seven Precious Things and Palaces and Pavilions are of no use. With this lonely cottage of mine, this hut of one room, I am quite content. If I go out to the Capital I may feel shame at looking like a mendicant priest, but when I come back home here I feel compassion for

19. The three "Worlds" are the world of desire and the suffering which is attendant on it, the impermanence of phenomena (the world of form), and the absence of a permanent soul which distinguishes one living thing from another (the world of no-form).

those who are still bound by the attraction of earthly things. If any doubt me let them consider the fish. They do not get tired of the water; but if you are not a fish you cannot understand their feelings.[20] Birds too love the woods, but unless you are yourself a bird you cannot know how they feel. It is just so with the life of a hermit: How can you understand unless you experience it?

Now the moon of my life has reached its last phase and my remaining years draw near to their close. When I soon approach the Three Ways of the Hereafter what shall I have to regret? The Law of Buddha teaches that we should shun all clinging to the world of phenomena, so that the affection I have for this thatched hut is in some sort a sin, and my attachment to this solitary life may be a hindrance to enlightenment. Thus I have been babbling, it may be, of useless pleasures, and spending my precious hours in vain.

In the still hours of the dawn I think of these things, and to myself I put these questions: "Thus to forsake the world and dwell in the woods, has it been to discipline my mind and practise the Law of Buddha or not? Have I put on the form of a recluse while yet my heart has remained impure? Is my dwelling but a poor imitation of that of the Saint Vimalakirrti while my merit is not even equal to that of Suddhipanthaka the most stupid of the followers of Buddha? Is this poverty of mine but the retribution for the offences of a past existence, and do the desires of an impure heart still arise to hinder my enlightenment? And in my heart there is no answer. The most I can do is to murmur two or three times a perchance unavailing invocation to Buddha."

The last day of the third month of the second year of the era Kenryaku. By me the Sramana Ren-in in my hut on Toyama Hill.

Sad am I at heart
When the moon's bright silver orb
Sinks behind the hill.
But how blest 't will be to see
Amida's perpetual light.

20. looks like an echo of the well-known passage in the Chuang-tzu. [Sadler's note.]

SIX *NŌ* PLAYS

It is worth noticing that Japanese literature has a considerable dramatic content apart from the *nō* play, the Japanese dramatic form which has most intrigued the West. The *nō* play is neither comedy nor tragedy, but the Japanese have tragedy, though not Aristotelian tragedy, in their *kabuki* and *jōrūri*, and farce in the *kyōgen*, which were played on the same bill with the *nō*. Though it runs to eleven acts, the *Loyal League of the Forty-Seven Ronin* (*Kanadehon Chūshingura*) (1748) has affinities with Western historical tragedy from Marlowe's *Tamburlaine* to the present. The great master of *kabuki* (done with live actors) and also of *jōrūri* (puppet plays) was Chikamatsu Monzaemon (1653–1724), who excelled both in "historical tragedy" and in "domestic tragedy" (using both phrases—loosely—as they are used in the West). His *Battles of Coxinga* (*Kokusen'ya Kassen*) has as its hero a Sino-Japanese general who continued a guerilla warfare against the Ch'ing dynasty in China (ca. 1644) after the Ch'ing overthrow of the Ming. The hero, after many military adventures and some attention to love, unhistorically restores the Ming dynasty. More important are Chikamatsu's domestic dramas. His *Love Suicide at Amijima* (*Shinjū ten no Amijima*) has a young merchant and a courtesan for its hero and heroine. Their ill-fated love affair, based on an actual incident in 1720, is complicated by his wife and children and the presence of a man who is ready to buy the heroine from her house of prostitution for his wife. Curiously, these late seventeenth—and early eighteenth—century military and domestic plays of Chikamatsu may remind the Western reader of English drama from Nicholas Rowe (1674–1718) to the end of the eighteenth century.

To regard the *kabuki*, *jōrūri*, and *kyōgen* as dramatic types approximating Western ones is an oversimplification, but a useful one if it serves to force the reader to regard the *nō* as having no Western counterpart, though its poetry and its subtlety have inspired Westerners, especially William Butler Yeats. Indeed, the *nō*, in an Aristotelian analysis, might not qualify as drama at all: it lacks a strong plot line, lacks moments of intense passion, and might better be described as the recollection of an action as a state of feeling rather than the imitation of an action.

The fourteenth and fifteenth centuries are the great period of the *nō* play. The word itself means "talent" or "exhibition of talent" or—as Ernest Fenollosa and Ezra Pound chose to translate it—"accomplishment." The word *nō*, in any case, is a later term for what was known in the days of its earliest practitioners as *sarugaku*, "monkey music." Originally a Shinto song and dance recital, the beginnings of which are dim, the *sarugaku* and a rival dance form, the *dengaku*, which had folkloristic origins, struggled for mastery in the thirteenth century and the *sarugaku nō* moved from a mere entertainment to a subtle art form through the achievement of Zeami Motokiyo (1363–1444) and his father Kanami Kiyotsugu (1333–1384). The "monkey music" (*sarugaku*) under the refining influence of these two masters, retained its essential music and dance quality. The dance, the chorus, and the rhythmical recitation of lines are, of course, characteristics of Greek drama, but, if we had to make the choice, we would elect to read a Greek drama without the performance and to see and hear a *nō* drama with only a summary knowledge of the text. This last is an extreme statement, but in comparison to the *nō*, Western drama (with some exceptions, like the commedia dell' arte) is more literary than theatrical. The *nō* play exists as a harmony of all theatrical elements: dance, music, poetry, setting, costume, mask, and the interaction of performers and audience.

The *nō* theater of the fifteenth century was circular, with the stage almost in the center of the audience. One part of the circle was interrupted by the backstage section which included the actors' dressing room and the "scenery," which was simple wood paneling, perhaps with a painting, and non-functional. Directly opposite the stage, on the far side of the circle, sat the royal party—the *shōgun* and his attendants. The musicians clustered around the stage, and the audience completed the circle. The later and modern *nō* stage is somewhat different; it has a longer runway from the dressing room for the actors to enter upon, which occupies much of the space to one side of the stage. The actors enter from the side. (The actor's entrance is important; Zeami discusses it in his theoretical works on the drama.) The plays, as the reader will observe, are brief. Shortly after Zeami's time it became a tradition to present five plays in a prescribed arrangement: one play each about the gods, a warrior, a woman, a mad person, and devils. Aesthetic considerations dictate this arrangement. Any one of these subjects carried on at length might become monotonous or excessive. Just as an individual play had to have aesthetic balance, so with the entire performance: it must have variety to relieve the emotion engendered by these serious or tragic facets of human experience and this relief must be by the performance of *kyōgen* (farces) between the plays. The intermixing of tragedy and comedy in Western drama has sometimes made critics and audiences uneasy. The Japanese like this change of mood, and the farces often parody the serious plays. One could argue that this type of dramatic combination makes a more sophisticated aesthetic impact on its audiences than do Western plays. On this ground, "having no need of mob or press to pay its way" it appealed to William Butler Yeats. On the other hand, the *nō* cannot offer the sustained, massive, and immediate emotional experience of a play by Sophocles or Shakespeare. Indeed, the *nō* play is constructed to avoid excessive emotion and immediacy: the characters are often spirits of people long dead and the tone is one of recalling as if from a distance an experience long-forgotten.

Zeami and his father Kanami so revolutionized the *nō* play that they succeeded both in elevating it in respectability and in establishing an ideal for its final perfection. Zeami was an active playwright and performer. He received careful training from his father, who was the greatest performer of his generation and whose efforts obtained the patronage of the *shōgun* Yoshimitsu (1358–1408). Associated with Yoshimitsu, Zeami grew up in an élite social and intellectual milieu. He thus combined the qualities of the cultivated aristocrat of Heian times with a rigorous apprenticeship in practical theater. Zeami's theatrical art, as revealed in both his plays and a considerable number of theoretical treatises, encompassed every aspect of the theater in a fashion so complete that Western synthesizers like Wagner and Edward Gordon Craig seem amateurish by comparison. Zeami's focus is not on the text but on the perfect performance, and he demands a religious intensity of his students: "There is a natural limitation to life," he said, "but there must never be an end to the cultivation of the *nō*." The performer's training begins as a child, and it is not over when he steps on stage for he must sense, at every performance, the mood of the audience and alter his dramatic efforts accordingly. For illustrative materials by which to demonstrate the essence of the *nō*, Zeami draws ideas from poetry and poetic theory, Buddhism, brush-writing, both Chinese and Japanese literature, and, of course, Japanese history and legend with its close relations to nature and to the landscape of specific locales.

"Flower" or *hana* is the term Zeami uses to symbolize the effect of a play. *Hana* is a quality about a performance which gives to the audience an impression of novelty and charm. This involves a harmonious composite of dancing, chanting, narrative, and action, and exists at three levels of effectiveness: (1) the play should have immediate visual effectiveness, even to those in the audience who are not connoisseurs of the *nō;* (2) the play should be aurally effective through its quiet and graceful chanting—this effect might not be noticed by the novice members of the audience; and (3) the play should have the effect of "performance which comes from the soul," moving the audience though the audience does not know why. This last aim cannot be achieved if the dancing is brilliant at the expense of the chanting or if some similar imbalance occurs. Devotées of Western acting (especially of "the method") should note that subtlety and nuance, not the "all-out" performance, are the ideals of Japanese theater: if the hero is waving his sword ferociously with his arms in violent motion, his feet should, contrariwise, move slowly to provide aesthetic balance.

The *nō* play itself employs a "doer" or "actor" (the *shite*) and a subordinate character who explains what is happening (the *waki*, "assistant"). Both of these main characters can have assistants called *tsure*. The *shite* has the principal dancing part; during his dance his verbal part is taken by the chorus, which chants the lines to the accompaniment of a flute and drums. The *nō* stage is especially built to be resonant to the footsteps of the dancers. Besides elaborate and gorgeous costumes the actors wear masks which are in themselves works of art. Men play the feminine roles. And the performer—it is worth repeating—as he enters the walkway to the stage, instantly gauges the nature of the audience. If it is night, Zeami says, the audience is likely to be depressed, and a spirited play and performance are called for. If the nobles arrive too early, the play must begin though lesser people are still finding a place, and the actor must stamp louder and be vivacious to quiet the audience. Practical as these and similar suggestions are, Zeami connects them with the world of the spirit, with *In* and Yō (Chinese *yin* and *yang*), the passive and active, female and male principles of the universe. "All things are accomplished where *In* and Yō are in harmony," Zeami says in his work the *Book of Flower* (*Kadensho* or *Kwadensho*).

The language of the *nō* plays aims to be poetic and evocative. Chinese and Japanese poetry is frequently quoted and often suggested. Well-known songs and Buddhist hymns are quoted or alluded to. "Pivot words"—a kind of serious pun in which a word by having two meanings closes one sequence of images and opens another—are used, but Zeami recommends that one be sparing with them, and a favorite Japanese poetic device, puns on names and place names, is employed (see p. 756). Zeami wrote both the words and music for many of his plays.

ZEAMI MOTOKIYO

(1363–1443)

Atsumori*

Persons: THE PRIEST RENSEI, *formerly the warrior* KUMAGAI

A YOUNG REAPER, *who turns out to be the ghost of* ATSUMORI

HIS COMPANION

CHORUS

Place: *The countryside*

PRIEST. Life is a lying dream, he only wakes
Who casts the World aside.

I am Kumagai-no-Naozane, a man of the country of Musashi. I have left my home and call myself the priest Rensei; this I have done because of my grief at the death of Atsumori,[1] who

* From *The Nō Plays of Japan*, translated by Arthur Waley. Copyright 1957 by Grove Press, Inc. Reprinted by permission of Grove Press, Inc., and Allen & Unwin Ltd.

1. An aristocratic youth of the Taira clan. He died at the age of sixteen (see p. 685).

fell in battle by my hand. Hence it comes that I am dressed in priestly guise.

And now I am going down to Ichi-no-Tani[2] to pray for the salvation of Atsumori's soul.

[*He walks slowly across the stage, singing a song descriptive of his journey.*]

I have come so fast that here I am already at Ichi-no-Tani, in the country of Tsu.

Truly the past returns to my mind as though it were a thing of to-day.

But listen! I hear the sound of a flute coming from a knoll of rising ground. I will wait here till the flute-player passes, and ask him to tell me the story of this place.

REAPERS. [*Together*] To the music of the reaper's flute
No song is sung
But the sighing of wind in the fields.

YOUNG REAPER. They that were reaping,
Reaping on that hill,
Walk now through the fields
Homeward, for it is dusk.

REAPERS. [*Together*] Short is the way that leads
From the sea of Suma[3] back to my home.
This little journey, up to the hill
And down to the shore again, and up to the hill,—
This is my life, and the sum of hateful tasks.
If one should ask me
I too would answer
That on the shore of Suma
I live in sadness.
Yet if any guessed my name,
Then might I too have friends.
But now from my deep misery
Even those that were dearest
Are grown estranged. Here must I dwell abandoned
To one thought's anguish:
That I must dwell here.

PRIEST. Hey, you reapers! I have a question to ask you.

YOUNG REAPER. Is it to us you are speaking? What do you wish to know?

PRIEST. Was it one of you who was playing on the flute just now?

YOUNG REAPER. Yes, it was we who were playing.

2. Near Kyōto to the southwest in the province of Settsu.

3. The reapers remind us of the exile of Yukihira, a noble lord, banished for political reasons to Suma on the shores of the Inland Sea, near present-day Kobe. This is mentioned also at the beginning of the play *Matsukaze* by Kanami (Zeami's father) which Zeami revised.

PRIEST. It was a pleasant sound, and all the pleasanter because one does not look for such music from men of your condition.

YOUNG REAPER. Unlooked for from men of our condition, you say!
Have you not read:—
"Do not envy what is above you
Nor despise what is below you"?
Moreover the songs of woodmen and the flute-playing of herdsmen,
Flute-playing even of reapers and songs of wood-fellers
Through poets' verses are known to all the world.
Wonder not to hear among us
The sound of a bamboo-flute.

PRIEST. You are right. Indeed it is as you have told me.
Songs of woodmen and flute-playing of herdsmen . . .

REAPER. Flute-playing of reapers . . .

PRIEST. Songs of wood-fellers . . .

REAPERS. Guide us on our passage through this sad world.

PRIEST. Song . . .

REAPER. And dance . . .

PRIEST. And the flute . . .

REAPER. And music of many instruments . . .

CHORUS. These are the pastimes that each chooses to his taste.
Of floating bamboo-wood
Many are the famous flutes that have been made;
Little-Branch and Cicada-Cage,
And as for the reaper's flute,
Its name is Green-leaf;
On the shore of Sumiyoshi[4]
The Corean flute[5] they play.
And here on the shore of Suma
On Stick of the Salt-kilns
The fishers blow their tune.

PRIEST. How strange it is! The other reapers have all gone home, but you alone stay loitering here. How is that?

REAPER. How is it, you ask? I am seeking for a prayer in the voice of the evening waves. Perhaps *you* will pray the Ten Prayers for me?

PRIEST. I can easily pray the Ten Prayers for you, if you will tell me who you are.

REAPER. To tell you the truth—I am one of the family of Lord Atsumori.

4. In the far off province of Chikuzen in Kyūshū, southernmost of the Japanese islands.

5. The flute played in civilized society; the reaper plays on a carved stick.

PRIEST. One of Atsumori's family? How glad I am!

CHORUS. Then the priest joined his hands [*He kneels down*] and prayed:—

NAMU AMIDABU

Praise to Amida Buddha![6]
"If I attain to Buddhahood,
In the whole world and its ten spheres
Of all that dwell here none shall call on my name
And be rejected or cast aside."

CHORUS. "Oh, reject me not!
One cry suffices for salvation,
Yet day and night
Your prayers will rise for me.
Happy am I, for though you know not my name,
Yet for my soul's deliverance
At dawn and dusk henceforward I know that you will pray."
So he spoke. Then vanished and was seen no more.

[*Here follows the Interlude between the two Acts, in which a recitation concerning* ATSUMORI'S *death takes place. These interludes are subject to variation and are not considered part of the literary text of the play.*]

PRIEST. Since this is so, I will perform all night the rites of prayer for the dead, and calling upon Amida's name will pray again for the salvation of Atsumori.

[*The ghost of* ATSUMORI *appears, dressed as a young warrior.*]

ATSUMORI. Would you know who I am
That like the watchmen at Suma Pass
Have wakened at the cry of sea-birds roaming
Upon Awaji[7] shore?
Listen, Rensei. I am Atsumori.

PRIEST. How strange! All this while I have never stopped beating my gong and performing the rites of the Law. I cannot for a moment have dozed, yet I thought that Atsumori was standing before me. Surely it was a dream.

ATSUMORI. Why need it be a dream? It is to clear the karma of my waking life that I am come here in visible form before you.[8]

6. "Lord of the Boundless Light." A *bodhisattva* or mediator between Buddha and man, and a favorite with certain Japanese sects. The priest offers the prayer.

7. An island south of present-day Kobe.

8. He has not yet entirely shaken off his worldly sins and desires.

PRIEST. Is it not written that one prayer will wipe away ten thousand sins? Ceaselessly I have performed the ritual of the Holy Name that clears all sin away. After such prayers, what evil can be left? Though you should be sunk in sin as deep . . .

ATSUMORI. As the sea by a rocky shore,
Yet should I be salved by prayer.

PRIEST. And that my prayers should save you . . .

ATSUMORI. This too must spring
From kindness of a former life.[9]

PRIEST. Once enemies . . .

ATSUMORI. But now . . .

PRIEST. In truth may we be named . . .

ATSUMORI. Friends in Buddha's Law.

CHORUS. There is a saying, "Put away from you a wicked friend; summon to your side a virtuous enemy." For you it was said, and you have proven it true.

And now come tell with us the tale of your confession, while the night is still dark. . . .

CHORUS. He[10] bids the flowers of Spring
Mount the tree-top that men may raise their eyes
And walk on upward paths;
He bids the moon in autumn waves be drowned
In token that he visits laggard men
And leads them out from valleys of despair.

ATSUMORI. Now the clan of Taira,[11] building wall to wall,
Spread over the earth like the leafy branches of a great tree:

CHORUS. Yet their prosperity lasted but for a day;
It was like the flower of the convolvulus.
There was none to tell them
That glory flashes like sparks from flint-stone,
And after,—darkness.
Oh wretched, the life of men!

ATSUMORI. When they were on high they afflicted the humble;
When they were rich they were reckless in pride.
And so for twenty years and more
They ruled this land.
But truly a generation passes like the space of a dream.
The leaves of the autumn of Juyei
Were tossed by the four winds;
Scattered, scattered (like leaves too) floated their ships.
And they, asleep on the heaving sea, not even in dreams
Went back to home.

9. "Atsumori must have done Kumagai some kindness in a former incarnation." This would account for Kumagai's remorse. [Waley's note.]

10. The Buddha. [Waley's note.]

11. The Taira evacuated the capital in the second year of Juyei, 1188. [Waley's note.]

Caged birds longing for the clouds,—
Wild geese were they rather, whose ranks are broken
As they fly to southward on their doubtful journey.
So days and months went by; Spring came again
And for a little while
Here dwelt they on the shore of Suma
At the first valley.[12]
From the mountain behind us the winds blew down
Till the fields grew wintry again.
Our ships lay by the shore, where night and day
The sea-gulls cried and salt waves washed on our sleeves.
We slept with fishers in their huts
On pillows of sand.
We knew none but the people of Suma.
And when among the pine-trees
The evening smoke was rising,
Brushwood, as they called it,
Brushwood we gathered
And spread for carpet.
Sorrowful we lived
On the wild shore of Suma,
Till the clan Taira and all its princes
Were but villagers of Suma.
But on the night of the sixth day of the second month
My father Tsunemori gathered us together.
"To-morrow," he said, "we shall fight our last fight.
To-night is all that is left us."
We sang songs together, and danced.

PRIEST. Yes, I remember; we in our siege-camp
Heard the sound of music
Echoing from your tents that night;
There was the music of a flute . . .

ATSUMORI. The bamboo-flute! I wore it when I died.

PRIEST. We heard the singing . . .

ATSUMORI. Songs and ballads . . .

PRIEST. Many voices . . .

ATSUMORI. Singing to one measure.
[ATSUMORI *dances.*][13]
First comes the Royal Boat.

CHORUS. The whole clan has put its boats to sea.
He[14] will not be left behind;
He runs to the shore.

12. Ichi no Tani means "First Valley." [Waley's note.]

13. Although this is a "warrior-play," Atsumori performs a dance appropriate to a beautiful youth whose life has been cut short, not the usual warrior dance.

14. Atsumori.

But the Royal Boat and the soldiers' boats
Have sailed far away.

ATSUMORI. What can he do?
He spurs his horse into the waves.
He is full of perplexity.
And then . . .

CHORUS. He looks behind him and sees
That Kumagai pursues him;
He cannot escape.
Then Atsumori turns his horse
Knee-deep in the lashing waves,
And draws his sword.
Twice, three times he strikes; then, still saddled,
In close fight they twine; roll headlong together
Among the surf of the shore.
So Atsumori fell and was slain, but now the Wheel of Fate
Has turned and brought him back.
[ATSUMORI *rises from the ground and advances towards the* PRIEST *with uplifted sword.*]
"There is my enemy," he cries, and would strike,
But the other is grown gentle
And calling on Buddha's name
Has obtained salvation for his foe;
So that they shall be re-born together
On one lotus-seat.
"No, Rensei is not my enemy.
Pray for me again, oh pray for me again."

The Deserted Crone (*Obasute*) *

Persons: A TRAVELER *from the Capital*
TWO COMPANIONS TO THE TRAVELER
AN OLD WOMAN
THE GHOST OF THE OLD WOMAN
A VILLAGER

Place: *Mount Obasute in Shinano province*

Time: *The fifteenth night of the eighth month*

* From *Monumenta Nipponica*, XVIII (1963), translated by Stanleigh H. Jones, Jr. Reprinted by permission of *Monumenta Nipponica* and Professor Jones. The notes are by the translator.

[*A* TRAVELER *and two* COMPANIONS *from the Capital enter and face each other at stage center. They wear short swords and conical* kasa *hats made of reeds.*]

TOGETHER. Autumn's height,
The full moon's night is near,
Soon the full moon's glory.
Let us go and visit Mount Obasute.

[*The* TRAVELER *removes his hat and faces front.*]

TRAVELER. I am a man of the Capital. I have yet to see the moon of Sarashina and this autumn I have bestirred myself at last. I hurry now to Obasute Mountain.

[*He puts his hat back on and faces his* COMPANIONS.]

TOGETHER. On our journey—
Fleeting are the dreams at inns along the way,
Fleeting are the dreams at inns along the way,
And once again we take our leave;
Nights and days in lonely hostels
Bring us here to famed Sarashina,

[*The* TRAVELER *faces front and takes a few steps forward, then returns to his place.*]

TOGETHER. We have reached Obasute Mountain,
Reached Obasute Mountain.

[*His return indicates that he has arrived. He takes off his hat and faces front.*]

TRAVELER. We have traveled so swiftly that we are here already at Mount Obasute.

COMPANION. Indeed, that is so.

[*The* COMPANIONS *move to the* waki-*position. The* TRAVELER *goes to stage center.*]

TRAVELER. Now that I am here at Mount Obasute I see that all is just as I imagined it—the level crest, the infinite sky, the unimpeded thousands of leagues of night flooded by the moon so clear. Yes, here I will rest and tonight gaze upon the moon.

[*The* OLD WOMAN, *wearing the* fukai *mask, slowly starts down the bridgeway. The* TRAVELER *moves to the* waki-*position.*]

OLD WOMAN. You there, traveler, what is it you were saying?

[TRAVELER, *standing, goes downstage left.*]

TRAVELER. I have come from the Capital, and this is my first visit here. But tell me, where do you live?

OLD WOMAN. In this village, Sarashina. Tonight is that mid-autumn night for which all have waited.
The moon has hurried the dusk of day,
And now the high plain of heaven
Glows in mounting brilliance—

In all directions, the crystalline night.
How wonderful the moon this evening!

TRAVELER. Oh, are you from Sarashina? Can you tell me then the spot where in ancient days the old woman was left to die?

[*The Old Woman has reached the* shite-*position.*]

OLD WOMAN. You ask of the fate of the old woman of Obasute?—a thoughtless question. But if you mean the remains of the woman who sang:

"No solace for my heart at Sarashina
When I see the moon
Shining down on Mount Obasute,"

They are here in the shadow of the little laurel tree—the remains of an old woman long ago abandoned.

TRAVELER. Then here beneath this tree lie the woman's remains, the woman who was deserted?

OLD WOMAN. Yes, deep in the loam,
Buried in obscure grasses
Cut by the reaper.
Short-lived, they say, as in this world,
And already now . . .

TRAVELER. It is an ancient tale,
Yet perhaps attachments still remain.

OLD WOMAN. Yes, even after death . . . somehow . . .

TRAVELER. The dismal loneliness of this moor,

OLD WOMAN. The penetrating wind,

TRAVELER. The lonely heart of autumn.

CHORUS. [*For the* OLD WOMAN] Even now,
"No solace for my heart at Sarashina,
No solace for my heart at Sarashina."
At dusk of day on Mount Obasute
The green lingers in the trees,
The intermingled pines and laurels,
The autumn leaves so quickly tinged.
Thin mists drift over One-Fold Mountain—
Folds of faintly dyed cloth;
In a cloudless sky a doleful wind.
Lonely mountain vista,
Remote and friendless landscape.

OLD WOMAN. Traveler, from where have you come?

TRAVELER. I am from the Capital, as I told you, but I have long heard of the beauties of the moon at Sarashina, and I come here now for the first time.

OLD WOMAN. Are you indeed from the Capital? If that is so, then I will show myself with the moon tonight and entertain you here.

TRAVELER. Who are you that you should entertain me tonight?

OLD WOMAN. In truth, I am from Sarashina . . .

TRAVELER. But where do you live now?

OLD WOMAN. Where do I live? On this mountain . . .

TRAVELER. This famous mountain that bears the name . . .

OLD WOMAN. Obasute Mountain of the Deserted Crone.

CHORUS. [*For the* OLD WOMAN] Even to pronounce the name—
How shameful!
Long ago I was abandoned here.
Alone on this mountainside
I dwell, and every year
In the bright and full mid-autumn moon
I try to clear away
The dark confusion of my heart's attachment.
That is why tonight I have come before you.

CHORUS. [*Narrating*] Beneath the tree,
In the evening shadows,
She vanished like a phantom,
Like an apparition . . . disappeared . . .

[*She exits.*]

[*The* VILLAGER *enters and stands at the naming-place. He wears a short sword.*]

VILLAGER. I live at the foot of this mountain. Tonight the moon is full, and I think I will climb the mountain and gaze at the moon.

[*He sees the* TRAVELER.]

Ah! There's a gentleman I have never seen before. You sir, standing there in the moonlight, where are you from and where are you bound?

TRAVELER. I am from the Capital. I suppose you live in this neighborhood?

VILLAGER. Yes indeed, I do.

TRAVELER. Certainly.

[*He kneels ot stage center.*]

VILLAGER. You said you had something to ask. What might it be?

TRAVELER. You may be somewhat surprised at what I have to ask, but would you tell me anything you may know about the pleasures of moonviewing at Sarashina and the story of Obasute Mountain?

VILLAGER. That is indeed a surprising request. I do live in this vicinity, it is true, but I have no detailed knowledge of such matters. Yet, would it not appear inhospitable if, the very first time we meet, I should say I know nothing of these things you ask? I will tell you, then, what in general I have heard.

TRAVELER. That is most kind of you.

VILLAGER. Well then, here is the story of Mount Obasute: Long ago there lived at this place a man named Wada no Hikonaga. When he was still a child his parents died and he grew up under the care of an aunt. From the day of his marriage his wife hated his aunt and made many accusations against her. But Hikonaga would not listen to her. At length, however, his wife spoke out so strongly that he forgot his aunt's many years of kindness and bowing to his wife's demands, he said one day to the old woman: "Not far from this mountain is a holy image of the Buddha. Let us go there and make our offerings and prayers." So he brought her to this mountain and in a certain place he abandoned her. Later he looked back at the mountain where now the moon was bright and clear. He wanted to go back and fetch his aunt, but his wife was a crafty woman and she detained him until it was too late. The old woman died and her heart's attachment to this world turned her to stone. Hikonaga later went in search of her, and when he saw the stone he realized the dreadful thing he had done. He became a priest they say. Ever since then the mountain has been called Mount Obasute—Mountain of the deserted Old Woman. Long ago it seems that the mountain was known as Sarashina Mountain. Well, that is what I know of the story. But why do you ask? It seems such an unusual request.

TRAVELER. How kind of you to tell me this story! I asked you for this reason: As I said a little while ago, I am from the Capital, but I had heard about Sarashina and so I made a special journey here to view the moon. A short while ago, as I was waiting for the moon to rise, an old woman appeared to me from nowhere and recited to me the poem about Obasute Mountain. She promised to entertain me this night of the full moon, and I asked her who she was. Long ago, she told me, her home was in Sarashina, but now she dwelled on Mount Obasute. She had come here this night in order to dispel the dark confusion of her heart's attachment. No sooner had she spoken than here, in the shadows of this tree, she vanished.

VILLAGER. Oh! Amazing! It must be the old woman's spirit, still clinging to this world, who appeared and spoke with you. If so, then stay awhile; recite the holy scriptures and kindly pray for her soul's repose. I believe you will see this strange apparition again.

TRAVELER. I think so too. I will gaze at the moon and cleanse my heart. For somehow I feel certain I shall see this mysterious figure again.

VILLAGER. If you have any further need of me, please call.

TRAVELER. I will.

VILLAGER. I am at your service.

[*He exits.*]

TRAVELER *and* COMPANIONS. Evening twilight deepens,
And quickens on the moon which sheds
Its first light-shadows of the night.

How lovely:
Ten thousand miles of sky, every corner clear—
Autumn is everywhere the same.
Serene my heart, this night I shall spend in poetry.
"The color of the moon new-risen—
Remembrances of old friends
Two thousand leagues away."

[*The* GHOST OF THE OLD WOMAN *enters, using the* uba *mask. She stands at the* shite-*position.*]

GHOST. How strange and wonderful this moment,
Superb yet strange this moment out of time—
Is my sadness only for the moon tonight?
With the dawn
Half of autumn will have passed,[1]
And waiting for it seemed so long.
The brilliant autumn moon of Mount Obasute,
So matchless, flawless I cannot think
I have ever looked upon the moon before;
Unbearably beautiful—
Surely this is not the moon of long ago.

TRAVELER. Strange,
In this moonlit night already grown so late
A woman robed in white appears—
Do I dream?—Is it reality?

GHOST. Why do you speak of dreams?
That aged figure who came to you by twilight
In shame has come again.

TRAVELER. What need have you for apologies?
This place, as everybody knows is called . . .
Obasute—

GHOST. Mountain where an old hag dwells.

TRAVELER. The past returns,
An autumn night . . .

GHOST. Friends had gathered
To share the moon together . . .
Grass on the ground was our cushion . . .

TRAVELER. Waking, sleeping, among flowers,
The dew clinging to our sleeves. .

TOGETHER. So many varied friends
Reveling in the moonlight . . .
When did we first come together?
Unreal—like a dream.

1. *Half of autumn . . . :* Adaption of a poem by Fujiwara no Teika, no. 621 in the *Shincho-kusenshū:* "Is my sadness only for the sinking moon? With the dawn half of autumn will have passed." The fifteenth day of the eighth month was, according to the old Japanese lunar calendar, the midpoint of autumn.

CHORUS. [*For the* GHOST] Like the lady-flower nipped by time,
The lady-flower past its season,
I wither in robes of grass;
Trying to forget that long ago
I was cast aside, abandoned,
I have come again to Mount Obasute.
How it shames me now to show my face
In Sarashina's moonlight, where all can see!
Ah, well, this world is all a dream—
Best I speak not, think not,
But in these grasses of remembrance
Delight in flowers, steep my heart in the moon.

[*She gazes upward, then advances a few steps during the following passage.*]

CHORUS. [*For the* GHOST] "When pleasure moved me, I came;
The pleasure ended. I returned."[2]
Then, as now tonight, what beauty in the sky!

GHOST. Though many are the famous places
Where one may gaze upon the moon,
Transcending all—Sarashina.

CHORUS. [*For the* GHOST] A pure full disk of light,
Round, round, leaves the coastal rang,
Cloudless over Mount Obasute.

GHOST. Even though the vows of the many Buddhas

CHORUS. Cannot be ranked in terms of high or low,
None can match the light of Amida's Vow,[3]
Supreme and all-pervading in its mercy.

[*She dances.*]

And so it is, they say,
The westward movement of the sun, the moon, and stars
Serves but to guide all living things
Unto the Paradise of the West.
The moon, that guardian who stands on Amida's right,
Leads those with special bonds to Buddha:
Great Seishi,[4] "Power Supreme," he is called,
For he holds the highest power to lighten heavy crimes.
Within his heavenly crown a flower shines,

2. *When . . . returned:* Allusion to the words of one Wang Tzu-yu of the Chin dynasty (A.D. 265–420). On a bright moonlit night Wang had boarded a small boat and gone to visit Tai An-tao. He came up to the gate of Tai's house but then left without seeing him. Asked by a friend the reason for his action, Wang replied: "Moved by pleasure, I came; the pleasure ended, I returned. Why must I see An-tao?

3. *Amida's Vow:* The vow that all living beings would receive salvation.

4. *Seishi:* In Sanskrit, Māhāsthamaprāpta, third person in the Buddhist Trinity of Amida (Amitābha), with Kannon (Avalokitesvara), the *bodhisattva* of Mercy. Seishi, representative of the Buddha-wisdom, stands on Amida's right.

And its jeweled calyx reveals with countless leaves
The pure lands of all the other worlds.[5]
The sounds of the wind in the jeweled tower,
Tones of string and flute,
Variously bewitch the heart.
Trees by the Pond of Treasures,[6]
Where the lotus blooms red and white,
Scatter flowers along their avenues;
On the water's little waves—
A riot of sweet fragrances.

GHOST. The incomparable voices of the birds of paradise—

CHORUS. [*For the* GHOST] Peacocks and parrots call their notes
In harmonies of imitation.
Throughout that realm—unimpeded, all-pervading—
The radiance that gives his name—"Light without limit."[7]
But here the moon through its rift of clouds,
Now full and bright, now dimly seen,
Reveals the inconstancy of this world
Where all is perpetual change.

GHOST. My sleeves move again in dances
Of sweet remembered nights of long ago.

[*She continues to dance, her song alternating back and forth between herself and the* CHORUS.]

CHORUS. "No solace for my heart at Sarashina
When I see the moon
Shining down on Mount Obasute"
When I see the shimmering moon.

GHOST. No stranger to the moon,
I dally among the flowers
For these moments, brief as dew on autumn grasses . . .

CHORUS. Fleeting as the dew indeed . . .
Why should I have come here?
A butterfly at play . . .

GHOST. Fluttering . . .
Dancing sleeves . . .

CHORUS. Over and return, over and . . .

GHOST. . . . Return, return
Autumn of long ago.

CHORUS. My heart is bound by memories,
Unshakable delusions.
In this piercing autumn wind tonight

5. *other worlds:* The infinite Buddha paradises of the universe, here as distinct from that of Amida in the West.

6. *Pond of Treasures:* The pond of the Eight Virtues in Amida's Western Paradise.

7. *"Light without limit:* Muhenkōm, another name for Seishi.

I ache with longing for the past,
Hunger after the world I knew—
Bitter world,
  Autumn,
    Friends.
But even as I speak,
See how the night already pales,
And daylight whitens into morning.
I shall vanish,
The traveler will return.

[*The* TRAVELER *exits.*]

GHOST. Now, alone,
Deserted,
A moss-grown wintry hag.

[*She watches the* TRAVELER *depart, and weeps.*]

CHORUS. Abandoned again as long ago.
And once again all that remains—
Desolate, forsaken crag.
Mountain of the Deserted Crone.

[*She spreads her arms and remains immobile at the* shite-*position.*]

The Dwarf Trees (*Hachi no Ki*) *

Persons: THE PRIEST, LORD TOKIYORI *disguised*
TSUNEYO GENZAYEMON, *a former retainer of* TOKIYORI
GENZAYEMON'S WIFE
TOKIYORI'S MINISTER *and* FOLLOWERS
CHORUS
Place: *The countryside*
Time: *The winter season*

PRIEST. No whence nor whither know I, only onward,
Onward my way.

I am a holy man of no fixed abode. I have been travelling through the land of Shinano;[1] but the snow lies thick. I had

* From *The Nō Plays of Japan*, translated by Arthur Waley. Copyright 1957 by Grove Press, Inc. Reprinted by permission of Grove Press, Inc., and Allen & Unwin Ltd.

1. Province in a mountainous region in central Honoshū, about 100 miles northwest of Tokyo.

best go up to Kamakura[2] now and wait there. When Spring comes I will set out upon my pilgrimage.

[*He walks round the stage singing his song of travel.*]

Land of Shinano, Peak of Asama,
Thy red smoke rising far and near! Yet cold
Blows the great wind whose breath
From Greatwell Hill is fetched.
On to the Village of Friends—but friendless I,
Whose self is cast aside, go up the path
Of Parting Hill, that from the temporal world
Yet further parts me. Down the river, down
Runs my swift raft plank-nosed to Plank-nose Inn,
And to the Ford of Sano I am come.

I have travelled so fast that I am come to the Ford of Sano in the country of Kozuke.[3] Ara! It is snowing again. I must seek shelter here. [*Goes to the wing and knocks*] Is there any-one in this house?

TSUNEYO'S WIFE. [*Raising the curtain that divides the hashigakari*[4] *from the stage*] Who is there?

PRIEST. I am a pilgrim; pray lodge me here to-night.

WIFE. That is a small thing to ask. But since the master is away, you cannot lodge in this house.

PRIEST. Then I will wait here till he comes back.

WIFE. That must be as you please. I will go to the corner and watch for him. When he comes I will tell him you are here.

[*Enter* TSUNEYO *from the wing, making the gesture of one who shakes snow from his clothes.*]

TSUNEYO. Ah! How the snow falls! Long ago when I was in the World I loved to see it:

"Hither and thither the snow blew like feathers plucked from a goose;
Long, long I watched it fall, till it dressed me in a white coat."[5]

So I sang; and the snow that falls now is the same that I saw then. But I indeed am frost-white[6] that watch it!

Oh how shall this thin dress of Kefu-cloth
Chase from my bones the winter of to-day,
Oh pitiless day of snow!

[*He sees his* WIFE *standing waiting.*]

2. On Sagami Sea near Yokohama.

3. Borders on Shinano to the east; the priest passes through it as he journeys south.

4. The runway in backstage center between the dressing room and the stage.

5. "Hither . . . white coat": Po Chü-i's *Works*, iii. 13. [Waley's note.]

6. Alluding partly to the fact that he is snow-covered, partly to his gray hairs. [Waley's note.]

What is this! How comes it that you are waiting here in this great storm of snow?

WIFE. A pilgrim came this way and begged for a night's lodging. And when I told him you were not in the house, he asked if he might wait till you returned. That is why I am here.

TSUNEYO. Where is this pilgrim now?

WIFE. There he stands!

PRIEST. I am he. Though the day is not far spent, how can I find my way in this great storm of snow? Pray give me shelter for the night.

TSUNEYO. That is a small thing to ask; but I have no lodging fit for you; I cannot receive you.

PRIEST. No, no. I do not care how poor the lodging may be. Pray let me stay here for one night.

TSUNEYO. I would gladly ask you to stay, but there is scarce space for us two, that are husband and wife. How can we give you lodging? At the village of Yamamoto yonder, ten furlongs further, you will find a good inn. You had best be on your way before the daylight goes.

PRIEST. So you are resolved to turn me away?

TSUNEYO. I am sorry for it, but I cannot give you lodging.

PRIEST. [*Turning away*] Much good I got by waiting for such a fellow! I will go my way. [*He goes.*]

WIFE. Alas, it is because in a former life we neglected the ordinances[7] that we are now come to ruin. And surely it will bring us ill-fortune in our next life, if we give no welcome to such a one as this! If it is by any means possible for him to shelter here, please let him stay.

TSUNEYO. If you are of that mind, why did you not speak before? [*Looking after the* PRIEST] No, he cannot have gone far in this great snowstorm. I will go after him and stop him. Hie, traveller, hie! We will give you lodging. Hie! The snow is falling so thick that he cannot hear me. What a sad plight he is in. Old-fallen snow covers the way he came and snow new-fallen hides the path where he should go. Look, look! He is standing still. He is shaking the snow from his clothes; shaking, shaking. It is like that old song:

"At Sano Ferry
No shelter found we
To rest our horses,
Shake our jackets,
In the snowy twilight."

That song was made at Sano Ferry,
At the headland of Miwa on the Yamato Way.

7. Buddhist ordinances, such as hospitality to priests. [Waley's note.]

CHORUS. But now at Sano on the Eastern Way
Would you wander weary in the snow of twilight?
Though mean the lodging,
Rest with us, oh rest till day!
[*The* PRIEST *goes with them into the hut.*]

TSUNEYO. [*To his* WIFE] Listen. We have given him lodging, but have not laid the least thing before him. Is there nothing we can give?

WIFE. It happens that we have a little boiled millet;[8] we can give him that if he will take it.

TSUNEYO. I will tell him. [*To the* PRIEST] I have given you lodging, but I have not yet laid anything before you. It happens that we have a little boiled millet. It is coarse food, but pray eat it if you can.

PRIEST. Why, that's a famous dish! Please give it me.

TSUNEYO. [*To* WIFE] He says he will take some; make haste and give it to him.

WIFE. I will do so.

TSUNEYO. Long ago when I was in the World I knew nothing of this stuff called millet but what I read of it in poems and songs. But now it is the prop of my life.
Truly Rosei's dream of fifty years' glory
That he dreamed at Kántán on lent pillow propped
Was dreamed while millet cooked, as yonder dish now.
Oh if I might but sleep as he slept, and see in my dream
Times that have passed away, then should I have comfort;
But now through battered walls

CHORUS. Cold wind from the woods
Blows sleep away and the dreams of recollection.
[*While the* CHORUS *sings these words an* ATTENDANT *brings on to the stage the three dwarf trees.*]

TSUNEYO. How cold it is! And as the night passes, each hour the frost grows keener. If I had but fuel to light a fire with, that you might sit by it and warm yourself! Ah! I have thought of something. I have some dwarf trees. I will cut them down and make a fire of them.

PRIEST. Have you indeed dwarf trees?

TSUNEYO. Yes, when I was in the World I had a fine show of them; but when my trouble came I had no more heart for tree-fancying, and gave them away. But three of them, I kept, —plum, cherry and pine.[9] Look, there they are, covered with snow. They are precious to me; yet for this night's entertainment I will gladly set light to them.

8. Food of the poorest peasants. [Waley's note.]

9. These have an almost sacred status in Japanese life, and the cultivation of dwarf trees is a fine art.

PRIEST. No, no, that must not be. I thank you for your kindness, but it is likely that one day you will go back to the World again and need them for your pleasure. Indeed it is not to be thought of.

TSUNEYO. My life is like a tree the earth has covered;
I shoot no blossoms upward to the world.

WIFE. And should we burn for you
These shrubs, these profitless toys,

TSUNEYO. Think them the faggots of our Master's servitude.[10]

WIFE. For snow falls now upon them, as it fell

TSUNEYO. When he to hermits of the cold
Himalayan Hills was carrier of wood.

WIFE. So let it be.

CHORUS. "Shall I from one who has cast life aside,
Dear life itself, withhold these trivial trees?"
[TSUNEYO *goes and stands by the dwarf trees*]
Then he brushed the snow from off them, and when he looked,
"I cannot, cannot," he cried, "O beautiful trees,
Must I begin?
You, plum-tree, among bare boughs blossoming
Hard by the window, still on northward face
Snow-sealed, yet first to scent
Cold air with flowers, earliest of Spring;
'You first shall fall.'
You by whose boughs on mountain hedge entwined
Dull country folk have paused and caught their breath,[11]
Hewn down for firewood. Little had I thought
My hand so pitiless!"
[*He cuts down the plum-tree.*]
"You, cherry (for each Spring your blossom comes
Behind the rest), I thought a lonely tree
And reared you tenderly, but now
I, *I* am lonely left, and you, cut down,
Shall flower but with flame."

TSUNEYO. You now, O pine, whose branches I had thought
One day when you were old to lop and trim,
Standing you in the field, a football-post,[12]

10. Referring to Shākyamuni, who went through a period of servitude in his early life. Shākyamuni is a manifestation of the Buddha and the manifestation most likely to be revealed to us in this world. Buddhism officially began in Japan in 552 A.D., when a bronze image of Shākyamuni was presented to the emperor by Korea.

11. *Dull . . . breath:* using words

12. For Japanese football, see Waley, *Nō Plays*, p. 291. A considerable amount of religious ritual accompanies Japanese sport, it should be noted, even in our day; this is most apparent to Westerners in exhibitions of *judo* and *sumo* wrestling.

Such use shall never know.
Tree, whom the winds have ever wreathed
With quaking mists, now shimmering in the flame
Shall burn and burn.
Now like a beacon, sentinels at night
Kindle by palace gate to guard a king,
Your fire burns brightly.
Come, warm yourself.

PRIEST. Now we have a good fire and can forget the cold.

TSUNEYO. It is because you lodged with us that we too have a fire to sit by.

PRIEST. There is something I must ask you: I would gladly know to what clan my host belongs.

TSUNEYO. I am not of such birth; I have no clan-name.

PRIEST. Say what you will, I cannot think you a commoner. The times may change; what harm will you get by telling me your clan?

TSUNEYO. Indeed I have no reason to conceal it. Know then that Tsuneyo Genzayemon, Lord of Sano, is sunk to this!

PRIEST. How came it, sir, that you fell to such misery?

TSUNEYO. Thus it was: kinsmen usurped my lands, and so I became what I am.

PRIEST. Why do you not go up to the Capital and lay your case before the Shikken's court?

TSUNEYO. By further mischance it happens that Lord Saimyoji[13] himself is absent upon pilgrimage. And yet not all is lost; for on the wall a tall spear still hangs, and armour with it; while in the stall a steed is tied. And if at any time there came from the City news of peril to our master—

Then, broken though it be I would gird this armour on,
And rusty though it be I would hold this tall spear,
And lean-ribbed though he be I would mount my horse and ride
Neck by neck with the swiftest,
To write my name on the roll.
And when the fight began
Though the foe were many, yet would I be the first
To cleave their ranks, to choose an adversary
To fight with him and die.
[*He covers his face with his hands; his voice sinks again.*]
But now, another fate, worn out with hunger
To die useless. Oh despair, despair!

PRIEST. Take courage; you shall not end so. If I live, I will come to you again. Now I go.

13. Tokiyori. [Waley's note.]

TSUNEYO and WIFE. We cannot let you go. At first we were ashamed that you should see the misery of our dwelling; but now we ask you to stay with us awhile.

PRIEST. Were I to follow my desire, think you I would soon go forth into the snow?

TSUNEYO and WIFE. After a day of snow even the clear sky is cold, and to-night—

PRIEST. Where shall I lodge?

WIFE. Stay with us this one day.

PRIEST. Though my longing bides with you—

TSUNEYO and WIFE. You leave us?

PRIEST. Farewell, Tsuneyo!

BOTH. Come back to us again.

CHORUS. [*Speaking for* PRIEST] "And should you one day come up to the City, seek for me there. A humble priest can give you no public furtherance, yet can he find ways to bring you into the presence of Authority. Do not give up your suit." He said no more. He went his way,—he sad to leave them and they to lose him from their sight.

Interval of Six Months.

TSUNEYO. [*Standing outside his hut and seeming to watch travellers on the road*] Hie, you travellers! Is it true that the levies are marching to Kamakura? They are marching in great force, you say? So it is true. Barons and knights from the Eight Counties of the East all riding to Kamakura! A fine sight it will be. Tasselled breastplates of beaten silver; swords and daggers fretted with gold. On horses fat with fodder they ride; even the grooms of the relay-horses are magnificently apparelled. And along with them [*Miming the action of leading a horse*] goes Tsuneyo, with horse, armour and sword that scarce seem worthy of such names. They may laugh, yet I am not, I think, a worse man than they; and had I but a steed to match my heart, then valiantly—[*Making the gesture of cracking a whip*] you laggard!

CHORUS. The horse is old, palsied as a willow-bough; it cannot hasten. It is lean and twisted. Not whip or spur can move it. It sticks like a coach in a bog. He follows far behind the rest.

PRIEST. [*Again ruler*[14] *of Japan, seated on a throne*] Are you there?

ATTENDANT. I stand before you.

PRIEST. Have the levies of all the lands arrived?

ATTENDANT. They are all come.

PRIEST. Among them should be a knight in broken armour, carry-

14. Hōjō no Tokiyori ruled at Kamakura from 1246 till 1256. He then became a priest and travelled through the country incognito in order to acquaint himself with the needs of his subjects. [Waley's note.]

ing a rusty sword, and leading his own lean horse. Find him, and bring him to me.

ATTENDANT. I tremble and obey. [*Going to* TSUNEYO] I must speak with you.

TSUNEYO. What is it?

ATTENDANT. You are to appear immediately before my lord.

TSUNEYO. Is it I whom you are bidding appear before his lordship?

ATTENDANT. Yes, you indeed.

TSUNEYO. How can it be I? You have mistaken me for some other.

ATTENDANT. Oh no, it is you. I was told to fetch the most ill-conditioned of all the soldiers; and I am sure you are he. Come at once.

TSUNEYO. The most ill-conditioned of all the soldiers?

ATTENDANT. Yes, truly.

TSUNEYO. Then I am surely he.
Tell your lord that I obey.

ATTENDANT. I will do so.

TSUNEYO. I understand; too well I understand. Some enemy of mine has called me traitor, and it is to execution that I am summoned before the Throne. Well, there is no help for it. Bring me into the Presence.

CHORUS. He was led to where on a great daïs
All the warriors of this levy were assembled
Like a bright bevy of stars.
Row on row they were ranged,
Samurai and soldiers;
Swift scornful glances, fingers pointed
And the noise of laughter met his entering.

TSUNEYO. Stuck through his tattered, his old side-sewn sash,
His rusty sword sags and trails,—yet he undaunted,
"My Lord, I have come."
[*He bows before the Throne.*]

PRIEST. Ha! He has come, Tsuneyo of Sano!

Have you forgotten the priest whom once you sheltered from the snowstorm? You have been true to the words that you spoke that night at Sano:

"If at any time there came news from the City of peril to our master
Then broken though it be, I would gird this armour on,
And rusty though it be, I would hold this tall spear,
And bony though he be, I would mount my horse and ride
Neck by neck with the swiftest."

These were not vain words; you have come valiantly. But know that this levy of men was made to this purpose: to test the issue of your words whether they were spoken false or true; and to hear the suits of all those that have obeyed my summons, that if any among them have suffered injury, his wrongs may be righted.

And first in the case of Tsuneyo I make judgment. To him shall be returned his lawful estate, thirty parishes in the land of Sano.

But above all else one thing shall never be forgotten, that in the great snowstorm he cut down his trees, his treasure, and burnt them for firewood. And now in gratitude for the three trees of that time,—plum, cherry and pine,—we grant to him three fiefs, Plumfield in Kaga, Cherrywell in Etchū and Pine-branch in Kōzuke.

He shall hold them as a perpetual inheritance for himself and for his heirs; in testimony whereof we give this title-deed, by our own hand signed and sealed, together with the safe possession of his former lands.

TSUNEYO. Then Tsuneyo took the deeds.

CHORUS. He took the deeds, thrice bowing his head.
[*Speaking for* TSUNEYO]
"Look, all you barons!
[TSUNEYO *holds up the documents.*]
Look upon this sight
And scorn to envy turn!"
Then the levies of all the lands
Took leave of their Lord
And went their homeward way.

TSUNEYO. And among them Tsuneyo

CHORUS. Among them Tsuneyo,
Joy breaking on his brow,
Rides now on splendid steed
To the Boat-bridge of Sano, to his lands once torn
Pitiless from him as the torrent tears
That Bridge of Boats at Sano now his own.

Attributed to ZEAMI

Komachi at Sekidera (*Sekidera Komachi*) *

Persons: THE ABBOT OF SEKIDERA
TWO PRIESTS
A CHILD
ONO NO KOMACHI

Place: *Sekidera in Omi province*

* From *Twenty Plays of the Nō Theatre*, edited by Donald Keene, with the assistance of Royall Tyler. New York: Columbia University Press, 1970. Translated by Karen Brazell. Reprinted by permission of Columbia University Press. The notes are by the translator.

Time: *The beginning of autumn: the seventh day of the seventh month*

[*The stage assistants bring forward a simple construction representing a hut with a thatched roof. It is covered with a cloth. The* OLD MOWAN *is inside.*

As the music begins the CHILD, *the* ABBOT, *and two* PRIESTS *enter and face each other onstage. The* ABBOT *and the* PRIESTS *carry rosaries.*]

THREE PRIESTS. So long awaited, autumn has come at last,
So long awaited, the lovers' autumn meeting!
Now let us begin the Festival of Stars.[1]

[*The* ABBOT *faces front.*]

ABBOT. I am the child priest of Sekidera in Omi. Today, the seventh day of the seventh month, we come to celebrate the Festival of Stars here in the temple garden. People say that the old woman who has built her hut at the foot of the mountain knows all the secrets of the art of poetry. So, on this festive day dedicated to poetry, I am going to take the young people to hear her stories.

[*He turns to the* CHILD.]

THREE PRIESTS. Early autumn comes and brings a touch of chill.
We feel it in the wind and in our thinning locks.[2]
Soon, soon the Seventh Night will be on us.

[*The* ABBOT *faces front.*]

ABBOT. We bring offerings for the festival today,
The music of flutes and strings,

TWO PRIESTS. And many poems

ABBOT. Composed in our native tongue.[3]

[*He turns to the* CHILD.]

THREE PRIESTS. Our prayers for skill at poetry are decked
With brightly colored streamers:
Fluttering ribbons, each a token of prayer,
Like silk threads woven into rich brocades
On looms of autumn flowers
And pampas grass pearly with dew.
The winds in the pines

[*The* ABBOT *faces front, takes a few steps, then returns to his former position, indicating he has made a journey.*]

1. The Tanabata Festival, of Chinese origin, is still celebrated in Japan on the seventh day of the seventh month. Bamboo branches are decorated with five-colored streamers and with slips on which poems have been written commemorating the lovers' meeting of the two stars.

2. From some lines by Po Chü-i included in the *Wakan Rōei Shū*, no. 204: "Who could have arranged things so well? The sighing cool wind and my thinning locks at once anounce autumn is here." A parallel is drawn between the coming of autumn in the world and the coming of autumn to the person, evidenced by the thinning locks.

3. Many poets wrote in Chinese, especially on formal occasions, but the Japanese preferred their own language for their intimate feelings.

Blend with the strings of the *koto*
To make music for the offerings tonight,[4]
Our offerings for this festive night.

[*The* ABBOT *and his companions are now at their destination.*]

ABBOT. Here is the hut now. Let us call on the old woman. [*To the* CHILD] But first, please sit down.

[*All kneel. A stage assistant removes the cloth around the hut, revealing the* OLD WOMAN *seated inside. Paper strips inscribed with poems hang from the crossbars of the hut frame. The* OLD WOMAN *wears the* uba *mask.*]

OLD WOMAN. Days go by without a single bowl of food;
Whom can I ask for one?
At night my tattered rags fail to cover me,
But their is no way to patch the rents.
Each passing rain
Ages the crimson of the flowers;
The willows are tricked by the wind
And their green gradually droops:[5]
Man has no second chance at youth;
He grows old. The aged song thrush
Warbles again when spring has come,
But time does not revert to the past.
Oh, how I yearn for the days that are gone!
What would I do to recapture the past!

[*She weeps. The* ABBOT *and the* CHILD *rise, and go to kneel before her.*]

ABBOT. Old woman, we have come to speak with you.

OLD WOMAN. Who are you?

ABBOT. I am a priest from Sekidera. These young people are students of poetry. They have heard of your talent, and I have brought them here to question you about poetry and to learn something of your life.

OLD WOMAN. This is an unexpected visit! The log buried in the earth has been so long forgotten you must not expect it will put forth new sprouts.[6] Just remember this: If you will make your heart the seed and your words the blossoms,[7] if you will steep yourself in the fragrance of the art, you will not fail to accomplish true poetry. But how praiseworthy that mere boys should cherish a love of poetry!

ABBOT. May I ask you about a poem everyone knows, "The Harbor

4. The above three lines are based on a poem by the Consort Itsukinomiya in the *Shūishū*, no. 451.

5. Derived from an anonymous poem in Chinese found in a commentary to the historical work *Hyakurenshō*.

6. Quoted, with slight modifications, from the preface to the *Kokinshū*.

7. Also from the preface to the *Kokinshū*.

of Naniwa?"[8] Do you agree that it should be used as a first guide?

OLD WOMAN. Indeed I do. Poetry goes back to the Age of the Gods, but the meters were then irregular and the meanings difficult to understand. "The Harbor of Naniwa," however, belongs to the Age of Man. It was composed for the joyous occasion of an emperor's enthronement, and has long been beloved for that reason.[9]

ABBOT. The poem about Mount Asaka, which once soothed the heart of a prince, is also beautifully written.[10]

OLD WOMAN. Truly, you understand the art,
For those two poems are the parents of all poetry.

ABBOT. They serve as models for beginners.

OLD WOMAN. Noblemen and peasantry alike,

ABBOT. City dwellers and country folk,

OLD WOMAN. Even commoners like ourselves

ABBOT. Take pleasure in composing poetry

OLD WOMAN. Following the promptings of our hearts.

CHORUS. Though the sands lapped by the waves
Of the lake in Oni should run out,
Though the sands of the shore should melt away.

[*The* ABBOT *and the* CHILD *return to kneel with the* PRIESTS.]

The words of poetry will never fail.[11]
They are enduring as evergreen boughs of pine,
Continuous as trailing branches of willow;
For poetry, whose source and seed is found
In the human heart, is everlasting.
Though ages pass and all things vanish,
As long as words of poetry remain,
Poems will leave their marks behind,
And the traces of poetry will never disappear.

ABBOT. Thank you for your words of explanation. It is true that countless poems survive from the past, but they are rarely by

8. This is the "Naniwazu" poem: "In Naniwa Harbor/ The flowers have come to the trees;/ They slept through the winter,/ But now it is the spring—/ See how the blossoms have opened!" The preface to the *Kokinshū* characterizes this poem and the one on Asakayama, Mount Asaka, as the "father and mother of poetry." Both poems are given considerable attention in *The Reed Cutter.*

9. The poem was traditionally supposed to have been composed to encourage the future Emperor Nintoku, who reigned in the fourth century, A.D., to accept the throne.

10. The poem runs, literally: "Mount Asaka—/ Its reflection appears In the mountain spring/ That is not shallow, and of you/ My thoughts are not shallow either." The Prince of Kazuraki was sent to the distant province of Mutsu where he was badly received by the governor. He was so angry that he refused to eat, but the governor's daughter cheered him by offering saké and reciting this poem.

11. Based on lines from the *Kokinshū* preface: "Though you count up my love you could never come to the end, not even if you count every grain of sand on the shore of the wild sea."

women. Few women know as much as you about poetry. Tell me —the poem

> "I know my lover
> Is coming tonight—
> See how the spider
> Spins her web:
> That is a sure sign!"[12]

Was that not by a woman?

OLD WOMAN. Yes, that poem was written long ago by Princess Sotori, the consort of Emperor Ingyo. I tried, if only in form, to master her style.

ABBOT. Ah! You have studied the style of Princess Sotori? I have heard that Ono no Komachi, who's so much talked of these days, wrote in that style.[13]

> "Wretched that I am—
> A floating water weed,
> Broken from its roots—
> If a stream should beckon,
> I would follow it, I think."

That poem is by Komachi.

OLD WOMAN. Yes, once my husband, Ōe no Koreaki, took up with another woman, and I grieved at the fickleness of the world. Then, Funya no Yasuhide[14] invited me to accompany him to Mikawa, where he was to be the governor. I wrote that poem in response to his urging and to his promises that life in the country would bring solace.

> Alas, memories of the past!
> So long forgotten, they rise up again
> Before me as I talk to you.
> Tears well up from my suffering heart.

[*She weeps.*]

ABBOT. Strange! This old woman says she wrote the poem "Wretched that I am." And she says she wrote in the Sotori style, just as Komachi did. She must be nearly a hundred years old, and if Komachi were still alive today. . . . And is there any reason why she couldn't be? It *must* be so! [*To the* OLD WOMAN] You are what is left of Ono no Komachi. Do not deny it.

OLD WOMAN. Ah, I burn with shame to be called Komachi, I who wrote

> "With no outward sign

12. An anonymous poem, no. 1110 in the *Kokinshū*.

13. So stated in the preface to the *Kokinshū*.

14. An early Heian poet, one of the "Six Immortals of Poetry." The explanation of the "Wretched that I am" poem was traditional.

CHORUS. It withers—
The flower in the human heart."[15]
How ashamed I am to be seen!
"Wretched that I am—
A floating water weed,
Broken from its roots—
If a stream should beckon,
I would follow it, I think."
How ashamed I am!
[*She weeps.*]
"Hide them though I may,
The tears keep flowing,
Too many for my sleeves to hold—
A rain of tears dissolving
Everything except the past."[16]
Now that my life has reached its end,
Like a withered flower,
Why should there still be tears?

OLD WOMAN. "Longing for him,
I fell asleep,
Then he appeared before me . . ."[17]

CHORUS. The joy I felt when I composed those lines
Is gone forever, but still my life goes on,
Attending the months and years as they come and go.
The dews of spring depart, and autumn frosts appear,
The leaves and grasses turn, and insect voices fade.

OLD WOMAN. My life is over, and now I see

CHORUS. It was like a rose of Sharon that knows
Only a single day of glory.[18]
"The living go on dying,
The dead increase in number;
Left in this world, ah—
How long must I go on
Lamenting for the dead?"[19]
And how long must I, who wrote that poem,
Live on, like flowers fallen, like leaves scattered,
With nothing left but life—dewlike, they always said.
Oh, how I long for the past!

15. From poem no. 757 in the *Kokinshū*, by Komachi.

16. A poem by Abe no Kiyoyuki, no. 556 in the *Kokinshū*.

17. The first part of a poem by Komachi, no. 552 in the *Kokinshū*. The last two lines run: "If I had known it was a dream/ I should never have wakened."

18. These lines are based on verses by Po Chü-i, no. 291 in the *Wakan Rōei Shū*.

19. A poem by Komachi, no. 850 in the *Shinkokinshū*.

My middle years were spent in yearning
For the distant glory of my youth.
Now even those days of wistful recollection
Have become such ancient history
I find myself wishing, if not for youth,
At least for middle age.
Long ago, wherever I spent a single night
My room would be bright with tortoise shell,
Golden flowers hung from the walls,
And in the door were strings of crystal beads.[20]
Brilliant as the Emperor's chair in grand procession
The jewellike gowns I wore, a hundred colors.
I lay on bright brocaded quilts
Within a pillowed bridal chamber.
Look at it now, my mud-daubed hut!
Can this be my resplendent room?

OLD WOMAN. The temple bell of Sekidera

CHORUS. Tolls the vanity of all creation—
To ancient ears a needless lesson.
A mountain wind blows down Osaka's slope
To moan the certainty of death;
Its message still eludes me.
Yet, when blossoms scatter and leaves fall,
Still in this hut I find my pleasure:
Grinding ink, I dip my brush and write.
My words are all dry, like seaweed on the shore.
Touching, they once said, but lacking strength[21]—
My poems lacked strength because they were a woman's.
Now when I have grown decrepit
My poems are weaker still. Their life is spent.
How wretched it is to be old!

[*She weeps. The* CHILD *turns to the* ABBOT.]

CHILD. I'm afraid we'll be late for the Festival of Stars. Let's ask the old lady to come with us.

[*The* ABBOT *kneels before the* OLD WOMAN.]

ABBOT. Please join us on this Seventh Night, the Festival of Stars.

OLD WOMAN. Alas! An old woman should not intrude on such an occasion. I cannot go.

[*She takes down the paper poem cards.*]

20. This description is based on a passage in the *Tamatsukuri Komachi Sōsuisho*, a work in Chinese, apparently by a Buddhist priest of the Heian period, describing Komachi's decline and her eventual salvation.

21. The appraisal of Komachi's poetry given in the preface to the *Kokinshū*.

ABBOT. What harm could come of it? Please come with us.

[*He goes to the hut and helps the* OLD WOMAN *to stand.*]

CHORUS. The Seventh Night—

How many years since first I offered the gods
Bamboo tied with colored streamers?
How long has shriveled old Komachi lived?

[*Assisted by the* ABBOT *and leaning on a staff, the* OLD WOMAN *leaves the hut.*]

Has Ono no Komachi reached a hundred years?
Or even more?
I who used to watch the Festival of Stars,
Familiar of the noblest lords and ladies,

[*She kneels beside the* shite-*pillar. The* ABBOT *goes back beside the others.*]

Now stand in shamful hempen rags!
A sight too painful to eyes to bear!

[*The* ABBOT *weeps.*]

Still, tonight we hold the Festival of Stars,

[*The* CHILD *stands and mimes serving wine to the* OLD WOMAN.]

Tonight we celebrate the Seventh Night
With multitudes of offerings for the stars.
Prayer streamers hang from bamboo,

[*While the following lines are being sung the* CHILD *goes to the gazing-pillar, moves clockwise around the stage, then stands at the center preparatory to beginning his dance.*]

Music plays and cups of wine go round.
The young dancer—look how gracefully
He twirls his sleeves, like snow
Swirling in the moonlight.

[*The* OLD WOMAN, *still seated, watches the* CHILD *dance.*]

We celebrate the Festival of Stars,
Streamers flutter from the bamboos. . . .

OLD WOMAN. May it be celebrated through ages as many
As the joints of the bamboo!

[*The* OLD WOMAN, *hardly aware of what she does, taps the rhythm with her fan.*]

CHORUS. We pray for eternal prosperity;
We dance the "Ten Thousand Years."[22]

[*The* CHILD *completes his dance, then sits as before.*]

OLD WOMAN. How gracefully that boy has danced! I remember how, long ago in the Palace, the Gosechi dancing girls swirled

22. The name of a *gagaku* dance, *Manzairaku*.

their sleeves five times at the Harvest Festival. They say that if a madman runs, even the sane will run after him. But tonight the proverb is reversed! Enticed by the boy's floating sleeves, see how a madwoman prances!

[*She stands with the aid of her staff and begins her dance.*]

One hundred years—
The dance of the butterfly
Who dreamt he had spent
A hundred years enfolded
Within a flower petal.[23]

CHORUS. How sad it is! It breaks my heart!
A flowering branch on a withered tree!

OLD WOMAN. I have forgotten how to move my hands.

CHORUS. Unsteady feet, uncertain wave of sleeves,

OLD WOMAN. Billow after billow, floating wave on wave.

CHORUS. My dancing sleeves rise up,
But sleeves cannot wave back the past.

[*She goes before the hut.*]

OLD WOMAN. I miss those vanished days!

[*She kneels and weeps.*]

CHORUS. But as I dance the early autumn night,
The short night, gives way to dawn.
The temple bell of Sekidera tolls.

OLD WOMAN. A chorus of morning birdsong heralds

CHORUS. The coming dawn, the day's approaching light,
The dawn's fresh light that reveals my shame!

OLD WOMAN. Where is the forest of Hazukashi?[24]

[*She stands, propping herself on her staff.*]

CHORUS. Where is the forest of Hazukashi?
There is no forest here to hide my shame.
Farewell, I take my leave.
Now, leaning heavily on her stick,
She slowly returns to her straw hut.

[*She enters the hut, sits and weeps.*]

The hundred-year-old woman you have spoken to
Is all that remains of famed Komachi,
Is all that is left of Ono no Komachi.

23. A reference to a poem by Ōe no Masafusa in the collection *Horikawa-in Ontoki Hyakushu Waka:* "This world where I have dwelt a hundred years lodged in a flower is the dream of a butterfly." The poem in turn refers to a famous passage in Chuang Tzu. See *The Complete Works of Chuang Tzu* (New York, 1968), translated by Burton Watson, p. 49.

24. Hazukashi, the name of a wood near Kyoto, also has the meaning "ashamed."

ZENCHIKU UJINOBU

(1414–1499?)

Princess Hollyhock (*Aoi no Uye*) *

Persons: COURTIER
THE WITCH
ROKUJŌ, a princess
THE SAINT OF YOKAWA
CHORUS

Place: *The Palace of the Prime Minister*

COURTIER. I am a courtier in the service of the Emperor Shujaku. You must know that the Prime Minister's daughter, Princess Aoi, has fallen sick. We have sent for abbots and high priests of the Greater School and of the Secret School, but they could not cure her.

And now, here at my side, stands the witch of Teruhi,[1] a famous diviner with the bow-string. My lord has been told that by twanging her bow-string she can make visible an evil spirit and tell if it be the spirit of a living man or a dead. So he bad me send for her and let her pluck her string. [*Turning to the* WITCH, *who has been waiting motionless*] Come, sorceress, we are ready!

WITCH. [*Comes forward beating a little drum and reciting a mystic formula*]

Ten shōjō; chi shōjō.
Naige shōjō; rokon shōjō.
Pure above; pure below.
Pure without; pure within.
Pure in eyes, ears, heart and tongue.

[*She plucks her bow string, reciting the spell.*]

You whom I call
Hold loose the reins
On your grey colt's neck
As you gallop to me
Over the long sands!

[*The living phantasm of* ROKUJŌ *appears at the back of the stage.*]

* From *The Nō Plays of Japan*, translated by Arthur Waley. Copyright 1957 by Grove Press, Inc. Reprinted by permission of Grove Press, Inc., and Allen & Unwin Ltd.

1. A *miko* or witch called Teruhi is the subject of the play *Sanja Takusen*. [Waley's note.]

ROKUJŌ. In the Three Coaches
That travel on the Road of Law
I drove out of the Burning House . . .[2]
Is there no way to banish the broken coach
That stands at Yūgao's door?[3]
This world
Is like the wheels of the little ox-cart;
Round and round they go . . . till vengeance comes.
The Wheel of Life turns like the wheel of a coach;
There is no escape from the Six Paths and Four Births.[4]
We are brittle as the leaves of the *bashō*;
As fleeting as foam upon the sea.
Yesterday's flower, to-day's dream.
From such a dream were it not wiser to wake?
And when to this is added another's scorn
How can the heart have rest?
So when I heard the twanging of your bow
For a little while, I thought, I will take my pleasure;
And as an angry ghost appeared.
Oh! I am ashamed!
[*She veils her face.*]
This time too I have come secretly[5]
In a closed coach.
Though I sat till dawn and watched the moon,
Till dawn and watched,
How could I show myself,
That am no more than the mists that tremble over the fields?
I am come, I am come to the notch of your bow
To tell my sorrow.
Whence came the noise of the bow-string?

WITCH. Though she should stand at the wife-door of the mother-house of the square court . . .[6]

ROKUJŌ. Yet would none come to me, that am not in the flesh.[7]

2. Rokujō has left the "Burning House," i.e., her material body. The "Three Couches" are those of the famous "Burning House" parable in the *Hokkekyo*. Some children were in a burning house. Intent on their play, they could not be induced to leave the building; till their father lured them out by the promise that they would find those little toy coaches awaiting them. So Buddha, by partial truth, lures men from the "burning house" of their material lives. Owing to the episode at the Kamo Festival, Rokujō is obsessed by the idea of "carriages," "wheels," and the like. [Waley's note.]

3. One day Rokojō saw a coach from which all badges and distinctive decorations had been purposely stripped (hence, in a sense, a "broken" coach) standing before Yugao's door. She found out that it was Genji's. [Waley's note.] [Yugao supplanted Rokujō in Genji's affections. —Editor.]

4. Buddhist ways to enlightenment.

5. Rokujō went secretly to the Kamo Festival in a closed carriage. [Waley's note.]

6. Words from an old dance-song or *saibara*. [Waley's note.]

7. "That am a ghost," but also "that have lost my beauty." [Waley's note.]

WITCH. How strange! I see a fine lady whom I do not know riding in a broken coach. She clutches at the shafts of another coach from which the oxen have been unyoked. And in the second coach sits one who seems a new wife.[8] The lady of the broken coach is weeping, weeping. It is a piteous sight.

Can this be she?

COURTIER. It would not be hard to guess who such a one might be. Come, spirit, tell us your name!

ROKUJŌ. In this Sahā World[9] where days fly like the lightning's flash
None is worth hating and none worth pitying.
This I knew. Oh when did folly master me?

You would know who I am that have come drawn by the twanging of your bow? I am the angry ghost of Rokujō, Lady of the Chamber.

Long ago I lived in the world.
I sat at flower-feasts among the clouds.[10]
On spring mornings I rode out
In royal retinue and on autumn nights
Among the red leaves of the Rishis' Cave[11]
I sported with moonbeams,
With colours and perfumes
My senses sated.
I had splendour then;
But now I wither like the Morning Glory
Whose span endures not from dawn to midday.
I have come to clear my hate.

[*She then quotes the Buddhist saying, "Our sorrows in this world are not caused by others; for even when others wrong us we are suffering the retribution of our own deeds in a previous existence."*

But while singing these words she turns towards AOI's *bed: passion again seizes her and she cries*]

I am full of hatred.
I must strike; I must strike.

[*She creeps toward the bed.*]

WITCH. You, Lady Rokujō, you a Lady of the Chamber! Would you lay wait and strike as peasant women do?[12] How can this be? Think and forbear!

ROKUJŌ. Say what you will, I must strike. I must strike now. [*Describing her own action*] "And as she said this, she went over to

8. Alluding to Aoi's pregnancy. [Waley's note.]

9. A Sanskrit word for the "world of appearances." [Waley's note.]

10. I.e., at the palace. [Waley's note.]

11. Rishis are semi-divine spirits.

12. It was the custom for wives who had been put away to ambush the new wife and strike her "to clear their hate." [Waley's note.]

the pillow and struck at it." [*She strikes at the head of the bed with her fan.*]

WITCH. She is going to strike again. [*To* ROKUJŌ] You shall pay for this!

ROKUJŌ. And this hate too is payment for past hate.

WITCH. "The flame of anger

ROKUJŌ. Consumes itself only."[13]

WITCH. Did you not know!

ROKUJŌ. Know it then now.

CHORUS. O Hate, Hate!
Her[14] hate so deep that on her bed
Our lady[15] moans.
Yet, should she live in the world again,[16]
He would call her to him, her Lord
The Shining One, whose light
Is brighter than fire-fly hovering
Over the slime of an inky pool.

ROKUJŌ. But for me
There is no way back to what I was,
No more than to the heart of a bramble-thicket.
The dew that dries on the bramble-leaf
Comes back again;
But love (and this is worst)
That not even in dream returns,—
That, is grown to be an old tale,—
Now, even now waxes,
So that standing at the bright mirror
I tremble and am ashamed.

I am come in my broken coach. [*She throws down her fan and begins to slip off her embroidered robe.*] I will hide you in it and carry you away!

[*She stands right over the bed, then turns away and at the back of the stage throws off her robe, which is held by two attendants in such a way that she cannot be seen. She changes her* deigan *mask for a female demon's mask and now carries a mallet in her hand.*]

[*Meanwhile the* COURTIER, *who has been standing near the bed:*]

COURTIER. Come quickly, some one! Princess Aoi is worse. Go and fetch the Little Saint of Yokawa.[17]

MESSENGER. I tremble and obey.

13. From the [Buddhist sutra] *Sūtrālankāra Shāstra* (Cat. No. 1182). [Waley's note.]

14. Rokujō's. [Waley's note.]

15. Aoi. [Waley's note.]

16. The chorus voices the hope that Aoi will recover.

17. The hero of the "Finding of Ukifune," a later episode in the *Genji Monogatari*. [Waley's note.]

[*He goes to the wing and speaks to some one off the stage.*]

May I come in?

SAINT. [*Speaking from the wing*] Who is it that seeks admittance to a room washed by the moonlight of the Three Mysteries, sprinkled with the holy water of Yoga? Who would draw near to a couch of the Ten Vehicles, a window of the Eight Perceptions?[18]

MESSENGER. I am come from the Court. Princess Aoi is ill. They would have you come to her.

SAINT. It happens that at this time I am practising particular austerities and go nowhere abroad. But if you are a messenger from the Court, I will follow you.

[*He comes on the stage.*]

COURTIER. We thank you for coming.

SAINT. I wait upon you. Where is the sick person?

COURTIER. On the bed here.

SAINT. Then I will begin my incantations at once.

COURTIER. Pray do so.

SAINT. He said: "I will say my incantations."

Following in the steps of En no Gyōja,[19]
Clad in skirts that have trailed the Peak of Two Spheres,[20]
That have brushed the dew of the Seven Precious Trees,
Clad in the cope of endurance
That shields from the world's defilement,
"Sarari, sarari," with such sound
I shake the red wooden beads of my rosary
And say the first spell:
Namaku Samanda Basarada
Namaku Samanda Basarada.[21]

ROKUJŌ. [*During the incantation she has cowered at the back of the stage wrapped in her Chinese robe, which she has picked up again*] Go back, Gyoja, go back to your home; do not stay and be vanquished!

SAINT. Be you what demon you will, do not hope to overcome the Gyōja's subtle power. I will pray again.

[*He shakes his rosary whilst the* CHORUS, *speaking for him, invokes the first of the Five Kings.*][22]

18. These are all approaches to salvation in Buddhism.

19. Founder of the sect of ascetics called Yamabushi Mountaineers. [Waley's note.]

20. Mount Ōmine, near Yoshino, ritual ascents of which were made by Yamabushi. [Waley's note.] This is actually a range of mountains in the Yoshino district, now a national park, which extends from Nara to Wakayama.

21. Known as the Lesser Spell of Fudō. The longer one which follows is the Middle Spell. They consist of corrupt Sanskrit mixed with meaningless magic syllables. [Waley's note.]

22. The Myō-o are a group of gods especially sacred to the Shingon sect of Buddhism. The five major ones are listed here, beginning with Gō Sanze (or Sensei.)

CHORUS. In the east Go Sanze, Subduer of the Three Worlds.
ROKUJŌ. [*Counter-invoking*] In the south Gundari Yasha.
CHORUS. In the west Dai-itoku.
ROKUJŌ. In the north Kongo
CHORUS. Yasha, the Diamond King.
ROKUJŌ. In the centre the Great Holy
CHORUS. Fudo Immutable.
Namaku Samanda Basarada
Senda Makaroshana
Sohataya Untaratakarman.
"They that hear my name shall get Great Enlightenment;
They that see my body shall attain to Buddhahood."[23]

ROKUJŌ. [*Suddenly dropping her mallet and pressing her hands to her ears*] The voice of the Hannya Book! I am afraid. Never again will I come as an angry ghost.

GHOST. When she heard the sound of Scripture
The demon's raging heart was stilled;
Shapes of Pity and Sufferance,
The Bodhisats descend.
Her soul casts off its bonds,
She walks in Buddha's Way.

KOMPARU ZEMBŌ MOTOYASU

(1453–1532)

Early Snow (*Hatsuyuki*)*

Persons: EVENING MIST, *a servant girl*
A LADY, *the* ABBOT'S *daughter*
TWO NOBLE LADIES
THE SOUL OF THE BIRD KATSU-YUKI ("EARLY SNOW")
CHORUS

Place: *The Great Temple at Izumo*

SERVANT. I am a servant at the Nyoroku Shrine in the Great Temple of Izumo.[1] My name is Evening Mist. You must know that the Lord Abbot has a daughter, a beautiful lady and gentle as can be. And she keeps a tame bird that was given her a year ago, and because it was a lovely white bird she called it Hatsuyuki, Early Snow; and she loves it dearly.

23. From the Buddhist Sūtra known in Japan as the *Hannya Kyō*. It was supposed to have a particular influence over female demons, who are also called "Hannyas." [Waley's note.]

* From *The Nō Plays of Japan*, translated by Arthur Waley. Copyright 1957 by Grove Press, Inc. Reprinted by permission of Grove Press, Inc., and Allen & Unwin Ltd.

1. The oldest Shintō shrine in Japan, located in Shimane prefecture about twenty-five miles west of Matsue.

I have not seen the bird to-day. I think I will go to the bird-cage and have a look at it.

[*She goes to the cage.*]

Mercy on us, the bird is not there! Whatever shall I say to my lady? But I shall have to tell her. I think I'll tell her now. Madam, madam, your dear Snow-bird is not here!

LADY. What is that you say? Early Snow is not there? It cannot be true.

[*She goes to the cage.*]

It is true. Early Snow has gone! How can that be? How can it be that my pretty one that was so tame should vanish and leave no trace?

Oh bitterness of snows
That melt and disappear!
Now do I understand
The meaning of a midnight dream
That lately broke my rest.
A harbinger it was
Of Hatsuyuki's fate.

[*She bursts into tears.*]

CHORUS. Though for such tears and sighs
There be no cause,
Yet came her grief so suddenly,
Her heart's fire is ablaze;
And all the while
Never a moment are her long sleeves dry.
They say that written letters first were traced
By feet of birds in sand
Yet Hatsuyuki leaves no testament.

[*They mourn.*]

CHORUS. [Kuse *chant, irregular verse accompanied by dancing*]
How sad to call to mind
When first it left the breeding-cage
So fair of form
And coloured white as snow.
We called it Hatsuyuki, "Year's First Snow."
And where our mistress walked
It followed like the shadow at her side.
But now alas! it is a bird of parting[2]
Though not in Love's dark lane.

LADY. There's no help now. [*She weeps bitterly.*]

CHORUS. Still there is one way left. Stop weeping, Lady,
And turn your heart to him who vowed to hear.
The Lord Amida, if a prayer be said—

2. "*Wakeare no tori*," the bird which warns lovers of the approach of day. [Waley's note.]

Who knows but he can bring
Even a bird's soul into Paradise
And set it on the Lotus Pedestal?[3]

LADY. Evening Mist, are you not sad that Hatsuyuki has gone? . . . But we must not cry any more. Let us call together the noble ladies of this place and for seven days sit with them praying behind barred doors. Go now and do my bidding.

[EVENING MIST *fetches the* NOBLE LADIES *of the place.*]

TWO NOBLE LADIES. [*Together*]

A solemn Mass we sing
A dirge for the Dead;
At this hour of heart-cleansing
We beat on Buddha's gong.

[*They pray.*]

NAMU AMIDA BUTSU
NAMU NYORAI
Praise to Amida Buddha,
Praise to Mida our Saviour!

[*The prayers and gong-beating last for some time and form the central ballet of the play.*]

CHORUS. [*The bird's soul appears as a white speck in the sky*]

Look! Look! A cloud in the clear mid-sky!
But it is not a cloud.
With pure white wings beating the air
The Snow-bird comes!
Flying towards our lady
Lovingly he hovers,
Dances before her.

THE BIRD'S SOUL. Drawn by the merit of your prayers and songs

CHORUS. Straightway he was reborn in Paradise.
By the pond of Eight Virtues[4] he walks abroad:
With the Phoenix and Fugan his playtime passing.
He lodges in the sevenfold summit of the trees of Heaven.
No hurt shall harm him
For ever and ever.

Now like the tasselled doves we loose
From battlements on holy days
A little while he flutters;
Flutters a little while and then is gone
We know not where.

3. Turn into a Buddha. [Waley's note.]

4. The eight virtues are: right views, right aims, right speech, right action, right livelihood, right effort, right-mindfulness, and right posture. The phoenix and fugan are mythical birds associated with fire and longevity.

BASHŌ AND OTHERS

Twenty-five *Haiku*

Perhaps over a million *haiku* are composed in Japanese every year, and in 1957, Mr. Harold Henderson[1] counted some fifty monthly magazines devoted to *haiku* and *tanka*, most of them successful commercial ventures. They are composed on all occasions (there is one on the arrival of the *Graf Zeppelin* in Japan). In the form of *renga* ("linked verse") they are improvised by Japanese as they play cards, the subject matter of each poem being determined by the preceding one. Also, the *haiku* and its slightly longer twin, the *tanka*, are the Japanese verse forms which have most appealed to the West, especially to the Imagist school (Richard Aldington, Amy Lowell, Ezra Pound, and others). We should observe, however, that the *haiku* and *tanka* are by no means the only Japanese verse forms. There are long poems in the early anthologies, the *Manyōshū* and the *Kokinshū* (*ca.* 760 and 905, respectively), which are among the glories of Japanese literature. In these and even in the historical chronicles of the early eighth century, the poems are in a form called *waka*, an alternation of five- and seven-syllable lines. The seventeen-syllable versions of *waka* are the *haiku*, the thirty-one-syllable versions are the *tanka*, and longer works are known as *chōka*. The *waka* remained the norm until recent times, when the influence of the West became operative. We must also remind ourselves that from earliest times the Japanese aristocrats composed both verse and prose in Chinese with somewhat the same impetus and orientation as a medieval Englishman writing in Latin.

An admirer of such works as Wordsworth's *The Prelude* (there are no such poems in Japanese) might see the seventeen syllables of the *haiku* as too short a verbal span to convey, adequately, an emotion. But the devices for getting around this limitation are many and frequently clever. The great Bashō, for instance, when told of a poet who had mentioned all of the famous eight views of Lake Ōmi in a *tanka*, managed to do the same in a *haiku* by mentioning the sound of the temple bell of Mii-dera (the sound of the bell is a "view" as much as the sight of it would be) and then saying that mist hid the other views. This is intellectual gymnastics. Linguistic gymnastics are also available to the Japanese poet, for his language is rich in homophones (words which sound alike), and it is therefore possible to use a common noun which is also a place name and which evokes the image of a place where some event, legendary or historical, took place. Thus the miniature *haiku* can have, in various ways, sugges-

1. *An Introduction to Haiku* (New York, 1958), p. 1.

tions of meanings which increase its profundity.

Japanese poetry has many of the general functions that poetry has fulfilled in the West. It is used for messages between lovers (always with beautiful calligraphy), it solaces the warrior, it communicates with gods and spirits, it commemorates or immortalizes the passing phenomena of nature. With this last subject matter, the freezing of a moment of nature, the *haiku* is especially concerned. The *haiku* poet is not content, however, with merely a hard, clear picture, as were too often his Imagist imitators in the West. Something more was required. The poem must have nuances, must suggest a good deal more than it says. Also it should, at its best, make some metaphysical comment or connection. It should not only bring together two disparate things for implied comparison but also put us in momentary contact with a flash of truth that is greater than any "message" that might be paraphrased out of the poem. This can happen—in Japanese as well as in English—by means of a pun. The dying Mercutio in *Romeo and Juliet* mutters, as he faces his end, "Ask for me tomorrow, and you shall find me a grave man." Such word play, at once amusing and sad, is characteristic of the sort of Japanese humorous verse called *senryū*.

The commonest subject of *haiku,* as noted earlier, is nature in its many manifestations. Sometimes this nature is in a violent mood—a stormy sea—but usually it is not. It is a nature meant for aesthetic viewing, whether it be in the form of a single branch of blossoms in a vase in an elaborately plain room of one's home, or a series of views, prescribed by tradition, of Mount Fuji from different perspectives along a winding road. The *Diary of a Waning Moon* (*Izayoi Nikki*), for instance, is a travel account of a journey made by a woman, Abutsu, from Kyoto to Kamakura in the thirteenth century. It contains an itinerary of her trip, with remarks on where she stayed and also on her loneliness in being away from her loved ones. But it also contains—as its most important part—some dozens of *tanka* celebrating the natural phenomena, including the weather, at each stage of the trip, and it has been looked upon by Japanese as a minor classic suitable as a school text in the writing of poetry. The landscape of Japan has been arranged both by man and by nature to invite continuing contemplation of a certain kind. Gardens are planned to reveal an ever-changing artistic composition from various points of view. The Japanese is not interested in climbing a mountain to see everything at once, nor is he interested in the geometrical formality of a continental garden. He takes "moon watching" seriously. In painting he seeks to capture the essence of a few shoots of bamboo or a branch of plum blossoms with a few deft strokes of the brush. He builds cricket cages so that the chirp of the cricket can be close at hand. Nature serves the poet by providing a concrete object to draw out his emotions and a setting which intensifies them.

All of the poetic devices used in longer Japanese poems are used in the *haiku*, but the compression into seventeen syllables is a formidable challenge. The risks are greater in writing *haiku* and, of course, the chances of success or failure are greater. The basis of all Japanese verse, long or short, is the syllable count. The language has neither stress accent sufficient for prosodic purposes (a mainstay of English poetry) nor quantity (such as exists in Latin). Also, since all Japanese words end in vowels, rhyme is too monotonous a device to use artistically.

Most of the poems below are by Bashō (pseudonym of Matsuo Munefusa, 1644–1694), whose pilgrimage through life led him finally to a hermit's hut and to Zen Buddhism. There are Zen overtones to many of Bashō's poems, but nothing doctrinaire is evident.

Twenty-five *Haiku**

1 *By Bashō*

On a withered branch
a crow has settled—
autumn nightfall.

Kare-eda	*ni*	*karasu-no*	*tomari-keri*	*aki-no-kure*
Withered-branch	on	crow's	settling-*keri*	autumn-nightfall

Two shades of darkness are presented here: the small, precise body of the crow against the amorphous darkness of an autumn evening. *Keri* is a *kireji* ("cut word") which has no translatable meaning but which often indicates an unfinished sentence and is used as a form of punctuation. *Kana* (No. 10) is a similar word.

2 *By Bashō*

Old pond:
frog jump in
water-sound.

Furu-ike	*ya*	*kawazu*	*tobi-komu*	*mizu-no-oto*
Old-pond	:	frog	jump-in	water-sound

"Probably the best known *haiku* in the Japanese language" (Henderson).[1] There is Zen illumination in this poem in the contrast between the ancient pond and the immediacy of the splash, with the frog symbolizing the sudden leap to *satori* (enlightenment).

* From *An Introduction to Haiku*, with translations and commentary by Harold G. Henderson. Copyright 1958 by Harold G. Henderson. Reprinted by permission of Doubleday & Company, Inc. The notes are adapted from the translator's notes and text.

1. *An Introduction to Haiku*, p. 19.

3 *By Bashō*

Around existence twine
(Oh, bridge that hangs across the gorge!)
ropes of twisted vine.

Kakehashi	*ya*	*inochi*	*wo*	*karamu*	*tsuta-katsura*
Hanging-bridge	:	life	[acc.]	entwine	ivy-vines

Here Bashō depicts an aspect of an experience on a journey through the mountains of Kiso where he and his companions were forced to cross a high gorge on a fragile, vine-covered rope bridge. *Inochi wo karamu* can be interpreted as meaning the vines themselves are hanging on for dear life.

4 *By Bashō*

Octopus traps: how soon
they are to have an end—these dreams
beneath the summer moon.

Take-tsubo	*ya*	*hakanaki*	*yume*	*wo*	*natsu-no-tsuki*
Octopus-pots	:	ephemeral	dreams	[onto]	summer-moon

The octopus trap is a pot set in shallow water. The octopus enters this and cannot back out. The octopus is a delicacy in Japan and is not regarded with the fear it engenders in the West. Who is dreaming, the octopus or the human observer?

5 *By Bashō*

Eight Views?—Ah, well;
mist hid seven when I heard
Mii-dera's bell.

Shichi	*kei*	*wa*	*kiri-ni*	*kakurete*	*Mii-no-kane*
Seven	views	as-for	mist-in	being-hidden	Mii's bell

As stated in the headnote, there existed a well-known *tanka* (thirty-one syllables) which mentioned all the eight views of Lake Ōmi, and Bashō was challenged to compose a *haiku* on the same subject. This is his solution. The sound of the bell of the temple is considered a "view."

6 *By Bashō*

Altar of Benkei,
Yoshitsune's sword! . . . Oh, fly
the carp in May!

Oi	*mo*	*tachi*	*mo*	*satsuki*	*ni*	*kazare*	*kami-nobori*
Altar	[too]	sword	[too]	May	in	decorate!	paper-streamers

During his travels Bashō arrived at a village during a festival. In the local temple he found the portable altar carried about by the monk Benkei, strong-man retainer to the warrior-hero Yoshitsune, and Yoshitsune's sword (see p. 325). He contrasts the immortal relics with the paper carp flying on the streets for the festival. The carp is a symbol of longevity, but longevity in man is as nothing when compared with the relics. Also, the paper carp lasts but a day.

7 *By Bashō*

Summer grass:
of stalwart warriors' splendid dreams
the aftermath.

Natsu-gusa	*ya*	*tsuwamono-domo-no*	*yume-no*	*ato*
Summer-grasses	:	strong-ones' [plural]	dreams'	afterward

Shortly after the occasion of No. 6, Bashō comes to Takadate, the fortress where Yoshitsune and his retainers were killed. Bashō records that in thinking of the bygone glories of the site, he was moved to tears. "Strong ones" is a medieval, somewhat archaic term for warriors; "dreams" has overtones of "splendor" and "lives like dreams." *Ato* includes the idea of "trace" or "relic." Henderson notes that this is very difficult to translate: the original has a strong sense of grief.

8 *By Bashō*

On a journey, ill,
and over fields all withered, dreams
go wandering still.

Tabi	*ni*	*yamite*	*yume*	*wa*	*kare-no*	*wo*	*kake-meguru*
Journey	on	taken-ill	dreams	as-for	dried-up-fields	on	run-about

This is a poem of Bashō's old age, with a premonition of death.

9 *By Bashō*

PERSISTENCE

Did it yell
till it became *all* voice?
Cicada-shell!

Koe	*ni*	*mina*	*naki-shimaute*	*ya*	*semi-no-kara*
Voice	to	all	cry-itself-out	?	cicada-shell

10 *By Bashō*

THE AUTUMN STORM

Wild boars and all
are blown along with it—
storm-wind of fall!

Inoshishi	*mo*	*tomo-ni*	*fukaruru*	*nowake*	*kana*
Wild-boars	even	together-with	get-blown	autumn-storm	*kana*

Violent nature is unusual in Bashō's work.

11 *By Bashō*

A PAINTING OF A SAKE-DRINKER

No blossoms and no moon,
and he is drinking sake
all alone!

Tsuki	*hana*	*mo*	*nakute*	*sake*	*nomu*	*hitori*	*kana*
Moon	blossoms	also	not-being	sake	drink	alone	*kana*

Contrast this with No. 18.

12 *By Bashō*

THE STILLNESS

So still:
into rocks it pierces—
the locust-shrill.

Shizukasa	*ya*	*iwa*	*ni*	*shimi-iru*	*semi-no-koe*
Stillness	:	rocks	to	pierce-in	locust-voices

I.e., the silence is so deep that when the locust shrills its sharp tone is so loud in contrast that it pierces the rocks.

13 *By Bashō*

SUMA BEACH IN AUTUMN

Between the waves:
mixed in with little shells,
shreds of bush-clover.

Nami-no-ma	*ya*	*kogai*	*ni*	*majiru*	*hagi-no-chiri*
Wave-intervals	:	small-shells	with	mix-in	bush-clover-rubbish

The waves represent the fertility of the universe (the *yin,* or female principle, is symbolized by water). Ironically, their product in this instance is dead—empty shells. In contrast, the earth provides life in an atmosphere hostile to land plants.

14 *By Bashō*

THE "INN OF THE WORLD"

At this same inn
slept pleasure women too.
Bush-clover and the moon!

Hito-ie	*ni*	*yujō*	*mo*	*netari*	*tsuki*	*to*	*hagi*
Same-house	in	courtesans	also	slept	moon	and	bush-clover

Bashō finds as he departs in the morning that the inn in which he slept provided, for the customer's pleasure, courtesans as well as the moon and the shrubbery.

15 *By Bashō*

THE MONKEY'S RAINCOAT

The first cold showers pour.
  Even the monkey seems to want
    a little coat of straw.

Hatsu-shigure	*saru*	*mo*	*ko-mino wo*	*hoshige-nari*
First-cold-rain	monkey	even	small-straw-coat	seems-to-want

Straw raincoats are a common thing in Japan. The monkey is an important figure in Chinese and Japanese literature and graphic art (see p. 235) as a symbol of animal energy and curiosity, but here he is simply a manlike animal.

16 *By Bashō*

A COVE AT THE "LAKE OF THE VIEWS"

From all four quarters
  cherry petals blowing in
    to Biwa's waters!

Shihō	*yori*	*hana*	*fuki-irete*	*Niō-no-umi*
"Four-directions"	from	blossoms	blowing-entering	Niō-Lake

Niō is another name for Lake Biwa or Ōmi, the lake of the "Eight Views" northeast of Kyoto.

17 *By Bashō*

SUMMER VOICES

So soon to die,
  and no sign of it is showing—
    locust-cry.

Yagate	*shinu*	*keskiki*	*wa*	*mie-zu*	*semi-no*	*koe*
Soon	die	indication	as-for	appear-not	locust's	voices

18 *By Bashō*

A WISH

I'd like enough drinks
  to put me to sleep—on stones
    covered with pinks.

Youte	*nemu*	*nadeshiko*	*sakeru*	*ishi-no*	*ue*
Being-drunk	would-lie-down	pinks	bloomed-on	stone's	top

One should drink to celebrate, unlike the unfortunate in No. 11. The flowers would provide (as would the moon) sufficient reason for celebration. The drinker may be alone, but he should have this relation to nature.

19 *By Bashō*

ON NEW YEAR'S DAY

Spring that no man
has seen:—plum-bloom on the back
of the mirror.

Hito	*mo*	*minu*	*haru*	*ya*	*kagami-no*	*ura-no*	*ume*
Person	even	not-see	spring	:	mirror's	back's	plum tree

This refers to highly stylized plum branches engraved on the back of a bronze hand mirror. The mirror is frequently believed to have something occult about it, and a mirror was part of the regalia which the emperor had to indicate his position, like the scepter and the orb in the West (see p. 315).

20 *By Kikaku*

Bright the full moon shines:
on the matting of the floor,
shadows of the pines.

Meigetsu	*ya*	*tatami-no*	*ue*	*ni*	*matsu-no-kage*
Bright-moon	:	floor-mats'	top	on	pine-tree-shadows

Kikaku presumably refers to the harvest moon, and he is enjoying it indoors while other people would normally be out "moon-viewing."

21 *By Kikaku*

AT THE BACK OF THE BUDDHA (KAMAKURA)

The Great Buddha—oh,
his lap must be all filled with it—
cherry-blossom-snow!

Ō-botoke	*hiza*	*uzumuramu*	*hana-no-yuki*
Great-Buddha	lap	may-be-filled	blossom-snow

The poet stands behind the great Buddha of Kamakura, a bronze, forty feet high, made in 1252 A.D., and speaks before he passes to the front of the statue.

22 *By Kyoroku*

THE SUMMONS

Banked fires; night grows late—
then comes a sound of rapping
at the gate.

Umorebi	*ya*	*yo*	*fukete*	*mon*	*wo*	*tataku*	*oto*
Banked-fires	:	night	growing-late	gate	[acc.]	knock-at	sound

23 *By Bonchō*

Something makes a sound!
With no one near, a scarecrow
has fallen to the ground.

Mono no	*oto*	*hitori*	*taoruru*	*kagashi*	*kana*
Thing's	sound	alone	get-a-tumble	scarecrow	*kana*

24 *By Sora*

Up the barley rows,
stitching, stitching them together,
a butterfly goes.

Kurikaeshi	*mugi-no-une*	*nuu*	*kochō*	*kana*
Again-and-again	barley-rows	stitching	butterfly	*kana*

25 *By Hokushi*

MOON-VIEWING

The moon on the pine:
I keep hanging it—taking it off—
and gazing each time.

Tsuki-wo	*matsu-ni*	*kakitari*	*hazushi*	*temo*	*mitari*
Moon [acc.]	pine-tree-	hanging-on	taking-off	and-still	looking-at

CHIKAMATSU MONZAEMON

(1653–1725)

The Courier for Hell (*Meido no Hikyaku*)

The popular drama of seventeenth- and eighteenth-century Japan, as has been noted,[1] has little affinity with the aristocratic *nō* drama of feudal Japan and some resemblances to the middle-class European drama which arose at about the same time. Chikamatsu Monzaemon lived in a period which seems, at least, more like what we are familiar with in the West, an age of sophisticated verse forms, a new kind of novel of intrigue and manners, and a drama which sometimes drew its plots from scandals reported in newspapers. It is the age of Bashō, the great master of the *haiku;* Saikaku, perhaps the greatest Japanese novelist since Murasaki; and Chikamatsu, sometimes referred to as the "Shakespeare" of Japan, though he is a

1. See pp. 702–706.

Shakespeare of adventure, intrigue, and pathos, not of high tragedy. It was also a period of the flowering of the arts. This is the age of the great screen painter Korin and that master of the delicate woodblock print, Moronobu, to mention only two well-known artists.

The period is loosely called the Genroku (1680 to about 1730). Certain social changes, by this time, had created the world about which Chikamatsu, Saikaku, and others write. The country was governed by a military dictatorship which, whatever its defects were, ordained a peaceful, orderly, conservative society. It faced economic conditions similar to those of England at the beginning of the eighteenth century—conflict between a feudal ruling class (in Japan, the samurai) and a rising and increasingly important merchant class. The ruling class sought to control the newly rich businessman by various kinds of restrictions on conspicuous consumption—restrictions on fancy clothes, ostentatious dwellings, and free spending, enforced both by edict and by repression. This repression, as it tends to in all societies, channeled the natural interests of the group which is in a position to enjoy life into whatever pursuit met the least resistance. The American businessman, if discouraged from the large Cadillac, can solace himself with a small, $15,000 Mercedes. The Russian bureaucrat, forbidden Western decadence, may be happy with a state summer home. The Japanese, living in a small, plain house, may without criticism elect to adorn it with priceless art objects. In Genroku Japan, one of the outlets for the rich merchant class and for those who aspired to be in it was the world of entertainment, the twilight world of the teahouse and the geisha in the licensed quarters of the large cities. It offered a wide range of entertainment and the excitement of women from the highly cultivated, refined geisha, to the prostitute, with many gradations in rank in between. Sexual intrigue, though an important aspect of the licensed quarter, was not the chief function of this world. It provided an opportunity for men to talk to sophisticated and educated women, a role in which the Japanese wife at home had not been trained. Success in this world of free spending, of course, became a status symbol, as expensive dining and the country club are success symbols in America.

This "floating world" was expensive, and could lead the unwary merchant or poor samurai into hopeless debt and the ruin of his family. A great many of the plays of the period deal with this problem or the larger one of loyalties divided between the home and family and the Gay Quarter. The conflict is between love and passion, in the Gay Quarter, and duty to the family, both the immediate family and the larger one of relatives and in-laws, the social group, and the class. The crisis does not usually come about because of the jealousy of the wife over the husband's attention to his paramour, but because the husband neglects his duties at home. This brings down on him the wrath of the larger family or, if he is led into crime, as Chūbei is in *The Courier for Hell*, the cruel hand of the law. The conflict is between what the Japanese call *giri*, "obligation," and human feelings. The father of a mistreated wife has a right to intervene in the family's affairs. *Giri* may make it obligatory that a person insist that his brother kill his wife. As Donald Keene points out, in Chikamatsu's *Love Suicides at Amijima* (*Ten no Amijima*) the hero and the heroine in the final moments of the play talk of their obligation to his wife, and, as Keene says, a "positively exasperating" example is in *The Courier for Hell*.[2] After Chubei is condemned, Magoemon yearns for a glimpse of his son's face but decides that, however much he longs to see him—and he is assured that he will not be noticed—it is not possible because of his obligations to his family and to society. Passion versus duty, of course, are the themes of Western heroic tragedy, but they are often on so lofty a plane that the passion bounds to the heavens and the duty involves the imminent fall of empires. The passions and the *giri* of the *kabuki-jōruri* drama are intimate, near to home, well within the world of the ordinary man and his next-door neighbor.

The plays written in the Genroku era were created for two kinds of theaters—the *jōruri*, or puppet stage, and the *kabuki* theater, with live actors. The same plays were often performed on both stages. The requirements for a drama to be performed by puppets limit the drama in some ways and liberate it in others. The puppets themselves are large, doll-like creatures whose arms, legs, and heads move, and sometimes the eyes—the flashing eyes of the warrior puppet are guaranteed to get audience response. Unlike marionettes, they are moved bodily about the stage by the puppeteers. The handlers dress inconspicuously in black, and one is soon oblivious both to them and to the artificiality of the puppets. An advantage of the form is that everything on the puppet stage is equally realistic. While the cinema, through its special effects, can achieve great realism in its depiction of horrible and dangerous scenes, the live-actor stage is more limited. If the hero has to fight a lion, we have the choice of an actor dressed in a lion skin or a very tired, affable, aged lion taught to do tricks, neither of which is convincing. But the puppet lion (or the dragon, for that matter) is as real as the puppet hero and heroine, and the stage can use cinematographic tricks, like the rainbow-bridge in *The Battles of Coxinga*. (On the *kabuki* stage, the lion would be a man in an abstract and symbolic lion garb, and realism would not be attempted.) The effect of the puppet theater on the literary technique lies in the fact that a single narrator reads all the parts, and the playwright must attempt to distinguish characters stylistically to help the narrator differentiate between parts.

A special pleasure in Japanese literature is derived, as we have

2. *Major Plays of Chikamatsu*, translated by Donald Keene (New York, 1961), p. 33.

seen in the poetry, from references to well-known places. Japan is a small country, and every inch of ground has historical or romantic or religious associations. Also, it is easy to make plays on common words and place names through homophones. We could, of course, do this more extensively than we do in English and American literature, but while we might decide on what the five great views in New York City are, our opinions would not necessarily agree with those of other people. The Eight Views of Lake Ōmi (see Bashō's poem, below) are conventionalized and known to all. The Japanese like the historical and romantic associations of place-names and also the feeling of journeying, in literature, over familiar ground at home. There is often in the *kabuki-jōruri* plays a final journey by the lovers which takes us on a route traceable on the map of Edo or Osaka. This satisfies the need for a sense of place and provides a period of lowered tension before the climax, which is usually tragic or pathetic.

Chikamatsu was born Sugimori Nobumori in Echizen Province in 1653. He may have taken his pen name from the Chikamatsu Temple in Ōmi. His family were lesser samurai, and he tells us that he was not a great success at official life, or as a samurai, or in business. Some scholars think he began writing plays early, but the first known one was the puppet play *The Soga Successors,* written when he was about thirty. This was a great success, and he went on to write many plays for both the puppet and the live stage, though he clearly preferred the former. His plays fall into two classes, *sewamono,* or domestic plays, and *jidaimono,* or historical plays. The former, of which *The Courier for Hell* is one of the best examples, are more popular today, but the *jidaimono* tradition is also a great one and leads us to the popular samurai movies of the twentieth century. *The Battles of Coxinga* (*Kokusenya Kassen*) was Chikamatsu's great success in historical drama. It is "Shakespearian" in that it has a great hero, ruthless villains, and brave and beautiful women, and deals with threats to the state; one imagines it would have appealed to Shakespeare's audience. Except for his considerable dramatic output and a brief memoir in which he describes his life and ideas on drama, we do not know much about Chikamatsu's life. He died in 1725.

Powerful emotions not checked by reason or instinct carry Chūbei, the hero of *The Courier for Hell* (1711), rapidly along to disgrace and tragedy. If we like him, it is because he is impetuous and warm-hearted, and not self-serving. In contrast to him are the two women, the wife and the lover. They are driven slowly back and forth between love and duty—sometimes they seek to protect themselves and what they have, sometimes they are willing to sacrifice themselves nobly for the good of all. The iron cage in which these three characters are confined is the "establishment," the family and its codes and the world without which supports the codes. If the hero seems to us to be weak, well, people *are* in real life, and Chikamatsu does not ask us to sit in judgement on his characters. Suicide, however, is not a weakness but an honorable way out of an impossible situation. But even the suicide of the lovers has to be done in a way considerate of others—one has *giri* even in death.

The Courier for Hell *

Characters

CHŪBEI, *aged 24, proprietor of the Kame-ya, a courier service*
HACHIEMON, *his friend*
KATSUGI MAGOEMON, CHŪBEI'S *father*
CHŪZABURŌ, *a friend of* CHŪBEI *in Ninokuchi Village*
JINNAI, *a samurai*
IHEI, *a clerk*
GOHEI, *a servant*
CLERKS, MESSENGERS, APPRENTICES, POLICE
UMEGAWA, *aged 22, a courtesan of low rank*
MYŌKAN, CHŪBEI'S *foster mother*
KIYO, *proprietress of the Echigo House*
WIFE OF CHŪZABURŌ
MAN, *a maid*
TOYOKAWA, *a prostitute*
TAKASE, *a prostitute*
PROSTITUTES, MAIDS

Act One

SCENE: THE SHOP OF THE KAME-YA, A COURIER SERVICE IN OSAKA.

TIME: LATE IN THE ELEVENTH MOON (OF 1710?).

NARRATOR. In Naniwa of water-markers, in Naniwa where bloom these flowers,[1] three are the streets in the Quarter of Flowers, Sado and Echigo and Hyōtan in between.[2] To them from Awaji Street "visited by shore birds"[3] comes Chūbei, a frequent visitor, heir to the Kame-ya, a youth barely turned four and twenty, arrived from Yamato four years ago as an adopted son with a dowry. He is clever in business, at assigning packloads, and at

*From *Major Plays of Chikamatsu*, translated by Donald Keene. Copyright 1961 by Columbia University Press. Reprinted by permission of Columbia University Press. The notes, unless otherwise indicated, are the translator's.

1. The water-marker (*miotsukushi*) was used as an epithet for Naniwa (Psaka). It is today the emblem of the city. "Where bloom these flowers" is a quotation from an old song about Naniwa; the flower in question is the plum blossom, and may be an allusion to Umegawa, whose name contains the word "plum" (*ume*).

2. Three streets in the Shimmachi licensed quarter of Osaka.

3. Allusion to the poem by Minamoto no Kanemasa, no. 288 of *Kinyōshū* (A.D. 1128): "Guardian of the barrier at Suma, how many nights have you awakened to the crying of the shore birds that visit the isle of Awaji?"

managing the thrice-monthly couriers to Edo. Adept in the tea ceremony, poetry, chess, and backgammon, he writes an elegant hand. When it comes to saké, he can manage three, four, or at most five cups, and he wears with the proper assurance a heavy silk cloak with five crests. His plain sword guard, so cunningly inlaid one would never suspect it was of country workmanship, is rare as Chūbei among country lads. Knowing in the ways of love, familiar of the Quarter, he does not wait for evening to race thither on flying feet.

In his absence the courier shop, busy with packing and unpacking, is crowded front and back with clerks scratching in the ledgers and clicking their abacuses. The ease with which they handle tens of thousands of *ryō* and transact business with distant Kyushu and Edo without stirring from the shop makes you think the gold and silver pieces came with wings.

The collector has returned from his rounds of the city and begins to enter the commissions in the register, when a voice is heard at the door.

JINNAI. Could you tell me, is Chūbei at home?

NARRATOR. The visitor is a samurai from a daimyo household, a regular customer of the shop. The clerk answers politely.

IHEI. Ah, it's you, sir, Mr. Jinnai. Chūbei is out, but if you have anything to send to Edo, I am at your service. Boy, bring some tea!

NARRATOR. He speaks deferentially.

JINNAI. No, I have no commissions for you. A letter has come from the young master in Edo. Listen to what he writes.

NARRATOR. He unfolds a letter.

JINNAI. "I shall send you 300 *ryo* in gold with the courier leaving on the second of next month. Please collect this sum on the ninth or the tenth from Chūbei of the Kame-ya in Osaka, and settle the business which I have discussed with you. I enclose herewith the receipt from the courier service. Surrender it to Chūbei on delivery of the remittance."

These are his orders. Important business arrangements have been disrupted by the failure of the remittance to arrive by today. What is the explanation for this disgraceful negligence?

NARRATOR. He utters the words with a scowl.

IHEI. I don't wonder that you're upset, sir, but with all the rain we've been having lately, the rivers are swollen and it takes longer than usual to make the journey. The slowness of your remittance hasn't been our only problem. We've sustained considerable losses. But there's nothing for you to worry about. Even supposing the courier were set upon by robbers or cutthroats, or himself yielded to sudden temptation on the way, the eighteen courier houses would compensate you in full, regardless of the sum of money. You wouldn't suffer the loss of so much as a mustard seed.

NARRATOR. Jinnai interrupts.

JINNAI. That goes without saying. Chūbei's head would fly if my master suffered any loss. Any further delay with the remittance will seriously hamper my master's business. That is why I've come here today to investigate. Send a courier to meet the one from Edo, and see to it that the money is brought immediately.

NARRATOR. Foot soldier and stripling that he is, he brandishes with authority his sword, silvery-looking, though probably leaden as his heavy dialect. He departs, only to be followed by another visitor.

MESSENGER. Excuse me, please. I've been sent by Hachiemon of the Tamba-ya in Nakanoshima. He says that he's received notice of a remittance from a rice wholesaler in Kofuna Street in Edo, and he'd like to know why the money hasn't reached him yet. He wrote you a letter about it the other day, but hasn't had any answer, and when he sent a messenger, you gave him the runaround. He wonders when you intend to deliver the money. Anyway, my master says that you should turn over the money to me and send me back with an escort. I'll return your receipt. Well, I'm ready to collect the money now.

NARRATOR. He stands legs astraddle in the doorway, making a clamor. The clerk, Ihei, devoted to his master, answers in unruffled tones.

IHEI. Indeed? I can't believe that a gentleman like Hachiemon would order us around in such a high-handed manner. Your company's business is not the only concern of the Kame-ya. This house is entrusted with five or even seven thousand *ryō* of people's money at a time, and our couriers range at will the 130 leagues between Edo and Osaka. It would be strange if deliveries weren't delayed once in a while. The master is expected back at any moment. When he returns, I'm sure he'll send a reply. I'll thank you not to make such a commotion over what, after all, is less than fifty *ryō*.

NARRATOR. The messenger, taken aback by his asperity, leaves quietly. Chūbei's mother, Myōkan, who scarcely ever quits the *kotatsu*,[4] emerges from the back room.

MYŌKAN. What was the meaning of that? I'm sure that the money for the Tamba-ya arrived at least ten days ago. Why hasn't Chūbei delivered it? All morning long I've been hearing customer after customer demanding his money. Never since the days of my husband has the house received a demand for even a single piece of silver. We've yet to cause the guild the least trouble. In fact,

4. A low table covered with a quilt which reaches the floor; underneath the table is a small charcoal fire. A normal type of heating even today in a Japanese house.

the Kame-ya has always been considered the model among the eighteen courier houses. But haven't you noticed? Lately Chūbei's behavior has been very peculiar. Those of you who are recent employees may not know it, but Chūbei is actually not my son. He was the only son of a prosperous farmer from Ninokuchi Village in Yamato named Katsugi Magoemon. His mother died, and his father, afraid that desperation at being under a stepmother might make Chūbei turn to vicious pleasures, suggested that I take him here as successor to the business. I've had no fault to find with Chūbei's running of the household and the business, but of late he's seemed restless and unable to keep his mind on his work. I've wanted to admonish him about his behavior, but I was afraid that he might think that his foster mother is just as bad as a stepmother. Rather than complain, I've preferred to shame him by my silence. I've pretended not to notice, but I've followed everything deserving of my attention. He's become so extravagant. Why, he uses two or three sheets of fine quality tissue, whatever he happens to lay his hand on, just to blow his nose! My late husband always used to say, "Never trust a man who uses one paper handkerchief after another!" Chūbei takes three packs with him whenever he leaves the house. I wonder how he can blow his nose so often—he never has a single sheet left when he returns. He's young and healthy, but if he goes on blowing his nose that way, he's sure to come down with some sickness.

NARRATOR. Still murmuring complaints, she leaves. The apprentices and errand boys feel sorry for her.

APPRENTICE. I wish he would please hurry home.

NARRATOR. While they have been waiting, the sun has journeyed back to the west, and it is time to shut the shop gates.

Love for Umegawa, a bird in a cage, has turned Chūbei into a swallow,[5] ever winging to the Quarter, but now he trudges the streets, his thoughts tangled like a spider's web with schemes for raising money and fears of what may happen at home. He sees the ten-penny harlots emerging at the street corners, and realizes in dismay that day has drawn to a close. He hurries home now, so precipitiously that his feet barely touch the ground. He arrives at the shop entrance, but hesitates, worried about what may have happened during his absence. Perhaps there have been dunning messengers from his customers, and Myōkan has heard their complaints. If only someone would come out, so that he could learn the situation before he entered! This is his own house, but the threshold seems too high for him to cross. He peeps inside and sees the cook, Man, apparently preparing to visit the saké shop.

5. The cry of the swallow, "chū, chū," leads into mention of Chūbei.

She is a sullen, sharp-tongued[6] creature, unlikely to reveal anything free of charge. "I'll pretend I'm in love and trick her into talking," he thinks, when suddenly she appears. He firmly grips her hand that holds a saké cask. She cries out.

MAN. Master, is that you?

CHŪBEI. Don't make such an uproar! You know too much about love for that!—I'm head over heels in love with you. They say that when there's love inside, it's bound to show on the outside. Have you seen the look in my eyes? Why do you torture me so with that adorable face of yours? You'd be kinder if you killed me.

NARRATOR. He takes her in his arms.

MAN. I can tell you're fibbing. I've seen how you go off every single day to Shimmachi, and how you use two or three packs of tissue at a time. When you have such a lovely nose to blow, why should you want to wipe it on the likes of me? You're lying!

NARRATOR. She shakes herself free, but he takes her in his arms again.

CHŪBEI. What purpose could I have in lying? It's the truth!

MAN. If you really mean it, will you come to my bed tonight?

CHŪBEI. Of course. How happy you've made me! But there's something I'd like to ask while I'm at it.

MAN. Ask me when we're snug in bed together! You won't fool me, will you? Promise, and I'll take a hot bath before you come!

NARRATOR. She breaks off the conversation and, freeing herself, runs off. Chūbei is irritated, though he is not sure at whom. He looks up.

CHŪBEI. I wonder who's that swaggering this way from the north block? Oh—it's Hachiemon. It'd be a nuisance meeting him.

NARRATOR. He starts off to the east, hoping to dodge Hachiemon.

HACHIEMON. Chūbei! Don't try to avoid me!

CHŪBEI. Hachiemon—you're a stranger in these parts! Yesterday, then today, too, and come to think of it, the day before yesterday, I planned to send somebody to your place, but what with one thing and another, I put if off.—It's turned decidedly cold. How's your father's rheumatism and your mother's toothache? Oh—you positively reek of saké! You shouldn't overdo it, you know. I'll send someone tomorrow morning first thing. Oh yes, ee-shay[7] sent a message. She says she'd like to see you one of these days.

NARRATOR. He chatters on, hoping to humor Hachiemon.

6. The expression *ki de hana mogu* means "to treat disagreeably," but literally is "to wipe one's nose with a piece of wood."

7. The word *sore* for "she" is given as *reso,* reversing the syllables as in pig Latin.

HACHIEMON. Drop it. I'm not a man to dance to your tune. Am I mistaken in thinking you run a courier service? Why hasn't the remittance of fifty *ryō* from Edo reached me yet? I wouldn't mind waiting four or five days, but it's been over ten days and you still haven't delivered my money. Friendship and business are two different matters. After all, you charge me high enough rates, and the business must be valuable to you. Today I sent a messenger to your shop and your damned clerk gave him a surly answer. I can't believe you treat other customers that way. Are you amusing yourself at my expense? Remember, in Kitahama, Utsubo, Nakanoshima and even in the Temma greengrocers' market they call Hachiemon "The Boss."[8] Make fun of me all you like, but today I get my money. Or must I report you to the messenger guild? First, I'll have a word with your mother.

NARRATOR. Chūbei stops him from going inside. He whispers.

CHŪBEI. I'm sorry. I've bungled things. Here, I'm begging you on bended knees—please listen to just one word. I beseech you.

HACHIEMON. What, again! You seem to think you can settle anything with your clever tongue. If you try the same tricks on me you've used on Umegawa, you'll find a man's quite a different proposition. You've something to tell me? Very well, I'm listening.

NARRATOR. He rebukes him bitterly.

CHŪBEI. If my mother should hear you, nothing, not even my death, would restore my reputation. I beg you, as the supreme act of kindness of a lifetime, keep your voice down.—Ah, I feel so disgusted with myself!

NARRATOR. He weeps bitterly.

CHŪBEI. Why should I hide the truth from you? Your money arrived from Edo two weeks ago. As you know, Umegawa's customer from the country has been using his money to outbid me. I've been at a complete disadvantage with only the miserable sums, two or three hundred *me*, that I've managed to pilfer when my mother and the clerks weren't looking. I was feeling bad enough—more dead than alive—when I learned that her ransom had been decided on, and all that was left was the final striking of hands. Umegawa was heartbroken, and my honor at stake. We should have killed ourselves already. One night we even went so far as to touch the cold steel of our daggers to each other's throats but—perhaps it wasn't yet time for us to die—obstacles of one sort and another interfered, and that night we parted in tears. The following morning—it was the twelfth of this month

8. Kitahama was a section of rich merchants, Utsubo of fish markets, Nakanoshima of samurai residences and storehouses—all in Osaka.

—the money for you from Edo arrived unexpectedly. I slipped it into my kimono, hardly realizing what I did, and fairly flew to Shimmachi, I have no recollection how. Then, with much effort, I persuaded the owner of the house to break the contract with Umegawa's country customer. He agreed to ransom her to me. I managed to save Umegawa by turning over your fifty *ryō* as earnest money. Every morning and night since then I've faced north[9] and worshiped you, telling myself that saving her was possible only because I have a friend in Hachiemon. Yet I know that no matter how close we are, it is one thing using the money after first getting your permission—that's the same as borrowing—but quite another asking for it later on. While I was wondering what to do, you began to demand your money. One lie led to another, and now that my earlier excuses have proven false, I don't suppose that anything I can say will seem true to you. But other money ought to be coming from Edo in the next four or five days at the latest. Somehow I'll manage to send it to you. I promise you won't lose a penny. It will only make you angry if you think of me as a human being. Consider instead that you've saved a dog's life and forgive me, I beg you.—I see now why there are always people being executed for crimes. I have no choice from now on but to steal. Do you think it's easy for a man to confess such things? Try to imagine what it's like! Nothing could be as painful as this, not even if I had to cough up a sword from my throat.

NARRATOR. He weeps tears of anguish. Hachiemon, a man ready to tackle even demons, also sheds tears.

HACHIEMON. I admire you for making such a painful confession. I'm a man—I forgive you and I'll wait. Work out your problem as best you can.

NARRATOR. Chūbei touches his forehead to the ground.

CHŪBEI. Thank you. I've had five parents—two fathers and three mothers[10]—but it'd be harder to forget your kindness, Hachiemon, than theirs.

NARRATOR. Tears interrupt his words.

HACHIEMON. I am satisfied, if those are your feelings. Well—somebody may be watching. I'll see you soon.

NARRATOR. He is about to leave when Chūbei's mother calls from inside.

MYŌKAN. Is that Hachiemon? Chūbei, invite him in.

NARRATOR. Chubei has no choice; hesitantly he leads Hachiemon inside. The mother is incorruptible honesty itself.

9. Hachiemon's house in Nakanoshima was north of Chūbei's place in Awajimachi.

10. His real parents, his stepmother, and his foster parents.

MYŌKAN. You sent a messenger a while ago and now you've come yourself. I can see why you'd be impatient. Chūbei, you know his money arrived ten days ago. Why have you delayed delivering it? Stop and think a moment. What use is a courier service if money is delivered late? Remember the nature of your business. Give Hachiemon the money at once.

NARRATOR. But Chūbei has no money to give him. Hachiemon guesses Chūbei's thoughts.

HACHIEMON. It may sound as if I'm boasting, ma'am, but I'm not in any desperate need for fifty or seventy *ryō*.—I must leave now for Nagabori. Tomorrow will do just as well.

NARRATOR. He is about to go.

MYŌKAN. No, no. I won't be able to sleep at night for worry as long as we are holding your precious money. Chūbei, give Hachiemon the money immediately.

NARRATOR. Thus urged, Chūbei answers "Yes" and goes into the back room. He looks round blankly, but there is no sign of money. He goes through with the pretense of unlocking the cupboard, though he knows it is empty; even the squeaking of the key embarrasses him. Wild with anxiety, he prays in his heart that the gods will grant their help.

CHŪBEI. Thank heavens! There's a pomade jar[11] in this hairdressing kit. Thank you, god of my ancestors!

NARRATOR. He lifts the jar thrice to his brow in gratitude, then wraps it in paper as though it were a packet of gold pieces, and quickly inscribes in bold black characters "Fifty *Ryō* in Gold." How shameless his deceit—passing off a worthless pot for fifty *ryō* and tricking his mother too!

CHŪBEI. Here you are, Hachiemon. As you know, I'm under no obligation to deliver this money now, but I'm giving it to you anyway, to relieve my mother's worries and to show my respect for you as a gentleman. Please accept it without further ado and reassure my mother. I'm sure you won't need to undo the packet. You can tell merely by the feel that it contains fifty *ryō*. Have you any objections?

NARRATOR. He offers the packet. Hachiemon takes it in his hand.

HACHIEMON. Why, who do you take me for? I'm Hachiemon of the Tamba-ya, and as long as I get my money, I certainly won't raise any objections. There you are, ma'am. I acknowledge receipt of the remittance from Edo. I'll be expecting you on your visit to the Fudō Temple.[12]

11. *Bimmizuire* is a jar used in dressing the sidelocks (*bin*) in a man's coiffure. It was of an oval shape, about an inch thick, and therefore was roughly the dimensions of a packet of gold coins (*koban*).

12. A temple in the north of Osaka; to go there from Chūbei's house would normally take one by way of Nakanoshima, Hachiemon's place.

NARRATOR. He is about to leave when Myōkan, apparently convinced by their deception, calls out.

MYŌKAN. Chūbei, it's customary when a remittance has been paid to claim the receipt for it. If Hachiemon hasn't his receipt with him, you should ask him please to write a few words. One has to be careful about everything.

CHŪBEI. [*Whispers to* HACHIEMON] Mother is illiterate—she can't read a word. Please write something, for form's sake.

NARRATOR. He holds out a writing set and winks.

HACHIEMON. That's no problem. I'll be delighted. Here, Chūbei, see what I write!

NARRATOR. He scrawls a note as his fancy dictates: "Item. I am not in receipt of fifty *ryō* in gold. The above is positive guarantee that this evening, as previously promised, I will go drinking in the Quarter, and will accompany you as your clown. I engage always to be present whenever there is merrymaking. In witness thereof, I accept this pomade jar as token of my intention to appear on all festive days."[13]

He dashes off this stream of nonsense.

HACHIEMON. I'll be leaving now.

NARRATOR. As soon as he steps outside Myōkan speaks.

MYŌKAN. Get everything in writing—a written document always carries weight.

NARRATOR. Chūbei's mother, deceived again, is honest-hearted as the Buddha, but like the Buddha, she will grow angry if rubbed the wrong way once too often.[14]

The night spent waiting for word of the thrice-monthly courier from Edo has deepened when outside there is a jingling of horse bells and the loud cry, "The pack horses have come! Open the inside gates!" Men swarm in, shouldering wicker trunks. Chūbei and his mother are overjoyed.

CHŪBEI. Good luck has returned, and next year will be lucky too![15] Saké and tobacco for the drivers!

NARRATOR. The shop is in a turmoil as the clerks, inkstones at their elbows, frantically jot entries in the ledger. Ihei, the chief clerk, still wears a sour expression.

IHEI. Mr. Jinnai, a samurai, was here a while ago from the mansion in Dōjima. He said that notice of the expected arrival of three hundred *ryō* of gold on the ninth had reached him, and he couldn't understand why it was so late. He left in a huff. What was the trouble?

13. The terminology of this note is a parody of stereotyped phrases normally found in pledges.

14. From an old proverb, "Even Buddha will get angry if you rub his face three times."

15. Chūbei thinks of next year because it is already the end of the eleventh moon. The phrase *shiawaseuma* (good-luck horse) refers to the fact that it was customary to write the words "good luck" on the horse's saddle girth.

NARRATOR. The supervisor empties his money belt.

SUPERVISOR. Yes, I know about his three hundred *ryō*. The money's urgently needed. Please deliver it tonight.

NARRATOR. Eight hundred *ryō* in gold, remittances for various clients, are plopped down. Chūbei grows all the more elated.

CHŪBEI. Put the silver in the inner storehouse, and the gold in the safe. Mother, I'll take these three hundred *ryō* to the daimyo's mansion at once. [*To servants*] Remember, we're entrusted with other people's money. Keep watch on the gate and shut the doors soon. Be particularly careful about fire. I may be a little late returning, but I'll be traveling in a palanquin, so there's nothing to worry about. Finish your dinners and get to bed early.

NARRATOR. He puts the money into his kimono and ties the strings of his cloak. Frost is gathering this night on the gate as he steps outside. Though he fully intends to go north, his feet follow their accustomed path to the south.[16] Absent-mindedly he crosses West Yoko Canal, so absorbed in thoughts of the prostitute that he reaches Rice Merchants' Street before he realizes it.

CHŪBEI. What's this? I'm supposed to be on my way to the mansion in Dōjima. Have I been bewitched by a fox? Good heavens!

NARRATOR. He retraces a few steps, only to stop.

CHŪBEI. Perhaps the reason why I've come here without meaning to is that Umegawa needs me, and my protecting god is guiding me to her. I'll stop by her place a moment and look in on her.

NARRATOR. He turns back again.

CHŪBEI. No, this is disastrous. With this money on me, I'll surely want to spend it. Shall I stop while I can? Shall I go to her?—I'll go and have done with it!

NARRATOR. His first thought was sensible, his second insensate, his third sends him as a courier back and forth six times a month on the Six Roads, a courier for hell.[17]

Act Two

SCENE: THE ECHIGO HOUSE IN THE SHIMMACHI QUARTER.

TIME: LATER THE SAME EVENING.

NARRATOR. "*Ei-ei!*" cry the crows, the crows,
The wanton crows,
On moonlit nights and in the dark,
Looking for their chance;
"Let's meet!" they cry, "let's meet!"[18]

16. North would take him to Dōjima, south to the Shimmachi quarter.

17. The courier service went three times a month in both directions between Osaka and Edo, for a total of six trips. The Six Roads refer to the six ways before the soul when it reaches the afterworld.

18. The cry of the crows, "*ao, ao*," is interpreted as the future of the verb *au* (to meet).

Green customers are ripened each day, till evening comes and charcoal fires glow, by the love of courtesans of their choice: the love and sympathy these women give, regardless of rank, is in essence one.[19] The Plum blossoms are fragrant and the Pines are lofty, but leaving rank aside,[20] teahouse girls have the deepest affections. Here comes one now, guided by a maid in a cotton print kimono to Echigo House in Sadoya Street—"Oh for a bridge between Echigo and Sado!" the song goes. The owner here is a woman; no doubt this is the reason why the girls who call feel so at home and open their hearts' deepest secrets of love. Umegawa thinks of the Echigo House as her refuge in sorrow, and neglects her duties elsewhere to come here, hiding a while from the Island House—"island hiding," as Kakinomoto said.[21]

UMEGAWA. [*To* PROPRIETRESS] Kiyo, that blockhead of a country bumpkin has been bothering me all day and my head is splitting. Hasn't Chūbei showed up yet? I sneaked away from my customer, hoping at least to see you, my only connection with Chūbei.

NARRATOR. She slides open the *shoji* door as she enters, even as she will slide it tomorrow at dawning.

KIYO. I'm glad you've come. There's a crowd of girls upstairs relaxing. They're drinking and playing *ken*[22] to pass the time until their customers call. Why don't you join them in a game of *ken* and have a cup of saké? It'll cheer you up. Some of your friends are there.

NARRATOR. Umegawa goes upstairs. The room is draughty and the women—no men are present—are drinking saké warmed over a *hibachi,* their hands tired from the gestures of the game. "*Romase!*" "*Sai!*" "*Torai!*"[23] "A tie!" Takase of the high-pitched voices takes on Toyokawa, and her fingers flash. "*Hama!*" "*San!*" "*Kyū!*" "*Go!*" "*Ryū!*" "*Sumui!*"

TOYOKAWA. I win! You must drink another cup! You can manage one, can't you, Narutose?

TAKASE. Look, Umegawa's here. [*To* UMEGAWA] You couldn't have come at a better time. You're so good at *ken.* Chiyotose's been beating us all evening long, and we're furious. Do take her on. Oh, I'll get another bottle of saké for you.

19. Literally, "green wicker hats turn [the color of] scarlet leaves. . . ." Men visiting the Quarter concealed their faces with basket-like wicker hats. Some commentators take the passage to read that the men stay on until their green hats are reddened by the glow of charcoal fires.

20. Pines (*matsu*) were the highest rank of courtesan, and Plum Blossoms (*ume*) came next. Umegawa belongs to the humble class of *mise joro,* prostitutes who call to customers from their shops.

21. Kakinomoto no Hitomaro, the great poet of the early eighth century. The phrase occurs in poem no. 409 of the *Kokinshū.*

22. A game of Chinese origin. Each player holds out none to five fingers; the one who guesses the total held out by both wins.

23. Approximations of the Chinese pronunciations, with various suffixes: *romase* is "six," *sai* "seven," and *tōrai* "ten." The numbers later in the passage are, respectively, eight, three, nine, five, six, and four.

UMEGAWA. I hate saké and I'm in no mood for *ken*. What I would like from you is a few tears of sympathy. My customer from the country intends to ransom me. Why, just today at the Island House he was trying to badger me into consent. I lost my temper, I hate him so. All the same, he spoke first. Chūbei asked later on, and it took all the master's efforts to get Chūbei permission to put down the earnest money. The master even extended the deadline when Chūbei failed to pay the balance as he promised. We've managed to stay together so far but, after all, Chūbei has responsibilities. He must think of his foster mother, and he runs an important business between here and Edo, with commissions from the daimyo granaries and all the leading merchants. Anything at all might ruin our plans.

If I allow myself to be redeemed by that oaf, I could kill myself afterwards and still people would say, since I'm not a high-class courtesan, "Her head was turned by filthy lucre. What contemptible creatures those teahouse girls are!" I must think of my reputation and the feelings of my friend Kamon and the other girls of my class. Oh, I wish I could be together with Chūbei, as we've always planned, and free myself from this endless gossip!

NARRATOR. Her sleeve is soaked with tears as she speaks. Her listeners, the other prostitutes, compare their lot to hers, and nodding, share in her tears.

PROSTITUTE. I feel terribly depressed. Why don't we cheer ourselves with a little music? Will one of you maids run down and ask Takemoto Tanomo to come here?[24]

UMEGAWA. Don't bother—I was buying some hair oil at his shop a few minutes ago and I happened to hear that he went directly from the theater to the Fan House in Echigo Street.[25] But I am a pupil of Tanomo's. I'll show you how well I can imitate him! A samisen, please.

NARRATOR. She begins to play a piece about Yūgiri, using this old example to tell of the courtesan's fate today.

UMEGAWA. There's no truth in courtesans, people say, but they are deceived, and their words but confessions of ignorance in love. Truth and falsehood are essentially one. Consider the courtesan, so faithful to her lover that she is ready to throw away her life for him—when no word comes from the man and he steadily grows more distant, brood over it as she may, a woman of this profession cannot control her fate. She may be ransomed instead by a

24. A leading *jōruri* chanter of his day. He owned a hair oil shop in the Shimmachi Quarter.

25. The Fan House (*Ōgi-ya*) was famous as the scene of the loves of Yūgiri, the great courtesan, and Izaemon. The selection about Yūgiri which Umegawa sings is quoted from an early work by Chikamatsu, *Sanzesō* (1686).

man she does not love, and the vows she has pledged become falsehoods. But sometimes it happens that a man favored by a courtesan from the start with merely the false smiles of her trade may, when constant meetings have deepened their love, become her lifelong partner; then all her first falsehoods have proved to be truth. In short, there is neither falsehood nor truth in love. All that we can say for certain is that fate brings people together. The very courtesan who lies awake, sleepless at night with longing for the lover she cannot meet, may be cursed by him for her cruelty, if he knows not her grief.

If that country fellow curses me, let him. I can't help loving Chūbei, that's my sickness. I wonder if all women of our profession have the same chronic complaint?

NARRATOR. The story of one who all for love abandoned the world induces melancholy reveries, and even the effects of the saké wear off. Hachiemon of Nakanoshima, approaching from Nine House Street, hears the singing.

HACHIEMON. Ah-ha! I recognize the voices of those whores! Is the madam there?

NARRATOR. He charges in. He picks up a long-handled broom and, holding it by the sweeping end, bangs loudly on the ceiling with the handle.

HACHIEMON. You give yourselves away, girls! I've been listening to you down here. What kind of man do you miss so much? If it makes you lonely being without a man, there's one available here, though I don't suppose he's to your taste. How would you like him?

NARRATOR. He shouts up through the floor. Umegawa does not recognize him.

UMEGAWA. Of course I want to see my sweetheart! If it's wrong for me to say so, come up and beat me! [*To* KIYO] Who is that downstairs, Kiyo?

KIYO. Nobody to worry about. It's Hachi from Nakanoshima.

NARRATOR. Umegawa is alarmed.

UMEGAWA. Oh, dear, I don't want to see him. Please, all of you, go downstairs and don't let on, whatever you do, that I'm here.

PROSTITUTE. We'll be the souls of discretion.

NARRATOR. They nod and file downstairs.

HACHIEMON. Well, well—Chiyotose, Narutose, quite a distinguished gathering! They told me at the Island House that Umegawa left her room this evening and went off somewhere, but Chūbei doesn't seem to have showed up here yet. Madam, come closer. You too, girls, and the maids also. I have something to tell about Chūbei, for your ears only. Gather round.

NARRATOR. He whispers confidentially.

PROSTITUTE. What can it be? You have us worried.

NARRATOR. They are all anxious lest Umegawa upstairs hear some unfortunate rumor. Just at this moment Chūbei furtively runs up to the Echigo House, his body chilled by the night and the icy weight of the three hundred *ryō* on his heart. He peeps inside and sees Hachiemon sitting in the place of honor, spreading rumors about himself. Astonished, Chūbei eavesdrops, while upstairs Umegawa is listening with rapt attention. The walls have ears: Hachiemon's words heard through them are the source of disasters that follow, though he does not suspect it.

HACHIEMON. You may imagine from what I am going to say that I'm jealous of Chūbei, but—Heaven strike me down if I lie! —I feel sorry when I think of how he's going to end his days. Yes, it's true that he sometimes shelters under his roof for a time a thousand or even two thousand *ryō* of other people's money, but his own fortune, throwing in his house, property, and furniture, doesn't amount to fifteen or twenty *kamme*[26] at most. They say his father in Yamato is a rich man, after all, he's a farmer, and you can imagine the size of his fortune if he had to send Chūbei as an adopted son to the Kame-ya. I'm a young man myself, and like any other young man, I have to visit the teahouses every so often, though it costs me ten or twenty *ryō* a year. But Chūbei is so mad about Umegawa that he's bought her for himself most of the time since last June in competition with another customer at the Island House, though he can ill afford it. I gather that her ransom was recently arranged and Chūbei gave as his deposit fifty of the 160 *ryō* required. That's why the money he should have delivered to various customers hasn't been paid, and he's had to resort to outright lies in order to stave them off. He's caught in a terrible fix. Just supposing he decided to ransom Umegawa as of this minute—she must have her debts, and he could weep his head off, and the bill would still come to 250 *ryō*. Does he think the money will fall from heaven or gush up out of the ground? His only way to raise it is to steal. Where do you suppose the fifty *ryō* he gave for the deposit came from? He intercepted a remittance of mine from Edo and that's what he used. I suspected nothing of this, and when I went to claim my money, there was his foster mother, poor woman. She knew that the money had arrived from Edo and she urged Chūbei to deliver it immediately. Shall I show you the gold pieces Chūbei paid me?

NARRATOR. He takes out a packet.

HACHIEMON. See—it looks like fifty *ryō* on the outside, but I'll reveal what's actually inside. This is why Chūbei will end up on the block!

26. Fifteen *kamme* would make about 250 *ryo* and twenty *kamme* over 33 *ryō*. Twenty *kamme* would be worth about $10,000 U.S.

NARRATOR. He cuts open the packet and empties it: out drops a pottery pomade jar. The proprietress and all the prostitutes shrink back with cries of alarm. Upstairs, Umegawa, her face pressed against the *tatami*, weeps, stifling her sobs. Chūbei, whose short temper is his undoing, fumes.

CHŪBEI. Telling something to a prostitute is proclaiming it to the world. Such arrogance and insults on my manhood, all because he advanced me a paltry fifty *ryō*! I'm sure that if Umegawa hears of this she'll want to kill herself. I'll draw fifty *ryō* from the 300 in my wallet, throw them in his face, and tell him exactly what I think of him. It'll save my honor and wipe out the insult to Umegawa.—But this money belongs to a samurai, and besides, it's urgently needed. I must be patient.

NARRATOR. His hand goes to his wallet again and again as he disconsolately debates which way to turn, at cross purposes with himself like the crossbill's beak. Inevitably he fails to understand Hachiemon's intent.

Hachiemon holds up the pomade jar.

HACHIEMON. You can buy one of these for eighteen coppers. Gold may be cheap, but never since the days of Jimmu[27] has fifty *ryō* in gold gone for eighteen coppers. If this is the way he treats even a friend, you can imagine how he must cheat strangers. From now on you'll see how he goes step by step from cutpurse to cutthroat and finally to the block where his own head gets cut off. It's a shame. When a man is that corrupted, nothing can cure him—not the threat of disinheritance by his parents or master, nor the admonitions of Shaka or Daruma, nor even a personal lecture delivered by Prince Shōtoku himself.[28] I'd like you to spread this story throughout the Quarter and see to it that Chūbei isn't permitted here again. I wish you'd also persuade Umegawa to break with him and gracefully allow herself to be ransomed by her country customer at the Island House. Rascals like Chūbei never come to a good end. They either get involved in a love suicide or else they wind up stealing some prostitute's clothes. They're sure to briing disgrace on their friends by being exposed in the stocks at the Main Gate with one sidelock shaven.[29] That's what is meant by being outside the pale of human society. If you care for Chūbei, don't let him in here again.

NARRATOR. Umegawa, hearing his words, is torn by mingled grief and pity and a feeling of helplessness. Silent tears rack her breast.

UMEGAWA. I wish I had a knife or even a pair of scissors so I could cut out my tongue and die.

27. The legendary first emperor of Japan.

28. Shōtoku Taishi, one of the chief figures in the establishment of Buddhism in Japan (573–621?).

29. A punishment imposed by the authorities of the Quarter on customers who transgressed its regulations.

NARRATOR. The women downstairs can guess the agony she undergoes.

PROSTITUTE. Umegawa must be miserable. What an unlucky girl! Poor Umegawa, I feel sorriest for her!

NARRATOR. The servants, the cooks, and even the young maids wring their sleeves for the tears.

Chūbei, always hot-tempered, is unable to endure more. He bursts into the room and plops himself down almost in Hachiemon's lap.

CHŪBEI. Well, Mr. Hachiemon of the Tamba-ya. Just as eloquent as ever, I see. Ah, there's a man for you, a prince! A gathering of three is a public meeting, they say—how kind of you to make an inventory of my possessions before this assemblage!—Look here! This jar was an understanding between friends. I handed it to you only after first asking indirectly if you'd accept it in order to reassure my mother. You agreed. But are you so worried now you might lose the fifty *ryō* you lent me that you must blab it all over the Quarter and ruin my reputation? Or have you taken a bribe from that customer at the Island House to win over Umegawa and deliver her to him? I've had enough of your nonsense! You've nothing to worry about. Chūbei's not a man to cause a friend to lose fifty or a hundred *ryō*. My esteemed Mr. Hachiemon—damn you, Hachiemon! Here's your money! Give me back the pledge!

NARRATOR. He pulls out the money and is about to untie the packet when Hachiemon stops him.

HACHIEMON. Chūbei!—wait! Don't let your foolishness get the better of you. I know your character well enough to realize you'd never listen to any advice from me. I hoped that if I could persuade the people of the Quarter to keep you at a distance, you might pull yourself together and become a normal human being again. I acted out of kindness to a friend and for no other reason. If I had been afraid for my fifty *ryō*, I'd have said so before your mother. Why, I even wrote out a crazy receipt to humor your mother, though she can't read. And have I still, not been considerate enough?—That packet you've got there looks like 300 *ryō*. I don't suppose it belongs to you. No doubt it's money you'll have to account for. If you tamper with it, you won't find another Hachiemon to settle for a pomade jar! But perhaps you intend to give your head in exchange? I suggest that instead of flying off the handle you deliver the money to its owner. You unsettled lunatic!

NARRATOR. He roundly upbraids Chūbei, point for point.

CHŪBEI. Stop trying to act the part of the disinterested friend! What makes you so sure that this money belongs to somebody else? Do you think I haven't three hundred *ryō* of my own? Now that you've called my fortune into question before all these women, my honor demands all the more that I return your money.

NARRATOR. Unfastening the packet, he scoops out ten, twenty, thirty, forty, and then—the final step to disaster—fifty *ryō*. He quickly wraps the coins in paper.

CHŪBEI. Here's proof that nobody loses any money on account of Chūbei of the Kame-ya! Take your money!

NARRATOR. He flings it down.

HACHIEMON. What kind of insult is this? Say "thank you" politely and offer it again.

NARRATOR. He throws back the money.

CHŪBEI. What thanks do I owe you?

NARRATOR. Again he throws the money at Hachiemon, who throws it back. They roll up their sleeves and grapple. Umegawa, overcome by tears, runs downstairs.

UMEGAWA. I've heard everything. Hachiemon is entirely right. Hachiemon, please forgive Chūbei, for my sake.

NARRATOR. She raises her voice and weeps.

UMEGAWA. Shame on you, Chūbei! How can you lose your head that way? Men who come to the Quarter, even millionaires, are frequently pressed for money. A disgrace here is no disgrace at all. What do you hope to achieve by breaking the seal on someone else's money and scattering it around? Would you like to get arrested and dragged off to prison with a rope around you? Would you prefer such a disgrace to your present trouble? It wouldn't be only a matter of disgrace for you—what would happen to me? Calm yourself at once and apologize to Hachiemon. Then wrap up the money and deliver it as quickly as you can to its owner. I know you don't want to give me up to another man. I feel the same. I have plans all worked out in my mind if I should have to sacrifice myself. My contract has two years to run. Then, even if I have to sell myself to some country brothel—Miyajima, who knows?—or become a streetwalker on the Osaka docks, I'll look after you. I'll never let my man suffer. So calm yourself. You're acting shamefully.—But whose fault is it? Mine. And knowing it's entirely my fault, I feel grateful and sorry for you at the same time. Try to imagine what I am going though.

NARRATOR. She pleads with him, and her tears, falling on the pieces of gold, are like the dew settling on the primroses of Idé.

Chūbei, utterly carried away, has recourse to a desperate last resort; he remembers the money he brought with him as an adopted son.

CHŪBEI. Be quiet! Do you take me for such a fool? Don't worry about the money. Hachiemon himself knows that I brought it from Yamato when I came here as an adopted son. I was left in someone's keeping, but I've claimed it now in order to ransom you. Madam, come here!

NARRATOR. He summons her.

CHŪBEI. The other day I gave you a deposit of fifty *ryō*. Here are 110 *ryō* more. That makes a total of 160 *ryō*, the money needed to ransom Umegawa. These forty-five *ryō* ate what I owe you on account—you worked it out the other day. Five *ryō* are for the Chaser.[30] I believe that Umegawa's fees since October come to about fifteen *ryō* altogether, but I can't be bothered with petty calculations. Here're twenty *ryō*, and now please clear my account. These ten *ryō* are a present for you, by way of thanks for your trouble. One *ryō* each goes to Rin, Tama, and Gohei. Come get it!

NARRATOR. He showers gold and silver in the momentary glory of the dream of Kantan.[31]

CHŪBEI. Please arrange the ransom at once so that Umegawa can leave this evening.

NARRATOR. His words stir the proprietress into sudden animation.

KIYO. It's a strange thing with money—when you haven't got it, you haven't got it, but when it comes, it comes in a flood. There's nothing more to worry about. I hope you're happy, Umegawa. I'll take this precious money to the owner. Rin and Tama—come along.

NARRATOR. They hurry out together. Hachiemon looks unconvinced.

HACHIEMON. [*To himself*] I don't believe he's telling the truth, but it's money he owes me anyway, and it'd be foolish reticence to refuse. [*To* CHŪBEI] Yes, I acknowledge receipt of the fifty *ryo*. Here's your note!

NARRATOR. He throws it at Chūbei.

HACHIEMON. Umegawa, you're lucky to have such a fine man. Enjoy yourselves, girls.

NARRATOR. He departs, stuffing the money into his wallet.

PROSTITUTES. We should be going too. Congratulations, Umegawa.

NARRATOR. They leave for their respective houses. Chūbei is impatient.

CHŪBEI. Why is the madam taking so long? Gohei, go tell her to hurry.

NARRATOR. He urges the man frantically.

GOHEI. I'm sorry, sir, but when a woman is ransomed the owner's permission is necessary. Then the elders of the Quarter cancel the seals on her contract. Finally the manager of the Quarter for the

30. A teahouse employee who served as both a procuress and a guardian of the courtesans.

31. Reference to the *nō* play *Kantan* (originally based on a Chinese legend) which tells of Rosei, a man who slept on a magic pillow in Kantan, and dreamed of a lifetime of glory. He awoke to discover that scarcely an hour had passed since he went to sleep.

current month has to issue a pass or she can't go out the Main Gate. It'll take a bit longer.

CHŪBEI. Here, this is to speed them.

NARRATOR. He throws another gold piece.

GOHEI. Leave it to me, sir!

NARRATOR. He races off nimbly: a piece of gold is more effective in building strong legs than a moxa cure.[32]

CHŪBEI. [*To* UMEGAWA] You get ready in the meanwhile. You look a mess. Here, tighten your sash.

NARRATOR. He speaks with desperate urgency.

UMEGAWA. Why are you so excited? This is the most wonderful occasion of my life. I'd like to offer the other girls a drink and say good-by properly. Please give me more time before I leave.

NARRATOR. Her face is flushed with innocent high spirits. Chūbei bursts into tears.

CHŪBEI. My poor dear! Didn't you realize that something was wrong? That money was an urgent remittance for a samurai residence in Dōjima. I knew that once I touched the money my life was ended. I tried very hard to restrain myself, but I could tell how mortified you were to see your lover humiliated before your friends. I wanted so badly to cheer you that my hand went unconsciously to the money. Once a man goes that far, he can't back away. Please try to think of our troubles as the workings of fate.—Hachiemon is on his way now to tell my mother—it was written all over his face. People will be here any moment from the eighteen courier houses to question me. We are now one foot over the brink of hell. Run away with me!

NARRATOR. He clings to her and weeps. Umegawa moans and begins to tremble. Her voice shakes into tears.

UMEGAWA. There—isn't this what I've always predicted? Why should we cling any longer to life? To die together is all we can ask. I would gladly die this very moment. Calm yourself, please, and think.

CHŪBEI. Could I have committed such a terrible crime if I had planned to go on living? But let us stay alive and together as long as we can, though we are resolved that sooner or later we must kill ourselves.

UMEGAWA. Yes, we'll stay together in this world as long as it's possible. But someone may come at any moment. Hide here.

NARRATOR. She pushes him behind a screen.

UMEGAWA. Oh, I left my good-luck amulet in the chest of drawers in my room. I wish I had it.

CHŪBEI. How could we escape punishment for our crime, no matter

32. The burning of the herb *mogusa* (moxa) at various places in the skin is still believed to strengthen different parts of the body.

how powerful your amulet may be? Make up your mind to it—we are doomed to die. I will offer prayers for your repose. Please offer them for mine.

NARRATOR. He raises his head above the screen.

UMEGAWA. Ugh—how horrible! Please don't do that—you look too much like something I can't bear.[33]

NARRATOR. She throws her arms around the screen and chokes with tears.

The proprietress of the Echigo House and her servants return.

KIYO. Everything's been settled. I've had your pass sent round to the West gate. That's the shortest way for you.

NARRATOR. She speaks words of good cheer, but the husband and wife are trembling, and their voices shake as they repeat, "Good-by, good-by."

KIYO. You sound as if you're cold. How about a drink?

CHŪBEI. The saké wouldn't get down my throat.

KIYO. I don't know whether to congratulate you or to tell you how sorry I am to see you go. I could chatter on a thousand days and still not run out of things to say.

CHŪBEI. I wish you hadn't mentioned "Thousand Days."[34]

NARRATOR. They take their farewells as the cock is crowing. His extravagance has been with others' money; now all is scattered like sand. They pass Sand Bank,[35] and let their feet guide them, come fields or come mountains, along the road to Yamato.

Act Three

SCENE ONE: THE ROAD TO NINOKUCHI VILLAGE IN YAMATO.
TIME: THE NEXT DAY AND THE FOLLOWING THREE WEEKS.

NARRATOR.

The green curtains, the crimson bedding,
The chamber where once, under familiar coverlets,
They ranged pillows all night through
And heard the drum sound the Gate's closing—
All has now vanished, comes not again even in dreams.

UMEGAWA.

Yes, though my lover promised without fail
He'd ransom me before autumn, I waited in vain.[36]
I trusted the fickle world, I trusted people,
But now my ties with the world and people are broken.

33. His head appearing over the screen looks like the severed head of a criminal exposed on a wall.

34. Sennichi (Thousand Days) was an execution ground in Osaka.

35. Sunaba (Sand Bank was just outside the West Gate of the Quarter.

36. Most of the above description is taken almost word for word from the *nō* play *Hanjo*, though the phrases acquire a somewhat different meaning in this context.

Though once we shared midnight trysts at the Gate,
Now we are kept apart by the barrier of men's eyes.
His hair is uncombed since yesterday;
When I take my comb to smooth his twisted locks,
My fingers are frozen with tears.
We press our chilled limbs to each other's thighs,
Making a double *kotatsu*.
The bearers pause, a moment's breathing spell—
How strange that we still breathe, that our lives go on!

NARRATOR.
They weep at Spillway Gate.[37]
There's still a while before the dawn, they think,
And lift the blinds of their palanquin.
Their knees remain entwined; they remember
Meetings at night in her little room—so alike,
But when did charcoal ashes turn to morning frost?
When summoned by the night winds,
Only the maid-pines[38] of the fields respond,
Recalling nights gone by, a source of tears.

CHŪBEI. Why are you so distraught? This is our foretaste of rebirth on one lotus.[39]

NARRATOR. He comforts Umegawa and takes comfort himself in smoking a double pipe with her.[40] The thin smoke and the morning fog melt and clear; the wind blows wild through the wheat sprouts. Ashamed to be seen by the early-rising farmers or by some field watchman who might ask them for a light, they stop their palanquin and dismiss the bearers. They do not begrudge the bearers' fees, nor even their uncertain lives, much less the hardship of walking barefoot. All that they begrudge is their remembrance of this world.

Never before has she worn an old woman's wadded hat.

UMEGAWA. Here, please warm yourself with this. It's more important than that I hide my face.

NARRATOR. She offers her purple kerchief to protect him from the wind, but for them purple passion is a thing of the past; today they are truly husband and wife.

They worship at the Kōshin Shrine[41] where prayers are

37. Kobore-guchi, the gate leading to Hirano.

38. *Kaburomatsu* are low, thick-growing pines. *Kaburo* (or kamuro) is the name of a courtesan's maid; hence the contrast is made between the gay quarters where *kaburo* answered when summoned, and the windswept fields where only the *kaburomatsu* reply.

39. In Pure Land Buddhism, saved souls are born on lotuses in the Western Paradise. Lovers hope to be reunited on the same lotus, in the manner that Chūbei and Umegawa now share one palanquin.

40. A pipe with two stems leading to single bowl, smoked by lovers.

41. A shrine south of the South Gate of the Tennō-ji. Shōman Temple is northwest of the same group of buildings. The Guardian King Aizen was popular with courtesans, boy actors, and others who depended on *ai* (love).

answered. They turn back and see some boy actors praying for popularity before the Aizen of the Shōman Temple amid offerings from the Dōtombori players and the women of the familiar houses of the Quarter. Among the lanterns marked with crests she knows, she notices one—oh, painful memories!—from the Tsuchi-ya, her own house.

UMEGAWA. Look, here is your crest, the muskmelon, and next to it mine, the double pine cone. When we offered this lantern, we prayed for the pine's thousand years, but our vows were ill-fated.

CHŪBEI. Tonight, as the lanterns of our existence flicker out, let us consider the crested robes we wear are our mourning shrouds, and journey hand in hand to hell.

UMEGAWA. Yes, I will be led by you.

NARRATOR. Again they take each other's hands; the tears they shed glaze the ice on their sleeves.

Though no one bars their way, they advance but slowly, asking directions at every turn. Umegawa is still in this morning's attire;[42] her frozen sandals stick to her bare feet. A bank of clouds in the sky threatens sleet, and leaves flutter in a wind mixed with hail. They have reached Hirano.[43]

CHŪBEI. Many people know me here. Come this way.

NARRATOR. They cover their faces with their sleeves and twist their way through the back streets of the town and over rice field paths till they reach Wisteria Well Temple.[44]

CHŪBEI. Look—you see, even the remotest village belongs to the world of love!

NARRATOR: A girl of seventeen or so, picking vegetables behind her house, is singing:

"You, standing by the gate,
Are you my secret lover?
The field winds will do you harm,
Please come inside the house."

They envy others' words of tenderness.

CHŪBEI. Do you remember? When was it—that morning of the first snow when the early customers were arriving and you walked back with me, still in your night clothes, through the thin snow by the Great Gate? The snow today is no different, but our hopes have entirely changed. You poor dear—it was because of me that you were first made to suffer, step by step the white cloth was dyed deeper, from blue to indigo. If divine punishment should

42. She wears a courtesan's robes, conspicuous outside the quarter. Courtesans do not wear *tabi* (linen socks).

43. About five miles south of Osaka; today part of the city.

44. *Fujii-dera.* Twisting streets are associated with the twisting of a wisteria (*fuji*) vine.

strike for the vows we wrote, the Hachiman of Konda as our witness, may it spare you!

NARRATOR. He weeps.

> Though for a while I may escape
> The prying eyes of men. . . .

UMEGAWA. I'm as much to blame as you!

NARRATOR. Her words dissolve in endless tears that soak her folded handkerchiefs. Her skirts are torn by the dun-colored weeds. In the frost-withered fields the wind crackles through desolate stretches of pampas grass.

CHŪBEI. Was that rustling the sound of people coming after us?

NARRATOR. He stands over Umegawa, concealing her, but when he glances up, he realizes that the sounds were not of men.

CHŪBEI. For what crime are we being punished that we should be frightened by the flapping of pheasants' wings?

NARRATOR. Flocks of crows over the forest of Tonda harshly scold, weeping—or laughing?—to see the lovers attempt to comfort each other, unwilling to allow them even one untroubled night. At Takama Mountain—shades of the god of Katsuragi—[45] they hesitate to travel by daylight on their fugitive road, their road of love, their road through a world made narrow by themselves. At Within-the-Bamboos Pass their sleeves are soaked. Next they journey the stony road called Cavern Crossing. They struggle on, across fields, mountains, and villages, all for love.

The laws of a well-governed land are strict; pursuers have been despatched to the home provinces in search of the guilty pair. Yamato especially, as Chūbei's birthplace, is canvassed by men from the seventeen courier houses, some disguised as pilgrims, others as dealers in old clothes or itinerant performers. They peep into the houses and with peep shows and sweets beguile the children into furnishing clues. Umegawa and Chūbei are like birds in a snare or fish in a weir: they are doomed not to escape. Unfortunate Chūbei!—it is hard enough to conceal himself alone, but impossible to keep Umegawa's appearance from attracting attention. They spend days in hired sedan chairs, five nights at an inn in Nara, and three nights at a teahouse in Miwa. In a little over twenty days they have spent forty *ryō*, and only half a *ryō*, remains of the money. They pass by without stopping at Hatsuse Mountain—how misty the sound of its bell!—and finally reach Ninokuchi Village, his father's home.

45. The god of Katsuragi was so ashamed of his ugliness that he appeared only at night.

SCENE TWO: NINOKUCHI VILLAGE, OUTSIDE THE HUT OF CHŪZABURŌ.
TIME: THE END OF THE TWELFTH MOON.

CHŪBEI. O-ume,[46] this is the town where I was born and grew up. I spent my first twenty years here, but I can never remember having seen so many beggars and peddlers of every description at the end of the year, nor even at New Year, for that matter. Look—do you see those men standing there? There were a couple of others at the edge of the fields. I'm beginning to feel nervous. Another four or five hundred yards farther on and we'll be at my real father's—Magoemon's—house, but I daren't go there. I haven't heard from my father since I went away and, besides, there's my stepmother. This thatch-covered hut belongs to Chūzaburō, a tenant farmer with an allotment from my family. He's been a close friend ever since I was a boy, and I know I can trust him. Let's call on him.

NARRATOR. He leads her inside the hut.

CHŪBEI. Chūzaburō, are you at home? I haven't seen you in ages.

NARRATOR. He goes boldly in. A woman, apparently Chūzaburō's wife, meets him.

WIFE. Who is it, please? My husband's been at the headman's house since this morning, and he's still not come back.

CHŪBEI. Chūzaburō never used to have a wife. Who might you be, please?

WIFE. I came here as his bride three years ago, and I don't know any of my husband's old friends. Excuse me, but I wonder if you folks wouldn't happen to be from Osaka? People have been talking about our landlord Magoemon's stepson[47]—Chūbei's his name. He went to Osaka as an adopted son and took up with a prostitute. They say he stole some money and ran off with her. The magistrate's investigating now. Magoemon disowned his son long ago, and he says that whatever may happen to Chūbei is no concern of his, but all the same, they're father and son, and it must be hard on a man of his age. My husband's an old friend of Chūbei, and he has the idea that Chūbei may be wandering in this neighborhood. He'd be sorry to see him get caught, and he's been keeping watch everywhere. Today the village headman sent for my husband. What with meetings and papers to seal, the whole village is in an uproar—now, at the end of the year!—all on account of that prostitute. She's certainly causing a lot of trouble.

NARRATOR. The woman babbles unrestrainedly. Chūbei is stunned.

CHŪBEI. Yes, rumors about Chūbei are going around Osaka too. My wife and I are on our way to Ise for an end of the year

46. Umegawa's real name, presumably. Umegawa was her name as a courtesan.

47. Possibly called "stepson" because he is not the child of Magoemon's present wife.

retreat at the shrine. I stopped by for old times' sake, happening to be in the neighborhood. Would you please ask Chūzaburō to come here a moment? I'd like to see him before I leave, even if there isn't time to sit down. But please don't tell him we've come from Osaka.

WIFE. Are you in such a big hurry? I'll go fetch him at once. But you know, there's a priest from Kyoto who's been giving sermons every day at the temple in Kamada Village. My husband may have gone there directly from the headman's house. Please keep the fire going under the soup while I'm away.

NARRATOR. She rolls up her sleeves and runs out. Umegawa shuts the back gate and fastens the latch.

UMEGAWA. We're really in the midst of the enemy here. Do you think we'll be all right?

CHŪBEI. Chūzaburō has an unusually chivalrous nature for a farmer. I'll ask him to put us up for the night. If I'm to die, it's best that it be here, where my body will become the earth of my native soil. I'd like to be buried in the same grave with my real mother so that in the future world I can present to her my bride.

NARRATOR. His eyes grow heavy with tears.

UMEGAWA. How happy that would make me! My own mother lives at Rokujō in Kyoto. I'm sure that the authorities have gone to question her during these past days. She's always suffered from dizzy spells, and I wonder how she's taken the news. I'd like to go to Kyoto and see my mother again before I die.

CHŪBEI. I'm sure you would. I'd like to meet your mother too, and tell her I'm her son.

NARRATOR. They embrace, for no one can see. The rain of tears is too much for their sleeves to hold; a driving shower beats against the windows.

CHŪBEI. It seems to have started raining.

NARRATOR. He opens the patched paper *shōji* a crack. Through the lattice window facing west, he looks out on a windswept road across the fields. Worshipers are hurrying towards the temple, their umbrellas tilted to protect them from the rain slanting from behind.

CHŪBEI. I know them all—they're people of the village. The man in front is Sukezaburō from Taruibata, a leading man in the village. And that old woman is Den's mother, Den the humpbacked porter. What a tea drinker she is! That man over there with his head almost completely shaved used to be the poorest man in town. He had so much trouble paying his taxes that he sold his daughter to Shimabara Quarter in Kyoto. A rich paper merchant ransomed her and made her his wife. Now, thanks to his son-in-law, the old man is a property holder—five *chō* of ricelands and storehouses in two places. I've ransomed a courtesan too, just as the paper merchant did, but it breaks my heart to think of the unhappiness I've brought your mother.—That old man is Tōjibei the Leveler.[48] At eighty-eight he ate a quart and a half of rice and didn't leave a grain. This year he's turned ninety-five. That priest coming up after him is Dōan the needle-doctor.[49] He killed my mother with his needle. He's my mother's enemy, now that I think of it.

NARRATOR. His bitterness comes from grief.

CHŪBEI. Look! That's my father! You can see him now.

UMEGAWA. The man in the hemp jacket?[50] Yes, his eyes are just like yours.

CHŪBEI. To think that a father and son who look so much alike cannot even exchange a few words! This must be my father's punishment—He's grown old. How unsteady his legs are! Farewell, father, for this life!

NARRATOR. He joins his hands in prayer.

UMEGAWA. I see you for the first and last time. I am your son's wife. My husband and I are doomed not to know even our next moments, but I hope that when you have passed your hundred years we shall meet again in the future life.

NARRATOR. She murmurs the words to herself. The two join hands and, in voices choked with tears, lament.

Magoemon passes by their door, pausing again and again to rest his aged limbs. He slips on the ice of the ditch at the edge of the fields and, when he checks himself, the thong of his high *geta* snaps. He falls heavily on his side into the muddy field. Chūbei cries out in dismay. He writhes in anguish and alarm but, fugitive that he is, he dares not leave the house.

Umegawa rushes out. She lifts the old man in her arms, and wrings the muddy water from the skirt of his kimono.

UMEGAWA. You haven't hurt yourself anywhere, have you? What a dreadful thing to happen to an old gentleman! I'll wash your feet and mend the thong. Please don't feel the least embarrassed with me.

NARRATOR. She comforts him, massaging his back and knees. Magoemon raises himself.

MAGOEMON. Thank you, whoever you are. No, I haven't hurt myself. What a kind young lady! You've shown me a solicitude not even a daughter-in-law could match, merely because of my years. Some people go to the temple for the sermons, but if they are cruel here, in their hearts, they might just as well not go.

48. Tōjibei was asked, in reference to his auspicious old age, to make leveling rods rice measures. The eighty-eighth birthday is called the "rice anniversary" (*beiju*) because of a calligraphic pun on the character.

49. Acupuncture is still a branch of traditional Japanese medicine.

50. A sleeveless jacket worn by believers in Pure Land Buddhism when they went to worship.

Your kindness is an act of true piety. Please wash your hands now. Luckily there's some straw here. I'll use it to mend the thong myself.

NARRATOR. He takes some coarse paper from his wallet.

UMEGAWA. I have some good paper. I'll twist it into a cord for you.

NARRATOR. Magoemon is surprised to see how skillfully she tears the soft paper into strips.

MAGOEMON. You know, I don't recall ever having seen you before in this neighborhood. Who are you, and why are you so kind to me?

NARRATOR. He closely examines her face. Umegawa's breast feels all the more constricted.

UMEGAWA. I'm traveling through. I have a father-in-law just your age, and he looks exactly like you. I don't feel in the least as if I'm helping a stranger. It's a daughter-in-law's duty, after all, to serve and comfort her aged father when he is stricken. You can't imagine how happy it makes me to be of help! I'm sure that, if he could, my husband would all but fly to your side, taking you for his father. Please give me your paper in exchange for mine. I'll ask my husband to keep it next to his skin as a keepsake of an old gentleman who looks like his father.

NARRATOR. She tucks the coarse paper in her sleeve. Hide the tears as she will, her emotion betrays itself in her face.

Magoemon guesses everything from one word and another, and he cannot suppress his fatherly love. His aged eyes are blinded with tears.

MAGOEMON. You say you show me such devotion because I look like your father-in-law! That makes me happy and furious at the same time. I have a grown son with whom I broke off relations for certain reasons. I sent him to Osaka as an adopted son, but some devil got into him, and he laid his hands on a good deal of money belonging to other people. The upshot was that he ran away, and now the search for him has extended to this village. If you want to know who's to blame, it's all my daughter-in-law's fault. It's a foolish thing, I know, but just as in the old proverb this is a case of not hating the son who steals but resenting instead the people who involved him in the crime. Now that I've broken with him, I suppose I should feel utterly indifferent whether he comes to good or ill. But you can imagine how happy it used to make me, even when people said Magoemon was a fool, an idiot, to have disinherited a son so clever, intelligent and well-behaved that he'd made a fortune since going to Osaka as an adopted son. Now, when he is hunted and soon to be dragged off a prisoner, you can imagine my grief even when people praise my foresight and good luck in having disinherited him in good time. I shudder to think what will happen. I'm on my way now to worship before Amida and the Founder,[51] and to pray that I may die at least one day ahead of my son. I do not lie to the Buddha.

NARRATOR. He falls prostrate on the ground and weeps aloud. Umegawa sobs and Chūbei holds his hands out through the *shōji*, bowing in worship before his father. His body is shaken by grief. Magoemon again brushes away the tears.

MAGOEMON. There's no disputing blood. A child, even one disinherited for all eternity, is always dearer to his parent than the closest friend.—Why didn't he take me into his confidence before he embarked on his stealing and swindling? If he had sent me word privately that he was in love with such and such a courtesan and needed money, for whatever purpose it was, I would, of course, have come to his help. Trouble brings a family together, they say, and we are father and son. And he's a motherless son at that. I'd have sold the fields I've saved to support me in my old age to keep him from the jailer's rope. Instead, he has become notorious. He's brought hardship to Myōkan, his foster mother, and caused others losses and suffering. Could I still say, "You're Magoemon's son," and harbor him? Could I even offer him shelter for a single night?

It's all his own doing. He's suffering now, and society is too small to hold him. He's brought misery on his wife, and he must slink through the wide world hiding from his dearest friends, his acquaintances, and even his kin. I didn't bring him into the world so that he might die a disgraceful death! He's a scoundrel, I know, but I love him.

NARRATOR. He falls into uncontrollable weeping. How hard it is for those who share the same blood! Still weeping, he takes a piece of silver from his purse.

MAGOEMON. I happen to have this coin with me. I had intended to offer it for the building fund of the Naniwa Temple. I do not give you this money because I take you for my daughter-in-law, but by way of thanks for your kindness a while ago.—But if you wander about this neighborhood, people will notice your resemblance to the fugitive woman. They'll arrest you, and they'll certainly arrest your husband. Use this money for your journey. Take the Gosé Road and leave this place as fast as you can. I'd like a glimpse of your husband's face. No—that would be shirking my duty to society. Send me good news soon, that you're safe.

NARRATOR. He takes two or three steps, then turns back.

MAGOEMON. What do you think? Would there be any harm in my seeing him?

UMEGAWA. Who will ever know? Please go to him.

51. Shinran Shōnin (1173–1262), founder of the Shin Sect of Pure Land Buddhism.

MAGOEMON. No, I won't neglect my duty to his family in Osaka.[52] —Urge hin, I beg you, not to violate nature by making a father mourn his son.

NARRATOR. He chokes with emotion. They part at last, turning back again and again. Then the husband and wife collapse in tears and, forgetting that others might see, they abandon themselves to their grief. How pathetic the ties between this father and son!

Chūzaburō's wife returns, drenched with rain.

WIFE. I'm sorry to have kept you waiting. My husband went straight from the headman's house to the temple, and I couldn't get to see him. The rain is beginning to let up. I'm sure he'll be coming back soon.

NARRATOR. At that moment Chūzaburō runs up, all out of breath.

CHŪZABURŌ. Chūbei—your father's told me everything. Police agents have come to the village from Osaka to arrest you, and the magistrate is conducting a search. Your luck has run out. You're surrounded by swords in broad daylight. Somebody must've recognized you. They've suddenly started a top to bottom, house to house search. They're at your father's place now, and my house will be next. Your poor father—he was out of his mind with grief. He begged me to help you to get away quickly. You're in the jaws of the crocodile now. Hurry, make your escape. Take the road back of the house to the Gosé Highway and head for the mountains.

NARRATOR. Chūbei and Umegawa are at their wits' ends. Chūzaburō's wife does not realize what is going on.

WIFE. Shall I run away with them?

CHŪZABURŌ. Don't be a fool.

NARRATOR. Pushing her aside, he helps Chūbei and Umegawa into old straw raincoats and rainhats. Their hearts and footsteps are agitated like reeds in a driving rain, but this kindness will not be forgotten even though they die; profoundly touched, they secretly creep out.

Hardly has Chūzaburō breathed a sigh of relief than two parties of raiding constables from the magistrate's office, led by the headman and a village official, simultaneously break into Chūzaburō's house from front and back gates. They roll up the mats, break through the flooring, turn over cabinets, rice chests, and dustbins in their search. The hut is so small that there is nowhere for anyone to hide.

OFFICER. This house is all right. Search the roads through the fields.

NARRATOR. The men hunt for the couple among the tea bushes in the field. Magoemon rushes up, barefooted.

52. For *giri* (obligation) see p. 755.

MAGOEMON. What's happened, Chūzaburō? Tell me—they're all right, aren't they?

CHŪZABURŌ. They're all right. There's nothing to worry about. They've both managed to escape.

MAGOEMON. Thank you. I'm grateful to you. I owe this to Amida's grace. I must go to the temple again immediately and offer my thanks to the Founder. How happy and grateful I am!

NARRATOR. The two start off together.

VOICE. Chūbei of the Kame-ya and Umegawa of the Tsuchi-ya have been apprehended!

NARRATOR. A crowd mills north of the village. Soon the constables lead in the husband and wife, tightly bound. Magoemon loses consciousness and seems about to expire. Umegawa, seeing Magoemon, weeps till her eyes dim over, to think that she and her husband, bound prisoners, are powerless to help. Chūbei shouts.

CHŪBEI. I am guilty of the crime and I am ready for punishment! I know that I cannot escape death. I humbly request you to pray for my repose. But the sight of my father's anguish will prove an obstacle to my salvation. Please, as a kindness, cover my face.

NARRATOR. An officer takes the towel at Chūbei's waist and tightly binds his eyes, as though for blindman's buff. Umegawa weeps, a sanderling by a river whose flow is uncertain as human fate.

They leave behind in Naniwa the name of two who gave their lives for love.

FOUR MODERN MASTERS OF FICTION

RYŪNOSUKE AKUTAGAWA (1892–1927)

JUNICHIRO TANIZAKI (1886–1965)

YASUNARI KAWABATA (1899–1972)

YUKIO MISHIMA (1925–1970)

Japanese society went through a rapid Westernization after 1868—a transmutation of an ancient culture perhaps unparalleled in recent history. A flood of translations from foreign literatures inundated the highly literate Japanese middle and upper class. Perhaps in no language of the world is foreign literature so available in translation. One of the immediate effects of this was to establish fiction as a respectable art form. While fiction has always been taken more seriously in Japan than in China, the early great writers of fiction were often women (which reduced the intellectual stature of the achievement—a gentleman wrote poetry and perhaps wrote it even in Chinese), and the era of Japanese fiction immediately before Akutagawa's time is, in general, undistinguished. In the early modern period, some works, no longer read, slavishly imitated Western models. But this stage soon passed, and the Japanese modified Western forms and adapted them to their needs; their achievement is a new kind of fiction, blending Western forms and Japanese sensitivities, is considerable. A major message from modern Western fiction to Japan was that no aspects of human life were denied to the literary artist, and topics which the Japanese had been reluctant to put into literary form now were treated. One of these types was the personal confession (*shishōsetsu*). While it would seem that there is much that is personal in such works as the *Kōjōki* and in the *tanka* and *haiku*, this is not the case. The type of confession which stems from Rousseau in Western literature has in it everything that offended—prior to the twentieth century—the Japanese psychology. The emotions in such works as the *Kōjōki* and classical poetry, however delicate and self-expressive they may seem, are generalized and never violate a conventional decorum. Drawing their inspiration from French, German, Russian, and English writers, the Japanese now experimented with all of the subject matter of modern Western writing. The confessional novel became popular, and the other landmark movements of the West were studied—naturalism, the proletarian novel, symbolism. All subjects were now possible, including the bizarre and the deviant in human conduct. The result was an immensely skilled and varied new kind of fiction.

Akutagawa died by his own hand at the age of thirty-five. He was born in Tokyo, the son of a middle-class merchant whose family clung, in a middle-class Victorian fashion, to family traditions which were dying and which they could not afford. Akutagawa's mother died, insane, shortly after his birth, and all his life he was haunted by the idea that he might become insane. (We know that he read widely in European literature; one wonders if he had read Ibsen's *Ghosts*.) While in college he published his first fiction and also translations of Anatole France and Keats. *Rashōmon* appeared, causing no particular fanfare, in 1915. His subsequent career was conventional enough—much publication, including *haiku*; teaching; travel to China; art collecting; and, finally, a series of disasters which undermined his health. In 1922 he showed signs of a nervous breakdown. The loss of his art collection in the 1923 fire in Tokyo affected him greatly. Family troubles also dogged him. He killed himself in 1927 by taking an overdose of barbituates. This dismal career would not be hard to duplicate in the West, even including the Bible found by the author's body.

In Akutagawa's writing, he attempted to combine a subtle and complicated style with extreme objectivity of observation. Some critics of his age regarded him as a mere stylist, clever but superficial. His objectivity is visible in the multiple points of view of *In a Grove*. He does not tell us which of the narrators is telling the truth. Each witness is trying to tell the truth and tell it in a fashion that will place himself in a favorable light, not only with the law but with mankind at large and with his own conscience. And perhaps this kind of truth is all that we ever get. Akutagawa further offended the prevailing literary schools by borrowing themes from earlier Japanese life. The Rashōmon (Rasho-gate) dates from 789, when it was one of the glories of the the new capital. But it also stands for hundreds of such structures —gates, palaces, temples—all made of wood and regularly razed by warfare and fire, symbolizing the transitory nature of all things. In his absolute detachment lies Akutagawa's strength and weakness. His favorite device is the objective and emotionless observer, who stands to one side and tells us the story.

Junichiro Tanizaki was born into a merchant family in 1886 in Tokyo. Though his family had conservative ways, as a young person he was fascinated by the new influences from the West. He studied classical Japanese literature at the Imperial University but also turned his attention to the new wave in literature. *Tattoo* first appeared in a literary magazine called *New Thought* when he was a student. The influences on his early writings were writers such as Poe, Baudelaire, and Oscar Wilde, and he became a leader of a "romantic" school of young writers. His removal to Kyoto after the earthquake of 1923 projected him back into the Japanese past, and he developed a more subdued and realistic style. A nostalgia for the Japanese past fought with Western innovations in his mind. *Some Prefer Nettles* (1928) treats this theme. In the thirties he continued to be occupied by traditional themes and translations. His translation into modern Japanese of Murasaki's *Tale of Genji* is one of his great achievements. In what is perhaps his best-known work, *The Makioka Sisters* (1949–48), he creates a panorama of life in pre-war Osaka, much of it based on his own experiences. *The Key* (1956) marks a new versatility. It is a story of the love relationship of a middle-aged couple, with its bizarre and perverted elements. *The Diary of a Mad Old Man* (1961) continues the psychological mode with its nuances of the abnormal. Perhaps *The Makioka Sisters* remains his masterpiece, and it has been popular in the West. His stories, however, are often minor masterpieces. Touches of sadomasochism emerge in *Tattoo*. It is romantic, rather than naturalist, but the dark mysteries of beauty and cruelty pervade the story.

Yasunari Kawabata, who won the Nobel Prize for literature in 1968, has always seemed to Japanese readers to be the most "Japanese" of these four writers, and many Japanese marvelled that he was so appreciated in the West. He was born in Osaka in 1899, into a family with literary and artistic tastes. A precocious youth, he was interested in painting but decided to become a novelist at the age of fifteen. He studied English literature at Tokyo University and started a literary magazine which drew the attention of the influential critic Kikuchi Kan. He was then launched into a career of literary journalism. Some of his early stories are sentimental, but his mature work is characterized by depictions of the isolation of individuals from one another. *Snow Country* (1937) describes the subtle and often painful relationship of a Westernized Japanese man with a geisha in a mountain village, of an intellectual, artistic man, and a woman who has experienced the joys and loneliness of life directly. Kawabata's style is often reminiscent of earlier writers in his ability to suggest nuances and moods with great economy. Old age and approaching death are the themes of two later novels, *The Sound of the Mountain* (1954) and *Thousand Cranes* (1951–53). Perhaps an early consciousness of his own eventual death overshadows these works. He was pleased with the honor of the Nobel Prize, but modestly suggested that he was only a symbol of all modern Japanese achievement in modern literature. Though his works are often poetic and evocative and their moods melancholy, Kawabata socialized with Westerners with ease, though he refused to speak English with Westerners. His suicide may have been a rational man's response to declining health in old age, or perhaps it was a gesture of sympathy for his young friend Mishima.

Yukio Mishima's spectacular public suicide on November 25, 1970, attracted world-wide attention. At the end of his short life he was the leader of a group of Japanese right-wing patriots with all of the trappings of such groups—banners and boots, swords and uniforms. He was dedicated to restoring the traditional Japanese virtues of austerity, fidelity to one's country, and the cultivation of the martial arts. The *Tate no Kai* or Shield Society seized the headquarters of the commanding general of the Japanese military headquarters in downtown Tokyo as a gesture against the pacifist postwar Japanese constitution. His conspicuous gesture made, Mishima disemboweled himself with his own sword and his head was cut off by a follower, a tradition for heroes of the samurai class in Japan. Mishima had prepared himself for this dramatic end by a long period of mental and physical discipline, and had raised his traditionalism to the heights of a religious passion. He was no rabble-rouser, but a deeeply committed man, even if the commitment was to a way of life now quite out of fashion, and many Western admirers of his writings, who did not share his philosophical views, have paid him affectionate tributes.

Mishima was born into a family of high civil servants and attended an aristocratic private school. He failed the physical examination for service in World War II and spent the war years working in a factory.

He then studied law. Blood and death, suicide and the rejection of modern life as sterile and without meaning, and homosexuality pervade his works, including the partly autobiographical *Confessions of a Mask* (1948), his first major effort. *The Temple of the Golden Pavillion* (1959) may remain for many readers his major effort. It tells the story of a young monk obsessed with beauty who finally burns down the Kinkakuji, the Golden Pavillion temple in Kyoto. The actual burning of the temple by a demented monk is the inspiration for the story. *Sun and Steel* (1970) celebrates the cult of body-building and the martial spirit and laments the defeat of Japan in the war. The *Sea of Fertility* (Part One, 1969) draws its title and inspiration from the so-called Sea of Fertility on the moon, a cold, dark, lifeless sea on a dead planet. It symbolized for Mishima the sterility of modern man. With all of his obsession with death and virtue and with the Japanese past, Mishima was well-informed on modern literature and had a vast knowledge of Western literary criticism. He also won renown as a writer of short stories.

RYŪNOSUKE AKUTAGAWA

Rashōmon*

It was a chilly evening. A servant of a samurai stood under the Rashōmon,[1] waiting for a break in the rain.

No one else was under the wide gate. On the thick column, its crimson lacquer rubbed off here and there, perched a cricket. Since the Rashōmon stands on Sujaku Avenue, a few other people at least, in sedge hat or nobleman's headgear, might have been expected to be waiting there for a break in the rain storm. But no one was near except this man.

For the past few years the city of Kyōto had been visited by a series of calamities, earthquakes, whirlwinds, and fires, and Kyōto had been greatly devastated. Old chronicles say that broken pieces of Buddhist images and other Buddhist objects, with their lacquer, gold, or silver leaf worn off, were heaped up on roadsides to be sold as firewood. Such being the state of affairs in Kyōto, the repair of the Rashōmon was out of the question. Taking advantage of the devastation, foxes and other wild animals made their dens in the

* This and the next story are from *Rashōmon and Other Stories* by Akutagawa Ryūnosuke, translated by Takashi Kojima. Copyright 1952 by Liveright Publishing Corporation. Reprinted by permission of Liveright Publishing Corporation.

1. The "Rashōmon" was the largest gate in Kyōto, the ancient capital of Japan. It was 106 feet wide and 26 feet deep, and was topped with a ridge-pole; its stone wall rose 75 feet high. This gate was constructed in 789 when the then capital of Japan was transferred to Kyoto. With the decline of West Kyoto, the gate fell into bad repair, cracking and crumbling in many places, and became a hideout for thieves and robbers and a place for abandoning unclaimed corpses. [Kojima's note.]

ruins of the gate, and thieves and robbers found a home there too. Eventually it became customary to bring unclaimed corpses to this gate and abandon them. After dark it was so ghostly that no one dared approach.

Flocks of crows flew in from somewhere. During the daytime these cawing birds circled round the ridgepole of the gate. When the sky overhead turned red in the afterlight of the departed sun, they looked like so many grains of sesame flung across the gate. But on that day not a crow was to be seen, perhaps because of the lateness of the hour. Here and there the stone steps, beginning to crumble, and with rank grass growing in their crevices, were dotted with the white droppings of crows. The servant, in a worn blue kimono, sat on the seventh and highest step, vacantly watching the rain. His attention was drawn to a large pimple irritating his right cheek.

As has been said, the servant was waiting for a break in the rain. But he had no particular idea of what to do after the rain stopped. Ordinarily, of course, he would have returned to his master's house, but he had been discharged just before. The prosperity of the city of Kyōto had been rapidly declining, and he had been dismissed by his master, whom he had served many years, because of the effects of this decline. Thus, confined by the rain, he was at a loss to know where to go. And the weather had not a little to do with his depressed mood. The rain seemed unlikely to stop. He was lost in thoughts of how to make his living tomorrow, helpless incoherent thoughts protesting an inexorable fate. Aimlessly he had been listening to the pattering of the rain on the Sujaku Avenue.

The rain, enveloping the Rashōmon, gathered strength and came down with a pelting sound that could be heard far away. Looking up, he saw a fat black cloud impale itself on the tips of the tiles jutting out from the roof of the gate.

He had little choice of means, whether fair or foul, because of his helpless circumstances. If he chose honest means, he would undoubtedly starve to death beside the wall or in the Sujaku gutter. He would be brought to this gate and thrown away like a stray dog. If he decided to steal . . . His mind, after making the same detour time and again, came finally to the conclusion that he would be a thief.

But doubt returned many times. Though determined that he had no choice, he was still unable to muster enough courage to justify the conclusion that he must become a thief.

After a loud fit of sneezing he got up slowly. The evening chill of Kyōto made him long for the warmth of a brazier. The wind in the evening dusk howled through the columns of the gate. The cricket which had been perched on the crimson-lacquered column was already gone.

Ducking his neck, he looked around the gate, and drew up the shoulders of the blue kimono which he wore over his thin underwear. He decided to spend the night there, if he could find a secluded corner sheltered from wind and rain. He found a broad lacquered stairway leading to the tower over the gate. No one would be there, except the dead, if there were any. So, taking care that the sword at his side did not slip out of the scabbard, he set foot on the lowest step of the stairs.

A few seconds later, halfway up the stairs, he saw a movement above. Holding his breath and huddling cat-like in the middle of the broad stairs leading to the tower, he watched and waited. A light coming from the upper part of the tower shone faintly upon his right cheek. It was the cheek with the red, festering pimple visible under his stubbly whiskers. He had expected only dead people inside the tower, but he had only gone up a few steps before he noticed a fire above, about which someone was moving. He saw a dull, yellow, flickering light which made the cobwebs hanging from the ceiling glow in a ghostly way. What sort of person would be making a light in the Rashōmon . . . and in a storm? The unknown, the evil terrified him.

As quietly as a lizard, the servant crept up to the top of the steep stairs. Crouching on all fours, and stretching his neck as far as possible, he timidly peeped into the tower.

As rumor had said, he found several corpses strewn carelessly about the floor. Since the glow of the light was feeble, he could not count the number. He could only see that some were naked and others clothed. Some of them were women, and all were lolling on the floor with their mouths open or their arms outstretched showing no more signs of life than so many clay dolls. One would doubt that they had even been alive, so eternally silent they were. Their shoulders, breasts, and torsos stood out in the dim light; other parts vanished in shadow. The offensive smell of these decomposed corpses brought his hand to his nose.

The next moment his hand dropped and he stared. He caught sight of a ghoulish form bent over a corpse. It seemed to be an old woman, gaunt, gray-haired, and nunnish in appearance. With a pine torch in her right hand, she was peeping into the face of a corpse which had long black hair.

Seized more with horror than curiosity, he even forgot to breathe for a time. He felt the hair of his head and body stand on end. As he watched, terrified, she wedged the torch between two floor boards and, laying hands on the head of the corpse, began to pull out the long hairs one by one, as a monkey kills the lice of her young. The hair came out smoothly with the movement of her hands.

As the hair came out, fear faded from his heart, and his hatred toward the old woman mounted. It grew beyond hatred, becoming a consuming antipathy against all evil. At this instant if anyone had brought up the question of whether he would starve to death or become a thief—the question which had occurred to him a little while ago—he would not have hesitated to choose death. His hatred toward evil flared up like the piece of pine wood which the old woman had stuck in the floor.

He did not know why she pulled out the hair of the dead. Accordingly, he did not know whether her case was to be put down as good or bad. But in his eyes, pulling out the hair of the dead in the Rashōmon on this stormy night was an unpardonable crime. Of course it never entered his mind that a little while ago he had thought of becoming a thief.

Then, summoning strength into his legs, he rose from the stairs and strode, hand on sword, right in front of the old creature. The hag turned, terror in her eyes, and sprang up from the floor, trembling. For a small moment she paused, poised there, then lunged for the stairs with a shriek.

"Wretch! Where are you going?" he shouted, barring the way of the trembling hag who tried to scurry past him. Still she attempted to claw her way by. He pushed her back to prevent her . . . they struggled, fell among the corpses, and grappled there. The issue was never in doubt. In a moment he had her by the arm, twisted it, and forced her down to the floor. Her arms were all skin and bones, and there was no more flesh on them than on the shanks of a chicken. No sooner was she on the floor than he drew his sword and thrust the silver-white blade before her very nose. She was silent. She trembled as if in a fit, and her eyes were open so wide that they were almost out of their sockets, and her breath came in hoarse gasps. The life of this wretch was his now. This thought cooled his boiling anger and brought a calm pride and satisfaction. He looked down at her, and said in a somewhat calmer voice:

"Look here, I'm not an officer of the High Police Commissioner. I'm a stranger who happened to pass by this gate. I won't bind you or do anything against you, but you must tell me what you're doing up here."

Then the old woman opened her eyes still wider, and gazed at his face intently with the sharp red eyes of a bird of prey. She moved her lips, which were wrinkled into her nose, as though she were chewing something. Her pointed Adam's apple moved in her thin throat. Then a panting sound like the cawing of a crow came from her throat:

"I pull the hair . . . I pull out the hair . . . to make a wig."

Her answer banished all unknown from their encounter and brought disappointment. Suddenly she was only a trembling old woman there at his feet. A ghoul no longer: only a hag who makes wigs from the hair of the dead—to sell, for scraps of food. A cold contempt seized him. Fear left his heart, and his former hatred entered. These feelings must have been sensed by the other. The old creature, still clutching the hair she had pulled off the corpse, mumbled out these words in her harsh broken voice:

"Indeed, making wigs out of the hair of the dead may seem a great evil to you, but these that are here deserve no better. This woman, whose beautiful black hair I was pulling, used to sell cut and dried snake flesh at the guard barracks, saying that it was dried fish. If she hadn't died of the plague, she'd be selling it now. The guards liked to buy from her, and used to say her fish was tasty. What she did couldn't be wrong, because if she hadn't, she would have starved to death. There was no other choice. If she knew I had to do this in order to live, she probably wouldn't care."

He sheathed his sword, and, with his left hand on its hilt, he listened to her meditatively. His right hand touched the big pimple on his cheek. As he listened, a certain courage was born in his heart—the courage which he had not had when he sat under the gate a little while ago. A strange power was driving him in the opposite direction of the courage which he had had when he seized the old woman. No longer did he wonder whether he should starve to death or become a thief. Starvation was so far from his mind that it was the last thing that would have entered it.

"Are you sure?" he asked in a mocking tone, when she finished talking. He took his right hand from his pimple, and, bending forward, seized her by the neck and said sharply:

"Then it's right if I rob you. I'd starve if I didn't."

He tore her clothes from her body and kicked her roughly down on the corpses as she struggled and tried to clutch his leg. Five steps, and he was at the top of stairs. The yellow clothes he had wrested off her were under his arm, and in a twinkling he had rushed down the steep stairs into the abyss of night. The thunder of his decending steps pounded in the hollow tower, and then it was quiet.

Shortly after that the hag raised up her body from the corpses. Grumbling and groaning, she crawled to the top stair by the still flickering torchlight, and through the gray hair which hung over her face, she peered down to the last stair in the torch light.

Beyond this was only darkness . . . unknowing and unknown.

RYŪNOSUKE AKŪTAGAWA

In a Grove

THE TESTIMONY OF A WOODCUTTER QUESTIONED BY A HIGH POLICE COMMISSIONER

Yes, sir. Certainly, it was I who found the body. This morning, as usual, I went to cut my daily quota of cedars, when I found the body in a grove in a hollow in the mountains. The exact location? About 150 meters off the Yamashina stage road.[1] It's an out-of-the-way grove of bamboo and cedars.

The body was lying flat on its back dressed in a bluish silk kimono and a wrinkled head-dress of the Kyōto style. A single sword-stroke had pierced the breast. The fallen bamboo-blades around it were stained with bloody blossoms. No, the blood was no longer running. The wound had dried up, I believe. And also, a gad-fly was stuck fast there, hardly noticing my footsteps.

You ask me if I saw a sword or any such thing?

No, nothing, sir. I found only a rope at the root of a cedar near by. And . . . well, in addition to a rope, I found a comb. That was all. Apparently he must have made a battle of it before he was murdered, because the grass and fallen bamboo-blades had been trampled down all around.

"A horse was near by?"

No, sir. It's hard enough for a man to enter, let alone a horse.

THE TESTIMONY OF A TRAVELING BUDDHIST PRIEST QUESTIONED BY A HIGH POLICE COMMISSIONER

The time? Certainly, it was about noon yesterday, sir. The unfortunate man was on the road from Sekiyama to Yamashina. He was walking toward Sekiyama with a woman accompanying him on horseback, who I have since learned was his wife. A scarf hanging from her head hid her face from view. All I saw was the color of her clothes, a lilac-colored suit. Her horse was a sorrel with a fine mane. The lady's height? Oh, about four feet five inches. Since I am a Buddhist priest, I took little notice about her details. Well, the man was armed with a sword as well as a bow and arrows. And I remember that he carried some twenty odd arrows in his quiver.

Little did I expect that he would meet such a fate. Truly human life is as evanescent as the morning dew or a flash of lightning. My words are inadequate to express my sympathy for him.

1. The action takes place in the vicinity of Kyōto.

THE TESTIMONY OF A POLICEMAN QUESTIONED BY A HIGH POLICE COMMISSIONER

The man that I arrested? He is a notorious brigand called Tajomaru. When I arrested him, he had fallen off his horse. He was groaning on the bridge at Awataguchi. The time? It was in the early hours of last night. For the record, I might say that the other day I tried to arrest him, but unfortunately he escaped. He was wearing a dark blue silk kimono and a large plain sword. And, as you see, he got a bow and arrows somewhere. You say that this bow and these arrows look like the ones owned by the dead man? Then Tajomaru must be the murderer. The bow wound with leather strips, the black lacquered quiver, the seventeen arrows with hawk feathers —these were all in his possession I believe. Yes, sir, the horse is, as you say, a sorrel with a fine mane. A little beyond the stone bridge I found the horse grazing by the roadside, with his long rein dangling. Surely there is some providence in his having been thrown by the horse.

Of all the robbers prowling around Kyoto, this Tajomaru has given the most grief to the women in town. Last autumn a wife who came to the mountain back of the Pindora of the Toribe Temple, presumably to pay a visit, was murdered, along with a girl. It has been suspected that it was his doing. If this criminal murdered the man, you cannot tell what he may have done with the man's wife. May it please your honor to look into this problem as well.

THE TESTIMONY OF AN OLD WOMAN QUESTIONED BY A HIGH POLICE COMMISSIONER

Yes, sir, that corpse is the man who married my daughter. He does not come from Kyoto. He was a samurai in the town of Kokufu in the province of Wakasa. His name was Kanazawa no Takehiko, and his age was twenty-six. He was of a gentle disposition, so I am sure he did nothing to provoke the anger of others.

My daughter? Her name is Masago, and her age is nineteen. She is a spirited, fun-loving girl, but I am sure she has never known any man except Takehiko. She has a small, oval, dark-complected face with a mole at the corner of her left eye.

Yesterday Takehiko left for Wakasa with my daughter. What bad luck it is that things should have come to such a sad end! What has become of my daughter? I am resigned to giving up my son-in-law as lost, but the fate of my daughter worries me sick. For heaven's sake leave no stone unturned to find her. I hate that robber Tajomaru, or whatever his name is. Not only my son-in-law, but my daughter . . .(Her later words were drowned in tears.)

TAJOMARU'S CONFESSION

I killed him, but not her. Where's she gone? I can't tell. Oh, wait a minute. No torture can make me confess what I don't know. Now things have come to such a head, I won't keep anything from you.

Yesterday a little past noon I met that couple. Just then a puff of wind blew, and raised her hanging scarf, so that I caught a glimpse of her face. Instantly it was again covered from my view. That may have been one reason; she looked like a Bodhisattva.[2] At that moment I made up my mind to capture her even if I had to kill her man.

Why? To me killing isn't a matter of such great consequence as you might think. When a woman is captured, her man has to be killed anyway. In killing, I use the sword I wear at my side. Am I the only one who kills people? You, you don't use your swords. You kill people with your power, with your money. Sometimes you kill them on the pretext of working for their good. It's true they don't bleed. They are in the best of health, but all the same you've killed them. It's hard to say who is a greater sinner, you or me. (An ironical smile.)

But it would be good if I could capture a woman without killing her man. So, I made up my mind to capture her, and do my best not to kill him. But it's out of the question on the Yamashina stage road. So I managed to lure the couple into the mountains.

It was quite easy. I became their traveling companion, and I told them there was an old mound in the mountain over there, and that I had dug it open and found many mirrors and swords. I went on to tell them I'd buried the things in a grove behind the mountain, and that I'd like to sell them at a low price to anyone who would care to have them. Then . . . you see, isn't greed terrible? He was beginning to be moved by my talk before he knew it. In less than half an hour they were driving their horse toward the mountain with me.

When he came in front of the grove, I told them that the treasures were buried in it, and I asked them to come and see. The man had no objection—he was blinded by greed. The woman said she would wait on horseback. It was natural for her to say so, at the sight of a thick grove. To tell you the truth, my plan worked just as I wished, so I went into the grove with him, leaving her behind alone.

The grove is only bamboo for some distance. About fifty yards ahead there's a rather open clump of cedars. It was a convenient spot for my purpose. Pushing my way through the grove, I told him a plausible lie that the treasures were buried under the cedars. When

2. A Buddhist holy person.

I told him this, he pushed his laborious way toward the slender cedar visible through the grove. After a while the bamboo thinned out, and we came to where a number of cedars grew in a row. As soon as we got there, I seized him from behind. Because he was a trained, sword-bearing warrior, he was quite strong, but he was taken by surprise, so there was no help for him. I soon tied him up to the root of a cedar. Where did I get a rope? Thank heaven, being a robber, I had a rope with me, since I might have to scale a wall at any moment. Of course it was easy to stop him from calling out by gagging his mouth with fallen bamboo leaves.

When I disposed of him, I went to his woman and asked her to come and see him, because he seemed to have been suddenly taken sick. It's needless to say that this plan also worked well. The woman, her sedge hat off, came into the depths of the grove, where I led her by the hand. The instant she caught sight of her husband, she drew a small sword. I've never seen a woman of such violent temper. If I'd been off guard, I'd have got a thrust in my side. I dodged, but she kept on slashing at me. She might have wounded me deeply or killed me. But I'm Tajomaru. I managed to strike down her small sword without drawing my own. The most spirited woman is defenseless without a weapon. At least I could satisfy my desire for her without taking her husband's life.

Yes, . . . without taking his life. I had no wish to kill him. I was about to run away from the grove, leaving the woman behind in tears, when she frantically clung to my arm. In broken fragments of words, she asked that either her husband or I die. She said it was more trying than death to have her shame known to two men. She gasped out that she wanted to be the wife of whichever survived. Then a furious desire to kill him seized me. (Gloomy excitement.)

Telling you in this way, no doubt I seem a crueler man than you. But that's because you didn't see her face. Especially her burning eyes at that moment. As I saw her eye to eye, I wanted to make her my wife even if I were to be struck by lightning. I wanted to make her my wife . . . this single desire filled my mind. This was not only lust, as you might think. At that time if I'd had no other desire than lust, I'd surely not have minded knocking her down and running away. Then I wouldn't have stained my sword with his blood. But the moment I gazed at her face in the dark grove, I decided not to leave there without killing him.

But I didn't like to resort to unfair means to kill him. I untied him and told him to cross swords with me. (The rope that was found at the root of the cedar is the rope I dropped at the time.) Furious with anger, he drew his thick sword. And quick as thought, he sprang at me ferociously, without speaking a word. I needn't tell you how our fight turned out. The twenty-third stroke . . . please remember this. I'm impressed with this fact still. Nobody under the sun has ever clashed swords with me twenty strokes. (A cheerful smile.)

When he fell, I turned toward her, lowering my blood-stained sword. But to my great astonishment she was gone. I wondered to where she had run away. I looked for her in the clump of cedars. I listened, but heard only a groaning sound from the throat of the dying man.

As soon as we started to cross swords, she may have run away through the grove to call for help. When I thought of that, I decided it was a matter of life and death to me. So, robbing him of his sword, and bow and arrows, I ran out to the mountain road. There I found her horse still grazing quietly. It would be a mere waste of words to tell you the later details, but before I entered town I had already parted with the sword. That's all my confession. I know that my head will be hung in chains anyway, so put me down for the maximum penalty. (A defiant attitude.)

THE CONFESSION OF A WOMAN WHO HAS COME TO THE *Shimizu* TEMPLE

That man in the blue silk kimono, after forcing me to yield to him, laughed mockingly as he looked at my bound husband. How horrified my husband must have been! But no matter how hard he struggled in agony, the rope cut into him all the more tightly. In spite of myself I ran stumblingly toward his side. Or rather I tried to run toward him, but the man instantly knocked me down. Just at that moment I saw an indescribable light in my husband's eyes. Something beyond expression . . . his eyes make me shudder even now. That instantaneous look of my husband, who couldn't speak a word, told me all his heart. The flash in his eyes was neither anger nor sorrow . . . only a cold light, a look of loathing. More struck by the look in his eyes than by the blow of the thief, I called out in spite of myself and fell unconscious.

In the course of time I came to, and found that the man in blue silk was gone. I saw only my husband still bound to the root of the cedar. I raised myself from the bamboo-blades with difficulty, and looked into his face; but the expression in his eyes was just the same as before.

Beneath the cold contempt in his eyes, there was hatred. Shame, grief, and anger . . . I didn't know how to express my heart at that time. Reeling to my feet, I went up to my husband.

"Takejiro," I said to him, "since things have come to this pass, I cannot live with you. I'm determined to die, . . . but you must die, too. You saw my shame. I can't leave you alive as you are."

This was all I could say. Still he went on gazing at me with loathing and contempt. My heart breaking, I looked for his sword. It must have been taken by the robber. Neither his sword nor his bow and arrows were to be seen in the grove. But fortunately my small sword was lying at my feet. Raising it over head, once more I said, "Now give me your life. I'll follow you right away."

When he heard these words, he moved his lips with difficulty. Since his mouth was stuffed with leaves, of course his voice could not be heard at all. But at a glance I understood his words. Despising me, his look said only, "Kill me." Neither conscious nor unconscious, I stabbed the small sword through the lilac-colored kimono into his breast.

Again at this time I must have fainted. By the time I managed to look up, he had already breathed his last—still in bonds. A streak of sinking sunlight streamed through the clump of cedars and bamboos, and shone on his pale face. Gulping down my sobs, I untied the rope from his dead body. And . . . and what has become of me since I have no more strength to tell you. Anyway I hadn't the strength to die. I stabbed my own throat with the small sword, I threw myself into a pond at the foot of the mountain, and I tried to kill myself in many ways. Unable to end my life, I am still living in dishonor. (A lonely smile.) Worthless as I am, I must have been forsaken even by the most merciful Kwannon.[3] I killed my own husband. I was violated by the robber. Whatever can I do? Whatever can I . . . I . . . (Gradually, violent sobbing.)

THE STORY OF THE MURDERED MAN, AS TOLD THROUGH A MEDIUM

After violating my wife, the robber, sitting there, began to speak comforting words to her. Of course I couldn't speak. My whole body was tied fast to the root of a cedar. But meanwhile I winked at her many times, as much as to say "Don't believe the robber." I wanted to convey some such meaning to her. But my wife, sitting dejectedly on the bamboo leaves, was looking hard at her lap. To all appearances, she was listening to his words. I was agonized by jealousy. In the meantime the robber went on with his clever talk, from one subject to another. The robber finally made his bold, brazen proposal. "Once your virtue is stained, you won't get along well with your husband, so won't you be my wife instead? It's my love for you that made me be violent toward you."

While the criminal talked, my wife raised her face as if in a trance. She had never looked so beautiful as at that moment. What did my beautiful wife say in answer to him while I was sitting

3. The Buddhist goddess of mercy.

bound there? I am lost in space, but I have never thought of her answer without burning with anger and jealousy. Truly she said, . . . "Then take me away with you wherever you go."

This is not the whole of her sin. If that were all, I would not be tormented so much in the dark. When she was going out of the grove as if in a dream, her hand in the robber's, she suddenly turned pale, and pointed at me tied to the root of the cedar, and said, "Kill him! I cannot marry you as long as he lives." "Kill him!" she cried many times, as if she had gone crazy. Even now these words threaten to blow me headlong into the bottomless abyss of darkness. Has such a hateful thing come out of a human mouth ever before? Have such cursed words ever struck a human ear, even once? Even once such a . . . (A sudden cry of scorn.) At these words the robber himself turned pale. "Kill him," she cried, clinging to his arms. Looking hard at her, he answered neither yes or no . . . but hardly had I thought about his answer before she had been knocked down into the bamboo leaves. (Again a cry of scorn.) Quietly folding his arms, he looked at me and said, "What will you do with her? Kill her or save her? You have only to nod. Kill her?" For these words alone I would like to pardon his crime.

While I hesitated, she shrieked and ran into the depths of the grove. The robber instantly snatched at her, but he failed even to grasp her sleeve.

After she ran away, he took up my sword, and my bow and arrows. With a single stroke he cut one of my bonds. I remember his mumbling, "My fate is next." Then he disappeared from the grove. All was silent after that. No, I heard someone crying. Untying the rest of my bonds, I listened carefully, and I noticed that it was my own crying. (Long silence.)

I raised my exhausted body from the root of the cedar. In front of me there was shining the small sword which my wife had dropped. I took it up and stabbed it into my breast. A bloody lump rose to my mouth, but I didn't feel any pain. When my breast grew cold, everything was as silent as the dead in their graves. What profound silence! Not a single bird-note was heard in the sky over this grave in the hollow of the mountains. Only a lonely light lingered on the cedars and mountains. By and by the light gradually grew fainter, till the cedars and bamboo were lost to view. Lying there, I was enveloped in deep silence.

Then someone crept up to me. I tried to see who it was. But darkness had already been gathering round me. Someone . . . that someone drew the small sword softly out of my breast in its invisible hand. At the same time once more blood flowed into my mouth. And once and for all I sank down into the darkness of space.

JUNICHIRO TANIZAKI

The Tattooer*

It was an age when men honored the noble virtue of frivolity, when life was not such a harsh struggle as it is today. It was a leisurely age, an age when professional wits could make an excellent livelihood by keeping rich or wellborn young gentlemen in a cloudless good humor and seeing to it that the laughter of Court ladies and geisha was never stilled. In the illustrated romantic novels of the day, in the Kabuki theater, where rough masculine heroes like Sadakuro and Jiraiya were transformed into women—everywhere beauty and strength were one. People did all they could to beautify themselves, some even having pigments injected into their precious skins. Gaudy patterns of line and color danced over men's bodies.

Visitors to the pleasure quarters of Edo preferred to hire palanquin bearers who were splendidly tattooed; courtesans of the Yoshiwara and the Tatsumi quarter fell in love with tattooed men. Among those so adorned were not only gamblers, firemen, and the like, but members of the merchant class and even samurai. Exhibitions were held from time to time; and the participants, stripped to show off their filigreed bodies, would pat themselves proudly, boast of their own novel designs, and criticize each other's merits.

There was an exceptionally skillful young tattooer named Seikichi. He was praised on all sides as a master the equal of Charibun or Yatsuhei, and the skins of dozens of men had been offered as the silk for his brush. Much of the work admired at the tattoo exhibitions was his. Others might be more noted for their shading, or their use of cinnabar, but Seikichi was famous for the unrivaled boldness and sensual charm of his art.

Seikichi had formerly earned his living as an ukiyoye painter of the school of Toyokuni and Kunisada, a background which, in spite of his decline to the status of a tattooer, was evident from his artistic conscience and sensitivity. No one whose skin or whose physique failed to interest him could buy his services. The clients he did accept had to leave the design and cost entirely to his discretion—and to endure for one or even two months the excruciating pain of his needles.

Deep in his heart the young tattooer concealed a secret pleasure, and a secret desire. His pleasure lay in the agony men felt as he

* From *Seven Japanese Tales*, by Junichiro Tanizaki. Translated by Howard Hibbett. Copyright © 1963 by Alfred A. Knopf, Inc. Reprinted by permission of the publisher.

drove his needles into them, torturing their swollen, blood-red flesh; and the louder they groaned, the keener was Seikichi's strange delight. Shading and vermilioning—these are said to be especially painful—were the techniques he most enjoyed.

When a man had been pricked five or six hundred times in the course of an average day's treatment and had then soaked himself in a hot bath to bring out the colors, he would collapse at Seikichi's feet half dead. But Seikichi would look down at him coolly. "I dare say that hurts," he would remark with an air of satisfaction.

Whenever a spineless man howled in torment or clenched his teeth and twisted his mouth as if he were dying, Seikichi told him: "Don't act like a child. Pull yourself together—you have hardly begun to feel my needles!" And he would go on tattooing, as unperturbed as ever, with an occasional sidelong glance at the man's tearful face.

But sometimes a man of immense fortitude set his jaw and bore up stoically, not even allowing himself to frown. Then Seikichi would smile and say: "Ah, you are a stubborn one! But wait. Soon your body will begin to throb with pain. I doubt if you will be able to stand it. . ."

For a long time Seikichi had cherished the desire to create a masterpiece on the skin of a beautiful woman. Such a woman had to meet various qualifications of character as well as appearance. A lovely face and a fine body were not enough to satisfy him. Though he inspected all the reigning beauties of the Edo gay quarters he found none who met his exacting demands. Several years had passed without success, and yet the face and figure of the perfect woman continued to obsess his thoughts. He refused to abandon hope.

One summer evening during the fourth year of his search Seikichi happened to be passing the Hirasei Restaurant in the Fukagawa district of Edo, not far from his own house, when he noticed a woman's bare milk-white foot peeping out beneath the curtains of a departing palanquin. To his sharp eye, a human foot was as expressive as a face. This one was sheer perfection. Exquisitely chiseled toes, nails like the iridescent shells along the shore at Enoshima, a pearl-like rounded heel, skin so lustrous that it seemed bathed in the limpid waters of a mountain spring—this, indeed, was a foot to be nourished by men's blood, a foot to trample on their bodies. Surely this was the foot of the unique woman who had so long eluded him. Eager to catch a glimpse of her face, Seikichi began to follow the palanquin. But after pursuing it down several lanes and alleys he lost sight of it altogether.

Seikichi's long-held desire turned into passionate love. One morning late the next spring he was standing on the bamboo-floored veranda of his home in Fukagawa, gazing at a pot of *omoto* lilies, when he heard someone at the garden gate. Around the corner of the inner fence appeared a young girl. She had come on an errand for a friend of his, a geisha of the nearby Tatsumi quarter.

"My mistress asked me to deliver this cloak, and she wondered if you would be so good as to decorate its lining," the girl said. She untied a saffron-colored cloth parcel and took out a woman's silk cloak (wrapped in a sheet of thick paper bearing a portrait of the actor Tojaku) and a letter.

The letter repeated his friend's request and went on to say that its bearer would soon begin a career as a geisha under her protection. She hoped that, while not forgetting old ties, he would also extend his patronage to this girl.

"I thought I had never seen you before," said Seikichi, scrutinizing her intently. She seemed only fifteen or sixteen, but her face had a strangely ripe beauty, a look of experience, as if she had already spent years in the gay quarter and had fascinated innumerable men. Her beauty mirrored the dreams of the generations of glamorous men and women who had lived and died in this vast capital, where the nation's sins and wealth were concentrated.

Seikichi had her sit on the veranda, and he studied her delicate feet, which were bare except for elegant straw sandals. "You left the Hirasei by palanquin one night last July, did you not?" he inquired.

"I suppose so," she replied, smiling at the odd question. "My father was still alive then, and he often took me there."

"I have waited five years for you. This is the first time I have seen your face, but I remember your foot. . . . Come in for a moment, I have something to show you."

She had risen to leave, but he took her by the hand and led her upstairs to his studio overlooking the broad river. Then he brought out two picture scrolls and unrolled one of them before her.

It was a painting of a Chinese princess, the favorite of the cruel Emperor Chou of the Shang Dynasty. She was leaning on a balustrade in a languorous pose, the long skirt of her figured brocade robe trailing halfway down a flight of stairs, her slender body barely able to support the weight of her gold crown studded with coral and lapis lazuli. In her right hand she held a large wine cup, tilting it to her lips as she gazed down at a man who was about to be tortured in the garden below. He was chained hand and foot to a hollow copper pillar in which a fire would be lighted. Both the princess and her victim—his head bowed before her, his eyes closed, ready to meet his fate—were portrayed with terrifying vividness.

As the girl stared at this bizarre picture her lips trembled and her eyes began to sparkle. Gradually her face took on a curious resemblance to that of the princess. In the picture she discovered her secret self.

"Your own feelings are revealed here," Seikichi told her with pleasure as he watched her face.

"Why are you showing me this horrible thing?" the girl asked, looking up at him. She had turned pale.

"The woman is yourself. Her blood flows in your veins." Then he spread out the other scroll.

This was a painting called "The Victims." In the middle of it a young woman stood leaning against the trunk of a cherry tree: she was gloating over a heap of men's corpses lying at her feet. Little birds fluttered about her, singing in triumph; her eyes radiated pride and joy. Was it a battlefield or a garden in spring? In this picture the girl felt that she had found something long hidden in the darkness of her own heart.

"This painting shows your future," Seikichi said, pointing to the woman under the cherry tree the very image of the young girl "All these men will ruin their lives for you."

"Please, I beg of you to put it away!" She turned her back as if to escape its tantalizing lure and prostrated herself before him, trembling. At last she spoke again. "Yes, I admit that you are right about me—I *am* like that woman. . . . So please, please take it away."

"Don't talk like a coward," Seikichi told her, with his malicious smile. "Look at it more closely. You won't be squeamish long."

But the girl refused to lift her head. Still prostrate, her face buried in her sleeves, she repeated over and over that she was afraid and wanted to leave.

"No, you must stay—I will make you a real beauty," he said, moving closer to her. Under his kimono was a vial of anesthetic which he had obtained some time ago from a Dutch physician.

The morning sun glittered on the river, setting the eight-mat studio ablaze with light. Rays reflected from the water sketched rippling golden waves on the paper sliding screens and on the face of the girl, who was fast asleep. Seikichi had closed the doors and taken up his tattooing instruments, but for a while he only sat there entranced, savoring to the full her uncanny beauty. He thought that he would never tire of contemplating her serene masklike face. Just as the ancient Egyptians had embellished their magnificent land with pyramids and sphinxes, he was about to embellish the pure skin of this girl.

Presently he raised the brush which was gripped between the thumb and last two fingers of his left hand, applied its tip to the girl's back, and, with the needle which he held in his right hand, began pricking out a design. He felt his spirit dissolve into the charcoal-black ink that stained her skin. Each drop of Ryukyu cinnabar that he mixed with alcohol and thrust in was a drop of his lifeblood. He saw in his pigments the hues of his own passions.

Soon it was afternoon, and then the tranquil spring day drew toward its close. But Seikichi never paused in his work, nor was the girl's sleep broken. When a servant came from the geisha house to inquire about her, Seikichi turned him away, saying that she had left long ago. And hours later, when the moon hung over the mansion across the river, bathing the houses along the bank in a dreamlike radiance, the tattoo was not yet half done. Seikichi worked on by candlelight.

Even to insert a single drop of color was no easy task. At every thrust of his needle Seikichi gave a heavy sigh and felt as if he had stabbed his own heart. Little by little the tattoo marks began to take on the form of a huge black-widow spider; and by the time the night sky was paling into dawn this weird, malevolent creature had stretched its eight legs to embrace the whole of the girl's back.

In the full light of the spring dawn boats were being rowed up and down the river, their oars creaking in the morning quiet; roof tiles glistened in the sun, and the haze began to thin out over white sails swelling in the early breeze. Finally, Seikichi put down his brush and looked at the tattooed spider. This work of art had been the supreme effort of his life. Now that he had finished it his heart was drained of emotion.

The two figures remained still for some time. Then Seikichi's low, hoarse voice echoed quaveringly from the walls of the room:

"To make you truly beautiful I have poured my soul into this tattoo. Today there is no woman in Japan to compare with you. Your old fears are gone. All men will be your victims."

As if in response to these words a faint moan came from the girl's lips. Slowly she began to recover her senses. With each shuddering breath, the spider's legs stirred as if they were alive.

"You must be suffering. The spider has you in its clutches."

At this she opened her eyes slightly, in a dull stare. Her gaze steadily brightened, as the moon brightens in the evening, until it shone dazzlingly into his face.

"Let me see the tattoo," she said, speaking as if in a dream but with an edge of authority to her voice. "Giving me your soul must have made me very beautiful."

"First you must bathe to bring out the colors," whispered Seikichi compassionately. "I am afraid it will hurt, but be brave a little longer."

"I can bear anything for the sake of beauty." Despite the pain that was coursing through her body, she smiled.

"How the water stings! . . . Leave me alone—wait in the other room! I hate to have a man see me suffer like this!"

As she left the tub, too weak to dry herself, the girl pushed aside the sympathetic hand Seikichi offered her, and sank to the floor in agony, moaning as if in a nightmare. Her disheveled hair hung over her face in a wild tangle. The white soles of her feet were reflected in the mirror behind her.

Seikichi was amazed at the change that had come over the timid, yielding girl of yesterday, but he did as he was told and went to wait in his studio. About an hour later she came back, carefully dressed, her damp, sleekly combed hair hanging down over her shoulders. Leaning on the veranda rail, she looked up into the faintly hazy sky. Her eyes were brilliant; there was not a trace of pain in them.

"I wish to give you these pictures too," said Seikichi, placing the scrolls before her. "Take them and go."

"All my old fears have been swept away—and you are my first victim!" She darted a glance at him as bright as a sword. A song of triumph was ringing in her ears.

"Let me see your tattoo once more," Seikichi begged.

Silently the girl nodded and slipped the kimono off her shoulders. Just then her resplendently tattooed back caught a ray of sunlight and the spider was wreathed in flames.

YASUNARI KAWABATA

The Moon on the Water*

It occurred to Kyōko one day to let her husband, in bed upstairs, see her vegetable garden by reflecting it in her hand mirror. To one who had been so long confined, this opened a new life. The hand mirror was part of a set in Kyōko's trousseau. The mirror stand was not very big. It was made of mulberry wood, as was the frame of the mirror itself. It was the hand mirror that still reminded her of the bashfulness of her early married years when, as she was looking into it at the reflection of her back hair in the stand mirror, her sleeve would slip and expose her elbow.

When she came from the bath, her busband seemed to enjoy reflecting the nape of her neck from all angles in the hand mirror. Taking the mirror from her, he would say: "How clumsy you are! Here, let me hold it." Maybe he found something new in the mirror. It was not that Kyōko was clumsy, but that she became nervous at being looked at from behind.

* From *Modern Japanese Stories*, edited by Ivan Morris. Copyright © 1961 by Charles E. Tuttle Co., Inc. Reprinted by permission of the publishers.

Not enough time had passed for the color of the mulberry-wood frame to change. It lay in a drawer. War came, followed by flight from the city and her husband's becoming seriously ill; by the time it first occurred to Kyōko to have her husband see the garden through the mirror, its surface had become cloudy and the rim had been smeared with face powder and dirt. Since it still reflected well enough, Kyōko did not worry about this cloudiness—indeed she scarcely noticed it. Her husband, however, would not let the mirror go from his bedside and polished it and its frame in his idleness with the peculiar nervousness of an invalid. Kyōko sometimes imagined that tuberculosis germs had found their way into the imperceptible cracks in the frame. After she had combed her husband's hair with a little camellia oil, he sometimes ran the palm of his hand through his hair and then rubbed the mirror. The wood of the mirror stand remained dull, but that of the mirror grew lustrous.

When Kyōko married again, she took the same mirror stand with her. The hand mirror, however, had been buried in the coffin of her dead husband. A hand mirror with a carved design had now taken its place. She never told her second husband about this.

According to custom, the hands of her dead husband had been clasped and his fingers crossed, so that it was impossible to make them hold the hand mirror after he had been put into the coffin. She laid the mirror on his chest.

"Your chest hurt you so. Even this must be heavy."

Kyōko moved the mirror down to his stomach. Because she thought of the important role that the mirror had played in their marital life, Kyōko had first laid it on his chest. She wanted to keep this little act as much as possible from the eyes even of her husband's family. She had piled white chrysanthemums on the mirror. No one had noticed it. When the ashes were being gathered after the cremation, people noticed the glass which had been melted into a shapeless mass, partly sooty and partly yellowish. Someone said: "It's glass. What is it, I wonder?" She had in fact placed a still smaller mirror on the hand mirror. It was the sort of mirror usually carried in a toilet case, a long, narrow, double-faced mirror. Kyōko had dreamed of using it on her honeymoon trip. The war had made it impossible for them to go on a honeymoon. During her husband's lifetime she never was able to use it on a trip.

With her second husband, however, she went on a honeymoon. Since her leather toilet case was now very musty, she bought a new one—with a mirror in it too.

On the very first day of their trip, her husband touched Kyōko and said: "You are like a little girl. Poor thing!" His tone was not in the least sarcastic. Rather it suggested unexpected joy. Possibly it was good for him that Kyōko was like a little girl. At this remark,

Kyōko was assailed by an intense sorrow. Her eyes filled with tears and she shrank away. He might have taken that to be girlish too.

Kyōko did not know whether she had wept for her own sake or for the sake of her dead husband. Nor was it possible to know. The moment this idea came to her, she felt very sorry for her second husband and thought she had to be coquettish.

"Am I so different?" No sooner had she spoken than she felt very awkward, and shyness came over her.

He looked satisfied and said: "You never had a child . . ."

His remark pierced her heart. Before a male force other than her former husband Kyōko felt humiliated. She was being made sport of.

"But it was like looking after a child all the time."

This was all she said by way of protest. It was as if her first husband, who had died after a long illness, had been a child inside her. But if he was to die in any case, what good had her continence done?

"I've only seen Mori from the train window." Her second husband drew her to him as he mentioned the name of her home town. "From its name[1] it sounds like a pretty town in the woods. How long did you live there?"

"Until I graduated from high school. Then I was drafted to work in a munitions factory in Sanjō."

"Is Sanjō near, then? I've heard a great deal about Sanjō beauties. I see why you're so beautiful."

"No, I'm not." Kyōko brought her hand to her throat.

"Your hands are beautiful, and I thought your body should be beautiful too."

"Oh no."

Finding her hands in the way, Kyōko quietly drew them back.

"I'm sure I'd have married you even if you had had a child. I could have adopted the child and looked after it. A girl would have been better," he whispered in Kyōko's ear. Maybe it was because he had a boy, but his remark seemed odd even as an expression of love. Possibly he had planned the long, ten-day honeymoon so that she would not have to face the stepson quite so soon.

Her husband had a toilet case for traveling, made of what seemed to be good leather. Kyōko's did not compare with it. His was large and strong, but it was not new. Maybe because he often traveled or because he took good care of it, the case had a mellow luster. Kyōko thought of the old case, never used, which she had left to mildew. Only its small mirror had been used by her first husband, and she had sent it with him in death.

1. *Mori* means "grove."

The small glass had melted into the hand mirror, so that no one except Kyōko could tell that they had been separate before. Since Kyōko had not said that the curious mass had been mirrors, her relatives had no way of knowing.

Kyōko felt as if the numerous worlds reflected in the two mirrors had vanished in the fire. She felt the same kind of loss when her husband's body was reduced to ashes. It had been with the hand mirror that came with the mirror stand that Kyōko first reflected the vegetable garden. Her husband always kept that mirror beside his pillow. Even the hand mirror seemed to be too heavy for the invalid, and Kyōko, worried about his arms and shoulders, gave him a lighter and smaller one.

It was not only Kyōko's vegetable garden that her husband had observed through the two mirrors. He had seen the sky, clouds, snow, distant mountains, and nearby woods. He had seen the moon. He had seen wild flowers, and birds of passage had made their way through the mirror. Men walked down the road in the mirror and children played in the garden.

Kyōko was amazed at the richness of the world in the mirror. A mirror which had until then been regarded only as a toilet article, a hand mirror which had served only to show the back of one's neck, had created for the invalid a new life. Kyōko used to sit beside his bed and talk about the world in the mirror. They looked into it together. In the course of time it became impossible for Kyōko to distinguish between the world that she saw directly and the world in the mirror. Two separate worlds came to exist. A new world was created in the mirror and it came to seem like the real world.

"The sky shines silver in the mirror," Kyōko said. Looking up through the window, she added: "When the sky itself is grayish." The sky in the mirror lacked the leaden and heavy quality of the actual sky. It was shining.

"Is it because you are always polishing the mirror?"

Though he was lying down, her husband could see the sky by turning his head.

"Yes, it's a dull gray. But the color of the sky is not necessarily the same to dogs' eyes and sparrows' eyes as it is to human eyes. You can't tell which eyes see the real color."

"What we see in the mirror—is that what the mirror eye sees?"

Kyōko wanted to call it the eye of their love. The trees in the mirror were a fresher green than real trees, and the lilies a purer white.

"This is the print of your thumb, Kyōko. Your right thumb."

He pointed to the edge of the mirror. Kyōko was somehow startled. She breathed on the mirror and erased the fingerprint.

"That's all right, Kyōko. Your fingerprint stayed on the mirror when you first showed me the vegetable garden."

"I didn't notice it."

"You may not have noticed it. Thanks to this mirror, I've memorized the prints of your thumbs and index fingers. Only an invalid could memorize his wife's fingerprints."

Her husband had done almost nothing but lie in bed since their marriage. He had not gone to war. Toward the end of the war he had been drafted, but he fell ill after several days of labor at an airfield and came home at the end of the war. Since he was unable to walk, Kyōko went with his elder brother to meet him. After her husband had been drafted, she stayed with her parents. They had left the city to avoid the bombings. Their household goods had long since been sent away. As the house where their married life began had been burned down, they had rented a room in the home of a friend of Kyōko's. From there her husband commuted to his office. A month in their honeymoon house and two months at the house of a friend—that was all the time Kyōko spent with her husband before he fell ill.

It was then decided that her husband should rent a small house in the mountains and convalesce there. Other families had been in the house, also fugitives from the city, but they had gone back to Tokyo after the war ended, Kyōko took over their vegetable garden. It was only some six yards square, a clearing in the weeds. They could easily have bought vegetables, but Kyōko worked in the garden. She became interested in vegetables grown by her own hand. It was not that she wanted to stay away from her sick husband, but such things as sewing and knitting made her gloomy. Even though she thought of him always, she had brighter hopes when she was out in the garden. There she could indulge her love for her husband. As for reading, it was all she could do to read aloud at his bedside. Then Kyōko thought that by working in the garden she might regain that part of herself which it seemed she was losing in the fatigue of the long nursing.

It was in the middle of September that they moved to the mountains. The summer visitors had almost all gone and a long spell of early autumn rains came, chilly and damp.

One afternoon the sun came out to the clear song of a bird. When she went into the garden, she found the green vegetables shining. She was enraptured by the rosy clouds on the mountain tops. Startled by her husband's voice calling her, she hurried upstairs, her hands covered with mud, and found him breathing painfully.

"I called and called. Couldn't you hear me?"

"I'm sorry. I couldn't."

"Stop working in the garden. I'd be dead in no time if I had to keep calling you like that. In the first place, I can't see where you are and what you're doing."

"I was in the garden. But I'll stop."

He was calmer.

"Did you hear the lark?"

That was all he had wanted to tell her. The lark sang in the nearby woods again. The woods were clear against the evening glow. Thus Kyōko learned to know the song of the lark.

"A bell will help you, won't it? How about having something you can throw until I get a bell for you?"

"Shall I throw a cup from here? That would be fun."

It was settled that Kyōko might continue her gardening; but it was after spring had come to end the long, harsh mountain winter that Kyōko thought of showing him the garden in the mirror.

The single mirror gave him inexhaustible joy, as if a lost world of fresh green had come back. It was impossible for him to see the worms she picked from the vegetables. She had to come upstairs to show him. "I can see the earthworms from here, though," he used to say as he watched her digging in the earth.

When the sun was shining into the house, Kyōko sometimes noticed a light and, looking up, discovered that her husband was reflecting the sun in the mirror. He insisted that Kyōko remake the dark-blue kimono he had used during his student days into pantaloons for herself. He seemed to enjoy the sight of Kyōko in the mirror as she worked in the garden, wearing the dark blue with its white splashes.

Kyōko worked in the garden half-conscious and half-unconscious of the fact that she was being seen. Her heart warmed to see how different her feelings were now from the very early days of her marriage. Then she had blushed even at showing her elbow when she held the smaller glass behind her head. It was, however, only when she remarried that she started making up as she pleased, released from the long years of nursing and the mourning that had followed. She saw that she was becoming remarkably beautiful. It now seemed that her husband had really meant it when he said that her body was beautiful.

Kyōko was no longer ashamed of her reflection in the mirror—after she had had a bath, for instance. She had discovered her own beauty. But she had not lost that unique feeling that her former husband had planted in her toward the beauty in the mirror. She did not doubt the beauty she was in the mirror. Quite the reverse: she could not doubt the reality of that other world. But between her skin as she saw it and her skin as reflected in the mirror she could not find the difference that she had found between that leaden sky and the silver sky in the mirror. It may not have been only the difference in distance. Maybe the longing of her first husband confined to his bed had acted upon her. But then, there was now no way of knowing how beautiful she had looked to him in the mirror as she worked in the garden. Even before his death, Kyōko herself had not been able to tell.

Kyōko thought of, indeed longed for, the image of herself working in the garden, seen through the mirror in her husband's hand, and for the white of the lilies, the crowd of village children playing in the field, and the morning sun rising above the far-off snowy mountains—for that separate world she had shared with him. For the sake of her present husband, Kyōko suppressed this feeling, which seemed about to become an almost physical yearning, and tried to take it for something like a distant view of the celestial world.

One morning in May, Kyōko heard the singing of wild birds over the radio. It was a broadcast from a mountain near the heights where she had stayed with her first husband until his death. As had become her custom, after seeing her present husband off to work, Kyōko took the hand mirror from the drawer of the stand and reflected the clear sky. Then she gazed at her face in the mirror. She was astonished by a new discovery. She could not see her own face unless she reflected it in the mirror. One could not see one's own face. One felt one's own face, wondering if the face in the mirror was one's actual face. Kyōko was lost in thought for some time. Why had God created man's face so that he might not see it himself?

"Suppose you could see your own face, would you lose your mind? Would you become incapable of acting?"

Most probably man had evolved in such a way that he could not see his own face. Maybe dragonflies and praying mantises could see their own faces.

But then perhaps one's own face was for others to see. Did it not resemble love? As she was putting the hand mirror back in the drawer, Kyōko could not even now help noticing the odd combination of carved design and mulberry. Since the former mirror had burned with her first husband, the mirror stand might well be compared to a widow. But the hand mirror had had its advantages and disadvantages. Her husband was constantly seeing his face in it. Perhaps it was more like seeing death itself. If his death was a psychological suicide by means of a mirror, then Kyōko was the psychological murderer. Kyōko had once thought of the disadvantages of the mirror, and tried to take it from him. But he would not let her.

"Do you intend to have me see nothing? As long as I live, I want to keep loving something I can see," her husband said. He would have sacrificed his life to keep the world in the mirror. After heavy rains they would gaze at the moon through the mirror, the reflection of the moon from the pool in the garden. A moon which could hardly be called even the reflection of a reflection still lingered in Kyōko's heart.

"A sound love dwells only in a sound person." When her second husband said this, Kyōko nodded shyly, but she could not entirely agree with him. When her first husband died, Kyōko wondered what good her continence had done; but soon the continence became a poignant memory of love, a memory of days brimming with love, and her regrets quite disappeared. Probably her second husband regarded woman's love too lightly. "Why did you leave your wife, when you are such a tender-hearted man?" Kyōko would ask him. He never answered. Kyōko had married him because the elder brother of her dead husband had insisted. After four months as friends they were married. He was fifteen years older.

When she became pregnant, Kyōko was so terrified that her very face changed.

"I'm afraid. I'm afraid." She clung to her husband. She suffered intensely from morning sickness and she even became deranged. She crawled into the garden barefooted and gathered pine needles. She had her stepson carry two lunch boxes to school, both boxes filled with rice. She sat staring blankly into the mirror, thinking that she saw straight through it. She rose in the middle of night, sat on the bed, and looked into her husband's sleeping face. Assailed by terror at the knowledge that man's life is a trifle, she found herself loosening the sash of her night robe. She made as if to strangle him. The next moment she was sobbing hysterically. Her husband awoke and retied her sash gently. She shivered in the summer night.

"Trust the child in you, Kyōko." Her husband rocked her in his arms.

The doctor suggested that she be hospitalized. Kyōko resisted, but was finally persuaded.

"I will go to the hospital. Please let me go first to visit my family for a few days."

Some time later her husband took her to her parents' home. The next day Kyōko slipped out of the house and went to the heights where she had lived with her first husband. It was early in September, ten days earlier than when she had moved there with him. Kyōko felt like vomiting. She was dizzy in the train and obsessed by an impulse to jump off. As the train passed the station on the heights, the crisp air brought her relief. She regained control of herself, as if the devil possessing her had gone. She stopped, bewildered, and looked at the mountains surrounding the high plateau. The outline of the blue mountains where the color was not growing darker was vivid against the sky, and she felt in them a living world. Wiping her eyes, moist with warm tears, she walked toward the house where he and she had lived. From the woods which had loomed against the rosy evening glow that day there came again the song of a lark. Someone was living in the house and a white lace curtain hung at the window upstairs. Not going too near, she gazed at the house.

"What if the child should look like you?" Startled at her own words, she turned back, warm and at peace.

YUKIO MISHIMA

The Priest and His Love*

According to Eshin's "Essentials of Salvation," the Ten Pleasures are but a drop in the ocean when compared to the joys of the Pure Land. In that land the earth is made of emerald and the roads that lead across it are lined by cordons of gold rope. The surface is endlessly level and there are no boundaries. Within each of the sacred precincts are fifty thousand million halls and towers wrought of gold, silver, lapis lazuli, crystal, coral, agate, and pearls; and wondrous garments are spread out on all the jeweled daises. Within the halls and above the towers a multitude of angels is forever playing sacred music and singing paeans of praise to the Tathagata Buddha. In the gardens that surround the halls and the towers and the cloisters are great gold and emerald ponds where the faithful may perform their ablutions; and gold ponds are lined with silver sand, and the emerald ponds are lined with crystal sand. The ponds are covered with lotus plants which sparkle in variegated colors and, as the breeze wafts over the surface of the water, magnificent lights crisscross in all directions. Both day and night the air is filled with the songs of cranes, geese, mandarin ducks, peacocks, parrots, and sweet-voiced Kalavinkas, who have the faces of beautiful women. All these and the myriad other hundred-jeweled birds are raising their melodious voices in praise of the Buddha. (However sweet their voices may sound, so immense a collection of birds must be extremely noise.)

The borders of the ponds and the banks of the rivers are lined with groves of sacred treasure trees. These trees have golden stems and silver branches and coral blossoms, and their beauty is mirrored in the waters. The air is full of jeweled cords, and from these cords hang the myriad treasure bells which forever ring out the Supreme Law of Buddha; and strange musical instruments, which play by themselves without ever being touched, also stretch far into the pellucid sky.

If one feels like having something to eat, there automatically

* From *Modern Japanese Stories*, edited by Ivan Morris. Copyright © 1961 by Charles E. Tuttle Co., Inc. Reprinted by permission of the publishers.

appears before one's eyes a seven-jeweled table on whose shining surface rest seven-jeweled bowls heaped high with the choicest delicacies. But there is no need to pick up these viands and put them in one's mouth. All that is necessary is to look at their inviting colors and to enjoy their aroma; thereby the stomach is filled and the body nourished, while one remains oneself spiritually and physically pure. When one has thus finished one's meal without any eating, the bowls and the table are instantly wafted off.

Likewise, one's body is automatically arrayed in clothes, without any need for sewing, laundering, dyeing, or repairing. Lamps, too, are unnecessary, for the sky is illumined by an omnipresent light. Furthermore, the Pure Land enjoys a moderate temperature all year round, so that neither heating nor cooling is required. A hundred thousand subtle scents perfume the air, and lotus petals rain down constantly.

In the chapter on the Inspection Gate we are told that, since uninitiated sightseers cannot hope to penetrate deep into the Pure Land, they must concentrate, first, on awakening their powers of "external imagination" and, thereafter, on steadily expanding these powers. Imaginative power can provide a short cut for escaping from the trammels of our mundane life and for seeing the Buddha. If we are endowed with a rich, turbulent imagination, we can focus our attention on a single lotus flower and from there can spread out to infinite horizons.

By means of microscopic observation and astronomical projection the lotus flower can become the foundation for an entire theory of the universe and an agent whereby we may perceive Truth. And first we must know that each of the petals has eighty-four thousand veins and that each vein gives off eighty-four thousand lights. Furthermore, the smallest of these flowers has a diameter of two hundred and fifty *yojana*. Thus, assuming that the *yojana* of which we read in the Holy Writings correspond to seventy-five miles each, we may conclude that a lotus flower with a diameter of nineteen thousand miles is on the small side.

Now such a flower has eighty-four thousand petals and between each of the petals there are one million jewels, each emitting one thousand lights. Above the beautifully adorned calyx of the flower rise four bejeweled pillars and each of these pillars is one hundred billion times as great as Mount Sumeru, which towers in the center of the Buddhist universe. From the pillars hang great draperies and each drapery is adorned with fifty thousand million jewels, and each jewel emits eighty-four thousand lights, and each light is composed of eighty-four thousand different golden colors, and each of those golden colors in its turn is variously transmogrified.

To concentrate on such images is known as "thinking of the

Lotus Seat on which Lord Buddha sits"; and the conceptual world that hovers in the background of our story is a world imagined on such a scale.

The Great Priest of Shiga Temple was a man of the most eminent virtue. His eyebrows were white, and it was as much as he could do to move his old bones along as he hobbled on his stick from one part of the temple to another.

In the eyes of this learned ascetic, the world was a mere pile of rubbish. He had lived away from it for many a long year, and the little pine sapling that he had planted with his own hands on moving into his present cell had grown into a great tree whose branches swelled in the wind. A monk who had succeeded in abandoning the Floating World for so long a time must feel secure about his afterlife.

When the Great Priest saw the rich and the noble, he smiled with compassion and wondered how it was that these people did not recognize their pleasures for the empty dreams that they were. When he noticed beautiful women, his only reaction was to be moved with pity for men who still inhabited the world of delusion and who were tossed about on the waves of carnal pleasure.

From the moment that a man no longer responds in the slightest to the motives that regulate the material world, that world appears to be a complete repose. In the eyes of the Great Priest the world showed only repose; it had become a mere picture drawn on a piece of paper, a map of some foreign land. When one has attained a state of mind from which the evil passions of the present world have been so utterly winnowed, fear too is forgotten. Thus it was that the priest no longer could understand why Hell should exist. He knew beyond all peradventure that the present world no longer had any power left over him; but, as he was completely devoid of conceit, it did not occur to him that this was the effect of his own eminent virtue.

So far as his body was concerned, one might say that the priest had well nigh been deserted by his own flesh. On such occasions as he observed it—when taking a bath, for instance—he would rejoice to see how his protruding bones were precariously covered by his withered skin. Now that his body had reached this stage, he felt that he could come to terms with it, as if it belonged to someone else. Such a body, it seemed, was already more suited for the nourishment of the Pure Land than for terrestrial food and drink.

In his dreams he lived nightly in the Pure Land, and when he awoke he knew that to subsist in the present world was to be tied to a sad and evanescent dream.

In the flower-viewing season large numbers of people came from the Capital to visit the village of Shiga. This did not trouble the priest in the slightest, for he had long since transcended that state in which the clamors of the world can irritate the mind. One spring evening he left his cell, leaning on his stick, and walked down to the lake. It was the hour when dusky shadows slowly begin to thrust their way into the bright light of the afternoon. There was not the slightest ripple to disturb the surface of the water. The priest stood by himself at the edge of the lake and began to perform the holy rite of Water Contemplation.

At that moment an ox-drawn carriage, clearly belonging to a person of high rank, came round the lake and stopped close to where the priest was standing. The owner was a court lady from the Kyōgoku district of the Capital who held the exalted title of Great Imperial Concubine. This lady had come to view the springtime scenery in Shiga and now on her return she stopped the carriage and raised the blind in order to have a final look at the lake.

Unwittingly the Great Priest glanced in her direction and at once he was overwhelmed by her beauty. His eyes met hers and, as he did nothing to avert his gaze, she did not take upon herself to turn away. It was not that her liberality of spirit was such as to allow men to gaze on her with brazen looks; but the motives of this austere old ascetic could hardly, she felt, be those of ordinary men.

After a few moments the lady pulled down the blind. Her carriage started to move and, having gone through the Shiga Pass, rolled slowly down the road that led to the Capital. Night fell and the carriage made its way toward the city along the Road of the Silver Temple. Until the carriage had become a pinprick that disappeared between the distant trees, the Great Priest stood rooted to the spot.

In the twinkling of an eye the present world had wreaked its revenge with terrible force on the priest. What he had imagined to be completely safe had collapsed in ruins.

He returned to the temple, faced the main image of Buddha, and invoked the Sacred Name. But impure thoughts now cast their opaque shadows about him. A woman's beauty, he told himself, was but a fleeting apparition, a temporary phenomenon composed of flesh—of flesh that was soon to be destroyed. Yet, try as he might to ward it off, the ineffable beauty which had overpowered him at that instant by the lake now pressed on his heart with the force of something that has come from an infinite distance. The Great Priest was not young enough, either spiritually or physically, to believe that this new feeling was simply a trick that his flesh had played on him. A man's flesh, he knew full well, could not alter so rapidly. Rather, he seemed to have been immersed in some swift, subtle poison which had abruptly transmuted his spirit.

The Great Priest had never broken his vow of chastity. The inner fight that he had waged in his youth against the demands of the flesh had made him think of women as mere carnal beings. The only real flesh was the flesh that existed in his imagination. Since, therefore, he regarded the flesh as an ideal abstraction rather than as a physical fact, he had relied on his spiritual strength to subjugate it. In this effort the priest had achieved success—success, indeed, that no one who knew him could possibly doubt.

Yet the face of the woman who had raised the carriage blind and gazed across the lake was too harmonious, too refulgent, to be designated as a mere object of flesh, and the priest did not know what name to give it. He could only think that, in order to bring about that wondrous moment, something which had for a long time lurked deceptively within him had finally revealed itself. That thing was nothing other than the present world, which until then had been at repose, but which had now suddenly lifted itself out of the darkness and begun to stir.

It was as if he had been standing by the highway that led to the Capital, with his hands firmly covering both ears, and had watched two great ox-carts rumble past each other. All of a sudden he had removed his hands and the noise from outside had surged all about him.

To perceive the ebb and flow of passing phenomena, to have their noise roaring in one's ears, was to enter into the circle of the present world. For a man like the Great Priest who had severed his relations with all outside things, this was to place himself once again into a state of relationship.

Even as he read the sutras he would time after time hear himself heaving great sighs of anguish. Perhaps nature, he thought, might serve to distract his spirit, and he gazed out the window of his cell at the mountains that towered in the distance under the evening sky. Yet his thoughts, instead of concentrating on the beauty, broke up like tufts of cloud and drifted away. He fixed his gaze on the moon, but his thoughts continued to wander as before; and when once again he went and stood before the main image in a desperate effort to regain his purity of mind, the countenance of the Buddha was transformed and looked like the face of the lady in the carriage. His universe had been imprisoned within the confines of a small circle: at one point was the Great Priest and opposite him was the Great Imperial Concubine.

The Great Imperial Concubine of Kyōgoku had soon forgotten about the old priest whom she had noticed gazing so intently at her by the lake at Shiga. After some time, however, a rumor came to her ears and she was reminded of the incident. One of the villagers happened to have caught sight of the Great Priest as he had stood watching the lady's carriage disappear into the distance. He had mentioned the matter to a Court gentleman who had come to Shiga for flower-viewing, and had added that since that day the priest had behaved like one crazed.

The Imperial Concubine pretended to disbelieve the rumor. The virtue of this particular priest, however, was noted throughout the Capital, and the incident was bound to feed the lady's vanity.

For she was utterly weary of the love that she received from the men of this world. The Imperial Concubine was fully aware of her own beauty, and she tended to be attracted by any force, such as religion, that treated her beauty and her high rank as things of no value. Being exceedingly bored with the present world, she believed in the Pure Land. It was inevitable that Jodo Buddhism, which rejected all the beauty and brilliance of the visual world as being mere filth and defilement, should have a particular appeal for someone like the Imperial Concubine who was thoroughly disillusioned with the superficial elegance of court life—an elegance that seemed unmistakably to bespeak the Latter Days of the Law and their degeneracy.

Among those whose special interest was love, the Great Imperial Concubine was held in honor as the very personification of courtly refinement. The fact that she was known never to have given her love to any man added to this reputation. Though she performed her duties toward the Emperor with the most perfect decorum, no one for a moment believed that she loved him from her heart. The Great Imperial Concubine dreamed of a passion that lay on the boundary of the impossible.

The Great Priest of Shiga Temple was famous for his virtue, and everyone in the Capital knew how this aged prelate had totally abandoned the present world. All the more startling, then was the rumor that he had been dazzled by the charms of the Imperial Concubine and that for her sake he had sacrificed the future world. To give up the joys of the Pure Land which were so close at hand—there could be no greater sacrifice than this, no greater gift.

The Great Imperial Concubine was utterly indifferent to the charms of the young rakes who flocked about the court and of the handsome noblemen who came her way. The physical attributes of men no longer meant anything to her. Her only concern was to find a man who could give her the strongest and deepest possible love. A woman with such aspirations is a truly terrifying creature. If she is a mere courtesan, she will no doubt be satisfied with wordly wealth. The Great Imperial Concubine, however, already enjoyed all those things that the wealth of the world can provide. The man whom she awaited must offer her the wealth of the future world.

The rumors of the Great Priest's infatuation spread throughout the court. In the end the story was even told half-jokingly to the Emperor himself. The Great Concubine took no pleasure in this bantering gossip and preserved a cool, indifferent mien. As she was well aware, there were two reasons that the people of the court could joke freely about a matter which would normally have been forbidden: first, by referring to the Great Priest's love they were paying a compliment to the beauty of the woman who could inspire even an ecclesiastic of such great virtue to forsake his meditations; secondly, everyone fully realized that the old man's love for the noblewoman could never possibly be requited.

The Great Imperial Concubine called to mind the face of the old priest whom she had seen through her carriage window. It did not bear the remotest resemblance to the face of any of the men who had loved her until then. Strange it was that love should spring up in the heart of a man who did not have the slightest qualification for being loved. The lady recalled such phrases as "my love forlorn and without hope" that were widely used by poetasters in the palace when they wished to awaken some sympathy in the hearts of their indifferent paramours. Compared to the hopeless situation in which the Great Priest now found himself, the state of the least fortunate of these elegant lovers was almost enviable, and their poetic tags struck her now as mere trappings of wordly dalliance, inspired by vanity and utterly devoid of pathos.

At this point it will be clear to the reader that the Great Imperial Concubine was not, as was so widely believed, the personification of courtly elegance, but, rather, a person who found the real relish of life in the knowledge of being loved. Despite her high rank, she was first of all a woman; and all the power and authority in the world seemed to her empty things if they were bereft of this knowledge. The men about her might devote themselves to struggles for political power; but she dreamed of subduing the world by different means, by purely feminine means. Many of the women whom she had known had taken the tonsure and retired from the world. Such women struck her as laughable. For, whatever a woman may say about abandoning the world, it is almost impossible for her to give up the things that she possesses. Only men are really capable of giving up what they possess.

That old priest by the lake had at a certain stage in his life given up the Floating World and all its pleasures. In the eyes of the Imperial Concubine he was far more of a man than all the nobles whom she knew at court. And, just as he had once abandoned this present Floating World, so now on her behalf he was about to give up the future world as well.

The Imperial Concubine recalled the notion of the sacred lotus flower, which her own deep faith had vividly imprinted upon her mind. She thought of the huge lotus with its width of two hundred and fifty *yojana*. That preposterous plant was far more fitted to her tastes than those puny lotus flowers which floated on the ponds of the Capital. At night when she listened to the wind soughing through the trees in her garden, the sound seemed to her extremely insipid when compared to the delicate music in the Pure Land when the wind blew through the sacred treasure trees. When she thought of the strange instruments that hung in the sky and that played by themselves without ever being touched, the sound of the harp that echoed through the palace halls seemed to her a paltry imitation.

The Great Priest of Shiga Temple was fighting. In the fight that he had waged against the flesh in his youth he had always been buoyed up by the hope of inheriting the future world. But this desperate fight of his old age was linked with a sense of irreparable loss.

The impossibility of consummating his love for the Great Imperial Concubine was as clear to him as the sun in the sky. At the same time he was fully aware of the impossibility of advancing toward the Pure Land so long as he remained in the thralls of this love. The Great Priest, who had lived in an incomparably free state of mind, had in a twinkling been enclosed in darkness, and the future was totally obscure. It may have been that the courage which had seen him through his youthful struggles had grown out of self-confidence and pride in the fact that he was voluntarily depriving himself of pleasure that could not have been his for the asking.

The Great Priest once more possessed himself of fear. Until that noble carriage had approached the side of Lake Shiga, he had believed that what lay in wait for him, close at hand, was nothing less than the final release of Nirvana. But now he had awakened into the darkness of the present world, where it is impossible to see what lurks a single step ahead.

The various forms of religious meditation were all in vain. He tried the Contemplation of the Chrysanthemum, the Contemplation of the Total Aspect, and the Contemplation of the Parts; but each time that he started to concentrate, the beautiful visage of the concubine appeared before his eyes. Water Contemplation, too, was useless, for invariably her lovely face would float up shimmering from beneath the ripples of the lake.

This, no doubt, was a natural consequence of his infatuation. Concentration, the priest soon realized, did more harm than good, and next he tried to dull his spirit by dispersal. It astonished him that spiritual concentration should have the paradoxical effect of leading him still deeper into his delusions; but he soon realized that to try the contrary method of dispersing his thoughts meant that he was, in effect, admitting these very delusions. As his spirit began to yield under the weight, the priest decided that, rather than pursue a futile struggle, it were better to escape from the effort of escaping by deliberately concentrating his thoughts on the figure of the Great Imperial Concubine.

The Great Priest found a new pleasure in adorning his vision of the lady in various ways, just as though he were adorning a Buddhist statute with diadems and baldachins. In so doing, he turned the object of his love into an increasingly replendent, distant, impossible being; and this afforded him particular joy. But why? Surely it would be more natural for him to envisage the Great Imperial Concubine as an ordinary female, close at hand and possessing normal human frailties. Thus he could better turn her to advantage, at least in his imagination.

As he pondered this question, the truth dawned on him. What he was depicting in the Great Imperial Concubine was not a creature of flesh, nor was it a mere vision; rather, it was a symbol of reality, a symbol of the essence of things. It was strange, indeed, to pursue that essence in the figure of a woman. Yet the reason was not far to seek. Even when falling in love, the Great Priest of Shiga had not discarded the habit, to which he had trained himself during his long years of contemplation, of striving to approach the essence of things by means of constant abstraction. The Great Imperial Concubine of Kyōgoku had now become uniform with his vision of the immense lotus of two hundred and fifty *yojana.* As she reclined on the water supported by all the lotus flowers, she had become vaster than Mount Sumeru, vaster than an entire realm.

The more the Great Priest turned his love into something impossible, the more deeply was he betraying the Buddha. For the impossibility of this love had become bound up with the impossibility of attaining enlightnment. The more he thought of his love as hopeless, the firmer grew the fantasy that supported it and the deeper rooted became his impure thoughts. So long as he regarded his love as being even remotely feasible, it was paradoxically possible for him to resign himself; but now that the Great Concubine had grown into a fabulous and utterly unattainable creature, the priest's love became motionless like a great, stagnant lake which firmly, obdurately, covers the earth's surface.

He hoped that somehow he might see the lady's face once more, yet he feared that when he met her that figure, which had now become like a giant lotus, would crumble away without a trace. If that were to happen, he would without doubt be saved. Yes, this time he was bound to attain enlightenment. And the very prospect filled the Great Priest with fear and awe.

The priest's lonely love had begun to devise strange, self-deceiving guiles, and when at length he reached the decision to go and see the lady, he was under the delusion that he had almost recovered from the illness that was searing his body. The bemused priest even mistook the joy that accompanied his decision for relief at having finally escaped from the trammels of his love.

None of the Great Concubine's people found anything especially strange in the sight of an old priest standing silently in the corner of the garden, leaning on a stick and gazing somberly at the residence. Ascetics and beggars frequently stood outside the great houses of the Capital and waited for alms. One of the ladies in attendance mentioned the matter to her mistress. The Great Imperial Concubine casually glanced through the blind that separated her from the garden. There in the shadow of the fresh green foliage stood a withered old priest with faded black robes and bowed head. For some time the lady looked at him. When she realized that this was without any question the priest whom she had seen by the lake at Shiga, her pale face turned paler still.

After a few moments of indecision, she gave orders that the priest's presence in her garden should be ignored. Her attendants bowed and withdrew.

Now for the first time the lady fell prey to uneasiness. In her lifetime she had seen many people who had abandoned the world, but never before had she laid eyes on someone who had abandoned the future world. The sight was ominous and inexpressibly fearful. All the pleasure that her imagination had conjured up from the idea of the priest's love disappeared in a flash. Much as he might have surrendered the future world on her behalf, that world, she now realized, would never pass into her own hands.

The Great Imperial Concubine looked down at her elegant clothes and at her beautiful hands, and then she looked across the garden at the uncomely features of the old priest and at his shabby robes. There was a horrible fascination in the fact that a connection should exist between them.

How different it all was from the splendid vision! The Great Priest seemed now like a person who had hobbled out of Hell itself. Nothing remained of that man of virtuous presence who had trailed the brightness of the Pure Land behind him. The brilliance which had resided within him and which had called to mind the glory of the Pure Land had vanished utterly. Though this was certainly the man who had stood by Shiga Lake, it was at the same time a totally different person.

Like most people of the court, the Great Imperial Concubine tended to be on her guard against her own emotions, especially when she was confronted with something that could be expected to affect her deeply. Now on seeing this evidence of the Great Priest's love, she felt disheartened at the thought that the consummate passion of which she had dreamed during all these years should assume so colorless a form.

When the priest had finally limped into the Capital leaning on his stick, he had almost forgotten his exhaustion. Secretly he made his way into the grounds of the Great Imperial Concubine's residence at Kyōgoku and looked across the garden. Behind those blinds, he thought, was sitting none other than the lady whom he loved.

Now that his adoration had assumed an immaculate form, the future world once again began to exert its charm on the Great Priest. Never before had he envisaged the Pure Land in so immaculate, so poignant an aspect. His yearning for it became almost sensual. Nothing remained for him but the formality of meeting the Great Concubine, of declaring his love, and of thus ridding himself once for all of the impure thoughts that tied him to this world and prevented him from attaining the Pure Land. That was all that remained to be done.

It was painful for him to stand there supporting his old body on his stick. The bright rays of the May sun poured through the leaves and beat down on his shaven head. Time after time he felt himself losing consciousness and without his stick he would certainly have collapsed. If only the lady would realize the situation and invite him into her presence, so that the formality might be over with! The Great Priest waited. He waited and supported his ever-growing weariness on his stick. At length the sun was covered with the evening clouds. Dusk gathered. Yet still no word came from the Great Imperial Concubine.

She, of course, had no way of knowing that the priest was looking through her, beyond her, into the Pure Land. Time after time she glanced out through the blinds. He was standing there immobile. The evening light thrust its way into the garden. Still he continued standing there.

The Great Imperial Concubine became frightened. She felt that what she saw in the garden was an incarnation of that "deep-rooted delusion" of which she had read in the sutras. She was overcome by the fear of tumbling into Hell. Now that she had led astray a priest of such high virtue, it was not the Pure Land to which she could look forward, but Hell itself, whose terrors she and those about her knew in such detail. The supreme love of which she had dreamed had already been shattered. To be loved as she was—that in itself represented damnation. Whereas the Great Priest looked beyond her into the Pure Land, she now looked beyond the priest into the horrid realms of Hell.

Yet this haughty noblewoman of Kyōgoku was too proud to succumb to her fears without a fight, and she now summoned forth all the resources of her inbred ruthlessness. The Great Priest, she told herself, was found to collapse sooner or later. She looked through the blind, thinking that by now he must be lying on the ground. To her annoyance, the silent figure stood there motionless.

Night fell and in the moonlight the figure of the priest looked like a pile of chalk-white bones.

The lady could not sleep for fear. She no longer looked through the blind and she turned her back to the garden. Yet all the time she seemed to feel the piercing gaze of the Great Priest on her back.

This, she knew, was no commonplace love. From fear of being loved, from fear of falling into Hell, the Great Imperial Concubine prayed more earnestly than ever for the Pure Land. It was for her own private Pure Land that she prayed—a Pure Land which she tried to preserve invulnerable within her heart. This was a different Pure Land from the priest's and it had no connection with his love. She felt sure that if she were ever to mention it to him, it would instantly disintegrate.

The priest's love, she told herself, had nothing to do with her. It was a one-sided affair, in which her own feelings had no part, and there was no reason that it should disqualify her from being received into her Pure Land. Even if the Great Priest were to collapse and die, she would remain unscathed. Yet, as the night advanced and the air became colder, this confidence began to desert her.

The priest remained standing in the garden. When the moon was hidden by the clouds, he looked like a strange, gnarled old tree.

"That form out there has nothing to do with me," thought the lady, almost beside herself with anguish, and the words seemed to boom within her heart. "Why in Heaven's name should this have happened?"

At that moment, strangely, the Great Imperial Concubine completely forgot her own beauty. Or perhaps it would be more correct to say that she had made herself forget it.

Finally, faint traces of white began to break through the dark sky and the priest's figure emerged in the dawn twilight. He was still standing. The Great Imperial Concubine had been defeated. She summoned a maid and told her to invite the priest to come in from the garden and to kneel outside her blind.

The Great Priest was at the very boundary of oblivion when the flesh is on the verge of crumbling away. He no longer knew whether it was for the Great Imperial Concubine that he was waiting or for the future world. Though he saw the figure of the maid approaching from the residence into the dusky garden, it did not occur to him that what he had been awaiting was finally at hand.

The maid delivered her mistress' message. When she had finished, the priest uttered a dreadful, almost inhuman, cry. The maid tried to lead him by the hand, but he pulled away and walked by himself toward the house with fantastically swift, firm steps.

It was dark on the other side of the blind and from outside it was impossible to see the lady's form. The priest knelt down and, covering his face with his hands, he wept. For a long time he stayed there without a word and his body shook convulsively.

Then in the dawn darkness a white hand gently emerged from behind the lowered blind. The priest of the Shiga Temple took it in his own hands and pressed it to his forehead and cheek.

The Great Imperial Concubine of Kyōgoku felt a strange, cold hand touching her hand. At the same time she was aware of a warm moisture. Her hand was being bedewed by someone else's tears. Yet when the pallid shafts of morning light began to reach her through the blind, the lady's fervent faith imbued her with a wonderful inspiration: she became convinced that the unknown hand which touched hers belonged to none other than the Buddha.

Then the great vision sprang up anew in the lady's heart: the emerald earth of the Pure Land, the millions of seven-jeweled towers, the angels playing music, the golden ponds strewn with silver sand, the resplendent lotus, and the sweet voices of the Kalavinkas—all this was born afresh. If this was the Pure Land that she was to inherit—and so she now believed—why should she not accept the Great Priest's love?

She waited for the man with the hands of Buddha to ask her to raise the blind that separated her from him. Presently he would ask her; and then she would remove the barrier and her incomparably beautiful body would appear before him as it had on that day by the edge of the lake at Shiga; and she would invite him to come in.

The Great Imperial Concubine waited.

But the priest of Shiga Temple did not utter a word. He asked her for nothing. After a while his old hands relaxed their grip and the lady's snow-white hand was left alone in the dawn light. The priest departed. The heart of the Great Imperial Concubine turned cold.

A few days later a rumor reached the Court that the Great Priest's spirit had achieved its final liberation in his cell at Shiga. At this news the lady of Kyōgoku set to copying the sutras in roll after roll of beautiful writing.

Guide to Pronunciation

The following notes on pronunciation are intended to guide the reader to an approximate rendition of the original words without his learning sounds difficult for an American or a European to pronounce. Needless to say, many of the sounds in Asian languages have no real approximations in English or European languages and can be learned only by repeated drill with a native speaker.

ARABIC

Words of two syllables are accented on the first syllable. Three-syllable words are accented on the first syllable, unless the syllable is "closed" (*i.e.*, consists of a consonant, a short vowel, and a vowelless consonant). The short vowels are: *a* as in *cat, i* as in *admit, u* as in *good.* The long vowels are: *ā* as in *father, ū* as in *boot* (but longer), and *ī* as in *machine* (but longer and not diphthongized). There are two diphthongs: *aw* as in *owl* and *ay* as in *eye.*

The consonants present considerable difficulty. Besides *t, d, s,* and *z,* there are *ṭ, ḍ, ṣ,* and *ẓ,* which are "emphatic" velarized sounds, made by placing the tongue in a position for the English sounds and then raising the back of the tongue towards the velum. Both ' and ' are sounds, not diacritical marks. The former is a glottal stop sometimes heard in English at the beginning of a word with an initial vowel, and more frequently in Scottish English. The latter is a most difficult sound to master. It is something like an emphatic *h,* but with vibration of the vocal chords. Double consonants must be pronounced double.

Persian is similar to Arabic but has fewer difficult consonants. Where the acute accent in Arabic or Persian transliteration (in older systems) signifies a long vowel, I have substituted the macron.

SANSKRIT

Sanskrit is a classical language of great antiquity with no body of colloquial material to provide stress patterns based on actual usage. It is the custom of Western scholars to accent Sanskrit as if it were Latin. Long vowels are stressed, especially the final long vowel in a polysyllabic word: thus *Rāmáyana, Mahābhárata.* There are three vowels, *a, i,* and *u,* which occur both long and short: *a* as in *far, ā* as in *father; i* as in *pin, ī* as in *machine; u* as in *pull, ū* as in *rule.*

The consonants present no particular difficulty in approximating, except for a smooth or untrilled *r* and an *l* (transliterated *ṛ* and *ḷ*). These have not been indicated in this volume.

CHINESE

Chinese words are generally monosyllabic, and hence there is no problem of stress accent within words. Meaning is distinguished in Chinese by musical tone. There are four or five tones, depending on the dialect used, "sung" to rising, falling, or steady pitch, which differentiate meanings. The tones require much practice and are ignored here. The standard transliteration system has been the Wade-Giles, and most translations from the Chinese and literary scholarship has used it, but a more modern system is rapidly replacing it. Wade-Giles is accurate, but it does not represent English equivalents very adequately. Thus the modern Chinese statesman Chou En-lai is not Mr. Chew but more like Mr. Joe, as is the name of the dynasty. The concept of *tao* is not "tay-oh" but something like "Dow" in Dow-Jones.

In Chinese, each word consists of an initial and a final.[1]

Initials

ch	*j* as in *jay*	p'	*p* in *spill*
ch'	*ch* in *charm*	s	*s*
f	*f*	sh	*sh*
h	guttural *h*	ss *or* sz	*s;* used only before *u*
hs	*sh*	t	*d*
j	*r*	t'	*t*
k	*g* in *gay*	ts	*dz*
k'	*k* in *skill*	ts'	*ts*
l	*l*	tz	*dz;* used only before *u*
m	*m*	tz'	*ts;* used only before *u*
n	*n*	w	*w* in *way*
p	*b* in *bait*	y	*y* in *you*

Finals

a	*ah*	iao	*yow; ow* in *how*
ai	*eye*	ieh	*yeah*
an	*on* in *yon*	ien	*yen*
ang	*ang* in German *lang*	ih	*rr,* not trilled
ao	*ow* in *how*	in	*in*

1. For Chinese I have used the examples given by Harold Shadick in his *Travels of Lao Ts'an* (Ithaca, New York, 1952), pp. 275-77.

e *or* ê	*u* in *cup*	ing	*ing*
ei	*ay* in *say*	iu	*ew* in *mew*
en *or* ên	*un* in *bun*	iung	*ee* + *ung;* German *jung*
eng *or* êng	*ung* in *bung*		
erh *or* êrh	*er* in *ermine*	o[3]	*aw* in *law*
i[2]	*ee*	o[4]	*u* in *cup*
ia	*yah*	ou (ow)	*ow* in *low*
iang	*yahng*	u[5]	*oo*
u *or* ŭ *or* e[6]	indicates prolonged buzz produced by voicing the consonant	ui (wei)	*way*
		un	*un* in German *und*
		ung	*ung* in German *bung*
		uo	*uaw* in *squaw*
ua	*wa* in *wand*	ü	ü in German *über*
uai	*wi* in *wine*	üan	ü + *ann* in German *mann*
uan	*wan* or in Spanish *Don Juan*	üeh (io)	ü + *eah* in *yeah*
uang	*oo* + *ang;* German *lang*	ün	French *une*

The above approximates the Peking or Mandarin dialect of Chinese.

JAPANESE

Westerners should endeavor to pronounce Japanese without stress accent (*i.e.*, by giving each syllable equal stress). The name of the poet Bashō is not accented on the second syllable—the *o* is merely prolonged in sound. Indeed, to Westerners, the name may seem to be stressed on the first syllable. Vowels should always be pronounced in conjunction with the preceding consonant, thus *ki-mo-no* rather than keem-oh-noh (and especially not "kuh-MON-uh." The lack of the common English unstressed vowel in Japanese and the heavy stress accent in English present difficulties for the beginner.

The short vowels are *a* as in *father, e* as in *enemy, i* as in *machine* or *beet* but as short as the vowel in *bit, o* as in *original* (but not *uh*), *u* as in *pull* or *full*. The long vowels are *ā* as in *park, ē* as in *fame* (usually transliterated *ei*), *ō* as in *so* or *old, ū* as in *soon, ī* as in *key* (usually transliterated *ii*). The vowels are precise, as in Italian. The consonants are similar to English except that the *r* sounds to Western ears like an *l*. It is a very briefly trilled *r* made far forward in the mouth at about the point where *d* and *n* are formed. Japanese has no equivalent for either the English *r* or the English *l*.

Double consonants must be pronounced: *hasshi* ("to parry") must be distinguished from *hashi* ("chopsticks").

2. Sometimes written *yi* when there is no other initial.
3. After initials other than *h* and *k*.
4. After *h* and *k* or without initial.
5. After initials other than *ss* or *sz, tz, tz'*.
6. After *ss* or *sz, tz, tz'*.

Note on Proper Names

Arabic and Persian names, like Spanish ones, are often complicated. If in doubt about a surname, the reader is referred to the indexes of the literary histories of Nicholson, Browne, and Arberry. The alphabetizing name often comes after *ibn* or *abu*. Sanskrit names present no difficulties.

Chinese names usually consist of two or three monosyllables. Li Po is Mr. Li. Lin Yutang is Mr. Lin, whether spelled Lin Yutang, Lin Yu Tang, or Lin Yu-tang. Some early Japanese names include the particle *no*, which means "of," as in Kamo no Chōmei, and is analogous to the "of" in John of Gaunt or William of Malmesbury. For later names I use the name by which the writer is commonly discussed in literary history and criticism: Sōseki for Sōseki Natsume. (The reader is warned that library catalogues do exactly the reverse!) After the Meiji restoration in the nineteenth century, Western order is used: Mishima for Yukio Mishima.

Bibliographical Note

A comprehensive, classified bibliography of books and articles on Far Eastern subjects (including India) is edited by Howard Linton annually in the *Journal of Asian Studies* (formerly *Far Eastern Quarterly*). Herbert Franke's *Sinologie* (Bern, 1953; Wissenschaftliche Forschungsberichte, Geisteswissenschaftliche Reihe, Band 19) is an annotated guide to Sinological study. An excellent and inexpensive bibliography of Japanese literature is *Japanese Literature in European Languages* (Tokyo: Japan P.E.N. Club, 1960). A general guide with some annotations is Hugh Borton, *et al., Selected List of Books and Articles on Japan* (Cambridge, Mass., 1954). A very complete *Bibliography of the Japanese Empire,* edited successively by Friedrich von Wenckstern, Oskar Nachod, and Hans Praesent and Wolf Haenisch, covers the years 1859-1937. For China see Tung-li Yuan's *China in Western Literature* (New Haven, 1958).

For Islamic literature see J. D. Pearson, *Index Islamicus* (with supplements, it covers 1906–1965) (1958, 1962, 1967), and Jean Sauvaget, *Introduction to the History of the Muslim East, a Bibliographical Guide* (1965). The *Dictionary of Oriental Literature,* edited by Jaroslav Průšek (3 vols., 1974), includes Islamic materials as well as the Far East.

Index

Akutagawa, Ryunosuke, 786
Analects, The, 391
Aoi no Uye (Princess Hollyhock), 737
Atsumori, 706

Bashō, 745
Bhagavad Gītā (The Song of God), 153
Book of Kings, The (Shāhnāma), 31
Book of Songs, The (Shih Ching), 371

Chikamatsu Monzaemon, 753
Chou Shu-jen, *see* Lu Hsün
Chuang-tzu, 407
Collection of Ten Thousand Leaves, The (Manyōshū), 598
Confucius, 389
Courier for Hell, The (Meido no Hikyaku), 757

Deserted Crone, The (Obasute), 712
Dwarf Trees, The (Hachi no Ki), 720

Early Snow (Hatsuyuki), 742

Financial Expert, The, 348
Firdausī, 29

Ghazals, 91
Golden Odes, The (Mu'allaqāt), 6
Gulistān (The Rose Garden), 67

Hachi no Ki (The Dwarf Trees), 720

Hāfiz, 90
Haiku, 747
Hatsuyuki (Early Snow), 742
Heike Monogatari (Tales of the Heike), 668
Hōjōki (Life in a Ten-Foot-Square Hut), 691
Hsi Yu Chi (Monkey), 478

In a Grove (Yabu no Naka), 795

Kālidāsa, 232
Kamo no Chōmei, 690
Kawabata, Yasunari, 786
Komachi at Sekidera (Sekidera Komachi), 728
Komparu Zembo Motoyasu, 742
K'ung Fu-tzi, *see* Confucius

Lady Who Loved Worms, The (Mushi Mezuru Himegimi), 660
Lao-ts'an Yu-chi (The Travels of Lao Ts'an), 498
Li Po, 455
Life in a Ten-Foot-Square Hut (Hōjōki), 691
Liu T'ieh-yun, 498
Lu Hsün, 531
Lu Ki, 422

Madman's Dairy, A, 533
Makura no Sōshi (The Pillow Book), 626
Manyōshū (Collection of Ten Thousand Leaves), 598
Mathnawī, 58
Medicine, 541
Meido no Hikyaku (The Courier for Hell), 757

Mishima, Yukio, 786
Monkey (Hsi Yu Chi), 478
Moon on the Water, The, 807
Mu'allaqāt (The Golden Odes), 6
Mushi Mezuru Himegini (The Lady Who Loved Worms), 660

Narayan, R. K., 346
Nō plays, 702

Obasute (The Deserted Crone), 712

Pillow Book, The (Makura no Sōshi), 626
Po Chü-i, 463
Post Office, The, 329
Priest and His Love, The, 815
Princess Hollyhock (Aoi no Uye), 737

Rāmāyana, 170
Rashōmon, 790
Red Lantern, The 556
Rhymeprose on Literature (Wen Fu), 424
Rigveda, 134
Rose Garden, The (Gulistan), 67
Rūmī, 56

Sa'dī, 66
Sei Shōnagon, 625
Sekidera Komachi (Komachi at Sekidera), 725
Shāhnāma (The Book of Kings), 31
Shakuntalā, 234
Shih Ching (The Book of Songs), 371
Soap, 548
Song of God, The (Bhagavad Gita), 153
Stream of Days, The, 103
Subhāsitaratnakosa (Treasury of Well-Turned Verse), 318

Tagore, Rabindranath, 328
Tāhā Hussein, 102
Tales of the Heike (Heike Monogatari), 668
Tales of the Middle Counselor of the Embankment (Tsutsumi Chunagon Monogatari), 659
Tanizaki, Junichiro, 786
T'ao Ch'ien, 434
Tattooer, The, 802
Travels of Lao Ts'an, The (Lao-ts'an Yu-chi), 498
Treasury of Well-Turned Verse, The (Subhāsitaratnakosa), 318
Tsutsumi Chunagon Monogatari (Tales of the Middle Counselor of the Embankment), 659

Vālmīki, 168
Vidyākara, 316

Wen Fu (Rhymeprose on Literature), 424
Wu Ch'eng-en, 477

Yabu no Naka (In a Grove), 795

Zeami Motokiyo, 702
Zenchiki Ujinobu, 737

593-595

598-625